my BusinessCourse

D0071286

FREE WITH NEW COPIES OF THIS TEXTBOOK*

Start using myBusinessCourse Today: www.mybusinesscourse.com

myBusinessCourse is a web-based learning and assessment program intended to complement your textbook and faculty instruction.

Student Benefits

- **eLectures**: These videos review the key concepts of each Learning Objective in each chapter.
- **Guided examples**: These videos provide step-by-step solutions for select problems in each chapter.
- **Auto-graded assignments**: Provide students with immediate feedback on select assignments. (**with Instructor-Led course ONLY**).
- **Quiz and Exam preparation**: myBusinessCourse provides students with additional practice and exam preparation materials to help students achieve better grades and content mastery.

You can access myBusinessCourse 24/7 from any web-enabled device, including iPads, smartphones, laptops, and tablets.

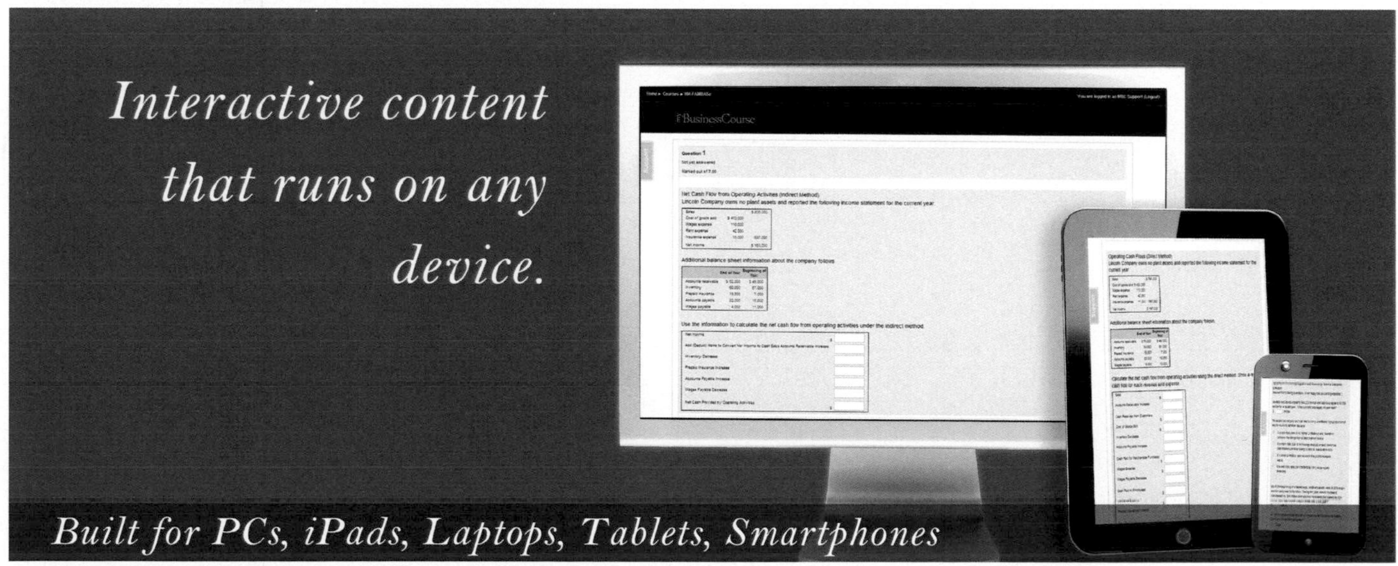

***Each access code is good for one use only.** If the textbook is used for more than one course or term, students will have to purchase additional myBusinessCourse access codes. In addition, students who repeat a course for any reason will have to purchase a new access code. If you purchased a used book and the protective coating that covers the access code has been removed, your code may be invalid.

Access to myBusinessCourse is free ONLY with the purchase of a new textbook.

THIRD EDITION

Financial Accounting for Decision Makers

MARK DEFOND
Leventhal School of Accounting
Marshall School of Business
University of Southern California

Cambridge
BUSINESS PUBLISHERS

DEDICATION

To my wife Carol, my secret co-author on this book and in life.

Photo Credits
Chapter 1 Opener: © Getty Images
Chapter 1 p. 5 (left): © istockphoto.com/monkeybusinessimages
Chapter 1 p. 5 (middle): © istockphoto.com/mtmphoto
Chapter 1 p. 5 (right): © shutterstock/leungchopan
Chapter 1 p. 6 (top left): © istockphoto.com
Chapter 1 p. 6 (bottom middle): © istockphoto.com
Chapter 1 p. 6 (top right): © istockphoto.com
Chapter 1 p. 6 (bottom right): © istockphoto.com
Chapter 1 p. 7: (top) © istockphoto.com
Chapter 1 p. 7: (middle) © istockphoto.com
Chapter 1 p. 7: (bottom) © istockphoto.com
Chapter 1 p. 8: (top) © istockphoto.com
Chapter 1 p. 8: (middle) © istockphoto.com
Chapter 1 p. 8 (bottom): © istockphoto.com/porcorex
Chapter 1 p. 11 (middle): © shutterstock/BCFC
Chapter 1 p. 11: © shutterstock/hxdbzxy
Chapter 2 Opener: © shutterstock
Chapter 2 p. 44: © istockphoto.com
Chapter 3 Opener: © istockphoto.com
Chapter 3 p. 76: © istockphoto.com
Chapter 4 Opener: © shutterstock
Chapter 4 p. 120 (top): © istockphoto.com
Chapter 4 p. 120 (bottom): © istockphoto.com
Chapter 5 Opener: © shutterstock
Chapter 5 p. 153: © istockphoto.com
Chapter 5 p. 154: © istockphoto.com
Chapter 6 Opener: © istockphoto.com
Chapter 6 p. 184: © shutterstock
Chapter 6 p. 185: © shutterstock
Chapter 6 p. 189: © shutterstock
Chapter 6 p. 195: © istockphoto.com
Chapter 7 Opener: © shutterstock
Chapter 7 p. 216 (left): © shutterstock/4045
Chapter 7 p. 216 (middle): © shutterstock/Harry Thomas Flower
Chapter 7 p. 216 (right): © shutterstock/QualityHD
Chapter 7 p. 217 (left): © istockpohoto.com/adventtr
Chapter 7 p. 217 (middle): © shutterstock/asharkyu
Chapter 7 p. 217 (right): © shutterstock/Hadrian
Chapter 7 p. 236: © istockphoto.com/style-photography
Chapter 8 Opener: © shutterstock
Chapter 8 p. 258: © istockphoto.com/Mindstyle
Chapter 8 p. 258 © shutterstock/FotograFFF
Chapter 8 p. 259: © istockphoto.com/ManuelGonzalezOlaecheaFranco
Chapter 8 p. 259: © istockphoto.com/nojustice
Chapter 9 Opener: © shutterstock
Chapter 10 Opener: © shutterstock
Chapter 11 Opener: © shutterstock
Chapter 12 Opener: © shutterstock

Acknowledgment: I wish to thank Ken Ferris, Jim Wallace, and Ted Christensen, whose Financial Accounting textbook provided the initial basis for this book.

Financial Accounting for Decision Makers, Third Edition, by Mark DeFond.

ISBN: 978-1-61853-443-9

Bookstores & Faculty: To order this book, contact the company via email **customerservice@cambridgepub.com** or call 800-619-6473.

Students & Retail Customers: To order this book, please visit the book's Website and order directly online.

Printed in Canada.
10 9 8 7 6 5 4 3 2 1

About the Author

Mark DeFond is the Associate Dean of Faculty and the A.N. Mosich Chair in Accounting in the Leventhal School of Accounting at the University of Southern California. He has taught financial accounting to a variety of audiences, including undergraduates, MBAs, and Executive MBAs. Mark earned his Ph.D. from the University of Washington and prior to that worked for several years as an auditor at a Big Eight accounting firm. His B.A. is from San Francisco State University. He is widely published and his research is highly cited. Professor DeFond has served on the editorial boards of several leading academic journals and is a recipient of several research awards, including the Notable Contribution to Auditing Literature Award and the Mellon Award for Excellence in Mentoring Faculty. He has held visiting professorships at universities in Hong Kong, Italy, and Singapore. He is also a four time winner of the MBA Golden Apple teaching award, and was ranked among the ten most outstanding USC MBA faculty by *BusinessWeek*.

Preface

Welcome to the third edition of *Financial Accounting for Decision Makers.* It is difficult to imagine being successful in today's business world without having a solid understanding of how to read and understand financial accounting reports. The overarching objective of this text is to prepare students for careers in business by providing them with a solid foundation in financial accounting and reporting without overloading them with the mechanics and procedures more appropriate for future accountants. This book makes extensive use of real-world companies to help students understand how to use accounting information. To further aid student success in the course, we provide a wealth of resources through our online learning and homework system, myBusinessCourse (MBC). Access to MBC is included for free with the purchase of each new copy of the text and can be purchased separately. (For more information on MBC see page x of the preface.)

TARGET AUDIENCE

Financial Accounting for Decision Makers is an ideal text for use in the first financial accounting course at both the *undergraduate* and the *graduate* level. With a strong emphasis on the interpretation of real-world financial statements, the book teaches students how to read, analyze, and interpret financial accounting data to make informed business decisions without using the traditional debit/credit paradigm. The book is filled with examples that use financial reports from actual companies, an approach that students find engaging.

TRANSACTION ANALYSIS TEMPLATE

The most important difference between this textbook and traditional introductory financial accounting texts is that this textbook does not use debits and credits to teach accounting. While Appendix C, The Language of Accountants: Debits and Credits, describes the system of debits and credits, students are not required to learn this system and it is not discussed in the body of the text. Knowledge of debits and credits is not required because the focus is on teaching students how to understand and analyze the financial statements. This contrasts sharply with traditional introductory textbooks, which focus primarily on teaching students how to prepare financial statements.

In place of debits and credits, the book uses a creative new tool that is designed to teach students how economic transactions translate into the financial reports. This tool is called the "Transaction Analysis Template," or TAT for short. The TAT is an abbreviated version of a horizontal worksheet and provides students with a "shorthand" way of understanding and interpreting accounting reports. Once students learn the basic structure of a balance sheet and income statement, the TAT becomes a simple and highly intuitive technique for learning financial accounting.

Transaction: *DataForce made an $11,000 sale, paid in cash.*

Balance Sheet							*Income Statement*				
Assets	=	**Liabilities**	+	**Stockholders' Equity**							
				Contrib. Capital	+	**Retained Earnings**	***Revenues***	–	***Expenses***	=	***Net Income***
11,000 Cash	=					11,000	11,000 Sales	–		=	11,000

Dropping the use of debits and credits in an introductory class has many advantages. One is that it frees up time for the instructor to focus on what the financial reports and accounting actually mean. Learning the system of debits and credits is time consuming for even the brightest student, and a significant amount of the instructor's time can be spent explaining mechanical rules. Replacing debits and credits with the TAT allows time for deeper class discussions of important accounting concepts. Most students will not go on to become accountants, and for them, learnings the system of debits and credits is of limited value. The TAT is a mechanism that allows these students to get much more out of their introductory financial accounting course. Rather than take up precious course time learning a set of mechanical rules, students are allowed to concentrate on the concepts that underlie the accounting, and what the accounting information means.

The author stopped teaching debits and credits in his introductory accounting classes many years ago. Over the years, he has used versions of the TAT for undergraduate students, graduate students, and executive audiences. As compared with teaching using debits and credits, his experience is that students learn much more, and learn it more quickly, using the TAT. Importantly, they also seem to gain a much greater understanding of the "big picture" concepts that underlie the financial reports.

REAL COMPANIES' FINANCIAL STATEMENTS

A feature that really brings accounting alive for students is seeing the accounting practices and reports of companies with which they are familiar. To this end, each chapter incorporates examples using real companies that students know. For example, we discuss accounting issues related to **Google**, **Apple**, **Microsoft**, **Amazon**, **Target**, **Krispy Kreme**, **MGM Resorts**, and many others.

Real Data and Examples

Each chapter includes an assignment called **Beyond the Numbers** that requires students to use year-end financial statements of **Columbia Sportswear** and **Under Armour**.

REPORTING AND ANALYSIS

Columbia Sportswear Company

BTN4-1. Financial Reporting Problem: Columbia Sportswear Company The financial statements for **Columbia Sportswear** can be found in Appendix A at the end of this textbook.

Required

Answer the following questions using the Consolidated Balance Sheet and the Notes to the consolidated financial statements:

a. What were the combined totals of Columbia's liabilities and stockholders' equity for each of the two years presented?

b. How do these amounts compare with Columbia's total assets for each year?

c. What was the largest, in dollar value, of Columbia's assets each year? What does this asset represent?

d. What is the balance of accrued liabilities made up of?

Accounting in Practice

Boxed inserts are included throughout the text to help bridge the gap between the classroom and what students encounter in the real world. **Accounting In Practice** illustrations document situations a reader is likely to encounter and present the choices that companies make in reporting financial results.

A.K.A. *Junk bonds* are often referred to as high-yield bonds because of the higher yield rates that typically accompany this type of debt investment.

ACCOUNTING IN PRACTICE

Bond Risk Ratings The relative riskiness of different bonds may vary considerably. Bond investors who want to know the relative quality of a particular bond issue can consult a bond-rating service. Two major firms that rate the riskiness of bonds are **Standard & Poor's Corporation** (S&P) and **Moody's Investors Service** (Moody's). The rating categories used by these firms are similar. The following schedule shows the relationship between the ratings and the degree of risk using Standard & Poor's rating system:

Low Risk							High Risk
AAA	AA	A	BBB	BB	B	CCC	D
Investment Grade Bonds				Junk Bonds			

Investment grade bonds are highly-rated bonds with little risk that the issuing company will fail to pay interest as scheduled or fail to repay the principal at a bond's maturity. Junk bonds, on the other hand, are low-quality, high-yield bonds. In the S&P rating system, junk bonds are any bond rated BB and lower. Generally, bonds with poor credit ratings must offer higher interest rates than highly-rated bonds to attract potential buyers.

Environmental, Social, and Governance (ESG)

Increasingly, companies have found that "doing good" leads to a more successful, profitable enterprise. These boxed inserts help students understand how corporate reporting on ESG is being embraced by forward-thinking enterprises as part of their long-term business models.

ENVIRONMENTAL, SOCIAL, AND GOVERNANCE

Intangible assets include items such as patents that provide protection from competitors using the patented device or process for up to 20 years. It is not uncommon for firms to vigorously defend their patents through aggressive lawsuits. Tesla believes so strongly in what electric vehicles can do for the planet that the company has chosen to freely share its patents. This allows Tesla's competitors, along with any engineers who wish to use these patents, to work with the technology with the aim, according to Tesla, of strengthening the development of sustainable technology.

DATA ANALYTICS & EXCEL SKILL DEVELOPMENT FOR CAREER READINESS

The basics of accounting haven't changed much in hundreds of years, but businesses have experienced significant change in the last decade due to the increased use of new technologies ranging from data analytics and Blockchain to machine learning and artificial intelligence. Technology is rapidly altering how accounting is performed and what can be done with the data once they are collected. In response to the changing demands of the business world, the AACSB has incorporated data analytics requirements within its educational framework. More recently, the AICPA and NASBA have underscored the importance of data analytics by making it a significant element in the CPA Evolution Model Curriculum. The consensus suggests that today's business students need an understanding and working knowledge of data analytics and data visualization to compete for the best jobs.

In addition to data analytics skills, employers expect prospective employees to be proficient with Excel. In recognition of the increasing importance of data analytics and the need for Excel proficiency, the Third Edition includes several new features to enhance students' career readiness.

- We include Data Analytics boxes throughout the text to expose students to techniques that are used by businesses in areas related to the topic being discussed. The following box appears in the chapter on inventory.

DATA ANALYTICS Data Analytics Can Make Order Fulfillment Faster and More Efficient

Many large retailers, such as Amazon, use data analytics to make order fulfillment faster and more efficient. Using automated shipping rules, an order is assigned to the fulfillment center nearest to the order destination, thereby reducing transportation time and cost. Inventory management software also optimizes warehousing by dictating inventory locations within a facility to ensure efficient product picking routes. Through the use of data analytics, retailers can optimize good flows within the warehouse, which leads to faster order fulfillment and lower operating costs.

- Each chapter includes assignments that require students to use **Excel** and **Tableau** to hone data analysis and data visualization skills.

DA11-1. Preparing and Interpreting Excel Visualizations Created from Income and Cash Flow Data

The Excel file associated with this exercise includes data extracted from Form 10-K reports for CVS Health Corporation (CVS) and Walgreens Boots Alliance (Walgreens Boots) for six years. In this exercise, we analyze changes to and the relations between net income and operating cash flows over a six-year period.

REQUIRED

1. Download Excel file DA11-1 found in myBusinessCourse.
2. Prepare a line chart for the six-year period for each company showing net income and operating cash flows. *Hint:* Highlight your data; click on Insert, Select line chart. There should be a separate line for net income and a separate line for operating cash flows. If necessary, edit the chart by opening the Chart Design tab and clicking Select Data. There should be two series.
3. Use the visualizations to answer the following questions.
   a. In what year(s) does net income exceed operating cash flows for CVS?
   b. In what year(s) does operating cash flows exceed net income for Walgreens Boots?
   c. Over the six-year period, which year showed the largest difference between net income

- **Appendix F** at the end of the book provides an overview of data analytics, data visualization, and best practices for the effective display of data.

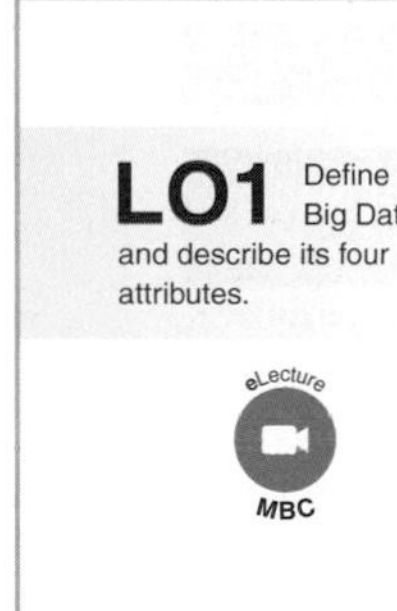

DATA ANALYTICS

Data analytics can broadly be defined as the process of examining sets of data with the goal of discovering useful information from patterns found in the data. Increasingly, this process is aided by computers running programs ranging from basic spreadsheet software, such as **Microsoft Excel** and **Google Sheets**, to specialized software, such as **Tableau** or **Power BI**. This technology can reveal trends and insights that would otherwise be lost in the overwhelming amount of data.

Big Data

The concept of data analytics is intertwined with the concept of **big data**. Although no precise definition exists for big data, a commonly accepted definition is that big data is a collection of data that is both extremely large and also extremely complex, thus making its analysis beyond the scope of traditional tools. Important attributes of big data, commonly referred to as the four

- **myBusinessCourse** *(MBC)* now contains a series of short videos that demonstrate the basic functions of Excel. These videos can be accessed within MBC as part of your MBC course.

ORGANIZING FOR STUDENT SUCCESS

To help students succeed in the course, we include many features that provide direction to students and require them to recall and apply the financial accounting techniques and concepts described in each chapter.

Putting Each Chapter in Context

Often, students lose sight of the big picture. The Past/Present/Future feature provides students with an overview of where the chapter fits within the whole course.

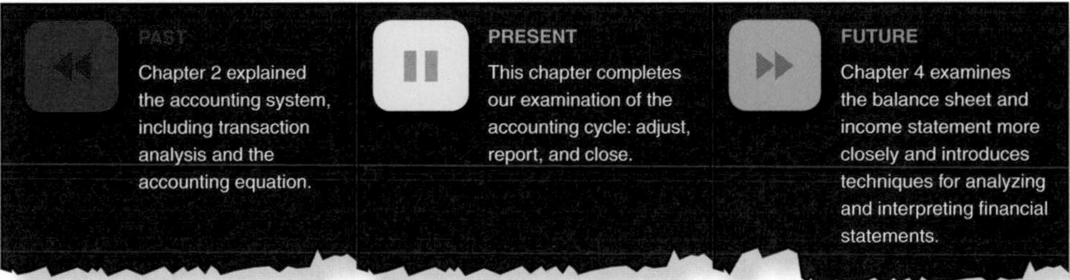

PAST
Chapter 2 explained the accounting system, including transaction analysis and the accounting equation.
PRESENT
This chapter completes our examination of the accounting cycle: adjust, report, and close.
FUTURE
Chapter 4 examines the balance sheet and income statement more closely and introduces techniques for analyzing and interpreting financial statements.

Mapping Each Chapter

Each chapter begins with a Road Map highlighting the chapter's learning objectives and corresponding eLecture videos, Guided Example videos, and assignments. The Chapter Organization chart provides an overview that visually depicts the layout of the chapter.

Road Map

LO	Learning Objective	Page	eLecture	Review	Assignments
LO1	**Discuss the nature of long-lived assets.**	259	E8-1	8.1	SE1, E1, P1, P4, P8
LO2	**Discuss the nature of depreciation, illustrate three depreciation methods, and explain impairment losses.**	261	E8-2	8.2	SE2, SE3, SE4, E2, P2, P3, P4, P8
LO3	**Discuss the distinction between revenue expenditures and capital expenditures.**	267	E8-3	8.3	E3, P4, P8
LO4	**Explain the accounting for disposals of property, plant and equipment.**	269	E8-4	8.4	SE5, SE11, E4, P5
LO5	**Discuss the nature of intangible assets.**	271	E8-5	8.5	SE6, SE7, E5, P6
LO6	**Illustrate the balance sheet presentation of long-lived assets.**	274	E8-6	8.6	SE12, E7, P7
LO7	**Define the return on assets ratio and the asset turnover ratio and explain their use.**	275	E8-7	8.7	SE8, SE9, SE10, E6

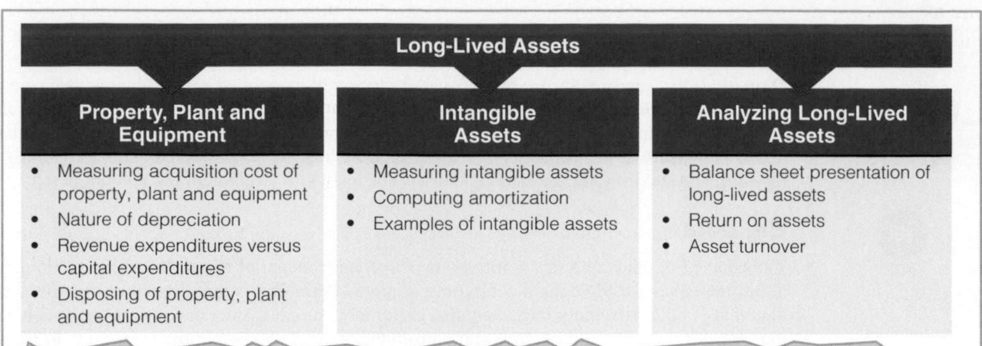

Review

Review boxes are integrated throughout each chapter as a means of reinforcing the material just presented. Solutions are provided at the end of the chapter so students can check their work. The reviews are also illustrated through "Guided Example" videos accessible directly from the eBook and via MBC.

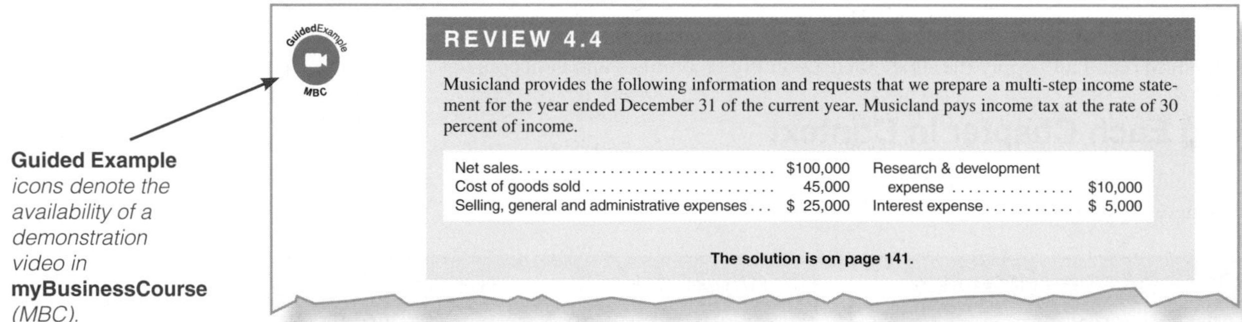

REVIEW 4.4

Musicland provides the following information and requests that we prepare a multi-step income statement for the year ended December 31 of the current year. Musicland pays income tax at the rate of 30 percent of income.

Net sales	$100,000	Research & development expense	$10,000
Cost of goods sold	45,000	Interest expense	$ 5,000
Selling, general and administrative expenses	$ 25,000		

The solution is on page 141.

Guided Example *icons denote the availability of a demonstration video in* **myBusinessCourse** *(MBC).*

A.K.A. Sidebars

A.K.A. (Also Known As) notations inform students of commonly used alternative terms that they may encounter.

Stockholders' equity is the residual ownership interest in the assets of a business after its liabilities have been paid off. The stockholders' equity of a corporation is divided into two main categories: amounts invested by stockholders (common stock) and the cumulative net income of a business that has not yet been distributed to its stockholders as a dividend (retained earnings).

A.K.A. Stockholders' equity is also referred to as *shareholders' equity*.

Takeaways

These in-chapter summaries ensure that students grasp key concepts before proceeding to the next topic.

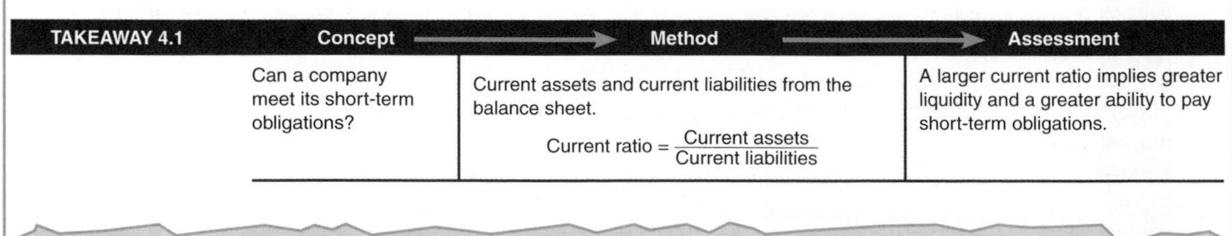

TAKEAWAY 4.1	Concept	Method	Assessment
	Can a company meet its short-term obligations?	Current assets and current liabilities from the balance sheet. $\text{Current ratio} = \frac{\text{Current assets}}{\text{Current liabilities}}$	A larger current ratio implies greater liquidity and a greater ability to pay short-term obligations.

Ethics

In today's post-Sarbanes-Oxley world, ethical decision-making has never been more pertinent to business and students studying accounting. We discuss ethics where appropriate in the text, and we have included at least one assignment in each chapter that raises an ethical issue. Assignments involving ethics are identified by the icon in the margin.

BTN3-7. **Accounting Ethics Case** It is the end of an accounting year for Juliet Kravetz, controller of a medium-sized, publicly held corporation specializing in toxic waste cleanup. Within the corporation, only Kravetz and the president know that the firm has been negotiating for several months to land a very large contract for waste cleanup in Western Europe. The president has hired another firm with excellent contacts in Western Europe to help with the negotiations. The outside firm charges an hourly fee plus expenses but has agreed not to submit a bill until the negotiations are in their final stages (expected to occur in another three to four months). Even if the contract falls through, the outside firm is entitled to receive payment for its services. Based

THINKING GLOBALLY

Thinking Globally inserts emphasize the similarities and differences in accounting practices between the United States and other countries.

THINKING GLOBALLY

U.S. GAAP and IFRS are substantially aligned when it comes to the reporting of liabilities. Under both accounting systems, for example, current liabilities (Accounts Payable) are reported at their settlement or future value, or the amount of money required to satisfy the obligation when it becomes due. Similarly, both systems require that long-term liabilities, like Bonds Payable, be reported at their present value, or the amount of money necessary to currently satisfy the obligation. Where the two systems diverge is in regards to the reporting of some contingent liabilities (to be discussed shortly).

NEW TO THIS EDITION

- **myBusinessCourse:** We have increased the number of assignments and videos in myBusinessCourse (MBC).
- **Chapter 1 has been updated:** Due to the increasing interest in data analysis technology, the section on Big Data has been expanded to include discussion and descriptions of Business Intelligence, Data Analytics, and Data Visualization. In order to eliminate redundancies, the Conceptual Framework appendix has been removed from this chapter and much of that discussion is now included in Chapter 4.
- **Chapter 2 has been revised:** The horizontal worksheet used to record transactions and adjustments now includes columns that identify the impact of transactions on the income statement. This not only improves students' understanding of the spreadsheet, it also allows for an easier and more intuitive transition to the Transaction Analysis Template (TAT).
- **Chapter 3 has been revised:** The discussion of deferrals and accruals has been reorganized and refined. Students should now find it easier to conceptually link these concepts to the end-of-period adjustments shown in the examples.
- **Chapter 8 has been revised:** The straight-line depreciation method is now emphasized as the depreciation method used by most companies, while discussion of the declining balance and units of production methods have been retained along with numerical examples and end of chapter materials.
- **Chapter 9 has been expanded:** Discussion of the amortization of bond discounts and premiums has been expanded to include a section on the straight-line method. The expanded section includes numerical examples and new end of chapter materials. The discussion and examples of the effective interest method have been retained.
- **Chapter 10 has been expanded:** The discussion of stock repurchases has been expanded to include discussion of the retirement of stock. This reflects a current trend in which many companies are retiring stock rather than holding the repurchased stock in treasury.
- **Chapter 12 has been revised:** The summary of the ratios is better integrated with the rest of the text by including a reference to the chapter of original discussion for each ratio.
- **Appendix C has been revised:** The debit and credit discussion of adjusting entries has been reorganized to reflect and mirror the adjustments in Chapter 3.
- **Appendix D has been revised:** The accounting for investment securities has been updated to include the most recent authoritative pronouncements (ASU 2016-01).
- For an expanded introduction to Data Analytics and Blockchain Technology, we added a new **Appendix F** that provides more detail and assignments that require the use of Excel and Tableau.

TECHNOLOGY THAT IMPROVES LEARNING AND COMPLEMENTS FACULTY INSTRUCTION

95% of students who used MBC, responded that MBC helped them learn accounting.*

myBusinessCourse is an online learning and assessment program intended to complement your textbook and faculty instruction. Access to **myBusinessCourse** is FREE ONLY with the purchase of a new textbook, but access can be purchased separately.

MBC is ideal for faculty seeking opportunities to augment their course with an online component. MBC is also a turnkey solution for online courses. The following are some of the features of MBC.

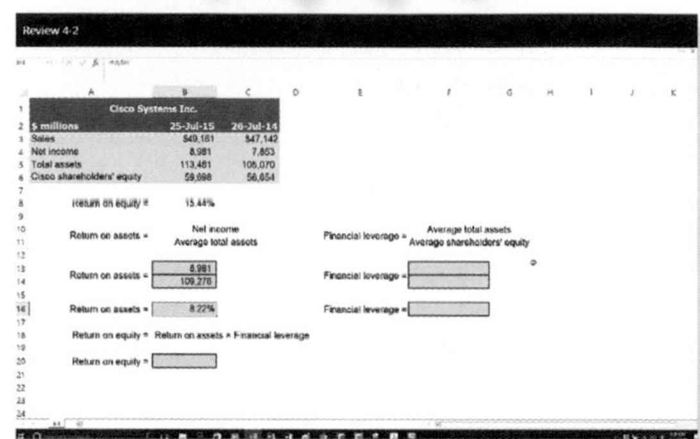

Increase Student Readiness

- **eLectures** cover each chapter's learning objectives and concepts. Consistent with the text and created by the authors, these videos are ideal for remediation and online instruction.
- **Guided Examples** are narrated video demonstrations created by the authors that show students how to solve select problems from the textbook.
- Immediate feedback with **auto-graded homework**.
- **Test Bank** questions that can be incorporated into your assignments.
- Instructor **gradebook** with immediate grade results.

86% of students said they would encourage their professor to continue using MBC in future terms.*

Make Instruction Needs-Based

- Identify where your students are struggling and customize your instruction to address their needs.
- Gauge how your entire class or individual students are performing by viewing the easy-to-use gradebook.
- Ensure your students are getting the additional reinforcement and direction they need between class meetings.

Provide Instruction and Practice 24/7

- Assign homework from your Cambridge Business Publishers' textbook and have MBC grade it for you automatically.
- With our Videos, your students can revisit accounting topics as often as they like or until they master the topic.
- Make homework due before class to ensure students enter your classroom prepared.
- For an additional fee, upgrade MBC to include the eBook and you have all the tools needed for an online course.

Integrate with LMS

myBusinessCourse integrates with many learning management systems, including **Canvas**, **Blackboard**, **Moodle**, **D2L**, **Schoology**, and **Sakai**. Your gradebooks sync automatically.

ADDITIONAL RESOURCES

Financial Accounting Bootcamp

This interactive tutorial is intended for use in programs that either require or would like to offer a preterm tutorial that creates a baseline of accounting knowledge for students with little to no prior exposure to financial accounting. This product can be used as a refresher of topics introduced in the first financial accounting course. It is designed as an asynchronous, interactive, self-paced experience for students. Available Learning Modules (You Select) follow.

---

* These statistics are based on the results of two surveys in which 2,330 students participated.

1. Introducing Financial Accounting (approximate completion time 2 hours)
2. Constructing Financial Statements (approximate completion time 4 hours)
3. Adjusting Entries and Completing the Accounting Cycle (approximate completion time 4 hours)
4. Reporting and Analyzing Cash Flows (approximate completion time 3.5 hours)
5. Analyzing and Interpreting Financial Statements (approximate completion time 3.5 hours)
6. Excel and Time-Value of Money Basics (approximate completion time 2 hours)

This is a separate, saleable item. Contact your sales representative to receive more information or email customerservice@cambridgepub.com.

Companion Casebook

Cases in Financial Reporting, 8th edition by Michael Drake (Brigham Young University), Ellen Engel (University of Illinois—Chicago), D. Eric Hirst (University of Texas—Austin), and Mary Lea McAnally (Texas A&M University). This book comprises 27 cases and is a perfect companion book for faculty interested in exposing students to a wide range of real financial statements. The cases are current and cover companies from Japan, Sweden, Austria, the Netherlands, the UK, India, as well as from the United States. Many of the U.S. companies are major multinationals. Each case deals with a specific financial accounting topic within the context of one (or more) company's financial statements. Each case contains financial statement information and a set of directed questions pertaining to one or two specific financial accounting issues. This is a separate, saleable casebook (ISBN 978-1-61853-122-3). Contact your sales representative to receive a desk copy or email customerservice@cambridgepub.com.

TEACHING SUPPLEMENTS

Solutions Manual: Created by the authors, the solutions manual contains complete solutions to all assignments.

Test Bank: Written by the authors, the test bank includes multiple choice items, true/false, exercises, and problems.

PowerPoint: Created by the authors, the PowerPoint slides outline key elements of each chapter.

myBusinessCourse: An online learning and assessment program intended to complement your textbook and classroom instruction (see page x for more details.) Access to myBusinessCourse is FREE with the purchase of a new textbook and can also be purchased separately.

ACKNOWLEDGMENTS

This book benefited greatly from the valuable feedback of focus group attendees, reviewers, students, and colleagues. We are extremely grateful to them for their help in making this project a success.

Tony Aaron
Robert Bloom
Bryan Bouchard
Carolyn Callahan
Cheryl Corke
Amanda Cromartie
Somnath Das
Doris Donovan
Stephan Fafatas
Susan Ferguson
Charlene Foley-Deno
Michael Gallagher
Charles Goodman
Rita Grant
Darla Honn
Bambi Hora
Julie Huang
Vicki Jobst
Staci Kenno
Michael Maier
Ariel Markelevich
Mary Lea McAnally
Susan Minke
Joseph Onyeocha
Timothy Pearson
Pamela Rouse
Bruce Samuelson
Delvin Seawright
Kevin Smith
Nancy Snow
Daria Squyres
Hakjoon Song
George Starbuck
Mark Vargas
Scott Whisenant
Gayle Williams
Scott White
Ivy Zhang

In addition, we are grateful to George Werthman, Lorraine Gleeson, Jill Sternard, Marnee Fieldman, Dana Zieman, Jocelyn Mousel, Debbie McQuade, Terry McQuade, and the entire team at Cambridge Business Publishers for their encouragement, enthusiasm, and guidance. Feedback is always welcome. Please feel free to contact us with your suggestions or questions.

Mark DeFond
January 2022

Brief Contents

Contents

Chapter 4
Understanding Accounting Information 108

Chapter 5
Internal Control and Cash 144

Chapter 6
Receivables 178

Chapter 7
Inventory 214

Chapter 8
Long-Lived Assets 256

Chapter 9
Liabilities 290

Chapter 10
Stockholders' Equity 334

Chapter 11
Statement of Cash Flows 372

Chapter 12
Analysis and Interpretation of Financial Statements 414

Appendix A
Columbia Sportswear: Financial Statements A-1

Appendix B
Under Armour Financial Statements B-1

Appendix C
The Language of Accountants: Debits and Credits C-1

Appendix D
Accounting for Investments and Consolidated Financial Statements D-1

CHAPTER

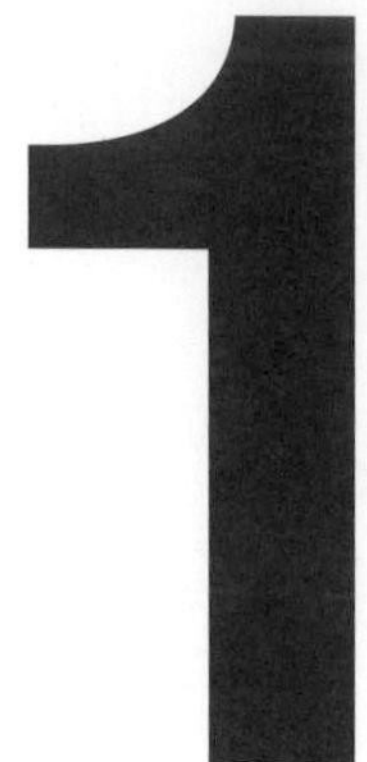

Financial Accounting and Business Decisions

Past/Present/Future *provides an overview of where the chapter fits within the context of the whole book.*

PRESENT

This chapter explains business formation, the use and users of accounting information, the types of activities companies pursue, and financial statements that report on businesses.

FUTURE

The next chapters more fully explain financial statements, including how they are prepared, constructed, analyzed, and interpreted.

A **Focus Company** *provides business context for the topics introduced in each chapter.*

WHAT THE NUMBERS MEAN

If it's true that accounting is the language of business, then this textbook is crucial to your future livelihood. All of us confront accounting issues in our daily lives. We must control our cash, monitor our paychecks, and live within our budgets.

It is no surprise then that businesses such as **Columbia Sportswear Company** (Columbia.com), a maker of clothing for dedicated lovers of the greater outdoors, must also rely upon accounting for its success. It uses financial reports to judge its performance and that of its managers. It uses accounting controls to monitor its inventory. Accounting impacts not only our lives, but also the business activities of all companies worldwide.

This first chapter introduces the basic relations and principles underlying financial accounting reports. It also identifies many key users of accounting information and how that information is useful in businesses globally.

*The **Road Map** summarizes each chapter's resources and categorizes them by learning objective.*

***eLectures** are videos available in MBC that provide 3-5 minute reviews of each learning objective.*

***Assignments** reinforce learning and can be completed by hand or within MBC.*

Road Map

LO	Learning Objective	Page	eLecture	Review	Assignments
LO1	**Explain business organization and its three forms.**	4	E1-1	1.1	SE1, E1, P1
LO2	**Describe business activities.**	5	E1-2	1.2	SE5, SE10, E6
LO3	**Indicate who uses accounting information.**	6	E1-3	1.3 & 1.4	SE3, SE8, E3, E14, P8
LO4	**Explain the accounting process and generally accepted accounting principles.**	10	E1-4	1.5	SE2, SE4, SE9, E2, E5, E15
LO5	**Describe the accounting equation and each financial statement.**	12	E1-5	1.6	SE6, SE11, SE12, SE13, SE14, E4, E7, E8, E9, E10, E11, E12, P2, P3, P4, P5, P6, P7, P9, P10, P11
LO6	**Explain additional disclosures that accompany financial statements.**	18	E1-6	1.7	SE7, E13, P11
LO7	**Discuss technology in accounting.**	20	E1-7	1.8	SE15, SE16

Learning Objectives *identify the key learning goals of the chapter.*

***Reviews** follow each learning objective and require students to apply what they have just learned. **Guided Examples** videos accompany many of the Reviews and demonstrate how to solve various types of problems. The videos are available in MBC.*

Chapter Organization charts visually depict the key topics and their sequence within the chapter.

Financial Accounting and Business Decisions

Forms of Business Organization	Activities of Business	Accounting Information and Its Use	Information Dissemination	Annual Report Components	Accounting and Technology
• Sole proprietorship • Partnership • Corporation	• Financing activities • Investing activities • Operating activities	• External users of accounting • Internal users of accounting • Business ethics and accounting	• Accounting process • Generally Accepted Accounting Principles • International Financial Reporting Standards	• Financial statements • Management's Discussion and Analysis • Notes to financial statements • Independent auditor's report	• Business intelligence (BI) • Data analytics and data visualization • Big data • Blockchain

Learning *Objectives are repeated at the start of the section covering that topic.*

LO1 Explain business organization and its three forms.

eLecture icons denote the availability of an instructional video in **myBusinessCourse** *(MBC). See the Preface for more on MBC.*

Key Terms *are highlighted in bold, red font.*

BUSINESS ORGANIZATION

The three principal forms of business organization are the:

- Sole proprietorship
- Partnership
- Corporation

Although each of these organizational forms is treated as an accounting entity, only the corporation is viewed under the law as a legal entity separate and distinct from its owners.

A **sole proprietorship** is a business owned by one person. It is the simplest and most common form of business organization. The primary advantage of the sole proprietorship is its ease of formation. As the only owner, the sole proprietor makes all of the decisions affecting the business. Sole proprietorships also enjoy an important income tax advantage relative to corporations in that the income of the business is not taxed; instead, its income is included as part of the owner's income that is reported to the taxation authorities. A disadvantage of sole proprietorships is that the owner has "unlimited liability" for the debts of the business. This means that if the business does not have enough assets to meet its obligations, its creditors are able to claim the owner's personal assets.

A **partnership** is a voluntary association of two or more persons for the purpose of conducting a business. The principal difference between a partnership and a proprietorship is the number of owners. Partnerships are also easy to create. Because a partnership involves multiple owners, it is important that the partners clearly establish the rights and obligations of each partner to avoid any misunderstandings that might lead to disputes and lawsuits. An advantage of the partnership form over the sole proprietorship is the broader skill set that multiple partners can bring to a business. Partnerships also enjoy the same income tax advantage as sole proprietorships. Like sole proprietorships, a disadvantage of partnerships is that they impose unlimited liability on their owners.

A **corporation** is a legal entity created under the laws of a state or the federal government. The owners of a corporation receive shares of stock as evidence of their ownership interest in the business, and consequently are referred to as **stockholders** (or *shareholders*). Since corporations are a separate legal entity, they must pay income taxes on any earned profits. This leads to double taxation because the income of the corporation is taxed and stockholders also pay taxes on dividends they receive from the corporation. A major advantage of corporations is "limited liability" for the stockholders. Creditors of the corporation have no claim on the assets of the stockholders, so stockholders are only liable for the amount of their investment. The corporation is the dominant organizational form in terms of the volume of business activity conducted in the United States and worldwide.

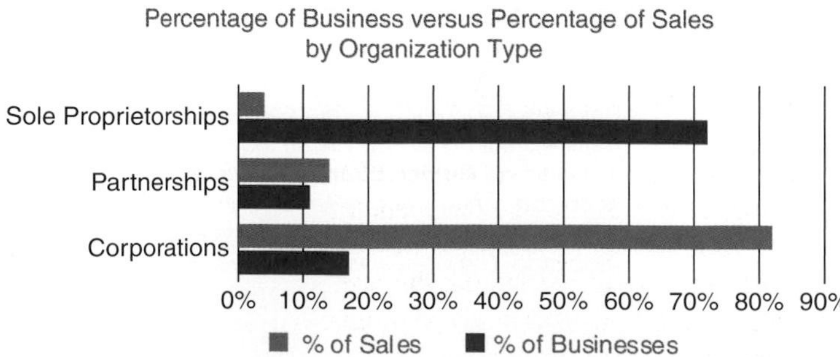

Source: Recent IRS Statistics

While most businesses start off as either a sole proprietorship or a partnership, some outgrow these organizational forms and convert to the corporate form. For example, the **Columbia Sportswear Company** was incorporated in 1961 after beginning as a sole proprietorship in 1938. One advantage of converting a sole proprietorship or a partnership to the corporate form of business is the limited liability afforded to stockholders. Another advantage of the corporate form is the relative ease of transferring ownership. Stock exchanges, such as the **New York Stock Exchange (NYSE)**, exist to enable stockholders of publicly traded corporations to readily buy and sell their ownership shares. No such exchanges exist for sole proprietors or partners, and thus, selling an ownership interest in a sole proprietorship or a partnership is a more difficult, time-consuming event.

Proprietorship	Partnership	Corporation

• One owner controlled	• Shared owner control	• All types of owner control
• Business not taxed, but owner taxed	• Business not taxed, but owners taxed	• Business taxed **and** owners taxed
• Unlimited liability for owner	• Unlimited liability for owners	• Limited liability for owners
• Relatively difficult to transfer ownership and raise new capital	• Relatively difficult to transfer ownership and raise new capital	• Relatively easy to transfer ownership and raise new capital

REVIEW 1.1

Identify two characteristics for each of the three principal forms of business organizations.

1. sole proprietorship **2.** partnership **3.** corporation

The solution is on page 37.

ACTIVITIES OF A BUSINESS

Every business, regardless of its organizational form, its industry, or its size, is involved in three types of business activities:

- Operating
- Investing
- Financing

Operating Activities

The day-to-day activities of producing and selling a product or providing a service are referred to as **operating activities**. Operating activities refer to the activities the business engages in to produce profits for the owners. Operations are critical, because if a company is unable to generate profits from its operations, the business eventually will fail. If creditors and stockholders do not believe that a company is able to generate a profit, they are unlikely to provide the financing needed to start, or maintain, its operations.

Investing Activities

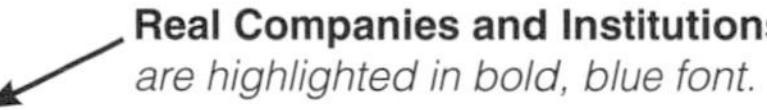

Real Companies and Institutions
are highlighted in bold, blue font.

For a company to undertake its business, it needs to purchase long-term resources necessary to conduct its business. For example, **Starbucks** must purchase equipment to roast its coffee. Purchases of these resources are known as **investing activities**. Companies can obtain the money needed to make an investment in such items as land, buildings, and equipment from either the financing activities discussed below or from cash that is accumulated from running the business profitably.

Most investing activities involve acquisition and disposition of items used to carry out the business plan, such as factories, office furniture, computer and data systems, and delivery vehicles. These items are referred to as *assets*. Investing decisions regarding these assets are known as *asset management*.

Financing Activities

Before a company can begin operations, it must acquire cash to support its operations. The company may need to hire employees, build or lease a work place, purchase inventory or raw materials, and engage in other start-up activities, all of which require cash. Companies can obtain the necessary funds to undertake these activities in several ways. These **financing activities** are generally categorized as either debt financing or equity financing.

Debt financing involves borrowing money from sources such as a bank by signing a note payable, or directly from investors by issuing bonds payable. The individuals and financial institutions that lend money to companies are called their **creditors**. Debt financing involves an obligation to repay a creditor both the amount initially borrowed, called the **principal**, and a fee for the use of the funds, referred to as **interest**.

Equity financing involves selling shares of stock to investors. In contrast to creditors who lend money to a business and expect to receive that money back with interest, investors who purchase shares of stock are actually buying an ownership interest in the company. Investors hope that their stock will increase in value so that they can earn a profit when the stocks are sold. Stockholders may also receive **dividend** payments when the company decides to distribute some of its net income.

Exhibit 1-1 provides a summary of the three types of business activities. Arrows are pointing both toward, and away from, operating activities. This is because financing and investing activities are necessary to carry out a company's operating activities; however, if a company's operating activities generate excess cash, then the excess cash can be used to either finance additional investments or repay the company's creditors.

EXHIBIT 1-1 Business Activities

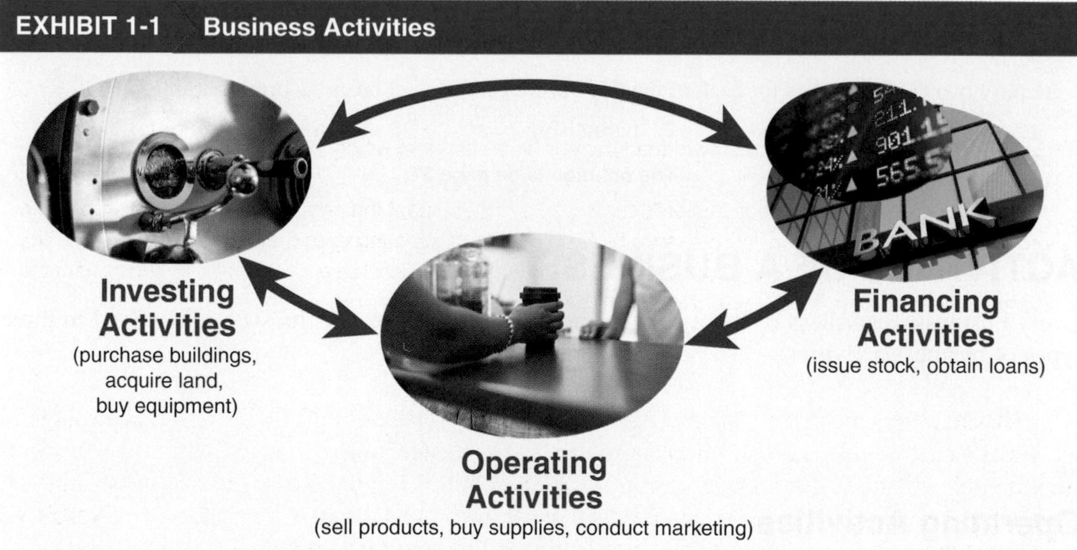

REVIEW 1.2

Classify each of the following activities as a financing, investing, or operating activity.

1. Receiving a loan from a bank.
2. Selling merchandise online.
3. Purchasing a delivery truck.
4. Purchasing merchandise for resale to customers.
5. Issuing shares of stock in exchange for cash.
6. Paying employee salaries.

The solution is on page 37.

LO3 Indicate who uses accounting information.

ACCOUNTING INFORMATION AND ITS USE

Accounting can be defined as the process of measuring the economic activity of an entity in monetary terms and communicating the results to users. In today's society, many individuals and agencies are involved in the economic life of a business. The information needs of these parties are fulfilled, in part, by accounting information. Information users are classified by their relation to a business as either *external users* or *internal users*.

External Users of Accounting

An important function of the accounting process is to report financial information that details a business's results of operations, cash flows, and financial position. U.S. publicly owned corporations are required by law to publish financial statements annually and quarterly. Accounting information that is designed for use by external users is referred to as **financial accounting**.

Financial accounting information serves a variety of users. Potential investors and investment professionals find financial accounting information useful in making investment decisions. Creditors use financial statements to assess the financial strength of a business before lending it funds, and stockholders use it to evaluate whether to remain invested in a business, buy more shares, or sell their existing shares of stock.

The financial statements issued by a company are the main source of financial information for these external users. Because financial statements are typically used to evaluate the management team running the business, their objectivity is sometimes called into question because the reports are prepared by the management team itself. To provide assurances that the information is credible, publicly held corporations are required to have their financial statements audited by an independent public accountant. The independent public accountant, or independent auditor, examines the systems and procedures that produce financial statements and expresses a professional opinion as to whether the financial statements are "fairly presented in conformity with generally accepted accounting principles." External users have greater confidence in financial statements that have been audited by an independent certified public accountant (CPA).

Accounting in Practice *boxes describe how accounting is used in real companies.*

ACCOUNTING IN PRACTICE

The Big Four Independent auditors are licensed by the state in which they do their auditing work and are identified as **certified public accountants (CPAs)**. To qualify as a CPA, an individual must pass a rigorous examination that is administered nationally and must meet the educational and work experience requirements set by each state to ensure high standards of accounting and auditing performance. The four largest U.S. public accounting firms, referred to as the *Big Four*, have offices located throughout the world and employ thousands of auditors. These firms are **PricewaterhouseCoopers**, **Deloitte**, **Ernst & Young**, and **KPMG**.

There are many other external users of a company's accounting information. For example, a business's customers may want information to help them determine if a company like **Whirlpool** will be able to honor its product warranties. Labor unions require information to determine the level of pay raises that they can demand from companies like **United Parcel Service**. **Exhibit 1-2** illustrates the kind of accounting information that is required by a company's external users.

EXHIBIT 1-2 Accounting Information Needs of External Users

User Group	Accounting Information Needed to Answer Questions such as:
Potential investors and stockholders	How does the profitability of **Target** compare to that of **Walmart**? How does **Bank of America** compare with **Wells Fargo** in terms of firm size?
Creditors and lenders	Will **Tesla Motors** be able to repay its creditors in a timely fashion? Is it safe to provide a bank loan to **FedEx**?
Customers and suppliers	Will **AECOM** remain solvent long enough to complete construction of our downtown highrise? Is it safe to make sales to **Best Buy** on credit?

Internal Users of Accounting

A major function of accounting is to provide the internal management with the information needed for decision-making. While managers have an interest in the information reported to external users in the financial statements, managers also require additional information, such as the cost of its products, estimates of the income to be earned from a sales campaign, cost comparisons of alternative courses of action, and long-range budgets. Because of the strategic nature of much of this information, it is usually only available to top-level management and is not included in the financial statements issued to external users. Accounting information that is designed for use by managers within the company is referred to as **managerial accounting**. **Exhibit 1-3** illustrates the various types of accounting information that are required by a company's internal users.

EXHIBIT 1-3 Accounting Information Needs of Internal Users

User Group		Accounting Information Needed to Address Questions such as:
Marketing Department		What is the optimal price to sell the Samsung Galaxy phone to maximize the company's profits? Has Steph Curry's endorsement contract with Under Armour been successful in promoting the company's brand?
Management Team		How much is Taco Bell, the fast food restaurant chain, contributing to the overall profitability of its parent company, the YUM! Brands? What is the projected profitability of General Motors's Chevrolet Bolt EV brand for the coming year?
Finance Department		Is there sufficient cash available for Hewlett Packard to buy back a large amount of its outstanding common stock? Will General Electric have sufficient cash flow to pay its short-term expenses?

REVIEW 1.3

1. Are financial statements the main source of financial information for external or internal users of accounting information? Explain.
2. Identify at least two internal users and explain why they need accounting information.
3. Identify at least two external users and explain why they need accounting information.

The solution is on page 37.

Hints *help explain difficult concepts.*

Hint: *To find out more about the AICPA's Professional Code of Conduct see https://www.aicpa.org/research/standards/codeofconduct.html*

Ethics and Accounting

Ethics deals with the values, rules, and justifications that govern one's way of life. Although fundamental ethical concepts such as right and wrong, good and evil, justice and morality are abstract, many issues in our daily lives have ethical dimensions. The way that we respond to these issues defines our ethical profile. In both our personal and our professional lives, our goal is to act ethically and responsibly.

Ethical behavior has not always been the rule in business. Business history reveals unethical activities such as using inside information for personal gain, paying bribes to government officials for favors, ignoring health and safety regulations, selling arms and military equipment to aggressor governments, polluting the environment, and issuing misleading financial information. Recent accounting scandals at such companies as Enron, WorldCom, and Lehman Brothers are examples of companies that engaged in unethical behavior by issuing fraudulent or misleading financial statements.

Increasingly, business managers recognize the importance and value of ethical behavior by their employees. It is now commonplace for businesses to develop a written code of ethics to help guide the behavior of employees. Similarly, professional organizations of accountants have written ethics codes. The **American Institute of Certified Public Accountants (AICPA)**, for example, has a professional code of ethics to guide the conduct of its member CPAs. Similarly, the **Institute of Management Accountants (IMA)** has written standards of ethical conduct for accountants employed in the private sector.

A.K.A *(Also Known As) identify commonly used alternative terms.*

Unethical behavior that results in misleading financial statements such as those at Enron and WorldCom has the potential to erode public confidence and trust in accounting information. In response to this decline in public confidence, the U.S. Congress passed the **Sarbanes-Oxley Act** in 2002 with the goal of restoring investor trust by reducing the likelihood of future accounting scandals. Among the many changes required by this legislation is that a company's top management must certify in writing that the financial statements are "fairly presented," and these executives risk criminal prosecution for fraudulent certification. In addition, companies must now report on the effectiveness of the company's internal controls, which are designed to prevent errors in the financial reporting process and to detect them should they occur. In the years since SOX was enacted, researchers have found that compliance with required internal control measures has resulted in fewer financial statement restatements. A 2017 poll found that 85% of CFOs believe their companies have benefited from the internal control measures mandated by SOX.

A.K.A. The *Sarbanes-Oxley Act* of 2002 is often referred to as SOX.

Accounting Ethics *boxes discuss ethical issues relevant to the material being discussed.*

ACCOUNTING ETHICS

Accountant as Detective—CSI in Real Life Law enforcement personnel are not the only people who perform criminal investigations. A branch of accounting known as **forensic accounting** is vitally important in many types of criminal investigations, from financial statement fraud, to money laundering, to massive investment frauds such as the one perpetrated by Bernard Madoff (who was sentenced to a 150-year prison term).

The financial reporting environment is characterized by several factors that pose a threat to ethical accounting. These threats include the following:

1. Management Pressures: Management may impose pressure on the accountant to "improve" the reported results. The amount of a bonus to be received by an employee and the amount of money to be distributed to a business's owners are examples of situations in which the financial implications can lead to efforts to influence the outcome. *Ethical behavior mandates that accountants ignore these pressures.*
2. Confidentiality: Accountants have access to confidential, sensitive information. Tax returns, salary data, details of financial arrangements, planned acquisitions, and proposed price changes illustrate this type of information. *Ethical behavior mandates that accountants respect the confidentiality of information.*
3. Management Myopia: A criticism of U.S. business practices is that they focus too much on short-term profit. This orientation can lead to unethical actions by management to increase reported profits. Because accountants measure and report a firm's profit, they must be particularly concerned about these ethical breakdowns. *Both accountants and management must recognize the importance of a long-run perspective.*

REVIEW 1.4

As an accountant for the Madoff Corporation, you are responsible for measuring and reporting the company's net income. It appears that actual results are going to be less than was expected by Wall Street analysts. Your supervisor has asked that you report some of next period's sales revenue early so that the current period's net income will be in line with analyst expectations. You know that reporting revenue like this represents a violation of generally accepted accounting principles. He states that you will not really be doing anything wrong because the sales revenues are real—the company will just be reporting the revenue earlier than accounting guidelines allow. What should you do?

The solution is on page 38.

THE ACCOUNTING PROCESS

LO4 **Explain** the accounting process and generally accepted accounting principles.

eLecture MBC

As previously noted, accounting is *the process of measuring economic activity of an entity in monetary terms and communicating results to users*. The accounting process consists of two principal activities:

- Measurement
- Communication

The **measurement process** must (1) identify the relevant economic activities of a business, (2) quantify these economic activities, and (3) record the resulting measures in a systematic manner. Measurement is done in monetary terms. In the United States, measurements are stated in U.S. dollars. In other countries, measurements are expressed in the local currency. In Mexico, for example, measurements are stated in pesos, and in most European countries, they are stated in euros.

The purpose of accounting is to provide useful financial information, and the **communication process** is extremely important. Accordingly, the accounting process (1) prepares financial reports to meet the needs of the user and (2) helps interpret the financial results for that user. In order for the communication to be effective, managers must be aware of how the financial information will be used. Businesses generate significant amounts of data, both financial and non-financial, and users analyze this data through ratio analysis and trend analysis. Data visualization tools, such as charts, graphs, and maps, help users understand the trends and patterns through graphical representation.

Thinking Globally *boxes emphasize the similarities and differences in business practices between companies in the U.S. and companies in other countries.*

THINKING GLOBALLY

Companies measure their operating performance using the currency of their principal place of business. **Columbia Sportswear** is headquartered in Oregon and reports its financial results using the U.S. dollar. On the other hand, **Adidas**, the largest sportswear manufacturer in Europe, is headquartered in Germany and reports its financial results using the euro. Some companies prepare "convenience translations" of their financial statements in the currency and language of other countries so that potential foreign investors can more readily understand the company's financial performance and condition.

Generally Accepted Accounting Principles

It is important that financial statements be prepared under a common set of rules that is understood by the users of reports. Imagine if every business were free to determine exactly how it measured and communicated its financial health and operating performance. How would a user of this information be able to compare one company's results to another if each played by a different set of rules? Financial statement users expect that all companies will follow the same standards and procedures when preparing their financial statements. In the United States, these standards and procedures are called **generally accepted accounting principles (GAAP)**.

A.K.A. *Generally accepted accounting principles* are often referred to as GAAP (pronounced like the clothing store "Gap").

Generally accepted accounting principles are the standards, procedures, and rules that accountants follow when preparing financial statements. Sometimes specific accounting principles must be altered or new principles formulated to fit a changing set of economic circumstances or changes in business practices. For instance, there existed no generally accepted accounting principles to account for internet-based companies when they first emerged; and consequently, the business community had to create a set of guidelines for companies such as **Amazon.com** and **eBay** to measure and communicate their financial results.

Financial Accounting Oversight

Organizations such as the **Financial Accounting Standards Board (FASB)**, the American Institute of Certified Public Accountants (AICPA), and the **U.S. Securities and Exchange Commission (SEC)** have been instrumental in the development of generally accepted accounting principles in the United States. As a federal agency, the SEC's primary focus is to regulate the interstate sale of stocks and bonds. The SEC requires companies under its jurisdiction to submit audited annual financial statements to the agency, which are then made available to the general public. The SEC has the power to set the accounting principles used by these companies, but the agency has largely delegated that responsibility to the FASB.

The FASB is a nongovernmental entity whose pronouncements establish U.S. GAAP. (See the discussion in Chapter 4 for additional information on the conceptual framework the FASB has developed to formulate accounting standards.) The FASB[1] consists of a seven-member board and follows a process that allows for input from interested parties as it considers a new or changed accounting principle. A new or changed principle requires the support of a majority of the board members. More recently, the **Public Company Accounting Oversight Board (PCAOB)** was established by the Sarbanes-Oxley Act of 2002. The PCAOB creates auditing standards, known as **generally accepted auditing standards (GAAS)**, and monitors the quality of financial statement audits. **Exhibit 1-4** illustrates the relationships between financial accounting oversight bodies.

EXHIBIT 1-4 Financial Accounting Oversight

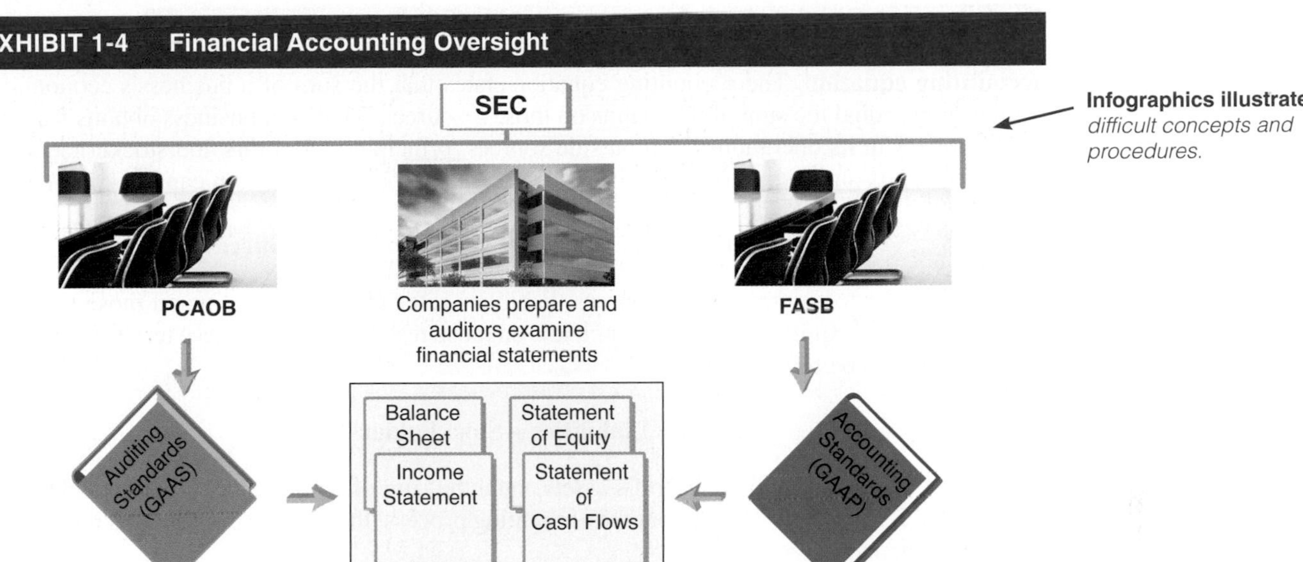

Infographics illustrate *difficult concepts and procedures.*

International Financial Reporting Standards

The increasing globalization of business over the past few decades has created a demand for a single set of accounting principles that can be used worldwide. The arguments for the need for international financial reporting standards revolve around the increase in companies raising capital in more than one country and the high cost of complying with multiple accounting standards. A common set of standards aids investors in comparing the financial performance of companies from different countries. Multinational companies with subsidiaries in multiple countries are able to lower their reporting costs by using a common set of accounting standards company-wide.

Although several organizations are working to increase international harmonization in accounting, the organization that has taken the lead in formulating international accounting principles is the **International Accounting Standards Board (IASB)**. The accounting standards formulated by the IASB are referred to as the **International Financial Reporting Standards (IFRS)**. More than 140 nations or reporting jurisdictions either require or permit the use of IFRS. This includes the European Union, Australia, New Zealand, Israel, and Canada. The United States, however, has chosen not to adopt IFRS. One reason is that many believe that making its own standards gives the United States greater flexibility in creating new standards when they are needed. However, this is a hotly debated issue, and many believe that U.S. companies and investors would be better served by adopting IFRS.

A.K.A. *International financial reporting standards* are often referred to as IFRS (pronounced "eye furs").

REVIEW 1.5

The accounting process consists of two principal activities—measurement and communication. What are the activities involved in the measurement process?

The solution is on page 38.

---

[1] Paralleling the FASB structure, the Governmental Accounting Standards Board (GASB) was organized in 1984 to formulate the generally accepted accounting principles for state and local governments.

FINANCIAL STATEMENTS

LO5 Describe the accounting equation and each financial statement.

A.K.A. The *balance sheet* is also referred to as the statement of financial position.

A.K.A. The *accounting equation* is also called the balance sheet equation.

There are four basic financial statements: the balance sheet, the income statement, the statement of stockholders' equity, and the statement of cash flows. Each financial statement begins with the name of the company, the name of the financial statement, and the date or time period of the statement.

Balance Sheet

The **balance sheet** is a listing of a firm's assets, liabilities, and stockholders' equity as of a given date, usually the end of an accounting period. The balance sheet reflects a framework called the **accounting equation**. The accounting equation states that the sum of a business's economic resources must equal the sum of the claims on those resources. That is, a business obtains resources that it utilizes in its operations from outside sources, principally creditors and stockholders, who maintain claims on those resources. Consequently, the accounting equation can be written as:

Resources of a company = Claims on the resources

Assets refer to a company's resources, liabilities refer to creditor claims on those resources, and stockholders' equity refers to owner claims on those resources. Using these terms, the accounting equation can be reformulated as:

Assets = Liabilities + Stockholders' equity

This equation states that the firm's assets equal the sum of its liabilities plus its stockholders' equity—see **Exhibit 1-5**. Throughout the accounting process, the accounting equation must always remain in balance.

EXHIBIT 1-5 Accounting Equation for a Business

Economic Terms	Resources	=	Creditor claims on resources	+	Stockholder (owner) claims on resources
Business Terms	Assets	=	Liabilities	+	Stockholders' equity

Hint: Accountants are only able to record resources with monetary values that are verifiable. There exist some assets with values that are very difficult to verify, such as the value of a company's workforce, and, therefore, are not reported on a balance sheet.

Assets are the economic resources owned by the business that can be expressed in monetary terms. Assets take many forms. Cash is an asset, as are claims to receive cash payments from customers for goods or services provided on credit, called accounts receivable. Other types of assets include inventory, supplies, land, buildings, and equipment. The key characteristic of any asset is that it represents a probable future economic benefit to a business.

Liabilities are the obligations or debts that a business must pay in cash or in goods and services at some future time as a consequence of past transactions or events. For example, a business can borrow money from a bank for six months. The business reports this obligation as a liability called notes payable. Similarly, if a business owes money to various suppliers for goods or services already provided, it is called accounts payable, or if it owes wages to its employees for work already performed, it is called wages payable. The business reports these obligations on its balance sheet.

Stockholders' equity refers to the ownership (stockholder) claims on the assets of the business. Stockholders' equity represents a *residual claim* on a business's assets; that is, it is a claim on the assets of a business that remain after all liabilities to creditors have been satisfied. For this reason, stockholders' equity is sometimes referred to as a business's **net assets**, where net assets equal the difference between the total assets and total liabilities. In equation format,

Assets − Liabilities = Stockholders' equity

and,

Net assets = Stockholders' equity

Columbia's balance sheet is shown in **Exhibit 1-6** and reports the company's assets, liabilities, and stockholders' equity. (All Columbia Sportswear amounts are in thousands of dollars.) Columbia's assets totaled $2,836,571 at year-end, with the largest asset being cash of $790,725. Total assets of $2,836,571 **(A)** are equal to the sum of liabilities $1,003,800 **(L)** and stockholders' equity $1,832,771 **(SE)**. This equality is required by the accounting equation and must always exist.

Real financial data *for focus companies illustrate key concepts of each chapter.*

EXHIBIT 1-6 Columbia Sportswear Balance Sheet

COLUMBIA SPORTSWEAR COMPANY
Balance Sheet
December 31, 2020
(In thousands)

Assets	
Cash	$ 790,725
Investments	1,224
Accounts receivable	452,945
Inventories	556,530
Prepaid expenses and other current assets	54,197
Property, plant, and equipment, net	649,036
Intangibles and other non-current assets	331,914
Total assets	$2,836,571 **(A)**
Liabilities and Stockholders' Equity	
Liabilities	
Accounts payable	$ 206,697
Income taxes payable	73,103
Other liabilities	724,000
Total liabilities	1,003,800 **(L)**
Stockholders' Equity	
Common stock	20,165
Retained earnings*	1,812,606
Total stockholders' equity	1,832,771 **(SE)**
Total liabilities and stockholders' equity	$2,836,571

*For ease of presentation, retained earnings includes accumulated other comprehensive income and non-controlling interest.

Hint: *Final totals in the financial statements are double underlined. Follow this format whenever asked to prepare a financial statement.*

Takeaways *summarize the key concepts before proceeding to the next topic.*

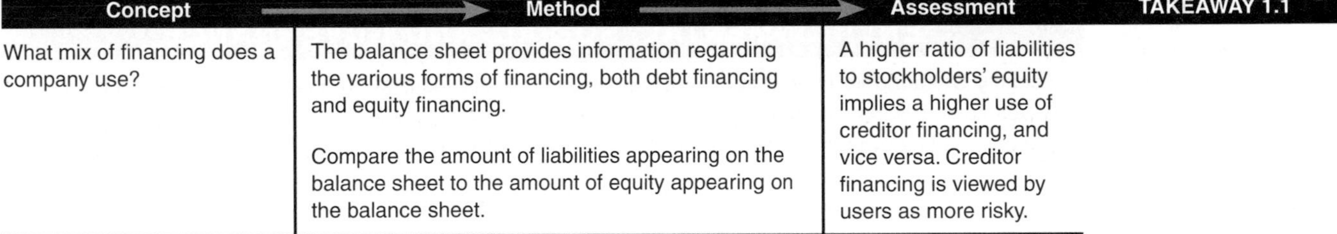

Concept	Method	Assessment	TAKEAWAY 1.1
What mix of financing does a company use?	The balance sheet provides information regarding the various forms of financing, both debt financing and equity financing. Compare the amount of liabilities appearing on the balance sheet to the amount of equity appearing on the balance sheet.	A higher ratio of liabilities to stockholders' equity implies a higher use of creditor financing, and vice versa. Creditor financing is viewed by users as more risky.	

Income Statement

The **income statement** reports the results of operations for a business for a given time period, usually a quarter or a year. The income statement lists the revenues and expenses of the business. **Sales revenues** are increases to a company's resources or decreases to its obligations that result when goods or services are provided to customers. The amount of sales revenue earned is measured by the value of the assets received in exchange for the goods or services delivered.

Expenses are decreases in a company's resources from generating revenue. Expenses are generally measured by the value of the assets used up or exchanged as a result of a business's operating activities. Common examples of expenses include the cost of the items sold, referred to as cost of goods sold, selling expenses, marketing expenses, administrative expenses, interest expense, and income taxes. When total revenue exceeds total expenses, the resulting amount is called **net income**; when total expenses exceed sales revenue, the resulting amount is called a **net loss**.

A.K.A. The *income statement* is also called the statement of operations, profit and loss statement (or P&L), the statement of income, and the earnings statement.

A.K.A. *Sales revenue* is also referred to as revenue, sales, net sales, or net revenue.

A.K.A. *Net income* is also referred to as net earnings or net profit.

Columbia's income statement is presented in **Exhibit 1-7**. The statement begins with the business's name, statement title, and time period to which the statement applies. For Columbia, total revenue for the year presented is $2,513,662 (**R**). Remember that amounts are rounded to the nearest $1,000. Next, Columbia subtracts a series of expenses totaling $2,405,649 (**E**), yielding net income of $108,013 (**NI**).

EXHIBIT 1-7 Columbia Sportswear Income Sheet

COLUMBIA SPORTSWEAR COMPANY
Income Statement
For Year Ended December 31, 2020
(In thousands)

Revenue		
Sales	$2,501,554	
Other revenue	12,108	
Total revenue	2,513,662	**(R)**
Expenses		
Cost of sales	1,277,665	
Selling, general, and administrative expense	1,098,948	
Income tax expense	31,510	
Other (income) and expenses	(2,474)	
Total expenses	2,405,649	**(E)**
Net income	$ 108,013	**(NI)**

TAKEAWAY 1.2	Concept	Method	Assessment
	Is a company profitable?	The income statement reports a company's performance for a given period of time. Deduct reported expenses from reported sales revenue.	Sales revenue in excess of expenses yields net income, which means the company is profitable. If expenses exceed revenue, the company has a net loss.

Environmental, Social, and Governance (ESG) *boxes showcase how forward-thinking companies are embracing ESG as part of their long-term business models.*

ENVIRONMENTAL, SOCIAL, AND GOVERNANCE

Socially Sustainable Investing Companies worldwide are focused on more than just the bottom line. Research shows that corporate environmental and social awareness is associated with many positive outcomes, perhaps even higher profitability. Financial statements are not designed to measure social performance. As a result, many large corporations now issue sustainability reports. Investors now look to these reports and a series of criteria known as **Environmental, Social, and Governance (ESG)** ratings when developing a sustainable investment strategy.

Statement of Stockholders' Equity

The **statement of stockholders' equity** reports the events causing an increase or decrease in a business's stockholders' equity during a given time period, including both the changes in a company's common stock and changes in its retained earnings. The statement of stockholders' equity consists of two parts—contributed capital and earned capital. **Contributed capital** is a measure of the capital contributed by the stockholders of a company when they purchase ownership shares from the company. Ownership shares are called *common shares* or *common stock*. As explained in a later chapter, a portion of the amount paid for the shares may be allocated to *additional paid-in capital*. **Earned capital** is a measure of the capital that is earned by the company, reinvested in the business, and not distributed to its stockholders. In corporations, earned capital is usually referred to as *retained earnings*.

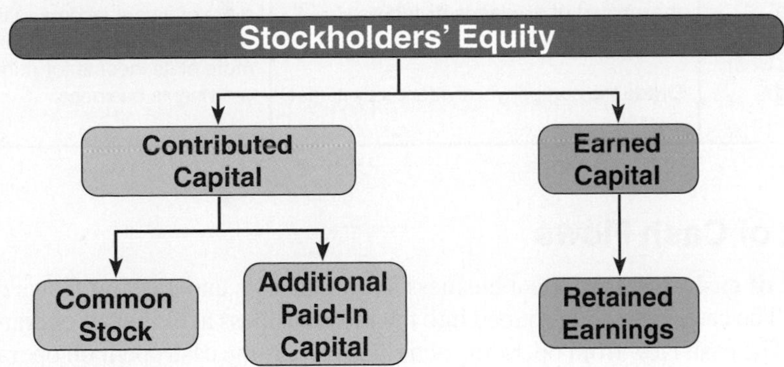

Retained earnings are increased when operations produce net income and decreased when operations produce a net loss. Retained earnings also decrease when a company pays a dividend to its stockholders. A company's retained earnings for a period are determined as follows (sometimes called *statement of retained earnings*):

Retained earnings, beginning of period	$1,844,510
Add: Net income (loss)	108,013
Less: Common stock repurchased	(127,953)
Dividends and other	(11,964)
Retained earnings, end of period	$1,812,606

Columbia's statement of stockholders' equity appears in **Exhibit 1-8**. We focus here on Columbia's retained earnings from its statement of stockholders' equity to emphasize two important concepts: (1) the relationship between the income statement and the balance sheet and (2) the factors that explain the change in retained earnings. The retained earnings column in Columbia's statement of stockholders' equity in **Exhibit 1-8** begins with its prior year ending retained earnings of $1,844,510. Its net income for the current year of $108,013 is then added. Can you find this amount on Columbia's income statement in **Exhibit 1-7**? Next, Columbia repurchased a portion of its outstanding common stock during the year, resulting in a distribution of $127,953. Additionally, the portion of earnings that was distributed to Columbia's stockholders as a dividend ($11,964) is subtracted to yield an ending retained earnings balance of $1,812,606 as of December 31. Can you find this amount on Columbia's balance sheet in **Exhibit 1-6**?

EXHIBIT 1-8 Columbia Sportswear Statement of Stockholders' Equity

COLUMBIA SPORTSWEAR COMPANY
Statement of Stockholders' Equity
For Year Ended December 31, 2020

(In thousands)	Common Stock	Retained Earnings	Total
Balance, December 31, 2019	$ 4,937	$1,844,510	$1,849,447
Add: Common stock issued	20,164		20,164
Net income		108,013	108,013
Less: Common stock repurchased	(4,936)	(127,953)	(132,889)
Dividends and other		(11,964)	(11,964)
Balance, December 31, 2020	$20,165	$1,812,606	$1,832,771

TAKEAWAY 1.3 Concept	Method	Assessment
What portion of a company's current period net income is distributed to its stockholders, and what portion is retained?	The statement of stockholders' equity reports both a company's net income and the amount of dividends distributed to stockholders. Divide the company's dividends by its net income.	A higher ratio of dividends to net income implies that a company is distributing more of its net income to its stockholders, whereas a lower ratio implies it is retaining more of its income for purposes such as growing its business.

Statement of Cash Flows

The **statement of cash flows** reports a business's cash inflows and cash outflows during a given period of time. The cash flows are grouped into the three business activities of operating, investing, and financing. The cash flow from operating activities reveals the cash spent on operating expenses and the cash received from the sale of goods or services. The cash flow from investing activities includes the cash payments and receipts when a business buys and sells long-lived assets that it uses in its operations. The cash flow from financing activities reports the issuances and repurchases of shares in the company's own business and the amounts borrowed and repaid to creditors.

Columbia's statement of cash flows is in **Exhibit 1-9**. This statement shows that Columbia's cash balance increased during the year by $104,716 from $686,009 at the beginning of the year to $790,725 at the end of the year. Can you find the ending cash balance on Columbia's balance sheet in **Exhibit 1-6**?

The statement of cash flows reveals how Columbia acquired its cash and how it was used. We see that its day-to-day operations generated operating cash flows **(OCF)** of $276,077. So if Columbia's operations generated all this cash, why did its cash balance increase by just $104,716? The statement reveals that uses of cash included investing cash flows **(ICF)** of $27,171 for investing activities and financing cash flows **(FCF)** of $144,190 for financing activities. We devote considerable time to understanding and analyzing financial statements such as those of Columbia's in later chapters.

EXHIBIT 1-9 Columbia Sportswear Statement of Cash Flows

COLUMBIA SPORTSWEAR COMPANY
Statement of Cash Flows
For Year Ended December 31, 2020
(In thousands)

Cash flows provided by operating activities	$276,077	**(OCF)**
Cash flows used in investing activities	(27,171)	**(ICF)**
Cash flows used in financing activities	(144,190)	**(FCF)**
Net increase (decrease) in cash	104,716	
Cash at beginning of year	686,009	
Cash at end of year	$790,725	

TAKEAWAY 1.4 Concept	Method	Assessment
What are the major sources and uses of a company's cash?	The statement of cash flows reports a company's sources and uses of cash separated into three activities: operating, investing, and financing. Identify a company's sources and uses of cash as reported in the statement of cash flows.	Sources of cash are reported as positive numbers and uses of cash as negative numbers. Larger positive numbers represent major cash sources and larger negative numbers represent major cash uses.

Relations Among the Financial Statements

The income statement, the statement of stockholders' equity, the balance sheet, and the statement of cash flows are linked to one another. That is, the financial statements *articulate*. To illustrate the linkages, refer to the financial statements of Columbia Sportswear in **Exhibit 1-10**. Observe that:

Ⓐ The company's net income (or net loss) for a period is an input to the statement of stockholders' equity.

Ⓑ The ending common stock, retained earnings, and total equity are inputs to the balance sheet.

Ⓒ The statement of cash flows explains the change in the cash balance on the balance sheet for a period.

EXHIBIT 1-10 Financial Statements for Columbia Sportswear Company

Columbia Sportswear Company
Income Statement
For Year Ended December 31, 2020

Revenue	
Sales	$2,501,554
Other revenue	12,108
Total revenue	2,513,662
Expenses	
Cost of sales	1,277,665
Selling, general, and administrative	1,098,948
Income tax expense	31,510
Other (income) and expenses	(2,474)
Total expenses	2,405,649
Net income	$ 108,013 Ⓐ

Columbia Sportswear Company
Statement of Stockholders' Equity
For Year Ended December 31, 2020

(in thousands)	Common Stock	Retained Earnings	Total
Balance, December 31, 2019	$ 4,937	$1,844,510	$1,849,447
Add: Common stock issued	20,164		20,164
Net income		108,013	108,013
Less: Common stock repurchased	(4,936)	(127,953)	(132,889)
Dividends and other		(11,964)	(11,964)
Balance, December 31, 2020	$20,165	$1,812,606	$1,832,771

Columbia Sportswear Company
Balance Sheet
December 31, 2020

Assets		**Liabilities**	
Cash	$ 790,725	Accounts payable	$ 206,697
Investments	1,224	Income taxes payable	73,103
Accounts receivable	452,945	Other liabilities	724,000
Inventories	556,530	Total liabilities	1,003,800
Prepaid expenses and other current assets	54,197	**Stockholders' Equity**	
Property, plant, and equipment, net	649,036	Common stock	20,165 Ⓑ
Intangibles and other non-current assets	331,914	Retained earnings	1,812,606 Ⓑ
		Total stockholders' equity	1,832,771 Ⓑ
Total assets	$2,836,571	Total liabilities and stockholders' equity	$2,836,571

Columbia Sportswear Company
Statement of Cash Flows
For Year Ended December 31, 2020

Cash flows provided by operating activities	$276,077
Cash flows used in investing activities	(27,171)
Cash flows used in financing activities	(144,190)
Net increase (decrease) in cash	104,716
Cash at beginning of year	686,009
Cash at end of year Ⓒ	$790,725

Three of these financial statements present information covering a specific period of time: the income statement, the statement of stockholders' equity, and the statement of cash flows. For this reason, these financial statements are referred to as **period-of-time statements**. In contrast, the balance sheet reports information as of a specific date. The balance sheet, therefore, is referred to as a **point-in-time statement**. **Exhibit 1-11** illustrates these links across time.

EXHIBIT 1-11 Financial Statement Links Across Time

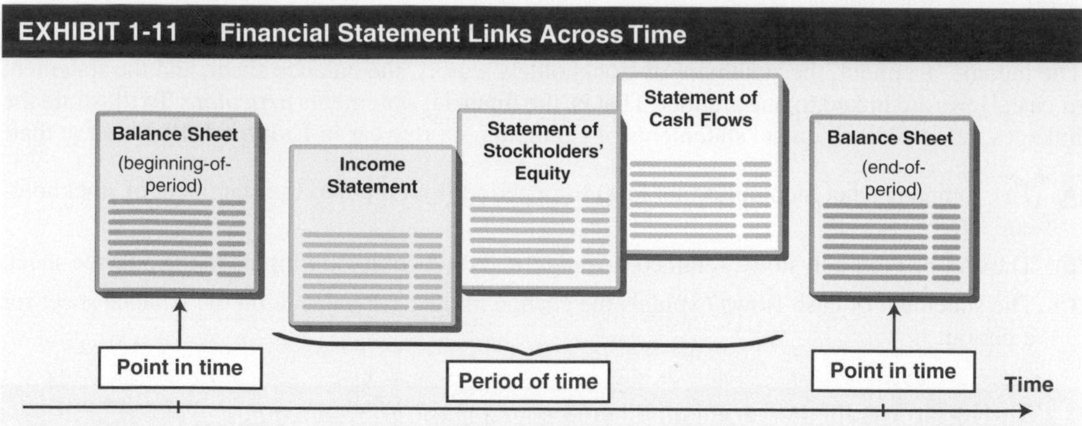

Guided Example *icons denote the availability of a demonstration video in* **myBusinessCourse** *(MBC). See the Preface for more on MBC.*

REVIEW 1.6

You have been approached by Jane Jones about helping her assemble a set of December 31 financial statements for her new business. Jane began the operations of her bakery shop on January 1 of the current year. Jane decided that she did not want to risk any personal liability resulting from operating the business; consequently, she organized the bakery, called Jane's Cakes and Chocolate, as a corporation.

REQUIRED

Use the format of **Exhibits 1-6** through **1-9** to prepare an income statement, statement of stockholders' equity, balance sheet, and statement of cash flows for Jane's Cakes and Chocolate as of December 31. Use the account titles and balances provided below. Be sure to use proper underlining and double underlining.

Sales of goods	$200,000	Dividends	$ 10,000
Cash	99,000	Bank loan payable	20,000
Rent expense	16,000	Accounts receivable	40,000
Interest payable	1,600	Cash flows provided by operating activities	66,000
Cash flows provided by financing activities	60,000	Salary expense	40,000
Insurance expense	20,000	Interest expense	1,600
Cash flows used in investing activities	27,000	Administrative expense	18,000
Equipment	27,000		
Common stock	50,000		

The solution is on page 38.

ADDITIONAL INFORMATION

LO6 Explain additional disclosures that accompany financial statements.

Columbia Sportswear Company, like all publicly traded companies in the United States, must file an **annual report** called a Form **10-K** with the U.S. Securities and Exchange Commission (SEC). Some companies also prepare a less detailed version of their annual report, which they make available to their stockholders at their Website. The four financial statements explained in this chapter are essential components of this report. Additional components of the annual report are the Management Discussion and Analysis, the notes to the financial statements, and the auditor's report.

eLecture MBC

Hint: *To view Columbia Sportswear's annual report visit the SEC website: https://www.sec.gov/edgar.shtml or Columbia's website: https://investor.columbia.com/sec-filings/annual-reports*

Management Discussion and Analysis

The **Management Discussion and Analysis**, or **MD&A**, contains management's interpretation of the company's recent performance and financial condition. This interpretation helps financial statement users gain a context within which to place their own analysis and interpretation of the numbers that appear in the financial statements.

The MD&A is also where a company's management provides its opinion regarding what the future holds for its business. Discussions of future opportunities and risks are called "forward-looking" and are helpful to any financial statement user interested in learning about such things as potential new markets for the company's products or potential new competitors. Obviously these forward-looking statements are subjective in nature, and the statement users must do an independent analysis of the financial statements.

The following is a short excerpt from Columbia's MD&A.

Excerpts *from recent financial statements and notes are used to illustrate and reinforce concepts.*

Our Business

We connect active people with their passions through our four well-known brands, Columbia, SOREL, Mountain Hardwear, and prAna, by designing, developing, marketing, and distributing our outdoor, active and everyday lifestyle apparel, footwear, accessories and equipment products to meet the diverse needs of our customers and consumers. We sell our products in approximately 90 countries and operate in four geographic segments: U.S., LAAP, EMEA, and Canada.

Our business is affected by the general seasonal trends common to the industry, including seasonal weather and discretionary consumer shopping and spending patterns. Our products are marketed on a seasonal basis, and our sales are weighted substantially toward the third and fourth quarters, while our operating costs are more equally distributed throughout the year. In 2020, approximately 65% of our net sales and the majority of our operating income were realized in the second half of the year. Although impacts from the ongoing COVID-19 pandemic exacerbated seasonal net sales and profitability patterns, this still illustrates our dependence upon sales results in the second half of the year, as well as the less seasonal nature of our operating costs.

Notes to Financial Statements

A skilled financial statement user wants to know more than just the raw numbers reported in financial statements. That user also wants to know assumptions and estimates that were used in preparing the statements, the measurement procedures that were followed, and the details behind certain summary numbers. **Notes to the financial statements**, which are both quantitative as well as qualitative, provide a great deal more information than just the numbers alone. For example, notes usually contain a description regarding how the company determined the value of its inventory, a detailed chart to explain the property, plant, and equipment account, and a description of pending lawsuits. No analysis of the annual report is complete without a careful reading of the notes to the financial statements. The following is a short excerpt from Columbia's notes:

Accounts receivable Accounts receivable have been reduced by an allowance for doubtful accounts. The Company maintains the allowance for estimated losses resulting from the inability of the Company's customers to make required payments.

Auditor's Report

The report of the independent auditor, commonly referred to as the **auditor's report**, describes the activities undertaken by a company's independent auditor and reports that auditor's opinion regarding whether the financial statements fairly present the results of the company's operations and financial health. A short excerpt from the auditor's report included with Columbia Sportswear's annual report follows. **Deloitte & Touche**, which is Columbia's independent auditor, reports that the financial statements of Columbia are, in its opinion, fairly presented. The audit report is not a "guarantee" that the financial statements are error-free. Instead, the auditor provides "reasonable assurance" to readers of the financial reports that the financial statements "present fairly" the company's financial position and the results of its operations.

Report of Independent Registered Public Accounting Firm

In our opinion, the financial statements present fairly, in all material respects, the financial position of the Company as of December 31, 2020 and 2019, and the results of its operations and its cash flows for each of the three years in the period ended December 31, 2020, in conformity with accounting principles generally accepted in the United States of America.

DELOITTE & TOUCHE LLP

REVIEW 1.7

Match each of the items in the left column with the appropriate annual report component where we would find that item, from the right column.

1. An opinion regarding the fair presentation of financial statements.	*a.* Management Discussion and Analysis
2. Information regarding the procedures followed to value a company's assets.	*b.* Notes to the Financial Statements
3. A discussion of new markets that a company plans to enter.	*c.* Auditor's report

The solution is on page 39.

ACCOUNTING AND TECHNOLOGY

Data Analytics and Data Visualization

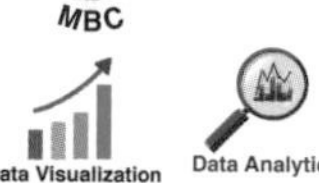

Business intelligence, or BI, refers to the tools that companies use to make data-based business decisions. BI tools include data analytics and data visualization, which are used to reveal patterns and trends in data and how they relate to human behavior. **Data analytics** addresses questions about *what and why things happened*, as well as *what will happen* in the future and *what should be done*, using methodology such as data mining, data management, and statistical analysis.

Once the data is analyzed, the answers to the above questions must be communicated to users. **Data visualization** is a tool used to explain and disseminate the results of data analysis. Data visualization incorporates graphs, charts, and maps, often in interactive ways. Data visualization tools include Tableau and Excel's Pivot charts, which are powerful tools for helping users understand data analysis and its implications.

Traditionally, the term **big data** has referred to very large and often complex data sets. More recently, this term has also come to refer to the methods used by companies to analyze big data sets. Companies use data analysis in a variety of ways in efforts to boost sales and improve performance. An early pioneer in the use of big data is the online retailer Amazon. Amazon uses big data to track customer search histories in order to target its advertising efforts. Amazon also uses the information it collects about its customers to personalize the sales experience and improve customer relations. Netflix is also a trailblazer in the use of big data. Netflix collects information on the entertainment streaming habits of millions of customers around the world and uses that information to customize viewing options and to predict trends in consumer behavior.

Big data has also become a powerful tool for accounting and finance professionals. Financial professionals such as stock analysts use data analysis to detect trends in company performance and predict future behavior. For example, American Express uses big data and data analytics to predict when customers are likely to close their credit card accounts. This allows for better planning and the opportunity to take actions that improve customer retention.

Big data has had a transformative effect on the methods used by auditors to ensure financial reporting quality. For example, both internal and external auditors now use big data and data analytics to enable year-round auditing, rather than waiting until the end of a quarter or year to perform auditing procedures. In addition, while auditing procedures used to rely on the analysis of relatively small samples from large populations, access to big data now allows auditors to observe the entire population of a company's transactions. In the case of large multinationals like Walmart, the number of these transactions can run into the hundreds of millions.

Blockchain

If you have been following the Bitcoin craze, you are doubtless familiar with the term "blockchain." **Blockchain** is a "distributed ledger" accounting system that allows participants, such as customers and suppliers, to keep track of transactions without the need for centralized record keeping. A distributed ledger differs from a traditional ledger in that no single party to the transaction controls it. All entries are made simultaneously in each copy of the ledger, and each entry must be agreed to by all of the members who share it.

Each transaction in the ledger is referred to as a "block," which is added chronologically to prior blocks, forming a "blockchain" of recorded transactions. The blocks are recorded using encryption technology, which means that they cannot be changed or tampered with. Copies of the ledgers are simultaneously stored by each member of the peer-to-peer network of users. The result is a highly secure record of business transactions with an audit trail that is permanent and "tamper proof."

While blockchain was originally developed as the accounting platform for the cryptocurrency Bitcoin, it is now seeing wide use in a variety of business settings. **Walmart** currently uses blockchain technology to track 1.1 million items from the manufacturer to its store shelves. The giant shipping concern, **Maersk**, now uses blockchain to track shipping containers on the open sea and claims that the approach streamlines the ability to get through customs. Other multinational companies who use blockchain to track their merchandise include **Unilever**, **Nestle**, **Kroger**, and **Tyson Foods**.

One industry in which Blockchain's potential for cost savings is particularly high is financial services. Blockchain's peer-to-peer approach and high degree of security means that the "middleman" in many financial transactions can be completely eliminated. **Goldman Sachs** estimates that the widespread implementation of blockchain technology could ultimately result in annual cost savings of over $6 billion dollars in the global financial services industry.

See Appendix F: Data Analytics and Blockchain Technology for an in depth discussion of these important technologies.

DATA ANALYTICS Data Analytics Adds Discipline to Columbia's Supply Chain

Columbia Sportswear is a leading company in the outdoor sportswear industry, but until recently it failed badly in its supply chain management. Luckily, after implementing data analytics, things have turned around. According to an article reported in the *Wall Street Journal*:

> "The company says the [FusionOps] software, which tracks open purchase orders, product fill rate, sales, as well as where products are in the supply chain, helped boost the share of merchandise delivered on-time and in-full, considered a core metric among retailers, from 28% to 78%. The analytics include a diagnostic component, showing Columbia why products are late, such as a ship delay at a port . . . When TurboDown jackets "took off" in the U.S. in December and January, the FusionOps software automatically notified Columbia staff to order more. Such data enabled Columbia to increase supply to minimize out-of-stock issues, reducing the amount of apparel the company marked down as sales waned."

Data Analytics

Data Analytics *boxes describe how data analytics tools and techniques are used in companies.*

REVIEW 1.8

Match these accounting technology concepts with their definition.

1. Business intelligence
2. Data analytics
3. Data visualization
4. Big data
5. Blockchain

a. Use of graphs, charts, and maps to explain and disseminate results of data analysis.
b. The methods used by companies to analyze large, often complex data sets.
c. A distributed ledger system that allows participants to keep track of transactions without the need for centralized record keeping.
d. The tools companies use to make data-based business decisions.
e. Uses methodology such as data mining, data management, and statistical analysis to determine what and why things happened and to anticipate what will happen or what should be done in the future.

The solution is on page 39.

Summaries *review key bullets points for each Learning Objective and summarize each section's takeaway.*

SUMMARY OF LEARNING OBJECTIVES

Explain business organization and its three forms. (p. 4) LO1

- There are three primary organizational forms that a business can take. They are the sole proprietorship, the partnership, and the corporation.
- A sole proprietorship consists of a single owner. It is the most common form of business and the easiest to establish.

- A partnership is similar to a sole proprietorship except that there is more than one owner. Partnerships are also relatively easy to establish. An advantage of the partnership form over the sole proprietorship is the broader set of skills and resources that multiple partners can bring to an enterprise.
- A corporation is the most complex of the three organizational forms. The advantages of the corporate form of business include the ease of transferring ownership interests and the ease of raising funds. Another advantage is the limited liability protection it offers its owners. A disadvantage of the corporate form is the possibility of double taxation of the company's net income.

LO2 Describe business activities. (p. 5)

- Companies engage in three types of business activities: operating, investing, and financing.
- Operating activities consist of selling products or providing services to generate sales revenue and using economic resources to manufacture goods or provide services.
- Investing activities consist of those activities needed to provide the infrastructure to run a company's operations. Also included in this activity category are investments of excess cash.
- Financing activities consist of both debt financing and equity financing. Debt financing involves the procurement of a bank loan, whereas equity financing involves the sale of shares of stock to investors.

LO3 Indicate who uses accounting information. (p. 6)

- Accounting information is important to both internal and external users.
- The process of generating and analyzing data for internal management use is referred to as managerial accounting.
- Business leaders recognize the importance of ethical behavior.
- Financial accounting produces publicly available financial statements for external users including investors, creditors, taxation authorities, regulatory agencies, labor unions, and customers.

LO4 Explain the accounting process and generally accepted accounting principles. (p. 10)

- Accounting is the process of measuring the economic activities of an enterprise in money terms and communicating the results to interested parties.
- The basic purpose of accounting is to provide financial information that is useful in making economic decisions.
- The Financial Accounting Standards Board (FASB) is an organization in the private sector that has responsibility for formulating generally accepted accounting principles in the United States.
- Generally accepted accounting principles (GAAP) are the standards and procedures that guide the preparation of financial statements.
- The International Accounting Standards Board (IASB) has taken the lead role in formulating International Financial Reporting Standards (IFRS).
- A common set of standards such as the IFRS benefits multinational companies, investors, and accounting professionals.

LO5 Describe the accounting equation and each financial statement. (p. 12)

- The accounting equation, Assets = Liabilities + Stockholders' Equity, is the fundamental framework within which accounting analysis takes place.
  - Assets are the economic resources of a business that can be expressed in money terms.
  - Liabilities are the obligations that a business must pay in money or services in the future as a consequence of past transactions or events.
  - Stockholders' equity is the residual interest of the owners in the assets of a business.
- *Income statement:* Presents a company's sales revenues and expenses for a period of time.
- *Statement of stockholders' equity:* Reports the financial events causing a change in stockholders' equity during a period of time, and includes retained earnings and common stock.
- *Balance sheet:* Presents a company's assets, liabilities, and stockholders' equity as of a given date.
- *Statement of cash flows:* Reports a company's cash inflows and outflows during a period of time.

LO6 Explain additional disclosures that accompany financial statements. (p. 18)

In addition to the basic financial statements, the annual report includes Management Discussion and Analysis, notes to the financial statements, and an auditor's report.

- The Management Discussion and Analysis (MD&A) provides management with an opportunity to both analyze past performance and discuss future opportunities and concerns involving a company.
- The notes to the financial statements provide both a quantitative and a qualitative description of a company's financial statements and explain the numbers reported in those financial statements.
- The auditor's report, issued by an independent auditor, provides a degree of assurance that a company's financial statements are presented fairly and can be relied upon for decision-making purposes.

Discuss technology in accounting. (p. 20) **LO7**

- Business intelligence refers to tools such as data analytics and data visualization that companies use to reveal patterns, trends, and associations in human behavior and to communicate their findings.
- Big data refers to very large and often complex data sets and the methods companies use to analyze them.
- Blockchain is a distributed ledger accounting system where encrypted transactions are stored by each member of the peer-to-peer network of users.

Concept	Method	Assessment	SUMMARY
What form of financing does a company use?	The balance sheet provides information regarding the various forms of financing, both debt financing and equity financing. Compare the amount of liabilities appearing on the balance sheet to the amount of equity appearing on the balance sheet.	A higher ratio of liabilities to stockholders' equity implies a higher use of creditor financing, and vice versa. Creditor financing is viewed by users as more risky.	TAKEAWAY 1.1
Is a company profitable?	The income statement reports a company's performance for a given period of time. Deduct reported expenses from reported sales revenue.	Sales revenue in excess of expenses yields net income, which means the company is profitable. If expenses exceed revenue, the company has a net loss.	TAKEAWAY 1.2
What portion of a company's current period net income is distributed to its stockholders, and what portion is retained?	The statement of stockholders' equity reports both a company's net income and the amount of dividends distributed to stockholders. Divide the company's dividends by its net income.	A higher ratio of dividends to net income implies that a company is distributing more of its net income to it stockholders, whereas a lower ratio implies that it is retaining more of its income for purposes such as growing its business.	TAKEAWAY 1.3
What are the major sources and uses of a company's cash?	The statement of cash flows reports a company's sources and uses of cash separated into three activities: operating, investing, and financing. Identify a company's sources and uses of cash as reported in the statement of cash flows.	Sources of cash are reported as positive numbers and uses of cash as negative numbers. Larger positive numbers represent major cash sources and larger negative numbers represent major cash uses.	TAKEAWAY 1.4

KEY TERMS

10-K (p. 18)
Accounting (p. 6)
Accounting equation (p. 12)
American Institute of Certified Public Accountants (AICPA) (p. 9)
Annual report (p. 18)
Assets (p. 12)
Auditor's report (p. 19)
Balance sheet (p. 12)
Big data (p. 20)
Blockchain (p. 20)
Business intelligence (p. 20)
Certified public accountants (CPAs) (p. 7)
Communication process (p. 10)
Contributed capital (p. 14)
Corporation (p. 4)
Creditors (p. 6)
Data analytics (p. 20)
Data visualization (p. 20)
Debt financing (p. 6)
Dividend (p. 6)
Earned capital (p. 14)
Environmental, Social, and Governance (ESG) (p. 14)
Equity financing (p. 6)
Ethics (p. 8)
Expenses (p. 13)
Financial accounting (p. 7)
Financial Accounting Standards Board (FASB) (p. 10)
Financing activities (p. 6)
Forensic accounting (p. 9)
Generally accepted accounting principles (GAAP) (p. 10)
Generally accepted auditing standards (GAAS) (p. 11)
Income statement (p. 13)
Institute of Management Accountants (IMA) (p. 9)
Interest (p. 6)
International Accounting Standards Board (IASB) (p. 11)
International Financial Reporting Standards (IFRS) (p. 11)
Investing activities (p. 5)
Liabilities (p. 12)
Management Discussion and Analysis (MD&A) (p. 18)
Managerial accounting (p. 8)
Measurement process (p. 10)
Net assets (p. 12)
Net income (p. 13)
Net loss (p. 13)
New York Stock Exchange (NYSE) (p. 5)

Notes to the financial statements (p. 19)
Operating activities (p. 5)
Partnership (p. 4)
Period-of-time statements (p. 17)
Point-in-time statement (p. 17)
Principal (p. 6)
Public Company Accounting Oversight Board (PCAOB) (p. 11)
Retained earnings (p. 15)
Sales revenues (p. 13)
Sarbanes-Oxley Act (SOX) (p. 9)
Sole proprietorship (p. 4)
Statement of cash flows (p. 16)
Statement of stockholders' equity (p. 14)
Stockholders (p. 4)
Stockholders' equity (p. 12)
U.S. Securities and Exchange Commission (SEC) (p. 10)

Self-Study Questions *in multiple-choice format with answers provided at the end of each chapter.*

Assignments with the MBC logo in the margin are available in myBusinessCourse. See the Preface of the book for details.

SELF-STUDY QUESTIONS

(Answers to Self-Study Questions are at the end of this chapter.)

Homework *icons indicate which assignments are available in* **myBusinessCourse** *(MBC). This feature is only available when the instructor incorporates MBC in the course.*

LO1 

1. **Which form of business organization is characterized by limited liability?**
   a. Sole proprietorship
   b. Partnership
   c. Corporation
   d. Both sole proprietorship and partnership

LO4 

2. **Which of the following processes best defines accounting?**
   a. Measuring economic activities
   b. Communicating results to interested parties
   c. Preventing fraud
   d. Both *a* and *b*.

LO4 

3. **Generally accepted accounting principles are:**
   a. A set of guidelines to aid in the financial reporting process
   b. A set of laws to prevent financial fraud
   c. A set of standards for ethical conduct
   d. A set of voluntary "best business practices"

LO4 

4. **To which area of accounting are generally accepted accounting principles primarily relevant?**
   a. Managerial accounting
   b. Financial accounting
   c. Tax accounting
   d. Financial reporting to all regulatory agencies

LO2 

5. **Which of the following is not one of the three types of business activities?**
   a. Investing
   b. Financing
   c. Marketing
   d. Operating

LO5 

6. **If assets total $70,000 and liabilities total $40,000, how much are net assets?**
   a. $30,000
   b. $40,000
   c. $70,000
   d. $110,000

LO5 

7. **What are increases in resources that a firm earns by providing goods or services to its customers?**
   a. Assets
   b. Revenues
   c. Expenses
   d. Liabilities

LO6 

8. **Which of the following items is not required to be included as part of a company's annual report?**
   a. Notes to the financial statements
   b. Management discussion and analysis
   c. Detailed history of the company
   d. Auditor's report

LO3 

9. **Which of the following situations presents ethical challenges to accountants?**
   a. Pressure by superiors to produce a "good" number
   b. Avoiding the disclosure of confidential information
   c. An emphasis on short-term results
   d. All the above present ethical challenges to accountants

LO1

10. **Match the following organizational attributes in the left column with the organizational form in the right column that the attribute is most often associated with.**

1. Tax advantages	*a.* Sole proprietorship
2. Unlimited liability	*b.* Partnership
3. Shared control	*c.* Corporation
4. Most complex to set up	
5. Easiest to raise a large amount of funds	
6. Single owner	

11. The financial statements of Bower Company contain the following. How much is its net income? LO5 Homework MBC

Accounts payable	$10,000
Revenues	17,000
Accounts receivable	12,000
Expenses	9,000
Cash	5,000

a. $15,000
b. $8,000
c. $17,000
d. $7,000

12. If Ross Company reports its year-end total liabilities to be $75,000, and its year-end stockholders' equity to be $85,000, how much is Ross Company's year-end total assets? LO5 Homework MBC

a. $10,000
b. $160,000
c. $85,000
d. Cannot be determined from the given information

13. Huff Company began the year with a retained earnings balance of $20,000, reported net income for the year of $60,000, and reported ending retained earnings of $70,000. How much dividends did Huff Company report for the year? LO5 Homework MBC

a. $150,000
b. $20,000
c. $10,000
d. $30,000

QUESTIONS

1. Define *accounting.* What is the basic purpose of accounting?
2. What is the distinction between *financial* accounting and *managerial* accounting?
3. Who are some of the outside groups that may be interested in a company's financial data, and what are their particular interests?
4. What are *generally accepted accounting principles,* and what organization has primary responsibility for their formulation in the United States?
5. What are the main advantages and disadvantages of the corporate form of business?
6. What role does financial accounting play in the allocation of society's financial resources?
7. What is the accounting equation? Define *assets, liabilities,* and *stockholders' equity.*
8. What are the three principal business activities, and how do they differ?
9. What is meant by corporate social responsibility?
10. What is the difference between generally accepted accounting principles (GAAP) and international financial reporting standards (IFRS)?
11. What are *revenues* and *expenses*?
12. What is the purpose of an income statement? The statement of stockholders' equity? The balance sheet? The statement of cash flows?
13. What is a *period-of-time statement*? Give three examples.
14. What is a *point-in-time statement*? Give one example.
15. On December 31, the Miller Company had $700,000 in total assets and owed $220,000 to creditors. If the corporation's common stock amounted to $300,000, what amount of retained earnings should appear on its December 31 balance sheet?
16. What are three aspects of the accounting environment that may create ethical pressure on an accountant?
17. What type of information might you find in the Management Discussion and Analysis (MD&A) section of the annual report?
18. What is the purpose of having the financial statements audited by an independent auditor?
19. Determine whether the following statements are true or false and explain why:
    a. The accounting process is only interested in communicating economic activity.
    b. There are few potential users of accounting information.
    c. Financial accounting is primarily used to communicate to outside users.
    d. Auditors ensure the validity of a company's financial statements.

DATA ANALYTICS

The assignments in this Data Analytics section are designed to familiarize you with the tools used in analyzing data and communicating the results. Appendix F provides an in-depth discussion of data analytics and blockchain technology.

DA1-1. Preparing Data Visualizations in Excel Using Doughnut Charts
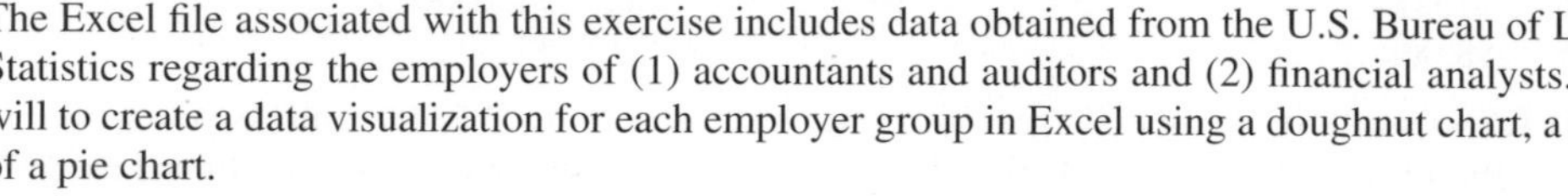
The Excel file associated with this exercise includes data obtained from the U.S. Bureau of Labor Statistics regarding the employers of (1) accountants and auditors and (2) financial analysts.[2] We will to create a data visualization for each employer group in Excel using a doughnut chart, a form of a pie chart.

REQUIRED

1. Download Excel file DA1-1 found in myBusinessCourse.
2. Create a new row in each dataset for "Other employers."
3. Add the applicable percentage to the new category, "Other employers." *Hint:* When creating a doughnut chart, we are showing proportions of a total. The total of the percentages for each dataset must add up to 100%.
4. Create a doughnut chart for each dataset. *Hint:* Highlight dataset, click on Insert, click on the Pie icon, click Doughnut. Do not include the dataset title when highlighting the dataset.
5. Update the features of your doughnut charts by either choosing one of the chart design templates or updating manually. *Hint:* You can add elements and change the chart style by using the Chart Layouts and Chart Styles tools on the Chart Design tab. The Chart Design tab appears when you click inside a chart.
6. Add percentages to each proportion of the doughnut charts. *Hint:* Right-click on your chart; click on Add data labels. Click on your chart labels to allow editing of color or font size.
7. Calculate the difference between the largest and smallest proportion in the doughnut chart for Dataset A.
8. Calculate the difference between the largest and smallest proportion in the doughnut chart for Dataset B.
9. List any employer categories that overlap between the two occupations.
10. List the formula type associated with the chart. *Hint:* Double-click on the doughnut chart in Dataset A, which will allow the formula to be visible in the formula bar.

DA1-2. Preparing Executive Compensation Visualizations with Tableau: Part I, Part II, Part III
Refer to PF-17, PF-18, and PF-19 in Appendix F. This three-part problem uses Tableau to analyze compensation of chief executive officers and chief financial officers of S&P 500 companies.

Data Analytics

Assignments with the MBC logo in the margin are available in myBusinessCourse. See the Preface of the book for details.

SHORT EXERCISES

LO1
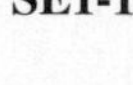

LOs *link assignments to the Learning Objectives of each chapter.*

SE1-1. Forms of Business Organization Match the following forms of business organization with the set of attributes that best describes that form of business: sole proprietorship, partnership, or corporation.

a. Shared control, unlimited liability, tax advantages, increased skills and resources
b. Best for raising large amounts of funds, double taxation, limited liability, easiest to transfer ownership interests
c. Sole ownership, easiest to establish, tax advantages, unlimited liability

LO4

SE1-2. Accounting Processes Identify the following processes as either measuring or communicating.

a. Prepare financial statements for the entity
b. Identify relevant economic activities of the entity
c. Record relevant economic activities of the entity
d. Interpret financial results of the entity
e. Quantify relevant economic activities of the entity

---

[2] Bureau of Labor Statistics, U.S. Department of Labor, Occupational Outlook Handbook, Accountants and Auditors, at https://www.bls.gov/ooh/business-and-financial/accountants-and-auditors.htm (visited August 18, 2021).

SE1-3. Types of Statements Match the following type of report with the most likely statement user: management, taxation authority, regulatory agency, or investor. LO3 Homework MBC

a. Financial statements
b. Tax return
c. Annual budget
d. Special report on a bank's financial health

SE1-4. Accounting Organizations Match the following organizations with the set of accounting guidelines: Financial Accounting Standards Board (FASB), International Accounting Standards Board (IASB). LO4 Homework MBC

a. Generally accepted accounting principles (GAAP)
b. International financial reporting standards (IFRS)

SE1-5. Business Activities Match the following activities with the type of activity: Operating, Investing, Financing. LO2 Homework MBC

a. Day-to-day business activities
b. Purchase of land for a new warehouse
c. Sale of merchandise inventory
d. Obtain a new bank loan
e. Payment of dividends
f. Invest excess cash
g. Purchase office supplies
h. Sell old equipment that is no longer needed

SE1-6. Financial Statement Items Identify the financial statement in which each of the following items would appear: income statement (IS), statement of retained earnings (SRE), balance sheet (BS), or statement of cash flows (SCF). LO5 Homework MBC

a. Assets
b. Revenues
c. Cash flow from investing activities
d. Stockholders' equity
e. Expenses
f. Net change in cash
g. Net income
h. Liabilities

SE1-7. Annual Report Components Which of the following would not be part of the notes to the financial statements in a company's annual report? LO6 Homework MBC

a. Qualitative information about potential lawsuits
b. Additional information about the reported total of notes payable
c. Details about potential new products to be introduced during the next year
d. Details of estimates used to compute the expected amount of warranty expense

SE1-8. Sarbanes-Oxley Act The Sarbanes-Oxley Act was enacted to help restore confidence in financial reporting. Which of the following was not part of the legislation? LO3 Homework MBC

a. Severe penalties for fraudulent reporting
b. A requirement for certification of the financial statements by top management
c. A new statement of social responsibility
d. A report on controls to help prevent and detect errors in the reporting process

SE1-9. Financial Accounting and Generally Accepted Accounting Principles Answer the following multiple-choice questions: LO4 Homework MBC

1. What is not a primary function of financial accounting in society?
   a. Provide comedy material for late-night talk shows.
   b. Aid in the proper allocation of financial resources in a free enterprise economic system.
   c. Aid users to make better investing decisions.
2. IFRS refers to:
   a. A random set of letters.
   b. A set of standards and procedures that form guidelines for international financial accounting.
   c. A set of standards and procedures that form guidelines for international managerial accounting.
3. GAAP:
   a. Is the distance between two objects.
   b. Is a set of guidelines for preparing managerial reports in the United States.
   c. Is a set of guidelines for preparing financial reports in the United States.

SE1-10. Cash Flow Activity Classification Classify each activity as financing, investing, or operating: LO2 Homework MBC

1. Repay a loan from a bank.
2. Sell merchandise from a storefront operation.
3. Dispose of an old delivery truck.
4. Pay rent on a company warehouse.
5. Repurchase shares of stock from stockholders.
6. Pay utilities.

LO5 

SE1-11. Using the Basic Accounting Equation Use the basic accounting equation to answer the following:

a. Kendrick Company has total assets of $100,000 and total liabilities of $60,000. How much is the company's total stockholders' equity?

b. Gassol Company has total liabilities of $80,000 and total stockholders' equity of $75,000. What are the company's total assets?

c. If Brown Company's total assets increased by $15,000 during the year, and its total liabilities decreased during the same year by $10,000, what was the change in the company's total stockholders' equity?

LO5

SE1-12. Using the Basic Accounting Equation Henderson Company had beginning-of-the-year total assets of $200,000 and total liabilities of $120,000.

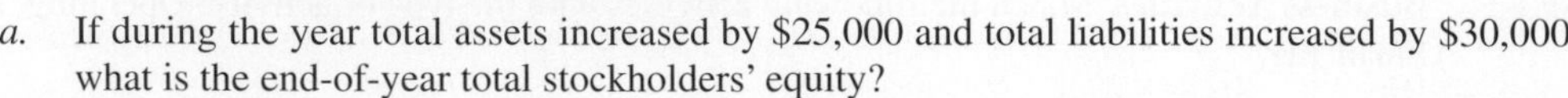

a. If during the year total assets increased by $25,000 and total liabilities increased by $30,000, what is the end-of-year total stockholders' equity?

b. If during the year total assets increased by $50,000 and total liabilities decreased by $10,000, what is the end-of-year total stockholders' equity?

c. If during the year total liabilities increased by $20,000 and total stockholders' equity increased by $30,000, what are the end-of-year total assets?

LO5

SE1-13. Financial Statements Indicate which statement(s) you would examine to locate the following items: balance sheet (BS), income statement (IS), statement of stockholders' equity (SE), or statement of cash flows (CF).

a. Expenses for the period
b. Cash at year-end
c. Cash used to purchase new equipment
d. Dividends for the period

LO5

SE1-14. Financial Statements Indicate which statement(s) you would examine to locate the following items: balance sheet (BS), income statement (IS), statement of retained earnings (RE), or statement of cash flows (CF).

a. Revenues for the period
b. Cash at year-end
c. Cash used to pay back borrowings
d. Dividends for the period

LO7 

SE1-15. Data Analytics Which of the following best describes data analytics?

a. Use of double-entry accounting to analyze transactions.
b. Computational techniques that companies use to reveal patterns, trends, and associations in human behavior.
c. Analysis of bitcoin transactions.
d. None of the above.

LO7 

SE1-16. Blockchain The advantages of a distributed ledger include all items listed except:

a. Does not require centralized record keeping.
b. No single party to the transaction controls the ledger.
c. The ledger is distributed by mail.
d. Data is encrypted for a high degree of security.

EXERCISES

LO1

E1-1. Forms of Business Organization Match the following organizational attributes in the left column with the organizational form in the right column. More than one organizational form may be associated with a given attribute.

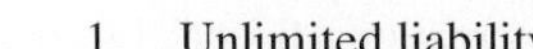

1. Unlimited liability
2. Full control
3. Business income combined with owner(s) income for income tax purposes
4. Relatively more difficult to establish
5. Easier to raise funds

a. Sole proprietorship
b. Partnership
c. Corporation

LO4 

E1-2. Accounting Process Establish the correct sequence of steps in the accounting measurement process.

a. Record in a systematic fashion
b. Identify relevant economic activity
c. Quantify economic activity

E1-3. Types of Accounting Identify the type of accounting associated with each type of report: Managerial, Financial, Tax, combination as needed. LO3 Homework MBC

a. Budget for internal use by management
b. Tax return for state income taxes
c. Audited financial statements
d. Special reports for regulators of a public utility

E1-4. Environmental, Social, and Governance Which of the following is not part of the triple bottom line reporting framework? LO5 Homework MBC

a. Economic bottom line
b. Social bottom line
c. Competitive bottom line
d. Environmental bottom line

E1-5. Generally Accepted Accounting Principles Identify whether the following statements are true or false: LO4 Homework MBC

a. U.S. GAAP is universally accepted in all countries in the world.
b. U.S. GAAP is established by the IASB.
c. Once established, U.S. GAAP is rarely, if ever, modified.
d. The international counterpart to the FASB is the IASB.

E1-6. Business Activities Identify each of the following activities as operating (O), investing (I), or financing (F): LO2 Homework MBC

a. Payment of employee salaries
b. Repayment of a loan
c. Issuance of common stock
d. Purchase of equipment to manufacture a company's products
e. Sale of merchandise inventory
f. Investment of excess cash in the shares of another company

E1-7. The Accounting Equation Determine the missing amount in each of the following cases: LO5 Homework MBC

Assets	Liabilities	Stockholders' Equity
$150,000	$92,000	?
?	$21,000	$42,000
$87,000	?	$61,000

E1-8. Determining Net Income The beginning and ending balances of retained earnings for the year were $30,000 and $35,000, respectively. If dividend payments from stockholders' equity exceed new capital contributions during the year by $3,000, determine the net income or net loss for the year. LO5 Homework MBC

a. $8,000 net loss
b. $14,000 net income
c. $2,000 net income
d. $8,000 net income

E1-9. Determining Retained Earnings and Net Income The following information appears in the records of Bock Corporation at year-end: LO5 Homework MBC

Accounts receivable	$ 23,000	Retained earnings	$?
Accounts payable	11,000	Supplies	9,000
Cash	8,000	Equipment, net	138,000
Common stock	110,000		

a. Calculate the balance in retained earnings at year-end.
b. If the amount of the retained earnings at the beginning of the year was $30,000, and $12,000 in dividends is paid during the year, calculate net income for the year.

E1-10. Determining Stockholders' Equity Determine the following: LO5 Homework MBC

a. The stockholders' equity of a corporation that has assets of $450,000 and liabilities of $326,000.
b. The assets of a corporation that has liabilities of $400,000, common stock of $200,000, and retained earnings of $185,000.

E1-11. Financial Statements Karl Flury operates a golf driving range. For each of the following financial items related to his business, indicate the financial statement (or statements) in which the item would be reported: LO5 Homework MBC

a. Accounts receivable
b. Cash received from the sale of land
c. Net income
d. Cash invested in the business by Flury
e. Notes payable
f. Supplies expense
g. Land
h. Supplies

LO5 Homework MBC **E1-12. Omitted Financial Statement Data** For the following four unrelated situations, A through D, calculate the unknown amounts appearing in each column:

	A	B	C	D
Beginning				
Assets	$28,000	$12,000	$28,000	$?
Liabilities	18,600	5,000	19,000	9,000
Ending				
Assets	30,000	26,000	34,000	40,000
Liabilities	17,300	?	15,000	19,000
During Year				
Sales revenue	?	23,500	28,000	24,000
Expense	8,500	21,000	11,000	17,000
Dividends	3,000	1,500	?	3,000

LO6 Homework MBC **E1-13. Other Components of the Annual Report** Identify where the following items will appear in a company's annual report: Management Discussion and Analysis (MD&A), notes to the financial statements, or the auditor's report.

a. A comment that the financial statements appear to be fairly presented
b. A discussion about new competition likely to occur next year
c. A quantitative summary of notes payable appearing on the balance sheet
d. The "secret" ingredients in the company's special sauce

LO3 **E1-14. Ethics** In each of the following cases, (a) identify the aspect of the accounting environment primarily responsible for the ethical pressure on the accountant and (b) indicate the appropriate behavioral response for the accountant.

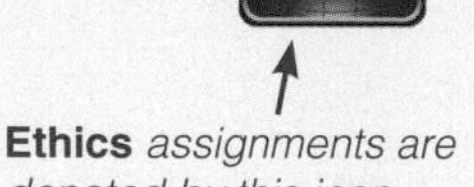

Ethics *assignments are denoted by this icon.*

1. James Jehring, a tax accountant, is preparing an income tax return for a client. The client asks Jehring to take a sizable deduction on the tax return for business-related travel even though the client states that he has no documentation to support the deduction. "I don't think the IRS will audit my return," declares the client.
2. Willa English, an accountant for Dome Construction Company, has just finished putting the numbers together for a construction project on which the firm is going to submit a bid next month. At a social gathering that evening, a friend casually asks English what Dome's bid is going to be. Ms. English knows that the friend's brother works for a competitor of Dome.
3. The manager of Cross Department Store is ending his first year with the firm. December's business was slower than expected, and the firm's annual results are trailing last year's results. The manager instructs Kyle Tarpley, the store accountant, to include sales revenues from the first week of January in the December data. "This way, we'll show an increase over last year," declares the manager.

LO4 IFRS **E1-15. International Accounting Principles** The worldwide acceptance of a global set of international accounting principles will provide certain benefits.

a. Which group has taken the lead in developing a set of international accounting principles?
b. Identify and briefly discuss two major benefits that would result from the adoption of a global set of international accounting principles.

PROBLEMS

LO1 **P1-1. Forms of Business Organization** Presented below are four independent situations:

a. Kali Kane, a senior in college looking for summer employment, decided to start a dog-walking business. Each morning and evening she picks up a group of dogs and walks them around the city park.

b. Brothers Joe and Jay Simmons each owned a separate electronics repair shop. They decided to combine their talents and resources in order to expand the amount of business they could undertake.

c. Three chemists at a large engineering company decided to start their own business based on an experimental chemical process they had developed outside the company. The process had the potential to be very successful; however, it was quite dangerous and could result in large legal problems.

d. Jack Prince ran a small, but successful holistic healing spa. The spa has gained a strong reputation beyond the community where it is located. Jack decided to open a chain of similar spas across the state to capitalize on his reputation. This will require a substantial investment in supplies and employee training. In addition, since Jack will not be able to closely supervise each location, he is worried about potential liability.

REQUIRED

Explain the form of organization that would be best in each situation—sole proprietorship, partnership, or corporation. Explain what factors you considered important in each situation.

P1-2. Financial Statements While each of the financial statements is likely to aid in any business decision, it is often the case that a particular financial statement may be best suited to help in a particular decision. Consider each decision below independently:

LO5

a. You are trying to determine whether a particular firm is a good investment. You understand that share price increases are impacted heavily by a company's earnings potential.

b. You are employed in the lending department of a large bank. You are trying to determine if you should lend to a potential customer. If you do make the loan you are especially concerned that the company will have sufficient collateral in the event that it is unable to repay the loan.

c. You wish to invest in a firm that provides you with a steady source of income. You especially want a firm that pays out a large part of its net income as dividends.

d. You are trying to determine if a particular firm will have sufficient cash flow in order to keep expanding without relying too heavily on external sources of financing.

REQUIRED

Determine which of the financial statements contains the most useful information to help in your decision. Explain what information you used from each statement to help you make your decision.

P1-3. Balance Sheet The following balance sheet data are for Normandy Catering Service, a corporation, at May 31 of the current year:

LO5

Accounts receivable	$18,300	Accounts payable	5,200
Notes payable	20,000	Cash	12,200
Equipment, net	55,000	Common stock	42,500
Supplies	16,400	Retained earnings	?

REQUIRED

Prepare a balance sheet for Normandy as of May 31.

P1-4. Statement of Stockholders' Equity and Balance Sheet The following is balance sheet information for Lynch Janitorial Service, Inc., at the end of the current year and prior year:

LO5

	December 31, Current Year	December 31, Prior Year
Accounts payable	$ 6,000	$ 9,000
Cash	23,000	20,000
Accounts receivable	42,000	33,000
Land	40,000	40,000
Building, net	250,000	260,000
Equipment, net	43,000	45,000
Mortgage payable	90,000	100,000
Supplies	20,000	18,000
Common stock	220,000	220,000
Dividends	10,000	0
Retained earnings	?	?

REQUIRED

a. Prepare a balance sheet as of December 31 of each year.

b. Prepare a statement of stockholders' equity for the current year. (*Hint:* The increase in retained earnings is equal to the net income less the dividend.)

LO5 **P1-5.** **Statement of Retained Earnings and Balance Sheet** The following is balance sheet information for House Janitorial Service, Inc., at the end of the current year and prior year:

	December 31, Current Year	December 31, Prior Year
Accounts payable	$ 12,000	$ 18,000
Cash	46,000	40,000
Accounts receivable	84,000	66,000
Land	80,000	80,000
Building, net	500,000	520,000
Equipment, net	86,000	90,000
Mortgage payable	180,000	200,000
Supplies	40,000	36,000
Common stock	440,000	440,000
Dividends	20,000	0
Retained earnings	?	?

REQUIRED

a. Prepare a balance sheet as of December 31 of each year.

b. Prepare a statement of retained earnings for the current year. (*Hint:* The increase in retained earnings is equal to the net income less the dividend.)

LO5 **P1-6.** **Income Statement and Balance Sheet** On March 1, Amy Dart began Dart Delivery Service, which provides delivery of bulk mailings to the post office, neighborhood delivery of weekly newspapers, data delivery to computer service centers, and various other delivery services using leased vans. On February 28, Dart invested $15,000 of her own funds in the firm and borrowed $6,000 from her father on a six-month, non-interest-bearing note payable. The following information is available at March 31:

Accounts receivable	$9,700	Delivery fees earned	$19,300
Rent expense	1,500	Cash	12,900
Advertising expense	900	Supplies	6,500
Supplies expense	2,700	Notes payable	6,000
Accounts payable	1,200	Insurance expense	800
Salaries expense	6,300	Common stock	15,000
Miscellaneous expense	200	Retained earnings	?

REQUIRED

a. Prepare an income statement for the month of March.

b. Prepare a balance sheet as of March 31.

LO5 **P1-7.** **Statement of Cash Flows** Shown below is selected information from the financial records of Mantle Corporation as of December 31:

Inventory	$ 72,000	Cash purchase of equipment	$ 27,000
Cash collected from customers	330,000	Buildings, net	440,000
Equipment, net	125,000	Sales revenue	475,000
Retained earnings	275,000	Cash paid for operating activities	210,000
Cash dividends paid	42,000	Principal payments on existing note payable	47,000
Salary expense	110,000	Common stock	155,000

REQUIRED

a. Determine which of the above items will appear on the statement of cash flows and then prepare the statement for Mantle Corporation for the year ended December 31.

b. Comment on the adequacy of Mantle's operations to provide cash for its investing and financing activities.

LO3 **P1-8.** **Ethics** In each of the following cases, (a) identify the aspect of the accounting environment primarily responsible for the ethical pressure on the accountant and (b) indicate the appropriate behavioral response that the accountant should take.

1. Patricia Kelly, an accountant for Wooden Company, is reviewing the costs charged to a government contract that Wooden worked on this year. Wooden is manufacturing special parts for the government and is allowed to charge the government for its actual manufacturing costs plus a fixed fee. Kelly notes that $75,000 worth of art objects purchased for the president's

office is buried among the miscellaneous costs charged to the contract. Upon inquiry, the firm's vice president replies, "This sort of thing is done all the time."

2. Barry Marklin, accountant for Smith and Wesson partnership, is working on the 2019 year-end financial data. The partnership agreement calls for Smith and Wesson to share the firm's 2019 net income equally. In 2020, the partners will share the net income 60 percent to Smith and 40 percent to Wesson. Wesson plans to cut back his involvement in the firm. Smith wants Marklin to delay recording sales revenue from work done at the end of 2019 until January 2020. "We haven't received the cash yet from those services," declares Smith.
3. The St. Louis Wheelers, a professional football franchise, just signed its first-round draft pick to a multiyear contract that is reported in the newspapers as a four-year, $20 million contract. Johanna Factor, the Wheelers' accountant, receives a call from an agent of another team's first-round pick. "Just calling to confirm the contract terms reported in the papers," states the agent. "My client should receive a similar contract, and I'm sure you don't want him to get shortchanged."

P1-9. Income Statement, Statement of Stockholders' Equity, and Balance Sheet Napolean Corporation started business on January 1. The following information was compiled by Napolean's accountant at year-end, December 31: **LO5**

Sales revenue	30,000	Building, net	60,000
Expenses	18,000	Accounts payable	6,000
Dividends	4,500	Notes payable	49,500
Cash	2,250	Common stock	30,000
Accounts receivable	3,750	Retained earnings	?
Inventory	4,500		
Equipment, net	22,500		

REQUIRED

a. You have been asked to assist the accountant for the Napolean Corporation in preparing year-end financial statements. Use the above information to prepare an income statement, statement of stockholders' equity, and a balance sheet as of December 31.

b. Comment on the decision to pay a $4,500 dividend.

P1-10. Income Statement, Statement of Stockholders' Equity, Balance Sheet, and Statement of Cash Flows Gregg Corporation started business on January 1. The following information was compiled by Gregg as of December 31. **LO5**

Homework MBC

Sales revenue	$20,000	Accounts payable	$ 4,000
Expenses	12,000	Notes payable	33,000
Dividends	3,000	Common stock	20,000
Cash	1,500	Retained earnings	?
Accounts receivable	2,500	Cash flow from operating activities	6,500
Inventory	3,000	Cash flow from investing activities	(55,000)
Equipment	15,000	Cash flow from financing activities	50,000
Building	40,000		

REQUIRED

Prepare the company's year-end financial statements: an income statement, a statement of stockholders' equity, a balance sheet, and a statement of cash flows.

P1-11. Financial Statements and Other Components Match each of the items in the left column with the appropriate annual report component from the right column: **LO5, 6**

1. The company's total liabilities
2. An opinion regarding whether the financial statements followed GAAP
3. Information regarding the estimates used in the financial statements
4. The cash from operations during the period
5. The company's total revenues for the period
6. A discussion of potential risks that a company may encounter in the future
7. The amount of a company's earnings that are distributed to the company's stockholders

a. Income Statement
b. Statement of Stockholders' Equity
c. Balance Sheet
d. Statement of Cash Flows
e. Management Discussion and Analysis (MD&A)
f. Notes to the Financial Statements
g. Auditor's report

SERIAL PROBLEM: ANGEL CITY GREETINGS

Angel City Greetings *is a continuous problem that requires students to apply the concepts from the current chapter. There is an Angel City Greetings assignment in each chapter.*

SP1. Kate Collins has always been good at putting together rhymes for any occasion. Recently, Kate's financial assistance for college was cut back due to budget problems in the state where she lives. Kate determined that the best way to raise enough money to stay in school and still have enough time for her studies was to start a greeting card business. She feels that this will not only help her to raise money, but supplement what she is learning at school as a business major.

Kate decided that she would start small and work out of her dorm room, designing the cards on a new Apple iMac that she was planning to purchase. Kate also decided to offer classes in greeting card design to other aspiring greeting card producers. After much thought, Kate decided to name her business "Angel City Greetings."

REQUIRED

a. What form of business—sole proprietorship, partnership, or corporation—should Kate choose? Discuss why the organizational form that you selected is most appropriate for Kate.

b. What accounting information will Kate need to run her business?

c. What balance sheet accounts—assets, liabilities, and stockholders' equity—and income statement accounts—revenues and expenses—will Kate likely need to use?

d. Should Kate use her personal bank account or open a separate business bank account?

Beyond the Numbers *assignments require use of real world financial statements and critical thinking skills.*

BEYOND THE NUMBERS

REPORTING AND ANALYSIS

Columbia Sportswear Company

BTN1-1. Financial Reporting Problem: Columbia Sportswear Company Financial statements for the **Columbia Sportswear Company** are reported in Appendix A at the end of the textbook.

Required

Refer to Columbia Sportswear's financial statements to answer the following questions:

a. How much did Columbia's total assets increase or decrease from December 31, 2019, to December 31, 2020?

b. How much did Columbia's cash and cash equivalents increase or decrease from December 31, 2019, to December 31, 2020, and how much cash did Columbia report on its December 31, 2020, balance sheet?

c. How much accounts receivable and accounts payable did Columbia report on December 31, 2020? Does it appear that Columbia is able to collect from its customers as well as pay its own bills?

d. Did Columbia experience revenue growth in 2020?

e. Was Columbia profitable in 2020? How does the company's 2020 profit compare to 2019?

Columbia Sportswear Company
Under Armour

BTN1-2. Comparative Analysis Problem: Columbia Sportswear Company vs. Under Armour, Inc. Simplified financial statements for the **Columbia Sportswear Company** are reported in **Exhibit 1-10** and **Under Armour**'s financial statements are presented in Appendix B at the end of this book.

Required

1. Based on the information in these financial statements, compare the following for each company as of December 31, 2020:
   a. Total assets
   b. Sales
   c. Net income
   d. Cash flow from operations
2. From this information, what can you conclude about the relative size and operating performance of each company?

BTN1-3. Business Decision Problem Paul Seale, a friend of yours, is negotiating the purchase of an exterminating company called Total Pest Control. Seale has been employed by a national pest control service and knows the technical side of the business. However, he knows little about accounting, so he asks for your assistance. The owner of Total Pest Control, Greg Krey, provided Seale with income statements for the past three years, which showed an average net income of $72,000 per year. The latest balance sheet shows total assets of $285,000 and liabilities of $45,000. Seale brings the following matters to your attention:

1. Krey is asking $300,000 for the firm. He told Seale that because the firm has been earning a 30 percent return on stockholders' equity, the price should be higher than the net assets reported on the balance sheet. (Note: The return on stockholders' equity is calculated as net income divided by total stockholders' equity.)
2. Seale noticed that there was no salary expense reported for Krey on the income statements, even though he worked half-time in the business. Krey explained that, because he had other income, he withdrew only $18,000 each year from the firm for personal use. If he purchases the firm, Seale will hire a full-time manager to run the firm at an annual salary of $36,000.
3. Krey's tax returns for the past three years report a lower net income for the firm than the amounts shown in the financial statements. Seale is skeptical about the accounting principles used in preparing the company's financial statements.

Required

a. If Seale accepts Krey's average annual income figure of $72,000, what would Seale's percentage return on stockholders' equity be, assuming that the net income remained at the same level and that the firm was purchased for $300,000?

b. Should Krey's withdrawals of $18,000 per year affect the net income reported in the financial statements? What will Seale's percentage return be if he takes into consideration the $36,000 salary he plans to pay a full-time manager?

c. Could there be legitimate reasons for the difference between net income as shown in the financial statements and net income as reported on the tax returns, as mentioned in point 3? How might Seale obtain additional assurances about the propriety of the company's financial statements?

BTN1-4. Financial Analysis Problem Todd Jansen is deciding among several job offers. One job offer he is considering is in the marketing department at **Columbia Sportswear Company**. Before he makes his decision, he decides to review the financial reports of the company.

Columbia Sportswear Company

Required

Use the Columbia Sportswear annual report located in Appendix A at the end of this book to answer the following questions:

a. Were the financial statements of Columbia audited? If so, what firm performed the audit?

b. What was the amount of Columbia's 2020 net income? How does this compare with 2019 net income?

c. How much cash was provided or used for financing activities? What were the major sources and uses of cash from financing activities?

d. How much were accrued liabilities in 2020? What makes up this balance?

e. What are some of the more significant estimates used in the preparation of the company's financial statements?

f. To what amount are the financial statements rounded?

CRITICAL THINKING

BTN1-5. Accounting Research Problem The annual report of **General Mills, Inc.**, for the year ending May 31, 2020 (fiscal year 2020), can be found at: https://investors.generalmills.com/financial-information/annual-reports/default.aspx.

General Mills, Inc.

Required

a. Refer to the company's balance sheet.

1. What form of business organization does General Mills use? What evidence supports your answer?
2. What is the date of the most recent balance sheet?
3. For the most recent balance sheet, what is the largest asset reported? the largest liability?

b. Refer to the company's income statement.

1. What time period is covered by the most recent statement of earnings?
2. What total amount of sales revenues did General Mills generate in the most recent period? What is the change in sales revenues from last year to the current report year?
3. What is the net income (i.e., net earnings, including earnings attributable to noncontrolling interests) for the most recent period?

c. Refer to the company's statement of cash flows.
1. For the most recent period, what is the amount and trend of the cash flow from operating activities?
2. For the most recent period, what is the amount and trend of the cash flow from investing activities?
3. For the most recent period, what is the amount and trend of the cash flow from financing activities?

Writing *assignments are denoted by this icon.*

BTN1-6. Accounting Communication Activity Jasper Simmons is an intern for the Newby Company. He knows the company's balance sheet is supposed to balance, but he is not having much luck getting it to balance. Jasper knows that you are taking a course in accounting, so he asks for your help. Jasper provides you with the following balance sheet that is currently out of balance:

NEWBY COMPANY
Balance Sheet
December 31

Assets		Liabilities	
Cash	15,000	Inventory	20,000
Accounts receivable	30,000	Notes payable	38,000
Equipment, net	28,000	**Stockholders' Equity**	
Accounts payable	(22,000)	Dividends	(11,000)
		Common stock	10,000
		Retained earnings, beginning of year	10,000
Total	51,000	Total	67,000

In addition, Jasper provides you with a correct income statement that reports net income for the year of $24,000.

Required

a. Prepare a corrected balance sheet for the Newby Company.
b. Write a memo to Jasper explaining what he did wrong.
c. In the memo explain the purpose of the balance sheet.

BTN1-7. Accounting Ethics Case Jack Hardy, CPA, has a brother, Ted, in the retail clothing business. Ted ran the business as a sole proprietor for 10 years. During this 10-year period, Jack helped Ted with various accounting matters. For example, Jack designed the accounting system for the company, prepared Ted's personal income tax returns (which included financial data about the clothing business), and recommended various cost control procedures. Ted paid Jack for all of these services. A year ago, Ted expanded the business and incorporated. Ted is president of the corporation and also chairs the corporation's board of directors. The board of directors has overall responsibility for corporate affairs. When the corporation was formed, Ted asked Jack to serve on its board of directors. Jack accepted. In addition, Jack now prepares the corporation's income tax returns and continues to advise his brother on accounting matters.

Recently, the corporation applied for a large bank loan. The bank wants audited financial statements for the corporation before it will decide on the loan request. Ted asked Jack to perform the audit. Jack replied that he cannot do the audit because the code of ethics for CPAs requires that he be independent when providing audit services.

Required

Why is it important that a CPA be independent when providing audit services? Which of Jack's activities or relationships impair his independence?

Columbia Sportswear Company

BTN1-8. Environmental, Social, and Governance Problem Go to the **Columbia Sportswear Company** Website (https://www.columbia.com) and find the section on their commitment to corporate responsibility. This section can be found near the bottom of their home page under the section "About Us."

Required

Answer the following questions.

a. How does Columbia describe the company's efforts at corporate responsibility?
b. What is the stated purpose of Columbia's sustainability efforts?
c. What featured initiative has Columbia embarked upon?

d. Why do you think that Columbia makes these efforts to be a good corporate citizen? Why do you think they devote so much space on their Website to promote these efforts?

BTN1-9. Accounting Ethics Problem Go to the Association of Certified Fraud Examiners Website (www.acfe.com) and find their description of a forensic accountant. This can be found under the Career tab, Career Paths, then click on Accounting, and then on Forensic Accountant.

Required
Answer the following questions.

a. What type of engagements do forensic accountants work on?
b. What are some of the useful skills that a forensic accountant should possess?
c. How might the knowledge learned from this course help you to become a forensic accountant?

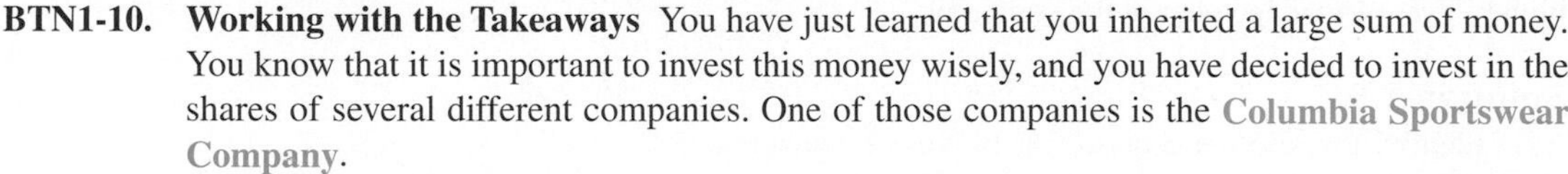

BTN1-10. Working with the Takeaways You have just learned that you inherited a large sum of money. You know that it is important to invest this money wisely, and you have decided to invest in the shares of several different companies. One of those companies is the **Columbia Sportswear Company**.

Columbia Sportswear Company

Required
Answer the following questions regarding your potential investment in Columbia Sportswear shares:

a. Should you request financial statements from the company, and if so, which ones?
b. Is it important that the financial statements be audited by an independent auditor? Explain.
c. What does each of the four financial statements tell you about Columbia's financial health or operating performance?

ANSWERS TO SELF-STUDY QUESTIONS

1. c **2.** d **3.** a **4.** b **5.** c **6.** a **7.** b **8.** c **9.** d
10.
1. Sole proprietorship and partnership (a & b)
2. Sole proprietorship and partnership (a & b)
3. Partnership (b)
4. Corporation (c)
5. Corporation (c)
6. Sole proprietorship (a)

11. b **12.** b **13.** c

REVIEW SOLUTIONS

Solution 1.1

Sole proprietorship: Single owner controlled, business is not taxed but owners are, unlimited liability of owners, more difficult to transfer ownership and raise capital compared to a corporation.

Partnership: Multiple owner controlled, business is not taxed but owners are, unlimited liability of owners, more difficult to transfer ownership and raise capital compared to a corporation.

Corporations: Business taxed on profits and owners taxed on dividends, limited liability of owners, easier to transfer ownership and raise capital compared to a sole proprietorship or partnership.

Solution 1.2

1. Financing
2. Operating
3. Investing
4. Operating
5. Financing
6. Operating

Solution 1.3

1. The financial statements are the main source of financial information for external users of accounting information. External users require information on a business's performance and financial position. This is the type of information provided by the financial statements.

2. Internal users include management, the marketing department, the human resources department, and the finance department, among others. Each of these groups requires data for decision-making.
3. External users include, among others, investors, lenders, and customers. These external groups require accounting information to help them make decisions regarding a company's performance and financial position.

Solution 1.4

Your supervisor is asking you to participate in the preparation of fraudulent financial statements. This is not only unethical, but illegal and could subject you to criminal prosecution. By reporting the sales revenue early, the financial statements will mislead users into thinking the company is doing better than it actually is. This in turn may lead them to make erroneous investment decisions. You should not follow your supervisor's request. Instead, you should explain to your supervisor why reporting sales revenue prior to when it is earned is unethical. If your supervisor continues to pressure you, you should report your supervisor's request to a higher level of management in the company.

Solution 1.5

1. Identify the relevant economic activities of a business
2. Quantify these economic activities
3. Record the resulting measures in a systematic manner

Solution 1.6

JANE'S CAKES AND CHOCOLATE, INC.
Income Statement
For Year Ended December 31

Revenue		
Sales of goods		$200,000
Expenses		
Rent expense	$16,000	
Insurance expense	20,000	
Salary expense	40,000	
Administrative expense	18,000	
Interest expense	1,600	
Total expenses		95,600
Net income		$104,400

JANE'S CAKES AND CHOCOLATE, INC.
Statement of Stockholders' Equity
For Year Ended December 31

	Common Stock	Retained Earnings	Total
Balance, January 1	$ 0	$ 0	$ 0
Add: Common stock issued	50,000		50,000
Net income		104,400	104,400
Less: Dividends		(10,000)	(10,000)
Balance, December 31	$50,000	$ 94,400	$144,400

JANE'S CAKES AND CHOCOLATE, INC.
Balance Sheet
December 31

Assets		Liabilities	
Cash	$ 99,000	Bank loan payable	$ 20,000
Accounts receivable	40,000	Interest payable	1,600
Equipment	27,000	Total liabilities	21,600
		Stockholders' Equity	
		Common stock	50,000
		Retained earnings	94,400
		Total stockholders' equity	144,400
Total assets	$166,000	Total liabilities and stockholders' equity	$166,000

JANE'S CAKES AND CHOCOLATE, INC.
Statement of Cash Flows
For Year Ended December 31

Cash provided by operating activities	$66,000
Cash used in investing activities	(27,000)
Cash provided by financing activities	60,000
Net increase of cash	99,000
Cash at January 1	0
Cash at December 31	$99,000

Solution 1.7

1. c
2. b
3. a

Solution 1.8

1. Business intelligence — *d.* The tools companies use to make data-based business decisions.
2. Data analytics — *e.* Uses methodology such as data mining, data management, and statistical analysis to determine what and why things happened and to anticipate what will happen or what should be done in the future.
3. Data visualization — *a.* Use of graphs, charts, and maps to explain and disseminate results of data analysis.
4. Big data — *b.* The methods used by companies to analyze large, often complex data sets.
5. Blockchain — *c.* A distributed ledger system that allows participants to keep track of transactions without the need for centralized record keeping.

Processing Accounting Information

PAST

Chapter 1 described the environment of financial accounting. It also introduced the financial statements and basic analysis of them.

PRESENT

This chapter explains the accounting system, including transaction analysis and the accounting equation.

FUTURE

Chapter 3 describes accounting adjustments, the construction of financial statements, and the period-end closing process.

SCORE!

Celebrity endorsements can generate significant sums for both advertisers and celebrities. Nowhere are endorsements more lucrative than in the athletic sportswear industry. Companies like **Under Armour** and **Nike** have multi-million dollar contracts with professional athletes such as NBA stars Steph Curry and LeBron James. However, when celebrities and star athletes run afoul of acceptable norms by engaging in unethical behavior, companies are quick to cancel their endorsement contracts to ensure their brand is not tarnished.

Accounting firms such as **PricewaterhouseCoopers**, **Ernst and Young**, **KPMG**, and **Deloitte** have reputations that are built on honesty and ethical conduct—attributes critical to the accounting profession. Many consider ethics the most fundamental principle underlying financial accounting and independent accounting firms.

While auditing work is not as glamorous as winning an NBA Championship, it is crucial for well-functioning capital markets. Companies as varied as **Under Armour**, **Lowe's**, **Alphabet**, and **McDonald's** all require reliable, audited financial statements for making good business decisions.

Road Map

LO	Learning Objective	Page	eLecture	Review	Assignments
LO1	**Identify the five major steps in the accounting cycle.**	42	E2-1	2.1	SE1
LO2	**Analyze and record transactions using the accounting equation.**	43	E2-2	2.2	SE2, SE3, SE4, E1, E2, E3, E4, E5, E6, E10, E11, E12, P1, P2, P3, P4, P5, P6, P8, P9, P10, P11, P12
LO3	**Introduce the Transaction Analysis Template.**	51		2.3	SE5, SE6, E8, E9, P7
LO4	**Explain the nature and purpose of an account, the chart of accounts, and the general ledger.**	52	E2-3	2.4	E7

Processing Accounting Information

Accounting Cycle	Analyzing and Recording Transactions	Transaction Analysis Template	The Account
• Five major steps • Accounting period	• Using the accounting equation • Expanding the accounting equation • Record transactions	• Objective of the Transaction Analysis Template (TAT) • An illustration of the use of the TAT	• The role of accounts • Chart of accounts • General ledger

ACCOUNTING CYCLE

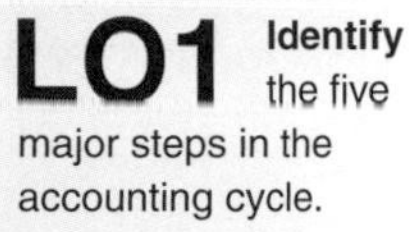

Businesses engage in economic activities. The role of accounting is to analyze these activities for their impact on a company's accounting equation and then enter the results of that analysis in the company's accounting system. When a company's management team needs financial data for decision-making purposes and for reports to external parties, the company's financial statements are prepared and communicated. At the end of the accounting period, the "books are closed," a process that prepares the accounting records for the next accounting period. The accounting activities described constitute major steps in the **accounting cycle**—a sequence of activities undertaken by accountants to accumulate and report the financial information of a business. Stated succinctly, these steps are analyze transactions, record transactions, adjust accounts, prepare financial statements, and close temporary accounts. **Exhibit 2-1** shows the sequence of the major steps in the accounting cycle.

EXHIBIT 2-1 Five Major Steps in the Accounting Cycle

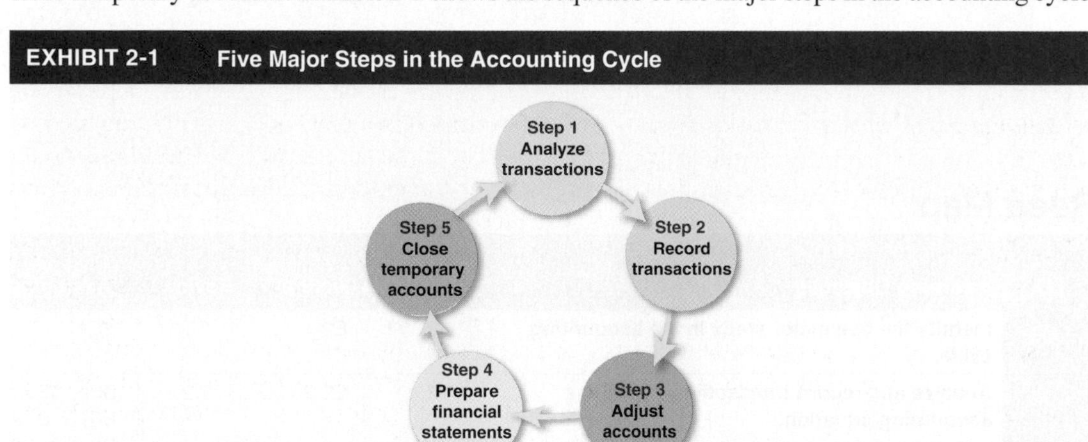

The five steps in the accounting cycle do not occur with equal frequency. A business analyzes and records financial transactions daily during the accounting period. It adjusts and reports accumulated financial data whenever management needs financial information, usually at weekly, monthly, or quarterly intervals, but at least annually. Closing the books occurs just once, at the end of the accounting period. This chapter focuses on the first two steps of the accounting cycle—analyze transactions and record transactions. In Chapter 3, we examine the final three steps of the cycle.

ACCOUNTING IN PRACTICE

Accounting Periods The annual accounting period is known as a **fiscal year**. Businesses with fiscal year-ends on December 31 are said to be on a **calendar year**. About 60 percent of U.S. businesses are on a calendar year. Many companies prefer to have their accounting year coincide with their "natural" year—that is, at a point in time when business activity is at a low point. For example, many retailers conclude their fiscal year when inventory quantities are low and easier to count, as year-end accounting procedures are more efficiently accomplished when there is less inventory. The "natural" year does not necessarily coincide with the calendar year. For example, **Gap**, a retailer, ends its fiscal year on the Friday nearest January 31. The company's busiest period is November through January, when its customers are holiday shopping. Similarly, the **Boston Celtics**, a professional basketball team, concludes its fiscal year on June 30, following completion of the NBA finals.

REVIEW 2.1

Place the following five major steps in the accounting cycle in the proper order:

a. Prepare financial statements
b. Record transactions
c. Close temporary accounts
d. Analyze transactions
e. Adjust accounts

The solution is on page 68.

ANALYZE TRANSACTIONS

LO2 Analyze and record transactions using the accounting equation.

Virtually all companies use computer-based accounting systems to record their financial transactions and prepare financial statements. The sophistication of these systems can vary greatly depending upon the size of the company and the complexity of its business. A small sole-proprietorship might record its transactions on a laptop, while large corporations like Under Armour require advanced information systems. Regardless of the size of the company, however, the underlying accounting process is the same. Importantly, a fundamental concept that is common to all accounting systems is the accounting equation.

The accounting equation is written as:

Assets = Liabilities + Stockholders' equity

Step 1 Analyze transactions

The accounting equation provides a convenient, and quite powerful, way to analyze and summarize a company's financial transactions and data. The first step in the accounting cycle—analyze—is to determine just what information (if any) must be recorded in a company's accounting records. The **monetary unit concept** requires that a monetary unit is used to measure an entity's economic activity (for example, the dollar in the United States or the euro in the European Union). Only items that can be expressed in monetary terms are recorded in financial statements. For example, the payment of wages to an employee is recorded because it can be expressed in monetary terms.

An **accounting transaction** is an economic event that must be recorded in the company's accounting records. In general, any event that affects any of the elements of the accounting equation—assets, liabilities, or stockholders' equity—must be recorded in a company's accounting records. Some activities—for example, ordering supplies, bidding on a contract, or negotiating the purchase of an asset—may represent a business activity, but an accounting transaction does not occur until such activities result in a change to an asset, liability, or stockholders' equity account.

An accounting transaction impacts the accounting equation. However, that equation always remains in balance, and at least two accounts are always affected. This is where the term **double-entry accounting** comes from. For example, if an asset account such as Cash is increased, one of the following financial events must also occur to keep the accounting equation in balance:

a. Another asset, such as accounts receivable, must decrease; or

b. A liability, such as notes payable, must increase; or

c. An account that affects stockholders' equity, such as sales revenue, must increase.

Accounting Equation Expanded

Stockholders' equity has two components—the amount invested by stockholders (common stock) and the cumulative net income of the business that has not yet been distributed to stockholders as a dividend (retained earnings). Common stock is increased when the company issues shares of stock, and retained earnings is increased by a company's net income (or decreased by a net loss) and decreased by a company's payment of dividends. Incorporating these two components into stockholders' equity, the *expanded accounting equation* is illustrated in **Exhibit 2-2**.

EXHIBIT 2-2 The Accounting Equation Expanded

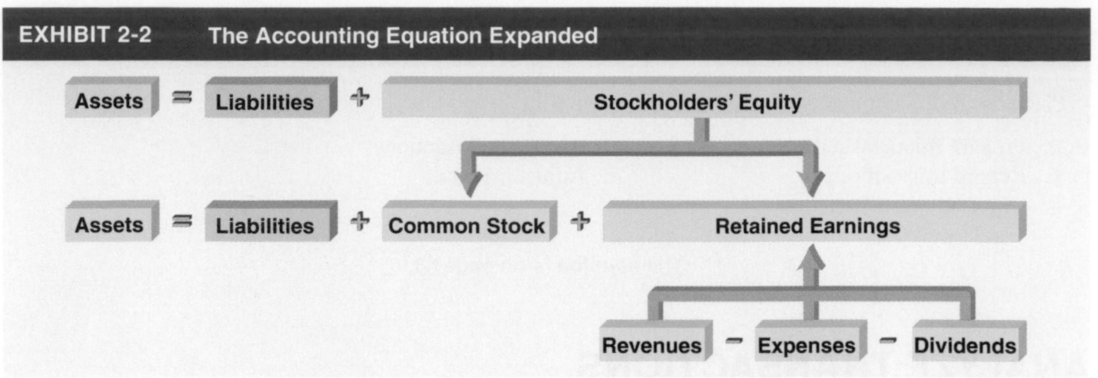

ACCOUNTING ETHICS

Fraudulent Reporting Verifying that the accounting equation is in balance for all transactions is not sufficient to guarantee accuracy of financial records. A case in point is **WorldCom**, which was the largest fraud (and bankruptcy) in history at the time of its demise. To inflate its net income, WorldCom improperly increased an asset account (property, plant, and equipment) when they should have increased an expense account. While WorldCom's accounting equation was in balance, assets were overstated and expenses were understated by almost $7 billion.

RECORD TRANSACTIONS

Step 2 Record transactions

We now consider the transactions of DataForce, Inc., a developer of cloud-based data security applications, to illustrate how various economic activities and events lead to financial statements.

Steve Gates established DataForce on December 1 of the current year. The company's transactions for December, the first month of operations, are analyzed on the following pages. The accounting equation for DataForce is shown after each transaction so that the financial effects of each transaction can be examined. Note that the accounting equation remains in balance following each transaction. This is not a coincidence; it is the result of the fundamental structure of the accounting system.

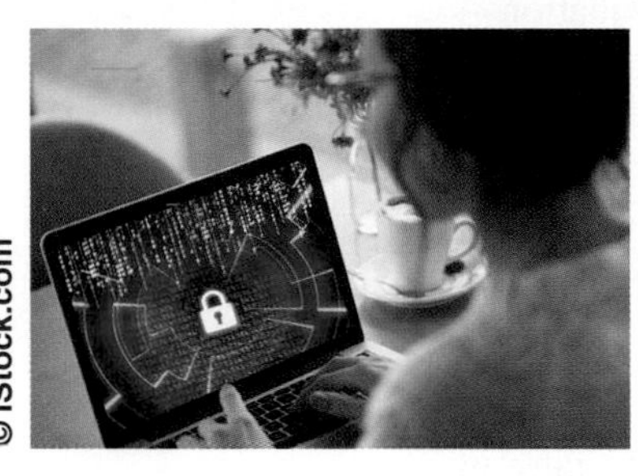
© iStock.com

The following pages illustrate eleven transactions that occurred during December at DataForce. Avoid the temptation to skip any of these transactions because each transaction is included to illustrate a particular concept or approach to recording an economic event utilizing the accounting equation.

Transaction 1. Issued Stock

On December 1, Steve Gates invested $30,000 cash in exchange for the company's common stock. This transaction increased the company's assets, Cash, by $30,000 and increased its stockholders' equity, Common Stock, by $30,000, as illustrated below using the accounting equation.

	Balance Sheet			
Trans.	Assets	= Liabilities	+	Stockholders' Equity
	Cash	=		Common Stock
(1)	+30,000			+30,000
	$30,000			$30,000

It is important to verify the equality of the accounting equation following each transaction. After the above transaction is recorded, both sides of the equation increase by $30,000.

Transaction 2. Paid Rent in Advance

On December 1, DataForce prepaid its office rent for the next six months, December through May of the following year. DataForce's rent is $1,800 per month, therefore it paid a total of $10,800 cash (6 × $1,800). This transaction decreased Cash by $10,800 and increased Prepaid Rent by $10,800.

	Balance Sheet				
Trans.	Assets		= Liabilities	+	Stockholders' Equity
	Cash	+ Ppd. Rent =		+	Common Stock
Bal.	30,000				30,000
(2)	**−10,800**	**+10,800**			
	19,200 +	10,800 =			30,000
	$30,000				$30,000

The expenditure for prepaid rent is recorded as an asset because the advance payment is a future economic benefit to the company. This outlay of cash has value to the business beyond the current accounting period, and any rent that is used up in the current accounting period will be recorded as an expense for the month of December.

A.K.A. Prepaid rent is also referred to as *advances to landlord.*

Transaction 3. Purchased Office Supplies on Account

On December 1, DataForce purchased office supplies on account totaling $2,850. Businesses often extend credit to their customers. Credit allows businesses to pay for goods or services at a later date. When credit is used to purchase goods or services, the purchase is said to be made *on account*. This transaction increased Office Supplies by $2,850, and it increased Accounts Payable, a liability, by the same amount.

	Balance Sheet					
Trans.	Assets			= Liabilities	+	Stockholders' Equity
	Cash	+ Office Supp.	+ Ppd. Rent =	Accts Pay.	+	Common Stock
Bal.	19,200		10,800			30,000
(3)		**+2,850**		**+2,850**		
	19,200 +	2,850 +	10,800 =	2,850	+	30,000
	$32,850			$32,850		

Office supplies are recorded as an asset because they are expected to be used by the business in future periods beyond the current accounting period. Any supplies that are used up in the current accounting period will be recorded as an expense for the month of December. Following the purchase of office supplies, assets total $32,850, which is equal to the sum of total liabilities of $2,850 plus stockholders' equity of $30,000.

Transaction 4. Signed Bank Note in Exchange for Cash

On December 1, DataForce obtained a two-year bank loan in the amount of $36,000, after signing a note payable. Annual interest charges on the note amount to 10 percent and are due each November 30. As a consequence of this loan, the company's Cash account increased by $36,000 and the Notes Payable account, a liability, increased by $36,000.

Balance Sheet						
Trans.	Assets			= Liabilities		+ Stockholders' Equity
	Cash +	Office Supp. +	Ppd. Rent =	Accts. Pay. +	Notes Pay. +	Common Stock
Bal.	19,200	2,850	10,800	2,850		30,000
(4)	**+36,000**				**+36,000**	
	55,200 +	2,850 +	10,800 =	2,850 +	36,000 +	30,000
	$68,850			$68,850		

Transaction 5. Purchased Equipment with Cash

On December 2, DataForce used cash to purchase office equipment costing $32,400. This transaction decreased Cash by $32,400 and increased Office Equipment by the same amount. The accounting equation remains in balance because an equal amount, $32,400, is both added to and subtracted from total assets.

Balance Sheet							
Trans.	Assets				= Liabilities		+ Stockholders' Equity
	Cash +	Office Supp. +	Ppd. Rent +	Equip-ment =	Accts Pay. +	Notes Pay. +	Common Stock
Bal.	55,200	2,850	10,800		2,850	36,000	30,000
(5)	**–32,400**			**+32,400**			
	22,800 +	2,850 +	10,800 +	32,400 =	2,850 +	36,000 +	30,000
	$68,850				$68,850		

Transaction 6. Received Customer Prepayment

On December 5, DataForce received a prepayment in the amount of $3,000 for services to be performed over the next few months. The **revenue recognition principle** (explained in Chapter 3) states that revenue should be recorded when the services are performed or the goods are delivered. Because DataForce has not yet performed the services, the revenue has not been earned, and it does not record the $3,000 payment as revenue. Instead, a liability account, **Unearned revenue**, is increased by $3,000, and the company's Cash account is increased by $3,000. Unearned revenue is a liability because the company accepted payment for goods or services have not yet been provided; therefore, the amount cannot be recorded as earned revenue.

A.K.A. *Unearned revenue* is also called *deferred revenue* or *advances from customers.*

Balance Sheet								
Trans.	Assets				= Liabilities			+ Stockholders' Equity
	Cash +	Office Supp. +	Ppd. Rent +	Equip-ment =	Accts Pay. +	Unearn. Rev. +	Notes Pay. +	Common Stock
Bal.	22,800	2,850	10,800	32,400	2,850		36,000	30,000
(6)	**+3,000**					**+3,000**		
	25,800 +	2,850 +	10,800 +	32,400 =	2,850 +	3,000 +	36,000 +	30,000
	$71,850				$71,850			

Transaction 7. Provided Services for Customers

On December 6, DataForce performed services for several customers and in exchange was paid \$13,510 cash. This transaction increased Cash by \$13,510 and increased Fee Revenue by the same amount. Because this transaction affects revenue, we now extend the horizontal worksheet to include the income statement. This income statement shows that revenues minus expenses equal net income. In addition, we add retained earnings to the balance sheet as a component of stockholders' equity, because net income affects retained earnings.

	Balance Sheet									Income Statement		
Trans.	Assets				= Liabilities			+ Stockholders' Equity				
	Cash	+ Office Supp.	+ Ppd. Rent	+ Equipment	= Accts Pay.	+ Unearn. Rev.	+ Notes Pay.	+ Common Stock	+ Retained Earnings	Rev.	− Exp.	= Net Income
Bal.	25,800	2,850	10,800	32,400	2,850	3,000	36,000	30,000				
(7)	+13,510								+13,510	+13,510		+13,510
	39,310 +	2,850 +	10,800 +	32,400 =	2,850 +	3,000 +	36,000 +	30,000 +	13,510	13,510 −		= 13,510
	\$85,360				\$85,360							

Transaction 8. Performed Services for Both Cash and on Account

On December 8, DataForce performed \$4,740 of services and received \$1,000 in cash, with the remaining \$3,740 to be paid to DataForce by customers within 90 days. Businesses often extend credit to customers, allowing them to pay for goods or services at a later date. Under accrual accounting, revenue must be recorded when earned, regardless of when payment is received. Consequently, this transaction increased Cash by \$1,000, it increased Accounts Receivable by \$3,740, and it increased Fee Revenue by \$4,740. The accounting equation in the balance sheet remains in balance because both sides of the equation are increased by \$4,740.

A.K.A. Delivering goods or services in advance of payment is referred to as providing goods or services "*on account*" or "on credit."

	Balance Sheet										Income Statement		
Trans.	Assets					= Liabilities			+ Stockholders' Equity				
	Cash	+ Accts. Rec.	+ Office Supp.	+ Ppd. Rent	+ Equipment	= Accts Pay.	+ Unearn. Rev.	+ Notes Pay.	+ Common Stock	+ Retained Earnings	Rev.	− Exp.	= Net Income
Bal.	39,310		2,850	10,800	32,400	2,850	3,000	36,000	30,000	13,510	13,510		13,510
(8)	+1,000	+3,740								+4,740	+4,740		+4,740
	40,310 +	3,740 +	2,850 +	10,800 +	32,400 =	2,850 +	3,000 +	36,000 +	30,000 +	18,250	18,250 −		= 18,250
	\$90,100					\$90,100							

Non-Accounting Transaction. Hired an Employee

On December 9, DataForce hired an employee to provide administrative help in the office. The employee will be paid \$1,620 every two weeks and begins work Monday, December 12. At the time the employee is hired there is no immediate financial effect on the assets, liabilities, or stockholders' equity of the company. There is only an employment agreement between the employee and the company. The employee has not yet performed any work, nor has the employee received any wages.

Transaction 9. Paid Employee Wages

On December 23, DataForce paid the employee after she completed her first two weeks on the job. This transaction decreased Cash by \$1,620, and it increased Wage Expense by \$1,620. Note that the income statement includes a negative sign in front of expenses. Thus, the increase in expenses, indicated by +\$1,620, is deducted from revenues to compute net income.

	Balance Sheet										Income Statement		
Trans.	Assets					= Liabilities			+ Stockholders' Equity				
	Cash +	Accts. Rec. +	Office Supp. +	Ppd. Rent +	Equipment =	Accts Pay. +	Unearn. Rev. +	Notes Pay. +	Common Stock +	Retained Earnings	Rev. –	Exp. =	Net Income
Bal.	40,310	3,740	2,850	10,800	32,400	2,850	3,000	36,000	30,000	18,250	18,250		18,250
(9)	**–1,620**									**–1,620**		**+1,620**	**–1,620**
	38,690 +	3,740 +	2,850 +	10,800 +	32,400 =	2,850 +	3,000 +	36,000 +	30,000 +	16,630	18,250 –	1,620 =	16,630
	$88,480					$88,480							

Transaction 10. Received Payment on Account from Customer

On December 27, DataForce received a payment of $2,400 cash from a customer that had previously received services performed on account (see Transaction 8). This transaction increased Cash by $2,400 and decreased Accounts Receivable by $2,400.

	Balance Sheet										Income Statement		
Trans.	Assets					= Liabilities			+ Stockholders' Equity				
	Cash +	Accts. Rec. +	Office Supp. +	Ppd. Rent +	Equipment =	Accts Pay. +	Unearn. Rev. +	Notes Pay. +	Common Stock +	Retained Earnings	Rev. –	Exp. =	Net Income
Bal.	38,690	3,740	2,850	10,800	32,400	2,850	3,000	36,000	30,000	16,630	18,250	1,620	16,630
(10)	**+2,400**	**–2,400**											
	41,090 +	1,340 +	2,850 +	10,800 +	32,400 =	2,850 +	3,000 +	36,000 +	30,000 +	16,630	18,250 –	1,620 =	16,630
	$88,480					$88,480							

The balance in Accounts Receivable becomes $1,340. This represents the amount still owed to DataForce for services that were previously performed on account but remain unpaid.

Transaction 11. Paid Cash Dividend

On December 30, DataForce paid a cash dividend. Dividends are not a business expense and are not included in the calculation of net income. Rather, dividends are a distribution of the company's accumulated net income to its stockholders. Payment of the dividend decreases Cash by $500 and increases Dividends by $500. Note that an increase in dividends results in a decrease in Retained Earnings.

	Balance Sheet										Income Statement		
Trans.	Assets					= Liabilities			+ Stockholders' Equity				
	Cash +	Accts. Rec. +	Office Supp. +	Ppd. Rent +	Equipment =	Accts Pay. +	Unearn. Rev. +	Notes Pay. +	Common Stock +	Retained Earnings	Rev. –	Exp. =	Net Income
Bal.	41,090	1,340	2,850	10,800	32,400	2,850	3,000	36,000	30,000	16,630	18,250	1,620	16,630
(11)	**–500**									**–500**			
	40,590 +	1,340 +	2,850 +	10,800 +	32,400 =	2,850 +	3,000 +	36,000 +	30,000 +	16,130	18,250 –	1,620 =	16,630
	$87,980					$87,980							

Transaction Summary

Exhibit 2-3 provides a summary of the eleven accounting transactions for DataForce for the month of December. The exhibit uses a horizontal worksheet to illustrate the financial effect of each transaction using the accounting equation. It is important that the accounting equation remains in balance at all times and that the equality between total assets and the sum of total liabilities and stockholders' equity is maintained following each transaction. From this worksheet it is possible to prepare an unadjusted balance sheet and income statement, as shown on the next page.

The totals in the bottom row of the spreadsheet in **Exhibit 2-3** are the account balances at the end of December, prior to making the adjustments that are needed to prepare the final financial

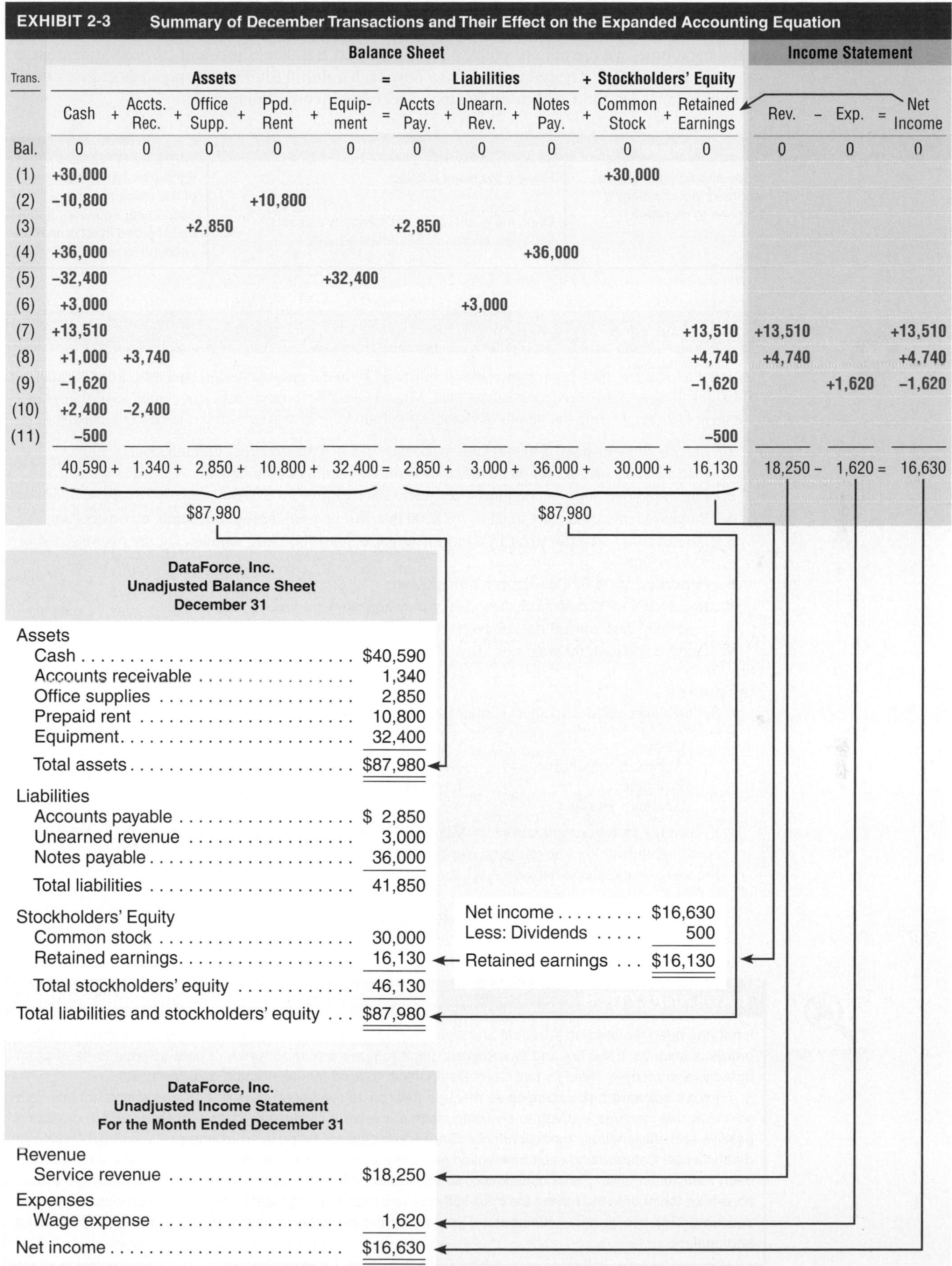

EXHIBIT 2-3 Summary of December Transactions and Their Effect on the Expanded Accounting Equation

	Balance Sheet										Income Statement		
	Assets					= Liabilities			+ Stockholders' Equity				
Trans.	Cash +	Accts. Rec. +	Office Supp. +	Ppd. Rent +	Equip-ment =	Accts Pay. +	Unearn. Rev. +	Notes Pay. +	Common Stock +	Retained Earnings	Rev. −	Exp. =	Net Income
Bal.	0	0	0	0	0	0	0	0	0	0	0	0	0
(1)	+30,000								+30,000				
(2)	−10,800			+10,800									
(3)			+2,850			+2,850							
(4)	+36,000							+36,000					
(5)	−32,400				+32,400								
(6)	+3,000						+3,000						
(7)	+13,510									+13,510	+13,510		+13,510
(8)	+1,000	+3,740								+4,740	+4,740		+4,740
(9)	−1,620									−1,620		+1,620	−1,620
(10)	+2,400	−2,400											
(11)	−500									−500			
	40,590 +	1,340 +	2,850 +	10,800 +	32,400 =	2,850 +	3,000 +	36,000 +	30,000 +	16,130	18,250 −	1,620 =	16,630
	$87,980					$87,980							

DataForce, Inc.
Unadjusted Balance Sheet
December 31

Assets	
Cash	$40,590
Accounts receivable	1,340
Office supplies	2,850
Prepaid rent	10,800
Equipment	32,400
Total assets	$87,980
Liabilities	
Accounts payable	$ 2,850
Unearned revenue	3,000
Notes payable	36,000
Total liabilities	41,850
Stockholders' Equity	
Common stock	30,000
Retained earnings	16,130
Total stockholders' equity	46,130
Total liabilities and stockholders' equity	$87,980

Net income	$16,630
Less: Dividends	500
Retained earnings	$16,130

DataForce, Inc.
Unadjusted Income Statement
For the Month Ended December 31

Revenue	
Service revenue	$18,250
Expenses	
Wage expense	1,620
Net income	$16,630

statements. Further adjustments are needed in order to properly reflect the company's operating performance during the month of December, and we will prepare these adjustments in Chapter 3. In the meantime, we are able to prepare an Unadjusted Balance Sheet and Income Statement, as shown in **Exhibit 2-3**. The red arrows show how each column total in the spreadsheet gives us the account balances in the Unadjusted Balance Sheet and Income Statement.

TAKEAWAY 2.1 Concept	Method	Assessment
When should an event be recorded in a company's accounting records?	Review the event details. Does the event affect the company's assets, liabilities, and/or stockholders' equity?	If the event affects any of the elements of the accounting equation, it must be recorded in a company's accounting records.

REVIEW 2.2

Miguel Rios acted upon his entrepreneurial spirit and started a graphic design business called Miguel's Designs. Based on an excellent business plan, Miguel was able to raise sufficient capital to begin operations in October. During the month of October, the following events occurred related to the business.

1. Stockholders invested $40,000 cash in the business in exchange for common stock.
2. Paid $2,500 cash for rent on an office suite for the month of October.
3. Purchased two desktop computers, software, and a printer for $10,000 cash.
4. Purchased miscellaneous supplies for $500 that will be used during the month, all on account.
5. Purchased an advertisement in a local newspaper for $300 cash, announcing the opening of his new business.
6. Performed $7,800 of design work on account.
7. Received $3,500 cash from customers for design work previously completed.
8. Paid $350 cash toward the company's accounts payable balance.
9. Paid $2,500 cash for wages of Miguel Rios.

REQUIRED

a. Set up a horizontal worksheet similar to **Exhibit 2-3** using the following accounts.

Cash	Common Stock
Accounts Receivable	Revenue
Equipment	Expense
Accounts Payable	

Record the October transactions of Miguel's Designs. Total all of the columns to show that assets equal liabilities plus stockholders' equity as of October 31.

b. Prepare an unadjusted balance sheet and income statement as of October 31.

The solution is on page 68.

Data Analytics

DATA ANALYTICS — Data Science Projects at Intuit

Intuit has been focused on personal and small business finance for nearly 40 years with industry-leading products such as TurboTax and QuickBooks. Intuit realizes the importance of data science to its product portfolio and recently hired its first Chief Data Officer to lead Intuit's 60-plus data scientists.

Intuit's software helps companies manage their cashflow, taxes, payroll, and accounting. Intuit's data scientists use machine learning to eliminate much of the work involved in these processes, which creates a positive and efficient customer experience. Transaction categorization is an example of Intuit's application of data science. Categorizing each transaction is a common task in any accounting system. Manually labeling each transaction is very time consuming, so Intuit offers users the option of directly downloading transactions from their bank and having the Intuit software use algorithms to classify the transactions into the proper accounts. This use of data science frees up time for the customer to perform more value-added activities and analysis.

TRANSACTION ANALYSIS TEMPLATE

LO3 Introduce the Transaction Analysis Template.

The objective of this text is to help users understand how to read and interpret financial statements. The focus is not on financial statement preparation, which requires knowledge of the system of debits and credits. Debits and credits are explained in **Appendix C** but are not required for moving forward in the text. In place of debits and credits, we use a "Transaction Analysis Template." The Transaction Analysis Template (or TAT for short) is a short-hand way of communicating how a transaction or event affects the financial statements.

To illustrate, let's take a look at how the TAT is used to reflect Transaction 7 from the DataForce example covered earlier in this chapter. Recall that on December 6, DataForce performed services for several customers and was paid $13,510 cash. This transaction increased Cash by $13,510 and increased Fee revenue by the same amount. Below, we reproduce the horizontal worksheet for Transaction 7 and show its relation to the TAT.

The TAT is an alternative to using a horizontal worksheet. While the horizontal worksheet shows all of the balance sheet accounts, the TAT focuses only on the accounts affected by the transaction being analyzed. In the case of Transaction 7, the TAT shows that Cash and Retained Earnings increase in the balance sheet and that Fee Revenue increases in the income statement. The red arrow in the TAT shows that the increase in Retained Earnings results from the increase in Net Income.

Horizontal Worksheet for Transaction 7

	Balance Sheet									Income Statement		
Trans.	Assets				= Liabilities			+ Stockholders' Equity				
	Cash	+ Office Supp.	+ Ppd. Rent	+ Equipment	= Accts Pay.	+ Unearn. Rev.	+ Notes Pay.	+ Common Stock	+ Retained Earnings	Revenues	– Expenses	= Net Income
Bal.	25,800	2,850	10,800	32,400	2,850	3,000	36,000	30,000				
(7)	+13,510								+13,510	+13,510		+13,510
	39,310	2,850	10,800	32,400 =	2,850	3,000	36,000 +	30,000	13,510	13,510 –		= 13,510
	$85,360				$85,360							

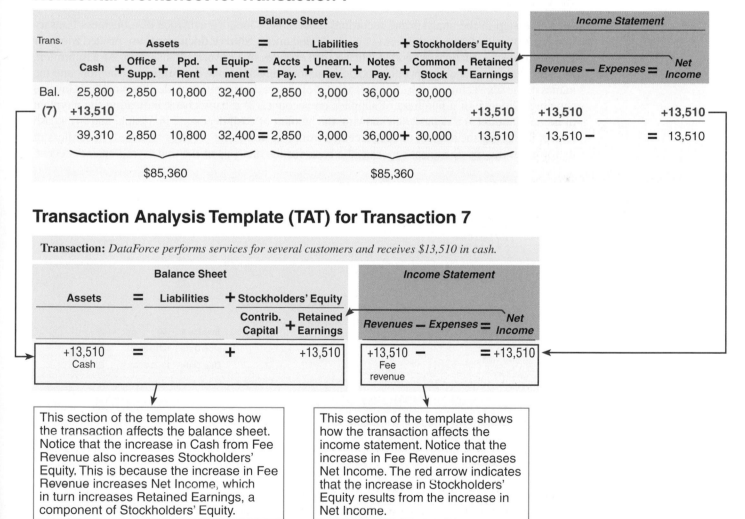

Transaction Analysis Template (TAT) for Transaction 7

Transaction: *DataForce performs services for several customers and receives $13,510 in cash.*

Balance Sheet					Income Statement		
Assets	= Liabilities	+ Stockholders' Equity					
		Contrib. Capital	+	Retained Earnings	Revenues	– Expenses	= Net Income
+13,510 Cash	=		+	+13,510	+13,510 Fee revenue	–	= +13,510

This section of the template shows how the transaction affects the balance sheet. Notice that the increase in Cash from Fee Revenue also increases Stockholders' Equity. This is because the increase in Fee Revenue increases Net Income, which in turn increases Retained Earnings, a component of Stockholders' Equity.

This section of the template shows how the transaction affects the income statement. Notice that the increase in Fee Revenue increases Net Income. The red arrow indicates that the increase in Stockholders' Equity results from the increase in Net Income.

REVIEW 2.3

Crystal Martin, who owns a high-end hair boutique, wants to understand how the following events may affect her financial statements. Using the accounting equation, record each of the transactions using the Transaction Analysis Template.

1. Purchased supplies of $500 on account.
2. Performed services and billed her client for $1,250.
3. Paid her assistant $2,000 in wages for cash.

The solution is on page 69.

THE "ACCOUNT" SYSTEM

LO4 Explain the nature and purpose of an account, the chart of accounts, and the general ledger.

The basic component of an accounting system is the **account**, which is an individual record of the increases and decreases in a specific asset, liability, or stockholders' equity item. An account is created for each asset, liability, and stockholders' equity item on a company's financial statements. Some common account titles are Cash, Accounts Receivable, Notes Payable, Fee Revenue, and Rent Expense.

Source Documents

An initial step in the analysis and recording process is to identify evidence of a business transaction. This usually comes in the form of a source document. **Source documents** are printed forms or computer records that are generated when a firm engages in a business transaction. At a minimum, a source document usually specifies the dollar amount involved, the date of the transaction, and the names of the transacting parties. Some examples of source documents include (1) a supplier's invoice showing evidence of a purchase of supplies on account, (2) a bank check indicating the payment of an obligation, (3) a deposit slip showing the amount of cash deposited in a bank, and (4) a cash receipt indicating the amount of cash received from a customer for services rendered. Regardless of its form, the source document serves as the basis for the analysis of the underlying business event.

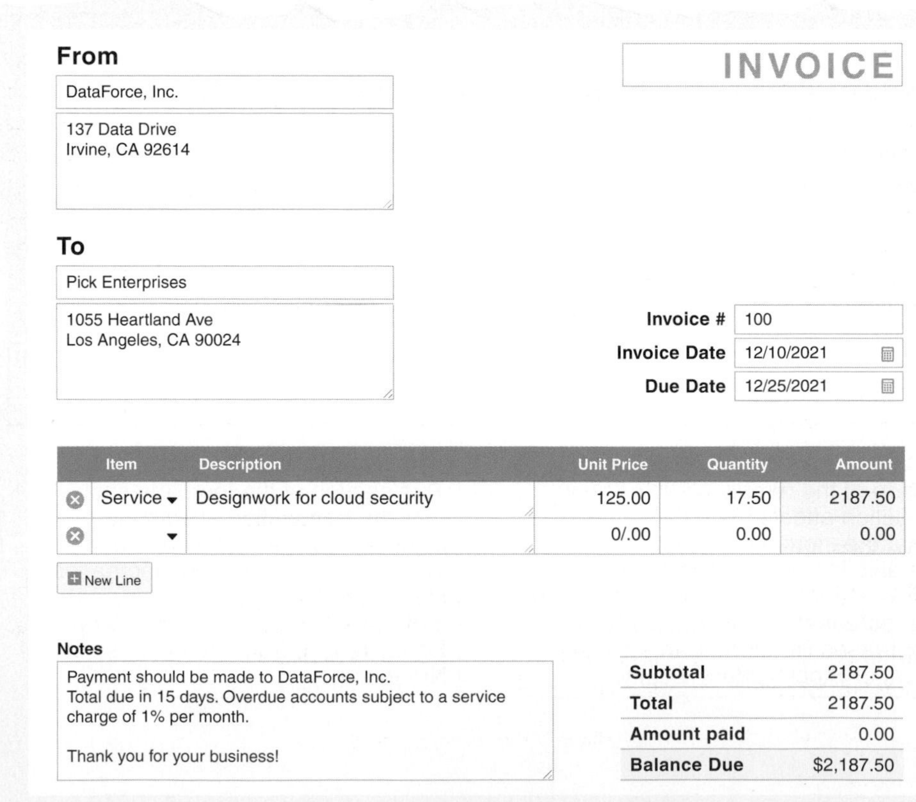

From

DataForce, Inc.

137 Data Drive
Irvine, CA 92614

INVOICE

To

Pick Enterprises

1055 Heartland Ave
Los Angeles, CA 90024

Invoice # 100
Invoice Date 12/10/2021
Due Date 12/25/2021

Item	Description	Unit Price	Quantity	Amount
Service	Designwork for cloud security	125.00	17.50	2187.50
		0/.00	0.00	0.00

New Line

Notes

Payment should be made to DataForce, Inc.
Total due in 15 days. Overdue accounts subject to a service charge of 1% per month.

Thank you for your business!

Subtotal	2187.50
Total	2187.50
Amount paid	0.00
Balance Due	$2,187.50

Chart of Accounts

Businesses maintain a chart of accounts. A **chart of accounts** is a list of the titles of all accounts in a business's accounting system. Account titles are grouped by, and in the order of, the five major components of the expanded accounting equation: assets, liabilities, stockholders' equity, revenues, and expenses. **Exhibit 2-4** shows the chart of accounts for DataForce and indicates the account numbers that they use. Each company maintains its own unique set of accounts and its own numbering system.

EXHIBIT 2-4 Chart of Accounts for DataForce

Assets	Equity
110 Cash	310 Common Stock
120 Accounts Receivable	320 Retained Earnings
130 Office Supplies	330 Dividends
150 Prepaid Rent	
170 Office Equipment	**Revenues**
175 Accumulated Depreciation—Office Equipment	410 Fee Revenue
	Expenses
Liabilities	510 Supplies Expense
210 Accounts Payable	520 Wage Expense
220 Interest Payable	530 Rent Expense
230 Wages Payable	540 Depreciation Expense—Office Equipment
250 Unearned revenue	550 Interest Expense
260 Notes Payable	

The General Ledger

Although businesses can use various ledgers to accumulate detailed accounting information, all firms have a general ledger. A **general ledger** is a listing of each of a company's accounts and the amounts from all transactions recorded during the period. The ending balances in the accounts are used in preparing the financial statements.

ENVIRONMENTAL, SOCIAL, AND GOVERNANCE

What to Record? An important principle in accounting is the monetary unit concept, which states that only those items that can be expressed in monetary terms are reported in financial statements. This causes many items of interest to be excluded from financial statements. Reporting of a company's social responsibility activities, for example, would be compromised if it were constrained to the activities that can be expressed in monetary terms. Reporting guidelines established by the Global Reporting Initiative, the organization that pioneered the world's most widely used sustainability reporting framework, allow for a wider range of activities to be measured and reported. For example, Bayer Group, a global healthcare company, reports such items as greenhouse emissions, net water usage, and employee safety records in its annual sustainable development report. Bayer's sustainability report can be found at the Bayer website.

REVIEW 2.4

Match the following key words with the correct definition.

a. Account
b. Source documents
c. Chart of accounts
d. General ledger

1. A list of titles of all accounts in a business's accounting system.
2. Printed forms or computer records that are generated when a firm engages in a business transaction.
3. A list of accounts and amounts of all transactions recorded during the period.
4. The basic component of an accounting system.

The solution is on page 69.

SUMMARY OF LEARNING OBJECTIVES

LO1 Identify the five major steps in the accounting cycle. (p. 42)

- The five major steps in the accounting cycle are:
  1. Analyze transactions.
  2. Record transactions.
  3. Adjust accounts.
  4. Prepare financial statements.
  5. Close temporary accounts.

LO2 Analyze and record transactions using the accounting equation. (p. 43)

- The accounting equation can be stated as: Assets = Liabilities + Stockholders' Equity.
- The accounting equation provides a convenient way to summarize the recording of financial information.
- An initial step in the accounting process—analyze—is to determine just which transactions (if any) need to be recorded.
- An *accounting transaction* is an economic event that requires accounting recognition. An event that affects any of the elements of the basic accounting equation (assets, liabilities, or stockholders' equity) must be recorded.
- All accounting transactions are analyzed using one or more of the basic account categories: (1) assets, (2) liabilities, (3) common stock, (4) dividends, (5) revenues, and (6) expenses. Retained earnings can also be included here.

LO3 Introduce the Transaction Analysis Template. (pg. 51)

- The Transaction Analysis Template is a way of communicating how a transaction or event affects the financial statements.

LO4 Explain the nature and purpose of an account, the chart of accounts, and the general ledger. (p. 52)

- An account is an individual record of the increases and decreases in specific assets, liabilities, stockholders' equity, dividends, revenues, or expenses.
- A general ledger is a grouping of all of the accounts that are used to prepare the basic financial statements.

SUMMARY	Concept	Method	Assessment
TAKEAWAY 2.1	When should an event be recorded in a company's accounting records?	Review the event details. Does the event affect the company's assets, liabilities, or stockholders' equity?	If the event affects any of the elements of the accounting equation, it must be recorded in a company's accounting records.

KEY TERMS

Account (p. 52)
Accounting cycle (p. 42)
Accounting transaction (p. 43)
Calendar year (p. 42)
Chart of accounts (p. 53)
Double-entry accounting (p. 43)
Fiscal year (p. 42)
General ledger (p. 53)
Monetary unit concept (p. 43)
Revenue recognition principle (p. 46)
Source documents (p. 52)
Unearned revenue (p. 46)

SELF-STUDY QUESTIONS

(Answers to Self-Study Questions are at the end of this chapter.)

LO2

1. **Which of the following transactions does not affect the balance sheet?**
   a. Purchased $500 supplies on account
   b. Paid off a $3,000 note payable
   c. Received $4,000 cash from a bank after signing a note payable
   d. Ordered a new machine that will be paid for upon its delivery in two months

2. Tobias Company purchased inventory on account. This transaction will affect: LO2 Homework MBC

a. Only the balance sheet
b. Only the income statement
c. The income statement and the statement of retained earnings
d. The income statement, balance sheet, and statement of retained earnings

3. If assets increase by $100 and liabilities decrease by $30, stockholders' equity must: LO2 Homework MBC

a. Remain unchanged
b. Increase by $130
c. Decrease by $70
d. Decrease by $130

4. If an asset value is increased, which of the following is true? LO2 Homework MBC

a. The value of a liability must decrease.
b. Either the value of a liability or stockholders' equity must decrease.
c. Either the value of a liability or stockholders' equity must increase or another asset must decrease.
d. Nothing more needs to occur.

5. Which of the following is an economic event and should be recorded in a company's accounting records? LO2 Homework MBC

a. The owner of the company purchases a Tesla automobile for personal use.
b. The company hires three new employees who will start work the following week.
c. The company is negotiating a contract to provide consulting services to a client.
d. The company makes a down payment on the purchase of a building site.

6. Which of the following is not one of the five steps in the accounting cycle? LO1 Homework MBC

a. Analyze transactions
b. Adjust accounts
c. Eliminate transactions
d. Prepare financial statements

7. The purchase of $500 of supplies on account will: LO2 Homework MBC

a. Increase both assets and stockholders' equity by $500
b. Increase assets and decrease liabilities by $500
c. Increase assets and decrease stockholders' equity by $500
d. Increase both assets and liabilities by $500

QUESTIONS

1. List the five major steps in the accounting cycle in their proper order.
2. Define the term *fiscal year*.
3. Provide three examples of source documents that underlie business transactions.
4. Provide an example of a transaction that would:
   a. Increase one asset account but not change the amount of total assets.
   b. Decrease an asset account and a liability account.
   c. Decrease an asset account and increase an expense account.
   d. Increase an asset account and a liability account.
5. Explain the financial effect (increase, decrease, or no effect) of each of the following transactions on stockholders' equity:
   a. Purchased supplies for cash.
   b. Paid an account payable.
   c. Paid salaries.
   d. Purchased equipment for cash.
   e. Invested cash in business.
   f. Rendered services to customers, on account.
   g. Rendered services to customers, for cash.
6. The retained earnings on a balance sheet are $80,000. Without seeing the rest of the balance sheet, can you conclude that stockholders should be able to receive a dividend in the amount of $80,000 cash from the business? Justify your answer.
7. On December 31, the Miller Company had $700,000 in total assets and owed $220,000 to creditors. If the corporation's common stock amounted to $300,000, what amount of retained earnings should appear on the company's December 31 balance sheet?
8. What type of account—asset, liability, stockholders' equity, revenue, or expense—is each of the following accounts?

   Professional Fees Earned
   Accounts Receivable
   Accounts Payable
   Cash
   Common Stock
   Advertising Expense
   Supplies
   Dividends
9. What is a chart of accounts?

10. Explain how it is possible for a balance sheet to be in balance but still be in error.
11. Is it possible for an accounting transaction to only affect the left side of the accounting equation and still leave the equation in balance? If so, provide an example.
12. Would a company record a transaction in its general ledger when an order is placed for the purchase of a machine that will be paid for at the time of its delivery in three months? Explain your answer.
13. What is an account?

DATA ANALYTICS

The assignments in this Data Analytics section are designed to familiarize you with the tools used in analyzing data and communicating the results. Appendix F provides an in-depth discussion of data analytics and blockchain technology.

DA2-1. Preparing Basic Data Visualization in Excel of the Balance Sheet
The Excel file associated with this exercise includes total liabilities, common stock, and retained earnings balances as of December 31 for Monona Inc. We will prepare data visualizations focusing on how these amounts relate to each other and how the relations are expressed through proportions.

REQUIRED

1. Download Excel file DA2-1 found in myBusinessCourse.
2. Prepare a doughnut chart showing total liabilities, total common stock, and total retained earnings as components of total liabilities plus stockholders' equity. *Hint:* Highlight the dataset and open the Insert tab. Click on the Pie icon in the Charts group and click on Doughnut.
3. Display a percentage label in each section of your chart. *Hint:* Right-click inside the doughnut, select Format data labels, select Percentage. Deselect Value if necessary.
4. List the formula for the chart data range. *Hint:* Click inside the chart. Open the Chart Design tab and click Select Data. The formula is in the Chart data range field.
5. List the percentage amount (or combination of percentage amounts) on the doughnut chart that reflect the stockholders' equity proportion.
6. List the larger percentage: either the total liabilities proportion or the total equity proportion of the pie chart.
7. List the percentage amount (or combination of percentage amounts) on the doughnut chart that reflect the total assets proportion.
8. List the dollar amount of total assets.

DA2-2. Preparing Tableau Visualizations of Basic Financial Information
Refer to PF-20 in Appendix F. This problem requires the creation of Tableau visualizations of financial information of S&P 500 companies from balance sheet, income statement, and statement of cash flows data.

Assignments with the MBC logo in the margin are available in myBusinessCourse. See the Preface of the book for details.

SHORT EXERCISES

LO1 **SE2-1. The Accounting Cycle** Which of the following is the correct order of the five steps in the accounting cycle?

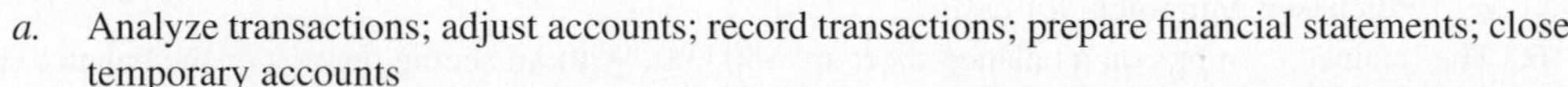

a. Analyze transactions; adjust accounts; record transactions; prepare financial statements; close temporary accounts
b. Analyze transactions; record transactions; adjust accounts; prepare financial statements; close temporary accounts
c. Analyze transactions; record transactions; adjust accounts; close temporary accounts; prepare financial statements
d. Analyze transactions; prepare financial statements; adjust accounts; record transactions; close temporary accounts

LO2 **SE2-2. Analyze a Transaction** Identify the accounts that will be affected in each of the following transactions. Indicate whether the accounts increase or decrease:

a. Issued common stock for cash
b. Borrowed money from a bank
c. Provided services on account
d. Purchased inventory on account
e. Collected cash from customers that owed a balance due

SE2-3. Determine a Transaction The Pearce Company recorded a transaction by increasing Accounts Receivable and increasing Sales Revenue. What event was being recorded? LO2

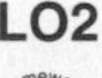

SE2-4. Determine the Cash Balance The beginning-of-the-period cash balance for the Travis Company was $10,000. Cash sales for the month were $5,000 and sales on account were $6,000. The company paid $3,500 cash for current-period purchases and paid $2,000 cash for amounts due from last month. What is the ending balance in the Cash account? LO2

SE2-5. Recording Transactions with the Accounting Equation During the year, the Decker Company experienced the following accounting transactions: LO3

1. Issued common stock in the amount of $100,000
2. Paid a $30,000 cash dividend
3. Borrowed $25,000 from a bank
4. Made a principal payment of $2,500 on an outstanding bank loan
5. Made an interest payment of $1,200 on an outstanding bank loan

Using the accounting equation, record each of the transactions using the Transaction Analysis Template:

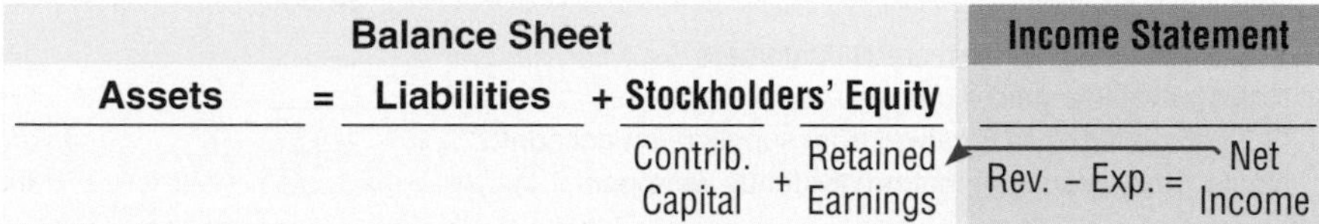

SE2-6. Recording Transactions with the Accounting Equation During the year, the Decker Company experienced the following accounting transactions: LO3

1. Purchased equipment with cash in the amount of $100,000
2. Purchased supplies on account in the amount of $10,000
3. Collected $21,000 cash from customers
4. Paid a cash dividend of $15,000

Using the accounting equation, record each of the transactions using the Transaction Analysis Template:

Balance Sheet					Income Statement		
Assets	=	Liabilities	+	Stockholders' Equity			
				Contrib. Capital + Retained Earnings	Rev.	– Exp. =	Net Income

EXERCISES

E2-1. Accounting Equation Determine the missing amount in each of the following cases: LO2

	Assets	Liabilities	Stockholders' Equity
a.	$200,000	$85,000	?
b.	?	$32,000	$28,000
c.	$93,000	?	$52,000

E2-2. Transaction Analysis Following the example shown in (a) below, indicate the accounting effects of the listed transactions on the assets, liabilities, and stockholders' equity of Martin & Company, a corporation: LO2

a. Purchased, for cash, a desktop computer for use in the office.
ANSWER: Increase assets (Office Equipment)
Decrease assets (Cash)

b. Rendered services and billed the client.

c. Paid rent for the month.

d. Rendered services to a client for cash.

e. Received amount due from a client in Transaction (b).

f. Purchased an office desk on account.

g. Paid employees' salaries for the month.
h. Paid for desk purchased in Transaction (f).
i. The company paid a dividend.

LO2 **E2-3. Analysis of Accounts** Calculate the unknown amount in each of the following five independent situations. The answer to situation *(a)* is given as an example.

Homework MBC

	Account	Beginning Balance	Ending Balance	Other Information
a.	Cash	$ 6,100	$ 5,250	Total cash disbursed, $5,400.
b.	Accounts receivable	8,500	9,300	Services on account, $16,500.
c.	Notes payable	15,000	20,000	Borrowed funds by issuing a note, $30,000.
d.	Accounts payable	3,280	1,720	Payments on account, $2,900.
e.	Stockholders' equity	32,000	46,000	Capital contribution, $5,000.

	Unknown Amounts Required	
a.	Total cash received	$4,550
b.	Total cash collected from credit customers	_____
c.	Notes payable repaid during the period	_____
d.	Goods and services received from suppliers on account	_____
e.	Net income, assuming that no dividends were paid	_____

LO2 **E2-4. Transaction Analysis** The accounts below are from the general ledger of The Bast Company. For each letter, describe the type of business transaction(s) or event(s) that would most likely be reflected by entries to the account. For example, the answer to *(a)* is amounts for services performed for clients on account.

a. An increase to Accounts Receivable
b. A decrease to Accounts Receivable
c. An increase to Notes Payable
d. An increase to Office Equipment
e. A decrease to Accounts Payable
f. An increase to Accounts Payable
g. An increase to Professional Fees Earned
h. An increase to Dividends
i. An increase to Common Stock
j. An increase to Wage Expense

LO2 **E2-5. Transaction Analysis** Match each of the following transactions of Lesch & Company with the appropriate letters, indicating the financial effect of the transaction. The key for the letters follows the list of transactions. The correct answer for Transaction (1) is given as an illustration:

Homework MBC

		Answer
1.	Purchased supplies on account.	*a, d*
2.	Paid interest on note payable.	_____
3.	Cash dividend was paid to stockholders.	_____
4.	Returned some defective supplies and received a reduction in the amount owed.	_____
5.	Made payment to settle note payable.	_____
6.	Received an invoice for utilities used.	_____
7.	Received payment in advance from client for work to be done next month.	_____
8.	The stockholders contributed additional capital to the business.	_____

Financial Effect of Transaction

a. Increase an asset
b. Decrease an asset
c. Decrease a liability
d. Increase a liability
e. Decrease common stock
f. Increase common stock
g. Increase dividends
h. Decrease dividends
i. Decrease revenue
j. Increase revenue
k. Increase an expense
l. Decrease an expense

E2-6. Recording Transactions Creative Designs, a firm providing art services for advertisers, began business on June 1. Prepare a horizontal worksheet using the format in Exhibit 2-3 with the following column headings: Cash; Accounts Receivable; Supplies; Office Equipment; Accounts Payable; Common Stock; Revenue; Expense; and Dividends. Record the following transactions and total the columns to show that assets equal liabilities plus stockholders' equity as of June 30. LO2 Homework MBC

June 1 Lisa Ryan invested $12,000 cash to begin the business; she received common stock for her investment.
2 Paid rent for June, $950.
3 Purchased office equipment on account, $6,400.
6 Purchased art materials and other supplies costing $3,800; paid $1,800 down with the remainder due within 30 days.
11 Billed clients for services, $4,700.
17 Collected $3,250 from clients on account.
19 Paid $3,000 on account to office equipment company (see June 3 transaction).
25 Lisa Ryan received a $2,000 dividend.
30 Paid utility bill for June, $350.
30 Paid salaries for June, $2,500.

E2-7. Source Documents For each transaction in E2-6, indicate the related source document or documents that provide evidence supporting the transaction. LO4

E2-8. Transaction Analysis Template Determine the financial effect on the balance sheet and income statement for each of the following independent events using the Transaction Analysis Template (use the format in SE2-5). LO3 Homework MBC

a. Purchased inventory on account, $10,000.
b. Rendered services to clients on account, $12,000.
c. Paid wages for the week, $1,600.
d. Collected $8,000 from clients on account.

E2-9. Transaction Analysis Template Determine the financial effect on the balance sheet and income statement for each of the following independent events using the Transaction Analysis Template (use the format in SE2-5). LO3 Homework MBC

a. Paid $4,000 for six months rent, in advance.
b. Borrowed $50,000 from a bank.
c. Received an invoice for utilities used during the current month, $800.
d. Paid dividends to stockholders, $25,000.

E2-10. Transaction Analysis Match each of the following transactions of L. Boyd & Company with the appropriate letters, indicating the financial effect of the transaction. The key for the letters follows the list of transactions. The correct answer for Transaction 1 is given as an illustration: LO2 Homework MBC

		Answer
1.	Stockholders contributed cash to the business.	*a, f*
2.	Purchased equipment on account.	____
3.	Received and immediately paid advertising bill.	____
4.	Purchased supplies for cash.	____
5.	Borrowed money from a bank, giving a note payable.	____
6.	Billed customers for services rendered.	____
7.	Made a partial payment on account for equipment.	____
8.	Paid employee's salary.	____
9.	Collected amounts due from customers billed in Transaction 6.	____

Financial Effect of Transaction

a. Increase an asset	*g.* Increase dividends
b. Decrease an asset	*h.* Decrease dividends
c. Decrease a liability	*i.* Decrease revenue
d. Increase a liability	*j.* Increase revenue
e. Decrease common stock	*k.* Increase an expense
f. Increase common stock	*l.* Decrease an expense

LO2 **E2-11. Recording Transactions** Daniel Kelly, an attorney, opened his law practice on October 1. Prepare a horizontal worksheet using the format in Exhibit 2-3 with the following column headings: Cash; Accounts Receivable; Office Equipment; Legal Database Subscription; Accounts Payable; Common Stock; Revenue; Expense; and Dividends and record the following October transactions. Total the columns to show that assets equal liabilities plus stockholders' equity as of October 31.

1. Kelly started his law practice by contributing $19,500 cash to the business on October 1, receiving shares of common stock in the company.
2. Purchased office equipment on account, $10,400.
3. Paid office rent for October, $700.
4. Paid $9,600 to access online legal database for two years.
5. Billed clients for services rendered, $11,300.
6. Made $6,000 payment on account for the equipment purchased on October 2.
7. Paid legal assistant's salary, $2,800.
8. Collected $9,400 from clients previously billed for services.
9. Received invoice for October utilities, $180; it will be paid in November.
10. The company paid stockholders $1,500 as a cash dividend.

LO2 **E2-12. Recording Transactions** Mead Pet Hospital, owned by R. Mead, a veterinarian, opened for business on December 1 of the current year. Prepare a horizontal worksheet using the format in Exhibit 2-3 with the following column headings: Cash; Accounts Receivable; Supplies; Office Equipment; Accounts Payable; Common Stock; Revenue; Expense; and Dividends. Record the following December transactions. Total the columns to show that assets equal liabilities plus stockholders' equity as of December 31.

1. Mead opened a checking account on December 1 at United Bank in the name of Mead Pet Hospital and deposited $20,000 cash. Mead received common stock for his investment.
2. Paid rent for December, $1,100.
3. Purchased office equipment on account, $2,900.
4. Purchased supplies for cash, $1,700.
5. Billed clients for services rendered, $7,300.
6. Paid secretary's salary, $1,950.
7. Paid $1,500 on account for the equipment purchased on December 3.
8. Collected $5,800 from clients previously billed for services.
9. The company paid stockholders $2,200 as a cash dividend.

PROBLEMS

LO2 **P2-1. Transaction Analysis** The accounting equation of L. Chen & Company as of the beginning of the accounting period is given below, followed by seven transactions whose effects on the accounting equation are shown. Describe each transaction that occurred.

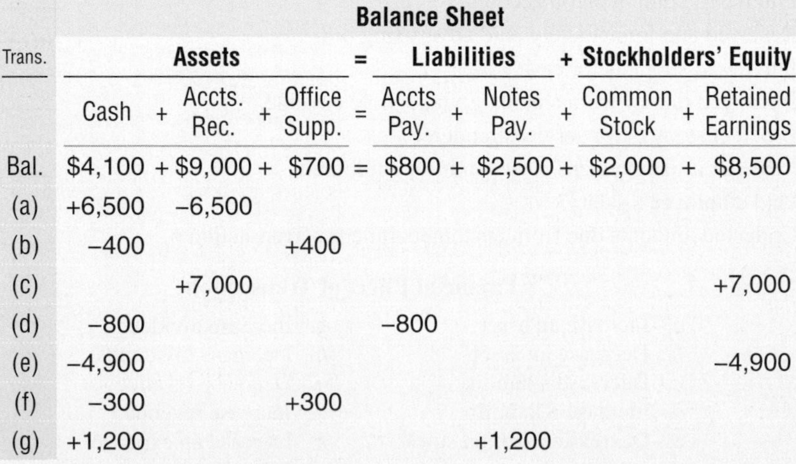

	Balance Sheet						
Trans.	Assets			= Liabilities		+ Stockholders' Equity	
	Cash +	Accts. Rec. +	Office Supp. =	Accts Pay. +	Notes Pay. +	Common Stock +	Retained Earnings
Bal.	$4,100 +	$9,000 +	$700 =	$800 +	$2,500 +	$2,000 +	$8,500
(a)	+6,500	−6,500					
(b)	−400		+400				
(c)		+7,000					+7,000
(d)	−800			−800			
(e)	−4,900						−4,900
(f)	−300		+300				
(g)	+1,200				+1,200		

P2-2. Transaction Analysis An analysis of the transactions of Hewitt Detective Agency for the month of May appears below. Line 1 summarizes the company's accounting equation data as of May 1; lines 2–10 represent the transactions for May: LO2

	Balance Sheet							
Trans.	Assets				= Liabilities		+ Stockholders' Equity	
	Cash	+ Accts. Rec.	+ Office Supp.	+ Equipment	= Accts Pay.	+ Notes Pay.	+ Common Stock	+ Retained Earnings
(1)	$2,400	+ $7,600	+ $500	+ $8,000	= $300	+ $5,000	+ $10,000	+ $3,200
(2)	+2,000					+2,000		
(3)	+6,100	−6,100						
(4)			+980		+980			
(5)		+6,800						+6,800
(6)	−300				−300			
(7)	+1,500							+1,500
(8)	−800							−800
(9)	−750			+750				
(10)	−2,500					−2,500		

REQUIRED

a. Show that assets equal liabilities plus stockholders' equity as of May 1.

b. Describe the apparent transaction indicated by each line. (For example, line 2: Borrowed $2,000, giving a note payable.) If any line could reasonably represent more than one type of transaction, describe each type.

c. Show that assets equal liabilities plus stockholders' equity as of May 31.

P2-3. Recording Transactions Grant Appraisal Service provides commercial and industrial appraisals and feasibility studies. On January 1, the assets and liabilities of the business were the following: Cash, $9,700; Accounts Receivable, $14,800; Accounts Payable, $600; and Notes Payable, $2,500. Common Stock had a balance of $18,400. Assume that Retained Earnings as of January 1, were $3,000. The following transactions occurred during the month of January: LO2

1. Paid rent for January, $950.
2. Received $8,800 payment on customers' accounts.
3. Paid $500 on accounts payable.
4. Received $1,600 for services performed for cash customers.
5. Borrowed $5,000 from a bank and signed a note payable for that amount.
6. Billed the city $6,200 for a feasibility study performed; billed various other credit customers, $1,900.
7. Paid the salary of an assistant, $4,000.
8. Received invoice for January utilities, $410.
9. Paid $6,000 cash for employee salaries.
10. Purchased a van (on January 31) for business use, $9,800.
11. Paid $50 to bank as January interest on the outstanding notes payable.

REQUIRED

a. Prepare a horizontal worksheet with the following individual assets, liabilities, and stockholders' equity accounts: Cash, Accounts Receivable, Van, Accounts Payable, Notes Payable, Common Stock, and Retained Earnings. Enter the January 1 balances below each item. (*Note:* The beginning Van account balance is $0.)

b. Show the impact (increase or decrease) of transactions 1–11 on the beginning balances, and total the columns to show that assets equal liabilities plus stockholders' equity as of January 31.

P2-4. Recording Transactions On June 1, a group of bush pilots in Thunder Bay, Ontario, Canada, formed the Outpost Fly-In Service, Inc., by selling $50,000 of common stock for cash. The group then leased several amphibious aircraft and docking facilities, equipping them to transport campers and hunters to outpost camps owned by various resorts. The following transactions occurred during June: LO2

1. Sold common stock for cash, $50,000.
2. Paid June rent for aircraft, dockage, and dockside office, $4,800.
3. Received invoice for the cost of a reception the firm gave to entertain resort owners, $1,600.

4. Paid for June advertising in various sports magazines, $900.
5. Paid insurance premium for June, $1,800.
6. Rendered fly-in services for various groups for cash, $22,700.
7. Billed the Canadian Ministry of Natural Resources for transporting mapping personnel, $2,900, and billed various firms for fly-in services, $13,000.
8. Paid $1,500 on accounts payable.
9. Received $13,200 on account from clients.
10. Paid June wages, $16,000.
11. Received invoice for the cost of fuel used during June, $3,500.
12. Paid a cash dividend, $3,000.

REQUIRED

Prepare a horizontal worksheet with the following column headings: Cash, Accounts Receivable, Accounts Payable, Common Stock, and Retained Earnings. Show how the June transactions affect the items in the accounting equation, and total all columns to show that assets equal liabilities plus stockholders' equity as of June 30. (*Note:* Revenues, expenses, and dividends affect Retained Earnings.)

LO2 **P2-5.** **Accounting Equation** Determine the following:

a. The stockholders' equity of a company that has assets of $450,000 and liabilities of $326,000.
b. The retained earnings of a company that has assets of $618,000, liabilities of $225,000, and common stock of $165,000.
c. The assets of a corporation that has liabilities of $400,000, common stock of $200,000, and retained earnings of $185,000.

LO2 **P2-6.** **Transaction Analysis** Following the example shown in (*a*) below, indicate the effects of the listed transactions on the assets, liabilities, and stockholders' equity of Martin Andrews & Company.

a. Rendered legal services to clients for cash.
ANSWER: Increase assets (Cash)
Increase stockholders' equity (Revenue)
b. Purchased office supplies on account.
c. Andrews invested cash into the firm and received stock for his investment.
d. Paid amount due on account for office supplies purchased in (*b*).
e. Borrowed cash from a bank and signed a six-month note payable.
f. Rendered services and billed clients.
g. Purchased, for cash, a desk lamp for the office.
h. Paid interest on a note payable to the bank.
i. Received invoice for the current month's utilities.

LO3 **P2-7.** **Transaction Analysis Template** On October 1, Alice Bloom started a consulting firm. Using the Transaction Analysis Template from SE2-5, determine the financial effect on the balance sheet and income statement of each of the following transactions.

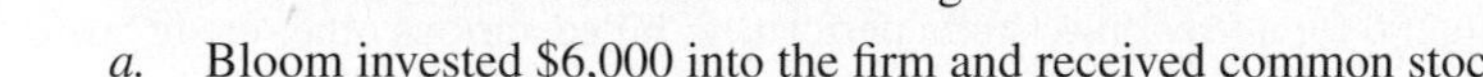

a. Bloom invested $6,000 into the firm and received common stock.
b. Purchased supplies for $2,000 cash.
c. Borrowed $3,500 from a bank and signed a note payable.
d. Purchased $5,000 worth of equipment.
e. Rendered services and billed clients for $1,000.
f. Collected $500 on account from clients.

LO2 **P2-8.** **Determination of Omitted Financial Statement Data** For the four unrelated situations, A-D, calculate the unknown amounts indicated by the letters appearing in each column:

	A	B	C	D
Beginning				
Assets	$28,000	$12,000	$28,000	$ (d)
Liabilities	18,600	5,000	19,000	9,000
Ending				
Assets	30,000	26,000	34,000	40,000
Liabilities	17,300	(b)	15,000	19,000
During the Year				
Common stock	2,000	4,500	(c)	3,500
Sales revenues	(a)	28,000	18,000	24,000
Dividends	5,000	1,500	1,000	6,500
Expenses	8,500	21,000	11,000	17,000

P2-9. Transaction Analysis Appearing below is an analysis of the June transactions for Rhode Consulting Services. Line 1 summarizes Rhode's accounting equation data as of June 1; lines 2 through 10 are the transactions for the month of June: LO2

Balance Sheet

Trans.	Assets				=	Liabilities		+	Stockholders' Equity	
	Cash	+ Accts. Rec.	+ Office Supp.	+ Equip-ment	=	Accts Pay.	+ Notes Pay.	+	Common Stock	+ Retained Earnings
(1)	$3,500	+ $5,200	+ $820	+ $9,000	=	$600	+ $3,000	+	$10,920	+ $4,000
(2)			+670			+670				
(3)				+5,000			+5,000			
(4)	+4,200	−4,200								
(5)		+7,800								+7,800
(6)	−600					−600				
(7)	−200		+200							
(8)	−4,600									−4,600
(9)	+2,000						+2,000			
(10)				+750					+750	

REQUIRED

a. Show that assets equal liabilities plus stockholders' equity as of June 1.

b. Describe the transaction indicated by each line. For example, line 2: Purchased supplies on account, $670. If any line could reasonably represent more than one type of transaction, describe each type.

c. Show that assets equal liabilities plus stockholders' equity as of June 30.

P2-10. Recording Transactions Grace Main began the Main Answering Service in December of the prior year. The firm provides services for professional people and is currently operating with leased equipment. On January 1 of the current year, the assets and liabilities of the business were: Cash, $4,400; Accounts Receivable, $6,900; Accounts Payable, $600; and Notes Payable, $1,500. Assume that Retained Earnings as of January 1 of the current year were zero. The balance of Common Stock was $9,200. The following transactions occurred during the month of January: LO2

1. Paid rent on office and equipment for January, $800.
2. Collected $4,500 on account from clients.
3. Borrowed $2,000 from a bank and signed a note payable for that amount.
4. Billed clients for work performed on account, $9,500.
5. Paid $400 on accounts payable.
6. Received invoice for January advertising, $550.
7. Paid January salaries, $3,800.
8. Paid January utilities, $430.
9. Paid stockholders a dividend of $2,600 cash.
10. Purchased fax machine (on January 31) for business use, $1,400.
11. Paid $30 to the bank as January interest on the outstanding notes payable.

REQUIRED

a. Prepare a horizontal worksheet with the following individual assets, liabilities, and stockholders' equity accounts: Cash, Accounts Receivable, Equipment, Accounts Payable, Notes Payable, Common Stock, and Retained Earnings. Enter the January 1 balances below each item. (*Note:* The beginning Equipment account balance is $0.)

b. Show the impact (increase or decrease) of the January transactions on the beginning balances, and total all columns to show that assets equal liabilities plus stockholders' equity as of January 31.

P2-11. Recording Transactions On December 1, Peter Allen started Career Services Inc., providing career and vocational counseling services. The following transactions took place during the month of December: LO2

Homework MBC

1. Allen invested $7,000 in the business, receiving common shares.
2. Paid rent for December on furnished office space, $750.

3. Received invoice for December advertising, $500.
4. Borrowed $15,000 from a bank and signed a note payable for that amount.
5. Received $1,200 for counseling services rendered for cash.
6. Billed certain governmental agencies and other clients for counseling services, $6,800.
7. Paid secretary's salary, $2,200.
8. Paid December utilities, $370.
9. Paid stockholders a dividend of $900 cash.
10. Purchased land for cash to use as a site for a new facility, $13,000.
11. Paid $100 to the bank as December interest on a note payable.

REQUIRED

a. Prepare a horizontal worksheet with the following column headings: Cash, Accounts Receivable, Land, Accounts Payable, Notes Payable, Common Stock, and Retained Earnings.

b. Show how the December transactions affect the items in the accounting equation, and total all columns to show that assets equal liabilities plus stockholders' equity as of December 31.

LO2 Homework MBC

P2-12. Recording Transactions and Balance Sheet Mary Aker opened a tax practice on June 1. The following transactions occurred during the month of June:

1. Aker opened a business checking account at a local bank, investing $16,000 in her practice in exchange for common stock.
2. Purchased office furniture and fixtures for $9,800, paid $2,800 cash, and gave a note payable for the balance.
3. Purchased books and software for a tax library on account, $3,700.
4. Purchased office supplies for cash, $560.
5. Paid rent for June, $750.
6. Returned $300 of books with defective bindings. The return reduced the amount owed to the supplier.
7. Billed clients for professional services rendered, $7,600.
8. Paid $1,700 on account for the library items purchased on June 3.
9. Collected $5,900 on account from clients billed on June 7.
10. Paid June salaries, $2,900.
11. Received invoice for June advertising, to be paid in July, $300.
12. Paid stockholders $800 cash as a dividend.
13. Paid utilities for June, $160.
14. Paid interest for June on note payable, $60.

REQUIRED

a. Prepare a horizontal worksheet using the format in **Exhibit 2-3** with the following column headings: Cash; Accounts Receivable; Office Supplies; Tax Library; Office Furniture and Fixtures; Accounts Payable; Notes Payable; Common Stock; Revenues; Expenses; and Dividends. Record the above transactions.

b. Prepare an unadjusted balance sheet as of June 30.

SERIAL PROBLEM: ANGEL CITY GREETINGS

Homework MBC

(Note: This is a continuation of the Serial Problem: Angel City Greetings from Chapter 1.)

SP2. In September of the current year, Kate incorporated Angel City Greetings after investigating different organizational forms, and began the process of getting her business up and running. The following events occurred during the month of September:

1. Kate deposited $10,000 that she had saved into a newly opened business checking account. She received common stock in exchange.
2. Kate designed a brochure that she will use to promote her greeting cards at local stationery stores.
3. Kate paid Fred Simmons $50 to critique her brochure before undertaking her final design and printing.

4. Kate purchased a new iMac computer tablet, specialized graphic arts software, and commercial printer for the company, paying $4,800 in cash. She decided to record all of these items under the same equipment account.
5. Kate purchased supplies such as paper and ink for $350 at the local stationery store. She opened a business account with the store and was granted 30 days credit on all purchases, including the one she just made.
6. Kate designed her first five cards and prepared to show them to potential customers.
7. The owner of the stationery store where Kate opened her account was impressed with Kate's work and ordered 1,000 of each of the five card designs at a cost of $1 per card, or $5,000 total. Kate tells the customer that she will have them printed and delivered within the week.
8. Kate purchased additional supplies, on account, in the amount of $1,500.
9. Kate delivered the 5,000 cards. Because the owner knows that Kate is just starting out, he paid her immediately in cash. He informed her that if the cards sell well he will be ordering more, but would expect a 30-day credit period like the one he grants to his own business customers.
10. The cost to Kate for the order was $1,750 of the supplies she had purchased. (*Hint:* This cost should be recorded as an expense called Cost of Goods Sold.)
11. Kate paid her balance due for the supplies in full.
12. Kate decided that she should have special renters' insurance to cover the business equipment she now owns. She purchased a one-year policy with coverage beginning on October 1, for $1,200, paying the entire amount in cash.
13. Kate determined that all of her equipment will have a useful life of 4 years (48 months), at which time it will not have any resale or scrap value. (*Hint:* Kate will expense 1/48th of the cost of the equipment each month to Depreciation Expense. This will increase Accumulated Depreciation.)
14. Kate paid herself a salary of $1,000 for the month.

REQUIRED

a. Prepare a horizontal worksheet using the format in **Exhibit 2-3** with the following column headings: Cash; Accounts Receivable; Supplies Inventory; Prepaid Insurance; Equipment; Accumulated Depreciation; Accounts Payable; Notes Payable; Common Stock; Revenue; Expense; and Dividends.

b. Record the accounting transactions for the month of September.

c. Prepare a balance sheet for Kate's Cards as of September 30.

BEYOND THE NUMBERS

REPORTING AND ANALYSIS

BTN2-1. Financial Reporting Problem: Columbia Sportswear Company The financial statements for the Columbia Sportswear Company can be found in Appendix A at the end of this book. The following selected accounts and their balances, in thousands, are from those statements:

Columbia Sportswear Company

Common stock	$ 20,165
Accounts payable	206,697
Accounts receivable	452,945
Inventories	556,530
Prepaid expenses and other current assets	54,197
Property, plant, and equipment	309,792
Net sales	2,501,554

Required

a. For each of these accounts, give an example of a likely event that would occur to increase its balance.

b. What other account is likely involved when:
1. Accounts receivable is increased?
2. Accounts payable is decreased?
3. Net sales are increased?

Columbia Sportswear Company
Under Armour, Inc.

BTN2-2. Comparative Analysis Problem: Columbia Sportswear Company vs. Under Armour, Inc. The financial statements for the **Columbia Sportswear Company** can be found in Appendix A, and **Under Armour, Inc.**'s financial statements can be found in Appendix B at the end of this book.

Required

Each of the following accounts is listed in the company's financial statements:

Accounts receivable	Inventories
Property, plant, and equipment	Cash
Accounts payable	Long-term debt
Income taxes payable	Retained earnings
Cost of goods sold	Income tax expense

Identify the probable other account involved when:

1. Cost of goods sold is increased.
2. Accounts payable is increased.
3. Accounts receivable is decreased.
4. Income taxes payable is increased.
5. Property, plant, and equipment is increased.

BTN2-3. Business Decision Problem Sarah Penney operates the Wildlife Picture Gallery, selling original art and signed prints received on consignment (rather than purchased) from recognized wildlife artists throughout the country. The firm receives a 30 percent commission on all art sold and remits 70 percent of the sales price to the artist. All art is sold on a cash basis.

Sarah began the business on March 1. She received a $10,000 loan from a relative to help her get started. Sarah signed a note agreeing to repay the loan in one year. No interest is being charged on the loan, but the relative does expect to receive a set of financial statements each month. On April 1, Sarah asks for your help in preparing the financial statements for the first month.

Sarah has carefully kept the firm's checking account up to date and provides you with the following complete listing of the cash receipts and disbursements for the month of March:

Cash Receipts	
Original investment by Sarah Penney in exchange for common stock	$ 6,500
Loan from relative	10,000
Sales of art	95,000
Total cash receipts	$111,500
Cash Disbursements	
Payments to artists for sales made	$ 54,000
Payment of March rent for gallery space	900
Payment of March staff wages	4,900
Payment of airfare for personal vacation of Sarah Penney (vacation will be taken in April)	500
Total cash disbursements	60,300
Cash balance, March 31	$ 51,200

Sarah also gives you the following documents she has received:

1. A $350 invoice for March utilities; payment is due by April 15.
2. A $1,700 invoice from Careful Express for the shipping of the artwork sold during March; payment is due by April 10.
3. The one-year lease she signed for the gallery space; as an incentive to sign the lease, the landlord reduced the first month's rent by 25 percent; the monthly rent starting in April is $1,200.

In your discussions with Sarah, she tells you that she has been so busy that she is behind in sending artists their share of the sales proceeds. She plans to catch up within the next week.

Required

From the above information, prepare the following financial statements for Wildlife Picture Gallery: (a) income statement for the month of March; (b) statement of stockholders' equity for the month of March; and (c) balance sheet as of March 31. Use a horizontal worksheet as in Exhibit 2-3.

CRITICAL THINKING

BTN2-4. **Accounting Research Problem** The annual report of General Mills, Inc., for the year ending May 31, 2020 (fiscal year 2020), can be found at: https://investors.generalmills.com/financial-information/annual-reports/default.aspx.

General Mills, Inc.

Required
What other account is likely involved when the effect of a single transaction causes:

1. Receivables to increase?
2. Accounts payable to decrease?
3. Revenues to increase?

BTN2-5. **Accounting Communication Activity** Fred Jones is struggling with some accounting concepts and has come to you for help. In particular, he does not understand what is meant by an economic event and a business event. He was especially confused when he learned that only one of them would be considered an accounting transaction.

Required
Write a short memorandum to Fred that explains the difference between an economic event and a business event.

BTN2-6. **Accounting Ethics Case** Andy Frame and his supervisor are sent on an out-of-town assignment by their employer. At the supervisor's suggestion, they stay at the Spartan Inn, across the street from the Luxury Inn. After three days of work, they settle their lodging bills and leave. On the return trip, the supervisor gives Andy what appears to be a copy of a receipt from the Luxury Inn for three nights of lodging. Actually, the supervisor indicates that he prepared the Luxury Inn receipt on his office computer and plans to complete his expense reimbursement request using the higher lodging costs from the Luxury Inn.

Required
What are the ethical considerations that Andy faces when he prepares his expense reimbursement request?

BTN2-7. **Environmental, Social, and Governance Problem** The Global Reporting Initiative (GRI) is a network-based organization that has pioneered the development of the world's most widely used sustainability reporting framework. The GRI website is located at http://www.globalreporting.org/. Sustainability reporting differs from financial reporting in several areas. One difference that is readily apparent is that sustainability reports contain performance metrics that are measured in units other than dollars. For example, greenhouse emissions may be measured in metric tons and employee in-kind volunteering may be measured in hours.

Required
Go to the GRI website and scroll down to the Latest News. Select an article of interest to you. What are some of the areas that GRI reports on?

BTN2-8. **Accounting Ethics Problem** Accrual accounting is based on the idea that revenue should be recognized when earned and that any resources consumed in the revenue-generating process (expenses) should be matched with those revenues in the same period. Another basic principle on which GAAP is based is that of the accounting period. This principle sets the time period for which the revenues and expenses are to be measured and matched. For many firms, this date is December 31. Revenues earned after December 31 are to be reported in the following period, and expenses in the following period are then matched to those revenues. One way that companies have been found to misrepresent their reported performance is to violate these principles by "holding the books open" beyond December 31. In other words, the firm will improperly record revenue earned after year-end as if it were earned in the current year, and at the same time, fail to properly match the expenses associated with those revenues. How might a forensic accountant who has been hired to investigate improper financial reporting catch this type of activity?

ANSWERS TO SELF-STUDY QUESTIONS

1. d **2.** a **3.** b **4.** c **5.** d **6.** c **7.** d

REVIEW SOLUTIONS

Solution 2.1

d, b, e, a, c

Solution 2.2

	Balance Sheet						Income Statement			
Trans.	Assets			= Liabilities +	Stockholders' Equity					
	Cash +	Accts. Rec. +	Equipment	= Accts Pay. +	Common Stock +	Retained Earnings	Rev. −	Exp. =	Net Income	
(1)	+40,000				+40,000					
(2)	−2,500					−2,500		+2,500	−2,500	Rent expense
(3)	10,000		+10,000							
(4)				+500		−500		+500	−500	Supplies expense
(5)	−300					−300		+300	−300	Advertising exp
(6)		+7,800				+7,800	+7,800		+7,800	
(7)	+3,500	−3,500								
(8)	−350			−350						
(9)	−2,500					−2,500		+2,500	−2,500	Wages exp
	27,850 +	4,300 +	10,000 =	150 +	40,000 +	2,000	7,800 −	5,800 =	2,000	
			$42,150			$42,150				

Miguel's Designs Unadjusted Balance Sheet October 31	
Assets	
Cash	$27,850
Accounts Receivable	4,300
Equipment	10,000
Total Assets	$42,150
Liabilities	
Accounts Payable	$ 150
Total Liabilities	150
Stockholders' Equity	
Common Stock	40,000
Retained Earnings	2,000
Total Stockholders' Equity	42,000
Total Liabilities and Stockholders' Equity	$42,150

Miguel's Designs Unadjusted Income Statement For the Month Ended October 31	
Revenue	
Service Revenue	$7,800
Expenses	
Rent Expense	2,500
Supplies Expense	500
Advertising Expense	300
Wage Expense	2,500
Total Expenses	5,800
Net Income (Loss)	$2,000

Solution 2.3

	Balance Sheet					Income Statement		
Trans.	Assets	=	Liabilities	+ Stockholders' Equity				
				Contrib. Capital	+ Retained Earnings	Rev.	– Exp.	= Net Income
1.	+500 Supplies	=	+500 Accounts payable	+			–	=
2.	+1,250 Accounts receivable				+1,250	+1,250 Service revenue	–	= +1,250
3.	−2,000 Cash				−2,000		– +2,000 Wages expense	= −2,000

Solution 2.4

a. 4 *b.* 2 *c.* 1 *d.* 3

CHAPTER

Accrual Basis of Accounting

PAST

Chapter 2 explained the accounting system, including transaction analysis and the accounting equation.

PRESENT

This chapter completes our examination of the accounting cycle: adjust, report, and close.

FUTURE

Chapter 4 examines the balance sheet and income statement more closely and introduces techniques for analyzing and interpreting financial statements.

MAKING DOUGH

Panera Bread was a trailblazer in the "fast-casual" restaurant segment. They began as a cookie store in 1980 and now have more than 2,300 bakery-cafes in the US and Canada. Panera is known for its additive-free food items and for being one of the first companies to display calorie information on its menu. More recently, they have introduced a "Cool Food Menu," which consists of foods with a low carbon footprint. Currently, more than half of Panera's menu items fall into this climate-friendly category.

In 2017, Panera Bread was purchased by JAB Holding Company and is no longer a public company. JAB, which also owns Krispy Kreme, is a private equity firm that invests in companies that exhibit strong brands, growth potential, and strong cash flow. Panera Bread's financial statements prior to the acquisition provided JAB important information about the financial strength of Panera.

Road Map

LO	Learning Objective	Page	eLecture	Review	Assignments
LO1	**Explain the accrual basis of accounting.**	72	E3-1	3.1	SE1, SE2, SE10, SE11, SE12, E11, P2, P9
LO2	**Describe the adjusting process and illustrate the four major types of adjusting entries.**	76	E3-2	3.2	SE3, SE4, SE5, SE6, SE7, E1, E2, E3, E5, E6, E7, E8, E9, P1, P3, P4, P5, P6, P7
LO3	**Prepare the financial statements.**	84	E3-3	3.3	SE8, E4, P1, P4, P8, P10, P11
LO4	**Describe the closing process and summarize the accounting cycle.**	88	E3-4	3.4	SE9, E10

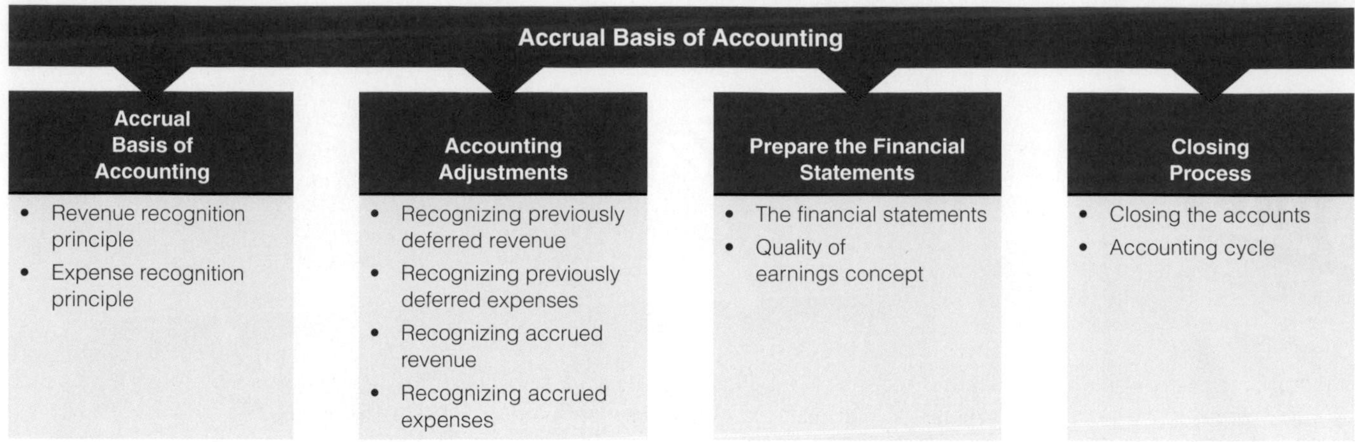

ACCRUAL BASIS OF ACCOUNTING

LO1 **Explain** the accrual basis of accounting.

Accountants use the **accrual basis of accounting** to decide when to recognize revenues and expenses. The overarching goal of accrual-based accounting is to make sure that net income is reported during the period in which it is earned. The two principles that guide accountants in measuring accrual-based income are the **revenue recognition principle** and the **expense recognition (matching) principle**, which are described in the following sections. Importantly, the decision to recognize revenues and expenses is based on whether the related income has been earned, and not upon whether the cash has been received for the reported sales or disbursed for the reported expenses.

PRINCIPLE ALERT

The FASB provides a five-step process for companies to follow in evaluating the timing and amount of revenue to be recognized. The five-step process consists of:

Step 1. Identify the contract with the customer.
Step 2. Identify the separate performance obligations in the contract.
Step 3. Determine the transaction price.
Step 4. Allocate the transaction price to the separate performance obligations in the contract.
Step 5. Recognize revenue when or as the entity satisfies a performance obligation.

Revenue Recognition Principle

The revenue recognition principle requires companies to recognize revenues in the period in which the company satisfies its obligation to provide goods or services to the customer, in the amount the company expects to receive. For most companies, this means that sales revenues are recognized during the period in which the goods or services are delivered to the customer in an amount equal to the sales price. However, a critical feature of accrual-based accounting is that revenues may also be recognized either before or after the cash is received for the sale. The following examples illustrate each of these situations.

Cash Received *When* Revenue Is Earned

For most sales, **Panera Bread** receives cash at the same time the customer receives the item they purchase, such as a loaf of freshly baked bread. In these cases, Panera will recognize sales revenue at the same time they receive the cash payment. This will result in Panera increasing both Cash and Sales Revenue at the time the sale is made. For example, a $100 cash sale is reflected in our Transaction Analysis Template as follows:

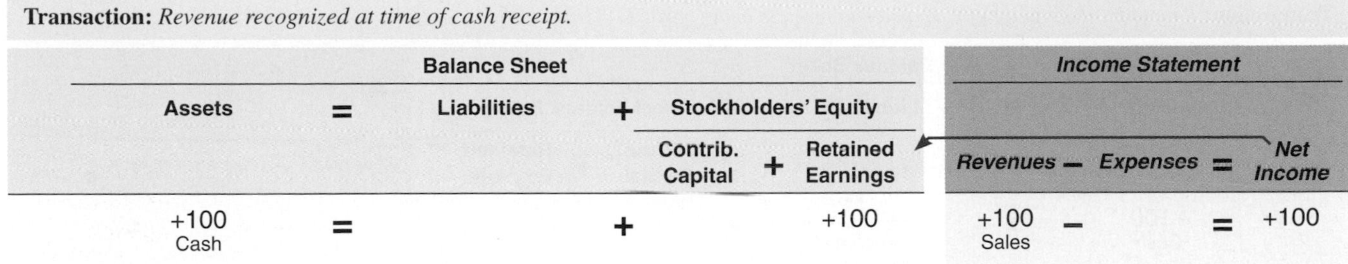

Transaction: *Revenue recognized at time of cash receipt.*

Assets	=	Liabilities	+	Contrib. Capital	+	Retained Earnings	Revenues	−	Expenses	=	Net Income
+100 Cash	=		+			+100	+100 Sales	−		=	+100

Cash Received *After* Revenue Is Earned

Panera Bread offers certain specialty food items for sale in grocery stores through its Panera At Home division. Assume that ShopRite purchases large quantities of Panera food items for resale in their grocery stores and agrees to pay for the items within thirty days following each purchase. Even though Panera has not received payment for the delivered items, they have earned the right to receive the cash. Consequently, Panera must recognize the sales revenue at the time of the sale, which is before they receive the cash. In this case, Panera will increase Accounts Receivable and increase Sales Revenue. Later, when the cash is subsequently received from ShopRite, Panera will increase Cash and reduce Accounts Receivable.

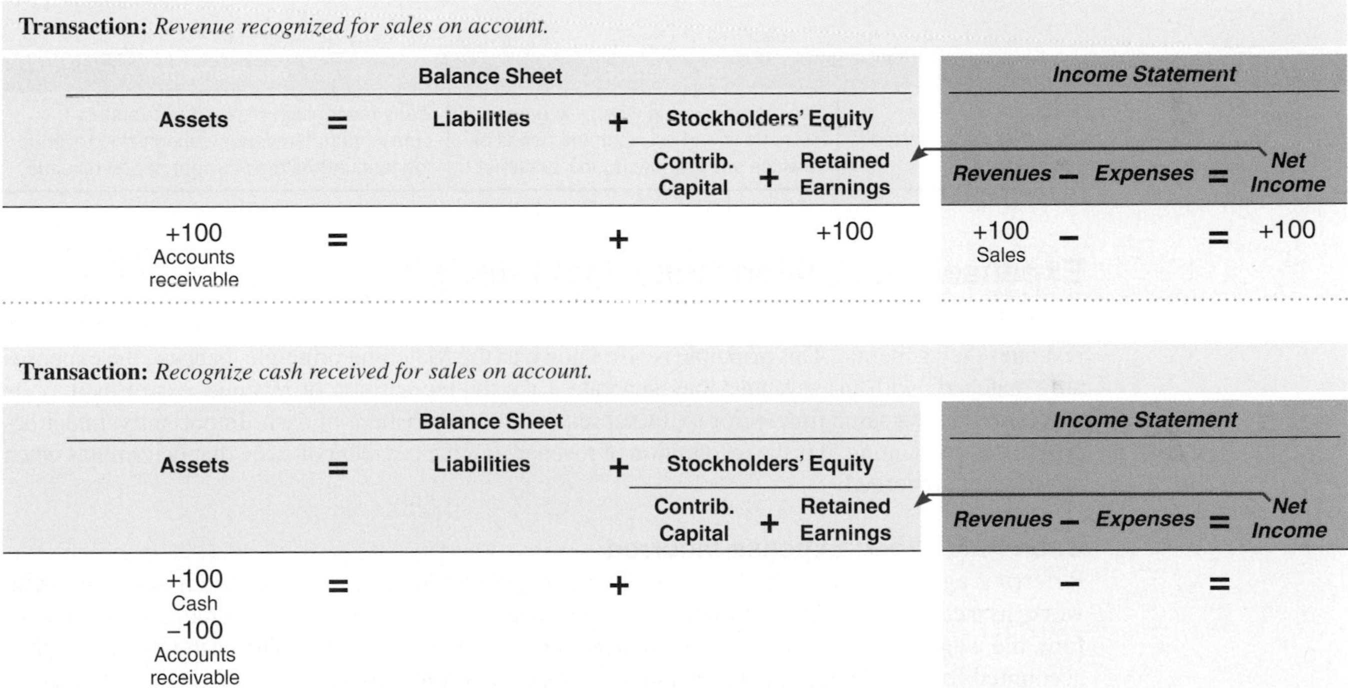

Transaction: *Revenue recognized for sales on account.*

Assets	=	Liabilities	+	Contrib. Capital	+	Retained Earnings	Revenues	−	Expenses	=	Net Income
+100 Accounts receivable	=		+			+100	+100 Sales	−		=	+100

Transaction: *Recognize cash received for sales on account.*

Assets	=	Liabilities	+	Contrib. Capital	+	Retained Earnings	Revenues	−	Expenses	=	Net Income
+100 Cash −100 Accounts receivable	=		+					−		=	

Cash Received *Before* Revenue Is Earned

Panera offers both plastic and eCard gift cards for sale through their cafes and website. While Panera receives payment at the time the gift card is purchased, they have not yet earned the revenue. Therefore, they will defer the recognition of sales revenue until it is earned, which is when the gift card is redeemed at a Panera restaurant. Upon receipt of the cash, Panera records an increase in Cash and an increase in a liability account, Unredeemed Gift Cards. When the gift card is used to make a purchase, Panera will record a reduction in Unredeemed Gift Cards and an increase in Sales Revenue. As these examples demonstrate, it is the earning of sales revenue that determines when revenue is recognized, not the timing of the cash collection.

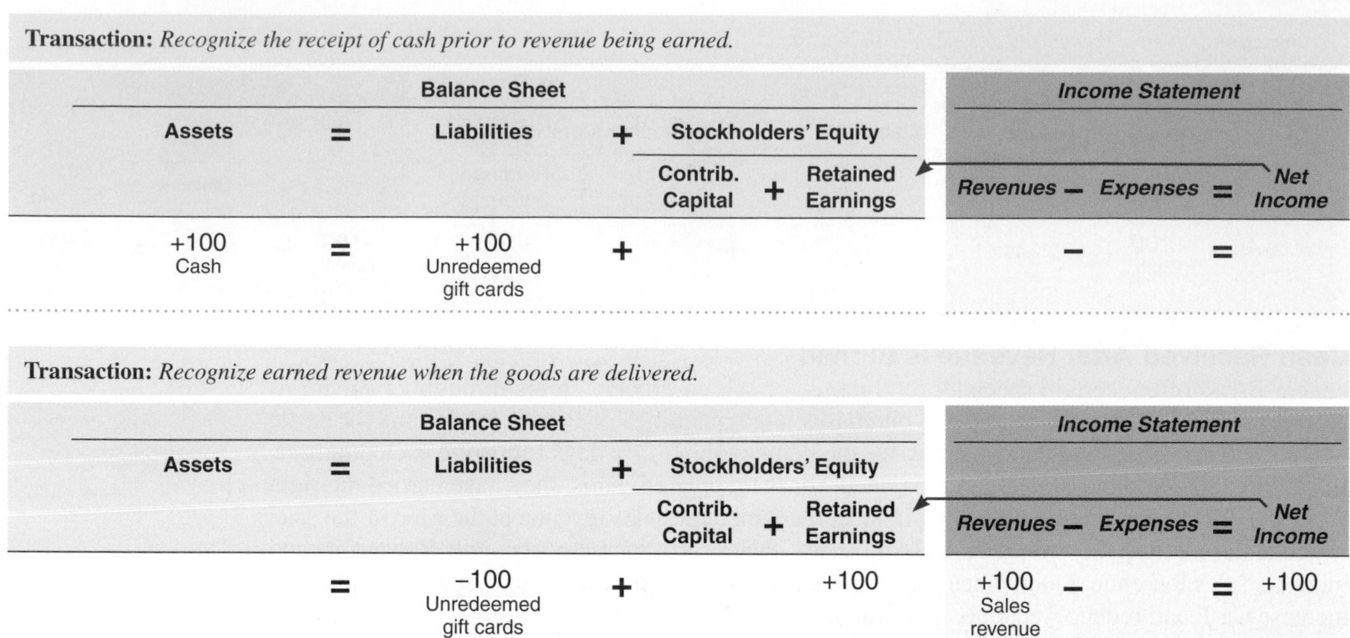

TAKEAWAY 3.1	Concept	Method	Assessment
	When should sales revenue be recognized?	Recognize revenue when it is earned. Revenue is earned when the goods or services are provided to the customer.	Early recognition of revenue overstates current period revenue; recognizing revenue too late understates current period revenue.

Expense Recognition (Matching) Principle

The Expense Recognition Principle requires expenses to be recognized during the same period as the revenues they generate. This principle is also known as the Matching principle, because the expenses are "matched" with the revenues they generate. Like the recognition of revenue, expenses may be recognized at the same time, prior to, or subsequent to the payment of cash. Importantly, under accrual basis accounting, it is the recognition of revenue, not the payment of cash, that determines when expenses are recorded.

Cash Paid *When* Expense Incurred

Referring again to Panera, assume the company pays $150 cash in wages to an employee who works as a cashier in a cafe. Revenue is recognized as the cashier sells Panera's menu items. Therefore, the wages should be recognized as an expense in the same period. The cash payment is thus accounted for as a decrease in Cash and an increase in Wage Expense.

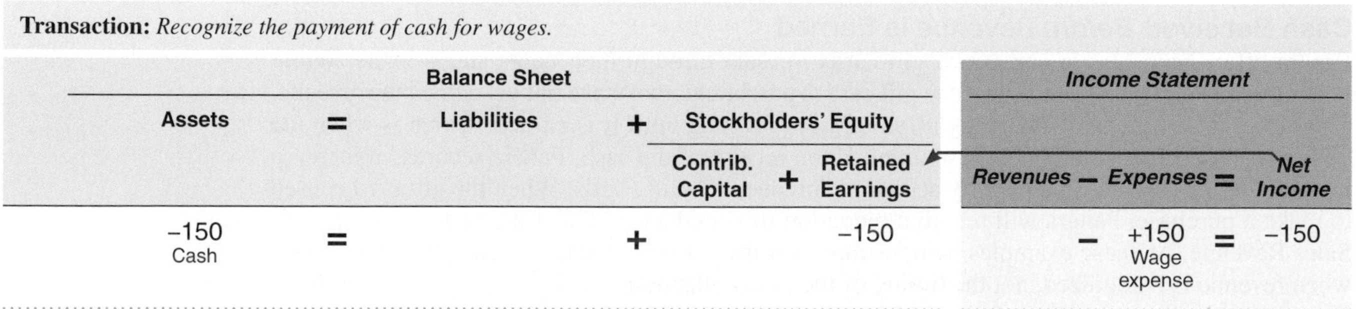

Cash Paid *Before* Expense Incurred

Assume Panera pays $50 cash to acquire baking supplies for its bread. This purchase is not recognized as an expense until Panera sells the bread it produces. The cash payment occurs before the revenue is recognized, and thus is not expensed at the time of the cash disbursement. The cash purchase of the supplies prior to the sale is accounted for as a decrease in Cash and an increase in Supplies, both assets.

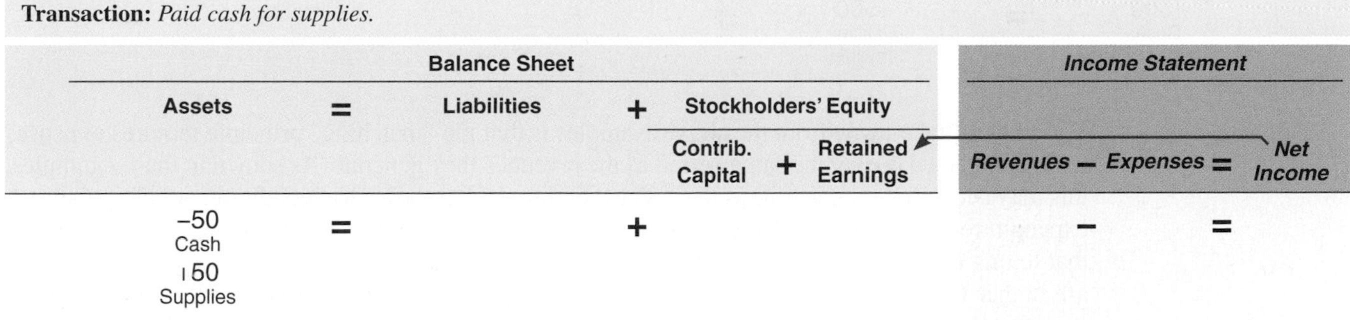

The expense related to supplies is subsequently recognized during the same period in which the revenues from the sale of the bread are recognized. At that point, Supplies Expense increases and Supplies decreases.

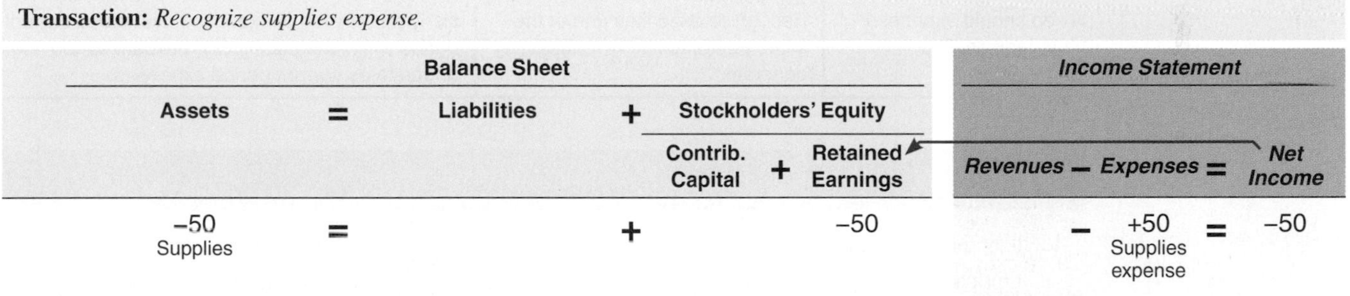

Cash Paid *After* Expense Incurred

In the normal course of business, Panera needs to keep the lights on and its ovens hot in order to welcome customers and sell its freshly baked bread. Utility companies typically bill after the utilities are provided, so companies will pay for their utilities after the expense is incurred. Assume Panera owes $500 for the month and the utility company allows a payment period of 14 days. Panera will increase Utilities Expense and Utilities Payable, a liability, during the period in which the utilities are provided.

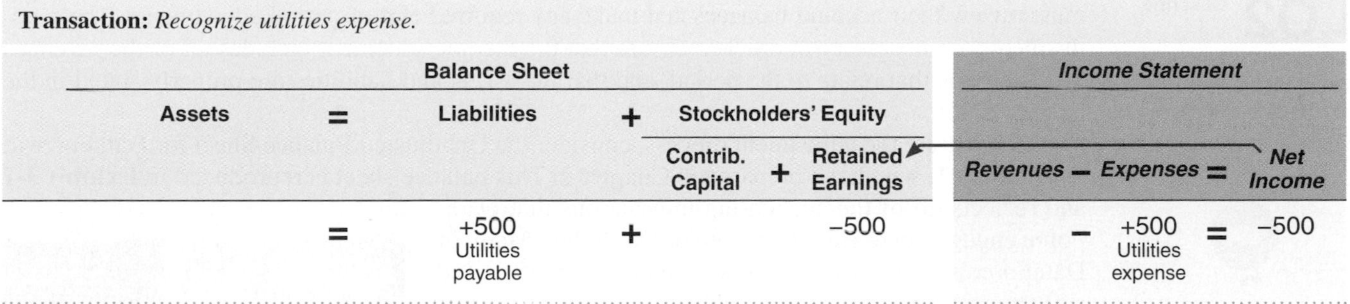

The subsequent payment of the utilities bill during the following period will decrease Utilities Payable and Cash by $500.

Transaction: *Payment of utilities payable.*

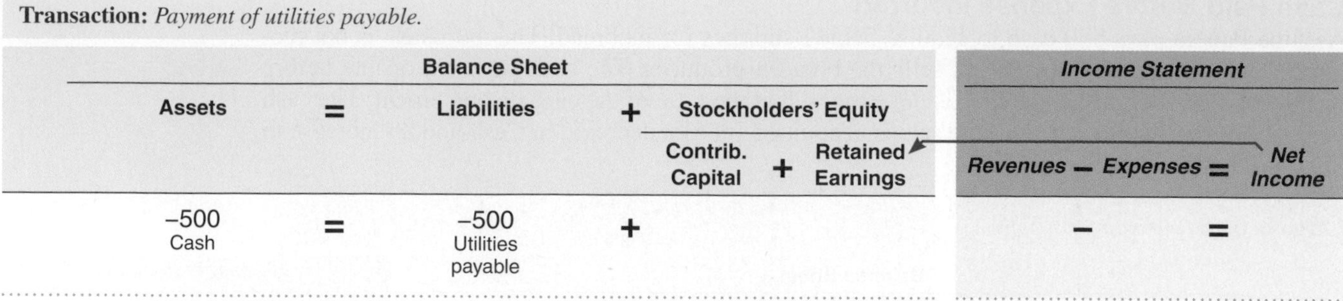

Balance Sheet								Income Statement				
Assets	=	Liabilities	+	Stockholders' Equity								
				Contrib. Capital	+	Retained Earnings		Revenues	–	Expenses	=	Net Income
–500 Cash	=	–500 Utilities payable	+						–		=	

The primary take-away from the above examples is that the "matching" principle requires expenses to be recognized during the same period as the revenues they generate. As shown in these examples, this may occur at the same time as the cash expenditure, after the cash expenditure, or before the cash expenditure. An appealing feature of the matching principle is that it results in net income numbers that tell us whether the company's business model is profitable. Specifically, if the revenues earned are higher than the expenses incurred to generate them, the company is profitable. This contrasts with the cash basis of accounting, which records revenues when the cash is received, and expenses when the cash is paid. Over the life of the company, both cash basis and accrual basis accounting will result in identical total income, but the amount of income in any given period is likely to be different.

TAKEAWAY 3.2	Concept →	Method →	Assessment
	When should expenses be recognized?	Recognize expenses during the same period as the revenues they generate.	Early recognition of expenses overstates current period expenses; recognizing expenses too late understates current period expenses.

REVIEW 3.1

Identify the proper point in time to recognize revenue for each of the following transactions.

a. Optical Systems sells and delivers equipment in March with payment due in May.

b. In May, George Smalls collects $12,000 from tenants, which represents six months' rent in advance for the period June through November.

c. Gregg Company delivers signage to an advertising agency in January and receives payment.

The solution is on page 103.

ACCOUNTING ADJUSTMENTS

LO2 Describe the adjusting process and **illustrate** the four major types of adjusting entries.

Step 3 Adjust accounts

At the end of each accounting period, when it is time to prepare the financial statements, companies must review their account balances and make any required end-of-period adjustments. These adjustments are necessary in order to ensure that the income statement includes all of the revenues and expenses that relate to the period, and that the assets and liabilities are properly stated in the balance sheet.

To illustrate the adjustment process, consider the Unadjusted Balance Sheet for DataForce at December 31, which we prepared in Chapter 2. This balance sheet is reproduced in **Exhibit 3-1** and reflects all of the accounting transactions that DataForce engaged in during the month of December. Many of DataForce's account balances will require end-of-period adjustments before they prepare their December financial statements. For example, recall that DataForce prepaid six months of rent for its office space on December 1. At the time of the payment, DataForce reduced cash by $10,800 and increased an asset called Prepaid Rent by $10,800. As of December 31 one month's rent has expired, equal to $1,800 (1 month/6 months × $10,800). Thus, Prepaid

Rent in the December 31 Balance Sheet must be reduced by $1,800, so that it reflects the remaining five months of rent that are still prepaid at the end of the month. In addition, DataForce will prepare an Income Statement for the month of December that will include one month's rent expense of $1,800. In the following section we will use the Transaction Analysis Template to show how DataForce will record this adjustment, as well as the other required adjustments at the end of December.

EXHIBIT 3-1 Unadjusted Balance Sheet for DataForce, Inc.

DATAFORCE, INC.
Unadjusted Balance Sheet
December 31

Assets	
Cash	$40,590
Accounts receivable	1,340
Office supplies	2,850
Prepaid rent	10,800
Equipment	32,400
Total assets	$87,980
Liabilities	
Accounts payable	$ 2,850
Unearned revenue	3,000
Notes payable	36,000
Total liabilities	$41,850
Stockholders' equity	
Common stock	30,000
Retained earnings	16,130
Total stockholders' equity	46,130
Total liabilities and stockholders' equity	$87,980

Types of Adjustments

There are four types of accounting adjustments made at the end of an accounting period:

ADJUSTMENTS RELATED TO:	DEFERRALS *Cash BEFORE Revenue/Expense Recognition*	ACCRUALS *Cash AFTER Revenue/Expense Recognition*
REVENUES	**Deferred Revenues** Recognize revenue earned on products or services for which cash was received in a prior period.	**Accrued Revenues** Recognize revenue earned on sales for which the cash will be received in a later period.
EXPENSES	**Deferred Expenses** Recognize expenses incurred for cash expenditures made in a prior period.	**Accrued Expenses** Recognize expenses incurred for which cash will be paid in a later period.

Each of the four types of adjustments is an application of the revenue and expense principles discussed previously in this chapter. The purpose of the period-end adjustments are to assure that revenues are recognized during the period in which they are earned, and that expenses are recognized during the same period as the revenues they generate. Two types of adjustments relate to **deferrals** and two types relate to **accruals**. As explained in more detail below, deferrals arise when cash is received or paid *before* the period in which the related revenues or expenses are recognized; and accruals arise when cash is received or paid *after* the period in which the related revenues or expenses are recognized. Each type of adjustment increases or decreases a balance sheet account (an asset or liability) and increases an income statement account (a revenue or expense). In the following sections, we illustrate each of the four types of adjustments using the December 31 Unadjusted Balance Sheet from DataForce.

Deferred Revenues

Recognizing Previously Deferred Revenue

Deferred Revenues arise when companies receive cash from the sale of services or products *before* the period in which the services or products are delivered to their customers. In the period that the cash is received, companies account for deferred revenues by increasing Cash and increasing a liability account, usually labeled **Unearned Revenue** (but sometimes labeled **Deferred Revenue** or **Advances from Customers**). The Unearned Revenue account represents an obligation to perform a service, or provide a product, in a future period. Once the service is provided or the products are delivered, the revenue is earned, and a period-end adjustment is necessary to recognize the revenue in that period. The adjustment reduces the Unearned Revenue account in the balance sheet and increases the related revenue account in the income statement. The purpose of the adjustment is to recognize revenues during the period in which they are earned.

Companies compute the required period-end adjustments by analyzing the Unadjusted Balance Sheet at the end of each accounting period. For example, the December 31 Unadjusted Balance Sheet of DataForce (shown in **Exhibit 3-1**) indicates that a period-end adjustment is required to recognize fee revenue related to Unearned Revenue on the balance sheet. The next section illustrates this adjustment.

Deferred Service Revenue

On December 5, DataForce signed a four-month contract to perform work for $750 per month, with the entire contract price of $3,000 received in advance. At that time, DataForce increased cash and recorded a liability of $3,000 in Unearned Revenue, as illustrated in Chapter 2. On December 31, the following adjustment transfers $750, the revenue earned in December, to Fee Revenue and reduces the liability Unearned Revenue by the same amount:

Transaction: *Adjustment to recognize portion of revenue earned in December.*

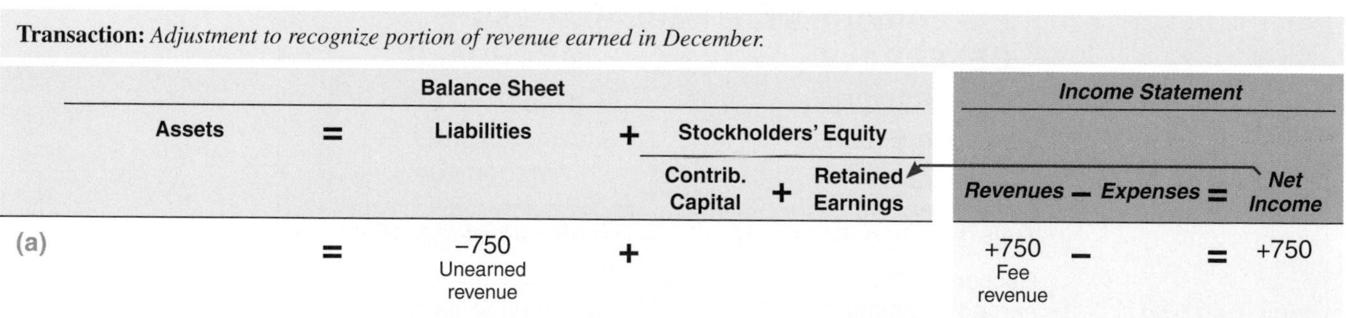

	Balance Sheet								Income Statement				
	Assets	=	Liabilities	+	Stockholders' Equity								
					Contrib. Capital	+	Retained Earnings		Revenues	−	Expenses	=	Net Income
(a)		=	−750 Unearned revenue	+					+750 Fee revenue	−		=	+750

After this adjustment, the income statement properly reflects the $750 fees earned during December, and the balance sheet properly reflects the remaining balance of $2,250 (the $3,000 contract price minus the $750 of fees earned during December) in the Unearned revenue account as of December 31.

Other examples of revenues received in advance include rental prepayments by real estate management companies, insurance premiums received in advance by insurance companies, subscription revenues received in advance by magazine and newspaper publishers, and membership fees received in advance by health and fitness clubs. In each case, a liability account is established when the prepayment is initially received. Later, an adjustment is made to reflect the revenues earned from the services provided or products delivered during the current accounting period.

Recognizing Previously Deferred Expenses

Deferred Expenses

Deferred expenses arise when companies make cash expenditures *before* the period in which the related expense is recognized. Common examples include purchases of buildings, equipment, and supplies; prepayments of rent and advertising; and payments of insurance premiums covering more than one period. During the period in which the cash is paid, these expenditures are accounted for by reducing cash and increasing an asset account. Then, at the end of each accounting period, the portion of the expenditure that has expired during the period is recognized as an expense. The adjustment reduces the asset account and increases an expense. The purpose of these period-end adjustments are to recognize expenses during the period that they benefit.

Turning again to DataForce's December 31 Unadjusted Balance Sheet (**Exhibit 3-1**), we observe that adjustments are required to recognize expenses related to the use of office supplies, the expiration of prepaid rent, and the use of the office equipment that relates to the current period (December). The next three sections illustrate those adjustments.

Office Supplies

At the beginning of December, DataForce purchased office supplies of $2,850 on account and recorded the expenditure in an asset account, Office Supplies, as illustrated in Chapter 2. During December, office supplies were used as services were provided. The cost of office supplies used is an expense for December that reduces the amount of supplies available. Companies do not record an expense as each individual supply item, such as a printer ink cartridge or post-it note pad, is used. Instead, at the end of each accounting period, the company physically counts the supplies still available and then subtracts that amount from the total amount purchased to determine the amount used during the period. For example, assume that a physical count of the office supplies indicates that $1,530 worth of DataForce's office supplies are available at the end of the month. This implies that $1,320 ($2,850 of Office Supples purchased minus the ending balance of $1,530) worth of supplies were used during December. An adjustment is needed to transfer this amount to an expense account, Office Supplies Expense.

Transaction: *Expense office supplies used in December.*

	Balance Sheet							Income Statement				
	Assets	=	Liabilities	+	Stockholders' Equity							
					Contrib. Capital	+	Retained Earnings	*Revenues*	–	*Expenses*	=	*Net Income*
(b)	−1,320 Office supplies	=		+			−1,320		–	+1,320 Office supplies expense	=	−1,320

After this adjustment, the income statement properly reflects the $1,320 expense for office supplies for the month of December, and the balance sheet reflects the remaining balance of $1,530 in the Office Supplies account as of December 31 obtained during the physical count.

Prepaid Rent

On December 1, DataForce paid six months' rent in advance and recorded the $10,800 payment to Prepaid Rent, an asset account. As each day passes, rent expense is being incurred, and the balance of the prepaid rent is decreasing. It is unnecessary to record rent expense on a daily basis because financial statements are not prepared daily; however, at the end of the accounting period, an adjustment is necessary to recognize the correct amount of rent expense for the month of December and to decrease the Prepaid Rent account. Specifically, on December 31, one month of DataForce's prepaid rent has expired; consequently, DataForce will transfer $1,800 ($10,800/6 months) from Prepaid Rent to Rent Expense.

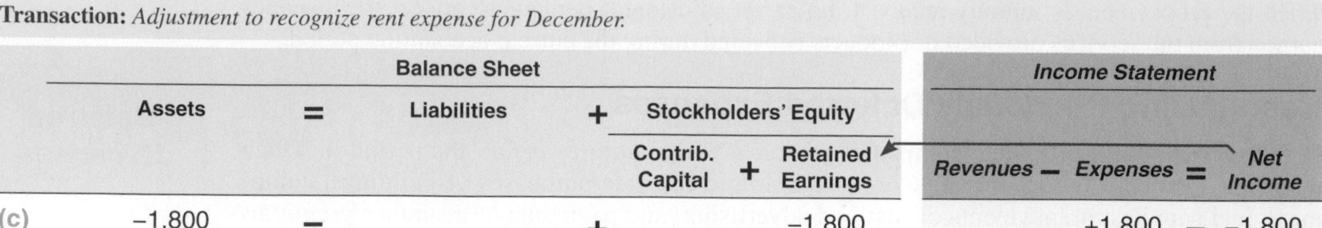

Transaction: *Adjustment to recognize rent expense for December.*

	Assets	=	Liabilities	+	Contrib. Capital	+	Retained Earnings	Revenues	−	Expenses	=	Net Income
(c)	−1,800 Prepaid rent	=		+			−1,800		−	+1,800 Rent expense	=	−1,800

After this adjustment, the income statement properly reflects the $1,800 rent expense for the month of December, and the balance sheet properly reflects the remaining balance of $9,000 (the $10,800 payment minus the amount expired of $1,800) in the Prepaid Rent account as of December 31. Examples of other prepaid expenses for which similar adjustments are made include prepaid insurance and prepaid advertising.

Property, Plant, and Equipment

The process of allocating the cost of buildings, equipment, and vehicles to the periods that benefit from their use is called **depreciation**. Because these long-lived assets help generate revenue for a company over many years, a portion of their cost is expensed each accounting period. This periodic expense is known as *depreciation expense*. The allocation of the costs of these assets over the period they benefit is an application of the "matching" principle for recognizing expense.

Because there is no exact way to measure the amount by which these assets have benefitted each period, depreciation expense is an estimate. The procedure used in this chapter estimates the annual amount of depreciation expense by dividing the acquisition cost of the asset by its estimated useful life in years. This method is called **straight-line depreciation**. (We will explore other depreciation methods in a later chapter.)

When recording depreciation expense, the asset account is not reduced directly. Instead, the reduction is recorded in a contra account called **Accumulated Depreciation**. **Contra accounts** are used to record reductions in, or offsets against, another account. The Accumulated Depreciation account appears in the balance sheet as a reduction of the Office equipment account. Using a contra account allows the original cost of the related asset to be reported in the company's balance sheet, followed by the accumulated amount of depreciation taken to date. Users of financial statements want to see both of these amounts so that they can estimate how much benefit an asset has provided and how much remains to benefit the business in future periods.

To illustrate, assume that the office equipment purchased by DataForce for $32,400 is expected to last six years. Straight-line depreciation is $5,400 per year ($32,400/6 years), or $450 per month ($5,400/12 months). At the end of December, DataForce would make the following adjustment.

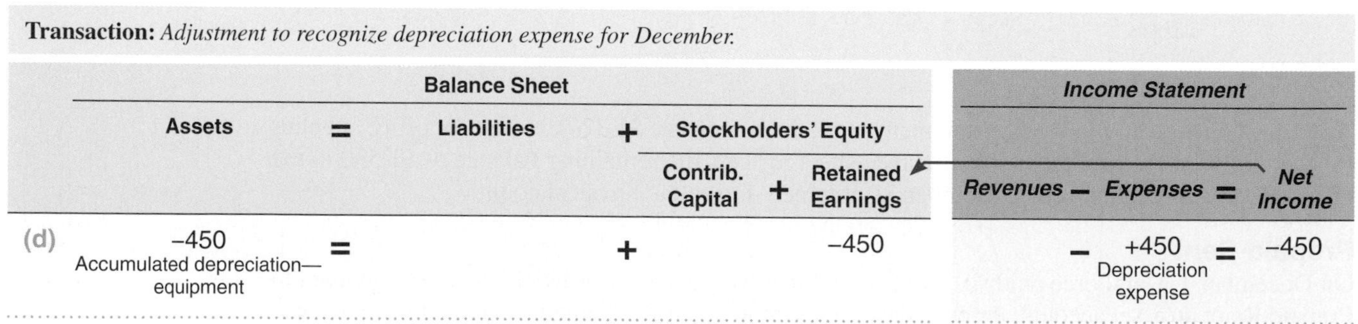

Transaction: *Adjustment to recognize depreciation expense for December.*

	Assets	=	Liabilities	+	Contrib. Capital	+	Retained Earnings	Revenues	−	Expenses	=	Net Income
(d)	−450 Accumulated depreciation—equipment	=		+			−450		−	+450 Depreciation expense	=	−450

As a result of this adjustment, the estimated cost of using the asset during December is reported as depreciation expense ($450) in the company's income statement. On the balance sheet, the accumulated depreciation is subtracted from the related asset account (Office Equipment). The resulting amount (acquisition cost less accumulated depreciation) is the balance in Office Equipment "net" of the Accumulated Depreciation. This amount is also known as the asset's **book value** and represents the unexpired asset cost to be applied as an expense against future periods. For example,

A.K.A. Book value is also called *carrying value.*

the December 31 balance sheet shows DataForce's office equipment with a book value of $31,950, presented as follows:

Office equipment	$32,400
Less: Accumulated depreciation.	450
Office equipment, net	$31,950

Recognizing Accrued Revenue

Accrued Revenues

Accrued revenues arise when companies sell goods or services and the cash is received *after* the period in which the related goods are delivered or the services are rendered. This period-end adjustment is required in order to recognize the revenues during the period in which they are earned, which is when the goods or services are delivered. The adjustment increases a receivable in the balance sheet, and increases a revenue account in the income statement. At December 31, DataForce must accrue Fee Revenue, as illustrated in the next section.

Accrued Fees

DataForce entered into a contract with a local company on December 2 that requires a December 31 adjusting entry to accrue revenue. Under the one-year contract, DataForce agreed to maintain that company's website in exchange for a monthly fee of $150, payable at the end of every three months. By December 31, DataForce has earned one month of fee revenue. This is recorded by making an adjustment that increases an asset account, Accounts Receivable, and increases Fee Revenue, as follows:

Transaction: *Accrue fee revenue earned in December.*

	Balance Sheet							Income Statement				
	Assets	=	Liabilities	+	Stockholders' Equity							
					Contrib. Capital	+	Retained Earnings	*Revenues*	−	*Expenses*	=	*Net Income*
(e)	+150 Accounts receivable	=		+			+150	+150 Fee revenue	−		=	+150

When DataForce receives the first $450 payment at the end of February 29, the company increases cash by $450. This represents payment for fees earned during the month of December in the current year, decreasing Accounts Receivable by $150; and payment for revenues earned during January and February of the subsequent year, increasing Fee Revenue by $300. (For ease of presentation, this assumes DataForce makes adjusting entries at the end of each year, not monthly.)

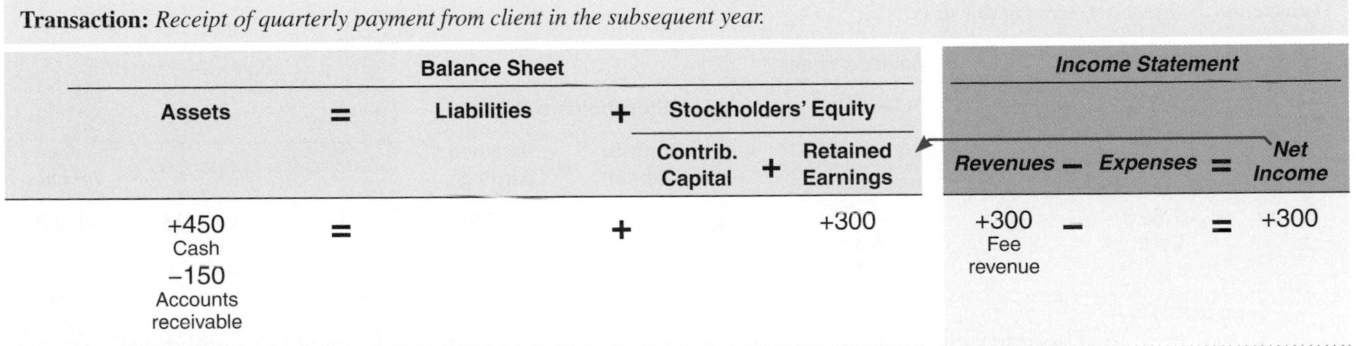

Transaction: *Receipt of quarterly payment from client in the subsequent year.*

Balance Sheet							Income Statement				
Assets	=	Liabilities	+	Stockholders' Equity							
				Contrib. Capital	+	Retained Earnings	*Revenues*	−	*Expenses*	=	*Net Income*
+450 Cash −150 Accounts receivable	=		+			+300	+300 Fee revenue	−		=	+300

After recording this transaction, the income statement properly reflects the $300 of fees earned (and received) during the first two months of the subsequent year; and the balance sheet properly reflects a zero balance in Accounts Receivable as of the end of February 29.

Accrued Expenses

Recognizing Accrued Expenses

Accrued expenses arise when the cash paid for an expense occurs *after* the period in which the expense is incurred and recognized. Examples of expenses that are typically incurred before the period in which they are paid include employee wages, utilities, and income taxes. Often the cash expenditures related to these expenses are made at regular time intervals, such as weekly, monthly, or quarterly. If the accounting period ends on a date that does not coincide with the cash payment, a period-end adjustment is required in order to recognize the expenses during the accounting period in which they are incurred. The period-end adjustments to recognize accrued expenses increase a payable account, which is a liability in the balance sheet, and increase the related expense account in the income statement. The following two sections illustrate the required adjustments to accrue wages and interest expense for DataForce for the period ended December 31.

Accrued Wages

DataForce's employee is paid every two weeks at the rate of $810 per week. The employee was paid $1,620 on Friday, December 27. At the close of business on Tuesday, December 31, the employee has worked two days during December for which wages are not paid until January. Thus, an additional two days of wage expense must be reflected in DataForce's income statement for December. Wages equal $162 per day ($810 divided by a five-day work week). This means that $324 of additional wage expense must be accrued on December 31 ($162 times 2 days). The adjustment at the end of December to accrue two days of wage expense follows:

Transaction: *Accrue wages for the last two days of December.*

	Balance Sheet							Income Statement				
	Assets	=	Liabilities	+	Stockholders' Equity							
					Contrib. Capital	+	Retained Earnings	Revenues	−	Expenses	=	Net Income
(f)		=	+324 Wages payable	+			−324		−	+324 Wage expense	=	−324

After this adjustment, the income statement properly reflects the $324 of wage expense incurred (but not yet paid) during the last two days of December, and the balance sheet properly reflects the $324 liability in Wages Payable as of December 31.

When the employee is paid on the next regular payday in January, DataForce decreases cash by $1,620. This includes payment for wages earned during the last two days of December, decreasing Wages Payable by $324; and payment for wages earned during the beginning of January, increasing Wages Expense in January by $1,296 ($1,620 – $324). Thus, the following adjustment will be made on Friday, January 10:

Transaction: *Subsequent payment of wages.*

Balance Sheet							Income Statement				
Assets	=	Liabilities	+	Stockholders' Equity							
				Contrib. Capital	+	Retained Earnings	Revenues	−	Expenses	=	Net Income
−1,620 Cash	=	−324 Wages payable	+			−1,296		−	+1,296 Wage expense	=	−1,296

This entry eliminates the liability recorded in Wages Payable at the end of December and expenses the portion of the wages paid that were earned by the employee in January.

Accrued Interest Expense

Another example of accrued expense is interest expense that has been incurred during the accounting period, but not paid as of the end of the period. To properly measure income for the period, the matching principle requires the interest expense to be recorded during the period it is incurred. The amount of the accrued interest is computed based on three factors: (1) the principal amount of the loan; (2) the rate of interest expressed as an annual rate; and (3) the amount of time the loan is outstanding during the period. On December 1, DataForce obtained a bank loan in the amount of $36,000 and signed a two-year note payable. The annual interest rate on the note is 10 percent per year, with interest payable each November 30. The first year's interest payment of $3,600 ($36,000 × 10 percent) is due on November 30 of the following year. Because interest accumulates as time passes, an adjustment is needed on December 31, to record the interest expense that has been incurred during December. December's interest expense is $300 ($3,600/12 months).

Transaction: *Accrue interest expense for December.*

	Balance Sheet							Income Statement				
	Assets	=	Liabilities	+	Stockholders' Equity							
					Contrib. Capital	+	Retained Earnings	Revenues	−	Expenses	=	Net Income
(g)		=	+300 Interest payable	+			−300		−	+300 Interest expense	=	−300

After this adjustment, the income statement properly reflects the $300 interest expense incurred (but not yet paid) during the month of December; and the balance sheet properly reflects the $300 liability in Interest Payable as of December 31.

When the first year's interest of $3,600 is paid on November 30 of the following year, DataForce decreases cash by $3,600. This represents payment for interest expense incurred during the month of December of the current year, decreasing Interest Payable by $300; and payment for interest expense incurred during January through November of the next year, increasing Interest Expense by $3,300. (For ease of presentation, this assumes DataForce makes adjusting entries at the end of each year, not monthly.) On November 30 of the following year, the interest payment is recorded as follows:

Transaction: *Payment of annual interest.*

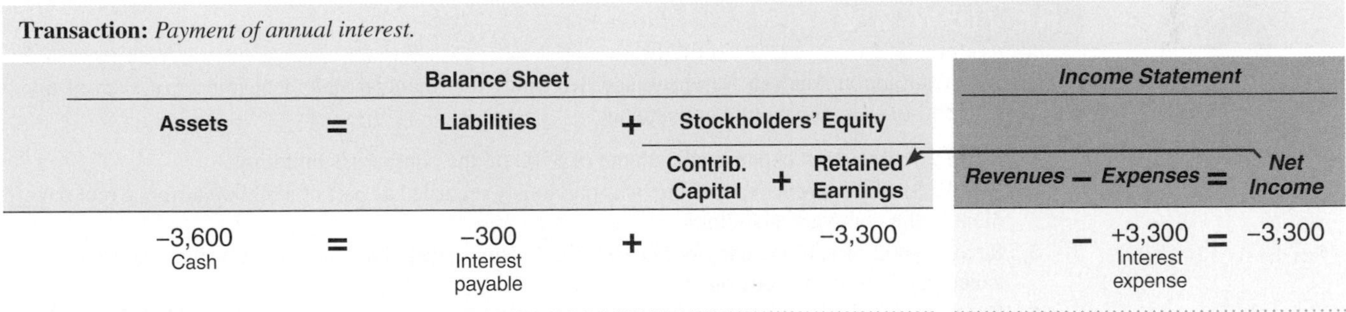

Balance Sheet							Income Statement				
Assets	=	Liabilities	+	Stockholders' Equity							
				Contrib. Capital	+	Retained Earnings	Revenues	−	Expenses	=	Net Income
−3,600 Cash	=	−300 Interest payable	+			−3,300		−	+3,300 Interest expense	=	−3,300

After this transaction is recorded, the income statement properly reflects the $3,300 interest expense incurred (and paid) during the first eleven months of the subsequent year; and the balance sheet properly reflects a zero balance in Interest Payable as of November 30 of that year.

Summary of Accounting Adjustments

Exhibit 3-2 summarizes the four types of accounting adjustments along with examples of how each type of adjustment arises and its effect on the financial statements. As explained, each adjustment affects at least one balance sheet (asset or liability) account and at least one income statement account (expense or revenue).

EXHIBIT 3-2 Four Types of Accounting Adjustments

Accounting Adjustment	Examples	Adjustment	Financial Statement Effect If the Adjustment Is NOT Made: Balance Sheet	Financial Statement Effect If the Adjustment Is NOT Made: Income Statement
Deferrals				
Deferred revenue	Recognize revenue earned on products or services for which cash was received in a prior period, such as unearned fee revenue.	**Increase Revenue** **Decrease Liability**	Liability overstated Equity understated	Revenue understated
Deferred expenses	Recognize expenses incurred for cash expenditures made in a prior period, such as depreciation of buildings and expiration of prepaid rent and insurance.	**Increase Expense** **Decrease Asset**	Asset overstated Equity overstated	Expense understated
Accruals				
Accrued revenue	Recognize revenue earned on sales for which the cash will be received in a later period, such as sales of products or services, and interest income.	**Increase Revenue** **Increase Asset**	Asset understated Equity understated	Revenue understated
Accrued expenses	Recognize expenses incurred for which cash will be paid in a later period, such as wages or interest.	**Increase Expense** **Increase Liability**	Liability understated Equity overstated	Expense understated

TAKEAWAY 3.3	Concept	Method	Assessment
	When should an adjustment be made?	Knowledge of the proper account balance is needed. Adjustments are required to (1) recognize previously deferred revenue, (2) recognize previously deferred expenses, (3) accrue revenue, and (4) accrue expenses.	Record an adjustment so that accounts are correctly reported; otherwise, the balance sheet and income statement accounts are incorrectly reported.

REVIEW 3.2

Prepare a Transaction Analysis Template and determine the financial statement impact of each of the following end-of-year accounting adjustments.

1. Record depreciation expense adjustment of $700 on the company's buildings.
2. Record $1,500 for rent expense that was previously recorded as part of a $2,000 advance rent payment to the company's landlord.
3. Record $400 of revenue earned that was previously recorded as unearned revenue due to an advance payment from a customer.
4. Record $500 of accrued interest expense that applies to the company's bank loan. The $500 is part of the company's annual cash interest payment that is due next period.

The solution is on page 103.

LO3 Prepare the financial statements.

PREPARING THE FINANCIAL STATEMENTS

After the end-of-period adjustments are recorded, the company prepares financial statements. The adjustments in the preceding section are summarized in a horizontal worksheet in **Exhibit 3-3**. The first line of Exhibit 3-3 reports the unadjusted balance sheet and income statement of DataForce from Exhibit 2-3 in Chapter 2. The above adjustments are then recorded in the worksheet to arrive at the adjusted trial balance. The adjusted trial balance is then used to prepare the income

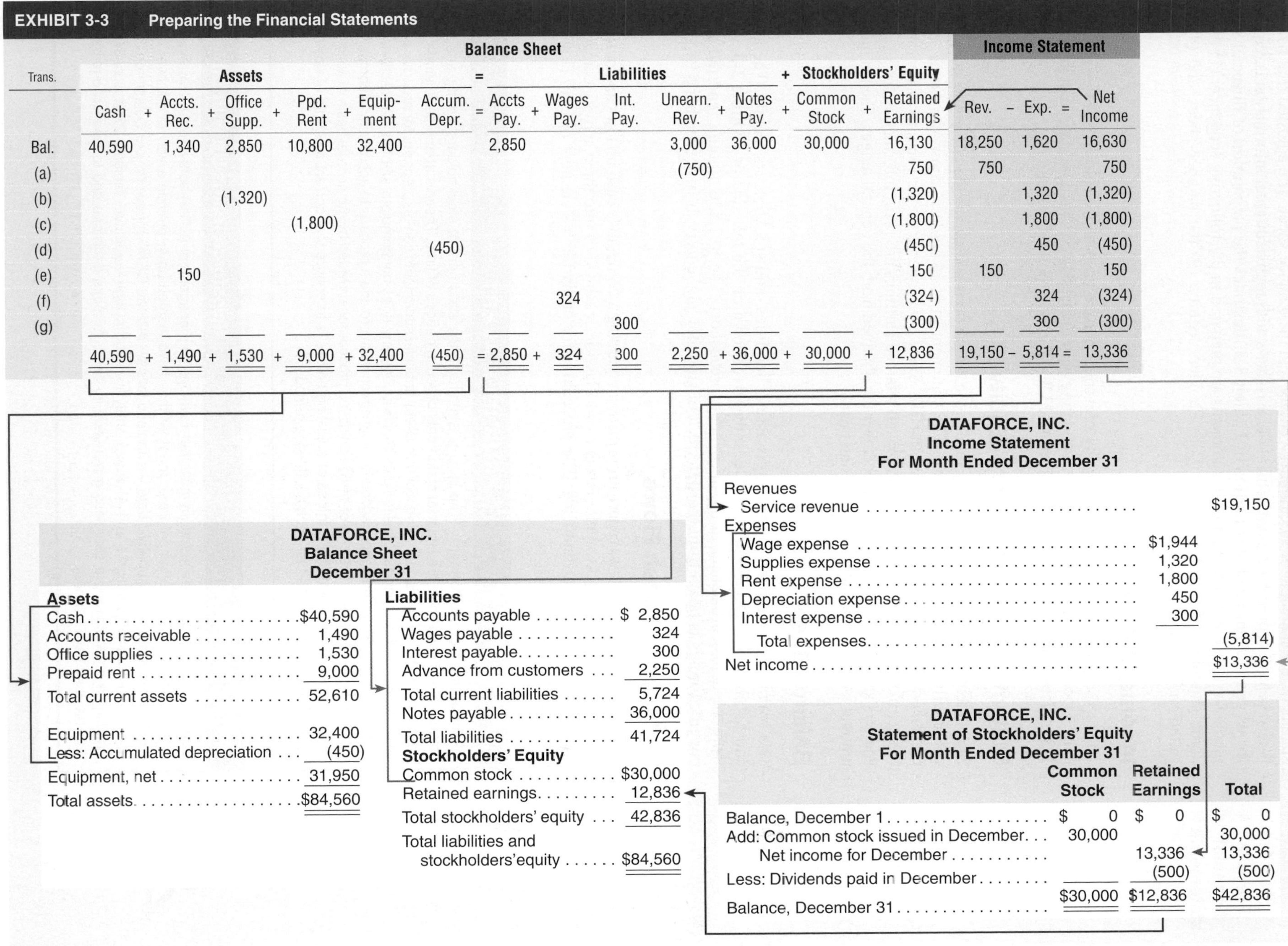

EXHIBIT 3-3 Preparing the Financial Statements

Trans.	Cash	Accts. Rec.	Office Supp.	Ppd. Rent	Equipment	Accum. Depr.	Accts Pay.	Wages Pay.	Int. Pay.	Unearn. Rev.	Notes Pay.	Common Stock	Retained Earnings	Rev.	Exp.	Net Income
	Balance Sheet: Assets						**= Liabilities**					**+ Stockholders' Equity**		**Income Statement**		
Bal.	40,590	1,340	2,850	10,800	32,400		2,850			3,000	36,000	30,000	16,130	18,250	1,620	16,630
(a)										(750)			750	750		750
(b)			(1,320)										(1,320)		1,320	(1,320)
(c)				(1,800)									(1,800)		1,800	(1,800)
(d)						(450)							(450)		450	(450)
(e)		150											150	150		150
(f)								324					(324)		324	(324)
(g)									300				(300)		300	(300)
	40,590 +	1,490 +	1,530 +	9,000 +	32,400	(450) =	2,850 +	324	300	2,250 +	36,000 +	30,000 +	12,836	19,150 −	5,814 =	13,336

DATAFORCE, INC.
Balance Sheet
December 31

Assets		**Liabilities**	
Cash	$40,590	Accounts payable	$ 2,850
Accounts receivable	1,490	Wages payable	324
Office supplies	1,530	Interest payable	300
Prepaid rent	9,000	Advance from customers	2,250
Total current assets	52,610	Total current liabilities	5,724
		Notes payable	36,000
Equipment	32,400	Total liabilities	41,724
Less: Accumulated depreciation	(450)	**Stockholders' Equity**	
Equipment, net	31,950	Common stock	$30,000
Total assets	$84,560	Retained earnings	12,836
		Total stockholders' equity	42,836
		Total liabilities and stockholders'equity	$84,560

DATAFORCE, INC.
Income Statement
For Month Ended December 31

Revenues		
Service revenue		$19,150
Expenses		
Wage expense	$1,944	
Supplies expense	1,320	
Rent expense	1,800	
Depreciation expense	450	
Interest expense	300	
Total expenses		(5,814)
Net income		$13,336

DATAFORCE, INC.
Statement of Stockholders' Equity
For Month Ended December 31

	Common Stock	Retained Earnings	Total
Balance, December 1	$ 0	$ 0	$ 0
Add: Common stock issued in December	30,000		30,000
Net income for December		13,336	13,336
Less: Dividends paid in December		(500)	(500)
Balance, December 31	$30,000	$12,836	$42,836

Step 4 Prepare financial statements

statement, the statement of stockholders' equity, and the balance sheet. The adjusted trial balance is also helpful in preparing the statement of cash flows, although additional information is required for its preparation. The lower portion of Exhibit 3-3 illustrates the preparation of financial statements for DataForce. The financial statements are prepared in the following sequence: (1) the income statement, (2) the statement of stockholders' equity, (3) the balance sheet, and (4) the statement of cash flows.

Income Statement

The income statement presents a company's revenues and expenses and discloses whether the company reported a profit or a loss for the accounting period. DataForce's income statement in Exhibit 3-3 indicates that it reported net income of $13,336 for the month of December.

Statement of Stockholders' Equity

The statement of stockholders' equity reports the transactions and events that affect the stockholders' equity accounts during the period. The statement of stockholders' equity for DataForce is presented in the lower right side of Exhibit 3-3. Since December is the first month of operations, the beginning balances in common stock and retained earnings are zero. Information for stock issuances and dividends paid during December are obtained from the general ledger. The net income amount is obtained from the income statement.

Balance Sheet

The balance sheet reports a company's assets, liabilities, and stockholders' equity. The assets and liabilities for DataForce as of December 31, shown on the left side of **Exhibit 3-3**, come from the adjusted balances in the horizontal spreadsheet. The $12,836 amount reported as retained earnings is taken from the statement of stockholders' equity as of December 31.

Statement of Cash Flows

The statement of cash flows reports information regarding a company's cash inflows and outflows during the period. The statement of cash flows classifies cash flows into three activity categories: operating, investing, and financing. The procedures for preparing a statement of cash flows are discussed in Chapter 11.

PRINCIPLE ALERT

Accounting Period Concept The income statement, the statement of stockholders' equity, and the statement of cash flows are financial statements covering periods of time. These statements illustrate the *accounting period concept*, the concept that useful financial statements can be prepared for arbitrary time periods within a company's total life span. Since a company does not complete all of its transactions by the end of an accounting period, accounting principles must provide a process to account for a company's continuing transactions. The end-of-period adjusting procedures provided by the accrual basis of accounting are that process. A major purpose of adjusting entries is to ensure that correct amounts of revenue and expense are reported for each accounting period.

Data Analytics

DATA ANALYTICS — Salesforce Teams Up with Tableau

Salesforce is a worldwide leader in customer relationship management (CRM) software, and Tableau is a leader in data visualization software. Together they have teamed up to provide a way to discover what can be learned from a company's data. As Tableau tells it, "Tableau CRM empowers your Salesforce CRM users with actionable insights and AI-driven analytics right in their workflow." Tableau CRM is native to Salesforce, thus allowing a seamless experience for users to make decisions and to take actions based on what they have learned.

REVIEW 3.3

The account balances of Cassi Company are provided below to assist in the preparation of its December 31 year-end financial statements.

CASSI COMPANY December 31	Adjusted Balances
Assets	
Cash	$ 8,000
Supplies	14,000
Inventory	17,000
Prepaid rent	3,000
Equipment	50,000
Accumulated depreciation	(10,000)
Total assets	$82,000
Liabilities	
Accounts payable	$ 9,000
Salaries payable	2,000
Interest payable	1,000
Unearned revenue	5,000
Long-term debt	35,000
Stockholders' equity	
Common stock	15,000
Retained earnings (January 1)	5,000
Dividends	(2,000)
Revenue	
Sales revenue	60,000
Expenses	
Supplies expense	(26,000)
Salaries expense	(9,000)
Rent expense	(6,000)
Depreciation expense	(5,000)
Interest expense	(2,000)
Total liabilities and stockholders' equity	$82,000

REQUIRED

Prepare an income statement and a statement of stockholders' equity for the year ended December 31, and a balance sheet for Cassi Company as of December 31. There were no changes in stockholders' equity during the year other than for net income and dividends.

The solution is on page 104.

QUALITY OF ACCOUNTING NUMBERS

Earnings quality refers to the degree to which a company's financial statements fairly present its true underlying financial performance. The better the statements are at portraying the company's underlying financial performance, the higher the earnings quality.

While many end-of-period adjustments discussed in this chapter are objectively determined, such as the time remaining for a prepaid insurance policy and the interest rate on an outstanding loan, many other adjustments that we discuss in later chapters involve significant judgments on the part of the company's management. Examples of judgments leading to adjusting entries are the amount of future warranty work associated with a company's product, the amount of a company's accounts receivable that will not be collected, and the estimated depreciable lives of a company's plant and equipment. Each of these items involves estimates of future events that cannot be known with certainty. Consequently, each of these estimates can have a material effect on a company's reported financial results in any given period.

Wall Street analysts often evaluate a company's quality of earnings by the degree to which these estimates are considered conservative or aggressive. Conservative estimates are those that are more pessimistic, leading to lower reported net income and net asset values, while aggressive estimates are those that result in higher reported net income and net asset values. Conservative estimates (within reason) are generally considered to be a feature of high-quality financial reporting. Investors may punish a company that is judged to have low-quality earnings by bidding down the price of their stock. This is because a company that uses aggressive accounting can surprise investors with poor future performance that will cause the company's stock price to fall.

CLOSE TEMPORARY ACCOUNTS

LO4 **Describe** the closing process and **summarize** the accounting cycle.

eLecture

MBC

A.K.A. Closing procedures are also known as *closing the books*.

Step 5 Close temporary accounts

All accounts can be identified as either permanent accounts or temporary accounts. **Permanent accounts** are the accounts presented on the balance sheet. They consist of the asset, liability, and stockholders' equity accounts. The distinguishing feature of a permanent account is that any balance in the account at the end of an accounting period is carried forward to the following accounting period. **Temporary accounts** are used to gather information for a particular accounting period. Revenue, expense, and dividend accounts are temporary accounts. At the end of the accounting period, temporary account balances are transferred to Retained Earnings, which is a permanent stockholders' equity account. The process of transferring the balances in temporary accounts to Retained Earnings is referred to as the **closing process** or **closing procedures**.

A temporary account is *closed* when its balance is transferred to Retained Earnings, a permanent account. The closing process adjusts the temporary account balances to zero, and they are then ready to start accumulating data for the next accounting period. The following summarizes the classification of permanent and temporary accounts.

Permanent Accounts	Temporary Accounts
Assets	Revenues
Liabilities	Expenses
Common Stock	Dividends
Retained Earnings	

Summary of the Accounting Cycle

The sequence of accounting procedures known as the *accounting cycle* occurs each fiscal period and represents a systematic process for accumulating and reporting the financial data of a business. **Exhibit 3-4** summarizes the five major steps in the accounting cycle, as described in this and the preceding chapter.

EXHIBIT 3-4 The Accounting Cycle: A Summary

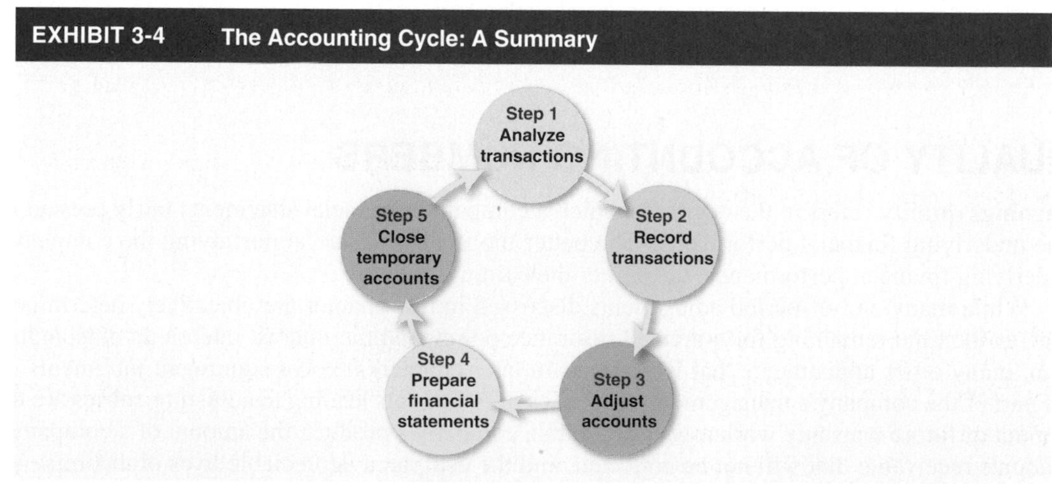

REVIEW 3.4

Balke Laboratory began operations two years ago on July 1 and provides diagnostic services for physicians and medical clinics. The company's fiscal year ends on June 30, and the accounts are adjusted annually on this date. Balke's unadjusted balance sheet as of June 30 of the current year is as follows:

BALKE LABORATORY
Unadjusted Balance Sheet
June 30 of the current year

Assets		
Cash	$ 1,000	
Accounts receivable	9,200	
Prepaid insurance	6,000	
Supplies	31,300	
Laboratory equipment	270,000	
Accumulated depreciation	(30,000)	
Total assets		$287,500
Liabilities and stockholders' equity		
Accounts payable	3,100	
Diagnostic fees received in advance	4,000	
Total liabilities		7,100
Common stock	90,000	
Retained earnings (beginning of year)	50,000	
Diagnostic fees revenue	220,400	
Wage expense	(58,000)	
Rent expense	(22,000)	
Total stockholders' equity		280,400
Total liabilities and stockholders' equity		$287,500

The following information is also available:

1. The Prepaid Insurance account balance represents a premium paid on January 1 of the current year for two years of fire and casualty insurance coverage. Balke Laboratory had no insurance protection prior to this time.
2. The supplies were physically counted at June 30. The count totaled $6,300.
3. All laboratory equipment was purchased on July 1 two years prior. It is expected to last nine years.
4. Balke Laboratory received a $4,000 cash payment on April 1 of the current year from Boll Clinic for diagnostic services to be provided uniformly over the four months beginning April 1. Balke credited the payment to Diagnostic Fees Received in Advance. The services for April, May, and June have been provided to Boll Clinic.
5. Unpaid wages at June 30 were $600.
6. Balke Laboratory performed lab tests in the last two days of June totaling $500, which were not billed.

REQUIRED

Using the Transaction Analysis Template, show the effect of each adjustment on the financial statements as of June 30 of the current year.

The solution is on pages 105–106.

SUMMARY OF LEARNING OBJECTIVES

Explain the accrual basis of accounting. (p. 72) LO1

- Revenue is recognized on an accrual basis at the time that it is earned. This may be prior to the receipt of cash, at the same time as the receipt of cash, or following the receipt of cash.

- Expenses are matched against revenues in the same accounting period that the associated revenue is recognized. This may be prior to cash payment, at the same time as cash payment, or following cash payment.
- Revenue recognition and the corresponding matching of expenses may differ in timing on an accrual basis versus on a cash basis.

LO2 Describe the adjusting process and illustrate the four major types of adjustments. (p. 76)

- Adjusting entries are made to achieve the appropriate recognition of revenues and matching of expenses with revenues, and consist of four general types of adjustments:
  1. Recognize revenue earned on products or services for which cash was received in a prior period.
  2. Recognize expenses incurred for cash expenditures made in a prior period.
  3. Recognize revenue earned on sales for which the cash will be received in a later period.
  4. Recognize expenses incurred for which cash will be paid in a later period.

LO3 Prepare the financial statements. (p. 84)

- An income statement, statement of stockholders' equity, balance sheet, and statement of cash flows may be prepared from adjusted balances and other information.

LO4 Describe the closing process and summarize the accounting cycle. (p. 88)

- *Closing the books* means closing the revenue, expense and dividends, and all temporary accounts to Retained Earnings, a permanent account.

SUMMARY	Concept	Method	Assessment
TAKEAWAY 3.1	When should sales revenue be recognized?	Recognize revenue when it is earned. Revenue is earned when the goods and services are provided to the customer.	Early recognition of revenue overstates current period revenue; recognizing revenue too late understates current period revenue.
TAKEAWAY 3.2	When should expenses be recognized?	Recognize expenses during the same period as the revenue they generate.	Early recognition of expenses overstates current period expenses; recognizing expenses too late understates current period expenses.
TAKEAWAY 3.3	When should an adjustment be made?	Knowledge of the proper account balance is needed. Adjustments are required to (1) recognize previously deferred revenue, (2) recognize previously deferred expenses, (3) accrue revenue, and (4) accrue expenses.	Record an adjustment so that accounts are correctly reported; otherwise, balance sheet and income statement accounts are incorrectly reported.

KEY TERMS

Accrual basis of accounting (p. 72)
Accruals (p. 78)
Accrued expenses (p. 82)
Accrued revenues (p. 81)
Accumulated depreciation (p. 80)
Advances from Customers (p. 78)
Book value (p. 80)
Closing procedures (p. 88)
Closing process (p. 88)
Contra accounts (p. 80)
Deferrals (p. 78)
Deferred expenses (p. 79)
Deferred Revenues (p. 78)
Depreciation (p. 80)
Earnings quality (p. 87)
Expense recognition (matching) principle (p. 72)
Permanent accounts (p. 88)
Revenue recognition principle (p. 72)
Straight-line depreciation (p. 80)
Temporary accounts (p. 88)
Unearned revenue (p. 78)

SELF-STUDY QUESTIONS

(Answers to the Self-Study Questions are available at the end of the chapter.)

LO2

1. Which of the following is an example of an adjustment?

a. Recording the purchase of supplies on account
b. Recording depreciation expense on a truck
c. Recording the billing of customers for services rendered
d. Recording the payment of wages to employees

2. An adjustment to record utilities used during a month for which no bill has yet been received is an example of LO2 Homework MBC

a. Allocating assets to expense to reflect the actual operating expenses incurred during the accounting period
b. Allocating revenues received in advance to revenue to reflect actual revenues earned during the accounting period
c. Accruing expenses to reflect expenses incurred during the accounting period that are not yet paid or recorded
d. Accruing revenues to reflect revenues earned during the accounting period that are not yet received or recorded

3. Which of the following would not occur during the closing process? LO4 Homework MBC

a. Close each revenue account to the Retained Earnings account
b. Close each expense account to the Retained Earnings account
c. Close the Dividends account to the Retained Earnings account
d. Close Unearned Revenue to Retained Earnings

4. Jones Company started business on November 1. On that date it paid $12,000 in advance for three months rent. What is the balance in the prepaid rent account at December 31? LO2 Homework MBC

a. $0 *c.* $4,000
b. $12,000 *d.* $8,000

5. Current Electric Company employees earned wages of $14,000 during the last week of December but were not paid until January 5. The Company did not make an accrual at December 31. What is the financial statement effect of NOT making this adjustment? LO2 Homework MBC

a. Assets are overstated, expenses understated
b. Liabilities are overstated, revenue understated
c. Assets are understated, revenues understated
d. Liabilities are understated, expenses understated

6. What is the financial statement effect of an adjustment to record revenue when payment has not been received by the end of the accounting period? LO2 Homework MBC

a. Assets are decreased, expenses are increased
b. Assets and revenues are increased
c. Liabilities and expenses are increased
d. Liabilities are decreased and revenues are increased

7. Kelly Corporation received an advance payment of $20,000 in Year 1 from Rufus Company for consulting services. Kelly performed half of the consulting in Year 1 and the remainder in Year 2. Kelly reports using the accrual basis of accounting. How much revenue from this consulting project will Kelly report in Year 1? LO2 Homework MBC

a. $20,000 *c.* $0
b. $10,000 *d.* $15,000

QUESTIONS

1. Why is the adjusting step of the accounting cycle necessary?
2. What four different types of adjustments are frequently necessary at the end of an accounting period? Provide an example of each type.
3. On January 1, Prepaid Insurance was increased for the cost of a two-year premium in the amount of $1,872. What adjustment should be made on January 31 before the January financial statements are prepared?
4. What is a contra account? What contra account is used in reporting the book value of a depreciable asset?
5. At the beginning of January, the Supplies account had a balance of $825. During January, purchases of $260 of supplies were made on account. Although only $630 of supplies were on hand at the end of January, the necessary adjustment was omitted. How will the omission affect (a) the income statement for January and (b) the balance sheet prepared as of January 31?
6. The publisher of *International View*, a monthly magazine, received two-year subscriptions totaling $9,720 on January 1. (a) What is the financial effect of the receipt of the $9,720? (b) What adjustment should be made at the end of January before financial statements are prepared for the month?

7. Globe Travel Agency pays an employee $475 in wages each Friday for a five-day work week ending on that day. The last Friday of January falls on January 27. What adjustment should be made on January 31, the fiscal year-end?
8. The Bayou Company earns interest amounting to $360 per month on its investments. The company receives the interest every six months, on December 31 and June 30. Monthly financial statements are prepared. What adjustment should be made on January 31?
9. Define *permanent account.* Provide an example.
10. Define *temporary account.* Provide an example.
11. Which group of accounts is closed at the end of the accounting year? Why?

DATA ANALYTICS

The assignments in this Data Analytics section are designed to familiarize you with the tools used in analyzing data and communicating the results. Appendix F provides an in-depth discussion of data analytics and blockchain technology.

DA3-1. Matching Chart Types and Aims to Data Measures
In the process of preparing a data visualization, determine which chart would be best suited for each data measure and determine what is the aim of that particular chart. Refer to Appendix F for a description of each chart type.

Data Measure	Chart Type	Aim of Chart
a. Relation of daily clicks on digital ads with daily online sales	__ Bar chart	__ Compare different categories
b. Sales by major city for a company's best-selling product	__ Pie chart	__ Analyze changes over time
c. Level of eight types of digital marketing expenses for the year	__ Line chart	__ Show parts that make up a whole
d. Common stock and retained earnings portions of total equity	__ Scatter Plot	__ Show correlation between two variables
e. Ten-year trend in digital marketing expense	__ Map chart	__ Show differences across geographic locations

DA3-2. Preparing Basic Visualization in Excel of Changes in Sales Data Over Time
The Excel file associated with this exercise includes daily sales for the month of December for Strickland Inc. In this exercise, we determine which sales amounts appear to be outliers which means that they differ significantly from the other daily sales amounts.

REQUIRED

1. Download Excel file DA3-2 found in myBusinessCourse.
2. Prepare a line chart for the month of December. *Hint:* Highlight the data and open the Insert tab. Click the Line chart in the Charts group and select one of the 2-D lines. Do not include the column titles or the total row when highlighting the data.
3. Add a trendline to the chart. *Hint:* Right-click on the line in your chart to view option to add a linear trendline.
4. Describe the position of the trendline on the chart on December 18.
5. List the point(s) (if any) on the chart that are positioned over +/−$1,200 beyond the trendline. *Hint:* Use the gridlines on the chart to help you visually detect outliers.

Assignments with the MBC logo in the margin are available in myBusinessCourse. See the Preface of the book for details.

SHORT EXERCISES

LO1 **SE3-1. Revenue Recognition** Jeff Martin performed web design services totaling $5,000 in the current month. By the end of the month he had received payment for half of this amount. Determine the amount of revenue to be recognized in the current period.

LO1 **SE3-2. Accrual Accounting** Evan Corporation provided consulting services for Kensington Company in year 1. Evan incurred costs of $60,000 associated with the consulting and billed Kensington $90,000. Evan paid $40,000 of its costs in year 1 and the remaining $20,000 in year 2. Evan received $45,000 of its billing in year 1. Kensington paid the remaining $45,000 in year 2. Evan reports on the accrual basis of accounting. How much is Evan's year 1 and year 2 profit related to the Kensington consulting?

SE3-3. **Adjusting Accounts** MacKenzie Enterprises has the following accounts in its general ledger. Explain why each of these accounts may need to be adjusted. LO2

a. Rent Payable
b. Unearned Revenue
c. Prepaid Subscriptions
d. Depreciation Expense

SE3-4. **Adjustment for Depreciation** Cowley Company just completed its first year of operations. The December 31 equipment account has a balance of $20,000. There is no balance in the Accumulated Depreciation—Equipment account or in the Depreciation Expense account. The accountant estimates the yearly equipment depreciation to be $4,000. Prepare the required adjustment to record the yearly depreciation for equipment. LO2

SE3-5. **Adjustment for Prepaid Insurance** Cooper Inc. recorded the purchase of a three-year insurance policy on July 1 in the amount of $3,600 by increasing Prepaid Insurance and decreasing Cash. Prepare the necessary December 31 year-end adjustment. LO2

SE3-6. **Accrual Adjustments** Prepare the necessary adjustments for Sparky Electronics for the following items: LO2

a. Salaries for employees in the amount of $2,500 have been incurred but have not been paid.
b. Interest expense of $1,200 has been incurred but not yet paid for an outstanding note.
c. Work performed but not yet billed for $3,500.

SE3-7. **Analyze Adjustments** Fisher Supplies has the following balance sheet accounts that require adjustment. Identify the likely income statement account that will be used to adjust these accounts. LO2

a. Prepaid Insurance
b. Accumulated Depreciation
c. Supplies
d. Unearned Revenue
e. Interest Payable

SE3-8. **Prepare an Income Statement from Adjusted Balances** The Century Company's adjusted balances as of December 31 follow: Sales $20,000; Cost of Goods Sold $8,000; Selling and Administrative Expenses $3,000; Interest Expense $1,500. Prepare an income statement for the year. LO3

SE3-9. **Temporary Accounts** Use the data from SE3-8 to determine the ending Retained Earnings balance for The Century Company. Beginning retained earnings were $8,500 and dividends paid during the year were $2,000. LO4

SE3-10. **Revenue Recognition** Michael Julius received an $18,000 payment in advance on a three-month contract to install a water purification system. By month-end the project was one-third completed. Determine the amount of revenue to be recognized in the current period. LO1

SE3-11. **Revenue Recognition** Ashley Garrett operates a flight training school. On occasion she will provide introductory flight simulator sessions. This month, she performed introductory sessions and received $2,000. The sessions are paid for at the time they are delivered. Determine the amount of revenue to be recognized in the current period. LO1

SE3-12. **Expense Recognition (Matching)** Jane's Party~Party provides party planning services. Jane purchased office supplies for $500 on account. Supplies were used as the services were provided. A physical count of the supplies at the end of the month found $100 in supplies still on hand. Determine the amount of expense to be recognized in the current period. Would your answer be different if Jane had paid for the supplies with cash? LO1

EXERCISES

E3-1. **Transaction Analysis and Adjustments** Deluxe Building Services offers janitorial services on both a contract basis and an hourly basis. On January 1, Deluxe collected $20,100 in advance on a six-month contract for work to be performed evenly during the next six months. Using the Transaction Analysis Template, determine the financial statement effect of the following: LO2

a. The January 1 receipt of $20,100 for contract work
b. The adjustment to be made on January 31, for the contract work done during January
c. At January 31, a total of 30 hours of hourly rate janitor work was unbilled. The billing rate is $19 per hour. Provide the accrual needed on January 31. (*Note:* The firm uses the account Fees Receivable to reflect amounts due.)

E3-2. **Transaction Analysis and Adjustments** Selected accounts of Ideal Properties Inc., a real estate management firm, are shown below as of January 31, before any adjustments have been made: LO2

	Unadjusted Balances
Prepaid insurance	$ 6,660
Supplies	1,930
Office equipment	5,952
Unearned rent revenue	5,250
Salaries expense	3,100
Rent revenue	15,000

Monthly financial statements are prepared. Using the Transaction Analysis Template, determine the financial statement effect of the following adjustments as of January 31:

a. Prepaid Insurance represents a three-year premium paid on January 1.
b. Supplies of $850 were on hand January 31.
c. Office equipment is expected to last eight years. Depreciation is recorded monthly.
d. On January 1, the firm collected six months' rent in advance from a tenant renting space for $875 per month.
e. Accrued salaries not recorded as of January 31 are $490.

LO2  **E3-3. Transaction Analysis and Adjustments** For each of the following unrelated situations, determine the financial statement effect using the Transaction Analysis Template:

a. Unrecorded depreciation on equipment is $610.
b. The Supplies account has a balance of $2,990. Supplies on hand at the end of the period totaled $1,100.
c. On the date for preparing financial statements, an estimated utilities expense of $390 has been incurred, but no utility bill has been received.
d. On the first day of the current month, rent for four months was paid and recorded as a $2,800 increase to Prepaid Rent and a $2,800 decrease in Cash. Monthly statements are now being prepared.
e. Nine months ago, Solid Insurance Company sold a one-year policy to a customer and recorded the receipt of the premium by increasing Cash and Unearned Premium Revenue for $624. No adjusting entries have been prepared during the nine-month period. Annual financial statements are now being prepared.
f. At the end of the accounting period, employee wages of $965 have been incurred but not paid.
g. At the end of the accounting period, $300 of interest has been earned but not yet received on notes receivable.

LO3  **E3-4. Statement of Stockholders' Equity** On January 1, the balance of the Retained Earnings account was $48,000. The company's Common Stock account had an opening balance of $70,000, and $6,000 in new capital contributions were made during the year. During the year, dividends of $9,700 were paid. The income statement shows net income of $29,900. Prepare a statement of stockholders' equity for Strife & Company, architectural design firm.

LO2  **E3-5. Transaction Analysis and Adjustments** For each of the following unrelated situations, determine the financial statement effect using the Transaction Analysis Template:

a. Equipment purchased at the beginning of the month for $12,000 on account has an estimated useful life of 5 years. One-month's depreciation on the equipment is unrecorded.
b. An estimated utilities expense of $545 has been incurred in the current month, but the utility bill has not been received.
c. On the first day of the current month, payment was made for four months, rent in advance in the amount of $8,000. Monthly statements are now being prepared for the current month-end.
d. Taylor Medical Equipment provides medical equipment for rent. A local nursing home pays $3,600 in advance for a three-month rental of hospital beds. At the end of the current period, one month has passed.

LO2  **E3-6. Transaction Analysis and Adjustments** For each of the following unrelated situations, determine the financial statement effect using the Transaction Analysis Template:

a. The Inventory account had a beginning balance of $8,900. Purchases of inventory during the month were $6,000. Inventory on hand at the end of the period totaled $7,100.
b. Siewald Tutorials provides group SAT tutoring sessions of six months. Fees collected in advance totaled $5,400. At the end of the current period, one month of instruction has been given.
c. At the end of the accounting period, employee wages of $1,800 have been incurred but not paid.
d. At the end of the accounting period, $400 of interest has been earned but not yet received on notes receivable.

E3-7. **Financial Statement Effect** For the following unrelated situations, determine whether the assets, liabilities, stockholders' equity, income and/or expense are overstated, understated, or properly stated: LO2

a. The supplies account has a balance of $900. Supplies on hand at the end of the period totaled $400. No adjustment has been made.

b. Employees worked the last three days of the month for which they have not been paid. No accrual has been made.

c. An employment contract has been signed with an accountant to start working next month. No adjustment has been made.

E3-8. **Analysis of Adjusted Data** Selected adjusted balances for Coyle Company are shown below as of January 31. The firm uses a calendar-year accounting period and makes monthly adjustments. LO2

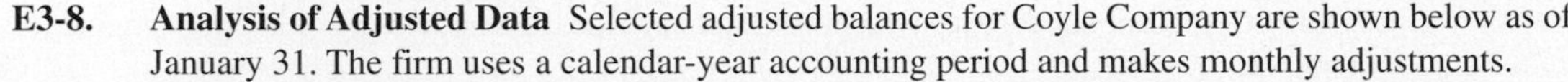

Adjusted Balances as of January 31	
Supplies	$ 800
Supplies expense	960
Prepaid insurance	574
Insurance expense	82
Wages payable	500
Wages expense	3,200
Truck	8,700
Accumulated depreciation	2,610

a. If the amount in Supplies Expense represents the January 31 adjustment for the supplies used in January, and $620 worth of supplies were purchased during January, what was the January 1 balance of Supplies?

b. The amount in the Insurance Expense account represents the adjustment made at January 31 for January insurance expense. If the original insurance premium was for one year, what was the amount of the premium, and on what date did the insurance policy start?

c. If we assume that no balance existed in Wages Payable or Wages Expense on January 1, how much cash was paid as wages during January?

d. If the truck has a useful life of five years, what is the monthly amount of depreciation expense, and how many months has Coyle owned the truck?

E3-9. **Analysis of the Impact of Adjustments on Financial Statements** At the end of the first month of operations, the Bradley Company's accountant prepared financial statements that showed the following amounts: LO2

Assets	$60,000
Liabilities	20,000
Stockholders' equity	40,000
Net income	9,000

In preparing the statements, the accountant overlooked the following items:

a. Depreciation for the month, $1,000.

b. Service revenue earned but not recorded at month-end, $1,500.

c. Employee wages earned but unpaid at month-end, $250.

Determine the correct amounts of assets, liabilities, and stockholders' equity at month-end and net income for the month.

E3-10. **Closing Process** Selected adjusted balances of the Rose Corporation, prepared as of December 31, are as follows: LO4

	Adjusted Balances
Service fees earned	$92,500
Interest income	2,200
Salaries expense	41,800
Advertising expense	4,300
Depreciation expense	8,700
Income tax expense	9,900
Common stock	75,000
Retained earnings, beginning balance	57,700
Cash dividends	15,000

Identify the temporary accounts that will be closed to Retained Earnings. Once the closing process is completed, what is the ending balance in the Retained Earnings account?

LO1 **E3-11. Revenue Recognition** Identify the proper point to recognize revenue for each of the following transactions.

a. Napoleon Industries sells and delivers a machine in January with terms of no payment due until six months later.

b. Emma Company collects an advance deposit of $700 in July toward the purchase of a $3,000 piece of equipment that is delivered to the customer the following September.

c. Ashley Corporation receives payment in October at the time of delivery of a rebuilt engine for a tractor.

PROBLEMS

LO2, 3 **P3-1. Transaction Analysis and Adjustments** Mark Ladd opened Ladd Roofing Service on April 1. The unadjusted account balances as of April 30 are as follows:

Cash	$5,645	Accounts payable	3,140
Accounts receivable	4,600	Unearned revenue	1,800
Supplies	1,200	Common Stock	11,500
Prepaid insurance	2,880	Retained earnings (beginning)	0
Truck	6,000	Roofing fee revenue	9,500
Less: Accumulated depreciation	0	Fuel expense	75
Equipment	2,940	Advertising expense	100
Less: Accumulated depreciation	0	Wages expense	2,500

REQUIRED

a. Using the Transaction Analysis Template, determine the financial statement effect of each of the necessary adjustments as of April 30.

1. Supplies on hand on April 30 amounted to $400.
2. A two-year insurance policy was purchased on April 1.
3. The used truck was purchased on April 1 and has an estimated useful life of 4 years.
4. The items in the Equipment account were purchased on April 1 and have an estimated useful life of 7 years.
5. One-fourth of the roofing fees received in advance (in Unearned revenue) were earned by April 30.

b. Prepare the income statement for the month of April and balance sheet as of April 30.

LO1 **P3-2. Cash Basis versus Accrual Basis** Armor Company is in the business of buying pencils and reselling them to department stores. During the month of May they purchased 500,000 pencils for $20,000 cash. During that same month, sales reps for Armor Company made a presentation to Walmart and sold them 400,000 pencils for twice what they paid for them (100% mark-up). They shipped the pencils to Walmart on the 25th of the month, and Walmart has 30 days to pay for them. The sales reps earn a commission of 15% on the sales, which is paid on the shipping date and charged to Compensation expense in the income statement.

Cash basis income statements for Armor Company	May	June
Sales Revenue	$ 0	$32,000
Inventory	20,000	
Compensation expense	4,800	
Net income (loss)	(24,800)	32,000

REQUIRED

Restate the Armor Company income statements to the accrual basis.

LO2 **P3-3. Transaction Analysis and Adjustments** Photomake, Inc., a commercial photography studio, has just completed its first full year of operations on December 31. The general ledger account balances before year-end adjustments follow. No adjustments have been made to the accounts at any time during the year.

Cash	$ 2,150	Accounts payable	$ 1,910
Accounts receivable	3,800	Unearned photography fees	2,600
Prepaid rent	12,600	Common stock	24,000
Prepaid insurance	2,970	Photography fees earned	34,480
Supplies	4,250	Wages expense	11,000
Equipment	22,800	Utilities expense	3,420

An analysis of the firm's records discloses the following items:

1. Photography services of $925 have been rendered, but customers have not yet been billed. The firm uses the account Fees Receivable to reflect amounts due but not yet billed.
2. The equipment, purchased January 1, has an estimated life of 10 years.
3. Utilities expense for December is estimated to be $400, but the bill will not arrive until January of next year.
4. The balance in Prepaid Rent represents the amount paid on January 1, for a two-year lease on the studio.
5. In November, customers paid $2,600 in advance for pictures to be taken for the holiday season. When received, these fees increased Unearned Photography Fees. By December 31, all fees are earned.
6. A three-year insurance premium paid on January 1 increased Prepaid Insurance.
7. Supplies on hand at December 31 are $1,520.
8. At December 31, wages expense of $375 has been incurred but not paid.

REQUIRED

Using the Transaction Analysis Template, determine the financial statement effect of each of the necessary adjustments as of December 31.

P3-4. Transaction Analysis and Adjustments Dole Carpet Cleaners ended its first month of operations on June 30. Monthly financial statements will be prepared. The unadjusted account balances are as follows: **LO2, 3**

DOLE CARPET CLEANERS
Unadjusted Balances
June 30

Cash	$ 1,180
Accounts receivable	450
Prepaid rent	3,100
Supplies	2,520
Equipment	4,440
Accounts payable	760
Common stock	2,500
Retained earnings (June 1)	5,000
Dividends	200
Service fees earned	4,650
Wages expense	1,020
	$12,910

The following information is also available:

1. The balance in Prepaid Rent was the amount paid on June 1 for the first four months' rent.
2. Supplies on hand at June 30 were $820.
3. The equipment, purchased June 1, has an estimated life of five years.
4. Unpaid wages at June 30 were $210.
5. Utility services used during June were estimated at $300. A bill is expected early in July.
6. Fees earned for services performed but not yet billed on June 30 were $380. The firm uses the account Fees Receivable to reflect amounts due but not yet billed.

REQUIRED

a. Determine the financial statement effect of the adjustments needed at June 30.
b. Prepare the income statement for the month of June and balance sheet as of June 30.

P3-5. Transaction Analysis and Adjustments The following information relates to December 31 adjustments for Finest Print, a printing company. The firm's fiscal year ends on December 31. **LO2**

1. Weekly salaries for a five-day week total $1,800, payable on Fridays. December 31 of the current year is a Tuesday.

2. Finest Print has $20,000 of notes payable outstanding at December 31. Interest of $200 has accrued on these notes by December 31 but will not be paid until the notes mature next year.
3. During December, Finest Print provided $900 of printing services to clients who will be billed on January 2. The firm uses the account Fees Receivable to reflect amounts due but not yet billed.
4. Starting December 1, all maintenance work on Finest Print's equipment is handled by Prompt Repair Company under an agreement whereby Finest Print pays a fixed monthly charge of $90. Finest Print paid six months' service charge in advance on December 1, increasing Prepaid Maintenance by $540.
5. The firm paid $900 on December 15 for a series of radio commercials to run during December and January. One-third of the commercials have aired by December 31.
6. Starting December 16, Finest Print rented 400 square feet of storage space from a neighboring business. The monthly rent of $0.80 per square foot is due in advance on the first of each month. Nothing was paid in December, however, because the neighbor agreed to add the rent for one-half of December to the January 1 payment.
7. Finest Print invested $5,000 in securities on December 1 and earned interest of $38 on these securities by December 31. No interest will be received until January.
8. The annual depreciation on the firm's equipment is $2,175. No depreciation has been recorded during the year.

REQUIRED

Using the Transaction Analysis Template, determine the financial statement effect of the required adjustments on December 31.

LO2 **P3-6.** **Adjustments** The following selected accounts of the Shaw Company have unadjusted balances as of December 31, the end of the fiscal year:

Prepaid advertising	$ 1,200	Unearned service fees	$ 5,400
Wages expense	43,800	Service fees earned	87,000
Prepaid insurance	3,420	Rental income	4,900

REQUIRED

Using the Transaction Analysis Template, determine the financial statement effect of the necessary adjustments as of December 31, assuming the following:

1. Prepaid advertising at December 31 is $800.
2. Unpaid wages earned by employees in December are $1,300.
3. Prepaid insurance at December 31 is $2,280.
4. Unearned service fees at December 31 are $3,000.
5. Rent revenue of $1,000 owed by a tenant is not recorded at December 31.

LO2 **P3-7.** **Adjustments** The following selected accounts of Birch Company have unadjusted balances as of December 31, the end of the fiscal year:

Prepaid maintenance	$2,700	Commission fees earned	$84,000
Supplies	8,400	Rent expense	10,800
Unearned commission fees	8,500		

REQUIRED

Using the Transaction Analysis Template, determine the financial statement effect of the necessary adjustments as of December 31, assuming the following:

1. On September 1, the company entered into a prepaid equipment maintenance contract. Birch Company paid $2,700 to cover maintenance service for six months, beginning September 1.
2. Supplies on hand at December 31 are $3,200.
3. Unearned commission fees at December 31 are $4,000.
4. Commission fees earned but not yet billed at December 31 are $2,800.
5. Birch Company's lease calls for rent of $900 per month payable on the first of each month, plus an annual amount equal to 1 percent of annual commissions earned. This additional rent is payable on January 10 of the following year. (*Note:* Be sure to use the adjusted amount of commissions earned in computing the additional rent.)

LO3 **P3-8.** **Financial Statements** The adjusted balances shown below are for Fine Consulting Service as of December 31. Byran Fine made no capital contributions during the year.

Cash	$ 2,700	Retained earnings	$ 5,205
Accounts receivable	3,270	Dividends	2,900
Supplies	3,060	Service fees earned	58,400
Prepaid insurance	1,500	Rent expense	12,000
Equipment	6,400	Salaries expense	33,400
Accumulated depreciation—Equipment	1,080	Supplies expense	4,700
Accounts payable	845	Insurance expense	3,250
Long-term notes payable	7,000	Depreciation expense—Equipment	720
Common stock	2,000	Interest expense	630

REQUIRED

Prepare an income statement and a statement of stockholders' equity for the year, and a balance sheet as of December 31.

P3-9. **Revenue Recognition** Jensen Publishing prints and markets lifestyle publications. Their initial offer of $60 for a three-year subscription was well received. They sold 10,000 subscriptions for cash. They purchased state-of-the-art computers and copiers that should last for 5 years for $100,000 cash. Printing supplies and postage are expected to be $25,000 per year. Salaries will be $90,000 per year. Assume no additional subscriptions are sold. **LO1**

Cash basis income statements for Jensen Publishing	Year 1	Year 2	Year 3
Subscription Revenue	$600,000		
Equipment	100,000		
Printing supplies expense	25,000	25,000	25,000
Salaries expense	90,000	90,000	90,000
Net income (loss)	$385,000	(115,000)	(115,000)

REQUIRED

Restate the Jensen Publishing income statements to the accrual basis.

P3-10. **Financial Statements** The following account balances were taken (out of order) from the general ledger of R. Ladd & Company as of January 31. Ladd trains dogs for competitive championship field trials. The firm's accounting year began on January 1. **LO3**

Land	$21,000	Office rent expense	$ 800
Maintenance expense	460	Supplies expense	760
Supplies	1,640	Utilities expense	200
Advertising expense	350	Fees earned	16,470
Common stock	20,000	Accounts receivable	8,200
Retained earnings	9,000		
Cash	7,300	Salaries expense	4,480
Accounts payable	820	Dividends	1,100

REQUIRED

Prepare an income statement and statement of stockholders' equity for the month of January and a balance sheet as of January 31.

P3-11. **Financial Statements** The following account balances, in alphabetical order, are from the general ledger of Morgan's Waterproofing Service at January 31. The firm began business on January 1. **LO3**

Accounts payable	$ 2,600	Notes payable	$ 6,000
Accounts receivable	21,000	Rent expense	1,700
Advertising expense	420	Salaries expense	8,000
Cash	10,400	Service fees earned	25,760
Common stock	29,740	Supplies	8,960
Dividends	3,000	Supplies expense	10,250
Interest expense	50	Utilities expense	320

REQUIRED

Prepare an income statement and statement of stockholders' equity for the month of January and a balance sheet as of January 31.

SERIAL PROBLEM: ANGEL CITY GREETINGS

(Note: This is a continuation of the Serial Problem: Angel City Greetings from Chapters 1 and 2.)

SP3. Getting ready for the upcoming holiday season is traditionally a busy time for greeting card companies, and it was no exception for Kate. The following transactions occurred during the month of October:

1. Hired an assistant at an hourly rate of $10 per hour to help with some of the computer layouts and administrative chores.
2. Supplements her business by teaching a class to aspiring card designers. She charges and receives a total of $450.
3. Delivers greeting cards to several new customers. She bills them a total of $1,500.
4. Pays a utility bill in the amount of $250 for the month of October that she determines is the business portion of her utility bill.
5. Receives an advance deposit of $500 for a new set of cards she is designing for a new customer.
6. Pays her assistant $200 for the work done this month.
7. Determines that the assistant has worked 10 additional hours this month that have not yet been paid.
8. Orders and receives additional supplies in the amount of $1,000. These were paid for during the month.
9. Counts her remaining inventory of supplies at the end of the month and determines the balance to be $300. Don't forget to consider the supplies inventory balance at September 30, from Chapter 2. (*Hint:* This expense will be an increase to Cost of Goods Sold.)
10. Records the adjusting entries for depreciation and insurance expense for the month. From the information provided in Chapter 2, we know that depreciation expense is $100 per month and insurance expense is also $100 per month.
11. Pays herself a salary of $1,000.
12. Deciding she needs a little more cash, Kate pays herself a $500 dividend.
13. Receives her next utility bill during November and determines $85 applies to October's operations.

ANGEL CITY GREETINGS
Balance Sheet
September 30

Assets		Liabilities and Stockholders' Equity	
Cash	$ 6,100	Accounts Payable	$ 0
Account Receivable	0	Notes Payable	0
Supplies Inventory	100		
Prepaid Insurance	1,200	Total Liabilities	0
Equipment	4,800		
Accumulated Depreciation	(100)	Common Stock	10,000
		Retained Earnings	2,100
		Total Stockholders' Equity	12,100
Total Assets	$12,100	Total Liabilities and Stockholders' Equity	$12,100

REQUIRED

Using the September 30 Balance Sheet for Angel City Greetings plus the new information above, complete the following:

a. Using the Transaction Analysis Template, determine the financial statement effect of the above transactions and adjustments.

b. Prepare an income statement and a statement of stockholders' equity for the month ending October 31, and a balance sheet as of October 31.

BEYOND THE NUMBERS

REPORTING AND ANALYSIS

Columbia Sportswear Company

BTN3-1. Financial Reporting Problem: Columbia Sportswear Company The financial statements for the Columbia Sportswear Company can be found in Appendix A at the end of this book.

Required

Answer the following questions using Columbia's Consolidated Financial Statements and the Notes to the consolidated financial statements:

a. Identify an item that likely requires adjustments for prepayments.
b. Identify an item that likely requires an adjusting accrual.
c. Identify the items that will require closing entries. What account will they be ultimately closed to?

Columbia Sportswear Company

Under Armour, Inc.

BTN3-2. Comparative Analysis Problem: Columbia Sportswear Company vs. Under Armour, Inc. The financial statements for the Columbia Sportswear Company can be found in Appendix A, and Under Armour, Inc.'s financial statements can be found in Appendix B at the end of this book.

Required

a. Examine the balance sheet of Columbia Sportswear and identify three items that indicate that the company uses the accrual method of accounting. In each case, identify the likely income statement account that is affected by these accruals.
b. Examine the balance sheet of Under Armour, Inc., and identify three items that indicate the company uses the accrual method of accounting. In each case, identify the likely income statement account that is affected by these accruals.

BTN3-3. Business Decision Problem Wyland Consulting Services, a firm started three years ago by Bruce Wyland, offers consulting services for material handling and plant layout. The balance sheet prepared by the firm's accountant at the end of the year is shown here.

WYLAND CONSULTING SERVICES
Balance Sheet
As of December 31

Assets			Liabilities	
Cash		$ 3,400	Notes payable	$30,000
Accounts receivable		22,875	Accounts payable	4,200
Supplies		13,200	Unearned consulting fees	11,300
Prepaid insurance		4,500	Wages payable	400
Equipment	$68,500		Total Liabilities	45,900
Less: Accumulated depreciation	(23,975)	44,525	**Stockholders' Equity**	
			Common stock	20,000
			Retained earnings	22,600
			Total Stockholders' Equity	42,600
Total Assets		$88,500	Total Liabilities and Stockholders' Equity	$88,500

Earlier in the year, Wyland obtained a bank loan of $30,000 for the firm. One of the provisions of the loan is that the year-end debt-to-equity ratio (ratio of total liabilities to total stockholders' equity) shall not exceed 1.0. Based on the above balance sheet, the ratio at the end of the year is 1.08 ($45,900/$42,600).

Wyland is concerned about being in violation of the loan agreement and asks your assistance in reviewing the situation. Wyland believes that his rather inexperienced accountant may have overlooked some items at year-end.

In discussions with Wyland and the accountant, you learn the following:

1. On January 1, the firm paid a $4,500 insurance premium for two years of coverage. The amount in Prepaid Insurance has not been adjusted.
2. Depreciation on the equipment should be 10 percent of cost per year. The accountant inadvertently recorded 15 percent for the current year.

3. Interest on the bank loan has been paid through the end of the year.
4. The firm concluded a major consulting engagement in December, doing a plant layout analysis for a new factory. The $6,000 fee has not been billed or recorded in the accounts.
5. On December 1, the firm received an $11,300 advance payment from Croy Corporation for consulting services to be rendered over a two-month period. This payment increased the Unearned Consulting Fees account. One-half of this fee was earned by December 31.
6. Supplies costing $4,800 were on hand on December 31. The accountant filed the record of the count but made no entry in the accounts.

Required

a. What is the correct debt-to-equity ratio at December 31? Is the firm in violation of the loan agreement? Prepare a schedule to support your computation of the correct total liabilities and total stockholders' equity as of December 31.

b. Why might the loan agreement have contained the debt-to-equity provision?

BTN3-4. Financial Analysis Problem Purpose: To learn more about the Financial Accounting Standards Board (FASB), visit http://www.fasb.org

Required

Use the information on the FASB site to answer the following questions:

a. When was the FASB established?

b. What is the mission of the FASB?

c. Who has oversight responsibility for the FASB?

d. What are some of the current projects of the FASB?

CRITICAL THINKING

General Mills, Inc.

BTN3-5. Accounting Research Problem Refer to the annual report of **General Mills, Inc.**, for the year ending May 31, 2020 (fiscal year 2020), which can be found at https://investors.generalmills.com/financial-information/annual-reports/default.aspx. Review the consolidated balance sheets.

Required

a. Identify two assets listed in the consolidated balance sheets that indicate that General Mills uses the accrual basis of accounting. Which income statement accounts of General Mills are affected by adjustments to these assets accounts?

b. Identify two liabilities listed in the consolidated balance sheets that indicate that General Mills uses the accrual basis of accounting. Which income statement accounts of General Mills are affected by these adjustments?

BTN3-6. Accounting Communications Activity Many people do not understand the concept of accrual accounting and how it differs from accounting on a cash basis. In particular, they are confused as to why a company's results in any one accounting period can differ so much between the two methods of accounting. Because the cash basis is understood to a far larger degree, many people argue that the cash basis should be the primary basis of accounting.

Required

Write a short memorandum that explains the difference between accrual accounting and the cash basis of accounting. In your memo give a simple example of how the accrual basis can give a clearer picture of a company's performance in a given period.

BTN3-7. Accounting Ethics Case It is the end of an accounting year for Juliet Kravetz, controller of a medium-sized, publicly held corporation specializing in toxic waste cleanup. Within the corporation, only Kravetz and the president know that the firm has been negotiating for several months to land a very large contract for waste cleanup in Western Europe. The president has hired another firm with excellent contacts in Western Europe to help with the negotiations. The outside firm charges an hourly fee plus expenses but has agreed not to submit a bill until the negotiations are in their final stages (expected to occur in another three to four months). Even if the contract falls through, the outside firm is entitled to receive payment for its services. Based upon her discussion with a member of the outside firm, Kravetz knows that its charge for services provided to date will be $150,000. This is a material amount for the company.

Kravetz knows that the president wants the negotiations to remain as secret as possible so that competitors will not learn of the European contract that the company is pursuing. Indeed, the president recently stated to her, "This is not the time to reveal our actions in Western Europe to other staff members, our auditors, or readers of our financial statements; securing this contract is crucial to our future growth." No entry has been made in the accounting records for the cost of the contract negotiations. Kravetz now faces an uncomfortable situation. The company's outside auditor has just asked her if she knows of any year-end adjustments that have not yet been recorded.

Required

What are the ethical considerations that Kravetz faces in answering the auditor's question? How should she respond to the question?

BTN3-8. **Environmental, Social, and Governance Problem** Unlike financial reporting that requires all reported amounts to be expressed in monetary terms, sustainability reporting is often more qualitative than quantitative. This has caused some individuals to discount these reports as too subjective.

Required

a. Can you identify any subjective areas within a financial statement prepared under GAAP?

b. Discuss the reasons both financial reporting, and to a larger extent sustainability reporting, allow subjective estimates to be part of the report.

BTN3-9. **Accounting Ethics Problem** Most employees who choose to commit fraud against their employers feel justified in doing so. For example, a demotion with a corresponding pay cut can provide motivation to produce what is called "wages in kind," where the employee creates his or her own wages.

Required

What actions might an organization take to prevent "wages in kind"?

ANSWERS TO SELF-STUDY QUESTIONS

1. b **2.** c **3.** d **4.** c **5.** d **6.** b **7.** b

REVIEW SOLUTIONS

Solution 3.1

a. At the time of sale and delivery—March (before cash is received).

b. As it is earned over the six-month period. 1/6 of $12,000 in each month from June to November (after cash is received).

c. At the time of delivery in January.

Solution 3.2

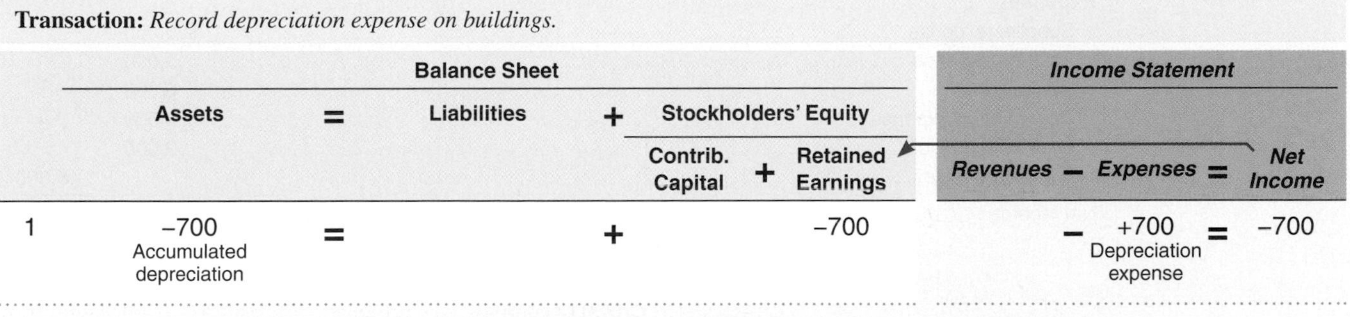

Transaction: *Record depreciation expense on buildings.*

	Balance Sheet							Income Statement				
	Assets	=	Liabilities	+	Stockholders' Equity							
					Contrib. Capital	+	Retained Earnings	*Revenues*	−	*Expenses*	=	*Net Income*
1	−700 Accumulated depreciation	=		+			−700		−	+700 Depreciation expense	=	−700

Transaction: *Record rent expense.*

	Assets	=	Liabilities	+	Contrib. Capital	+	Retained Earnings	Revenues	−	Expenses	=	Net Income
2	−1,500 Prepaid rent	=		+			−1,500		−	+1,500 Rent expense	=	−1,500

Transaction: *Recognize revenue earned on a previously recorded advance payment from customer.*

	Assets	=	Liabilities	+	Contrib. Capital	+	Retained Earnings	Revenues	−	Expenses	=	Net Income
3		=	−400 Unearned revenue	+			+400	+400 Revenue	−		=	+400

Transaction: *Accrue interest expense payable in the next period.*

	Assets	=	Liabilities	+	Contrib. Capital	+	Retained Earnings	Revenues	−	Expenses	=	Net Income
4		=	+500 Interest payable	+			−500		−	+500 Interest expense	=	−500

Solution 3.3

CASSI COMPANY
Income Statement
For the Year Ended December 31

Sales revenues		$60,000
Expenses		
Supplies expense	$26,000	
Salaries expense	9,000	
Rent expense	6,000	
Depreciation expense	5,000	
Interest expense	2,000	
Total expenses		48,000
Net income		$12,000

CASSI COMPANY
Statement of Stockholders' Equity
For the Year Ended December 31

	Common Stock	Retained Earnings	Total
Balance, January 1	$15,000	$ 5,000	$20,000
Add: Net income		12,000	12,000
Less: Dividends		(2,000)	(2,000)
Balance, December 31	$15,000	$15,000	$30,000

CASSI COMPANY
Balance Sheet
As of December 31

Assets			**Liabilities**		
Current assets			Current liabilities		
Cash	$ 8,000		Accounts payable	$ 9,000	
Accounts receivable	14,000		Salaries payable	2,000	
Supplies	17,000		Interest payable	1,000	
Prepaid rent	3,000		Unearned revenue	5,000	
Total current assets		$42,000	Total current liabilities		$17,000
			Long-term debt		35,000
Equipment	50,000		Total liabilities		52,000
Less: Accumulated depreciation	(10,000)	40,000	**Stockholders' Equity**		
			Common stock	15,000	
			Retained earnings	15,000	
			Total stockholders' equity		30,000
Total Assets		$82,000	Total Liabilities and Stockholders' Equity		$82,000

Solution 3.4

Transaction: *Adjustment to recognize 6 months' insurance expense ($6,000/4 = $1,500)*

	Balance Sheet: Assets	=	Liabilities	+	Stockholders' Equity: Contrib. Capital	+	Retained Earnings	Income Statement: Revenues	−	Expenses	=	Net Income
1	−1,500 Prepaid insurance	=		+			−1,500		−	+1,500 Insurance expense	=	−1,500

Transaction: *Adjustment to recognize supplies expense for the year. ($31,300 – $6,300 = $25,000)*

	Balance Sheet: Assets	=	Liabilities	+	Stockholders' Equity: Contrib. Capital	+	Retained Earnings	Income Statement: Revenues	−	Expenses	=	Net Income
2	−25,000 Supplies	=		+			−25,000		−	+25,000 Supplies expense	=	−25,000

Transaction: *Adjustment to recognize depreciation expense for the year. ($270,000/9 years = $30,000)*

	Balance Sheet: Assets	=	Liabilities	+	Stockholders' Equity: Contrib. Capital	+	Retained Earnings	Income Statement: Revenues	−	Expenses	=	Net Income
3	−30,000 Accumulated depreciation	=		+			−30,000		−	+30,000 Depreciation expense	=	−30,000

Transaction: *Recognize revenue earned. ($4,000 × 3/4 = $3,000)*

	Balance Sheet							Income Statement				
	Assets	=	Liabilities	+	Stockholders' Equity: Contrib. Capital	+	Retained Earnings	Revenues	−	Expenses	=	Net Income
4		=	−3,000 Diagnostic fees received in advance	+			+3,000	+3,000 Diagnostic fees revenue	−		=	+3,000

Transaction: *Accrue wages payable at June 30.*

	Balance Sheet							Income Statement				
	Assets	=	Liabilities	+	Stockholders' Equity: Contrib. Capital	+	Retained Earnings	Revenues	−	Expenses	=	Net Income
5		=	+600 Wages payable	+			−600		−	+600 Wages expense	=	−600

Transaction: *Accrue revenue for unbilled lab tests.*

	Balance Sheet							Income Statement				
	Assets	=	Liabilities	+	Stockholders' Equity: Contrib. Capital	+	Retained Earnings	Revenues	−	Expenses	=	Net Income
6	+500 Accounts receivable	=		+			+500	+500 Diagnostic fees revenue	−		=	+500

Understanding Accounting Information

PAST

Chapters 1 through 3 explained the accounting system including transaction analysis, the accounting equation, and accrual accounting.

PRESENT

This chapter explains financial reporting quality, introduces classified financial statements, and computes some key financial statement ratios.

FUTURE

Later chapters discuss further the ratios that are computed from the financial statements. Chapter 5 focuses on a current asset, cash. In addition, it explains how firms' internal control systems are designed to prevent and detect accounting errors and fraud.

IDENTIFYING A WIN-WIN COMPANY

After a visit to one of **Apple**'s many retail stores, you will likely find it hard to believe that the company ever faced financial difficulties. The company has a cult-like following for its products but things have not always been so good for the company. In fact, Apple suffered crippling financial losses and record low stock prices in the mid-1990s. Steve Jobs was instrumental in leading Apple back to profitability through creative technological innovations.

Being a profitable company has allowed Apple to benefit from what some refer to as a virtuous cycle in which the company is able to both do good financially and do good socially. Apple believes that a win-win situation can be obtained through its commitment to social responsibility.

But what if we decide to consider investing in a company like Apple? How should we go about determining whether Apple is a good investment? We first want to do some research to determine if the company is profitable and financially sound.

Road Map

LO	Learning Objective	Page	eLecture	Review	Assignments
LO1	**Describe the qualities that make financial reporting useful.**	110	E4-1	4.1	SE4-9, SE4-10
LO2	**Explain where you can find accounting information.**	112	E4-2	4.2	SE4-11
LO3	**Describe a classified balance sheet.**	113	E4-3	4.3, 4.7	SE1, E1, E4, P1, P2, P4
LO4	**Describe a classified income statement.**	118	E4-4	4.4, 4.7	SE8, E2, E6, P3, P6, P10
LO5	**Discuss the use of a balance sheet and ratios to assess liquidity and solvency.**	121	E4-5	4.5	SE3, SE4, SE6, E3, E5, P5, P8, P9
LO6	**Discuss the use of the income statement and ratios to assess profitability.**	123	E4-6	4.5	SE2, SE7, E3, E5, E8, P5, P6, P8, P9
LO7	**Explain the components of the statement of stockholders' equity.**	124	E4-7	4.6	E7, E9, P7
LO8	**Explain the purpose of the statement of cash flows.**	125	E4-8	4.7	SE5, E10, P4

Understanding Accounting Information

Financial Reporting	Balance Sheet Classification	Income Statement Classification	Working with Financial Statements
• Financial reporting quality • Objectives of financial reporting • Qualities of useful accounting information • Availability of accounting information	• Balance sheet components • Current assets and liabilities • Long-term assets and liabilities	• Income statement components • Income statement format	• Analysis using ratios • Balance sheet • Income statement • Statement of stockholders' equity • Statement of cash flows

FINANCIAL REPORTING QUALITY

LO1 Describe the qualities that make financial reporting useful.

The earliest accounting records date back more than 7,000 years, when the peoples of ancient Mesopotamia kept track of receipts and disbursements to account for crops and calculate taxes. Over the intervening millennia, financial accounting reports have evolved into the financial statements that this text is teaching you how to read. Currently, the structure and content of the financial reports of U.S. public companies are guided by the **conceptual framework**, a document created by the Financial Accounting Standards Board (FASB). The FASB's conceptual framework defines the objectives and fundamental characteristics of financial accounting and reporting. This section discusses the conceptual framework's views on the objectives of modern financial accounting reports, and the qualitative characteristics that make accounting information useful.

Objectives of Financial Reporting

The overarching goal of financial accounting is to facilitate the efficient allocation of resources. This includes the creation of financial reports that provide investors (including creditors and other lenders) with information that is useful in making investment decisions. For example, investors in common stock want to know whether the firm's stock is likely to appreciate in value, how management performed during the period, and about the firm's ability to pay dividends. Creditors want to know whether the firm will be able to make timely interest payments and repay the principal when it is due.

Existing and potential investors who are outside the firm must rely on publicly available financial reports to obtain this information. Insiders, such as managers, have access to financial information about the firm and thus are not reliant on external financial reports. Thus, the FASB considers outside investors to be the primary users of external financial reports, and financial reports are designed primarily for the needs of these users. While other parties, such as regulators and members of the public other than investors may also find accounting information useful, financial reports are not specifically designed to serve these users. It is notable, however, that outside investors need more than just the financial reports to make informed investment decisions. They also need industry and economy-wide information, such as future demand for the firm's products, expected interest rates, and political events.

The financial reports help with investment decisions by providing information about the company's resources, claims against those resources, and how effectively and efficiently a company deploys its resources. The company's resources are reported in the asset section of the balance sheet, while the claims against those resources are reported in the liabilities section of the balance sheet. The effectiveness and efficiency of management's use of those resources are reflected in the income statement.

As discussed in Chapter 3, a defining feature of financial accounting reports is that they use accrual basis accounting, which captures the effects of events and transactions during the period in which those effects occur, which is not necessarily the period in which the related cash receipts or disbursements occur. This is a crucial advantage of accounting information because research shows that information about an entity's accounting resources and claims is a better basis for assessing past and future performance than information solely about cash receipts and disbursements.

Qualities of Useful Accounting Information

Several qualitative characteristics help make accounting information useful to investors for making investment decisions. Most importantly, the information must be relevant to the investment decision, and it must faithfully represent what it purports to represent. Other characteristics that enhance the quality of financial information include comparability, verifiability, timeliness, and understandability. Further, accounting information is only useful when it is material. In addition, while not considered by the FASB's conceptual framework to be a characteristic that enhances the quality of financial reports, research finds that accounting conservatism is a factor that improves the quality of accounting reports.

Relevance Accounting information is relevant if it makes a difference in users' decisions. Generally, information makes a difference when it has **predictive value** or **confirmatory value**. Information with predictive value is useful in predicting future events, while information has confirmatory value if it provides feedback about whether financial expectations are met. These features are typically interrelated. For example, for most companies, current year's revenues are useful in predicting future revenues, and for evaluating whether past performance met expectations.

Faithful Representation Financial statements are faithfully representational when they faithfully report the events and transactions they purport to represent. Faithful representation is related to the notion of *substance over form*, which means that the financial statements report the *substance* of the economic phenomenon rather than merely representing its legal *form*. Faithful representation also means that the financial statements are *fairly presented*. Additionally, faithful representation means that the information is *complete*, presenting all of the necessary details required to capture the underlying economic phenomenon reported. Faithful representation also implies the information is *neutral* and free from bias that might slant the information to be perceived as favorable or unfavorable by users. While accuracy is an important feature of faithful representation, it does not mean the information is absolutely free from error. Accounting information necessarily contains numerous estimates and judgments, which by their nature may turn out differently than expected.

Comparability Financial statements are comparable when they allow users to identify similarities in, and differences between, two or more items or companies. Comparability should make like items look alike, and different items look different. Comparability should not be confused with uniformity. Uniformity simply means requiring firms to apply the same set of standards, while comparability is a characteristic of the relation between two or more items of information. Comparability is also not the same as consistency. Consistency refers to using the same methods over time or across companies. Comparability is the goal, while consistency helps achieve that goal. Of course, regardless of how comparable information may be, it is useless unless it faithfully represents (i.e., fairly presents) the information it purports to represent.

Verifiability Financial information is verifiable if different knowledgeable and independent observers would reach a consensus that the phenomenon being reported is faithfully represented. Verification can be either direct or indirect. For example, counting the ending balance in the cash account is a direct verification of the cash balance. Indirect verification means checking the inputs to a model or formula using the same formula. An example is checking the inputs to measure ending inventory (the costs and quantities), and then recalculating ending inventory using the same cost flow assumptions (as described in more detail in Chapter 7).

Timeliness Financial information is timely when it is available to users in time to influence their decisions. While some information must be very recent to be timely, older information also may have value. For example, financial reports typically report information spanning several years, because investors are interested in trends over time.

Understandability Accounting reports are understandable when they present information clearly and concisely. However, this does not mean that complex information, which is inherently difficult to understand, should be excluded from financial reports. That would make the information incomplete and hence potentially misleading. It is also worth noting that even sophisticated and knowledgeable users may require the advice of an expert with a greater understanding of the complex economic phenomena being reported.

Conservatism As noted above, conservatism is not considered by the FASB's conceptual framework to be a characteristic that enhances financial reporting quality. This is because conservative accounting numbers may result in reported earnings that are biased downward. Nevertheless, a large body of academic research suggests that many financial statement users value conservatively reported financial statements. Financial information is said to be conservative when losses are recorded in a timelier fashion than gains. The notion is that accountants are quick to report bad news but slow to report good news. Research finds that some users, especially creditors, value accounting conservatism because they are primarily interested in the downside risk of not receiving their principal or interest payments, and conservative accounting numbers alert them to potential problems on a more timely basis. Research also shows that conservative accounting reduces the tendency for management to report overly optimistic earnings. Management has incentives to report favorable earnings because their compensation is typically tied to their company's accounting performance.

Materiality An item is considered material if its omission or misstatement is expected to mislead investors. Unlike the other characteristics discussed in this section, however, materiality can only be determined based on the financial situation of the specific company being accounted for. For example, because Starbucks has billions of dollars in total assets, misstating total assets by $1,000 is unlikely to mislead investors, and thus would be immaterial. By contrast, for a small enterprise, with assets in the tens of thousands, a $1,000 misstatement may make an important difference, and therefore would be considered material.

REVIEW 4.1

Which of the following is NOT a quality of useful financial reporting?

a. Liquidity
b. Comparability
c. Timeliness
d. Verifiability

The solution is on page 140.

FINDING FINANCIAL ACCOUNTING INFORMATION

LO2 Explain where you can find accounting information.

Where do investors and prospective investors find the accounting information they need to make informed investment decisions? There are a variety of sources. Publicly traded corporations (those with shares traded on the major stock exchanges) are required to provide shareholders and potential shareholders with financial statements on a periodic basis. In the U.S., the Securities and Exchange Commission (SEC) mandates that public companies issue quarterly reports every three months, as well as an annual financial statement at the end of each fiscal year. Quarterly reports are often referred to as "**10-Q's**" and annual reports are often referred to as "**10-K's**," in reference to the names of the forms filed with the SEC. These reports contain all of the primary financial statements, as well as footnotes and discussion by management of any major changes in the company's financial condition. An outside independent auditor must audit the annual reports, while the quarterly reports only need to be reviewed by the auditor. An audit provides greater assurance than a review that the financial statements are fairly presented.

The SEC makes the filed annual reports freely available to the public on the internet at http://www.sec.gov/edgar/searchedgar/webusers.htm. You can use the search engine at this website to locate the quarterly and annual reports for any U.S. publicly-traded company. This website also includes all of the other forms and documents the company is required to file with the SEC. For example, companies also must file a **Form 8-K** (simply referred to as an "8-K"), which discloses events that are expected to affect the value of the company's shares. For example, companies must file 8-Ks if they land a major contract, or if the outside auditor resigns or is dismissed. Public companies must also hold annual shareholder meetings and must issue **proxy statements** prior to those meetings. Proxy statements contain information about voting for directors, shareholder proposals, and executive compensation.

Companies also typically make their SEC filings available at their websites, often under a section titled Investor Relations. For example, you can find Apple's quarterly and annual reports at http://investor.apple.com/financials.cfm. Apple's website also includes press releases made by the company that announce various events that are of interest to shareholders. For example, companies typically announce their earnings a few weeks prior to the publication of their complete financial statements. Managers also often forecast earnings for the coming quarters or year. **Management earnings forecasts** are designed to help investors set expectations regarding company performance.

Accounting reports as well as other financial information can also be found at the websites of companies that specialize in providing investment information. For example, information extracted from Apple's financial reports, as well as analysis of some key ratios and other financial indicators can be found at the **Yahoo Finance** website at http://finance.yahoo.com/q?s=AAPL, and at **The Motley Fool** website at http://www.fool.com/quote/nasdaq/apple/aapl.

REVIEW 4.2

Which of the following is NOT a true statement?

a. The SEC mandates that public companies issue audited annual financial statements.
b. An annual report filed with the SEC is often called 10-K.
c. The SEC mandates that private companies issue audited annual financial statements.
d. The SEC makes filed annual reports freely available to the public on the internet.

The solution is on page 140.

BALANCE SHEET CLASSIFICATION

LO3 Describe a classified balance sheet.

A **classified balance sheet** presents the assets and liabilities of a business in separate subgroups. Such classification aids in financial analysis and business decision making. **Exhibit 4-1** presents a list of the typical components of a classified balance sheet. A company need not use all of the components, and each company will use only those components necessary to report its financial position. **Exhibit 4-1** shows that a company's assets are commonly classified into two subgroups: current assets and long-term assets. Similarly, liabilities are classified into two subgroups: current liabilities and long-term liabilities. Classified balance sheets are presented by most businesses.

EXHIBIT 4-1 Typical Components of a Classified Balance Sheet

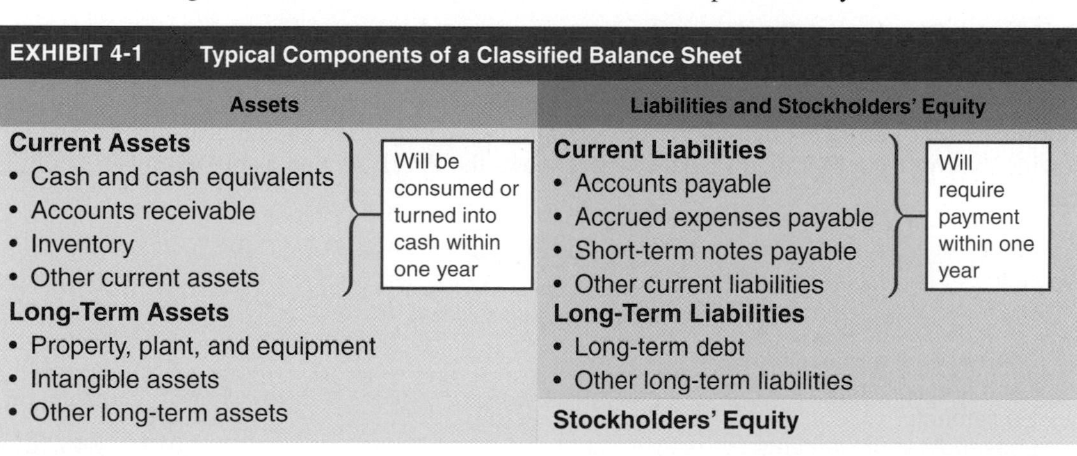

Assets		Liabilities and Stockholders' Equity	
Current Assets • Cash and cash equivalents • Accounts receivable • Inventory • Other current assets	Will be consumed or turned into cash within one year	**Current Liabilities** • Accounts payable • Accrued expenses payable • Short-term notes payable • Other current liabilities	Will require payment within one year
Long-Term Assets • Property, plant, and equipment • Intangible assets • Other long-term assets		**Long-Term Liabilities** • Long-term debt • Other long-term liabilities	
		Stockholders' Equity	

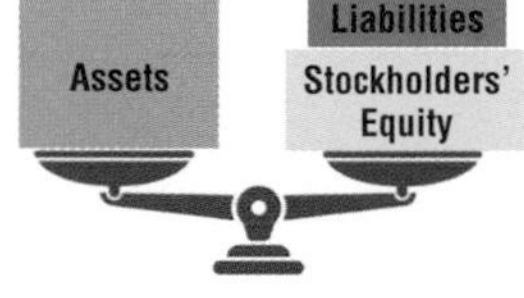

To illustrate the components of a classified balance sheet and multi-step income statement, we will use the financial information of a fictitious company, Meridian, Inc., a large, multi-national technology company. Meridian develops and supports various software, hardware, and cloud-based products and services designed for large organizations and individuals.

Current Assets

Current assets consist of cash and other assets that will be converted into cash or consumed within the normal operating cycle of a business or one year, whichever is longer. The **normal operating**

cycle of a business is the average period of time between the use of cash to deliver a service or to buy goods for resale and the subsequent collection of cash from customers who purchase those services or products. For most businesses, the normal operating cycle is less than one year. For example, the normal operating cycle for a grocery store chain like **Safeway** might be as short as a week or two, on average, and only a day or two for perishable products like bread and fresh vegetables.

Current assets are listed on a classified balance sheet in the order of their expected liquidity. **Liquidity** refers to the speed with which an asset will be converted into cash. **Exhibit 4-1** lists four examples of current assets in the order of their expected liquidity: cash and cash equivalents, accounts receivable, inventory, and other current assets. Accounts receivable and inventory are converted into cash as part of the normal operations of a business; that is, inventory is sold for cash or on credit (accounts receivable) that is subsequently collected as cash from customers. Other current assets, such as supplies, are consumed during the normal operating cycle rather than converted into cash, and thus, represent the least liquid of the current assets. The following excerpt from Meridian's balance sheet shows the current asset section as of December 31 of the current year.

MERIDIAN, INC.
Balance Sheet (Partial)
December 31 (in millions)

Current assets	
Cash and cash equivalents	$ 7,963
Accounts receivable	17,792
Inventory	2,101
Other current assets	127,835
Total current assets	$155,691

Assets that will be converted into cash or used within the normal operating cycle of a business or one year, whichever is longer.

Long-Term Assets

Long-term assets are assets that the company does not expect to convert into cash or consume within the next year or the normal operating cycle, whichever is longer. Long-term assets include property, plant, and equipment, intangible assets, and other long-term assets.

Property, Plant, and Equipment

Property, plant, and equipment consists of the land, buildings, equipment, vehicles, furniture, and fixtures that a company uses in its day-to-day operations. Investments in property, plant, and equipment, or PP&E, are often referred to as *capital expenditures* or capital investments. The following excerpt from Meridian's balance sheet shows the PP&E section as of December 31 of the current year.

MERIDIAN, INC.
Balance Sheet (Partial)
December 31 (in millions)

Property, plant, and equipment		
Land and buildings	$18,191	
Equipment	24,158	
Leasehold improvements	4,013	$46,362
Less: accumulated depreciation and amortization		22,179
Total property, plant, and equipment, net		$24,183

Intangible Assets

Intangible assets consist of brand names, copyrights, patents, and trademarks that a company acquires. These assets are referred to as "intangible" because, unlike buildings and equipment, they lack physical substance. But, like buildings and equipment, intangible assets enable a company to generate revenue from its customers who recognize the quality associated with products bearing a brand name or trademark. The following excerpt from Meridian's balance sheet shows the intangible assets section as of December 31 of the current year.

MERIDIAN, INC. Balance Sheet (Partial) December 31 (in millions)	
Intangible assets	
Goodwill	$29,122
Acquired technology	9,106
Total intangible assets	$38,228

Other Long-Term Assets

Other long-term assets consist of resources that a company consolidates into a single miscellaneous category. The following excerpt from Meridian's balance sheet shows the other long-term assets section as of December 31 of the current year.

MERIDIAN, INC. Balance Sheet (Partial) December 31 (in millions)	
Other long-term assets	
Long-term marketable securities	$ 8,023
Other assets	9,250
Total other long-term assets	$17,273

Current Liabilities

Current liabilities consist of liabilities that must be settled within the normal operating cycle or one year, whichever is longer. **Exhibit 4-1** lists four types of current liabilities: accounts payable, accrued expenses payable, short-term notes payable, and other current liabilities. Accounts payable reflects the amounts owed to vendors and other suppliers for purchases made on credit. Accrued expenses payable include wages, utilities, interest, income tax, and property taxes that are legally owed by a company but which have not yet been paid. Short-term notes payable represent amounts owed that are specified in a formal contract called a note. Other current liabilities consist of current obligations that the company aggregates into a single miscellaneous category. One example is the advance payments received from customers (unearned revenue), such as for goods under a layaway plan that will be earned as revenue within the normal operating cycle or one year, whichever is longer. The following excerpt from Meridian's balance sheet shows the current liabilities section as of December 31 of the current year.

MERIDIAN, INC. Balance Sheet (Partial) December 31 (in millions)	
Current liabilities	
Accounts payable	$ 8,390
Accrued expenses	33,921
Other current liabilities	16,216
Total current liabilities	$58,527

Liabilities that must be settled within the normal operating cycle or one year, whichever is longer.

Long-Term Liabilities

A.K.A. Long-term liabilities are also referred to as *noncurrent liabilities*.

Long-term liabilities consist of debt obligations not due to be settled within the normal operating cycle or one year. Long-term notes payable and bonds payable are two examples of long-term liabilities. Other long-term liabilities include unfunded employee retirement plans that will be funded by the company in the future. The following excerpt from Meridian's balance sheet shows the current liabilities section as of December 31 of the current year.

MERIDIAN, INC. Balance Sheet (Partial) December 31 (in millions)	
Long-term liabilities	
Long-term debt	$ 77,073
Other liabilities	29,092
Total long-term liabilities	$106,165

Stockholders' Equity

A.K.A. Stockholders' equity is also referred to as *shareholders' equity*.

Stockholders' equity is the residual ownership interest in the assets of a business after its liabilities have been paid off. The stockholders' equity of a corporation is divided into two main categories: amounts invested by stockholders (common stock) and the cumulative net income of a business that has not yet been distributed to its stockholders as a dividend (retained earnings). The following excerpt from Meridian's balance sheet shows the current liabilities section as of December 31 of the current year.

MERIDIAN, INC. Balance Sheet (Partial) December 31 (in millions)	
Stockholders' equity	
Common stock	$67,315
Retained earnings	2,967
Other equity	401
Total stockholders' equity	$70,683

Presentation Format

***Hint:** According to* Accounting Trends and Techniques*, a recent survey of 600 large U.S. companies shows 88% use the* report form *for their balance sheet while 12% use the* account form.

There are two generally accepted formats for presenting a classified balance sheet—the account form and the report form. For the **account form**, assets are displayed on the left side and liabilities and stockholders' equity are displayed on the right side. For the **report form**, assets are displayed at the top, with liabilities displayed below the assets, and stockholders' equity displayed below liabilities. Meridian's balance sheet as of December 31 of the current year in report form is presented in **Exhibit 4-2**. The report form is the more widely used format.

EXHIBIT 4-2 Report Form of a Classified Balance Sheet

MERIDIAN, INC.
Balance Sheet
December 31

(in millions)	Current Year
Assets	
Current assets	
Cash and cash equivalents	$ 7,963
Accounts receivable	17,792
Inventory	2,101
Other current assets	127,835
Total current assets	155,691
Long-term assets	
Property, plant and equipment, net	24,183
Intangible assets	38,228
Other long-term assets	17,273
Total long-term assets	79,684
Total assets	$235,375
Liabilities	
Current liabilities	
Accounts payable	$ 8,390
Accrued expenses	33,921
Other current liabilities	16,216
Total current liabilities	58,527
Long-term liabilities	106,165
Total liabilities	164,692
Stockholders' Equity	
Common stock	67,315
Retained earnings	2,967
Other equity	401
Total stockholders' equity	70,683
Total liabilities and stockholders' equity	$235,375

REVIEW 4.3

The President of Musicland Company requests that you prepare a classified balance sheet in report form for the company. The following financial data are available from the company's accounting records as of December 31 of the current year.

Cash	$ 300	Accounts payable	$ 2,500
Accounts receivable	3,000	Other current liabilities	2,000
Inventory	12,200	Long-term notes payable	20,000
Other current assets	1,500	Stockholders' equity	17,500
Property, plant, & equipment, net	25,000		

The solution is on page 140.

DATA ANALYTICS The Next Frontier: Data Analytics and the Audit

Auditors use data analytics to gain a deeper understanding of the companies they audit and to perform the audit more efficiently and effectively. Some of the ways that data analytics could improve financial statement auditing include the testing of complete data sets rather than sampling and risk assessment through the identification of anomalies and trends. To achieve the full potential of data analytics in auditing, several things must happen, including broadening the education of accountants. The auditors of the future will need a better understanding of data science, information technology, statistics, modeling, and machine learning. With a staff knowledgeable in these areas, CPA firms will be able to expand their services to include areas such as data quality, cybersecurity, fraud prevention and detection, and internal controls.

Source: *Journal of Accountancy* online, Data analytics helps auditors gain deep insight, Murphy and Tysiac

INCOME STATEMENT CLASSIFICATION

LO4 **Describe** a classified (single-step and multi-step) income statement.

A **single-step income statement** is the simplest form of an income statement. The name originates from the way the statement is constructed. The sum of the expenses is subtracted from the sum of the revenues in a single step to arrive at net income. An example of a single-step income statement for Meridian, Inc. is shown in **Exhibit 4-3**.

EXHIBIT 4-3 Single-Step Income Statement

MERIDIAN, INC.
Income Statement
For Year Ended December 31

(in millions)	Current Year
Revenues	
Net sales	$87,650
Other income (expense), net	897
Total revenues	88,547
Expenses	
Cost of goods sold	33,061
Research and development expenses	12,560
Selling, general and administrative	21,826
Income tax expense	1,925
Total expenses	69,372
Net income	$19,175

For the current year, Meridian reported revenues of $88,547 million. Next, expenses of $69,372 million are totaled and subtracted from total revenues to yield net income of $19,175 million.

A.K.A A multi-step income statement is also known as a *classified income statement*.

A **multi-step income statement** presents revenues and expenses in distinct categories to facilitate financial analysis and management decision making. A multi-step income statement provides financial statement users with more information, and thus, enables them to make better and more informed decisions about a business. The format of a multi-step income statement will differ depending on whether the company is a service firm or a merchandising firm. The difference in format between service firms and merchandising firms results because service firms do not sell a physical product and therefore do not have cost of goods sold. Examples of service companies include accounting firms, health care providers, and architects. In contrast, merchandising companies sell goods to customers. For a service company, income from operations is computed by subtracting total operating expenses from service revenues. Operating expenses are those expenses that relate to the primary operating activities of a business. Operating expenses are commonly classified as selling, general and administrative expenses. Revenue and expense items that do not relate to the primary operating activities of the company appear in a separate category called *Other Income and Expense.* The net amount of other income and expense is either added to or subtracted from income from operations to compute income before income taxes.

A.K.A. Gross profit is often referred to as *gross margin*.

For a merchandising company, the cost of goods sold is subtracted from the firm's net sales to determine its gross profit on sales. **Gross profit**, or gross profit on sales, is computed as the difference between net sales and cost of goods sold and indicates the amount of sales revenue remaining after subtracting the cost of products sold. **Net sales** are total sales less an amount to record **sales returns and allowances** and **sales discounts**. Sales returns and allowances represent the amount given to the customer for the return of merchandise or an amount given in lieu of a return. Sales discounts represent an amount allowed to the buyer for early payment. Gross profit indicates how much sales revenue remains, after deducting the cost of goods sold, to cover a business's operating expenses. The remainder of the structure of a merchandising company's multi-step income statement (following gross profit) is the same as the structure of the service company's multi-step income statement.

A.K.A. Income before income tax is also known as *pretax income*.

Exhibit 4-4 presents a multi-step income statement for Meridian, Inc., which provides more detail to the financial statement user with four measures of company performance: gross profit on sales, income from operations, income before income taxes, and net income. Gross profit on sales indicates just how well the company performed in terms of purchasing goods, warehousing those goods, and pricing the goods for sale. Income from operations reports a company's performance after considering the cost of running its stores, paying its employees, advertising to its customers, and administering the business. The income before income taxes reports the company's performance after considering various nonoperating items like interest expense and interest income but before subtracting income taxes. Income tax is then subtracted from income before income taxes in order to compute net income. Income tax is computed as a percentage of income before income taxes.

EXHIBIT 4-4 Multi-Step Income Statement for a Merchandising Company

MERIDIAN, INC.
Income Statement
For Year Ended December 31

(in millions)	Current Year
Net sales	$87,650
Less cost of goods sold	33,061
Gross profit on sales	54,589
Operating expenses	
Research and development expenses	12,560
Selling, general and administrative expenses	21,826
Total operating expenses	34,386
Income from operations	20,203
Other income and expenses	
Other income (expense), net	897
Income before income taxes	21,100
Income tax expense	1,925
Net income	$19,175

A multi-step income statement for a service firm will not have cost of goods sold nor will it have a subtotal for gross profit on sales

Net income reports the bottom-line performance—that is, after all costs of running the business are subtracted. Net sales for Meridian consists primarily of sales of hardware, software, digital content, and support contracts. The company records reductions from these amounts for future product returns. Cost of goods sold represents the cost of the items sold. Cost of goods sold is typically the largest expense for a retail company such as Meridian. Cost of goods sold is subtracted directly from net sales to highlight the gross profit on sales. The gross profit on sales is an important financial indicator for investment professionals who follow retail companies. Analysts compare the gross profit on sales between retailers as a way to assess the effectiveness of the retailer's pricing and purchasing policies.

The operating expenses section includes those expenses that relate to the primary operating activities of a business. Operating expenses consist primarily of selling expenses and administrative expenses. Examples of Meridian's selling, general and administrative expenses include sales salaries expense, delivery expense, advertising expense, depreciation expense, rent expense, office salaries expense, and supplies expense.

The other income and expense section of the income statement is sometimes labeled nonoperating activities. Examples of revenues and expenses that do not relate to the primary operating activities of a merchandising firm include:

Other Expenses and Losses	Other Revenues and Gains
• Interest expense	• Interest revenue
• Losses on asset sales	• Gains on asset sales
	• Dividend income

These items are reported in the other income and expense section that follows the financial information regarding a business's primary operating activities.

Exhibit 4-5 compares the components of a classified income statement for DataForce (a service company) and Meridian (a merchandising company). Notice that the income statement for DataForce, a service company, does not include a line-item for cost of goods sold and does not compute the gross profit on sales. Otherwise, the income statement formats are identical.

EXHIBIT 4-5 Classified Income Statements for Service and Merchandising Companies

DATAFORCE, INC. Income Statement For Year Ended December 31		MERIDIAN, INC. Income Statement For Year Ended December 31	
Revenues	$19,150	Net sales	$87,650
		Less cost of goods sold	**33,061**
		Gross profit on sales	**54,589**
Operating expenses		Operating expenses	
Wage, rent and supplies expenses	5,064	Research and development expenses	12,650
Depreciation expense	450	Selling, general and administrative expenses	21,826
Total operating expenses	5,514	Total operating expenses	34,386
Income from operations	13,636	Income from operations	20,203
Other income (expense), net	(300)	Other income (expense), net	897
Income before income taxes	13,336	Income before income taxes	21,100
Income tax expense	4,005	Income tax expense	1,925
Net income	$ 9,331	Net income	$19,175

REVIEW 4.4

Musicland provides the following information and requests that we prepare a multi-step income statement for the year ended December 31 of the current year. Musicland pays income tax at the rate of 30 percent of income.

Net sales	$100,000	Research & development expense	$10,000
Cost of goods sold	45,000	Interest expense	$ 5,000
Selling, general and administrative expenses	$ 25,000		

The solution is on page 141.

WORKING WITH FINANCIAL STATEMENTS

The basic financial statements were introduced in Chapter 1. We now extend that discussion by demonstrating how financial statements are used to address questions about a company's operating performance and financial health.

Ratio Analysis

In 2020, Apple, Inc. reported net income of $57,411 million. Based on that information should we conclude that the company had a good year or a bad year? While $57,411 million is a large number, some frame of reference is needed before we can conclude that this amount represents a good, bad, or mediocre level of performance. For example, $57,411 million is a phenomenal performance if the company had only $100 million in assets to operate with during the year. But it is not as exceptional if the company had $500 billion in assets to operate with during the year. Apple, Inc.'s 2020 financial statements can be found at https://investor.apple.com/investor-relations.

Investment professionals use a variety of methods to understand how to interpret net income. One such method involves ratio analysis. **Ratio analysis** expresses the relation of one relevant accounting number to another relevant accounting number through the process of division. The result of the division is expressed as a percentage, a rate, or as a proportion.

To illustrate how a ratio can provide additional meaning to Apple's net income of $57,411 million, we can divide Apple's net income by its total assets of $323,888 million, to compute its **return on assets (ROA)**.

$$\textbf{Return on assets} = \frac{\textbf{Net income}}{\textbf{Total assets}}$$

The result is 17.7 percent and tells us that Apple earned a rate of return of 17.7 cents on each dollar of assets invested in the business at the end of 2020. We can also compare this return with that of other technology companies to help us evaluate Apple's performance.

A single ratio, however, is difficult to interpret without some point of reference or benchmark. Business professionals often use one of two techniques to interpret ratios. **Trend analysis** compares a company's results, or the results of a ratio, over time. This technique helps the financial statement user identify trends in a company's performance. **Benchmarking analysis** compares a company's performance, or a ratio, to that of its competitors, or to an industry average. The objective is to compare the company's performance against similar companies, or against an industry standard. Trend analysis and benchmarking analysis are powerful tools for evaluating a firm's performance and are discussed in greater detail in Chapter 12.

Working with the Balance Sheet

LO5 **Discuss** use of a balance sheet and ratios to assess liquidity and solvency.

The balance sheet helps users evaluate a company's financial health. The balance sheet also provides information on how much debt and equity was used to finance the acquisition of the company's assets.

Liquidity and solvency measure a firm's financial well-being. For a company to remain in business it must be able to pay its bills when they come due. Before a bank such as **Bank of America** will commit to extend a loan to a company, it needs to assess the likelihood that it will be repaid the amount borrowed and related interest, both in a timely manner. This assessment involves evaluating the company's *liquidity*, the ability to pay obligations that come due in the current year, and *solvency*, the ability to pay obligations over the long term.

Liquidity

Liquidity refers to a company's ability to pay its short-term financial obligations. It depends on several factors, including the level of cash a company has and how quickly it can generate cash from operations or its assets.

Current Ratio One widely-used measure of liquidity is the current ratio. The current ratio is defined as current assets divided by current liabilities. Current assets provide a measure of the cash that is currently available, and which will become available, during the current period. Current liabilities provide a measure of the cash that will be needed in the current period to pay existing and accrued obligations.

$$\textbf{Current ratio} = \frac{\textbf{Current assets}}{\textbf{Current liabilities}}$$

A current ratio greater than one indicates that a company has more cash and current assets than needed to pay off its current and accrued obligations, and a ratio less than one implies the opposite. While this interpretation is overly simplistic, it does provide an easily understood assessment of a company's liquidity. In general, the greater the current ratio, the more liquid a company is, and the less concern a lender has in extending a loan to the company.

One of Apple's competitors is **Samsung Electronics Co., Ltd (Samsung)**, which provides smart phones, tablets and other electronic components to individuals and businesses. Samsung is a multinational company headquartered in South Korea and prepares its financial statements according to IFRS. Financial statements for Samsung can be found at https://www.samsung.com/global/ir/financial-information/audited-financial-statements/. The current ratios for both Apple and Samsung are shown in **Exhibit 4-6**. Both Apple and Samsung report current ratios greater than one in both years; however, both companies report a decline in their current ratios over the two years. Based on these ratios, we would conclude that both companies appear to be sufficiently liquid to satisfy their current obligations.

EXHIBIT 4-6 Current Ratio

(in millions)	2020	2019
Apple	$\frac{\$143,713}{\$105,392} = 1.36$	$\frac{\$162,819}{\$105,718} = 1.54$
Samsung	$\frac{\$167,914}{\$61,047} = 2.62$	$\frac{\$153,657}{\$54,032} = 2.84$

TAKEAWAY 4.1

Concept	Method	Assessment
Can a company meet its short-term obligations?	Current assets and current liabilities from the balance sheet. $\text{Current ratio} = \frac{\text{Current assets}}{\text{Current liabilities}}$	A larger current ratio implies greater liquidity and a greater ability to pay short-term obligations.

Solvency

Lenders often provide loans that have repayment terms that extend over several years. In such cases the lender is interested in evaluating a company's solvency. **Solvency** refers to a company's ability to pay its long-term financial obligations. It depends on several factors, including the level of assets a company has. Solvency, therefore, is a measure of a company's ability to survive over the long term. Both liquidity and solvency are important indicators of financial health; but, a company must first be liquid. If a company is unable to pay its bills in the short term, it is irrelevant whether it is solvent in the long term.

Debt-to-Total-Assets Ratio In general, the more debt a company uses to finance its assets and day-to-day operations, the riskier it is. This follows because the amount borrowed and the interest on that amount must be paid on a regular schedule. If a company is unable to meet the cash outflows required to satisfy its debt repayment schedule or meet its regular interest payments, a lender can legally demand immediate repayment of a loan, potentially forcing a company into bankruptcy if it is unable to repay that amount. The debt-to-total-assets ratio, calculated as total liabilities divided by total assets, provides a measure of this risk and is one ratio used to assess a company's solvency.

$$\textbf{Debt-to-total-assets ratio} = \frac{\textbf{Total liabilities}}{\textbf{Total assets}}$$

The greater the debt-to-total-assets ratio, the greater the company's risk of not being able to pay its interest payments or principal repayments on a timely basis, and the lower is the company's solvency. Like the current ratio, the debt-to-total-assets ratio should not be used in isolation. There are many factors that must be considered when judging a company's solvency.

Exhibit 4-7 shows the debt-to-total-assets ratio for Apple and Samsung. This exhibit reveals that in 2020, Samsung used considerably less debt to finance its assets than did Apple (27.0 percent versus 79.8 percent). One reason for this difference is that recently, Apple has increased its debt in order to return capital to its shareholders. Another reason is that Samsung has a very low dividend payout, which results in higher retained earnings and thus higher stockholders' equity.

EXHIBIT 4-7 Debt-to-Total-Assets Ratio

(in millions)	2020	2019
Apple	$\frac{\$258,549}{\$323,888} = 79.8\%$	$\frac{\$248,028}{\$338,516} = 73.3\%$
Samsung	$\frac{\$86,651}{\$320,415} = 27.0\%$	$\frac{\$75,974}{\$298,668} = 25.4\%$

TAKEAWAY 4.2

Concept	Method	Assessment
Can a company meet its long-term obligations?	Total assets and total liabilities from the balance sheet. Debt-to-total-assets ratio = $\frac{\text{Total liabilities}}{\text{Total assets}}$	A larger ratio implies less solvency and a lower ability to repay outstanding obligations over the long term.

Working with the Income Statement

LO6 Discuss use of the income statement and ratios to assess profitability.

Apple generates income by selling computers, iPads, iPods, iPhones, peripherals, and downloads from its iTunes store. The company's income statement reports how much net income Apple was able to generate from these activities. The analysis of a company's income and its components is called profitability analysis. Apple's net income of $57,411 million for fiscal year 2020 indicates that Apple sold these products at a price that exceeded the cost of manufacturing as well as the cost of operations.

Apple's net income increased by $2,155 million, from $55,256 million in 2019 to $57,411 million in 2020. During a similar period, Samsung's net income increased by $3,955 million, from $18,416 million in 2019 to $22,371 million in 2020.

Profitability Analysis Measures

There are many ways to measure a company's success. One such measure is profitability. Profitability indicates whether or not a company is able to bring its products or services to the market efficiently, and whether it produces products or services that are valued by the market. The more profitable a company is, the higher it is valued, and the better its long-term prospects. Conversely, unprofitable companies risk going out of business unless they eventually become profitable.

Profit Margin (Return on sales) It is somewhat unfair, and potentially misleading, to compare two companies of differing size on the basis of net income. A larger company is expected to generate a larger net income. But a larger net income does not necessarily indicate that a company is performing more efficiently than a company with a smaller net income. One measure that facilitates a comparison of the profitability between companies of different size is the return on assets ratio, which we explained earlier in this chapter. Another useful measure is the profit margin, calculated as net income divided by net sales.

A.K.A Profit margin is often referred to as *return on sales*.

$$\textbf{Profit margin} = \frac{\textbf{Net income}}{\textbf{Net sales}}$$

Exhibit 4-8 shows the calculation of profit margin for both Apple and Samsung. Apple is larger than Samsung based on sales generated in 2020 ($274,515 million for Apple versus $200,606 million for Samsung). Apple also generated more net income than Samsung ($57,411 million for Apple versus $22,371 million for Samsung). This translates into a higher profit margin for Apple (20.9 percent versus 11.2 percent for Samsung). A profit margin of 20.9 percent indicates Apple has 20.9 cents left over from each dollar of sales revenue after subtracting all of its expenses. Samsung increased its profit margin from 9.4 percent in 2019 to 11.2 percent in 2020 suggesting it has improved efficiency in its operations.

EXHIBIT 4-8 Profit Margin		
(in millions)	2020	2019
Apple	$\frac{\$57,411}{\$274,515} = 20.9\%$	$\frac{\$55,256}{\$260,174} = 21.2\%$
Samsung	$\frac{\$22,371}{\$200,606} = 11.2\%$	$\frac{\$18,416}{\$195,179} = 9.4\%$

TAKEAWAY 4.3 Concept	Method	Assessment
How much net income does a company generate from each dollar of sales revenue?	Net sales and net income from the income statement. $\text{Profit margin} = \frac{\text{Net income}}{\text{Net sales}}$	A larger ratio indicates that a company is more profitable on each sales dollar; this is because it commands a premium price for its products and/or is more operationally efficient.

REVIEW 4.5

The following information is available from the financial statements of the Philips Company.

	Year 2	Year 1
Net sales	$120,000	$110,000
Net income	20,000	15,000
Current assets	75,000	65,000
Current liabilities	50,000	45,000
Total assets	220,000	190,000
Total liabilities	150,000	145,000

Compute the following ratios and comment on any trends observed between Year 1 and Year 2: (1) profit margin, (2) current ratio, and (3) debt-to-total-assets ratio.

The solution is on page 141.

Working with the Statement of Stockholders' Equity

LO7 Explain the components of the statement of stockholders' equity.

Chapter 1 introduced the statement of stockholders' equity, which summarizes the changes in a company's stockholders' equity during the period. The statement of stockholders' equity consists of two parts—contributed capital and earned capital. **Contributed capital** reports the capital contributed by the stockholders of a company when they purchase ownership shares in the company. Ownership shares are called common shares or common stock. **Earned capital** reports the capital that is earned by the company and reinvested in the business. These are earnings that have not been distributed to shareholders and thus represent retained earnings. Retained earnings at the end of a fiscal period are calculated as retained earnings at the start of the period, plus net income for the period, less any dividends paid during the period.

Retained earnings, beginning of period
+ Net income
– Dividends
Retained earnings, end of period

Meridian's statement of stockholders' equity is presented in **Exhibit 4-9**. The column labeled Common Stock represents the change in contributed capital during the period covered by the statement. The change to common stock resulted from the issuance of additional shares. The newly issued shares may have been sold to Meridian's existing stockholders, to new stockholders, or possibly to its employees.

The column labeled Retained Earnings in **Exhibit 4-9** represents Meridian's earned capital. Adjustments to this column include the addition of net income for the period, the reduction for dividends, and reduction for the repurchase of common stock. Meridian's management began a program to repurchase common stock as a mechanism for returning capital to its shareholders. Why would management decide to repurchase shares? While many factors contribute to this decision, one is that the company has made profits that have generated large amounts of cash. If management does not have an immediate use for this cash, they may consider distributing it to shareholders in the form of stock repurchases.

EXHIBIT 4-9 Statement of Stockholders' Equity

MERIDIAN, INC.
Statement of Stockholders' Equity

($ in millions)	Common Stock	Retained Earnings	Other Equity	Total Equity
December 31, prior year	$65,064	$ 4,487	$1,185	$70,736
Issuance of common stock	793			793
Net income		19,175		19,175
Dividends		(9,845)		(9,845)
Repurchase of common stock	(1,786)	(10,850)		(12,636)
Other adjustments	3,244		(784)	2,460
Balance as of December 31, current year	$67,315	$ 2,967	$ 401	$70,683

ENVIRONMENTAL, SOCIAL, AND GOVERNANCE

Investing with a Social Conscience A segment of the investing community believes that companies that follow sustainable practices will see improved financial performance. **Socially responsible investing (SRI)**, also known as sustainable investing, considers a firm's environmental stewardship, consumer protection, human rights and diversity, along with its financial performance. SRI funds incorporate Environmental, Social, and Governance (ESG) measures in developing investment strategies. Investments in SRI funds totaled $17.1 trillion in assets in the United States at the start of 2020, amounting to 1 in 3 dollars in professionally managed investments according to the U.S. SIF Foundation's 2020 "Report on US Sustainable and Impact Investing Trends."

REVIEW 4.6

GuidedExample MBC

You have been asked to assist with the preparation of a statement of stockholders' equity for Palatin Company for the current year ended December 31. You determine the following balances:

Beginning-of-year common stock	$45,000
Beginning-of-year retained earning	17,500
Net income	22,500
Dividends	9.250
Issuance of common stock	4,000

REQUIRED

Prepare a sttement of stockholder's equity for Palatin Company for the current year.

The solution is on page 141.

Working with the Statement of Cash Flows

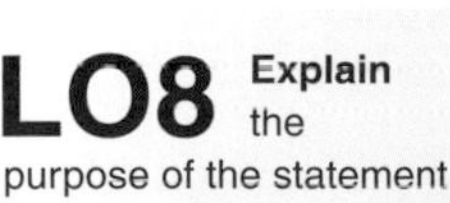

LO8 **Explain** the purpose of the statement of cash flows.

A common refrain heard from business people is that we do not pay bills with net income, we pay bills with cash! While net income is eventually converted into cash, it is the cash available that a company uses to run its business and pay its bills. Where can we find information about a company's cash resources? The answer is the statement of cash flows, which provides information on a company's sources and uses of cash.

The statement of cash flows aids us in understanding the change in cash reported by a company over a period of time, telling us how the cash is generated, and how it is being spent. The statement explains the change in cash over the accounting period, classifying all of the company's

eLecture MBC

business activities into three broad categories: (1) cash flow from operating activities, (2) cash flow from investing activities, and (3) cash flow from financing activities. These categories help in understanding how the company is being managed. For example, it is useful to know whether the company's operations generate cash, or if the company is making large cash investments.

Exhibit 4-10 shows a simplified version of Meridian's statement of cash flows. The balance in Meridian's cash account decreased by $491 million during the current year, from $8,454 million at the beginning of the year to $7,963 million at the end of the year. Meridian's cash flows during the current year were generated from operating activities ($37,507 million) and from financing activities through the issuance of debt. Meridian used much of its cash flow for investing activities, including $22,644 million for purchases of investments.

EXHIBIT 4-10 Statement of Cash Flows

MERIDIAN, INC.
Statement of Cash Flows
For Year Ended December 31

($ in millions)	Current Year
Cash flow provided by operating activities	
Cash receipts less cash disbursements from operating activities	$37,507
Net cash provided by operations	37,507
Cash flow provided by investing activities	
Net purchases of investments	(22,644)
Net payments for property, plant, and equipment	(8,326)
Other cash payments	(11,230)
Net cash used in investing activities	(42,200)
Cash flow provided by financing activities	
Issuance of common stock	793
Dividends paid	(9,845)
Repurchase common stock	(12,636)
Proceeds from issuance of long-term debt	26,422
Other	(532)
Cash provided by financing activities	4,202
Net decrease in cash	(491)
Cash at beginning of year	8,454
Cash at end of year	$ 7,963

REVIEW 4.7

Following are items reported on the financial statements of Megacorp, Inc., as of December 31 of the current year. (Some of the reported accounts have been combined for simplicity.) Amounts given are in millions of dollars.

Cash flow provided by operating activities	$ 305	Operating expenses	$ 794
Cash, beginning of the year	657	Other income	8
Cash, end of the year	620	Intangible assets	463
Revenue	2,750	Other long-term assets	132
Cash flow from investing activities	(173)	Income tax expense	14
Inventory	293	Accounts payable	299
Accounts receivable	383	Other current liabilities	434
Cost of goods sold	1,731	Long-term liabilities	130
Cash flow from financing activities	(169)	Common stock	87
Other current assets	69	Retained earnings (end of year)	1,120
Property, plant, and equipment	79	Other stockholders' equity	(31)

Prepare a multi-step income statement, a classified balance sheet, and a statement of cash flows using the accounts listed above.

The solution is on page 142.

SUMMARY OF LEARNING OBJECTIVES

LO1

Describe the qualities that make financial reporting useful. (p. 110)

- Financial reports are designed with the objective of providing existing and potential investors with information that is useful in making investment decisions.
- Qualitative characteristics help make accounting information useful to investors for the purpose of making investment decisions.

LO2

Explain where you can find accounting information. (p. 112)

- The Securities and Exchange Commission mandates that public companies issue quarterly reports, as well as an annual financial statement at the end of each fiscal year.
- Companies also typically make their SEC filings available at their websites, often under a section titled Investor Relations.
- Accounting reports as well as other financial information can also be found at the websites of companies that specialize in providing investment information.

LO3

Describe a classified balance sheet. (p. 113)

- A classified balance sheet contains two subgroups of assets (current assets and long-term assets) and two subgroups of liabilities (current liabilities and long-term liabilities).

LO4

Describe a classified income statement. (p. 118)

- A multi-step income statement classifies items into subgroups in order to facilitate analysis and decision making.
- A multi-step income statement for a merchandising firm often includes one section for sales revenue; two sections for expenses: cost of goods sold and operating expenses; and a section for other income and expenses.
- A multi-step income statement for a service firm is similar, but does not have a section for cost of goods sold, and therefore no gross profit subtotal.

LO5

Discuss use of a balance sheet and ratios to assess liquidity and solvency. (p. 121)

- Ratio analysis involves expressing the relation of one relevant accounting number with another relevant accounting number through the process of division. Ratios are useful for interpreting financial accounting numbers.
- Two techniques that are often used in ratio analysis are (1) trend analysis where ratios are examined over time and (2) benchmarking analysis where a company's ratios are compared to those of another company or to industry averages.
- Liquidity refers to a company's ability to pay those obligations that are expected to come due in the next year.
- The current ratio, or current assets divided by current liabilities, provides a measure of a company's liquidity.
- Solvency refers to a company's ability to repay its debts over the long term.
- The debt-to-total-assets ratio, calculated as total liabilities divided by total assets, provides one measure of a company's solvency.

LO6

Discuss use of the income statement and ratios to assess profitability. (p. 123)

- Profit margin, or net income divided by net sales, provides a measure of a company's profitability by indicating how much net income a company earns on each dollar of sales revenue.

LO7

Explain the components of the statement of stockholders' equity. (p. 124)

- Stockholders' equity comprises two parts: (1) contributed capital and (2) earned capital.
- Contributed capital is the capital contributed to a firm by stockholders when they purchase ownership shares in the company.
- Earned capital represents the net income that has been earned by a company and not distributed to stockholders as a dividend.

LO8

Explain the purpose of the statement of cash flows. (p. 125)

- The statement of cash flows provides information regarding a company's sources and uses of cash.

SUMMARY	Concept	Method	Assessment
TAKEAWAY 4.1	Can a company meet its short-term obligations?	Current assets and current liabilities from the balance sheet. $$\text{Current ratio} = \frac{\text{Current assets}}{\text{Current liabilities}}$$	A larger current ratio implies greater liquidity and a greater ability to pay short-term obligations.
TAKEAWAY 4.2	Can a company meet its long-term obligations?	Total assets and total liabilities from the balance sheet. $$\text{Debt-to-total-assets ratio} = \frac{\text{Total liabilities}}{\text{Total assets}}$$	A larger ratio implies less solvency and a lower ability to repay outstanding obligations over the long term.
TAKEAWAY 4.3	How much net income does a company generate from each dollar of sales revenue?	Net sales and net income from the income statement. $$\text{Profit margin} = \frac{\text{Net income}}{\text{Net sales}}$$	A larger ratio indicates that a company is more profitable on each sales dollar; this is because it commands a premium price for its products and/or is more operationally efficient.

KEY TERMS

10-K (p. 112)
10-Q (p. 112)
Account form (p. 116)
Benchmarking analysis (p. 121)
Classified balance sheet (p. 113)
Comparability (p. 111)
Conceptual framework (p. 110)
Confirmatory value (p. 111)
Conservatism (p. 112)
Contributed capital (p. 124)
Current assets (p. 113)
Current liabilities (p. 115)
Current ratio (p. 121)
Debt-to-total-assets ratio (p. 122)
Earned capital (p. 124)
Faithful Representation (p. 111)
Form 8-K (p. 112)
Gross profit (p. 118)
Intangible assets (p. 114)
Liquidity (p. 114, 121)
Long-term liabilities (p. 116)
Management earnings forecasts (p. 113)
Materiality (p. 112)
Multi-step income statement (p. 118)
Net sales (p. 118)
Normal operating cycle (p. 113)
Predictive value (p. 111)
Profit margin (p. 123)
Property, plant, and equipment (p. 114)
Proxy statements (p. 112)
Ratio analysis (p. 121)
Relevance (p. 111)
Report form (p. 116)
Return on assets (ROA) (p. 121)
Sales discounts (p. 118)
Sales returns and allowances (p. 118)
Single-step income statement (p. 118)
Socially responsible investing (SRI) (p. 125)
Solvency (p. 122)
Stockholders' equity (p. 116)
Timeliness (p. 111)
Trend analysis (p. 121)
Understandability (p. 111)
Verifiability (p. 111)

SELF-STUDY QUESTIONS

(Answers to the Self-Study Questions are available at the end of the chapter.)

LO1 

1. **According to the FASB's Conceptual Framework, who are the primary users of external financial reports?**
   a. Existing and potential investors
   b. Managers
   c. Bankers and hedge fund managers
   d. Accounting professors

LO1 

2. **Which of the following is NOT a quality of useful financial reporting?**
   a. Relevance
   b. Faithful representation
   c. Comparability
   d. Solvency

LO1  

3. **Which of the following best describes the quality comparability in financial reporting?**
   a. Faithfully reporting the events and transactions it purports to represent.
   b. Allowing users to identify similarities in, and differences between, two or more items or companies.
   c. Making a difference in users' decisions.
   d. Making information available in a timely fashion.

4. Which of the following best describes the quality relevance in financial reporting? LO1 Homework MBC

a. Faithfully reporting the events and transactions it purports to represent.
b. Allowing users to identify similarities in, and differences between, two or more items or companies.
c. Making a difference in users' decisions.
d. Making information available in a timely fashion.

5. Where might one find 10-Q and 10-K financial accounting reports for publicly held U.S. companies? LO2 Homework MBC

a. At the SEC's website where the reports are filed.
b. At the website of the company who files the reports.
c. At websites of companies who specialize in providing investment information, such as Yahoo Finance and The Motley Fool.
d. All of the above.

6. Which of the following items will not be reported on a classified balance sheet? LO3 Homework MBC

a. Current assets
b. Net income
c. Total liabilities
d. Common stock

7. Which of the following would not be considered a current asset? LO3 Homework MBC

a. Inventory
b. Accounts receivable
c. Property, plant, and equipment
d. Cash

8. For the balance sheet to be in balance, the following must exist: LO3 Homework MBC

a. Total assets must be greater than total liabilities
b. Total assets must be less than total liabilities
c. Total assets must equal total liabilities plus stockholders' equity
d. Total liabilities must equal total stockholders' equity

9. Which of the following would be considered an intangible asset? LO3 Homework MBC

a. Cash
b. Land
c. Accounts payable
d. Patents

10. Which of the following would most likely be classified as a long-term liability? LO3 Homework MBC

a. Accounts payable
b. Notes payable
c. Accounts receivable
d. Common stock

11. Ratio analysis always involves which type of arithmetic operation? LO4 Homework MBC

a. Addition
b. Subtraction
c. Multiplication
d. Division

12. Which of the following is not a true statement? LO4 Homework MBC

a. Benchmarking analysis involves comparing a company to its industry's averages.
b. Benchmarking analysis involves comparing a company to its competitors.
c. Trend analysis involves comparing a company's ratios over time.
d. Benchmarking analysis involves comparing a company's ratios over time.

13. A company reported net income of $200 on net sales of $2,000. The company's profit margin is: LO6 Homework MBC

a. $1,800
b. 10 percent
c. 0.1 percent
d. None of the above

14. The profit margin does not provide insight on which of the following: LO6 Homework MBC

a. A company's net income per dollar of sales.
b. A measure of a company's financial performance.
c. A measure of a company's cash flow flexibility.
d. A measure of a company's operating efficiency.

15. Which of the following is not shown on the statement of stockholders' equity? LO7 Homework MBC

a. Contributed capital
b. Retained earnings
c. Common stock
d. Total liabilities

16. The following data appear in the financial statements of a company. Calculate its current ratio. LO5 Homework MBC

Current assets	$10,000
Current liabilities	$5,000

a. 2:1
b. 1:2
c. $5,000
d. ($5,000)

LO7 **17. The following data pertain to Smith Consulting, Inc. Compute its ending retained earnings.**

Beginning-of-year retained earnings	$120,000
Net income	37,500
Dividends paid	5,000

a. $157,500 *c.* $162,500
b. $152,500 *d.* $115,000

LO4 **18. A merchandising company's multi-step income statement differs from that of a service company in what way?**

MBC

a. There is no difference.
b. A service company does not include a line for cost of goods sold.
c. A service company has a line for selling expenses whereas a merchandising company does not.
d. A merchandising company will have a line for income from operations whereas a service company will not.

QUESTIONS

1. List three subgroups of assets that may be found in the asset section of a classified balance sheet.
2. Define *current asset* and *normal operating cycle.*
3. Which of the following are current assets: land, cash, prepaid expense, building, accounts receivable, inventory, equipment?
4. What is meant by corporate social responsibility?
5. Define the following ratios: current ratio, debt-to-total-assets ratio, and profit margin.
6. What is meant by socially responsible investing?
7. Which of the following measures are best computed using a classified balance sheet?
   a. Liquidity *c.* Profit margin
   b. Solvency *d.* Both a. and b.
8. Which of the following is a correct statement?
   a. The current ratio is a measure of firm solvency.
   b. The current ratio is a measure of firm liquidity.
   c. The debt-to-total-assets ratio is a measure of firm liquidity.
   d. None of the above is correct.
9. Profit margin is measured using information from which financial statement?
   a. Balance sheet *c.* Statement of cash flows
   b. Income statement *d.* Statement of retained earnings
10. Socially responsible investing
    a. Means making as much money on your investments as you can as your only goal.
    b. Means investing in companies that adhere to environmental and social policies in their operations.
    c. Is too small of a concept to matter much.
    d. Means investing time using social media.

DATA ANALYTICS

The assignments in this Data Analytics section are designed to familiarize you with the tools used in analyzing data and communicating the results. Appendix F provides an in-depth discussion of data analytics and blockchain technology.

DA4-1. Preparing a Basic Data Visualization in Excel to Highlight Changes in Expenses Over Time
The Excel file associated with this exercise includes three years of operating expenses of **Starbucks Corporation** reported in recent reports on Form 10-K. We will use data visualizations to analyze the trends of expenses over this three-year period.

REQUIRED

1. Download Excel file DA4-1 found in myBusinessCourse.
2. Create a data visualization within the worksheet in Excel, through the Sparkline feature: Line option. *Hint:* Highlight the cells with numeric data and click on Insert, click on Sparklines, click on Line. Next, select where to place Sparklines by highlighting the empty cells in the column to the right of your last column of data.

3. Format the Sparklines by adding color markers to the high and low points of your chart and adding thickness to the chart lines. *Hint:* Highlight your Sparkline and under the Sparkline tab, click on High Point and Low Point and choose your desired color scheme from the options listed in the Style Group. To add thickness, click on Sparkline Color and Weight to make an adjustment.
4. Determine which Sparkline (and, thus, pattern of activity) is most similar to the Sparkline for Product and distribution.
5. Determine which Sparkline is most similar to the Sparkline for Store operating expenses.

DA4-2. Analyzing the Liquidity of Companies by Industry Segments in Excel
The Excel file associated with this exercise includes Compustat data for S&P 500 companies for five years. In this exercise, we will prepare the data in the Excel file and convert the information in the data file to a PivotTable. Lastly, we will prepare a PivotChart to discern data trends in liquidity by industry segment, measured through the current ratio.

REQUIRED

PART 1 PREPARING DATA; CREATING A PIVOTTABLE; MINING DATA

1. Download Excel file DA4-2 found in myBusinessCourse.
2. Add a column to the worksheet in the Excel file that computes the current ratio per each row of data.
3. Sort data in the current ratio column in ascending order to group together rows where errors appear. *Hint:* Use the filter button in the column heading field to sort the data.
4. Identify the industry that had the most instances in which current assets and current liabilities were not provided which resulted in errors in the current ratio column. *Hint:* Use the filter button in the current ratio column heading field and select only those rows with errors (#DIV/0 rows). Then use the filter button in the column heading of the Segment field to sort the column in alphabetical order.
5. Delete all rows in the worksheet where errors appeared in the current ratio calculated cell. *Hint:* Start by clearing the filter in the Current Ratio column. If necessary, re-sort Current Ratio column in ascending order.
6. Create a PivotTable displaying the average current ratio for years 1 through 5 by industry segment. *Hint:* To create a PivotTable, click anywhere inside the table. Open Insert tab and select PivotTable in the Tables group. Add the PivotTable to a new worksheet. Drag Segment to Columns, drag Year to Rows, and drag Current ratio to Values. Select Value Field Settings in the dropdown menu next to Current Ratio in the Values box. Select Average in the Summarize Value Field box.
7. List for each year the industry that has the highest and lowest current ratio.
8. List the company with the highest and lowest current ratio for the Health Care segment in Year 4. *Hint:* Double-click on the average current ratio for Health Care in Year 4 to automatically open up a new sheet that holds the supporting details.

PART 2 CREATING A PIVOTCHART AND ANALYZING TRENDS

1. Create a visualization through a PivotChart in the form of a line chart of the current ratio by industry segment over the five-year period. *Hint:* Click anywhere inside the PivotTable created in Part 1. Open the PivotTable Analyze tab and click PivotChart in the Tools group. Click Line.
2. Based only on the visualization, answer the following questions.
   a. What two industries appear to have had the least fluctuation from year to year?
   b. What three industries appear to have had the most fluctuation from year to year?
3. Describe the trend in liquidity from Year 1 to Year 5 for the Consumer Staples segment.

DA4-3. Preparing Tableau Visualizations to Analyze Liquidity Through the Current Ratio
Refer to PF-27 in Appendix F. This problem uses Tableau to analyze liquidity of S&P 500 companies through the current ratio. The visualization is exported to PowerPoint for communication purposes.

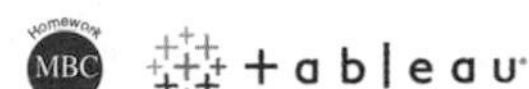

Assignments with the MBC logo in the margin are available in myBusinessCourse.
See the Preface of the book for details.

SHORT EXERCISES

SE4-1. Preparing a Classified Balance Sheet Dino Company, a merchandising firm, reports the following data as of January 31: **LO3**

Cash	$ 400
Accounts receivable	1,200
Inventory	2,500
Property, plant, and equipment	10,000
Accounts payable	800
Other current liabilities	600
Long-term notes payable	8,000
Stockholders' equity	4,700

Prepare a classified balance sheet for Dino Company as of January 31.

LO6 Homework MBC

SE4-2. Evaluating Firm Profitability The following financial information is taken from the annual reports of the Smith Company and the Wesson Company:

	Smith	Wesson
Net income	$10,000	$100,000
Net sales	50,000	400,000

Calculate the profit margin ratio for each company and determine which firm is more profitable.

LO5 Homework MBC

SE4-3. Evaluating Firm Liquidity The following financial information is taken from the balance sheets of the Drucker Company and the Ito Company:

	Drucker	Ito
Current assets	$250,000	$50,000
Current liabilities	100,000	15,000

Calculate the current ratio for each company and determine which firm has the higher level of liquidity.

LO5 Homework MBC

SE4-4. Evaluating Firm Solvency The following financial information is taken from the balance sheets of the Lambeth Company and the Maritza Company:

	Lambeth	Maritza
Total debt	$350,000	$ 850,000
Total assets	550,000	1,000,000

Calculate the debt-to-total-assets ratio and determine which firm has the higher level of solvency.

LO8 Homework MBC

SE4-5. Statement of Cash Flows Which of the following would not appear on a company's statement of cash flows?

a. Cash flow from operating activities
b. Net change in cash
c. Total assets
d. Cash flow for investing activities

LO5 Homework MBC

SE4-6. Debt-to-Total-Assets Ratio Ruby Company's balance sheet reports the following totals: Assets = $40,000; Liabilities = $25,000; Stockholders' Equity = $15,000. Determine the company's debt-to-total-assets ratio.

a. 37.5%
b. 62.5%
c. $15,000
d. 166.7%

LO6 Homework MBC

SE4-7. Profit Margin The following data are from the financial statements of Burkee Wines, Inc. Compute Burkee's profit margin.

Total revenues: $3,500,000
Total expenses: $2,800,000

a. 125%
b. 80%
c. 25%
d. 20%

LO4 Homework MBC

SE4-8. The Multi-step Income Statement Dino Company, a merchandising firm, reports the following data for the month ended January 31:

Net sales	$10,000
Cost of goods sold	4,000
Operating expenses	3,000
Other income	500
Income tax expense	1,200

Prepare a multi-step income statement for Dino Company for the month of January.

SE4-9. Qualities of Useful Accounting Information Which of the following best describes the quality "faithful representation" in financial reporting? **LO1** Homework MBC

a. Making a difference in users' decisions.
b. Allowing users to identify similarities in, and differences between, two or more items or companies.
c. Faithfully reporting the events and transactions it purports to represent.
d. Making information available in a timely fashion.

SE4-10. Objectives of Financial Reporting The overarching goal of financial accounting is to facilitate the efficient allocation of resources. This includes the creation of financial reports that provide useful information to users. Which of the following is not a user of financial information? **LO1** Homework MBC

a. Suppliers
b. Stockholders and potential stockholders
c. Lenders
d. None of the above

SE4-11. Finding Financial Accounting Information Identify three sources which provide financial statement information on public companies. **LO2**

EXERCISES

E4-1. Preparing a Classified Balance Sheet From the following accounts, listed in alphabetical order, prepare a classified balance sheet for Berkly Wholesalers as of December 31. **LO3**

Accounts payable	$ 43,000	Inventory	$117,000
Accounts receivable	40,000	Land	45,000
Building	67,000	Mortgage payable (long term)	78,000
Cash	26,000	Office supplies	2,000
Common stock	111,000	Retained earnings	?
		Salaries payable	7,000

E4-2. Multi-step Income Statement From the following accounts, listed in alphabetical order, prepare a multi-step income statement for Karlman Distributors for the year ended December 31. **LO4**

Selling, general and administrative expense	$186,000	Sales revenue	$550,000
Cost of goods sold	330,000	Income tax expense	10,000
Interest expense	3,000		

E4-3. Evaluating the Liquidity, Solvency, and Profitability of a Company Identify whether the following statements are true or false. **LO5, 6**

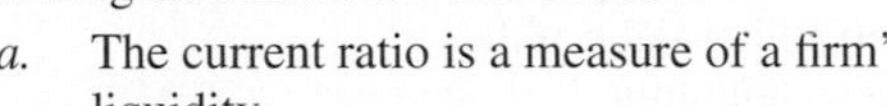

a. The current ratio is a measure of a firm's liquidity.
b. The return on assets ratio is a measure of a firm's solvency.
c. The profit margin is a measure of a firm's liquidity.
d. The debt-to-total-assets ratio is a measure of a firm's liquidity.

E4-4. Classified Balance Sheet The Werthman Company collected the following information for the preparation of its December 31 classified balance sheet: **LO3** Homework MBC

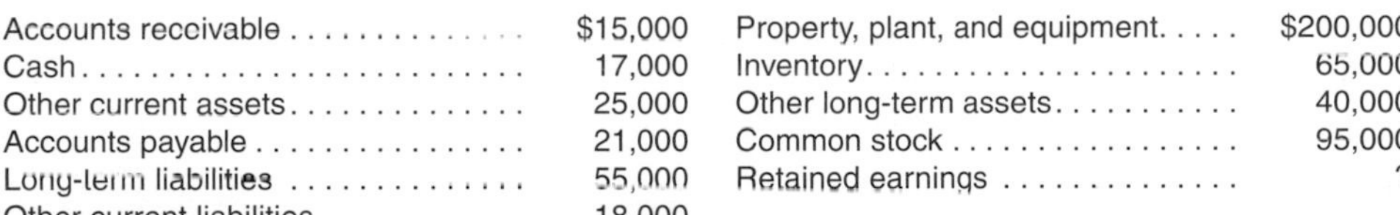

Accounts receivable	$15,000	Property, plant, and equipment	$200,000
Cash	17,000	Inventory	65,000
Other current assets	25,000	Other long-term assets	40,000
Accounts payable	21,000	Common stock	95,000
Long-term liabilities	55,000	Retained earnings	?
Other current liabilities	18,000		

Prepare a classified balance sheet for Werthman Company.

LO5, 6 **E4-5. Profitability, Liquidity, and Solvency Ratios** Shannon Corporation gathered the following information from its financial statements:

Net sales	$180,000	Current liabilities	$ 27,000
Net income	25,200	Total assets	130,000
Current assets	40,500	Total liabilities	97,500

Using the above data, calculate the following: (1) profit margin, (2) current ratio, (3) debt-to-total-assets ratio, and (4) return on assets ratio.

LO4 **E4-6. Return on Assets** The following information was taken from recent Apple Inc. financial statements. Numbers are in millions.

	2020	2019
Net income	$ 57,411	$ 55,256
Total assets	323,888	338,516

REQUIRED

a. What was Apple's return on assets for each year?

b. Based on your answer from part a., how did the company's performance change from year to year?

LO7 **E4-7. Statement of Stockholders' Equity** You have been asked to assist with the preparation of a statement of stockholders' equity for Maxx Company for the current year ended December 31. You determine the following balances:

Beginning-of-year common stock	$5,000
Beginning-of-year retained earnings	7,500
Net income	2,500
Dividends paid	250
Issuance of common stock	400

REQUIRED

Prepare a statement of stockholders' equity for Maxx Company for the current year.

LO6 **E4-8. Profit Margin** Kuyu Co.'s sales rose 10 percent over prior year sales of $100,000; however, net income increased by only 5 percent over the prior year's net income. If Kuyu's prior year profit margin was 10 percent, what is the current year profit margin?

LO7 **E4-9. Statement of Stockholders' Equity** Prag Co. reported the following financial data for its most current year:

Beginning-of-year common stock	$ 80,000
Beginning-of-year retained earnings	175,400
Net income	32,250
Dividends paid	8,500
Issuance of common stock	15,000

Compute Prag's end-of-year total stockholders' equity.

LO8 **E4-10. Statement of Cash Flows** Identify whether the following statements are true or false.

a. The statement of cash flows reveals whether a firm is profitable.

b. The statement of cash flows reveals a firm's financial health.

c. The statement of cash flows reveals a firm's liquidity.

d. The statement of cash flows reveals a firm's solvency.

PROBLEMS

LO3 **P4-1. Preparing a Classified Balance Sheet** The following financial data for Crane Distributors was collected as of December 31.

Cash	$ 15,200	Delivery equipment	$ 80,000
Accounts receivable	110,200	Accumulated depreciation	35,000
Inventory	114,000	Accounts payable	70,000
Prepaid insurance	2,400	Common stock	100,000
Supplies	6,400	Retained earnings	?

REQUIRED

Prepare a classified balance sheet as of December 31 for Crane Distributors.

P4-2. Preparing a Classified Balance Sheet The following financial data for the Marshall Corporation was collected as of December 31. LO3

Homework MBC

Cash	$46,400	Furniture and equipment	$ 97,000
Accounts receivable	95,200	Accumulated depreciation—furniture and equipment	38,800
Inventory	90,000	Accounts payable	17,400
Prepaid insurance	300	Common stock	200,000
		Retained earnings	?

REQUIRED

Prepare a classified balance sheet as of December 31.

P4-3. Multi-step Income Statements The adjusted balances of Fletcher Distributors on December 31 are shown below. LO4

FLETCHER DISTRIBUTORS
Adjusted Balances
December 31

Cash	$ 15,200
Accounts receivable	110,200
Inventory	84,000
Prepaid insurance	2,400
Supplies	6,400
Delivery equipment	80,000
Accumulated depreciation	35,000
Accounts payable	70,000
Common stock	100,000
Retained earnings	42,000
Sales revenue	785,800
Cost of goods sold	513,400
Salaries expense	118,000
Rent expense	40,000
Supplies expense	8,400
Utilities expense	4,000
Depreciation expense	16,000
Insurance expense	4,800
Income tax expense	30,000

REQUIRED

Prepare a multi-step income statement for the year ended December 31. Combine all the operating expenses into one line on the income statement for selling, general and administrative expenses.

P4-4. Preparing the Financial Statements Listed below are items reported on the financial statements of the Huntington Company as of June 30: LO3, 8

Cash flow provided by operating activities	$21,000	Other long-term assets	$17,500
Cash, beginning-of-year	9,000	Cash flow from financing activities	1,300
Cash, end-of-year	16,000	Current liabilities	22,000
Inventory	5,500	Long-term liabilities	18,250
Accounts receivable	12,200	Intangible assets	9,500
Cash flow from investing activities	(15,300)	Common stock	51,000
Other current assets	1,500	Retained earnings	?
Property, plant and equipment	40,000		

REQUIRED

Prepare a classified balance sheet as of June 30 and statement of cash flows for the current year.

LO5, 6 **P4-5. Assessing a Firm's Profitability, Liquidity, and Solvency** Presented below is financial data for the Forrester Company as of the current and prior year-ends:

	Current Year	Prior Year		Current Year	Prior Year
Current assets	$ 55,000	$ 35,000	Total liabilities	112,000	72,000
Total assets.	170,000	120,000	Net sales.	187,000	132,000
Current liabilities. . .	70,000	29,000	Net income	25,200	17,500

REQUIRED

Calculate Forrester's current ratio, debt-to-total-assets ratio, and profit margin. Comment on the trend in the company's profitability, liquidity, and solvency over the two years.

LO4, 6 **P4-6. Profitability and the Income Statement** Presented below is income statement data for Longo & Company as of the current year-end:

Income tax expense	$ 5,400	Net revenue	58,500
Cost of goods sold	12,300	Operating expenses	26,000
Other expenses	700		

REQUIRED

Prepare a multi-step income statement for the current year and calculate the company's profit margin. If Longo's profit margin was 20 percent in the prior year, is the company's profitability improving or declining?

LO7 **P4-7. Preparing the Statement of Stockholders' Equity** Presented below is financial data for Likert & Co. as of the current year-end:

Cash	$ 6,000	Accumulated depreciation	$(14,000)
Retained earnings, beginning of the year. . .	13,000	Net income	30,000
Intangible assets.	22,000	Stockholders' equity, beginning of the year. . .	63,000
Common stock	50,000	Retained earnings, December 31.	?
Accounts payable	4,000	Stockholders' equity, December 31	81,000
Dividends paid	12,000		

REQUIRED

Prepare a statement of stockholders' equity for Likert & Co. as of December 31.

LO5, 6 **P4-8. Interpreting Liquidity, Solvency, and Profitability Ratios** Presented below are financial data for two retail companies:

	Company A	Company B
Profit margin	15.5%	13.9%
Current ratio	0.5	2.0
Debt-to-total-assets	65%	30%

REQUIRED

Consider the financial ratio data for the two companies. Which company represents the better investment opportunity in your view and why?

LO5, 6 **P4-9. Ratio Analysis** The following balances were reported in the financial statements for Nafooz Company.

	Current Year	Prior Year		Current Year	Prior Year
Net sales.	$800,000	$700,000	Current liabilities. . .	$ 80,000	$100,000
Net income	80,000	65,000	Total liabilities	250,000	225,000
Current assets	200,000	175,000	Total assets.	750,000	600,000

REQUIRED

1. Compute the following ratios for each year for Nafooz Company.
   a. Profit margin
   b. Current ratio
   c. Debt-to-total-assets ratio
2. Comment on changes to Nafooz Company's profitability, liquidity, and solvency.

P4-10. Multi-step Income Statement and Adjustments The Boston Trading Company, whose accounting year ends on December 31, had the following balances in its general ledger at December 31: LO4

Homework MBC

Cash	$13,000	Sales revenue	$630,000
Accounts receivable	56,600	Cost of goods sold	404,000
Inventory	73,000	Utilities expense	4,800
Prepaid insurance	6,000	Salaries expense	138,000
Office supplies	4,200	Delivery expense	10,800
Furniture and fixtures	21,000	Advertising expense	5,600
Accumulated depreciation— furniture and fixtures	5,000	Rent expense	14,400
Delivery equipment	84,000	Income tax expense	9,000
Accumulated depreciation— delivery equipment	12,000		
Accounts payable	41,000		
Long-term notes payable	30,000		
Common stock	75,000		
Retained earnings	51,400		

During the year, the accounting department prepared monthly statements but no adjustments were made. Data for the year-end procedures are as follows:

1. Prepaid insurance, December 31, was $1,200
2. Depreciation expense on furniture and fixtures for the year was $1,800
3. Depreciation expense on delivery equipment for the year was $13,000
4. Salaries payable, December 31, was $3,000
5. Unused office supplies on December 31 were $1,000

REQUIRED

a. Determine the financial statement effect of the necessary adjustments at December 31.

b. Prepare a multi-step income statement for the year. Combine all the operating expenses into one line on the income statement for selling, general and administrative expenses.

SERIAL PROBLEM: ANGEL CITY GREETINGS

(Note: This is a continuation of the Serial Problem: Angel City Greetings from Chapter 3.)

SP4. In order to learn more about the industry and to meet people who could give her advice, Kate attended several industry trade shows. At the most recent trade show, Kate was introduced to Fred Abbott, operations manager of "Sentiments," a national card distributor. After much discussion, Fred asked Kate to consider being one of Sentiments' card suppliers. He provided Kate with a copy of the company's recent financial statements. Fred indicated that he expects that Kate will need to supply Sentiments with approximately 50 card designs per month. Kate is to send Sentiments a monthly invoice, and she will be paid approximately 30 days from the date the invoice is received in Sentiments' corporate office. Naturally, Kate was thrilled with this offer, since this will certainly give her business a big boost.

REQUIRED

Kate has several questions. Answer the following questions for Kate.

a. What type of information does each of Sentiments' financial statements provide to Kate?

b. What financial statements would Kate need to evaluate whether Sentiments will have enough cash to meet its current liabilities? Explain what to look for.

c. What financial statement would Kate need to evaluate whether Sentiments will be able to survive over a long period of time? Explain what to look for.

d. What financial statement would Kate need to evaluate Sentiments' profitability? Explain what to look for.

e. Where can Kate find out whether Sentiments has outstanding debt? How can Kate determine whether Sentiments will be able to meet its interest and principal payments on any debts that it has?

f. How could Kate determine whether Sentiments pays a dividend?

g. In deciding whether to go ahead with this opportunity, are there other areas of concern that Kate should be aware of?

BEYOND THE NUMBERS

REPORTING AND ANALYSIS

Columbia Sportswear Company

BTN4-1. Financial Reporting Problem: Columbia Sportswear Company The financial statements for **Columbia Sportswear** can be found in Appendix A at the end of this textbook.

Required

Answer the following questions using the Consolidated Balance Sheet and the Notes to the consolidated financial statements:

a. What were the combined totals of Columbia's liabilities and stockholders' equity for each of the two years presented?
b. How do these amounts compare with Columbia's total assets for each year?
c. What was the largest, in dollar value, of Columbia's assets each year? What does this asset represent?
d. What is the balance of accrued liabilities made up of?

Columbia Sportswear Company
Under Armour, Inc.

BTN4-2. Comparative Analysis Problem: Columbia Sportswear Company vs. Under Armour, Inc. The financial statements for **Columbia Sportswear** can be found in Appendix A and **Under Armour**'s financial statements can be found in Appendix B at the end of this textbook.

Required

a. Calculate the following ratios for each company for the most current year presented:
1. Current ratio
2. Debt-to-total-assets ratio
3. Profit margin

b. Comment on the companies' relative profitability, liquidity, and solvency.

Western Digital

BTN4-3. Business Decision Problem **Western Digital** is a global data storage devices and solutions provider. "We create environments for data to thrive. We drive the innovation needed to help customers capture, preserve, access, and transform an ever-increasing diversity of data." Western reports the following information in its financial statements. Assume that you are a loan officer at a major bank and have been assigned the task of evaluating whether to extend a loan for a plant expansion to the company.

(in millions)	2020	2019	(in millions)	2020	2019
Current assets	$ 9,048	$ 8,477	Retained earnings . . .	$ 6,725	$ 7,449
Total assets.	25,662	26,370	Net sales.	16,736	16,569
Current liabilities.	4,406	3,817	Cost of goods sold . . .	12,955	12,817
Total liabilities	16,111	16,403	Net income (loss)	(250)	(754)

Required

a. Calculate the company's current ratio, debt-to-total-assets ratio, and profit margin for each year.
b. Comment on Western Digital's liquidity, solvency, and profitability.
c. Based on what you have learned about Western Digital, would you recommend offering the company a loan?

BTN4-4. Financial Analysis Problem As part of your internship at Walleys Inc. you have been assigned the job of developing a few important ratios from the company's financial statements. This information is intended to be used by the company to help Walleys obtain a large bank loan. In particular, the data will need to convince the bank that Walleys is a good loan risk based on its liquidity, solvency, and profitability. Below are the data you pulled together:

	Current year	Prior year
Current ratio	2.2:1	1.5:1
Debt-to-total-assets ratio	55 percent	63 percent
Profit margin.	9.3 percent	9.1 percent
Net income	Up 15 percent	Down 12 percent

Required

Prepare brief comments that discuss how each of these items can be used to support the argument that Walleys is showing improving financial health.

CRITICAL THINKING

BTN4-5. **Accounting Research Problem** The annual report of General Mills, Inc., for the year ending May 31, 2020 (fiscal year 2020) , can be found at: https://investors.generalmills.com/financial-information/annual-reports/default.aspx. General Mills, Inc.

Required

1. Calculate the company's profit margin for each of the most recent two years presented. What is the trend?
2. Calculate the company's current asset ratio for each of the two years presented. What is the trend?
3. Calculate the company's debt-to-total-assets ratio for each of the two years presented. What is the trend?

BTN4-6. **Accounting Communication Activity** V. J. Simmons is the President of Forward Engineering Associates. He is a very good engineer, but his accounting knowledge is quite limited.

Required

V. J. has heard that ratio analysis can help him determine the financial condition of his company. In particular, he would like you to explain to him in a memo how to calculate and interpret the following three ratios: (1) profit margin, (2) current ratio, and (3) debt-to-total-assets ratio. Prepare a memo for V.J.

BTN4-7. **Accounting Ethics Case** In the post-Enron environment, and with the enactment of the Sarbanes-Oxley legislation, many firms are proactively portraying themselves as being "ethical." Ethical behavior is, for example, part of the Corporate Social Responsibility movement. This behavior includes many dimensions, from the ethical treatment of employees and the environment, to ethical financial reporting. Some academic research suggests that ethical behavior may be associated with financial success. What do you think would explain this relationship?

BTN4-8. **Accounting Ethics Problem** Debra Day, a business major at a local college, was recently hired for the summer at Sweet Delights, a popular ice cream parlor near the campus. Debra spent most of her time tending the cash register where she noticed that most of the customers paid in cash and never seemed to care about getting a receipt. Debra soon figured out that she could ring up a much lesser amount on the register, charge the customer the full amount, then toss the receipt. For example, on a $7 order she would charge and collect the full $7 from the customer, but only ring up $5. She would then deposit $5 in the register so that it would agree with the register tape and pocket the $2.

Required

a. What type of fraud is Debra committing?

b. The store manager recently hired you as a forensic accountant to critique the controls at Sweet Delights. He has noticed that while the store seems as busy as ever, and the cash in the register agrees with the tapes, the store is not as profitable as it previously was. What control would you recommend to help prevent the type of fraud being committed by Debra?

BTN4-9. **Working with the Takeaways** Earlier in this chapter, we analyzed select financial data of Apple, Inc. and Samsung. Utilize these same tools to analyze the financial data of Logitech International, a manufacturer of computer peripherals. The following information was reported by Logitech in the company's financial statements as of year-end March 31, 2020 and 2019: Logitech International

March 31 (in millions)	2020	2019
Current assets	$1,414	$1,350
Total assets	2,363	2,024
Current liabilities	714	718
Total liabilities	874	848
Net sales	2,976	2,788
Net income	450	258

Required

1. Calculate the profit margin for each year and comment on Logitech's profitability.
2. Calculate the current ratio for each year and comment on Logitech's liquidity.
3. Calculate the debt-to-total-assets ratio for each year and comment on Logitech's solvency.
4. Apple's fiscal year-end occurs near the end of September, whereas Logitech uses a March year-end. How might this affect a comparison of the financial results of the two companies?

ANSWERS TO SELF-STUDY QUESTIONS

1. a **2.** d **3.** b **4.** c **5.** d **6.** b **7.** c **8.** c **9.** d **0.** b **11.** d **12.** d **13.** b **14.** c **15.** d **16.** a **17.** b **18.** b

REVIEW SOLUTIONS

Solution 4.1

a. Liquidity is not a quality of useful financial reporting.

Solution 4.2

b. The SEC does NOT mandate that private companies issue audited annual financial statements.

Solution 4.3

MUSICLAND COMPANY Balance Sheet December 31	
Assets	
Current assets	
Cash	$ 300
Accounts receivable	3,000
Inventory	12,200
Other current assets	1,500
Total current assets	17,000
Property, plant, & equipment	25,000
Total assets	$42,000
Liabilities and Stockholders' Equity	
Current liabilities	
Accounts payable	$ 2,500
Other current liabilities	2,000
Total current liabilities	4,500
Long-term notes payable	20,000
Total liabilities	24,500
Stockholders' equity	17,500
Total liabilities and stockholders' equity	$42,000

Solution 4.4

MUSICLAND COMPANY Income Statement For Year Ended December 31	
Net sales	$100,000
Less Cost of goods sold	45,000
Gross profit on sales	55,000
Operating expenses	
Selling, general and administrative	25,000
Research and development expenses	10,000
Total operating expenses	35,000
Income from operations	20,000
Other income and expense	
Interest expense	5,000
Income before income taxes	15,000
Income tax expense	4,500
Net income	$ 10,500

Solution 4.5

	Year 2	Year 1
Profit margin	$\frac{\$20,000}{\$120,000} = 16.7\%$	$\frac{\$15,000}{\$110,000} = 13.6\%$
Current ratio	$\frac{\$75,000}{\$50,000} = 1.50:1$	$\frac{\$65,000}{\$45,000} = 1.44:1$
Debt-to-total-assets ratio	$\frac{\$150,000}{\$220,000} = 68.2\%$	$\frac{\$145,000}{\$190,000} = 76.3\%$

The Philips Company has improved its performance. The company is earning a higher amount of net income on every dollar of sales revenue as indicated by its profit margin. In addition, both its liquidity as reflected by the current ratio and its solvency as reflected by the debt-to-total-assets ratio are trending in a positive direction.

Solution 4.6

PALATIN COMPANY
Statement of Stockholders' Equity

	Common Stock	Retained Earnings	Total Equity
Dcember 31, prior year	$45,000	$17,500	$62,500
Issuance of common stock	4,000		4,000
Net income		22,500	22,500
Dividends		(9,250)	(9,250)
Balance as of December 31, current year	$49,000	$30,750	$79,750

Solution 4.7

MEGACORP, INC. Income Statement For Year Ended December 31 (in millions)	
Net sales	$2,750
Less cost of goods sold	1,731
Gross profit on sales	1,019
Operating expenses	794
Income from operations	225
Other income	8
Income before income taxes	233
Income tax expenses	14
Net income	$ 219

MEGACORP, INC. Balance Sheet December 31 (in millions)		
Assets		
Current assets		
Cash	$ 620	
Accounts receivable	383	
Inventory	293	
Other current assets	69	
Total current assets		$1,365
Property, plant, and equipment		79
Intangible assets		463
Other long-term assets		132
Total assets		$2,039
Liabilities and Stockholders' Equity		
Current liabilities		
Accounts payable	$ 299	
Other current liabilities	434	
Total current liabilities		$ 733
Long-term liabilities		130
Total liabilities		863
Stockholders' equity		
Common stock	87	
Retained earnings	1,120	
Other stockholders' equity	(31)	
Total stockholders' equity		1,176
Total liabilities and stockholders' equity		$2,039

MEGACORP, INC. Statement of Cash Flows For Year Ended December 31 (in millions)	
Cash flow provided by operations	$305
Cash flow used by investing activities	(173)
Cash flow from financing activities	(169)
Net increase in cash	(37)
Cash at beginning of the year	657
Cash at end of the year	$620

Internal Control and Cash

PAST

Chapters 1 through 4 explained the accounting system, including transaction analysis, classified financial statements, and ratio analysis.

PRESENT

In this chapter, we focus our attention on a current asset, cash. In addition, we study how internal controls can be used to prevent errors and fraud associated with assets such as cash and inventory.

FUTURE

Chapter 6 explains the accounting for accounts and notes receivable. We will explain the reporting of uncollectible accounts and how managers monitor such accounts.

WIRECARD FRAUD

Wirecard was a highflying fintech company worth more than €24 billion before it went bankrupt in one of Germany's largest accounting frauds in history. In its heyday Wirecard was on the cutting edge of the electronic payment services industry, facilitating credit and debit card transactions around the globe. But investigators discovered that over €1.9 billion in cash ($2.3 billion) reported on the balance sheet did not exist. Police also found that high-level employees carried away plastic bags filled with millions of dollars-worth of cash from Wirecard's Munich headquarters. Several Wirecard executives are now behind bars, and the Chief Operating Officer, who fled the country, is being pursued by Interpol. Wirecard is a textbook example of what can go wrong when companies have poor internal controls over cash that fail to prevent employee fraud.

Road Map

LO	Learning Objective	Page	eLecture	Review	Assignments
LO1	**Define the three elements of fraud.**	146	E5-1	5.1	SE1
LO2	**Discuss how the COSO framework prevents fraud, identify potential internal control failures, and discuss SOX regulations.**	147	E5-2	5.2	SE2, SE3, SE10, E1, E8, P1, P2, P6, P7
LO3	**Define cash and discuss the accounting for cash.**	150	E5-3	5.3	SE6, SE7, E7, P5
LO4	**Describe the internal controls for cash.**	151	E5-4	5.4	SE8, E1, E2, P1, P2, P7
LO5	**Describe the four primary activities of effective cash management.**	154	E5-5	5.5	SE9, E9, P8
LO6	**Appendix 5A Describe financial statement audits and operational audits.**	156	E5-6	5.6	SE4, SE5, E5, E6
LO7	**Appendix 5B Illustrate the bank reconciliation process.**	158	E5-7	5.7	E3, E4, P3, P4

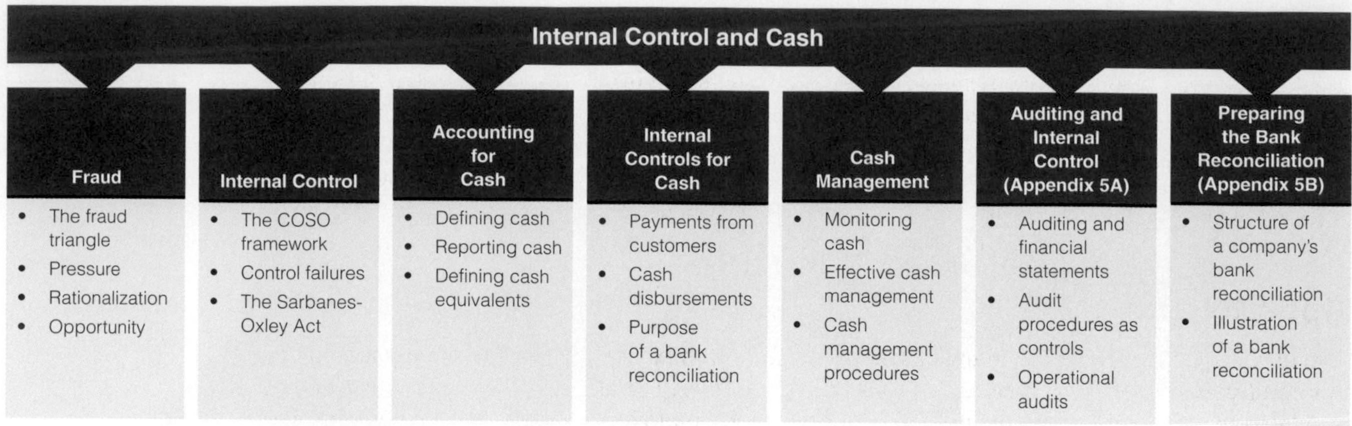

FRAUD

The Wirecard fraud appears to have been perpetrated by a group of determined insiders who were seeking to enrich themselves at the expense of the company's shareholders. While a fraud the size of Wirecard is relatively unusual, fraud on a smaller scale is all too common. In fact, researchers have found that, under the right circumstances, most individuals are capable of committing fraud. While this does not mean that most employees will end up committing fraud, it does mean that it is very difficult to predict which employees will be the ones who eventually commit fraud.

Fraud refers to any act by the management or employees of a business engaged in intentional deception for personal gain. Fraud may include, among other acts, embezzlement of a business's cash, theft of assets, filing false insurance claims, filing false health claims, and financial statement fraud. Fraud is a punishable crime and a violation of civil law. Research has shown that three elements are almost always present when a fraud occurs. These elements are often referred to as the **fraud triangle** and consist of (1) a perceived pressure on the individual committing the fraud, (2) some way to rationalize the fraudulent act, and (3) a perceived opportunity. Reducing or suppressing any of the three elements of the fraud triangle reduces the likelihood of fraud occurring in a business.

The first two elements of the fraud triangle are the most challenging because they are often the result of the individual's particular life circumstances or personality. As a consequence, nearly all fraud prevention efforts by businesses are devoted to the third element—reducing the opportunity to commit fraud. As we will discuss in this chapter, this often involves implementing a system of internal control, including such measures as physical control over cash and proper authorization over cash disbursements.

Pressure

Pressure can be divided into several categories, but research has shown that nearly all frauds are committed by individuals who feel perceived pressure from some sort of financial need. Financial pressure could come from living beyond one's means and being unable to pay one's bills, experiencing large medical bills, or the financial pressure from vices like gambling, drugs, and alcohol. The latter pressure is sometimes referred to as vice pressure.

Financial statement fraud, such as the overstatement of revenues or the understatement of expenses, usually occurs because of pressure on management to "make the numbers," either to satisfy Wall Street analyst expectations or to qualify for an earnings-based bonus.

While it is difficult to counter this element, companies can take actions to reduce the likelihood of its occurence. An obvious action is to perform careful personnel screening before hiring any employee to reduce the likelihood of employing individuals with known histories of fraud.

Rationalization

Most people who commit fraud recognize that it is wrong. In order to overcome feelings of guilt, most employees need to come up with some form of rationalization so that they can live with the knowledge of what they did. Common rationalizations include convincing themselves that (1) I am underpaid and the company owes it to me; (2) Everyone else is doing it; or (3) I am only borrowing the money and I will pay it back later.

One way to reduce this element of fraud is to create an environment in which it is difficult to rationalize unethical behavior. A company that promotes a culture of honesty and integrity, within which unethical behavior is considered unacceptable, is much less likely to encounter fraudulent behavior by management or its employees. The key to building organization-wide attitudes regarding ethical behavior starts with the "tone at the top"—that is, the behaviors and attitudes displayed by a company's CEO or president.

Opportunity

The third element of the fraud triangle is perceived opportunity. An individual will only attempt to commit fraud if he or she perceives that there is an opportunity to succeed. Of course, this element is related to the other two elements. For example, if an employee is under tremendous pressure either at work or outside the workplace, he may attempt to commit a fraud even if he perceives only a small chance of success, while an individual under much less pressure will likely only attempt the fraud if it is perceived to be easy to commit.

REVIEW 5.1

The three elements of the fraud triangle include perceived pressure, rationalization, and perceived opportunity. Nearly all fraud prevention efforts by businesses focus on which element?

The solution is on page 175.

INTERNAL CONTROL

Reducing the opportunity to commit fraud often involves implementing a system of internal controls, including such measures as physical control over cash and proper authorization over cash disbursements.

LO2 **Discuss** how the COSO framework prevents fraud, **identify** potential internal control failures, and **discuss** SOX regulations.

COSO Framework

In 1992, the Committee on Sponsoring Organizations of the Treadway Commission (COSO) released a framework to help companies structure and evaluate their internal controls. Twenty years later, in 2013, COSO updated its framework to reflect changes in business environments brought about by developments such as technological advancements and increasing globalization.

The COSO framework identifies five internal control components: (1) the control environment, (2) risk assessment, (3) control activities, (4) information and communication, and (5) monitoring activities.

Hint: Visit COSO's website at https://www.coso.org/Pages/ic.aspx for their 2020 guidance on how Blockchain technology intersects with an entity's internal control.

1. Control Environment

The **control environment** sets the tone of the organization. An environment of ethical values and integrity is crucial to keeping employees from feeling that it is acceptable to commit fraud. The control environment provides the foundation for all other components of internal control. Included in the control environment are management's philosophy and management style; the organizational structure and assignment of authority and responsibility; the process for attracting and developing competent employees; and the rewards to drive accountability for performance.

ACCOUNTING ETHICS

Despite the regulations in place with the 2002 Sarbanes Oxley Act, **Lehman Brothers** fraudulently kept billions of dollars worth of debt off its balance sheet through the improper accounting for securities repurchase agreements. By inappropriately classifying loan obligations as sales revenue, it caused its shareholders to lose hundreds of billions of dollars. At the time of its collapse, in September 2008, it was the fourth largest U.S. investment bank, with over 25,000 employees. Now it goes down in history as one of the ten largest accounting scandals of all time.

2. Risk Assessment

Every organization faces a variety of different risks from both internal and external sources. Risk is defined as the possibility that an event will occur that has a negative impact on the organization's objectives. **Risk assessment** involves identifying and analyzing risks that may adversely affect the organization's objectives. Because items external to the organization, such as the economic conditions, industry competitors, and regulations, along with internal items such as operating conditions, are constantly changing, risk assessment must be an ongoing and iterative process.

3. Control Activities

The accounting system represents a cornerstone of the control environment that is necessary to reduce the opportunity for, and success of, fraudulent behavior. A critical aspect of the accounting system is a strong system of internal controls. **Internal controls** are the measures undertaken by a business to ensure the reliability of its accounting data, protect its assets from theft or unauthorized use, ensure that employees are following the company's policies and procedures, and evaluate the performance of employees, departments, divisions, and the company as a whole. Management is responsible for designing, installing, and monitoring internal controls throughout the business with the objective of attaining "reasonable assurance," rather than "absolute assurance," that the controls will meet their objectives.

Control activities are the specific policies and procedures designed to reduce risk. A control activity can be either a prevention control or a detection control. A **prevention control** is intended to deter a problem before it arises. A **detection control**, on the other hand, is designed to discover a problem shortly after it arises. Prevention controls are more desirable and preferred than detection controls, modifying an old saying that "an ounce of prevention is worth a pound of detection."

A company should incorporate the following elements when it designs its prevention and detection controls:

- Establish clear lines of authority and responsibility.
- Implement segregation of duties. **Segregation of duties** requires that no single employee be assigned duties that would allow him or her to misappropriate company assets. In particular, management should separate the following three functions: authorization, recording, and custody.
- Hire competent personnel. Employees should be adequately trained to perform their duties.
- Require mandatory vacations for employees. This is an excellent control for detecting fraud.
- All business documents, such as purchase orders, sales invoices, credit memos, and checks, should have **control numbers** preprinted on them.
- Develop plans and budgets. The observation of variances when comparing actual outcomes to planned performance should be investigated by management.
- Maintain adequate accounting records. One important control is the use of double-entry accounting, whereby assets must equal liabilities plus stockholders' equity.
- Provide physical and electronic controls. Physical controls such as locks on doors, safes, and security cameras are a means of safeguarding assets.

Data Analytics

DATA ANALYTICS IN ACCOUNTING — **Benford's Law**

Benford's Law provides an example of how data analytics has been used to uncover fraud in a national call center. Forensic accountants utilized their knowledge of Benford's Law to form evidence of a problem by observing patterns in the data. According to Benford's Law, in any list of financial transactions, the number 1 should occur as the first digit 30.1 percent of the time, with each successive number occurring as the first digit in lesser percentages, with the number 9 occurring less than 5 percent of the time. Forensic accountants examined issued refunds and noticed an excessively high occurrence of the number 4. The forensic accountants learned that the company had a policy that required supervisor approval of refunds that exceeded $50. The accountants were able to identify a small group of operators who had been issuing fraudulent refunds to family, friends, and themselves. These fraudulent $40 refunds totaled several hundred thousand dollars.

4. Information and Communication

The fourth control component of the COSO framework involves communication. It is important that individuals receive a clear message from senior management that control responsibilities must be taken seriously. To do this management must obtain or generate relevant and quality information from both internal and external sources.

5. Monitoring Activities

It is necessary for the internal control system to be monitored in order to assess the quality of the system's performance over time. **Monitoring activities** involve ongoing evaluations, special evaluations, or some combination of each.

Internal Audits

Internal audits are one type of monitoring activity. In a small company, internal auditing is a function typically assigned to an employee who has other duties as well. In a large company, internal auditing is an activity assigned to an independent department that reports to top management or the board of directors of the corporation. An **internal audit** provides independent appraisals of the company's financial statements, its internal controls, and its operations.

DATA ANALYTICS IN ACCOUNTING Blockchain and the Future of Accounting

When most people hear the word *blockchain*, they likely think of Bitcoin. What makes blockchain so important for cybercurrencies like Bitcoin also makes it likely to revolutionize the future of accounting. Blockchain technology, which is also known as distributed ledger technology, allows multiple parties to a transaction to securely share a database. Blockchain has the potential to create a completely traceable audit trail and could potentially automate the entire financial audit. While the future possibilities appear endless, current applications in addition to auditing include cybersecurity and financial planning and analysis.

Data Analytics

Control Failures

Occasionally, internal controls fail. For example, an employee may forget to lock an exterior door, and a thief will steal some merchandise. Or, an employee with custody responsibilities steals cash received from customers. A company cannot completely prevent these types of incidents from occurring. Consequently, many businesses purchase insurance that helps mitigate the cost of these events. Casualty insurance provides financial reimbursement for losses from fire, natural disasters, and theft. A fidelity bond is an insurance policy that covers losses from employee theft by employees who are covered by the insurance.

Another reason that internal controls fail is **employee collusion**. When two or more employees work together to circumvent or avoid prescribed internal controls, this act is known as *employee collusion*. For example, an employee with custody of an asset (like cash) can work with an employee with recording responsibilities to steal the asset and cover up the theft in the accounting records. Employee collusion is especially difficult to prevent or detect. Hiring high-quality employees and paying them market wages is one approach to avoid collusion.

As with employee collusion, senior management can also circumvent internal controls. Additionally, in small companies where proper segregation of duties is not possible, the owner may serve as a mitigating control. However, this is not an ideal control since it requires the owner to be present most of the time and provides an opportunity for the owner to circumvent internal controls.

The Sarbanes-Oxley Act

The **Sarbanes-Oxley Act** of 2002 (SOX) is generally considered to be the most far-reaching securities legislation since the Securities and Exchange Commission was created in 1934. SOX is first and foremost an anti-fraud bill, which was passed in the wake of a series of high-profile accounting scandals that occurred during the early 2000's. These financial meltdowns, which included high flying companies such as **Enron** and **WorldCom**, destroyed hundreds of billions of dollars in shareholder value and resulted in some of the largest bankruptcies in U.S. history.

SOX attempts to prevent future accounting failures with a wide variety of reforms, most of which are designed to strengthen corporate governance and the accountability of top management.

For example, one notable reform requires corporate executive officers to sign a statement certifying the accuracy of financial statements, with penalties ranging from 10 to 20 years in prison for a knowingly false certification. SOX also requires corporate boards to include a majority of directors who are independent of top management.

One of the most controversial SOX reforms is what is commonly known as "Section 404," which requires external auditors to issue a formal opinion on the effectiveness of their client's internal controls over financial reporting. This requirement has resulted in public companies making large investments in beefing up their internal control systems and has increased the cost of external audits. While the academic literature generally concludes that the Section 404 internal control audits have been effective in curtailing misreporting, critics argue that their benefits may not exceed their costs.

Many of the changes brought about by SOX focused on reforming the auditing profession, whose failures were generally seen as responsible for the accounting scandals that spurred the adoption of SOX. The most impactful reform to the audit market was the creation of the **Public Company Accounting Oversight Board (PCAOB)**, a new governmental agency tasked with overseeing the audits of public companies. The PCAOB is responsible for establishing auditing standards, inspecting the auditing practices of independent audit firms, and disciplining those firms that fail to maintain acceptable audit standards and practices. While academic research provides evidence that the PCAOB and its inspection program have improved the quality of financial reporting in the U.S. capital markets, the inspections have been harshly criticized by some as expensive and ineffective.

TAKEAWAY 5.1

Concept	Method	Assessment
Are the internal controls adequate?	The COSO framework identifies five internal control components: (1) the control environment, (2) risk assessment, (3) control activities, (4) information and communication, and (5) monitoring activities.	Monitoring activities include appraisals of the company's internal control system. If weaknesses are reported, be cautious in relying on the reported financial statements.

REVIEW 5.2

Identify which control activity within the COSO framework is being violated and explain how this may cause an opportunity for fraud to occur within a business:

1. The supervisor for the purchasing department has not taken a vacation in three years.
2. Inventory is left in a receiving area at the back of the store by an open door.
3. The purchasing supervisor has the authority to order a purchase and to receive the merchandise, record its receipt, and authorize the accounting department to issue a check.

The solution is on page 175.

ACCOUNTING FOR CASH

LO3 Define cash and **discuss** the accounting for cash.

Cash includes coins, currency (paper money), checks, money orders, traveler's checks, and funds on deposit at a financial institution in a company's checking and savings accounts. An item is considered to be an element of cash if (1) it is accepted by a bank or other financial institution (brokerage firm or credit union) for deposit, and (2) it is free from restrictions that would prevent its use for paying debts.

Many near-cash items such as certificates of deposit, non-sufficient funds checks, and IOUs are not considered to be cash. **Certificates of deposit (CDs)** are securities issued by a bank when cash is invested for a short period of time, typically three months to one year. CDs pay a fixed rate of interest on the deposited funds. A **non-sufficient-funds check (NSF check)** is a check from an individual or company that had an insufficient cash balance in the bank when the holder of the check presented it to the bank for payment. IOU is a slang term for a note receivable—that is, a written document that states that one party promises to pay another party a certain amount of cash on a certain date. CDs are accounted for as investments, whereas NSF checks and IOUs are accounted for as Other Receivables.

Reporting Cash

Cash is a current asset and is shown first in the balance sheet listing of assets. A company may have only one Cash account, or it may have multiple cash accounts, such as Cash in Bank, Cash on Hand, and Petty Cash. Cash in Bank includes any cash held in a company's checking accounts and savings accounts, while Cash on Hand includes cash items not yet deposited in the bank. Petty Cash is an example of cash on hand that is used for small disbursements and is maintained at the company's business location.

Cash and Cash Equivalents

A company may combine certain short-term, highly liquid investments with cash, and then present a single amount called **cash and cash equivalents** on the balance sheet. Cash equivalents are highly liquid, short-term investments of 90 days maturity or less in such risk-free securities as U.S. Treasury bills and money market funds. A company presents this combined amount on the balance sheet so that it reconciles with the change in cash and cash equivalents appearing on the company's statement of cash flows. The statement of cash flows explains the changes in a firm's total cash and cash equivalents during an accounting period.

ACCOUNTING IN PRACTICE

The FASB has not yet issued official rules for the accounting treatment of cryptocurrencies such as Bitcoin and Ethereum. However, the AICPA has guidelines that suggest these currencies do not meet the definition of cash or cash equivalents since they are not legal tender or issued by a sovereign government. Instead, owners of cryptocurrency should report it on the balance sheet as an intangible asset with an indefinite life.

REVIEW 5.3

Identify each of the following items as cash, cash equivalents, or neither:

a. Money market funds
b. Euros
c. NSF check
d. Savings account
e. Bitcoin

The solution is on page 176.

INTERNAL CONTROLS OVER CASH

LO4 Describe the internal controls for cash.

Cash is highly desired, easily concealed, and quickly convertible into other assets. In addition, large amounts of cash flow in and out of companies on a regular basis, and many companies keep large amounts of cash on hand and in the bank. Together, this makes cash an especially attractive target for theft and fraud. While internal controls over cash should be tailored to the firm's particular financial reporting system, the following elements underlie all strong cash internal control systems:

1. **Written policies and procedures** over the handling and accounting for cash. Examples include the following:
   a. Cash received must be deposited with the bank on a daily basis. Keeping unnecessarily large amounts of cash on hand exposes a company to a heightened risk of theft. Any cash that must be kept on hand should be kept physically secure, such as in a safe, or a locked cash register.
   b. Bank statements must be reconciled monthly by someone who is not involved with the physical custody of the cash, or whose duties are to record or authorize cash transactions. The detailed process of reconciling the firm's bank account is discussed in Appendix 5B.
2. **Segregation of duties.** Some examples where segregation of duties are particularly important are as follows:
   a. When cash payments are received from customers, whether it is in cash, through the mail, or electronically, the person responsible for depositing the funds cannot have responsibility for recording the transaction in the company's books. By keeping these du-

ties segregated, both individuals would have to collude in order to misappropriate cash. Segregation of duties also applies to cash disbursements. That is, the person responsible for disbursing the cash cannot have responsibility for recording the disbursement in the company's books. In small "mom and pop" businesses, which typically have few employees, this control is often difficult to implement.

b. The person responsible for approving company purchases must not be the same person who is responsible for disbursing the cash for those purchases. Segregating these activities reduces the ability of employees to authorize payments that would enrich themselves.

c. The person responsible for depositing cash receipts should not also be responsible for making cash disbursements. When the same individual makes cash deposits and cash disbursements, it provides an opportunity to misappropriate cash.

Payments from Customers

Depending on a firm's business model, companies receive payments for goods and services in a variety of ways. Most payments by customers, however, occur in one of these five forms: (1) electronic; (2) cash; (3) check; (4) credit card; or (5) debit card. **Exhibit 5-1** reports the results of a 2019 study by the U.S. Federal Reserve that examined the payment methods used by the average American consumer. The exhibit indicates that in terms of the total number of payments in 2019, cash, credit, and debit are the largest categories. However, when looking at the data based on payment amount, cash is far and away the leader for purchases under $10 at 47%, but electronic payments are the leader in purchases over $100 at 36%. The large number of electronic payments (and payments by debit and credit cards) is partially a reflection of the dramatic growth in online shopping.

EXHIBIT 5-1 Shares of Transactions by Payment Instrument

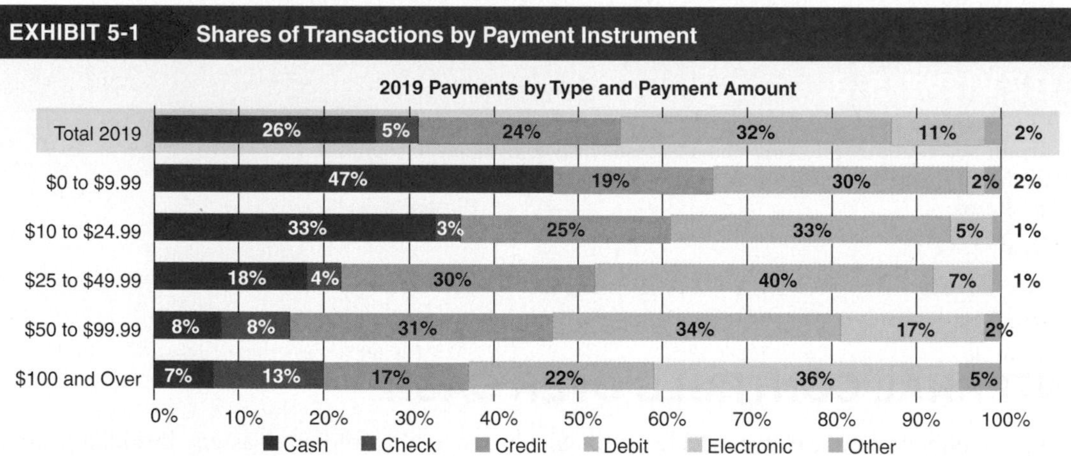

Electronic Payments

Electronic payments are a fast growing payment method that includes **electronic funds transfers (EFT)**. EFT refers to funds that are moved from one bank account to another electronically, thereby eliminating the physical handling of cash or checks. Companies use EFT for many types of payments, including to suppliers and employees (payroll direct deposits). Consumers use EFT in the form of online banking bill pay, ATM transactions, and services such as PayPal. EFT involves sending an electronic message from one computer to another to cause a transfer of money within a financial institution, from one financial institution to another, or directly to a company. The internal control concerns surrounding electronic payments primarily involve online security and customer privacy. Controls over payment authorization should be consistent with those used for any type of disbursement.

Payments by Cash or Check

The primary control challenge for companies that receive cash in the form of currency or check is physical security to guard against theft. While checks are not as liquid as cash, they can easily be converted to cash (by forging a signature), and thus must be secured in a similar fashion. Companies that deal primarily in cash transactions, such as fast-food restaurants, typically have elaborate controls in place to prevent employee theft. For example, the uniforms of fast food employees usually do not have pockets, and access to cash registers is limited and heavily monitored. Payments by check are often received via mail and are typically made to pay off accounts receivable. These payments require additional layers of controls to ensure the mail is not diverted to unauthorized employees.

Payments by Credit or Debit Cards

When a customer pays using a credit card, the funds are electronically transferred to the selling company from the customer's credit card company. As with EFTs, this eliminates the physical handling of cash or checks. The customer then makes the payment to the credit card company, often with a substantial amount of interest. From the customer's perspective, debit cards work much differently. With debit cards, the customer makes a pre-paid deposit of funds with a debit card provider (typically a bank), prior to the purchase. At the time of purchase, the debit card provider electronically transfers the funds to the selling company. As with EFTs, the internal controls issues related to credit and debit card sales primarily involve online security and customer privacy.

Cash Disbursements

Checks

A **check** is a written order signed by a checking account owner (also known as the *maker*) directing the bank (called the *payer*) to pay a specified amount of money to the person or company named on the check (called the *payee*). A check is a negotiable instrument; it can be transferred to another person or company by writing "pay to the order of" and the name of the other person or company on the back of the check and then signing the back of the check.

When a company opens a checking account at a bank, the bank requires each company employee who will sign checks to sign a signature card. Occasionally, a bank employee compares the signatures on the checks presented for payment by various parties to the authorized signatures on the signature cards. This comparison provides an internal control for the bank that it is not cashing a check written by an unauthorized employee. The bank is responsible for any amounts erroneously paid out of a company's checking account.

The Petty Cash Fund

Businesses find it inconvenient and expensive to write checks for small expenditures. Instead, these businesses establish a petty cash fund. A **petty cash fund** is a small amount of cash that is placed in a secure location on a business's premises to be used to pay for small expenditures such as postage, delivery service charges, and minor purchases of supplies.

Internal control over petty cash can be maintained by handling the fund on an imprest basis with documented procedures. An imprest fund contains a fixed amount of cash. A business establishes a petty cash fund by writing a check against the firm's checking account and cashing the check at the bank. All replenishments of the petty cash fund are also made by check. As a result, all expenditures are ultimately controlled by check, providing a paper trail of all cash transfers to the petty cash fund.

Bank Reconciliation

At the end of each month, a business's bank prepares a bank statement for each checking account that the company maintains and sends the statement to the internal audit department of the company that owns the checking account. An example of a bank statement from Anchor National Bank for the Wilson Corporation's checking account is shown in **Exhibit 5B-2** in Appendix 5B.

The internal audit department prepares a bank reconciliation as of the end of each month. A **bank reconciliation** is a schedule that (1) accounts for all differences between the ending cash balance on the bank statement and the ending cash balance in the company's Cash account and (2) determines the reconciled cash balance as of the end of the month. A detailed illustration of the bank reconciliation process is presented in Appendix 5B.

REVIEW 5.4

Edwards Company operates a retail department store. Most customers pay cash for their purchases. Edwards has asked you to help it design procedures for processing cash received from customers for cash sales. Briefly describe the procedures that should be used to safeguard cash.

The solution is on page 176.

EFFECTIVE CASH MANAGEMENT

LO5 Describe the four primary activities of effective cash management.

Cash is a critically important asset. Without cash, a company would be unable to pay its employees or its suppliers. In short, a company would be unable to continue operating. As a consequence, managers spend considerable time and effort managing and monitoring this key asset. Similarly, investors and lenders spend considerable time understanding where a company's cash came from and how the company spent it.

Monitoring Cash

The most effective tool for external parties to monitor a company's cash is the statement of cash flows.[1] As discussed in Chapter 1, the statement of cash flows identifies a company's cash inflows and cash outflows, segmenting them into the three business activities of operating, investing, and financing. **Exhibit 5-2** presents the statement of cash flows for DataForce Inc. for the month ended December 31.

The positive numbers on the statement of cash flows represent a company's cash inflows, and the negative numbers represent a company's cash outflows. DataForce's primary cash inflows arose from the issuance of stock ($30,000) and its bank borrowings ($36,000). The company's primary uses of cash resulted from the purchase of office equipment ($32,400) and the payment of rent ($10,800). Not only does the statement of cash flows identify the sources and uses of cash, but it identifies whether a company's cash balance increased or decreased for the period. **Exhibit 5-2** indicates that DataForce's cash account increased by $40,590 in the month of December.

EXHIBIT 5-2 Statement of Cash Flows for DataForce, Inc.

DATAFORCE, INC.
Statement of Cash Flows
For Month Ended December 31

Cash flow from operating activities		
Cash received from clients	$19,910	
Cash paid to employees and suppliers	(1,620)	
Cash paid for rent	(10,800)	
Cash provided by operating activities		$ 7,490
Cash flow from investing activities		
Purchase of office equipment	(32,400)	
Cash used by investing activities		(32,400)
Cash flow from financing activities		
Stock issued	30,000	
Borrowing from bank	36,000	
Cash dividends	(500)	
Cash provided by financing activities		65,500
Net increase in cash		40,590
Cash at December 1		0
Cash at December 31		$40,590

[1] The statement of cash flows provides an after-the-fact monitoring of cash sources and uses. Many companies use a cash budget in order to plan anticipated cash inflows and outflows so that they are able to manage the amount of cash on hand at an appropriate level. Cash budgets are covered in most managerial accounting textbooks.

While having some cash on hand is important to enable a company to pay its employees and its suppliers on a timely basis, having too much cash on hand may indicate that a company is not maximizing the return on its assets. Thus, it is important for managers to not only monitor a company's cash but also manage it effectively to ensure that the company is earning an adequate return on this key asset.

Primary Activities of Effective Cash Management

Effective cash management generally involves four primary activities:

1. **Managing accounts receivable.** Since accounts receivable rarely include interest charges for late payment, managers should attempt to collect this cash as soon as possible.
2. **Managing inventory levels.** If inventory levels are too low, companies may not have enough inventory on hand to meet customer demands. Alternatively, if inventory levels are too high, the company will unnecessarily tie up costly resources. Thus, managers should try to keep inventory levels as low as possible without losing any sales.
3. **Managing accounts payable.** Since accounts payable rarely include an interest charge for late payment, companies benefit from delaying payment as long as feasibly possible. However, they should not be delayed beyond the point that their credit rating may be harmed. Where accounts payable have credit terms that provide a discount for prompt payment, managers must evaluate the trade-off involved by delaying the payment of accounts payable versus the reduced purchase price that results from timely payment.
4. **Investing excess cash.** Since cash on hand or in a bank account yields a very low rate of return, it is important to invest excess cash. Thus, an important management activity is forecasting a company's cash needs by constructing a cash budget each period. Only a sufficient amount of cash necessary to cover a company's day-to-day needs should be kept on hand; any excess amounts should be invested in an effort to earn an adequate rate of return on this asset.

REVIEW 5.5

Presented below is the statement of cash flows for Los Altos, Inc., for the month ended December 31. Identify (a) the major sources of cash, (b) the major uses of cash, and (c) the change in the cash balance during the month.

LOS ALTOS, INC.
Statement of Cash Flows
For the Month Ended December 31

Cash flows from operating activities	
Cash receipts from customers	$13,275
Cash payments for operating activities	(11,131)
Cash provided by operating activities	2,144
Cash flows from investing activities	
Net purchases of investments	(140)
Net capital expenditures	(30,000)
Cash used by investing activities	(30,140)
Cash flows for financing activities	
Repurchase of common stock	(7,300)
Cash dividends paid	(6,000)
Cash used in financing activities	(13,300)
Net decrease in cash	(41,296)
Cash at beginning of month	95,000
Cash at end of month	$53,704

The solution is on page 176.

APPENDIX 5A: Auditing and Internal Control

LO6 Describe financial statement audits and operational audits.

An internal control concept previously discussed was conducting internal company audits. Internal audits provide appraisals of a company's financial statements, its internal controls, and its operations. Internal auditors, who are employees of the company that they audit, conduct internal audits under the direction of top management or a company's board of directors. Parties outside the company, such as bankers and stockholders, prefer independent appraisals of a company's performance. These parties are usually unwilling to accept an audit report prepared by company-employed internal auditors because of possible bias and conflicts of interest.

Consequently, creditors and stockholders usually require that an independent, professional auditing firm conduct an audit of the annual financial statements. Moreover, U.S. securities law requires that all corporations whose common stock is publicly traded have an independent firm of certified public accountants (CPAs) audit the company's annual financial statements.

Financial Statement Audits

A **financial statement audit** is an examination of a company's annual financial statements by a firm of independent certified public accountants. The independent audit firm conducts this examination so it can prepare a report that expresses an opinion regarding whether (or not) the financial statements present fairly, in all material respects, the results of operations, cash flows, and financial position of a company.

PRINCIPLE ALERT

Going Concern Concept The *going concern concept* assumes that a business entity will continue to operate indefinitely. As part of the annual audit, a company's independent auditors must assess the likelihood that the company that they are auditing will continue as a going concern for a reasonable period. Events such as recurring losses, pending litigation, and the loss of a major customer or supplier may raise concern about a firm's ability to maintain its going-concern status. In such cases, the independent auditors should assess management's response to the problem and the type of financial statement disclosure being made about the problem. When substantial doubt exists about a company's going-concern status, the independent auditors may include a paragraph in the audit report expressing their concern regarding this issue.

Audit Procedures

The independent audit firm conducts the annual financial statement audit of public companies according to standards established by the Public Company Accounting Oversight Board (PCAOB), a quasi-governmental agency established by the Sarbanes-Oxley Act. The annual financial statement audit includes many different stages of work. During the early stage of an audit, the independent auditor reviews and evaluates the internal controls imbedded in a company's accounting system and other systems. This review and evaluation helps the auditor determine what additional investigative steps, if any, should be included in the audit. The auditor then collects and analyzes data that substantiates the amounts in the financial statements. The auditor obtains most of these data from accounting records (such as journals and ledgers), business documents (such as purchase orders, sales invoices, and payment approval forms), and outside sources (such as banks, insurance companies, customers, and suppliers).

The Audit Report

The **audit report** issued by the independent accountant specifies the financial statements that were audited, summarizes the audit process, and states the auditor's opinion regarding the financial statement data. The opinion usually states that the financial statements "present fairly" the results of operations, cash flow, and financial position of the company in accordance with GAAP. It would be too costly for the auditor to provide assurance that the financial statements were absolutely correct. Instead, the audit provides "reasonable assurance" that the financial statements are fairly presented.

The primary purpose of the annual financial statement audit is not the discovery of fraudulent acts by management or employees of the company. Many audit procedures use statistical samples of transactions and data rather than examining the complete population of transactions. The auditors use samples to minimize the time required to conduct the audit, and consequently, to minimize its cost. As a result, there is the possibility that some errors or irregularities will exist in the transactions and data that the auditor does not review or evaluate. However, the independent auditor carefully designs the sampling procedures to detect errors and irregularities that are material in relation to the financial statements. Although auditing procedures continue to utilize statistical sampling, due to both big data and blockchain, auditors are more often able to evaluate nearly 100% of certain transactions.

Report of Independent Registered Public Accounting Firm
In our opinion, such consolidated financial statements present fairly, in all material respects, the financial position of the Company as of December 31, 2020 and 2019, and the results of its operations and its cash flows for each of the three years in the period ended December 31, 2020, in conformity with accounting principles generally accepted in the United States of America. Also, in our opinion, such a financial statement schedule, when considered in relation to the basic consolidated financial statements taken as a whole, presents fairly, in all material respects, the information set forth therein.
DELOITTE & TOUCHE LLP

Operational Audits

Both internal audit departments and independent audit firms perform operational audits. An **operational audit** is an evaluation of activities, systems, and internal controls within a company to determine their efficiency, effectiveness, and economy. Operational auditing goes beyond accounting records and financial statements to obtain a full understanding of the operations of a company. Companies dedicated to continuous quality improvement often use operational audits to identify specific areas where they need to improve the quality of their operations or products.

Auditors design operational audits to assess the quality and efficiency of operational performance, identify opportunities for improvement, and develop specific recommendations for improvement. The scope of an operational audit can be very narrow, such as a review and evaluation of the procedures for processing cash receipts, or quite broad, such as a review and evaluation of all of the internal controls in a computerized accounting system.

REVIEW 5.6

Match the description in the left-hand column with the type of audit in the right-hand column:

1. Conducted by company employees
2. Conducted by independent auditors
3. Conducted by both independent auditors and internal auditors
4. Primary purpose is to report on the fairness of a company's financial statements
5. Evaluation of the efficiency and effectiveness of company activities

a. Internal audit
b. Financial statement audit
c. Operational audit

The solution is on page 176.

APPENDIX 5B: Preparing the Bank Reconciliation

LO7 **Illustrate** the bank reconciliation process.

Exhibit 5B-1 outlines the structure of a company's bank reconciliation. The bank reconciliation is really two schedules prepared side by side. The schedule on the left includes bank items, and the schedule on the right includes items related to the company's cash account balance.

EXHIBIT 5B-1 Structure of a Company's Bank Reconciliation

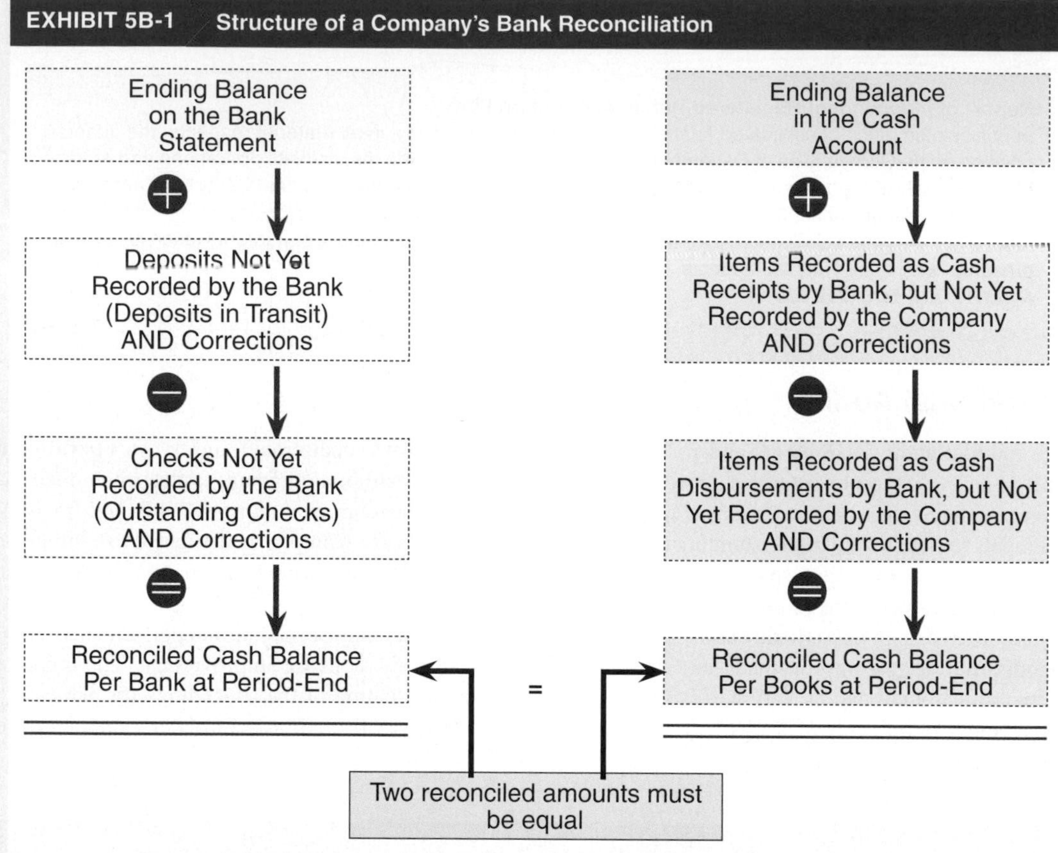

The schedule on the left begins with the ending cash balance from the bank statement (the month-end balance according to the bank's records). The internal audit department employee preparing the reconciliation adds (1) deposits not yet recorded by the bank, called **deposits in transit**, and (2) any corrections not yet made by the bank that will increase the bank balance. The preparer then subtracts (1) checks not yet recorded by the bank, called **outstanding checks**, and (2) any corrections not yet made by the bank that will decrease the bank balance. The resulting total is the *reconciled cash balance per bank at period-end.*

The schedule on the right begins with the ending balance in the Cash account in the company's general ledger. The internal audit department employee adds (1) items recorded as cash receipts by the bank but not yet recorded in the company's journals and (2) any corrections not yet made by the company that will increase the general ledger cash balance. The preparer subtracts (1) items recorded as cash disbursements by the bank but not yet recorded in the company's journals and (2) any corrections not yet made by the company that will decrease the general ledger cash balance. The resulting total is the *reconciled cash balance per books at period-end.* The totals of the two schedules should be the same.

EXHIBIT 5B-2 Wilson Corporation Bank Statement

ANCHOR NATIONAL BANK
123 Center Street
Madison, Wisconsin 53701

Wilson Corporation
1847 Elmwood Avenue
Madison, Wisconsin 53712

Account Number 27-31020558
Statement Date November 30

Deposits and Credits		Checks and Debits			Daily Balance	
Date	**Amount**	**Number**	**Date**	**Amount**	**Date**	**Amount**
Nov. 01	420.00	149	Nov. 02	125.00	Nov. 01	6,060.30
Nov. 02	630.00	154	Nov. 03	56.25	Nov. 02	6,565.30
Nov. 07	560.80	155	Nov. 10	135.00	Nov. 03	6,509.05
Nov. 10	480.25	156	Nov. 08	315.10	Nov. 07	6,801.19
Nov. 14	525.00	157	Nov. 07	233.26	Nov. 08	6,486.09
Nov. 17	270.25	158	Nov. 11	27.14	Nov. 10	6,831.34
Nov. 21	640.20	159	Nov. 18	275.00	Nov. 11	6,804.20
Nov. 26	300.00CM	160	Nov. 15	315.37	Nov. 14	7,329.20
Nov. 26	475.00	161	Nov. 17	76.40	Nov. 15	7,013.83
Nov. 30	471.40	162	Nov. 21	325.60	Nov. 17	7,207.68
		163	Nov. 21	450.00	Nov. 18	6,932.68
		164	Nov. 23	239.00	Nov. 21	6,731.58
		165	Nov. 21	65.70	Nov. 23	6,492.58
		166	Nov. 28	482.43	Nov. 26	7,262.58
		169	Nov. 28	260.00	Nov. 28	6,520.15
		170	Nov. 30	122.50	Nov. 30	6,488.95
		171	Nov. 30	370.10		
			Nov. 07	35.40RT		
			Nov. 26	5.00DM		
			Nov. 30	10.00SC		

Beginning Balance	+	Deposits and Credits	–	Checks and Debits	=	Ending Balance
$5,640.30	+	$4,772.90	–	$3,924.25	=	$6,488.95

Item Codes: EC: Error Correction DM: Debit Memo CM: Credit Memo SC: Service Charge OD: Overdraft RT: Returned Item IN: Interest Earned

Bank Reconciliation Illustrated The bank statement from Anchor National Bank for the Wilson Corporation's checking accounts as of November 30 of the current year is presented in **Exhibit 5B-2**.

In the body of the bank statement, the bank lists Wilson's deposits and other credits on the left, Wilson's checks (in numerical order) and other debits in the center, and Wilson's daily account balance on the right. From the bank's perspective, credits represent increases to Wilson's account, while debits equal decreases. The daily account balance is the balance in the account as of the end of each day listed. The bank presents a summary calculation of Wilson's ending account balance near the bottom of the statement.

The bank may make adjustments to the checking account. These adjustments may include: corrections of errors made by the bank; automatic loan payments and bank charges for items such as collecting notes; amounts collected by the bank for the depositor; fees charged by the bank for the checking account; fees for an overdraft (a negative balance in the account); NSF (non-sufficient funds) checks for which the bank could not collect cash; and interest earned added to the account.

Assume that the internal auditor of the Wilson Corporation is preparing the November 30 bank reconciliation. She uses the following procedures to reconcile the November 30 bank statement balance of $6,488.95 (see **Exhibit 5B-2**) to the November 30 general ledger Cash account balance of $4,872.69:

1. **Trace outstanding items on the bank reconciliation for the previous month to the current bank statement.** Any items on the previous bank reconciliation that have still not been processed by the bank must appear on the current bank reconciliation. The October 31 reconciliation included the following:

Deposit in transit		$420.00
Outstanding checks:	Number 149	$125.00
	Number 154	56.25
	Number 155	135.00

   The November 30 bank statement includes the $420 deposit and all three checks listed above. Therefore, none of these items will appear on the November 30 bank reconciliation.

2. **Compare the deposits made during the month to the deposits on the bank statement.** The Wilson Corporation made the following deposits during November:

November 2	$630.00	November 21	$640.20
November 7	560.80	November 26	475.00
November 10	480.25	November 29	471.40
November 14	525.00	November 30	225.00
November 17	270.25		

   All of these deposits appear on the bank statement except for the November 30 deposit of $225. The $225 deposit will appear on the left side of the November 30 bank reconciliation as a deposit in transit.

3. **Compare the checks issued during the month to the checks on the bank statement.** The Wilson Corporation issued the following checks during November:

Number 156	$315.10	Number 165	$ 65.70
Number 157	233.26	Number 166	482.43
Number 158	27.14	Number 167	301.66
Number 159	275.00	Number 168	149.50
Number 160	315.37	Number 169	260.00
Number 161	76.40	Number 170	122.50
Number 162	325.60	Number 171	370.10
Number 163	450.00	Number 172	450.00
Number 164	239.00	Number 173	240.50

   Four of the checks—numbers 167, 168, 172, and 173—do not appear on the bank statement. These four checks will appear on the left side of the November 30 bank reconciliation as outstanding checks.

4. **Scan the bank statement for bank adjustments not yet reflected in the general ledger.** The Wilson Corporation's bank statement contains a charge of $35.40 for a returned item, a debit memo of $5.00, and a service charge of $10.00 in the checks and other debits column. The deposits and other credits column contains a credit memo for $300.00. Supplemental information sent by the bank with the bank statement reveals that the bank charged a $35.40 NSF check against Wilson's account, collected a $300.00 note for Wilson and charged a $5.00 collection fee, and that the service charge for the month of November was $10.00. These four items have not yet been recorded by Wilson Corporation. Therefore, they must be listed on the right side of the bank reconciliation.

5. **Check for errors.** The Wilson Corporation recorded check number 159 as $725.00. The correct amount of $275.00 appears on the bank statement. The check was written to pay for office supplies. The correction of the transposition in the amount of $450 must be listed on the right side of the bank reconciliation.

After the five preceding procedures have been completed, the November 30 bank reconciliation for the Wilson Corporation appears as shown in **Exhibit 5B-3**. Note that both the left side and the right side of the reconciliation end with a reconciled cash balance and that the two amounts are the same. This reconciled cash balance is the amount that will appear on the November 30 balance sheet for the company.

EXHIBIT 5B-3 Bank Reconciliation for Wilson Corporation

WILSON CORPORATION
Bank Reconciliation
November 30

Ending balance from bank statement		$6,488.95	Balance from general ledger		$4,872.69
Add: Deposits in transit.		225.00	Add: Check 159 for $275 recorded as $725 .		450.00
			Collection of note . . .	$300.00	
		6,713.95	Less: Collection fee	5.00	295.00
					5,617.69
Less: Outstanding checks:					
No. 167	$301.66		Less: NSF check	35.40	
No. 168	149.50		Service charge	10.00	45.40
No. 172	450.00				
No. 173	240.50	1,141.66			
Reconciled cash balance per bank . . .		$5,572.29	Reconciled cash balance per books.		$5,572.29

Before the Wilson Corporation prepares its financial statements for November, Wilson must make adjusting entries to bring the balance in the Cash account into agreement with the reconciled cash balance on the bank reconciliation. The Transaction Analysis for each adjustment follows:

Transaction: *Bank reconcilation adjustments.*

Assets	=	Liabilities	+	Contrib. Capital	+	Retained Earnings	Revenues	−	Expenses	=	Net Income
+450 Cash	=		+			+450.00		−	−450.00 Office supplies expense	=	+450.00
Correct recording error on check number 159.											
+295.00 Cash −300.00 Notes receivable	=		+			−5.00		−	+5.00 Miscellaneous expense	=	−5.00
Record a note collected by the bank, less a collection fee.											
+35.40 Accounts receivable −35.40 Cash	=		+					−		=	
Reclassify an NSF check as an account receivable.											
−10.00 Cash	=		+			−10.00		−	+10.00 Miscellaneous expense	=	−10.00
Record bank service charge for November.											

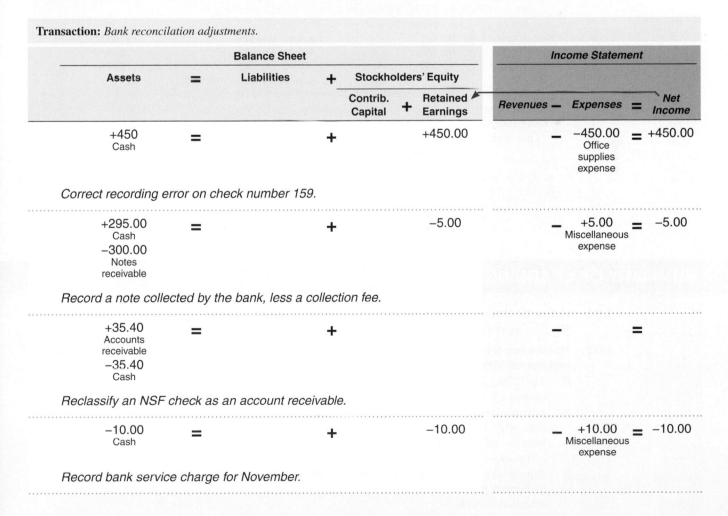

(Balance Sheet: Assets = Liabilities + Stockholders' Equity; Income Statement: Revenues − Expenses = Net Income, Net Income flows to Retained Earnings.)

ACCOUNTING IN PRACTICE

Accounting Trick to Catch Transpositions Transposing numbers is one of the most frequent causes of errors in bank reconciliations. Transposing numbers occurs when they are written in the wrong sequence. Recording 87 instead of 78 or 149 instead of 194 are examples of transposition errors. Fortunately, there is an easy way to detect transposition errors. If you find that the number you arrive at differs from the bank's number by a multiple of 9, chances are it is a transposition error because all transpositions, no matter what numbers are transposed, will cause an error evenly divisible by 9.

REVIEW 5.7

At December 31 the Cash account in the Tyler Company's general ledger had a balance of $18,434.27. The December 31 bank statement showed a balance of $19,726.40. In reconciling the two amounts, you discover the following:

1. Bank deposits made by Tyler on December 31 amounting to $2,145.40 do not appear on the bank statement.
2. A non-interest-bearing note receivable from the Smith Company for $2,000, left with the bank for collection, was collected by the bank at the end of December. The bank credited the proceeds, less a $5 collection charge, on the bank statement. Tyler Company has not recorded the collection.
3. Accompanying the bank statement is a debit memorandum indicating that John Miller's check for $450 was charged against Tyler's bank account on December 30 because of insufficient funds.
4. Check No. 586, written for advertising expense of $869.10, was recorded as $896.10 by Tyler Company.
5. A comparison of the paid checks returned by the bank with the recorded disbursements revealed that the following checks are still outstanding as of December 31:

No. 561	$306.63	No. 591	$190.00
No. 585	440.00	No. 592	282.50
No. 588	476.40	No. 593	243.00

6. The bank mistakenly charged Tyler Company's account for check printing costs of $30.50, which should have been charged to Taylor Company.
7. The bank charged Tyler Company's account $42.50 for the rental of a safe deposit box. No entry has been made in Tyler's records for this expense.

Required

a. Prepare a bank reconciliation as of December 31.

b. Using the TAT, identify the adjustments Tyler Company will record at December 31.

The solution is on pages 176–177.

SUMMARY OF LEARNING OBJECTIVES

LO1 Define the three elements of fraud. (p. 146)

- The fraud triangle consists of three parts: (1) pressure, (2) rationalization, and (3) opportunity.

LO2 Discuss how the COSO framework helps prevent fraud, identify potential internal control failures, and discuss SOX regulations. (p. 147)

- The COSO framework identifies five internal control components: (1) the control environment; (2) risk assessment; (3) control activities; (4) information and communication; and (5) monitoring activities.
- Internal controls are the measures undertaken by a company to ensure the reliability of its accounting data, protect its assets from theft or unauthorized use, ensure that employees follow the company's policies and procedures, and evaluate the performance of employees, departments, divisions, and the company as a whole.
- A prevention control is designed to deter problems before they arise. A detection control is designed to discover problems soon after they arise. Prevention controls are generally more desirable than detection controls.

- A company should incorporate the following concepts when it designs its internal control:
  - Establish clear lines of authority and responsibility.
  - Implement segregation of duties.
  - Hire competent personnel.
  - Use control numbers on all business documents.
  - Develop plans and budgets.
  - Maintain adequate accounting records.
  - Provide physical and electronic controls.
- The internal control system must be monitored in order to assess the quality of the system's performance over time. One type of monitoring activity is an internal audit.
- Occasionally, internal controls fail. To compensate, many businesses purchase a fidelity bond, an insurance policy that provides financial compensation for theft by employees specifically covered by the insurance.
- For public companies, strong internal controls are required by law. The Sarbanes-Oxley Act (SOX) mandates that all publicly traded U.S. corporations maintain an adequate system of internal controls, that top management ensures the reliability of these controls, and that outside independent auditors attest to the adequacy of the controls. Failing to do so can result in prison sentences of up to 20 years and/or monetary fines of up to $5 million.

Define cash and discuss the accounting for cash. (p. 150) LO3

- Cash includes coins, currency (paper money), checks, money orders, traveler's checks, and funds on deposit at a financial institution in a company's checking accounts and savings accounts.
- A company can have one or more cash accounts. Cash is a current asset.
- A company may combine certain short-term, highly liquid investments with cash and present a single amount called *cash and cash equivalents.*

Describe the internal controls for cash. (p. 151) LO4

- Two broad elements underlie all strong cash internal control systems:
  - Written policies and procedures over the handling and accounting for cash.
  - Segregation of duties.
- Most payments by customers occur in one of these five forms: (1) electronic; (2) cash; (3) check; (4) credit card; or (5) debit card.
  - The single largest form of consumer transactions in terms of numbers is cash.
  - The single largest form of consumer transactions in terms of dollar volume is electronic.
  - Controls over Electronic funds transfers (EFT) are primarily concerned with security and customer privacy.
  - The primary control challenges for companies that receive cash in the form of currency or check is physical security to ensure against theft.
  - As with EFTs, the internal control concerns regarding debit and credit cards primarily involve security and customer privacy.
- Internal controls over checks include signature cards held by the bank, which guard against forgery. Internal controls over petty cash include replenishment of the fund by check, thereby leaving a paper trail.

Describe the four primary activities of effective cash management. (p. 154) LO5

- Cash should be monitored using the statement of cash flows.
- Effective cash management includes monitoring and managing accounts receivable, inventory, and accounts payable, and investing any excess cash.

Appendix 5A: Describe financial statement audits and operational audits. (p. 156) LO6

- A financial statement audit is an examination of a company's financial statements by a firm of independent certified public accountants. The firm issues an audit report upon completion of the audit.
- An operational audit is an evaluation of activities, systems, and internal controls within a company to determine their efficiency, effectiveness, and economy.

Appendix 5B: Illustrate the bank reconciliation process. (p. 158) LO7

- A bank reconciliation is a schedule that (1) accounts for all differences between the ending cash balance of the bank statement and the ending cash balance of the Cash account in a company's general ledger and (2) determines the reconciled cash balance as of the end of the month.
- The procedure used to prepare the bank reconciliation involves five steps:
  - Trace outstanding items on the bank reconciliation from the previous month to the current bank statement.

- Compare the deposits made during the month to the deposits on the bank statement.
- Compare the checks issued during the month to the checks on the bank statement.
- Scan the bank statement for charges and credits not yet reflected in the general ledger.
- Check for errors.

SUMMARY	Concept	Method	Assessment
TAKEAWAY 5.1	Are the internal controls adequate?	The COSO framework identifies five internal control components: (1) the control environment, (2) risk assessment, (3) control activities, (4) information and communication, and (5) monitoring activities.	Monitoring activities include appraisals of the company's internal control system. If weaknesses are reported, be cautious in relying on the reported financial statements.

KEY TERMS

Audit report (p. 156)
Bank reconciliation (p. 153)
Cash (p. 150)
Cash and cash equivalents (p. 151)
Certificates of deposit (CDs) (p. 150)
Check (p. 153)
Control activities (p. 148)
Control environment (p. 147)
Control numbers (p. 148)
Deposits in transit (p. 158)
Detection control (p. 148)
Electronic funds transfers (EFT) (p. 152)
Employee collusion (p. 149)
Financial statement audit (p. 156)
Fraud (p. 146)
Fraud triangle (p. 146)
Internal audit (p. 149)
Internal controls (p. 148)
Monitoring activities (p. 149)
Non-sufficient funds check (NSF check) (p. 150)
Operational audit (p. 157)
Outstanding checks (p. 158)
Petty cash fund (p. 153)
Prevention control (p. 148)
Public Company Accounting Oversight Board (PCAOB) (p. 150)
Risk assessment (p. 148)
Sarbanes-Oxley Act (p. 149)
Segregation of duties (p. 148)

SELF-STUDY QUESTIONS

(Answers to the Self-Study Questions are at the end of the chapter.)

LO1 Homework MBC

1. Which of the following is not one of the three elements of the fraud triangle?
a. Pressure
b. Rationalization
c. Embezzlement
d. Opportunity

LO2 Homework MBC

2. Which of the following is not a common internal control concept?
a. Establish clear lines of responsibility
b. Provide physical and electronic controls
c. Collusion among employees
d. Separate work functions

LO2 Homework MBC

3. Which of the following are considered good internal control practices?

a. Job rotation
b. Required vacations
c. Only promoting from within
d. Both *a* and *b*

LO2 Homework MBC

4. Burton Company should utilize all except one of the following concepts related to placing control numbers on business documents. Which concept should Burton not use?
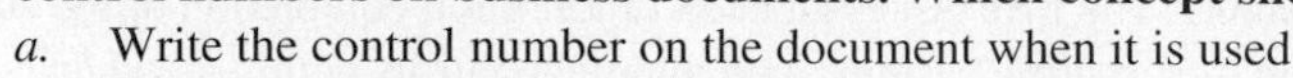
a. Write the control number on the document when it is used.
b. Place control numbers on all business documents.
c. Use the documents in strict numerical sequence.
d. Periodically account for all numbers used.

LO6 (Appendix 5A) Homework MBC

5. An operational audit is:
a. Just another word for a financial statement audit
b. Only performed by independent auditors
c. Used to assess the quality and efficiency of operational performance
d. Usually reported to the public along with the financial statements

6. Which of the following statements is correct regarding the reporting of cash? LO3

a. Money market funds are always shown as a noncurrent asset
b. Cash is shown as the first asset on the balance sheet
c. US Treasury bills are never considered cash or cash equivalent.
d. If a company maintains more than one bank account, each must be shown separately on the balance sheet

7. Which of the following is not a common form of cash payment? LO4

a. Electronic
b. Gold bullion
c. Check
d. Credit card

8. What is a bank reconciliation? LO5

a. A formal financial statement that lists all of a firm's bank account balances
b. A merger of two banks that previously were competitors
c. A statement sent monthly by a bank to a depositor that lists all deposits, checks paid, and other credits and charges to the depositor's account for the month
d. A schedule that accounts for differences between a firm's cash balance as shown on its bank statement and the balance shown in its general ledger Cash account

9. In a bank reconciliation, outstanding checks are: LO7 **(Appendix 5B)**

a. Deducted from the bank balance
b. Added to the bank balance
c. Deducted from the general ledger balance
d. Added to the general ledger balance

10. Which of the following statements about a petty cash fund is not true? LO5

a. The fund is managed on an imprest basis.
b. The fund is used to pay for minor items such as postage and delivery charges.
c. The fund should have a balance large enough to support one replenishment per year.
d. All replenishments are made by check.

QUESTIONS

1. Describe the three elements of the fraud triangle and how they relate to each other.
2. Explain why supervision is an important internal control.
3. Define and contrast prevention controls and detection controls. Which are more desirable?
4. Yates Company is reviewing its internal procedures to try to improve the company's internal control. It specifically wants to separate work functions. What three types of work functions must be separated to improve internal control?
5. Janet Jones is considered one of the rising stars at Finch Company. Janet is very hard working and has not taken a vacation in three years. Explain why this is a violation of good internal control.
6. Kwong Industries is redesigning its business documents. What three rules should Kwong follow relative to the use of control numbers on business documents?
7. In what way did the Sarbanes-Oxley Act impact the need for internal control?
8. How are a financial statement audit and an operational audit similar and different?
9. What types of items are included in cash? What are the two important characteristics of an item of cash?
10. Which of the following are considered to be cash: paper money, certificates of deposit, traveler's checks, funds in a checking account, and money orders?
11. What is electronic funds transfer (EFT)?
12. What is the purpose of a bank reconciliation?
13. In preparing a bank reconciliation, how should you determine (a) deposits not recorded in the bank statement and (b) outstanding checks?
14. Indicate whether the following bank reconciliation items should be (1) added to the bank statement balance, (2) deducted from the bank statement balance, (3) added to the ledger account balance, or (4) deducted from the ledger account balance:
    a. Bank service charge.
    b. NSF check.
    c. Deposit in transit.
    d. Outstanding check.
    e. Bank error charging company's account with another company's check.
    f. Difference of $270 in amount of check written for $410 but recorded by the company as $140.

15. Name two concepts that underlie strong internal controls over cash.

16. What is an imprest petty cash fund? How is such a fund established and replenished?

17. Carter Manufacturing Company makes a variety of consumer products. For the year just ended (and the two prior years), sales of private-label product to Mega-Mart (1,200 stores nationwide) have made up 60 to 65 percent of total sales. On December 31 of the year just ended, Mega-Mart informed Carter that it would be buying all private-label products from another manufacturer under a five-year contract. Losing this business will result in a 50 to 55 percent reduction in total gross profit for Carter.

a. What is the going concern concept and how does it apply to this situation?

b. How should the full disclosure principle be applied when preparing the annual report for the year just ended?

c. What is the independent auditor's responsibility in this situation?

DATA ANALYTICS

The assignments in this Data Analytics section are designed to familiarize you with the tools used in analyzing data and communicating the results. Appendix F provides an in-depth discussion of data analytics and blockchain technology.

DA5-1. Differentiating Between Different Types of Data Analytics

For CPAs, we commonly consider four types of data analytics: descriptive analytics, diagnostic analytics, predictive analytics, and prescriptive analytics. To understand the differences between these four types, review Appendix F to this text and refer to *The Next Frontier in Data Analytics* by N. Tschakert, J. Kokina, S. Kozlowski, and M. Vasarhelyi in the *Journal of Accountancy* found at https://www.journalofaccountancy.com/issues/2016/aug/data-analytics-skills.html.

REQUIRED

For each of the following ten examples, indicate which type of data analytics best applies (descriptive, diagnostic, predictive, or prescriptive).

1. Analyzing the trends of collections over the past three years for a customer and using that information to estimate the customer's collection schedule over the upcoming year.
2. Preparing a horizontal analysis, showing changes in expenses over the prior year.
3. Analyzing a significant change in operating expenses over the prior year by drilling down to specific categories that were over budget, down to specific departments, down to specific time periods.
4. An analysis of inventory turns by product in conjunction with an analysis of web clicks for the related product resulted in a list of products to phase out over the next year.
5. Preparing a forecast of sales by major segment using a regression analysis.
6. The relations of a digital marketing campaign and resulting sales is used to budget sales in the following year given the plan for upcoming digital marketing campaigns.
7. An analysis of the relations between the costs of five recent digital marketing campaigns and resulting sales was used to recommend digital marking campaigns to pursue in the future.
8. Preparing monthly unaudited financial statements by department.
9. Examining trends in gross margin at a product level to understand the cause of a drop in overall gross margin.
10. Preparing a data visualization showing how many of the company's current customers are self-employed.

DA5-2. Displaying Key Performance Indicators in Excel

A key performance indicator (KPI) is a quantifiable measure used to track a company's overall performance. Managers can create a KPI dashboard, which is a data visualization that displays all indicators in one central location. This allows a manager to conveniently track and monitor key operational data. Information in KPI dashboards may even be updated in real time. For this exercise, we use the data included in the Excel file associated with this exercise for Wakeboards Inc. to create a data visualization (dashboard). Wakeboards Inc. manufactures and sells three types of wakeboards to 50 customers located primarily in oceanside cities in the U.S.

REQUIRED

1. Download Excel file DA5-2 found in myBusinessCourse.
2. Create the following six PivotCharts arranged as one KPI dashboard using the data included in file DA5-2.

a. Top five customers for Model 1 in a bar chart. *Hint:* Click anywhere inside the data table and open the Insert tab. Click PivotTable in the Tables group. Add the PivotTable to a new worksheet. Drag Customer Name to Rows; Model 1 Sales Units to Values. In the PivotTable, open the dropdown menu next to RowLabels and select Top 10 in the Values Filter menu. Change to Top 5. Click anywhere inside the PivotTable and open the PivotTable Analyze tab. Click PivotChart in the Tools group. Select Bar. Click inside the bars and click Format Data Labels.

b. Top five customers for Model 2 in a bar chart. *Hint:* Highlight all cells in the PivotTable created in part *a*. Right-click and select Copy. Move to another location on the same worksheet. Right-click and select Paste. Make the appropriate changes to the second PivotTable.

c. Top five customers for Model 3 in a bar chart.

d. Sales in units by model by month in a line chart. *Hint:* Months in Rows; Model 1, 2, and 3 Sales Units fields to Values.

e. Most recent monthly sales (December) in a pie chart showing the proportion by Model number. *Hint:* Months in Columns; Model 1, 2, and 3 Sales Units fields to Values.

f. Sales in units by customer by month with a slicer for Customer name and Months. *Hint:* Customer Name and Months fields to Rows; Model 1, 2, and 3 Sales Units fields to Values. Click inside the chart and open the PivotTable Analyze tab. Click Insert Slicer and select Customer Name and Months. Slicers are used to filter the data included in PivotTables.

3. Use the visualizations to answer the following questions.

a. List the third largest customer for Model 1.

b. List the first largest customer for Model 2.

c. List the fifth largest customer for Model 3.

d. List the peak month for sales of Model 1.

e. List the quantity of sales in December for Model 2.

f. List the quantity of sales of Model 1, Model 2, and Model 3 for Marina Inc. in June.

DA5-3. Using Tableau for Fraud Detection
Refer to PF-25 in Appendix F. This problem uses Tableau to apply Benford's Law to detect fraud in reimbursement request data from an actual court case.

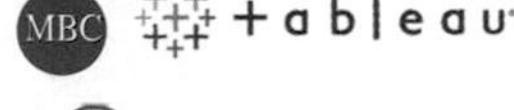

Assignments with the MBC logo in the margin are available in myBusinessCourse. See the Preface of the book for details.

SHORT EXERCISES

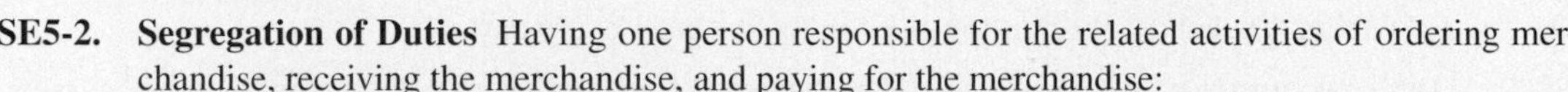

SE5-1. The Fraud Triangle Each of the following is part of the fraud triangle except: LO1

a. pressure.
b. opportunity.
c. concealment.
d. rationalization.

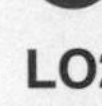

SE5-2. Segregation of Duties Having one person responsible for the related activities of ordering merchandise, receiving the merchandise, and paying for the merchandise: LO2

a. provides increased security over the firm's assets.
b. is an example of good internal control.
c. is a good example of segregation of duties.
d. increases the potential of fraud.

SE5-3. Internal Control Internal controls do each of the following except: LO2

a. protect assets from theft.
b. evaluate the performance of employees.
c. guarantee the accuracy of the accounting records.
d. increase the likelihood that any errors will be caught.

SE5-4. Auditors Which of the following is true? LO6 (Appendix 5A)

a. Internal auditors are independent of the company they audit.
b. Internal audits provide appraisals of a company's internal control.
c. The company being audited cannot pay the external auditing firm since this would violate their independence.
d. Outside parties prefer appraisals by internal auditors over those of external auditors since they know more about the company being audited.

LO6 (Appendix 5A) **SE5-5. Financial Statement Audit** The financial statement audit of public companies is:

a. conducted by the internal auditors.
b. conducted by auditors overseen by the American Institute of Certified Public Accountants.
c. conducted by auditors overseen by the Public Company Accounting Oversight Board.
d. only necessary if fraud is suspected.

LO3 **SE5-6. Cash** Cash includes each of the following except:

a. an NSF check.
b. currency.
c. money orders.
d. funds in a checking account.

LO3 **SE5-7. Cash Equivalents** Cash equivalents:

a. include crypto currencies.
b. must be shown as a noncurrent asset.
c. are shown as a liability.
d. include certain short-term, highly liquid investments.

LO4 **SE5-8. Electronic Funds Transfer** Electronic funds transfer (EFT) involves transferring cash from one location to another using:

a. armored trucks.
b. computers.
c. bicycle messengers.
d. the mail service.

LO5 **SE5-9. Cash Management** Effective cash management involves all the following except:

a. manage accounts receivable.
b. manage inventory.
c. invest excess cash.
d. conduct internal audits.

LO2 **SE5-10. COSO Framework** The COSO framework identifies five internal control components. The internal control components include each of the following except:

a. segregation of duties.
b. risk assessment.
c. monitoring activities.
d. control activities.

EXERCISES

LO2, 4 **E5-1. Internal Control** Explain how each of the following procedures strengthens a company's internal control:

a. After preparing a check for a cash disbursement, the accountant for Travis Lumber Company cancels the supporting business documents (purchase order, receiving report, and invoice) by stamping them PAID.
b. The salespeople for Davis Department Store give each customer a cash register receipt along with the proper change. A sign on each cash register states that no refunds or exchanges are allowed without the related cash register receipt.
c. The ticket-taker at the Esquire Theater tears each admission ticket in half and gives one half back to the ticket purchaser. The seat number is printed on each half of the ticket.
d. John Renaldo's restaurant provides servers with prenumbered customers' checks. The servers are to void checks with mistakes on them and issue new ones rather than make corrections on them. Voided checks must be given to the manager every day.

LO4 **E5-2. Internal Controls for Cash Received on Account** Hudson Company sells supplies to restaurants. Most sales are made on account. Hudson has requested your help in designing procedures for processing checks received from its customers. Briefly describe the procedures that should be used to safeguard cash.

LO7 (Appendix 5B) **E5-3. Bank Reconciliation** Use the following information to prepare a bank reconciliation for Young Company at June 30:

1. Balance per Cash account, June 30, $7,055.80.
2. Balance per bank statement, June 30, $7,300.25.
3. Deposits not reflected on bank statement, $725.
4. Outstanding checks, June 30, $1,260.45.
5. Service charge on bank statement not recorded in books, $11.
6. Error by bank—Yertel Company check charged on Young Company's bank statement, $550.
7. Check for advertising expense, $250, incorrectly recorded in books as $520.

E5-4. Bank Reconciliation Components Identify the requested amount in each of the following situations: LO7 (Appendix 5B)

a. Munsing Company's May 31 bank reconciliation shows deposits in transit of $1,400. The general ledger Cash account shows total cash receipts during June of $57,300. The June bank statement shows total cash deposits of $55,900. What amount of deposits in transit should appear in the June 30 bank reconciliation?

b. Sandusky Company's August 31 bank reconciliation shows outstanding checks of $2,100. The general ledger Cash account shows total cash disbursements (all by check) during September of $50,300. The September bank statement shows $49,200 of checks clearing the bank. What amount of outstanding checks should appear in the September 30 bank reconciliation?

c. Fremont Corporation's March 31 bank reconciliation shows deposits in transit of $800. The general ledger Cash account shows total cash receipts during April of $38,000. The April bank statement shows total cash deposits of $37,100 (including $1,300 from the collection of a note; the note collection has not yet been recorded by Fremont). What amount of deposits in transit should appear in the April 30 bank reconciliation?

E5-5. External versus Internal Audit Explain why parties outside the company, such as bankers and stockholders, prefer an independent appraisal of the company's financial results rather than relying on the work of internal auditors. LO6 (Appendix 5A)

E5-6. Operational Audits Explain the nature of an operational audit. LO6 (Appendix 5A)

E5-7. Cash and Cash Equivalents Identify each of the following items as either cash (C), cash equivalents (CE), or neither (N): LO3

a. Coin
b. U.S. treasury bills
c. Checks
d. Six-month certificate of deposit
e. Currency

E5-8. Internal Control Explain how each of the following actions strengthens a company's system of internal control: LO2

a. Separate work functions.
b. Hire competent personnel.
c. Develop plans and budgets.
d. Use control numbers on all business documents.

E5-9. Effective Cash Management Explain how each of the following activities can improve a company's cash management: LO5

a. Manage accounts receivable.
b. Manage inventory.
c. Manage accounts payable.
d. Invest excess cash.

PROBLEMS

P5-1. Internal Control Regent Company encountered the following situations: LO2, 4

a. The person who opens the mail for Regent, Bill Stevens, stole a check from a customer and cashed it. To cover up the theft, he increased Sales Returns and Allowances and decreased Accounts Receivable in the general ledger. He also posted the amount to the customer's account in the accounts receivable subsidiary ledger.

b. The purchasing agent, Susan Martin, used a company purchase order to order building materials from Builders Mart. Later, she telephoned Builders Mart and changed the delivery address to her home address. She told Builders Mart to charge the material to the company. At month-end, she approved the invoice from Builders Mart for payment.

c. Nashville Supply Company sent two invoices for the same order: the first on June 10 and the second on July 20. The accountant authorized payment of both invoices, and both were paid.

d. On January 1, Jack Monty, a junior accountant for Regent, was given the responsibility of recording all general journal entries. At the end of the year, the auditors discovered that Monty had made 150 serious errors in recording transactions. The chief accountant was unaware that Monty had been making mistakes.

REQUIRED

For each situation, describe any violations of good internal control procedures and identify the steps that you would take to prevent each situation.

LO2, 4 **P5-2.** **Internal Control** Each of the following lettered paragraphs briefly describes an independent situation involving some aspect of internal control.

REQUIRED

Answer the following questions.

a. Robert Flynn is the office manager of Oswald Company, a small wholesaling company. Flynn opens all incoming mail, makes bank deposits, and maintains both the general ledger and the accounts receivable subsidiary ledger. An assistant records transactions in the credit sales journal and the cash receipts journal. The assistant also prepares a monthly statement for each customer and mails the statements to the customers. These statements list the beginning balance, credit sales, cash receipts, adjustments, and ending balance for the month.

1. If Flynn stole Customer A's $200 check (payment in full) and made no effort to conceal his embezzlement in the ledgers, how would the misappropriation be discovered?
2. What routine accounting procedure would disclose Flynn's $200 embezzlement in part (1), even if Flynn destroyed Customer A's subsidiary ledger account?
3. What circumstances might disclose Flynn's theft if he posted a payment to Customer A's account in the accounts receivable subsidiary ledger and set up a $200 account for a fictitious customer?
4. In part (3), why might Flynn be anxious to open the mail himself each morning?
5. In part (3), why might Flynn want to have the authority to write off accounts considered uncollectible?

b. A doughnut shop uses a cash register that produces a printed receipt for each sale. The register also prints each transaction on a paper tape that is locked inside the cash register. Only the supervisor has access to the cash-register tape. A prominently displayed sign promises a free doughnut to any customer who is not given a cash-register receipt with his or her purchase. How is this procedure an internal control device for the doughnut shop?

c. Jason Miller, a swindler, sent several businesses invoices requesting payment for office supplies that had never been ordered or delivered to the businesses. A five percent discount was offered for prompt payment. What internal control procedures should prevent this swindle from being successful?

d. The cashier for Uptown Cafeteria is located at the end of the food line. After customers have selected their food items, the cashier rings up the prices of the food and the customer pays the bill. The customer line frequently stalls while the person paying searches for the correct amount of cash. To speed things up, the cashier often collects money from the next customer or two who have the correct change without ringing up their food on the register. After the first customer finally pays, the cashier rings up the amounts for the customers who have already paid. What is the internal control weakness in this procedure? How might the internal control over the collection of cash from the cafeteria customers be strengthened?

LO7 (Appendix 5B) **P5-3.** **Bank Reconciliation** On July 31, Sullivan Company's Cash account had a balance of $7,216.60. On that date, the bank statement indicated a balance of $9,098.55. A comparison of returned checks and bank advices revealed the following:

1. Deposits in transit July 31 amounted to $3,576.95.
2. Outstanding checks July 31 totaled $1,467.90.
3. The bank erroneously charged a $325 check of Solomon Company against the Sullivan bank account.
4. A $25 bank service charge has not yet been recorded by Sullivan Company.
5. Sullivan neglected to record $4,000 borrowed from the bank on a ten percent six-month note. The bank statement shows the $4,000 as a deposit.
6. Included with the returned checks is a memo indicating that J. Martin's check for $640 had been returned NSF. Martin, a customer, had sent the check to pay an account of $660 less a $20 discount.
7. Sullivan Company recorded a $109 payment for repairs as $1,090.

REQUIRED

a. Prepare a bank reconciliation for Sullivan Company at July 31.

b. Using the TAT, identify the adjustments necessary to bring the Cash account into agreement with the reconciled cash balance on the bank reconciliation.

P5-4. Bank Reconciliation The bank reconciliation made by Winton, Inc., on August 31 showed a deposit in transit of $1,280 and two outstanding checks, No. 597 for $830 and No. 603 for $640. The reconciled cash balance on August 31 was $14,110. LO7 (Appendix 5B)

The following bank statement is available for September:

Bank Statement

TO Winton, Inc. St. Louis, MO — September 30 STATE BANK

Date	Deposits	Date	No.	Charges	Date	Balance
					Aug. 31	$14,300
Sept. 1	$1,280	Sept. 1	597	$ 830	Sept. 1	14,750
2	1,120	5	607	1,850	2	15,870
5	850	5	608	1,100	5	13,770
9	744	9	609	552	8	13,130
15	1,360	8	610	640	9	13,322
17	1,540	17	611	488	15	14,008
25	1,028	15	612	674	17	15,060
30	680	25	614	920	25	15,168
		29	NSF	1,028	29	14,140
		30	SC	36	30	14,784

Item Codes: EC: Error Correction; SC: Service Charge; IN: Interest Earned; DM: Debit Memo; OD: Overdraft; NSF: Non-sufficient Funds; CM: Credit Memo; RT: Returned Item

A list of deposits made and checks written during September is shown below:

Deposits Made		Checks Written	
Sept. 1	$1,120	No. 607	$1,850
4	850	608	1,100
8	744	609	552
12	1,360	610	640
16	1,540	611	488
24	1,028	612	746
29	680	613	310
30	1,266	614	920
	$8,588	615	386
		616	420
			$7,412

The Cash account balance on September 30 was $15,286. In reviewing checks returned by the bank, the accountant discovered that check No. 612, written for $674 for advertising expense, was recorded in the cash disbursements journal as $746. The NSF check for $1,028, which Winton deposited on September 24, was a payment on account from customer D. Walker.

REQUIRED

a. Prepare a bank reconciliation for Winton, Inc., at September 30.

b. Using the TAT, identify the adjustments necessary to bring the Cash account into agreement with the reconciled cash balance on the bank reconciliation.

P5-5. Reporting Cash Jenkins Company has the following items at year-end. LO3

Currency and coin in safe	$ 3,500
Funds in savings account	25,250
Funds in checking account	6,750
Traveler's checks	500
Non-sufficient funds check	850
Money market fund	32,400

REQUIRED

Identify the amount of the above items that should be reported as cash and cash equivalents on Jenkins Company's balance sheet.

P5-6. Internal Control Bart Simons has worked for Dr. Homer Spring for many years. Bart has been a model employee. He has not taken a vacation in over four years, always stating that work was too LO2 important. One of Bart's primary jobs at the clinic is to open mail and list the checks received. He also collects cash from patients at the cashier's window as patients leave. There are times that things are so hectic that Bart does not bother to give the patient a receipt; however, he assures them that he will make sure their account is properly credited. When things slow down at the clinic Bart often offers to help Lisa post payments to the patients' accounts receivable ledger. Lisa is always happy to receive help since she is also quite busy and because Bart is such a careful worker.

REQUIRED

Identify any internal control principles that may be violated in Dr. Spring's clinic.

LO2, 4 **P5-7.** **Internal Control** Listed below are (a) four potential errors or problems that could occur in the processing of cash transactions and (b) internal control principles. Review each error or problem and identify an internal control principle that could reduce the chance of the error or problem occurring. You may also cite more than one principle if more than one applies, or write none if none of the principles will correct the error or problem.

1. An employee steals cash collected from a customer's accounts receivable and hides the theft by issuing a credit memorandum indicating the customer returned the merchandise.
2. An official with authority to sign checks is able to steal blank checks and issue them without detection.
3. Due to a labor shortage many employees are hired without sufficient skills with the thought they can "learn on the job."
4. A salesperson often rings up a sale for less than the actual amount and then pockets the additional cash collected from the customer.

Internal control principles:

a. Establish clear lines of authority and responsibility.
b. Segregate duties.
c. Hire competent personnel.
d. Use control numbers on all business documents.
e. Develop plans and budgets.
f. Maintain adequate accounting records.
g. Provide physical and electronic controls.
h. Conduct internal audits.

LO5 **P5-8.** **Effective Cash Management** Longo LLP is a new law firm struggling to manage its cash flow. Like all new businesses, the firm has not yet developed a sufficient client base to cover its operating costs. Additionally, the firm faced a number of large initial, but nonrecurring, start-up costs at the beginning of the year. Ongoing monthly costs include office rent and salary for a paralegal staff member. Another problem that the firm faces is that several of its major clients have failed to pay their current, but overdue, bills. Mick Longo, one of the two founding partners, has not taken any salary since the firm began operations over eight months ago, and has decided to maintain a part-time job bartending on weekends at a local resort to ensure that he has some cash to cover day-to-day expenses like travel.

REQUIRED

What suggestions would you make to Mick Longo to improve his firm's cash management practices?

SERIAL PROBLEM: ANGEL CITY GREETINGS

(Note: This is a continuation of the Serial Problem: Angel City Greetings from Chapters 1 through 4.)

SP5. On February 15, Kate Collins, owner of Angel City Greetings, asks you to investigate the cash handling activities in her business. She believes that a new employee might be stealing funds. "I have no proof," she says, "but I'm fairly certain that the January 31 undeposited receipts amounted to more than $12,000, although the January 31 bank reconciliation prepared by the cashier (who works in the treasurer's department) shows only $7,238.40. Also, the January bank reconciliation doesn't show several checks that have been outstanding for a long time. The cashier told me that these checks needn't appear on the reconciliation because he had notified the bank to stop payment on them and he had made the necessary adjustment on the books. Does that sound reasonable to you?"

At your request, Kate shows you the following January 31 bank reconciliation prepared by the cashier:

ANGEL CITY GREETINGS
Bank Reconciliation
January 31

Ending balance from bank statement. .		$ 4,843.69	Balance from general ledger		$10,893.89
Add: Deposits in transit.		7,238.40			
		$12,082.09			
Less:			Less:		
Outstanding checks:			Bank service charge	$ 60.00	
No. 2351	$1,100.20		Unrecorded credit	1,200.00	(1,260.00)
No. 2353	578.32				
No. 2354	969.68	(2,448.20)			
Reconciled cash balance per bank. . . .		$ 9,633.89	Reconciled cash balance per books. . . .		$ 9,633.89

You discover that the $1,200 unrecorded bank credit represents a note collected by the bank on Kate's behalf; it appears in the deposits column of the January bank statement. Your investigation also reveals that the December 31 bank reconciliation showed three checks that had been outstanding longer than 10 months: No. 1432 for $600, No. 1458 for $466.90, and No. 1512 for $253.10. You also discover that these items were never added back into the Cash account in Kate's books. In confirming that the checks shown on the cashier's January 31 bank reconciliation were outstanding on that date, you discover that check No. 2353 was actually a payment of $1,658.32 and had been recorded on the books for that amount.

To confirm the amount of undeposited receipts at January 31, you request a bank statement for February 1–12 (called a cutoff bank statement). This indeed shows a January 1 deposit of $7,238.40.

REQUIRED

a. Calculate the amount of funds stolen by the employee.
b. Describe how the employee concealed the theft.
c. What suggestions would you make to Kate about cash control procedures?

BEYOND THE NUMBERS

REPORTING AND ANALYSIS

BTN5-1. Financial Reporting Problem: Columbia Sportswear Company The financial statements for the Columbia Sportswear Company can be found in Appendix A at the end of this book.

Columbia Sportswear Company

Required
Use the financial statements and the accompanying notes to the financial statements to answer the following questions about Columbia Sportswear:

a. What title is used on Columbia's consolidated balance sheet for cash?
b. According to the information given in Note 2, what is the makeup of the cash and cash equivalents account?
c. According to information in Item 9A. Controls and Procedures, who is responsible for establishing and maintaining adequate internal control over financial reporting?
d. Deloitte and Touche, the independent auditor of Columbia Sportswear, issued a report on their audit of Columbia's internal control. What did they conclude?

BTN5-2. Comparative Analysis Problem: Columbia Sportswear Company vs. Under Armour, Inc. The financial statements for Columbia Sportswear Company can be found in Appendix A, and Under Armour, Inc.'s financial statements can be found in Appendix B at the end of this book.

Columbia Sportswear Company
Under Armour, Inc.

Required
Use the information in the companies' financial statements to answer the following questions:

a. What is the balance in cash and cash equivalents as of December 31, 2020?
b. What percentage of each company's total assets is made up of cash and cash equivalents as of December 31, 2020?
c. How much did cash and cash equivalents change during 2020 for each firm?
d. For each company, how did the change in cash for 2020 compare to its cash provided by operating activities?

BTN5-3. **Business Decision Problem** Qualitec Electronics Company is a distributor of microcomputers and related electronic equipment. The company has grown rapidly. It is located in a large building near Chicago, Illinois. Jack Flanigan, the president of Qualitec, has hired you to perform an internal control review of the company. You conduct interviews of key employees, tour the operations, and observe various company functions. You discover the following:

1. Qualitec has not changed its ordering procedures since it was formed eight years ago. Anyone in the company can prepare a purchase order and send it to the vendor without getting any managerial approval. When the invoice arrives from the vendor, it is compared only to the purchase order before authorizing payment.
2. Qualitec does not have an organization chart. In fact, employees are encouraged to work on their own, without supervision. Flanigan believes that this approach increases creativity.
3. Business documents have been carefully designed by the controller. When the printer prints the documents, no control numbers are printed on them. Instead, employees using a form write the next sequential number on the form. The controller believes that this approach ensures that a proper sequencing of numbers will be maintained.
4. No budgets are prepared for the company.
5. All doors to the building remain unlocked from 7:00 a.m. to 11:00 p.m. Employees normally work from 7:30 a.m. to 5:00 p.m. A private security firm drives to the building to unlock it each morning and lock it each night. The security firm's employee leaves immediately after unlocking or locking. The company does not use time clocks or employee badges.
6. Flanigan believes that audits (either external or internal) are a waste of time. He has resisted the bank president's urging to hire a CPA firm to conduct an audit.

Required
Analyze the findings listed above. Then list all the internal control weaknesses that you can identify. For each weakness, describe one or more internal controls that Qualitec should install to overcome the weakness.

BTN5-4. **Financial Analysis Problem** The **Public Company Accounting Oversight Board (PCAOB)** was created as part of the Sarbanes-Oxley legislation to provide oversight to U.S. accounting firms. The PCAOB's address is http://www.pcaobus.org

Required
Answer the following questions:

a. What is the mission of the PCAOB?
b. What is the title of auditing standard AS 2201 issued by the PCAOB?
c. According to the rules section of the site, what is required for a PCAOB rule to take effect? (*Hint:* Select "About" followed by "Rulemaking Docket")

CRITICAL THINKING

General Mills, Inc.

BTN5-5. **Accounting Research Problem** Refer to the consolidated balance sheets in the fiscal year 2020 annual report of **General Mills, Inc.**, which can be found at https://investors.generalmills.com/financial-information/annual-reports/default.aspx.

Required

a. What was the amount of cash and cash equivalents as of May 31, 2020?
b. By what amount did cash and cash equivalents increase or decrease during the year?
c. What statement elsewhere in the annual report contains an explanation of the increase or decrease in the cash and cash equivalents amount? In that statement, what amount of cash was provided or used by (1) operating activities, (2) investment activities, and (3) financing activities?
d. What firm conducted the audit of General Mills?
e. What opinion did the accounting firm express about General Mills' financial statements?
f. In addition to their audit of the financial statements, what else did the auditing firm audit?

BTN5-6. **Accounting Communication Activity** You were recently hired as the head of a company's ethics division. As one of your first acts, you decide to prepare a letter to the company's Chairman of the Board explaining the importance of ethics within the company. What are some of the items that should be included in your letter?

BTN5-7. **Accounting Ethics Case** Gina Pullen is the petty cash cashier for a large family-owned restaurant. She has been presented on numerous occasions with properly approved receipts for

reimbursement from petty cash that she believes are personal expenses of one of the five owners of the restaurant. She reports to the controller of the company. The controller is also a family member and is the person who approves the receipts for payment out of petty cash.

Required
What are the accounting implications if Pullen is correct? What alternatives should she consider?

BTN5-8. **Environmental, Social, and Governance Problem** Social sustainability and fraud prevention are often related. One way that the two are connected is in the creation of a culture of honesty and the ethical treatment of employees. This is often the result of the tone from the top, where the company leaders not only talk about these concepts, but also practice them.

Required
Discuss how a culture of honesty and the ethical treatment of employees can reduce the risk of fraud.

BTN5-9. **Accounting Ethics Problem** Internal control follows the concept of reasonable assurance. Pete Simmons, the chief compliance officer of Salem Company, stated that he does not want simply reasonable assurance. He wants absolute assurance in all aspects that apply to the financial statements of the company. Specifically, Pete stated, "As long as I am working here, we will run a perfectly tight system that ensures absolutely no fraud in our financial statements." Betty Flint, the controller, disagreed with Pete and argued that anything more than reasonable assurance is both financially and practically impossible.

Required
Do you agree with Pete or Betty, and why?

BTN5-10. **Working with the Takeaways** The following conditions of material weaknesses were reported in a prior year independent auditors' report on internal control of the U.S. Department of Transportation Highway Trust Fund (HTF):

1. Weaknesses with respect to journal entry preparation:
   a. Lack of indication of preparer
   b. Lack of supporting documentation
   c. Lack of proper review and approval
2. Weaknesses with respect to the consolidated financial statement preparation and analysis process:
   a. Inadequate analysis of abnormal balances
   b. Inadequate analysis of account relationships
   c. Inadequate controls over journal entry processing
   d. Lack of oversight related to allocation transfers

Required
a. What is the possible negative effect of these material weaknesses?
b. If you were the reporting auditor, what would you recommend be done?

ANSWERS TO SELF-STUDY QUESTIONS

1. c **2.** c **3.** d **4.** a **5.** c **6.** b **7.** b **8.** d **9.** a **10.** c

REVIEW SOLUTIONS

Solution 5.1

Businesses typically focus on reducing the *opportunity* to commit fraud by implementing a system of internal controls.

Solution 5.2

1. This is a human resources control violation. The supervisor may be committing a fraud and covering up his acts. If the supervisor were forced to take a vacation, the employee filling in might observe some suspicious activity and uncover the fraud.
2. This is a physical control violation. The unattended inventory could be stolen through the open door.

3. This is a segregation of duties violation. The supervisor is in a position to order an improper purchase, receive the goods for his own purposes, record the goods as received by the company, and then have the company pay for the purchase.

Solution 5.3

a. Cash equivalent
b. Cash
c. Neither
d. Cash
e. Neither

Solution 5.4

While internal controls over cash should be tailored to the firm's particular financial reporting system, all strong cash internal control systems include written policies and procedures, as well as segregation of duties.

Solution 5.5

a. The major source of cash for Los Altos is cash receipts from customers ($13,275).
b. The major uses of cash include (a) net capital expenditures ($30,000), (b) cash payments for operating activities ($11,131), (c) the repurchase of common stock ($7,300), and (d) the payment of cash dividends ($6,000).
c. The cash account declined by $41,296 during the month of December.

Solution 5.6

1. (a) Internal audit
2. (b) Financial statement audit
3. (c) Operational audit
4. (b) Financial statement audit
5. (c) Operational audit

Solution 5.7

a.

TYLER COMPANY
Bank Reconciliation
December 31

Ending balance from bank statement		$19,726.40	Balance from general ledger		$18,434.27
Add: Deposits in transit		2,145.40	Add: Collection of note	$2,000.00	
Error by bank (Check printing charge of Taylor Co.)		30.50	Less: Collection charge	5.00	1,995.00
			Error in recording check No. 586		27.00
		21,902.30			20,456.27
Less: Outstanding checks:			Less:		
No. 561	$306.63		NSF check	450.00	
No. 585	440.00		Charge for safe deposit box	42.50	492.50
No. 588	476.40				
No. 591	190.00				
No. 592	282.50				
No. 593	243.00	1,938.53			
Reconciled cash balance per bank		$19,963.77	Reconciled cash balance per books		$19,963.77

b.

Transaction: *Tyler Company bank reconciliation adjustments on December 31.*

Balance Sheet							Income Statement				
Assets	=	Liabilities	+	Stockholders' Equity							
				Contrib. Capital	+	Retained Earnings	Revenues	–	Expenses	=	Net Income
+27.00 Cash	=		+			+27.00		–	–27.00 Advertising expense	=	+27.00
Correct recording error on check number 586.											
+1,995.00 Cash –2,000.00 Notes receivable	=		+			–5.00		–	+5.00 Miscellaneous expense	=	–5.00
Record a note collected by the bank, less a collection fee.											
+450.00 Accounts receivable –450.00 Cash	=		+					–		=	
Reclassify an NSF check as an account receivable.											
–42.50 Cash	=		+			–42.50		–	+42.50 Miscellaneous expense	=	–42.50
Record bank service charge for December.											

Receivables

PAST

In Chapter 5 we studied how companies can prevent errors and fraud with the use of internal controls.

PRESENT

In this chapter we turn our attention to the accounting for two important assets—accounts and notes receivable.

FUTURE

In Chapter 7 we will continue our study of a company's assets and describe the accounting for inventory, including cost assumptions, the lower of cost or net realizable value and inventory analysis.

MGM RESORTS INTERNATIONAL—MANAGING CREDIT FOR BIGGER PROFITS

MGM Resorts International is among the largest gaming companies in the world. The company owns 29 hotels and casino resorts in the United States and Macau, including Bellagio, MGM Grand Las Vegas, and The Mirage.

Casino credit is an important marketing tool for gaming companies like MGM Resorts International. Granting credit to gamblers can result in significant increases in revenue since casinos like Bellagio and The Mirage rely heavily on clientele who gamble on credit. Credit also increases player loyalty because gamblers are inclined to play at casinos where they have a line of credit. A casino grants credit to its clientele with the expectation that the more a gambler uses the line of credit, the more likely the casino is to win.

While credit lines provide a boost to a casino's revenue, it is critical that the casino carefully manage receivables. MGM Resorts International, for example, maintains strict controls over the issuance of markers and "aggressively pursues collection from those customers who fail to repay their markers on a timely basis." GAAP requires MGM Resorts International to recognize the likelihood that a casino may be unable to collect all of its outstanding markers on its financial statements. At year-end 2020, despite aggressive collection efforts, MGM Resorts International reported nearly $127 million dollars in doubtful collections, almost 29% of total accounts receivable. This percentage is a significant increase over prior years as the gaming industry was hit hard by closures due to the pandemic. Although MGM's accounts receivable has declined, more of the accounts are deemed uncollectible.

Road Map

LO	Learning Objective	Page	eLecture	Review	Assignments
LO1	**Define accounts receivable and describe the allowance method of accounting for doubtful accounts.**	180	E6-1	6.1	SE1, SE4, E2, E3, E8, E9, E14, P2, P3, P7, P8
LO2	**Describe the percentage of net sales method and the accounts receivable aging method for estimating bad debt expense.**	184	E6-2	6.2, 6.3, 6.6	SE1, SE2, SE3, E1, E2, E8, E9, P1, P2, P3, P5, P6, P7, P8, P9
LO3	**Discuss the accounting treatment for credit card sales.**	189	E6-3	6.4	SE6, E4, E10, P4
LO4	**Illustrate a promissory note receivable and discuss the calculation of interest on notes receivable.**	191	E6-4	6.5, 6.6	SE7, SE8, E5, E6, E11, E12, P5, P9
LO5	**Define accounts receivable turnover and average collection period and explain their use in the analysis and management of receivables.**	195	E6-5	6.7	SE5, SE9, E7, E13

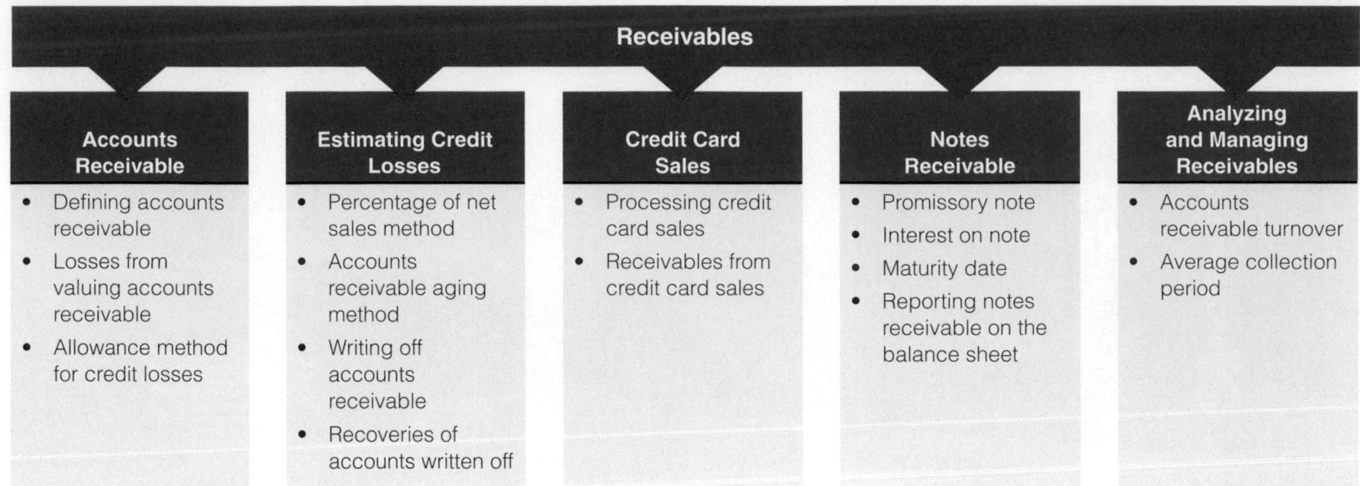

RECEIVABLES

Receivables are assets representing the right to receive cash or other assets in the future. Receivables may be classified as either a current asset or a noncurrent asset, depending upon the date of the expected receipt of cash or other assets. The most common types of receivables are accounts and notes receivable, which arise when a company sells its products or services to its customers on credit. Other types of receivables include loans to employees, loans to other companies, and any interest receivable on outstanding loans.

ACCOUNTING IN PRACTICE

Accounts Receivable Accounts receivable can amount to a large percentage of total assets for a company. Below are representative accounts receivable as a percentage of total assets appearing on the recent balance sheets of five well known companies in different industries.

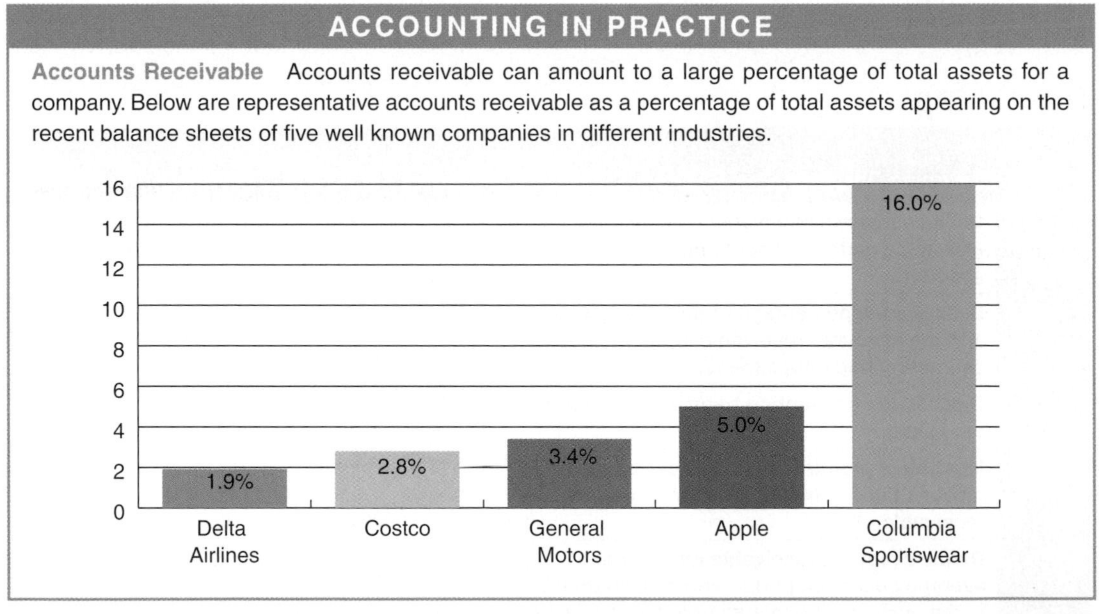

LO1 Define accounts receivable and **describe** the allowance method of accounting for doubtful accounts.

ACCOUNTS RECEIVABLE

Many businesses sell goods and services to their customers on credit, allowing customers to pay for their purchases over a period of time called the credit period. **Accounts receivable** is the current asset created when a company sells goods or services on credit.

When a company makes a credit sale, the transaction increases both the Accounts Receivable account and the Sales Revenue account. To illustrate, assume that on December 1, the Claremont Company sells $20,000 of merchandise on account. The effect of this transaction on the financial statements is as follows:

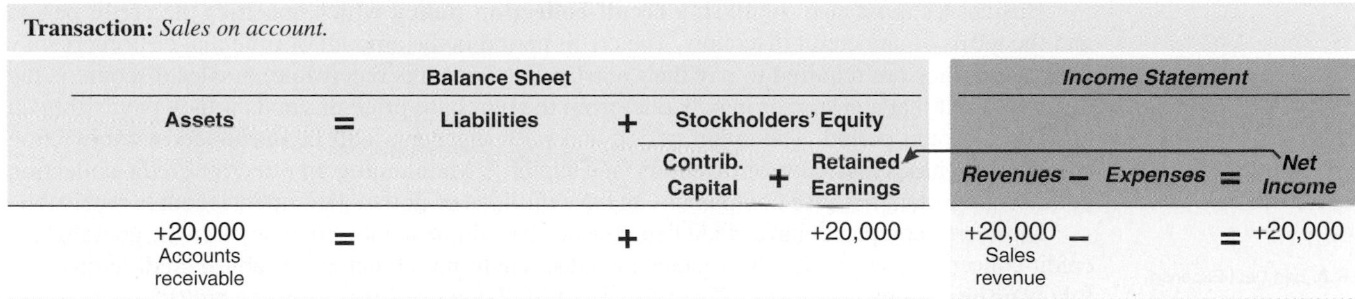

Transaction: *Sales on account.*

Assets	=	Liabilities	+	Stockholders' Equity: Contrib. Capital	+	Stockholders' Equity: Retained Earnings	Revenues	−	Expenses	=	Net Income
+20,000 Accounts receivable	=		+			+20,000	+20,000 Sales revenue	−		=	+20,000

When the credit sale is collected on December 20, the accounts receivable is converted to cash, with the following effect on the financial statements.

Transaction: *Cash collections.*

Assets	=	Liabilities	+	Stockholders' Equity: Contrib. Capital	+	Stockholders' Equity: Retained Earnings	Revenues	−	Expenses	=	Net Income
+20,000 Cash −20,000 Accounts receivable	=		+					−		=	

Accounts receivable includes only those amounts relating to credit sales of goods or services. Other receivables, such as those that arise from advancing cash to employees or loaning money to affiliated companies, should be included with the Other Receivables account on the balance sheet. Other Receivables may be either a current asset or a noncurrent asset.

A.K.A. Accounts receivable are also sometimes referred to as *trade receivables*.

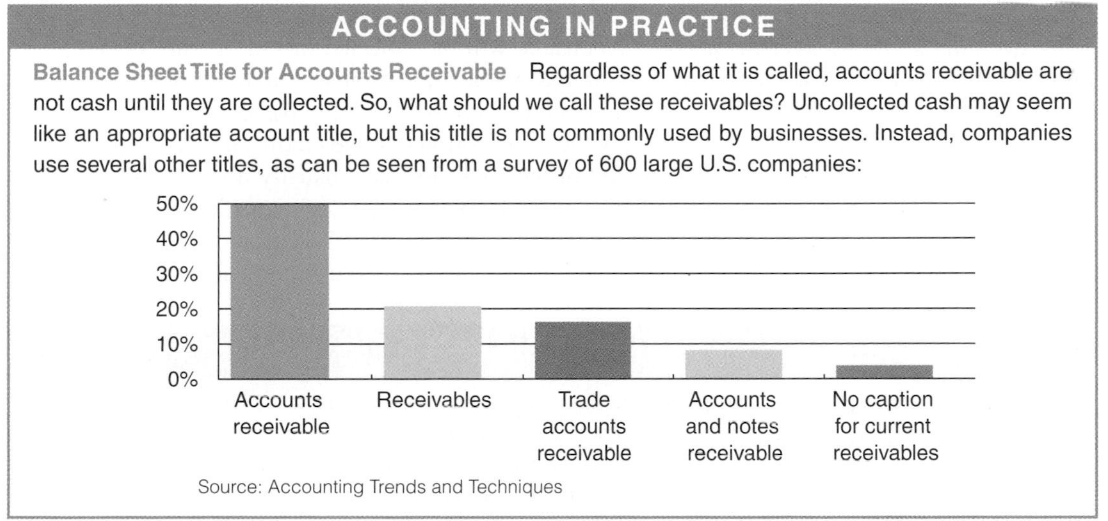

ACCOUNTING IN PRACTICE

Balance Sheet Title for Accounts Receivable Regardless of what it is called, accounts receivable are not cash until they are collected. So, what should we call these receivables? Uncollected cash may seem like an appropriate account title, but this title is not commonly used by businesses. Instead, companies use several other titles, as can be seen from a survey of 600 large U.S. companies:

Source: Accounting Trends and Techniques

LOSSES FROM VALUING ACCOUNTS RECEIVABLE

Businesses that extend credit to their customers anticipate some amount of credit losses—that is, losses from customers who fail to pay for their credit purchases. The magnitude of these losses is usually closely related to a firm's credit-granting policy. A **credit-granting policy** is established to decide which customers should be allowed to purchase on credit, and how much credit they should be granted. Companies often base their credit-granting policy on a computerized credit score. (See Accounting in Practice: Credit Scoring Systems, p. 182.) A company may deliberately relax its credit-granting policy to increase its sales, fully anticipating that it will result in an increase in credit losses.

Businesses must also establish a **credit-collection policy** which specifies the credit period and the terms of any credit discounts. The credit period is the amount of time that customers may take before they are required to pay their outstanding accounts receivable. A sales discount is the dollar amount that a customer may deduct from the purchase price of goods if they pay within an allowed discount period. The credit period and sales discounts will be discussed in conjunction with the purchases and sales of inventory in Chapter 7. Maintaining an effective credit-collection policy is important because companies can have millions of dollars tied up in accounts receivable.

Most large companies have credit departments that administer the company's credit-granting and credit-collection policies. Credit personnel conduct credit investigations, establish credit limits, and follow up on any unpaid accounts. They also decide, following written collection procedures, when an account receivable is uncollectible, and consequently, when an account receivable should be written off a company's balance sheet as uncollectible.

A.K.A. Bad Debt Expense is also sometimes referred to as the ***Provision for Bad Debts***, the ***Loss from Uncollectible Accounts***, or the *Uncollectible Accounts Expense*.

Credit losses are an operating expense called **Bad Debt Expense**. Normally, the Bad Debt Expense account is classified as a selling expense on the income statement, although some companies include it as part of their administrative expenses.

ACCOUNTING IN PRACTICE

Credit Scoring Systems Most companies use a computerized credit scoring system to decide whether to extend credit to their customers. The credit scoring system is based on a set of formulas with multiple variables. Data from a customer's credit application and from credit reporting agencies are used by the system to calculate a credit score. The system then compares the score to predetermined limits and recommends whether or not credit be extended.

If credit is extended, the scoring system often recommends an upper limit on the amount of credit to be extended. Scoring systems focus on a customer's ability to generate net income and cash flow, the customer's current level of debt and required repayment schedule, and current assets. Many of the financial statement ratios discussed throughout this text are incorporated into credit scoring systems.

Allowance Method

Credit losses are a cost of extending credit to customers. At the time that a credit sale is made, the seller does not know whether the account receivable will be collected in full, in part, or not at all. Further, any loss from an uncollectible account may not be known for several months, or even a year or more, following the credit sale. In order to comply with the matching principle, companies must recognize the costs of their credit sales during the same period that the credit sales are recognized in the income statement. Since the exact amount of the credit losses is usually not known at the time the credit sales are recognized, companies must estimate the amount of the credit losses they expect to incur. This estimate is reported in an end-of-period adjusting entry. The process of estimating and recording the bad debt expense for a business is most often executed using the **allowance method**.

PRINCIPLE ALERT

Matching Principle The *matching principle* states that expenses should be linked with, or matched with, the revenues that they help to generate. A company sells its goods and services on credit because this business practice attracts more customers and, therefore, more sales revenue than if the company only permitted cash transactions. One of the costs associated with extending credit to customers is bad debt expense. The matching principle requires that this expense be reported in the same accounting period as the related sales revenue. To accomplish the appropriate matching of sales revenue and expenses, accountants must estimate the bad debt expense because the specific accounts that will be uncollectible are not known until a later time period.

Recording Estimated Bad Debt Expense Under the Allowance Method

A.K.A. The **Allowance for Doubtful Accounts** is also often referred to as the *Allowance for Uncollectible Accounts*.

The allowance method receives its name because the end-of-period adjustment increases a contra-asset account called the **Allowance for Doubtful Accounts**. The allowance method matches credit losses with the related credit sales in the same time period in which the sale occurs, and also reports accounts receivable at their estimated realizable value in the end-of-period balance sheet. To illustrate, assume that the Claremont Corporation estimates its bad debt expense for the year to be $4,000 and makes the following adjustment:

Transaction: *Bad debt expense for the year.*

Balance Sheet							Income Statement				
Assets	=	Liabilities	+	Stockholders' Equity							
				Contrib. Capital	+	Retained Earnings	*Revenues*	–	*Expenses*	=	*Net Income*
−4,000 Allowance for doubtful accounts	=		+			−4,000		–	+4,000 Bad debt expense	=	−4,000

Note that an increase in the Allowance for Doubtful Accounts (a contra asset) results in a decrease in total assets.

Notice that the entry is made to the Allowance for Doubtful Accounts rather than directly against the Accounts Receivable account. This is because when a firm records its estimate of the amount of its uncollectible accounts, it does not know precisely which of its customer accounts will be uncollectible. Thus, the company is unable to reduce the specific receivables that will be uncollectible. Instead, the company uses the Allowance for Doubtful Accounts, which is a contra-asset account.

To report the expected collectible amount of accounts receivable on the balance sheet, the Allowance for Doubtful Accounts is subtracted from the Accounts Receivable account. Assuming that the Claremont Corporation had $100,000 of accounts receivable (and a zero balance in the Allowance for Doubtful Accounts prior to the December 31 adjustment), the year-end balance sheet presentation would appear as follows:

Current Assets		
Cash		$ 52,000
Accounts receivable	$100,000	
Less: Allowance for doubtful accounts	4,000	96,000
Inventory		125,000
Other current assets		31,000
Total Current Assets		$304,000

PRINCIPLE ALERT

Going Concern Concept Accounts receivable are reported on the balance sheet at the amount that a company expects to collect in the future from its credit customers. This presentation assumes that the company will be in existence long enough to collect its accounts receivable, and therefore, it is an example of the *going concern concept*. As a principle of accounting, the going concern concept assumes that a business entity will continue to operate indefinitely in the future.

REVIEW 6.1

The allowance method of accounting for credit losses is

a. Not in accordance with GAAP
b. Designed to achieve a proper matching of sales revenue and expenses
c. The process of estimating and recording bad debt expense
d. Both *b.* and *c.*

The solution is on page 210.

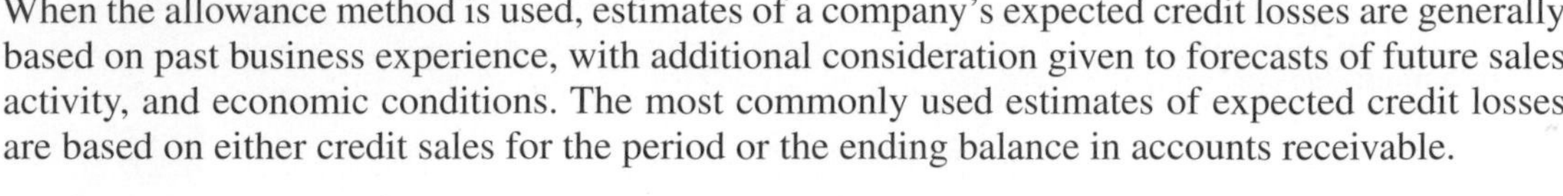

ESTIMATING CREDIT LOSSES

LO2 Describe the percentage of net sales method and the accounts receivable aging method for estimating bad debt expense.

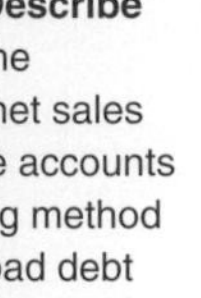

When the allowance method is used, estimates of a company's expected credit losses are generally based on past business experience, with additional consideration given to forecasts of future sales activity, and economic conditions. The most commonly used estimates of expected credit losses are based on either credit sales for the period or the ending balance in accounts receivable.

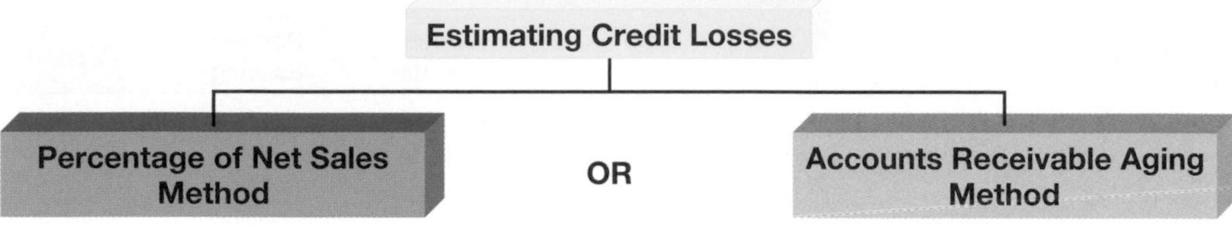

Percentage of Net Sales Method

The **percentage of net sales method** computes bad debt expense for the period by estimating the amount of credit sales that will be uncollectible. The adjustment to bad debt expense then results in a corresponding adjustment to the allowance for doubtful accounts. By focusing on the estimation of bad debt expense, this method takes an income statement approach to estimating net realizable accounts receivable.

This method uses the company's history of credit losses to compute the percent of credit sales that are expected to be uncollectible. Credit sales for the period are then multiplied by the historical percentage of credit losses to compute the bad debt expense for the period. For example, suppose that credit sales for the year for the Claremont Corporation are $500,000 and that past experience indicates that the company is likely to sustain a two percent loss on its credit sales. Claremont's expected credit losses for the year of $10,000 (2 percent × $500,000) would increase the Allowance for Doubtful Accounts and Bad Debt Expense, as shown below:

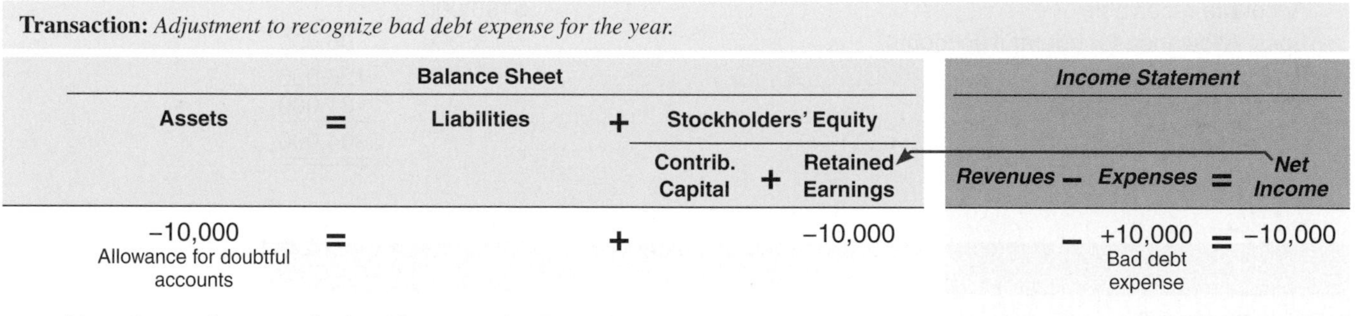

Transaction: *Adjustment to recognize bad debt expense for the year.*

Balance Sheet							Income Statement				
Assets	=	Liabilities	+	Stockholders' Equity							
				Contrib. Capital	+	Retained Earnings	Revenues	–	Expenses	=	*Net Income*
−10,000 Allowance for doubtful accounts	=		+			−10,000		–	+10,000 Bad debt expense	=	−10,000

Note that an increase in the Allowance for Doubtful Accounts (a contra asset) results in a decrease in total assets.

Because the periodic estimate for doubtful accounts under this procedure is related to credit sales, a firm should review its allowance account regularly to ensure that the account maintains a reasonable balance. If the allowance account balance is too large or too small, the percentage used to estimate the periodic credit losses should be revised accordingly.

A company that uses the percentage of net sales method applies the estimated uncollectible percentage only to its credit sales, excluding cash sales, since only credit sales are subject to credit losses. Further, any sales discounts and sales returns and allowances should be deducted from total credit sales before applying the historical uncollectible percentage.

It is quite common for companies to use the percentage of net sales method for interim reporting periods, and then apply the aging method (discussed next) at the end of the year. This is because the aging method generally results in a more precise estimate of the amount of accounts receivable that will be uncollectible but is more costly to implement.

REVIEW 6.2

Taylor Company estimates three percent of its $600,000 credit sales will prove uncollectible. Determine the amount of the year-end adjustment and, using the TAT, determine the financial statement effect.

The solution is on page 210.

Accounts Receivable Aging Method

The **accounts receivable aging method** computes the desired ending balance in the Allowance for Doubtful Accounts. The adjustment needed to properly state the Allowance for Doubtful Accounts then results in a corresponding adjustment to Bad Debt Expense. By focusing on the estimation of the Allowance for Doubtful Accounts, this method takes a balance sheet approach to estimating net realizable accounts receivable.

The aging method computes the desired ending balance in the allowance account by analyzing the age of the accounts receivable balances. An aging schedule similar to the one in **Exhibit 6-1** is typically used. An **aging schedule** analyzes the amount of time that has elapsed since a credit sale originally occurred, which indicates how long a customer's account receivable has remained unpaid. Assume, for example, that the firm whose aging schedule appears in **Exhibit 6-1** sells its goods on credit with a credit period of 30 days. The aging schedule in the exhibit, which is prepared as of December 31, indicates that the Alton account is current, which means that the $320 billing was made within the last 30 days; however, the Bailey account is 1–30 days *past due,* which means that the account receivable is from 31 to 60 days old. The aging schedule also reveals that the Wall balance consists of a $50 billing that is 61 to 120 days past due, and a $100 billing that is 121 days to 6 months past due, and so on.

EXHIBIT 6-1 Aging Schedule of Customer Balances, December 31

			Past Due				
Customer	Account Balance	Current	1–30 Days	31–60 Days	61–120 Days	121 Days to 6 Mos.	Over 6 Mos.
Alton, J.	320	$ 320					
Bailey, C.	400		$ 400				
many more accts	...	...	...	...	...	...	...
Wall, M.	150				50	100	
Zorn, W.	210			210			
	$50,000	$42,000	$4,000	$2,000	$1,000	$800	$200

The company uses the aging schedule to compute the probability-of-noncollection for the receivables in each age category. These percentages are based on past collection experience for similar accounts as well as current economic conditions. The probability-of-noncollection percentages are applied to the totals of each age category to determine the appropriate allowance account balance for a given category. For our example, these percentages are shown in the table below. Applying the percentages to the totals in our aging schedule, we can calculate the required balance for the Allowance for Doubtful Accounts—that is, $1,560:

	Amount	Probability of Noncollection	Allowance Required
Current	$42,000	2%	$ 840
1–30 days past due	4,000	3%	120
31–60 days past due	2,000	5%	100
61–120 days past due	1,000	20%	200
121 days to 6 mos. past due	800	25%	200
Over 6 mos. past due	200	50%	100
Total allowance required			$1,560

The aging analysis is used to estimate the balance in Accounts Receivable that the company estimates will not be collected. This estimate is then used to adjust the balance in the Allowance for Doubtful Accounts at the end of the year, December 31. Because the aging method is an estimation process, estimation errors are likely to occur, causing the allowance account to sometimes be over or underestimated. For example, suppose that the Allowance for Doubtful Accounts has an existing balance of $400 at December 31, before the adjustment for the above aging analysis is made. This would suggest that management overestimated the Allowance for Doubtful Accounts in the prior year, since $400 was not written off by year end. The aging analysis indicates that the balance in the Allowance for Doubtful Accounts at December 31 should be $1,560, which is the amount of Accounts Receivables on the balance sheet at December 31 that the company estimates it will be unable to collect. Thus, the adjustment resulting from the aging analysis, which is made in order to properly reflect the balance that should appear in the Allowance for Doubtful Accounts, will increase the Allowance for Doubtful Accounts, and Bad Debt Expense, by $1,160 ($1,560 – $400).

Transaction: *Adjustment to recognize bad debt expense for the year.*

Balance Sheet							Income Statement				
Assets	=	Liabilities	+	Stockholders' Equity							
				Contrib. Capital	+	Retained Earnings	*Revenues*	–	*Expenses*	=	*Net Income*
−1,160 Allowance for doubtful accounts	=		+			−1,160		–	+1,160 Bad debt expense	=	−1,160

Note that an increase in the Allowance for Doubtful Accounts (a contra asset) results in a decrease in total assets.

This brings the balance in the Allowance for Doubtful Accounts account to the required amount—$1,560, as shown below:

Hint: *In contrast to the percentage of net sales method, the accounts receivable aging method takes into account the beginning balance in the Allowance for Doubtful Accounts.*

Balance prior to adjustment	$ 400
Year end adjustment.	1,160
Required Allowance for doubtful accounts . . .	$1,560

It is also possible to have underestimated the allowance account in the prior period. This would occur whenever the write-off of specific accounts receivable during the year exceeded the balance in the account as of the beginning of the year. Assume, for example, that the Allowance for Doubtful Accounts had a $350 negative balance prior to the recording of the December 31 adjustment, and that the aging schedule showed that the allowance account should have a $1,560 balance. The year-end adjustment would then increase the Allowance for Doubtful Accounts and Bad Debt Expense by $1,910 ($1,560 + $350).

Transaction: *Adjustment to recognize bad debt expense for the year.*

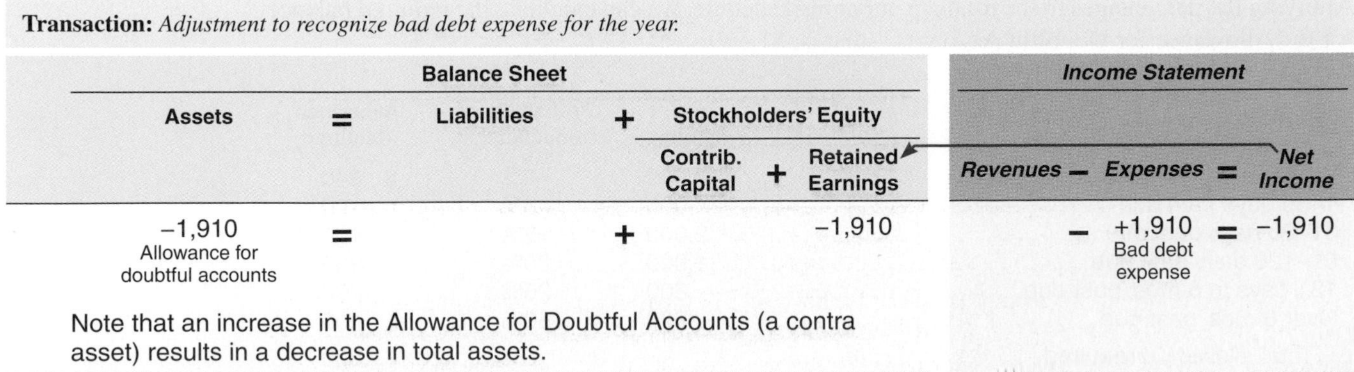

The balance in the Allowance for Doubtful Accounts after the adjustment has the desired year-end balance of $1,560 as shown below:

Balance prior to adjustment	$ (350)
Year end adjustment.	1,910
Required Allowance for doubtful accounts . . .	$1,560

Concept →	Method →	Assessment	TAKEAWAY 6.1
Are the accounts receivable being collected in a timely manner?	List the accounts receivable along with how long they have been outstanding. Prepare an aging schedule.	Accounts that are past due have not been collected in a timely manner and require additional collection attention.	

WRITING OFF SPECIFIC ACCOUNTS RECEIVABLE UNDER THE ALLOWANCE METHOD

A company's credit department manager is usually the employee with the authority to determine when an account receivable is uncollectible. When a customer's receivable is deemed uncollectible, it is written off and removed from the balance sheet. Assume, for example, that in the period following the above balance sheet date, the credit manager of the Claremont Corporation determines that a $300 account receivable from the Monroe Company is uncollectible. The adjustment to write off the Monroe receivable affects the financial statements as follows:

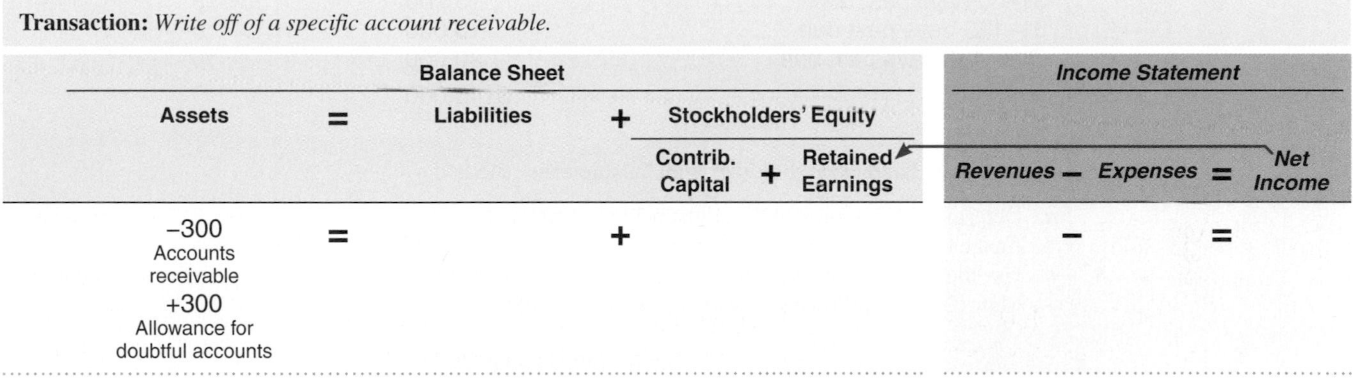

The entry to write off an account receivable does not affect a company's net income or total assets. This is appropriate because the estimated bad debt expense is reported in the period when the related sales revenue is recorded. Because the Allowance for Doubtful Accounts is deducted from the Accounts Receivable account on the balance sheet, the *net* realizable value of accounts receivable is unchanged by the account write off. The table below shows how the write off affects the Accounts Receivable, the Allowance Account, and the net realizable value of Claremont's accounts receivable.

	Before Write Off		After Write Off
Accounts receivable	$100,000	($100,000 – $300)	$99,700
Less Allowance for doubtful accounts . . .	(4,000)	(4,000 – 300)	(3,700)
Net accounts receivable	$ 96,000	← same →	$96,000

As shown in the above table, the net realizable value of Claremont's accounts receivable is unchanged as a result of the write off. The balance prior to the write off is $96,000 ($100,000 less $4,000 allowance for doubtful accounts). Following the write off, the net realizable value of the Claremont

Corporation's accounts receivable remains $96,000 ($99,700 less $3,700 allowance for doubtful accounts) since both the Accounts Receivable account and the Allowance for Doubtful Accounts are reduced by the same amount ($300). The following table summarizes the allowance method.

Action	Balance Sheet Effect (Increase/Decrease)	Income Statement Effect (Increase/Decrease)
Recording Estimated Bad debt expense (In period when sale occurred)	↑ Allowance for doubtful accounts ↓ Accounts receivable, net	↑ Bad debt expense ↓ Net income
Writing-Off Bad Debt (When receivable is determined uncollectible)	↓ Accounts receivable ↓ Allowance for doubtful accounts **No Change** Accounts receivable, net	**No Change**

REVIEW 6.3

Phisher, Inc., analyzed its accounts receivable at the end of its first year of operations, and arrived at the aged balances listed below, along with the percentage that is estimated to be uncollectible:

Age Group	Balance	Estimated Loss Percentage
1–30 days past due	$100,000	1
31–60 days past due	15,000	3
61–120 days past due	10,000	5
Over 120 days past due	20,000	10
	$145,000	

The company handles credit losses with the allowance method.

a. Determine the amount of the adjustment for estimated credit losses and, using the TAT, determine its financial statement effect at year end.

b. Use the TAT to show the financial statement effect of the write off of Phorest Company's account on May 12 of the following year in the amount of $480.

The solution is on page 211.

RECOVERIES OF ACCOUNTS WRITTEN OFF UNDER THE ALLOWANCE METHOD

Occasionally, an account that was written off will later be paid, in whole or in part, by the customer. This is accounted for by first reinstating the customer's account receivable for the amount collected. This is done by increasing accounts receivable and the allowance account by the amount collected, which reverses the adjustment that was made to write off the account. Then the cash payment is recorded as it would be with the collection of a normal account receivable, by increasing cash and reducing the accounts receivable account. For example, assume that the Claremont Corporation is using the allowance method and wrote off the Monroe Company's $300 account on January 5, but subsequently received a $200 payment on April 20. The following illustrates the financial statement effect of the recovery:

Transaction: *Write off and subsequent recovery of account written off.*

Balance Sheet: Assets	=	Liabilities	+	Stockholders' Equity: Contrib. Capital	+	Retained Earnings	Income Statement: Revenues	−	Expenses	=	Net Income
−300 Accounts receivable +300 Allowance for doubtful accounts	=		+					−		=	
Write off the account.											
+200 Accounts receivable −200 Allowance for doubtful accounts	=		+					−		=	
Reinstate the account to the extent of the recovery.											
+200 Cash −200 Accounts receivable	=		+					−		=	
Record the subsequent recovery.											

The first entry shows the write off of $300, which reduced both accounts receivable and the allowance account. When the $200 is received from Monroe, the company reinstates this portion of the receivable by increasing accounts receivable and the allowance account by the $200. This adjustment reverses the write off of $200 of the receivable from Monroe. Then the company treats the collection of the $200 as it would any other collection of an account receivable by increasing cash and reducing accounts receivable. The financial statement effect of the recovery is the same even if the recovery occurs more than a year following the period in which the account was originally written off.

ACCOUNTING ETHICS

Lapping Lapping is a technique that a fraudster uses to cover up a fraud, typically involving the theft of funds. Using lapping, an employee who has access to incoming payments from the collection of accounts receivable will steal cash received from credit customers. The employee then applies another customer's payment to the outstanding balance of the first account in order to cover up the theft. The process is repeated in an effort to cover up the original misappropriation. One audit procedure that may detect a lapping scheme involves the confirmation of accounts receivable. As part of the year-end independent audit, or a regular internal audit, a company's accountant will send out confirmation letters to a sample of customers from the list of outstanding accounts receivable and pay particular attention to replies from customers disputing the timing of their payments.

CREDIT CARD SALES

LO3 Discuss the accounting treatment for credit card sales.

Many businesses, especially retailers, allow their customers to pay using credit cards. Popular credit cards include VISA, MasterCard, Discover, and American Express. When a customer uses a credit card to make a purchase, the seller collects cash from the credit card company, and the customer pays cash to the credit card company when billed at a later date. To facilitate this process, the transaction, along with the credit card information, is electronically transmitted to a financial institution. The financial institution authorizes the transaction based on the available credit along with other criteria.

The issuer of a credit card, frequently a financial institution like **Chase Bank** or **Citibank**, will charge the seller a fee each time a card is used. The **credit card fee** usually ranges from 1.5 percent to 3.5 percent of the amount of the credit card purchase. Businesses are willing to incur this fee because credit cards provide considerable benefits to a seller. For example, the seller does not have to evaluate the creditworthiness of the customer using a credit card, and the business avoids any risk of noncollection of the account since this risk remains with the credit card issuer. Finally, the seller typically receives the cash from the credit card issuer faster than if the customer were directly granted credit by the seller.

Depending upon the type of credit card, there are two ways that a seller may collect from the credit card issuer: (1) immediately or (2) on a delayed basis. For example, assume a $1,000 credit card sale with a three percent credit card fee. If the cash is received immediately, the transaction would increase Sales Revenue by $1,000, increase Cash by $970 ($1,000 less 3%) and increase Credit Card Fee Expense by $30 ($1,000 × 3%). The financial statement effect is as follows:

Transaction: *Credit card sales with immediate collection.*

Balance Sheet							Income Statement				
Assets	=	Liabilities	+	Stockholders' Equity: Contrib. Capital	+	Retained Earnings	Revenues	−	Expenses	=	Net Income
+970 Cash	=		+			+970	+1,000 Sales revenue	−	+30 Credit card fee	=	+970

If, instead, there is a delay in the cash settlement, the $1,000 credit card sale with subsequent collection would reflect an increase in Accounts Receivable rather than Cash. When the cash is ultimately received from the credit card company, the receivable is reduced and cash is increased. This is illustrated below:

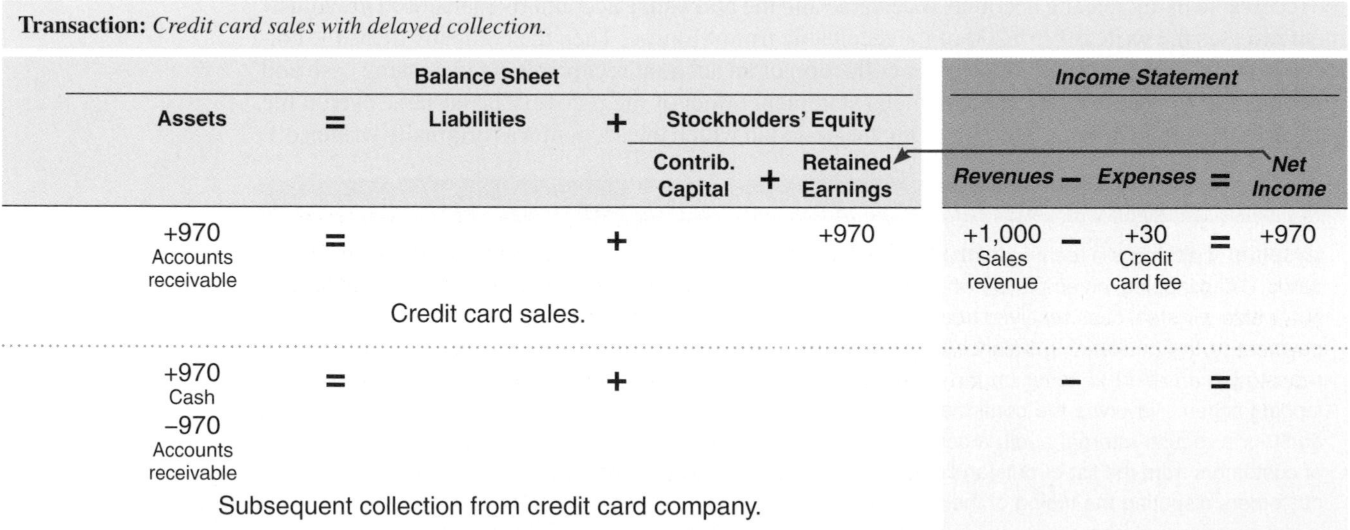

Transaction: *Credit card sales with delayed collection.*

Balance Sheet							Income Statement				
Assets	=	Liabilities	+	Stockholders' Equity: Contrib. Capital	+	Retained Earnings	Revenues	−	Expenses	=	Net Income
+970 Accounts receivable	=		+			+970	+1,000 Sales revenue	−	+30 Credit card fee	=	+970
Credit card sales.											
+970 Cash −970 Accounts receivable	=		+					−		=	
Subsequent collection from credit card company.											

REVIEW 6.4

Nafooz Company pays a two percent credit card fee on all credit sales, and receives a cash deposit immediately following each credit card transaction. If credit sales for the company total $50,000, determine the financial statement effect of the receipt of cash and the credit card fee expense using the TAT.

The solution is on page 211.

NOTES RECEIVABLE

LO4 **Illustrate** a promissory note receivable and **discuss** the calculation of interest on notes receivable.

Promissory notes receivable are often used in sale transactions when the credit period is longer than the 30- to 60-day credit period that is typical for accounts receivable. Promissory notes are also used frequently in sales involving equipment and property because the dollar amount of these transactions can be quite large. Occasionally, a note will be substituted for an account receivable when an extension of the usual credit period is granted. Also, promissory notes are normally used when financial institutions make a loan to a business or an individual.

A **promissory note** is a written promise to pay a certain sum of money on demand or at a fixed (or determinable) future date. The note is signed by the **maker** and made payable to the order of either a specific **payee** or to the **bearer**. The interest rate specified on the note is typically an annual rate. **Exhibit 6-2** illustrates a promissory note.

EXHIBIT 6-2 A Promissory Note

$2,000.00 Los Angeles, CA May 3, 20XX

Sixty days after date

I promise to pay to the order of Susan Robinson

Two thousand and no/100 .... dollars

for value received with interest at 9%

payable at First Bank of Los Angeles, CA

James Stone

A note from a debtor is called a **note receivable** by the noteholder. A note is usually regarded as a stronger claim against a debtor than an account receivable because the terms of payment are specified in writing.

Interest on Notes Receivable

Interest is a charge for the use of money over time. Interest incurred on a promissory note receivable is interest income to the noteholder or payee of the note and interest expense to the maker of the note. Businesses are required to distinguish between operating and nonoperating items in their income statements; consequently, they classify interest expense and interest income as "other income and expense" in the income statement. Interest expense is a financing expense, not an operating expense, and interest income is financing income, not operating income.

Interest on a short-term promissory note is paid at the maturity date of the note. The formula for determining the amount of interest expense to the maker and interest income to the noteholder is as follows:

Interest = Principal × Interest rate × Time

The principal is the face amount of a note; the interest rate is the annual rate of interest specified in the note agreement. Time is the fraction of a year that a note receivable is outstanding.

When a note is written for a certain number of months, interest is expressed in twelfths of a year. For example, interest on a six-month note for $2,000 with a nine percent annual interest rate is calculated as:

Interest = $2,000 × 0.09 × 6/12 = $90

When a note's duration, or time to maturity, is given in days, interest is expressed as a fraction of a year; the numerator is the number of days that the note receivable will be outstanding and the denominator is 360 days. (Some lenders use 360 days, while others use 365 days; we use 360 days in our examples, exercises, and problems.) For example, interest on a 60 day note for $2,000 with a nine percent annual interest rate is:

Interest = $2,000 × 0.09 × 60/360 = $30

Determining Maturity Date

When a note's duration is expressed in days, it is customary to count the exact number of days in each calendar month to determine the note's **maturity date**. For example, a 90 day note dated July 21 has an October 19 maturity date, which is determined as follows:

10	days in July (remainder of month—31 days minus 21 days)
31	days in August
30	days in September
19	days in October (number of days required to total 90)
90	

If the duration of a note is expressed in months, the maturity date is calculated simply by counting the number of months from the date of issue. For example, a two-month note dated January 31 would mature on March 31, a three-month note of the same date would mature on April 30 (the last day of the month), and a four-month note would mature on May 31.

Recording Notes Receivable and Interest

When a note is exchanged to settle an account receivable, an adjustment is made to reflect the note receivable and to reduce the balance of the related account receivable. For example, suppose that Jordon Company sold $12,000 of merchandise on account to Bowman Company. On October 1, after the regular credit period had elapsed, the Bowman Company gave the Jordon Company a 60 day, nine percent note receivable for $12,000. Jordon Company makes the following adjustment to record receiving the note:

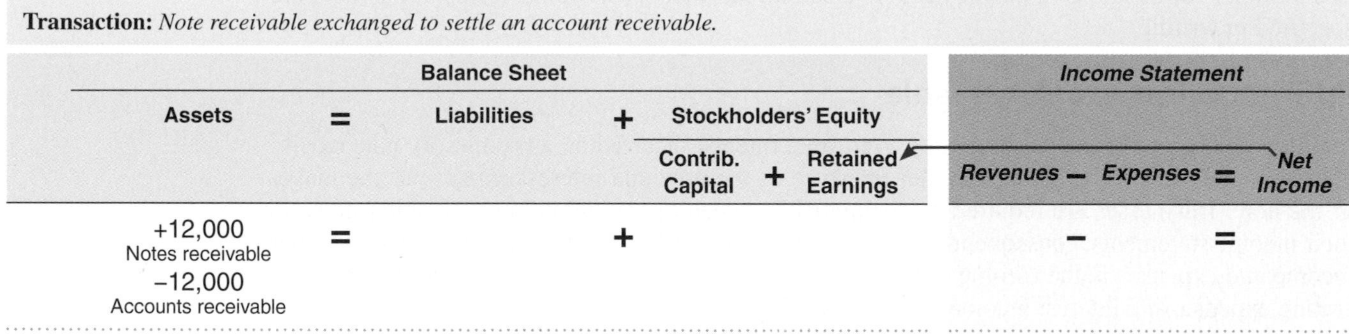

Transaction: Note receivable exchanged to settle an account receivable.
Balance Sheet
Income Statement
Assets = Liabilities + Stockholders' Equity
Contrib. Capital + Retained Earnings
Revenues − Expenses = Net Income
+12,000 Notes receivable
−12,000 Accounts receivable

If the Bowman Company pays its note receivable on the November 30 maturity date, the financial statement impact to Jordon Company is as follows:

Transaction: *Collection of note receivable on maturity date.*

Assets	=	Liabilities	+	Contrib. Capital	+	Retained Earnings	Revenues	−	Expenses	=	Net Income
+12,180 Cash −12,000 Notes receivable	=		+			+180	+180 Interest income	−		=	+180

$12,000 × 0.09 × 60/360 = $180

Adjusting Entry for Interest

When the term of a promissory note extends beyond the end of an accounting period, a period-end adjusting entry is necessary to reflect the interest earned. To illustrate, assume that Jordon Company has a note receivable outstanding at December 31, Year 1. The note receivable from the Garcia Company is dated December 21, Year 1, has a principal amount of $6,000, an interest rate of 12 percent, and a maturity date of February 19, Year 2. The adjustment that Jordon Company makes at December 31, Year 1, to record the interest that is earned but uncollected at year end, is as follows:

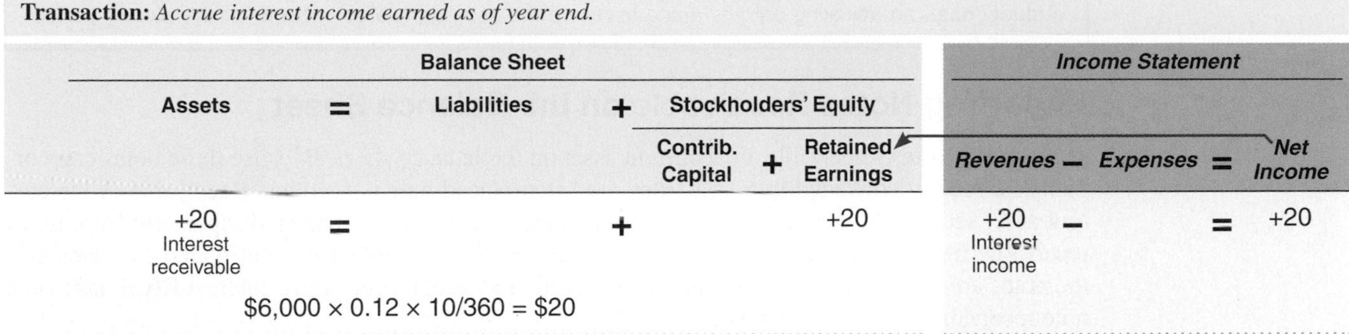

Transaction: *Accrue interest income earned as of year end.*
Balance Sheet
Assets = Liabilities + Stockholders' Equity
Contrib. Capital + Retained Earnings
Income Statement
Revenues − Expenses = Net Income
+20 Interest receivable = + +20
+20 Interest income − = +20
$6,000 × 0.12 × 10/360 = $20

When the note is subsequently paid on February 19, Year 2, Jordon Company makes the following adjustment:

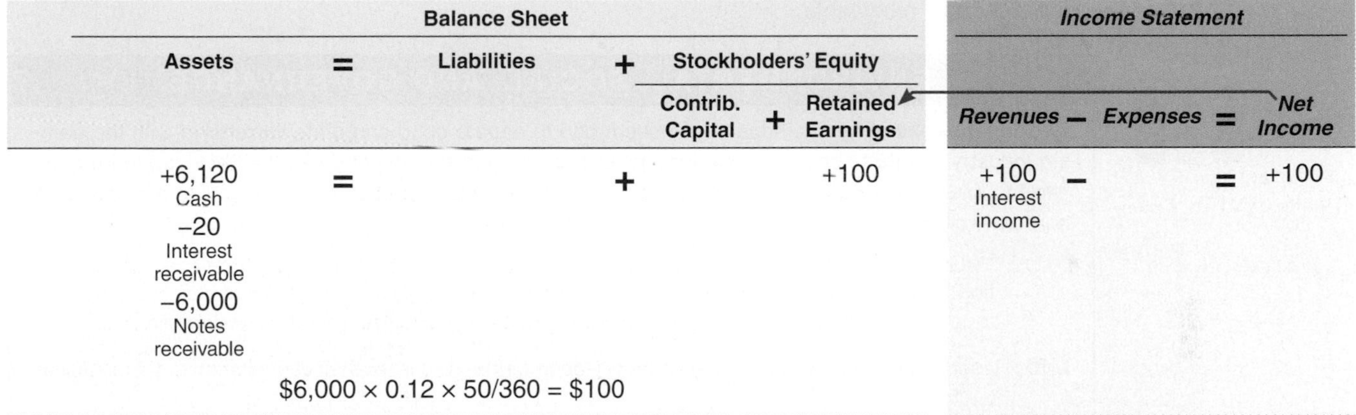

Transaction: *Collection of note receivable on maturity date, assuming no interest accrual in January.*
Balance Sheet
Assets = Liabilities + Stockholders' Equity
Contrib. Capital + Retained Earnings
Income Statement
Revenues − Expenses = Net Income
+6,120 Cash
−20 Interest receivable
−6,000 Notes receivable
= + +100
+100 Interest income − = +100
$6,000 × 0.12 × 50/360 = $100

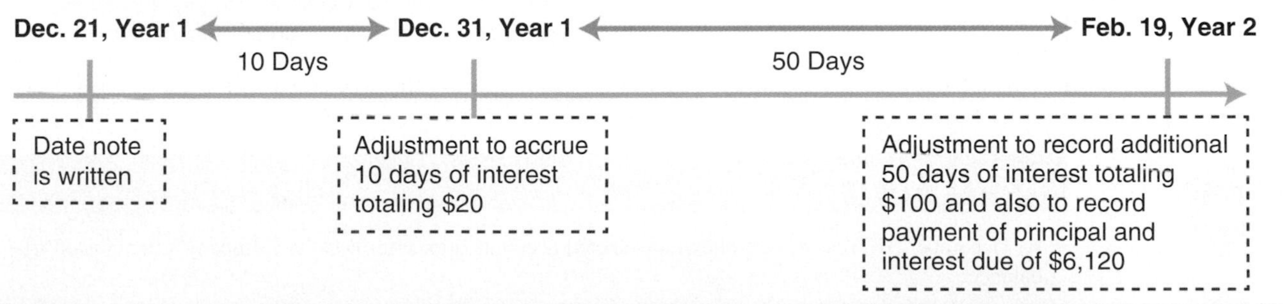

Dec. 21, Year 1

Feb. 19, Year 2

Adjustment to accrue 10 days of interest totaling $20
Adjustment to record additional 50 days of interest totaling $100 and also to record payment of principal and interest due of $6,120

REVIEW 6.5

Ruby Company received a four month, five percent note receivable for $40,000 on October 1. How much interest income should be accrued on December 31?

The solution is on page 211.

PRINCIPLE ALERT

Revenue Recognition Principle The adjusting entry to accrue interest income on an outstanding promissory note receivable at year-end illustrates the *revenue recognition principle.* This principle requires companies to recognize revenues when services are performed or goods are sold. The holder of a promissory note provides the maker of the note with a service: the use of money for a specified time period. This service is provided each day that a note is outstanding; and, interest is the payment for this service. Interest income is not recorded each day. Normally, interest income for a note's full term is recorded when it is collected at the note's maturity. If the accounting period ends before a note's maturity date, an adjusting entry is made to record the accrued interest income for the current period.

Reporting Notes Receivable on the Balance Sheet

Short-Term Notes Receivable are a current asset on the balance sheet. Because these notes can normally be readily converted into cash, they are often placed below Accounts Receivable in the current asset section. As with accounts receivable, notes receivable are reported separately from notes receivable from officers and employees and notes representing advances to affiliated companies. If the notes are not short term, they should be classified as noncurrent assets. Interest Receivable on a note receivable is also a current asset.

Sometimes companies with a large volume of notes receivable must provide for possible losses on the outstanding notes. Frequently, the Allowance for Doubtful Accounts also covers potential credit losses on notes as well. In such cases, the Allowance for Doubtful Accounts account is deducted from the aggregate total of Accounts Receivable and Notes Receivable on the balance sheet. Estimating the potential credit losses on outstanding notes receivable follows the same procedures as for accounts receivable.

ENVIRONMENTAL, SOCIAL, AND GOVERNANCE

Responsible Gaming Perhaps it may seem odd to equate good corporate citizenship with the gaming industry, but that does not mean that gaming companies should not do all that they can to be good citizens. MGM Resorts International's mission statement aims to portray the company as a responsible corporate citizen:

> "MGM Resorts International is the leader in entertainment & hospitality—a diverse collection of extraordinary people, distinctive brands and best in class destinations. Working together, we create partnerships and experiences that engage, entertain and inspire."

MGM Resorts International's 2019 Sustainability Report further discusses their commitment to sustainability:

> "In 2019, we introduced *Focused on What Matters: Embracing Humanity and Protecting the Planet*—MGM Resorts' commitment to making an impact in society for the benefit of our employees, shareholders and communities. Guided by our values of integrity, teamwork, inclusion and excellence, *Focused on What Matters* is an expression of what we stand for and who we are."

REVIEW 6.6

At December 31, Year 1, the following selected accounts appeared in Delta Company's unadjusted trial balance:

Accounts receivable	$81,000
Allowance for doubtful accounts.	1,200
Notes receivable (Jason, Inc.)	12,000

Net credit sales for Year 1 were $250,000. The $12,000 note receivable was a 90 day, eight percent note dated December 13, Year 1. The following adjustments and transactions occurred at the end of Year 1 and during Year 2:

continued

continued from previous page

Year 1

Dec. 31 Recorded the adjustment for the bad debt expense, at $1\frac{1}{2}$ percent of net credit sales.
31 Recorded the adjustment for interest on the $12,000 note receivable.

Year 2

Mar. 12 Received payment on the $12,000 note receivable from Jason, Inc., plus interest.
Apr. 5 Wrote off the account of Abilene Company, $2,850.
July 9 Wrote off the account of Acme Suppliers, $1,450.
Sept. 5 Received payment from Acme Suppliers, which is in bankruptcy proceedings, for $450 in final settlement of the account written off on July 9.
Dec. 6 Wrote off the account of Walton, Inc., $1,300.
31 Changed from the percentage-of-net-sales method of providing for uncollectible accounts to an estimate based on the accounts receivable aging method. The account analysis indicated a desired credit balance of $4,500 in the Allowance for Doubtful Accounts.

Required

Using the TAT, determine the financial statement effect of these adjustments and transactions.

The solution is on pages 211–213.

ANALYZING AND MANAGING RECEIVABLES

LO5 **Define** accounts receivable turnover and average collection period and **explain** their use in the analysis and management of receivables.

eLecture MBC

Most companies transact the majority of their sales on credit, and doing so creates accounts receivable. Management and financial analysts closely monitor a company's accounts receivable using a variety of financial measures, including the accounts receivable turnover ratio and the average collection period. **Accounts receivable turnover** indicates how many times a year a firm collects its average accounts receivable, and thus, measures how fast accounts receivable are being converted into cash. Accounts receivable turnover is calculated as follows:

$$\textbf{Accounts receivable turnover} = \frac{\textbf{Net sales}}{\textbf{Average accounts receivable (net)}}$$

The numerator in this ratio is net sales. Ideally, the numerator should be net credit sales, but financial information available to financial statement users does not usually divide net sales into credit sales and cash sales. For many businesses, particularly those that sell primarily to other businesses, it is common to assume that a company's net sales is a good proxy for its credit sales. Average accounts receivable (net of the allowance for doubtful accounts) is calculated by summing the beginning and ending accounts receivable (net) balances and dividing the sum by two.

To illustrate these financial indicators, consider the financial results for the Claremont Corporation.

	Year 2	Year 1
Net sales	$40,831	$33,548
Beginning accounts receivable (net)	1,848	1,948
Ending accounts receivable (net)	1,799	1,848
Accounts receivable turnover	22.39	17.68

Claremont's accounts receivable turnover for Year 2 is 22.39, or $40,831/[($1,848 + $1,799)/2], and for Year 1 is 17.68, or $33,548/[($1,948 + $1,848)/2]. In general, the higher the accounts receivable turnover ratio, the faster a company is converting its receivables into cash. The increase in accounts receivable turnover from Year 1 to Year 2 is a positive sign regarding how well the Claremont Corporation is managing its accounts receivable.

An extension of the accounts receivable turnover ratio is the **average collection period**, calculated as follows:

$$\textbf{Average collection period} = \frac{\textbf{365}}{\textbf{Accounts receivable turnover}}$$

This ratio indicates how many days it takes, on average, to collect an account receivable. During Year 2, Claremont's average collection period was 16.3 days, or 365/22.39. During Year 1, Claremont's average collection period was 20.6 days, or 365/17.68. The ratio reveals that Claremont is taking four fewer days to collect its accounts receivable in Year 2 than in Year 1, another sign of improved accounts receivable management.

The average collection period may also be used to evaluate the effectiveness of a company's credit policies. One rule of thumb states that the average collection period should not exceed a business's allowed credit period by more than 15 days. Thus, if a firm grants credit terms of 30 days to its customers, its average collection period should not exceed 45 days.

REVIEW 6.7

The Forrester Corporation disclosed the following financial information (in millions) in its recent annual report:

	Current Year
Net sales	$30,000
Beginning accounts receivable (net)	2,800
Ending accounts receivable (net)	3,200

a. Calculate the accounts receivable turnover ratio for the year.
b. Calculate the average collection period for the year.

The solution is on page 213.

TAKEAWAY 6.2 Concept	Method	Assessment
Are any of the existing accounts receivable in need of further attention?	Net sales and average accounts receivable Accounts receivable turnover = $\frac{\text{Net sales}}{\text{Average accounts receivable}}$ Average collection period = $\frac{365}{\text{Accounts receivable turnover}}$	Compare the average collection period to the company credit policy. Longer collection periods suggest the need for management attention.

Data Analytics

DATA ANALYTICS Tesla Uses Customer Data to Refine the Cars It Builds

Many consider **Tesla** a pioneer in the manufacturing of electric vehicles (EVs); however, Tesla was not the first to build EVs. It is more accurate to think of Tesla as a pioneer in the use of big data and data analytics to build and improve its cars. One of Tesla's goals is to collect as much user data as possible from the owners of its cars. Tesla collects data from various sources. One such source is its optional technology package, which, for example, includes cameras and sensors to help warn drivers of potential road hazards. Although this option provides a valuable service to Tesla owners, it also provides Tesla access to a trove of data which Tesla compiles and analyzes to improve its cars.

SUMMARY OF LEARNING OBJECTIVES

LO1 Define accounts receivable and describe the allowance method of accounting for doubtful accounts. (p. 180)

- Accounts receivable is a current asset created when a sales transaction is executed on a credit basis.
- Accounts receivable does not include such receivables as loans to affiliate companies or advances to employees.
- The credit department of a company is responsible for conducting credit investigations of customers, establishing credit limits, and following up on overdue accounts.

- The allowance method is designed to record the bad debt expense in the same accounting period as the related credit sale.

Describe the percentage of net sales method and the accounts receivable aging method for estimating bad debt expense. (p. 184) LO2

- The percentage of net sales method is used to determine estimated credit losses directly. Estimated credit losses are determined by multiplying credit sales (net of any sales discounts and sales returns and allowances) times the estimated percentage of uncollectible credit sales.
- The accounts receivable aging method determines the estimated credit loss indirectly. The balance in the Accounts Receivable account is segmented into age categories. Then the balance of each category is multiplied by the estimated uncollectible percentage for that age category. The results are added to obtain the desired balance in the Allowance for Doubtful Accounts. The desired balance is then compared to the existing balance in the Allowance for Doubtful Accounts to determine the estimated credit losses and bad debt expense for the period.
- When the allowance method is used, specific accounts are written off by decreasing both the Allowance for Doubtful Accounts and Accounts Receivable.
- Occasionally, accounts written off against the Allowance for Doubtful Accounts later prove to be wholly or partially collectible. When this happens, the Accounts Receivable account is first reinstated to the extent of the recovery, and then the cash collection is recorded.

Discuss the accounting treatment for credit card sales. (p. 189) LO3

- The credit card issuer can reimburse the merchant accepting the credit card immediately upon the electronic transmission of the transaction.
- The credit card fee expense is recognized when the credit card transactions are transmitted to the credit card issuer.

Illustrate a promissory note receivable and discuss the calculation of interest on notes receivable. (p. 191) LO4

- Interest on a short-term promissory note is determined using the following formula:

$$\text{Interest} = \text{Principal} \times \text{Interest rate} \times \text{Time}$$

- When a note is received in payment of an account receivable balance, the Notes Receivable account is increased and the Accounts Receivable account is decreased.
- The noteholder recognizes interest income at the maturity date or in an end-of-period adjustment if the financial statements are prepared before the note matures.

Define accounts receivable turnover and average collection period and explain their use in the analysis and management of receivables. (p. 195) LO5

- Accounts receivable turnover = Net sales/Average accounts receivable
- Average collection period = 365/Accounts receivable turnover
- *Accounts receivable turnover* indicates how many times a year, on average, that a firm collects its accounts receivable. *Average collection period* indicates how many days it takes, on average, to collect an account receivable.

Concept	Method	Assessment	SUMMARY
Are the accounts receivable being collected in a timely manner?	List the accounts receivable along with how long they have been outstanding. Prepare an aging schedule.	Accounts that are past due have not been collected in a timely manner and require additional collection attention.	TAKEAWAY 6.1
Are any of the existing accounts receivable in need of further attention?	Net sales and average accounts receivable Accounts receivable turnover = $\frac{\text{Net sales}}{\text{Average accounts receivable}}$ Average collection period = $\frac{365}{\text{Accounts receivable turnover}}$	Compare the average collection period to the company credit policy. Longer collection periods suggest the need for management attention.	TAKEAWAY 6.2

KEY TERMS

- **Accounts receivable** (p. 180)
- **Accounts receivable aging method** (p. 185)
- **Accounts receivable turnover** (p. 195)
- **Aging schedule** (p. 185)
- **Allowance for Doubtful Accounts** (p. 182)
- **Allowance method** (p. 182)
- **Average collection period** (p. 195)
- **Bad Debt Expense** (p. 182)
- **Bearer** (p. 191)
- **Credit card fee** (p. 190)
- **Credit-collection policy** (p. 182)
- **Credit-granting policy** (p. 181)
- **Maker** (p. 191)
- **Maturity date** (p. 192)
- **Note receivable** (p. 191)
- **Payee** (p. 191)
- **Percentage of net sales method** (p. 184)
- **Promissory note** (p. 191)

SELF-STUDY QUESTIONS

(Answers to the Self-Study Questions are at the end of the chapter.)

LO2 

1. A firm, using the allowance method of recording credit losses, wrote off a customer's account in the amount of $500. Later, the customer paid the account. The firm reinstated the account and then recorded the collection. What is the result of these procedures?

a. Increases total assets by $500
b. Decreases total assets by $500
c. Decreases total assets by $1,000
d. Has no effect on total assets

LO2 

2. A firm has accounts receivable of $90,000 and a negative balance of $900 in the Allowance for Doubtful Accounts. Two-thirds of the accounts receivable are current and one-third is past due. The firm estimates that two percent of the current accounts and five percent of the past due accounts will prove to be uncollectible. The adjustment to provide for the bad debt expense under the aging method should be for what amount?

a. $2,700
b. $3,600
c. $1,800
d. $4,500

LO4 

3. A firm receives a six-month note from a customer. The note has a face amount of $4,000 and an interest rate of nine percent. What is the total amount of interest to be received?

a. $1,080
b. $30
c. $360
d. $180

LO5 

4. A business has net sales of $60,000, a beginning balance in Accounts Receivable of $5,000, and an ending balance in Accounts Receivable of $7,000. What is the company's accounts receivable turnover?

a. 10.0
b. 12.0
c. 8.6
d. 9.2

LO5  

5. A business has an accounts receivable turnover of ten. What is the company's average collection period?

a. 36.0
b. 30.8
c. 34.6
d. 36.5

LO4  

6. Miller Company received a 90 day, six percent note receivable for $10,000 on December 1. How much interest should be accrued on December 31?

a. $150
b. $90
c. $50
d. $25

LO1, 2 Homework MBC

7. Smith Company uses the allowance method to record its expected credit losses. It estimates its losses at one percent of credit sales, which were $750,000 during the year. The Accounts Receivable balance was $220,000 and the Allowance for Doubtful Accounts had a balance of $1,000 at year-end. What amount is the adjustment to the Bad debt expense for the year?

a. $7,500
b. $8,500
c. $6,500
d. $3,200

8. Rankine & Company pays a three percent credit card fee on all credit sales, and receives a cash deposit immediately following each credit card transaction. If credit sales for the company total $15,000 on December 13, what is the amount of cash received and the credit card fee expense? LO3

a. Cash $14,550; Credit Card Fee Expense $450.
b. Cash $15,000; Credit Card Fee Expense $450.
c. Cash $15,450; Credit Card Fee Expense $450.

9. Which of the following statements is true? LO1, 2

a. Generally accepted accounting principles do not require companies use the allowance method.
b. The percentage of net sales method is based on the cash flow statement.
c. The accounts receivable aging method estimates the bad debt expense based on a balance sheet approach.
d. None of the above is true.

QUESTIONS

1. What are accounts receivable?
2. How does a credit scoring system work?
3. What generally accepted accounting principle is being implemented when a company estimates its potential credit losses from its outstanding accounts receivable?
4. When a firm provides for credit losses under the allowance method, why is the adjustment made to the Allowance for Doubtful Accounts rather than Accounts Receivable?
5. What are the two most commonly used methods of estimating the bad debt expense when the allowance method is employed? Describe them.
6. Murphy Company estimates its bad debt expense by aging its accounts receivable and applying percentages to various age groups of the accounts. Murphy calculated a total of $2,100 in possible credit losses as of December 31. Accounts Receivable has a balance of $98,000, and the Allowance for Doubtful Accounts has a balance of $500 before adjustment at December 31. What is the amount of the December 31 adjustment to provide for credit losses? What is the net amount of accounts receivable that should be included in current assets?
7. On June 15, Rollins, Inc. sold $750 worth of merchandise to Dell Company. On November 20, Rollins, Inc., wrote off Dell's account. On March 10 of the following year, Dell Company paid the account in full. What is the effect on total assets of the write-off and the recovery assuming that Rollins, Inc., uses the allowance method of handling credit losses?
8. Wood Company sold a $675 refrigerator to a customer who charged the sale using a VISA credit card. Wood Company electronically transmits credit card transactions at the time of the sale. Wood Company receives payment from VISA upon approval of the transaction. Wood Company's bank charges a credit card fee of four percent of sales revenue. What is the financial statement effect of this sale?
9. Volter Inc. received a 60 day, nine percent note for $15,000 on March 5 from a customer. What is the maturity date of the note?
10. Stanley Company received a 150 day, eight percent note for $15,000 on December 1. What is the amount of accrued interest due on December 31?
11. Define *accounts receivable turnover* and explain its use. How is the *average collection period* determined?
12. At a recent board of directors meeting of Ascot, Inc., one of the directors expressed concern over the Allowance for Doubtful Accounts appearing on the company's balance sheet. "I don't understand this account," he said. "Why don't we just show accounts receivable at the amount we would receive if we sold them to a financial institution and get rid of that allowance account?"

    Prepare a written response to the director. Include in your response (1) an explanation of why the company has an allowance account, (2) what the balance sheet presentation of accounts receivable is supposed to show, and (3) how the basic principles of accounting relate to the analysis and presentation of accounts receivable.
13. When a previously written-off account receivable is collected, it must first be reinstated by increasing both the Accounts Receivable account and the Allowance for Doubtful Accounts. Explain the reason for adjusting the Allowance for Doubtful Accounts.

DATA ANALYTICS

The assignments in this Data Analytics section are designed to familiarize you with the tools used in analyzing data and communicating the results. Appendix F provides an in-depth discussion of data analytics and blockchain technology.

DA6-1. Preparing Accounts Receivable Aging Using Excel

A review of open invoices of Sketchers Inc. results in a schedule shown in the Excel file associated with this exercise. For this exercise, we convert the list of open invoices into an accounts receivable aging schedule.

PART 1 CLEANING THE DATA

1. Download Excel file DA6-1 found in myBusinessCourse.
2. Separate the items listed in one column in the worksheet into three columns using Text to Columns feature under the Data tab.
3. Determine which method to use to divide the data into columns, delimited or fixed width.
4. List the invoice that required a manual adjustment after applying the Text to columns feature.
5. Create a new column in your worksheet that calculates the number of days the invoices are outstanding. *Hint:* Enter: Dec 31 (the date of reference) in a new cell; next, in a new column, for each invoice, subtract the cell holding each invoice date from the cell holding Dec 31 (using an absolute reference). Add $ before the column and row cell reference in a formula to make it absolute. Absolute references don't change when formulas are copied. Change the format in your new column to Number, if necessary. Add headings to your columns.
6. Determine how many days invoice #204 is outstanding based upon data included in your worksheet.

PART 2 CREATING A PIVOTTABLE

1. Create a PivotTable which results in an aging schedule that lists invoices in categories of (1) less than 30 days due, (2) 31–60 days due, (3) 60–90 days due, and (4) greater than 90 days due. *Hint:* After selecting your data and creating a PivotTable, drag Days outstanding to Rows, and drag Amount to Values. PivotTables are created by highlighting the data, including column titles, and clicking PivotTable on the Insert tab. To group your PivotTable into 30-day increments, right-click on the first column, select Group, and enter 1 for "starting," enter 90 for "ending," and enter 30 for "by." Lastly, drag Invoice to Rows to show invoices within each aging category.
2. Determine the total amount in each category, 1–30, 31–60, 61–90, and >91 based on data in the PivotTable.
3. Determine how many invoices are in the 61–90 day category based on data in the PivotTable. *Hint:* Copy the PivotTable from 1. Remove Invoice number from Rows. Open the dropdown menu next to Sum of Amount in the Values box and select Value Field Settings. Select Count in the Summarize value field by box.
4. Create a new PivotTable, updating the aging categories to show aging categories by 30 days through 180 days past due.
5. Determine the total amount in each category, 1–30, 31–60, 61–90, 91–120, 121–150, 151–180 and >181.
6. Determine how many invoices are in the 151–180 category.

DA6-2. Preparing Excel Visualizations to Analyze Industry Trends Over Time

The file associated with this exercise includes data extracted from the Estimates of Monthly Retail and Food Services Sales by Kind of Business obtained at the United States Census Bureau at https://www.census.gov/retail/index.html. In this exercise, we will analyze the trends in sales of *automobile and other motor vehicles* over a five-year period.

REQUIRED

1. Download Excel file DA6-2 found in myBusinessCourse.
2. Transpose the data so that it is shown in a column instead of a long row. *Hint:* Copy, Paste Special, Transpose.
3. Prepare a line chart showing trends in the sales of automobile and other motor vehicle dealers from 2017 to 2021. *Hint:* Highlight data and open Insert tab. Click Line graph in Charts group and select one of the 2-D graphs.
4. Answer the following questions using the visualization for reference.
   a. What was the lowest month of sales during the period of January 2017 to June of 2021?
   b. What was the peak month of sales during the period of January 2017 to June of 2021?
   c. How would you describe the trends in 2020 through the first half of 2021?
   d. What is a likely cause of the low point described in part *a*?

DA6-3. Preparing Tableau Visualizations of Accounts Receivable Aging
Refer to PF-23 in Appendix F. This problem uses Tableau to create accounts receivable aging visualizations based on invoice data provided for Hugo Enterprises.

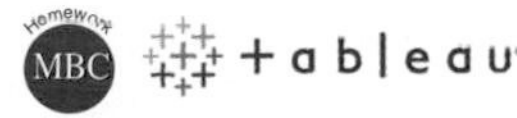

Data Analytics

Assignments with the MBC logo in the margin are available in myBusinessCourse. See the Preface of the book for details.

SHORT EXERCISES

SE6-1. Accounting for Doubtful Accounts Rankine Company estimates its bad debt expense by aging its accounts receivable and applying percentages to various age groups of the accounts. Rankine calculated a total of $4,000 in possible credit losses as of December 31. Accounts Receivable has a balance of $128,000, and the Allowance for Doubtful Accounts has a balance of $500 before adjustment at December 31. What is the amount of the December 31 adjustment to provide for credit losses? What is the net amount of accounts receivable that should be included in current assets? **LO1, 2**

SE6-2. Reinstating Written-Off Accounts The Watergate Company uses the allowance method of recording credit losses and wrote off a customer's account in the amount of $800. Later, the customer paid the account. The company reinstated the account and then recorded the collection. What is the result of these procedures? **LO2**

a. Increases total assets by $800
b. Decreases total assets by $800
c. Decreases total assets by $1,600
d. Has no effect on total assets

SE6-3. Estimating the Bad Debt Expense Winstead & Company has accounts receivable of $120,000 and a negative balance of $1,000 in the Allowance for Doubtful Accounts. Two-thirds of the accounts receivable are current and one-third are past due. The firm estimates that two percent of the current accounts and five percent of the past due accounts will prove to be uncollectible. The adjustment to provide for the bad debt expense under the aging method should be for what amount? **LO2**

a. $3,600
b. $4,600
c. $2,600
d. $1,600

SE6-4. The Financial Statement Effects of Write-Offs Jeffrey Company wrote off $500 in accounts receivable owed from Michael Company. Before the write-off, Net Accounts Receivable for Jeffrey Company were $144,000, which consisted of Accounts Receivable of $150,000, and an Allowance for Doubtful Accounts of $6,000. Which of the following effects did this write-off have on the financial statements of Jeffrey Company? **LO1**

a. Net Accounts Receivable declined by $500
b. Total Assets declined by $500
c. All of the above
d. None of the above

SE6-5. Average Collection Period Los Altos, Inc. has an accounts receivable turnover of 20. What is the company's average collection period? **LO5**

a. 18.25 days
b. 20.0 days
c. 22.25 days
d. 24.25 days

SE6-6. Accounting for Credit Card Sales Chassoul & Company pays a three percent credit card fee on all credit sales, and receives a cash deposit immediately following each credit card transaction. If credit sales for the company total $30,000 on January 15, what amounts should be recorded to recognize the receipt of cash and the credit card fee expense? **LO3**

a. Increase Cash $29,100; increase Credit Card Fee Expense $900.
b. Increase Cash $29,100; decrease Credit Card Fee Expense $900.
c. Increase Cash $30,900; increase Credit Card Fee Expense $900.
d. Increase Cash $30,900; decrease Credit Card Fee Expense $900.

SE6-7. Calculating Accrued Interest Income on Promissory Notes Receivable Likert Company received a 90 day, six percent note receivable for $20,000 on November 1. How much interest income should be accrued on December 31? **LO4**

a. $100
b. $200
c. $300
d. $400

LO4 

SE6-8. Calculating Interest on Promissory Notes Receivable Dallas Company receives a six-month note from a customer. The note has a face amount of $8,000 and an interest rate of nine percent. What is the total amount of interest income to be received?

a. $720
b. $540
c. $360
d. $180

LO5

SE6-9. Accounts Receivable Turnover Tarrant Company has net sales of $120,000, a beginning balance in Accounts Receivable of $10,000, and an ending balance in Accounts Receivable of $14,000. What is the company's accounts receivable turnover?

a. 10.0
b. 12.0
c. 8.6
d. 9.2

EXERCISES

LO2

E6-1. Credit Losses Based on Percentage of Credit Sales Lewis Company uses the allowance method for recording its expected credit losses. It estimates credit losses at 1 percent of credit sales, which were $900,000 during the year. On December 31, the Accounts Receivable balance was $150,000, and the Allowance for Doubtful Accounts had a balance of $10,200 before adjustment.

a. Determine the amount and the financial statement effect of the adjustment to record the credit losses for the year.
b. Show how Accounts Receivable and the Allowance for Doubtful Accounts would appear in the December 31 balance sheet.

LO1, 2

E6-2. Credit Losses Based on Accounts Receivable Aging Hunter, Inc., analyzed its accounts receivable balances at December 31, and arrived at the aged balances listed below, along with the percentage that is estimated to be uncollectible:

Age Group	Balance	Probability of Noncollection
0–30 days past due	$ 90,000	1
31–60 days past due	20,000	2
61–120 days past due	11,000	5
121–180 days past due	6,000	10
Over 180 days past due	4,000	25
	$131,000	

The company handles credit losses using the allowance method. The balance of the Allowance for Doubtful Accounts is $520 on December 31, before any adjustments.

a. Determine the amount of the adjustment for estimated credit losses on December 31.
b. Determine the financial statement effect of a write off of the Rose Company's account on April 10 of the following year in the amount of $425.

LO1

E6-3. Allowance Method On March 10, Gardner, Inc., declared a $900 account receivable from the Gates Company as uncollectible and wrote off the account. On November 18, Gardner received a $400 payment on the account from Gates.

a. Assume that Gardner uses the allowance method of handling credit losses. What are the adjustments to record the write-off and the subsequent recovery of Gates's account?
b. Assume that the payment from Gates arrives on February 5 of the following year rather than on November 18 of the current year. Is there any difference in the financial statement impact?

LO3

E6-4. Credit Card Sales Ruth Anne's Fabrics accepts cash, personal checks, and two credit cards when customers buy merchandise. With the Great American Bank Card, Ruth Anne's Fabrics receives an immediate deposit in its checking account for credit card sales. The bank charges a four percent fee. With the United Merchants Card, Ruth Anne's Fabrics receives a deposit after 3 days, net of a three percent fee. Use the Transaction Analysis Template to record the following:

a. Sales for March 15 were as follows:

Cash and checks	$ 850
Great American Bank Card	1,100
United Merchants Card	700
	$2,650

b. Received a check for $3,978 from United Merchants on March 20.

E6-5. Maturity Dates of Notes Receivable Determine the maturity date and compute the amount of interest at maturity for each of the following notes: **LO4**

Homework MBC

	Date of Note	Principal	Interest Rate (%)	Term
a.	August 5	$ 6,000	8	120 days
b.	May 10	16,800	7	90 days
c.	October 20	24,000	9	45 days
d.	July 6	4,500	10	60 days
e.	September 15	9,000	8	75 days

E6-6. Computing Accrued Interest Compute the interest accrued on each of the following notes receivable held by Northland, Inc., on December 31: **LO4**

Maker	Date of Note	Principal	Interest Rate (%)	Term
Maple	11/21	$18,000	10	120 days
Wyman	12/13	14,000	9	90 days
Nahn	12/19	21,000	8	60 days

E6-7. Accounts Receivable Turnover and Average Collection Period The Forrester Corporation disclosed the following financial information (in millions) in its recent annual report: **LO5**

	Year 1	Year 2
Net sales	$67,096	$81,662
Beginning accounts receivable (net)	3,896	3,696
Ending accounts receivable (net)	3,696	3,598

a. Calculate the accounts receivable turnover ratio for both years.
b. Calculate the average collection period for both years.
c. Is the company's accounts receivable management improving or deteriorating?

E6-8. Credit Losses Based on Percentage of Credit Sales Los Altos, Inc. uses the allowance method of handling its credit losses. It estimates credit losses at one percent of credit sales, which were $1,800,000 during the year. On December 31, the Accounts Receivable balance was $300,000, and the Allowance for Doubtful Accounts had a credit balance of $20,400 before adjustment. **LO1, 2**

a. Determine the amount and financial statement effect of the adjustment to record the credit losses for the year.
b. Show how Accounts Receivable and the Allowance for Doubtful Accounts would appear in the December 31 balance sheet.

E6-9. Credit Losses Based on Accounts Receivable Aging Miller, Inc., analyzed its accounts receivable balances at December 31 and arrived at the aged balances listed below, along with the percentage that is estimated to be uncollectible: **LO1, 2**

Age Group	Balance	Probability of Noncollection
0–30 days past due	$180,000	1
31–60 days past due	40,000	2
61–120 days past due	22,000	5
121–180 days past due	12,000	10
Over 180 days past due	8,000	25
	$262,000	

The company handles credit losses using the allowance method. The credit balance of the Allowance for Doubtful Accounts is $1,040 on December 31, before any adjustments.

a. Determine the amount of the adjustment for estimated credit losses on December 31.
b. Determine the financial statement effect of a write off of the Lyons Company's account on April 10 of the following year in the amount of $425.

LO3 **E6-10. Credit Card Sales** The Tin Roof accepts cash, personal checks, and two credit cards when customers buy merchandise. With the Great American Bank Card, The Tin Roof receives an immediate deposit in its checking account for credit card sales. The bank charges a four percent fee. With the United Merchants Card, The Tin Roof receives a deposit after 3 days, net of a three percent fee. Use the Transaction Analysis Template to record the following:

a. Sales for March 15 were as follows:

Cash and checks	$1,700
Great American Bank Card	2,200
United Merchants Card	1,400
	$5,300

b. Received a check for $7,956 from United Merchants on March 20.

LO4 **E6-11. Maturity Dates of Notes Receivable** Determine the maturity date and compute the amount of interest at maturity for each of the following notes:

	Date of Note	Principal	Interest Rate (%)	Term
a.	August 10	$12,000	8	120 days
b.	May 15	33,600	7	90 days
c.	October 25	48,000	9	45 days
d.	July 11	9,000	10	60 days
e.	September 10	18,000	8	75 days

LO4 **E6-12. Computing Accrued Interest** Compute the interest accrued on each of the following notes receivable held by Kierland, Inc., on December 31:

Maker	Date of Note	Principal	Interest Rate (%)	Term
Abel	11/16	$36,000	10	120 days
Baker	12/8	28,000	9	90 days
Charlie	12/19	42,000	8	60 days

LO5 **E6-13. Accounts Receivable Turnover and Average Collection Period** VanPoole Corporation disclosed the following financial information (in millions) in its recent annual report:

	Year 1	Year 2
Net sales	$167,096	$181,662
Beginning accounts receivable (net)	13,896	13,696
Ending accounts receivable (net)	13,696	13,598

a. Calculate the accounts receivable turnover ratio for both years.
b. Calculate the average collection period for both years.
c. Is the company's accounts receivable management improving or deteriorating?

LO1 **E6-14. Recognizing Accounts Receivable** On June 7, Bixby Co. sells $750 of merchandise to Jasmine Co. on account. Jasmine Co. pays for this merchandise on June 21.

a. Use the Transaction Analysis Template to record the sale.
b. Use the Transaction Analysis Template to record the receipt of payment.

PROBLEMS

LO2 **P6-1. Allowance Method** Fullerton Company, which has been in business for three years, makes all of its sales on account and does not offer cash discounts. The firm's credit sales, collections from customers, and write-offs of uncollectible accounts for the three-year period are summarized below:

Year	Sales	Collections	Accounts Written Off
1	$300,000	$287,000	$2,100
2	385,000	380,000	3,350
3	420,000	407,000	3,650

REQUIRED

a. If Fullerton Company had used the allowance method of recognizing credit losses and had provided for such losses at the rate of 1.2 percent of credit sales, what amounts in accounts receivable and the allowance for doubtful accounts would appear on the firm's balance sheet at the end of Year 3? What total amount of bad debt expense would have appeared on the firm's income statement during the three year period?

b. Comment on the use of the 1.2 percent rate to provide for credit losses in part *a.*

P6-2. Accounts Receivable and Credit Losses At the beginning of the year, Whitney Company had the following accounts on its books: **LO1, 2**

Accounts receivable	$122,000
Allowance for doubtful accounts	7,900

During the year, credit sales were $1,173,000 and collections on account were $1,150,000. The following transactions, among others, occurred during the year:

Feb. 17 Wrote off R. Lowell's account, $3,600.
May 28 Wrote off G. Boyd's account, $2,400.
Oct. 13 Received $600 from G. Boyd, who is in bankruptcy proceedings, in final settlement of the account written off on May 28. This amount is not included in the $1,150,000 collections.
Dec. 15 Wrote off K. Marshall's account, $1,500.
31 Adjusted the allowance for doubtful accounts at 0.8 percent of credit sales for the year.

REQUIRED

a. What is the amount of the Bad Debt Expense for the year?

b. Determine the ending balances of Accounts Receivable and Allowance for Doubtful Accounts using the above information.

c. Show how Accounts Receivable and the Allowance for Doubtful Accounts would appear on the December 31 balance sheet.

P6-3. Credit Losses Based on Accounts Receivable Aging At December 31, Schuler Company had a balance of $375,000 in its Accounts Receivable account and a balance of $4,200 in the Allowance for Doubtful Accounts account. The company aged its accounts as follows: **LO1, 2**

Current	$304,000
0–60 days past due	44,000
61–180 days past due	18,000
Over 180 days past due	9,000
	$375,000

In the past, the company has experienced credit losses as follows: one percent of current balances, five percent of balances 0–60 days past due, 15 percent of balances 61–180 days past due, and 40 percent of balances over six months past due. The company bases its allowance for doubtful accounts on an aging analysis of accounts receivable.

REQUIRED

a. Determine the amount of the adjustment to record the allowance for doubtful accounts for the year.

b. Show how Accounts Receivable and the Allowance for Doubtful Accounts would appear on the December 31 balance sheet.

P6-4. Credit Card Sales Valderi's Gallery sells quality art work. The following two credit card transactions occurred during the first day of June. **LO3**

Sold three framed etchings totaling $2,400 to Maria Alvado, who used the United Merchants Card to charge the cost of the etchings. Valderi transmitted the transaction to United Merchants the same day. United Merchants will credit the company's checking account within seven days after deducting a one percent fee.

Sold a $2,000 watercolor to Julie and John Malbie, who used their Great American Bank Card to charge the purchase of the painting. Valderi transmitted the transaction the same day and received immediate credit in the company's checking account. The bank charged a two percent fee.

REQUIRED

Use the Transaction Analysis Template to show how sales revenues were recorded for these credit card transactions for the Valderi Gallery.

LO2, 4 **P6-5.** **Accounting for Accounts and Notes Receivable** Lancaster Inc. began business on January 1. Certain transactions for the year follow:

Homework MBC

June 8 Received a $15,000, 60 day, eight percent note on account from R. Elliot.
Aug. 7 Received payment from R. Elliot on her note (principal plus interest).
Sept. 1 Received an $18,000, 120 day, nine percent note from B. Shore Company on account.
Dec. 16 Received a $14,400, 45 day, ten percent note from C. Judd on account.
30 B. Shore Company failed to pay its note.
31 Wrote off B. Shore's account as uncollectible. Lancaster, Inc. uses the allowance method of providing for credit losses.
31 Accounts written off during this first year have exceeded the balance in the Allowance for Doubtful Accounts by $22,600. An analysis of aged receivables indicates that the desired balance of the allowance account should be $19,500.

REQUIRED

a. Determine the balance in Notes Receivable.
b. Determine the amount of the year end adjustment to the Allowance for Doubtful Accounts.
c. Determine the amount of the Accrued Interest at year end.

LO2 **P6-6.** **Allowance Method** The Huntington Company, which has been in business for three years, makes all of its sales on account and does not offer cash discounts. The firm's credit sales, collections from customers, and write-offs of uncollectible accounts for the three-year period are summarized below:

Year	Sales	Collections	Accounts Written Off
1	$600,000	$574,000	$4,200
2	770,000	760,000	6,700
3	840,000	814,000	7,300

REQUIRED

a. If the Huntington Company had used the allowance method of recognizing credit losses and had provided for such losses at the rate of 1.2 percent of credit sales, what amounts in Accounts Receivable and the Allowance for Doubtful Accounts would appear on the firm's balance sheet at the end of Year 3? What total amount of bad debt expense would have appeared on the firm's income statement during the three year period?
b. Comment on the use of the 1.2 percent rate to provide for credit losses in part *a.*

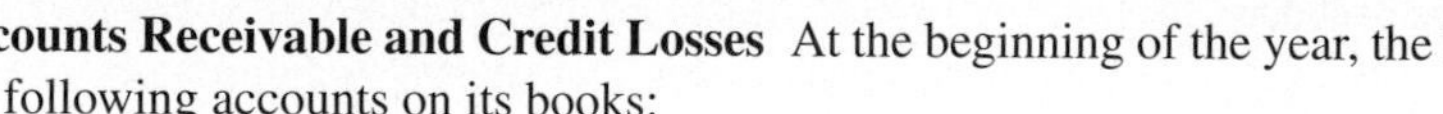

LO1, 2 **P6-7.** **Accounts Receivable and Credit Losses** At the beginning of the year, the Houston Company had the following accounts on its books:

Accounts receivable	$244,000
Allowance for doubtful accounts	15,800

During the year, credit sales were $2,346,000 and collections on account were $2,300,000. The following transactions, among others, occurred during the year:

Feb. 17 Wrote off R. St. John's account, $7,200.
May 28 Wrote off G. Herberger's account, $4,800.
Oct. 13 Received $1,200 from G. Herberger, who is in bankruptcy proceedings, in final settlement of the account written off on May 28. This amount is not included in the $2,300,000 collections.
Dec. 15 Wrote off R. Clancy's account, $3,000.
31 Adjusted the allowance for doubtful accounts to 0.8 percent of credit sales for the year.

REQUIRED

a. What is the amount of Bad Debt Expense for the year?
b. Determine the balance in Accounts Receivable and the Allowance for Doubtful Accounts.
c. Show how Accounts Receivable and the Allowance for Doubtful Accounts would appear on the December 31 balance sheet.

P6-8. **Credit Losses Based on Accounts Receivable** At December 31, the Selling Company had a balance of $750,000 in its Accounts Receivable account and a balance of $8,400 in the Allowance for Doubtful Accounts account. The company aged its accounts as follows: LO1, 2

Current	$608,000
0–60 days past due	88,000
61–180 days past due	36,000
Over 180 days past due	18,000
	$750,000

In the past, the company has experienced credit losses as follows: one percent of current balances, five percent of balances 0–60 days past due, 15 percent of balances 61–180 days past due, and 40 percent of balances over six months past due. The company bases its allowance for doubtful accounts on an aging analysis of accounts receivable.

REQUIRED

a. Determine the amount of the adjustment to record the allowance for doubtful accounts for the year.

b. Show how Accounts Receivable and the Allowance for Doubtful Accounts would appear on the December 31 balance sheet.

P6-9. **Accounts and Notes Receivable** Pittsburgh, Inc., began business on January 1. Certain transactions for the year follow: LO2, 4

June 8 Received a $30,000, 60 day, eight percent note on account from J. Albert.
Aug. 7 Received payment from J. Albert on his note (principal plus interest).
Sept. 1 Received a $36,000, 120 day, nine percent note from R.T. Matthews Company on account.
Dec. 16 Received a $28,800, 45 day, ten percent note from D. LeRoy on account.
30 R.T. Matthews Company failed to pay its note.
31 Wrote off R.T. Matthews' account as uncollectible. Pittsburgh, Inc., uses the allowance method of providing for credit losses.
31 Accounts written off during this first year have exceeded the balance in the allowance for doubtful accounts by $45,200. An analysis of aged receivables indicates that the desired balance of the allowance account should be $39,000.
31 Adjusted for accrued interest.

REQUIRED

a. Determine the balance in Notes Receivable at December 31.

b. Determine the amount of interest income from these notes receivable.

c. Determine the amount of the adjustment for credit losses.

SERIAL PROBLEM: ANGEL CITY GREETINGS

(Note: This is a continuation of the Serial Problem: Angel City Greetings from Chapters 1 through 5.)

SP6. Kate has put a lot of time and effort into streamlining the process to design and produce a greeting card. She has documented the entire process in a QuickTime video she produced on her iMac. The video takes the viewer through the step-by-step process of selecting hardware and software, and shows how to design and produce the card. Kate has met many people who would like to get into the production of greeting cards, but are overwhelmed by the process. Kate has decided to sell the entire package (hardware, software, and video tutorial) to aspiring card producers. The cost of the entire package to Kate is $4,500 and she plans to mark it up by $500 and sell it for $5,000.

John Stevens, an individual Kate met recently at a greeting card conference, would like to buy the package from Kate. Unfortunately, John does not have this much cash and would like for Kate to extend credit.

Kate believes that many of her customers will not be able to pay cash and, therefore, she will need to find some way to provide financing. One option she is exploring is to accept credit cards. She learned that the credit card provider charges a 2.5 percent fee and provides immediate cash upon receiving the sales receipts.

Kate would like you to answer the following questions:

1. What are the advantages and disadvantages of offering credit?
2. What precautions should she take before offering credit to people like John?

3. If Kate grants credit to John, the terms will be 2/10, n/30. Assuming the payment is made during the 10-day discount period, what would be the financial statement effect of the sale and then the subsequent payment?
4. If instead of paying early, John pays in 25 days, what would be the financial statement effect of the payment?
5. Rather than providing the financing directly, assume that Kate decides to allow the use of credit cards. Further, assume that during the month there is $15,000 worth of credit card sales. What is the financial statement effect of the sales, along with the associated credit card fee? The cost of the goods sold total $13,500.

BEYOND THE NUMBERS

REPORTING AND ANALYSIS

Columbia Sportswear Company

BTN6-1. **Financial Reporting Problem: Columbia Sportswear Company** The financial statements of the **Columbia Sportswear Company** are presented in Appendix A at the end of this book.

a. What was the amount of the Accounts Receivables and the Allowance for Doubtful Accounts at the end of each of the two years presented?

b. What percent of total accounts receivables was the allowance for doubtful accounts at the end of each of the two years presented?

Columbia Sportswear Company
Under Armour, Inc.

BTN6-2. **Comparative Analysis Problem: Columbia Sportswear Company vs. Under Armour, Inc.** The financial statements of the **Columbia Sportswear Company** are presented in Appendix A and of **Under Armour, Inc.**, in Appendix B.

Required

a. Calculate the accounts receivable turnover and the average collection period for Columbia Sportswear and Under Armour, Inc. for each of the two years presented. (To calculate the accounts receivable turnover, use the ending net accounts receivable balance as the denominator rather than average net accounts receivable.)

b. Compare the average collection periods for the two companies and comment on possible reasons for the difference in the average collection periods for the two companies.

BTN6-3. **Business Decision Problem** Sally Smith owned a dance studio in San Francisco, California. Students could buy access to the dance classes by paying a monthly fee. Unfortunately, many of Sally's students were struggling actors and actresses who lacked the ability to pay their bills in a timely manner. And, although the students were expected to pay for classes in advance, Sally had begun offering credit to many of her students in order to grow her business. This, however, created a serious liquidity problem for Sally.

Age Classification	Trade Receivables Outstanding Balance	Historical Estimate of Noncollection
0–30 days	$44,000	4%
31–60 days	31,000	8%
61–90 days	22,000	12%
91–120 days	13,000	14%
121–150 days	9,000	20%
> 150 days	5,000	50%

Sally's accountant, Matt Thomas, had tried to help her get a handle on the receivable problem, but to little avail. One trick he had successfully used in the past to make Sally realize the seriousness of the problem was to overestimate the extent of Sally's bad debt problem; consequently, there currently existed a balance in the Allowance for Uncollectible Accounts totaling $2,700.

Required

1. The first step to help get Sally's business back on track is to write off all receivables having a very low probability of collection (i.e., those accounts over 150 days). Which accounts are affected and by what amount, to execute this action?
2. Prepare an aging of Sally's remaining accounts receivable. What should be the balance in the Allowance for Uncollectible Accounts?
3. Sally is in need of an immediate cash infusion and Matt has advised her to sell some of her receivables. A local bank has offered her two alternatives:

a. Factor $40,000 of "current" receivables (i.e., 0–30 days old) on a without-recourse basis at a flat fee of eleven percent of the receivables sold.

b. Factor $40,000 of "current" receivables on a recourse basis at a flat fee of six percent of the receivables sold.

Which option should Sally choose? Why?

Abbott Laboratories
Pfizer Inc.

BTN6-4. Financial Analysis Problem Abbott Laboratories is a diversified health care company devoted to the discovery, development, manufacture, and marketing of innovative products that improve diagnostic, therapeutic, and nutritional practices. Abbott markets products worldwide and employs 99,000 people. Pfizer Inc. is a research-based, global health care company. Its mission is to discover and develop innovative, value-added products that improve the quality of life of people around the world. Pfizer manufactures products in 58 sites worldwide and markets them in more than 125 countries. These two companies reported the following information in their financial reports:

(in millions)	2020	2019
Abbott Laboratories		
Net sales	$34,608	$31,904
Beginning accounts receivable (net)	5,425	5,182
Ending accounts receivable (net)	6,414	5,425
Pfizer Inc.		
Net sales	$41,908	$41,172
Beginning accounts receivable (net)	6,772	8,025
Ending accounts receivable (net)	7,930	6,772

Required

a. Calculate the accounts receivable turnover and the average collection period for Abbott Laboratories and Pfizer Inc. for both years.

b. Compare the average collection periods for the two companies and comment on possible reasons for the difference in average collection periods for the two companies.

CRITICAL THINKING

General Mills, Inc.

BTN6-5. Accounting Research Problem Access the fiscal year 2020 annual report of General Mills, Inc., which can be found at: https://investors.generalmills.com/financial-information/annual-reports/default.aspx.

Required

a. What was the amount of total Accounts Receivables and the Allowance for Doubtful Accounts at the end of each fiscal year? (Note: This information can be found in note 18.)

b. What percent of total accounts receivables was the allowance for doubtful accounts at the end of each fiscal year?

c. Calculate the accounts receivable turnover and the average collection period for General Mills for each year. (For purposes of calculating the accounts receivable turnover, use the ending total accounts receivable balance as the denominator rather than the average total accounts receivable.)

d. Comment on whether General Mills' management of accounts receivable improved (or not) over the two year period.

BTN6-6. Accounting Communications Activity You have been hired as the accounting manager of Taylor, Inc., a provider of custom furniture. The company recently switched its method of paying its salespeople from a straight salary to a commission basis in order to encourage them to increase sales. The salespeople receive ten percent of the sales price at the time of the sale. You have noticed that the company's accounts receivable balance is growing because the salespeople are granting more credit to their customers.

Required

Draft a memorandum explaining why it is important to closely monitor the company's accounts receivable balance and why a large balance could lead to cash flow problems.

BTN6-7. Accounting Ethics Case Tractor Motors' best salesperson is Marie Glazer. Glazer's largest sales have been to Farmers Cooperative, a customer she brought to the company. Another salesperson, Bryan Blanchard, has been told in confidence by his cousin (an employee of Farmers

Cooperative) that Farmers Cooperative is experiencing financial difficulties and may not be able to pay Tractor Motors what is owed.

Both Glazer and Blanchard are being considered for promotion to a new sales manager position.

Required

What are the ethical considerations that face Bryan Blanchard? What alternatives does he have?

MGM Resorts International

BTN6-8. Environmental, Social, and Governance Problem MGM Resorts International is committed to responsible gaming and strictly adheres to the Code of Conduct established by the American Gaming Association. The company's efforts include employee training, public awareness, and support for research initiatives through the National Center for Responsible Gaming.

Because MGM Resorts International makes money when people gamble, and the more people gamble, the more money the company makes, why would MGM Resorts International work to curtail gambling by some of the people they could make a lot of money from? Does this form of good citizenship run counter to the company's responsibilities to its stockholders?

BTN6-9. Accounting Ethics Problem The chapter highlight on accounting ethics discussed the technique of covering up receivables theft by lapping (see Accounting Ethics: Lapping on page 189), where one account is credited with the receipt from another account. The highlight stated that lapping may be detected by an auditor through the confirmation of accounts receivables. While detection is important, it is far better to prevent lapping from occurring in the first place. Can you think of any controls that can be put in place to help prevent lapping?

MGM Resorts International

BTN6-10. Working with the Takeaways Below are selected data from MGM Resorts International 2020 financial statements. Amounts are in thousands.

Net sales	$5,162,082
Beginning of year accounts receivable	612,717
End of year accounts receivable	316,502

Required

Calculate the MGM Resorts International (a) accounts receivable turnover, and (b) average collection period.

ANSWERS TO SELF-STUDY QUESTIONS

1. d **2.** b **3.** d **4.** a **5.** d **6.** c **7.** a **8.** a **9.** c

REVIEW SOLUTIONS

Solution 6.1

d. Both *b.* and *c.* are correct. The allowance method follows the matching principle which states that expenses should be matched with the revenues they help generate and the amount of bad debt expense is an estimate.

Solution 6.2

Transaction: *Bad debt expense for the year.*

Balance Sheet							Income Statement				
Assets	=	Liabilities	+	Stockholders' Equity							
				Contrib. Capital	+	Retained Earnings	Revenues	−	Expenses	=	Net Income
−18,000 Allowance for doubtful accounts	=		+			−18,000		−	+18,000 Bad debt expense	=	−18,000

$600,000 × 3%

Solution 6.3

Transaction: *Bad debt expense for the year and subsequent write off of accounts receivable.*

	Balance Sheet							Income Statement				
	Assets	=	Liabilities	+	Stockholders' Equity							
					Contrib. Capital	+	Retained Earnings	Revenues	−	Expenses	=	Net Income
a.	−3,950 Allowance for doubtful accounts	=		+			−3,950		−	+3,950 Bad debt expense	=	−3,950
	Bad debt expense for the year.											
b.	+480 Allowance for doubtful accounts −480 Accounts receivable	=		+					−		=	
	Write off Phorest Company uncollectible account.											

Solution 6.4

Transaction: *Credit card sales and collection, less a two percent fee.*

Balance Sheet							Income Statement				
Assets	=	Liabilities	+	Stockholders' Equity							
				Contrib. Capital	+	Retained Earnings	Revenues	−	Expenses	=	Net Income
+49,000 Cash	=		+			+49,000	+50,000 Sales revenue	−	+1,000 Credit card fee expense	=	+49,000

Solution 6.5

$40,000 × .05 × 3/12 = $500

Solution 6.6

	Balance Sheet							Income Statement				
	Assets	=	Liabilities	+	Stockholders' Equity							
					Contrib. Capital	+	Retained Earnings	Revenues	−	Expenses	=	Net Income
Year 1 31 Dec.	−3,750 Allowance for doubtful accounts	=		+			−3,750		−	+3,750 Bad debt expense	=	−3,750
	Provide for bad debt expense at 1.5% of net credit sales ($250,000 × 0.015)											
31 Dec.	+48 Interest receivable	=		+			+48	+48 Interest income	−		=	+48
	Accrue interest on Jason, Inc. note receivable ($12,000 × 0.08 × 18/360)											

continued

continued from previous page

	Balance Sheet							Income Statement				
	Assets	=	Liabilities	+	Stockholders' Equity							
					Contrib. Capital	+	Retained Earnings	*Revenues*	−	*Expenses*	=	*Net Income*
Year 2 12 Mar.	+12,240 Cash −12,000 Notes receivable −48 Interest receivable	=		+			+192	+192 Interest income	−		=	+192
	Receipt of payment of Jason, Inc. note receivable ($12,000 × 0.08 × 72/360 = $192)											
5 Apr.	+2,850 Allowance for doubtful accounts −2,850 Accounts receivable	=		+					−		=	
	Write off the account of Abilene Company as uncollectible.											
9 Jul.	+1,450 Allowance for doubtful accounts −1,450 Accounts receivable	=		+					−		=	
	Write off the account of Acme Suppliers as uncollectible.											
5 Sep.	+450 Accounts receivable −450 Allowance for doubtful accounts	=		+					−		=	
	Reinstate $450 of the account of Acme Suppliers.											
5 Sep.	+450 Cash −450 Accounts receivable	=		+					−		=	
	Payment of Acme Suppliers' account.											
6 Dec.	+1,300 Allowance for doubtful accounts −1,300 Accounts receivable	=		+					−		=	
	Write off the account of Walton, Inc. as uncollectible.											

continued

continued from previous page

	Balance Sheet						Income Statement		
	Assets	=	Liabilities	+	Stockholders' Equity				
					Contrib. Capital	+ Retained Earnings	Revenues	− Expenses	= Net Income
31 Dec.	−4,700 Allowance for doubtful accounts	=		+		−4,700		− +4,700 Bad debt expense	= −4,700

Provide for bad debt expense.

Allowance for bad debts—activity	
Beginning	1,200
Year 1 provision	3,750
Abilene Company w/o	(2,850)
Acme Suppliers w/o	(1,450)
Acme Suppliers settlement . . .	450
Walton, Inc. w/o	(1,300)
Balance before adjustment . . .	(200)
Year 2 provision	4,700
Ending Balance	4,500

Solution 6.7

a. Accounts receivable turnover = \$30,000/[(\$2,800 + \$3,200)/2] = 10

b. Average collection period = 365/10 = 36.5 days

Inventory

PAST

In Chapter 6 we studied how to account for accounts and notes receivable.

PRESENT

This chapter focuses on the accounting for inventory and cost flow assumptions.

FUTURE

In Chapter 8 we will continue our study of a company's assets by looking at property, plant and equipment, and intangible assets.

COSTCO

With the advent of the COVID-19 pandemic in 2020, Americans felt the need to purchase large quantities of bottled water and paper products. Who better to provide buying opportunities than **Costco Wholesale**? Costco members lined up in cold temperatures with oversized shopping carts to panic-purchase these items, resulting in a 9% increase in net sales for Costco in fiscal 2020.

Costco's business model is "based on the concept that offering our members low prices on a limited selection of nationally-branded and private-label products in a wide range of categories will produce high sales volumes and rapid inventory turnover. When combined with the operating efficiencies achieved by volume purchasing, efficient distribution and reduced handling of merchandise in no-frills, self-service warehouse facilities, these volumes and turnover enable us to operate profitably at significantly lower gross margins (net sales less merchandise costs) than most other retailers. We generally sell inventory before we are required to pay for it, even while taking advantage of early payment discounts." *Source:* Costco 2020 Form 10K.

Road Map

LO	Learning Objective	Page	eLecture	Review	Assignments
LO1	**Explain how inventories differ between merchandisers, manufacturers, and wholesalers.**	216	E7-1	7.1	SE1, E2
LO2	**Describe inventory costing under specific identification, weighted-average cost, FIFO, and LIFO.**	221	E7-2	7.2, 7.6	SE4, SE8, SE9, SE11, E3, E5, E8, E9, P2, P4, P5
LO3	**Analyze the effects of different inventory costing methods on company profit.**	225	E7-3	7.2, 7.6	SE12, E13, P4, P6
LO4	**Apply the lower of cost or net realizable value rule.**	230	E7-4	7.3	SE3, SE6, E7, E12
LO5	**Define the gross profit percentage and explain its use.**	231	E7-5	7.4, 7.6	SE2, E1, P1
LO6	**Define inventory turnover and days' sales in inventory and explain their use.**	233	E7-6	7.5, 7.6	SE7, E10, E12, P7
LO7	**Appendix 7A: Describe inventory costing under a perpetual inventory system.**	235	E7-7		SE10, E4, E6, P3
LO8	**Appendix 7B: Define the LIFO reserve and explain its use.**	239	E7-8		SE5, E11, P8

Inventory					
The Nature of Inventory	Inventory Costing Methods	Lower of Cost or Net Realizable Value	Inventory Analysis	Inventory Costing Using a Perpetual System (Appendix 7A)	LIFO Reserve (Appendix 7B)
• Categories of inventory • Costs included • Inventory management • Cost of goods sold • Physical inventory counts • Inventory costing systems	• Goods flow vs. cost flow • Specific identification • First-in, first-out • Last-in, first-out • Weighted-average cost • Effects of inventory method choice • How managers choose an inventory method	• What is net realizable value • Apply the net realizable value rule	• Gross profit percentage • Inventory turnover • Days' sales in inventory	• Specific identification method • First-in, first-out • Last-in, first-out • Weighted-average cost • Comparison of costing methods	• What is a LIFO inventory reserve • How can the use of a LIFO reserve impact ending inventory, net earnings, and the current ratio

eLecture
MBC

THE NATURE OF INVENTORY

LO1 Explain how inventories differ between merchandisers, manufacturers, and wholesalers.

Manufacturers, wholesalers, and retailers are companies that sell products rather than services. Wholesalers and retailers are both merchandising firms. **Merchandising firms** buy finished products, warehouse the products for varying periods of time, and then resell the products. Merchandising firms do not manufacture products nor do they consume the products that they purchase. Merchandising firms provide additional services to their customers, but their primary business is the resale of goods produced by other companies. **Exhibit 7-1** illustrates the typical relationship among these three types of companies and the final consumer.

EXHIBIT 7-1 Distribution of Products to Individual Consumers

Walmart
Manufacturer
Wholesaler and/or Retailer
Consumer
Manufacturers convert raw materials into finished goods as part of their business activities.
Merchandisers resell the inventory they purchase; they do not manufacture or consume products as part of their business activities.

A.K.A. Business-to-business transactions, such as Del Monte's sale of canned peaches to Safeway, are often referred to simply as *B2B transactions*.

Manufacturers convert raw materials and component parts into a finished product through the application of skilled labor and machine operations. **Ford Motor Company**, for example, converts raw materials such as sheets of steel and components such as tires into automobiles and trucks. Similarly, **Del Monte** converts such raw materials as fresh peaches and such components as metal cans into canned peaches. Manufacturers typically only sell their products to wholesale distributors. This process is referred to as a business-to-business (B2B) transaction.

Wholesalers buy finished products from manufacturing firms in large quantities and sell and ship the product to various retailers in smaller quantities. **Retailers** typically buy products from wholesale distributors and resell the finished products to individual consumers in what is referred to as a business-to-consumer transaction (a B2C transaction).

Categories of Inventory

Merchandise inventory consists of finished goods that a merchandising company buys from a manufacturing company and makes available for sale to its customers. Unlike merchandising firms, manufacturing firms purchase raw materials and components and convert them into salable merchandise in their factories. At any point in time, manufacturing firms have merchandise at various stages of completion. Consequently, a manufacturing firm usually maintains three categories of inventory: raw materials inventory, work-in-process inventory, and finished goods inventory.

The **raw materials inventory** includes raw materials and components that have been purchased for use in the production of a product but that have not yet been placed into the production process. Sheets of steel are an example of raw material, and computer chips are an example of a component. A component is an item in the raw materials inventory account that was a finished product for the manufacturer that produced it. For example, **Intel Corporation** manufactures computer chips that other manufacturers incorporate into their final products. **Dell Inc.**, a computer manufacturer, is an example of a company that incorporates the finished goods of Intel into the computers that it manufactures.

The **work-in-process inventory** consists of units of product that have been placed into production in a factory but that are not fully assembled. All of the costs related to raw materials, human labor in the factory, factory utilities, and other factory-related resources are included in the work-in-process inventory. Items in this inventory category are not ready for sale because they are not yet a finished product.

The **finished goods inventory** includes all units that have been fully manufactured and are ready to be sold to customers. The cost of each item in the finished goods inventory is accumulated in the work-in-process inventory account and is transferred to the finished goods inventory when the inventory is ready for sale.

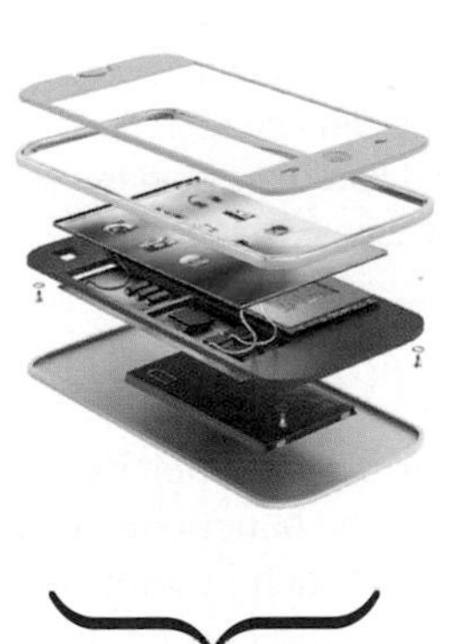

Raw Materials

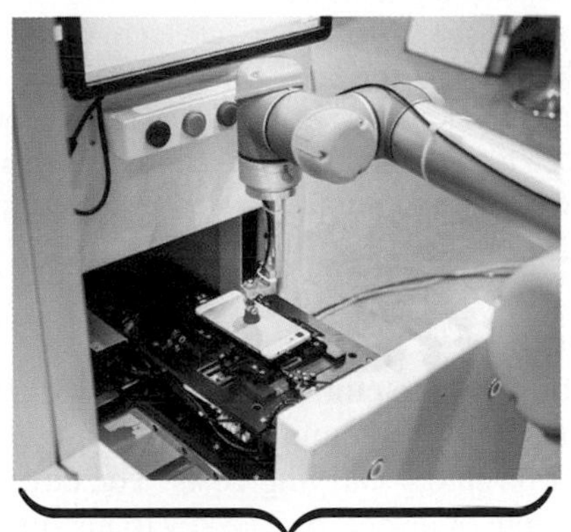

Work-in-Process

Finished Goods

Costs Included in Inventory

All necessary costs incurred to acquire the inventory and deliver it to the buyer's place of business are included in the buyer's cost of inventory. These costs usually consist primarily of the inventory's **purchase price**, but also include other costs, such as taxes and shipping costs. The inventory cost is reduced by **purchase returns and allowances** and by any **purchase discounts** that are earned by the purchaser. Returns and allowances occur, for example, when the seller ships the wrong inventory, or the inventory is damaged during shipping. In the case of a purchase return, the buyer ships the unsatisfactory inventory back to the seller and the amount owed to the seller is reduced by the purchase price. In the case of a purchase allowance, the buyer retains the inventory, and the amount owed to the seller is reduced by the purchase price. Purchase discounts are sometimes offered by sellers when purchasers buy on credit and pay the seller before the contractually agreed due date. Such discounts reduce the cost of the inventory.

PRINCIPLE ALERT

Cost Principle The inclusion of taxes and transportation costs in the acquisition cost of inventory is consistent with the **cost principle**. The cost principle states that an asset is initially recorded at the amount paid to acquire the asset. There can be multiple expenditures associated with an asset acquisition, and all expenditures that are reasonable and necessary to acquire an asset are added to the asset's initial recorded cost.

Inventory Management

Merchandising and manufacturing companies often find it desirable to maintain a large and varied inventory of merchandise to satisfy the diverse needs and preferences of their customers.

Just-in-Case Inventory

Manufacturing companies have traditionally maintained inventories as a buffer against unforeseen shipping delays and unforeseen demand by customers. This extra quantity is known as **just-in-case inventory**. While just-in-case inventories reduce the chances of running out of inventory, the downside is that they result in **inventory carrying costs**, which include insurance, building usage costs, and the cost of the capital invested in the inventory.

ACCOUNTING IN PRACTICE

Quick Response Systems Many retailers have installed point-of-sale checkout systems to assist in inventory management. These systems either read Universal Product Code bar codes or specially-formed characters using either a plate scanner built into the checkout counter or a handheld scanner (or "wand") to identify the product being sold. Retailers also use a quick response system to optimize their inventory. A **quick response system** is designed to ensure that the retailer quickly reorders items that are being sold and quickly eliminates from inventory any items that are not selling. Special software on a business's computer identifies fast-selling and slow-selling items. The retailer reviews the list and orders more of the highly desirable items that are selling quickly. A retailer typically uses one (or both) of the following approaches to eliminate slow-moving items: (1) return the item to the supplier (if possible) and (2) reduce the unit selling price to (hopefully) induce a quick sale. Quick response systems tend to reduce both the size of inventory that a company must maintain and increase the dollar amount of its sales revenue.

Just-in-Time Manufacturing

Just-in-time (JIT) manufacturing seeks to eliminate or minimize inventory quantities by ordering and stocking only enough material to meet immediate demand. This can be beneficial because smaller inventories result in lower inventory carrying costs. The downside of such systems is that they increase the chance of running out of inventory. The key to just-in-time manufacturing involves careful raw material purchase planning and careful management of the manufacturing and sales processes.

Cost of Goods Sold

Revenues from the sale of inventory in the income statement equal the number of units sold times the selling price. The costs of the inventory for merchandisers all flow through its accounting system as diagrammed below. Specifically, a company records its *costs of goods purchased* and adds this to any *beginning inventory* it might have. These two components make up the company's **cost of goods available for sale**. From that total, a company sells part or all of this inventory, which is recorded in *cost of goods sold*. The remaining inventory is referred to as the *ending inventory*, and becomes the next period's beginning inventory. Thus, as shown in **Exhibit**

7-2, beginning inventory plus cost of goods purchased equals cost of goods available for sale; deducting ending inventory from cost of goods available for sale equals **cost of goods sold**.

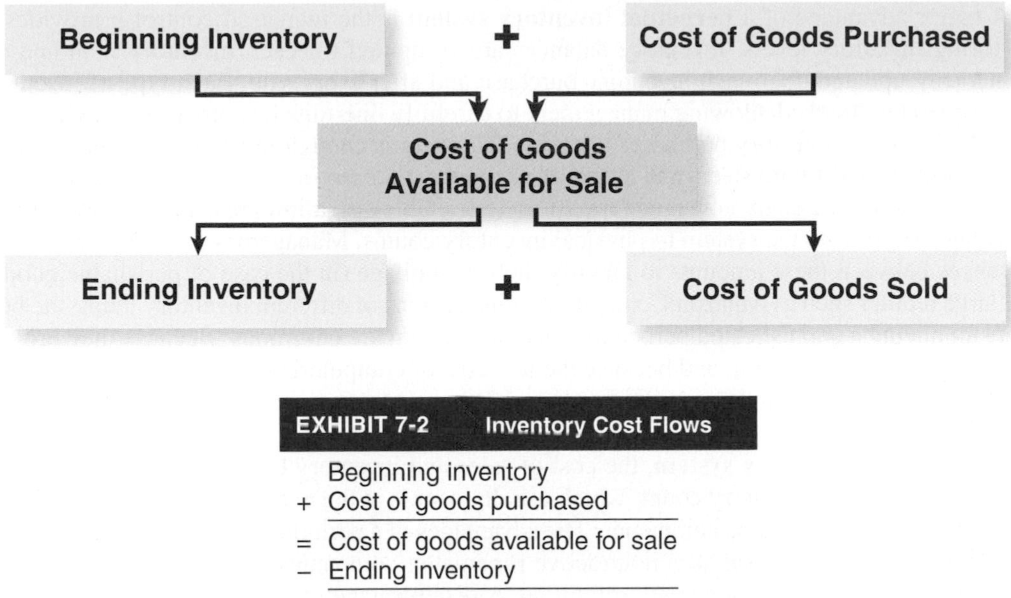

EXHIBIT 7-2 Inventory Cost Flows

	Beginning inventory
+	Cost of goods purchased
=	Cost of goods available for sale
−	Ending inventory
=	Cost of goods sold

Physical Count of Inventory

It is important for companies to take a **physical count of inventory** at the end of each accounting period. This is because changes in the quantity of particular items could have taken place without a transaction being recognized. For example, items may have been stolen, damaged, or destroyed. Also, the seller might have shipped an incorrect quantity to a customer even though the seller reflected the correct quantity in recording the sale. The physical count of inventory is usually taken at year-end and consists of the following steps:

1. Count the number of individual items of inventory available at the end of the period.
2. Determine the unit cost of each individual item and multiply the unit cost times the quantity to obtain the total cost for each individual inventory item.
3. Add the total cost of all the individual inventory items to obtain the total cost of the aggregate inventory available.

In a perpetual inventory system, if the physical count of inventory results in a total that does not agree with the balance in the Inventory account, the company makes a year-end adjustment. If the physical inventory total is less than the Inventory account balance, the company makes an adjustment to increase Cost of Goods Sold and decrease Inventory for the difference between the physical inventory total and the balance in the Inventory account. The cost associated with an inventory shortage is known as **inventory shrinkage**. Shrinkage for U.S. retailers during 2020 is estimated at over $60 billion, or 1.62%, according to the 2020 National Retail Security Survey, the largest part resulting from theft.

If the physical inventory total is greater than the Inventory account balance, the company makes an adjustment to increase Inventory and decrease Cost of Goods Sold for the difference between the physical inventory and the Inventory account balance. This entry increases the balance in the Inventory account and subtracts the cost of this **inventory overage** from Cost of Goods Sold.

Inventory Costing Systems

Companies typically use one of two systems to account for inventory: a **perpetual inventory system** or a **periodic inventory system**. The difference between the two methods is how frequently the cost of inventory sold and ending inventory are calculated. Under a perpetual system, the cost of inventory sold is calculated immediately after each sale. Consequently, the inventory balance is kept "perpetually" up-to-date. Under a periodic system, the cost of inventory sold is only calculated "periodically," at the end of the accounting period. Consequently, the inventory balance is only computed at the end of the accounting period.

A major advantage of a **perpetual inventory system** is the increased control it provides in monitoring inventory levels. Inventory balances are computed for each inventory item and are continuously updated after each inventory purchase and after every sale. Each type of inventory item is separately tracked allowing management to carefully fine-tune inventory levels. This facilitates the timing of inventory purchases to assure that there is enough inventory on hand to cover pending or expected future sales, and at the same time avoid carrying excess inventory. Having a "real-time" record of exactly how much inventory is available also allows management to compare the inventory counts in the system to physical inventory counts. Management can then investigate differences between these amounts to identify theft or spoilage (in the case of perishable goods). For a large retailer such as Amazon.Com, which sells millions of different inventory items, the benefits from having a sophisticated perpetual inventory system are enormous. Because they provide up-to-the-minute information, and because the low cost of computerization has made them easier to implement, perpetual inventory systems have become the most popular inventory accounting system in use.

In a **periodic inventory system**, the cost of sales and inventory balances are typically computed after a physical inventory count, which usually occurs at the end of the fiscal year, but may occur more frequently in some companies. The advantages of a periodic system are that it is simple and easy to implement. This makes it attractive for smaller companies, where sophisticated computerized perpetual systems are cost prohibitive. A disadvantage of a periodic inventory system is that inventory levels and cost of sales are harder to track on a day-to-day basis. This makes managing inventory levels more difficult, increasing the risk of both running out of inventory and of being overstocked.

PRINCIPLE ALERT

Revenue and Expense Recognition The revenue recognition principle requires revenues to be recorded when they are earned, which is usually when control of the goods or services is transferred to the buyer. The amount recorded equals the amount received (for cash sales), or the amount expected to be received (for sales on credit). The *expense recognition (matching) principle* requires the cost of goods sold to be recorded in the same accounting period as the revenues they help generate.

ENVIRONMENTAL, SOCIAL, AND GOVERNANCE

Governance and Conflicts of Interest An important component of good corporate responsibility is strong corporate governance. **Target** publishes a Business Conduct Guide for its employees as part of its governance program. Included in this handbook are guidelines concerning conflicts of interest. The list below provides examples of potential conflicts of interest:

- Owning a substantial amount of stock in any competing business or in any organization that does business with us.
- Serving as a director, manager, consultant, employee or independent contractor for any organization that does business with us, or is a competitor—except with our company's specific prior knowledge and consent.
- Accepting or receiving gifts of any value or favors, compensation, loans, excessive entertainment or similar activities from any individual or organization that does business or wants to do business with us, or is a competitor.
- Representing the company in any transaction in which you or a related person has a substantial interest.
- Disclosing or using for your benefit confidential or non-public information about Target or other organizations with which we do business.
- Taking personal advantage of a business opportunity that is within the scope of Target's business—such as by purchasing property that Target is interested in acquiring.

REVIEW 7.1

Gold's Snack Foods, Inc., reports the following information regarding its inventory for the current year:

Beginning inventory	$ 57,000
Cost of goods purchased	650,000
Ending inventory	43,000

Compute (a) cost of goods available for sale and (b) cost of goods sold.

The solution is on page 254.

INVENTORY COSTING METHODS

LO2 **Describe** inventory costing under specific identification, weighted-average cost, FIFO, and LIFO.

In general, the value of a company's inventory is entered into the accounting records at its acquisition cost. Inventory costing is simple when the purchase price per unit is constant over time. For example, assume that Nikola's Electric Motor Company had no beginning inventory, and made four purchases of inventory during the year, as shown in **Exhibit 7-3**:

EXHIBIT 7-3 Illustration of Cost Flows When Prices Do Not Change

February 10 purchase	100 motors at $180 each
April 25 purchase	150 motors at $180 each
July 16 purchase	150 motors at $180 each
October 8 purchase	200 motors at $180 each
December 31 ending inventory	40 motors at $_?_ each

The December 31 ending inventory for Nikola's Electric Motor Company includes 40 electric motors, some from the July 16 purchase and some from the October 8 purchase. In this case, it is easy to determine the cost to be assigned to the 40 motors (40 × $180 = $7,200) since all of the inventory purchases were made at the same purchase price of $180. In real business situations, however, the purchase price often changes over the course of the accounting period. The trend is usually toward increasing prices, but some prices may decline. When purchase prices change during the year, a company must either keep track of the acquisition cost of each specific unit or make an assumption about which units have been sold and which units remain in inventory. Because the cost of keeping track of exactly which units have been sold can be prohibitively costly, most companies choose to make an assumption about which units have sold and which are still in inventory.

Goods Flow vs. Cost Flow

Two concepts that are helpful in understanding the problem of assigning a cost to inventory when purchase prices are changing are goods flow and cost flow. **Goods flow** describes the actual physical movement of inventory through a business. **Cost flow** is the assumed assignment of costs to goods sold and to ending inventory. The cost flow need not, and often does not, reflect the actual goods flow through a business.

Generally accepted accounting principles permit businesses to use a cost flow that does not reflect the company's actual goods flow. For example, the goods flow in a grocery store chain like Safeway will almost always be such that the goods brought in first will be the first goods to be sold. This physical goods flow results in the least amount of loss due to spoilage. However, just because Safeway operates with this physical goods flow through its stores does not mean that the company is required to adopt a similar cost flow to calculate the value of its inventory. The *cost flow assumption* adopted could be one in which the most recent goods added to inventory are assumed to be the first goods sold.

Data for Illustration of Cost Flow Assumptions

In this section, we illustrate four generally accepted methods of costing inventories: (1) specific identification, (2) first-in, first-out (FIFO), (3) last-in, first-out (LIFO), and (4) weighted-average cost. Following this illustration, a comparative analysis of the financial results of the methods is presented. To facilitate a comparison of their results, we use a common set of data. Assume that the Causeway Bay Company had purchases and sales of inventory during the year, as shown in **Exhibit 7-4**.

EXHIBIT 7-4 Purchases and Sales for Application of Inventory Methods

Date		Event	No. of Units	Unit Cost		Total Cost
Jan.	1	Beginning inventory	60	@ $10	=	$ 600
Mar.	27	Purchase inventory.	90	@ $11	=	$ 990
May	**2**	**Sell inventory**	**(130)**			
Aug.	15	Purchase inventory.	100	@ $13	=	$1,300
Nov.	6	Purchase inventory.	50	@ $16	=	$ 800
Dec.	**10**	**Sell inventory**	**(90)**			
Dec.	31	Ending inventory.	80			

The four inventory costing methods differ in the way they assign costs to the 80 units in ending inventory and the 220 units in cost of goods sold. Under the periodic inventory system, the Inventory account and the Cost of Goods Sold account are updated only at the end of the period, following a physical count of the ending inventory. Once the total cost of ending inventory is determined, the ending inventory amount is subtracted from cost of goods available for sale to derive the period's cost of goods sold.

Specific Identification Method

This information is used to compute ending inventory

The **specific identification method** involves (1) keeping track of the purchase cost of each specific unit available for sale and (2) costing the ending inventory at the actual costs of the specific units not sold. Assume that the 80 unsold units consist of 10 units from beginning inventory, 20 units from the August 15 purchase, and all 50 of the units purchased on November 6. The cost assigned to the ending inventory and cost of goods sold is shown in **Exhibit 7-5**. Observe that the entire $3,690 of cost of the goods available for sale is assigned as either ending inventory or as cost of goods sold.

EXHIBIT 7-5 Specific Identification Method (Periodic Inventory System)

	Goods Available					Ending Inventory				
Date Event	Units		Cost		Total	Units		Cost		Total
Jan. 1 Beginning inventory	60	@	$10	=	$ 600	10	@	$10	=	$ 100
Mar. 27 Purchase	90	@	11	=	990					
Aug. 15 Purchase	100	@	13	=	1,300	20	@	13	=	260
Nov. 6 Purchase	50	@	16	=	800	50	@	16	=	800
	300				$3,690	80				$1,160
Cost of goods available for sale .					$3,690					
Less: Ending inventory					1,160					
Cost of goods sold					**$2,530**					

Ending Inventory $1,160

$100 $500 $990 $260 $1,040 $800

Cost of Goods Sold $2,530

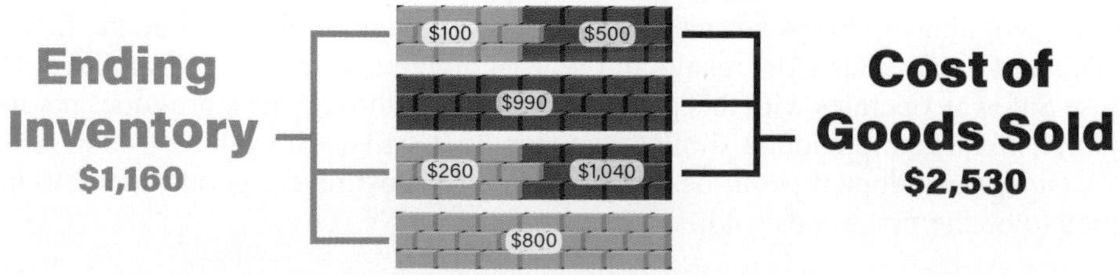

First-In, First-Out (FIFO) Method

The **first-in, first-out (FIFO) method** assumes that the oldest goods (in other words, the earliest purchases) are sold first. This means that ending inventory is *always* made up of the most recent purchases. **Exhibit 7-6** shows how cost of goods sold are calculated using the FIFO method. This method assumes that the oldest 220 units are sold first and that the most recent 80 units purchased are those remaining.

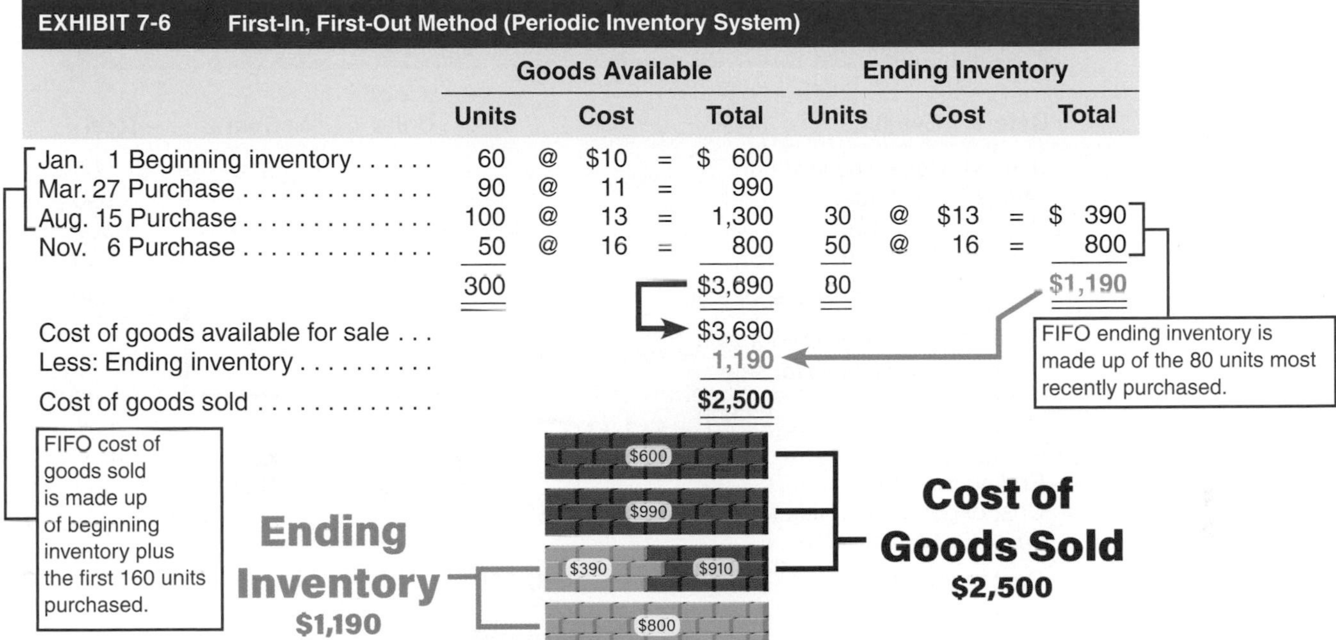

EXHIBIT 7-6 First-In, First-Out Method (Periodic Inventory System)

	Goods Available					Ending Inventory				
	Units		Cost		Total	Units		Cost		Total
Jan. 1 Beginning inventory	60	@	$10	=	$ 600					
Mar. 27 Purchase	90	@	11	=	990					
Aug. 15 Purchase	100	@	13	=	1,300	30	@	$13	=	$ 390
Nov. 6 Purchase	50	@	16	=	800	50	@	16	=	800
	300				$3,690	80				$1,190
Cost of goods available for sale					$3,690					
Less: Ending inventory					1,190					
Cost of goods sold					**$2,500**					

FIFO ending inventory is made up of the 80 units most recently purchased.
FIFO cost of goods sold is made up of beginning inventory plus the first 160 units purchased.
$600
$990
$390
$910
$800
Ending Inventory $1,190
Cost of Goods Sold $2,500

Last-In, First-Out (LIFO) Method

The **last-in, first-out (LIFO) method** assumes that the most recent purchases are sold first. **Exhibit 7-7** shows how cost of goods sold are calculated using the LIFO method. LIFO assumes that the 220 units most recently purchased are sold first, and that the 80 oldest units available for sale remain in inventory at the end of the period.

EXHIBIT 7-7 Last-In, First-Out Method (Periodic Inventory System)

	Goods Available					Ending Inventory				
	Units		Cost		Total	Units		Cost		Total
Jan. 1 Beginning inventory	60	@	$10	=	$ 600	60	@	$10	=	$600
Mar. 27 Purchase	90	@	11	=	990	20	@	11	=	220
Aug. 15 Purchase	100	@	13	=	1,300					
Nov. 6 Purchase	50	@	16	=	800					
	300				$3,690	80				$820
Cost of goods available for sale					$3,690					
Less: Ending inventory					820					
Cost of goods sold					**$2,870**					

LIFO cost of goods sold is made up of the last 220 purchases.

LIFO ending inventory is made up of beginning inventory plus the first 20 units purchased.

$600 | $220 | $770 | $1,300 | $800

Ending Inventory $820

Cost of Goods Sold $2,870

Weighted-Average Cost Method

A.K.A. The **weighted-average cost method** is often referred to as the *average cost method*.

The **weighted-average cost method** spreads the total dollar cost of the goods available for sale equally among all units. In our illustration below, the weighted-average cost per unit is $12.30, computed as $3,690/300. **Exhibit 7-8** shows how cost of goods sold are calculated using the weighted-average cost method. The entire cost of goods available for sale is allocated between ending inventory and cost of goods sold.

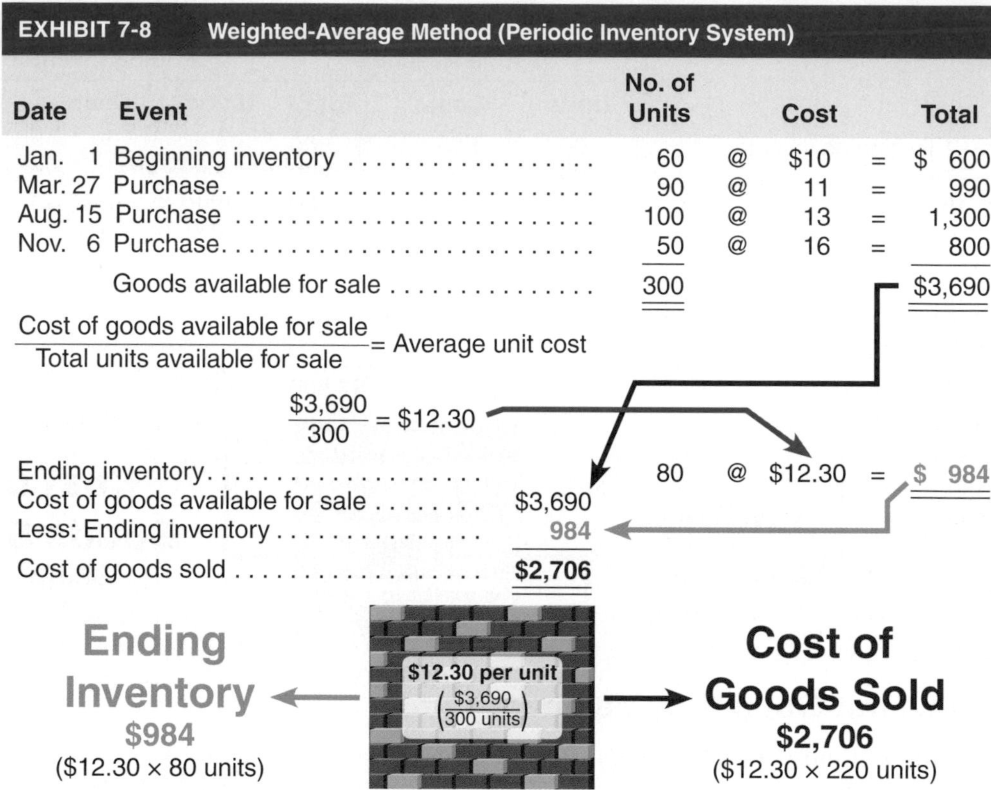

EXHIBIT 7-8 Weighted-Average Method (Periodic Inventory System)

Date	Event	No. of Units		Cost		Total
Jan. 1	Beginning inventory	60	@	$10	=	$ 600
Mar. 27	Purchase	90	@	11	=	990
Aug. 15	Purchase	100	@	13	=	1,300
Nov. 6	Purchase	50	@	16	=	800
	Goods available for sale	300				$3,690

$$\frac{\text{Cost of goods available for sale}}{\text{Total units available for sale}} = \text{Average unit cost}$$

$$\frac{\$3{,}690}{300} = \$12.30$$

Ending inventory		80	@	$12.30	=	$ 984
Cost of goods available for sale	$3,690					
Less: Ending inventory	984					
Cost of goods sold	**$2,706**					

It would be incorrect to use a *simple* average of the unit costs. The simple average unit cost is $12.50, or [($10 + $11 + $13 + $16)/4]. The simple average fails to take into account the different number of units purchased and available at the various prices. The simple average cost yields the same result as the weighted-average cost only when the same number of units is purchased at each unit price.

ACCOUNTING IN PRACTICE

Inventory Costing Methods The following chart identifies the inventory costing method used by a sample of 600 U.S. firms. The most frequently used method is FIFO, followed by LIFO and then weighted-average cost. (The total exceeds 100% because some firms use more than one method to value their inventory, which is permitted under GAAP.) [Source: Accounting Trends and Techniques]

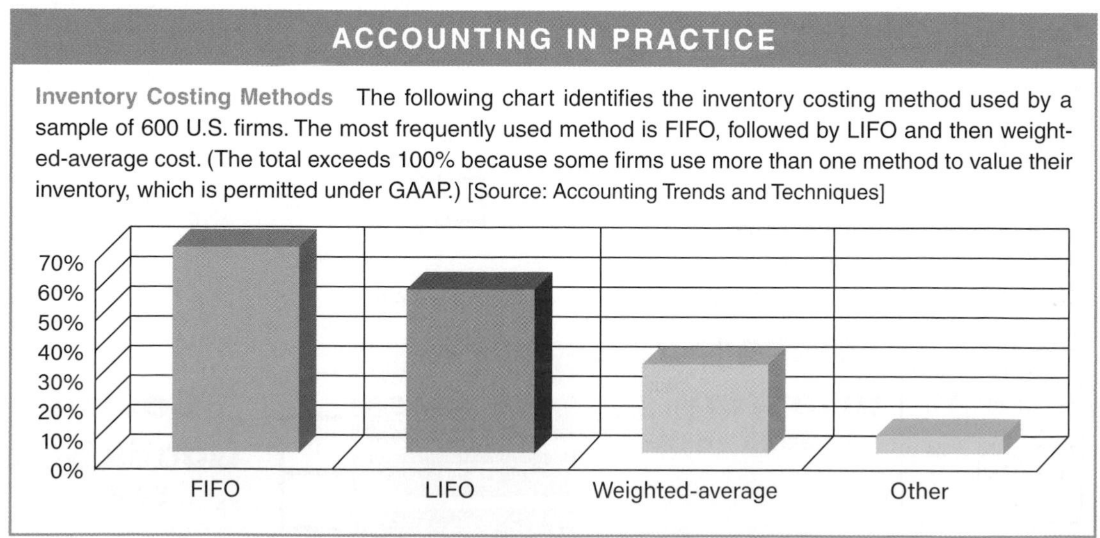

Inventory Costing Under the Perpetual Versus the Periodic Method

Cost of goods sold in this section is computed assuming the company uses a periodic inventory system. This means that the cost of goods sold are computed "as if" all of the purchases for the period have already been made. Many companies, however, use a perpetual inventory system, which computes cost of goods sold after each sale, not just at the end of the accounting period. Appendix 7A shows how to compute cost of goods sold for the examples in this chapter under the perpetual method, and compares the results under a periodic versus perpetual system. It is worth noting, as shown in that appendix, that for companies using FIFO, cost of goods sold is identical whether the company uses the periodic or the perpetual system. It is also useful to know that LIFO users with perpetual inventory systems usually compute cost of goods sold "assuming" they had used a periodic system. This is because LIFO users typically track their inventory during the accounting period using the FIFO or weighted average cost method, and then make an adjustment at the end of the period to convert cost of goods sold to a LIFO basis. Because the adjustment occurs at the end of the accounting period, cost of goods sold for these companies is equivalent to cost of goods sold computed using a periodic system. Thus, in the real world, for most FIFO and LIFO users, cost of goods sold is reported as we compute it in this section, regardless of whether the company uses a periodic or a perpetual inventory system.

How Inventory Methods Affect the Financial Statements

LO3 Analyze the effects of different inventory costing methods on company profit.

The purchase price data used in the Causeway Bay Company illustration has an important characteristic: the purchase price of the inventory increased each time that a purchase was made, from $11 per unit to $13 per unit to $16 per unit. Increasing inventory prices are frequently encountered in the real world where price inflation is common and price deflation is uncommon. **Exhibit 7-9** summarizes the results of applying the four inventory costing methods to the Causeway Bay Company data and finds that the FIFO method produces the lowest cost of goods sold ($2,500), while the LIFO method produces the highest cost of goods sold ($2,870). The exhibit also indicates that FIFO produces the highest year-end value of ending inventory ($1,190), while LIFO produces the lowest year-end value of ending inventory ($820). Specific identification and weighted-average cost produce ending inventory values and cost of goods sold values that fall in between the results obtained using FIFO and LIFO.

These results, however, are highly dependent on the purchase prices for the inventory. If the inventory's purchase price had been decreasing rather than increasing, the financial effects would have been just the opposite, with LIFO producing the lowest cost of goods sold and FIFO the highest. If, on the other hand, the purchase prices had been perfectly stable (and equal to the beginning inventory cost per unit), there would be no difference between the cost of goods sold or the ending inventory for any of the four methods.

EXHIBIT 7-9 Results of Different Inventory Costing Methods (Periodic Inventory System)

	Specific Identification	FIFO	LIFO	Weighted-Average
Cost of goods sold	$2,530	$2,500	$2,870	$2,706
Ending inventory.	1,160	1,190	820	984

How Managers Choose an Inventory Method

Generally accepted accounting principles allow managers to choose the inventory method they prefer. In principle, the overriding criterion for choosing among alternative accounting methods should be the method that is best at faithfully representing the firm's financial condition, whenever this is possible. With inventory, however, all of the methods involve trade-offs and thus there is no "correct choice."

Specific Identification Method

Specific identification is typically used by companies that manufacture a small volume of products with relatively high unit values. Airplanes, jewelry, and construction equipment are examples of products that would justify the cost of tracking the specific unit cost of each inventory item. Specific identification is usually not cost-justified for companies that manufacture products that have a low unit cost or involve high volumes of production. It can be very expensive to trace the exact costs of producing a product, especially a product manufactured in high volumes.

FIFO Method

Many companies, especially those with perishable, time-dated, or style-affected merchandise, attempt to sell their oldest merchandise first. This is especially true for companies that sell food products, chemicals, and drugs. For these types of companies, the cost flow produced by the FIFO method most closely matches the actual goods flow. However, this does not mean that this method necessarily is the best method for such companies. When costs are rising, FIFO will result in the lowest cost of goods sold, and therefore, the highest net income (as shown in **Exhibit 7-9**). This may be one reason for its popularity

LIFO Method

Although LIFO does not reflect the actual goods flow for most businesses, its popularity is primarily explained by the tax benefits it can provide. For some industries, however, LIFO does depict the actual goods flow. For example, in industries that extract natural resources, such as mining, the product is frequently dumped onto a storage pile from an overhead trestle, and sold inventory is taken from the top of the pile. One disadvantage of using LIFO when beginning inventories have been maintained or increased is that a firm's ending inventory can be substantially undervalued since old purchase prices tend to be retained on a company's books under the LIFO method. This, in turn, will cause a firm's current assets and total assets to likewise be undervalued. However, companies that use LIFO are required to also disclose what their ending inventory would have been (approximately) under FIFO.

Weighted-Average Cost Method

Weighted-average cost is best suited for businesses that warehouse a large volume of undifferentiated goods in a common area. Liquid fuels, grains, and other commodities are examples. Weighted-average cost typically generates a cost of goods sold amount that is neither high nor low as compared to the other methods, as indicated in **Exhibit 7-9**.

Summary of Impacts

We can broadly summarize the impacts of the cost flow assumptions as follows:

1. Specific identification most closely identifies the actual composition of cost of goods sold and ending inventory.
2. FIFO approximates the actual physical goods flow for most firms.
3. LIFO is popular because of the income tax savings it provides.
4. Weighted-average cost is most often associated with businesses in which undifferentiated goods are commingled in a common area like a warehouse.

The Effects of Inventory Method Choice on Gross Profit Analysis

Managers, investment professionals, and stockholders closely monitor a company's **gross profit margin**, which for a merchandising firm, is computed as Sales minus the Cost of Goods Sold. To illustrate the financial effects of the different inventory costing methods, assume that the 220 units sold by the Causeway Bay Company were sold for $20 each, producing sales of $4,400 ($20 × 220). **Exhibit 7-10** shows the difference in gross profit under each of the four inventory costing methods. Remember that the difference in reported gross profit results from the assumptions made about cost flow, not from any difference in actual goods flow. In each case, 220 units were sold and 80 units remained. While each inventory costing method is allowed under generally accepted accounting principles, they each result in a different measure of gross profit.

EXHIBIT 7-10 Gross Profit Using Alternative Inventory Costing Methods

	Specific Identification	FIFO	LIFO	Weighted-Average
Sales (220 units @ $20)	$4,400	$4,400	$4,400	$4,400
Cost of goods sold	2,530	2,500	2,870	2,706
Gross profit	$1,870	$1,900	$1,530	$1,694
Increased gross profit compared with LIFO	$ 340	$ 370		$ 164

Income Statement and Balance Sheet Effects

As **Exhibit 7-10** indicates, LIFO results in the smallest gross profit ($1,530), with FIFO producing the highest gross profit ($1,900). This result occurs because the purchase price of inventory is increasing throughout the year, from $11 per unit to $13 per unit to $16 per unit. Most agree that when costs are rising, FIFO tends to overstate gross profit (and income) because older, lower unit costs are included in the cost of goods sold and matched with current sales prices. In other words, in the illustration, all of the units sold are charged to costs of goods sold under FIFO at unit costs of $10, $11, and $13. If the latest purchase price reflects the inventory's current acquisition cost, the units sold must be replaced by units costing $16 (or more if costs continue to rise). However, while net income tends to be overstated (by including older, lower cost inventory), the ending inventory balance under FIFO tends to be more accurately stated, in terms of capturing the inventory's current fair value, because it reflects the more recent inventory costs.

In contrast to FIFO, LIFO provides a better matching of current costs with current revenues since the most recent purchases are included in cost of goods sold under LIFO. While LIFO associates the current, higher unit costs with cost of goods sold, it assigns costs to ending inventory using the older, lower unit costs. As a consequence, the value of the LIFO ending inventory on the balance sheet is often undervalued relative to the inventory's current value. When inventory quantities are maintained or increased, the LIFO method prevents older costs from appearing in the cost of goods sold. In summary, when prices are rising, FIFO tends to overstate net income, while ending inventory on the balance sheet is closer to the inventory's current fair value; in contrast, LIFO tends to more accurately value net income, while ending inventory in the balance sheet is lower than the inventory's current fair value.

PRINCIPLE ALERT

Consistency and Full Disclosure Inventory costing requires the application of *consistency* and *full disclosure*. Because of the possible variation in gross profit and ending inventory values that results from the use of different inventory costing methods, it is important that a firm use the same inventory costing method from one fiscal period to the next. This application of consistency enhances the comparability of a firm's cost of goods sold, gross profit, net income, inventory, current assets, and total assets over time. In addition, a firm should disclose which inventory costing method it is using, either in its financial statements or in the notes to the statements. This information is required by the full disclosure principle and is important to users who compare financial data across firms.

Income Tax Effects

During periods of rising purchase prices, LIFO results in a lower gross profit than any of the alternative inventory costing methods. A lower gross profit, and net income, means that lower amounts of income taxes need to be paid. Hence, the desire to reduce current income tax payments is a major reason for widespread use of LIFO.

To illustrate LIFO's income tax advantage, assume that the Huntington Corporation has beginning inventory of 10 units costing $500 each, and that only two transactions occur. In the first transaction, it purchases 10 more units costing $630 each, for a total cash purchase price of $6,300. In the second transaction, it sells 10 units for $700 each, for a total cash sale of $7,000. Both transactions are for cash and, for simplicity, we assume that the company's operating expenses are zero and the applicable income tax rate is 35 percent. **Exhibit 7-11** presents the income statements and cash flows for Huntington under both FIFO and LIFO.

EXHIBIT 7-11 FIFO vs. LIFO Comparison: Phantom Profit Effect and Tax Benefit

	FIFO		LIFO	
	Income Statement	**Cash In (Out)**	**Income Statement**	**Cash In (Out)**
Sales (10 @ $700)	$ 7,000	$7,000	$ 7,000	$7,000
Cost of goods sold				
Beginning inventory (10 @ $500)	5,000		5,000	
Purchases (10 @ $630)	6,300	(6,300)	6,300	(6,300)
Goods available (20 units)	11,300		11,300	
Ending inventory				
10 @ FIFO	6,300			
10 @ LIFO			5,000	
Cost of goods sold	5,000		6,300	
Protax income	2,000		700	
Income tax (at 35%)	700	(700)	245	(245)
Net income	$ 1,300		$ 455	
Net cash proceeds		$ 0		$ 455

Under FIFO, Huntington reports $1,300 of net income, but cash from sales ($7,000) is only enough to replace the inventory sold ($6,300) and pay the income tax ($700) on the $2,000 in FIFO pretax income. The net income of $1,300 is not realized in cash, and consequently, is unavailable to pay dividends, or be reinvested in the business, or replace the sold inventory. As a consequence, FIFO net income is sometimes referred to as *phantom profit.*

Under LIFO, Huntington reports net income of $455, because of its larger cost of goods sold ($6,300). With a lower net income, it incurs a smaller cash outflow ($245) for income taxes. The attractiveness of LIFO during periods of rising inventory purchase prices is due to LIFO's effect on taxes, which results in a higher net cash flow ($455) as compared with FIFO ($0). Use of LIFO during times of falling inventory purchase prices, however, has the opposite income tax effect.

Management is usually free to select different accounting treatments for financial reporting to shareholders and for income tax reporting to the Internal Revenue Service (IRS). For example, it is acceptable for a business to use different methods of computing inventory when reporting under GAAP on the income statement and for reporting under income tax regulations on a company's income tax return. This means that U.S. corporations effectively maintain two sets of financial records—one for reporting to shareholders and one for reporting to the IRS. An exception to this flexibility occurs when a company chooses to use LIFO for income tax reporting. A U.S. federal tax regulation known as the **LIFO conformity rule** requires companies that choose to use LIFO for income tax reporting to also use LIFO for financial reporting to shareholders. Thus, it is not possible to report lower taxable income to the IRS using LIFO while also reporting higher net income to shareholders using FIFO. The elimination of LIFO for income tax purposes has often been proposed as a way to generate additional tax revenues to help close the U.S. budget deficit.

REVIEW 7.2

The following inventory information is gathered from the accounting records of a company:

Beginning inventory	4,000 units at $5 each
Purchases	6,000 units at $7 each
Sales	9,000 units at $10 each

Calculate (a) ending inventory, (b) cost of goods sold, and (c) the gross profit using each of the following methods (i) FIFO, (ii) LIFO, and (iii) weighted-average cost.

The solution is on page 254.

Errors in the Inventory Count

A physical count of inventory is necessary to determine the value of ending inventory, regardless of what inventory method is used. Unfortunately, errors in the inventory count, for example failing to count some items or counting some items twice, can occur. These errors affect not only the value of ending inventory reported on the balance sheet in the period of the error, but also cost of goods sold and current net income. Further, the error is not limited to only the current period—net income in the following period is also affected. To illustrate, assume that the Arrow Company began operations in Year 1. **Exhibit 7-12** summarizes Arrow's transactions for Years 1 and 2. For simplicity, assume that the only expense that it incurs is its cost of goods sold.

EXHIBIT 7-12 Inventory Transactions for Arrow Company

		Inventory Units	Inventory Balance	Sales
Year 1	Beginning inventory	0	0	
	Purchased 1,000 units of merchandise inventory for $3 per unit	1,000	$3,000	
	Sold 400 units of merchandise inventory for $7 per unit	(400)	(1,200)	$ 2,800
	Ending inventory	600	$1,800	
Year 2	Beginning inventory	600	$1,800	
	Purchased 2,000 units of merchandise inventory for $3 per unit	2,000	6,000	
	Sold 1,500 units of merchandise inventory for $7 per unit	(1,500)	(4,500)	$10,500
	Ending inventory	1,100	$3,300	

Assume that Arrow Company made an error in its physical count of inventory at the end of Year 1, mistakenly double-counting 40 units. This error would result in an ending inventory count of 640 units (600 units + 40 units), with an ending inventory balance of $1,920 (640 × $3), which overstates Year 1 ending inventory by $120 ($1,920 – $1,800; or 40 units × $3). As illustrated in **Exhibit 7-13**, an ending inventory balance of $1,920 in Year 1 would result in cost of goods sold of $1,080, understating Year 1 cost of goods by $120 ($1,200 – $1,080). Further, because ending inventory in Year 1 becomes beginning inventory in Year 2, cost of goods sold in Year 2 becomes $4,620, which overstates Year 2 cost of goods sold by $120 ($4,620 – $4,500). **Exhibit 7-13** illustrates these effects on both the Year 1 and Year 2 Arrow Company income statements.

EXHIBIT 7-13 Inventory Error Effects

Cost of goods sold	=	Beginning Inventory	+	Purchases	–	Ending Inventory
Year 1: $1,080 (instead of $1,200)	=	$ 0	+	$ 3,000	–	$1,920*
Year 2: $4,620 (instead of $4,500)	=	$ 1,920	+	$ 6,000	–	$3,300

* $1,920 = (600 units + 40 units) × $3

Key figures	No Error		With Error
Year 1			
Sales	$ 2,800		$ 2,800
Cost of goods sold	1,200	–120	1,080 ↓
Net income	$ 1,600	+120	$ 1,720 ↑
Year 2			
Sales	$10,500		$10,500
Cost of goods sold	4,500	+120	4,620 ↑
Net income	$ 6,000	–120	$ 5,880 ↓

The example in **Exhibit 7-13** generalizes to both overstatements and understatements in ending inventory. An over (under) statement of ending inventory in the current year results in an under (over) statement of cost of goods sold, and an over (under) statement of net income. Further, the error "reverses" in the following year, having the opposite effect on cost of goods sold and net income in the following year. Thus, net income summed over the current and following year is equivalent whether the error occurs or not. To show this using the information for Arrow Company in **Exhibit 7-13**, notice that the combined net income summed over both years is $7,600, without the error ($1,600 + $6,000) or with the error ($1,720 + $5,880). Further, we see that ending inventory is overstated in Year 1 by $120, which results in: Year 1 cost of goods sold being understated by $120, and Year 1 net income being overstated by $120. The same $120 error is carried through to Year 2 where it causes cost of goods sold to be overstated by $120 (because of the overstatement of beginning inventory), and net income to be understated by $120.

A company that overstates inventory is sometimes said to have a "bloated balance sheet." As shown in the above illustration, companies with bloated balance sheets report earnings that are overstated during the year (or years) when the balance sheet is overstated, and then report reduced earnings in the years when the overstatement is corrected. This phenomenon illustrates an important relationship between the balance sheet and the income statement: overstating operating assets results in overstated earnings. But when the overstated assets are ultimately corrected, earnings will decline. Companies can have bloated balance sheets due to the overstatement of any operating asset, including receivables and fixed assets. Interestingly, academic research has found that bloated balance sheets often fool investors into overvaluing the stock prices of public companies during the periods in which the operating assets are overstated.

ACCOUNTING ETHICS

Fraudulent Reporting Most errors in inventory result from honest mistakes; however, there are inventory counts that have been intentionally overstated. One famous case involved a retail company called **Crazy Eddie**, which was a discount electronics store. Crazy Eddie's accountants reportedly inflated earnings by $10–$12 million dollars by overstating the balance in ending inventory. The U.S. Securities and Exchange Commission ultimately charged Eddie with securities fraud and he was sentenced to 8 years in prison and ordered to pay more than $150 million in fines.

LOWER OF COST OR NET REALIZABLE VALUE

LO4 **Apply** the lower of cost or net realizable value rule.

When inventory is purchased, it is initially recorded on the balance sheet at its acquisition cost. However, if the value of the inventory subsequently declines below its **net realizable value**, it must be *written down* to its net realizable value. This accounting principle is known as the **lower of cost or net realizable value (LCNRV)** rule in accounting for inventories.

Inventory usually declines in value for one of two reasons: (1) it has been damaged or becomes obsolete, such that it cannot be sold at its normal selling price; or (2) market forces, such as lower demand, drive down the value of the inventory, which may also result in a lower sales price. At the end of each accounting period, management evaluates whether there is evidence of a decline in the value of the ending inventory.

Net Realizable Value

Net realizable value is an inventory item's estimated selling price less the expected selling costs. For example, assume that an inventory item cost $300 but can be sold for only $200, either because it is damaged or because the selling price of the item has declined. If the related selling costs are estimated to be $20, the inventory should be written down to $180 ($200 estimated selling price less $20 estimated selling costs). This would result in recording a $120 inventory loss ($300 – $180) reported on the income statement, with a corresponding $120 reduction in inventory in the balance sheet.

The lower of cost or net realizable value adjustments can be made separately for each individual inventory item, or they can be based on the aggregate value of the inventory as a whole. It is notable that when the write-down is based on the aggregate inventory value, any increases in inventory value are essentially offset against the losses in value, which often results in a smaller write-down as compared with a separate write-down for each individual inventory item.

The lower of cost or net realizable value rule does not apply to companies using the LIFO method of accounting for inventories. Instead, LIFO companies must use the lower of cost or "market" rule. The computation of market values is somewhat technical and hence is typically the subject of more advanced accounting courses.

REVIEW 7.3

Determine the proper total inventory value for each of the following items in Viking Company's ending inventory:

a. Viking has 200 bottles of sunscreen that are past the expiration date marked on the container. The sunscreen cost $5.50 each and normally sold for $9.95. To clear out the old sunscreen, Viking will drop the selling price to $4.00. There are no related selling costs.

b. Viking has twelve hair dryers in stock that have not sold because the supplier has been advertising its new improved model. The older model dryers cost $35 and normally sold for $60. In order to move the older model dryers, Viking has set the selling price at $20 each. Expected selling costs are $2 per dryer. New models of the dryer will cost Viking $40 and will be priced to sell at $75.

The solution is on page 254.

PRINCIPLE ALERT

Conservatism The lower of cost or net realizable value rule is an example of accounting conservatism, which requires the timely recognition of losses, but does not allow for the anticipation of gains. Companies must write down inventory when its cost exceeds the amount of cash the company expects to receive when the inventory is sold. However, U.S. GAAP does not allow companies to write up the value of their inventory above its original cost.

THINKING GLOBALLY

Inventory accounting is one area where International Financial Reporting Standards (IFRS) differs from U.S. GAAP. One important difference is that LIFO is not allowed under IFRS. In fact, even U.S. companies cannot use LIFO in accounting for the inventories in their foreign operations. Another difference is that, unlike U.S. GAAP, IFRS permits inventory to be revalued up to its original acquisition cost if the inventory's fair value appreciates after a previous write down. When inventory is revalued upward under IFRS a parallel increase is made to an equity account called *asset revaluation reserve.*

INVENTORY ANALYSIS

Gross Profit Analysis

LO5 **Define** the gross profit percentage and **explain** its use.

The gross profit margin is commonly recognized as an important indicator of a company's financial health, because a decline from one year to the next may indicate that the company is having difficulty selling its inventory at a price that will cover its costs. Thus, a declining gross profit margin can signal a deterioration in current and future net income.

The **gross profit percentage** indicates how much the company earns, on average, for each dollar of sales revenue. A merchandising company measures its gross profit percentage as follows:

$$\textbf{Gross profit percentage} = \frac{\textbf{Gross profit on sales}}{\textbf{Net sales}}$$

The 2020 gross profit percentage for Costco is 11.2 percent, computed as $18,281/$163,220. This tells us that for every dollar of sales, the company had 11.2 cents left, after paying for the cost of sales, to cover its other expenses and provide a profit for its shareholders. The previous year, Costco's gross profit was 11.0 percent, slightly less than the current year. Costco's financial data for the two years are presented below.

($ millions)	2020	2019
Gross profit on sales	$ 18,281	$ 16,465
Net sales	163,220	149,351
Gross profit percentage	11.2%	11.0%

Financial analysis of the gross profit percentage frequently involves benchmarking the company against competitor companies. Gross profit percentages are presented in **Exhibit 7-14** for Costco Warehouse and two of its chief competitors, Walmart Inc. and Target Corporation.

EXHIBIT 7-14 Gross Profit Percentage

($ millions)	Costco*	Walmart**	Target***
Gross profit on sales	$ 18,281	$134,918	$26,223
Net sales	163,220	555,233	92,400
Gross profit percentage	11.2%	24.3%	28.4%

*FYE August 30, 2020 ** FYE January 31, 2021 *** FYE January 30, 2021

Both Walmart and Target have significantly higher gross profit percentages than Costco. An explanation for the large differences between the gross profit percentage of these companies is their different business strategies. Costco attempts to sell its higher quality products at low prices to ensure high sales volume but results in lower profit margins than other retailers. Walmart focuses more on low prices and less on product quality. Target, on the other hand, attempts to sell higher quality products at reasonable prices.

TAKEAWAY 7.1

Concept	Method	Assessment
Is a company able to maintain prices on its goods consistent with changes in the cost of its inventory?	Gross profit and net sales $\text{Gross profit percentage} = \frac{\text{Gross profit on sales}}{\text{Net sales}}$	A higher ratio is consistent with the company selling goods at a higher mark-up over cost. A lower ratio is consistent with a company attempting to compete by charging lower prices.

REVIEW 7.4

The President of Musicland has asked for help to evaluate the company's performance during the current year. In particular, we are requested to calculate Musicland's gross profit percentage and its profit margin (described in Chapter 4 as the ratio of net income to net sales) and then explain what these measures indicate. The following information is from Musicland's financial statements:

Net sales	$100,000
Cost of goods sold	45,000
Net income	10,500

The solution is on page 254.

DATA ANALYTICS Data Analytics Can Make Order Fulfillment Faster and More Efficient

Many large retailers, such as Amazon, use data analytics to make order fulfillment faster and more efficient. Using automated shipping rules, an order is assigned to the fulfillment center nearest to the order destination, thereby reducing transportation time and cost. Inventory management software also optimizes warehousing by dictating inventory locations within a facility to ensure efficient product picking routes. Through the use of data analytics, retailers can optimize good flows within the warehouse, which leads to faster order fulfillment and lower operating costs.

Inventory Turnover and Days' Sales in Inventory

The **inventory turnover ratio** indicates how many times a year, on average, a firm sells its inventory, and it is calculated as:

LO6 Define inventory turnover and days' sales in inventory and **explain** their use.

eLecture MBC

$$\textbf{Inventory turnover} = \frac{\textbf{Cost of goods sold}}{\textbf{Average inventory}}$$

This ratio relates data from two financial statements: the income statement and the balance sheet. Cost of goods sold is taken from the income statement, while the average inventory is calculated from balance sheet data—that is, the beginning and ending inventories are summed and the total is divided by two.

In general, the faster a company can turn over its inventory, the more profitable the company will be. Further, the higher the inventory turnover ratio, the less time a firm has its funds tied up in its inventory and the less risk the firm faces from trying to sell out-of-date merchandise. What is considered to be a satisfactory inventory turnover varies from industry to industry. A grocery store chain like **Safeway**, for example, should have a much higher inventory turnover than a jewelry store like **Zales**.

To illustrate the inventory turnover ratio, **Costco** reported the following financial data:

($ millions)	2020	2019
Cost of goods sold	$144,939	$132,886
Beginning inventory	11,395	11,040
Ending inventory	12,242	11,395

Costco's inventory turnover in FYE 2020 was 12.26 computed as $144,939/[($11,395 + $12,242)/2]. A similar calculation indicates that Costco's inventory turnover in 2019 was 11.85 computed as $132,886/[($11,040 + $11,395)/2]. Thus, Costco had a relatively stable ratio over these two years.

The inventory turnover ratio can be influenced by a firm's choice of inventory costing method. Inventory amounts calculated using LIFO, for example, will typically be smaller than the same inventory calculated using FIFO. An investor comparing inventory turnover ratios between different firms will need to verify that the firms are using the same inventory costing method; otherwise, any ratio comparisons will be apples-to-oranges rather than apples-to-apples.

An extension of the inventory turnover ratio is the **days' sales in inventory**, calculated as:

$$\textbf{Days' sales in inventory} = \frac{\textbf{365}}{\textbf{Inventory turnover}}$$

This ratio indicates how many days it takes, on average, for a firm to sell its inventory. In FYE 2020 Costco's days' sales in inventory was 29.8 days, or 365/12.26; meaning it took nearly 30 days to sell its inventory. Looking at the prior year, it took 30.8 days for Costco to sell its inventory (365/11.85). Do these ratios indicate that Costco is doing a good job of managing its investment in inventory? Without comparable ratio data from competitors, it would be difficult to conclude whether Costco's inventory turnover or days' sales in inventory are indicative of good or bad inventory management. The inventory turnover and days' sales in inventory for **Costco**, **Target** and **Walmart** are presented in **Exhibit 7-15**. Notice that Costco turned its inventory over 12 times or

A.K.A. The **days' sales in inventory ratio** is also referred to as the *days' inventory-on-hand ratio* and the *inventory-on-hand period*.

EXHIBIT 7-15 Inventory Turnover and Days' Sales in Inventory Comparison

($ millions)	Costco*	Walmart**	Target***
Cost of goods sold	$144,939	$420,315	$66,177
Beginning inventory	11,395	44,435	8,992
Ending inventory	12,242	44,949	10,653
Inventory turnover	12.26	9.40	6.74
Days' sales in inventory	29.8	38.8	54.2

*FYE August 30, 2020 ** FYE January 31, 2021 *** FYE January 30, 2021

once per month in the year presented. Walmart turned its inventory just over 9 times or about every 40 days. Target has the lowest turnover at about 7 times or about 54 days. Again, these ratios are consistent with each company's business strategy.

TAKEAWAY 7.2 Concept	Method	Assessment
How long, on average, does it take to sell the inventory?	Cost of goods sold, beginning inventory, and ending inventory $\text{Inventory turnover} = \dfrac{\text{Cost of goods sold}}{\text{Average inventory}}$ $\text{Days' sales in inventory} = \dfrac{365}{\text{Inventory turnover}}$	A higher inventory turnover or a lower days' sales in inventory indicates that the company is able to sell its inventory more quickly.

REVIEW 7.5

Flip Company installed a new inventory management system at the beginning of the current year. Shown below are financial data from the company's accounting records:

	Prior Year	Current Year
Sales revenue	$4,000,000	$4,400,000
Cost of goods sold	2,000,000	2,300,000
Beginning inventory	450,000	430,000
Ending inventory	430,000	320,000

Calculate the inventory turnover and days' sales in inventory for each year. Discuss your findings.

The solution is on page 254.

ENVIRONMENTAL, SOCIAL, AND GOVERNANCE

Target and an Ethical Supply Chain Many businesses strive to not only do well financially, but also to do good environmentally and socially. **Target** serves as the ultimate seller of many products manufactured by other companies, such as TVs by **Samsung**, cameras by **Nikon**, and iPads by **Apple**. Target also sells its own brands. As the manufacturer of these products, Target faces decisions on how and where these products are produced. Target's Corporate Responsibility Report states, "Apparel is one of Target's largest product categories, and textile production represents one of our most significant environmental impacts due to its use of water, chemicals and energy." Target has adopted a program called Clean by Design to reduce waste and emissions that it has introduced to its suppliers worldwide. In addition Target has stringent labor and human rights policies in place to mitigate the occurrence of underage and forced labor practices. Target also has a factory audit program to identify environmental and social problems at its suppliers.

REVIEW 7.6

The Montclair Corporation had the following inventory transactions for its only product during the current year:

Purchases	
February 15	2,000 units @ $27.00 each
April 20	3,000 units @ $28.40 each
October 25	1,200 units @ $31.25 each
Sales	
March 1	1,200 units @ $50.00 each
June 12	2,000 units @ $52.00 each
August 10	1,000 units @ $53.00 each
December 14	1,600 units @ $55.00 each

continued

continued from previous page

The Montclair Corporation had 1,000 units in its January 1 beginning inventory with a unit cost of $24 each. Montclair uses the periodic inventory system.

Required

a. Determine the cost assigned to Montclair's December 31 ending inventory and Montclair's cost of goods sold for the year under each of the following inventory costing methods:

1. Weighted-average cost 2. FIFO 3. LIFO

b. Determine Montclair's gross profit for the year under each of the following inventory costing methods:

1. Weighted-average cost 2. FIFO 3. LIFO

c. Determine Montclair's inventory turnover and days' sales in inventory for the year under each of the following inventory costing methods:

1. Weighted-average cost 2. FIFO 3. LIFO

The solution is on pages 254–255.

APPENDIX 7A: Inventory Costing using a Perpetual Inventory System

LO7 Appendix 7A: **Describe** inventory costing under a perpetual inventory system.

In this chapter, the periodic inventory system was used to illustrate inventory costing methods. This appendix illustrates the accounting for inventories using the perpetual inventory system, and compares accounting using the periodic versus perpetual system under the four costing methods: (1) specific identification; (2) first-in, first-out; (3) last-in, first-out; and (4) weighted-average cost. All four methods are illustrated using the following data for the Causeway Bay Company.

Date	Event	No. of Units		Unit Cost		Total Cost
Jan. 1	Beginning inventory	60	@	$10	=	$ 600
Mar. 27	Purchase inventory	90	@	11	=	990
Aug. 15	Purchase inventory	100	@	13	=	1,300
Nov. 6	Purchase inventory	50	@	16	=	800
	Goods available for sale	300				$3,690
May 2	Sell inventory	(130)				
Dec. 10	Sell inventory	(90)				
Dec. 31	Ending inventory	80				

Under all four inventory costing methods, the Inventory account is increased each time a purchase occurs for the amount of the purchase and is decreased each time a sale occurs by an amount equal to the cost of goods sold. The methods differ only in the computation of cost of goods sold, consisting of 220 units (130 + 90 = 220), and the year-end Inventory account balance, consisting of 80 units remaining.

Specific Identification Method

Under the **specific identification method**, the actual cost of the specific units sold is identified and used to compute the cost of goods sold. To illustrate, assume that (1) 50 of the 130 units sold on May 2 came from the beginning inventory of 60 units and the remaining 80 units sold (50 + 80 = 130) came from the purchase of 90 units on March 27, and that (2) 10 of the 90 units sold on December 10 came from the purchase of 90 units on March 27 and the remaining 80 units sold (10 + 80 = 90) came from the purchase of 100 units on August 15. **Exhibit 7A-1** illustrates the calculation of cost of goods sold and ending inventory using specific identification. The cost of goods sold is $2,530 (sum of the Sold Total column), and the ending inventory of 80 units is valued at $1,160 (final amount in the Inventory Balance Total column).

EXHIBIT 7A-1 Specific Identification Method (Perpetual Inventory System)

	Purchased			Sold			Inventory Balance		
Date	**Units**	**Unit Cost**	**Total**	**Units**	**Unit Cost**	**Total**	**Units**	**Unit Cost**	**Total**
Jan. 1							60	$10	$ 600
Mar. 27	90	$11	$ 990				60	10	1,590
							90	11	
May 2				**50**	**$10**	**$ 500**	10	10	210
				80	**11**	**880**	10	11	
Aug. 15	100	13	1,300				10	10	1,510
							10	11	
							100	13	
Nov. 6	50	16	800				10	10	2,310
							10	11	
							100	13	
							50	16	
Dec. 10				**10**	**11**	**110**	**10**	**10**	**1,160**
				80	**13**	**1,040**	**20**	**13**	
							50	**16**	
Total						**$2,530**			

First-In, First-Out (FIFO) Method

Under the **first-in, first-out (FIFO) method**, each time that a sale is made the cost of the oldest goods are charged to cost of goods sold. Visually, the FIFO method appears like a conveyor belt. Items of inventory are placed on the belt and then move along to the end. As items reach the end of the conveyor belt, they are assumed to be sold. Those items still on the belt (which are the last items placed on the belt) are assumed to remain in inventory until they reach the end of the conveyor belt. This visualization is illustrated in **Exhibit 7A-2**.

EXHIBIT 7A-2 First-In, First-Out

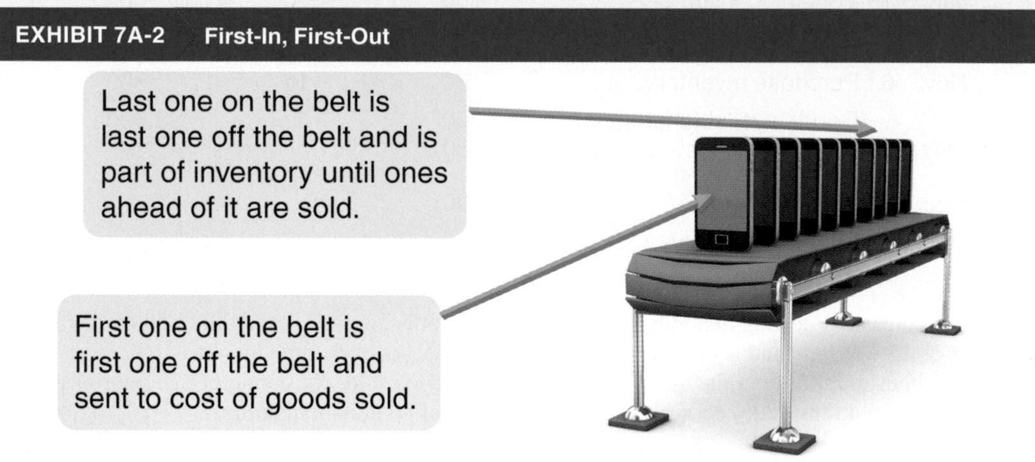

Last one on the belt is last one off the belt and is part of inventory until ones ahead of it are sold.
First one on the belt is first one off the belt and sent to cost of goods sold.

Results of the FIFO method are in **Exhibit 7A-3**. FIFO handles the May 2 sale of 130 units as follows: The oldest units are the units in the January 1 beginning inventory. These are the first 60 units assumed to be sold. The next oldest units are the units purchased on March 27 and 70 units are needed from this purchase (130 sold – 60 from January 1) to provide all of the units sold on May 2. After the May 2 sale, only 20 units remain, all from the March 27 purchase.

The December 10 sale of 90 units is handled in a similar manner. The oldest units at December 10 are the 20 units remaining from the March 27 purchase. These are the first units assumed to be sold. The next oldest units are the 100 units purchased on August 15 and 70 additional units are needed for the sale (90 sold – 20 from the March 27 purchase). Therefore, 70 of the 100 units purchased on August 15 are assumed to be included in the units sold on December 10. After the December 10 sale, 30 units remain from the August 15 purchase and 50 units remain from the November 6 purchase.

Cost of goods sold using the FIFO method is $2,500 (sum of the Sold Total column), and the ending inventory is $1,190 (final amount in the Inventory Balance Total column).

EXHIBIT 7A-3 First-In, First-Out Method (Perpetual Inventory System)

	Purchased			Sold			Inventory Balance		
Date	Units	Unit Cost	Total	Units	Unit Cost	Total	Units	Unit Cost	Total
Jan. 1 . . .							60	$10	$ 600
Mar. 27 . . .	90	$11	$ 990				60 90	10 11	1,590
May 2 . . .				**60** **70**	**$10** **11**	**$ 600** **770**	20	11	220
Aug. 15 . . .	100	13	1,300				20 100	11 13	1,520
Nov. 6 . . .	50	16	800				20 100 50	11 13 16	2,320
Dec. 10 . . .				**20** **70**	**11** **13**	**220** **910**	**30** **50**	**13** **16**	**1,190**
Total						$2,500			

Last-In, First-Out (LIFO) Method

When the **last-in, first-out (LIFO) method** is used, the cost of the most recent inventory purchased is charged to cost of goods sold when a sale occurs. Visually, the LIFO method appears like a stack of bricks. Each new brick entered into inventory is placed on top of the existing stack of bricks. When a brick is sold, the last brick placed on the stack is pulled from the top of the stack and given to the customer. The bricks at the bottom of the stack are assumed to remain in inventory until the newer bricks from the top of the stack are first sold. This visualization is illustrated in **Exhibit 7A-4**.

EXHIBIT 7A-4 Last-In, First-Out

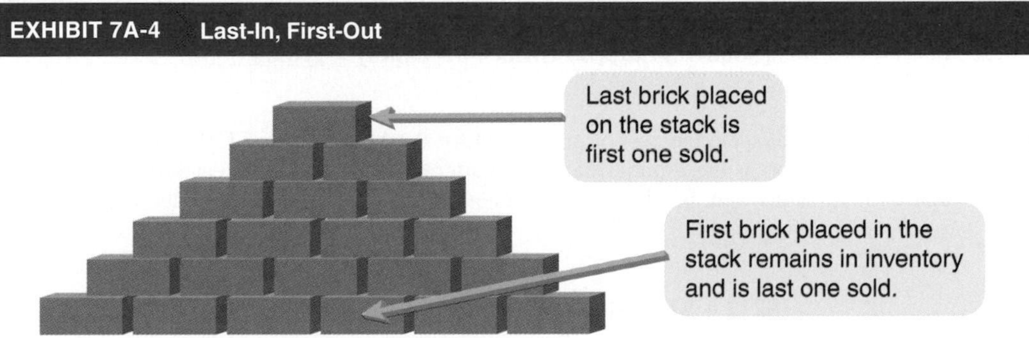
Last brick placed on the stack is first one sold.
First brick placed in the stack remains in inventory and is last one sold.

Exhibit 7A-5 illustrates the results using LIFO. The LIFO method handles the May 2 sale of 130 units as follows: The most recently purchased units (newest units) are the units from the March 27 purchase. These are the first 90 units assumed to be sold. The next newest units are the units in the January 1 beginning inventory and 40 units from the January 1 units are needed (130 sold – 90 from the March 27 purchase) to provide all of the units sold on May 2. After the May 2 sale, only 20 units remain, all from the January 1 beginning inventory.

The December 10 sale of 90 units is handled in a similar manner. The newest units at December 10 are the 50 units purchased on November 6. These are the first units assumed to be sold. The next newest units are the 100 units purchased on August 15 and 40 additional units are needed for the sale (90 sold – 50 from the November 6 purchase). Therefore, 40 of the 100 units purchased on August 15 are assumed to be included in the units sold on December 10. After the sale, 20 units remain from the January 1 inventory and 60 units remain from the August 15 purchase.

Cost of goods sold using LIFO is $2,710 (sum of the Sold Total column), and the ending inventory is $980 (final amount in the Inventory Balance Total column).

EXHIBIT 7A-5 Last-In, First-Out Method (Perpetual Inventory System)

	Purchased			Sold			Inventory Balance		
Date	Units	Unit Cost	Total	Units	Unit Cost	Total	Units	Unit Cost	Total
Jan. 1 . . .							60	$10	$ 600
Mar. 27 . . .	90	$11	$ 990				60 90	10 11	1,590
May 2 . . .				**90** **40**	**$11** **10**	**$ 990** **400**	20	10	200
Aug. 15 . . .	100	13	1,300				20 100	10 13	1,500
Nov. 6 . . .	50	16	800				20 100 50	10 13 16	2,300
Dec. 10 . . .				**50** **40**	**16** **13**	**800** **520**	**20** **60**	**10** **13**	**980**
Total						**$2,710**			

Weighted-Average Cost Method

When the **weighted-average cost method** is used, a new weighted-average unit cost is calculated for the goods (**total cost divided by total units**) each time that goods are purchased and added to inventory. The cost of goods sold for each sale is calculated by multiplying the weighted-average unit cost at the time of sale by the number of units sold. **Exhibit 7A-6** illustrates the calculation of cost of goods sold and ending inventory under the weighted-average cost method. The weighted-average unit cost is calculated three times in **Exhibit 7A-6**. On March 27, 90 units were purchased at a unit cost of $11, and the updated weighted-average unit cost on this date is:

[$600 + $990]/[60 Units + 90 Units] = $10.60

This unit cost is used to calculate the cost of goods sold for the May 2 sale of 130 units. 130 × $10.60 = $1,378. The ending inventory is the 20 units that remain after that sale, also valued at $10.60 per unit.

On August 15, 100 units were purchased at a unit cost of $13. The updated weighted-average unit cost on this date is:

[$212 + $1,300]/[20 Units + 100 Units] = $12.60

This unit cost is used to calculate the ending inventory balance of $1,512 ($12.60 × 120).

On November 6, 50 units were purchased at a unit cost of $16. The updated weighted-average unit cost on this date is:

[$1,512 + $800]/[120 Units + 50 Units] = $13.60

This unit cost is used to calculate the cost of goods sold for the Dec. 10 sale of 90 units. 90 × $13.60 = $1,224. The ending inventory is the 80 units that remain after that sale, also valued at $13.60 per unit.

The cost of goods sold is $2,602 (sum of the Sold Total column), and the ending inventory is $1,088 (final amount in the Inventory Balance Total column).

EXHIBIT 7A-6 Weighted-Average Cost Method (Perpetual Inventory System)

	Purchased			Sold			Inventory Balance		
Date	Units	Unit Cost	Total	Units	Unit Cost	Total	Units	Unit Cost	Total
Jan. 1 . . .							60	$10.00	$ 600
Mar. 27 . . .	90	$11	$ 990				150	10.60	1,590
May 2 . . .				**130**	**$10.60**	**$1,378**	20	10.60	212
Aug. 15 . . .	100	13	1,300				120	12.60	1,512
Nov. 6 . . .	50	16	800				170	13.60	2,312
Dec. 10 . . .				**90**	**13.60**	**1,224**	**80**	**13.60**	**1,088**
Total						**$2,602**			

Comparison of Inventory Costing Methods

Exhibit 7A-7 summarizes the results of applying the periodic and perpetual costing methods to the same Causeway Bay data. The specific identification method and the FIFO method yield the exact same results for ending inventory and cost of goods sold regardless of whether the periodic or the perpetual method is being used. Only the LIFO and weighted-average methods produce different results under the periodic and perpetual systems.

EXHIBIT 7A-7 Summary Results of Different Inventory Costing Methods

Costing Method	Ending Inventory	Cost of Goods Sold
Specific identification		
Periodic.	$1,160	$2,530
Perpetual.	1,160	2,530
FIFO		
Periodic.	1,190	2,500
Perpetual.	1,190	2,500
LIFO		
Periodic.	820	2,870
Perpetual.	980	2,710
Weighted-Average		
Periodic.	984	2,706
Perpetual.	1,088	2,602

Choice of a periodic vs perpetual system does *not* impact specific identification or FIFO

Choice of a periodic vs perpetual system does impact LIFO and weighted-average results

APPENDIX 7B: LIFO Reserve

LO8 Appendix 7B: **Define** the LIFO reserve and **explain** its use.

As shown in this chapter, the LIFO inventory costing method can produce significantly different results relative to other inventory costing methods for both cost of goods sold, and therefore gross profit and net income, and ending inventory. The difference is greatest when compared to FIFO. When costs are rising, FIFO will result in higher reported ending inventory, lower cost of goods sold, and higher net income.

To make comparisons between companies using LIFO and companies using FIFO, we need to use the **LIFO inventory reserve**, or simply the *LIFO reserve*. Companies that use LIFO are required under generally accepted accounting principles to report the difference between ending inventory using LIFO and the inventory that would have been reported under FIFO. This difference is called the LIFO inventory reserve and is disclosed in the notes to the financial statements.

Referring again to **Exhibit 7-9**, FIFO ending inventory is valued at $1,190 and LIFO ending inventory at $820 when the periodic method is used. The LIFO reserve is $370 ($1,190 – $820). Use of LIFO can have a material impact on many ratios, and one way to compensate for these effects is to use the LIFO reserve to restate the reported inventory. To illustrate, assume that Causeway Bay Company, whose inventory costing method results are contrasted in **Exhibit 7-9**, has current assets of $2,100 and current liabilities of $1,400 under the LIFO method. **Exhibit 7B-1** calculates the current ratio (current assets divided by current liabilities) under both LIFO and FIFO. (The current ratio is discussed in Chapter 4.)

EXHIBIT 7B-1 Impact of the LIFO Inventory Reserve on the Current Ratio

	LIFO	FIFO
Current ratio	$\frac{\$2,100}{\$1,400} = 1.50$	$\frac{(\$2,100 + \$370)}{\$1,400} = 1.76$

As shown in **Exhibit 7B-1**, the current ratio is much higher under FIFO (1.76) than under LIFO (1.50). Differences occur between LIFO and FIFO companies for many ratios, with FIFO resulting in more favorable ratios in most cases since FIFO generally results in higher inventory values and higher net earnings. For some ratios, however, LIFO produces more favorable results. Two examples are the inventory turnover ratio and the days' sales in inventory ratio. Because LIFO results in lower inventory values, the inventory turnover (and consequently, the days' sales in inventory) under LIFO appears higher (lower) than it does under FIFO. The LIFO reserve also affects cost of goods sold and therefore the numerator of the inventory turnover ratio; in most cases the adjustment to cost of goods sold is much smaller than the adjustment to average inventory, leading to a higher inventory turnover under LIFO than under FIFO.

TAKEAWAY 7.3

Concept	Method	Assessment
What effect does the use of LIFO have on ending inventory relative to the use of FIFO?	Examine the difference between ending inventory under LIFO and FIFO, defined as the LIFO reserve.	If the LIFO reserve is material it can have a significant impact on many ratios when compared to FIFO. The calculation of these ratios can be adjusted using the LIFO inventory reserve to provide a more comparable set of results.

SUMMARY OF LEARNING OBJECTIVES

LO1 Explain how inventories differ between merchandisers, manufacturers, and wholesalers. (p. 216)

- Merchandising firms sell merchandise. There are two types of merchandising firms: wholesale distributors and retailers.
- Manufacturing companies convert raw materials and components into finished products through the application of skilled labor and machine operations.
- Merchandise inventory is inventory that a merchandising company buys from a manufacturer and makes available for sale to its customers.
- A manufacturing firm maintains three different inventory categories: raw materials inventory, work-in-process inventory, and finished goods inventory.
- Traditionally, manufacturers have maintained just-in-case inventories of raw materials and components to provide for unplanned production or delayed raw material shipments, resulting in high levels of inventory carrying costs.
- Today, many manufacturers have adopted the just-in-time (JIT) manufacturing philosophy which is designed to eliminate or minimize raw materials, work-in-process, and finished goods inventories. The key to JIT manufacturing is careful inventory order planning and sophisticated production management.
- The year-end physical count of inventory is taken to verify the inventory balance.
- Periodic vs. perpetual inventory systems

LO2 Describe inventory costing under specific identification, weighted-average cost, FIFO, and LIFO. (p. 221)

- To assign cost to units sold (cost of goods sold) and units available (inventory), a company must either keep track of the cost of each specific unit (specific identification method) or make an assumption about which units have been sold (weighted-average cost, FIFO, and LIFO methods).
- The weighted-average cost method assumes that a mix of the goods available is sold; the FIFO method assumes that the oldest goods are sold first; and, the LIFO method assumes that the newest goods are sold first.

LO3 Analyze the effects of different inventory costing methods on company profit. (p. 225)

- Each of the alternative inventory costing methods produces a different cost of goods sold and gross profit.
- When costs are rising, the LIFO method does the best job of matching current costs with revenues; LIFO also produces a lower gross profit and lower income taxes than either weighted-average cost or FIFO.

Apply the lower of cost or net realizable value rule. (p. 230) LO4

- The lower of cost or net realizable value rule requires the write-down of inventory when its original cost exceeds its net realizable value.
- Net realizable value is an inventory item's estimated selling price less the expected costs of selling the item.

Define the gross profit percentage and explain its use. (p. 231) LO5

- The gross profit percentage is the rate at which a company earns gross profit on net sales.
- The gross profit percentage is calculated as net sales less the cost of goods sold, all divided by net sales.

Define inventory turnover and days' sales in inventory and explain their use. (p. 233) LO6

- Inventory turnover and days' sales in inventory indicate, respectively, how many times, on average, during the year a firm sells its inventory and how many days, on average, it takes a firm to sell its inventory.
- Inventory turnover and days' sales in inventory provide evidence regarding a firm's ability to sell its inventory and its ability to effectively manage its investment in inventory.

Appendix 7A: Describe inventory costing under a perpetual inventory system. (p. 235) LO7

- To assign cost to units sold (cost of goods sold) and units available (inventory), a company must either keep track of the cost of each specific unit (specific identification method) or make an assumption about which units have been sold (weighted-average cost, FIFO, and LIFO methods).
- The weighted-average cost method assumes that a mix of the goods available is sold; the FIFO method assumes that the oldest goods are sold; and, the LIFO method assumes that the newest goods are sold.
- The specific identification method and the FIFO method yield the exact same results for ending inventory and for cost of goods sold regardless of whether the periodic or the perpetual method is being used. Only LIFO and weighted-average methods produce different results.

Appendix 7B: Define the LIFO reserve and explain its use. (p. 239) LO8

- The LIFO inventory reserve represents the difference between the value of LIFO ending inventory and what the ending inventory would have been valued at under FIFO.
- The LIFO inventory reserve can cause a material effect on many ratios. These ratios should be adjusted for the LIFO inventory reserve when comparing a company using LIFO with a FIFO company.

Concept	Method	Assessment	SUMMARY
Is a company able to maintain prices on its goods consistent with changes in the cost of its inventory?	Gross profit and net sales $\text{Gross profit percentage} = \dfrac{\text{Gross profit on sales}}{\text{Net sales}}$	A higher ratio is consistent with the company selling goods at a higher mark-up over cost. A lower ratio is consistent with a company attempting to compete by charging lower prices.	TAKEAWAY 7.1
How long, on average, does it take to sell the inventory?	Cost of goods sold, beginning inventory, and ending inventory $\text{Inventory turnover} = \dfrac{\text{Cost of goods sold}}{\text{Average inventory}}$ $\text{Days' sales in inventory} = \dfrac{365}{\text{Inventory turnover}}$	A higher inventory turnover or a lower days' sales in inventory indicates that the company is able to sell its inventory more quickly.	TAKEAWAY 7.2
What effect does the use of LIFO have on ending inventory relative to the use of FIFO?	Examine the difference between ending inventory under LIFO and FIFO, defined as the LIFO reserve.	If the LIFO reserve is material it can have a significant impact on many ratios when compared to FIFO. The calculation of these ratios can be adjusted using the LIFO inventory reserve to provide a more comparable set of results.	Solution 6.2

KEY TERMS

Cost flow (p. 221)
Cost of goods available for sale (p. 218)
Cost of goods sold (p. 219)
Cost principle (p. 218)
Days' sales in inventory (p. 233)
Finished goods inventory (p. 217)
First-in, first-out (FIFO) method (p. 223, 236)
Goods flow (p. 221)
Gross profit margin (p. 226)
Gross profit percentage (p. 231)
Inventory carrying costs (p. 218)
Inventory overage (p. 219)
Inventory shrinkage (p. 219)
Inventory turnover ratio (p. 233)
Just-in-case inventory (p. 218)
Just-in-time (JIT) manufacturing (p. 218)
Last-in, first-out (LIFO) method (p. 223, 237)
LIFO conformity rule (p. 228)
LIFO inventory reserve (p. 239)
Lower of cost or net realizable value (LCNRV) (p. 230)
Manufacturers (p. 216)
Merchandise inventory (p. 217)
Merchandising firms (p. 216)
Net realizable value (p. 230)
Periodic inventory system (p. 219)
Perpetual inventory system (p. 219)
Physical count of inventory (p. 219)
Purchase discounts (p. 217)
Purchase price (p. 217)
Purchase returns and allowances (p. 217)
Quick response system (p. 218)
Raw materials inventory (p. 217)
Retailers (p. 217)
Specific identification method (p. 222, 235)
Weighted-average cost method (p. 224, 238)
Wholesalers (p. 217)
Work-in-process inventory (p. 217)

SELF-STUDY QUESTIONS

(Answers to Self-Study Questions are at the end of this chapter.)

LO5 **1. The Arcadia Company is a merchandiser and reports the following data at year-end:**

Net sales	$100,000
Cost of goods sold	60,000
Net income	15,000

What is the company's gross profit percentage?

a. 40 percent
b. 60 percent
c. 15 percent
d. None of the above

LO1 **2. Which of the following statements regarding cost flows is true?**

a. Cost of goods available for sale is equal to beginning inventory minus cost of goods purchased.
b. Cost of goods available for sale is equal to beginning inventory plus cost of goods purchased.
c. CGAS = beginning inventory minus ending inventory.
d. CGAS = cost of goods sold minus cost of goods purchased.

LO1 **3. Which of the following concepts relates to the elimination or minimization of inventories by a manufacturing firm?**

a. Quick response
b. Just-in-time
c. Just-in-case
d. Specific identification

LO2 **4. Which inventory costing method assumes that the most recently purchased merchandise is sold first?**

a. Specific identification
b. Weighted-average cost
c. FIFO
d. LIFO

LO3 **5. Which inventory costing method results in the highest-valued ending inventory during a period of rising unit costs?**

a. Specific identification
b. Weighted-average cost
c. FIFO
d. LIFO

6. When should ending inventory be written down below its acquisition cost on the balance sheet? LO4 Homework MBC

a. When units are shipped to buyers.
b. When the inventory's net realizable value exceeds its acquisition cost.
c. When the inventory's net realizable value is below its acquisition cost.
d. None of the above.

7. Which inventory costing method results in the highest net income during a period of rising unit prices? LO3 Homework MBC

a. Specific identification *c.* FIFO
b. Weighted-average cost *d.* LIFO

8. Which inventory costing method is expensive to implement? LO2 Homework MBC

a. Specific identification *c.* FIFO
b. Weighted-average cost *d.* LIFO

9. Which inventory costing method is frequently used when undifferentiated units are stored in a common area? LO2 Homework MBC

a. Specific identification *c.* FIFO
b. Weighted-average cost *d.* LIFO

10. Which inventory costing method results in the lowest net income during a period of rising unit prices? LO3 Homework MBC

a. Specific identification *c.* FIFO
b. Weighted-average cost *d.* LIFO

11. Which inventory costing method does not require the use of the lower of cost or net realizable value rule? LO4 Homework MBC

a. Specific identification *c.* FIFO
b. Weighted-average cost *d.* LIFO

12. Tracker Corp. reported annual cost of goods sold of $30,000 and average inventory on hand during the year of $3,750. What was Tracker's inventory turnover? LO6 Homework MBC

a. 0.125 times *c.* $26,250
b. 8.0 times *d.* 8.0%

13. The Avner Company reports ending inventory under the LIFO method of $15,000. Had Avner used FIFO, the ending inventory would have been reported as $16,500. Avner's LIFO inventory reserve is: LO8 (Appendix 7B) Homework MBC

a. $31,500 *c.* $1,500
b. $15,000 *d.* 91%

14. The periodic inventory system differs from the perpetual inventory system: LO1, 7 Homework MBC

a. because the periodic system is not compatible with modern technology.
b. because the perpetual system continually updates inventory, while the periodic inventory system only updates inventory at the end of the period.
c. because the periodic system continually updates inventory, while the perpetual inventory system only updates inventory at the end of the period.
d. because the periodic system is more complex and costly.

QUESTIONS

1. Describe the differences between (a) a manufacturer, (b) a wholesale distributor, and (c) a retailer.
2. Explain how *gross profit on sales* is calculated.
3. Explain how *gross profit percentage* is calculated. How is this percentage used by analysts and investors?
4. When merchandisers and manufacturers prepare income statements for their annual reports to shareholders, they usually begin the statement with net sales. For internal reporting purposes, however, the income statements will show gross sales and the related contra-revenue accounts of sales returns and allowances and sales discounts. What might explain this difference in the financial information disclosed to external parties and management? Do you consider the more limited disclosure in the annual reports to be inconsistent with the full disclosure principle? Briefly explain your point of view.
5. What are the three inventory accounts maintained by a manufacturing firm? Define each.
6. ShopMart Stores uses point-of-sale equipment at its checkout counters to read universal bar codes. It also uses a quick response system. What is a quick response system?

7. What are *just-in-case inventory* and *inventory carrying costs?*

8. What is the *just-in-time manufacturing philosophy?* Describe it.

9. What is meant by *goods flow* and *cost flow?*

10. Describe how each of the following inventory costing methods is used: (a) Specific identification; (b) Weighted-average cost; (c) First-in, first-out; and (d) Last-in, first-out.

11. What is an appropriate operating situation (that is, goods flow corresponds with cost flow) for each of the following approaches to inventory costing: Specific identification, Weighted-average cost, FIFO, and LIFO?

12. Why do relatively stable purchase prices reduce the significance of the choice of an inventory costing method?

13. What is the nature of FIFO *phantom profits* during periods of rising inventory purchase prices?

14. If costs have been rising, which inventory costing method—weighted-average cost; first-in, first-out; or last-in, first-out—yields (a) the lowest ending inventory value? (b) the lowest net income? (c) the largest ending inventory value? (d) the largest net income?

15. Even though it does not represent their goods flow, why might firms adopt last-in, first-out inventory costing during periods when inventory costs are rising?

16. Describe two situations in which merchandise may be valued on the balance sheet at an amount less than its acquisition cost.

17. What is the effect on reported net income of applying the lower of cost or net realizable value rule to ending inventory?

18. How do the accounting principles of consistency and full disclosure apply to inventory costing?

19. What is a LIFO inventory reserve and how can it be useful to an analyst?

20. Moyer Company has an inventory turnover of 4.51. What is Moyer's days' sales in inventory?

DATA ANALYTICS

The assignments in this Data Analytics section are designed to familiarize you with the tools used in analyzing data and communicating the results. Appendix F provides an in-depth discussion of data analytics and blockchain technology.

DA7-1. Preparing Excel Visualizations of Gross Profit Data Over Time

Data Analytics | Homework MBC

Financial information for the following five retailers is included in the Excel file associated with this chapter: **The Home Depot, Inc.** (Home Depot), **Lowe's Companies, Inc.** (Lowe's), **Target Corporation** (Target), **The ODP Corporation** (ODP), and **Costco Wholesale Corporation** (Costco). In this problem we analyze the gross profit percentage of retail companies with different business models. The gross profit percentage measures a company's ability to cover its operating costs from revenues after allowing for costs of goods and services sold. A gross profit percentage will vary by industry (some industries require extensive manufacturing operations for example) and is also affected by a company's business strategy. For example, a company with a lower gross profit percentage (a grocery store) will make up for profits with higher sales volume. A company with a high gross profit percentage (high-end jewelry store) can afford to sell fewer products when each item has a higher gross profit percentage.

REQUIRED

1. Download Excel file DA7-1 found in myBusinessCourse.
2. Calculate the gross profit percentage for each of the three years (with Year 3 being the most recent year).
3. Create a line chart showing the trend of the gross profit percentage for each company over the three-year period.
4. List the companies in order from the highest to the lowest gross profit percentage for each of the three years.
5. Add a trendline to the line chart for each company and forecast one additional period. *Hint:* Right-click on each line in your chart and add trendline. In the format trendline area under Forecast, forward 1 period.
6. List the companies in order from the highest to the lowest gross profit percentage for the forecasted year.
7. Describe the trends in the line chart.
8. Describe the likely source of the difference between the company with the highest gross profit percentage and the lowest gross profit percentage.

Gross Profit Percentage

$$\frac{\text{Sales revenue} - \text{Cost of goods sold}}{\text{Sales revenue}}$$

DA7-2. Preparing and Interpreting Sales Data in Excel

Wakeboards Inc. manufactures and sells three types of wakeboards to 50 customers located primarily in oceanside cities in the U.S. The Excel file associated with this exercise contains daily sales data for its three different models over the past year. Using this file, we will drill down to and rank sales by model number, by customer name, by time period.

PART 1 CREATING PIVOTTABLE ONE

1. Download Excel file DA7-2 found in myBusinessCourse.
2. Prepare a PivotTable showing sales by customer by month. *Hint:* With your cursor on a cell in the worksheet, click on Insert, PivotChart. Drag month into Columns and Customer name into Rows, and desired Model (such as Model 1) into Values.
3. Answer the following questions based upon data in your PivotTable.
   a. How many units of Model 1 did Villager Store purchase for the year?
   b. How many units of Model 1 did Carmel Sports purchase in April?
   c. How many units of Model 2 did West Loop Inc. purchase during the year?
   d. How many units of Model 2 did Marina Inc. purchase in July?
   e. How many units of Model 3 did East Beach purchase in May? What dates were the purchases? *Hint:* Double-click on the total purchases by the customer in May and a worksheet will automatically open with the date details.
4. Apply conditional formatting to the PivotTable, highlighting all monthly orders > 50 units of Model 1. *Hint:* Highlight cells in the month column of the table; then under the Home tab, click on Conditional formatting in the Styles group. Click Highlight cell rules, Greater than and specify your rule.
5. List the companies with four or more orders that are greater than 50 units of Model 1.

PART 2 CREATING PIVOTTABLE TWO

1. Prepare a second PivotTable showing the total sales of Model 1 by month. *Hint:* Drag Months to Columns and Model 1 Sales Units to Values.
2. List the amount of the highest monthly sales and the month in which it occurs.
3. Calculate the number of months where unit sales fall below 500 units.

DA7-3. Preparing Tableau Visualizations to Analyze Gross Profit

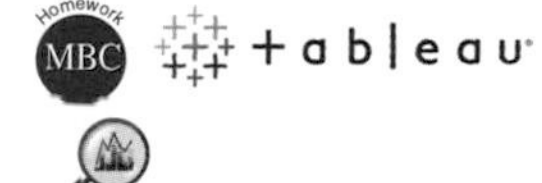

Refer to PF-21 in Appendix F. This problem uses Tableau to create and analyze visualizations of gross profit percentages of S&P 500 companies.

DA7-4. Preparing Tableau Visualizations to Analyze Inventory Management

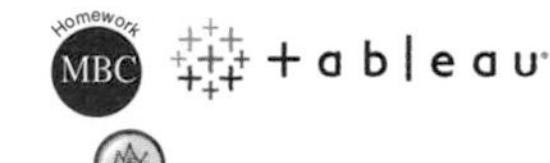

Refer to PF-22 in Appendix F. This problem uses Tableau to create and analyze visualizations of inventory ratios of certain market segments of S&P 500 companies.

Assignments with the MBC logo in the margin are available in myBusinessCourse. See the Preface of the book for details.

SHORT EXERCISES

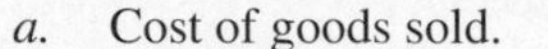

SE7-1. Merchandising versus Service Firm For each of the following accounts, indicate whether it would be found in the records of a merchandising firm, a service firm, or both. **LO1**

a. Cost of goods sold.
b. Service revenue.
c. Purchase returns and allowances.
d. Inventory.
e. Accounts receivable.
f. Accounts payable.
g. Sales revenue.
h. Freight-out.

SE7-2. Gross Profit Percentage Using the data below, compute Dino's gross profit percentage for the month of January. **LO5**

Net sales	$10,000
Cost of goods sold	4,000
Operating expenses	3,000
Other income	500
Income tax expense	1,200

LO4 Homework MBC

SE7-3. Departures from Acquisition Cost At year-end, The Appliance Shop has a refrigerator that has been used as a demonstration model. The refrigerator cost $350 and sells for $500 when new. In its present condition, the refrigerator will be sold for $325. Related selling costs are an estimated $15. At what amount should the refrigerator be carried in inventory?

a. $350
b. $335
c. $325
d. $310

LO2 Homework MBC

SE7-4. Inventory Costing Methods Which inventory costing method requires that a company keep track of the cost of each specific unit of inventory?

a. Specific identification
b. Lower of cost or net realizable value
c. LIFO
d. All of the above

LO8 (Appendix 7B) Homework MBC

SE7-5. LIFO Inventory Reserve Lamil Company reports ending inventory of $150,000 on a LIFO basis and also reports a LIFO inventory reserve of $27,000. If Lamil had used FIFO rather than LIFO, ending inventory would have been:

a. $123,000.
b. $150,000.
c. $177,000.
d. $182,500.

LO4 Homework MBC

SE7-6. Lower of Cost or Net Realizable Value Rule The Causeway Bay Company's ending inventory is composed of 50 units that had cost $20 each and 100 units that had cost $15 each. If the company can sell the 150 units at a price of $16 each, what value should be assigned to the company's ending inventory assuming that it applies LCNRV?

LO6 Homework MBC

SE7-7. Inventory Turnover and Days' Sales in Inventory W. Glass & Company reported the following information in its recent annual report:

	Year 1	Year 2
Cost of goods sold	$4,000,000	$4,600,000
Beginning inventory	900,000	860,000
Ending inventory.	860,000	640,000

Calculate the company's inventory turnover and days' sales in inventory for both years.

LO2 Homework MBC

SE7-8. Inventory Costing Methods and the Periodic Method Lambeth Company experienced the following events in January:

Date	Event	Units		Unit Cost	Total Cost
Jan. 10	Purchased inventory.	100	@	$12	$1,200
Jan. 20	Purchased inventory.	200	@	14	2,800
Jan. 30	Sold inventory.	150			

If the Lambeth Company uses the FIFO inventory costing method, calculate the company's cost of goods sold and its ending inventory as of January 31 assuming the periodic method.

LO2 Homework MBC

SE7-9. Inventory Costing Methods and the Periodic Method Lambeth Company experienced the following events in February:

Date	Event	Units		Unit Cost	Total Cost
Feb. 1	Purchased inventory.	100	@	$20	$2,000
Feb. 4	Sold inventory.	50			
Feb. 9	Purchased inventory.	100	@	$22	$2,200
Feb. 27	Sold inventory.	100			

If the Lambeth Company uses the LIFO inventory costing method, calculate the company's cost of goods sold and ending inventory as of February 28 assuming the periodic method.

LO7 (Appendix 7A) Homework MBC

SE7-10. Inventory Costing Methods and the Perpetual Method Refer to the information in SE7-9 and assume the perpetual inventory system is used. Use the LIFO inventory costing method to calculate the company's cost of goods sold and ending inventory as of February 28.

LO2 Homework MBC

SE7-11. Inventory Costing Methods and the Periodic Method McKay & Company experienced the following events in March:

Date	Event	Units		Unit Cost	Total Cost
Mar. 1	Purchased inventory.	100	@	$15	$1,500
Mar. 3	Sold inventory.	60			
Mar. 15	Purchased inventory.	100	@	$18	$1,800
Mar. 20	Sold inventory.	40			

If McKay & Company uses the weighted-average cost method, calculate the company's cost of goods sold and ending inventory as of March 31 assuming the periodic method.

SE7-12. Errors in Inventory Count Bow Corp. accidentally overstated its 2019 ending inventory by $750. Assume that ending 2020 inventory is accurately counted. The error in 2019 will have what effect on Bow Corp.? **LO3**

a. 2019 net income is understated by $750.
b. 2019 net income is overstated by $750.
c. 2020 net income is understated by $750.
d. Both *b* and *c* are correct.

EXERCISES

E7-1. Profitability Analysis Shannon Enterprises reports the following information on its year-end income statement: **LO5**

Net sales.	$150,000	Operating expenses	30,000
Cost of goods sold	90,000	Other income	10,000

REQUIRED

Calculate Shannon's gross profit percentage and profit margin.

E7-2. Just-in-Time Inventories Raymond Manufacturing Company plans to use raw materials costing $600,000 in manufacturing its products during the current year. Raymond will operate its factory 300 days during the current year. Currently, Raymond follows the just-in-case philosophy with its raw materials inventory, keeping raw materials costing $15,000 in its raw materials inventory. Raymond plans to switch to the just-in-time manufacturing philosophy by keeping only the raw materials needed for the next two days of production. Calculate the new raw materials inventory level after Raymond implements the just-in-time manufacturing philosophy in its factory. **LO1**

E7-3. Inventory Costing Methods The Lippert Company uses the periodic inventory system. The following July data are for an item in Lippert's inventory: **LO2**

July 1 Beginning inventory, 30 units @ $8 per unit.
10 Purchased 50 units @ $9 per unit.
15 Sold 60 units.
26 Purchased 25 units @ $10 per unit.

Calculate the cost of goods sold for July and ending inventory at July 31 using (a) first-in, first-out, (b) last-in, first-out, and (c) the weighted-average cost methods. Round your final answers to the nearest dollar.

E7-4. Inventory Costing Methods—Perpetual Method Refer to the information in E7-3 and assume the perpetual inventory system is used. Calculate the cost of goods sold for the July 15 sale using (a) first-in, first-out, (b) last-in, first-out, and (c) the weighted-average cost methods. Round your final answers to the nearest dollar. **LO7 (Appendix 7A)**

E7-5. Inventory Costing Methods Archer Company is a retailer that uses the periodic inventory system. On August 1, it had 80 units of product A at a total cost of $1,600. On August 5, Archer purchased 100 units of A for $2,116. On August 8, it purchased 200 units of A for $4,416. On August 11, it sold 150 units of A for $4,800. Calculate the August cost of goods sold and the ending inventory at August 31 using (a) first-in, first-out, (b) last-in, first-out, and (c) the weighted-average cost methods. Round your final answers to the nearest dollar. **LO2**

E7-6. Inventory Costing Methods—Perpetual Method Refer to the information in E7-5 and assume the perpetual inventory system is used. Calculate the inventory cost of product A on August 11 **LO7 (Appendix 7A)**

(after the sale) using (a) first-in, first-out, (b) last-in, first-out, and (c) the weighted-average cost methods. Round your final answers to the nearest dollar.

LO4 **E7-7. Lower of Cost or Net Realizable Value (LCNRV) Rule** Determine the proper total inventory value for each of the following items in Viking Company's ending inventory:

a. Viking has 300 rolls of camera film that are past the expiration date marked on the film's box. The films cost $1.65 each and are normally sold for $3.30. To clear out these old films, Viking will drop their selling price to $1.40. There are no related selling costs.

b. Viking has five cameras in stock that have been used as demonstration models. The cameras cost $180 and normally sell for $280. Because these cameras are in used condition, Viking has set the selling price at $160 each. Expected selling costs are $10 per camera. New models of the camera (on order) will cost Viking $200 and will be priced to sell at $320.

LO2 **E7-8. Inventory Costing Methods** The following information is for the Bloom Company for the current year; the company sells just one product:

		Units	Unit Cost
Beginning inventory		200	$10
Purchases:	Feb. 11	500	14
	May 18	400	16
	October 23	100	20

At December 31 there was an ending inventory of 360 units. Assume the use of the periodic inventory method. Calculate the value of ending inventory and the cost of goods sold for the year using (a) first-in, first-out, (b) last-in, first-out, and (c) the weighted-average cost method.

LO2 **E7-9. Inventory Costing Methods** The following data are for the Evans Company, which sells just one product:

		Units	Unit Cost
Beginning inventory, January 1		200	$10
Purchases:	February 11	500	14
	May 18	400	16
	October 23	100	20
Sales	March 1	400	
	July 1	400	

Calculate the value of ending inventory and cost of goods sold using the periodic method and (a) first-in, first-out, (b) last-in, first-out, and (c) weighted-average cost method.

LO6  **E7-10. Inventory Turnover and Days' Sales in Inventory** The Southern Company installed a new inventory management system at the beginning of Year 1. Shown below are data from the company's accounting records as reported by the new system:

	Year 1	Year 2
Sales revenue	$8,000,000	$10,000,000
Cost of goods sold	4,000,000	4,900,000
Beginning inventory	500,000	530,000
Ending inventory	530,000	600,000

Calculate the company's (a) inventory turnover and (b) days' sales in inventory for both years. Comment on your results.

LO8 (Appendix 7B)  **E7-11. The LIFO Inventory Reserve** Midwestern Steel Company uses the LIFO inventory costing method to value its ending inventory. The following data were obtained from the company's accounting records:

Current assets (under FIFO)	$8,000,000
Current liabilities	5,500,000
Inventory under LIFO	2,000,000
Inventory under FIFO	2,700,000

Calculate the company's (a) LIFO inventory reserve and (b) the current ratio assuming (i) FIFO and (ii) LIFO.

E7-12. Applying IFRS LVMH is a Paris based manufacturer of luxury goods that prepares its financial statements using IFRS. During the year, the management of the company undertook a review of the fair value of its inventory and found that the inventory had appreciated above its book value of 10 million euros. According to the company's management, the inventory was undervalued by 1 million euros. How would the revaluation immediately affect the company's (a) current ratio, (b) inventory turnover, and (c) days' sales in inventory? **LO4, 6** LVMH

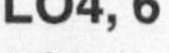

E7-13. Errors in Inventory Counts The following information was taken from the records of Taylor Enterprises: **LO3**

	Year 2	Year 1
Beginning inventory	$ 60,000	$ 50,000
Cost of goods purchased	420,000	400,000
Cost of goods available for sale	480,000	450,000
Ending inventory	55,000	60,000
Cost of goods sold	$425,000	$390,000

The following two errors were made in the physical inventory counts:

1. Year 1 ending inventory was understated by $10,000.
2. Year 2 ending inventory was overstated by $5,000.

Compute the correct cost of goods sold for both years.

PROBLEMS

P7-1. Profitability Analysis Kolby Enterprises reports the following information on its income statement: **LO5**

Net sales	$220,000	Administrative expenses	$10,000
Cost of goods sold	140,000	Other income	15,000
Selling expenses	40,000	Other expense	5,000

REQUIRED

Calculate Kolby's gross profit percentage and profit margin. Explain what each ratio tells us about Kolby's performance. Kolby is planning to add a new product and expects net sales to be $30,000 and cost of goods to be $25,000. No other income or expenses are expected to change. How will this affect Kolby's gross profit percentage and profit margin? What do you advise regarding the new product offering?

P7-2. Inventory Costing Methods Fortune Stores uses the periodic inventory system for its merchandise inventory. The April 1 inventory for one of the items in the merchandise inventory consisted of 120 units with a unit cost of $325. Transactions for this item during April were as follows: **LO2**

April 9 Purchased 40 units @ $345 per unit.
14 Sold 80 units @ $550 per unit.
23 Purchased 20 units @ $350 per unit.
29 Sold 40 units @ $550 per unit.

REQUIRED

a. Calculate the cost of goods sold and the ending inventory cost for the month of April using the weighted-average cost method. Round your final answers to the nearest dollar.

b. Calculate the cost of goods sold and the ending inventory cost for the month of April using the first-in, first-out method.

c. Calculate the cost of goods sold and the ending inventory cost for the month of April using the last-in, first-out method.

P7-3. Inventory Costing Methods—Perpetual Method Refer to the information in P7-2 and assume the perpetual inventory system is used. **LO7 (Appendix 7A)**

REQUIRED

a. Calculate the cost of goods sold and the ending inventory cost for the month of April using the weighted-average cost method.

b. Calculate the cost of goods sold and the ending inventory cost for the month of April using the first-in, first-out method.
c. Calculate the cost of goods sold and the ending inventory cost for the month of April using the last-in, first-out method.

LO2, 3 **P7-4. Inventory Costing Methods** Chen Sales Corporation uses the periodic inventory system. On January 1, Chen had 1,000 units of product A with a unit cost of $20 per unit. A summary of purchases and sales during the year follows:

	Unit Cost	Units Purchased	Units Sold
Feb. 2			400
Apr. 6	$22	1,800	
July 10			1,600
Aug. 9	26	800	
Oct. 23			800
Dec. 30	29	1,200	

REQUIRED

a. Assume that Chen uses the first-in, first-out method. Compute the cost of goods sold for the year and the ending inventory balance at December 31 for product A.
b. Assume that Chen uses the last-in, first-out method. Compute the cost of goods sold for the year and the ending inventory balance at December 31 for product A.
c. Assume that Chen uses the weighted-average cost method. Compute the cost of goods sold for the year and the ending inventory balance at December 31 for product A.
d. Assuming that Chen's products are perishable items, which of the three inventory costing methods would you choose to:
1. Reflect the likely goods flow through the business?
2. Minimize income taxes for the period?
3. Report the largest amount of net income for the period?

Explain your answers.

LO2 **P7-5. Inventory Costing Methods** The following data are for the Portet Corporation, which sells just one product:

		Units	Unit Cost
Beginning inventory, January 1.		1,200	$ 8
Purchases	February 11	1,500	9
	May 18	1,400	10
	October 23	1,100	12
Sales	March 1.	1,400	
	July 1	1,400	
	October 29	1,000	

Calculate the value of ending inventory and cost of goods sold at year-end using the periodic method and (a) first-in, first-out, (b) last-in, first-out, and (c) weighted-average cost method. Round the cost per unit to 3 decimal places and round your final answers to the nearest dollar.

LO3 **P7-6. Inventory Error** The following selected financial information is from Taylor and Company.

	Year 1	Year 2
Beginning inventory	$14,300	$14,000
Ending inventory.	14,000	13,400
Cost of goods sold	67,000	73,500

It was determined that due to errors in the physical inventory count, the Year 1 ending inventory was overstated by $2,300. At the end of Year 2, items costing $500 were in transit and not included in the physical inventory count; however, ownership had transferred to Taylor and Company.

a. Compute the correct cost of goods sold for both years.
b. What is the effect on net income for both years?

LO6 **P7-7. Inventory Turnover and Days' Sales in Inventory** The Eastern Corporation installed a new inventory management system at the beginning of Year 1. Shown below are data from the company's accounting records as reported by the new system:

	Year 1	Year 2
Sales revenue	$18,000,000	$20,000,000
Cost of goods sold	8,000,000	8,900,000
Beginning inventory	2,500,000	2,530,000
Ending inventory	2,530,000	2,600,000

Calculate the company's (a) inventory turnover and (b) days' sales in inventory for both years. Comment on your results.

P7-8. **The LIFO Inventory Reserve** Waterloo Manufacturing Company uses the LIFO inventory costing method to value its ending inventory. The following data were obtained from the company's accounting records for the current year:

LO8 (Appendix 7B)

Current assets (under FIFO)	$18,000,000
Current liabilities	15,500,000
Inventory under LIFO	7,000,000
Inventory under FIFO	7,700,000

Calculate the company's (a) LIFO inventory reserve and (b) current ratio assuming (i) FIFO and (ii) LIFO. If the company's LIFO gross profit was $10,000,000 and the change in the LIFO inventory reserve from the prior to current year was $1,200,000, calculate the company's gross profit under FIFO.

SERIAL PROBLEM: ANGEL CITY GREETINGS

(Note: This is a continuation of the Serial Problem: Angel City Greetings from Chapters 1 through 6.)

SP7. As expected, the holiday season was very busy for Kate and her greeting card company. In fact, most of her supplies were fully depleted by year-end, necessitating a restocking of inventory. Assume that Kate uses the periodic method of accounting for inventory and that her January beginning inventory was $0. The following transactions occurred for Angel City Greetings during January of the New Year:

Purchases	Units		Unit Cost	Total Cost
Jan. 10	400	@	$3.00 per unit	$1,200
Jan. 17	500	@	$3.50 per unit	1,750
Jan. 23	300	@	$4.00 per unit	1,200
Total	1,200			$4,150

Sales	Units
Jan. 15	360
Jan. 21	420
Jan. 27	380
Total	1,160

REQUIRED

Calculate the company's cost of goods sold and value of ending inventory for the month of January using (1) FIFO, (2) LIFO, and (3) the weighted-average cost method. Round the cost per unit to three decimal places and round your final answers to the nearest dollar.

BEYOND THE NUMBERS

REPORTING AND ANALYSIS

BTN7-1. **Financial Reporting Problem: The Columbia Sportswear Company** The financial statements for the Columbia Sportswear Company can be found in Appendix A at the end of this textbook.

Columbia Sportswear Company

Required

Answer the following questions using Columbia's Consolidated Financial Statements:

a. How much inventory does Columbia carry on its balance sheet? What percentage of Columbia's total assets does inventory represent in each year presented?

b. Compute the inventory turnover and days' sales in inventory for 2020 and 2019. Inventory at December 31, 2018, was $521.8 million.

c. Is Columbia's inventory management improving?

Columbia Sportswear Company
Under Armour, Inc.

BTN7-2. Comparative Analysis Problem: Columbia Sportswear Company vs Under Armour, Inc. The financial statements for Columbia Sportswear Company can be found in Appendix A at the end of this textbook, and the financial statements of Under Armour, Inc. can be found in Appendix B.

Required

a. Compare the dollar value of inventory carried on the balance sheet by each company in 2020 and 2019. Which company carries the greater dollar amount of inventory? Compare the ratio of inventory divided by total assets for each company for both years. Which company carries the larger relative investment in inventory?

b. Calculate the inventory turnover and days' sales in inventory for both years for each company. Inventory at December 31, 2018, for Columbia and Under Armour, Inc. was $521.8 million and $1,019.5 million, respectively.

c. Which company appears to be doing the better job of managing its investment in inventory?

BTN7-3. Business Decision Problem Northwestern Corporation started a retail clothing business on July 1 of the current year. During the year, Northwestern Corporation had the following summary transactions related to merchandise inventory:

	Purchases	Sales
July	$240,000	$ 360,000
August	384,000	696,000
September	312,000	576,000
October	360,000	660,000
November	900,000	1,020,000
December	264,000	1,344,000

On average, Northwestern's cost of goods sold is 50 percent of sales. Assume that there were no sales returns and allowances or purchases returns and allowances during this six-month time period.

Required

a. Calculate the ending merchandise inventory for each of the six months.

b. Northwestern's purchases peaked during November; its sales peaked during December. Did Northwestern plan its purchases wisely? Should Northwestern expect a similar pattern in future years?

Johnson & Johnson

BTN7-4. Financial Analysis Problem Johnson & Johnson is a worldwide manufacturer of health care products, including Band-Aid bandages and Mylanta antacid. It reported the following results for three recent years (Year 3 is the most recent):

(in millions)	Year 3	Year 2	Year 1
Net sales	$82,584	$82,059	$81,581
Cost of goods sold	28,427	27,556	27,091

Assume that similar-sized companies in the same basic industries have experienced an average gross profit percentage of 70 percent each year.

Required

a. Calculate the gross profit percentage for Johnson & Johnson for the three years.

b. Compare the three-year trend in gross profit percentage for Johnson & Johnson to the assumed industry average. Analyze the trend and evaluate the performance of Johnson & Johnson compared to the assumed industry average.

CRITICAL THINKING

General Mills, Inc.

BTN7-5. Accounting Research Problem The fiscal year 2020 annual report of General Mills, Inc. is available at: https://investors.generalmills.com/financial-information/annual-reports/default.aspx.

Required

a. What percentage of total assets are represented by General Mills' investment in inventory in 2020 and 2019?

b. Compute the inventory turnover and days' sales in inventory for General Mills for both years. In 2018, the ending inventory was $1,642.2 billion.
c. Is the company doing a better job of managing its investment in inventory in 2020?
d. What inventory costing method does General Mills use?
e. What is the value of the company's LIFO reserve at year-end 2020? (Appendix 7B)

BTN7-6. **Accounting Communication Activity** Nobel Company produces custom machinery that has few competitors. As such, Nobel is able to charge a large markup that is reflected in its large gross profit percentage. Recently the marketing director proposed offering a new set of products that are more generic in nature, and therefore will not allow large markups. The accounting department has, however, determined the products will add to Nobel's overall net income. The following table provides estimates of Nobel's profitability both with and without the new product:

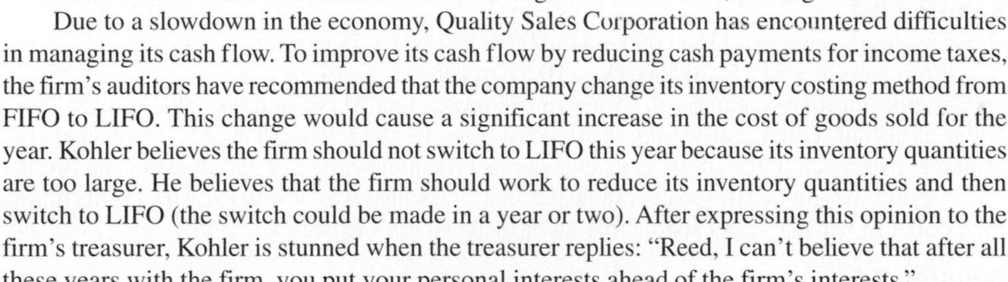

	Without New Product	With New Product
Net sales	$250,000	$350,000
Cost of goods sold	125,000	210,000
Net income	25,000	31,500

Required
The President of Nobel, Jack Towne, has asked you to write a memo answering the following questions.
a. How will the new product line affect the company's profitability as measured by its gross profit percentage and the profit margin?
b. How is it possible for net income to improve, while at the same time these profitability ratios may deteriorate?
c. Should the company expand by offering this new product line?

BTN7-7. **Accounting Ethics Case** Reed Kohler is in his final year of employment as controller for Quality Sales Corporation; he hopes to retire next year. As a member of top management, Kohler participates in an attractive company bonus plan. The overall size of the bonus is a function of the firm's net income before bonus and income taxes—the larger the net income, the larger the bonus.

Due to a slowdown in the economy, Quality Sales Corporation has encountered difficulties in managing its cash flow. To improve its cash flow by reducing cash payments for income taxes, the firm's auditors have recommended that the company change its inventory costing method from FIFO to LIFO. This change would cause a significant increase in the cost of goods sold for the year. Kohler believes the firm should not switch to LIFO this year because its inventory quantities are too large. He believes that the firm should work to reduce its inventory quantities and then switch to LIFO (the switch could be made in a year or two). After expressing this opinion to the firm's treasurer, Kohler is stunned when the treasurer replies: "Reed, I can't believe that after all these years with the firm, you put your personal interests ahead of the firm's interests."

Explain why Kohler may be viewed as holding a position that favors his personal interests. What can Kohler do to increase his credibility when the possible change to LIFO is discussed at a meeting of the firm's top management next week?

BTN7-8. **Environmental, Social, and Governance Problem** Target is one of a large growing number of companies that publish an annual corporate social responsibility report. Go to the Target Website and navigate to the section on corporate responsibility in order to download Target's latest corporate responsibility report. Discuss some of the ways that Target documents its good citizenship.

Target

BTN7-9. **Accounting Ethics Problem** The chapter highlights an inventory fraud case at Crazy Eddie. Unfortunately there have been many other serious inventory frauds where the auditors were fooled by illegal acts. A few of these cases include (1) Comptronix Corporation, (2) Leslie Fay Company, (3) Laribee Manufacturing Company, and (4) Phar-Mor drug stores.

Do a computer search of one of these cases and explain how inventory was used to commit the fraud. List some ways the auditors can lessen the chance such frauds could go undetected.

Crazy Eddie
Comptronix Corporation
Leslie Fay Company
Laribee Manufacturing Company
Phar-Mor

ANSWERS TO SELF-STUDY QUESTIONS

1. a **2.** b **3.** b **4.** d **5.** c **6.** c **7.** c **8.** a **9.** b **10.** d **11.** d **12.** b **13.** c **14.** b

REVIEW SOLUTIONS

Solution 7.1

Beginning inventory	$ 57,000
Add: Cost of goods purchased	650,000
(a) ***Cost of goods available for sale***	***$707,000***
Less: Ending inventory	43,000
(b) ***Cost of goods sold***	***$664,000***

Solution 7.2

a. Ending inventory in units = beginning inventory + purchases – sales (4,000 + 6,000 – 9,000 = 1,000)
Ending inventory balance using:
i. FIFO: 1,000 × $7 = $7,000
ii. LIFO: 1,000 × $5 = $5,000
iii. Weighted-average cost: 1,000 × [(4,000 × $5) + (6,000 × $7)]/10,000 = 1,000 × $6.20 = $6,200

b. Cost of goods sold using:
i. FIFO: (4,000 × $5) + (5,000 × $7) = $55,000
ii. LIFO: (6,000 × $7) + (3,000 × $5) = $57,000
iii. Weighted-average cost: 9,000 × [(4,000 × $5) + (6,000 × $7)]/10,000 = 9,000 × $6.20 = $55,800

c. Sales in dollars = 9,000 × $10 = $90,000.
Gross profit using:
i. FIFO: $90,000 – $55,000 = $35,000
ii. LIFO: $90,000 – $57,000 = $33,000
iii. Weighted-average cost: $90,000 – $55,800 = $34,200

Solution 7.3

a. 200 × $4.00 = $800. The inventory is valued at net realizable value.
b. 12 × $18 = $216. The inventory is valued at net realizable value ($20 – $2 per dryer).

Solution 7.4

Gross profit percentage = ($100,000 – $45,000)/$100,000 = 55 percent
Profit margin = $10,500/$100,000 = 10.5 percent

A gross profit percentage of 55 percent indicates that Musicland was able to earn 55 cents for each dollar of net sales after considering just its cost of goods sold. In other words, Musicland still has 55 cents available from each dollar of net sales to cover its remaining expenses and to earn a net profit.

A profit margin of 10.5 percent indicates that Musicland was able to earn 10.5 cents in net income from each dollar of net sales after subtracting all of the business's expenses.

Solution 7.5

	Prior Year	Current Year
Inventory turnover	$2,000,000 / (($450,000 + $430,000)/2) = 4.55	$2,300,000 / (($430,000 + $320,000)/2) = 6.13
Days' sales in inventory	365/4.55 = 80.22 days	365/6.13 = 59.54 days

The company increased its sales by $400,000 from the prior year to the current year, and at the same time, decreased its average inventory by $65,000 ($440,000 – $375,000) as a consequence of improved inventory management. This resulted in a significantly improved inventory turnover (6.13 versus 4.55) and 20.68 (80.22 – 59.54) fewer days' sales in inventory. It appears that the new inventory management system is a financial success.

Solution 7.6

a. Cost of goods available for sale:

1,000	units @ $24.00 =	$ 24,000
2,000	units @ $27.00 =	54,000
3,000	units @ $28.40 =	85,200
1,200	units @ $31.25 =	37,500
7,200		$200,700

Units in ending inventory = 1,400, computed as units in beginning inventory, plus units purchased, minus units sold [1,000 + (2,000 + 3,000 + 1,200) – (1,200 + 2,000 + 1,000 + 1,600)].

1. **Weighted-average cost:**

Weighted-average unit cost:	$200,700/7,200 units =	$ 27.875
Ending inventory:	1,400 units × $27.875 =	$ 39,025
Cost of goods sold:	$200,700 – $39,025 =	$161,675

2. **FIFO:**

Ending inventory:	1,200 units @ $31.25 =	$ 37,500
	200 units @ $28.40 =	5,680
	1,400	$ 43,180
Cost of goods sold:	$200,700 – $43,180 =	$157,520

3. **LIFO:**

Ending inventory:	1,000 units @ $24.00 =	$ 24,000
	400 units @ $27.00 =	10,800
	1,400	$ 34,800
Cost of goods sold:	$200,700 – $34,800 =	$165,900

b. Sales revenue:

1,200 units @ $50.00 =	$ 60,000
2,000 units @ $52.00 =	104,000
1,000 units @ $53.00 =	53,000
1,600 units @ $55.00 =	88,000
5,800	$305,000

1. Weighted-average gross profit = $305,000 – $161,675 = $143,325
2. FIFO gross profit = $305,000 – $157,520 = $147,480
3. LIFO gross profit = $305,000 – $165,900 = $139,100

c. Inventory Turnover

Weighted-average cost					
Cost of goods sold	$161,675.00	=	$161,675.00	=	5.13 times
Average ending inventory	($24,000 + $39,025)/2		$31,512.50		
FIFO:					
Cost of goods sold	$157,520.00	=	$157,520.00	=	4.69 times
Average ending inventory	($24,000 + $43,180)/2		$33,590.00		
LIFO:					
Cost of goods sold	$165,900.00	=	$165,900.00	=	5.64 times
Average ending inventory	($24,000 + $34,800)/2		$29,400.00		

Days' Sales in Inventory

Weighted-average cost	71.15 days
FIFO:.	77.83 days
LIFO:.	64.72 days

Long-Lived Assets

PAST

Chapter 7 explained the accounting for inventory. We described and applied the costing methods of specific identification, FIFO, LIFO, and weighted average.

PRESENT

This chapter focuses on another important set of assets—long-lived property, plant and equipment and intangible assets.

FUTURE

Chapter 9 begins our study of the nature of liabilities.

TESLA MOTORS INC.

Tesla Motors, Inc. is best known for its high-end electric vehicles. CEO Elon Musk's goal is to produce 20 million electric vehicles per year by the end of this decade. To achieve this goal, Tesla has opened a manufacturing plant near Shanghai and is building two additional plants, one near Berlin and the other in Austin, Texas. Along with its high-end passenger vehicles, Tesla will soon offer a Cybertruck and a big-rig truck called Semi.

One thing Tesla has in common with other automobile manufacturers such as Ford Motor Company and Bavarian Motor Works (BMW) is the need for large investments in plant assets such as land, buildings, and equipment to produce the products they sell. Companies like Tesla also typically maintain large investments in such intangible assets as trademarks and patents. Because of its large investment in these long-lived, revenue-producing assets, Tesla, like other automobile manufacturers, is referred to as a capital-intensive company. Wall Street analysts evaluate the capital intensity of companies by calculating a capital-intensity ratio, equal to the value of plant assets plus the value of intangible assets divided by the value of a company's total assets. Tesla's capital-intensity ratio is approximately 28 percent.

Road Map

LO	Learning Objective	Page	eLecture	Review	Assignments
LO1	**Discuss the nature of long-lived assets.**	259	E8-1	8.1	SE1, E1, P1, P4, P8
LO2	**Discuss the nature of depreciation, illustrate three depreciation methods, and explain impairment losses.**	261	E8-2	8.2	SE2, SE3, SE4, E2, P2, P3, P4, P8
LO3	**Discuss the distinction between revenue expenditures and capital expenditures.**	267	E8-3	8.3	E3, P4, P8
LO4	**Explain the accounting for disposals of property, plant and equipment.**	269	E8-4	8.4	SE5, SE11, E4, P5
LO5	**Discuss the nature of intangible assets.**	271	E8-5	8.5	SE6, SE7, E5, P6
LO6	**Illustrate the balance sheet presentation of long-lived assets.**	274	E8-6	8.6	SE12, E7, P7
LO7	**Define the return on assets ratio and the asset turnover ratio and explain their use.**	275	E8-7	8.7	SE8, SE9, SE10, E6

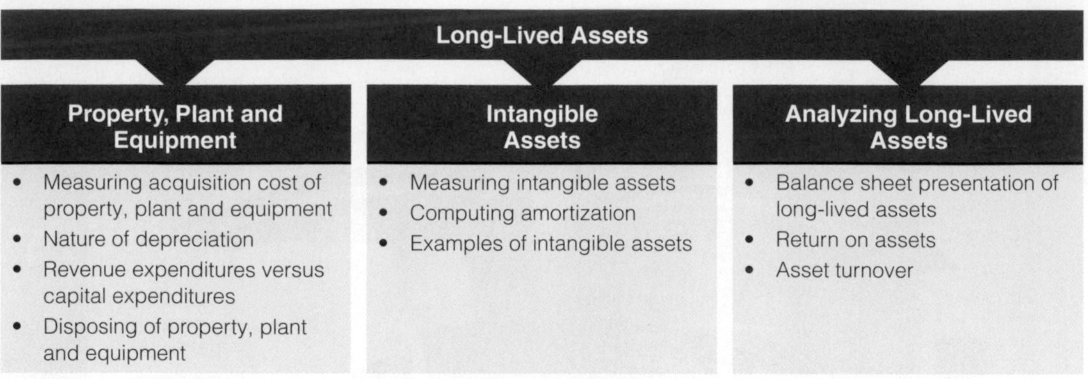

OVERVIEW OF LONG-LIVED ASSETS

A.K.A. Property, plant and equipment is often referred to as *fixed assets*, *plant assets* or simply as *PP&E*.

Consider for a moment the asset structure of Tesla Motors, Inc. Approximately 28 percent of the assets used to fulfill the company's mission of manufacturing and distributing power products are in the long-term asset categories: **property, plant and equipment** and **intangible assets**. Tesla reports property, plant and equipment of over $12.7 billion and intangible assets of over $500 million. Property, plant and equipment are sometimes referred to as fixed assets, because they are physical assets that cannot be easily liquidated. Examples of property, plant and equipment include land, machinery and buildings. Intangible assets, on the other hand, refer to assets that lack the physical substance that characterizes property, plant and equipment. Examples of intangible assets include copyrights, franchises, and patents. The benefits provided to a firm by its property, plant and equipment and its intangible assets extend over many accounting periods. In this chapter, we discuss the accounting for these long-lived assets.

The carrying value of long-lived assets is initially based on the asset's historical cost—that is, the cost incurred to acquire and place the asset into service. In order to properly measure income, the costs related to the use of long-lived assets must be matched with the revenues that they help to generate. The portion of an asset's cost that is consumed or used in any given period is called *depreciation expense, when referring to property, plant and equipment*, and *amortization expense, when referring to intangible assets*. Both of these terms have an equivalent meaning in accounting: that is, depreciation and amortization refer to the process of allocating a portion of an asset's acquisition cost to an expense on the income statement. These expenses reflect the consumption of the asset as it produces revenue for a business.

Exhibit 8-1 provides several examples of both categories of assets. The exhibit also identifies the appropriate term for the periodic consumption of the asset and its write-off to expense. Note that land has an indefinite useful life, and therefore, does not require a periodic write-off to expense. As discussed in Chapter 9, companies also report the carrying values of long-lived assets that are leased. These are referred to as **Right-of-use assets** and consist of assets such as land, buildings, furniture, and equipment. Thus, it is common for companies to include a category of long-lived assets labeled Right-of-use assets.

EXHIBIT 8-1 Long-Lived Assets That Require Periodic Write-Off

Asset Category	Examples	Term for the Periodic Write-Off to Expense
Property, Plant and Equipment	*Buildings, equiapment, tools, furniture, fixtures, vehicles Right-of-use assets*	Depreciation
Intangible Assets	*Patents, copyrights, leaseholds, franchises, trademarks, brand names*	Amortization

ACCOUNTING FOR LONG-LIVED ASSETS

Exhibit 8-2 is a graphic presentation of the accounting issues associated with long-lived assets during their useful lives. These include: ❶ Identifying the type, and amount of expenditures that were incurred to acquire the asset. ❷ Determining the amount of the asset's cost to periodically expense in the income statement. This involves estimating the asset's useful life and the salvage value expected to be received when the asset is disposed of. ❸ Differentiating between expenditures that are incurred to maintain the asset in good working order and expenditures that increase the asset's productive capacity or extend its useful life. ❹ Determining the gain or loss to be recognized when a long-lived asset is disposed of.

LO1 Discuss the nature of long-lived assets.

Acquisition Cost of Property, Plant and Equipment

Property, plant and equipment are initially recorded on the balance sheet at their acquisition cost. This is also called the asset's *historical cost* because it represents the original expenditure made to acquire the asset. In general, the acquisition cost of a long-lived asset equals the cash and/or cash equivalent given up to acquire the asset *and* to prepare it for its intended use.

EXHIBIT 8-2 Issues Associated with the Accounting for Long-lived Assets

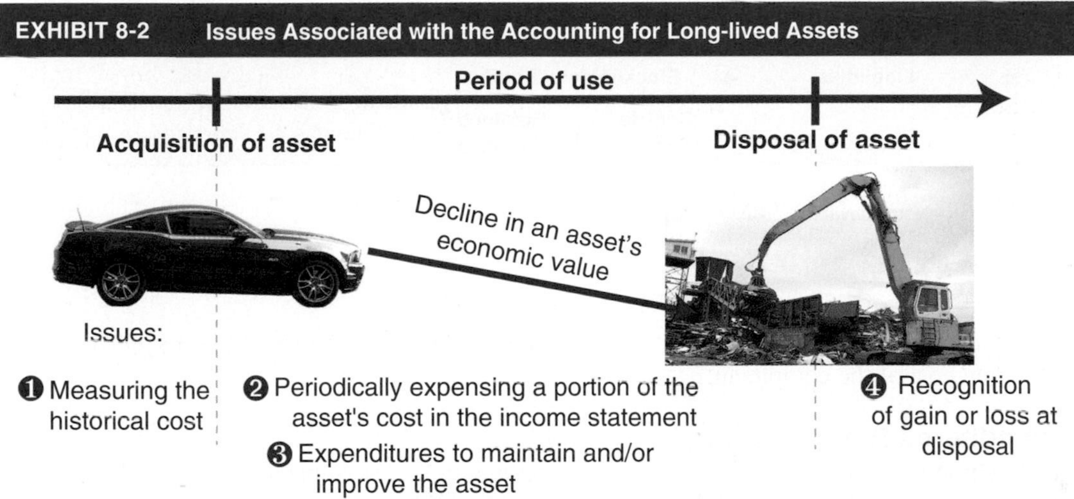

PRINCIPLE ALERT

Cost Principle The initial valuation of property, plant and equipment follows directly from the *cost principle*, meaning assets and liabilities are initially recorded at the amount paid or obligated to pay. To measure an asset's acquisition cost, accountants must identify the asset's purchase price and any additional costs incurred to transport the asset and to prepare it for service. All of these costs are added to the asset's balance sheet value and are considered part of the asset's acquisition cost.

Cash Purchases

An asset's acquisition cost is often simply the amount of cash paid when the asset is acquired and readied for use by a business. Consider, for example, the following expenditures for a piece of equipment purchased by Los Altos, Inc.:

Purchase price components:		
Gross invoice price	$10,000	
Less: Cash discount (1/10, n/30)	100	
Sales tax	500	$10,400
Related expenditures:		
Freight charges	200	
Installation costs	500	
Testing of installed machine	300	1,000
Acquisition cost of equipment		**$11,400**

The total acquisition cost of the equipment is $11,400, consisting of a cash purchase price of $10,400 and related preparation costs of $1,000. The sales tax is also a component of the purchase price and should be included in the asset's acquisition cost. Similarly, the costs of freight, installation, and testing are expenditures necessary to get the asset to the desired business location and prepare it for its intended use.

Deferred Payment Purchases

If an asset's purchase price is not immediately paid in cash, the cash-equivalent purchase price is used to compute its acquisition cost. Suppose, for example, that Los Altos, Inc. purchased its equipment under a financing plan requiring a $400 cash down payment and a nine percent, $10,000 note payable due in one year. The implied cash price remains $10,400 even though more than $10,400 is eventually paid under the financing plan [$400 down payment + $10,000 principal payment on note + $900 interest payment ($10,000 note payable × 9%) = $11,300]. Because the equipment is ready for immediate use, the extra $900 paid as interest is charged to interest expense and does not become part of its acquisition cost. The financial statement effect of this transaction is as follows:

Transaction: *Purchase equipment with $400 cash down payment and $10,000 note payable.*

Balance Sheet								Income Statement				
Assets	=	Liabilities	+	Stockholders' Equity: Contrib. Capital	+	Retained Earnings		*Revenues*	–	*Expenses*	=	*Net Income*
+10,400 Equipment −400 Cash	=	+10,000 Notes payable	+						–		=	

As in the case of a cash purchase, the expenditures for freight, installation, and testing increase the acquisition cost of the equipment.

Expenditures Related to Land

The purchase of land often raises a number of accounting issues. Suppose, for example, that Los Altos, Inc. retains a local real estate broker at a fee of $2,000 to locate an appropriate site for the company's new office building. The terms of the sale include a down payment of $40,000 to the seller, with the buyer paying off an existing mortgage of $10,000 and $300 of accrued interest. In addition, Los Altos, Inc. agrees to pay accrued real estate taxes of $800 owed by the seller. Other related expenditures include legal fees of $400 and a title insurance premium of $500. Assume, also, that the property selected for purchase has an existing building on it that will need to be razed. A local salvage company will be hired to raze the old building, paying Los Altos, Inc. $200 for reclaimed materials. Applying the cost principle, the acquisition cost of the land is calculated as follows:

Payment to the seller	$40,000
Commission to real estate agent	2,000
Payment of mortgage and accrued interest due at time of sale	10,300
Payment of property taxes owed by seller	800
Legal fees	400
Title insurance premium	500
	$54,000
Less: Net recovery from material reclamation	**200**
Cost of land	$53,800

The expenditures for the property taxes, insurance, and legal fees are capitalized, or added to, the acquisition cost of the land because they are necessary to complete the purchase transaction. Similarly, removing the old building also prepares the land for its intended use. The $200 net recovery from razing the existing structure, therefore, *reduces* the land's cost. A net payment to remove the old building would have *increased* the land's cost.

When land is acquired in an undeveloped area, a firm may pay a special assessment to the local government for such property improvements as streets, sidewalks, and sewers. These improvements are considered to be permanent improvements; and consequently, the special assessment is capitalized to (added to) the acquisition cost of the land.

A firm may also make property improvements that have limited lives. Classified as **land improvements**, they include such improvements as paved parking lots, driveways, private sidewalks, and fences. Expenditures for these assets are charged to a separate Land Improvement account on the balance sheet and depreciated over the estimated useful life of the improvements.

Leasehold Improvements

Expenditures made by a business to alter or improve leased property are called **leasehold improvements**. For example, a merchandising firm may make improvements, with the permission of the owner, to a leased building. **The Home Depot, Inc.**, a home improvement retail chain, leases a significant portion of its nearly 2,300 stores and reports more than $1.9 billion of leasehold improvements on its balance sheet. The improvements, or alterations, become part of the leased property and revert to the owner of the property at the end of the lease. The cost of the leasehold improvements is capitalized to the Leasehold Improvements account on the balance sheet and is depreciated over the life of the lease or the life of the improvements, whichever is shorter.

REVIEW 8.1

Kelly Company purchased manufacturing equipment for $20,000 cash. In addition to the $20,000 purchase price, Kelly paid sales tax of $1,600, freight costs of $400, installation costs of $600, testing costs of $100, and $300 for unrelated supplies from the same company. Explain the accounting treatment for each of the expenditures.

The solution is on page 289.

NATURE OF DEPRECIATION

LO2 Discuss the nature of depreciation, **illustrate** three depreciation methods, and **explain** impairment losses.

With the exception of land, the use of property, plant and equipment to generate revenues reduces their value. At some point—usually before they are totally worthless—these assets are disposed of, and often replaced. A diagram of a typical pattern of asset utilization is illustrated below:

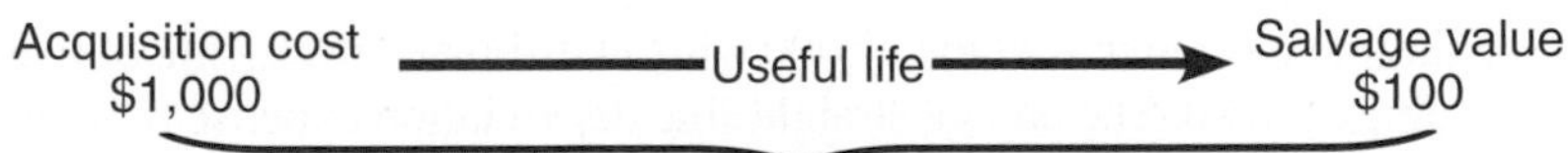

Decline in recorded value, $900

In this example, property, plant and equipment is acquired for $1,000, used for several accounting periods, and then sold for $100. The $900 decline in recorded value is called **depreciation** and is an expense of generating the revenues recognized during the periods that the asset was in use. Thus, $900 of expense must be allocated to the periods of asset use and matched with the sales revenue generated over those periods. Failure to do so would overstate the company's net income for these periods.

As part of this allocation process, it is first necessary to estimate the asset's useful life and its expected salvage value. **Useful life** is the period over which the asset will help generate revenues—that is, the period from the date of acquisition to the expected date of disposal. **Salvage value** is the expected net recovery (sales proceeds – disposal costs) when the asset is sold or removed from service. When the salvage value is insignificant, it may be ignored in computing depreciation under the materiality concept.

A.K.A. The **salvage value** of property, plant and equipment is often referred to as its *residual value* or *scrap value*.

Allocation versus Valuation: Depreciation Accounting

Accountants do not compute depreciation expense based on changes in the asset's market value or on the measured wear of the asset, primarily because a reliable, objective, and practical source for such data rarely exists. Rather, **depreciation accounting** is an attempt to allocate, in a *systematic* and *rational* manner, the difference between an asset's acquisition cost and its estimated salvage value over its *estimated* useful life. Consequently, depreciation accounting techniques should be viewed as convenient expedients for estimating asset utilization and should not be considered precise. Although imprecise, depreciation estimates facilitate a better assessment of a business's net income than would result from expensing the asset at either its date of acquisition or its date of disposal.

PRINCIPLE ALERT

Expense Recognition (Matching) Principle Depreciation accounting represents an application of the expense recognition principle, also known as the matching principle. Depreciable plant assets are used in a business's operating activities to help generate revenues. Each period that benefits from the use of an asset is assigned part of the asset's cost as depreciation expense. In so doing, the depreciation expense is matched with the sales revenue that the asset helps to generate.

Several factors are related to the periodic allocation of depreciation. Depreciation can be caused by wear from use, from natural deterioration, and from technical obsolescence. Each factor reduces the economic value of an asset. To some extent, maintenance (lubrication, adjustments, parts replacements, and cleaning) should partially arrest or offset wear and deterioration. When an asset's useful life and salvage value are estimated, it is assumed that maintenance expenditures will be incurred to keep the asset productive and in good working condition.

Calculating Depreciation Expense

Estimating the periodic depreciation of property, plant and equipment can be achieved in many ways. This section illustrates the most commonly-used depreciation method, known as the **straight-line method**.

Straight-Line Method

The straight-line method is the easiest depreciation method to understand and calculate. Consequently, this method is the most widely used depreciation method by U.S. businesses. Under the straight-line method, an equal amount of depreciation expense is allocated to each period of an asset's useful life. Straight-line depreciation is calculated as follows:

$$\textbf{Annual depreciation} = \frac{\textbf{(Acquisition cost – Salvage value)}}{\textbf{Estimated useful life (in years)}}$$

Assume that equipment is purchased for $1,000 with an estimated useful life of five years and an estimated salvage value of $100. The annual straight-line depreciation expense for the equipment is:

$$\frac{\textbf{(\$1,000 – \$100)}}{\textbf{5 years}} = \textbf{\$180 per year}$$

And, the financial statement effect of the annual depreciation expense is:

Transaction: *Depreciation expense.*

Balance Sheet							Income Statement				
Assets	=	Liabilities	+	Stockholders' Equity							
				Contrib. Capital	+	Retained Earnings	*Revenues*	–	*Expenses*	=	*Net Income*
−180 Accumulated depreciation	=		+			−180		–	+180 Depreciation expense	=	−180

Like other expenses, Depreciation Expense is deducted from revenue on the income statement. The offsetting entry is posted to a contra-asset account, Accumulated Depreciation, which is deducted from the Equipment account on the balance sheet to calculate the asset's book value. This results in maintaining the original acquisition cost of the asset in the asset account, and the cumulative amount of depreciation taken to date reported in the contra-asset account.

A.K.A. The **book value of an asset** (acquisition cost less accumulated depreciation) is also referred to as the *net book value*.

The following table shows the balances related to the equipment account and its book value during the equipment's five-year life under the straight-line method:

	Income Statement	Balance Sheet End of Period		
Year of Useful Life	**Annual Depreciation Expense**	**Equipment Account**	**Accumulated Depreciation Account**	**Asset's Book Value**
1	**$180**	$1,000	$180	$820
2	**180**	1,000	360	640
3	**180**	1,000	540	460
4	**180**	1,000	720	280
5	**180**	1,000	900	100
Total	**$900**			

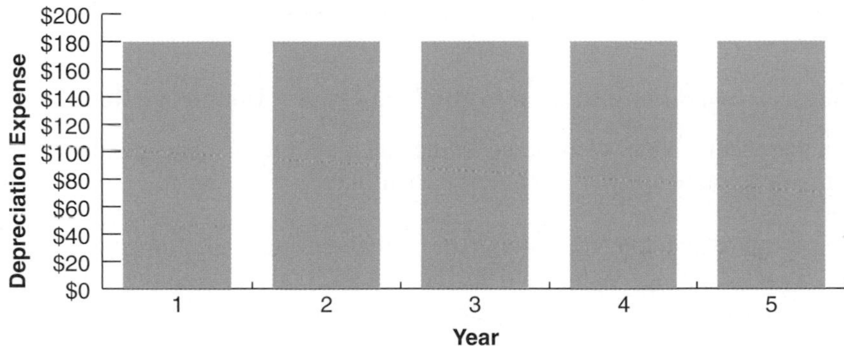

Notice that (1) the Equipment account always reflects the original acquisition cost ($1,000) of the asset; (2) $180 of depreciation expense is recorded in each period; (3) the Accumulated Depreciation account balance is cumulative and shows the portion of the acquisition cost taken as depreciation to date; (4) the asset's book value is the original acquisition cost of the asset less the accumulated depreciation taken to date ($1,000 – $180 = $820 at the end of the first year); and (5) the asset's book value at the end its useful life is equal to the asset's estimated salvage value ($100). Thus, an asset's book value declines to its estimated salvage value as the asset is depreciated over its useful life.

For periods of less than one year, straight-line depreciation amounts are simply proportions of the annual depreciation charge. For example, if an asset is acquired on April 1, depreciation for the period ended December 31 would be $135, or 9/12 × $180. Assets acquired or disposed of during the first half of any month are usually treated as if the acquisition or disposal occurred on the first day of the month. When either event occurs during the last half of any month, it is assumed that the event occurred on the first day of the following month.

PRINCIPLE ALERT

Going Concern Concept Absent evidence to the contrary, the *going concern concept* assumes that a business has an indefinite life. Depreciation accounting allocates an asset's acquisition cost to expense over the asset's useful life. Any depreciation method that allocates an asset's acquisition cost over many years—whether the useful life is five years or 25 years (or more)—implicitly assumes that a business will be in existence for at least that number of years.

Alternative Depreciation Methods

While straight-line is by far the most commonly used depreciation method, companies are also allowed to use several alternative methods. In this section we illustrate two of these methods: declining balance and units of production.

Declining-Balance Method

An **accelerated depreciation method**, as the name implies, accelerates the amount of depreciation expense recognized in the early years of an asset's life. These methods assume that the asset's productivity is greater, and therefore the revenue it generates would be greater, in the earlier years of the asset's life. The **declining-balance method** calculates depreciation expense as a constant percentage of an asset's book value. Recall that an asset's book value is the acquisition cost less accumulated depreciation. Over time, the book value declines as depreciation is recorded, yielding a decreasing depreciation expense.

There are many versions of the declining-balance method including *double-declining balance depreciation* which uses a depreciation rate that is twice the straight-line rate; similarly, *150 percent-declining balance depreciation* which uses a depreciation rate that is one and one-half times the straight-line rate.

For example, the straight-line depreciation rate for an asset with a five-year useful life is 20 percent per year (100 percent/5 years). Thus, to depreciate a five-year asset on an accelerated basis, the double-declining balance method uses a 40 percent depreciation rate (2 × 20 percent); and, the 150 percent declining-balance method uses a 30 percent depreciation rate (1.5 × 20 percent).

Under the double-declining balance method, the annual depreciation expense is calculated as follows:

Annual depreciation = Book value at beginning of year × Double-declining balance rate

An asset's salvage value is not considered in the calculation of declining-balance depreciation, except that the depreciation of an asset stops when the asset's book value equals its estimated salvage value.

Referring to our example of the equipment purchased for $1,000, with a useful life of five years and an expected salvage value of $100, the periodic double-declining balance depreciation would be calculated as follows (amounts rounded to the nearest dollar):

Year of Useful Life	Acquisition Cost	Beginning Accumulated Depreciation	Beginning Book Value		Twice Straight-line Percentage		Annual Depreciation Expense
1	$1,000	$ 0	$1,000	×	40 percent	=	**$400**
2	1,000	400	600	×	40 percent	=	**240**
3	1,000	640	360	×	40 percent	=	**144**
4	1,000	784	216	×	40 percent	=	**86**
5	1,000	870	130		**[exceeds limit]**		**30**
Total							**$900**

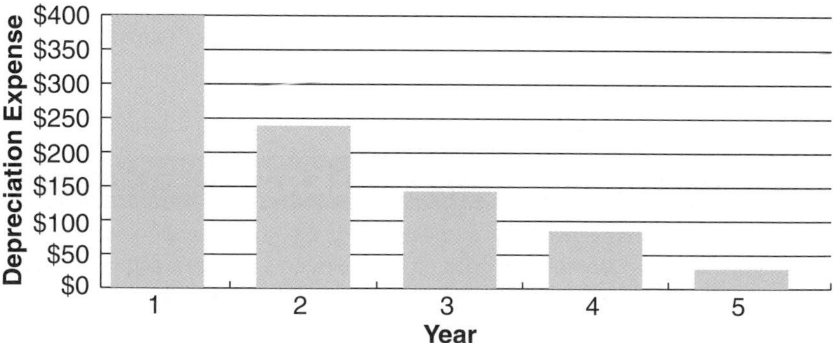

Hint: An asset's salvage value must be considered when calculating the depreciation expense for an asset using the straight-line method or the units-of-production method; but, an asset's salvage value is not considered when calculating declining balance depreciation, until the final year.

Notice in the fifth year that the depreciation expense is only $30, the amount that will reduce the asset's book value to its estimated salvage value of $100. Assets are not depreciated below their estimated salvage value.

Units-of-Production Method

The **units-of-production method** allocates depreciation in proportion to an asset's use in operations. Under this method, the depreciation per unit of production is first calculated by dividing the total depreciable cost of the asset (in our example, \$1,000 – \$100 = \$900) by the asset's projected units-of-production capacity:

$$\textbf{Depreciation per unit} = \frac{\textbf{(Acquisition cost – Salvage value)}}{\textbf{Total estimated units of production}}$$

The total estimated units of production may represent the total expected miles that an asset will be driven, the total tons expected to be hauled, the total hours expected to be used, or the total number of expected cuttings, drillings, or stampings of parts by a piece of equipment. To illustrate, assume that a drilling tool will drill an estimated 45,000 parts during its expected useful life. The tool is purchased for \$1,000 and has an expected salvage value of \$100. Consequently, the depreciation per unit of production is:

$$\frac{\textbf{(\$1,000 – \$100)}}{\textbf{45,000 parts}} = \textbf{\$0.02 per part}$$

To find the asset's annual depreciation expense, the depreciation per unit of production is multiplied by the number of units actually produced during a given year:

Annual depreciation = Depreciation per unit × Units of production for the period

Assuming that the number of parts drilled over the five years were 8,000, 14,000, 10,000, 4,000, and 9,000, respectively, in Year 1 through Year 5, the units-of-production depreciation expense is calculated as follows:

Year of Useful Life	Depreciation per Unit		Annual Units of Production		Annual Depreciation Expense
1	\$0.02	×	8,000	=	\$160
2	0.02	×	14,000	=	280
3	0.02	×	10,000	=	200
4	0.02	×	4,000	=	80
5	0.02	×	9,000	=	180
Total					\$900

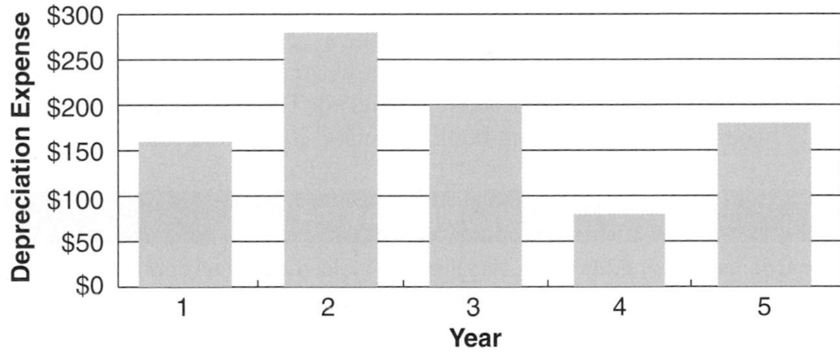

A Comparison of Depreciation Methods

The following chart compares the periodic depreciation expense from our equipment illustration for the straight-line, the double-declining balance, and the units-of-production methods. The chart visually displays the accelerated nature of the double-declining balance method relative to the straight-line method. Notice, for example, that the depreciation expense in Year 1 under the double-declining balance method is \$400 but is only \$180 under the straight-line method. In Year 2, the double-declining balance depreciation is \$240 but again is only \$180 for the straight-line method. It is not until Year 3 that the straight-line method produces a depreciation charge that exceeds the double-declining balance charge. The units-of-production method reflects the assumptions presented previously in the chapter. There is no general pattern for the annual depreciation expense under this method. The annual depreciation for the units-of-production method depends on the yearly productive activity of an asset, and this activity will vary from asset to asset. Note that the total depreciation over an asset's life is the same under each depreciation method.

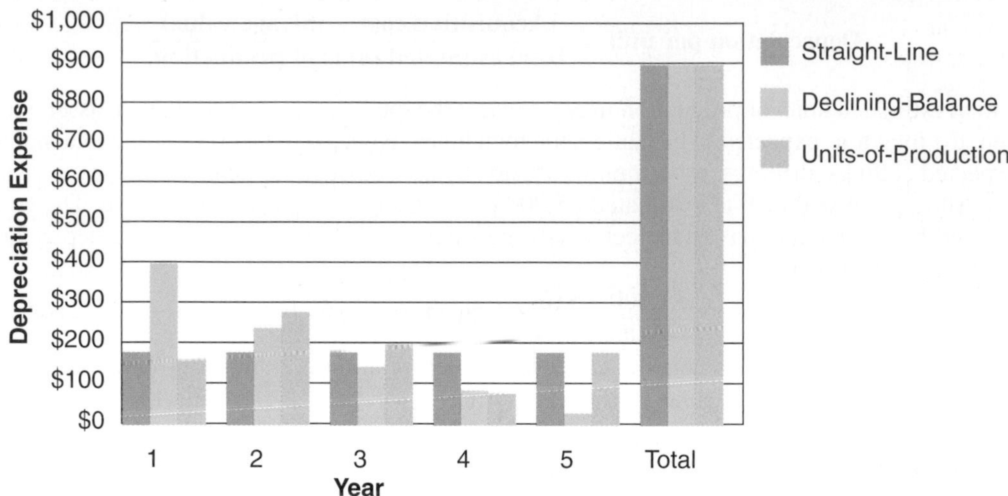

Depreciation Method Estimate Changes

Depreciation expense is based on estimates of both an asset's useful life and its salvage value. Circumstances change, however, and original estimates of both an asset's useful life and its salvage value may subsequently be found to be too high or too low. Once it is determined that the original estimates of either an asset's useful life or salvage value were incorrect, the calculation of the periodic depreciation expense for an asset's remaining useful life may be revised. When a depreciation estimate revision is warranted, the revision is executed by allocating the undepreciated balance of the asset's book value over the asset's revised remaining useful life.

Impairment Losses

Sometimes a depreciable asset can lose value, such that the expected future cash flows from the asset's use and disposal are *less* than its current book value. The loss in value can arise for a variety of reasons, including a drop in market value due to declining consumer demand and physical damage to the asset. If an asset's remaining book value cannot be recovered through the future cash flows expected to be generated from the asset's use, the asset's value is said to be *impaired.* Under these circumstances, an impairment loss is recorded on the income statement, and the asset's book value on the balance sheet is reduced. The **impairment loss** is calculated as the difference between the asset's current book value and its current fair value.

PRINCIPLE ALERT

Conservatism Concept U.S. GAAP mandates that asset values be written down when impaired, but prohibits the write-up of assets when their value appreciates. This is an example of the *conservatism concept,* which requires losses to be recognized on a timelier basis than gains. When the value of a plant asset is impaired, it is immediately written down to its current fair value. Unimpaired plant assets remain on the balance sheet at their book value, however, even if the current fair value is higher than the book value. Gains on unimpaired assets can only be recognized when the asset is sold and the gain is realized.

Depreciation for Income Tax Purposes

Depreciation expense may be deducted by a business on its federal income tax return as a normal business expense. As a consequence, some refer to the tax deductibility of depreciation as a "tax shield" since depreciation expense lowers a business's pre-tax net income, and hence, lowers the actual income taxes that must be paid. The depreciation expense deducted on a business's income tax return, however, is usually quite different from the depreciation expense deducted in a company's income statement. This is because the depreciation used for tax purposes must follow the **modified accelerated cost recovery system (MACRS)**. While companies can choose from several different depreciation methods for financial reporting purposes, such as straight-line or units of production, U.S. tax law requires them to use MACRS for tax reporting purposes.

MACRS establishes eight asset classes with prescribed useful lives ranging from three years to 31.5 years. Most machinery and equipment, for example, is in the seven-year asset class. When acquired, an asset is placed in the appropriate asset class (per MACRS guidelines) and depreciated over the prescribed useful life specified for that class.

MACRS was introduced into U.S. tax law to encourage companies to invest in plant assets. Because the useful life specified under MACRS is usually shorter than an asset's accounting useful life, this method provides larger depreciation deductions during an asset's early years than was previously possible, much like the declining-balance method used for financial statement reporting. In a sense, the accelerated deductions under MACRS provide an interest-free loan to a business because they allow the firm to pay less income tax in the early years of an asset's life and more in the later years. During the intervening time period, the firm can use the postponed income tax payments to support the business's operations, without incurring any interest charges.

Change and modification characterize U.S. tax law. Tax depreciation guidelines will likely be modified again in the future. Keep in mind, however, that depreciation changes in the tax law do not affect the depreciation method that is allowed for financial reporting purposes under U.S. GAAP.

REVIEW 8.2

The Salsbury Company purchased equipment costing $10,000 at the start of the year. The equipment has an estimated useful life of five years and a salvage value of $2,000. The CEO is unsure if the company should use the straight-line method or the double-declining balance method to depreciate the new equipment.

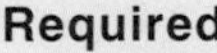

Required

Calculate the depreciation for the second year under each of the alternative depreciation accounting methods.

The solution is on page 289.

REVENUE EXPENDITURES VERSUS CAPITAL EXPENDITURES

LO3 Discuss the distinction between revenue expenditures and capital expenditures.

Revenue expenditures are expenditures relating to property, plant and equipment that are expensed when incurred. The following list identifies two common types of revenue expenditures:

1. Expenditures for ordinary maintenance and repairs of existing property, plant and equipment.
2. Expenditures to acquire low-cost items that benefit the firm for several periods.

Maintenance and Repairs

Companies routinely make expenditures for maintenance and repair on their property, plant and equipment in order to keep these assets productive and in good working order. Thus, accountants' estimates of asset lives and salvage values anticipate these expenditures. Without these expenditures asset lives would be shorter and salvage values lower. Thus, a company's periodic expenditures on routine maintenance and repairs are expensed as they are incurred.

Low-Cost Items

Most businesses purchase items that provide years of service at a relatively small cost, such as paperweights, staplers, and wastebaskets. Because of the small dollar amounts involved, establishing these items as assets on the balance sheet and depreciating them over their expected useful lives is inefficient. The effect on the financial statements is immaterial; and consequently, expensing these expenditures at the time of purchase is more efficient.

PRINCIPLE ALERT

Materiality Concept The practice of accounting for small dollar transactions in the most expedient fashion follows the *materiality concept*. Under this accounting concept, generally accepted accounting principles apply only to items of significance to the users of financial statements. Because the judgment of users will be unaffected by the accounting for immaterial dollar amounts, their immediate expensing does not diminish the usefulness of financial statements.

Capital Expenditures

Capital expenditures increase the book value of property, plant and equipment. To *capitalize* an amount means to classify the expenditure as an asset on the balance sheet. The following are two typical capital expenditures related to property, plant and equipment:

1. Initial acquisitions and additions.
2. Betterments.

Initial Acquisitions and Additions

As discussed previously, property, plant and equipment is originally recorded on the balance sheet at its historical cost, which equals the expenditures made to acquire the asset and put it into service. These expenditures on property, plant and equipment are commonly referred to as capital expenditures. These same accounting guidelines apply for additions to existing property, plant and equipment. Adding a new wing to a building or expanding the size of an asphalt parking lot are examples of additions. These capital expenditures increase the balance of the asset. If the useful life of the addition differs from the remaining useful life of the existing asset, the addition is depreciated using a separate depreciation schedule. A separate account (and depreciation schedule) should be used for an addition when its estimated useful life differs from the remaining useful life of the existing asset.

Betterments

Betterments are expenditures that (1) extend the useful life of an asset, (2) improve the quality and/or quantity of the asset's output, or (3) reduce the asset's operating expenses. Examples include overhauling the engine or adding a power winch to a highway service truck, improving the precision of a machining device to reduce defects, or converting a building to solar power. Expenditures for betterments generally increase the asset to which they relate, and the subsequent periodic depreciation expense is increased to allocate the additional cost over the asset's remaining useful life.

REVIEW 8.3

Hastings Company recorded the following expenditures during the year with regard to its delivery van:

1. Changed the engine oil
2. Repainted the van
3. Overhauled the engine that is expected to increase the useful life of the van
4. Repaired a dent in a fender
5. Converted the van to run on a biofuel with an estimated annual fuel cost savings of 30 percent.

Required

Determine whether each of the above expenditures is a revenue expenditure or a capital expenditure.

The solution is on page 289.

ACCOUNTING ETHICS

WorldCom's Bad Accounting On the surface, the decision to capitalize or expense an expenditure related to property, plant and equipment does not seem like the subject matter for one of the most infamous accounting scandals of all time. Unfortunately, to the many investors in **WorldCom** who saw the value of their investment disappear, this accounting decision had profound consequences.

WorldCom, under the direction of its CEO, CFO, Controller, and Director of General Accounting, used fraudulent accounting methods to portray a false picture of the company's financial health. The principal accounting gimmickry used by the company was to misclassify "line costs," a cost that should have been expensed each year, as a capital expenditure, thus, adding to WorldCom's assets rather than adding to its expenses.

A small team of internal auditors working in secret, mostly at night, to investigate and uncover this fraud, brought the fraud to the attention of the Securities and Exchange Commission. The final conclusion—WorldCom's assets and pre-tax net income had been inflated by nearly $11 billion! With $100 billion in assets, WorldCom, at the time, was the largest bankruptcy in history. Following a conviction for filing false financial reports with the SEC, WorldCom's CEO Bernard Ebbers was sentenced to 25 years in prison.

DISPOSALS OF PROPERTY, PLANT AND EQUIPMENT

LO4 Explain the accounting for disposals of property, plant and equipment.

A business may dispose of its property, plant and equipment in a variety of ways. An asset may be sold, retired, or exchanged as partial payment for a new asset. The asset's usefulness to a firm may also be ended by an unfavorable or unanticipated event—the asset may be stolen or destroyed by a natural disaster.

Depreciation must be recorded up to the disposal date, regardless of how the asset is disposed. Should the disposal date not coincide with the end of an accounting period, depreciation expense is reported for the partial period—that is, the period from the date that depreciation was last recorded to the asset's disposal date.

Sale of Property, Plant and Equipment

Most sales of property, plant and equipment involve the following factors:

1. The sale of the asset in exchange for cash. Because the asset sold is no longer on hand, the asset account and its related accumulated depreciation account are removed from the balance sheet. The asset account minus its accumulated depreciation account equals the asset's book value.
2. Because property, plant and equipment are often sold for an amount higher or lower than their book value, a gain or loss often results. If the sales proceeds exceed the asset's book value, the sale will result in a gain. If the proceeds are less than the asset's book value, the sale will result in a loss.

The following data is used to illustrate the disposal of property, plant and equipment.

Equipment's acquisition cost	$1,000
Estimated salvage value after five years	100
Annual straight-line depreciation	180

Asset Sales for More Than Book Value

Assume that the equipment is sold for $230 midway through its fifth year of use and that depreciation expense was last recorded at the end of the fourth year. The financial statement effects of the sale are:

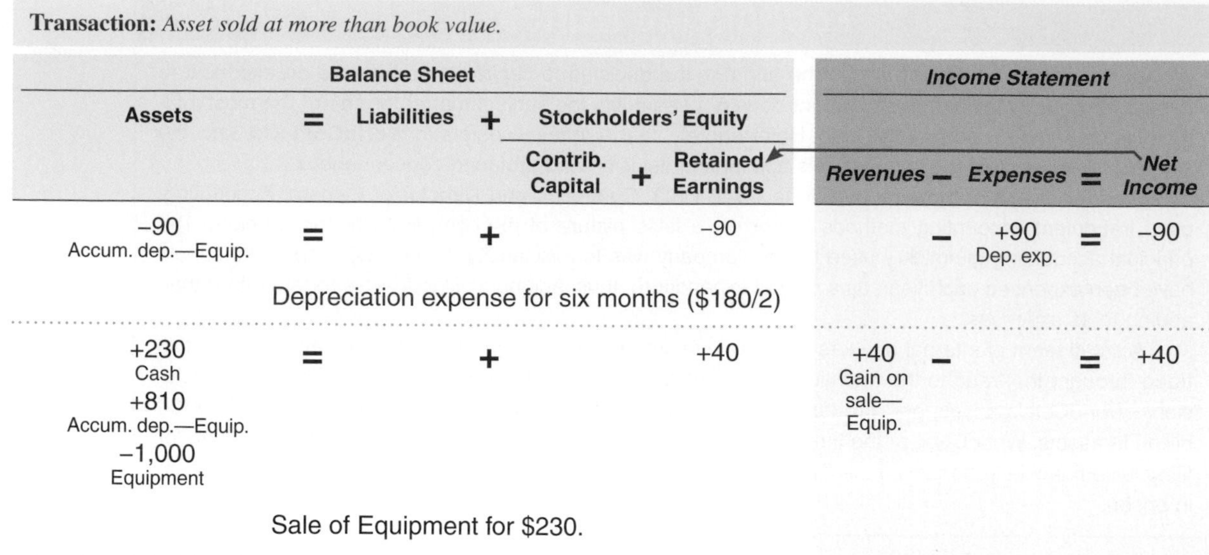

Transaction: *Asset sold at more than book value.*

Assets	=	Liabilities	+	Contrib. Capital	+	Retained Earnings	Revenues	−	Expenses	=	Net Income
−90 Accum. dep.—Equip.	=		+			−90		−	+90 Dep. exp.	=	−90
Depreciation expense for six months ($180/2)											
+230 Cash +810 Accum. dep.—Equip. −1,000 Equipment	=		+			+40	+40 Gain on sale—Equip.	−		=	+40
Sale of Equipment for $230.											

Note that the company first records depreciation expense for the first half of year 5, which equals $90 (6/12 × $180).This results in total accumulated depreciation at the date of the sale of $810, calculated as [(4 × $180) + $90]. Then the sales proceeds of $230 is recorded and both the accumulated depreciation at the date of the sale of $810 and the original cost of the asset of $1,000 are removed from the books. Finally, the gain on the sale of $40 is recorded, which equals the sale proceeds of $230 minus the asset's book value of $190 ($1,000 – $810).

Asset Sales for Less Than Book Value

Assume that the equipment is sold for $30 at the end of the fifth year. The financial statement effect of this sale is:

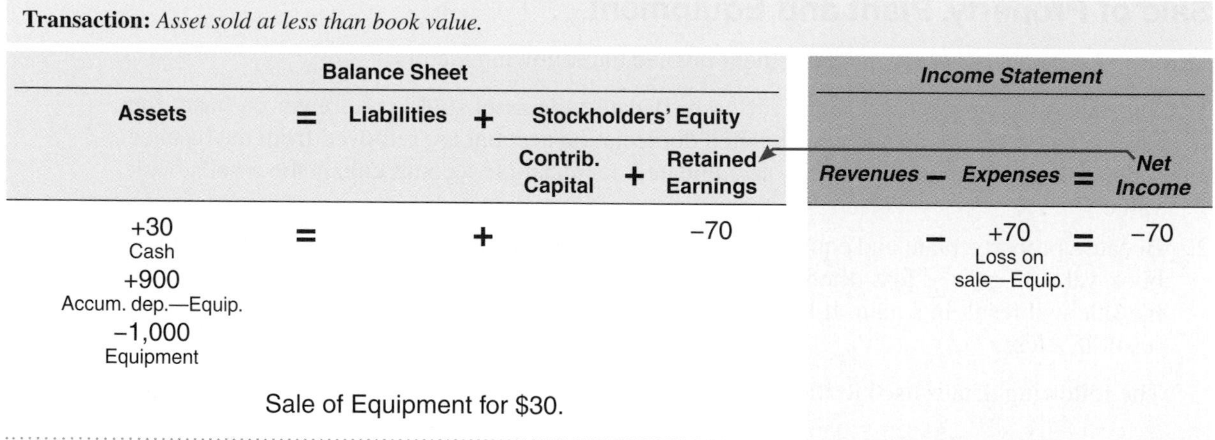

Transaction: *Asset sold at less than book value.*

Assets	=	Liabilities	+	Contrib. Capital	+	Retained Earnings	Revenues	−	Expenses	=	Net Income
+30 Cash +900 Accum. dep.—Equip. −1,000 Equipment	=		+			−70		−	+70 Loss on sale—Equip.	=	−70
Sale of Equipment for $30.											

At the end of year 5 total accumulated depreciation equals $900 (5 years × $180). The cash received of $30 is recorded, and the balances from both the Equipment account ($1,000) and the Accumulated Depreciation account ($900) are removed from the books. Then the loss on the sale of $70 is recorded, which equals the book value of $100 ($1,000 – $900) minus the sales proceeds of $30.

If the equipment is sold for an amount exactly equal to its book value, no gain or loss results. Should the equipment be abandoned, stolen, or destroyed (with no insurance coverage) before the end of its expected useful life, a loss equal to its book value is recorded.

Exchange of Property, Plant and Equipment

An asset may be exchanged for another asset. The accounting for property, plant and equipment exchanges can be complex depending upon the relationship between the new asset and the asset being traded in. Consequently, the accounting for asset exchanges is covered in intermediate accounting textbooks.

GuidedExample MBC

REVIEW 8.4

The Jones Company is self-insured; and consequently, the company does not receive any insurance payments if it is involved in an accident. One of the Jones Company trucks was involved in a major accident and the company decided to sell the truck for scrap. At the time of the accident, the truck had a cost basis of $22,500 and accumulated depreciation of $15,000. The proceeds from the sale totaled $750.

Required

Calculate the gain or loss on the disposal of the truck.

The solution is on page 289.

ACCOUNTING IN PRACTICE

Career Opportunities at Tesla When one thinks of a career at Tesla, one probably first thinks of somebody with an engineering or science background. While Tesla certainly hires people with these skills, the company is also constantly looking for people with accounting skills to support its manufacturing. A recent search of career opportunities on Tesla's Website highlighted many accounting positions, including a Technical Accounting Manager (Finance). Among the requirements is a bachelor's degree in accounting or finance, CPA certification and six to nine years of experience.

INTANGIBLE ASSETS

LO5 Discuss the nature of intangible assets.

Intangible assets are resources that benefit a business's operations, but which lack physical characteristics or substance. Intangible assets include, for example, the exclusive rights or privileges obtained from a governmental unit or by legal contract, such as patents, copyrights, franchises, trademarks, and leaseholds. Another intangible asset is goodwill, which reflects the beneficial synergies that arise from business combinations. Because intangible assets lack physical characteristics, the related accounting procedures are somewhat more subjective than for tangible assets such as property, plant and equipment.

It is important to note that the term *intangible asset*, as used in accounting, is not precisely defined. By convention, only certain assets are classified as intangible assets, while some assets that lack physical substance, such as prepaid insurance, accounts receivable, and investments, are not classified as intangible assets.

Measurement of Intangible Assets

In general, intangible assets that are purchased from outsiders are recorded at their historical acquisition cost. For example, the amount paid to purchase a patent from an outside party would increase a Patents account. Similarly, some intangible assets created internally are recorded at cost. For example, the costs to secure a trademark—such as attorney's fees, registration fees, and design costs—are charged to a Trademarks account. **Research and development costs** are not capitalized to the balance sheet as an intangible asset because it is highly uncertain whether these expenditures will ultimately result in developing a marketable product. As a consequence, many costs associated with developing products and processes are expensed as incurred. This is an example of accounting conservatism. The accounting treatment errs on the side of understating rather than overstating assets. However, one U.S. industry is allowed to capitalize research and development costs. Under U.S. GAAP, software development companies may capitalize the development of second generation software, although the cost of first generation software must be expensed as incurred.

THINKING GLOBALLY

The accounting for some intangible assets under IFRS differs significantly from the accounting under U.S. GAAP. For instance, under U.S. GAAP, research and development costs must be expensed when incurred; however, under IFRS, development costs may be capitalized if a commercially viable product results from the original research effort. A significant consequence of this alternative accounting treatment is that

continued

continued from previous page

IFRS-accounted companies typically include more intangible assets on their balance sheets as compared with companies that use U.S. GAAP.

To illustrate, assume that British Laboratories PLC, a biotechnology company, spends five million British pounds on research for a cure for diabetes. The research leads to a promising compound that is shown in tests to effectively control the disease. Further testing is needed, however; and consequently, the company spends an additional three million British pounds to develop and test the drug compound before receiving a patent from the British Patent Office. Under these circumstances, the company would record an expense for its initial research effort, and an asset for the subsequent expenditure to develop the drug.

In short, under IFRS, research costs must be expensed when incurred; however, development costs may be capitalized to the balance sheet when a commercially viable product is evident.

Amortization of Intangibles

Amortization refers to the periodic expensing of an intangible asset over its expected useful life. Because salvage values are rarely used, the amortization of intangible assets typically entails (1) determining the asset's cost, (2) estimating the asset's useful life (i.e., the period over which it benefits the company), and (3) allocating the cost over the asset's estimated useful life. Straight-line amortization is typically used to allocate the cost of intangible assets unless another method is shown to be more appropriate.

Amortization increases the Amortization Expense account, while the decrease in assets goes directly to the Intangible Asset account. An Accumulated Amortization account could be used but generally there is no particular benefit to financial statement users from accumulating amortization in a separate contra-asset account.

EXAMPLES OF INTANGIBLE ASSETS

Patents

A **patent** is an exclusive privilege granted to an inventor by the U.S. Patent Office for a period of 20 years from the date the patent application is filed. A patent gives the patent holder the right to exclude others from making, using, or selling the invention. Patent laws were originated to encourage inventors by protecting them from imitators who might usurp the invention for commercial gain. Even though patents have a legal life of 20 years from application date, changes in technology or consumer tastes may shorten their economic life. Because of their uncertain value, patents are accounted for conservatively by most businesses. For example, most businesses amortize patents over a shorter period than 20 years.

ENVIRONMENTAL, SOCIAL, AND GOVERNANCE

Intangible assets include items such as patents that provide protection from competitors using the patented device or process for up to 20 years. It is not uncommon for firms to vigorously defend their patents through aggressive lawsuits. **Tesla** believes so strongly in what electric vehicles can do for the planet that the company has chosen to freely share its patents. This allows Tesla's competitors, along with any engineers who wish to use these patents, to work with the technology with the aim, according to Tesla, of strengthening the development of sustainable technology.

Copyright

A **copyright** protects its owner against the unauthorized reproduction of a specific written work, recorded work, or artwork. A copyright lasts for the life of the author plus 70 years. The purchase price of valuable copyrights can be substantial, and proper measurement and amortization are necessary for valid business income determination.

Franchises

Franchises most often involve exclusive rights to operate or sell a specific brand of products in a given geographic area. Franchises may be for definite or indefinite periods. Although many franchises are agreements between two private firms, various governmental units award franchises to public utilities. The right to operate a **Kentucky Fried Chicken (KFC)** restaurant or to sell **Midas Mufflers** in a specific area illustrates franchise agreements in the private sector.

Trademarks

Trademarks and **trade names** represent the exclusive and continuing right to use certain terms, names, or symbols, usually to identify a brand or family of products. An original trademark or trade name can be registered with the U.S. federal government for a nominal cost. A company may spend considerable time and money to determine an appropriate name or symbol for a product. Also, the purchase of well-known, and thus valuable, trademarks or trade names may involve substantial amounts of money. When the cost of a trademark or trade name is material, the amount is an increase to the intangible asset account—Trademarks—and amortized over the period of its expected useful life.

Goodwill

Goodwill is an often misunderstood concept. In common usage, goodwill may represent the favorable reputation a firm has earned from its customers, quality of service, or positive product characteristics. The term goodwill, however, has a much different meaning when used in accounting and finance. Literally, goodwill is the amount paid by one company in the acquisition of another company that exceeds the fair value of the identifiable net assets of the acquired company. Thus, in accounting, goodwill can only arise from a business combination (i.e., when one company acquires another). Goodwill represents the perceived synergies between the acquiring company and the acquired company. Goodwill does not include assets that can be separately identified or separated from the combined entity, such as a brand name or a customer list. Unlike most intangible assets, goodwill is not subject to periodic amortization. Instead, goodwill is evaluated annually for any impairment in value. If a company's goodwill is found to be impaired, the Goodwill account is written down to its fair value and an Impairment Loss is recorded on the income statement.

ACCOUNTING IN PRACTICE

Goodwill Can Be a Significant Asset Although accountants only record goodwill when another business entity is purchased (to the extent that the purchase price exceeds the fair value of the identifiable net assets acquired), the balance sheets of many major corporations contain significant amounts of goodwill. Recent balance sheets, for example, show the following amounts of goodwill: **Bank of America Corporation**, $69.0 billion; **The Walt Disney Company**, $77.7 billion; **Microsoft Inc.**, $35.1 billion; **Pfizer Inc.**, $49.6 billion; **AT&T Inc.**, $135.3 billion; and **Procter & Gamble Company**, $39.9 billion. These amounts are evidence of the active acquisition efforts of these major corporations, and also of the large amounts that may be paid for goodwill in acquisition transactions.

ACCOUNTING IN PRACTICE

Crypto Assets Are Not Tangible According to Forbes Magazine, there are currently over 7,800 cryptocurrencies, and CoinBaseCap estimates that their combined market capitalization is $2 trillion dollars, with $1 trillion dollars attributable to Bitcoin alone. An important question for accounting standard setters is how cryptocurrency, referred to as crypto assets, should be reported in the financial statements. As mentioned in Chapter 5, current guidance by the AICPA suggests that crypto assets should not be classified as cash because they are not backed by a government or considered legal tender. In addition, because they are intangible, crypto assets cannot be classified as inventory, even if they are held for resale. Instead, the AICPA recommends that crypto assets be classified as intangible assets with an indefinite life.

While it is still not a widely accepted medium of exchange, several large corporations have indicated their willingness to accept payments in the form of crypto assets, including Microsoft, Starbucks, Whole Foods, and Tesla, who recently purchased $1.5 billion in bitcoin. But despite its growing popularity, crypto assets also have many critics. Berkshire Hathaway's Warren Buffett and current Treasury Secretary Janet Yellen complain that the sky-high value of crypto assets is a speculative bubble fueled by naïve investors. Crypto assets have also been criticized by environmentalists, with recent research concluding that Bitcoin mining consumes more energy in one year than the country of Sweden, and if continued at its current rate has the potential to increase the earth's temperature by 2 degrees.

REVIEW 8.5

Match the descriptive explanation below with the correct term:

Amortization	Patent	
Franchise	Trademark	Copyright

1. An exclusive right that protects an owner against the unauthorized reproduction of a specific written work.
2. The periodic write-off of an intangible asset to expense on the income statement.
3. An exclusive and continuing right to use a certain symbol to identify a brand or family of products.
4. An exclusive right to operate or sell a specific brand of products in a given geographic area.
5. An exclusive privilege granted to an inventor that gives the asset holder the right to exclude others from making, using, or selling the invention.

The solution is on page 289.

BALANCE SHEET PRESENTATION

LO6 Illustrate the balance sheet presentation of long-lived assets.

Property, plant and equipment and intangible assets are presented on the balance sheet below the current assets category. (Recall that the assets are listed on a classified balance sheet in descending order of liquidity.) For example, **Exhibit 8-3** reveals how these assets appear on the balance sheet of Tesla.

EXHIBIT 8-3 Tesla, Inc.

TESLA, INC.
Balance Sheet (asset section only)
December 31, 2020 and 2019
$ in millions

	2020	2019
Current Assets		
Cash and cash equivalents	$19,384	$ 6,268
Accounts receivable	1,886	1,324
Inventory	4,101	3,552
Other current assets	1,346	959
Total current assets	26,717	12,103
Property, plant, and equipment, net	12,747	10,396
Intangible assets and goodwill	520	537
Other noncurrent assets	12,164	11,273
Total assets	$52,148	$34,309

Long-lived Assets are presented on the balance sheet below the Current Assets category.

REVIEW 8.6

Smithson Corporation reported the following amounts for the year just ended:

Land	$ 5,000
Trademarks	400
Cash and cash equivalents	7,500
Equipment	2,000
Buildings	24,000
Accounts receivable	1,200
Inventory	5,000
Goodwill	750
Accumulated depreciation	12,000
Accumulated amortization	50
Other noncurrent assets	3,000

Prepare the asset section of the balance sheet using these amounts.

The solution is on page 289.

DATA ANALYTICS **Using Analytics for Starbucks' Site Selections**

Perhaps the only thing **Starbucks** has more of than beans is data. With more than 17 million active users for its mobile app and more than 13 million for its reward program, Starbucks knows what you buy, and where and when you make the purchase. This allows Starbucks to personalize your experience by knowing what you like and suggesting new products based on those preferences. In addition, Starbucks does not simply need to go with gut hunches on where to locate new stores. Instead, the company pulls from the enormous data they have collected and feed this data into a mapping and business intelligence tool called Atlas to determine optimal store locations.

Data Analytics

RETURN ON ASSETS AND ASSET TURNOVER

LO7 Define the return on assets ratio and the asset turnover ratio.

The ability of a firm to use its assets effectively and efficiently is a sign of a healthy, well-managed company. The rate of return generated on a company's assets, referred to as the *return on assets ratio,* is a widely used indicator of a firm's financial health. This ratio answers the question: "for every dollar of assets invested in the firm, how much is generated for the shareholders?" In practice, there is some variation in the calculation of this ratio; however, one commonly used definition of the **return on assets** is:

$$\textbf{Return on assets} = \frac{\textbf{Net income}}{\textbf{Average total assets}}$$

This ratio relates data from two financial statements—the income statement and the balance sheet. The numerator consists of the net income for the year from the income statement. The denominator in the ratio is the average balance of total assets for the year (sum the total assets at the beginning of the year with the total assets at the end of the year and divide the sum by two) obtained from the balance sheet.

Exhibit 8-4 illustrates the calculation of the return on assets ratio for Tesla. The company reported 2020 net income of $721 million, total assets at the beginning of the year of $34,309 million, and year-end total assets of $52,148 million. Tesla's return on assets for the year is 1.7 percent. This indicates that the company generated 1.7 cents for every dollar of assets invested in the firm.

To evaluate a firm's return on assets, it is useful to consider the trend in the ratio, the return for other firms in the same industry, the industry's average return on assets, and the company's economic environment. For example, in the same year that Tesla generated a 1.7 percent return on its assets, General Motors, a competitor of Tesla, generated a 2.8 percent return on assets. These results indicate that while both automotive manufacturers reported a seemingly low ROA, General Motors utilized its assets more efficiently and profitably than did Tesla.

EXHIBIT 8-4 **Return on Assets—Tesla**

($ in millions)		2020
Net income		$ 721
Beginning total assets		34,309
Ending total assets		52,148
ROA	$721 / [($34,309 + $52,148)/2] =	1.7%

TAKEAWAY 8.1

Concept	Method	Assessment
How efficiently is a company using its assets to produce net income?	Net income and average total assets Return on assets ratio = $\frac{\text{Net income}}{\text{Average total assets}}$	A higher ratio value implies a higher, more efficient level of asset utilization.

The **asset turnover** ratio is another ratio that evaluates a company's effective use of its assets. This ratio answers the question: "for every dollar of assets invested in the firm, how many dollars of sales are generated?" This ratio measures how effectively a firm uses its assets to generate sales revenue. The asset turnover ratio is calculated as follows:

$$\text{Asset turnover} = \frac{\text{Net sales}}{\text{Average total assets}}$$

EXHIBIT 8-5 Asset Turnover—Tesla

($ in millions)		2020
Net sales		$31,536
Beginning total assets		34,309
Ending total assets		52,148
Asset turnover	$31,536 / [($34,309 + $52,148)/2] =	0.73%

The calculation of Tesla's 2020 asset turnover is presented in **Exhibit 8-5**. The asset turnover of 0.73 {$31,536/[($34,309 + $52,148)/2]} indicates that the company was able to generate $0.73 of sales revenue for every dollar invested in assets.

General Motors had an asset turnover of 0.53 for the same period. When comparing the two companies it can be noted that Tesla used its assets more effectively to generate sales revenue than General Motors. When comparing both ratios it is interesting to note that General Motors used its assets more efficiently to generate *net income* where Tesla used its assets more efficiently to generate *sales revenue*. This is an indication that Tesla may not be effectively managing its expenses.

TAKEAWAY 8.2

Concept	Method	Assessment
How efficient is a company in generating sales revenue using its assets?	Average total assets and net sales $\text{Asset turnover ratio} = \frac{\text{Net sales}}{\text{Average total assets}}$	A higher ratio value implies a higher level of sales revenue generated for each dollar invested in assets, which suggests a more efficient use of assets.

REVIEW 8.7

Allied Systems reported the following financial data (in millions) in its annual report:

	Year 3	Year 2
Net income	$16,134	$18,052
Net sales	46,117	49,540
Total assets	78,128	68,734

If the company's total assets were $65,676 at the end of Year 1, calculate the company's (*a*) return on assets and (*b*) asset turnover for both years.

The solution is on page 289.

SUMMARY OF LEARNING OBJECTIVES

LO1 Discuss the nature of long-lived assets. (p. 259)

- The accounting for long-lived assets involves the determination of an asset's acquisition cost, periodic depreciation expense, subsequent capital expenditures, and disposal.
- The initial cost of a property, plant and equipment asset is its implied cash price plus any expenditure necessary to prepare the asset for its intended use.

LO2 Discuss the nature of depreciation, illustrate three depreciation methods, and explain impairment losses. (p. 261)

- Depreciation is a cost allocation process; it allocates a long-lived asset's depreciable cost (acquisition cost less salvage value) in a systematic manner over the asset's estimated useful life.
- The most commonly used depreciation method is straight-line. Alternative methods include units-of-production, and declining-balance.
- Revisions of depreciation estimates are accomplished by recalculating depreciation charges for current and subsequent periods.

- When a plant asset is impaired, a loss is recognized equal to the difference between the asset's book value and its current fair value.

Discuss the distinction between revenue expenditures and capital expenditures. (p. 267) **LO3**

- Revenue expenditures are expensed as incurred and include the cost of ordinary repairs and maintenance and the purchase of low-cost items.
- Capital expenditures, which increase an asset's book value, include initial acquisitions, additions, and betterments.

Explain the accounting for disposals of property, plant and equipment. (p. 269) **LO4**

- When a firm disposes of a fixed asset, depreciation must be recorded on the asset up to the disposal date.
- Gains and losses on property, plant and equipment dispositions are determined by comparing an asset's book value to the proceeds received.

Discuss the nature of intangible assets. (p. 271) **LO5**

- Intangible assets acquired from other entities are initially valued at their acquisition cost. Some internally created intangible assets are also measured at their cost.
- Research and development costs related to a firm's products and its production processes are expensed as incurred.
- Amortization is the periodic write-off to expense of an intangible asset's cost over the asset's useful life.
- Goodwill may be shown in the accounts only when it has been purchased as part of the acquisition of another business.
- Goodwill is not amortized.

Illustrate the balance sheet presentation of long-lived assets. (p. 274) **LO6**

- Plant assets and intangible assets are shown on the balance sheet below the current asset category.

Define the return on assets ratio and the asset turnover ratio. (p. 275) **LO7**

- The return on assets ratio is calculated by dividing net income by average total assets; it represents an overall measure of a firm's profitability and how efficiently a company is using its assets to generate net income.
- The asset turnover ratio is calculated by dividing net sales by average total assets; it provides an indication of the effective utilization of business assets to generate sales revenues.

Concept	Method	Assessment	SUMMARY
How efficiently is a company in using its assets to produce net income?	Net income and average total assets $\text{Return on assets ratio} = \frac{\text{Net income}}{\text{Average total assets}}$	A higher ratio value implies a higher, more efficient level of asset utilization.	TAKEAWAY 8.1
How efficient is a company at generating sales revenue using its assets?	Average total assets and net sales $\text{Asset turnover ratio} = \frac{\text{Net sales}}{\text{Average total assets}}$	A higher ratio value implies a higher level of sales revenue generated for each dollar invested in assets, which suggests a more efficient use of assets.	TAKEAWAY 8.2

KEY TERMS

Accelerated depreciation method (p. 264)
Amortization (p. 272)
Asset turnover (p. 275)
Betterments (p. 268)
Capital expenditures (p. 268)
Copyright (p. 272)
Declining-balance method (p. 264)
Depreciation (p. 261)
Depreciation accounting (p. 261)
Franchises (p. 272)
Goodwill (p. 273)
Impairment loss (p. 266)
Intangible assets (p. 258, 271)
Land improvements (p. 261)
Leasehold improvements (p. 261)
Modified accelerated cost recovery system (MACRS) (p. 266)
Patent (p. 272)
Property, plant and equipment (p. 258)
Research and development costs (p. 271)
Return on assets (p. 275)
Revenue expenditures (p. 267)
Right-of-use assets (p. 258)
Salvage value (p. 261)
Straight-line method (p. 262)
Trademarks (p. 273)
Trade names (p. 273)
Units-of-production method (p. 264)
Useful life (p. 261)

SELF-STUDY QUESTIONS

(Answers for the Self-Study Questions are available at the end of this chapter.)

LO1 Homework MBC

1. The acquisition cost of property, plant and equipment is equal to the asset's implied cash price and:
- *a.* The interest paid on any debt incurred to finance the asset's purchase.
- *b.* The market value of any noncash assets given up to acquire the asset.
- *c.* The reasonable and necessary costs incurred to prepare the asset for its intended use.
- *d.* The asset's estimated salvage value.

LO2 Homework MBC

2. On January 1, Rio Company purchased a delivery truck for $10,000. The company estimates the truck will be driven 80,000 miles over its eight-year useful life. The estimated salvage value is $2,000. The truck was driven 12,000 miles in its first year. Which method results in the largest depreciation expense for the first year?
- *a.* Units-of-production
- *b.* Straight-line
- *c.* Double-declining balance

LO4 Homework MBC

3. On the first day of the current year, Blakely Company sold equipment for less than its book value. Which of the following would result from the sale?
- *a.* An increase to Equipment
- *b.* An increase to Accumulated Depreciation—Equipment
- *c.* A Gain on Sale of Property, Plant and Equipment
- *d.* A Loss on Sale of Property, Plant and Equipment

LO5 Homework MBC

4. Accounting for the periodic amortization of intangible assets is similar to which depreciation method?
- *a.* Straight-line
- *b.* Units-of-production
- *c.* Double-declining balance

LO5 Homework MBC

5. An exclusive right to operate or sell a specific brand of products in a given geographic area is called:
- *a.* A franchise.
- *b.* Goodwill.
- *c.* A patent.
- *d.* A copyright.

LO5 Homework MBC

6. Which of the following statements is true?
- *a.* Goodwill is subject to amortization.
- *b.* Research and development costs may be capitalized to the balance sheet.
- *c.* Intangible assets are amortized to expense on the income statement.
- *d.* Goodwill arises because of a company's positive corporate image among its customers.

LO3 Homework MBC

7. Which of the following statements is false?
- *a.* Expenditures for ordinary repairs are a capital expenditure.
- *b.* Betterment expenditures are a capital expenditure.
- *c.* Expenditures to acquire low-cost assets are revenue expenditures.
- *d.* Material additions to a plant asset are capital expenditures.

LO6 Homework MBC

8. Which of the following statements is true?
- *a.* Intangible assets are shown on the balance sheet net of the Accumulated Amortization account.
- *b.* Goodwill is shown on the balance sheet net of the Accumulated Amortization account.
- *c.* The Accumulated Depreciation account need not be used for property, plant and equipment.
- *d.* Property, plant and equipment are shown on the balance sheet net of the Accumulated Depreciation account.

LO7 Homework MBC

9. A company reports net income of $6,000, net sales of $15,000, and total average assets of $24,000. What is the company's return on assets?
- *a.* 62.5 percent
- *b.* 25.0 percent
- *c.* 40.0 percent
- *d.* None of the above

LO7 Homework MBC

10. A company reports net income of $6,000, net sales of $15,000, and average total assets of $24,000. What is the company's asset turnover?
- *a.* 0.625
- *b.* 0.25
- *c.* 0.40
- *d.* None of the above

LO4 Homework MBC

11. Harley Company sold one of its worn out delivery trucks on December 31, Year 4. The truck was purchased on January 1, Year 1, for $50,000 and was depreciated on a straight-line basis

over a 5-year life. There was no salvage value associated with the truck. If the truck was sold for $14,000, what was the amount of gain or loss recorded at the time of the sale?

a. $4,000 loss *c.* $4,000 gain
b. $14,000 gain *d.* $6,000 loss

QUESTIONS

1. What are the two major types of long-lived assets that require a periodic write-off? Present examples of each, and indicate for each type of asset the term that denotes the periodic write-off to expense.
2. In what way is land different from other property, plant and equipment?
3. In general, what amounts constitute the acquisition cost of property, plant and equipment?
4. Why is the recognition of depreciation expense necessary to match revenue and expense properly?
5. What is the pattern of plant asset utilization (or benefit) that is appropriate for each of the following depreciation methods: (a) straight-line, (b) units-of-production, (c) double-declining balance?
6. How should a revision of depreciation charges due to a change in an asset's estimated useful life or salvage value be handled? Which periods—past, present, or future—are affected by the revision?
7. When is an asset considered to be impaired? How is an impairment loss calculated?
8. What is the benefit of accelerating depreciation for income tax purposes when the total depreciation taken is no more than if straight-line depreciation were used?
9. Identify two types of revenue expenditures. What is the proper accounting for revenue expenditures?
10. Identify two types of capital expenditures. What is the proper accounting for capital expenditures?
11. What factors determine the gain or loss on the sale of property, plant and equipment?
12. Folger Company installed a conveyor system that cost $192,000. The system can be used only in the excavation of gravel at a particular site. Folger expects to excavate gravel at the site for 10 years. Over how many years should the conveyor be depreciated if its physical life is estimated at (a) 8 years or (b) 12 years?
13. What are five different types of intangible assets? Briefly explain the nature of each type.
14. How should a firm account for research and development costs?
15. Under what circumstances is goodwill recorded?
16. How is the *return on assets* ratio calculated? What does this ratio reveal about a business?
17. How is the *asset turnover ratio* calculated? What does this ratio reveal about a business?

DATA ANALYTICS

The assignments in this Data Analytics section are designed to familiarize you with the tools used in analyzing data and communicating the results. Appendix F provides an in-depth discussion of data analytics and blockchain technology.

DA8-1. Preparing an Excel Visualization of Property and Equipment Components Over Time
The Excel file associated with this exercise includes information regarding **Fastenal Company**'s disclosures on its property and equipment in its Form 10-Ks over a six-year period. For this exercise, we analyze the changes in the composition of property and equipment over time.

REQUIRED

1. Download Excel file DA8-1 found in myBusinessCourse.
2. Create a Stacked Area chart showing the gross balances (before accumulated depreciation) of its property and equipment accounts. *Hint:* Highlight your data and open the Insert tab. Click Recommended Charts in the Charts group. Open the All Charts tab and click Area. Select the Stacked Area chart.
3. Answer the following questions based on the visualization.
   a. In which two years did total property and equipment rise at a slightly faster pace than the other years shown?
   b. From Year 1 to Year 6, which category of property and equipment showed the most growth?
   c. Which category of property and equipment appeared to drop (in proportion to the other categories) from Year 1 to Year 6?
   d. What is the largest category of property and equipment in Year 6?

4. Create two Pie charts, one for Year 1, and one for Year 6, showing gross balances (before accumulated depreciation) of property and equipment accounts.
5. If necessary, add chart titles to state the year. *Hint:* Click inside the chart and open the Chart Design tab. Click Add Chart Element in the Charts Layout group and select Chart Title.
6. Add data labels to the pie charts and edit data labels to only show percentages and not values. *Hint:* Right-click inside the pie and select Format Data Labels. Select Percentages under Label Options in the sidebar. Deselect Value, if necessary.
7. Answer the following questions based on the visualization.
   a. Which component has the highest proportion in Year 1? What is the percentage?
   b. Which component has the highest proportion in Year 6? What is the percentage?
   c. Which component had the greatest increase in proportion of the total from Year 1 to Year 6? What was the percentage difference?
   d. Which component had the greatest decrease in proportion from Year 1 to Year 6? What was the percentage difference?
   e. Which components showed a 2% or less difference in proportion of the total between Year 1 and Year 6?

Data Analytics

DA8-2. Determining the Method Used to Produce a Depreciation Visualization
The Excel file associated with this exercise includes four charts depicting depreciation under four different methods over the life of a fixed asset with a useful life of five years. In this exercise, we match each depreciation method provided to the appropriate depreciation chart based upon the trend in depreciation over the five-year period.

REQUIRED

1. Download Excel file DA8-2 found in myBusinessCourse.
2. Calculate the fixed asset's original cost if the residual value of the asset is $5,000.
3. Match each of the charts with the depreciation method used: straight-line, sum-of-the-years'-digits, declining-balance, or units-of-production methods.
4. Indicate which chart(s) can be prepared upon purchase of the fixed asset and which chart(s) can only be prepared over time.

Data Analytics

DA8-3. Using Excel Visualizations to Analyze Property and Equipment
The Excel file associated with this exercise includes data for Delta Air Lines, Inc., as reported in its Form 10-K reports over a 10-year period. The percent depreciated of depreciable fixed assets measures the age of the assets compared to useful life. A company that has made substantial investments in new fixed assets will have a lower ratio compared to a company with fixed assets nearing the end of their useful life. In this exercise, we review the trend of percent depreciated of gross property and equipment for Delta Airlines over a 10-year period.

Percent Depreciated

$$\frac{\text{Accumulated depreciation}}{\text{Cost of depreciable asset}}$$

REQUIRED

1. Download Excel file DA8-3 found in myBusinessCourse.
2. Compute the ratio of accumulated depreciation to gross property and equipment for each year. Assume all assets are depreciable.
3. Prepare the following three charts in Excel.
   - Chart 1: A bar chart showing accumulated depreciation and gross property and equipment per year over the 10-year period.
   - Chart 2: A line chart showing property and equipment additions over the 10-year period, with the earliest year on the left hand side. *Hint:* To reverse the order of the years, right-click inside the horizontal axis. A Format Axis sidebar will appear. Open the bar chart icon tab. Click Categories in reverse order under Axis options.
   - Chart 3: A line chart showing the ratio of accumulated depreciation to gross property and equipment over the 10-year period.
4. Answer the following questions based on your visualizations.
   a. In Chart 1, in what year(s) was the trend of increasing values not evident in the chart?
   b. In Chart 2, what year(s) showed a drop in property and equipment additions?
   c. In Chart 2, what year showed the most significant change?
   d. Describe the trend shown in Chart 3.
   e. What is the likely cause of the increase shown in Year 10 in Chart 3.

Assignments with the MBC logo in the margin are available in myBusinessCourse. See the Preface of the book for details.

SHORT EXERCISES

SE8-1. Calculate Amount to Capitalize The Miller Company paid $10,000 to acquire a 100 ton press. Freight charges to deliver the equipment amounted to $1,500 and were paid by Miller. Installation costs amounted to $570, and machine testing charges amounted to $250. Calculate the amount that should be capitalized to the Equipment account. LO1

SE8-2. Depreciation Expense Using the Straight-Line Method The Pack Company purchased an office building for $4,500,000. The building had an estimated useful life of 40 years and an expected salvage value of $500,000. Calculate the depreciation expense for the second year using the straight-line method. LO2

SE8-3. Depreciation Expense Using the Double-Declining Balance Method The Pack Company purchased an office building for $4,500,000. The building had an estimated useful life of 40 years and an expected salvage value of $500,000. Calculate the depreciation expense for the second year using the double-declining balance method. LO2

SE8-4. Depreciation Expense Using the Units-of-Production Method The Likert Company is a coal company based in West Virginia. The company recently purchased a new coal truck for $60,000. The truck had an expected useful life of 200,000 miles and an expected salvage value of $2,000. Calculate the depreciation expense using the units-of-production method assuming the truck travelled 40,000 miles on company business during the year. LO2

SE8-5. Sale of a Building The Miller Company sold a building for $400,000 that had a book value of $450,000. The building had originally cost the company $12,000,000 and had accumulated depreciation to date of $11,550,000. Calculate the gain or loss on the sale of the building. LO4

SE8-6. Goodwill Impairment Bruceton Farms Equipment Company had goodwill valued at $80 million on its balance sheet at year-end. A review of the goodwill by the company's CFO indicated that the goodwill was impaired and was now only worth $50 million. What is the financial statement effect of the goodwill impairment? LO5

SE8-7. Amortization Expense Los Altos, Inc. obtained a patent for a new optical scanning device. The fees incurred to file for the patent and to defend the patent in court against several companies that challenged the patent amounted to $45,000. Los Altos, Inc. concluded that the expected economic life of the patent was 12 years. Calculate the amortization expense that should be recorded in the second year. LO5

SE8-8. Return on Assets The Kingwood Company reported net income of $50,000 and average total assets of $450,000. Calculate the company's return on assets. LO7

SE8-9. Asset Turnover The Kingwood Company reported sales revenue of $520,000 and average total assets of $450,000. Calculate the company's asset turnover. LO7

SE8-10. Return on Assets and Asset Turnover Last year, the Miller Company reported a return on assets of 15 percent and an asset turnover of 1.6. In the current year, the company reported a return on assets of 19 percent but an asset turnover of only 1.2. If sales revenue remained unchanged from last year to the current year, what would explain the two ratio results? LO7

SE8-11. Sale of Equipment Calculate the gain or loss for the following transactions: (1) Geysler Company sold some old equipment that initially cost $30,000 and had $25,000 of accumulated depreciation and received cash in the amount of $3,000. (2) Assume the same facts except Geysler received $9,000. LO4

SE8-12. Financial Statement Placement Name the financial statement where each of the following will appear: (IS) Income Statement; (BS) Balance Sheet; (SCF) Statement of Cash Flows; (N) None. LO6

a. Book value of equipment purchased five years ago
b. Market value of equipment purchased five years ago
c. Cash proceeds from the sale of land
d. Gain on the sale of buildings
e. Accumulated depreciation on equipment
f. Impairment loss on land

EXERCISES

LO1 E8-1. Acquisition Cost of a Fixed Asset The following data relate to a firm's purchase of a machine used in the manufacture of its product:

Invoice price	$20,000
Applicable sales tax	1,200
Cash discount taken for prompt payment	400
Freight paid	260
Cost of insurance coverage on machine while in transit	125
Installation costs	1,000
Testing and adjusting costs	475
Repair of damages to machine caused by the firm's employees	550
Prepaid maintenance contract for first year of machine's use	300

Determine the acquisition cost of the machine.

LO2 E8-2. Depreciation Methods A delivery truck costing $18,000 is expected to have a $1,500 salvage value at the end of its useful life of four years or 125,000 miles. Assume that the truck was purchased on January 2. Calculate the depreciation expense for the second year using each of the following depreciation methods: (a) straight-line, (b) double-declining balance, and (c) units-of-production. (Assume that the truck was driven 28,000 miles in the second year.)

LO3 E8-3. Revenue and Capital Expenditures Shively Company built an addition to its chemical plant. Indicate whether each of the following expenditures related to the addition is a revenue expenditure or a capital expenditure:

a. Shively's initial application for a building permit was denied by the city as not conforming to environmental standards. Shively disagreed with the decision and spent $6,000 in attorney's fees to convince the city to reverse its position and issue the permit.

b. Due to unanticipated sandy soil conditions, and on the advice of construction engineers, Shively spent $58,000 to extend the footings for the addition to a greater depth than originally planned.

c. Shively spent $3,000 to send each of the addition's subcontractors a side of beef as a thank-you gift for completing the project on schedule.

d. Shively invited the mayor to a ribbon-cutting ceremony to open the plant addition. It spent $25 to purchase the ribbon and scissors.

e. Shively spent $4,100 to have the company logo sandblasted into the concrete above the entrance to the addition.

LO4 E8-4. Sale of Machinery Raine Company has a machine that originally cost $68,000. Depreciation has been recorded for five years using the straight-line method, with a $5,000 estimated salvage value at the end of an expected nine-year life. After recording depreciation at the end of the fifth year, Raine sells the machine.

a. Calculate the book value of the machine at the end of five years.

b. Calculate the gain/loss on the sale of the machine for:

i. $37,000 cash.
ii. $33,000 cash.
iii. $28,000 cash.

LO5 E8-5. Amortization Expense For each of the following unrelated situations, calculate the annual amortization expense:

a. A patent with a 15-year remaining legal life was purchased for $270,000. The patent will be commercially exploitable for another nine years.

b. A patent was acquired on a device designed by a production worker. Although the cost of the patent to date consisted of $42,300 in legal fees for handling the patent application, the patent should be commercially valuable during its entire remaining legal life of 18 years and is currently worth $378,000.

c. A franchise granting exclusive distribution rights for a new solar water heater within a three-state area for four years was obtained at a cost of $63,000. Satisfactory sales performance over the four years permits renewal of the franchise for another four years (at an additional cost determined at renewal).

E8-6. **Return on Assets Ratio and Asset Turnover Ratio** Campo Systems reported the following financial data (in millions) in its annual report: LO7

	Year 2	Year 3
Net income	$ 8,052	$ 6,134
Net sales	39,540	36,117
Total assets	58,734	68,128

If the company's total assets are $55,676 in Year 1, calculate the company's (a) return on assets and (b) asset turnover for Years 2 and 3.

E8-7. **Financial Statement Presentation** Vera Corp. reported the following amounts for the year just ended: LO6

Land	$120,000
Patents	25,000
Equipment	40,000
Buildings	150,000
Goodwill	35,000
Accumulated amortization	10,000
Accumulated depreciation	80,000

Prepare a partial balance sheet for these amounts.

PROBLEMS

P8-1. **Acquisition Cost of Property, Plant and Equipment** The following items represent expenditures (or receipts) related to the construction of a new home office for Lowrey Company. LO1

Cost of land site, which included an old apartment building appraised at $75,000	$ 165,000
Legal fees, including fee for title search	2,100
Payment of apartment building mortgage and related interest due at time of sale	9,300
Payment for delinquent property taxes assumed by the purchaser	4,000
Cost of razing the apartment building	17,000
Proceeds from sale of salvaged materials	(3,800)
Grading to establish proper drainage flow on land site	1,900
Architect's fees on new building	300,000
Proceeds from sales of excess dirt (from basement excavation) to owner of adjoining property (dirt was used to fill in a low area on property)	(2,000)
Payment to building contractor	5,000,000
Payment of medical bills of employee accidentally injured while inspecting building construction	1,400
Special assessment for paving city sidewalks (paid to city)	18,000
Cost of paving driveway and parking lot	25,000
Cost of installing lights in parking lot	9,200
Premium for insurance on building during construction	7,500
Cost of open house party to celebrate opening of new building	8,000

REQUIRED

From the given data, calculate the proper balances for the Land, Building, and Land Improvements accounts of Lowrey Company.

P8-2. **Depreciation Methods** On July 1, Small Company purchased most of the property, plant and equipment of a small trucking company that was going out of business. The purchase price was allocated as follows: LO2

Land	$120,000
Building	440,000
Trucks	144,000
Equipment	96,000
Total	$800,000

Small depreciated the assets using the straight-line method on the building and on the equipment, and the double-declining balance method on the trucks. Estimated useful lives and salvage values were as follows:

	Useful Life	Salvage Value
Building	20 years	$42,000
Trucks	4 years	15,000
Equipment	7 years	12,000

REQUIRED

Calculate the depreciation expense for the year on the building, trucks, and equipment. Assume a December 31 year end.

LO2 **P8-3.** **Depreciation Methods** On January 2, Roth, Inc. purchased a laser cutting machine to be used in the fabrication of a part for one of its key products. The machine cost $80,000, and its estimated useful life was four years or 1,000,000 cuttings, after which it could be sold for $5,000.

REQUIRED

Calculate the depreciation expense for each year of the machine's useful life under each of the following depreciation methods:

a. Straight-line.
b. Double-declining balance.
c. Units-of-production. Assume annual production in cuttings of 200,000; 350,000; 260,000; and 190,000.

LO1, 2, 3 **P8-4.** **Accounting for Property, Plant and Equipment** Basin Corporation had the following transactions related to its delivery truck:

Year 1

Jan. 5 Purchased for $14,300 cash a new truck with an estimated useful life of four years and a salvage value of $2,300.
Feb. 20 Installed a new set of side-view mirrors at a cost of $68 cash.
June 9 Paid $285 for an engine tune-up, wheel balancing, and a periodic chassis lubrication.
Aug. 2 Paid a $250 repair bill for the uninsured portion of damages to the truck caused by Basin's own driver.
Dec. 31 Recorded depreciation on the truck for the year.

Year 2

May 1 Installed a set of parts bins in the truck at a cost of $800 cash. This expenditure was not expected to increase the salvage value of the truck.
Dec. 31 Recorded depreciation on the truck for the year.

Year 3

Dec. 31 Recorded depreciation on the truck for the year.

Basin's depreciation policies include (1) using straight-line depreciation, (2) recording depreciation to the nearest whole month, and (3) expensing all truck expenditures of $75 or less.

REQUIRED

Based on these transactions:

a. Calculate the depreciation expense for each of the three years.
b. Calculate the book value of the delivery truck at the end of year 3.

LO4 **P8-5.** **Disposal of Property, Plant and Equipment** Citano Company has a used executive charter plane that originally cost $800,000. Straight-line depreciation on the plane has been recorded for six years, with an $80,000 expected salvage value at the end of its estimated eight-year useful life. The last depreciation entry was made at the end of the sixth year. Eight months into the seventh year, Citano disposes of the plane.

REQUIRED

Calculate:

a. Depreciation expense for the eight months in Year 7 to the date of disposal.
b. The book value of the plane at the date of the disposal.
c. The gain or loss on the sale of the plane for $215,000 cash.
d. The gain or loss on the sale of the plane for $195,000 cash.
e. The gain or loss on the destruction of the plane in a fire. Citano expects a $190,000 insurance settlement.

P8-6. Accounting for Intangible Assets Berdahl Company owns several retail outlets. During the year, it expanded operations and entered into the following transactions: LO5

Mar.	1	Paid $45,000 to obtain an exclusive area franchise for five years to distribute a new line of perfume.
July	1	Paid $38,000 to LogoLab, Inc., for designing a trademark for a new line of gourmet chocolates that Berdahl will distribute nationally. Berdahl will use the trademark for as long as the firm remains in business. Berdahl expects to be in business for at least another 50 years.
	1	Paid $25,000 for advertisement in a national magazine (June issue) introducing the new line of chocolates and the trademark.

REQUIRED

a. Determine the financial statement effects of these transactions.

b. Determine the annual amortization expense on December 31 for these transactions. Berdahl uses straight-line amortization.

P8-7. Preparation of Balance Sheet Dooley Company's December 31 balance sheet accounts contain the following balances: LO6

Cash	$ 9,000
Accounts payable	18,000
Building	439,500
Long-term notes payable	785,000
Common stock	900,000
Retained earnings	70,000
Accumulated depreciation—Equipment	180,000
Land	829,500
Accounts receivable	22,500
Accumulated depreciation—Building	135,000
Wages payable	6,000
Patent (net of amortization)	120,000
Notes payable (short term)	131,000
Inventory	206,000
Equipment	600,000
Allowance for doubtful accounts	1,500

REQUIRED

Prepare a December 31 classified balance sheet for Dooley Company.

P8-8. Accounting for Property, Plant and Equipment During the first few days of the year, Coast Company entered into the following transactions:

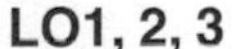

1. Purchased a parcel of land with a building on it for $900,000 cash. The building, which will be used in operations, has an estimated useful life of 25 years and a salvage value of $60,000. Of the purchase price, $810,000 is allocated to the cost of the building, and the remaining balance to the land.
2. Paid $30,000 for the construction of an asphalt parking lot for customers. The parking lot is expected to last 12 years and has no salvage value.
3. Paid $25,000 for the construction of a new entrance to the building.
4. Purchased store equipment, paying the invoice price (including seven percent sales tax) of $74,900 in cash. The estimated useful life of the equipment is eight years, and the salvage value is $6,000.
5. Paid $220 freight on the new equipment.
6. Paid $1,500 to repair damages to floor caused when the store equipment was accidentally dropped as it was moved into place.
7. Paid $40 for an umbrella holder to place inside front door (customers may place wet umbrellas in the holder). The holder is expected to last 20 years.

REQUIRED

a. Determine the acquisition cost associated with each asset based on these transactions.

b. Calculate the depreciation expense for the year. Double-declining balance depreciation is used for the equipment, and straight-line depreciation is used for the building and parking lot.

SERIAL PROBLEM: ANGEL CITY GREETINGS

(Note: This is a continuation of the Serial Problem: Angel City Greetings from Chapters 1 through 7.)

SP8. Kate's business is growing faster than she had predicted. In order to keep up, she will need to purchase improved computer hardware. Kate has learned that the software that she uses runs much faster if her computer has a lot of memory. In addition, her files are very large and she is running out of free space on her existing hard drive. Finally, Kate has heard horror stories about hard disk drive crashes and the possibility that all of her work will be destroyed. In order to protect against this possibility, she has decided to invest in a large commercial grade backup system.

The cost of the memory and hard disk drive upgrade to Kate's computer will total $420. The cost of the backup system is $3,000. The memory and hard disk upgrade will increase the productivity of Kate's current computer; however, it will not extend its useful life. The backup system is expected to have a five-year useful life.

Kate would like to know the following items:

1. How should the expenditure for the memory and hard disk drive upgrade be recorded?
2. Kate's current computer has 42 months remaining for depreciation purpose (under the straight-line method). The original cost of the computer was $4,800 and had a four-year useful life. The current monthly depreciation is $100. How will this current expenditure affect the monthly depreciation?
3. Kate would like to know how depreciation on the backup system under both the straight-line method and the double-declining method differ. She is assigning a $500 salvage value to the equipment. Construct a table showing yearly depreciation under both methods.

BEYOND THE NUMBERS

REPORTING AND ANALYSIS

Columbia Sportswear Company

BTN8-1. Financial Reporting Problem: Columbia Sportswear Company The financial statements for the Columbia Sportswear Company can be found in Appendix A at the end of this book.

Required

Answer the following questions.

a. What was the total cost of Columbia's property, plant and equipment at December 31, 2020?
b. What was the total accumulated depreciation at December 31, 2020?
c. What percentage of the total cost of property, plant and equipment at December 31, 2020, was from building and improvements?
d. How much depreciation and amortization expense was taken in 2020?
e. What amount of property, plant and equipment purchases (capital expenditures) occurred in 2020?

Columbia Sportswear Company
Under Armour, Inc.

BTN8-2. Comparative Analysis Problem: Columbia Sportswear Company vs. Under Armour, Inc. The financial statements for the Columbia Sportswear Company can be found in Appendix A at the end of this book, and the financial statements of Under Armour, Inc. can be found in Appendix B.

Required

a. Calculate the following ratios for Columbia Sportswear and for Under Armour, Inc. for 2020:
   1. Return on assets
   2. Asset turnover
b. Comment on your findings.

BTN8-3. Business Decision Problem Lyle Fleming, president of Fleming, Inc., wants you to resolve his dispute with Mia Gooden over the amount of a finder's fee due Gooden. Fleming hired Gooden to locate a new plant site to expand the business. By agreement, Gooden's fee was to be 15 percent of the "cost of the property (excluding the finder's fee), measured according to generally accepted accounting principles."

Gooden located Site 1 and Site 2 for Fleming to consider. Each site had a selling price of $150,000, and the geographic locations of both sites were equally acceptable to Fleming. Fleming employed an engineering firm to conduct the geological tests necessary to determine the relative quality of the two sites for construction. The tests, which cost $10,000 for each site, showed that Site 1 was superior to Site 2.

The owner of Site 1 initially gave Fleming 30 days—a reasonable period—to decide whether or not to buy the property. However, Fleming procrastinated in contracting the geological tests, and the results were not available by the end of the 30-day period. Fleming requested a two-week extension. The Site 1 owner granted Fleming the additional two weeks but charged him $6,000 for the extension (which Fleming paid). Fleming eventually bought Site 1.

Fleming sent Gooden a fee of $24,000, which was 15 percent of a cost computed as follows:

Sales price, Site 1	$150,000
Geological tests, Site 1	10,000
Total	$160,000

Gooden believes that she is entitled to $26,400, based on a cost computed as follows:

Sales price, Site 1	$150,000
Geological tests, Site 1	10,000
Geological tests, Site 2	10,000
Fee for time extension	6,000
Total	$176,000

Required
What fee is Gooden entitled to under the agreement? Explain.

BTN8-4. Financial Analysis Problem Microsoft Corporation is headquartered in Redmond, Washington. The company provides computer and software products and services to individuals and businesses. Selected financial data for Microsoft follow (amounts in millions):

Microsoft Corporation

	2020	2019
Total assets, beginning of year	$286,556	$258,848
Total assets, end of year	301,311	286,556
Revenues for the year	143,015	125,843
Net income for the year	44,281	39,240

Required
a. Calculate the return on assets and asset turnover for each year.
b. Comment on your findings.

CRITICAL THINKING

BTN8-5. Accounting Research Problem General Mills, Inc.'s 2020 annual report can be found at https://investors.generalmills.com/financial-information/annual-reports/default.aspx. Review the consolidated statements of earnings, the consolidated balance sheets, and Notes 2 and 18.

General Mills, Inc.

Required
a. What is General Mills' gross cost of land, buildings, and equipment at May 31, 2020?
b. What depreciation method is used in the financial statements?
c. How much depreciation and amortization were expensed in fiscal 2020?
d. How much depreciation has accumulated by May 31, 2020?
e. How much research and development cost was expensed in fiscal 2020?
f. What is General Mills' return on assets for fiscal 2020?

BTN8-6. Accounting Communication Activity Peggy Zimmer, a friend of yours taking her first accounting class, is confused as to why there is a separate accumulated depreciation account. She argues that it would be much simpler to just credit the asset that is being depreciated directly instead of crediting accumulated depreciation.

Required
Explain to your friend in an informal memo a possible advantage that keeping the cost and accumulated depreciation separate can have for an analyst.

BTN8-7. **Accounting Ethics Case** Linda Tristan, assistant controller for Ag-Growth, Inc., a biotechnology firm, has concerns about the accounting analysis for the firm's purchase of a land site and building from Hylite Corporation. The price for this package purchase was $1,800,000 cash. A memorandum from the controller, Greg Fister, stated that the cost allocation for this purchase should be Land for $1,350,000, and Building for $450,000. The building, a used laboratory facility, is to be depreciated over 10 years with a zero salvage value.

The source documents supporting the transaction include two appraisals of the property, one done for Ag-Growth and one done for Hylite Corporation. The appraisal for Ag-Growth valued the land at $1,000,000 and the building at $500,000. The appraisal for Hylite Corporation (done by a different appraiser) valued the land at $1,500,000 and the building at $750,000. Negotiations between the two firms finally settled on an overall price of $1,800,000 for the land and the building.

Tristan asked Fister how he arrived at the amounts to be recorded for the land and building since each appraisal valued the land at only twice the building's value. "Well," replied Fister, "I used the $1,500,000 land value from Hylite's appraiser and the $500,000 building value from our appraiser. That relationship shows the land to be worth three times the building's value. Using that relationship, I assigned 75 percent of our actual purchase price of $1,800,000 to the land and 25 percent of the purchase price to the building."

"But why do it that way?" asked Tristan.

"Because it will improve our profits, before income taxes, by $150,000 over the next decade," replied Fister.

"But it just doesn't seem right," commented Tristan.

Required

a. How does the accounting analysis by Fister improve profits before income taxes by $150,000 over the next decade?

b. Is the goal of improving profits a sufficient rationale to defend the accounting analysis by Fister?

c. Do you agree with Fister's analysis? Briefly explain.

d. What actions are available to Tristan to resolve her concerns with Fister's analysis?

Cummins Inc.

BTN8-8. **Environmental, Social, and Governance Problem** Unlike Tesla Motors' emphasis on electric engines, **Cummins, Inc.** is best known for its design and manufacturing of diesel engines. Go to the Cummins' Website at http://cummins.com and navigate to the section on sustainability.

Required

1. Articulate Cummins' approach to corporate responsibility.
2. Cummins states that "corporate responsibility contributes directly to the long-term health, growth and profitability of our company." Explain how being a good corporate citizen may lead to increased growth and profitability.

Waste Management, Inc.

BTN8-9. **Accounting Ethics Problem** **Waste Management** is a leading provider of comprehensive trash and waste removal, recycling, and waste management services. In 2002, the Securities and Exchange Commission sued several members and former members of Waste Management's management team for fraud. Go to the S.E.C. press release at: www.sec.gov/news/press/2002-44.txt to answer the following questions:

1. What does the complaint claim about Dean L. Buntrock, the company's founder, chairman of the board, and chief executive officer?
2. What accounting methods does the complaint claim were used by Waste Management in order to perpetuate the fraud?

Alphabet Inc.

BTN8-10. **Working with the Takeaways** The following data (in millions) is from **Alphabet Inc.'s (AKA Google)** 2020 financial statements:

	2020	2019
Net sales	$182,527	$161,857
Net income	40,269	34,343
Total assets	319,616	275,909

Calculate 2020 asset turnover and return on assets for Alphabet Inc.

ANSWERS TO SELF-STUDY QUESTIONS

1. c **2.** c **3.** d **4.** a **5.** a **6.** c **7.** a **8.** d **9.** b **10.** a **11.** c

REVIEW SOLUTIONS

Solution 8.1

All of the costs, with the exception of the unrelated supplies, are considered to be part of the equipment's acquisition cost, and therefore, should be capitalized to the equipment account. This includes the $20,000 purchase price, along with the $1,600 sales tax, $400 freight cost, $600 installation cost, and $100 testing cost, for a total acquisition cost of $22,700. The cost of the $300 of supplies should be accounted for as a supplies inventory (an asset) and allocated to expense on the income statement as it is used.

Solution 8.2

(a) Under the straight-line method, the annual depreciation expense is calculated as ($10,000 – $2,000)/5 years = $1,600 for each year.

(b) The depreciation rate for a five-year asset under the double-declining balance method is 40 percent, or [(100 percent/5 years) × 2]. And, the depreciation expense is calculated as 40 percent times the book value of the asset as of the beginning of the year. Thus, the first year depreciation is $4,000 (40 percent × $10,000) and the second year depreciation is $2,400 [40 percent × ($10,000 – $4,000)].

Solution 8.3

Items (1), (2), and (4) are revenue expenditures. Item (3) increases the van's useful life and item (5) reduces the van's operating costs; consequently, items (3) and (5) are capital expenditures.

Solution 8.4

Cost of truck	$22,500
Accumulated depreciation	15,000
Book value of truck	7,500
Proceeds from sale	750
Loss on disposal of truck	$ 6,750

Solution 8.5

1. Copyright
2. Amortization
3. Trademark
4. Franchise
5. Patent

Solution 8.6

Smithson Corporation
Partial Balance Sheet

Cash and cash equivalents	$ 7,500
Accounts receivable	1,200
Inventory	5,000
Current Assets	13,700
Property, plant & equipment, net	19,000
Goodwill	750
Intangibles, net	350
Other noncurrent assets	3,000
Total assets	$36,800

Solution 8.7

		Year 3	Year 2
	Average assets	(68,734 + 78,128)/2 = 73,431	(65,676 + 68,734)/2 = 67,205
(a)	Return on assets	(16,134/73,431) = 22.0 %	(18,052/67,205) = 26.9%
(b)	Asset turnover	(46,117/73,431) = 0.63	(49,540/67,205) = 0.74

Liabilities

PAST

Chapter 8 concluded our investigation of the accounting for assets.

PRESENT

In this chapter we turn our attention to the accounting for liabilities.

FUTURE

Chapter 10 examines the accounting for stockholders' equity.

MICROSOFT CORPORATION

Microsoft Corporation is one of the world's most well-recognized companies. In 2020, Microsoft had global annual revenue of $143 billion and employed nearly 163,000 employees worldwide.

Until 2009, Microsoft remained largely debt free. The company's business model was so successful that it was unnecessary for the company to utilize debt financing. The high profit margins on the company's products enabled Microsoft to finance its growth using internally generated operating cash flow. In 2009, however, the company issued its first bonds to the capital market. Wall Street analysts speculated that Microsoft really didn't need the cash provided by the debt issuance but rather sold the bonds to take advantage of the extremely low interest rates available at that time.

In this chapter, we examine how companies, like Microsoft, value and disclose liabilities on their balance sheets. We consider current liabilities, noncurrent liabilities, and contingent liabilities such as pending lawsuits and environmental cleanup obligations.

Road Map

LO	Learning Objective	Page	eLecture	Review	Assignments
LO1	**Describe the nature of liabilities and define current liabilities.**	292	E9-1	9.1	E1, E2, E3, E4, E5, E11, P1, P2, P3
LO2	**Define long-term liabilities.**	296	E9-2		SE2, E16, E17
LO3	**Explain bond pricing and illustrate two methods of amortizing bond discounts/premiums.**	299	E9-3	9.2, 9.3	SE8, SE9, SE10, E7, E8, E9, E10, E11, E12, E16, E17, P4, P5, P6, P7
LO4	**Describe the accounting for leases.**	309	E9-4		SE4, E13
LO5	**Define contingent liabilities and explain their disclosure in the financial statements.**	310	E9-5	9.4	SE1, SE3, E1, E6, E14, P3
LO6	**Define the current ratio, quick ratio, and times-interest-earned ratio.**	314	E9-6	9.5	SE5, SE6, SE7, E15, P8

Liabilities				
Current Liabilities	**Long-Term Liabilities**	**Leases**	**Contingent Liabilities**	**Analyzing Liabilities**
• Accounts payable • Notes and interest • Accrued interest payable • Current portion of long-term debt • Income tax • Unearned revenue	• Debt financing • Bonds and bond pricing • Bonds sold at a discount or premium • Straight-line method of amortization • Effective interest method of amortization • Retiring bonds • Notes payable	• Financing with leases • Finance leases • Operating leases	• Defining contingent liabilities • Reporting contingent liabilities • Types of contingent liabilities • Warranties • Lawsuits • Environmental risks • Guarantees	• Current ratio • Quick ratio • Times interest earned

CURRENT LIABILITIES

LO1 **Describe** the nature of liabilities and **define** *current liabilities.*

Liabilities are obligations resulting from past transactions or events that require a business to pay money, provide goods, or perform services in the future. **Current liabilities** are obligations, as of the balance sheet date, that will require, within the coming year or the normal operating cycle, whichever is longer, (1) the use of existing current assets or (2) the creation of other current liabilities. Most current liabilities are settled by using current assets, but sometimes a current liability is settled by the issuance of another current liability. A past due account payable, for example, may be settled by issuing a short-term note payable. Liabilities are classified as current using the same time frame used to classify current assets—the longer of one year or a firm's normal operating cycle. In the following section, we consider some typical current liabilities.

Accounts Payable

In a balance sheet listing of current liabilities, amounts due to short-term creditors on notes payable and accounts payable are commonly shown first. Short-term creditors send invoices specifying the amount owed for goods or services that they have provided. As a result, the amount of any account or note payable is easily determined because it is based on the invoices received from a creditor.

At the end of an accounting period, accountants need to know whether any goods are in transit and what the shipping terms are for such goods. If the goods are shipped F.O.B. shipping point, ownership of the goods has transferred to the buyer and an account payable should be recorded at year-end (as well as an increase in inventory) even though the goods and an invoice have not yet arrived.

DATA ANALYTICS **Power of Data Analytics for Managing Procurement**

In most large businesses, the accounts payable function represents a very large volume of transactions and a significant percentage of the business's costs. Although most business have a variety of controls in place to manage this process, payment errors still do occur. While these errors as a percentage of total invoices may be very small, the total dollar amounts can still be meaningful to the business's overall profitability. The accounting firm, Deloitte, believes using data analytics can help uncover invalid payments and at the same time protect the business from future erroneous invoices. They have developed a sophisticated software package that tests, scores, and then presents the findings to allow interactive views of all suspect vendors, invoices, or payments, thus helping manage this very important function.

Notes Payable and Interest

Promissory notes are often issued in transactions when the credit period is longer than the 30 or 60 days typical for accounts payable. Although promissory notes are commonly used in credit sales transactions involving equipment and real property, a note may sometimes be exchanged for merchandise. A note payable may also be substituted for an account payable when an extension of the usual credit period is granted. And, a promissory note is prepared when a loan is obtained from a bank.

Interest is a charge for the use of money. Consequently, interest incurred on a promissory note is an expense to the maker of the note. Since businesses are required under GAAP to distinguish between operating and nonoperating expenses in their income statements, interest expense is reported under the Other Income and Expense category to indicate that it is not considered to be an operating expense, and instead, is a financing expense of the business.

Interest on promissory notes can be structured in either of two ways: (1) as an amount paid in addition to the face amount of the note, called the *add-on interest method*, or (2) as an amount included in the face amount of the note, called the *discount method*. The add-on interest method is more commonly used, and consequently, we focus on that approach.

Add-On Interest Method

Interest on a short-term note payable using the *add-on interest method* is paid at the maturity date of the note. The formula for determining the amount of interest to be paid is as follows:

Interest = Principal × Interest rate × Time

The principal, or face amount, of a note is the amount borrowed. The **interest rate** is the annual rate of interest. Time is the fraction of a year that a note is outstanding.

When a note is written for a certain number of months, time is expressed in twelfths of a year. For example, interest on a three-month note for $4,000, with a nine percent annual interest rate is:

Interest = $4,000 × 0.09 × 3/12 = $90

When the length of the borrowing period is given in days, time is expressed as a fraction of a year; the numerator is the number of days that the note will be outstanding; and the denominator is 360 days. (Some lenders use 360 days, while others use 365 days; we will use 360 days in our examples.) For example, interest on a 60-day note for $3,000, with a nine percent annual interest rate is:

Interest = $3,000 × 0.09 × 60/360 = $45

Determining the Maturity Date of a Note

When the length of the borrowing period is expressed in days, the exact number of days in each calendar month is counted to determine the note's **maturity date**. For example, a 90-day note dated July 21 has an October 19 maturity date, determined as follows:

10	days in July (**remainder of month, 31 days minus 21 days**)
31	days in August
30	days in September
19	days in October (**number of days required to total 90**)
90	

If the length of the borrowing period is expressed in months, the maturity date is determined by counting the number of months from the date of issue. For example, a two-month note dated January 31 matures on March 31, a three-month note of the same date matures on April 30 (the last day of the month), and a four-month note matures on May 31.

Recording Notes Payable and Interest Expense

When a note payable is exchanged to settle an account payable, the effect on the financial statements is to increase a note payable and to reduce the balance of the related account payable. For example, suppose that the Jordon Company sold $12,000 of merchandise on account to Bowman Company. On October 1, after the regular credit period had expired, Bowman Company gave the Jordon Company a 60-day, nine percent note for $12,000. As a consequence, the financial statement effect to Bowman Company on October 1 is:

Transaction: *Note payable issued on October 1 in payment of an account payable (60-day, 9 percent note).*

Balance Sheet							Income Statement				
Assets	=	Liabilities	+	Stockholders' Equity: Contrib. Capital	+	Retained Earnings	*Revenues*	−	*Expenses*	=	*Net Income*
	=	+12,000 Note payable −12,000 Accounts payable	+					−		=	

If the Bowman Company pays the note on the November 30 maturity date, the financial statement effect is as follows:

Transaction: *Payment of note payable on November 30.*

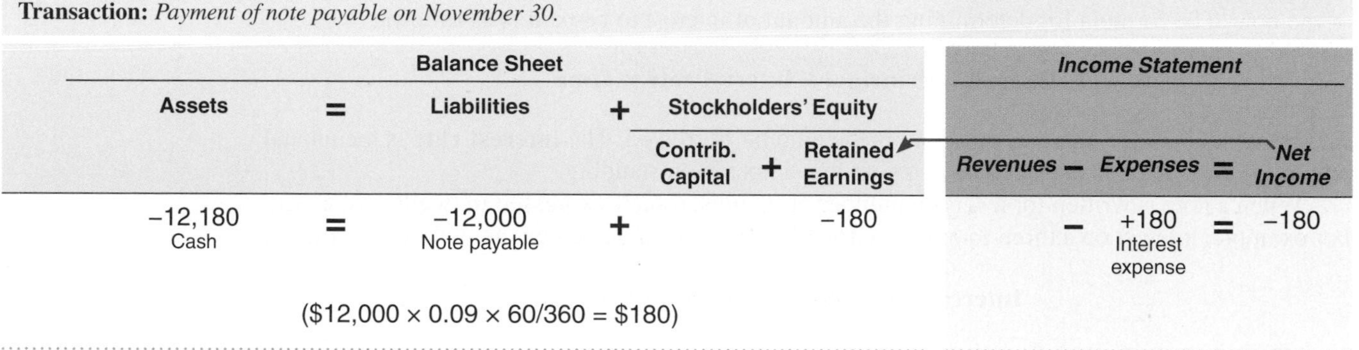

Balance Sheet							Income Statement				
Assets	=	Liabilities	+	Stockholders' Equity: Contrib. Capital	+	Retained Earnings	*Revenues*	−	*Expenses*	=	*Net Income*
−12,180 Cash	=	−12,000 Note payable	+			−180		−	+180 Interest expense	=	−180

($12,000 × 0.09 × 60/360 = $180)

Accrued Interest Payable

As discussed in Chapter 3, adjustments to accrue expenses and unearned revenues result in accrued liabilities. Additionally, at the end of the fiscal year, adjustments must be made to reflect any accrued, but unpaid, interest expense. For example, assume that the Bowman Company has one note payable outstanding at December 31, Year 1, to Garcia Company, which is dated December 21, Year 1, has a principal amount of $6,000, an interest rate of 12 percent, and a maturity date of February 19, Year 2. The financial statement effect of the adjustment that must be made to accrue interest expense through December 31, Year 1, is as follows:

Transaction: *December 31 interest expense accrued on the note payable to Garcia Company.*

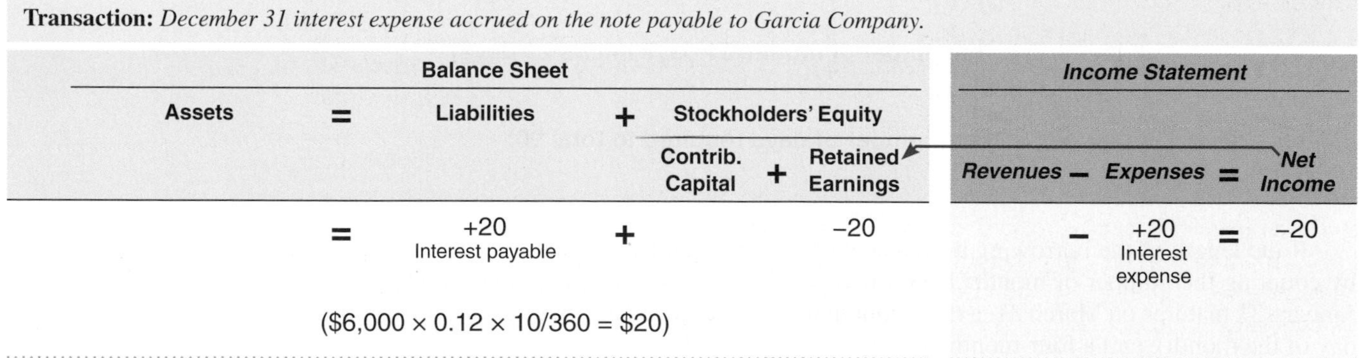

Balance Sheet							Income Statement				
Assets	=	Liabilities	+	Stockholders' Equity: Contrib. Capital	+	Retained Earnings	*Revenues*	−	*Expenses*	=	*Net Income*
	=	+20 Interest payable	+			−20		−	+20 Interest expense	=	−20

($6,000 × 0.12 × 10/360 = $20)

When the note payable to Garcia Company is subsequently paid on February 19, Year 2, the effect on the Bowman Company financial statements is:

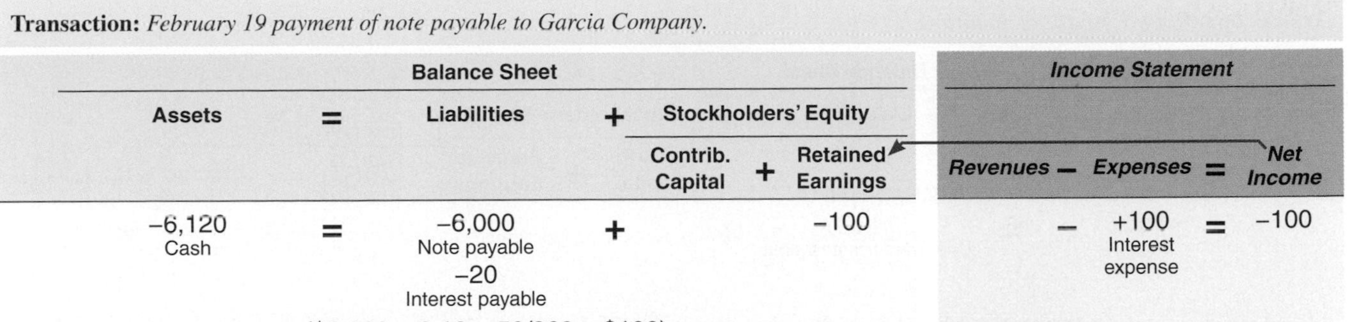

Transaction: February 19 payment of note payable to Garcia Company.
Balance Sheet
Assets = Liabilities + Stockholders' Equity
Contrib. Capital + Retained Earnings
Income Statement
Revenues − Expenses = Net Income
−6,120 Cash = −6,000 Note payable −20 Interest payable + −100
− +100 Interest expense = −100
($6,000 × 0.12 × 50/360 = $100)

REVIEW 9.1

Compute the maturity date and the amount of interest accrued on December 31 for each of the following notes payable owed by Standard Company.

	Date of Note	Principal	Interest Rate (%)	Term
a.	October 10	$20,000	8	120 days
b.	November 22	8,500	7	90 days
c.	December 15	16,000	9	75 days

The solution is on page 332.

Current Portion of Long-Term Debt

The repayment of many long-term obligations involves a series of principal payment installments over several years. To report liabilities involving installments, any principal due within one year (or the operating cycle, if longer) is reported as a current liability on the balance sheet. Failure to reclassify the currently maturing portion of any long-term debt due within the next year as a current liability can mislead readers regarding the total current obligations of a business.

Income Taxes Payable

The U.S. Federal Government, most states, and some municipalities levy income taxes against corporations, individuals, estates, and trusts. Sole proprietorships and partnerships are not taxable entities—their owners include any business income on their personal income tax return.

The tax due is determined in accordance with tax law, rulings by taxing agencies, and court decisions. Because the administration of tax law is quite complex and many honest differences exist in their interpretation, the tax obligation reported on a tax return is only an estimate until the government reviews and accepts a firm's (or individual's) calculations.

Because corporations are separate taxable entities, they incur a legal obligation for income taxes whenever income is earned. Therefore, corporate financial statements routinely include income tax liabilities and the related income tax expense.

Corporations usually pay their estimated income taxes quarterly, with final payment due within a few months following the end of a calendar year. Thus, any liability for income taxes in the financial statements is classified as a current liability because payment is expected in the short-term.

Unearned Revenue

Airline tickets, gift cards, cruise-line tickets, season football tickets, and cellular phone connection charges are examples of unearned revenue. A customer pays cash in advance for these services, and the service provider agrees to provide future services. As an example, assume that **Southwest Airlines Co.**, sells a ticket for $400 on March 20 for travel on May 25. Southwest increases cash for the amount of the ticket sale and increases a liability for the unearned revenue as follows:

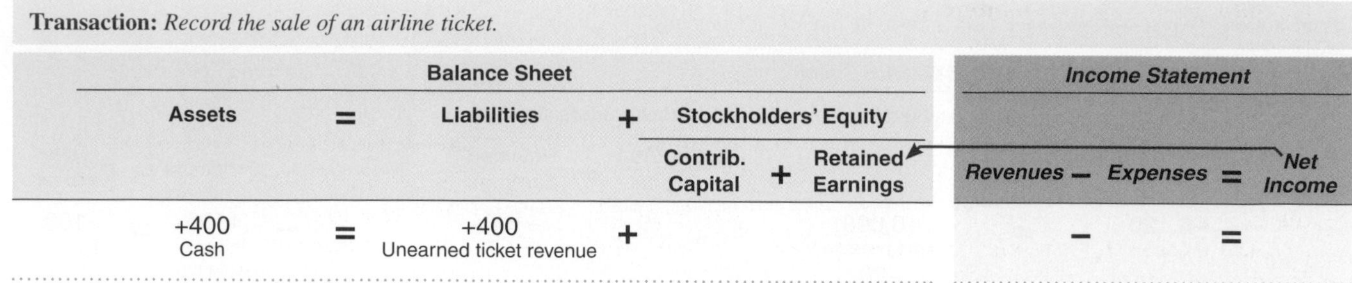

Transaction: *Record the sale of an airline ticket.*

Balance Sheet							Income Statement				
Assets	=	Liabilities	+	Stockholders' Equity							
				Contrib. Capital	+	Retained Earnings	*Revenues*	–	*Expenses*	=	*Net Income*
+400 Cash	=	+400 Unearned ticket revenue	+					–		=	

When the passenger takes the scheduled flight, the airline records the earned revenue as follows:

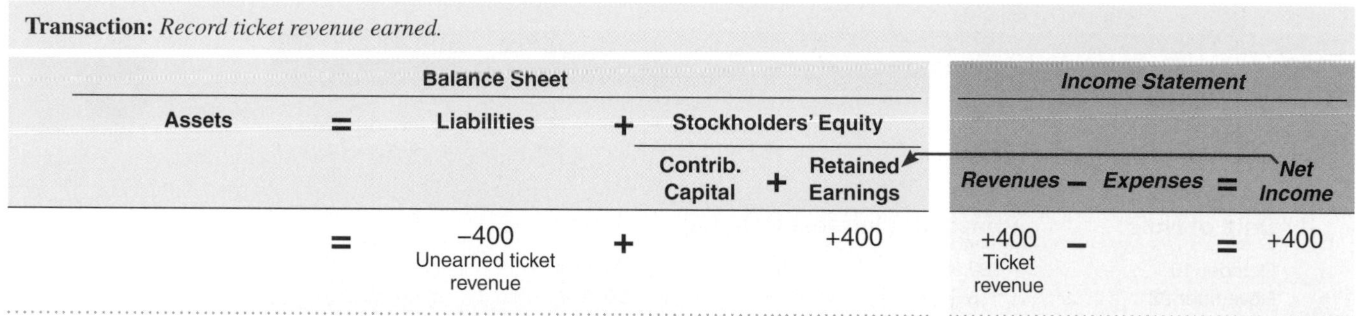

Transaction: *Record ticket revenue earned.*

Balance Sheet							Income Statement				
Assets	=	Liabilities	+	Stockholders' Equity							
				Contrib. Capital	+	Retained Earnings	*Revenues*	–	*Expenses*	=	*Net Income*
	=	–400 Unearned ticket revenue	+			+400	+400 Ticket revenue	–		=	+400

ENVIRONMENTAL, SOCIAL, AND GOVERNANCE

Aligning Business and Citizenship Being socially responsible does not mean simply trying to solve the world's problems single-handedly. To do things that one has no particular competence in is wasteful, and it makes far more sense and is far more responsible to do things to help others using one's strengths. Few would contest that one of Microsoft Corporation's strengths is technology. Although technology has led to phenomenal advances in productivity and economic growth in developed countries, much of the world still has little access to this technology. Microsoft's mission is "to empower every person and every organization on the planet to achieve more." Microsoft's Global Skills initiative combines Microsoft's technology, business strategies, and citizenship efforts with global nonprofit partners to take aim at the needs of local communities. The impact of these partnerships spans the world with people from 231 countries and all 50 states increasing their digital skills. Microsoft has made a $20 million investment in its global skills initiative, which they hope will make data analytics available globally. "We are committed to leveraging our range of resources to help people develop new digital skills and get back to work, secure a new job—or to maintain the job they already have."

LONG-TERM LIABILITIES

Businesses often require long-term funds to finance their operations and acquire long-term operating assets. Companies can use debt to meet their long-term financing needs by issuing bonds or long-term notes. A **bond** is a long-term debt instrument that promises to pay interest periodically as well as a principal amount at maturity, to the bond investor. In the United States, bond interest is usually paid semiannually. The principal amount is referred to as the bond's face value (because it is printed on the face of the bond certificate), par value, or maturity value. Whereas bonds are usually issued to the general public with a large number of buyers, long-term notes are usually arranged with a single lender. The borrower typically signs a note payable, and the debt is referred to as a **term loan**.

Advantages of Bonds and Long-Term Notes

Corporations can meet their long-term financing needs by issuing common stock or by issuing bonds or notes. The *advantages* of obtaining long-term funds by issuing bonds and notes instead of common stock include:

1. **No dilution of ownership interest.** Bondholders and noteholders are creditors of the corporation, not shareholders. Issuing bonds or notes does not change the proportionate ownership interest of any of the shareholders.
2. **Tax deductibility of interest expense.** Interest expense is deductible as an expense on a corporation's income tax return. Dividend payments to shareholders are not tax deductible.
3. **Income to common shareholders can increase. Leverage** refers to the use of borrowed funds, particularly long-term debt, to finance a business's growth. When a firm is able to earn a return on its borrowed funds that exceeds the cost of borrowing the funds, it creates income for the shareholders.

For example, assume that a firm can earn 15 percent on $5,000,000 obtained by issuing bonds and notes that have a 10 percent interest rate. If the firm pays income taxes at a 40 percent rate, its net income will increase $150,000 each year, as follows:

Earnings on funds borrowed: 15 percent × $5,000,000	$750,000
Interest cost on funds borrowed: 10 percent × $5,000,000	**(500,000)**
Increase in income before income tax expense	$250,000
Income tax expense on increase: 40 percent × $250,000	**(100,000)**
Increase in net income	$150,000

The $150,000 increase in net income accrues exclusively to the company's common stockholders.

Disadvantages of Bonds and Long-Term Notes

Not all aspects of issuing bonds and notes, however, are necessarily desirable for the borrowing company. Among the *disadvantages* of issuing bonds and notes are the following:

1. **Interest expense is a contractual obligation.** In contrast with dividends on common stock, interest represents a fixed periodic expenditure that the firm is contractually obligated to pay.
2. **Funds borrowed have a specific repayment date.** Borrowers have to repay the obligation at a specified maturity date. Firms that fail to make interest payments or repay their debt (perhaps due to poor performance), may be forced into bankruptcy.
3. **Borrowing agreement can restrict company actions.** The legal document setting forth the terms of a debt issue is called an *indenture.* Some of the provisions in an indenture may involve restrictions on dividend payments, restrictions on additional financing, and specification of minimum financial ratios that must be maintained. These provisions, called debt covenants, provide protection for debtholders but limit the company's ability to engage in various activities that could benefit its shareholders.

Types of Bonds

There are many types of bonds, the features of which may cater to certain lending situations, appeal to special investor groups, or provide special repayment patterns.

Secured bonds, for example, pledge specific property as security for meeting the terms of the bond agreement. The specific title of the bonds may indicate the type of property pledged—for example, real estate mortgage bonds (land or buildings), chattel mortgage bonds (machinery or equipment), and collateral trust bonds (negotiable securities).

Bonds that have no specific property pledged as security for their repayment are called **debentures**. Buyers of debentures rely on a borrower's general credit reputation. Because a lender's risk is usually greater than with secured bonds, debentures must offer a higher rate of interest in order to attract buyers.

The maturity dates of **serial bonds** are staggered over a series of years. For example, a serial bond issue of $15 million may provide for $1 million of the bonds to mature each year for 15 years. An advantage of serial bonds is that bond investors can choose bonds with maturity dates that correspond with their desired length of investment.

Convertible bonds grant the bondholder the right to convert the bonds into a company's common stock at some specific exchange (or conversion) ratio. This provision gives an investor the security of being a creditor during a certain stage of a firm's life, with the option of becoming a stockholder if the firm becomes sufficiently profitable. Because the conversion feature is attractive to potential investors, convertible bonds offer lower rates than similar bonds without the conversion feature.

A.K.A. *Junk bonds* are often referred to as high-yield bonds because of the higher yield rates that typically accompany this type of debt investment.

ACCOUNTING IN PRACTICE

Bond Risk Ratings The relative riskiness of different bonds may vary considerably. Bond investors who want to know the relative quality of a particular bond issue can consult a bond-rating service. Two major firms that rate the riskiness of bonds are **Standard & Poor's Corporation** (S&P) and **Moody's Investors Service** (Moody's). The rating categories used by these firms are similar. The following schedule shows the relationship between the ratings and the degree of risk using Standard & Poor's rating system:

Low Risk							High Risk
AAA	AA	A	BBB	BB	B	CCC	D
I- - - - - - - - Investment Grade Bonds - - - - - - - -				-I- - - - - - - - Junk Bonds - - -			I

Investment grade bonds are highly-rated bonds with little risk that the issuing company will fail to pay interest as scheduled or fail to repay the principal at a bond's maturity. Junk bonds, on the other hand, are low-quality, high-yield bonds. In the S&P rating system, junk bonds are any bond rated BB and lower. Generally, bonds with poor credit ratings must offer higher interest rates than highly-rated bonds to attract potential buyers.

Zero-coupon bonds are bonds that pay no periodic interest but are issued at a substantial discount from their face value. The face value is paid to the bondholder at maturity. The total interest implicit in the bond contract is the difference between the bond's original issue price and its face value at maturity. For example, a five-year, $1,000 face value zero-coupon bond issued for $713 will pay the lender $1,000 at the end of the five years. The total interest associated with this bond is $287 ($1,000 – $713). Zero-coupon bonds are helpful to borrowers when the project being financed with the bond proceeds provides no cash inflows until the bond maturity date. Zero-coupon bonds are popular with insurance companies and pension plans, who have expected pay-offs in the future and who do not wish to worry about reinvesting periodic interest payments.

Bond Features

Bonds with a **call provision** allow the bond issuer to repurchase (or "call") the bonds from the buyer at a pre-specified price. Usually, an extra amount or premium must be paid to the holders of a called bond. A call provision offers borrowers additional financing flexibility that may be significant if funds become available at interest rates substantially lower than those currently being paid on the bonds. Borrowers can, in effect, also "call" any of their bonds by buying them in the open market at the prevailing market price.

A **sinking fund provision** requires that a borrower retire a portion of its outstanding bonds each year or, in some bond issues, make payments each year to a trustee who is responsible for managing the funds needed to retire the bonds at maturity. The orderly retirement of bonds, or the accumulation of funds needed at maturity, as required by a sinking fund provision is generally viewed as making any bond safer (less risky) for the bondholders.

ACCOUNTING IN PRACTICE

Microsoft Bond Issuance and Company Value As noted in the opening feature story, **Microsoft** was essentially debt free until 2009. Following the $3.75 billion in bonds that Microsoft issued in late 2009, part of a larger $6 billion debt issue that the board of directors approved, analysts weighed in on why they thought this occurred. Noting that Microsoft also authorized a plan to buy back $40 billion of its own stock over the following five years, Sid Parakh, an analyst at McAdams Wright Ragen stated, "They said a few months ago they would like to leverage the balance sheets; that's what they're doing. Lowering the cost of capital will probably benefit shareholder value in the long term."

Bond Prices

LO3 **Explain** bond pricing and **illustrate** two methods of amortizing bond discounts/premiums.

Bonds are typically sold in units of $1,000 face (maturity) value, and the market price is expressed as a percentage of face value. Thus, a $1,000 face value bond that is quoted at 98 will sell for $980. Generally, bond prices fluctuate in response to changes in market interest rates, which are determined by government monetary policies (managing the demand and supply of money) and economic expectations. Bond prices also are affected by the financial outlook for the issuing firm.

A bond specifies a pattern of future cash flows, usually a series of interest payments and a single payment at maturity equal to the bond's face value. The amount of the periodic interest payment is determined by the **coupon rate** stated on the bond certificate. Interest rates are usually quoted as annual rates, so the coupon rate will need to be converted to a per period interest rate when interest is paid more than once a year. For example, in the United States, bond interest is usually paid semiannually, with the payments six months apart. Thus, the amount of interest paid semiannually is calculated by multiplying one-half the coupon rate of interest times the bond's face value.

A bond's market price is determined by discounting the bond's future cash flows (both its principal and interest payments) to the present using the current **market rate of interest** for the bond as the discount rate, a process known as *computing the bond's present value.* The market rate is the rate of return investors expect on their investment.

When issued, a bond's price may be equal to, less than, or greater than its face value. Bonds sell at *face value* when the market rate of interest equals the bond's coupon rate. Bonds sell at a *discount* (less than face value) when the market interest rate exceeds the bond's coupon rate; and, bonds sell at a *premium* (more than face value) when the market interest rate is less than the bond's coupon rate.

Since a bond's coupon rate is determined before the bonds are actually sold, and interest rates change over time, the market rate and coupon rate will often differ. Market rates and coupon rates are frequently stated in percentage terms, although increasingly, these rates are stated as "basis points." One percentage point is equal to one hundred basis points. Thus, a bond with a coupon rate of three percent is said to have a coupon rate of 300 basis points.

A.K.A. A bond's *face value* is also referred to as its maturity value, stated value, or settlement value.

A.K.A. A bond's *coupon rate* of interest is also referred to as its nominal rate or stated rate of interest.

A.K.A. A bond's *market rate of interest* is also referred to as its effective rate or its yield.

THINKING GLOBALLY

U.S. GAAP and IFRS are substantially aligned when it comes to the reporting of liabilities. Under both accounting systems, for example, current liabilities (Accounts Payable) are reported at their settlement or future value, or the amount of money required to satisfy the obligation when it becomes due. Similarly, both systems require that long-term liabilities, like Bonds Payable, be reported at their present value, or the amount of money necessary to currently satisfy the obligation. Where the two systems diverge is in regards to the reporting of some contingent liabilities (to be discussed shortly).

Exhibit 9-1 computes the issue price for bonds issued at three different market rates of interest. In this example, we look at the issuance of $100,000 face amount bonds, with an eight percent annual coupon rate payable semiannually, due in four years. The semiannual interest payment on the bonds is $4,000 ($100,000 × 0.08 × ½). Thus, this bond issue promises to pay the buyers a stream of cash payments that will consist of the eight semiannual interest payments of $4,000 every six months over the four years of the bonds' term, plus the $100,000 face amount of the bond at its maturity at the end of the four years. The selling price of the bonds will depend upon the market interest rates that prevail at the time the bonds are issued. Recall that the market interest rate at which the bonds are sold can differ from the coupon rate the company is paying on the bonds, because interest rates can increase or decrease between the time the company sets the coupon rate and the time the company actually issues the bonds. **Exhibit 9-1** computes the selling price using three different market (or effective) interest rates: (1) eight percent (which is equal to the coupon rate), (2) ten percent (which is above the coupon rate), and (3) six percent (which is below the coupon rate).

EXHIBIT 9-1 Calculating Bond Issue Price Using Present Value Tables*

Sold at Face Value

❶ $100,000 of eight percent, four-year bonds with interest payable semiannually sold to yield eight percent:

	Multiplier (Table III)	Multiplier (Table IV)	Present Values at 4% Semiannually (8% × ½)
A. Principal repayment, $100,000 (a single amount paid eight semiannual periods hence)	0.73069		$ 73,069
B. Interest payments, $4,000 at end of each of eight semiannual interest periods.		6.73274	26,931
C. Total present value (or issue price) of bonds			**$100,000** Face value

Sold at a Discount

❷ $100,000 of eight percent, four-year bonds with interest payable semiannually sold to yield ten percent:

	Multiplier (Table III)	Multiplier (Table IV)	Present Values at 5% Semiannually (10% × ½)
A. Principal repayment, $100,000 (a single amount paid eight semiannual periods hence)	0.67684		$ 67,684
B. Interest payments, $4,000 at end of each of eight semiannual interest periods.		6.46321	25,853
C. Total present value (or issue price) of bonds			**$ 93,537** Discount

Sold at a Premium

❸ $100,000 of eight percent, four-year bonds with interest payable semiannually sold to yield six percent:

	Multiplier (Table III)	Multiplier (Table IV)	Present Values at 3% Semiannually (6% × ½)
A. Principal repayment, $100,000 (a single amount paid eight semiannual periods hence)	0.78941		$ 78,941
B. Interest payments, $4,000 at end of each of eight semiannual interest periods		7.01969	28,079
C. Total present value (or issue price) of bonds			**$107,020** Premium

* See Tables III and IV in Appendix E "Accounting for the Time Value of Money."

To calculate the present values, **Exhibit 9-1** uses Appendix E, as follows:

A. Table III in Appendix E is used to calculate the present value of the future principal repayment at the bonds' effective rate of interest.
B. Table IV in Appendix E is used to calculate the present value of the future series of interest payments at the bonds' effective rate of interest.
C. The two present value calculations obtained in steps one and two are added together to arrive at the purchase price of the bonds.

As shown in the exhibit, the bond is:

1. Sold at ***face value*** when the market rate (eight percent) equals the coupon rate (eight percent).
2. Sold at a ***discount*** when the market rate (ten percent) exceeds the coupon rate (eight percent).
3. Sold at a ***premium*** when the market rate (six percent) is less than the coupon rate (eight percent).

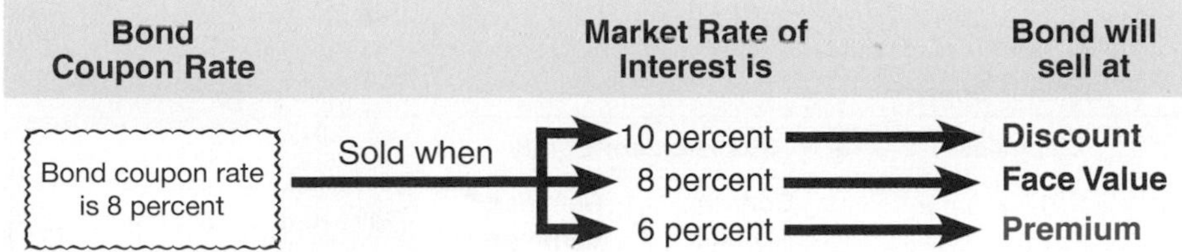

Financial Statement Effect of Issuing Bonds

Bonds Issued at Face Value

Face Value Bonds

To provide a simple illustration, we use a bond with a short period to maturity. Assume that on December 31, Year 1, Reid, Inc., issues at face value $100,000 of eight percent bonds that mature in four years with interest paid on June 30 and December 31. The following shows the effect on the financial statements of issuing the bonds, which are sold at face value:

Transaction: *Issuance of bonds at face value.*

Balance Sheet							*Income Statement*				
Assets	=	Liabilities	+	Stockholders' Equity: Contrib. Capital	+	Retained Earnings	*Revenues*	−	*Expenses*	=	*Net Income*
+100,000 Cash	=	+100,000 Bonds payable	+					−		=	

Interest of $4,000 ($100,000 × 0.08 × 6/12) will be paid on each of the eight payment dates (four years, semiannual payments). For example, on June 30, Year 2, the first interest payment date, the financial statement effect is:

Transaction: *Payment of semiannual interest on bonds.*

Balance Sheet							*Income Statement*				
Assets	=	Liabilities	+	Stockholders' Equity: Contrib. Capital	+	Retained Earnings	*Revenues*	−	*Expenses*	=	*Net Income*
−4,000 Cash	=		+			−4,000		−	+4,000 Bond interest expense	=	−4,000

When the bonds mature, Reid, Inc., records their retirement as follows (this assumes the December 31, Year 5, interest payment is separately recorded):

Transaction: *Retirement of bonds at maturity.*

Balance Sheet							*Income Statement*				
Assets	=	Liabilities	+	Stockholders' Equity: Contrib. Capital	+	Retained Earnings	*Revenues*	−	*Expenses*	=	*Net Income*
−100,000 Cash	=	−100,000 Bonds payable	+					−		=	

Bonds Issued at a Discount

Discounted Bonds

If the coupon rate of interest on the bonds issued is less than the current market rate, the bonds will be sold at a price less than their face value. In such cases, investors "discount" the price of the bonds to enable the buyer to earn the current market rate of interest. For example, assume that Reid, Inc.'s $100,000 issue of eight percent, four-year bonds is sold on December 31, Year 1, for $93,537. This price permits investors to earn an interest rate of ten percent. (For calculations, please see **Exhibit 9-1**.) The following records the issuance of the bonds at a discount:

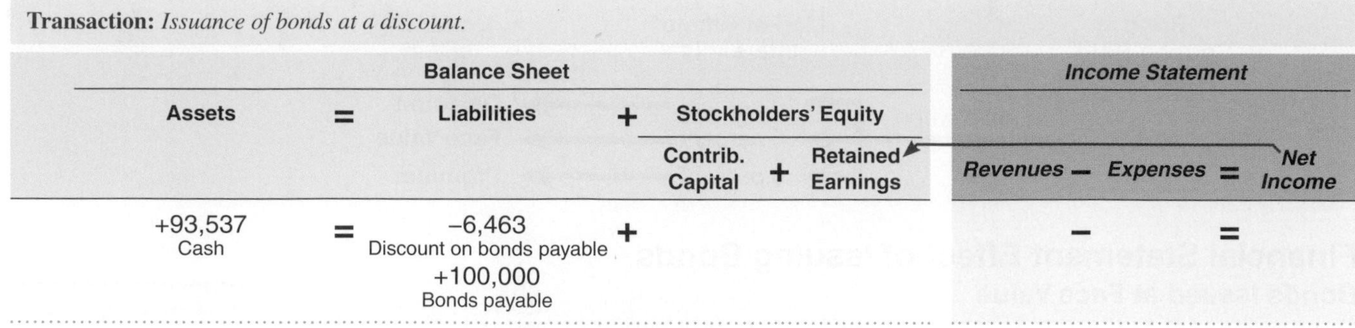

Transaction: *Issuance of bonds at a discount.*

Balance Sheet							Income Statement				
Assets	=	Liabilities	+	Stockholders' Equity							
				Contrib. Capital	+	Retained Earnings	Revenues	−	Expenses	=	Net Income
+93,537 Cash	=	−6,463 Discount on bonds payable +100,000 Bonds payable	+					−		=	

The $6,463 discount is not an immediate loss or expense to Reid, Inc. It represents an adjustment of interest expense over the life of the bonds. This can be illustrated by comparing the funds that Reid, Inc., receives with the funds it must pay to the bondholders. Regardless of their selling price, the bonds represent an agreement to pay $132,000 to the bondholders ($100,000 principal plus eight semiannual interest payments of $4,000 each).

Total funds paid to bondholders	$132,000
Total funds received from bond sale.	(93,537)
Difference equals total interest expense.	38,463
Total semiannual interest payments ([$100,000 × 8% = $8,000] × 4 years).	(32,000)
Increase in interest expense beyond semiannual interest payments (aka *bond discount*)	**$ 6,463**

The total interest expense for this four-year bond issue is $38,463, the difference between the total cash paid to the bondholders and the proceeds from the sale of the bonds. The semiannual interest payments to bondholders total $32,000, so an additional $6,463 must be recognized as interest expense over the life of the bonds. The $6,463 is the amount of the bond discount. To reflect the larger periodic interest expense, the bond discount is *amortized over the eight interest payment periods*. Amortization of a bond discount means that, periodically, an amount is transferred from the Discount on Bonds Payable account to the Bond Interest Expense account. The methods of calculating amortization will be discussed later in this chapter.

Premium Bonds

Bonds Issued at a Premium

If the market rate of interest had been below the eight percent offered by Reid, Inc., investors would have been willing to pay a premium to buy the bonds. Suppose that the market interest rate was six percent. Reid Inc.'s $100,000, eight percent, four-year bonds would sell for $107,020 (for calculations, please see **Exhibit 9-1**). The issuance of the bonds on December 31, Year 1, is recorded as follows:

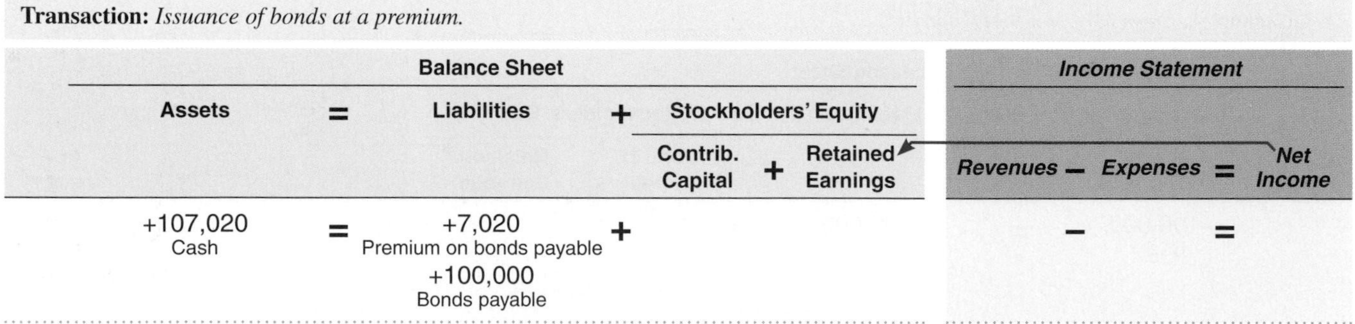

Transaction: *Issuance of bonds at a premium.*

Balance Sheet							Income Statement				
Assets	=	Liabilities	+	Stockholders' Equity							
				Contrib. Capital	+	Retained Earnings	Revenues	−	Expenses	=	Net Income
+107,020 Cash	=	+7,020 Premium on bonds payable +100,000 Bonds payable	+					−		=	

When bonds are issued at a premium, the book value of the bond liability is determined by adding the Premium on the Bonds Payable account balance to the Bonds Payable account balance.

Like a bond discount, a bond premium is considered an adjustment of interest expense over the life of the bonds. We saw that a bond discount represents the excess of total interest expense over the total semiannual interest payments. A similar analysis shows that a bond premium represents the amount by which the total semiannual interest payments exceed the total interest expense. The analysis begins by comparing the total funds that will be paid to the bondholders over the four years (again, it is $132,000) with the proceeds received when the bonds are issued:

Total funds paid to bondholders	$132,000
Total funds received from bond sale	(107,020)
Difference equals total interest expense	24,980
Total semiannual interest payments ([$100,000 × 8% = $8,000] × 4 years)	(32,000)
Decrease in interest expense below semiannual interest payments (aka *bond premium*)	**$ 7,020**

The total interest expense for this four-year bond issue is $24,980, an amount that is $7,020 less than the total semiannual interest payments to be made to bondholders. The $7,020 is the amount of the bond premium. The bond premium is amortized to cause the periodic interest expense to be less than the semiannual interest payment.

Interest Expense and Amortization

Each time an interest payment is made, a portion of the bond discount or premium is amortized to interest expense. There are two methods of bond amortization: the straight-line method and the effective interest method. Under the *straight-line method*, the amount of the amortization is the same each period. Under the effective interest method, the amount of the amortization varies each period. GAAP requires the *effective interest method*, except in cases in which the differences between the two methods is not material.

Straight-line Method of Amortization

A bond discount or premium can be amortized to interest expense using the straight-line method when the difference between it and the effective method are not material. The **straight-line method** amortizes an equal amount of interest expense from the bond discount or premium each interest period. In the case in which the bonds are sold at a discount, interest expense equals the amount of the coupon interest payment *plus* the discount divided by the number of interest periods. When issued at a premium, interest expense equals the amount of the coupon interest payment *less* the amount of the premium divided by the number of interest periods.

Straight-line Method of Discount Amortization

Exhibit 9-2 presents the bond accounts for Reid, Inc., at the issuance date and for each interest payment period, using the straight-line method of amortization. Column A lists the coupon interest payment for each six-month period, which equals the coupon interest rate times the bond's face value ($4,000 = 8% × 6/12 × $100,000). Column B lists the amount of the discount that is amortized each six-month period, which equals the amount of the discount when the bond was issued,

EXHIBIT 9-2 Bonds Sold at a Discount: Straight-line Method

$100,000 of 8%, four-year bonds with interest payable semiannually issued on December 31, Year 1, at $93,537 to yield 10%

Year	Interest Period	A Interest Paid (8% × 1/2 × face value)	B Straight-line Amortization ($6,463/8)	C Interest Expense (A + B)	D Balance of Unamortized Discount (D – B)	E Book Value of Bonds—End of Period ($100,000 – D)
At issue...					$6,463	$ 93,537
2........	1	$4,000	$808	$4,808	5,655	94,345
	2	4,000	808	4,808	4,847	95,153
3........	3	4,000	808	4,808	4,039	95,961
	4	4,000	808	4,808	3,231	96,769
4........	5	4,000	808	4,808	2,423	97,577
	6	4,000	808	4,808	1,615	98,385
5........	7	4,000	808	4,808	807	99,193
	8	4,000	807*	4,807	—	100,000

*Adjusted for cumulative rounding error of $1

divided by the number of interest payments ($808 = $6,463/8). Column C lists the total interest expense for each period, which equals the sum of the coupon interest payment (Column A) plus the discount amortization (Column B). Column D lists the balance of the unamortized discount at the end of each period, and Column E lists the book value of the bond at the end of each period, which equals the face value of the bond minus the ending balance of the discount.

The amounts recorded for each interest payment can be read directly from the amortization schedule. Interest expense and the amortization of the discount will be the same for each interest period. The financial statement effect of the first interest payment follows:

Transaction: *Semiannual interest payment and amortization of bond discount.*

Balance Sheet							Income Statement				
Assets	=	Liabilities	+	Stockholders' Equity							
				Contrib. Capital	+	Retained Earnings	Revenues	−	Expenses	=	Net Income
4,000 Cash	=	+808 Discount on bonds payable	+			−4,808		−	+4,808 Bond interest expense	=	−4,808

Amortizing the bond discount over the four-year life of the bonds leaves a zero balance in the Discount on Bonds Payable account on the maturity date of the bonds. The retirement of the bonds at maturity then is recorded by reducing Bonds Payable and Cash by $100,000, the amount of their face value.

Straight-line Method of Premium Amortization

The straight-line method for amortizing a bond premium is handled the same way as bond discount amortization. **Exhibit 9-3** shows the amortization schedule for Reid, Inc., when the bonds are issued at a premium, using the straight-line amortization method. Column A lists the coupon interest payment for each six-month period ($4,000 = 8% × 6/12 × $100,000), and Column B lists the amount of the premium that is amortized each six-month period ($878 = $7,020/8). Column C lists the total interest expense for each period. In the case of a premium, the amortization of the premium (Column B) is deducted from the coupon interest payment (Column A) to compute the total interest expense for the period (Column C). Column D lists the balance of the unamortized premium at the end of each period, and Column E lists the book value of the bond at the end of each period, which equals the face value of the bond plus the ending balance of the premium.

EXHIBIT 9-3 Bonds Sold at a Premium: Straight-line Method

$100,000 of 8%, four-year bonds with interest payable semiannually issued on December 31, Year 1, at $107,020 to yield 6%

Year	Interest Period	A Interest Paid (8% × 1/2 × face value)	B Straight-line Amortization ($7,020/8)	C Interest Expense (A – B)	D Balance of Unamortized Discount (D – B)	E Book Value of Bonds—End of Period ($100,000 + D)
At issue. . .					$7,020	$107,020
2.	1	$4,000	$878	$3,122	6,142	106,142
	2	4,000	878	3,122	5,264	105,264
3.	3	4,000	878	3,122	4,386	104,386
	4	4,000	878	3,122	3,508	103,508
4.	5	4,000	878	3,122	2,630	102,630
	6	4,000	878	3,122	1,752	101,752
5.	7	4,000	878	3,122	874	100,874
	8	4,000	874*	3,126	—	100,000

*Adjusted for cumulative rounding error of $4

Note that the periodic interest expense is less than the semiannual interest payment when bonds are issued at a premium. The financial statement effect of the first interest payment follows.

Transaction: *Semiannual interest payment and amortization of bond premium.*

Balance Sheet							Income Statement				
Assets	=	Liabilities	+	Stockholders' Equity							
				Contrib. Capital	+	Retained Earnings	*Revenues*	−	*Expenses*	=	*Net Income*
−4,000 Cash	=	−878 Premium on bonds payable	+			−3,122		−	+3,122 Bond interest expense	=	−3,122

Effective Interest Method of Amortization

The **effective interest method** of amortization recognizes a constant percentage of the book value of a bond as interest expense for each interest payment period. The book value of a bond is the balance in the Bonds Payable account less the balance in the Discount on Bonds Payable account, or plus the balance in the Premium on Bonds Payable account. To obtain a period's interest expense under the effective interest method, we multiply the bond's book value at the beginning of each period by the effective interest rate. The **effective interest rate** is the market rate of interest used to price the bonds when they are originally issued. The difference between this amount and the amount of interest paid (coupon interest rate × face value of bonds) is the amount of discount or premium amortized. When using the effective interest method of amortization, accountants often prepare an amortization schedule similar to the one in **Exhibit 9-4**. This schedule covers the four-year life of the Reid, Inc., bonds issued at a discount.

Effective Interest Method of Discount Amortization

Exhibit 9-4 presents the various components for the Reid, Inc., bonds for the six-month interest payment periods. The interest rates shown in columns A and B are one-half the annual rates. Column A lists the constant amounts of interest paid each six months—that is, the coupon interest rate times the face value (8 percent × 6/12 × $100,000). The amounts in Column B are obtained by multiplying the book value as of the beginning of each period, which equals the ending balance from the prior period as shown in (column E), by the effective interest rate of 5 percent for the six month period (10% × 6/12). For example, the $4,677 interest expense for the first period is 5 percent times $93,537; for the second period, it is 5 percent times $94,214, or $4,711, and so on. The reported value of the bonds changes each period. For discounted bonds, the value increases each period because the book value increases over the life of the bonds until it reaches the face value on the maturity date. The amount of discount amortization for each period, given in column C, is the difference between the corresponding amounts in columns A and B. Column D lists the amount of unamortized discount at the end of each period.

EXHIBIT 9-4 Bonds Sold at a Discount: Effective Interest Method

$100,000 of 8%, four-year bonds with interest payable semiannually issued on December 31, Year 1, at $93,537 to yield 10%

Year	Interest Period	A Interest Paid (8% × 1/2 × face value)	B Interest Expense (10% × 1/2 × bond book value)	C Periodic Amortization (B - A)	D Balance of Unamortized Discount (D - C)	E Book Value of Bonds, End of Period ($100,000 - D)
At issue. . .					$6,463	$ 93,537
2.	1	$4,000	$4,677	$677	5,786	94,214
	2	4,000	4,711	711	5,075	94,925
3.	3	4,000	4,746	746	4,329	95,671
	4	4,000	4,784	784	3,545	96,455
4.	5	4,000	4,823	823	2,722	97,278
	6	4,000	4,864	864	1,858	98,142
5.	7	4,000	4,907	907	951	99,049
	8	4,000	4,951*	951	0	100,000

*Adjusted for cumulative rounding error of $1

The amounts recorded for each interest payment can be read directly from the amortization schedule. The financial statement effect of the interest expense and discount amortization at the first interest payment follows:

Transaction: *Semiannual interest payment and amortization of bond discount.*

Balance Sheet							Income Statement				
Assets	=	Liabilities	+	Stockholders' Equity							
				Contrib. Capital	+	Retained Earnings	Revenues	−	Expenses	=	Net Income
−4,000 Cash	=	+677 Discount on bonds payable	+			−4,677		−	+4,677 Bond interest expense	=	−4,677

Amortizing the bond discount over the four-year life of the bonds leaves a zero balance in the Discount on Bonds Payable account on the maturity date of the bonds. The retirement of the bonds at maturity is then recorded by reducing Bonds Payable and Cash by $100,000, the amount of their face value.

PRINCIPLE ALERT

Materiality Concept Under U.S. GAAP, the effective interest method is the preferred method of bond amortization. It is generally accepted because it uses the actual market rate of interest when the bonds were originally issued to determine the amount of the periodic amortization. The effective interest method, however, is somewhat more complex than the straight-line method. Accounting standards permit the straight-line method of amortization to be used when the results are not materially different from those achieved under the effective interest method. This exception represents an application of the *materiality concept*. As previously discussed, the materiality concept permits insignificant accounting transactions to be recorded most expediently. Here, the materiality concept permits a simpler (and, thus, more expedient) straight-line method to be used when it results in insignificant differences from the theoretically superior effective interest method.

Effective Interest Method of Premium Amortization

The effective interest method of amortizing a bond premium is handled the same way as a bond discount amortization. Each interest period, a constant percentage of the bonds' book value as of the beginning of the period is recognized as interest expense; the difference between the interest expense and the semiannual interest payment is the amount of the premium amortization.

Exhibit 9-5 shows the amortization schedule for the four-year life of the Reid, Inc., bonds that were issued at a premium.

EXHIBIT 9-5 Bonds Sold at a Premium: Effective Interest Method

$100,000 of 8%, four-year bonds with interest payable semiannually issued on December 31, Year 1, at $107,020 to yield 6%

		A	B	C	D	E
Year	Interest Period	Interest Paid (8% × 1/2 × face value)	Interest Expense (6% × 1/2 × bond book value)	Periodic Amortization (A − B)	Balance of Unamortized Premium (D − C)	Book Value of Bonds, End of Period ($100,000 + D)
At issue. . .					$7,020	$107,020
2	1	$4,000	$3,211	$789	6,231	106,231
	2	4,000	3,187	813	5,418	105,418
3	3	4,000	3,163	837	4,581	104,581
	4	4,000	3,137	863	3,718	103,718
4	5	4,000	3,112	888	2,830	102,830
	6	4,000	3,085	915	1,915	101,915
5	7	4,000	3,057	943	972	100,972
	8	4,000	3,028*	972	0	100,000

*Adjusted for cumulative rounding error of $1

The amounts for each interest payment are taken directly from the amortization schedule. The financial statement effect of the first interest payment follows. Note that the periodic interest expense is less than the semiannual interest payment.

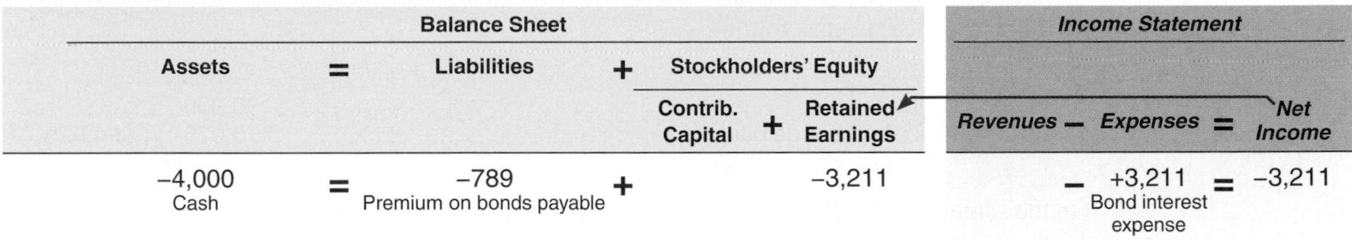

Transaction: *Semiannual interest payment and amortization of bond premium.*

Assets	=	Liabilities	+	Contrib. Capital	+	Retained Earnings	Revenues	−	Expenses	=	Net Income
−4,000 Cash	=	−789 Premium on bonds payable	+			−3,211		−	+3,211 Bond interest expense	=	−3,211

After amortizing the bond premium over the four-year life of the bonds, the balance in the Premium on Bonds Payable account is zero. When the bonds mature at the end of four years, the retirement reduces Bonds Payable and Cash for the $100,000 face value of the bonds.

REVIEW 9.2

The following are selected transactions for Tyler, Inc., for Year 1 and Year 2. The firm ends its fiscal year on December 31.

Year 1

Dec. 31 Issued $500,000 of 12 percent, ten-year bonds for $562,360, yielding an effective rate of ten percent. Interest is payable June 30 and December 31.

Year 2

June 30 Paid semiannual interest and recorded semiannual premium amortization on bonds.
Dec. 31 Paid semiannual interest and recorded semiannual premium amortization on bonds.

REQUIRED

a. Using Exhibit 9-5 as an example, prepare an effective interest amortization schedule for this bond issue.

b. Determine the financial statement effect of the transactions.

The solution is on pages 332–333.

Year-End Adjustments

When a periodic interest payment does not correspond with the fiscal year-end, an adjustment should be recorded reflecting the amount of interest expense incurred but not yet paid. The adjustment also includes a pro rata amortization of bond discount or bond premium for the portion of the year involved.

PRINCIPLE ALERT

Matching Concept The adjustment to record interest expense incurred but not yet paid is an application of the *expense recognition* (*matching*) *concept.* This accounting concept states that all expenses incurred to generate sales revenue must be recorded, regardless of when the expense is paid in cash. Interest is a charge for the use of money, and this charge is incurred every day that a borrower has use of, and benefits from, borrowed funds.

Bonds Payable Disclosed on the Balance Sheet

Bonds payable that mature more than one year in the future are classified as long-term liabilities on the balance sheet. Bonds payable maturing within the next year, on the other hand, are classified as current liabilities. The Discount on Bonds Payable is classified as a deduction from and Premium on Bonds Payable as an addition to the face value of the bonds reported in the balance sheet. Most companies do not separately disclose the Discount on Bonds Payable account or the Premium on Bonds Payable account on their publicly disseminated balance sheet, but rather net these amounts against the Bonds Payable account.

At December 31, Year 2, the Reid, Inc., bonds issued at a discount (see **Exhibit 9-4**) appear on Reid's balance sheet as follows:

Bonds payable	$100,000	
Less: Discount on bonds payable	5,075	$94,925

On the same date, the Reid, Inc., bonds issued at a premium (see **Exhibit 9-5**) appear as follows:

Bonds payable	$100,000	
Add: Premium on bonds payable	5,418	$105,418

REVIEW 9.3

Koby Company issued $300,000 of bonds for $325,000.

REQUIRED

a. Determine the financial statement effect of the issuance of the bonds.

b. Illustrate how the bonds will be shown on the Koby Company's balance sheet at the issuance date.

The solution is on page 333.

Long-Term Notes (Term Loans)

An obligation in the form of a written note due after the current period is referred to as a **term loan** or long-term note payable. Term loans are often repaid in equal periodic installments. The agreement may require installment payments to be made monthly, quarterly, or semiannually. Each payment contains an interest amount and a partial repayment of principal. Because the installment payments are equal, each installment payment contains different amounts of interest and principal repayment. These component amounts change with each installment because the interest is computed on the unpaid principal, and the unpaid principal is reduced with each payment.

To illustrate, assume that on December 31, Year 1, Reid, Inc., borrows $100,000 from a bank on a 12 percent, ten-year mortgage note payable. The note is to be repaid with equal quarterly installments of $4,326 (please see Appendix 9A, Example 4 for explanation on how to do this calculation). Thus, there will be 40 quarterly payments; and, the quarterly interest rate is three percent (12 percent/4 quarters). **Exhibit 9-6** presents the first eight quarterly payments (of the complete 40 quarterly payment schedule) and their division between interest expense and principal repayment.

EXHIBIT 9-6 Partial Mortgage Note Payment Schedule

$100,000 mortgage note payable with quarterly payments of $4,326 and quarterly interest rate of three percent

Payment Date	A Cash Payment	B Interest Expense (3% × D)*	C Principal Repaid (A − B)	D Book Value of Note (Unpaid Principal)
Year 1				
December 31 (issue date). . .				$100,000
Year 2				
March 31.	$4,326	$3,000	$1,326	98,674
June 30.	4,326	2,960	1,366	97,308
September 30.	4,326	2,919	1,407	95,901
December 31	4,326	2,877	1,449	94,452
Year 3				
March 31.	4,326	2,834	1,492	92,960
June 30.	4,326	2,789	1,537	91,423
September 30.	4,326	2,743	1,583	89,840
December 31	4,326	2,695	1,631	88,209

* 3 percent × Unpaid principal after previous payment (rounded to nearest dollar).

The financial statement effect of the first quarterly payment follows:

Transaction: *Quarterly mortgage loan payment.*

Assets	=	Liabilities	+	Contrib. Capital	+	Retained Earnings	Revenues	−	Expenses	=	Net Income
−4,326 Cash	=	−1,326 Mortgage note payable	+			−3,000		−	+3,000 Interest expense	=	−3,000

LEASES

Accounting for Leases

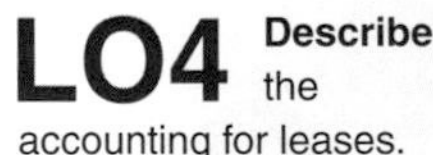

A firm may rent property for a specified period of time under a contract called a **lease**. The company acquiring the right to use the property is the **lessee**, while the owner of the property is the **lessor**.

The lessee's right to use the leased asset over the life of the lease is referred to as a **right-of-use asset**. Examples of leased assets include land, buildings, factory machinery, and office equipment. The present value of the future lease payments determines the dollar amount of the right-of-use asset and lease obligation. For example, assume that Reid, Inc., leases equipment under a lease for ten years at $40,000 per year, and that the present value of the ten lease payments is $226,009. Consequently, this transaction affects Reid's financial statements as follows:

Transaction: *Record 10-year capital lease.*

Assets	=	Liabilities	+	Contrib. Capital	+	Retained Earnings	Revenues	−	Expenses	=	Net Income
+226,009 Leased equipment	=	+226,009 Lease obligation	+					−		=	

The lessee's accounting for leases in the income statement depend upon whether the lease is a **finance lease** or an **operating lease**.

Finance Leases

A finance lease transfers *control* of the leased asset to the lessee. Economically, a finance lease is equivalent to an installment purchase. A lease that meets at least one of the following criteria is considered a finance lease:

1. The lease transfers ownership of the property to the lessee by the end of the lease term.
2. The lease contains a purchase option that enables the lessee to acquire the leased asset and the lessee is reasonably certain to exercise the option.
3. The lease term is a major part of the remaining estimated economic life of the leased asset.
4. The present value of the lease payments comprise substantially all of the fair value of the leased asset.
5. The leased asset is very specialized and would be of no use to the lessor at the end of the lease.

The leased equipment is amortized over the life of the lease and appears among the firm's plant assets in the balance sheet. The total lease obligation is divided between current liabilities and long-term liabilities in the balance sheet based on the settlement dates for the obligation. The accounting for each lease payment is similar to the accounting for an installment note payment illustrated in the previous section. Part of each lease payment made by the lessee is charged to interest expense, and the remainder reduces the lease obligation.

Operating Leases

A lease that transfers only the *use* of the leased asset is classified as an operating lease. The amortization of the asset is recorded as lease expense. No interest expense is related to the lease payments.

CONTINGENT LIABILITIES

LO5 Define *contingent liabilities* and **explain** their disclosure in the financial statements.

Recall that a *liability* is defined as an obligation resulting from past transactions or events that require a firm to pay money, provide goods, or perform services in the future. Even though a past transaction or event has taken place, the existence of some liabilities still depends on the occurrence of a future event. These types of liability are called **contingent liabilities**. Whether or not a contingent liability is recorded in the accounts depends on the likelihood of the future event occurring and the measurability of the obligation.

If the future event will *probably occur* and the amount of the liability can be *reasonably estimated,* an estimated liability should be recorded in the accounts. The estimated liability for product warranty, discussed below, is a good example of this situation. The analysis assumes that customers are likely to make claims under a warranty for goods that they had purchased, and that a reasonable estimate of the amount of the warranty obligation could be made.

Some contingent liabilities are not recorded in the accounts but must be disclosed in a note to the financial statements. Contingent liabilities disclosed in this manner are (1) those for which the likelihood of the future event occurring is probable but no reasonable estimate of the future obligation is determinable or (2) those for which the likelihood of the future event occurring is *reasonably possible* (but not probable), regardless of the ability to measure the future amount. When the future amount is not determinable, the note should state that the amount cannot be estimated.

If the likelihood of the future event occurring is *remote,* the contingent liability is not recorded in the accounts nor disclosed in the notes to the financial statements, regardless of the ability to measure the future amount. One exception to this guideline, however, is when a company guarantees the credit of others (discussed in the following section). Even remote contingent liabilities associated with credit guarantees must be disclosed in the notes to the financial statements.

PRINCIPLE ALERT

Measuring Unit Concept and Full Disclosure Principle The accounting guidelines for contingent liabilities illustrate the application of two principles of accounting: the *measuring unit concept* and the *full disclosure principle.* The measuring unit concept requires that information reported in the body of the financial statements be expressed in money terms. If a reasonable estimate of a contingent liability's dollar amount cannot be made, the measuring unit concept prevents the item from appearing in the balance sheet, even if its future occurrence is probable. However, the full disclosure principle requires that firms disclose all significant financial facts and circumstances to financial statement users. This principle leads to the reporting of likely, but unmeasurable contingent liabilities in the notes to the financial statements.

Examples of Contingent Liabilities

Situations that may create contingent liabilities are discussed in the following sections. In each of these situations, accountants must assess the likelihood of the future event occurring and the measurability of the future amount because these factors determine the proper accounting treatment of the contingent liability.

Product Warranties

Many firms guarantee their products for a period of time following their sale. A proper matching of sales revenue and expenses requires that the estimated cost of honoring and servicing these **product warranties** be recognized as an expense in the period of sale rather than in a later period when the warranty costs may actually be incurred and paid.

To illustrate, assume that a firm sells a product for $300 per unit, which includes a 30-day warranty against defects. Past experience indicates that three percent of the units will prove defective and that the average repair cost will be $40 per defective unit. Furthermore, during a particular month, product sales were $240,000, and 13 of the units sold during the month were defective and were repaired. Using this information, the accrued liability for product warranties at the end of the month can be calculated as follows:

Number of units sold ($240,000/$300)	800
Rate of projected defective units	× 0.03
Total units expected to fail	24
Less: Units that failed in the month of sale	**13**
Units expected to fail in the remainder of the warranty period	11
Average repair cost per unit	× $40
Estimated liability for product warranty at end of month	$440

This liability is accrued at the end of the month of sale as follows:

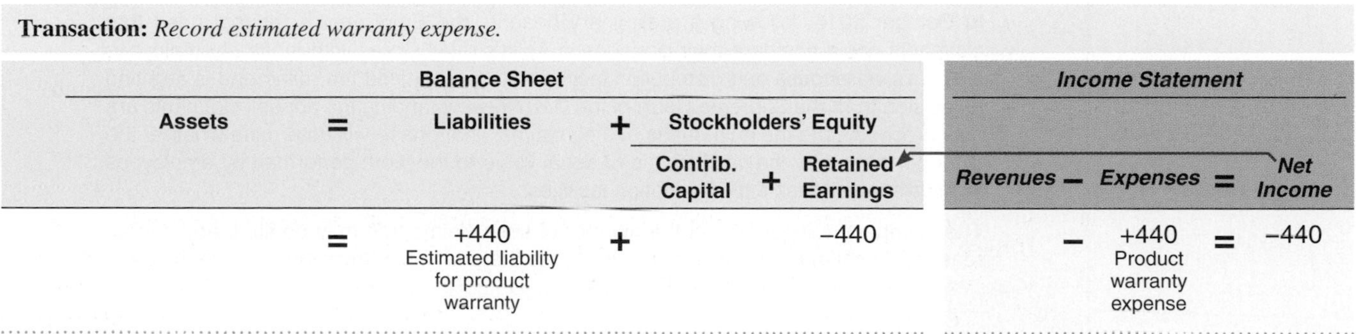

Transaction: *Record estimated warranty expense.*

Assets	=	Liabilities	+	Contrib. Capital	+	Retained Earnings	Revenues	−	Expenses	=	Net Income
	=	+440 Estimated liability for product warranty	+			−440		−	+440 Product warranty expense	=	−440

When a unit fails in a future period, the repair costs will be recorded by decreasing the Estimated Liability for Product Warranty account and Cash, Supplies, and so forth.

PRINCIPLE ALERT

Matching Concept The accounting for product warranties follows the *expense recognition* (*matching*) *concept.* This accounting concept states that expenses must be recorded in the same accounting period as the revenues they help generate. Product warranties make a company's products more attractive to buyers; consequently, product warranties help generate incremental sales revenues. Hence, one of the expenses that must be matched with sales revenues is the cost of honoring and servicing a product warranty. Because most warranty costs are incurred in periods following the period of sale, it is necessary to estimate these costs and record them in the same period when the sale of the product occurs, to achieve a proper matching of revenues and expenses.

Lawsuits

In the course of its operations, a firm may pursue a claim in a court of law by filing a **lawsuit**. At any point, a firm may also be a defendant in one or more lawsuits involving potentially material financial settlements. Examples of litigation issues include product liability, patent infringement, unfair labor practices (see the Accounting in Practice below), and environmental matters. The resolution of a lawsuit may take many years. During the time a lawsuit is pending, the defendant has a contingent liability for any future financial settlement.

ACCOUNTING IN PRACTICE

Estimated Liabilities Resulting from Lawsuits **Walmart Stores, Inc.**, is the world's largest retailer with more than 11,400 stores in 26 countries. Each week, 240 million customers visit a Walmart store to take advantage of the company's notorious low prices. Walmart expects its future growth will be in e-commerce sales rather than through opening more stores. But while Walmart may be cheered by consumers for its low prices, others are more critical of the company. Walmart, for example, has been criticized and sued by community groups, trade unions, and environmental groups for, among other things, its extensive foreign product sourcing, treatment of employees and product suppliers, environmental policies, and store impact on local communities. One such lawsuit alleges that female employees were discriminated against in pay. The following description of the lawsuit appeared in the company's 2020 annual report:

> Asda, a wholly-owned subsidiary of the Company which was sold in February 2021, is a defendant in over 40,000 "equal value" claims that began in 2008 and are proceeding before an Employment Tribunal in Manchester (the "Employment Tribunal") in the United Kingdom ("U.K.") on behalf of current and former Asda store employees, and further claims may be asserted in the future. The claimants allege that the work performed by employees in Asda's retail stores is of equal value in terms of, among other things, the demands of their jobs compared to that of employees working in Asda's warehouse and distribution facilities, and that the difference in pay between these job positions disparately impacts women because more women work in retail stores while more men work in warehouses and distribution facilities, and that the pay difference is not objectively justified. The claimants are requesting differential back pay based on higher wage rates in the warehouse and distribution facilities and higher wage rates on a prospective basis.
>
> In October 2016, following a preliminary hearing, the Employment Tribunal ruled that claimants could compare their positions in Asda's retail stores with those of employees in Asda's warehouse and distribution facilities. Asda appealed the ruling and is awaiting a decision from the Supreme Court of the U.K. Notwithstanding the appeal, claimants are now proceeding in the next phase of their claims. That phase will determine whether the work performed by the claimants is of equal value to the work performed by employees in Asda's warehouse and distribution facilities. . .
>
> The Company cannot predict the number of such claims that may be filed, and cannot reasonably estimate any loss or range of loss that may arise from these proceedings.

Walmart's description of its pending litigation illustrates a common problem with measuring and reporting lawsuit liabilities—it is impossible in most cases to arrive at a reasonable estimate of a company's possible losses. For this reason, lawsuit liabilities are most commonly disclosed in the notes to the financial statements and not on the face of the income statement or the balance sheet.

Environmental Cleanup Costs

Past actions by many companies in disposing of various types of industrial waste have caused subsequent environmental damage. Some estimates of the total cleanup costs for the United States run as high as $100 billion. Firms owning sites that require environmental remediation or that may require cleanup face a contingent liability for the remediation costs. Cleanup costs for a particular site may be very difficult to estimate. The party responsible for bearing the cost—the company or its insurance company—may also be at issue.

Credit Guarantees

To accommodate important, but less financially secure suppliers or customers, a firm may create a **credit guarantee** by cosigning a note payable. Until the original debtor satisfies the obligation, the cosigning firm is contingently liable for the debt. Even when the likelihood of default by a debtor is considered remote, the contingent liability associated with credit guarantees must be disclosed in the notes to the financial statements.

THINKING GLOBALLY

The accounting for some contingent liabilities under U.S. GAAP and IFRS differs significantly. For example, under U.S. GAAP, purchase commitments—that is, an agreement by one company to buy merchandise from another company at a future date—are not reported on the balance sheet but, if material in amount, are disclosed in the notes to the financial statements. Under IFRS, however, purchase commitments are reported on the balance sheet when a company has a clear and demonstrable commitment to a second company to buy its goods. In essence, IFRS adopts a broader definition of what constitutes an accounting liability than does U.S. GAAP. Under U.S. GAAP, while purchase commitments are acknowledged to be economic liabilities of a business, they do not constitute an accounting liability until an exchange of assets occurs between the two companies.

Exhibit 9-7 summarizes the accounting for different types of liabilities according to their unique characteristics.

EXHIBIT 9-7 Liabilities: Criteria and Financial Statement Treatment

Characteristics that Determine the Type of Liability and How it is Recorded	Reported on Balance Sheet			Disclosed in Footnote to Financial Statements		No Disclosure Required
	Noncontingent		Contingent	Contingent	Contingent	Contingent
Dependent on future event	No	No	Yes	Yes	Yes	Yes
Likelihood of future event	Already Occurred	Already Occurred	**Probable**	**Probable**	**Reasonably possible**	**Remote**
Amount of future obligation	Known	Reasonably estimable	Reasonably estimable	Not reasonably estimable	Known, or Reasonably estimable, or Not reasonably estimable	Known, or Reasonably estimable, or Not reasonably estimable
Common examples	Notes payable, Accounts payable, Dividends payable	Income tax payable, Estimated liability for frequent use awards	Estimated liability for product warranty	Lawsuits, Environmental cleanup, Guarantee of others' credit	Lawsuits, Environmental cleanup, Guarantee of others' credit	Lawsuits, Environmental cleanup

TAKEAWAY 9.1

Concept	Method	Assessment
Does the company have any contingent or off-balance-sheet liabilities?	Notes to the financial statements Read the notes to the financial statements to identify contingent liabilities and operating leases	Consider the likely outcome and size of contingent liabilities and the amount of operating leases. If significant, consider these items in the analysis of the firm's liabilities.

REVIEW 9.4

For each of the following scenarios determine if the firm should (a) record as a liability; (b) disclose as a contingent liability; or (c) neither:

1. The Anderson Co. has been sued by a group of individuals claiming the products they purchased from the company were defective and caused injuries. Anderson's lawyers have determined that the product in question could not possibly have caused the types of damages claimed and further that the same group of individuals has unsuccessfully sued several other companies claiming their products caused the same injuries. The likelihood of losing this lawsuit is deemed remote.
2. The Greene Co. has guaranteed the loan of a subsidiary that is suffering minor financial distress. The chance that the loan will not be repaid is deemed remote.
3. Stewart Inc. has acquired a defunct mining company and assumed all its liabilities. Toxic waste from the defunct company was recently discovered to have leaked into some nearby wells. The evidence that the waste came from the mining company is very strong and the cost of cleanup is estimated to be $4 million.

The solution is on page 333.

ANALYZING LIABILITIES

Current Ratio and Quick Ratio

LO6 **Define** the *current ratio, quick ratio, and times-interest-earned ratio.*

The **working capital** of a firm is the difference between the value of its current assets and the value of its current liabilities. In general, having a higher working capital position is preferred to having a lower working capital position. In analyzing the adequacy of a firm's working capital, the current ratio is a widely used financial metric. The **current ratio** is calculated as follows:

$$\textbf{Current ratio} = \frac{\textbf{Current assets}}{\textbf{Current liabilities}}$$

Historically, a current ratio of 2.00 has been considered an acceptable current ratio; however, this is a general guide only. Many businesses operate successfully with a current ratio below 2.00, particularly service firms, because they do not need to maintain large amounts of inventory among their current assets. Similarly, many fast-food franchises operate successfully with a negative working capital position. These businesses produce large amounts of operating cash flow, have no accounts receivable, and extensively utilize the trade credit (accounts payable) provided by their suppliers.

The **quick ratio** is another ratio used to evaluate a company's working capital position. The quick ratio is calculated as follows:

$$\textbf{Quick ratio} = \frac{\textbf{[Cash and cash equivalents + Short-term investments + Accounts receivable]}}{\textbf{Current liabilities}}$$

Cash and cash equivalents, short-term investments, and accounts receivable are also known as quick assets. Quick assets are converted to cash more quickly than inventory or prepaid assets.

Comparing the quick ratio to the current ratio, the main current assets omitted from the numerator when calculating the quick ratio are inventory and prepaid assets. Consequently, the quick ratio is often preferred by investment professionals because it gives a more accurate picture of a company's ability to pay current liabilities.

The following are examples of recent current and quick ratios for companies in different industries:

	Current Ratio	Quick Ratio
Verizon Communications (telecommunications)	0.64	0.52
Johnson & Johnson (health care products)	2.17	1.77
Duke Energy (utility)	0.73	0.14
Google (technology)	4.80	4.39

As can be seen from the above data, the recent current and quick ratios vary dramatically between industries.

Concept	Method	Assessment	TAKEAWAY 9.2
Can a firm pay its current liabilities?	Current assets, Quick assets, Current liabilities Current ratio = $\frac{\text{Current assets}}{\text{Current liabilities}}$ Quick ratio = $\frac{\text{Quick assets}}{\text{Current liabilities}}$	A higher current ratio and quick ratio indicates that a firm can readily pay its current liabilities.	

Times-Interest-Earned Ratio

A financial ratio of particular interest to current and potential long-term creditors is the times-interest-earned ratio. The **times-interest-earned ratio** is computed as follows:

$$\textbf{Times-interest-earned ratio} = \frac{\textbf{Income before interest expense and income taxes}}{\textbf{Interest expense}}$$

A.K.A. The **times-interest-earned ratio** is also referred to as the *interest coverage ratio*.

The principal on long-term debt, such as bonds payable, is not due until maturity, which may be many years into the future. Interest payments, however, are due every six months, and possibly monthly on term loans. Thus, creditors examine the times-interest-earned ratio to help assess the ability of a company to meet its periodic interest commitments. The ratio indicates the number of times that the fixed interest charges were earned during the year. Many investment professionals believe that the times-interest-earned ratio should be at least in the range of 3.0–4.0 for the extension of long-term credit to be considered a safe investment. The trend of the ratio in recent years and the nature of the industry (volatile or stable, for example) also influence the interpretation of this ratio.

Both the numerator and denominator in the times-interest-earned ratio are obtained from the income statement. The numerator uses income before interest expense and income taxes because that is the amount available to cover a business's current interest charges. The denominator is the business's total interest expense for the period. To illustrate, Reid, Inc., issued $100,000 of eight percent bonds at face value. The annual interest expense was $8,000. If this was Reid's only interest expense and Reid's income before interest expense and income taxes the first year were $28,000, Reid's times-interest-earned ratio for the year would be 3.5, or $28,000/$8,000.

The times-interest-earned ratio may differ substantially among industries and firms, depending upon a company's decision to use leverage to finance its assets and operations. The following are examples of recent times-interest-earned ratios for several companies in different industries:

Kellogg Company (grocery products)	4.4
WestRock (paper and paper products)	6.7
Amazon.com, Inc. (online retailing)	4.4
Cisco Systems, Inc. (computer communications equip.)	20.8

Concept	Method	Assessment	TAKEAWAY 9.3
Can a firm pay its current periodic interest payments?	Income before income taxes and interest expense, Interest expense Times-interest-earned ratio = $\frac{\text{Income before income taxes and interest expense}}{\text{Interest expense}}$	A higher times-interest-earned ratio indicates that a firm will have less difficulty paying its current interest expense.	

REVIEW 9.5

Hathaway Company reports the following in its current year financial statements:

Current assets	$200,000
Current liabilities	180,000
Cash and cash equivalents	15,000
Short-term investments	30,000
Accounts receivable	45,000
Income before income taxes	25,000
Interest expense	3,000

Compute the following ratios for Hathaway Company:

a. Current ratio *b.* Quick ratio *c.* Times-interest-earned ratio

The solution is on page 333.

APPENDIX 9A: Interest Calculations Using Excel

Using an Electronic Spreadsheet

In addition to formulas and tables, a third way to solve time value of money problems is with an electronic spreadsheet such as Excel. Excel has several built-in functions that allow calculation of time value of money problems. Depending upon the version of Excel, these functions are accessed differently. Within Microsoft 365 Excel, go to the Insert function *fx* (Insert Function) in the Formulas ribbon. The required functions are located under the FINANCIAL option. Following are examples of how to use Excel to solve the same problems we previously solved in Exhibit 9-1 using tables.

Example 1

Find the selling price (present value) of $100,000 of eight percent, four-year bonds with interest payable semiannually sold to yield eight percent. Use the PV function and enter the values as follows:

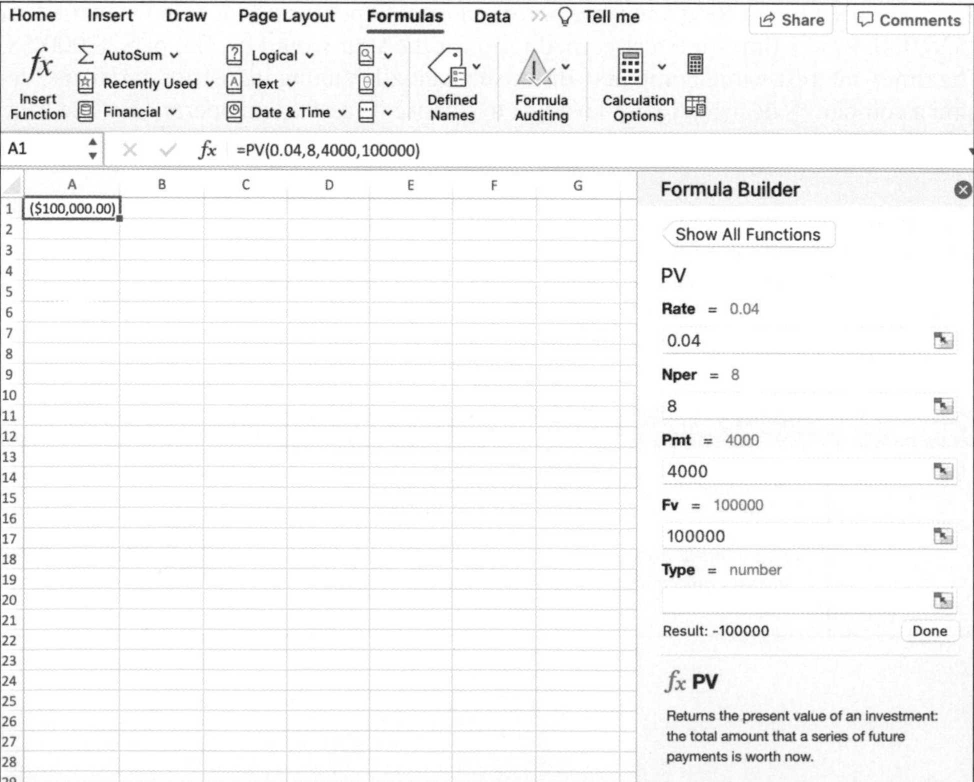

Example 2

Find the selling price (present value) of $100,000 of eight percent, four-year bonds with interest payable semiannually sold to yield ten percent. Use the PV function and enter the values as follows:

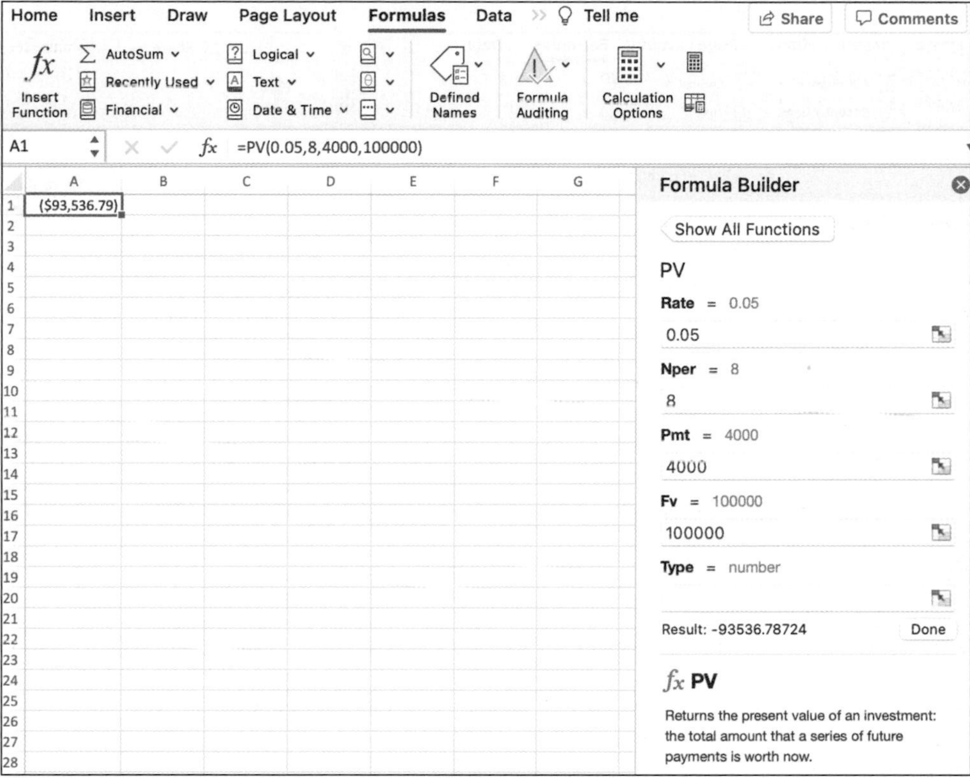

Example 3

Find the selling price (present value) of $100,000 of eight percent, four-year bonds with interest payable semiannually sold to yield six percent. Use the PV function and enter the values as follows:

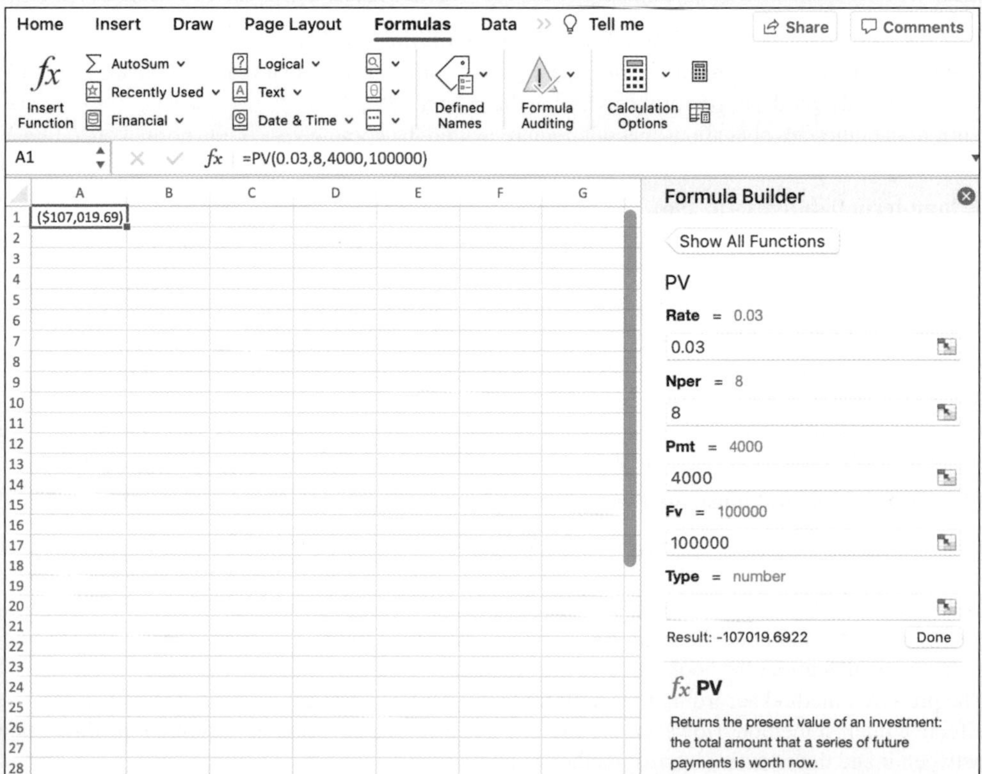

Example 4

Find the payment amount for a term loan of $100,000 at 12% for a ten-year term. The note is repaid with equal quarterly installments. Exhibit 9-6 presents a partial mortgage payment schedule using this example. Use the PMT function and enter the values as follows:

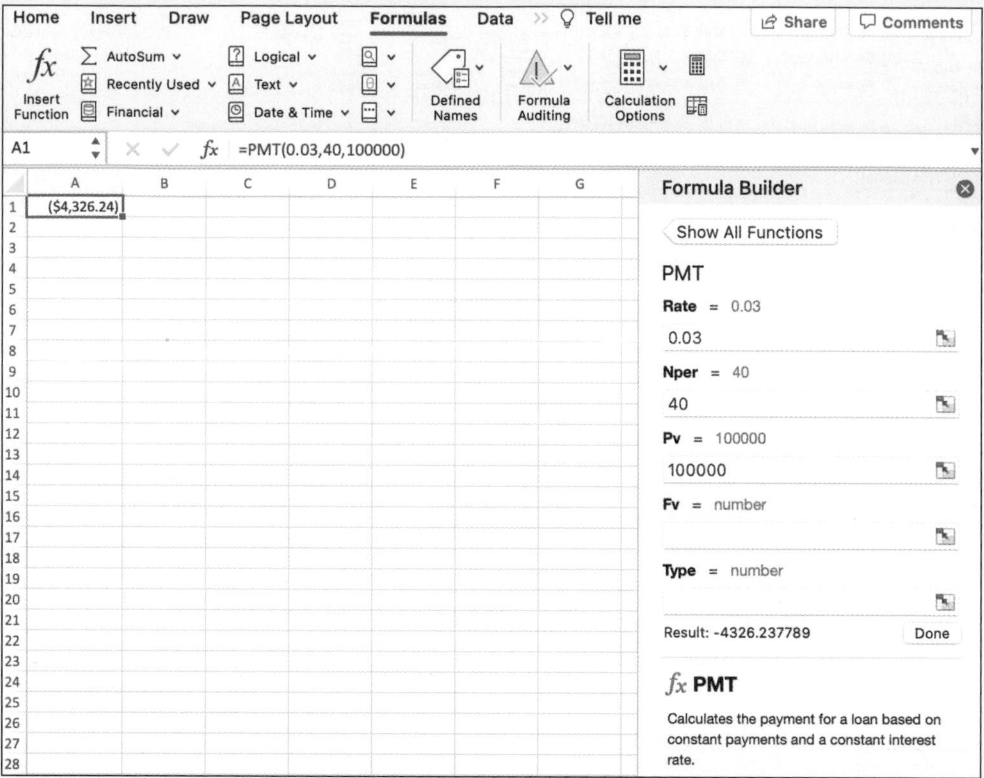

SUMMARY OF LEARNING OBJECTIVES

LO1 Describe the nature of liabilities and define current liabilities. (p. 292)

- Liabilities are obligations resulting from past transactions or events that require a business to pay money, provide goods, or perform services in the future.
- Current liabilities are obligations that will require, within the coming year or the normal operating cycle, whichever is longer, (1) the use of existing current assets or (2) the creation of other current liabilities.

LO2 Define long-term liabilities. (p. 296)

- A bond is a long-term debt instrument used by many businesses to provide financing for operations or asset purchases.
- There are a number of different types of bonds: secured, debenture, serial, convertible, and zero-coupon; all of which differ due to certain contractual characteristics.
- Advantages of long-term bonds and notes include: no dilution of ownership, the interest is tax deductible, and leverage.
- Disadvantages of long-term bonds and notes include: the interest payment is a contractual obligation, repayment is required on a specific date, and there may be restrictions on company actions.

LO3 Explain bond pricing and illustrate two methods of amortizing bond discounts/premiums. (p. 299)

- Because of the role played by interest, the selling price of the bond often differs from the face amount of the bond.
- We account for this difference by utilizing bond premium (when the market rate of interest is less than the coupon rate) and bond discount (when the market rate of interest is more than the coupon rate) accounts, which affect the book value of the liability.
- The preferred method according to GAAP for amortizing bond premiums and discounts is the effective interest method. However, the straight-line method is acceptable assuming the difference between it and the effective interest method is immaterial.

- Bonds payable are shown in the long-term liabilities section of the balance sheet, with any unamortized premium added or unamortized discount deducted.

Describe the accounting for leases. (p. 309) LO4

- A lease transfers most of the usual risks and rewards of property ownership to the lessee. At the inception of the lease, the lessee records an asset (a right-to-use asset) and a liability (a lease obligation).
- Under a finance lease, the asset is depreciated over its expected useful life, and the liability is reduced as the periodic lease payments are made.
- Under an operating lease, the lessor retains the usual risks and rewards of owning the property. The lessee amortizes the right-to-use asset generally on a straight-line basis.

Define contingent liabilities and explain their disclosure in the financial statements. (p. 310) LO5

- Even though a past transaction or event has taken place, the existence of some liabilities, called contingent liabilities, depends on the occurrence of a future event. Whether or not a contingent liability is recorded in the accounts depends on the likelihood of the future event occurring and the measurability of the obligation:
  1. If the future event will probably occur and the amount of the liability can be reasonably estimated, the contingent liability should be recorded in the accounts.
  2. If the likelihood of the future event occurring is probable, but no reasonable estimate of the future obligation is determinable, or the likelihood of the future event occurring is reasonably possible (but not probable), regardless of the ability to measure the future amount, the contingent liability should be disclosed in a note to the financial statements, but not recorded in the accounts.
  3. If the likelihood of the future event occurring is remote, the contingent liability is not recorded in the accounts or disclosed in a note to the financial statements. The only exception is a credit guarantee, which must be disclosed in a note to the financial statements.

Define the current ratio, quick ratio, and times-interest-earned ratio. (p. 314) LO6

- The current ratio is calculated as follows:

$$\text{Current ratio} = \frac{\text{Current assets}}{\text{Current liabilities}}$$

- The quick ratio is calculated as follows:

$$\text{Quick ratio} = \frac{[\text{Cash and cash equivalents} + \text{Short-term investments} + \text{Accounts receivable}]}{\text{Current liabilities}}$$

- Both ratios measure a firm's ability to pay its current liabilities, as well as the strength of its working capital position.
- The times-interest-earned ratio measures the ability of a firm to meet its periodic interest commitments, and is calculated as:

$$\text{Times-interest-earned ratio} = \frac{\text{Income before interest expense and income taxes}}{\text{Interest expense}}$$

Concept	Method	Assessment	SUMMARY
Does the company have any contingent or off-balance-sheet liabilities?	Notes to the financial statements Read the notes to the financial statements to identify contingent liabilities and operating leases	Consider the likely outcome and size of contingent liabilities and the amount of operating leases. If significant, consider these items in the analysis of the firm's liabilities.	TAKEAWAY 9.1
Can a firm pay its current liabilities?	Current assets, Quick assets, Current liabilities $\text{Current ratio} = \frac{\text{Current assets}}{\text{Current liabilities}}$ $\text{Quick ratio} = \frac{\text{Quick assets}}{\text{Current liabilities}}$	A higher current ratio and quick ratio indicates that a firm can readily pay its current liabilities.	TAKEAWAY 9.2
Can a firm pay its current periodic interest payments?	Income before income taxes and interest expense, Interest expense Times-interest-earned ratio = $\frac{\text{Income before income taxes and interest expense}}{\text{Interest expense}}$	A higher times-interest-earned ratio indicates that a firm will have less difficulty paying its current interest expense.	TAKEAWAY 9.3

KEY TERMS

Bond (p. 296)
Call provision (p. 298)
Contingent liabilities (p. 310)
Convertible bonds (p. 297)
Coupon rate (p. 299)
Credit guarantee (p. 313)
Current liabilities (p. 292)
Current ratio (p. 314)
Debentures (p. 297)
Effective interest method (p. 305)
Effective interest rate (p. 305)
Finance lease (p. 310)
Interest rate (p. 293)
Lawsuit (p. 312)
Lease (p. 309)
Lessee (p. 309)
Lessor (p. 309)
Leverage (p. 297)
Liabilities (p. 292)
Market rate of interest (p. 299)
Maturity date (p. 293)
Operating lease (p. 310)
Product warranties (p. 311)
Quick ratio (p. 314)
Right-of-use asset (p. 309)
Secured bonds (p. 297)
Serial bonds (p. 297)
Sinking fund provision (p. 298)
Straight-line method (p. 303)
Term loan (p. 296, 308)
Times-interest-earned ratio (p. 315)
Working capital (p. 314)
Zero-coupon bonds (p. 298)

SELF-STUDY QUESTIONS

(Answers for the Self-Study Questions are available at the end of this chapter.)

LO1 Homework MBC

1. **Goldsteen Corporation obtained a $5,000 loan from a bank on April 1. If the bank charges eight percent interest annually, how much interest will be accrued at December 31?**
   a. $400
   b. $300
   c. $275
   d. $250

LO5 Homework MBC

2. **Jansen Company sells a product for $400 per unit, which includes a 30-day warranty against product defects. Experience indicates that four percent of the units sold will prove defective, requiring an average repair cost of $50 per unit. During the first month of business, product sales were $320,000, and 20 of the units sold were found to be defective and repaired during the month. What is the accrued liability for product warranties at month-end?**
   a. $1,000
   b. $600
   c. $1,600
   d. $2,000

LO5 Homework MBC

3. **Which of the following is *not* considered to be a contingent liability?**
   a. Environmental cleanup costs
   b. Notes payable
   c. Credit guarantees
   d. Lawsuit

LO2, 3 Homework MBC

4. **On January 1, a firm issued $400,000 of 12-year, nine percent bonds payable at 96 1/2. The bonds are dated January 1, and interest is payable on January 1 and July 1 of each year. The amount the firm receives on January 1 from the sale of the bonds is:**
   a. $386,000.
   b. $422,000.
   c. $392,000.
   d. $398,000.

LO3 Homework MBC

5. **A firm issued $250,000 of ten-year, 12 percent bonds payable on January 1, for $281,180, yielding an effective rate of ten percent. Interest is payable on January 1 and July 1 each year. The firm records amortization on each interest date. Bond interest expense for the first six months using effective interest amortization is:**
   a. $15,000.
   b. $16,870.80.
   c. $14,059.
   d. $14,331.

LO3 Homework MBC

6. **In financial statement presentations, the Discount on Bonds Payable account is:**
   a. added to Bond Interest Expense.
   b. deducted from Bonds Payable.
   c. added to Bonds Payable.
   d. deducted from Bond Interest Expense.

LO6 Homework MBC

7. **Apolo Company reported year-end current assets of $75,000 and current liabilities of $25,000. The company's current ratio is:**
   a. 1/3.
   b. 3.
   c. 4.
   d. $50,000.

8. Cristo Company reported net income of $50,000 after subtracting $10,000 for interest expense and $20,000 for taxes. Compute the company's times-interest-earned ratio: LO6

a. 2.5
b. 5
c. 8
d. 3

QUESTIONS

1. For accounting purposes, how are liabilities defined?
2. At what amount are current liabilities presented on the balance sheet?
3. What does the term *current liabilities* mean?
4. What formula should Hardy Company use to calculate the total amount of interest on a note payable that uses add-on interest?
5. Gordon Company signed a note payable on November 20. Gordon has a December 31 year-end. It paid the note, including interest, on the maturity date, February 20. What is the financial statement effect of the transaction on February 20?
6. Jack Swanson gave a creditor a 90-day, eight percent note payable for $7,200 on December 16. Calculate the amount of interest Swanson should accrue on December 31.
7. What is the difference between accounting for product warranties on (a) failed units repaired in the month of sale and (b) failed units repaired in a subsequent month but that are still covered by warranty?
8. Apple, Inc., recently reported a current liability of $6.6 billion labeled Deferred Revenue. A note to the financial statements explained: Apple, Inc.

> The Company has identified up to three performance obligations regularly included in arrangements involving the sale of iPhone, Mac, iPad and certain other products. The first performance obligation, which represents the substantial portion of the allocated sales price, is the hardware and bundled software delivered at the time of sale. The second performance obligation is the right to receive certain product-related bundled services, which include iCloud, Siri and Maps. The third performance obligation is the right to receive, on a when-and-if-available basis, future unspecified software upgrades relating to the software bundled with each device. . . .
> . . . Revenue allocated to the product-related bundled services and unspecified software upgrade rights is deferred and recognized on a straight-line basis over the estimated period they are expected to be provided.

What basic principle of accounting guides Apple's handling of its deferred revenues and deposits?

9. What do the following terms mean? (a) term loan, (b) bonds payable, (c) trustee, (d) secured bonds, (e) serial bonds, (f) call provision, (g) convertible bonds, (h) face value, (i) coupon rate, (j) bond discount, (k) bond premium, and (l) amortization of bond premium or discount
10. What are the advantages and disadvantages of issuing bonds rather than common stock?
11. If the effective interest amortization method is used for bonds payable, how does the periodic interest expense change over the life of the bonds when they are issued (a) at a discount and (b) at a premium?
12. What are *contingent liabilities*? List three examples of contingent liabilities. When should contingent liabilities be recorded in the accounts?
13. What is the difference between an operating lease and a finance lease?
14. Define the terms *current ratio* and *quick ratio*. What does each ratio tell us?
15. Define the times-interest-earned ratio and explain how it is used.

DATA ANALYTICS

The assignments in this Data Analytics section are designed to familiarize you with the tools used in analyzing data and communicating the results. Appendix F provides an in-depth discussion of data analytics and blockchain technology.

DA9-1. Preparing Excel Schedules to Determine Compliance with Debt Agreements

Monroe Inc. (the Company) obtained financing from Pro Bank in Year 8. Associated with the debt agreement are debt covenants, which place restrictions on the Company's activities. The intention of the covenants are to protect the lender (Pro Bank) from a situation where the Company is unable to pay the debt when it is due. A debt agreement will include any debt covenants along with details on any calculations involved. From the debt agreement between Monroe Inc. and Pro Bank, the financial covenants are included below. Key definitions of certain terms are also included.

Financial Covenants

1. Total Leverage Ratio. The Company will not, as of the last day of any fiscal quarter, permit the Total Leverage Ratio to be greater than 2.00 to 1.00.
2. Minimum EBITDA. The Company will not, as of the last day of any fiscal quarter, permit EBITDA, for the period of the quarter ending on or immediately prior to such date to be less than $300 million.
3. Funded Debt. The Company will not, at any time, permit the aggregate outstanding principal amount of all Funded Debt to exceed an amount equal to 10% of the Company's total assets (as determined as of the last day of the most recently ended fiscal quarter for which financial statements have been provided).

Definitions

- Total Leverage Ratio: As of any date of determination, the ratio of (*a*) Funded Debt on such date to (*b*) EBITDA for the quarter ending on or immediately prior to such date.
- EBITDA: For any period, the sum of the following, for the Company in accordance with GAAP: Net income for such period plus (*b*) the sum of the following, to the extent deducted in determining net income for such period: (1) income tax expense during such period, (2) interest expense, net of interest income for such period, and (3) amortization and depreciation expense.
- Funded Debt: As of the date of determination with respect to the Company, the sum of all liabilities of the Company due to borrowing money.

The Excel file associated with this exercise includes quarterly financial information for Monroe Inc. from Quarter 1 of Year 10 to Quarter 2 of Year 12.

Required

1. Download Excel file DA9-1 found in myBusinessCourse.
2. Determine the key financial categories needed in order to determine whether the company is in compliance with the three financial covenants for each quarter presented.
3. Calculate the key financial amounts within the Excel worksheet.
4. Create an IF statement for each financial covenant per quarter that returns a "YES" if the company is in compliance at quarter end, or a "NO" if the company is not in compliance at quarter end.
5. List the formula for the IF statement for Q1 Year 10 for the first financial statement covenant.
6. Add a rule to your IF statement to shade the cell where YES is contained in green and a rule to shade the cell where NO is contained in red. *Hint:* Under the Home tab, click on Conditional formatting, Highlight cell rules, Text that contains, and then set up two rules.
7. Indicate the quarter ends (if any) where the company is not in compliance with the financial covenants.
8. Create What-if Scenario 1 by duplicating the original schedule created. Assume that Funded Debt increased by 10% each quarter-end. (*Hint:* Increase interest expense by 10% as well as Funded Debt.) Assume no other changes in the financial data provided.
9. Indicate the quarter ends (if any) where the company is not in compliance with the financial covenants based on the schedule created in part 8.
10. Create What-if Scenario 2 by duplicating the original schedule created. Assume that total assets decreased by 10% each quarter-end. Assume no other changes in the financial data provided.
11. Indicate the quarter ends (if any) where the company is not in compliance with the financial covenants based on the schedule created in part 10.
12. Determine the minimum required net income for each quarter in order to be in compliance with the second financial covenant, using the original data. Use 30% of earnings before tax as an estimate for tax expense. Round tax expense to one decimal place.
13. Determine the quarter where there is the smallest difference between net income reported and the minimum net income required to meet the second financial covenant.

Assignments with the MBC logo in the margin are available in myBusinessCourse. See the Preface of the book for details.

SHORT EXERCISES

LO5 **SE9-1. Contingent Liabilities** The CEO of Los Altos, Inc., negotiated with its principal supplier of raw materials to purchase 10,000 units for a total price of $100,000. The units are to be delivered in 90 days. The CEO is uncertain whether she should record the purchase commitment on the company's balance sheet as a liability or not. She asks for your advice. What would you advise her?

SE9-2. Determining Bond Premium or Discount Los Altos, Inc., decides to sell $1,000,000 in bonds to finance the construction of a new warehouse. The bonds will carry an annual coupon rate of interest of four percent, to be paid semiannually, and will mature in five years. (a) If the market rate of interest at the time of issuance is five percent, will the bonds sell at their face value, a discount, or a premium? (b) If the market rate of interest at the time of issuance is four percent, will the bonds sell at their face value, a discount, or a premium? (c) If the market rate of interest at the time of issuance is three percent, will the bonds sell at their face value, a discount, or a premium? **LO2**

SE9-3. Contingent Liabilities Los Altos, Inc., received notification from a local attorney that the company was being sued for $5,000,000 for patent infringement. A review of the situation by the company's CEO led to the conclusion that Los Altos had indeed infringed upon the other company's patented product. Nonetheless, the CEO thought the amount of $5,000,000 was excessive and intended to litigate the issue. How should the lawsuit be reported in Los Altos' annual report? **LO5**

SE9-4. Operating and Finance Leases The CEO of Los Altos, Inc., was considering a lease for a new administrative headquarters building. The building was old, but was very well located near the company's principal customers. The leasing agent estimated that the building's remaining useful life was ten years, and at the end of its useful life, the building would probably be worth $100,000. The proposed lease term was nine years, and as an inducement to Los Altos' CEO to sign the lease, the leasing agent indicated a willingness to include a statement in the lease agreement that would allow Los Altos to buy the building at the end of the lease for only $10,000. As the CEO considered whether or not to sign the lease, she wondered whether the lease could be accounted for as a financing lease or as an operating lease. What would you advise her? **LO4**

The following information relates to **Short Exercises SE9-5 through SE9-7**:

LOS ALTOS, INC.
Income Statement
For Years Ended December 31, Current Year and Prior Year

(in millions)	Current Year	Prior Year
Net sales	$10,000	$ 9,500
Cost of goods sold	5,500	5,200
Gross profit	4,500	4,300
Selling and administrative expenses	2,800	2,700
Income from operations	1,700	1,600
Interest expense	300	250
Income before income taxes	1,400	1,350
Income tax expense	420	400
Net income	$ 980	$ 950

LOS ALTOS, INC.
Balance Sheet
December 31, Current Year and Prior Year

(in millions)	Current Year	Prior Year
Assets		
Current assets		
Cash and cash equivalents	$ 200	$ 400
Accounts receivable	900	800
Inventory	500	650
Other current assets	400	250
Total current assets	2,000	2,100
Property, plant, & equipment (net)	2,600	2,500
Other assets	5,700	5,900
Total assets	$10,300	$10,500

continued

continued from previous page

LOS ALTOS, INC. Balance Sheet December 31, Current Year and Prior Year		
(in millions)	Current Year	Prior Year
Liabilities and Stockholders' Equity		
Current liabilities	$ 3,000	$ 2,900
Long-term liabilities	5,000	5,400
Total liabilities	8,000	8,300
Stockholders' equity—common	2,300	2,200
Total Liabilities and Stockholders' Equity	$10,300	$10,500

LO6 Homework MBC

SE9-5. Current Ratio Calculate the current ratio for Los Altos, Inc., for both years, and comment on the company's working capital position. Did the company's ability to pay its current liabilities improve over the two years?

LO6 Homework MBC

SE9-6. Quick Ratio Calculate the quick ratio for Los Altos, Inc., for both years, and comment on the company's working capital position. Did the company's ability to pay its current liabilities improve over the two years?

LO6 Homework MBC

SE9-7. Times-Interest-Earned Ratio Calculate the times-interest-earned ratio for Los Altos, Inc., for both years, and comment on the company's ability to pay its current interest payments. Did the company's ability to pay its current interest charges improve?

LO3 Homework MBC

SE9-8. Premium and Discount of a Bond or Debenture Slater-Johnson, Inc. reported the following borrowings in their annual report:

	Borrowing ($ in millions)	Amount	Effective Interest Rate (%)
a.	3.00 percent, zero-coupon bond, due 2024	$202	3.00
b.	4.95 percent debentures, due 2037	500	5.00
c.	3.80 percent debentures, due 2021	500	3.82
d.	6.95 percent bonds, due 2029	293	6.90

For each borrowing, indicate whether the bond or debenture was originally sold at its face value, a discount, or a premium.

LO3 Homework MBC

SE9-9. Bond Interest Expense Los Altos, Inc., sold $100,000 face value, six percent coupon rate, four-year bonds, for an aggregate issue price of $96,000. Calculate the total interest expense to be recorded by the company over the four-year life of the bonds.

LO3 Homework MBC

SE9-10. Bond Interest Expense Los Altos, Inc., issued $400 million of zero-coupon ten-year bonds. The proceeds from the bond issuance were $186.6 million. Calculate the total interest expense that the company will incur over the life of the bonds.

EXERCISES

LO1, 5 Homework MBC

E9-1. Liabilities on the Balance Sheet For each of the following situations, indicate the amount shown as a liability on the balance sheet of Kane, Inc., at December 31:

a. Kane has accounts payable of $110,000 for merchandise included in the year-end inventory.
b. Kane agreed to purchase a $28,000 drill press in the following January.
c. During November and December of the current year, Kane sold products to a firm and guaranteed them against product failure for 90 days. Estimated costs of honoring this provision next year are $2,200.
d. On December 15, Kane declared a $70,000 cash dividend payable on January 15 of the following year to shareholders of record on December 31.
e. Kane provides a profit-sharing bonus for its executives equal to five percent of the reported before-tax income for the current year. The estimated before-tax income for the current year is $600,000.

E9-2. Maturity Dates of Notes Payable Determine the maturity date and compute the interest for each of the following notes payable with add-on interest: **LO1**

	Date of Note	Principal	Interest Rate (%)	Term
a.	August 5	$15,000	8	120 days
b.	May 10	8,400	7	90 days
c.	October 20	12,000	9	45 days
d.	July 6	4,500	10	60 days
e.	September 15	13,500	8	75 days

E9-3. Accrued Interest Payable Compute the interest accrued on each of the following notes payable owed by Northland, Inc., on December 31: **LO1**

Lender	Date of Note	Principal	Interest Rate (%)	Term
Maple	11/21	$18,000	10	120 days
Wyman	12/13	14,000	9	90 days
Nahn	12/19	16,000	12	60 days

E9-4. Interest Accruals The following note transactions occurred during the year for Towell Company: **LO1**

Nov. 25 Towell issued a 90-day, nine percent note payable for $8,000 to Hyatt Company for merchandise.

Dec. 7 Towell signed a 120-day, $12,000 note at the bank at ten percent.

22 Towell gave Barr, Inc., a $12,000, ten percent, 60-day note in payment of account.

Calculate the amount of the necessary interest accrual for each note payable at December 31.

E9-5. Advance Payments for Goods The Chicago Daily Times Corporation (CDT) publishes a daily newspaper. A 52-week subscription sells for $208. Assume that CDT sells 100 subscriptions on January 1. None of the subscriptions are cancelled as of March 31. **LO1**

a. What is the financial statement effect of the receipt of the subscriptions on January 1?

b. What is the financial statement effect of one week of earned revenue on March 25?

E9-6. Warranty Costs Milford Company sells a motor that carries a 60-day unconditional warranty against product failure. Based on a reliable statistical analysis, Milford knows that between the sale and the end of the product warranty period, two percent of the units sold will require repair at an average cost of $50 per unit. The following data reflect Milford's recent experience: **LO5**

	October	November	December	Dec. 31 Total
Units sold	23,000	22,000	25,000	70,000
Known product failures from sales in:				
October	120	180	160	460
November		130	220	350
December			210	210

Calculate the estimated liability for product warranties at December 31. Assume that warranty costs of known failures have already been reflected in the records.

E9-7. Bonds Payable Sold at a Discount; Straight-line Interest Amortization On December 31, Blair Company issued $600,000 of 20-year, 11 percent bonds payable for $554,718, yielding an effective interest rate of 12 percent. Interest is payable semiannually on June 30 and December 31. Determine the financial statement effect of (a) the issuance of the bonds, (b) the first semiannual interest payment and discount amortization (straight-line interest method) on June 30, and (c) the second semiannual interest payment and discount amortization on December 31. Round amounts to the nearest dollar. **LO3**

E9-8. Bonds Payable Sold at a Discount; Effective Interest Amortization On December 31, Daggett Company issued $800,000 of ten-year, nine percent bonds payable for $750,232, yielding an effective interest rate of ten percent. Interest is payable semiannually on June 30 and December 31. Determine the financial statement effect of (a) the issuance of the bonds, (b) the first semiannual interest payment and discount amortization (effective interest method) on June 30, and (c) the second semiannual interest payment and discount amortization on December 31. Round amounts to the nearest dollar. **LO3**

LO3  **E9-9. Bonds Payable Sold at a Premium; Straight-line Interest Amortization** On December 31, Kay Company issued $400,000 of five-year, 13 percent bonds payable for $446,372, yielding an effective interest rate of ten percent. Interest is payable semiannually on June 30 and December 31. Determine the financial statement effect of (a) the issuance of the bonds, (b) the first semiannual interest payment and premium amortization (straight-line interest method) on June 30, and (c) the second semiannual interest payment and premium amortization on December 31. Round amounts to the nearest dollar.

LO3  **E9-10. Bonds Payable Sold at a Premium; Effective Interest Amortization** On December 31, Coffey Company issued $300,000 of 15-year, ten percent bonds payable for $351,780, yielding an effective interest rate of eight percent. Interest is payable semiannually on June 30 and December 31. Determine the financial statement effect of (a) the issuance of the bonds, (b) the first semiannual interest payment and premium amortization (effective interest method) on June 30, and (c) the second semiannual interest payment and premium amortization on December 31. Round amounts to the nearest dollar.

LO1, 3  **E9-11. Financial Statement Presentation of Bond Accounts** Indicate the proper financial statement classification for each of the following accounts:

Discount on Long-term Bonds Payable
Mortgage Notes Payable
Long-term Bonds Payable
Bond Interest Expense
Bond Interest Payable
Premium on Long-term Bonds Payable

LO3 **E9-12. Installment Term Loan** On December 31, Thomas, Inc., borrowed $700,000 on a 12 percent, 15-year mortgage note payable. The note is to be repaid in equal semiannual installments of $50,854 (payable on June 30 and December 31). Determine the financial statement effect of (a) the issuance of the mortgage note payable, (b) the payment of the first installment on June 30, and (c) the payment of the second installment on December 31. Round amounts to the nearest dollar.

LO4  **E9-13. Leases** On January 1, Spider, Inc., entered into two lease contracts. The first lease contract was a six-year lease for a computer with $15,000 annual lease payments due at the end of each year. Spider took possession of the computer on January 1. The second lease contract was a six-month lease, beginning January 1 for warehouse storage space with $1,000 monthly lease payments due the first of each month. Spider made the first month's payment on January 1. The present value of the lease payments under the first contract is $74,520. The present value of the lease payments under the second contract is $5,853.

a. Determine the financial statement effect of the first lease on January 1.
b. Determine the financial statement effect of the second lease on January 1.

LO5 **E9-14. Contingent Liabilities** Determine which of the following transactions represent contingent liabilities for Hermani Rental and indicate the proper accounting treatment at the company's fiscal year-end, by placing the letter of the correct accounting treatment in the space provided.

A. Accrue a liability and disclose in the financial statement notes
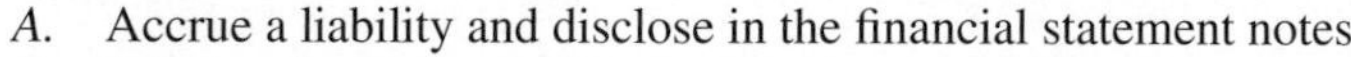
B. Disclose in the financial statement footnotes only
C. No disclosure

1. Hermani Rental cosigned a loan for $75,000 due in one year for Wyler Company. Wyler is a very profitable company and is very liquid, making it a remote chance Hermani will have to pay the loan.	
2. One of Hermani's rental tents collapsed at a wedding and injured the bride and groom. Hermani's legal counsel believes it is probable that Hermani will have to pay damages of $400,000.	
3. Hermani Rental is being audited by the Internal Revenue Service. Its tax returns for the past two years are being examined. At the company's year-end, the audit is still in process. Hermani's CPA believes that payment of significant taxes is possible.	

E9-15. Ratio Analysis Presented below are summary financial data from Pompeo's annual report: LO6

Amounts in millions	
Balance sheet	
Cash and cash equivalents	$ 1,808
Marketable securities	18,085
Accounts receivable (net)	9,367
Total current assets	39,088
Total assets	123,078
Current liabilities	37,724
Long-term debt	7,279
Shareholders' equity	68,278
Income Statement	
Interest expense	359
Net income before taxes	14,007

Calculate the following ratios:

a. Times-interest earned ratio
b. Quick ratio
c. Current ratio

E9-16. Issue Price of a Bond Conner Enterprises issued $100,000 of 10%, five-year bonds with interest payable semiannually. Determine the issue price if the bonds are priced to yield (a) 10%, (b) 8%, and (c) 12%. LO2, 3

E9-17. Issue Price of a Bond Lunar, Inc., plans to issue $900,000 of 10% bonds that will pay interest semiannually and mature in five years. Assume that the effective interest rate is 12 percent per year compounded semiannually. Calculate the selling price of the bonds. LO2, 3

PROBLEMS

P9-1. Accounts Payable and Notes Payable Logan Company had the following transactions: LO1

Apr.	8	Issued a $4,800, 75-day, eight percent note payable in payment of an account with Bennett Company.
May	15	Borrowed $36,000 from Lincoln Bank, signing a 60-day note at nine percent.
June	22	Paid Bennett Company the principal and interest due on the April 8 note payable.
July	6	Purchased $12,000 of merchandise from Bolton Company; signed a 90-day note with ten percent interest.
	14	Paid the May 15 note due Lincoln Bank.
Oct.	2	Borrowed $24,000 from Lincoln Bank, signing a 120-day note at 12 percent.
	4	Defaulted on the note payable to Bolton Company.

REQUIRED

a. Determine the financial statement effect of these transactions.
b. Determine the financial statement effect of the interest to be accrued on December 31, Logan Company's year-end.

P9-2. Interest Accruals At December 31, Year 1, Hoffman Corporation had two notes payable outstanding (notes A and B). At December 31, Year 2, Hoffman also had two notes payable outstanding (notes C and D). These notes are described below: LO1

	Date of Note	Principal Amount	Interest Rate	Number of Days
December 31, Year 1				
Note A	11/16/Year 1	$12,000	8%	120
Note B	12/4/Year 1	16,000	9	60
December 31, Year 2				
Note C	12/7/Year 2	9,000	9	60
Note D	12/21/Year 2	18,000	10	30

REQUIRED

a. Determine the financial statement effect of the interest accrual at December 31, Year 1.

b. Assume that the interest accruals were made at December 31, Year 1. Determine the financial statement effect of the payments made during Year 2 on the notes that were outstanding at December 31, Year 1.

c. Determine the financial statement effect of the interest accrual at December 31, Year 2.

LO1, 5 **P9-3. Noncontingent and Contingent Liabilities** The following independent situations represent various types of liabilities:

1. One of the employees of Martin Company was severely injured when hit by one of Martin's trucks in the parking lot. The 35-year-old employee will never be able to work again. Insurance coverage is minimal. The employee has sued Martin Company and a jury trial is scheduled.
2. A shareholder has filed a lawsuit against Sweitzer Corporation. Sweitzer's attorneys have reviewed the facts of the case. Their review revealed that similar lawsuits have never resulted in a cash award and it is highly unlikely that this lawsuit will either.
3. Armstrong Company signed a 60-day, ten percent note when it purchased merchandise from Fischer Company.
4. Richmond Company has been notified by the Department of Environment Protection (DEP) that a state where it has a plant is filing a lawsuit for groundwater pollution against Richmond and another company that has a plant adjacent to Richmond's plant. Test results have not identified the exact source of the pollution. Richmond's manufacturing process can produce by-products that pollute groundwater.
5. Fredonia Company has cosigned a note payable to a bank for one of its customers. The customer received all of the proceeds of the note. Fredonia will have to repay the loan if the customer fails to do so. Fredonia Company believes that it is unlikely that it will have to pay the note.
6. Holt Company manufactured and sold products to Z-Mart, a retailer that sold the products to consumers. The manufacturer's warranty offers replacement of the product if it is found to be defective within 90 days of the sale to the consumer. Historically, 1.2 percent of the products are returned for replacement.

REQUIRED

Prepare a multicolumn analysis that presents the following information for each of these situations:

a. Number of the situation.

b. Type of liability: (1) noncontingent or (2) contingent.

c. Accounting treatment: (1) record in accounts, (2) disclose in a note to the financial statements, or (3) neither record nor disclose.

LO3 **P9-4. Effective Interest Amortization** On December 31, Caper, Inc., issued $250,000 of eight percent, nine-year bonds for $220,900, yielding an effective interest rate of ten percent. Semiannual interest is payable on June 30 and December 31 each year. The firm uses the effective interest method to amortize the discount.

REQUIRED

a. Prepare an amortization schedule showing the necessary information for the first two interest periods. Round amounts to the nearest dollar.

b. Determine the financial statement effect of the bond issuance on December 31.

c. Determine the financial statement effect of the bond interest payment and discount amortization at June 30 of the following year.

d. Determine the financial statement effect of the bond interest payment and discount amortization at December 31 of the following year.

LO3 **P9-5. Straight-line Amortization** Using the information given in P9-4, complete the required items assuming Caper, Inc., uses the straight-line method to amortize the discount.

LO3 **P9-6. Effective Interest Amortization** On January 1, Eagle, Inc., issued $800,000 of nine percent, 20-year bonds for $878,948, yielding an effective interest rate of eight percent. Semiannual interest is payable on June 30 and December 31 each year. The firm uses the effective interest method to amortize the premium.

REQUIRED

a. Prepare an amortization schedule showing the necessary information for the first two interest periods. Round amounts to the nearest dollar.

b. Determine the financial statement effect of the bond issuance on January 1.

c. Determine the financial statement effect of the bond interest payment and premium amortization at June 30.

d. Determine the financial statement effect of the bond interest payment and premium amortization at December 31.

P9-7. **Straight-line Amortization** Using the information given in P9-6, complete the required items assuming Eagle, Inc., uses the straight-line method to amortize the premium. LO3

P9-8. **Current Ratio, Quick Ratio, and Times-Interest-Earned Ratio** The following data is from the current accounting records of Florence Company: LO6

Cash	$120
Accounts receivable (net of allowance of 40)	200
Inventory	150
Other current assets	80
Accounts payable	110
Other current liabilities	170

The president of the company is concerned that the company is in violation of a debt covenant that requires the company to maintain a minimum current ratio of 2.0. He believes the best way to rectify this is to reverse a bad debt write-off in the amount of $10 that the company just recorded. He argues that the write-off was done too early, and that the collections department should be given more time to collect the outstanding receivables. The CFO argues that this will have no effect on the current ratio, so a better idea is to use $10 of cash to pay accounts payable early.

REQUIRED

a. Which idea, the president's or the CFO's, is better for attaining a minimum 2.0 current ratio?

b. Will either the quick ratio or the times-interest-earned ratios be affected by either of these ideas?

SERIAL PROBLEM: ANGEL CITY GREETINGS

(Note: This is a continuation of the Serial Problem: Angel City Greetings from Chapters 1 through 8.)

SP9. Recall that Kate previously obtained a $15,000 bank loan, signing a note payable, on November 30. The note required semiannual interest payments at the rate of six percent. The entire principal balance was due two years from the origination date of the note. Kate has been accruing interest on a monthly basis in the amount of $75. Kate would like to know how she should record the interest in May, the month she makes the first interest payment. She is unsure how much expense will need to be recorded in May.

The upcoming interest payment is really not Kate's main concern right now. She was just notified by a lawyer that she is being sued for copyright infringement. Mega Cards Incorporated, one of the largest greeting card companies, believes that one of Kate's designs is too similar to one of Mega's designs for it to be coincidence, and has, therefore, decided to sue Angel City Greetings. Mega has a prior reputation for suing small companies and settling out of court for lesser damages. Kate, however, knows that her design is original and that she had never previously seen the Mega design that is the subject of the lawsuit. She has determined to fight the lawsuit, regardless of the cost. She doesn't know, however, how this will affect her financial statements.

1. How much interest expense is reported in May?
2. How should Kate report the copyright infringement lawsuit in her financial statements?

BEYOND THE NUMBERS

REPORTING AND ANALYSIS

BTN9-1. **Financial Reporting Problem: Columbia Sportswear Company** The financial statements for the Columbia Sportswear Company can be found in Appendix A at the end of this book. Columbia Sportswear Company

Required

Answer the following questions as they relate to December 31, 2020:

a. How much were Columbia's current liabilities?

b. What two items made up the largest percentage of Columbia's current liabilities?

c. What was the largest component of Columbia's accrued liabilities?

Columbia Sportswear Company
Under Armour, Inc.

BTN9-2. Comparative Analysis Problem: Columbia Sportswear Company vs Under Armour Inc. The financial statements for the Columbia Sportswear Company can be found in Appendix A, and the financial statements of Under Armour, Inc., can be found in Appendix B.

Required

Answer the following questions:

a. Compute the current ratio for Columbia Sportswear and Under Armour, Inc., as of December 31, 2020, and comment on what this ratio implies about each company's liquidity and working capital position.

b. Compute the debt-to-total assets ratio for Columbia Sportswear and Under Armour, Inc., as of December 31, 2020, and comment on what this ratio implies about each company's solvency.

BTN9-3. Business Decision Problem Kingston Corporation has total assets of $5,200,000 and has been earning an average of $800,000 before income taxes the past several years. The firm is planning to expand plant facilities to manufacture a new product and needs an additional $2,000,000 in funds, on which it expects to earn 18 percent before income tax. The income tax rate is expected to be 40 percent for the next several years. The firm has no long-term debt outstanding and presently has 75,000 shares of common stock outstanding. The firm is considering three alternatives:

1. Obtain the $2,000,000 by issuing 25,000 shares of common stock at $80 per share.
2. Obtain the $2,000,000 by issuing $1,000,000 of ten percent, 20-year bonds at face value and 12,500 shares of common stock at $80 per share.
3. Obtain the $2,000,000 by issuing $2,000,000 of ten percent, 20-year bonds at face value.

Required

As a shareholder of Kingston Corporation, which of the three alternatives would you prefer if your main concern is enhancing the firm's earnings per share? (Hint: Divide net income by the number of outstanding common shares to determine the company's earnings per share.)

Abbott Laboratories

BTN9-4. Financial Analysis Problem Abbott Laboratories is a diversified health care company devoted to the discovery, development, manufacture, and marketing of innovative products that improve diagnostic, therapeutic, and nutritional practices. The company's balance sheet for three recent years contains the following data ($ in millions):

	2020	2019	2018
Cash and cash equivalents	$ 6,838	$ 3,860	$ 3,844
Investment securities	310	280	242
Trade receivables (net of allowance)	6,414	5,425	5,182
Inventories	5,012	4,316	3,796
Other current assets	1,867	1,786	1,568
Total current assets	$20,441	$15,667	$14,632
Total current liabilities	$11,907	$10,863	$ 9,012

Required

a. Compute the current ratio for each year.

b. Compute the quick ratio for each year.

c. Comment on the three-year trend in these ratios.

CRITICAL THINKING

General Mills, Inc.

BTN9-5. Financial Analysis on the Web: General Mills, Inc. The fiscal year 2020 annual report of General Mills, Inc., can be found at: https://investors.generalmills.com/financial-information/annual-reports/default.aspx. Refer to the consolidated statement of earnings, the consolidated balance sheets, and Note 9.

Required

a. What was the total dollar amount of current liabilities as of May 31, 2020?

b. What percent of long-term debt was considered current as of May 31, 2020?

c. What were the current ratio and quick ratio as of May 31, 2020?

d. What is the total amount of long-term liabilities reported by General Mills as of May 31, 2020?

e. How much principal payments on the long-term debt is General Mills anticipating paying in fiscal year 2021?

BTN9-6. **Accounting Communication Activity** Cedric Salos is considering different ways to raise money for the expansion of his company's operations. Cedric is not sure about the advantages of issuing bonds versus issuing common stock. In addition, he is not sure which features he should consider including with the bonds if he selects that form of financing. He asks you to explain, in simple terms, the answers to his questions.

Required

Write a short memorandum to Cedric explaining the advantages of issuing bonds over issuing common stock and the features that should be considered for inclusion with the bonds.

BTN9-7. **Accounting Ethics Case** Sunrise Pools, Inc., is being sued by the Crescent Club for negligence when installing a new pool on Crescent Club's property. Crescent Club alleges that the employees of Sunrise Pools damaged the foundation of the clubhouse and part of the golf course while operating heavy machinery to install the pool.

The lawsuit is for $1.5 million. At the time of the alleged incident, Sunrise Pools carried only $600,000 of liability insurance.

While reviewing the draft of Sunrise Pools' annual report, its president deletes all references to this lawsuit. She is concerned that disclosure of this lawsuit in the annual report will be viewed by Crescent Club as admission of Sunrise's wrongdoing, even though she privately admits that Sunrise employees were careless and believes that Sunrise Pools will be found liable for an amount in excess of $1 million. The president sends the amended draft of the annual report to the vice president of finance with a note stating that the lawsuit will not be disclosed in the annual report and that the lawsuit will not be disclosed to the board of directors.

Required

Is the president's concern valid? What ethical problems will the vice president of finance face if he follows the president's instructions?

BTN9-8. **Environmental, Social, and Governance Problem** The chapter highlight on Microsoft's corporate social responsibility efforts (see page 296) discussed the Microsoft Global Skills Initiative. Go to Microsoft's website and navigate to the section "About Microsoft"; select Values, then navigate to the section on Corporate Social Responsibility. In addition to Microsoft Global Skills Initiative, what are some other ways that Microsoft demonstrates its commitment to being a good corporate citizen?

Microsoft

BTN9-9. **Accounting Ethics Problem** Billing schemes are frauds in which an employee causes the victim organization to issue fraudulent payments by submitting invoices for nonexistent goods or services, inflated invoices, or invoices for personal items. One type of billing scheme uses a shell company that is set up for the purpose of committing the fraud. The shell company is often nothing more than a fake corporate name and a post-office mailbox.

What are some of the ways that shell company invoices can be detected?

BTN9-10. **Working with the Takeaways** Below are selected data from Microsoft's 2020 financial statements ($ in millions):

	2020	2019
Net income	$ 44,281	$ 39,240
Tax expense	8,755	4,448
Interest expense	2,591	2,686
Cash and cash equivalents	13,576	11,356
Short-term investments	122,951	122,463
Accounts receivable	32,011	29,524
Other current assets	13,377	12,209
Current liabilities	72,310	69,420

Required

Calculate the following ratios for both years and comment on the trend:

a. Current ratio
b. Quick ratio
c. Times interest earned ratio

ANSWERS TO SELF-STUDY QUESTIONS

1. b **2.** b **3.** b **4.** a **5.** c **6.** b **7.** b **8.** c

REVIEW SOLUTIONS

Solution 9.1

Maturity date

a. 21 + 30 + 31 + 31 + 7: February 7
b. 8 + 31 + 31 + 20: February 20
c. 16 + 31 + 28: February 28

Accrued interest at December 31

a. \$20,000 × 0.08 × 82/360 = \$364.44
b. \$8,500 × 0.07 × 39/360 = \$64.46
c. \$16,000 × 0.09 × 16/360 = \$64.00

Solution 9.2

a.

Year	Interest Period	A Interest Paid 12% × ½ × \$500,000	B Interest Expense 10% × ½ of beginning year bond book value	C Periodic Amortization (A – B)	D Balance of Unamortized Premium (D – C)	E Book Value of Bonds (\$500,000 + D)
At issue. . .					\$62,360	\$562,360
2.	1	\$30,000	\$28,118	\$1,882	60,478	560,478
	2	30,000	28,024	1,976	58,502	558,502
3.	3	30,000	27,925	2,075	56,427	556,427
	4	30,000	27,821	2,179	54,248	554,248
4.	5	30,000	27,712	2,288	51,960	551,960
	6	30,000	27,598	2,402	49,558	549,558
5.	7	30,000	27,478	2,522	47,036	547,036
	8	30,000	27,352	2,648	44,388	544,388
6.	9	30,000	27,219	2,781	41,607	541,607
	10	30,000	27,080	2,920	38,687	538,687
7.	11	30,000	26,934	3,066	35,621	535,621
	12	30,000	26,781	3,219	32,402	532,402
8.	13	30,000	26,620	3,380	29,022	529,022
	14	30,000	26,451	3,549	25,473	525,473
9.	15	30,000	26,274	3,726	21,747	521,747
	16	30,000	26,087	3,913	17,834	517,834
10.	17	30,000	25,892	4,108	13,726	513,726
	18	30,000	25,686	4,314	9,412	509,412
11.	19	30,000	25,471	4,529	4,883	504,883
	20	\$30,000	\$25,244	\$4,883*	\$ —	\$500,000

*Increased by \$127 due to rounding.

continued from previous page

b.

	Assets	=	Liabilities	+	Contrib. Capital	+	Retained Earnings	Revenues	–	Expenses	=	Net Income
Dec. 31, Year 1	+562,360 Cash	=	+500,000 Bonds payable +62,360 Premium on bonds payable	+					–		=	
	Issued 10-year bonds at a premium.											
Jun. 30, Year 2	–30,000 Cash	=	–1,882 Premium on bonds payable	+			–28,118		–	+28,118 Bond interest expense	=	–28,118
	Semiannual interest payment and premium amortization. ($562,360 × 10% × 1/2 = $28,118)											
Dec. 31, Year 2	–30,000 Cash	=	–1,976 Premium on bonds payable	+			–28,024		–	+28,024 Bond interest expense	=	–28,024
	Semiannual interest payment and premium amortization. [($562,360 – $1,882) × 10% × 1/2 = $28,024]											

Solution 9.3

a.

Assets	=	Liabilities	+	Contrib. Capital	+	Retained Earnings	Revenues	–	Expenses	=	Net Income
+325,000 Cash	=	+300,000 Bonds payable +25,000 Premium on bonds payable	+					–		=	

The issuance of bonds payable at a premium.

b. Long-term liabilities

Bonds payable	$300,000	
Add: Premium on bonds payable	25,000	$325,000

Solution 9.4

1. Because the likelihood of losing the lawsuit is deemed remote, it does not need to be recognized or disclosed by Anderson Co.
2. Even though the contingency is remote, credit guarantees must be disclosed in the notes to the financial statements.
3. The liability should be recorded on the balance sheet because the likelihood of payment is both high and can be estimated.

Solution 9.5

a. $200,000/180,000 = 1.1
b. ($15,000 + 30,000 + 45,000)/180,000 = 0.5
c. (25,000 + 3,000)/3,000 = 9.3

10 Stockholders' Equity

PAST

Chapter 9 examined accounting for liabilities.

PRESENT

In this chapter, we turn our attention to accounting for stockholders' equity.

FUTURE

In Chapter 11, we shift our focus to the statement of cash flows.

AMAZON

Amazon.com, Inc., strives to be "Earth's most customer-centric company" by focusing on the customer rather than the competition. A company that started as an online bookstore with 158 employees now employs 1.3 million worldwide. Amazon's business includes online merchandising, smart devices such as Alexa, video streaming, content development and cloud-based services. It boasts 200 million Amazon Prime members around the world.

Where do firms get the necessary capital for expansion? One of the most important characteristics of the corporate form of organization is the ability to raise new capital by selling ownership shares in the company. Amazon had its initial public offering of its common shares in 1997.

Without a doubt, the modern corporation dominates the national and international economic landscape. In the United States, corporations generate well over three-fourths of the combined sales revenue of all forms of business organization, even though less than one of every five businesses is organized as a corporation.

Road Map

LO	Learning Objective	Page	eLecture	Review	Assignments
LO1	Define the corporate form of organization and discuss its principal characteristics.	336	E10-1	10.1	SE1, E10
LO2	Explain the difference between par value stock and no-par value stock.	339	E10-2		SE2, E2
LO3	Identify and discuss the two types of capital stock and their respective stockholder rights.	340	E10-3	10.2, 10.7	SE3, SE7, E1, E5, E7, P1
LO4	Describe the accounting for issuances of capital stock.	343	E10-4	10.3, 10.7	SE4, E2, E4, E11, P2, P3, P4, P5, P6, P7, P8
LO5	Define and discuss the accounting for stock splits.	345	E10-5		SE5, E3, E8, P4, P6, P7
LO6	Explain the accounting for stock repurchases.	346	E10-6	10.4, 10.7	SE6, SE12, E4, E11, P3, P4, P5, P6, P7, P8
LO7	Identify and distinguish between cash dividends and stock dividends.	349	E10-7	10.5, 10.7	E1, E5, P1
LO8	Illustrate the statement of retained earnings and the statement of stockholders' equity.	351	E10-8	10.6	SE11, E6, E11, P2, P3, P4, P7, P8
LO9	Define the return on common stockholders' equity, dividend yield, and dividend payout ratio.	353	E10-9	10.8	SE8, SE9, SE10, E9

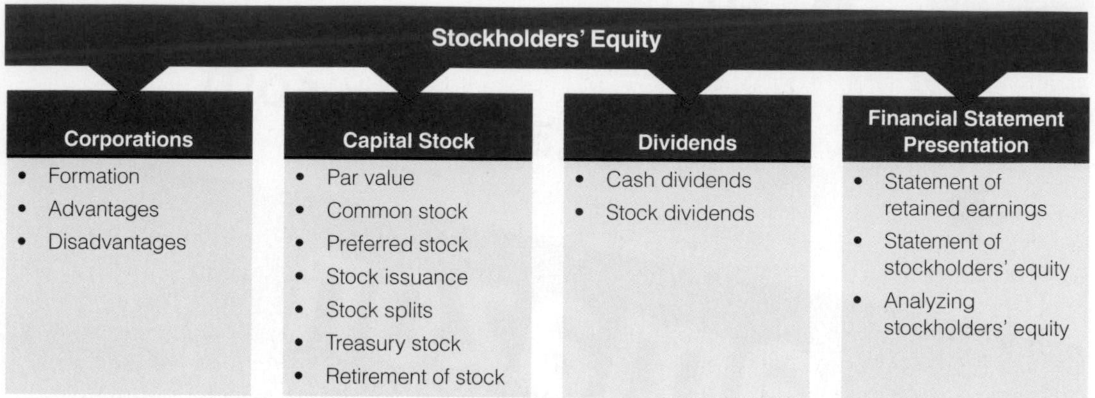

NATURE AND FORMATION OF A CORPORATION

LO1 **Define** the corporate form of organization and **discuss** its principal characteristics.

The right to conduct business as a **corporation** is a privilege granted by the state in which a corporation is formed (or chartered). All states have laws specifying the requirements for creating a corporation.

To form a corporation, the founders must apply for a charter by filing the **articles of incorporation**, which define the basic structure of the corporation, including the purpose for which it is formed and the amount of capital stock to be authorized. If all of the legal requirements are met, the state issues a charter or certificate of incorporation. After a charter has been granted, the founders hold an organizational meeting to elect the first board of directors and adopt the corporation's bylaws.

Corporations typically issue (or sell) *certificates of capital stock* to obtain the necessary funds to acquire its operating assets. As owners of a corporation, *stockholders* are entitled to a voice in the control and management of the company. Stockholders with voting stock may vote on specific issues at the annual shareholders' meeting and participate in the election of the board of directors. The board of directors establishes the overall policies of a corporation and declares dividends. Normally, the board also hires a group of corporate officers, including a president, a chief financial officer, one or more vice presidents, a controller (who is the top person in charge of accounting), a treasurer, and a secretary, to execute the day-to-day operations of the company. The officers implement the policies of the board of directors and actively manage the affairs of the corporation. **Exhibit 10-1** depicts the responsibilities of the corporation's stakeholders.

EXHIBIT 10-1 Responsibilities of Selected Corporate Stakeholders

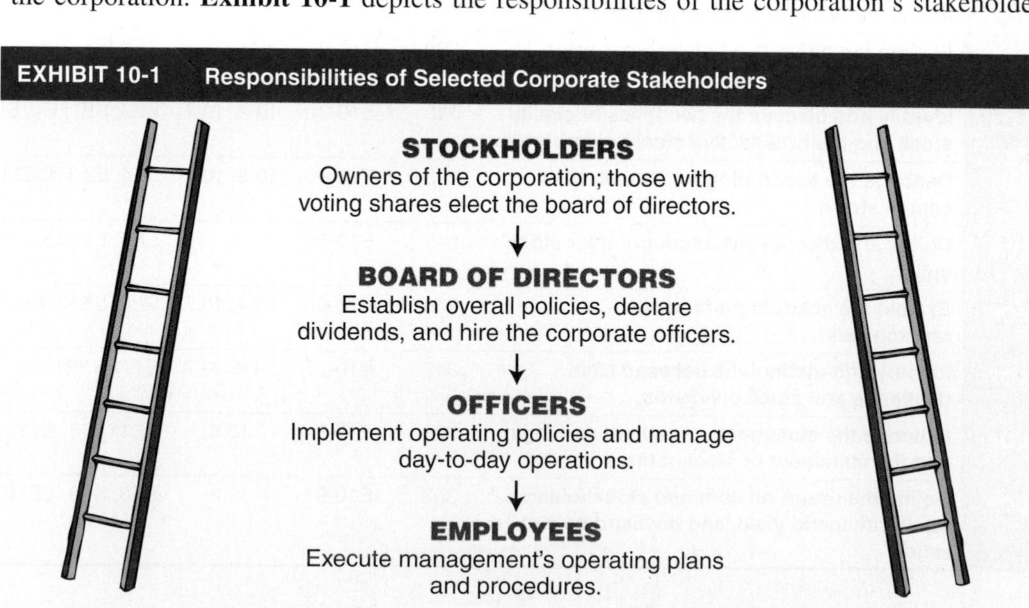

STOCKHOLDERS
Owners of the corporation; those with voting shares elect the board of directors.
BOARD OF DIRECTORS
Establish overall policies, declare dividends, and hire the corporate officers.
OFFICERS
Implement operating policies and manage day-to-day operations.
EMPLOYEES
Execute management's operating plans and procedures.

Advantages of the Corporate Form of Organization

A corporation has several advantages when compared with a sole proprietorship or partnership.

Separate Legal Entity

The corporation, as a separate legal entity, may acquire assets, incur debt, enter into contracts, sue, and be sued—all in its own name. The stockholders of a corporation, however, are separate and distinct from the corporation. This characteristic contrasts with proprietorships and partnerships, which are accounting entities but not legal entities apart from their owners.

Limited Liability

The shareholders' liability with respect to the corporation is usually limited to the value of their investment in the corporation. This limited liability is an advantage for the shareholders because it puts a cap on the amount they can lose on their investment. This contrasts with the owners of proprietorships and partnerships who can be held financially responsible, separately and collectively, for any unsatisfied obligations of the business. To protect a corporation's creditors, state laws limit the distribution of contributed capital. Distributions of retained earnings (undistributed profits) are not legal unless the board of directors formally votes to declare a dividend. Because of the legal constraints regarding the amount of stockholder capital available for distribution, corporations must maintain clear distinctions in the accounts to identify the various elements of stockholders' equity.

Transferability of Ownership

Shares in a corporation may be routinely transferred without affecting a company's operations. The corporation merely notes such transfers of ownership in the stockholder records. Although a corporation must have stockholder records to notify stockholders of meetings and to pay dividends, the price at which shares transfer between investors does not directly impact the corporation and, thus, are not recognized in the corporation's accounts.

Continuity of Existence

Because routine transfers of ownership do not directly affect the corporation, the corporation is said to have continuity of existence. This contrasts with a partnership, in which changes in ownership technically result in a discontinuation of the old partnership and the formation of a new one.

PRINCIPLE ALERT

Entity Concept and Going Concern Concept Two characteristics of the corporate form of organization mesh well with the basic principles of accounting. The separate legal status conferred upon a corporation conforms with the *entity concept*. When the corporation is the unit of focus for accounting purposes, the entity concept requires that the economic activity of the corporation be accounted for separately from the activities of its owners. Legally, the corporate entity is also distinct from its owners. Consequently, the corporation's continuity of existence also aligns with the *going concern concept*, which assumes that the company will continue indefinitely into the future.

Capital Raising Capability

The limited liability of stockholders and the ease with which shares of stock may be transferred from one investor to another are attractive features to potential stockholders. These characteristics enhance the ability of the corporation to raise large amounts of capital by issuing shares of stock. Because both large and small investors may acquire ownership interests in a corporation, there is a large pool of potential investors, and corporations with thousands of stockholders are not uncommon.

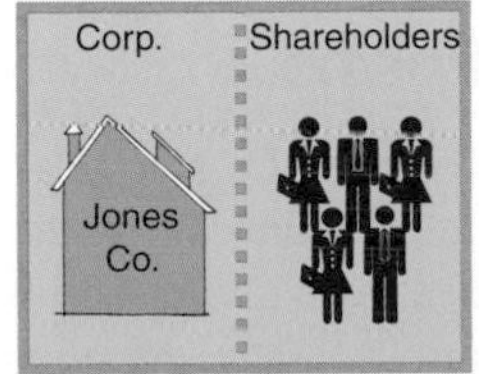

Separate Legal Entity

Limited Liability

Transferability of Ownership

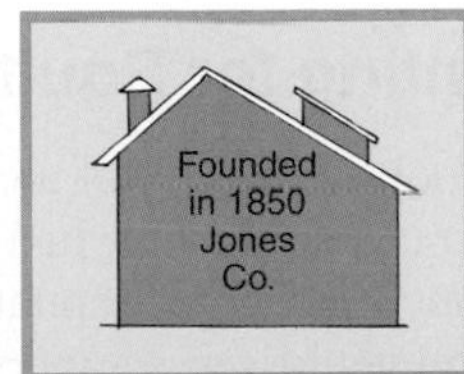

Continuous Existence

Capital Raising Capability

Disadvantages of the Corporate Form of Organization

There are some disadvantages to organizing as a corporation as compared with a proprietorship or partnership.

Organization Costs

Creating a corporation is more costly than organizing a proprietorship or partnership. The expenditures incurred to organize a corporation are charged to Organization Costs and expensed on the income statement when incurred. These costs include attorney's fees, fees paid to the state, and the costs of promoting the enterprise.

Taxation

As separate legal entities, corporations are subject to federal income taxes on their reported income. Stockholders are also subject to income taxes on the dividends they receive from the corporation. Thus, corporations are said to be subject to double taxation.

Usually, corporations are also subject to state income taxes in the states in which they are incorporated or are doing business. They also may be subject to real estate, personal property, and franchise taxes.

THINKING GLOBALLY

The equity ownership structure of most U.S. and United Kingdom companies is characterized by small diffuse investors, each of whom owns only a small fraction of the firm. But the ownership structure of public companies in most of the rest of the world is strikingly different and is more commonly characterized by the presence of a large investor who holds a controlling interest in the company's shares. These large owners usually consist of families and typically are involved directly in managing the company's operations. To illustrate, consider the following seven East Asian countries and the percentage of their public companies that are controlled by families. South Korea has the highest percentage of family-controlled public companies at 78 percent:

Country	Percentage of Family-Controlled Companies
Hong Kong	65%
Indonesia	75
Malaysia	71
Singapore	50
South Korea	78
Taiwan	55
Thailand	68

Regulation and Supervision

Corporations are subject to greater degrees of regulation and supervision than are proprietorships and partnerships. Each state maintains the right to regulate the corporations it charters. State laws also limit the powers a corporation may exercise, identify reports that must be filed by a corporation, and define the rights and liabilities of stockholders. If shares of stock are issued to the public, the corporation must comply with the securities laws governing the sale of corporate securities. Furthermore, corporations whose shares are listed and traded on organized security exchanges, such as the New York Stock Exchange, are subject to various reporting and disclosure requirements of these exchanges.

Accounting for Equity in Alternative Organizational Forms

The stockholders' equity of a corporation is accounted for differently than the equity of a sole proprietorship or partnership. In a sole proprietorship, only a single owner's capital account is needed to reflect increases from capital contributions and net income as well as decreases from owner withdrawals and net losses. Partnerships have multiple owners and typically maintain separate accounts that disclose the equity of each partner.

Because a corporation is a legal entity that is separate from its stockholders, it does not maintain equity accounts for each owner. Strict laws require corporations to distinguish between capital that is contributed by shareholders and capital from retained earnings.

REVIEW 10.1

The following attributes are associated with the corporate form of organization. Identify each one as either an advantage or a disadvantage of the corporate form over other forms of organization:

1. Taxation
2. Limited liability
3. Capital raising capability
4. Regulation
5. Cost to organize
6. Transferability of ownership

The solution is on page 370.

PAR VALUE STOCK AND NO-PAR VALUE STOCK

LO2 Explain the difference between par value stock and no-par value stock.

A corporate charter may specify a face value, or **par value**, for each share of capital stock. In the early days of corporate stock issuances, par value represented the market value of the stock when it was issued. In more recent times, however, par values typically have been set at amounts well below a stock's fair market value on the date of issue. As a consequence, a stock's par value has no economic significance today.

Par value, however, may have legal implications. In some states, par value may represent the minimum amount that must be contributed for each share of stock issued. If stock is issued at a *discount* (that is, at less than its par value), the stockholder may have a liability for the amount of the discount should any creditor claims remain unsatisfied following a company's liquidation. Issuing stock at a discount rarely occurs, however, because boards of directors have generally established par values far below fair market values at the time of issue. For example, **PepsiCo, Inc.**, set the par value of its common stock at $0.0167, and **Starbucks** set the par value of its common stock at $0.001.

Par value also may be used in some states to define a corporation's legal capital. *Legal capital* is the minimum amount of contributed capital that must remain in a corporation as a margin of protection for creditors. However, given the low par values typically assigned to common stock today, this protection has limited value for creditors. Still, given the role that par value may play in defining legal capital, accountants carefully segregate and record the par value of stock transactions in an appropriate capital stock account.

Most states permit the issuance of capital stock without a par value, called **no-par value stock**. The company's board of directors, however, usually sets a **stated value** for the no-par stock. In such cases, the stated value will determine the corporation's legal capital. For accounting purposes, stated value amounts are treated similarly to par value amounts. In the absence of a stated value, the entire proceeds from the issuance of no-par value stock will likely establish a corporation's legal capital.

ENVIRONMENTAL, SOCIAL, AND GOVERNANCE

Amazon To some, environmental and social responsibility means doing things for non-stockholder stakeholders, even if it means a lower rate of return for stockholders. This sort of thinking pits social responsibility against stockholder gains, as if the two were competitors for the corporate dollar. Companies that truly understand social responsibility have come to see it in a more strategic light, where doing good can lead to doing well. Further, these companies realize that they would not have the resources to do good if they were not making money. Amazon is not only a highly profitable company with 2020 profits of 21 billion U.S. dollars, but also a company "committed to building a sustainable business for our customers and the planet." The company has set goals such as powering is operations with 100% renewable energy by 2025 and achieving net-zero carbon emissions by 2040. The company also has programs in place to address recycling and diversity.

TYPES OF CAPITAL STOCK

LO3 Identify and **discuss** the two types of capital stock and their respective stockholder rights.

The amounts and kinds of capital stock that a corporation may issue are specified in a company's corporate charter. Providing for the sale of several classes of capital stock permits a company to raise capital from different types of investors with diverse risk preferences. The charter also specifies a corporation's **authorized shares**—the maximum number of shares of each class of capital stock that may be issued. Shares that have been sold and issued to stockholders constitute the **issued shares**. Some of these shares may be repurchased by the corporation. When shares are repurchased, they may be retired and cancelled or held for reissuance. Shares actually held by stockholders are called **outstanding shares**; whereas those reacquired by a corporation (and not cancelled) are called *treasury stock*. We will discuss treasury stock later in the chapter.

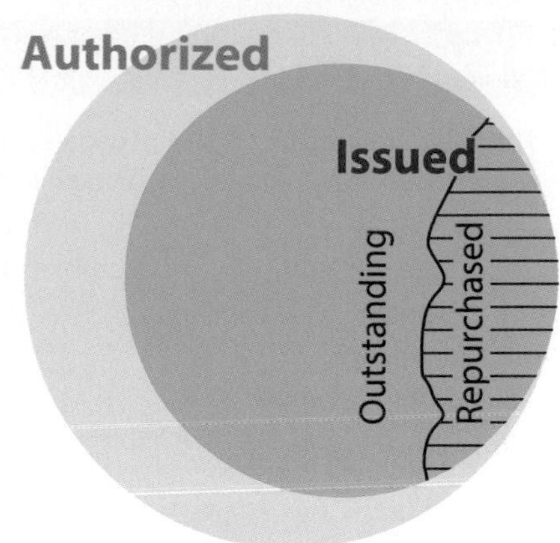

Common Stock

When only one class of stock is issued, it is called **common stock**. Common stockholders have the right to vote on corporate matters, to share in the corporation's net income, to participate in additional issuances of stock, and in the case of a corporate liquidation, to share in any asset distributions after paying the amounts owed to creditors.

As the owners of a corporation, the common stockholders elect the board of directors and vote on all matters requiring the approval of the owners. Common stockholders are entitled to one vote for each share of stock they own. Stockholders who do not attend the annual stockholders' meetings may vote by proxy.

A common stockholder has the right to a proportionate share of the corporation's earnings that are distributed as dividends. All earnings belong to the corporation, however, until the board of directors formally votes to declare a dividend.

Each stockholder of a corporation has a **preemptive right** to maintain his or her proportionate ownership interest in the corporation. If a company issues additional shares of stock, the current owners of that type of capital stock receive the first opportunity to acquire, on a pro rata basis, the new shares. In certain situations, management may request stockholders to waive their preemptive right. For example, a corporation may wish to issue additional shares of capital stock for use to acquire another company.

ACCOUNTING IN PRACTICE

Preemptive Right Prevents Wealth Transfer A major reason for the preemptive right is to protect stockholders against a transfer of their wealth to new stockholders. To illustrate, assume that a firm has 10,000 shares of common stock outstanding with a market price of $20 per share. Thus, the firm's total market value is $200,000 (10,000 shares × $20). If the firm sells another 10,000 common shares at $10 per share (a price below its current market value), the additional $100,000 cash received would raise the firm's total market value to $300,000. With a new market value of $15 per share ($300,000/20,000 shares), the new share issuance causes the old stockholders to lose $5 per share and the new stockholders to gain $5 per share—that is, the sale of the new shares at a lower price caused a wealth transfer from the old stockholders to the new stockholders. The preemptive right protects the existing stockholders from such wealth transfers by enabling them to purchase any newly issued shares.

When a corporation liquidates, it converts its assets to a form suitable for distribution, usually cash, which it then distributes to all parties having claims on the corporate assets. Any assets remaining after all claims have been satisfied belong to the residual owners of the corporation—that is, the common stockholders. Common stockholders are entitled to the final distribution of the balance of any remaining assets in a corporate liquidation.

A company may occasionally issue *classified* common stock; that is, it may issue more than one class of common stock. For example, when two classes of common stock are issued, they are often identified as Class A and Class B. The two classes usually differ in either their respective dividend rights or their respective voting powers. Usually, classified common stock is issued when the founders of a corporation wish to acquire funds from the public while retaining voting control of the corporation.

Preferred Stock

Preferred stock is a class of stock with characteristics that differentiate it from common stock. Preferred stock, for example, has one or more preferences over common stock, usually with reference to (1) the payment of dividends and (2) the distribution of assets when a corporation liquidates. Typical features associated with preferred stock are discussed below.

Dividend Preference

When the board of directors declares a distribution of the company's net income, preferred stockholders are entitled to an annual dividend before common stockholders may receive any dividend distribution. The amount usually is specified in the preferred stock contract as a percentage of the par value of the stock or in dollars per share if the stock lacks a par value. Thus, if the preferred stock has a $100 par value and a six percent dividend rate, the preferred stockholders receive $6 per share in dividends. However, the dividend is owed to the stockholders only if, and when, it is declared by the board of directors.

From both a legal and an accounting standpoint, preferred stock is disclosed as part of stockholders' equity on the balance sheet. Dividends are distributions of earnings and thus, unlike interest on bonds, are not shown as expenses on the income statement. Also, because of the legal classification of preferred stock as stockholders' equity, the company cannot deduct dividends as expenses for income tax purposes, whereas interest on debt is deducted as an expense.

Preferred dividends are usually **cumulative**—that is, regular dividends to preferred stockholders omitted in the past must be paid in addition to the current year's dividend before any dividend distribution can be made to the common stockholders. If a preferred stock is **noncumulative**, omitted dividends do not carry forward.

To illustrate the difference between cumulative and noncumulative preferred stock, assume that a company ending its second year of operations has 1,000 shares of $100 par value, six percent preferred stock and 100,000 shares of $1 par value common stock outstanding. The company declared no dividends last year. This year a dividend of $27,000 is declared. The distribution of the $27,000 between the two stockholder classes depends upon whether the preferred stock is cumulative or noncumulative. If the preferred stock is cumulative, preferred stockholders receive $12 per share before common stockholders receive anything, as illustrated below:

	Preferred	Common	Total
Total par value of outstanding shares	$100,000	$100,000	$200,000
Preferred stock is cumulative			
Preferred dividends in arrears (6 percent)	$ 6,000		$ 6,000
Regular preferred dividend (6 percent)	6,000		6,000
Remainder to common		$ 15,000	15,000
Total distribution	$ 12,000	$ 15,000	$ 27,000
Preferred stock is noncumulative			
Regular preferred dividend (6 percent)	$ 6,000		$ 6,000
Remainder to common		$ 21,000	21,000
Total distribution	$ 6,000	$ 21,000	$ 27,000

Dividends in arrears (that is, dividends omitted in past years) on cumulative preferred stock are not an accounting liability and do not appear in the liability section of the balance sheet. They do not become an obligation of the corporation until the board of directors formally declares such dividends. Any dividends in arrears are disclosed to investors in the notes to the financial statements.

Asset Distribution Preference

Preferred stockholders normally have a preference over common stockholders with respect to the receipt of assets in the event of a corporate liquidation. When a corporation liquidates, any creditor claims are settled first. Preferred stockholders then have the right to receive assets equal to the par value of their shares, or a larger stated liquidation value per share, before any assets are distributed to common stockholders. The preferred stockholders' preference to assets in liquidation also includes any dividends in arrears.

Other Preferred Stock Features

Although preferred stockholders do not ordinarily have the right to vote in the election of the board of directors, this right can be accorded by contract. Some state laws require that all capital stock issued by a corporation be given voting rights. Further, preferred stock may contain features that cause the shares to resemble common stock. Preferred stock may, for example, be **convertible** into common stock at a specified conversion rate. When this feature is present, the market price of the preferred shares often moves in a fashion consistent with the related common shares; that is, when the price of the common stock rises, the value of the conversion feature is enhanced, and consequently, the value of the preferred shares should also rise. When preferred stock is converted into a company's common stock, the newly issued common stock assumes the book value of the preferred stock; that is, the Preferred Stock—Par Value and the Paid-in Capital in Excess of Par Value—Preferred Stock are decreased while the Common Stock—Par Value and Paid-in Capital in Excess of Par Value—Common Stock are increased.

Preferred stock may be **participating**. A *participating preferred stock* shares any special dividend distributions with common stock beyond the regular preferred stock dividend rate. After receiving its regular dividend preference, preferred stock normally does not participate in any special dividend distribution until the common stock is allowed a dividend amount corresponding to the regular preferred stock dividend rate. At this point, the two classes of stock begin to share the special dividend distribution at the same rate. The preferred stock participation feature may be partial (which limits the participation to a certain amount) or full (which places no limit on the rate of participation).

Preferred stock may be **callable**, which means that a corporation can redeem the shares after a length of time and at a price specified in the stock contract. The call feature makes the preferred stock similar to a bond, because many bonds are callable or have a limited life. Most preferred stocks are callable, with the call or redemption price set slightly above the original preferred stock issuance price.

Data Analytics

DATA ANALYTICS **Facebook Insights**

When Mark Zuckerberg, the CEO of **Facebook**, was called to testify before Congress, he was asked how Facebook could prosper under a model in which its core business was given away for free. Zuckerberg smirked and replied, "Senator, we run ads." This comment is perhaps one of the largest understatements of all time. Facebook runs a lot of ads. Facebook is also on the cutting edge of how analytics, called Facebook Insights, are used to target the ads they run. Facebook Insights includes two analytics tools: Facebook Page Insights and Facebook Audience Insights. Page Insights helps organizations and individuals understand their audience, the success of posts, and the health of their Pages over time. Audience Insights gives organizations and individuals aggregated data about people connected to their Page and people on Facebook. Facebook Insights provides data that will help organizations and individuals make decisions about the content and strategy of their Page.

ACCOUNTING IN PRACTICE

Preferred Shares and the Capital Market Although legally, and from an accounting standpoint, preferred shares are considered to be part of a company's stockholders' equity, the capital market takes a different point of view. Most investment professionals consider a company's preferred stock to be part of the company's debt structure. Thus, from a capital market perspective, the only true stockholders of a business are its common stockholders. This point of view is apparent in the calculation of such ratios as the return on common stockholders' equity, discussed shortly, which excludes a company's preferred stockholders' equity.

REVIEW 10.2

Match the description in the right column with the appropriate term in the left column:

1. Authorized	*a.* The right to receive dividends omitted in prior years.
2. Outstanding	*b.* The most basic class of stock ownership.
3. Common stock	*c.* Stock with one or more preferences over common stock.
4. Preemptive right	*d.* The maximum number of shares of each class of stock that may be issued.
5. Preferred stock	*e.* Shares actually held by stockholders.
6. Cumulative	*f.* The right to maintain a proportionate ownership interest in a corporation.

The solution is on page 370.

STOCK ISSUANCES FOR CASH

LO4 Describe the accounting for issuances of capital stock.

When issuing capital stock to investors, a corporation may use the services of an investment bank, which specializes in helping companies market their securities to investors. The investment bank may *underwrite* a stock issue by agreeing to sell the shares on a firm commitment basis— that is, buying the shares from the corporation and then reselling them to investors. Under a firm commitment agreement, a corporation does not risk being unable to sell its stock. The underwriter bears this risk in return for the fees and profits generated by selling the shares to investors at a price higher than it paid to the corporation. An investment bank that is unwilling to underwrite a stock issue may handle the issuance of the shares on a *best efforts* basis. In this case, the investment bank agrees to sell as many shares as possible at a set price, but the corporation bears the risk of any unsold shares.

When capital stock is issued to investors, the appropriate capital stock account is increased for the par value of the stock issued, or if the stock is no-par value stock, with its stated value, if any. The asset received in exchange for the stock (usually cash) also is increased, and any difference is reflected as an increase to the Paid-in Capital in Excess of Par Value account.

To illustrate how various stock issuances in exchange for cash affect the financial statements, assume that Los Altos, Inc., issued two different types of capital stock during its first year of operations:

Issuing Stock at a Premium

1. Issued 1,000 shares of $100 par value, 9% preferred stock at $107 cash per share:

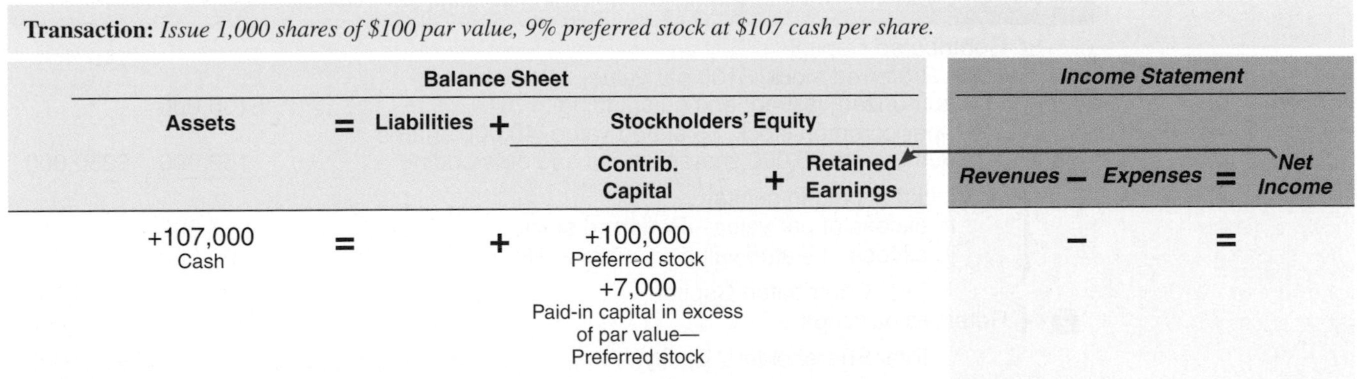

Transaction: *Issue 1,000 shares of $100 par value, 9% preferred stock at $107 cash per share.*

Balance Sheet							Income Statement				
Assets	=	Liabilities	+	Stockholders' Equity							
				Contrib. Capital	+	Retained Earnings	Revenues	−	Expenses	=	Net Income
+107,000 Cash	=		+	+100,000 Preferred stock +7,000 Paid-in capital in excess of par value—Preferred stock				−		=	

In this transaction, the preferred stock is issued at a price greater than its par value—that is, the shares were sold at a premium. The par value of the preferred stock issued is recorded as an increase to the Preferred Stock account and the $7,000 premium to the Paid-in Capital in Excess of Par Value account. If there is more than one class of par value stock, the account title may indicate the class of stock to which the premium relates, in this case Paid-in Capital in Excess of Par Value—Preferred Stock.

Issuing No-Par Stock

2. Issued 30,000 shares of no-par value common stock, stated value $5, at $8 cash per share:

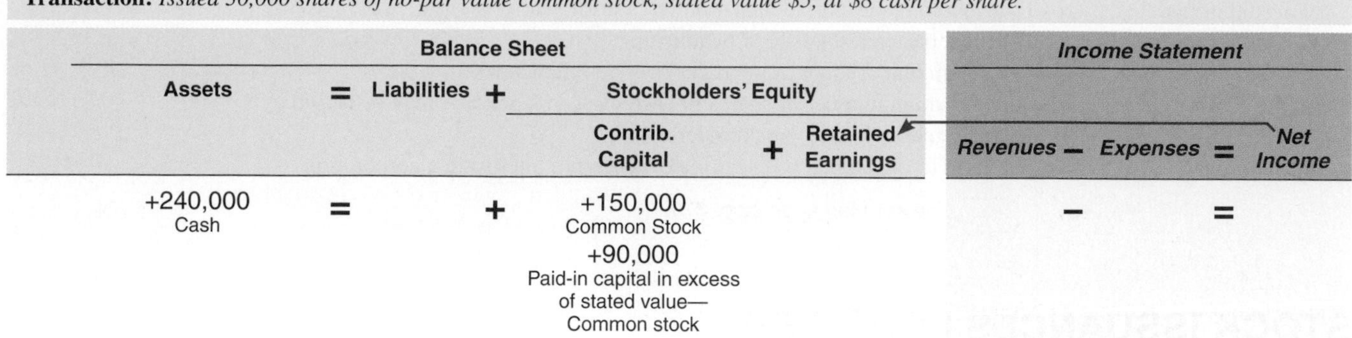

Assets	=	Liabilities	+	Contrib. Capital	+	Retained Earnings	Revenues	−	Expenses	=	Net Income
+240,000 Cash	=		+	+150,000 Common Stock +90,000 Paid-in capital in excess of stated value—Common stock				−		=	

When no-par value stock has a stated value, as in Entry 2, the stated value of the total shares issued is recorded in the proper capital stock account, and any additional amount received is an increase to the account Paid-in Capital in Excess of Stated Value. If there is no stated value for the no-par value stock, the entire proceeds are recorded in the appropriate capital stock account. For example, in the second transaction, if the common stock had no stated value, the entire $240,000 amount would have been an increase to the Common Stock account.

These two stock issuances are reflected in **Exhibit 10-2**, which presents the stockholders' equity section from Los Altos, Inc.'s year-end balance sheet. (It is assumed that the company is authorized to issue 1,000 shares of preferred stock and 40,000 shares of common stock, and that retained earnings are $25,000.) The stockholders' equity section is divided into two major categories: ❶ Contributed Capital and ❷ Retained Earnings. **Contributed capital** is the amount of capital contributed to the corporation from various capital stock transactions such as the issuance of preferred stock and common stock. The capital contributed by stockholders through the issuance of stock is divided between the legal capital (the par value or stated value of the stock) and the amounts received in excess of the legal capital. Later in this chapter we discuss treasury stock transactions that may affect a corporation's contributed capital. **Retained earnings** represent the cumulative net income and losses of the company that have not been distributed to stockholders as a dividend.

A.K.A. *Contributed Capital* is also referred to as Paid-in Capital.

EXHIBIT 10-2 Stockholders' Equity Section of the Balance Sheet

❶	Contributed Capital		
	9% Preferred stock, $100 par value, 1,000 shares authorized, issued, and outstanding	$100,000	
	No-par common stock, $5 stated value, 40,000 shares authorized; 30,000 shares issued and outstanding	150,000	$250,000
	Additional paid-in capital		
	In excess of par value—Preferred stock	7,000	
	In excess of stated value—Common stock	90,000	97,000
	Total Contributed Capital		347,000
❷	Retained earnings		25,000
	Total Shareholders' Equity		$372,000

Noncash Stock Issuances

Sometimes a corporation will exchange its common stock for services or operating assets. In these cases, the stock issuance is valued at the fair value of the assets or services received in exchange for the stock. For example, some start-up companies lacking cash will exchange their common stock for professional services provided by attorneys and accountants. When this occurs, the exchange is recorded as an increase to the Professional Services Expense account and an increase to Common Stock account for the fair value of the services received. When common stock is exchanged for operating assets, such as Equipment, a similar entry is made, except that the Equipment account is increased by the fair value of the equipment.

Corporations may also exchange their common stock for convertible bonds, as discussed in Chapter 9. When this occurs, the value of the newly issued stock is assumed to be equal to the book value of the bonds. An exchange of convertible bonds for common stock is reflected as a decrease in the Bonds Payable account and the Premium on Bonds Payable account (or the Discount on Bonds Payable account). The book value of the bond is allocated to the Common Stock account, and any excess over the par value increases Paid-In Capital in Excess of Par Value.

REVIEW 10.3

Wyatt Industries began operations on June 1 by issuing 10,000 shares of $1 par value common stock for cash at $9 per share. How much Additional Paid-in Capital will be reported by Wyatt Industries?

The solution is on page 370.

STOCK SPLITS

LO5 Define and **discuss** the accounting for stock splits.

Occasionally, a corporation may issue additional shares of common stock to its stockholders through a **forward stock split**. The principal reason that companies execute a forward stock split is to reduce the market price of their shares. Companies often wish to reduce the price of their shares in order to make them more affordable to a larger number of shareholders. A forward stock split increases the number of shares outstanding and is accounted for by reducing the par value or stated value of the stock affected. A forward stock split does not change the balances of any of the stockholders' equity accounts; however, a memorandum entry is made in the general journal to show the altered par value or stated value of the stock and to note the increase in the number of shares issued and outstanding. For example, if Los Altos, Inc., has 10,000 shares of $10 par value common stock outstanding and announces a 2-for-1 forward stock split, it would simply reduce the par value of its common stock to $5 per share and issue to its stockholders 10,000 new common shares. Thus, after the forward stock split, each stockholder would have twice the number of shares held prior to the split, and the value of the Common Stock account would remain unchanged at $100,000 (10,000 shares × $10 = 20,000 shares × $5 = $100,000). If you owned one share of Los Altos, Inc., $10 par value stock before the 2-for-1 forward stock split, you would own two shares of Los Altos, Inc., $5 par value stock after the stock split.

Before 2-for-1 forward stock split

Share #1–
$5 par value

Share #2–
$5 par value

After 2-for-1 forward stock split

Occasionally, a company may execute a *reverse stock split* by increasing the par value of the stock and reducing the number of shares outstanding. Reverse stock splits are designed to increase a company's stock price. Most major stock exchanges have a minimum trading price that a company must meet or exceed in order to be traded on the exchange. When a company's stock price falls below the minimum trading price, the shares may be delisted, making it difficult for stockholders to find buyers for their shares. Meeting and exceeding an exchange's minimum listing price is one of the principal reasons for reverse stock splits.

ACCOUNTING FOR STOCK REPURCHASES

LO6 Explain the accounting for stock repurchases.

Corporations repurchase their own outstanding stock for many reasons. Depending on the reason, repurchased shares may either be included in stockholders' equity as Treasury Stock, or they may be retired.

Accounting for Treasury Stock

When a corporation acquires its own outstanding shares and does not retire (cancel) those shares, the acquired shares are called **treasury stock**. Treasury stock may be purchased for a variety of reasons, including to reissue them to officers and employees in profit-sharing programs or employee stock option plans. Whatever the purpose, treasury stock purchases reduce a company's stockholders' equity. The repurchased shares do not carry voting privileges or preemptive rights, are not paid dividends, are not used to calculate earnings per share, and do not receive assets in the event of a corporation's liquidation.

Accountants record treasury stock at its acquisition cost, increasing the Treasury Stock account and decreasing the Cash account. The Treasury Stock account is a contra-stockholders' equity account, and its balance is deducted when computing total stockholders' equity on the balance sheet. To illustrate the affect on the financial statements of purchasing treasury stock, assume that Los Altos, Inc., had 20,000 shares of $10 par value common stock outstanding and then purchased 1,000 shares at its market price of $12 per share. The purchase reduces Cash by $12,000 and increases the contra-stockholders' equity account, Treasury Stock, by $12,000.

This is shown in the transaction analysis template below, which includes the newly created account in stockholders' equity, Treasury Stock.

Transaction: *Purchase 1,000 shares of treasury stock at $12 per share.*

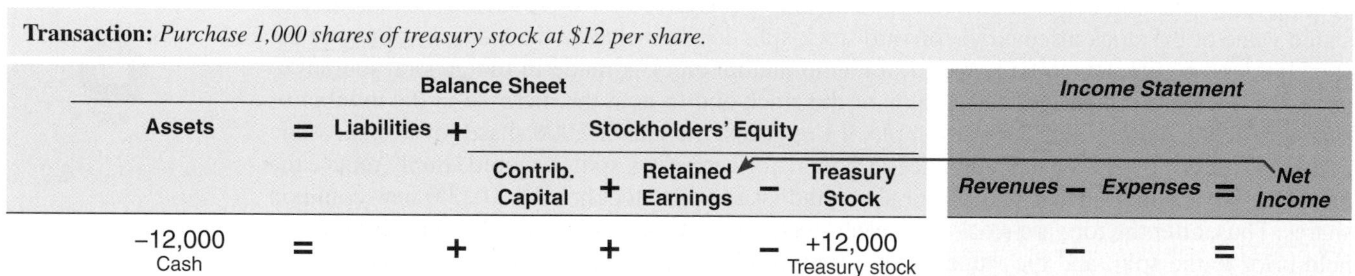

Assets	=	Liabilities	+	Contrib. Capital	+	Retained Earnings	−	Treasury Stock	Revenues	−	Expenses	=	Net Income
−12,000 Cash	=		+		+		−	+12,000 Treasury stock		−		=	

Following this transaction, the stockholders' equity section of Los Altos, Inc.'s balance sheet would appear as follows (the values for Paid-in Capital in Excess of Par Value and Retained Earnings are assumed):

LOS ALTOS, INC. Stockholders' Equity	
Contributed Capital	
Common stock, $10 par value, authorized and issued 20,000 shares; 1,000 shares in treasury, 19,000 shares outstanding	$200,000
Paid-in capital in excess of par value	20,000
Total Contributed Capital	220,000
Retained earnings	40,000
	260,000
Less: Treasury stock (1,000 shares) at cost	**12,000**
Total Stockholders' Equity	$248,000

Note that the $200,000 par value of all *issued* stock is disclosed, although the 1,000 treasury shares are no longer outstanding. The total cost of the 1,000 shares, however, is later deducted as the last component in the presentation of total stockholders' equity.

If Los Altos, Inc., subsequently resells 500 shares of its treasury stock at $14 per share (the market value at the time of the reissuance), the Treasury Stock account is reduced by the original cost of the treasury stock (500 × $12 per share = $6,000) and the excess [(500 × ($14 – $12) = $1,000] increases paid-in capital in excess of par value. This is shown in the transaction analysis template and the stockholders' equity section of Los Altos, Inc.'s balance sheet after recording this transaction.

Transaction: *Sale of 500 shares of treasury stock for $14 per share. The original cost of the treasury shares was $12.*

Balance Sheet										Income Statement				
Assets	=	Liabilities	+	Stockholders' Equity										
				Contrib. Capital	+	Retained Earnings	–	Treasury Stock		Revenues	–	Expenses	=	Net Income
+7,000 Cash	=		+	+1,000 Additional paid-in capital—Treasury stock	+		–	–6,000 Treasury stock			–		=	

LOS ALTOS, INC.
Stockholders' Equity
After Resale of Treasury Stock

Contributed Capital	
Common stock, $10 par value, authorized and issued 20,000 shares; 1,000 shares in treasury, 19,000 shares outstanding	$200,000
Paid-in capital in excess of par value ($20,000 + $1,000 treasury)	21,000
Total Contributed Capital	221,000
Retained earnings	40,000
	261,000
Less: Treasury stock (500 shares) at cost ($12,000 - (500 × $12))	**6,000**
Total Stockholders' Equity	$255,000

Note that the additional $1,000 received on the resale of the treasury stock is accounted for as an increase in contributed capital and not as net income. This is because the treasury stock is reissued at its market price, and, thus, does not result in a gain for the existing shareholders.

Accounting for Repurchase and Retirement of Stock

When a corporation acquires its own outstanding shares and retires them, the Common Stock account is reduced by the amount of the par value. The excess of the repurchase price over the par value is allocated to Additional Paid-In Capital and/or Retained Earnings. While management has some discretion in this allocation, companies typically reduce Additional Paid-In Capital by the amount related to the original issue price, and any remaining amount to Retained Earnings. Note, however, that the net effect on total stockholders' equity is the same as with the acquisition of Treasury Stock.

To illustrate, assume Los Altos, Inc., repurchased the 1,000 shares at $12 as discussed above, but retired them instead of holding them in the Treasury. The financial statement effect is a reduction to Common Stock of $10,000 (1,000 shares × $10 par), a reduction to Additional Paid-in Capital of $1,000 ((original issue price of $11 – $10 par) × 1,000 shares) and a reduction to Retained Earnings of $1,000 ($12,000 – $10,000 – $1,000). Note that the original issue price of $11 is calculated as total contributed capital divided by the number of issued shares ($220,000/20,000 shares). As with the treasury stock transaction, Cash is reduced by $12,000.

Transaction: *Repurchase and retirement of 1,000 shares of common for $12 per share. The shares had a par value $10; issue price $11.*

Balance Sheet							Income Statement		
Assets	=	Liabilities	+	Stockholders' Equity: Contrib. Capital	+	Stockholders' Equity: Retained Earnings	*Revenues*	− *Expenses*	= *Net Income*
−12,000 Cash	=		+	−10,000 Common stock −1,000 Additional paid-in capital		−1,000		−	=

Following this transaction, the stockholders' equity section of Los Altos, Inc.'s balance sheet would appear as follows. Note that the $190,000 par value of all issued and outstanding shares is reported. Note also that total stockholders' equity after the retirement is $248,000, which is the same as it was in the example when Los Altos held the repurchased shares in treasury.

LOS ALTOS, INC.
Stockholders' Equity

Contributed Capital	
Common stock, $10 par value, authorized 20,000 shares; 19,000 shares issued and outstanding	$190,000
Paid-in capital in excess of par value	19,000
Total Contributed Capital	209,000
Retained earnings	39,000
Total Stockholders' Equity	$248,000

ACCOUNTING IN PRACTICE

Negative Retained Earnings Generally, negative retained earnings result from operating losses, which may indicate that the company is in financial distress. However, many successful companies such as Starbucks currently report negative retained earnings. Starbucks reported a $7.8 billion deficit in retained earnings and total stockholders' equity in its fiscal 2020 balance sheet. Starbucks' negative retained earnings is the result of aggressively repurchasing its common shares for several years.

THINKING GLOBALLY

Under IFRS and U.S. GAAP, treasury stock is reported on the balance sheet as a contra stockholders' equity account; that is, the repurchase cost of any treasury stock is subtracted from total stockholders' equity. In addition, both IFRS and U.S. GAAP preclude the recognition of any gain or loss by a company from stock transactions involving its own shares—that is, any "gain" or "loss" from trading in a company's own shares is recorded as part of Paid-in Capital in Excess of Par Value. By way of contrast, some countries permit treasury stock to be reported on the asset side of the balance sheet as an investment in marketable securities. Under IFRS and U.S. GAAP, treasury stock does not satisfy the definition of an asset, and, therefore, cannot be reported on the balance sheet as marketable securities. It is also noteworthy that in some countries, treasury stock purchases are illegal because they are viewed as a form of stock price manipulation.

REVIEW 10.4

The Fullerton Corporation purchased 5,000 shares of its outstanding $2 par value common stock for $75,000 cash on November 1. Management anticipates holding the stock in the treasury until it resells the stock. How much would the Fullerton Corporation report as Treasury Stock for this purchase?

The solution is on page 370.

CASH DIVIDENDS AND STOCK DIVIDENDS

LO7 Identify and distinguish between cash dividends and stock dividends.

Dividends are a distribution of assets or shares of stock from a corporation to its stockholders. A corporation can distribute dividends to stockholders only after its board of directors has formally voted to declare a distribution. Dividends usually are paid in cash but also may be paid as property or additional shares of stock in the firm. Legally, declared dividends are an obligation of the firm, and an entry to record the dividend obligation is made on the *dividend declaration date*. Cash and property dividends payable are carried as liabilities, and stock dividends to be issued are shown in the stockholders' equity section of the balance sheet. At the date of declaration, a *record date* and *payment date* also are established. For example, assume that on April 25 (the declaration date), the board of directors of Los Altos, Inc., declares a cash dividend payable on June 1 (the payment date) to those investors who own shares of stock on May 15 (the record date). Stockholders owning stock on the record date receive the dividend even if they dispose of their shares before the payment date. Therefore, shares sold between the record date and the payment date are sold *ex dividend*—that is, they are sold without the right to receive the dividend.

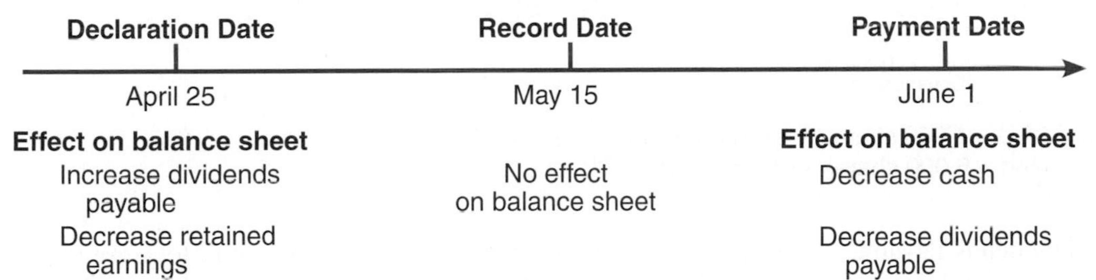

Most dividend declarations are accounted for by reducing retained earnings. Under certain conditions, however, state laws may permit distributions from additional paid-in capital. Stockholders should be informed of the source of such dividends, because, a dividend paid from a company's contributed capital is a nontaxable return of capital rather than a taxable distribution of earnings.

THINKING GLOBALLY

Although corporations principally distribute cash and/or stock dividends, property dividend distributions are common among corporations worldwide. For example, **Starbucks** is known for distributing a certificate for a free coffee with its annual report. And, **Lindt & Sprungli AG** distributes a box of its chocolates to certain shareholders. Companies that distribute their products or coupons for their products to stockholders as a property dividend believe that by making stockholders more familiar with the company's products, they will retain the investment commitment of their stockholders on a longer term basis than would otherwise be the case.

Cash Dividends

The majority of dividends distributed by corporations are paid in cash. Although companies may pay such dividends annually, many firms pay quarterly dividends. Dividends that are paid routinely are called regular dividends. The **Johnson & Johnson Company** and **PepsiCo, Inc.**, for example, pay regular quarterly dividends. Some companies occasionally pay a special dividend. Special dividends occur infrequently and represent the distribution of excess cash that has been accumulated by a business and for which the business has no immediate operational need.

When a company declares a cash dividend, the company must have the necessary amount of cash on hand. Uninformed investors often believe that a large retained earnings balance automatically permits generous dividend distributions. A company, however, may successfully accumulate earnings and at the same time not have enough cash to pay large cash dividends. Many companies, especially new firms in growth industries, finance their expansion from assets generated through earnings and pay out small cash dividends or none at all.

Cash dividends are based on the number of shares outstanding. When a company's directors declare a cash dividend, an entry is made to decrease Retained Earnings and increase a liability account, Dividends Payable. To illustrate, assume that Los Altos, Inc., has 1,000 shares of $100 par value, six percent preferred stock and 6,000 shares of $10 par value common stock outstanding. If the company declares the regular $6 dividend on the preferred stock and a $2 dividend on the common stock, the dividend payment totals $18,000. The following reflects the financial statement effect on the declaration date:

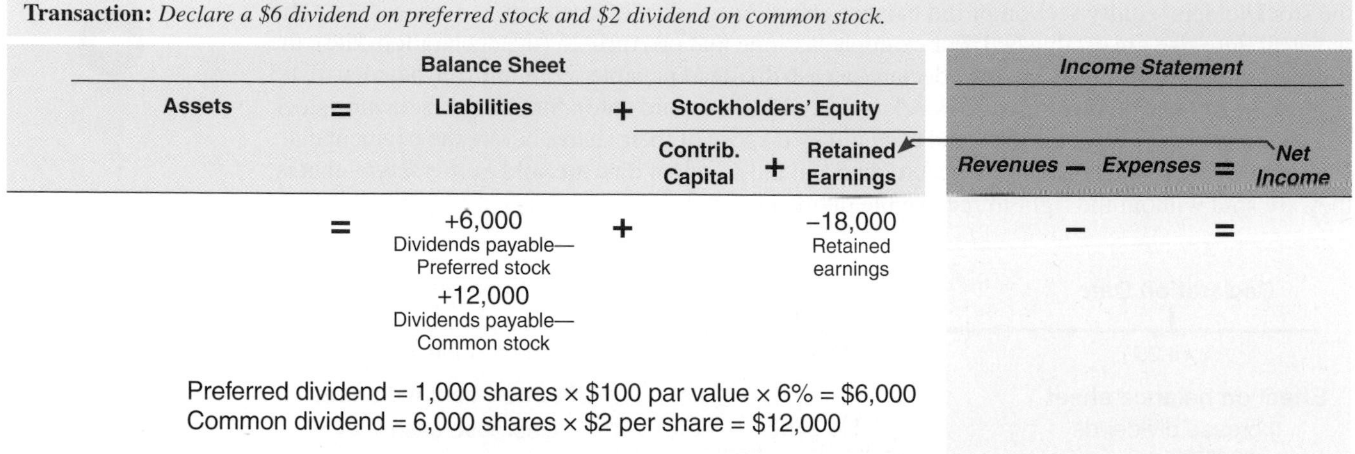

Dividends Payable—Preferred Stock and Dividends Payable—Common Stock are reported as current liabilities on the balance sheet until paid. On the dividend payment date, the financial statement effect is as follows:

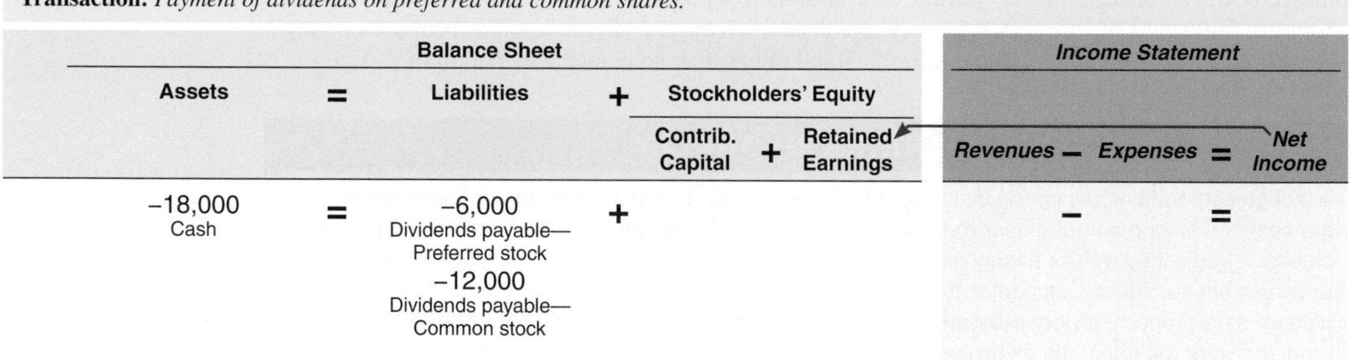

Stock Dividends

Companies frequently distribute shares of their own stock as dividends to stockholders in lieu of, or in addition to, cash dividends. A company may issue **stock dividends** when it does not wish to deplete its working capital by paying a cash dividend. Young and growing companies often issue stock dividends because cash is usually needed to acquire new facilities and to expand.

The accounting for a stock dividend results in a transfer of a portion of retained earnings to the contributed capital accounts. Thus, the distribution of a stock dividend signals to investors that management plans to "plow back" earnings into the company. Although stock dividends may take a number of forms, usually common shares are distributed to common stockholders. We limit our discussion to this type of stock dividend distribution.

ACCOUNTING IN PRACTICE

Small versus Large Stock Dividends Small stock dividends are share distributions that involve less than 25 percent of the total number of shares previously outstanding. Small stock dividends are *recorded at the market value* of the shares issued, causing retained earnings to decrease and contributed capital to increase by this amount. When the number of shares issued as a stock dividend is large enough to impact the stock's market value per share, the stockholders may not perceive the same benefits as they do for a small stock dividend. Accordingly, the accounting for large stock dividends (those greater than 25 percent) differs from the accounting for small stock dividends. To record a large stock dividend, Retained Earnings is decreased and the Common Stock account increased for the *par or stated value of the shares issued* (rather than the market value).

REVIEW 10.5

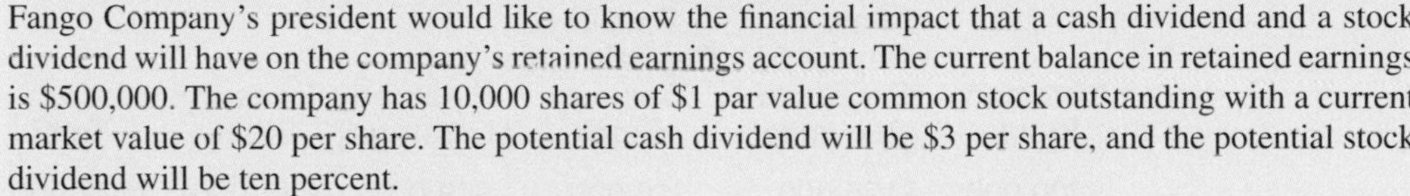
Fango Company's president would like to know the financial impact that a cash dividend and a stock dividend will have on the company's retained earnings account. The current balance in retained earnings is $500,000. The company has 10,000 shares of $1 par value common stock outstanding with a current market value of $20 per share. The potential cash dividend will be $3 per share, and the potential stock dividend will be ten percent.

Required

Compute the Fango Company retained earnings balance after

a. A $3 per share cash dividend
b. A ten percent stock dividend

The solution is on page 370.

RETAINED EARNINGS AND THE STATEMENT OF STOCKHOLDERS' EQUITY

LO8 Illustrate the statement of retained earnings and the statement of stockholders' equity.

A **statement of retained earnings** presents an analysis of the Retained Earnings account for a given accounting period. An example of a statement of retained earnings is presented in **Exhibit 10-3**. The statement begins with the retained earnings balance as of the beginning of the period ❶, then reports the items that caused retained earnings to change during the period ❷, and ends with the end-of-period balance in retained earnings ❸.

EXHIBIT 10-3 Statement of Retained Earnings

GEYSER CORPORATION
Statement of Retained Earnings
For Year Ended December 31

❶	Retained earnings, January 1	$48,000
❷	Add: Net income	32,000
		80,000
	Less: Cash dividends declared	19,000
❸	Retained earnings, December 31	$61,000

Statement of Stockholders' Equity

Rather than reporting a statement of retained earnings, most corporations integrate the information regarding retained earnings into a more comprehensive statement called a **statement of**

stockholders' equity. This statement shows an analysis of all of the stockholders' equity accounts for the period. **Exhibit 10-4** presents an example of a statement of stockholders' equity. The statement begins with the beginning balances of the various stockholders' equity accounts ❶, reports the items causing changes in these accounts ❷, and ends with the end-of-period balances ❸.

The statement of stockholders' equity in **Exhibit 10-4** reports all of the events affecting the Geyser Corporation's stockholders' equity during the year. These events are the issuance of common stock, the issuance of treasury stock, the earning of net income, the declaration of a cash dividend, and the acquisition of treasury stock. Note that the information in the retained earnings column (highlighted using a dotted red box) contains the same information as a statement of retained earnings.

EXHIBIT 10-4 Statement of Stockholders' Equity

GEYSER CORPORATION
Statement of Stockholders' Equity
For Year Ended December 31

		Common Stock	Paid-in Capital in Excess of Par Value	Paid-in Capital from Treasury Stock	Retained Earnings	Treasury Stock	Total
❶	Balance, January 1	$200,000	$120,000	$18,000	$48,000	$(14,000)	$372,000
❷	6,000 Common shares issued	30,000	24,000				54,000
	500 Treasury shares issued			2,000		3,500	5,500
	Net income				32,000		32,000
	Cash dividends declared				(19,000)		(19,000)
	200 Treasury shares acquired					(2,000)	(2,000)
❸	Balance, December 31	$230,000	$144,000	$20,000	$61,000	$(12,500)	$442,500

THINKING GLOBALLY

There exist a number of terminology differences between U.S. GAAP and IFRS with respect to the reporting of stockholders' equity.

U.S. GAAP	IFRS
Common stock	Share capital
Paid-in capital in excess of par value	Share premium
Retained earnings	Retained profits
Accumulated other comprehensive income	Other reserve accounts

REVIEW 10.6

Dior Company had beginning balances at January 1 of $100,000 Common Stock, $900,000 Paid-in Capital in Excess of Par Value, and $50,000 Retained Earnings, $(10,000) Treasury Stock. Net income for the year was $30,000. Dior paid a cash dividend of $8,000. Dior also issued 1,000 new $1 par value common shares for $15 each.

Required

Prepare a statement of stockholders' equity for the Dior Company for the year ending December 31.

The solution is on page 370.

REVIEW 10.7

Following is the stockholders' equity section of Bayside Corporation's December 31 balance sheet:

Contributed Capital		
7 percent preferred stock, $50 par value, 5,000 shares authorized, issued, and outstanding	$ 250,000	
Common stock, $6 par value, 700,000 shares authorized; 200,000 issued, of which 10,000 shares are in the treasury	1,200,000	$1,450,000
Additional Paid-in Capital		
In excess of par value—Preferred stock	80,000	
In excess of par value—Common stock	1,000,000	
From treasury stock	22,000	1,102,000
Total Contributed Capital		2,552,000
Retained earnings		2,223,000
		4,775,000
Less: Treasury stock (10,000 common shares) at cost		140,000
Total Stockholders' Equity		$4,635,000

Required

a. What is Bayside's legal capital at December 31?
b. What is the number of common shares outstanding at December 31?
c. What is the average amount per share received from the original issuance of common stock?
d. Assuming that the preferred stock is cumulative with no dividends in arrears, what total dollar amount of preferred dividends needs to be declared at December 31, before the common stockholders may receive a dividend?
e. Has Bayside ever sold treasury stock for more than the treasury stock cost when it was acquired? Briefly explain.
f. Assume that Bayside splits its common stock 3-for-1 on the following January 1. What is the total amount of contributed capital immediately after the split?

The solution is on page 371.

ANALYZING STOCKHOLDERS' EQUITY

Return on Common Stockholders' Equity

LO9 **Define** the return on common stockholders' equity, dividend yield, and dividend payout ratio.

A financial ratio of particular interest to common stockholders is the return on common stockholders' equity. This ratio measures the profitability of the common stockholders' investment in a company. The **return on common stockholders' equity** is calculated as follows:

$$\textbf{Return on common stockholders' equity} = \frac{\textbf{(Net income – Preferred stock dividends)}}{\textbf{Average common stockholders' equity}}$$

By subtracting the preferred stock dividends from net income, the numerator represents the net income available exclusively to the common stockholders. The denominator averages the common stockholders' equity for the year (sum the beginning and ending common stockholders' equity and then divide by 2). If a company has preferred stock outstanding, the common stockholders' equity is calculated by subtracting the preferred stockholders' equity (the sum of the preferred stock par value and the preferred stock paid-in capital in excess of par value) from total stockholders' equity.

To illustrate the calculation of the return on common stockholders' equity, we look at financial data from **Amazon.com, Inc.** The company's 2020 financial data are as follows (in millions of dollars):

Net income	$21,331
Preferred stock dividends	0
Preferred stockholders' equity, beginning of year	0
Preferred stockholders' equity, end of year	0
Common stockholders' equity, beginning of year	62,060
Common stockholders' equity, end of year	93,404

Amazon's return on common stockholders' equity for the year is 27.4 percent, calculated as \$21,331– \$0/[(\$62,060 + \$93,404)/2].

TAKEAWAY 10.1 Concept	Method	Assessment
How profitable is the stockholders' investment in a company?	Statement of stockholders' equity and the income statement. $\text{Return on common stockholders' equity} = \frac{\text{Net income} - \text{Preferred stock dividends}}{\text{Average common stockholders' equity}}$	The higher the return on common stockholders' equity, the higher the profitability of the stockholders' investment in a business.

Dividend Yield and Dividend Payout Ratio

Investors differ in their expectations regarding their investments—some investors are primarily interested in appreciation in the market value of their shares, while other investors focus on receiving current income in the form of dividends. Dividend yield and dividend payout ratio are ratios that are helpful to this latter group of investors.

Investors seeking income in the form of dividends would likely not invest in Amazon, since they have never paid dividends. CEO Jeff Bezos considers Amazon to be in "Day one" of the start-up phase. In a 2017 letter to shareholders, Bezos wrote, "Day 2 is stasis. Followed by irrelevance. Followed by excruciating, painful decline. Followed by death." For purposes of illustration, Microsoft, another tech giant, which was founded in 1975 and started paying dividends in 2003, will be used to demonstrate the dividend yield and dividend payout ratios.

Dividend Yield

Dividend yield measures the current rate of return in cash dividends from an investment in a company's shares. The ratio may be calculated for either common or preferred shares, and is calculated by dividing the latest annual dividend per share by the current market price of the stock:

$$\textbf{Dividend yield} = \frac{\textbf{Annual dividend per share}}{\textbf{Market price per share}}$$

To illustrate, in 2020, **Microsoft** declared cash dividends per common share of \$2.04. At its fiscal year-end, Microsoft's common stock had a market price of \$203.51 per share. Consequently, at year-end, the company's dividend yield was 1.0 percent, or \$2.04/\$203.51.

Dividend yields are included in the stock tables published in *The Wall Street Journal* and *Barrons,* as well as online resources such as Yahoo! Finance, so it is easy for investors to compare current dividend yields for different stocks. The following are recent dividend yields for several well-known companies:

The Coca-Cola Company	3.1 percent
AT&T	6.9 percent
IBM Corporation	4.5 percent
Chevron Corp.	5.1 percent
Wal-Mart Stores, Inc.	1.6 percent

TAKEAWAY 10.2 Concept	Method	Assessment
What is a company's current rate of return to stockholders in the form of dividends?	Statement of stockholders' equity and a company's current market price per share. $\text{Dividend yield} = \frac{\text{Annual dividend per share}}{\text{Market price per share}}$	The higher a company's dividend yield, the greater the rate of return to stockholders in the form of dividends.

Dividend Payout Ratio

The **dividend payout ratio** measures the percentage of net income available to common stockholders that is paid out as dividends. The ratio is calculated as follows:

$$\textbf{Dividend payout ratio} = \frac{\textbf{Annual dividend per share}}{\textbf{Earnings per share}}$$

Dividend payout ratios vary considerably among corporations. Companies that are considered "growth" companies often have low payout ratios because they use the net income generated by operations to help finance their growth. By way of contrast, "mature" companies that lack significant growth opportunities often distribute a high percentage of their net income as dividends. A good example of a mature company is the local utility company whose growth is limited by the net increase of new homes and businesses in the community and the approved rate increases by the local public utility commission.

Some corporations try to maintain a reasonably stable dividend payout ratio, so their payout ratios do not vary much from one year to the next. Other corporations try to keep their dividend per share either constant or increasing each year at a constant rate. If net income fluctuates quite a bit from year to year, these latter corporations will show dividend payout ratios that are quite variable over time.

The following are the dividend payout ratios for some well-known corporations:

Best Buy Co. Inc. (retail)	32 percent
Microsoft Corporation (technology)	35 percent
Procter & Gamble Co. (consumer goods)	61 percent

Concept	Method	Assessment	TAKEAWAY 10.3
What percentage of a company's net income is paid out to stockholders as a dividend?	Statement of stockholders' equity and the income statement. Dividend payout ratio = $\frac{\text{Annual dividend per share}}{\text{Earnings per share}}$	The higher the dividend payout ratio, the higher the percentage of net income paid to stockholders as a dividend.	

REVIEW 10.8

The following information relates to Litchfield, Inc.:

	Year 1	Year 2
Net income	$ 110,000	$ 150,000
Preferred stock dividends	15,000	15,000
Average common stockholders' equity	4,000,000	4,200,000
Dividend per common share	3.00	3.20
Earnings per share	5.80	5.90
Market price per common share, year-end	58.00	59.50

Required

a. Calculate the company's return on common stockholders' equity for both years.

b. Calculate the company's dividend yield for both years.

c. Calculate the company's dividend payout for both years.

The solution is on page 371.

SUMMARY OF LEARNING OBJECTIVES

Define the corporate form of organization and discuss its principal characteristics. (p. 336) LO1

- A corporation is a separate legal entity chartered by the state in which it is formed.
- The liability of corporate stockholders for the debts of a business is limited to the value of their ownership interest in a corporation; whereas claims against partners and sole proprietors may extend to their personal resources.

- Unlike proprietorships and partnerships, corporations must report contributed capital separately from the accumulated balance of retained earnings. Distributions to stockholders are limited by the amount of retained earnings and other capital as specified by state law.

LO2 Explain the difference between par value stock and no-par value stock. (p. 339)

- Par value is the face value printed on a stock certificate. It has no economic significance but may have legal significance.
- No-par value stock has no face value printed on the stock certificate, although generally the board of directors sets a stated value for a corporation's capital stock.

LO3 Identify and discuss the two types of capital stock and their respective stockholder rights. (p. 340)

- Common stock represents a corporation's basic ownership class of stock; common shares carry the right to vote and may or may not pay a dividend.
- Preferred stocks may differ from common stock in several ways. Typically, preferred stocks have, at a minimum, some type of dividend preference and a prior claim to assets in the event of a corporate liquidation, relative to common stock.

LO4 Describe the accounting for issuances of capital stock. (p. 343)

- When capital stock is issued, the appropriate capital stock account is increased by the par value or stated value of the shares issued. The asset received in exchange for the stock (usually cash) is increased by its fair value. Any difference is recorded in the Paid-in Capital in Excess of Par Value account.

LO5 Define and discuss the accounting for stock splits. (p. 345)

- Stock splits change the par or stated value of capital stock and affect the number of shares outstanding. Forward stock splits increase the number of shares outstanding and lower its par or stated value, while reverse stock splits do the opposite. The total amount of Paid In Capital does not change as a result of a stock split.

LO6 Explain the accounting for stock repurchases. (p. 346)

- Treasury stock represents reacquired shares of a firm's capital stock. It is commonly recorded at its acquisition cost and is deducted from total stockholders' equity on the balance sheet.
- Shares repurchased and retired also result in a reduction to stockholders' equity through a reduction to par value common stock, additional paid in capital and, if repurchased at a premium, retained earnings.

LO7 Identify and distinguish between cash dividends and stock dividends. (p. 349)

- Cash dividends reduce retained earnings and are a current liability when declared.
- Stock dividends are accounted for by a transfer of retained earnings to the appropriate capital stock and paid-in capital accounts at the fair market value of the shares distributed for small stock dividends and at par value for large stock dividends.

LO8 Illustrate the statement of retained earnings and the statement of stockholders' equity. (p. 351)

- A statement of retained earnings presents the financial effect of events causing retained earnings to change during an accounting period.
- A statement of stockholders' equity presents the financial effect of events causing each component of stockholders' equity (including retained earnings) to change during an accounting period.

LO9 Define the return on common stockholders' equity, dividend yield, and dividend payout ratio. (p. 353)

- The return on common stockholders' equity is computed as (net income – preferred stock dividends)/ average common stockholders' equity. It indicates the profitability of the common stockholders' investment in a company.
- Dividend yield is computed by dividing a stock's annual dividend per share by its current market price per share. For investors, this ratio identifies the annual rate of return in dividends from an investment in a company's shares.
- The dividend payout ratio is computed by dividing the annual dividend per share by a company's earnings per share.

Concept	Method	Assessment	SUMMARY
How profitable is the stockholders' investment in a company?	Statement of stockholders' equity and the income statement. $\text{Return on common stockholders' equity} = \frac{\text{Net income} - \text{Preferred stock dividends}}{\text{Average common stockholders' equity}}$	The higher the return on common stockholders' equity, the higher the profitability of the stockholders' investment in a business.	TAKEAWAY 10.1
What is a company's current rate of return to stockholders in the form of dividends?	Statement of stockholders' equity and a company's current market price per share. $\text{Dividend yield} = \frac{\text{Annual dividend per share}}{\text{Market price per share}}$	The higher a company's dividend yield, the greater the rate of return to stockholders in the form of dividends.	TAKEAWAY 10.2
What percentage of a company's net income is paid out to stockholders as a dividend?	Statement of stockholders' equity and the income statement. $\text{Dividend payout ratio} = \frac{\text{Annual dividend per share}}{\text{Earnings per share}}$	The higher the dividend payout ratio, the higher the percentage of net income paid to stockholders as a dividend.	TAKEAWAY 10.3

KEY TERMS

Articles of incorporation (p. 336)
Authorized shares (p. 340)
Callable (p. 342)
Common stock (p. 340)
Contributed capital (p. 344)
Convertible (p. 342)
Corporation (p. 336)
Cumulative (p. 341)
Dividend payout ratio (p. 354)
Dividends (p. 349)
Dividend yield (p. 354)
Forward stock split (p. 345)
Issued shares (p. 340)
Noncumulative (p. 341)
No-par value stock (p. 339)
Outstanding shares (p. 340)
Participating (p. 342)
Par value (p. 339)
Preemptive right (p. 340)
Preferred stock (p. 341)
Retained earnings (p. 344)
Return on common stockholders' equity (p. 353)
Stated value (p. 339)
Statement of retained earnings (p. 351)
Statement of stockholders' equity (p. 351)
Stock dividends (p. 350)
Treasury stock (p. 346)

SELF-STUDY QUESTIONS

(Answers for the Self-Study Questions are available at the end of this chapter.)

1. What is the usual liability of stockholders for corporation actions? LO1

   a. Unlimited
   b. Limited to the par value or stated value of the shares of stock they hold
   c. Limited to the amount of their investment in the corporation
   d. Limited to the amount of a corporation's retained earnings

2. Which type of stock may have dividends in arrears? LO3

   a. Cumulative preferred stock
   b. Common stock
   c. Noncumulative preferred stock
   d. Treasury stock

3. Wyler Company issued 20,000 shares of $10 par value common stock in exchange for a building with a current fair value of $1,000,000. In recording this transaction, what is the amount of the increase to the Paid-in Capital in Excess of Par Value account? LO4

   a. $1,000,000
   b. $200,000
   c. $800,000
   d. $980,000

4. Which of the following accounts is a reduction to Stockholders' Equity? LO6

   a. Common Stock
   b. Paid-in Capital in Excess of Stated Value
   c. Preferred Stock
   d. Treasury Stock

LO7 Homework MBC
5. Which of the following events decreases a corporation's stockholders' equity?
a. A payment of a previously declared cash dividend
b. A declaration of a six percent stock dividend
c. A 2-for-1 forward stock split
d. A declaration of a $1 cash dividend per share on preferred stock

LO5 Homework MBC
6. When a company wants to reduce the market price per share of its stock, what action should it take?
a. Issue a cash dividend
b. Issue a stock dividend
c. Do a reverse stock split
d. Do a forward stock split

LO9 Homework MBC
7. What type of company is typically characterized by a high dividend payout ratio?
a. Technology company
b. High-growth company
c. Mature, low-growth company
d. All of the above

LO3 Homework MBC
8. Preferred stock that may be converted into common stock has which of the following characteristics?
a. Call feature
b. Cumulative feature
c. Participation feature
d. Convertible feature

LO7 Homework MBC
9. A dividend that is paid every quarter or every year is called?
a. Regular dividend
b. Special dividend
c. Property dividend
d. Stock dividend

LO8 Homework MBC
10. The statement of stockholders' equity includes each of the following except:
a. Retained Earning
b. Treasury Stock
c. Paid-in Capital in Excess of Par Value
d. Accounts Receivable

QUESTIONS

1. What is the meaning of each of the following terms and, when appropriate, how do they interrelate: *corporation, articles of incorporation, corporate charter, board of directors, corporate officers,* and *organization costs*?
2. What is meant by the limited liability of a stockholder? Does this characteristic enhance or reduce a corporation's ability to raise capital?
3. Contrast the federal income taxation of a corporation with that of a sole proprietorship and a partnership. Which of the three types of organizations must file a federal income tax return?
4. Define *par value stock*. What is the significance of a stock's par value?
5. What is the preemptive right of a stockholder?
6. What are the basic differences between preferred stock and common stock? What are the typical features of preferred stock?
7. What features make preferred stock similar to debt? Similar to common stock?
8. What is meant by dividend in arrears? If dividends are two years in arrears on $500,000 of six percent preferred stock and dividends are declared this year, what amount of total dividends must preferred stockholders receive before any distributions can be made to common stockholders?
9. Distinguish between authorized shares and issued shares. Why might the number of shares issued be more than the number of shares outstanding?
10. What are two different sources of contributed capital?
11. Define a *forward stock split*. What is the major reason for a forward stock split?
12. Define *treasury stock*. Why might a corporation acquire treasury stock? How is treasury stock shown on the balance sheet?
13. If a corporation purchases 600 shares of its own common stock at $10 per share and resells the shares at $14 per share, where would the $2,400 [($14 – $10) × 600 shares] increase in capital appear in the financial statements? Why is no gain reported?
14. Assume that a corporation has preferred shares outstanding. How is the return on common stockholders' equity computed?
15. What is a stock dividend? How does a common stock dividend paid to common stockholders affect their respective ownership interests?

16. What is the difference between the accounting for a small stock dividend versus the accounting for a large stock dividend?

17. What information is presented in a statement of retained earnings? a statement of stockholders' equity?

18. Where do the following accounts (and their balances) appear in the balance sheet?
a. Dividends Payable—Common Stock
b. Stock Dividend Distributable

19. How is a corporation's dividend yield calculated?

20. Bleaker Company declares and pays its annual dividend near the end of its fiscal year. For the current year, Bleaker's dividend payout ratio was 40 percent, its earnings per common share were $5.80, and it had 50,000 shares of common stock outstanding all year. What total amount of dividends did Bleaker declare and pay in the current year?

21. What is the difference between the accounting for a treasury stock repurchase and a stock repurchase and retirement?

DATA ANALYTICS

The assignments in this Data Analytics section are designed to familiarize you with the tools used in analyzing data and communicating the results. Appendix F provides an in-depth discussion of data analytics and blockchain technology.

DA10-1. Constructing and Analyzing a Data Set on Share-Based Compensation in Excel For this exercise, we will create and analyze a data set in Excel of the changes in the composition of share-based compensation plans (restricted stock unit, performance share, and stock option plans) for Target Corporation over a 10-year period.

Required

1. Download Excel file DA10-1 found in myBusinessCourse.
2. Create a data set that will provide information on the composition of Target's share-based compensation plans over a 10-year period from fiscal year 2011 to fiscal year 2020.
   - In your data set, for each of the share-based awards (restricted stock unit, performance share, and stock options) include the following: number of units granted during the year and the unrecognized compensation expense at year-end.
   - Also include in your data set the total share-based compensation expense included on the income statement for each year and the fair value per unit at grant date of the restricted stock units for each year.
   - *Hints:*
     - o This information can be found in the note disclosures in the annual 10-K reports.
     - o When collecting your data, note that some amounts are in thousands, and some in millions.
     - o Fiscal years end in January or February of the following year; for example, Fiscal Year 2020 ends January 30, 2021.
3. Prepare a line chart in Excel over the 10-year period showing the trends in units granted of the three different types of share-based awards. *Hint:* Chart should show the earliest year on the left and the latest year on the right.
4. Based on the visualization prepared in part 2, match the 10-year trend in the data visualization for each of the three awards with the best description below.
   a. Units granted only in specific years, four times during the period.
   b. Units granted were on a decreasing pace during the first five years, and an increasing pace during the latter five year.
   c. Units were granted consistently over the years with a marked dip in a particular year.
   d. Units were granted consistently over the years with wider fluctuations between years then other method consistently used.
   e. Units granted in each year are increasing at a gradual, even pace each year.
   f. Units are granted only in specific years but only once in the last eight years.
5. Prepare a line chart in Excel showing the trend of share-based compensation expense over the 10-year period.
6. Indicate which year(s) in the data visualization prepared in part 5, showed a highly visible decline in share-based compensation expense.

7. Indicate which year seems to be the start of an increasing trend in the visualization created in part 5.
8. Prepare a line chart in Excel showing the trend of unrecognized share-based compensation expense over the 10-year period for all three share-based plan types.
9. Indicate which share-based plan type in the data visualization prepared in part 8 showed the highest value and lowest value in Fiscal Year 2011, 2015, and 2020.
10. Prepare a schedule for the total value of the restricted stock share awards at the date of grant for each of the 10 years. *Hint:* Multiply the number of restricted stock units by the unit price at the date of grant.
11. Indicate which year(s) showed a decrease in total value based on the data visualization prepared in part 9.
12. Indicate which description below best describes the trend shown from fiscal year 2016 to fiscal year 2020.
    a. Increasing
    b. Decreasing
    c. Volatile
    d. Stable
13. Summarize the result of your analysis by choosing the most accurate statement based on your visualizations considering the 10-year period. While total share-based compensation expense has generally increased, the mix of plan usage has changed:
    a. the use of performance share plans and stock option plans varies and is volatile and the use of restricted stock awards has remained steady.
    b. the use of performance share plans varies and is the most volatile, the use of restricted stock awards has increased, and the use of stock options has slightly increased.
    c. Stock options were once used most frequently, but were replaced with the restricted stock awards plan and to a lesser extent, the performance share plan.
    d. the use of performance share plans varies and is the most volatile, the use of restricted stock awards has increased, and the use of stock options has declined from much higher levels in the earlier years.

Data Analytics

DA10-2. Preparing Tableau Visualizations to Analyze Dividend Payout Policies through Ratios Refer to PF-28 in Appendix F. This problem uses Tableau to analyze dividend payout policies of S&P 500 companies through the dividend yield and dividend payout ratio.

Assignments with the MBC logo in the margin are available in myBusinessCourse. See the Preface of the book for details.

SHORT EXERCISES

LO1 **SE10-1. Issuance of Common Stock** Los Altos, Inc., is authorized to issue one million shares of $1 par value common stock. In the company's initial public offering, 500,000 shares are sold to the investing public at a price of $5 per share. One month following Los Altos, Inc.'s initial public offering, 1,000 of its common shares were sold by one investor to another at a price of $10 per share. How should this second transaction be recorded in the accounts of Los Altos, Inc.? Why?

LO2 **SE10-2. Issuance of No-Par Common Stock** Jackson & Company issued 100,000 shares of $1 par value common stock at a price of $5 per share and issued 10,000 shares of no-par value common stock at a price of $10 per share. How does the effect on Stockholders' Equity differ between the issuance of the no-par value common stock and the issuance of the $1 par value common stock?

LO3 Homework MBC **SE10-3. Allocating Liquidation between Common Stockholders and Preferred Stockholders** The Arcadia Company is liquidating. After paying off all of its creditors, the company has $1 million to distribute between its preferred stockholders and its common stockholders. The aggregate par value of the preferred stock is $900,000, and the aggregate par value of its common stock is $2 million. How much of the remaining $1 million in assets should be distributed to the preferred stockholders and how much should be distributed to the common stockholders?

LO4 Homework MBC **SE10-4. Issuance of Common Stock** Los Altos, Inc., is authorized to issue one million shares of $1 par value common stock. The company actually sells 500,000 shares at $10 per share. What are the amounts recorded as Common Stock—$1 par value and Additional Paid-in Capital in excess of par value related to the issuance of the 500,000 shares?

SE10-5. Outstanding Shares Pearce & Company has 10 million shares of $2 par value common stock outstanding. The company believes that its current market price of $100 per share is too high and decides to execute a 4-for-1 forward stock split to lower the price. How many shares will be outstanding following the stock split, and what will be the new par value per share? **LO5**

SE10-6. Treasury Stock Purchase Jackson & Company has no-par value common stock outstanding that is selling at $20 per share. The company's CEO believes that the stock price is undervalued and decides to buy back 10,000 shares. What is the financial statement effect of the purchase of the treasury stock? **LO6**

SE10-7. Dividends Paid and Dividends in Arrears The Arcadia Company has 100,000 shares of cumulative, six percent, $100 par value preferred stock outstanding. Last year the company failed to pay its regular dividend, but the board of directors would like to resume paying its regular dividend this year. Calculate the dividends in arrears and the total dividend that must be paid this year. **LO3**

The following information relates to SE10-8 through SE10-10:

Los Altos, Inc., disclosed the following information in a recent annual report:

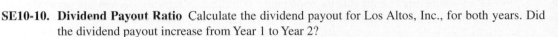

	Year 1	Year 2
Net income	$ 35,000	$ 55,000
Preferred stock dividends	3,000	3,000
Average common stockholders' equity	1,200,000	1,500,000
Dividend per common share	1.20	1.20
Earnings per share	1.90	2.05
Market price per common share, year-end	19.50	21.00

SE10-8. Return on Common Stockholders' Equity Calculate the return on common stockholders' equity for Los Altos, Inc., for both years. Did the return improve from Year 1 to Year 2? **LO9**

SE10-9. Dividend Yield Calculate the dividend yield for Los Altos, Inc., for both years. Did the dividend yield improve from Year 1 to Year 2? **LO9**

SE10-10. Dividend Payout Ratio Calculate the dividend payout for Los Altos, Inc., for both years. Did the dividend payout increase from Year 1 to Year 2? **LO9**

SE10-11. Change in Stockholders' Equity Nikron Corporation issued 10,000 shares of $0.50 par value common stock during the year for $20 each. Nikron also repurchased treasury stock for $15,000. Net income for the year was $120,000. The company also paid cash dividends of $25,000. What was the total change in Nikron's stockholders' equity for the year? **LO8**

SE10-12. Stock Retirements Holder & Company issued 50,000 shares of $5.00 par value common stock for $10.00 per share when they started business three years ago. Business has been successful, and currently total stockholders' equity is $860,000. Holder decides to repurchase and retire 5,000 shares at the market price of $18 per share. **LO6**

Required

Determine the balance in the following after the stock retirement transaction:

a. Common stock
b. Additional paid-in capital
c. Retained earnings
d. Total stockholders' equity

EXERCISES

E10-1. Dividend Distribution Lakeside Company has the following shares outstanding: 20,000 shares of $50 par value, six percent cumulative preferred stock and 80,000 shares of $10 par value common stock. The company declared cash dividends amounting to $160,000. **LO3, 7**

a. If no dividends in arrears on the preferred stock exist, how much in total dividends, and in dividends per share, is paid to each class of stock?

b. If one year of dividends in arrears exist on the preferred stock, how much in total dividends, and in dividends per share, is paid to each class of stock?

LO2, 4 

E10-2. **Share Issuances for Cash** Finlay, Inc., issued 8,000 shares of $50 par value preferred stock at $68 per share and 12,000 shares of no-par value common stock at $10 per share. The common stock has no stated value. All issuances were for cash.

a. Determine the financial statement effect of the share issuances.
b. Determine the financial statement effect of the issuance of the common stock assuming that it had a stated value of $5 per share.
c. Determine the financial statement effect of the issuance of the common stock assuming that it had a par value of $1 per share.

LO5 

E10-3. **Forward Stock Split** On March 1 of the current year, Sentry Corporation has 400,000 shares of $20 par value common stock that are issued and outstanding. The general ledger shows the following account balances relating to the common stock:

Common stock	$8,000,000
Paid-in capital in excess of par value	3,400,000

On March 2, Sentry Corporation splits its stock 2-for-1 and reduces the par value to $10 per share.

a. How many shares of common stock are issued and outstanding immediately following the stock split?
b. What is the balance in the Common Stock account immediately following the stock split?
c. What is the balance in the Paid-in Capital in Excess of Par Value account immediately following the stock split?
d. Is an entry required to record the forward stock split?

LO4, 6 

E10-4. **Treasury Stock** Coastal Corporation issued 25,000 shares of $5 par value common stock at $17 per share and 6,000 shares of $50 par value, eight percent preferred stock at $78 per share. Later, the company purchased 3,000 shares of its own common stock at $20 per share.

a. Determine the financial statement effect of the share issuances and the purchase of the common shares.
b. Assume that Coastal sold 2,000 shares of the treasury stock at $26 per share. Determine the financial statement effect of the sale of this treasury stock.
c. Assume that Coastal sold the remaining 1,000 shares of treasury stock at $19 per share. Determine the financial statement effect of the sale of this treasury stock.

LO3, 7 

E10-5. **Cash Dividends** Sanders Corporation has the following shares outstanding: 6,000 shares of $50 par value, six percent preferred stock and 40,000 shares of $1 par value common stock. The company has $328,000 of retained earnings. At year-end, the company declares its regular $3 per share cash dividend on the preferred stock and a $2.20 per share cash dividend on the common stock. Three weeks later, the company pays the dividends.

a. Determine the financial statement effect of the declaration of the cash dividends.
b. Determine the financial statement effect of the payment of the cash dividends.

LO8 

E10-6. **Statement of Retained Earnings** Use the following data to prepare a statement of retained earnings for Shepler Corporation.

Total retained earnings originally reported at January 1	$324,000
Cash dividends declared during the year	75,000
Net income for the year	193,000
Stock dividend declared during the year	30,000

LO3 

E10-7. **Conversion of Preferred Stock into Common Stock** Los Altos, Inc., has 12,000 shares of $100 par value, six percent preferred stock and 80,000 shares of $0.50 par value common stock outstanding. The preferred stock is convertible into the company's common stock at a conversion rate of 1-to-20; that is, each share of preferred stock is convertible into 20 shares of common stock. The preferred stock had been sold for its par value when issued. Prepare the entry to record the conversion of all of the company's preferred stock into common stock.

LO5 

E10-8. **Reverse Stock Split** Titanium Metals Company had 20,000,000 shares of $0.01 par value common stock outstanding, which had been sold for an aggregate amount of $300,000,000. The company's shares are traded on the New York Stock Exchange, which has a minimum listing price of $1 per share. Recently, the company's common stock has been trading on the exchange below $1 per share, and the exchange has notified the company that its common stock would be delisted in 30 days if the stock price did not rebound above its minimum listing price. In response to this notification, Titanium Metals authorized a 1-for-10 reverse stock split. Following the reverse stock split:

a. How many common shares will be outstanding?
b. What will be the new par value per share?
c. How will the reverse stock split be recorded in the company's accounts?

E10-9. Return on Common Stockholders' Equity, Dividend Yield, and Dividend Payout The following information relates to Waterloo Components, Inc.: LO9

	Year 1	Year 2
Net income	$ 55,000	$ 75,000
Preferred stock dividends	5,000	5,000
Average common stockholders' equity	2,000,000	2,100,000
Dividend per common share	1.50	1.60
Earnings per share	2.90	2.95
Market price per common share, year-end	29.50	30.00

a. Calculate the company's return on common stockholders' equity for both years.
b. Calculate the company's dividend yield for both years.
c. Calculate the company's dividend payout for both years.

E10-10. Characteristics of a Corporation Label each of the following characteristics of a corporation as either an (A) advantage, or a (D) disadvantage: LO1

a. Limited liability
b. Taxation
c. Regulations
d. Transferability of ownership

E10-11. Stock Retirements Harland Corporation began business on January 1 by issuing 25,000 shares of $10 par value stock for $15 per share. The stockholders' equity accounts of Harland Corporation at August 31 appear below: LO4, 6, 8

Common stock, $10 par value, 50,000 shares authorized 25,000 issued and outstanding	$250,000
Paid-in capital in excess of par value–Common stock	125,000
Retained earnings	238,000
Total Stockholders' Equity	$613,000

Assume that Harland Corporation purchased and retired 2,500 common shares at $18 per share on September 1.

Required
Prepare the stockholders' equity section of the balance sheet at September 1 after the stock repurchase and retirement.

PROBLEMS

P10-1. Dividend Distribution Rydon Corporation began business on January 1. At that time, it issued 20,000 shares of $60 par value, seven percent cumulative preferred stock, and 100,000 shares of $5 par value common stock. Through the end of Year 3, there had been no change in the number of preferred and common shares outstanding. LO3, 7

Required
a. Assume that Rydon declared dividends of $0 in Year 1, $183,000 in Year 2, and $200,000 in Year 3. Calculate the total dividends and the dividends per share paid to each class of stock in each of the 3 years.
b. Assume that Rydon declared dividends of $0 in Year 1, $84,000 in Year 2, and $150,000 in Year 3. Calculate the total dividends and the dividends per share paid to each class of stock in each of the 3 years.

P10-2. Stockholders' Equity: Transactions and Balance Sheet Presentation Tunic Corporation was organized on April 1, with an authorization of 25,000 shares of six percent, $50 par value preferred stock and 200,000 shares of $5 par value common stock. During April, the following transactions affecting stockholders' equity occurred: LO4, 8

Apr. 1 Issued 80,000 shares of common stock at $15 cash per share.
3 Issued 2,000 shares of common stock to attorneys and promoters in exchange for their services in organizing the corporation. The services were valued at $31,000.
8 Issued 3,000 shares of common stock in exchange for equipment with a fair market value of $48,000.
20 Issued 6,000 shares of preferred stock for cash at $55 per share.

Required

a. Using the TAT, determine the financial statement effect of the above transactions.

b. Prepare the stockholders' equity section of the balance sheet at April 30. Assume that the net income for April is $49,000.

LO4, 6, 8 **P10-3.** **Stockholders' Equity: Transactions and Balance Sheet Presentation** The stockholders' equity accounts of Windham Corporation at January 1 appear below:

8 Percent preferred stock, $25 par value, 50,000 shares authorized; 6,800 shares issued and outstanding	$170,000
Common stock, $10 par value, 200,000 shares authorized; 50,000 shares issued and outstanding	500,000
Paid-in capital in excess of par value—Preferred stock	68,000
Paid-in capital in excess of par value—Common stock	200,000
Retained earnings	270,000

During the year, the following transactions occurred:

Jan. 10 Issued 28,000 shares of common stock for $17 cash per share.
23 Purchased 8,000 shares of common stock as treasury stock at $19 per share.
Mar. 14 Sold one-half of the treasury shares acquired January 23 for $21 per share.
July 15 Issued 3,200 shares of preferred stock in exchange for equipment with a fair market value of $128,000.
Nov. 15 Sold 1,000 of the treasury shares acquired January 23 for $24 per share.
Dec. 31 Closed the net income of $59,000 to the Retained Earnings account.

Required

a. Set up a horizontal worksheet for the stockholders' equity accounts as of the beginning of the year and enter the January 1 balances. Add columns for Treasury Stock and Paid-in capital from Treasury stock.

b. Determine the ending balances for the stockholders' equity accounts after accounting for the above transactions.

c. Prepare the December 31 stockholders' equity section of the balance sheet.

LO4, 5, 6, 8 **P10-4.** **Stockholders' Equity: Transactions and Balance Sheet Presentation** The stockholders' equity of Summit Corporation at January 1 follows:

7 Percent preferred stock, $100 par value, 20,000 shares authorized; 5,000 shares issued and outstanding	$ 500,000
Common stock, $15 par value, 100,000 shares authorized; 40,000 shares issued and outstanding	600,000
Paid-in capital in excess of par value—Preferred stock	24,000
Paid-in capital in excess of par value—Common stock	360,000
Retained earnings	325,000
Total Stockholders' Equity	$1,809,000

The following transactions, among others, occurred during the year:

Jan. 12 Announced a 3-for-1 common stock split, reducing the par value of the common stock to $5 per share. The authorization was increased to 300,000 shares.
Mar. 31 Converted $40,000 face value of convertible bonds payable (the book value of the bonds was $43,000) to common stock. Each $1,000 bond converted to 125 shares of common stock.
June 1 Acquired equipment with a fair market value of $60,000 in exchange for 500 shares of preferred stock.
Sept. 1 Acquired 10,000 shares of common stock for cash at $10 per share.
Oct. 12 Sold 1,500 treasury shares at $12 per share.

Nov. 21 Issued 5,000 shares of common stock at $11 cash per share.
Dec. 28 Sold 1,200 treasury shares at $9 per share.
31 Closed net income of $83,000 to the Retained Earnings account.

Required

a. Set up a horizontal worksheet for the stockholders' equity accounts as of the beginning of the year and enter the January 1 balances. Add columns for Treasury Stock and Paid-in capital from Treasury stock.

b. Determine the ending balances for the stockholders' equity accounts after accounting for the above transactions.

c. Prepare the stockholders' equity section of the balance sheet at December 31.

P10-5. Stockholders' Equity: Analyze Information from Comparative Data Comparative stockholders' equity sections from two successive years of balance sheets from Smiley, Inc., are as follows: LO4, 6

Homework MBC

	Dec. 31, Current Year	Dec. 31, Prior Year
Contributed Capital		
8 Percent preferred stock, $50 par value, authorized 20,000 shares; issued and outstanding, 2019: 8,000 shares; 2020: 12,000 shares	$ 600,000	$ 400,000
Common stock, no-par value, $20 stated value, authorized 80,000 shares; issued, 2019: 32,000 shares; 2020: 40,000 shares	800,000	640,000
Additional Paid-in Capital		
In excess of par value—Preferred stock	224,000	144,000
In excess of stated value—Common stock	232,000	160,000
From treasury stock	21,000	
Retained earnings	300,000	229,000
		$1,573,000
Less: Treasury stock (7,000 shares common) at cost	0	196,000
Total Stockholders' Equity	$2,177,000	$1,377,000

No dividends were declared or paid during the current year.

Required

Using the TAT, analyze the transactions affecting stockholders' equity that occurred during the current year. Do not prepare the entry for closing net income to retained earnings. Assume that any share transactions were for cash.

P10-6. Stockholders' Equity Transactions The stockholders' equity of Fremantle Corporation at January 1 follows: LO4, 5, 6

Homework 

8 Percent preferred stock, $100 par value, 20,000 shares authorized; 4,000 shares issued and outstanding	$ 400,000
Common stock, $1 par value, 100,000 shares authorized; 40,000 shares issued and outstanding	40,000
Paid-in capital in excess of par value—Preferred stock	200,000
Paid-in capital in excess of par value—Common stock	800,000
Retained earnings	550,000
Total Stockholders' Equity	$1,990,000

The following transactions, among others, occurred during the year:

Jan. 1 Announced a 2-for-1 common stock split, reducing the par value of the common stock to $0.50 per share.
Mar. 31 Converted $80,000 face value of convertible bonds payable (the book value of the bonds was $83,000) to common stock. Each $1,000 bond converted to 125 shares of common stock.
June 1 Acquired equipment with a fair market value of $45,000 in exchange for 300 shares of preferred stock.
Sept. 1 Acquired 10,000 shares of common stock for cash at $20 per share.
Nov. 21 Issued 5,000 shares of common stock at $22 cash per share.
Dec. 28 Sold 1,000 treasury shares at $23 per share.
31 Closed net income of $103,000, to the Retained Earnings account.

Required

a. Set up a horizontal worksheet for the stockholders' equity accounts as of the beginning of the year and enter the January 1 balances. Add columns for Treasury Stock and Paid-in capital from Treasury stock.

b. Determine the ending balances for the stockholders' equity accounts after the above transactions.

LO4, 5, 6, 8 **P10-7.** **Stockholders' Equity Section of the Balance Sheet** Using your analysis from P10-6, prepare the stockholders' equity section of the Fremantle Corporation's balance sheet.

LO4, 6, 8 **P10-8.** **Stockholders' Equity: Transactions and Balance Sheet Presentation** The stockholders' equity accounts of Scott Corporation at January 1 follow:

Common stock, $5 par value, 350,000 shares authorized 150,000 shares issued and outstanding	$750,000
Paid-in capital in excess of par value	600,000
Retained earnings	346,000

During the year, the following transactions occurred:

Jan.	5	Issued 10,000 shares of common stock for $12 cash per share.
	18	Purchased and retired 4,000 shares of common stock at $14 cash per share.
Oct.	1	Issued 5,000 shares of eight percent, $25 par value preferred stock for $35 cash per share. These are the first preferred shares issued out of 50,000 authorized shares.
Dec.	31	Closed the net income of $72,500 to the Retained Earnings account.

Required

a. Set up a horizontal worksheet for the stockholders' equity accounts as of the beginning of the year and enter the January 1 balances.

b. Determine the ending balances for the stockholders' equity accounts after the above transactions.

c. Prepare the December 31 stockholders' equity section of the balance sheet.

LO4, 6 **P10-9.** **Stockholders' Equity Transactions** The stockholders' equity of Xeltron Corporation at January 1 follows:

9% preferred stock, $100 par value, 20,000 shares authorized; 6,000 shares issued and outstanding	$ 600,000
Common stock, $2 par value, 100,000 shares authorized; 40,000 shares issued and outstanding	80,000
Paid-in capital in excess of par value—Preferred stock	400,000
Paid-in capital in excess of par value—Common stock	800,000
Retained earnings	750,000
Total Stockholders' Equity	$2,630,000

The following transactions, among others, occurred during the year:

June	1	Acquired equipment with a fair market value of $30,000 in exchange for 200 shares of preferred stock.
Sept.	1	Acquired and retired 10,000 shares of common stock for cash at $26 per share.
Nov.	21	Issued 5,000 shares of common stock at $30 cash per share.
Dec.	31	Closed net income of $200,000 to the Retained Earnings account.

Required

a. Set up a horizontal worksheet for the stockholders' equity accounts as of the beginning of the year and enter the January 1 balances.

b. Determine the ending balances for the stockholders' equity accounts after entering the above transactions.

c. Prepare the Stockholders' Equity section of Xeltron Corporation's balance sheet.

SERIAL PROBLEM: ANGEL CITY GREETINGS

(Note: This is a continuation of the Serial Problem: Angel City Greetings from Chapters 1 through 9.)

SP10. Kate's business continues to flourish. It hardly seems that just eleven months ago, in September, that Kate started the business. She is especially pleased that she was able to successfully defend herself against what turned out to be a mistaken attempt to sue her for copyright infringement. She was able to clearly demonstrate that her card designs were unique and significantly different from the designs sold by Mega Cards.

Kate has decided to take on an investor. Taylor Kasey believes that Angel City Greetings represents a good investment and wishes to invest money to help Kate expand the business. Kate, however, is somewhat unsure how to structure Taylor's investment. Taylor wishes to be an equity investor rather than simply providing a loan to Kate. Kate wants to know whether she should issue Taylor common stock or preferred stock for her investment.

1. Discuss the difference between the two classes of stock and suggest which type is more appropriate for Kate to issue.

   Kate has decided that she does not want to give up voting control of Angel City Greetings. Since Taylor prefers to be a passive investor, but does wish to have a steady income from dividends, the decision is made to issue 50 shares of $100 par value, 6 percent cumulative preferred stock.

2. Using the TAT, analyze the effect on the financial statements of the issuance of the preferred stock for cash.

   Kate also wishes to pay dividends on both her common shares and the preferred stock. She is a little confused between cash and stock dividends.

3. Explain the difference between a cash dividend and a stock dividend. Since Kate is the only stockholder of the common stock, what would be the effect of issuing a 10 percent stock dividend?

   Kate decides to issue cash dividends on both the common stock and the preferred stock. Currently there are 50 outstanding preferred shares and 500 common shares outstanding. The dividends that Kate paid were $6 per share on the preferred shares and $2 per share on the common shares.

4. Using the TAT, analyze the effect on the financial statements of the payment of the cash dividends.

   Angel City Greetings has a net income of $1,500 for the current month of August. Kate had decided that the business will have a fiscal year-end of August 31, so this is the completion of the company's first year. Kate will be preparing her annual financial statements; however, she would also like to see a monthly statement of retained earnings for August. In addition, she would like to see how the stockholders' equity section of the balance sheet will look after the addition of the preferred stock. The stockholders' equity section from July is shown below:

Stockholders' Equity	
Common stock (5,000 shares authorized, 500 shares issued and outstanding)	$ 500
Paid-in capital in excess of par value—common stock	9,500
Retained earnings	15,000
Total stockholders' equity	$25,000

5. Prepare a statement of retained earnings for the month of August and the stockholders' equity section of the balance sheet as of August 31.

BEYOND THE NUMBERS

REPORTING AND ANALYSIS

Columbia Sportswear Company

BTN10-1. Financial Reporting Problem: Columbia Sportswear Company The financial statements for the Columbia Sportswear Company can be found in Appendix A at the end of this book.

Required

Answer the following questions as they relate to fiscal year 2020:

a. How many shares of common stock are authorized at the end of the year?
b. What percentage of the common shares authorized are outstanding at the end of the year?
c. Does Columbia Sportswear have any preferred shares outstanding at the end of the year?
d. How many shares of common stock did Columbia Sportswear repurchase during the year? What was the dollar amount of this repurchase?
e. What amount of dividends per share did Columbia Sportswear report for the three years presented?

Columbia Sportswear Company
Under Armour, Inc.

BTN10-2. Comparative Analysis Problem: Columbia Sportswear Company versus Under Armour, Inc. The financial statements for the Columbia Sportswear Company can be found in Appendix A, and the financial statements of Under Armour, Inc., can be found in Appendix B.

Required

Answer the following questions as they relate to fiscal year 2020:

a. Calculate the return on common stockholders' equity for each company for the year.
b. Calculate the dividend payout ratio for each company for the year.
c. Based on these ratios, which company performed better for its shareholders during the year?

BTN10-3. Business Decision Problem Egghead, Inc., was a software chain that had more than 100 stores across the United States. Initially, its founders and employees owned the company privately. The company eventually went public with an initial public offering (IPO) of 3.6 million shares (the company had 12 million shares prior to the IPO). The new shares were priced at $15 each. The company did not hold any treasury shares.

Required

a. Discuss whether you think Egghead's board of directors and existing shareholders had to approve the public issuance before it occurred.
b. Provide some reasons why Egghead wished to raise $54 million with equity rather than debt.

BTN10-4. Financial Analysis Problem Gregg Industries, Lynch & Jones, Inc., and Young-Listo Company are three fictitious firms in the personal care consumer products industry. During the year, the average return on common stockholders' equity for the personal care consumer products industry was 28.1 percent. The relevant financial data for Gregg, Lynch & Jones, and Young-Listo were as follows (in millions):

	Gregg	Lynch & Jones	Young-Listo
Preferred stockholders' equity, beginning	$ 99.2	$1,969.0	$ 418.3
Preferred stockholders' equity, ending	99.0	1,942.0	414.3
Preferred dividends	4.7	102.0	21.6
Common stockholders' equity, beginning	1,397.2	5,472.0	2,201.5
Common stockholders' equity, ending	1,380.0	6,890.0	1,460.7
Net income	426.9	2,211.0	548.1

Required

a. Calculate Gregg Industries return on common stockholders' equity.
b. Evaluate Gregg Industries return on common stockholders' equity by comparing it with the following:
   1. The average for the personal care consumer products industry.
   2. The return earned by the Lynch & Jones, Inc.
   3. The return earned by Young-Listo Company.

4. The return earned by Gregg Industries in the previous year (based on net income of \$513.4 million, preferred stock dividends of \$4.8 million, and average common stockholders' equity of \$1,227.3 million).

CRITICAL THINKING

BTN10-5. Financial Analysis on the Web: General Mills, Inc. The fiscal year 2020 annual report of **General Mills, Inc.**, can be found at: https://investors.generalmills.com/financial-information/annual-reports/default.aspx.

General Mills, Inc.

Required

a. How many shares of common stock is General Mills authorized to issue? How many common shares are issued as of the end of the fiscal year?
b. What is the par value of General Mills' common stock?
c. Does General Mills have any preferred shares? If so, how many shares of preferred stock are outstanding at the end of the fiscal year?
d. How many treasury shares did General Mills purchase on the open market during the fiscal year? What did General Mills pay to purchase these shares? How many common shares are in the treasury as of the end of the fiscal year?
e. What is General Mills' return on common stockholders' equity for the fiscal year?
f. What is the cash dividend per share declared by General Mills in each of the three years presented?
g. What are General Mills' basic earnings per share in each of the three years presented?
h. What is General Mills' dividend payout ratio for each of the three years presented?

BTN10-6. Accounting Communication Activity Your neighbor, Norman Vetter, has been tinkering in his garage with his inventions. He believes he has finally come up with one that could really sell well. He is a little concerned about some potential safety issues, but he believes those issues will be worked out. He wants to form a business to manufacture and sell his invention and has come to you for advice. In particular, he would like to know the advantages and disadvantages of forming a corporation, rather than simply organizing as a sole proprietor.

Required

Write a brief memorandum to your neighbor explaining the advantages and disadvantages of the corporate form of organization.

BTN10-7. Accounting Ethics Case Colin Agee, chairperson of the board of directors and chief executive officer of Image, Inc., is pondering a recommendation to make to the firm's board of directors in response to actions taken by Sam Mecon. Mecon recently informed Agee and other board members that he (Mecon) had purchased 15 percent of the voting stock of Image at \$12 per share and is considering an attempt to take control of the company. His effort to take control would include offering \$16 per share to stockholders to induce them to sell shares to him. Mecon also indicated that he would abandon his takeover plans if the company would buy back his stock at a price 50 percent over its current market price of \$13 per share.

Agee views the proposed takeover by Mecon as a hostile maneuver. Mecon has a reputation of identifying companies that are undervalued (that is, their underlying net assets are worth more than the price of the outstanding shares), buying enough shares to take control of the company, replacing top management, and, on occasion, breaking up the company (that is, selling off the various divisions to the highest bidder). The process has proven profitable to Mecon and his financial backers. Stockholders of the companies taken over have also benefited because Mecon paid them attractive prices to buy their shares.

Agee recognizes that Image is currently undervalued by the stock market but believes that eventually the company will significantly improve its financial performance to the long-run benefit of its stockholders.

Required

What are the ethical issues that Agee should consider in arriving at a recommendation to make to the board of directors regarding Mecon's offer to be "bought out" of his takeover plans?

BTN10-8. Environmental, Social, and Governance Problem In the environmental, social, and governance highlight regarding Amazon on page 339 in this chapter, it was stated that Amazon is committed to operating its business using 100% renewable energy by 2025 and to having a net-zero carbon footprint by 2040. Go to the Amazon website (https://sustainability.aboutamazon.com) and review

their most recent Sustainability Report. Identify how the company is doing with respect to these two metrics.

General Electric Company

BTN10-9. Working With The Takeaways The following data is from a recent General Electric Company annual report. All amounts, except per share data, are in $ millions.

Net income	$ 5,704
Preferred stock dividends	474
Average common stockholders' equity	33,461
Dividends per share	0.04
Earnings per share	0.58
Per share market price of common stock at year-end	10.80

Required

Compute the following ratios for the General Electric Company:

a. Return on common stockholders' equity
b. Dividend yield
c. Dividend payout

ANSWERS TO SELF-STUDY QUESTIONS

1. c **2.** a **3.** c **4.** d **5.** d **6.** d **7.** c **8.** d **9.** a **10.** d

REVIEW SOLUTIONS

Solution 10.1

1. Disadvantage
2. Advantage
3. Advantage
4. Disadvantage
5. Disadvantage
6. Advantage

Solution 10.2

1. d **2.** e **3.** b **4.** f **5.** c **6.** a

Solution 10.3

Paid-in capital in excess of par value = ($9 – $1) × 10,000 shares = $80,000

Solution 10.4

$75,000

Solution 10.5

a. A cash dividend will lower retained earnings by $30,000 ($3 × 10,000 shares) to $470,000.
b. A ten percent stock dividend will lower retained earnings by $20,000 (.10 × 10,000 × $20) to $480,000.

Solution 10.6

DIOR COMPANY
Statement of Stockholders' Equity
For Year Ended December 31

	Common Stock	Paid-in Capital in Excess of Par Value	Retained Earnings	Treasury Stock	Total
Balance, January 1	$100,000	$900,000	$50,000	$(10,000)	$1,040,000
1,000 common shares issued	1,000	14,000			15,000
Net income			30,000		30,000
Cash dividend			(8,000)		(8,000)
Balance, December 31	$101,000	$914,000	$72,000	$(10,000)	$1,077,000

Solution 10.7

a. $1,450,000 (the par value of the issued preferred stock and common stock).

b. 190,000 shares (200,000 issued common shares less 10,000 shares in the treasury).

c. $11 [($1,200,000 par value of issued shares + $1,000,000 paid-in capital in excess of par value)/200,000 issued shares].

d. $17,500 (7 percent × $250,000).

e. Yes, the stockholders' equity section shows additional paid-in capital of $22,000 from treasury stock. This type of paid in capital represents the excess of proceeds from the sale of treasury stock over that treasury stock's cost.

f. $2,552,000 (splitting the common stock does not change any of the account balances composing contributed capital; the common stock's par value will decrease to $2 per share, and the common shares issued will increase to 600,000).

Solution 10.8

a. Return on common stockholder equity
Year 1: ($110,000 – $15,000)/$4,000,000 = 2.38 percent
Year 2: ($150,000 – $15,000)/$4,200,000 = 3.21 percent

b. Dividend yield
Year 1: $3.00/$58.00 = 5.17 percent
Year 2: $3.20/$59.50 = 5.38 percent

c. Dividend payout
Year 1: $3.00/$5.80 = 51.7 percent
Year 2: $3.20/$5.90 = 54.2 percent

Statement of Cash Flows

PAST

Chapter 10 examined the accounting for stockholders' equity.

PRESENT

In this chapter, we turn our attention to the statement of cash flows.

FUTURE

Chapter 12 completes our study of financial accounting by looking at the analysis and interpretation of financial statements.

THE HOME DEPOT: A Company with a Vision

The Home Depot is the largest home improvement retailer in the United States. It was founded in 1978 in Atlanta, Georgia, and today, the company operates nearly 2,300 stores in the United States, Canada, and Mexico. The company's founders believed a company that considered the importance of values such as respect, customer service, and giving back to communities would be successful.

It takes a lot of cash to build and operate nearly 2,300 stores, especially when the average Home Depot store is about 104,000 square feet. In fiscal year 2020 Home Depot spent more than $2.4 billion on capital expenditures. This represents the eleventh year in a row that the company expended more than $1 billion dollars in capital expenditures. In the last three years the expenditures have exceeded $2.4 billion per year. How can a financial statement user determine where a company obtained the cash to fund such growth? Understanding the content, format, and construction of the statement of cash flows will enable a financial statement user to assess just how a company like The Home Depot was able to finance its capital expenditures for new store growth.

Road Map

LO	Learning Objective	Page	eLecture	Review	Assignments
LO1	**Discuss the content and format of the statement of cash flows.**	374	E11-1	11.1	SE1, SE2, SE3, E1, E2
LO2	**Explain the preparation of a statement of cash flows using the indirect method.**	380	E11-2	11.2, 11.3	SE1, SE2, SE3, E3, E4, E9, E10, P1, P2, P3, P4
LO3	**Define several ratios used to analyze the statement of cash flows.**	388	E11-3	11.4	SE8, SE9, SE10, E3, E11, P1, P5, P9
LO4	**Appendix 11: Explain the preparation of a statement of cash flows using the direct method.**	391	E11-4	11.5	SE4, SE5, SE6, SE7, E5, E6, E7, E8, P5, P6, P7, P8

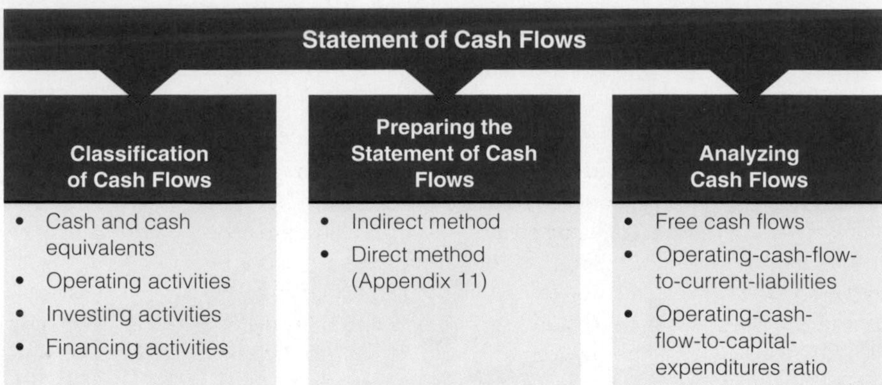

CASH AND CASH EQUIVALENTS

LO1 **Discuss** the content and format of the statement of cash flows.

Do you maintain a checkbook in which you record the checks you write and the bank deposits you make? If so, you are keeping a record of your cash flows—the checks you write are your cash outflows, and the bank deposits you make are your cash inflows. Businesses also experience cash inflows and outflows; but, they do more than just record their cash flows because GAAP requires that businesses prepare an entirely separate financial statement explaining where their cash flow came from and how it was used.

The statement of cash flows complements the balance sheet and the income statement. While a balance sheet reports a company's financial position as of a point in time, usually the end of a fiscal period, the statement of cash flows explains the change in one component of a company's financial position—its cash—from one balance sheet date to the next. The income statement, on the other hand, reveals the results of a company's operating activities for the period, and these operating activities are a major source and use of the cash reported in a company's statement of cash flows.

In the eyes of most creditors, investors, and managers, cash is a business's most important asset. Without cash, a business would be unable to pay its employees, its lenders, its suppliers, its service providers, or its shareholders. In short, cash is the only asset that a business can't operate without.

The dilemma for most managers, however, is knowing exactly how much cash to keep on hand. Although managers know that they need to keep some cash on hand in a checking account and/or petty cash fund to pay their immediate bills, they also know that cash is the lowest return-generating asset that a business has. Keeping too much cash on hand means that a business is not maximizing the value of its assets. For this reason, most managers spend considerable time assessing their cash needs—an activity called **cash management**. Because the science of cash management is inexact, managers have derived ways to help them minimize the amount of cash that they need to keep on hand while also maximizing the return on a business's assets. One such method is to invest any excess cash in alternative investments that are readily convertible back into cash and earn a higher rate of return than cash, but which do not place the invested cash at risk of loss. These alternative investments are known as cash equivalents.

Cash equivalents are short-term, highly liquid investments that are (1) easily convertible into cash and (2) close enough to maturity so that their market value is relatively insensitive to interest rate changes (generally, investments with maturities of three months or less). U.S. Treasury bills, certificates of deposit (CDs), commercial paper (short-term notes issued by corporations), and money market funds are examples of cash equivalents. Because there are differences across firms in the investments they classify as cash equivalents, GAAP requires that each firm disclose in the notes to the financial statements the company's policy regarding which investments are treated as cash equivalents.

When preparing a statement of cash flows, the cash and cash equivalents are added together and treated as a single amount. This is done because the purchase and sale of investments in cash equivalents are considered to be part of a firm's overall cash management strategy rather than a source or use of cash. As financial statement users evaluate a firm's cash flows, it should not matter whether the cash is on hand, deposited in a bank account, or invested in cash equivalents. Transfers back and forth between a firm's Cash account and its investments in cash equivalents, consequently, are not treated as cash inflows or outflows in the statement of cash flows.

When discussing the statement of cash flows, accountants often just use the word *cash* rather than the term *cash and cash equivalents.* We follow that practice in this chapter.

ACCOUNTING IN PRACTICE

Definition of Cash Equivalents There exist some differences between firms regarding the investments they classify as cash equivalents. For example, PepsiCo, Inc., the beverage and snack food company, states in the notes to its financial statements that "Cash equivalents are investments with original maturities of three months or less." International Game Technology, a manufacturer of gaming machines and proprietory gaming software systems, on the other hand, notes that "In addition to cash deposits at major banks, cash and equivalents include other marketable securities with original maturities of 90 days or less, primarily in U.S. Treasury-backed money market funds." The commonality among all firms, however, is that cash equivalents represent a temporary investment of excess cash in risk-free investments until such time as the cash is needed to support a business's operations.

ACTIVITY CLASSIFICATIONS IN THE STATEMENT OF CASH FLOWS

According to the Financial Accounting Standards Board, the primary objective of the cash flow statement is to provide users with relevant information about the receipts and payments of cash. This information, in turn, helps managers make better business decisions and investors make better investment decisions. To accomplish this, the statement of cash flows classifies a company's cash receipts and cash payments into three major business activity categories: operating activities, investing activities, and financing activities. Grouping cash flows into these categories identifies the effect on cash of each of the firm's major business activities (see Chapter 1). The combined effects on cash from all three categories explain the net change in cash for the period. The net change in cash then is reconciled with the beginning and ending balances of cash from the balance sheet. **Exhibit 11-1** illustrates the basic format for a statement of cash flows.

EXHIBIT 11-1 Format for the Statement of Cash Flows

SAMPLE COMPANY
Statement of Cash Flows
For Year Ended December 31

Cash Flow from Operating Activities		
(Details of cash flow from operating activities)	$###	
Cash provided (used) by operating activities		$###
Cash Flow from Investing Activities		
(Details of investing cash inflows and outflows)	###	
Cash provided (used) by investing activities		###
Cash Flow from Financing Activities		
(Details of financing cash inflows and outflows)	###	
Cash provided (used) by financing activities		###
Net increase (decrease) in cash		###
Cash at beginning of year		###
Cash at end of year		$###

Operating Activities

A company's income statement reflects the transactions and events that constitute its operating activities. The focus of a firm's operating activities involves selling goods or rendering services. The cash flow from **operating activities** is defined broadly, however, and includes any cash receipts or payments that are not classified as investing activities or financing activities. For example, cash received from a lawsuit settlement and cash payments to charity are treated as cash flow from operating activities. The following are examples of cash inflows and outflows relating to a firm's operating activities:

Cash Inflows

1. Receipts from customers for sales of goods or services
2. Receipts of interest and dividends
3. Other receipts that are not related to investing or financing activities, such as lawsuit settlements and refunds received from suppliers

Cash Outflows

1. Payments to suppliers
2. Payments to employees
3. Payments of interest to creditors
4. Payments of taxes to governmental agencies
5. Other payments that are not related to investing or financing activities, such as contributions to charity

Investing Activities

A firm's **investing activities** include those transactions involving (1) the acquisition or disposal of plant assets and intangible assets; (2) the purchase or sale of investments in stocks, bonds, and other securities (that are not cash equivalents); and (3) the lending and subsequent collection of cash from borrowers.[1] The related cash receipts and cash payments appear in the investing activities section of the statement of cash flows. Examples of these cash flows include:

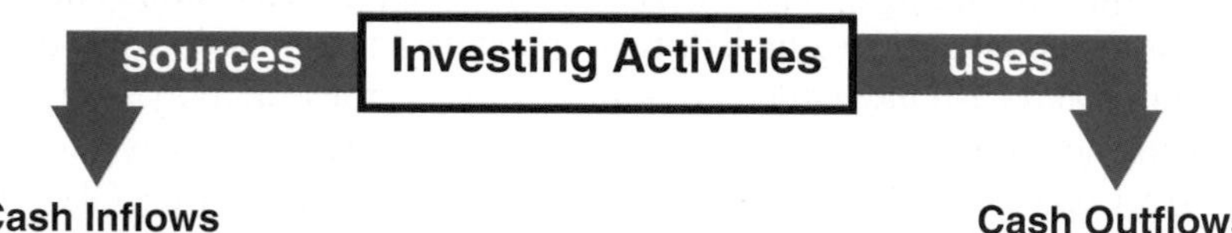

Cash Inflows

1. Receipts from sales of plant assets and intangible assets
2. Receipts from sales of investments in stocks, bonds, and other securities (other than cash equivalents)
3. Receipts from repayments of loans by borrowers

Cash Outflows

1. Payments to purchase plant assets and intangible assets
2. Payments to purchase investments in stocks, bonds, and other securities (other than cash equivalents)
3. Payments to lend money to borrowers

Financing Activities

A firm engages in **financing activities** when it obtains cash from shareholders, returns cash to shareholders, borrows from creditors, and repays amounts borrowed from creditors. Cash flows related to these events are reported in the financing activities section of the statement of cash flows. Examples of these cash flows include:

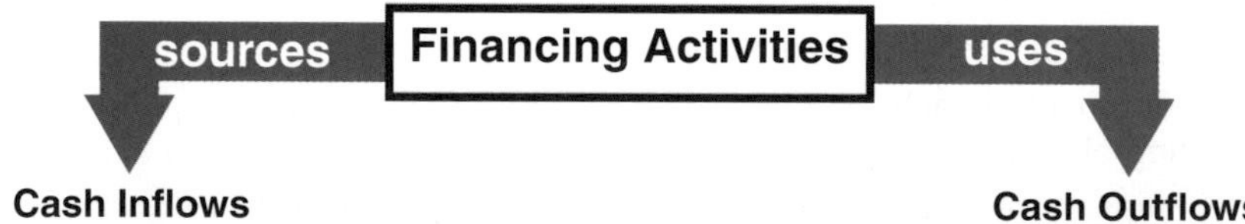

Cash Inflows

1. Receipts from issuing common stock and preferred stock and from sales of treasury stock
2. Receipts from issuing bonds payable, mortgage notes payable, and other notes payable

Cash Outflows

1. Payments to acquire treasury stock
2. Payments of dividends
3. Payments to settle outstanding bonds payable, mortgage notes payable, and other notes payable

[1] There are exceptions to the classification of these events as investing activities for financial institutions. For example, the purchase or sale of mortgage loans by a mortgage banker, like Bank of America, and the purchase or sale of securities in the trading account of a broker/dealer in financial securities, like Merrill Lynch, represent operating activities for these businesses.

Observe that paying cash to settle such obligations as accounts payable, wages payable, interest payable, and income tax payable are operating activities, not financing activities. Also observe that cash received as interest and dividends and cash paid as interest are classified as cash flows from operating activities, although cash paid as dividends to a company's stockholders is classified as a financing activity.

THINKING GLOBALLY

While cash flow statements prepared under both International Financial Reporting Standards (IFRS) and U.S. GAAP are quite similar, there are also important differences. One difference is that IFRS gives companies the option of classifying interest and dividends paid as either operating or financing activities, and interest and dividends received as either operating or investing activities. Under U.S. GAAP, companies have no options: interest paid and interest and dividends received are classified as operating activities, and dividends paid are classified as financing activities. These differences should be taken into account when investors compare cash flow statements prepared under IFRS and U.S. GAAP.

An Illustration of Activity Classification Usefulness

The classification of cash flows into the three business activity categories helps financial statement users analyze and interpret a company's cash flow data. To illustrate, assume that companies D, E, and F operate in the same industry, and that each company reported a $100,000 increase in cash during the period. Information from each company's statement of cash flows is summarized below:

	Company		
	D	E	F
Cash flow from operating activities	$100,000	$ 0	$ 0
Cash flow from investing activities:			
Sale of plant assets	0	100,000	0
Cash flow from financing activities:			
Issuance of notes payable	0	0	100,000
Net increase in cash	$100,000	$100,000	$100,000

Although each company's increase in cash was exactly $100,000, the source of the cash increase varied by company. This variation affects the analysis of the cash flow data, particularly for potential creditors who must evaluate the likelihood of the repayment of funds loaned to a company. Based only on this cash flow data, a potential creditor would feel more comfortable lending money to Company D than to either Company E or F. Company D's cash increase came from its operating activities, whereas E's cash increase came from the sale of plant assets, a source that is unlikely to recur, and F's cash increase came from borrowed funds. Company F faces additional future uncertainty when the interest and principal payments on the existing notes become due, and for this reason, a potential creditor would be less inclined to extend additional loans to Company F.

NONCASH INVESTING AND FINANCING ACTIVITIES

A secondary objective of the statement of cash flows is to present summary information about a firm's investing and financing activities. Although many of these activities affect cash and, therefore, are already included in the investing and financing sections of the statement of cash flows, some significant investing and financing events do not affect current cash flow. Examples of **noncash investing and financing activities** are the issuance of stock or bonds in exchange for plant assets or intangible assets, the exchange of long-term assets for other long-term assets, and the conversion of long-term debt into common stock. A common feature among each of these transactions is that no cash is exchanged between the parties involved in the transaction.

Noncash investing and financing transactions generally do, however, affect future cash flows. Issuing bonds in exchange for equipment, for example, requires future cash payments for interest and principal on the bonds. On the other hand, converting bonds into common stock eliminates the future cash payments related to the bonds' interest and principal. Knowledge of these types of events, therefore, should be helpful to financial statement users who wish to evaluate a firm's future cash flows.

Information regarding noncash investing and financing transactions is disclosed in a separate accounting schedule. The separate schedule may be placed immediately below the statement of cash flows, or it may be presented in the notes to the financial statements.

PRINCIPLE ALERT

Objectivity Principle The *objectivity principle* asserts that the usefulness of financial statements is enhanced when the underlying data are objective and verifiable. Measuring cash and the changes in cash are among the most objective measurements that accountants make. The statement of cash flows, therefore, is the most objective financial statement required under generally accepted accounting principles. This characteristic of the statement of cash flows is welcomed by investors and creditors interested in evaluating the quality of a firm's net income and assets. Financial statement users often feel more confident about the quality of a company's net income and assets when there is a high correlation between, or relationship with, a company's cash flow from operating activities and its net income.

USING THE STATEMENT OF CASH FLOWS

The Financial Accounting Standards Board believes that one of the principal objectives of financial reporting is to help financial statement users assess the amount, timing, and uncertainty of a business's future cash flows. These assessments, in turn, help users evaluate prospective future cash receipts from their investments in, or loans to, a business. Although the statement of cash flows describes a company's past cash flows, it is also useful for assessing future cash flows since the recent past is often a very good predictor of the future.

A statement of cash flows shows the cash effects of a firm's operating, investing, and financing activities. Distinguishing among these different categories of cash flows helps financial statement users compare, evaluate, and predict a business's future cash flows. With cash flow information, creditors and investors are better able to assess a company's ability to repay its liabilities and pay dividends. A firm's need for outside financing also can be evaluated using the statement of cash flows. Further, the statement enables users to observe and analyze management's investing and financing policies, plans, and strategies.

A statement of cash flows also provides information useful in evaluating a firm's financial flexibility. **Financial flexibility** is a company's ability to generate sufficient amounts of cash to respond to unanticipated needs and opportunities. Information about past cash flows, particularly the cash flow from operations, helps in assessing financial flexibility. An evaluation of a firm's ability to survive an unexpected drop in demand for its goods and services, for example, may include a review of its past cash flow from operations. The larger these past cash flows, the greater will be a firm's ability to withstand adverse changes in future economic conditions.

Some investors and creditors find the statement of cash flows useful in evaluating the "quality" of a firm's net income. As we saw in Chapter 3, determining net income under the accrual basis of accounting requires many accruals, deferrals, allocations, and valuations. These adjustment and measurement procedures often require a great deal of subjective judgment by management. Consequently, some financial statement users look at the difference between net income and cash flows from operations. To these users, the higher the relationship between a company's net income and the cash flow from operations, the higher is the quality of the firm's net income.

CASH FLOW FROM OPERATING ACTIVITIES

The first section of the statement of cash flows presents a firm's cash flow from operating activities. *Two alternative formats are available to present the cash flow from operating activities: the indirect method and the direct method. Both methods report the same amount of cash flow from operating activities and differ only in how the cash flow from operating activities is presented.*

The **indirect method** starts with net income using the accrual basis of accounting and applies a series of adjustments to convert it to net income under the cash basis of accounting, which is equivalent to the cash flow from operating activities. The adjustments to net income do not represent specific cash flows; consequently, the indirect method does not report any detail concerning individual revenues or expenses.

ACCOUNTING IN PRACTICE

Popularity of Method for Reporting the Cash Flow from Operations Do you think a direct approach in communicating with financial statement users is best, or should your approach be more indirect? When it comes to reporting the cash flow from operations, companies appear to favor the indirect approach by a wide margin as evidenced by the responses to a survey of 600 large U.S. companies.

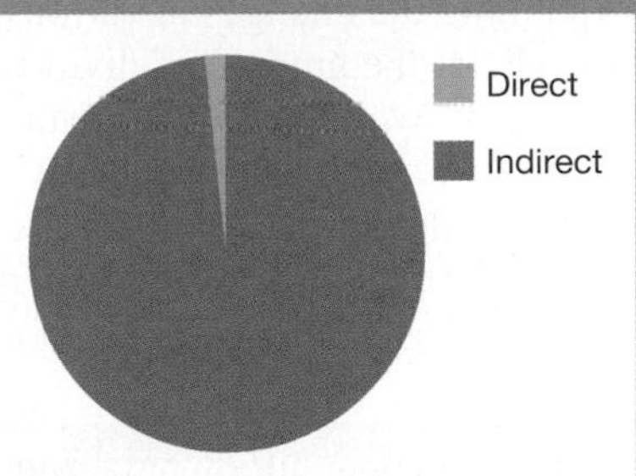

Source: Accounting Trends and Techniques

The **direct method** shows individual amounts of cash inflows and cash outflows for the major operating activities. The net difference between these inflows and outflows is the cash flow from operating activities.

The Financial Accounting Standards Board encourages companies to use the direct method but permits the use of the indirect method. Despite the FASB's preference for the direct method, *more than 95 percent of companies preparing the statement of cash flows use the indirect method.* The indirect method is popular because (1) it is easier and less expensive to prepare than the direct method and (2) the direct method requires a supplemental disclosure showing the indirect method.

ACCOUNTING IN PRACTICE

A Comparison of Accrual-Basis and Cash-Basis Amounts Accountants calculate net income on the income statement using the accrual basis of accounting. The cash flow from operating activities, presented on the statement of cash flows, represents a company's net income using the cash basis of accounting. No necessary relationship exists between the two numbers. Compared with net income, the cash flow from operating activities may be larger, smaller, or about the same amount. Financial data from recent annual reports of three well-known companies—**Under Armour**, **Logitech**, and **Netflix**—bear this out.

($ in thousands)	Net Income or (Loss)	Cash Flow Provided (Used) by Operating Activities
Under Armour.	$ (549,177)	$ 212,864
Logitech	$ 449,723	$ 425,000
Netflix	$1,866,916	$(2,887,322)

REVIEW 11.1

Classify each of the cash flow events listed below as either an (1) operating activity, (2) investing activity, or (3) financing activity:

1. Cash received from customers
2. Cash sale of land
3. Cash paid to suppliers
4. Cash purchase of equipment
5. Payment on note payable
6. Cash dividend payment
7. Cash wages paid
8. Purchase of treasury stock
9. Cash sale of investments

The solution is on page 410.

The following section on preparing the statement of cash flows uses the indirect method. Appendix 11 uses the direct method. Your instructor can choose to cover either one or both methods. If the indirect method is skipped, read Appendix 11 and return to the section titled "Analyzing Cash Flows" on page 390.

PREPARING THE STATEMENT OF CASH FLOWS USING THE INDIRECT METHOD

LO2 **Explain** the preparation of a statement of cash flows using the indirect method.

To prepare a statement of cash flows using the indirect method, the following information is needed: a company's income statement, the two most recent balance sheets, and additional data explaining the changes in various accounts, such as the book value of fixed assets sold during the period and the amount of dividends paid. **Exhibit 11-2** presents this information for the Bennett Company. We will use this data to prepare Bennett's statement of cash flows using the indirect method. As will be seen shortly, Bennett's statement of cash flows will explain the $25,000 increase in the company's cash account during the current year (from $10,000 at the beginning of the year to $35,000 at the end of the year) by classifying the firm's cash inflows and outflows into the three business activity categories of operating, investing, and financing.

EXHIBIT 11-2 Financial Data of Bennett Company

BENNETT COMPANY
Income Statement
For Year Ended December 31, Current Year

Sales revenue		$250,000
Cost of goods sold	$148,000	
Wages expense	52,000	
Insurance expense	5,000	
Depreciation expense	10,000	
Income tax expense	11,000	
Gain on sale of plant assets	(8,000)	218,000
Net income		$ 32,000

Additional Data for the Current Year

1. **Sold plant assets costing $20,000 for $28,000 cash.**
2. **Declared and paid cash dividends of $13,000.**

BENNETT COMPANY
Balance Sheets

As of December 31	Current Year	Prior Year
Assets		
Cash	$ 35,000	$ 10,000
Accounts receivable	39,000	34,000
Inventory	54,000	60,000
Prepaid insurance	17,000	4,000
Long-term investments	15,000	—
Plant assets	180,000	200,000
Accumulated depreciation	(50,000)	(40,000)
Patent	60,000	—
Total assets	$350,000	$268,000
Liabilities and Equity		
Accounts payable	$ 10,000	$ 19,000
Income tax payable	5,000	3,000
Common stock	260,000	190,000
Retained earnings	75,000	56,000
Total liabilities and equity	$350,000	$268,000

To see that the statement of cash flows can be prepared using only a company's income statement and the changes in its balance sheet accounts, consider again the balance sheet equation, equation (1), that was first introduced in Chapter 1:

$$\text{Assets (A)} = \text{Liabilities (L)} + \text{Stockholders' equity (SE)} \quad (1)$$

$$CA + NCA = L + SE \quad (2)$$

$$\Delta CA + \Delta NCA = \Delta L + \Delta SE \quad (3)$$

$$\Delta CA = \Delta L - \Delta NCA + \Delta SE \quad (4)$$

In equation (2), separate the firm's assets into its cash (CA) and noncash assets (NCA) and note that the equation remains in balance. In equation (3), rewrite the balance sheet equation in terms of changes in the accounts. Finally, in equation (4), subtracting the change in noncash assets from both sides of the equation shows that the change in cash (which is the end result of the statement of cash flows) can be computed from the change in all of the other accounts.

THINKING GLOBALLY

Currently, both U.S. GAAP and IFRS permit a company to present its statement of cash flows using either the direct method or the indirect method. A topic being considered by the FASB/IASB convergence project would limit the preparation of the statement of cash flows to just the direct method. The direct method is currently preferred by both the FASB and the IASB, although most U.S. firms present their statement of cash flows using the indirect method.

Five Steps to Preparing a Statement of Cash Flows

The indirect method of preparing the cash flow statement is based on the above observation that the change in cash is equal to the change in all of the other accounts in the balance sheet. This approach begins with first calculating the changes in each of the balance sheet accounts over the accounting period. We then classify each change into one of the three business categories (operating, investing, and financing). Next, we incorporate the information not contained in the balance sheet in order to refine the cash flows reported in each category. In the following example, we illustrate this process by breaking it down into five discrete steps using the financial statements found in **Exhibit 11-2**.

Step One Using just the beginning and ending balance sheets (see Columns 1 and 2 in **Exhibit 11-3**), calculate the change in each balance sheet account by subtracting the beginning balance sheet amount from the ending amount. The results of this step for the Bennett Company are presented in Column 3 of **Exhibit 11-3**. To simplify this step, the change in the Plant Assets account is combined with the Accumulated Depreciation account—that is, the change in the Plant Assets account is calculated based on the balance of Plant Assets, net of Accumulated Depreciation.

To verify the accuracy of the Step One calculations, simply compare the sum of the changes in the asset accounts ($82,000) with the sum of the changes in the liability and stockholders' equity accounts ($82,000). These totals must be equal. If not, there is a subtraction error that must be corrected before progressing to Step Two.

EXHIBIT 11-3 Preparing a Statement of Cash Flows: The Indirect Method

BENNETT COMPANY
Balance Sheet
December 31

	(1) Beginning of Year	(2) End of Year	(3) Change for Year	(4) Cash Flow Classification
Assets				
Cash	$ 10,000	$ 35,000	**$25,000**	**Cash flow increase**
Accounts receivable	34,000	39,000	5,000	Operating
Inventory	60,000	54,000	(6,000)	Operating
Prepaid insurance	4,000	17,000	13,000	Operating
Long-term investments	0	15,000	15,000	Investing
Plant assets (net)	160,000	130,000	(30,000)	Investing/Operating
Patent	0	60,000	60,000	Investing/Operating
Total assets	$268,000	$350,000	$82,000	
Liabilities and Equity				
Accounts payable	$ 19,000	$ 10,000	$ (9,000)	Operating
Income tax payable	3,000	5,000	2,000	Operating
Common stock	190,000	260,000	70,000	Financing
Retained earnings	56,000	75,000	19,000	Operating/Financing
Total liabilities and equity	$268,000	$350,000	$82,000	

An important amount identified during Step One is the change in the cash account. The highlighted area in **Exhibit 11-3** reveals that the cash account of the Bennett Company increased by

$25,000 from the beginning of the year to the end of the year. Hence, all of the various cash inflows and outflows for the company must aggregate to this amount.

Step Two Identify the appropriate business activity category—operating, investing, or financing—for each balance sheet account. The cash flow activity classifications are presented in Column 4 of **Exhibit 11-3**.

Although measuring the change in the balance sheet accounts in Step One is a straightforward arithmetic activity, there can be some confusion over the correct activity classification for some of the balance sheet accounts in Step Two. The changes in accounts receivable, inventory, prepaid insurance, accounts payable, and income tax payable are all easily identified as operating activities because they are associated with the day-to-day operations of a business. For example, changes in Accounts Receivable result from credit sales (which increase accounts receivable) and cash collections (which reduce accounts receivable). The change in common stock, on the other hand, is clearly a financing activity because it is associated with issuing stock to finance a business. The change in net plant assets, however, can result from both an investing activity and an operating activity. Purchases and sales of plant assets are investing activities that increase the balance in plant assets; but, depreciation expense is an operating activity because it appears in the income statement, and it reduces the balance in plant assets by increasing accumulated depreciation. Similarly, the change in intangible assets such as patents can result from both an investing activity and an operating activity because the acquisition or sale of intangibles is an investing activity, whereas the amortization of intangibles is an operating activity reflected in the income statement, which reduces the balance of the Patent account. Finally, the change in retained earnings results from both operating and financing activities. Retained earnings is increased by net income, an operating activity, and decreased by the payment of dividends, a financing activity.

As a general rule, the following cash flow activity classifications apply, although exceptions exist:

Balance Sheet Account	Cash Flow Activity Category
Current assets	Operating
Noncurrent assets	Investing/Operating
Current liabilities.	Operating
Noncurrent liabilities.	Financing
Capital stock.	Financing
Retained earnings	Operating/Financing

Examples of exceptions to the above classifications include the following:

- Marketable securities, a current asset, are an investing activity item.
- Current maturities of long-term debt, a current liability, are a financing activity item.
- Employee pension obligations, a noncurrent liability, are an operating activity item.

Step Three Having completed Steps One and Two, you are now ready to build a preliminary statement of cash flows using the calculated increases or decreases in the various balance sheet accounts from Step One and the identified activity classifications from Step Two. The preliminary statement of cash flows for the Bennett Company using the change values from Column 3 of **Exhibit 11-3** and the cash flow activity classifications from Column 4 is presented in **Exhibit 11-4**.

Because a statement of cash flows measures the inflows and outflows of cash for a business, it is important to note that the sign of the changes in the asset accounts that were calculated in Step One must be reversed when preparing the preliminary statement of cash flows in **Exhibit 11-4**. This is because changes in noncash assets are deducted in computing the change in cash, which can be seen in equation (4), on page 382, in which the change in noncash assets has a negative sign. For instance, **Exhibit 11-4** shows that the change in accounts receivable was an increase of $5,000, whereas the change in inventory was a decrease of $6,000. When preparing the indirect method statement of cash flows, a $5,000 increase in accounts receivable represents a subtraction from net income (a cash outflow), and a decline in inventory of $6,000 represents an addition to net income (a cash inflow), to arrive at the cash flow from operations. To illustrate why an increase in accounts receivable must be subtracted from net income to arrive at operating cash flow, consider how sales revenue is initially recorded. Assume that a $2,000 sale of goods is paid for with $1,200 in cash and the remaining amount recorded as an increase in accounts receivable.

$$\Delta CA = \Delta L - \Delta NCA + \Delta SE$$

+1,200	=		–	+800	+	+2,000
Increase in cash	=		–	Increase in accounts receivable	+	Increase in net income

In this example, net income increases by $2,000, but cash is increased by only $1,200. Therefore, net income must be reduced by the $800 increase in accounts receivable to reflect the amount of cash received from sales of $1,200. Hence, when preparing the preliminary statement of cash flows in Step Three, it is important to remember to reverse the sign of the change values for the asset accounts. This is unnecessary for the liability and stockholders' equity accounts as also can be seen from equation (4), on page 382.

Exhibit 11-4 presents the preliminary statement of cash flows for the Bennett Company as computed in Step Three. This preliminary statement suggests that the firm's cash flow from operating activities was $0, the cash flow from investing activities was negative $45,000, and the cash flow from financing activities was $70,000. As required, the cash inflows and outflows aggregate to the change in cash from the balance sheet, an increase of $25,000.

EXHIBIT 11-4 An Illustration of a Preliminary Statement of Cash Flows: The Indirect Method

BENNETT COMPANY
Preliminary Statement of Cash Flows
For Year Ended December 31

Operating Activities	
Retained earnings	$19,000
Accounts receivable	(5,000)
Inventory	6,000
Prepaid insurance	(13,000)
Accounts payable	(9,000)
Income tax payable	2,000
Cash flow from operating activities	0
Investing Activities	
Long-term investments	(15,000)
Plant assets (net)	30,000
Patent	(60,000)
Cash flow for investing activities	(45,000)
Financing Activities	
Common stock	70,000
Cash flow from financing activities	70,000
Change in cash (from the balance sheet)	$25,000

Step Four To this point we have used the balance sheet exclusively to compute the statement of cash flows. For most businesses, however, cash flows also will be generated by a firm's ongoing operations. Hence, it is now appropriate to introduce the operations-related data found on the company's income statement (see **Exhibit 11-2**).

In this step, we make two important adjustments to the preliminary statement of cash flows in **Exhibit 11-4**. First, the change in retained earnings from the balance sheet is replaced by net income from the income statement. For the Bennett Company, the change in retained earnings of $19,000 does not equal net income of $32,000. The difference of $13,000 ($32,000 – $19,000) represents a cash dividend paid to Bennett's shareholders, which reduced retained earnings. Thus, when we replace the change in retained earnings of $19,000 with net income of $32,000, it is also necessary to report the $13,000 cash dividend payment as a cash outflow under the financing activities section in **Exhibit 11-5**. Increasing the cash flow from operations and decreasing the cash flow from financing activities by an equivalent amount ($13,000) allows the statement of cash flows to remain in balance with the net change in cash of $25,000.

Second, we adjust the Bennett Company's net income for any **noncash expenses** such as the depreciation of plant assets and the amortization of intangibles that were deducted in the process of calculating the firm's accrual basis net income.[2] These noncash expenses must be added back to net income in the operating activities section to correctly measure the firm's operating cash flow. However, to keep the preliminary statement of cash flows in balance with an increase in cash of $25,000, it is also necessary to subtract equivalent amounts in the investing activities section.

To summarize, the adjustments to the Bennett Company's preliminary statement of cash flows in **Exhibit 11-4** are as follows:

1. Net income of $32,000 replaces the change in retained earnings of $19,000 in the operating activities section. This adjustment adds $13,000 to the cash flow from operating activities. To keep the statement of cash flows in balance with the change in cash of $25,000, it is necessary to subtract $13,000 elsewhere on the statement. Since retained earnings is calculated as follows:

   Retained earnings (beginning)
   \+ Net income for the period
   − Dividends declared
   = Retained earnings (ending)

   the outflow of $13,000 is also reflected as a cash dividend to shareholders under the financing activities section.
2. Depreciation expense of $10,000, a noncash deduction from net income, is added back to net income to avoid understating the cash flow from operations. However, to keep the statement of cash flows in balance with the change in cash of $25,000, a similar amount is subtracted from net plant assets under the investing activities section. This adjustment is necessary because the $10,000 in depreciation expense in the income statement also increased accumulated deprecation, which decreased net plant assets.

Step Five To provide the most useful cash flow data, a final step is required: Make any appropriate adjustments to the operating activities section to calculate a company's operating cash flow. As noted above, a firm's operating cash flow should include only the cash flows from operating activities. Consequently, it is necessary to review the income statement to identify and remove the financial effects of any nonoperating transactions included in net income.[3]

To illustrate this point, note that the Bennett Company sold plant assets during the year at a gain of $8,000 ($28,000 sales price less $20,000 cost). This event is an investing activity and, therefore, properly belongs under the investing activities. To correctly compute Bennett's operating cash flow, it is necessary to remove this gain from the operating activity section and add it to plant assets under the investing activities section. These actions allow us to correctly measure Bennett's cash flow from operating activities, as well as its cash flow from plant assets. Note that after making the adjustments from Steps Four and Five to Plant Assets in **Exhibit 11-4** ($30,000 − $10,000 + $8,000) the cash flows from Plant Assets equals $28,000, which is exactly the amount of cash received from selling plant assets during the year. Because the company did not purchase any plant assets, this represents the total increase in cash flows from investing activities related to Plant Assets.

[2] Depreciation expense and amortization expense are called noncash expenses because these expenses do not involve any current period cash outflow. Depreciation expense, for example, represents the allocation of the purchase price of plant assets over the many periods that these assets produce sales revenue for a business. The matching principle requires that the cost of plant assets be matched with the sales revenue produced by these assets, and this is accomplished on the income statement by the deduction of the periodic depreciation charge.

[3] An exception is interest expense, which most investment professionals view as a financing activity. Regardless, interest payments are required to be included in the cash flow from operating activities.

Exhibit 11-5 presents the final statement of cash flows for Bennett Company and includes not only the adjustments from Step Four, but also the adjustment to remove any nonoperating gains and losses from the cash flow from operating activities (Step Five). Bennett's statement of cash flows in **Exhibit 11-5**, using the indirect method, reveals that the cash flow from operating activities is $15,000, the cash flow used for investing activities is negative $47,000, and the cash flow provided by financing activities is $57,000. The resulting cash flow of $25,000 exactly equals the increase in cash on the balance sheet of $25,000, as required.

EXHIBIT 11-5 Statement of Cash Flows—The Indirect Method

BENNETT COMPANY
Statement of Cash Flows
For Year Ended December 31

Cash Flow from Operating Activities			
Net income	$32,000		← from the Income Statement
Add (deduct) items to convert net income to cash basis			
Depreciation	10,000		
Gain on sale of plant assets	(8,000)		
Accounts receivable increase	(5,000)		
Inventory decrease	6,000		
Prepaid insurance increase	(13,000)		
Accounts payable decrease	(9,000)		
Income tax payable increase	2,000		
Cash provided by operating activities		$15,000	
Cash Flow from Investing Activities			
Purchase of long-term investments	(15,000)		
Sale of plant assets	28,000		
Purchase of patent	(60,000)		
Cash used by investing activities		(47,000)	
Cash Flow from Financing Activities			
Issuance of common stock	70,000		
Payment of dividends	(13,000)		
Cash provided by financing activities		57,000	
Net increase in cash		25,000	
Cash at beginning of year		10,000	← from the Balance Sheet
Cash at end of year		$35,000	← from the Balance Sheet

ENVIRONMENTAL, SOCIAL, AND GOVERNANCE

According to **Home Depot**, "Our values are our beliefs, principles and standards that do not change over time. Values are the resources we draw on when asked to make decisions. They form the groundwork for our ethical behavior. All that we do at The Home Depot must be consistent with the values of the Company. We believe in *Doing the Right Thing*, having *Respect for all People*, building *Strong Relationships*, *Taking Care of Our People*, *Giving Back*, providing *Excellent Customer Service*, *Encouraging Entrepreneurial Spirit* and providing strong *Shareholder Returns*."

Home Depot believes that "Doing the Right Thing" leads to doing well for all its stakeholders, including its shareholders. As Home Depot states, "We are steadfast in this commitment" to return value to our shareholders, "while also recognizing that exercising corporate responsibility and being informed by the needs of our other stakeholders, including our customers, associates, supplier partners, and communities, creates value for all stakeholders, including our shareholders." There seems to be a lot of truth in this as Home Depot has managed to stay profitable and produce cash flows from operating activities each year.

The following illustration summarizes the five-step process to prepare an indirect method statement of cash flows:

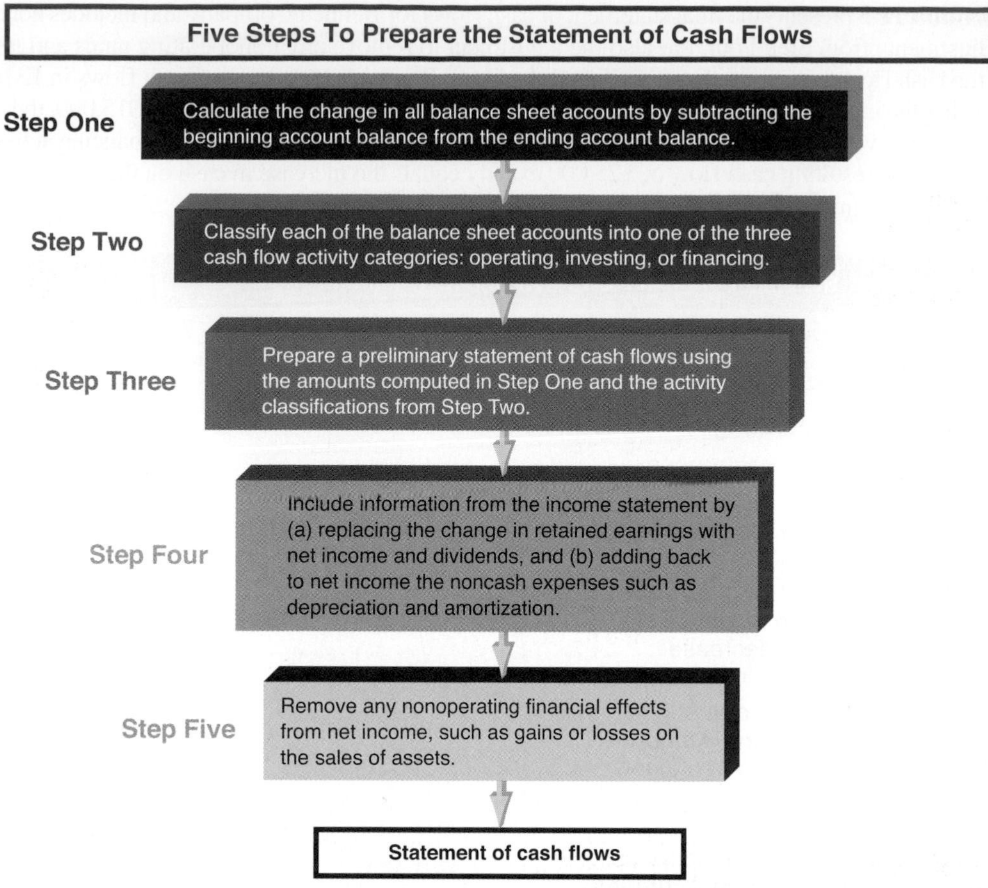

Five Steps To Prepare the Statement of Cash Flows
Step One
Calculate the change in all balance sheet accounts by subtracting the beginning account balance from the ending account balance.
Step Two
Classify each of the balance sheet accounts into one of the three cash flow activity categories: operating, investing, or financing.
Step Three
Prepare a preliminary statement of cash flows using the amounts computed in Step One and the activity classifications from Step Two.
Step Four
Include information from the income statement by (a) replacing the change in retained earnings with net income and dividends, and (b) adding back to net income the noncash expenses such as depreciation and amortization.
Step Five
Remove any nonoperating financial effects from net income, such as gains or losses on the sales of assets.
Statement of cash flows

REVIEW 11.2

Husky Company's income statement from the current year ended December 31 and comparative balance sheets as of December 31 of the current and prior years are shown below:

HUSKY COMPANY
Income Statement
For the Current Year Ended December 31

Sales revenue		$1,270,000
Cost of goods sold	$860,000	
Wages expense	172,000	
Insurance expense	16,000	
Depreciation expense	34,000	
Interest expense	18,000	
Income tax expense	58,000	1,158,000
Net income		$ 112,000

HUSKY COMPANY
Balance Sheets

	December 31	
	Current Year	Prior Year
Assets		
Cash	$ 22,000	$ 10,000
Accounts receivable	82,000	64,000
Inventory	180,000	120,000
Prepaid insurance	10,000	14,000
Plant assets	500,000	390,000
Accumulated depreciation	(136,000)	(102,000)
Total assets	$658,000	$496,000

continued

continued from previous page

HUSKY COMPANY
Balance Sheets

	December 31	
	Current Year	**Prior Year**
Liabilities and Stockholders' Equity		
Accounts payable	$ 14,000	$ 20,000
Wages payable	18,000	12,000
Income tax payable	14,000	16,000
Bonds payable	260,000	150,000
Common stock	180,000	180,000
Retained earnings	172,000	118,000
Total liabilities and stockholders' equity	$658,000	$496,000

Cash dividends of $58,000 were declared and paid during the current year. Plant assets were purchased for cash, and bonds payable were issued for cash. Accounts payable relate to merchandise purchases.

Required

Prepare a statement of cash flows for the current year ended December 31 for the Husky Company using the indirect method.

The solution is on page 411.

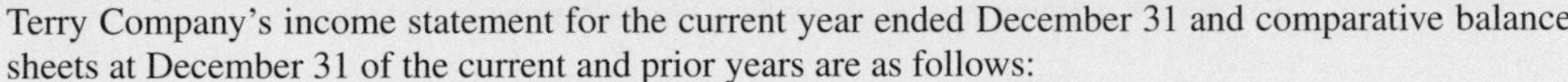

REVIEW 11.3

Terry Company's income statement for the current year ended December 31 and comparative balance sheets at December 31 of the current and prior years are as follows:

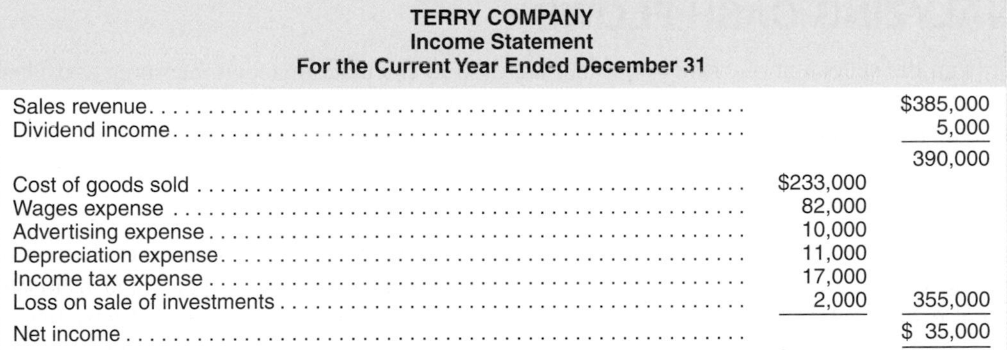

TERRY COMPANY
Income Statement
For the Current Year Ended December 31

Sales revenue		$385,000
Dividend income		5,000
		390,000
Cost of goods sold	$233,000	
Wages expense	82,000	
Advertising expense	10,000	
Depreciation expense	11,000	
Income tax expense	17,000	
Loss on sale of investments	2,000	355,000
Net income		$ 35,000

TERRY COMPANY
Balance Sheets

	December 31	
	Current Year	**Prior Year**
Assets		
Cash	$ 8,000	$ 12,000
Accounts receivable	22,000	28,000
Inventory	94,000	66,000
Prepaid advertising	12,000	9,000
Long-term investments—available for sale	30,000	41,000
Fair value adjustment to investments	—	(1,000)
Plant assets	178,000	130,000
Accumulated depreciation	(72,000)	(61,000)
Total assets	$272,000	$224,000

continued

continued from previous page

TERRY COMPANY Balance Sheets	December 31	
	Current Year	Prior Year
Liabilities and Stockholders' Equity		
Accounts payable	$ 27,000	$ 14,000
Wages payable	6,000	2,500
Income tax payable	3,000	4,500
Common stock	139,000	125,000
Retained earnings	97,000	79,000
Unrealized loss on investments	—	(1,000)
Total liabilities and stockholders' equity	$272,000	$224,000

Cash dividends of $17,000 were declared and paid during the current year. Plant assets were purchased for cash, and, later in the year, additional common stock was issued for cash. Investments costing $11,000 were sold for cash at a $2,000 loss; an unrealized loss of $1,000 on these investments had been recorded in the prior year (at December 31 of the current year, the cost and fair value of the unsold investments are equal).

Required

a. Calculate the change in cash that occurred during the year.

b. Prepare a statement of cash flows for the current year ended December 31 using the indirect method.

The solution is on pages 411–412.

For readers skipping the indirect method, please resume reading here.

ANALYZING CASH FLOWS

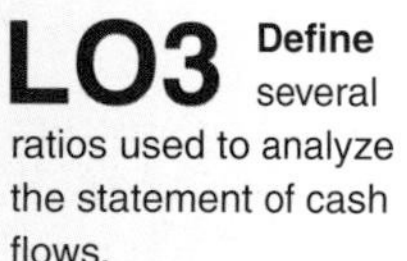

LO3 Define several ratios used to analyze the statement of cash flows.

Data from the statement of cash flows often are used to calculate financial measures to evaluate a company's cash flow health. Three such measures include a company's free cash flow, the operating-cash-flow-to-current-liabilities ratio, and the operating-cash-flow-to-capital-expenditures ratio.

Free Cash Flow

Free cash flow (FCF) often is used by investment professionals and investors to evaluate a company's cash-flow strength. Intuitively, FCF represents the amount of cash generated from operations, in addition to (or short of) the amount of capital expenditures for investing activities. FCF is an important reference point because over the life of the company, FCF represents the amount of cash that can be paid in dividends to shareholders. FCF excludes cash from financing activities because that cash does not represent cash generated for payment of dividends.

FCF = Cash flow from operating activities – Capital expenditures

In recent financial statements, **The Home Depot** reported cash flows from operating activities of $18,839 million and capital expenditures of $2,463 million. Home Depot has FCF of $16,376 million ($18,839 million – $2,463 million), which is available to be paid out in dividends to its shareholders.

As discussed in Chapter 8, capital expenditures refer to the required reinvestment in a business's plant and intangible assets necessary to enable a firm to remain a going concern. A firm with strong FCF will carry a higher stock value than one with weak (or no) FCF.

TAKEAWAY 11.1 Concept	Method	Assessment
Does a company generate cash flows in excess of its capital expenditure needs?	Statement of cash flows. FCF = Cash flow from operating activities – Capital expenditures	The higher the free cash flow, the greater is a company's ability to generate cash for needs other than capital expenditures.

Operating-Cash-Flow-to-Current-Liabilities Ratio

Two measures previously introduced—the current ratio and the quick ratio—emphasize the relationship of a company's current or quick assets to its current liabilities in an attempt to measure the ability of a firm to pay its current liabilities. The **operating-cash-flow-to-current-liabilities ratio** is another measure of a company's ability to pay its current liabilities. Although the current and quick ratios focus on a firm's ability to pay liabilities using existing current or quick assets, the operating-cash-flow-to-current-liabilities highlights a firm's ability to pay its current liabilities using its operating cash flow. The ratio is calculated as follows:

$$\textbf{Operating-cash-flow-to-current-liabilities ratio} = \frac{\textbf{Cash flow from operating activities}}{\textbf{Average current liabilities}}$$

The cash flow from operating activities is obtained from the statement of cash flows. The denominator is the average of the beginning and ending current liabilities for the year from the balance sheet.

The following amounts were reported by The Home Depot in recent financial statements ($ in millions):

Cash flow from operating activities	$18,839
Current liabilities at beginning of the year	18,375
Current liabilities at end of the year	23,166

The operating cash-flow-to-current-liabilities ratio for the The Home Depot is calculated as follows:

$$\frac{\$18{,}839}{\left[\frac{(\$18{,}375 + \$23{,}166)}{2}\right]} = 0.91$$

The higher this ratio, the greater is a firm's ability to pay current liabilities using its operating cash flow. As a rough rule of thumb, a ratio of 0.5 is considered a strong ratio; consequently, The Home Depot's ratio of 0.91 would be interpreted as very strong. A ratio of 0.91 indicates that The Home Depot generates $0.91 of operating cash flow for every dollar of current liabilities.

TAKEAWAY 11.2

Concept	Method	Assessment
Will a company have sufficient cash to pay its current liabilities as they become due?	Statement of cash flows and balance sheet. Operating-cash-flow-to-current-liabilities ratio = Cash flow from operating activities / Average current liabilities	The higher the ratio, the higher the probability that a company will have sufficient operating cash flow to pay its current liabilities as they become due.

Operating-Cash-Flow-to-Capital-Expenditures Ratio

To remain competitive, a business must be able to replace, and expand when appropriate, its property, plant, and equipment. A ratio that evaluates a firm's ability to finance its capital investments from operating cash flow is the **operating-cash-flow-to-capital-expenditures ratio**. This ratio is calculated as follows:

$$\textbf{Operating-cash-flow-to-capital-expenditures ratio} = \frac{\textbf{Cash flow from operating activities}}{\textbf{Annual net capital expenditures}}$$

The numerator in this ratio comes from the statement of cash flows. Information for the denominator may be found in one or more places in the financial statements. Data on capital expenditures are part of the required industry segment disclosures in the notes to the financial statements. Data regarding a company's capital expenditures also are presented in the investing activities section of the statement of cash flows. (When capital expenditures are reported in the statement of cash flows, the amount often is broken into two figures—(1) Proceeds from the sale of property, plant, and equipment and (2) Purchases of property, plant, and equipment. The appropriate "capital expenditures" figure for the purpose of calculating this ratio is the net of the two amounts.) Finally, management's discussion and analysis of the financial statements may identify a company's annual capital expenditures.

A ratio in excess of 1.0 indicates that a firm's current operating activities are providing cash in excess of the amount needed to fund its desired investment in plant and intangible assets and normally would be considered a sign of financial strength. The interpretation of this ratio is influenced by the trend in recent years, the ratio being achieved by other firms in the same industry, and the stage of a firm's life cycle. A firm in the early stages of its life cycle—when periods of rapid expansion may occur—may be expected to experience a lower ratio than a firm in the later stage of its life cycle—when maintenance of plant capacity may be more likely than an expansion of plant capacity.

To illustrate the ratio's calculation, **The Home Depot** reported capital expenditures of $2,463 million in its financial statements and cash flow from operating activities of $18,839 million. Thus, Abbott's operating-cash-flow-to-capital-expenditures ratio for the year was 7.65, or ($18,839/$2,463). The following are recent operating-cash-flow-to-capital-expenditures ratios for other well-known companies:

PepsiCo Inc. (Consumer foods and beverages)	2.54
Lockheed Martin Corporation (Aerospace).	4.63
Norfolk Southern Corporation (Freight transportation services).	3.13

TAKEAWAY 11.3 Concept	Method	Assessment
Does a company generate sufficient operating cash flows to finance its capital expenditure needs?	Statement of cash flows. $$\text{Operating-cash-flow-to-capital-expenditures ratio} = \frac{\text{Cash flow from operating activities}}{\text{Annual net capital expenditures}}$$	The higher the ratio, the higher the probability that a company will generate sufficient operating cash flow to finance its capital expenditure needs.

REVIEW 11.4

The following selected data were obtained from the financial statements of Blake Enterprises:

Cash flow from operating activities.	$40,000
Annual net capital expenditures	12,500
Average current liabilities	30,000

Calculate the following financial measures for Blake Enterprises:

1. Free cash flow
2. Operating-cash-flow-to-current-liabilities ratio
3. Operating-cash-flow-to-capital-expenditures ratio

The solution is on page 412.

DATA ANALYTICS Using Analytics to Improve Cash Flow Management

A firm's financial transactions can be complex, and with complexity comes risk. There is the risk of missing data, the risk of data duplication, and the risk that the information used for decisions is dated and doesn't reflect the current state of the firm's financial health. Business intelligence software such as Tableau can be of tremendous benefit by bringing clarity to the complexity and providing a clear understanding of a company's cash flow.

A shortcoming of using the traditional approach of reviewing month-end bank statements in a general ledger and then analyzing operating, investing, and financing activities is that this perspective is static and often untimely. In addition, it does not consider outliers and multiple touchpoints. In contrast, business intelligence software allows for real-time analysis from multiple sources. Further, the ability to display the data in easier to understand visualizations, and the ability to drill down into the data as needed provides business managers with a far better way to understand and manage cash flows.

APPENDIX 11: Preparing the Statement of Cash Flows Under the Direct Method

LO4 Explain the preparation of a statement of cash flows using the direct method.

Although it is quite straightforward to create a direct method statement of cash flows given access to a company's internal accounting records, such access is rarely available to anyone except a company's management team. All that is necessary is to pull the numbers directly off the Cash general ledger account and place them in the appropriate section of the statement of cash flows. This is why, in fact, the direct method is referred to as "direct." The cash flow from operations is taken directly from the company's general ledger, rather than being indirectly computed from net income. Unfortunately, investment professionals, lenders, and stockholders rarely have access to such proprietary internal data. Thus, it is necessary to be able to create direct method cash flow information using only such publicly available data as the indirect method statement of cash flows. Thus, a firm using the direct method must also separately disclose the reconciliation of net income to cash flow from operating activities (i.e., the indirect method).

The process to convert an indirect method statement of cash flows to the direct method requires two steps. First, replace net income (the first line item under the operating activities section of the indirect method statement format) with the line items appearing on a firm's income statement. For instance, Bennett Company's income statement in **Exhibit 11-2** contains the following line items:

Sales revenue	$250,000
Cost of goods sold	(148,000)
Wages expense	(52,000)
Insurance expense	(5,000)
Depreciation expense	(10,000)
Income tax expense	(11,000)
Gain on sale of plant assets	8,000
Net income	$ 32,000

Thus, for the Bennett Company, we begin by replacing the net income of $32,000 under the operating activities section in **Exhibit 11-5** with the seven income statement line items shown above, which aggregate to $32,000.

The second step involves adjusting the income statement line items identified in Step One with the remaining line items from the operating activities section of the indirect method statement of cash flows. **Exhibit 11A-1** summarizes the procedures for converting individual income statement items to the corresponding cash flows from operating activities.

EXHIBIT 11A-1 Direct Method Conversion Schedule: Adjustments to Convert Income Statement Items to Operating Activity Cash Flows

Income Statement Item	Adjustment to Cash Flow	Operating Activity Cash Flow
Sales revenue	+ Decrease in accounts receivable *or* − Increase in accounts receivable	= Receipts from customers
Cost of goods sold	+ Increase in inventory *or* − Decrease in inventory **and** + Decrease in accounts payable *or* − Increase in accounts payable	= Payments for merchandise
Operating expenses Interest expense Income tax expense (excluding items listed below)	+ Increase in related prepaid expense *or* − Decrease in related prepaid expense **and** + Decrease in related accrued liability *or* − Increase in related accrued liability	= Payments for expenses
Depreciation expense Depletion expense Amortization expense	+ Depreciation expense + Depletion expense + Amortization expense	= 0
Gains (investing/financing) Losses (investing/financing)	Omit: Not related to operating activities	= 0

Using Bennett Company's data in **Exhibit 11-5**, those adjustments would appear as follows:

Income Statement Line Items		Operating Activities Line Items	Direct Method Cash Flow	
Sales revenue	$250,000	**Less $ 5,000 accounts receivable**	Cash received from customers	$245,000
Cost of goods sold	(148,000)	Add $ 6,000 inventory **Less $ 9,000 accounts payable**	Cash paid for merchandise	(151,000)
Wage expense	(52,000)		Cash paid to employees	(52,000)
Insurance expense	(5,000)	**Less $13,000 prepaid insurance**	Cash paid for insurance	(18,000)
Depreciation expense	(10,000)	Add $10,000 depreciation		
Income tax expense	(11,000)	Add $ 2,000 income tax payable	Cash paid for income taxes	(9,000)
Gain on sale of plant assets	8,000	**Less $ 8,000 gain on sale of plant assets**		
Net income	$ 32,000		Cash flow from operations	$ 15,000

Exhibit 11A-2 presents the Bennett Company's direct method statement of cash flows after undertaking the above two steps. As expected, the direct method cash flow from operating activities of $15,000 is exactly equivalent to the indirect method result of $15,000 as reported in **Exhibit 11-5**. Note that the cash flow from investing activities and the cash flow from financing activities are exactly the same in both **Exhibit 11-5** and **Exhibit 11A-2**. The only difference between the two exhibits is the manner in which the cash flow from operating activities is calculated. In **Exhibit 11-5**, the cash flow from operating activities is calculated by beginning with net income and then adjusting for various noncash expenses (depreciation expense) and nonoperating transactions (gain on sale of plant assets), as well as adjusting for the changes in the various working capital accounts (accounts receivable, inventory, prepaid insurance, accounts payable, and taxes payable). In **Exhibit 11A-2**, net income is replaced with the income statement line items, and the noncash expenses and working capital adjustments are disaggregated to the individual line items. But in each case, the operating cash flow of $15,000 remains the same.

EXHIBIT 11A-2 Statement of Cash Flows Under the Direct Method

BENNETT COMPANY
Statement of Cash Flows
For the Current Year Ended December 31

Cash Flow from Operating Activities		
Cash received from customers		$245,000
Cash paid for merchandise purchased	$(151,000)	
Cash paid to employees	(52,000)	
Cash paid for insurance	(18,000)	
Cash paid for income taxes	(9,000)	(230,000)
Cash provided by operating activities		15,000
Cash Flow from Investing Activities		
Purchase of long-term investments	(15,000)	
Sale of plant assets	28,000	
Purchase of patent	(60,000)	
Cash used by investing activities		(47,000)
Cash Flow from Financing Activities		
Issuance of common stock	70,000	
Payment of dividends	(13,000)	
Cash provided by financing activities		57,000
Net increase in cash		25,000
Cash at beginning of year		10,000
Cash at end of year		$ 35,000

REVIEW 11.5

Husky Company's income statement for the current year ended December 31, and comparative balance sheets as of December 31 of the current and prior years are shown below:

continued

continued from previous page

HUSKY COMPANY
Income Statement
For the Current Year Ended December 31

Sales revenue		$1,270,000
Cost of goods sold	$860,000	
Wages expense	172,000	
Insurance expense	16,000	
Depreciation expense	34,000	
Interest expense	18,000	
Income tax expense	58,000	1,158,000
Net income		$ 112,000

HUSKY COMPANY
Balance Sheets

	December 31	
	Current Year	**Prior Year**
Assets		
Cash	$ 22,000	$ 10,000
Accounts receivable	82,000	64,000
Inventory	180,000	120,000
Prepaid insurance	10,000	14,000
Plant assets	500,000	390,000
Accumulated depreciation	(136,000)	(102,000)
Total assets	$658,000	$496,000
Liabilities and Stockholders' Equity		
Accounts payable	$ 14,000	$ 20,000
Wages payable	18,000	12,000
Income tax payable	14,000	16,000
Bonds payable	260,000	150,000
Common stock	180,000	180,000
Retained earnings	172,000	118,000
Total liabilities and stockholders' equity	$658,000	$496,000

Cash dividends of $58,000 were declared and paid during the year. Plant assets were purchased for cash, and bonds payable were issued for cash. Bond interest is paid semiannually on June 30 and December 31. Accounts payable relate to merchandise purchases.

Required

Prepare a statement of cash flows for the current year ended December 31 using the direct method.

The solution is on pages 412–413.

SUMMARY OF LEARNING OBJECTIVES

Discussion the content and format of the statement of cash flows. (p. 374) LO1

- A statement of cash flows explains the net increase or decrease in cash and cash equivalents during the period.
- A statement of cash flows separates cash flows into operating, investing, and financing activity categories.
- A secondary objective of cash flow reporting is to provide information regarding a firm's investing and financing activities. A required supplemental disclosure reports noncash investing and financing activities.
- A statement of cash flows should help users compare, evaluate, and predict a firm's cash flows and also help evaluate its financial flexibility.

LO2 Explain the preparation of a statement of cash flows using the indirect method. (p. 380)

- The indirect method reconciles net income to cash flow from operating activities.

LO3 Define several ratios used to analyze the statement of cash flows. (p. 388)

- Free cash flow is defined as a company's cash flow from operations less its capital expenditures. Over the life of the company, the free cash flows approximate the total cash that can be paid out in dividends to shareholders.
- The operating-cash-flow-to-current-liabilities ratio is calculated by dividing a company's cash flow from operating activities by its average current liabilities for the year; the ratio reveals a firm's ability to repay current liabilities from operating cash flow.
- The operating-cash-flow-to-capital-expenditures ratio is calculated by dividing a firm's cash flow from operating activities by its annual net capital expenditures; the ratio evaluates a firm's ability to fund its capital investment using operating cash flow.

LO4 Appendix 11: Explain the preparation of a statement of cash flows using the direct method. (p. 391)

- The direct method shows the major categories of operating cash receipts and payments.
- The FASB encourages use of the direct method but permits use of either the direct or the indirect method.
- A firm using the direct method must separately disclose the reconciliation of net income to cash flow from operating activities.

Summary	Concept	Method	Assessment
TAKEAWAY 11.1	Does a company generate cash flows in excess of its capital expenditure needs?	Statement of cash flows. FCF = Cash flow from operating activities – Capital expenditures	The higher the free cash flow, the greater is a company's ability to generate cash for needs other than capital expenditures.
TAKEAWAY 11.2	Will a company have sufficient cash to pay its current liabilities as they become due?	Statement of cash flows and balance sheet. $\text{Operating-cash-flow-to-current-liabilities ratio} = \frac{\text{Cash flow from operating activities}}{\text{Average current liabilities}}$	The higher the ratio, the higher the probability that a company will have sufficient operating cash flow to pay its current liabilities as they become due.
TAKEAWAY 11.3	Does a company generate sufficient operating cash flows to finance its capital expenditure needs?	Statement of cash flows. $\text{Operating-cash-flow-to-capital-expenditures ratio} = \frac{\text{Cash flow from operating activities}}{\text{Annual net capital expenditures}}$	The higher the ratio, the higher the probability that a company will generate sufficient operating cash flow to finance its capital expenditure needs.

KEY TERMS

Cash equivalents (p. 374)
Cash management (p. 374)
Direct method (p. 379)
Financial flexibility (p. 378)
Financing activities (p. 376)
Free cash flow (FCF) (p. 388)
Indirect method (p. 378)
Investing activities (p. 376)
Noncash expenses (p. 384)
Noncash investing and financing activities (p. 377)
Operating activities (p. 375)
Operating-cash-flow-to-capital-expenditures ratio (p. 389)
Operating-cash-flow-to-current-liabilities ratio (p. 389)

SELF-STUDY QUESTIONS

(Answers for the Self-Study Questions are available at the end of this chapter.)

1. Which of the following is not disclosed in a statement of cash flows? LO1 Homework MBC

a. A transfer of cash to a cash equivalent investment
b. The amount of cash at year-end
c. Cash outflows from investing activities during the period
d. Cash inflows from financing activities during the period

2. Which of the following events will appear in the cash flows from investing activities section of the statement of cash flows? LO1 Homework MBC

a. Cash received as interest
b. Cash received from issuance of common stock
c. Cash purchase of truck
d. Cash payment of dividends

3. Which of the following events will appear in the cash flows from financing activities section of the statement of cash flows? LO1 Homework MBC

a. Cash purchase of equipment
b. Cash purchase of bonds issued by another company
c. Cash received as repayment for funds loaned
d. Cash purchase of treasury stock

4. Tyler Company has net income of $49,000 and the following related items: LO2 Homework MBC

Depreciation expense	$ 5,000
Accounts receivable increase	2,000
Inventory decrease	10,000
Accounts payable decrease	4,000

Using the indirect method, what is Tyler's cash flow from operations?

a. $42,000 *c.* $58,000
b. $46,000 *d.* $38,000

5. Which of the following methods will disclose the cash received from customers in the statement of cash flows? LO4 (Appendix 11) Homework MBC

a. Indirect method *c.* Direct method
b. Reconciliation method *d.* Both direct and indirect methods

6. Which of the following events will not appear in the cash flows from financing activities section of the statement of cash flow? LO1 Homework MBC

a. Borrowing cash from a bank
b. Issuance of stock in exchange for plant assets
c. Sales of common stock
d. Payment of dividends on preferred stock

7. Los Altos, Inc., reports sales revenue of $1,000,000 on its income statement. Its balance sheet reveals beginning and ending accounts receivable of $60,000 and $92,000, respectively. What is the amount of cash collected from customers of the company? LO4 (Appendix 11) Homework MBC

a. $1,032,000 *c.* $1,060,000
b. $968,000 *d.* $1,092,000

8. Which of the following is not a cash equivalent? LO1 Homework MBC

a. Short-term U.S. Treasury bill *c.* Money-market account
b. Short-term certificate of deposit *d.* IBM common stock

9. Which of the following expenses are not added back to net income when using the indirect method to prepare a statement of cash flows? LO2 Homework MBC

a. Amortization expense *c.* Interest expense
b. Depletion expense *d.* Depreciation expense

LO4 (Appendix 11)

10. Los Altos, Inc., reports interest expense of $90,000 on its income statement. The beginning and ending balances for interest payable reported on its balance sheet are $10,000 and $15,000, respectively. How much cash did Los Altos, Inc., pay for interest expense this period?

a. $85,000
b. $95,000
c. $100,000
d. $105,000

LO3

11. Free cash flow is a measure of a firm's

a. debt.
b. ability to generate net income.
c. ability to generate cash from operations beyond the amount required for investments.
d. ability to collect accounts receivable in a timely manner.

LO3

Homework MBC

12. Taylor Company reports free cash flow of $15,000, total cash of $18,000, net income of $50,000, current assets of $90,000, average current liabilities of $60,000, and cash flow from operating activities of $48,000. Compute the operating-cash-flow-to-current-liabilities ratio for Taylor Company.

a. 0.83
b. 0.80
c. 0.30
d. 1.25

QUESTIONS

1. What is the definition of *cash equivalents?* Give three examples of cash equivalents.
2. Why are cash equivalents included with cash in a statement of cash flows?
3. What are the three major types of activities classified on a statement of cash flows? Give an example of a cash inflow and a cash outflow in each classification.
4. In which of the three activity categories of a statement of cash flows would each of the following items appear? Indicate for each item whether it represents a cash inflow or a cash outflow
   a. Cash purchase of equipment
   b. Cash collection on loans
   c. Cash dividends paid
   d. Cash dividends received
   e. Cash proceeds from issuing stock
   f. Cash receipts from customers
   g. Cash interest paid
   h. Cash interest received
5. Why is a statement of cash flows a useful financial statement?
6. What is the difference between the direct method and the indirect method of presenting the cash flow from operating activities?
7. In determining the cash flow from operating activities using the indirect method, why is it necessary to add depreciation back to net income? Give an example of another item that is added back to net income under the indirect method.
8. Vista Company sold land for $98,000 cash that originally had cost $70,000. The company recorded a gain on the sale of $28,000. How is this event reported in a statement of cash flows using the indirect method?
9. A firm uses the indirect method. Using the following information, what is its cash flow from operating activities?

Net income	$88,000
Accounts receivable decrease	13,000
Inventory increase	9,000
Accounts payable decrease	3,500
Income tax payable increase	1,500
Depreciation expense	6,000

10. If a business had a net loss for the year, under what circumstances would the statement of cash flows show a positive cash flow from operating activities?
11. A firm is converting its accrual revenues to corresponding cash amounts using the direct method. Sales revenue on the income statement are $925,000. Beginning and ending accounts receivable on the balance sheet are $58,000 and $44,000, respectively. What is the amount of cash received from customers?
12. A firm reports $86,000 wages expense in its income statement. If beginning and ending wages payable are $3,900 and $2,800, respectively, what is the amount of cash paid to employees?
13. A firm reports $43,000 advertising expense in its income statement. If beginning and ending prepaid advertising are $6,000 and $7,600, respectively, what is the amount of cash paid for advertising?

14. Rusk Company sold equipment for $5,100 cash that had cost $35,000 and had $29,000 of accumulated depreciation. How is this event reported in a statement of cash flows using the direct method?

15. What separate disclosures are required for a company that reports a statement of cash flows using the direct method?

16. How is the *operating-cash-flow-to-current-liabilities ratio* calculated? Explain its use.

17. How is the *operating-cash-flow-to-capital-expenditures ratio* calculated? Explain its use.

18. The statement of cash flows provides information that may be useful in predicting future cash flows, evaluating financial flexibility, assessing liquidity, and identifying a company's financing needs. It is not, however, the best financial statement for learning about a firm's financial performance during a period. Information about a company's financial performance is provided by the income statement. Two basic principles—the revenue recognition principle and the matching concept—work to distinguish the income statement from the statement of cash flows. (a) Define the revenue recognition principle and the matching concept. (b) Briefly explain how these two principles work to make the income statement a better report regarding a firm's periodic financial performance than the statement of cash flows.

DATA ANALYTICS

The assignments in this Data Analytics section are designed to familiarize you with the tools used in analyzing data and communicating the results. Appendix F provides an in-depth discussion of data analytics and blockchain technology.

DA11-1. Preparing and Interpreting Excel Visualizations Created from Income and Cash Flow Data

The Excel file associated with this exercise includes data extracted from Form 10-K reports for **CVS Health Corporation** (CVS) and **Walgreens Boots Alliance** (Walgreens Boots) for six years. In this exercise, we analyze changes to and the relations between net income and operating cash flows over a six-year period.

REQUIRED

1. Download Excel file DA11-1 found in myBusinessCourse.
2. Prepare a line chart for the six-year period for each company showing net income and operating cash flows. *Hint:* Highlight your data; click on Insert, Select line chart. There should be a separate line for net income and a separate line for operating cash flows. If necessary, edit the chart by opening the Chart Design tab and clicking Select Data. There should be two series.
3. Use the visualizations to answer the following questions.
   a. In what year(s) does net income exceed operating cash flows for CVS?
   b. In what year(s) does operating cash flows exceed net income for Walgreens Boots?
   c. Over the six-year period, which year showed the largest difference between net income and operating cash flows for CVS?
   d. What is a likely cause of the difference shown between net income and operating cash flows for the year identified in part *c*?
   e. For Walgreens Boots, in what year were net income and operating cash flows most similar?
   f. For CVS, in what year were net income and operating cash flows most similar?
   g. How would you compare the trend of operating cash flows for CVS vs. Walgreens Boots?

DA11-2. Analyzing Cash Flow Ratio Trends by Industry Segment

The Excel file associated with this exercise includes Compustat data for S&P 500 companies for Year 1 through Year 5. For this exercise, we analyze trends in cash flow ratios by industry segment. The current cash debt coverage ratio is a liquidity ratio that measures whether a company can pay its *current* debts with cash provided from operating activities. The cash debt coverage ratio is a solvency ratio that measures a company's ability to pay *all* debts with cash provided from operating activities. In both cases, an increase in the ratio is generally viewed as favorable because it indicates that the company has a stronger ability to pay off obligations.

PART 1 PREPARING THE DATA

1. Download Excel file DA11-2 found in myBusinessCourse.
2. Format the worksheet as a table. *Hint:* Highlight data in worksheet by clicking on keys Alt and A simultaneously. Select Insert, Table.
3. Sort data in table by Segment and delete all rows in the Financials and Real Estate Segments. Companies in these industries rarely report current assets or liabilities. *Hint:* Because this

worksheet is formatted as a table, you can sort by any row using the dropdown at the column head.

4. Add a column to calculate average current liabilities for Years 2 through 5. *Hint:* Use the IF function to calculate the amount (the average current liabilities for that year). If the company name agrees to the company name in the previous cell (Company Name column), then calculate the average; otherwise, put "n/a" in the cell. Year 1 will always be n/a.
5. Copy and Paste Special—Values back into the same cells. This will allow you to sort by other columns in the table without causing a recalculation error. *Hint:* To quickly highlight a long column, double-click on the bottom right corner of the first cell in the column.
6. Add a column to calculate average liabilities for Years 2 through 5. *Hint:* Use similar steps as in part 4.

Current Cash Debt Coverage

$$\frac{\text{Cash provided by operating activities}}{\text{Average current liabilities}}$$

Cash Debt Coverage

$$\frac{\text{Cash provided by operating activities}}{\text{Average total liabilities}}$$

7. Create a ratio column to calculate the current cash debt coverage ratio and a ratio column to calculate the cash debt coverage ratio. Sort your worksheet in ascending order by each ratio column and eliminate any rows with errors due to incomplete information (such as a Year 1 calculation) or where the answer is zero and it indicates an error or missing information.
8. Eliminate extreme outliers by deleting any company's information where it shows a ratio over +/–60. Be sure to eliminate all years of data of any company considered an outlier.
9. Check your output by answering the following questions:
   a. What is the Current cash debt coverage ratio for XRX for Year 3?
   b. What is the Cash debt coverage ratio for GD for Year 2?
   c. What is Cash flow from operations for HD for Year 5?
   d. How many rows are included for the Materials segment? *Hint:* Sort your worksheet by segment and then by the Materials column and view the "Count" at the bottom right of your screen.

PART 2 CREATING A PIVOTTABLE

1. Create a PivotTable showing the average current cash debt coverage ratio and cash debt coverage ratio by segment by year. *Hint:* Drag Year then Segment to Rows and Current cash debt coverage and Cash debt coverage to Values. *Hint:* Right-click on a numeric field, select Value Field Settings, and change to Average.
2. Format your table to show two decimal places. *Hint:* Right-click on any item in the column to format and click on Number Format to update.
3. Eliminate totals from your chart. *Hint:* Click on the Design tab (it will be highlighted when you click anywhere in your PivotTable), Grand totals, Off for rows & columns.
4. Answer the following questions:
   a. Which industry segment has the highest average current cash debt coverage ratio in Year 2?
   b. Which industry segment has the lowest average current cash debt coverage ratio in Year 3?
   c. Which industry segment has the highest average cash debt coverage ratio in Year 5?
   d. Which industry segment has the lowest average cash debt coverage ratio in Year 5?
   e. What company had the largest current cash debt coverage ratio listed in the Telecommunications segment in Year 5? *Hint:* Double-click on the ratio amount in the PivotTable for Telecommunications, Year 5 to open up a new sheet with the supporting detail.

PART 3 PREPARING AND ANALYZING A PIVOTCHART

1. Create a PivotChart of the Cash Debt Coverage Ratio using a line chart.
2. Add a Slicer for Segment. *Hint:* Click inside the chart, click PivotChart Analyze, and click Add Slicer.
3. Describe the trend in each segment from Year 2 through Year 5.

Assignments with the MBC logo in the margin are available in myBusinessCourse. See the Preface of the book for details.

SHORT EXERCISES

Use the following information regarding the Seville Corporation to answer Short Exercises 11-1 through 11-3:

Accounts payable increase	$ 9,000
Accounts receivable increase	4,000
Accrued liabilities decrease	3,000
Amortization expense	6,000
Cash balance, January 1	22,000
Cash balance, December 31	15,000
Cash paid as dividends	29,000
Cash paid to purchase land	90,000
Cash paid to retire bonds payable at par	60,000
Cash received from issuance of common stock	35,000
Cash received from sale of equipment	17,000
Depreciation expense	29,000
Gain on sale of equipment	4,000
Inventory decrease	13,000
Net income	76,000
Prepaid expenses increase	2,000

SE11-1. Cash Flow from Operating Activities Using the information for the Seville Corporation above, calculate the cash flow from operating activities. **LO1, 2** Homework MBC

SE11-2. Cash Flow from Investing Activities Using the information for the Seville Corporation above, calculate the cash flow from investing activities. **LO1, 2** Homework MBC

SE11-3. Cash Flow from Financing Activities Using the information for the Seville Corporation above, calculate the cash flow for financing activities. **LO1, 2** Homework MBC

SE11-4. Direct Method Using the following data for Los Altos, Inc., calculate the cash paid for rent: **LO4 (Appendix 11)** Homework MBC

Rent expense	$80,000
Prepaid rent, January 1	10,000
Prepaid rent, December 31	8,000

SE11-5. Direct Method Using the following data for Los Altos, Inc., calculate the cash received as interest: **LO4 (Appendix 11)** Homework MBC

Interest income	$26,000
Interest receivable, January 1	3,000
Interest receivable, December 31	3,700

SE11-6. Direct Method Using the following data for Los Altos, Inc., calculate the cash paid for merchandise purchased: **LO4 (Appendix 11)** Homework MBC

Cost of goods sold	$108,000
Inventory, January 1	19,000
Inventory, December 31	22,000
Accounts payable, January 1	11,000
Accounts payable, December 31	7,000

SE11-7. Converting Sales Revenue to Cash Los Altos, Inc., is converting its sales revenues to corresponding cash amounts using the direct method. Sales revenue on the income statement is $1,025,000. Beginning and ending accounts receivable on the balance sheet are $58,000 and $34,000, respectively. Calculate the amount of cash received from customers. **LO4 (Appendix 11)** Homework MBC

The following information for Los Altos, Inc., relates to Short Exercises 11-8 through 11-10:

Cash flow from operating activities	$1,500,000
Capital expenditures	850,000
Current liabilities, beginning of year	300,000
Current liabilities, end of year	360,000

LO3 **SE11-8.** **Free Cash Flow** Using the above data, calculate the free cash flow for Los Altos, Inc.

LO3 **SE11-9.** **Operating-Cash-Flow-to-Current-Liabilities Ratio** Using the above data, calculate the operating-cash-flow-to-current-liabilities ratio for Los Altos, Inc.

LO3 **SE11-10.** **Operating-Cash-Flow-to-Capital-Expenditures Ratio** Using the above data, calculate the operating-cash-flow-to-capital-expenditures ratio for Los Altos, Inc.

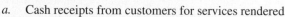

EXERCISES

LO1 **E11-1.** **Classification of Cash Flows** For each of the items below, indicate whether the cash flow item relates to an operating activity, an investing activity, or a financing activity:

a. Cash receipts from customers for services rendered
b. Sale of long-term investments for cash
c. Acquisition of plant assets for cash
d. Payment of income taxes
e. Bonds payable issued for cash
f. Payment of cash dividends declared in previous year
g. Purchase of short-term investments (not cash equivalents) for cash

LO1 **E11-2.** **Classification of Cash Flows** For each of the items below, indicate whether it is (1) a cash flow from an operating activity, (2) a cash flow from an investing activity, (3) a cash flow from a financing activity, (4) a noncash investing and financing activity, or (5) none of the above:

a. Paid cash to retire bonds payable at a loss
b. Received cash as settlement of a lawsuit
c. Acquired a patent in exchange for common stock
d. Received advance payments from customers on orders for custom-made goods
e. Gave large cash contribution to local university
f. Invested cash in 60-day commercial paper (a cash equivalent)

LO2, 3 **E11-3.** **Statement of Cash Flows (Indirect Method)** Use the following information regarding the Lund Corporation to (a) prepare a statement of cash flows using the indirect method and (b) compute Lund's operating-cash-flow-to-current-liabilities ratio.

Accounts payable increase	$ 9,000
Accounts receivable increase	4,000
Accrued liabilities decrease	3,000
Amortization expense	6,000
Cash balance, January 1	22,000
Cash balance, December 31	15,000
Cash paid as dividends	29,000
Cash paid to purchase land	90,000
Cash paid to retire bonds payable at par	60,000
Cash received from issuance of common stock	35,000
Cash received from sale of equipment	17,000
Depreciation expense	29,000
Gain on sale of equipment	4,000
Inventory decrease	13,000
Net income	76,000
Prepaid expenses increase	2,000
Average current liabilities	100,000

E11-4. Cash Flow from Operating Activities (Indirect Method) The Lincoln Company owns no plant assets and had the following income statement for the year: **LO2**

Sales revenue		$750,000
Cost of goods sold	$470,000	
Wages expense	110,000	
Rent expense	42,000	
Insurance expense	15,000	637,000
Net income		$113,000

Additional information about the company includes:

	End of Year	Beginning of Year
Accounts receivable	$54,000	$49,000
Inventory	60,000	66,000
Prepaid insurance	8,000	7,000
Accounts payable	22,000	18,000
Wages payable	9,000	11,000

Use the preceding information to calculate the cash flow from operating activities using the indirect method.

E11-5. Operating Cash Flows (Direct Method) Calculate the cash flow in each of the following cases: **LO4 (Appendix 11)**

a. Cash paid for advertising:

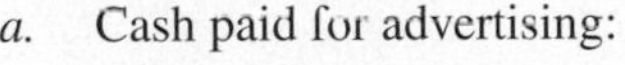

Advertising expense	$62,000
Prepaid advertising, January 1	11,000
Prepaid advertising, December 31	15,000

b. Cash paid for income taxes:

Income tax expense	$29,000
Income tax payable, January 1	7,100
Income tax payable, December 31	4,900

c. Cash paid for merchandise purchased:

Cost of goods sold	$180,000
Inventory, January 1	30,000
Inventory, December 31	25,000
Accounts payable, January 1	10,000
Accounts payable, December 31	12,000

E11-6. Statement of Cash Flows (Direct Method) Use the following information regarding the cash flows of Mason Corporation to prepare a statement of cash flows using the direct method: **LO4 (Appendix 11)**

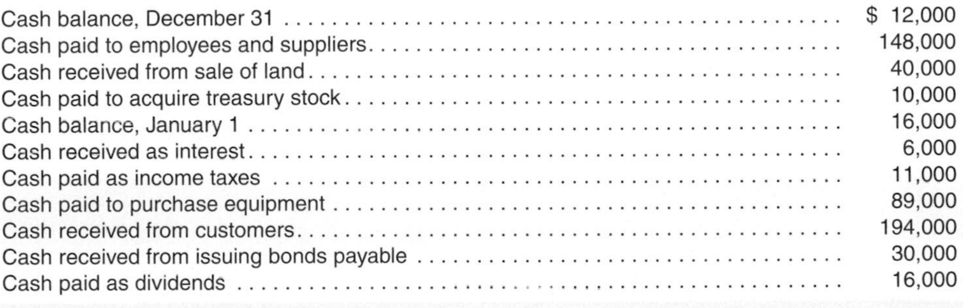

Cash balance, December 31	$ 12,000
Cash paid to employees and suppliers	148,000
Cash received from sale of land	40,000
Cash paid to acquire treasury stock	10,000
Cash balance, January 1	16,000
Cash received as interest	6,000
Cash paid as income taxes	11,000
Cash paid to purchase equipment	89,000
Cash received from customers	194,000
Cash received from issuing bonds payable	30,000
Cash paid as dividends	16,000

E11-7. Operating Cash Flows (Direct Method) Refer to the information in Exercise E11-3. Calculate the cash flow from operating activities using the direct method. Show a related cash flow for each revenue and expense. **LO4 (Appendix 11)**

E11-8. Investing and Financing Cash Flows During the year, Paxon Corporation's Long-Term Investments account (at cost) increased $15,000, the net result of purchasing stocks costing $80,000 and selling stocks costing $65,000 at a $6,000 loss. Also, the Bonds Payable account decreased by $40,000, the net result of issuing $100,000 of bonds at 103 and retiring bonds with a face **LO2, 4 (Appendix 11)**

value (and book value) of $140,000 at a $9,000 gain. What items and amounts will appear in the (a) cash flows from investing activities and the (b) cash flows from financing activities sections of Paxon's statement of cash flows?

LO2 **E11-9. Cash Flow from Operating Activities (Indirect Method)** The Arcadia Company owns no plant assets and had the following income statement for the year:

Sales revenue		$950,000
Cost of goods sold	$670,000	
Wages expense	210,000	
Rent expense	42,000	
Utilities expense	15,000	937,000
Net income		$ 13,000

Additional information about the company includes:

	End of Year	Beginning of Year
Accounts receivable	$64,000	$59,000
Inventory	60,000	86,000
Prepaid rent	8,000	7,000
Accounts payable	22,000	28,000
Wages payable	9,000	6,000

Use the preceding information to calculate the cash flow from operating activities using the indirect method.

LO2 **E11-10. Statement of Cash Flows (Indirect Method)** Use the following information regarding the Newcastle Corporation to prepare a statement of cash flows using the indirect method:

Accounts payable decrease	$ 5,000	Cash paid to retire bonds payable at par	$75,000
Accounts receivable increase	7,000	Cash received from issuance of common stock	45,000
Wages payable decrease	3,000	Cash received from sale of equipment	12,000
Amortization expense	16,000	Depreciation expense	39,000
Cash balance, January 1	30,000	Gain on sale of equipment	14,000
Cash balance, December 31	7,000	Inventory increase	13,000
Cash paid as dividends	6,000	Net income	96,000
Cash paid to purchase land	100,000	Prepaid expenses increase	8,000

LO3 **E11-11. Cash Flow Ratios** Spencer Company reports the following amounts in its annual financial statements:

Cash flow from operating activities	$50,000	Capital expenditures	$ 35,000*
Cash flow from investing activities	(40,000)	Average current assets	80,000
Cash flow from financing activities	(5,000)	Average current liabilities	60,000
Net income	25,000	Total assets	150,000

* This amount is a cash outflow

a. Compute Spencer's free cash flow.
b. Compute Spencer's operating-cash-flow-to-current-liabilities ratio.
c. Compute Spencer's operating-cash-flow-to-capital-expenditures ratio.

PROBLEMS

LO2, 3 **P11-1. Statement of Cash Flows (Indirect Method)** The Wolff Company's income statement and comparative balance sheets at December 31 are shown below:

WOLFF COMPANY
Income Statement
For the Year Ended December 31

Sales revenue		$635,000
Cost of goods sold	$430,000	
Wages expense	86,000	
Insurance expense	8,000	
Depreciation expense	17,000	
Interest expense	9,000	
Income tax expense	29,000	579,000
Net income		$ 56,000

WOLFF COMPANY
Balance Sheets

	Dec. 31, Current Year	Dec. 31, Prior Year
Assets		
Cash	$ 11,000	$ 5,000
Accounts receivable	41,000	32,000
Inventory	90,000	60,000
Prepaid insurance	5,000	7,000
Plant assets	250,000	195,000
Accumulated depreciation	(68,000)	(51,000)
Total assets	$329,000	$248,000
Liabilities and Stockholders' Equity		
Accounts payable	$ 7,000	$ 10,000
Wages payable	9,000	6,000
Income tax payable	7,000	8,000
Bonds payable	130,000	75,000
Common stock	90,000	90,000
Retained earnings	86,000	59,000
Total liabilities and stockholders' equity	$329,000	$248,000

Cash dividends of $29,000 were declared and paid during the current year. Plant assets were purchased for cash and bonds payable were issued for cash. Bond interest is paid semi-annually on June 30 and December 31. Accounts payable relate to merchandise purchases.

Required

a. Calculate the change in cash that occurred during the current year.
b. Prepare a statement of cash flows using the indirect method.
c. Compute free cash flow.
d. Compute the operating-cash-flow-to-current-liabilities ratio.
e. Compute the operating-cash-flow-to-capital-expenditures ratio.

P11-2. **Statement of Cash Flows (Indirect Method)** Arctic Company's income statement and comparative balance sheets as of December 31 follow: **LO2**

ARCTIC COMPANY
Income Statement
For the Year Ended December 31

Sales revenue		$728,000
Cost of goods sold	$534,000	
Wages expense	190,000	
Advertising expense	31,000	
Depreciation expense	22,000	
Interest expense	18,000	
Gain on sale of land	(25,000)	770,000
Net loss		$ (42,000)

ARCTIC COMPANY
Balance Sheets

	Dec. 31, Current Year	Dec. 31, Prior Year
Assets		
Cash	$ 49,000	$ 28,000
Accounts receivable	42,000	50,000
Inventory	107,000	113,000
Prepaid advertising	10,000	13,000
Plant assets	360,000	222,000
Accumulated depreciation	(78,000)	(56,000)
Total assets	$490,000	$370,000
Liabilities and Stockholders' Equity		
Accounts payable	$ 17,000	$ 31,000
Interest payable	6,000	—
Bonds payable	200,000	—
Common stock	245,000	245,000
Retained earnings	52,000	94,000
Treasury stock	(30,000)	—
Total liabilities and stockholders' equity	$490,000	$370,000

During the year, Arctic sold land for $70,000 cash that originally had cost $45,000. Arctic also purchased equipment for cash, acquired treasury stock for cash, and issued bonds payable for cash. Accounts payable relate to merchandise purchases.

Required

a. Calculate the change in cash that occurred during the year.

b. Prepare a statement of cash flows using the indirect method.

LO2 **P11-3. Statement of Cash Flows (Indirect Method)** The Dairy Company's income statement and comparative balance sheets as of December 31 follow:

DAIRY COMPANY
Income Statement
For the Year Ended December 31

Sales revenue		$700,000
Cost of goods sold	$440,000	
Wages and other operating expenses	95,000	
Depreciation expense	22,000	
Goodwill amortization expense	7,000	
Interest expense	10,000	
Income tax expense	36,000	
Loss on bond retirement	5,000	615,000
Net income		$ 85,000

DAIRY COMPANY
Balance Sheets

	Dec. 31, Current Year	Dec. 31, Prior Year
Assets		
Cash	$ 27,000	$ 18,000
Accounts receivable	53,000	48,000
Inventory	103,000	109,000
Prepaid expenses	12,000	10,000
Plant assets	360,000	336,000
Accumulated depreciation	(87,000)	(84,000)
Goodwill	43,000	50,000
Total assets	$511,000	$487,000

DAIRY COMPANY Balance Sheets	Dec. 31, Current Year	Dec. 31, Prior Year
Liabilities and Stockholders' Equity		
Accounts payable	$ 32,000	$ 26,000
Interest payable	4,000	7,000
Income tax payable	6,000	8,000
Bonds payable	60,000	120,000
Common stock	252,000	228,000
Retained earnings	157,000	98,000
Total liabilities and stockholders' equity	$511,000	$487,000

During the year, the company sold for $17,000 cash old equipment that had cost $36,000 and had $19,000 accumulated depreciation. New equipment worth $60,000 was acquired in exchange for $60,000 of bonds payable. Bonds payable of $120,000 were retired for cash at a loss. A $26,000 cash dividend was declared and paid. All stock issuances were for cash.

Required

a. Compute the change in cash that occurred during the year.

b. Prepare a statement of cash flows using the indirect method.

P11-4. Statement of Cash Flows (Indirect Method) The Rainbow Company's income statement and comparative balance sheets as of December 31 follow: **LO2**

RAINBOW COMPANY Income Statement For Year Ended December 31		
Sales revenue		$750,000
Dividend income		15,000
		765,000
Cost of goods sold	$440,000	
Wages and other operating expenses	130,000	
Depreciation expense	39,000	
Patent amortization expense	7,000	
Interest expense	13,000	
Income tax expense	44,000	
Loss on sale of equipment	5,000	
Gain on sale of investments	(10,000)	668,000
Net income		$ 97,000

RAINBOW COMPANY Balance Sheets	Dec. 31, Current Year	Dec. 31, Prior Year
Assets		
Cash and cash equivalents	$ 19,000	$ 25,000
Accounts receivable	40,000	30,000
Inventory	103,000	77,000
Prepaid expenses	10,000	6,000
Long-term investments—available for sale	—	50,000
Fair value adjustment to investments	—	7,000
Land	190,000	100,000
Buildings	445,000	350,000
Accumulated depreciation—Buildings	(91,000)	(75,000)
Equipment	179,000	225,000
Accumulated depreciation—Equipment	(42,000)	(46,000)
Patents	50,000	32,000
Total assets	$903,000	$781,000

RAINBOW COMPANY Balance Sheets	Dec. 31, Current Year	Dec. 31, Prior Year
Liabilities and Stockholders' Equity		
Accounts payable	$ 20,000	$ 16,000
Interest payable	6,000	5,000
Income tax payable	8,000	10,000
Bonds payable	155,000	125,000
Preferred stock ($100 par value)	100,000	75,000
Common stock ($5 par value)	379,000	364,000
Paid-in-capital in excess of par value—Common	133,000	124,000
Retained earnings	102,000	55,000
Unrealized gain on investments	—	7,000
Total liabilities and stockholders' equity	$903,000	$781,000

During the year, the following transactions occurred:

1. Sold long-term investments costing $50,000 for $60,000 cash. Unrealized gains totaling $7,000 related to these investments had been recorded in earlier years. At year-end, the fair value adjustment and unrealized gain account balances were eliminated.
2. Purchased land for cash.
3. Capitalized an expenditure made to improve the building.
4. Sold equipment for $14,000 cash that originally cost $46,000 and had $27,000 accumulated depreciation.
5. Issued bonds payable at face value for cash.
6. Acquired a patent with a fair value of $25,000 by issuing 250 shares of preferred stock at par value.
7. Declared and paid a $50,000 cash dividend.
8. Issued 3,000 shares of common stock for cash at $8 per share.
9. Recorded depreciation of $16,000 on buildings and $23,000 on equipment.

Required

a. Calculate the change in cash and cash equivalents that occurred during the year.
b. Prepare a statement of cash flows using the indirect method.

LO3, 4 (Appendix 11)

P11-5. Statement of Cash Flows (Direct Method) Refer to the data given for the Wolff Company in Problem P11-1.

Required

a. Calculate the change in cash that occurred during the year.
b. Prepare a statement of cash flows using the direct method.
c. Compute free cash flow.
d. Compute the operating-cash-flow-to-current-liabilities ratio.
e. Compute the operating-cash-flow-to-capital-expenditures ratio.

LO4 (Appendix 11)

P11-6. Statement of Cash Flows (Direct Method) Refer to the data given for the Arctic Company in Problem P11-2.

Required

a. Calculate the change in cash that occurred during the year.
b. Prepare a statement of cash flows using the direct method.

LO4 (Appendix 11)

P11-7. Statement of Cash Flows (Direct Method) Refer to the data given for the Dairy Company in Problem P11-3.

Required

a. Compute the change in cash that occurred in the year.
b. Prepare a statement of cash flows using the direct method. Use one cash outflow for "cash paid for wages and other operating expenses." Accounts payable relate to inventory purchases only.

LO4 (Appendix 11)

P11-8. Statement of Cash Flows (Direct Method) Refer to the data given for the Rainbow Company in Problem P11-4.

Required

a. Calculate the change in cash that occurred in the year.
b. Prepare a statement of cash flows using the direct method. Use one cash outflow for "cash paid for wages and other operating expenses." Accounts payable relate to inventory purchases only.

P11-9. Analyzing Cash Flow Ratios Molly Enterprises reported the following information for the past year of operations: LO3

Transaction	Free Cash Flow $250,000	Operating-Cash-Flow-to-Current-Liabilities Ratio 1.0 times	Operating-Cash-Flow-to-Capital-Expenditures Ratio 3.0 times
a. Recorded credit sales of $5,000.			
b. Collected $3,000 owed from customers.			
c. Purchased $20,000 of equipment on long-term credit.			
d. Purchased $15,000 of equipment for cash.			
e. Paid $4,000 of wages with cash.			
f. Recorded utility bill of $1,500 that has not been paid.			

For each transaction, indicate whether the ratio will (I) increase, (D) decrease, or (N) have no effect.

SERIAL PROBLEM: ANGEL CITY GREETINGS

(Note: This is a continuation of the Serial Problem: Angel City Greetings from Chapter 1 through Chapter 10.)

SP11. Kate has just completed her first year running Angel City Greetings. She has been preparing monthly income statements and balance sheets, so she knows that her company has been profitable and that there is cash in the bank. She has not, however, prepared a statement of cash flows. Kate provides you with the year-end income statement and balance sheet and asks that you prepare a statement of cash flows for Angel City Greetings.

Additional information:

1. There were no disposals of equipment during the year.
2. Dividends in the amount of $1,300 were paid in cash during the year.
3. Prepaid expenses relate to operating expenses.

Required

a. Prepare a statement of cash flows for Angel City Greetings for the year ended August 31 using the indirect method. *Hint:* Since this was Kate's first year of operations, the beginning balance sheet account balances were zero.

b. Prepare a statement of cash flows for Angel City Greetings for the year ended August 31 using the direct method. (Appendix 11)

ANGEL CITY GREETINGS Income Statement Year Ended August 31	
Sales revenue	$135,000
Cost of goods sold	72,000
Gross profit	63,000
Operating expenses	
Wages	18,000
Consulting	11,850
Insurance	1,200
Utilities	2,400
Depreciation	3,250
Total operating expenses	36,700
Income from operations	26,300
Interest expense	900
Income before income tax	25,400
Income tax expense	8,900
Net income	$ 16,500

ANGEL CITY GREETINGS
Balance Sheet
As of August 31

Assets		**Liabilities**	
Current assets		Current liabilities	
Cash	$12,300	Accounts payable	$ 6,200
Accounts receivable	11,000	Unearned revenue	1,250
Inventory	16,000	Other current liabilities	1,900
Prepaid insurance	1,000	Total current liabilities	9,350
Total current assets	40,300	Note payable	15,000
Equipment	17,500	Total liabilities	24,350
Accumulated depreciation	3,250	Stockholders' equity	
		Common stock	500
		Additional paid-in-capital	9,500
		Preferred stock	5,000
		Retained earnings	15,200
		Total stockholders' equity	30,200
Total assets	$54,550	Total liabilities and stockholders' equity	$54,550

BEYOND THE NUMBERS

REPORTING AND ANALYSIS

Columbia Sportswear Company

BTN11-1. Financial Reporting Problem: Columbia Sportswear Company The financial statements for the Columbia Sportswear Company can be found in Appendix A at the end of this book.

Required

Answer the following questions as they relate to 2020:

a. How much did Columbia Sportswear's cash and cash equivalents increase during the year?
b. What was the largest source of cash and cash equivalents during the year?
c. What was the single largest use of cash and cash equivalents during the year?
d. How much dividends were paid during the year?
e. Why do depreciation and amortization, both noncash items, appear on Columbia's statement of cash flows?

Columbia Sportswear Company
Under Armour, Inc.

BTN11-2. Comparative Analysis Problem: Columbia Sportswear Company vs. Under Armour, Inc. The financial statements for the Columbia Sportswear Company can be found in Appendix A at the end of this book, and the financial statements of Under Armour, Inc., can be found in Appendix B.

Required

Answer the following questions as they relate to 2020:

a. Compute the free cash flow for both Columbia Sportswear and Under Armour, Inc.
b. Compute the operating cash flows to capital expenditures for both Columbia Sportswear and Under Armour, Inc.
c. Comment on the ability of each company to finance its capital expenditures.

BTN11-3. Business Decision Problem Recently hired as assistant controller for Finite, Inc., you are sitting next to the controller as she responds to questions at the annual stockholders' meeting. The firm's financial statements contain a statement of cash flows prepared using the indirect method. A stockholder raises his hand.

Stockholder: "I notice that depreciation expense is shown as an addition in the calculation of the cash flow from operating activities."

Controller: "That's correct."

Stockholder: "What depreciation method do you use?"

Controller: "We use the straight-line method for all plant assets."

Stockholder: "Well, why don't you switch to an accelerated depreciation method, such as double-declining balance, increase the annual depreciation amount, and, thus, increase the cash flow from operating activities?"

The controller pauses, turns to you, and replies, "My assistant will answer your question."

Required

Prepare an answer to the stockholder's question.

BTN11-4. Financial Analysis Problem Parker Hannifin Corporation, headquartered in Cleveland, Ohio, manufactures motion control and fluid system components for a variety of industrial users. The firm's financial statements contain the following data (Year 3 is the most recent year; dollar amounts are in thousands):

Parker Hannifin Corporation

	Year 3	Year 2	Year 1
Current assets at year-end	$4,885,204	$7,673,086	$5,085,238
Current liabilities at year-end	3,148,373	3,151,773	3,197,483
Current liabilities at beginning of year	3,151,773	3,197,483	3,395,860
Cash provided by operating activities	2,070,949	1,730,140	1,596,700
Capital expenditures, net	206,246	148,497	165,786

a. Calculate Parker Hannifin's current ratio (current assets/current liabilities) for Years 1, 2, and 3.

b. Calculate Parker Hannifin's operating-cash-flow-to-current-liabilities ratio for Years 1, 2, and 3.

c. Comment on the three-year trend in Parker Hannifin's current ratio and operating-cash-flow-to-current-liabilities ratio. Do the trends in these two ratios reinforce each other or contradict each other as indicators of Parker Hannifin's ability to pay its current liabilities?

d. Calculate Parker Hannifin's operating-cash-flow-to-capital-expenditures ratio for Years 1, 2, and 3. Comment on the strength of this ratio over the three-year period.

CRITICAL THINKING

BTN11-5. Accounting Research Problem: General Mills, Inc. The fiscal year 2020 annual report of General Mills, Inc., can be found at: https://investors.generalmills.com/financial-information/annual-reports/default.aspx.

General Mills, Inc.

Required

a. Refer to Note 2. How does General Mills define its cash equivalents?

b. What method does General Mills use to report its cash provided by operating activities?

c. What is the change in cash and cash equivalents experienced by General Mills during fiscal 2020? What is the amount of cash and cash equivalents as of May 31, 2020?

d. What is General Mills' operating-cash-flow-to-capital-expenditures ratio for fiscal year 2020?

e. Calculate General Mills' 2020 operating-cash-flow-to-current-liabilities ratio.

BTN11-6. Accounting Communication Activity Susan Henderson, the vice president of marketing, was told by the CEO that she needs to understand the numbers because the company's existence depends on making money. It has been a long time since Susan took a class in accounting. She recalls that companies report net income and cash flows in two separate statements. She feels pretty comfortable with the income statement, but is somewhat lost looking at the statement of cash flows. She asks you to help explain this statement.

Required

Write a brief memo to Susan explaining the form and content of the statement of cash flows, along with a short discussion of how to analyze the statement.

BTN11-7. Accounting Ethics Case Due to an economic recession, Anton Corporation faces severe cash flow problems. Management forecasts that payments to some suppliers will have to be delayed for several months. Jay Newton, controller, has asked his staff for suggestions on selecting the suppliers for which payments will be delayed.

"That's a fairly easy decision," observes Tim Haslem. "Some suppliers charge interest if our payment is late, but others do not. We should pay those suppliers that charge interest and delay payments to the ones that do not charge interest. If we do this, the savings in interest charges will be quite substantial."

"I disagree," states Tara Wirth. "That position is too 'bottom line' oriented. It's not fair to delay payments only to suppliers who don't charge interest for late payments. Most suppliers in that category are ones we have dealt with for years; selecting these suppliers would be taking advantage of the excellent relationships we have developed over the years. The fair thing to do is to make pro-rata payments to each supplier."

"Well, making pro-rata payments to each supplier means that *all* our suppliers will be upset because no one receives full payment," comments Sue Myling. "I believe it is most important to maintain good relations with our long-term suppliers; we should pay them currently and delay payments to our newer suppliers. The interest costs we end up paying these newer suppliers is the price we must pay to keep our long-term relationships solid."

Required

Which suppliers should Jay Newton select for delayed payments? Discuss.

The Home Depot, Inc.

BTN11-8. Environmental, Social, and Governance Problem The environmental, social, and governance highlighted in this chapter (see page 385) mentions that **Home Depot** believes in giving back. One of the ways the company has done this is through its Team Depot program of employee volunteerism. Under this program, Home Depot employees volunteer their own time to work together on projects that benefit communities in which the company does business. Each year the program provides millions of hours of employee volunteerism.

One of the groups that benefits from Team Depot is veterans. Do a computer search and report how Team Depot has helped veterans.

BTN11-9. Accounting Ethics Problem Cash larceny involves the fraudulent stealing of an employer's cash. These schemes often target the company's bank deposits. The fraudster steals the money after the deposit has been prepared, but before the deposit is taken to the bank. Most often these schemes involve a deficiency in the internal control system in which segregation of duties is not present. The perpetrator is often in charge of recording receipts, preparing the deposit, delivering the deposit to the bank, and verifying the receipted deposit slip. Without proper segregation of duties, the fraudster is able cover up the theft.

In addition to segregation of duties, what internal control procedures might help deter and detect cash larceny?

BTN11-10. Working with the Takeaways Logitech recently reported (in thousands) cash provided by operating activities of $425,000. For the same period, average current liabilities were reported to be $715,982, and annual capital expenditures were $38,447. Calculate the free cash flow, operating-cash-flow-to-current-liabities ratio, and the operating-cash-flow-to-capital-expenditures ratio for Logitech and comment on the results.

ANSWERS TO SELF-STUDY QUESTIONS

1. a **2.** c **3.** d **4.** c **5.** c **6.** b **7.** b **8.** d **9.** c **10.** a **11.** c **12.** b

REVIEW SOLUTIONS

Solution 11.1

1. Operating
2. Investing
3. Operating
4. Investing
5. Financing
6. Financing
7. Operating
8. Financing
9. Investing

Solution 11.2

HUSKY COMPANY Statement of Cash Flows For the Current Year Ended December 31		
Cash Flow from Operating Activities		
Net income	$112,000	
Add (deduct) items to convert net income to cash basis		
Depreciation	34,000	
Accounts receivable increase	(18,000)	
Inventory increase	(60,000)	
Prepaid insurance decrease	4,000	
Accounts payable decrease	(6,000)	
Wages payable increase	6,000	
Income tax payable decrease	(2,000)	
Cash provided by operating activities		$ 70,000
Cash Flow from Investing Activities		
Purchase of plant assets		(110,000)
Cash Flow from Financing Activities		
Issuance of bonds payable	110,000	
Payment of dividends	(58,000)	
Cash provided by financing activities		52,000
Net increase in cash		12,000
Cash at beginning of year		10,000
Cash at end of year		$ 22,000

Solution 11.3

a. $8,000 ending balance – $12,000 beginning balance = $4,000 decrease in cash

b. 1. Use the indirect method to determine the cash flow from operating activities.
   - The adjustments to convert Terry Company's net income of $35,000 to the cash provided by operating activities of $38,000 are shown in the following statement of cash flows.

2. Analyze changes in remaining noncash asset (and contra asset) accounts to determine cash flows from investing activities.
   - Long-term investments: $11,000 decrease resulted from sale of investments for cash at a $2,000 loss. Cash received from sale of investments = $9,000 ($11,000 cost – $2,000 loss).
   - Fair value adjustment to investments: $1,000 decrease resulted from the elimination of this account balance (and the unrealized loss of investments) at the end of the year. No cash flow effect.
   - Plant assets: $48,000 increase resulted from purchase of plant assets for cash. Cash paid to purchase plant assets = $48,000.
   - Accumulated depreciation: $11,000 increase resulted from the recording of depreciation expense. No cash flow effect.

3. Analyze changes in remaining liability and stockholders' equity accounts to determine cash flows from financing activities.
   - Common stock: $14,000 increase resulted from the issuance of stock for cash. Cash received from issuance of common stock = $14,000.
   - Retained earnings: $18,000 increase resulted from net income of $35,000 and dividend declaration of $17,000. Cash paid as dividends = $17,000.
   - Unrealized loss on investments: $1,000 decrease resulted from the elimination of this account balance (and the fair value adjustment to investments) at the end of the year. No cash flow effect.

The statement of cash flows (indirect method) is as follows:

TERRY COMPANY Statement of Cash Flows For the Current Year Ended December 31		
Cash Flow from Operating Activities		
Net income	$35,000	
Add (deduct) items to convert net income to cash basis		
Depreciation	11,000	
Loss on sale of investments	2,000	
Accounts receivable decrease	6,000	
Inventory increase	(28,000)	
Prepaid advertising increase	(3,000)	
Accounts payable increase	13,000	
Wages payable increase	3,500	
Income tax payable decrease	(1,500)	
Cash provided by operating activities		$38,000
Cash Flow from Investing Activities		
Sale of investments	9,000	
Purchase of plant assets	(48,000)	
Cash used by investing activities		(39,000)
Cash Flow from Financing Activities		
Issuance of common stock	14,000	
Payment of dividends	(17,000)	
Cash used by financing activities		(3,000)
Net decrease in cash		(4,000)
Cash at beginning of year		12,000
Cash at end of year		$ 8,000

Solution 11.4

Free cash flow: $40,000 – $12,500 = $27,500

Operating-cash-flow-to-current-liabilities-ratio: $40,000/$30,000 = 1.33

Operating-cash-flow-to-capital-expenditures-ratio: $40,000/$12,500 = 3.20

Solution 11.5

Supporting Calculations:

Cash received from customers:
$1,270,000 Sales revenue – $18,000 Accounts receivable increase = $1,252,000

Cash paid for merchandise purchased:
$860,000 Cost of goods sold + $60,000 Inventory increase + $6,000 Accounts payable decrease = $926,000

Cash paid to employees:
$172,000 Wages expense – $6,000 Wages payable increase = $166,000

Cash paid for insurance:
$16,000 Insurance expense – $4,000 Prepaid insurance decrease = $12,000

Cash paid for interest:
Equal to the $18,000 balance in interest expense

Cash paid for income taxes:
$58,000 Income tax expense + $2,000 Income tax payable decrease = $60,000

Purchase of plant assets:
$500,000 Ending plant assets – $390,000 Beginning plant assets = $110,000

Issuance of bonds payable:
$260,000 Ending bonds payable – $150,000 Beginning bonds payable = $110,000

Payment of dividends
$58,000 given in problem data

Other Analysis

Accumulated depreciation increased by $34,000, which is the amount of depreciation expense.

Common stock account balance did not change.

Retained earnings increased by $54,000, which is the difference between the net income of $112,000 and the dividends declared of $58,000.

HUSKY COMPANY Statement of Cash Flows (Direct Method) For the Current Year Ended December 31		
Cash Flow from Operating Activities		
Cash received from customers		$1,252,000
Cash paid for merchandise purchased	$(926,000)	
Cash paid to employees	(166,000)	
Cash paid for insurance	(12,000)	
Cash paid for interest	(18,000)	
Cash paid for income taxes	(60,000)	(1,182,000)
Cash provided by operating activities		70,000
Cash Flow from Investing Activities		
Purchase of plant assets		(110,000)
Cash Flow from Financing Activities		
Issuance of bonds payable	110,000	
Payment of dividends	(58,000)	
Cash provided by financing activities		52,000
Net increase in cash		12,000
Cash at beginning of year		10,000
Cash at end of year		$ 22,000

Analysis and Interpretation of Financial Statements

PAST

In Chapter 11, we examined the statement of cash flows.

PRESENT

In this chapter we complete our study of financial accounting by looking at the analysis and interpretation of financial statements.

FMCG

Companies in the fast-moving consumer goods (FMCG) industry produce and sell products that are sold quickly and at low cost. These products include packaged foods, toiletries, and many other consumables. The top 40 companies in the FMCG industry had combined sales in excess of $1 trillion in a recent year. **Nestle**, **Proctor & Gamble**, and **PepsiCo** make up the largest three FMCG companies based on sales.

The FMCG industry has continued to grow and was seen to be strong as the world experienced the COVID pandemic. Although some of this growth has come from internally developed brands, referred to as organic growth, a significant portion has come from mergers and acquisitions (M&A). M&A are complex transactions, and perhaps the hardest part of any merger or acquisition is to determine the appropriate price to pay. Many factors go into such an analysis, but a key determinant is usually an assessment of the acquiree's financial health and profitability. Much of this analysis consists of examining the financial ratios that we cover in this chapter.

Road Map

LO	Learning Objective	Page	eLecture	Review	Assignments
LO1	**Identify persistent earnings and discuss the content and format of the income statement.**	416	E12-1	12.1	SE11, E1, P1, P3
LO2	**Identify the sources of financial information used by investment professionals and explain horizontal financial statement analysis.**	419	E12-2	12.2	SE12, E3, P4, P6, P10
LO3	**Explain vertical financial statement analysis.**	424	E12-3	12.3	SE13, E4, P6
LO4	**Define and discuss financial ratios for analyzing a firm.**	425	E12-4	12.4, 12.5, 12.6, 12.7, 12.8	SE1, SE2, SE3, SE4, SE5, SE6, SE7, SE8, SE9, SE10, E2, E5, E6, E7, E8, E9, P2, P3, P5, P6, P7, P8, P9, P10
LO5	**Discuss the limitations of financial statement analysis.**	438	E12-5		SE14, E10
LO6	**Appendix 12A: Describe financial statement disclosures.**	440	E12-6		SE15, E11

Analysis and Interpretation of Financial Statements

Persistent Earnings	Analytical Techniques
• Persistent earnings • Discontinued operations • Changes in accounting principles • Comprehensive income	• Sources of information • Horizontal analysis • Vertical analysis • Ratio analysis • Limitations of financial analysis • Financial statement disclosures (Appendix 12A)

PERSISTENT EARNINGS AND THE INCOME STATEMENT

LO1 Identify persistent earnings and **discuss** the content and format of the income statement.

A.K.A Persistent earnings also are referred to as sustainable earnings or permanent earnings.

A.K.A Transitory earnings are also referred to as non-persistent earnings.

Net income is the "bottom line" measure of firm performance. Financial statement users have historically emphasized the importance of accounting earnings because past accounting earnings are usually a good predictor of a firm's future operating cash flow. Modern valuation theory tells us that the economic value of a company is the present value of the company's future operating cash flows. Thus, an important role for accounting numbers is their use by investment professionals when assessing the economic value of a company.

One of the determinants of the ability of historical accounting earnings to predict future cash flow is the extent to which earnings recur over time, referred to as *earnings persistence*. Since the value of a share of common stock today is a function of a firm's ability to consistently generate earnings year in and year out, the persistence (or sustainability) of a company's operating earnings is closely linked to its economic value. **Persistent earnings** are also sometimes referred to as *sustainable earnings* or *permanent earnings*, whereas non-persistent earnings are often referred to as **transitory earnings**. In general, transitory earnings include such single-period events as special items, restructuring charges, changes in accounting principle, and discontinued operations.

To assist investors in their assessment of a company's persistent earnings, and hence in assessing a firm's economic value, companies are required under GAAP to classify income statement accounts in a manner that aids a financial statement user in assessing persistent earnings. In Chapter 4, we discussed the classified and multi-step income statement. In this chapter, we discuss a refinement of the multi-step income statement.

Exhibit 12-1 illustrates the basic format of the multi-step income statement. While a single-step income statement derives the net income of a business in one step by subtracting total expenses from total revenues, a multiple-step income statement derives one or more intermediate performance measures before net income is reported. Examples of such intermediate performance measures are gross profit, net operating income, and net income from continuing operations before taxes.

The income statement is organized in such a way that items with greater persistence are reported higher up in the income statement, whereas items considered more transitory, less predictable, and/or less central to the core operations of the business are reported further down in the statement. Thus, operating revenues and expenses are reported first. These items arise from the activities that are central to the company's core business and day-to-day operations. They consist of accounts such as sales revenue, cost of goods sold, and selling, general and administrative expenses. These activities are expected to recur regularly and are generally persistent over time. After reporting the individual operating and revenue and expense items, companies then report a subtotal, referred to as **net operating income**. Net operating income is important information for users because it indicates the total earnings that result from the company's primary operating activities.

Following net operating income, companies report nonoperating revenues and expenses that tend to recur over time. These items are often referred to as "below the line" items. Common examples include interest income and expense, gains and losses on the sales of fixed assets, and income tax expense. Although these activities are generally expected to recur over time, they are not considered to be part of the company's core operating activities. For example, while most companies incur interest expense, borrowing is not central to a company's operating activities. Further, a wide variation in financing choices exist across companies and within companies over time. Thus, accountants report interest expense separately from operating income. Similarly, while it is common for companies to sell equipment and pay income taxes, these activities are not central to the company's core operating activities. After reporting the recurring non-operating items, companies compute two subtotals: **net income from continuing operations before taxes** and **net income from continuing operations** (after deducting income taxes).

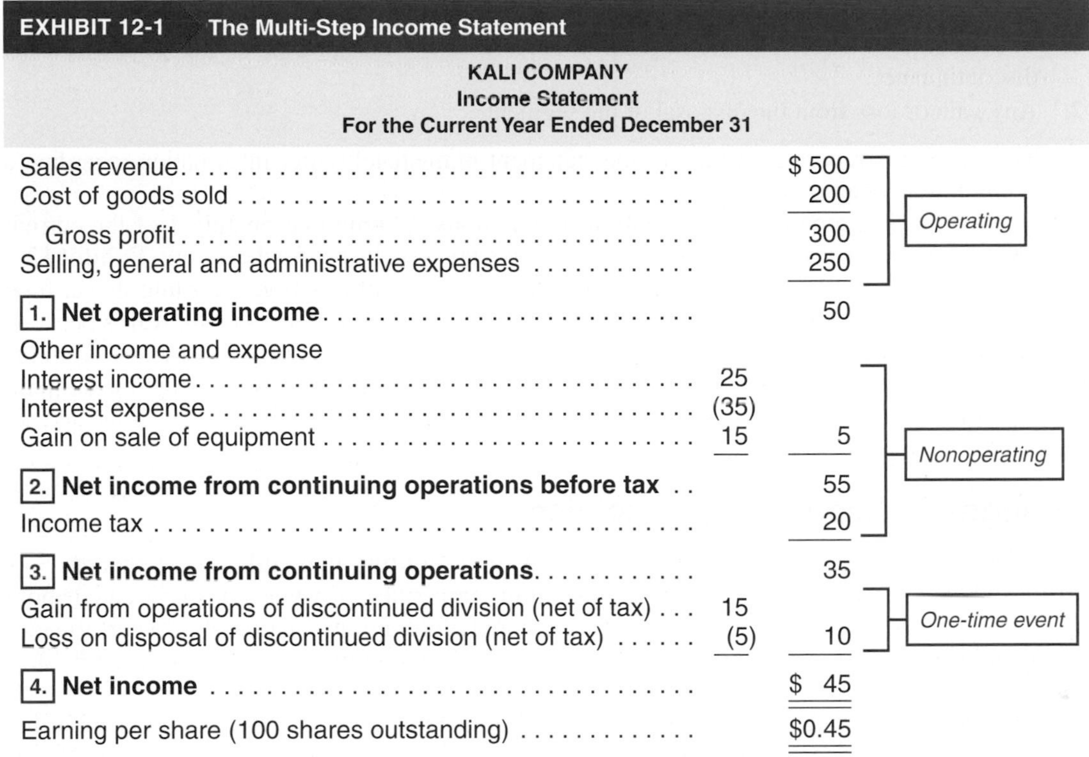

EXHIBIT 12-1 The Multi-Step Income Statement

KALI COMPANY
Income Statement
For the Current Year Ended December 31

Sales revenue		$ 500	Operating
Cost of goods sold		200	Operating
Gross profit		300	Operating
Selling, general and administrative expenses		250	Operating
1. **Net operating income**		50	
Other income and expense			
Interest income	25		Nonoperating
Interest expense	(35)		Nonoperating
Gain on sale of equipment	15	5	Nonoperating
2. **Net income from continuing operations before tax**		55	Nonoperating
Income tax		20	Nonoperating
3. **Net income from continuing operations**		35	
Gain from operations of discontinued division (net of tax)	15		One-time event
Loss on disposal of discontinued division (net of tax)	(5)	10	One-time event
4. **Net income**		$ 45	
Earning per share (100 shares outstanding)		$0.45	

Following income from continuing operations, companies report the gains or losses that arise from events that are unlikely to recur on a regular basis, sometimes referred to as one-time events. However, unlike the individual revenue and expense items used to compute income from continuing operations, one-time items are computed net of the income tax expense attributable to those items. Examples of one-time items include the net operating activities of a business segment that the company intends to sell, the net effect of a change in accounting principle, and comprehensive income. Each of these are discussed in the following sections.

One-time items are added to or deducted from income from continuing operations to arrive at **net income**. Thus, the income statement, depending on the activities in which the firm engages, reports four different income numbers, which are generally in descending order of persistence:

1. Net operating income
2. Income from continuing operations before tax
3. Income from continuing operations
4. Net income

In addition, all public companies are required to report net income per common share, referred to as **earnings per share (EPS)**, on the income statement immediately following net income.

THINKING GLOBALLY

Like U.S. GAAP, IFRS encourages companies to use a multi-step income statement when presenting a company's periodic performance. An income statement prepared under IFRS presents four measures of firm performance: gross profit, operating profit, profit before tax, and profit for the year. These indicators correspond to the four performance measures reported by the Kali Company in **Exhibit 12-1**: gross profit, net operating income, net income from continuing operations before tax, and net income. The income statements under U.S. GAAP and IFRS are very similar, with only minor labeling differences—like using "profit" instead of "income."

Discontinued Operations

Discontinued Operations

When a company sells, abandons, or otherwise disposes of a segment of its operations, a **discontinued operations** section of the income statement reports information about the discontinued business segment. The discontinued operations section presents two categories of information:

1. The income or loss from the segment's operations for the portion of the year before its discontinuance.
2. Any gain or loss from the disposal of the segment.

This section is reported on the income statement immediately after information regarding a firm's continuing operations.

To illustrate the reporting of discontinued operations, assume that on July 1 of the current year, Kali Company, a diversified manufacturing company, sold its pet food division. **Exhibit 12-1** illustrates the income statement for Kali Company, including information regarding its pet food division in the discontinued operations section. From January 1 through June 30, Kali's pet food division operated at a profit, net of income taxes, of $15. The loss, net of income taxes, from the sale of the division's assets and liabilities was $5. Note that when there is a discontinued operations section, the difference between a firm's continuing sales revenues and expenses is labeled net income from continuing operations.

Changes in Accounting Principles

Occasionally, a company may implement a **change in accounting principle**. These changes may arise from changes in Generally Accepted Accounting Principles, or when a business can demonstrate that the new accounting method results in a more faithful representation of firm performance as compared with the replaced method. These include changes in inventory costing methods, such as changing from FIFO to weighted-average cost.

Changing accounting principles can present a problem for financial statement users analyzing a company's performance over time because different accounting principles are likely to produce different financial statement results. Consequently, such changes must be reported retroactively. That is, the financial statements of prior years, issued in comparative form with current year financial statements, also must be presented using the new accounting principles as if the new method had been used all along.

Companies may also implement a **change in accounting estimate**. For example, a company may determine that changing from the declining balance method to the straight-line method of estimating depreciation expense results in a more accurate estimation. Unlike changes in principle, changes in estimates are reported prospectively. That is, the change is only reflected in the current and future financial statements.

PRINCIPLE ALERT

Consistency Principle The *consistency principle* states that, unless otherwise disclosed, financial statements use the same accounting methods from one period to the next. A consistent use of accounting methods enhances the comparability of financial data across time. The consistency principle impacts the accounting for a change in accounting principles in several ways. First, to change an accounting principle, a company must be able to justify that the reported results under the new principle are preferable. Second, a company must present its prior year financial statements as though the new principle had been in use all along. In actual practice, only the prior year financial statements presented with the current year financial statements must be presented using the new accounting method. For all financial statements prior to those presented with the current statements, a lump sum adjustment is made to retained earnings on the statement of retained earnings and the statement of stockholders' equity.

Comprehensive Income

Most items that generate wealth changes in a business are required to be shown on the income statement. There are, however, a few items that do not appear as part of the regular content of the income statement and instead are classified under a category labeled **comprehensive income**. A business's comprehensive income includes its net income, any changes in the market value of certain marketable securities (see Appendix D at the end of this book), and any unrealized gains and losses from translating foreign currency denominated financial statements into U.S. dollars. This latter topic is covered in more advanced accounting textbooks.

Companies are given some flexibility in how they report their comprehensive income. They are allowed to utilize two alternative formats under GAAP: (1) appending comprehensive income to the bottom of the income statement; or (2) creating a separate statement of comprehensive income. In addition to comprehensive income for the current period, GAAP requires a company to report accumulated other comprehensive income as part of stockholders' equity on the balance sheet. Accumulated other comprehensive income serves the same role for comprehensive income as retained earnings serves for regular net income—it reports the cumulative amount of comprehensive income as of the balance sheet date.

REVIEW 12.1

Conner Company, a retail company, entered into the following transactions during the year:

1. Sold merchandise to customers
2. Settled a major lawsuit
3. Wrote down the book value of a closed warehouse
4. Paid employee wages
5. Disposed of a line of discount stores
6. Paid income taxes

Required

Classify each of the above items as either persistent earnings or transitory earnings.

The solution is on page 465.

SOURCES OF INFORMATION

LO2 **Identify** the sources of financial information used by investment professionals and **explain** horizontal financial statement analysis.

Publicly-traded companies are required to publish their financial statements at least annually. Most large companies also issue quarterly financial statements. Normally, annual financial statements are attested to by a certified public accountant, and investment professionals review the independent accountant's opinion to assess the reliability of the published financial data. Companies listed on stock exchanges must also submit financial statements, called a 10-K for the annual report and 10-Q for the quarterly report, to the U.S. Securities and Exchange Commission (SEC).

Investment professionals also may want to compare the performance of a particular firm with that of the other firms in the same industry. Data on industry norms, median financial ratios by industry, and other relationships are available from such data collection services as Dun & Bradstreet, Moody's, and Standard and Poor's. In addition, some brokerage firms compile industry norms and financial ratios from their own computer databases.

ACCOUNTING IN PRACTICE

SEC EDGAR Database An example of a financial database is **EDGAR**, the Electronic Data Gathering, Analysis, and Retrieval system, maintained by the U.S. SEC (www.sec.gov/edgar.shtml). This computer database aids financial statement analysis by performing automated data collection, validation, indexing, acceptance, and forwarding of submissions by companies and others who are required by law to file forms with the U.S. Securities and Exchange Commission. The primary intent of the SEC in creating EDGAR was to increase the efficiency of the securities market for the benefit of investors, corporations, and the economy, by accelerating the receipt, acceptance, dissemination, and analysis of corporate information filed with the agency. An "efficient" securities market means that investors are able to make the best possible decisions regarding where and when to invest their funds.

Analytical Techniques

The absolute dollar amounts of net income, sales revenue, total assets, and other key data are usually not meaningful when analyzed in isolation. For example, knowing that a company's annual net income is $1 million is of little informational value unless the amount of the income can be related to other factors. A $1 million profit might represent excellent performance for a company with less than $10 million in invested capital. On the other hand, $1 million in net income would be considered meager for a firm that had several hundred million dollars in invested capital. Thus, it is important to evaluate net income in relation to other accounts, such as total assets or stockholders' equity. To describe these relationships clearly and to make comparisons easy, the relationships are often expressed in terms of ratios or percentages.

For example, we might express the relationship of $15,000 in net income to $150,000 in sales revenue as a ten percent ($15,000/$150,000) rate of return on sales. To describe the relationship between sales revenue of $150,000 and inventory of $20,000, we might use a ratio or a percentage; ($150,000/$20,000) may be expressed as 7.5, 7.5:1, or 750 percent.

Changes in selected financial statement items compared in successive financial statements are often expressed as percentages. For example, if a firm's net income increased from $40,000 last year to $48,000 this year, the $8,000 increase related to last year (the base year) is expressed as a 20 percent increase ($8,000/$40,000) in net income. To express a dollar increase or decrease as a percentage, however, the analyst must make the base year amount a positive figure. If, for example, a firm had a net loss of $4,000 in one year and net income of $20,000 in the next, the $24,000 increase cannot be meaningfully expressed as a percentage. Similarly, if a firm reported no marketable securities in last year's balance sheet but showed $15,000 of such securities in this year's statement, the $15,000 increase cannot be expressed as a meaningful percentage.

When evaluating a firm's financial statements for two or more years, analysts often use **horizontal analysis**. Horizontal analysis is a technique that can be useful for detecting an improvement or deterioration in a firm's performance and for spotting trends regarding a firm's financial well-being. The term **vertical analysis** is used to describe the analysis of a single year of financial data.

HORIZONTAL ANALYSIS

The type of horizontal analysis most often used by investment professionals is **comparative financial statement analysis** for two or more years, showing dollar and/or percentage changes for important financial statement items and totals. Dollar increases and decreases are divided by data from the base year to obtain percentage changes. To illustrate, financial statements of PureBrands Group, Inc. (PBG), a fictitious, mature consumer products company, are presented in **Exhibits 12-2, 12-3**, and **12-4**. We will use the data in these statements throughout this chapter to illustrate various analytical techniques.

EXHIBIT 12-2 PureBrands Group Income Statement

PUREBRANDS GROUP, INC.
Consolidated Income Statements

(in millions)	Current Year	Common-Size	Prior Year	Common-Size	$ Change	% Change
Net sales	$65,058	100.0%	$65,299	100.0%	$ (241)	(0.4)%
Cost of goods sold	32,535	50.0%	32,909	50.4%	(374)	(1.1)%
Gross profit	32,523	50.0%	32,390	49.6%	133	0.4%
Selling, general, and administrative expense	18,568	28.5%	18,949	29.0%	(381)	(2.0)%
Operating income	13,955	21.5%	13,441	20.6%	514	3.8%
Interest expense	465	0.7%	579	0.9%	(114)	(19.7)%
Other non-operating income (expense)	(233)	(0.4)%	507	0.8%	(740)	(146.0)%
Income before taxes	13,257	20.4%	13,369	20.5%	(112)	(0.8)%
Income taxes	3,063	4.7%	3,342	5.1%	(279)	(8.3)%
Net income	$10,194	15.7%	$10,027	15.4%	$ 167	1.7%
Earnings per share	$3.69		$3.49		$0.20	5.7%
Dividends per share	$2.70		$2.66		$0.04	1.5%

When analyzing financial statements, the investment professional is likely to focus his or her immediate attention on those financial statement items or percentages that are significant in amount. Although percentage changes are helpful in identifying significant items, they can sometimes be misleading. An unusually large percentage change may occur simply because the dollar amount of the base year is small. For example, PBG had a decrease in other non-operating income (expense) of $740, from $507 in the prior year to a loss of ($233) in the current year (see **Exhibit 12-2**). This represents a decrease of 146.0 percent, yet the dollar amount of this line item is quite small and insignificant relative to the other reported dollar amounts on PBG's income statement. The financial statement user's attention should be directed first to changes in key financial statement totals: sales revenue, operating income, net income, total assets, total liabilities, and so on. Next, the changes in significant individual items, such as accounts receivable, inventory, and property, plant and equipment should be examined.

Exhibit 12-3 shows that PBG's total assets decreased by 5.3 percent from the prior year. This decrease is primarily the result of the sale of investments held for sale as well as the purchase of treasury stock. Note that while **Exhibit 12-2** indicates that sales declined slightly (by 0.4 percent), net income actually increased by 1.7 percent. This suggests that despite a small sales decline, PBG has increased the profitability of its operations. Two factors that seem to be partially responsible for this improvement are the decline in cost of goods of 1.1 percent, and the decline in selling, general, and administrative expenses of 2.0 percent.

EXHIBIT 12-3 PureBrands Group Balance Sheet

PUREBRANDS GROUP, INC.
Consolidated Balance Sheets

(in millions)	Current Year End	Common-Size	Prior Year End	Common-Size	$ Change	% Change
Assets						
Current assets						
Cash and cash equivalents	$ 5,569	4.6%	$ 7,102	5.6%	$ (1,533)	(21.6)%
Short-term investments	9,568	7.9%	6,246	4.9%	3,322	53.2%
Accounts receivable	4,594	3.8%	4,373	3.4%	221	5.1%
Inventories	4,624	3.8%	4,716	3.7%	(92)	(2.0)%
Other current assets	2,139	1.8%	11,345	8.9%	(9,206)	(81.1)%
Total current assets	26,494	22.0%*	33,782	26.6%*	(7,288)	(21.6)%
Property, plant, and equipment, net	19,893	16.5%	19,385	15.2%	508	2.6%
Intangible assets	68,886	57.2%	68,877	54.2%	9	0.0%
Other noncurrent assets	5,133	4.3%	5,092	4.0%	41	0.8%
Total assets	$120,406	100.0%	$127,136	100.0%	$ (6,730)	(5.3)%
Liabilities and Stockholders' Equity						
Current liabilities						
Accounts payable	$ 9,632	8.0%	$ 9,325	7.3%	$ 307	3.3%
Other current liabilities	20,578	17.1%	21,445	16.9%	(867)	(4.0)%
Total current liabilities	30,210	25.1%	30,770	24.2%	(560)	(1.8)%
Long-term debt	18,038	15.0%	18,945	14.9%	(907)	(4.8)%
Other noncurrent liabilities	16,380	13.6%	19,438	15.3%	(3,058)	(15.7)%
Total liabilities	64,628	53.7%	69,153	54.4%	(4,525)	(6.5)%
Preferred stock	1,006	0.8%	1,038	0.8%	(32)	(3.1)%
Common stock	4,009	3.3%	4,009	3.2%	0	0.0%
Additional paid-in capital	63,641	52.9%	63,714	50.1%	(73)	(0.1)%
Treasury stock	(93,715)	(77.8)%	(87,389)	(68.7)%	(6,326)	(7.2)%
Retained earnings	96,124	79.8%	93,166	73.3%	2,958	3.2%
Other stockholders' equity	(15,287)	(12.7)%	(16,555)	(13.0)%	1,268	(7.7)%
Total stockholders' equity	55,778	46.3%	57,983	45.6%*	(2,205)	(3.8)%
Total liabilities and stockholders' equity	$120,406	100.0%	$127,136	100.0%	$ (6,730)	(5.3)%

*Does not foot due to rounding.

We can see from PBG's statement of cash flows (**Exhibit 12-4**) that cash flow from operations declined in the current year compared to the prior year by 17.4 percent, which was due in part to a small decrease in liabilities in the current year compared to a large increase in liabilities in the prior year. Despite the decline in operating cash flows, however, PBG increased the cash used in its investing activities by 2.0 percent. In addition, PBG decreased the cash used in financing activities by 10.4 percent, primarily by cutting dividends and stock repurchases.

EXHIBIT 12-4 PureBrands Group Statement of Cash Flows

PUREBRANDS GROUP, INC.
Consolidated Statements of Cash Flows

(in millions)	Current Year	Prior Year	$ Change	% Change
Operating activities				
Net earnings	$10,194	$10,027		
Depreciation and amortization	2,820	3,078		
Changes in accounts receivable	(322)	35		
Changes in inventories	71	116		
Change liabilities	(149)	1,285		
Change in other operating activities	139	894		
Net cash flow provided by operating activities	12,753	15,435	(2,682)	(17.4)%
Investing activities				
Capital expenditures	(3,384)	(3,314)		
Investments	(3,355)	(1,461)		
Other cash flows from investing activities	1,050	(800)		
Net cash flow used by investing activities	(5,689)	(5,575)	(114)	2.0%
Financing activities				
Dividends	(7,236)	(7,436)		
Net stock purchases	(5,204)	(5,734)		
Net borrowings	1,399	1,285		
Other cash flows from financing activities	2,444	2,291		
Net cash used by financing activities	(8,597)	(9,594)	997	(10.4)%
Change in cash and cash equivalents	(1,533)	266		
Beginning cash and cash equivalents	7,102	6,836		
Ending cash and cash equivalents	$ 5,569	$ 7,102		

From this limited analysis of comparative financial statements, an investment professional might conclude that PBG's profitability improved in the current year compared to the prior year. Some of the techniques summarized later in the chapter will help us dig deeper into these changes, and cause that opinion to be either affirmed or modified.

PRINCIPLE ALERT

Consistency Principle Horizontal analysis is a process of analyzing a firm's financial data across two or more years by examining dollar changes, percentage changes, and/or trend percentages. The utility of horizontal analysis, however, is dependent upon the effective implementation of the *consistency principle.* This accounting principle requires that a firm use the same accounting methods from one period to the next or, if a firm finds it necessary (or required) to change an accounting method, that the financial effects of any change be fully disclosed in the financial statements. The consistency principle assures financial analysts that, unless otherwise noted, changes in the accounts over time represent underlying economic changes in a business, and not the result of an accounting method change.

TREND ANALYSIS

To observe percentage changes over time in selected financial data, investment professionals often calculate **trend percentages**. Most companies provide summaries of their key financial data for the past five or ten years in their annual reports. With such information, the financial statement user can examine changes over periods longer than just the past two years. For example, suppose an analyst is interested in the trend in sales and net income for PBG for the past five years. The following table reports PBG's sales revenue and net income for the most recent five years:

PUREBRANDS GROUP COMPANY
Annual Performance

	Base Year		Base Year +1		Base Year +2		Prior Year		Current Year	
	Millions of Dollars	Percentage of Base Year	Millions of Dollars	Percentage of Base Year	Millions of Dollars	Percentage of Base Year	Millions of Dollars	Percentage of Base Year	Millions of Dollars	Percentage of Base Year
Net sales......	$73,910	100%	$74,401	101%	$70,749	96%	$65,299	88%	$65,058	88%
Net income....	10,346	100%	10,658	103%	8,287	80%	10,027	97%	10,194	99%

The pattern of changes from year to year can be determined more precisely by calculating trend percentages. To do this, we select a base year and then divide the data for each of the remaining years by the base year. The result is an index of the changes occurring throughout the period. The data for the years subsequent to the base year will be a proportion of the base year amounts, which is represented as 100 percent.

To create the table of data displayed above, we divide each year's net sales by $73,910, the base year net sales (in millions of dollars). Similarly, PBG's net income for the subsequent years is divided by $10,346, the company's base year net income (in millions of dollars).

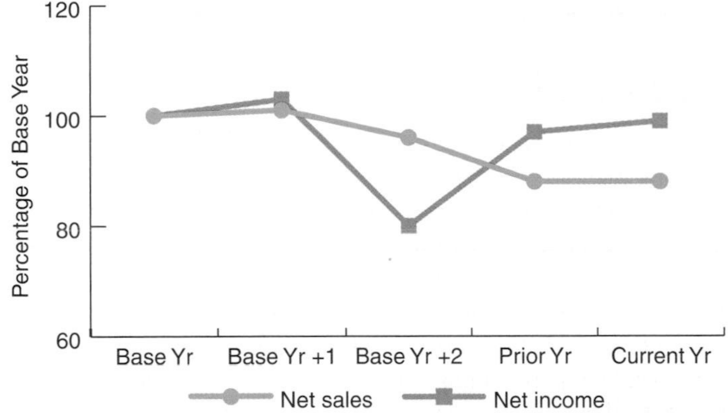

PBG's trend percentages indicate that both net sales and net income increased slightly from base year to base year +1. Then both dropped significantly in base year +2, the first year of PBG's restructuring, with net income falling further than net sales. Net sales continued to decline in the prior year, while net income rebounded significantly. In the current year, net sales were flat, while net income continued growing by two percent. PureBrands implemented a cost cutting program beginning in late base yr +2. Thus, looking at only the trend analysis, it appears as if the company is becoming more efficient, as evidenced by its making 99 percent of its base-period net income, on only 88 percent of the sales.

It is important to note that care must be exercised when interpreting trend percentages. Since all index percentages are related to a base year, it is important to select a good representative base year. If it was an unusual period for the firm, perhaps because of some large transitory items, its use in the trend analysis would be of limited value.

Other data items that an investment professional may relate to sales revenue and net income over multiple years include total assets, a company's investment in plant assets, and its cash flow from operations, among others.

REVIEW 12.2

The following data pertain to the Farrow Company:

	Current Year	Prior Year
Sales revenue	$800,000	$750,000
Net income	120,000	100,000
Total assets	300,000	290,000

Calculate both the amount in dollars and the percentage change in the current year using horizontal analysis and the prior year as the base year.

The solution is on page 465.

TAKEAWAY 12.1	Concept →	Method →	Assessment
	How does a company's current performance compare with the prior year?	Income statement and balance sheet for current and prior year. The income statement and balance sheet should be compared using the prior year as the base. Percentage changes in financial statement amounts can be computed as the change between years divided by the base year amount.	Significant changes should be analyzed to determine their reason.

VERTICAL ANALYSIS

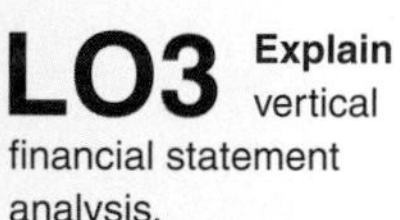

LO3 Explain vertical financial statement analysis.

The relative importance of various accounts in a company's financial statements for a single year can be highlighted by showing them as a percentage of a key financial statement figure. A financial statement that presents the various account balances as a percentage of a key figure is called a **common-size financial statement**. Sales revenue (or net sales) is the key figure used to construct a common-size income statement, whereas total assets is the key figure used to construct a common-size balance sheet.

A financial statement may present both the dollar amounts and common-size percentages. For example, **Exhibit 12-2** presents PBG's current year income statement in dollars and common-size percentages. The common-size percentages show each item in the income statement as a percentage of the company's net sales.

The common-size income statement allows financial statement users to readily compare PBG's ability to manage and control its various expenses while the level of its sales revenue changes over time. For example, PBG's net income increased from 15.4 percent of net sales in the prior year to 15.7 percent of net sales in the current year. Common-size income statements are also useful when comparing across firms, especially when the firms are significantly different in size. We would expect firms of different sizes to report different levels of sales revenues and expenses on a dollar basis. But, we would expect far more similarities when the comparison is done on a common-size basis.

Common-size percentages can also be used to analyze balance sheet data. For example, by examining a firm's current assets and long-term assets as a percentage of total assets, we can determine whether a company is becoming more or less liquid over time. Another use of common-size percentages with balance sheet data is to evaluate the changing sources of financing used by a business. For example, the proportion of total assets supplied by short-term creditors, long-term creditors, preferred stockholders, and common stockholders of PBG is shown in **Exhibit 12-3**. PBG's common-size balance sheets indicate that PBG is relying slightly less on debt financing than equity financing in the current year compared to the prior year. Specifically, the percent of assets financed by total liabilities moved from 54.4 percent in the prior year to 53.7 percent in the current year. We also see that the proportion of total assets that consist of current assets declined from 26.6 percent in the prior year to 22.0 percent in the current year.

REVIEW 12.3

The Sanford Company reported the following income statement for the current year:

SANFORD COMPANY
Income Statement
For the Year Ended December 31

Sales revenue	$13,500
Cost of goods sold	5,400
Gross profit	8,100
Selling and administrative expenses	1,350
Income from operations	6,750
Interest expense	675
Other expense	135
Income before income taxes	5,940
Income tax expense	2,295
Net income	$ 3,645

Hint: When preparing common-size income statements, expenses are expressed as a positive percentage of net sales even though they are subtractions on the income statement.

Required

Prepare a common-size income statement for Sanford Company.

The solution is on page 465.

TAKEAWAY 12.2

Concept	Method	Assessment
How do the relationships within a company's income statement and balance sheet compare to those of prior years?	Income statement and balance sheet for current and prior year. Each income statement item should be presented as a percentage of sales revenue, and each balance sheet item should be presented as a percentage of total assets. Financial statements in this form are called common-size statements.	The percentages should be analyzed for differences between years, and significant changes should be analyzed to determine the reason for any change.

THINKING GLOBALLY

Financial statement analysis is executed, worldwide, in the same way. Common-size financial statements and the financial ratios discussed below are currency neutral and can be effectively used anywhere in the world. Not all ratios are relevant, however, in all countries. For example, in emerging countries that lack the financial infrastructure to support a credit system, ratios involving accounts receivable and accounts payable may be irrelevant since sales transactions in those countries are only executed on a cash basis. Similarly, solvency ratios like the times-interest-earned ratio (discussed shortly) are irrelevant since bank financing in lesser-developed countries is rare (although it is becoming more prevalent with the advent of micro-finance in these countries).

RATIO ANALYSIS

LO4 **Define and discuss** financial ratios for analyzing a firm.

In prior chapters, a number of financial ratios were introduced. At this juncture, we classify those ratios by their analytical objective and review their analysis and interpretation by calculating them for a single company. PBG's financial statements in **Exhibit 12-2**, **Exhibit 12-3**, and **Exhibit 12-4** provide the data for these calculations (all amounts are in millions). Also, representative industry averages are presented for comparison purposes where available. Some of the financial ratios that are commonly calculated by investment professionals, lenders, and managers are presented and explained in **Exhibit 12-5**, along with a reference to the chapter in which they were first introduced.

EXHIBIT 12-5 Key Financial Ratios

Ratio	Definition	Explanation
Analyzing Firm Profitability		
• Gross profit percentage (Chapter 7)	Gross profit on sales / Net sales	The amount remaining from each dollar of sales after deducting the cost of goods sold.
• Profit margin (Chapter 4)	Net income / Net sales	The amount earned for the shareholders from each dollar of sales after subtracting all expenses.
• Asset turnover (Chapter 8)	Net sales / Average total assets	Amount of sales generated from each dollar invested in assets.
• Return on assets (Chapter 8)	Net income / Average total assets	The amount earned for the shareholders from each dollar invested in assets.
• Return on common stockholders' equity (Chapter 10)	(Net income – Preferred stock dividends) / Average common stockholders' equity	The amount earned for the common shareholders from every dollar of the common shareholders' investment.
Analyzing Short-Term Firm Liquidity		
• Working capital (Chapter 9)	Current assets – Current liabilities	The difference between a firm's current assets and its current liabilities.
• Current ratio (Chapter 4)	Current assets / Current liabilities	Amount of current assets available to service current liabilities.
• Quick ratio (Chapter 9)	(Cash and cash equivalents + Short-term investments + Accounts receivable) / Current liabilities	Amount of liquid assets available to service current liabilities.
• Operating-cash-flow-to-current-liabilities ratio (Chapter 11)	Cash flow from operating activities / Average current liabilities	Amount of cash flow from operating activities available to service current liabilities.
• Accounts receivable turnover (Chapter 6)	Net sales / Average accounts receivable (net)	Number of sales/collection cycles experienced by a firm during the period.
• Average collection period (Chapter 6)	365 / Accounts receivable turnover	Number of days required, on average, to collect an outstanding accounts receivable.
• Inventory turnover (Chapter 7)	Cost of goods sold / Average inventory	Number of production/sales cycles experienced by a firm during the period.
• Days' sales in inventory (Chapter 7)	365 / Inventory turnover	Number of days, on average, required to sell the inventory currently on hand.
Analyzing Long-Term Firm Solvency		
• Debt-to-equity ratio (Chapter 12)	Total liabilities / Total stockholders' equity	The amount of debt financing for every dollar of equity financing.
• Times-interest-earned ratio (Chapter 9)	Income before interest expense and income taxes / Interest expense	Extent to which current operating income covers current debt service charges.
• Operating-cash-flow-to-capital-expenditures ratio (Chapter 11)	Cash flow from operating activities / Annual net capital expenditures	The ability of a firm's operations to provide sufficient cash to replace and expand its property, plant, and equipment.
Financial Ratios for Common Stockholders		
• Earnings per share (Chapter 12)	(Net income – Preferred stock dividends) / Weighted-average number of common shares outstanding	The net income available to common shareholders calculated on a per share basis.
• Price-earnings ratio (Chapter 12)	Market price per share / Earnings per share	A measure of the price of a share of common stock relative to the share's annual earnings.
• Dividend yield (Chapter 10)	Annual dividend per share / Market price per share	The earnings on an investment in stock coming from dividends.
• Dividend payout ratio (Chapter 10)	Annual dividend per share / Earnings per share	The percentage of net income paid out to shareholders as dividends.

Analyzing Firm Profitability

Several ratios assist in evaluating how efficiently a firm has performed in its quest for profits, or what is referred to as firm profitability. These ratios include (1) gross profit percentage, (2) profit margin, (3) asset turnover, (4) return on assets, and (5) return on common stockholders' equity.

Gross Profit Percentage

The **gross profit percentage** is a closely watched ratio for both retailers and manufacturers, among other industries. The ratio is calculated as:

$$\textbf{Gross profit percentage} = \frac{\textbf{Gross profit on sales}}{\textbf{Net sales}}$$

A.K.A Gross profit is often referred to as *gross margin.*

This ratio tells us, for every dollar of sales, after the company covers its direct costs, how much is left over to cover indirect costs and leave a profit. **Gross profit**, or **gross profit on sales**, is the difference between net sales and cost of goods sold and reports the amount of sales revenue remaining after subtracting the cost of products sold.

PBG's common-size income statements (see **Exhibit 12-2**) indicate that its gross profit percentage increased from 49.6 percent in the prior year to 50.0 percent in the current year. These percentages are derived using the following figures:

	Current Year	Prior Year
Gross profit	$32,523	$32,390
Net sales	65,058	65,299
Gross profit percentage	**50.0%**	**49.6%**
Industry average	54.6%	

These figures show an upward trend in the amount of profits PBG has, after deducting cost of sales, to cover overhead costs (i.e., the remaining costs included in the income statement). In addition, we also note that PBG's ratio is below the industry average of 54.6 percent.

Profit Margin (Return on Sales)

Another important measure of firm profitability is the **profit margin**. This ratio tells us, for every dollar of sales, after covering all of the company's costs, how much was generated for the shareholders. The profit margin is calculated as follows:

A.K.A Profit margin is often referred to as *return on sales.*

$$\textbf{Profit margin} = \frac{\textbf{Net income}}{\textbf{Net sales}}$$

When common-size income statements are available, the profit margin equals the net income percentage. PBG's common-size income statements in **Exhibit 12-2** indicate that its profit margin increased from 15.4 percent in the prior year to 15.7 percent in the current year. These percentages are calculated using the following figures:

	Current Year	Prior Year
Net income	$10,194	$10,027
Net sales	65,058	65,299
Profit margin	**15.7%**	**15.4%**
Industry average	16.9%	

PBG's current year profit margin of 15.7% tells us that for every dollar of sales $0.157 was generated for the shareholders. Additionally, a profit margin of 15.7% is somewhat lower than the industry average.

The profit margin and gross profit percentages should be used only when analyzing companies from the same industry or when comparing a firm's performance across multiple time periods (as we did above) since the ratio may vary widely across industries. Retail jewelers, for example, have much larger gross profit percentages (an industry average of 45.0 percent) than do retail grocers (an industry average of 23.0 percent). Industry averages for the asset turnover ratio, discussed next, would also be expected to vary significantly from one industry to another.

Asset Turnover

The **asset turnover ratio** tells us, for every dollar of assets invested in the company, how many dollars in sales were generated. This ratio is calculated as follows:

$$\textbf{Asset turnover} = \frac{\textbf{Net sales}}{\textbf{Average total assets}}$$

PBG's asset turnover is calculated as (total assets were $129,495 at the beginning of the prior year):

		Current Year	Prior Year
Net sales		$ 65,058	$ 65,299
Total assets			
Beginning of year	(a)	127,136	129,495
End of year	(b)	120,406	127,136
Average [(a + b)/2]		123,771	128,316
Asset turnover		**0.53**	**0.51**
Industry average		0.65	

PBG's asset turnover increased slightly over the two years, indicating that the company is more effective in using its assets to generate sales revenue. Specifically, the company generated $0.53 in net sales for every dollar invested in total assets in the current year, compared to $0.51 in the prior year. However, PBG's asset turnover ratio is below the industry average of $0.65.

Industries that are characterized by low gross profit percentages generally have relatively high asset turnover ratios. Retail grocery chains, for example, typically turnover their assets five to six times per year. This is largely due to the low profit margins earned by retail grocers, which requires them to produce a high sales volume in order to stay in business.

Return on Assets

The rate of return on total assets, called the **return on assets**, is an overall measure of a firm's profitability. This ratio tells us, for every dollar of assets invested in the firm, how much is generated for the shareholders. The return on assets is calculated as follows:

$$\textbf{Return on assets} = \frac{\textbf{Net income}}{\textbf{Average total assets}}$$

PBG's return on assets is calculated as:

	Current Year	Prior Year
Net income	$ 10,194	$ 10,027
Average total assets	123,771	128,316
Return on assets	**8.2%**	**7.8%**
Industry average	11.03%	

PBG's return on assets increased from 7.8 percent in the prior year to 8.2 percent in the current year. The industry average is somewhat higher.

The return on asset ratio summarizes the financial impact of two component ratios: the profit margin and asset turnover; that is, the return on assets is the multiplicative product of these latter two ratios, as follows:

Ratio:	Profit margin	×	Asset turnover	=	Return on assets
Ratio calculation:	$\frac{\text{Net income}}{\text{Net sales}}$	×	$\frac{\text{Net sales}}{\text{Average total asset}}$	=	$\frac{\text{Net income}}{\text{Average total assets}}$
PBG:	**15.7 percent**	×	**0.53**	=	**8.2 percent (with rounding)**

Return on Common Stockholders' Equity

The **return on common stockholders' equity** tells us, for every dollar of shareholders' equity invested in the firm, how much is generated for the shareholders. The ratio shows the percentage of income available to common stockholders—that is, net income less any preferred stock dividends—for each dollar of common stockholder equity invested in a business, as follows:

$$\textbf{Return on common stockholders' equity} = \frac{\textbf{(Net income − Preferred stock dividends)}}{\textbf{Average common stockholders' equity}}$$

The return on common stockholders' equity for PBG is calculated as (common stockholders' equity was $61,973 at the beginning of the prior year; and Preferred stock dividends were $247 and $255 for the current and prior years, respectively):

		Current Year	Prior Year
Net income		$10,194	$10,027
Less: Preferred stock dividends		247	255
Common stock earnings		9,947	9,772
Common stockholders' equity:			
Beginning of year	(a)	56,945	61,973
End of year	(b)	54,772	56,945
Average [(a + b)/2]		55,858	59,459
Return on common stockholders' equity		**17.8%**	**16.4%**
Industry average		28.7%	

PBG's return on common stockholders' equity increased from 16.4 percent in the prior year to 17.8 percent in the current year. We note that this is much lower than PBG's industry peers.

REVIEW 12.4

The following data was obtained from the current financial statements for Kelly Corporation:

Net sales	$30,000	Average total assets	$50,000
Cost of goods sold	10,500	Average common stockholders' equity	35,000
Net income	4,500	Preferred dividends	500

Required

Calculate the following ratios for Kelly Corporation:

a. Gross profit percentage
b. Profit margin
c. Asset turnover
d. Return on assets
e. Return on common stockholders' equity

The solution is on page 465.

TAKEAWAY 12.3

Concept	Method	Assessment
How much profit is a company generating relative to the amount of assets invested in the company?	Income statement and balance sheet. Calculate the return on assets by dividing net income by the average total assets for the year.	The higher the return on assets, the better a company is doing in terms of generating profits utilizing the assets under its control.

Analyzing Short-Term Firm Liquidity

A firm's **working capital** is the difference between its current assets and current liabilities. Maintaining an adequate working capital enables a firm to repay its current obligations on a timely basis and to take advantage of any available purchase discounts associated with the timely payment of accounts payable. Shortages of working capital, on the other hand, can force a company into borrowing at inopportune times and unfavorable interest rates. As a consequence, many long-term debt contracts contain provisions that require the borrowing firm to maintain an adequate working capital position. A firm's working capital is calculated as follows:

Working capital = Current assets − Current liabilities

Analysis of a firm's short-term liquidity utilizes several financial ratios that relate to various aspects of a company's working capital. These ratios are (1) the current ratio, (2) the quick ratio, (3) operating-cash-flow-to-current-liabilities ratio, (4) accounts receivable turnover and average collection period, and (5) inventory turnover and days' sales in inventory.

Current Ratio

The **current ratio** is calculated as a firm's current assets divided by its current liabilities:

$$\textbf{Current ratio} = \frac{\textbf{Current assets}}{\textbf{Current liabilities}}$$

This ratio is a widely used measure of a firm's ability to meet its current obligations and to have funds available for use in daily operations. The following calculations reveal that PBG's current ratio declined from 1.10 in the prior year to 0.88 (or 0.88:1) in the current year:

	Current Year	Prior Year
Current assets	$26,494	$33,782
Current liabilities	30,210	30,770
Current ratio	**0.88**	**1.10**
Industry average	1.1	

In essence, PBG had $0.88 in current assets for every $1 in current liabilities at the end of the current year.

In the past, a generally accepted rule of thumb was that a firm's current ratio should be approximately 2:1, indicating that a company should maintain twice the dollar amount of current assets as was needed to satisfy its current liabilities. Improved cash flow management techniques and alternate forms of short-term financing (such as bank lines of credit) have reduced the need for businesses to maintain such a high current ratio. Still, many creditors prefer to see a higher current ratio and consider a low ratio as a potential warning sign of short-term liquidity problems.

Evaluating the adequacy of a firm's current ratio may involve comparing it with the recent past (PBG's current ratio declined over the two years presented) or with an industry average (PBG's ratio is below the industry average of 1.1). What is considered an appropriate current ratio varies by industry. A service firm with little or no inventory, such as a car wash service, would be expected to have a smaller current ratio than would a firm carrying a large inventory, such as a hardware retailer. The composition (or mix) of a firm's current assets significantly influences any evaluation of a firm's short-term liquidity. The quick ratio, discussed next, explicitly considers the composition of a firm's current assets when evaluating short-term liquidity.

Quick Ratio

A.K.A. The quick ratio is also referred to as the *acid-test ratio*.

The **quick ratio** is an indicator of the relationship between a firm's liquid, or quick, assets and its current liabilities. Quick assets include cash and cash equivalents, short-term investments, and accounts receivable. The quick ratio omits a company's inventory and prepaid assets, which may not be particularly liquid. Consequently, the quick ratio may give a more accurate picture of a company's ability to meet its current obligations since the ratio ignores a firm's potentially illiquid inventory and prepaid expenses.

Comparing the quick ratio and the current ratio indicates the financial impact of a company's inventory on its working capital. For example, a company might have an acceptable current ratio, but if its quick ratio falls to an unacceptable level, a financial analyst is likely to be concerned about the amount of inventory on hand, and consequently, analyze the company's inventory position more thoroughly.

The quick ratio is calculated as follows:

$$\textbf{Quick ratio} = \frac{\textbf{(Cash and cash equivalents + Short-term investments + Accounts receivable)}}{\textbf{Current liabilities}}$$

The quick ratio for PBG is calculated as:

	Current Year	Prior Year
Cash and cash equivalents, short-term investments, and accounts receivable	$19,731	$17,721
Current liabilities	30,210	30,770
Quick ratio	**0.65**	**0.58**
Industry average	0.40	

PBG's quick ratio increased from 0.58 in the prior year to 0.65 in the current year and is well above the industry average in both years. PBG's increased quick ratio is mainly due to a large increase in short-term investments in the current year.

Operating-Cash-Flow-to-Current-Liabilities Ratio

Ultimately, cash will be needed to settle a business's current liabilities. Another ratio indicating a firm's ability to pay its current liabilities as they come due focuses on a company's operating cash flow. The **operating-cash-flow-to-current-liabilities ratio** is calculated as follows:

$$\textbf{Operating-cash-flow-to-current-liabilities ratio} = \frac{\textbf{Cash flow from operating activities}}{\textbf{Average current liabilities}}$$

The operating-cash-flow-to-current-liabilities ratio relates the net cash available as a result of operating activities to the average current liabilities outstanding during the period. A higher ratio indicates that a firm has a greater ability to settle its current liabilities using its operating cash flow.

PBG's operating-cash-flow-to-current-liabilities ratio is calculated as (current liabilities at the beginning of the prior year was $29,790; no industry average is available):

		Current Year	Prior Year
Cash flow from operating activities		$12,753	$15,435
Current liabilities			
Beginning of year	(a)	30,770	29,790
End of year	(b)	30,210	30,770
Average [(a + b)/2]		30,490	30,280
Operating-cash-flow-to-current-liabilities ratio		**0.42**	**0.51**

PBG's operating-cash-flow-to-current-liabilities ratio declined over the two years, a result of a decline in cash provided by operating activities and an increase in average current liabilities.

Accounts Receivable Turnover

The speed with which accounts receivable are collected is of considerable interest to investment professionals when evaluating a firm's short-term liquidity. **Accounts receivable turnover** indicates how many times a year a firm collects its average outstanding accounts receivable, and, thus, measures how fast a firm converts its accounts receivable into cash. The quicker a firm is able to convert its accounts receivables into cash, the less cash the company needs to keep on hand to satisfy its current liabilities. Accounts receivable turnover is calculated as follows:

$$\textbf{Accounts receivable turnover} = \frac{\textbf{Net sales}}{\textbf{Average accounts receivable (net)}}$$

Recall from Chapter 6 that accounts receivable less the allowance for doubtful accounts—that is, the net balance of accounts receivable—is the amount of receivables that the company expects to collect from customers. The accounts receivable turnover for PBG is calculated as (accounts receivable at the beginning of the prior year were $4,568):

		Current Year	Prior Year
Net sales		$65,058	$65,299
Average accounts receivable (net)			
Beginning of year	(a)	4,373	4,568
End of year	(b)	4,594	4,373
Average [(a + b)/2]		4,484	4,470
Accounts receivable turnover		**14.51**	**14.61**
Industry average		10.16	

The higher the accounts receivable turnover, the faster a company is able to convert its accounts receivable into cash. PBG's accounts receivable turnover decreased slightly from 14.61 in the prior year to 14.51 in the current year. However, PBG's accounts receivable turnover is well above the industry average of 10.16 for both years.

Average Collection Period

A.K.A. The average collection period is also referred to as the *days' sales outstanding, or DSO.*

An extension of the accounts receivable turnover is the **average collection period**. The average collection period reveals how many days it takes, on average, for a company to collect an account receivable. The ratio is calculated as follows:

$$\textbf{Average collection period} = \frac{\textbf{365}}{\textbf{Accounts receivable turnover}}$$

PBG's average collection period is calculated as:

	Current Year	Prior Year
Average collection period		
Current yr: 365/14.51; Prior yr: 365/14.61	**25.2 days**	**25.0 days**
Industry average	35.9 days	

PBG's average collection period increased slightly from year to year. This may have resulted from such actions as PBG relaxing the credit standards they apply to their customers or by extending the allowed credit period. Alternatively, it may reflect that PBG's customers have experienced deteriorating cash flows, and, thus, they are not able to pay their accounts as promptly. Knowledge of PBG's credit terms would permit a more complete analysis of these results. If, for example, the company's credit terms are *n*/20, then an average collection period of 25.2 days indicates that the company has a problem with slow-paying customers. If, on the other hand, their credit terms are *n*/30, then the the current year average collection period shows no particular problem with the company's speed of receivable collection. We also note that PBG's collection period is consistently better than the industry average of 35.9 days.

Inventory Turnover

An analyst concerned about a company's inventory position is likely to evaluate the company's **inventory turnover**. This ratio indicates whether the inventory on hand is disproportionate to the amount of sales revenue. Excessive inventories not only tie up company funds and increase storage costs but may also lead to subsequent losses if the goods become outdated or unsalable. In general, a higher turnover is preferred to a lower turnover. The calculation of inventory turnover is as follows:

$$\textbf{Inventory turnover} = \frac{\textbf{Cost of goods sold}}{\textbf{Average inventory}}$$

PBG's inventory turnover is calculated as (inventory at the beginning of the prior year was $4,979):

		Current Year	Prior Year
Cost of goods sold		$32,535	$32,909
Inventory			
Beginning of year	(a)	4,716	4,979
End of year	(b)	4,624	4,716
Average [(a + b)/2]		4,670	4,848
Inventory turnover		**6.97**	**6.79**
Industry average		11.28	

PBG's inventory turnover increased from 6.79 in the prior year to 6.97 in the current year. In addition, the company's inventory turnover is below the industry average of 11.28.

The cost of goods sold is used in the calculation of inventory turnover because the inventory measure in the denominator is a *cost* figure; consequently, it is appropriate to also use a cost figure in the numerator. By way of contrast, accounts receivable turnover uses net sales in the calculation because accounts receivable is based on sales revenue, which includes a markup for the company's expected profit.

A low inventory turnover can result from an overextended inventory position or from inadequate sales volume. For this reason, an appraisal of a firm's inventory turnover should be accompanied by a review of the quick ratio and an analysis of trends in both inventory and sales revenue.

Days' Sales in Inventory

The **days' sales in inventory** ratio is derived from a firm's inventory turnover ratio and reveals how many days it takes, on average, for a firm to sell its inventory on hand. The ratio is calculated as follows:

$$\textbf{Days' sales in inventory} = \frac{\textbf{365}}{\textbf{Inventory turnover}}$$

PBG's days' sales in inventory is calculated as:

	Current Year	Prior Year
Current yr: 365/6.97; Prior yr: 365/6.79	**52.4 days**	**53.8 days**
Industry average	32.3 days	

PBG's days' sales in inventory reveals that the average amount of time required to sell its inventory improved by 1.4 days from 53.8 days in the prior year to 52.4 days in the current year. However, this is well above the industry average of 32.3 days.

By combining the days' sales in inventory with the average collection period, it is possible to estimate the average time period from the acquisition of inventory, to the sale of inventory, to the eventual collection of cash. The sum of the days' sales in inventory plus the average collection period measures the length of the company's **operating cycle**. Although operating cycles will naturally vary across different industries, a shorter operating cycle is preferred as it is an indicator of the operating efficiency and working capital management of the company. In the current year, for example, it took PBG 77.6 days (52.4 days' sales in inventory + 25.2 days average collection period) to sell its average inventory and collect the related cash from its customers. We note, however, that this operating cycle is somewhat less efficient than the industry average of 68.2 days (32.3 days + 35.9 days).

TAKEAWAY 12.4

Concept	Method	Assessment
How financially capable is a company to pay its current liabilities as they come due?	Income statement, balance sheet, and statement of cash flows. Calculate the current ratio, the quick ratio, and the operating-cash-flow-to-current-liabilities ratio.	The higher the ratios, the higher the probability that a company will have the ability to pay its current liabilities as they become due.

REVIEW 12.5

The following selected data was obtained from the financial statements of Justin Corporation:

Current assets	$ 60,000	Average accounts receivable (net)	$15,000
Current liabilities for both current and prior year	40,000	Cost of goods sold	70,000
Cash flow from operating activities	55,000	Average inventory	9,000
Net sales	100,000		

Required

Calculate the following financial measures and ratios for Justin Corporation:

a. Working capital
b. Current ratio
c. Operating-cash-flow-to-current-liabilities ratio
d. Accounts receivable turnover
e. Days' sales in inventory

The solution is on page 466.

Analyzing Long-Term Firm Solvency

The preceding set of ratios examined a firm's short-term liquidity. A separate set of ratios analyzes a firm's long-term solvency, or its long-term debt repayment capability. Ratios in this latter group include (1) the debt-to-equity ratio, (2) the times-interest-earned ratio, and (3) the operating-cash-flow-to-capital-expenditures ratio.

Debt-to-Equity Ratio

The **debt-to-equity ratio** evaluates the financial structure of a firm by relating a company's total liabilities to its total stockholders' equity. This ratio considers the extent to which a company relies on creditors versus stockholders to provide financing. The debt-to-equity ratio is calculated as follows:

$$\textbf{Debt-to-equity ratio} = \frac{\textbf{Total liabilities}}{\textbf{Total stockholders' equity}}$$

This ratio uses year-end balances for the ratio's components, rather than averages, since we are interested in the firm's capital structure as of a particular point in time. The total stockholders' equity for a business is its total assets minus its total liabilities.

The debt-to-equity ratio gives creditors an indication of the margin of protection available to them (creditors' claims to assets have priority over stockholders' claims). The lower the ratio, the greater the protection being provided to creditors. A firm with a low ratio also has greater flexibility when seeking additional borrowed funds at a low rate of interest than does a firm with a high ratio.

PBG's debt-to-equity ratio is calculated as:

	Current Year	Prior Year
Total liabilities (year-end)	$64,628	$69,153
Total stockholders' equity (year-end)	55,778	57,983
Debt-to-equity ratio	**1.16**	**1.19**
Industry average	1.6	

PBG's debt-to-equity ratio decreased from 1.19 to 1.16 at the current year end, indicating a small decrease in reliance on debt to finance its operations. Still, PBG is far less leveraged than its industry peers, who have an average ratio of 1.6.

A.K.A. The times-interest-earned ratio is also referred to as the *interest coverage ratio.*

Times-Interest-Earned Ratio

To evaluate the ability of a company to make its interest payments, an analyst may investigate the relationship between the company's current interest charges and its net income. For example, an extremely high debt-to-equity ratio for a company may indicate excessive borrowing by the company; however, if its operating earnings are sufficient to meet the interest charges on the debt several times over, an analyst may regard the situation quite favorably.

Analysts, particularly long-term credit analysts, almost always consider the **times-interest-earned ratio** of a company with interest-bearing debt. This ratio is calculated by dividing the income before interest expense and income taxes by the annual interest expense:

$$\textbf{Times-interest-earned ratio} = \frac{\textbf{Income before interest expense and income taxes}}{\textbf{Interest expense}}$$

PBG's times-interest-earned ratio is calculated as:

	Current Year	Prior Year
Income before interest expense and income taxes	$13,722	$13,948
Interest expense	465	579
Times-interest-earned ratio	**29.5**	**24.1**
Industry average	25.9	

Income before interest expense and income taxes equals net income before income taxes, plus interest expense (e.g., $13,257 + $465 = $13,722 for the current year). PBG's operating income available to meet its interest charges increased from 24.1 times in the prior year to 29.5 times in the current year. Generally speaking, a company that earns its interest charges several times over is regarded as a satisfactory risk by long-term creditors.

Operating-Cash-Flow-to-Capital-Expenditures Ratio

The ability of a firm's operations to provide sufficient cash to replace and expand its property, plant, and equipment is revealed by the **operating-cash-flow-to-capital-expenditures ratio**. To the extent that acquisitions of plant assets can be financed using cash provided by operating activities, a firm does not have to use other financing sources, such as long-term debt. This ratio is calculated as follows:

$$\textbf{Operating-cash-flow-to-capital-expenditures ratio} = \frac{\textbf{Cash flow from operating activities}}{\textbf{Annual net capital expenditures}}$$

A ratio in excess of 1.0 indicates that a company has more than sufficient operating cash flow to fund any needed expansion in plant capacity.

The operating-cash-flow-to-capital-expenditures ratio for PBG is:

	Current Year	Prior Year
Cash flow from operating activities	$12,753	$15,435
Annual net capital expenditures	3,384	3,314
Operating-cash-flow-to-capital-expenditures ratio	**3.8**	**4.7**

In the current year, PBG's operating-cash-flow-to-capital-expenditures ratio was 3.8, a decrease from 4.7 in the prior year. It appears that PBG is generating plenty of operating cash flow to cover its net capital expenditures in each year.

TAKEAWAY 12.5

Concept	Method	Assessment
How solvent is a company?	Income statement, balance sheet, and statement of cash flows. Calculate the debt-to-equity ratio, the times-interest-earned ratio, and the operating-cash-flow-to-capital-expenditures ratio.	The higher the times-interest-earned and the operating-cash-flow-to-capital-expenditures ratios, and the lower the debt-to-equity ratio, the greater is a company's solvency.

REVIEW 12.6

The following selected data was obtained from the financial statements for the Hartford Corporation:

Total liabilities	$180,000	Net income	$55,000
Total stockholders' equity	600,000	Interest expense	5,000
Cash flow from operating activities	100,000	Income tax expense	25,000
Annual capital expenditures	30,000		

Required

Calculate the following ratios for Hartford Corporation:

a. Debt-to-equity ratio
b. Times-interest-earned ratio
c. Operating-cash-flow-to-capital-expenditures ratio

The solution is on page 466.

Financial Ratios for Common Stockholders

Present and potential common stockholders share an interest with a business's creditors in analyzing the profitability, short-term liquidity, and long-term solvency of a company. There are also other financial ratios that are primarily of interest to common stockholders. These ratios include (1) earnings per share, (2) the price-earnings ratio, (3) dividend yield, and (4) the dividend payout ratio.

Earnings per Share

Because stock market prices are quoted on a per-share basis, the reporting of earnings per share of common stock is useful to investors. **Earnings per share (EPS)** is calculated by dividing the net income available to common stockholders by the weighted average number of common shares outstanding during a year. The net income available to common stockholders is a company's net income less any preferred stock dividends. Preferred stock dividends are subtracted from net income to arrive at the net income available exclusively to a company's common stock stockholders. Thus, earnings per share is calculated as follows:

$$\textbf{Earnings per share} = \frac{\textbf{(Net income – Preferred stock dividends)}}{\textbf{Weighted-average number of common shares outstanding}}$$

Since earnings per share is a required disclosure on a company's income statement, investment professionals do not have to calculate this financial metric. PBG's income statements reveal the following earnings per share (see **Exhibit 12-2**):

	Current Year	Prior Year
Earnings per share	**$3.69**	**$3.49**

PBG's earnings per share increased from $3.49 in the prior year to $3.69 in the current year, an increase of 5.7 percent.

Price-Earnings Ratio

A.K.A. The price-earnings ratio is also referred to as the *P/E multiple.*

The **price-earnings ratio** is calculated by dividing the market price per share of common stock by a company's earnings per share:

$$\textbf{Price-earnings ratio} = \frac{\textbf{Market price per share}}{\textbf{Earnings per share}}$$

For many analysts and investors, this ratio is an important tool for assessing a stock's valuation. However, it should be interpreted with a great deal of caution and in the context of the firm's accounting policies and events. For example, a large transitory gain is not likely to be priced at the same value as earnings that are expected to recur in the future.

When calculating the price-earnings ratio, it is customary to use the latest market price per share and the earnings per share for the last four quarters of a company's operations. PBG's price-earnings ratios as of the end of the two fiscal years are:

	Current Year	Prior Year
Market price per share (at year-end)	$87.15	$84.67
Earnings per share	3.69	3.49
Price-earnings ratio	**23.6**	**24.3**
Industry average	19.1	

The market price of a share of PBG's common stock at the current year year-end was 23.6 times the company's earnings per share.

Dividend Yield

Investor expectations vary greatly with personal economic circumstances and with the overall economic outlook. Some investors are more interested in the potential share price appreciation of a stock than in any dividends that a company may pay on its outstanding shares. When shares are disposed of in the future, the capital gains provision of U.S. income tax law generally taxes capital gains at a rate that is lower than the tax rate applied to dividend income. Some investors, on the other hand, are more concerned with dividends than with stock price appreciation. These investors desire a high **dividend yield** on their investments. Dividend yield is calculated by dividing a company's current annual dividend per share by the current market price per share:

$$\textbf{Dividend yield} = \frac{\textbf{Annual dividend per share}}{\textbf{Market price per share}}$$

PBG's dividend yield per common share is calculated as (the dividend per share is disclosed in **Exhibit 12-2**):

	Current Year	Prior Year
Annual dividend per share	$ 2.70	$ 2.66
Market price per share (at year-end)	87.15	84.67
Dividend yield	**3.1%**	**3.1%**
Industry average	2.51%	

PBG's dividend yield remained the same over the two years, and is somewhat above the industry average of 2.51 percent.

Dividend Payout Ratio

Investors who emphasize the yield on their investments may also be interested in a firm's **dividend payout ratio**—that is, the percentage of net income paid out as dividends to stockholders. The payout ratio indicates whether a firm has a conservative or a liberal dividend policy, and may also indicate whether a firm is conserving funds for internal financing of its growth. The dividend payout ratio is calculated as follows:

$$\textbf{Dividend payout ratio} = \frac{\textbf{Annual dividend per share}}{\textbf{Earnings per share}}$$

PBG's dividend payout ratio is calculated as:

	Current Year	Prior Year
Annual dividends per share	$2.70	$2.66
Earnings per share	3.69	3.49
Dividend payout ratio	**73.2%**	**76.2%**
Industry average	44.7%	

PBG's dividend payout ratio decreased from 76.2 percent in the prior year to 73.2 percent in the current year. A higher payout ratio is consistent with the payout ratio for most comparable mature U.S. industrial corporations.

Payout ratios for mature industrial corporations vary between 40 percent and 60 percent of net income. Many corporations, however, need funds for internal financing of growth and pay out little (if any) of their net income as dividends. At the other extreme, some companies—principally utility companies—may pay out as much as 70 percent of their net income as dividends.

REVIEW 12.7

The following selected data was obtained from financial statements for Baylor Corporation:

Earnings per share	$ 4.50
Market price per share of common stock	54.00
Dividends per share of common stock	1.50

Required

Calculate the following ratios for Baylor Corporation:

a. Dividend yield
b. Dividend payout ratio

The solution is on page 466.

TAKEAWAY 12.6	Concept	Method	Assessment
	How much dividends are common stockholders likely to receive?	Earnings per share, dividends per share, and market price of common stock. Calculate the dividend yield and dividend payout ratio.	The higher the dividend yield and the dividend payout ratio, the greater the company's dividend distribution policy.

ACCOUNTING IN PRACTICE

Accounting as an Aid to Investing The days of corporations offering traditional pension plans where the employee is guaranteed certain benefits at retirement are numbered. More and more employers are switching to plans such as a 401(k) where the employee is responsible for deciding what the plan invests in. Having a knowledge of the accounting techniques demonstrated in this chapter can certainly provide a better understanding of the risks and rewards of investing.

LO5 Discuss the limitations of financial statement analysis.

LIMITATIONS OF FINANCIAL STATEMENT ANALYSIS

The ratios, percentages, and other relationships described in this chapter reflect the analytical techniques used by investment professionals and experienced investors. Nonetheless, they must be interpreted with due consideration of the general economic conditions, the conditions of the industry in which a company operates, and the relative position of individual companies within an industry.

Financial statement users also must be aware of the inherent limitations of financial statement data. Problems of comparability are frequently encountered. Companies within the same industry may use different accounting methods that can cause problems in comparing certain key relationships. For instance, inventory turnover can be quite different for a company using LIFO than for one using FIFO. Inflation may also distort certain financial data and ratios, especially those resulting from horizontal analysis. For example, trend percentages calculated from data unadjusted for inflation may be deceptive.

Financial statement users also must be careful when comparing companies within a particular industry. Factors such as firm size, diversity of product line, and mode of operations can make firms within the same industry dissimilar in their reported results. Moreover, some firms, particularly conglomerates, are difficult to classify by industry. If segment information is available, the financial statement user may compare the statistics for several industries. Often, trade associations prepare industry statistics that are stratified by size of firm or type of product, facilitating financial statement analysis.

REVIEW 12.8

Knox Instruments, Inc., is a manufacturer of various medical and dental instruments. Financial statement data for the firm follow:

(thousands of dollars, except per-share amount)	Current Year
Sales revenue	$200,000
Cost of goods sold	98,000
Net income	10,750
Dividends	4,200
Cash provided by operating activities	7,800
Earnings per share	3.07

KNOX INSTRUMENTS, INC.
Balance Sheets

	December 31	
(thousands of dollars)	Current Year	Prior Year
Assets		
Cash	$ 3,000	$ 2,900
Accounts receivable (net)	28,000	28,800
Inventory	64,000	44,000
Total current assets	95,000	75,700
Plant assets (net)	76,000	67,300
Total Assets	$171,000	$143,000
Liabilities and Stockholders' Equity		
Current liabilities	$ 45,200	$ 39,750
10% Bonds payable	20,000	14,000
Total Liabilities	65,200	53,750
Common stock, $10 par value	40,000	30,000
Retained earnings	65,800	59,250
Total Stockholders' Equity	105,800	89,250
Total Liabilities and Stockholders' Equity	$171,000	$143,000

Required

a. Using the given data, calculate the nine financial ratios below for the current year. Compare the ratio results for Knox Instruments, Inc., with the following industry averages and comment on its operations.

Median Ratios for the Industry

1. Current ratio	2.7
2. Quick ratio	1.6
3. Average collection period	73 days
4. Inventory turnover	2.3
5. Operating-cash-flow-to-current-liabilities ratio	0.22
6. Debt-to-equity ratio	0.50

continued

continued from previous page

7. Return on assets 4.9 percent
8. Return on common stockholders' equity 10.2 percent
9. Profit margin 4.1 percent

b. Calculate the dividends paid per share of common stock. (Use the average number of shares outstanding during the year.) What was the dividend payout ratio?

c. If the current year-end market price per share of Knox's common stock is $25, what is the company's (1) price-earnings ratio and (2) dividend yield?

The solution is on page 466.

APPENDIX 12A: Financial Statement Disclosures

LO6 Describe financial statement disclosures.

Disclosures related to a company's financial statements fall into one of three categories: (1) parenthetical disclosures on the face of the financial statements, (2) notes to the financial statements, and (3) supplementary information. Most disclosures amplify or explain aggregated information contained in the financial statements. Some disclosures, however, provide additional information.

Parenthetical Disclosures

Parenthetical disclosures are placed next to an account title or other descriptive label in the financial statements. Their purpose is to provide additional detail regarding the item or account.

An example of parenthetical disclosures indicating the amount of the allowance for doubtful accounts follows:

	Current Year	Prior Year
Accounts receivable, less allowances for doubtful accounts ($7,545 and $7,098, respectively).	$351,538	$300,181

Instead of using a parenthetical disclosure, companies may choose to present the additional detail in the notes to the financial statements.

Notes to the Financial Statements

Although much information is gathered, summarized, and reported in a company's financial statements, the financial statements alone are limited in their ability to convey a complete picture of a company's financial status. **Notes to the financial statements** are added to help fill in these gaps. Notes may cover a wide variety of topics. Typically, they deal with significant accounting policies, explanations of complex or special transactions, details of reported amounts, commitments, contingencies, business segments, quarterly data, and subsequent material events.

Significant Accounting Policies

GAAP contains a number of instances for which alternative accounting procedures are equally acceptable. For example, there are several generally accepted depreciation and inventory valuation methods. The particular accounting policies selected by a company affect the financial data presented. Knowledge of a firm's specific accounting principles and methods of applying these principles helps users more fully understand a company's financial statements. Accordingly, these principles and methods are disclosed in a **summary of significant accounting policies**, which is typically the first note to the financial statements.

For example, the annual report of the **Columbia Sportswear Company** contains the following description of its inventory policy:

> Inventories consist primarily of finished goods and are carried at the lower of cost or net realizable value. Cost is determined using the first-in, first-out method. The Company periodically reviews its inventories for excess, close-out or slow moving items and makes provisions as necessary to properly reflect inventory value.

Explanations of Complex or Special Transactions

The complexity of certain transactions means that not all important aspects are likely to be reflected in the accounts. Financial statement notes, therefore, report additional relevant details about such transactions.

Typical examples include notes discussing the financial aspects of pension plans, profit-sharing plans, acquisitions of other companies, borrowing agreements, stock option and other incentive plans, and income taxes.

Transactions with related parties are special transactions requiring disclosure in the financial statement notes. Related party transactions include transactions between a firm and its (1) principal owners, (2) members of management, (3) subsidiary companies, or (4) affiliate companies.

Details of Reported Amounts

Financial statements often summarize several groups of accounts into a single aggregate dollar amount. For example, a balance sheet may show one asset account labeled *Property, Plant, and Equipment,* or it may list *Long-Term Debt* as a single amount among the liabilities. Notes report more detail, presenting schedules that list the types and amounts of property, plant, and equipment and long-term debt. Other items that may be summarized in the financial statements and detailed in the notes include inventories, other current assets, notes payable, accrued liabilities, stockholders' equity, and a company's income tax expense.

The notes to Columbia Sportswear Company's 2020 annual report contain several examples of financial statement items that are detailed, including property, plant, and equipment **(Note 5)**; intangible assets, net, and goodwill **(Note 6)**; short-term borrowing and credit lines **(Note 7)**; accrued liabilities **(Note 8)**; leases **(Note 9)**; and income taxes **(Note 10)**.

Commitments

A firm may have contractual arrangements existing as of a balance sheet date in which both parties to the contract still have acts yet to be completed. If performance under these **commitments** will have a significant financial impact on a firm, the existence and nature of the commitments should be disclosed in the notes to the financial statements. Examples of commitments reported in the notes include contracts to purchase materials or equipment, contracts to construct facilities, salary commitments to executives, commitments to retire or redeem stock, and commitments to deliver goods.

Columbia Sportswear Company reports the following commitments in its annual report:

> During its normal course of business, the Company has made certain indemnities, commitments and guarantees under which it may be required to make payments in relation to certain transactions. These include (i) intellectual property indemnities to the Company's customers and licensees in connection with the use, sale and/or license of Company products, (ii) indemnities to various lessors in connection with facility leases for certain claims arising from such facility or lease, (iii) indemnities to customers, vendors and service providers pertaining to claims based on the negligence or willful misconduct of the Company, (iv) executive severance arrangements and (v) indemnities involving the accuracy of representations and warranties in certain contracts. The duration of these indemnities, commitments and guarantees varies, and in certain cases, may be indefinite. The majority of these indemnities, commitments and guarantees do not provide for any limitation of the maximum potential for future payments the Company could be obligated to make. The Company has not recorded any liability for these indemnities, commitments and guarantees in the accompanying Consolidated Balance Sheets.

Contingencies

Contingent liabilities were discussed in Chapter 9. As noted there, if the future event that would turn a contingency into an obligation is not likely to occur, or if the liability cannot be reasonably estimated, the **contingency** is disclosed in a note to the financial statements. Typical contingencies disclosed in the notes include pending lawsuits, environmental cleanup costs, possible income tax assessments, credit guarantees, and discounted notes receivable.

Columbia reports the following regarding contingencies in its annual report:

> The Company is involved in litigation and various legal matters arising in the normal course of business, including matters related to employment, retail, intellectual property, contractual agreements, and various regulatory compliance activities. Management has considered facts related to legal and regulatory matters and opinions of counsel handling these matters, and does not believe the ultimate resolution of these proceedings will have a material adverse effect on the Company's financial position, results of operations or cash flows.

Segments

Many firms diversify their business activities and operate in several different industries. A firm's financial statements often combine information from all of a company's operations into aggregate amounts. This complicates the financial statement user's ability to analyze the statements because the interpretation of financial data is influenced by the industry in which a firm operates. Different industries face different types of risk and have different rates of profitability. In making investment and lending decisions, financial statement users evaluate risk and required rates of return. Having financial data available by industry segment is helpful to such evaluations.

The FASB recognizes the usefulness of industry data to investors and lenders. Public companies with significant operations in more than one industry must report certain financial information by industry **segment**. Typically, these disclosures are in the financial statement notes. The major disclosures by industry segment are sales revenue, operating profit or loss, identifiable assets (the assets used by the segment), capital expenditures, and depreciation.

Other types of segment data may also be disclosed. Business operations in different parts of the world are subject to different risks and opportunities for growth. Thus, public companies with significant operations in foreign countries must report selected financial data by foreign geographic area. The required data disclosures include sales revenue, operating profit or loss (or other profitability measure), and identifiable assets. Also, if a firm has export sales or sales revenue to a single customer that are ten percent or more of total sales revenue, the amount of such sales revenue must be separately disclosed.

Note 17 to **Columbia Sportswear's** financial statements in its annual report illustrates segment disclosures by foreign versus domestic segments.

Quarterly Data

Interim financial reports cover periods shorter than one year. Companies that issue interim reports generally do so quarterly. These reports provide financial statement users with timely information on a firm's progress and are useful in predicting a company's annual financial results. The SEC requires that certain companies disclose selected quarterly financial data in their annual reports to stockholders. Included among the notes, the data reported for each quarter include sales revenue, gross profit, net income, and earnings per share. **Quarterly data** permit financial statement users to analyze such things as the seasonal nature of operations, the impact of diversification on quarterly activity, and whether the firm's activities lead or lag general economic trends.

The Columbia Sportswear Company provides quarterly financial information as supplemental data in its annual report.

Subsequent Events

If a company issues a large amount of securities or suffers a casualty loss after the balance sheet date, this information should be reported in a note, even though the situation arose subsequent to the balance sheet date. Firms are responsible for disclosing any significant events that occur between the balance sheet date and the date the financial statements are issued. This guideline recognizes that it takes several weeks for financial statements to be prepared and audited before they are issued. Events occurring during this period may have a material effect on a firm's operations and should be disclosed. Other examples of **subsequent events** requiring disclosure are sales of assets, significant changes in long-term debt, and acquisitions of other companies.

For example, **Tesla, Inc.**, reported the following subsequent event in its annual report:

> In January 2021, we updated our investment policy to provide us with more flexibility to further diversify and maximize returns on our cash that is not required to maintain adequate operating liquidity. As part of the policy, we may invest a portion of such cash in certain specified alternative reserve assets. Thereafter, we invested an aggregate $1.50 billion in bitcoin under this policy. Moreover, we expect to begin accepting bitcoin as a form of payment for our products in the near future, subject to applicable laws and initially on a limited basis, which we may or may not liquidate upon receipt.

Supplementary Information

Supplementing the financial statements are several additional disclosures—management's discussion and analysis of the financial statements and selected financial data covering a five- to ten-year period along with possible other supplementary disclosures that are either required of certain companies by the SEC or recommended (but not required) by the FASB.

Management Discussion and Analysis

Management may increase the usefulness of financial statements by sharing some of their knowledge about a company's financial condition and operations. This is the purpose of the disclosure devoted to the **management discussion and analysis (MD&A)**. In this supplement to the financial statements, management identifies and comments on events and trends influencing a company's liquidity, operating results, and financial resources. Management's position within a company not only provides it with insights unavailable to outsiders, but also may introduce certain biases into the analysis. Nonetheless, management's comments, interpretations, and explanations should contribute to a better understanding of a company's financial statements.

Comparative Selected Financial Data

The analysis of a company's financial performance is enhanced when financial data for several years are available. By analyzing trends over time, it is possible for a financial statement user to learn much more about a company than would be possible by analyzing only a single year of data. Year-to-year changes may give clues as to a firm's future growth or may highlight areas for concern. Corporate annual reports to stockholders present complete financial statements in comparative form, showing the current year and one or two preceding years. Beyond this, however, the financial statements are supplemented by a summary of selected key financial statistics for a five- or ten-year period. The financial data presented in this historical summary usually include sales revenue, net income, dividends, earnings per share, working capital, and total assets.

SUMMARY OF LEARNING OBJECTIVES

Identify persistent earnings and discuss the content and format of the income statement. (p. 416) LO1

- Persistent earnings are earnings that are likely to recur, while transitory earnings are unlikely to recur.
- The continuing income of a business may be reported in a single-step format or in a multiple-step format.
- Gains and losses from discontinued operations are reported in a special income statement section following income from continuing operations.
- The effect of most changes in accounting principle requires restatement of prior financial statements as if the new method had been applied all along.
- Companies are required to report other comprehensive income in addition to regular income in their financial statements.

Identify the sources of financial information used by investment professionals and explain horizontal financial statements analysis. (p. 419) LO2

- Data sources for investment professionals include published financial statements, filings with the U.S. Securities and Exchange Commission, and statistics available from financial data services.
- A common form of horizontal analysis involves analyzing dollar and percentage changes in comparative financial statements for two or more years.
- Analyzing trend percentages of key figures, such as sales revenue, net income, and total assets for a number of years, related to a base year, is often useful.

Explain vertical financial statement analysis. (p. 424) LO3

- Vertical analysis deals with the relationship of financial statement data for a single year.
- Common-size statements express financial statement items as a percentage of another key item, such as expressing income statement items as a percentage of sales revenue and balance sheet items as a percentage of total assets.

Define and discuss financial ratios for analyzing a firm. (p. 425) LO4

- Ratios for analyzing firm profitability include the gross profit percentage, the profit margin, asset turnover, the return on assets, and the return on common stockholders' equity.
- Ratios for analyzing short-term firm liquidity include the current ratio, quick ratio, operating-cash-flow-to-current-liabilities ratio, accounts receivable turnover, average collection period, inventory turnover, and days' sales in inventory.
- Ratios for analyzing long-term firm solvency include the debt-to-equity ratio, the times-interest-earned ratio, and the operating-cash-flow-to-capital-expenditures ratio.
- Ratios of particular interest to common stockholders include a company's earnings per share, the price-earnings ratio, dividend yield, and the dividend payout ratio.

Discuss the limitations of financial statement analysis. (p. 438) LO5

- When analyzing financial statements, financial statement users must be aware of a firm's accounting methods, the effects of inflation, and the difficulty of currently identifying a firm's industry classification.

Appendix 12A: Describe financial statement disclosures. (p. 440) LO6

- Parenthetical disclosures on the face of the financial statements provide additional detail regarding the item or account.
- Notes to the financial statements provide information on significant accounting policies, explanations of complex or special transactions, details of reported amounts, commitments, contingencies, segments, quarterly data, and subsequent events.
- Supplemental information includes the management discussion and analysis, and comparable selected financial information.

SUMMARY OF FINANCIAL STATEMENT RATIOS

Analyzing Firm Profitability

$$\text{Gross profit percentage} = \frac{\text{Gross profit on sales}}{\text{Net sales}}$$

$$\text{Profit margin} = \frac{\text{Net income}}{\text{Net sales}}$$

$$\text{Asset turnover} = \frac{\text{Net sales}}{\text{Average total assets}}$$

$$\text{Return on assets} = \frac{\text{Net income}}{\text{Average total assets}}$$

$$\text{Return on common stockholders' equity} = \frac{(\text{Net income} - \text{Preferred stock dividends})}{\text{Average common stockholders' equity}}$$

Analyzing Short-Term Firm Liquidity

$$\text{Working capital} = \text{Current assets} - \text{Current liabilities}$$

$$\text{Current ratio} = \frac{\text{Current assets}}{\text{Current liabilities}}$$

$$\text{Quick ratio} = \frac{(\text{Cash and cash equivalents} + \text{Short-term investments} + \text{Accounts receivable})}{\text{Current liabilities}}$$

$$\text{Operating-cash-flow-to-current-liabilities ratio} = \frac{\text{Cash flow from operating activities}}{\text{Average current liabilities}}$$

$$\text{Accounts receivable turnover} = \frac{\text{Net sales}}{\text{Average accounts receivable (net)}}$$

$$\text{Average collection period} = \frac{365}{\text{Accounts receivable turnover}}$$

$$\text{Inventory turnover} = \frac{\text{Cost of goods sold}}{\text{Average inventory}}$$

$$\text{Days' sales in inventory} = \frac{365}{\text{Inventory turnover}}$$

Analyzing Long-Term Firm Solvency

$$\text{Debt-to-equity ratio} = \frac{\text{Total liabilities}}{\text{Total stockholders' equity}}$$

$$\text{Times-interest-earned ratio} = \frac{\text{Income before interest expense and income taxes}}{\text{Interest expense}}$$

$$\text{Operating-cash-flow-to-capital-expenditures ratio} = \frac{\text{Cash flow from operating activities}}{\text{Annual net capital expenditures}}$$

Financial Ratios for Common Stockholders

$$\text{Earnings per share} = \frac{(\text{Net income} - \text{Preferred stock dividends})}{\text{Weighted-average number of common shares outstanding}}$$

$$\text{Price-earnings ratio} = \frac{\text{Market price per share}}{\text{Earnings per share}}$$

$$\text{Dividend yield} = \frac{\text{Annual dividend per share}}{\text{Market price per share}}$$

$$\text{Dividend payout ratio} = \frac{\text{Annual dividend per share}}{\text{Earnings per share}}$$

Concept	Method	Assessment	SUMMARY
How does a company's current performance compare with the prior year?	Income statement and balance sheet for current and prior year. The income statement and balance sheet should be compared using the prior year as the base. Percentage changes in financial statement amounts can be computed as the change between years divided by the base year amount.	Significant changes should be analyzed to determine their reason.	TAKEAWAY 12.1
How do the relationships within a company's income statement and balance sheet compare to those of prior years?	Income statement and balance sheet for current and prior year. Each income statement item should be presented as a percentage of sales revenue and each balance sheet item should be presented as a percentage of total assets. Financial statements in this form are called common-size statements.	The percentages should be analyzed for differences between years and significant changes should be analyzed to determine the reason for any change.	TAKEAWAY 12.2
How much profit is a company generating relative to the amount of assets invested in the company?	Income statement and balance sheet. Calculate the return on assets by dividing net income by the average total assets for the year.	The higher the return on assets, the better a company is doing with respect to generating profits utilizing the assets under its control.	TAKEAWAY 12.3
How financially capable is a company to pay its current liabilities as they come due?	Income statement, balance sheet, and statement of cash flows. Calculate the current ratio, the quick ratio, and the operating-cash-flow-to-current-liabilities ratio.	The higher the ratios, the higher the probability that a company will have the ability to pay its current liabilities as they come due.	TAKEAWAY 12.4
How solvent is a company?	Income statement, balance sheet, and statement of cash flows. Calculate the debt-to-equity ratio, the times-interest-earned ratio, and the operating-cash-flow-to-capital-expenditures ratio.	The higher the times-interest-earned and the operating-cash-flow-to-capital-expenditures ratios, and the lower the debt-to-equity ratio, the greater is a company's solvency.	TAKEAWAY 12.5
How much dividends are common stockholders likely to receive?	Earnings per share, dividends per share, and market price of common stock. Calculate the dividend yield and dividend payout ratio.	The higher the dividend yield and the dividend payout ratio, the greater the company's dividend distribution policy.	TAKEAWAY 12.6

KEY TERMS

Accounts receivable turnover (p. 431)
Asset turnover ratio (p. 428)
Average collection period (days' sales outstanding, or DSO) (p. 432)
Change in accounting estimate (p. 418)
Change in accounting principle (p. 418)
Commitments (p. 441)
Common-size financial statement (p. 424)
Comparative financial statement analysis (p. 420)
Comprehensive income (p. 418)
Contingency (p. 441)
Current ratio (p. 430)
Days' sales in inventory (p. 433)
Debt-to-equity ratio (p. 434)
Discontinued operations (p. 418)
Dividend payout ratio (p. 437)
Dividend yield (p. 437)
Earnings per share (EPS) (p. 417, 436)
Gross profit (gross margin) (p. 427)
Gross profit on sales (p. 427)
Gross profit percentage (p. 427)
Horizontal analysis (p. 420)
Inventory turnover (p. 432)
Management discussion and analysis (MD&A) (p. 442)
Notes to the financial statements (p. 440)
Operating-cash-flow-to-capital-expenditures ratio (p. 435)
Operating-cash-flow-to-current-liabilities ratio (p. 431)

Operating cycle (p. 433)
Parenthetical disclosures (p. 440)
Persistent earnings (p. 416)
Price-earnings ratio (P/E multiple) (p. 436)
Profit margin (return on sales) (p. 427)
Quarterly data (p. 442)
Quick ratio (acid-test ratio) (p. 430)
Return on assets (p. 428)
Return on common stockholders' equity (p. 429)
Segment (p. 442)
Subsequent events (p. 442)
Summary of significant accounting policies (p. 440)
Times-interest-earned ratio (interest coverage ratio) (p. 435)
Transitory earnings (p. 416)
Trend percentages (p. 422)
Vertical analysis (p. 420)
Working capital (p. 429)

SELF-STUDY QUESTIONS

(Answers for the Self-Study Questions are available at the end of this chapter.)

LO1 Homework MBC

1. **Assume that an income statement contains each of the three sections listed below. Which will be the last section presented in the income statement?**
   a. Gross profit
   b. Income from continuing operations
   c. Discontinued operations

LO3 Homework MBC

2. **When constructing a common-sized income statement, all amounts are expressed as a percentage of:**
   a. net income.
   b. gross profit.
   c. net sales.
   d. income from operations.

Questions 3–9 of the Self-Study Questions are based on the following data:

HYDRO COMPANY
Balance Sheet
December 31

Cash	$ 40,000	Current liabilities	$ 80,000
Accounts receivable (net)	80,000	10% Bonds payable	120,000
Inventory	130,000	Common stock	200,000
Plant and equipment (net)	250,000	Retained earnings	100,000
Total Assets	$500,000	Total Liabilities and Stockholders' Equity	$500,000

Sales revenues for the year were $800,000, gross profit was $320,000, and net income was $36,000. The income tax rate was 40 percent. One year ago, accounts receivable (net) were $76,000, inventory was $110,000, total assets were $460,000, and stockholders' equity was $260,000. The bonds payable were outstanding all year and the interest expense for the year was $12,000.

LO4 Homework MBC

3. **The current ratio of Hydro Company at December 31, calculated using the above data, was 3.13, and the company's working capital was $170,000. Which of the following would happen if the firm paid off $20,000 of its current liabilities on January 1 of the following year?**
   a. Both the current ratio and working capital would decrease.
   b. Both the current ratio and working capital would increase.
   c. The current ratio would increase, but working capital would remain the same.
   d. The current ratio would increase, but working capital would decrease.

LO4 Homework MBC

4. **What was the firm's inventory turnover for the year?**
   a. 6.67
   b. 4
   c. 6
   d. 3.69

LO4 Homework MBC

5. **What was the firm's return on common stockholders' equity for the year?**
   a. 25.7 percent
   b. 12.9 percent
   c. 17.1 percent
   d. 21.4 percent

LO4 Homework MBC

6. **What was the firm's average collection period for the year?**
   a. 36.5 days
   b. 37.4 days
   c. 35.6 days
   d. 18.3 days

LO4 

7. **What was the firm's times-interest-earned ratio for the year?**
   a. 4
   b. 3
   c. 5
   d. 6

8. What was the firm's profit margin for the year? LO4 Homework MBC

a. 4.0 percent
b. 4.5 percent
c. 5.0 percent
d. 5.5 percent

9. What was the firm's return on assets for the year? LO4 Homework MBC

a. 6.0 percent
b. 7.0 percent
c. 7.5 percent
d. 8.0 percent

10. When performing trend analysis, each line item is expressed as a percentage of: LO2 Homework MBC

a. net income.
b. the base year amount.
c. the prior year amount.
d. total assets.

11. Recognized limitations of financial statement analysis include each of the following except: LO5 Homework MBC

a. companies in the same industry using different accounting methods.
b. inflation.
c. different levels of profitability between companies.
d. difficulty of classifying by industry conglomerates.

12. Financial statement disclosures include each of the following except: LO6 (Appendix 12A) Homework MBC

a. notes to the financial statements.
b. parenthetical disclosures.
c. supplementary information.
d. promotional giveaways.

QUESTIONS

1. What is the difference between a single-step income statement and a multiple-step income statement?

2. Which of the following amounts would appear only in a multiple-step income statement?

a. Income from continuing operations
b. Income from discontinued operations
c. Gross profit on sales
d. Net income

3. What is a business segment? Why are gains and losses from a discontinued segment reported in a separate section of the income statement?

4. How do horizontal analysis and vertical analysis of financial statements differ?

5. "Financial statement users should focus attention on each item showing a large percentage change from one year to the next." Is this statement correct? Why?

6. What are trend percentages, and how are they calculated? What pitfalls must financial statement users avoid when preparing trend percentages?

7. What are common-size financial statements, and how are they used?

8. What item is the key figure (that is, 100 percent) in a common-size income statement? A common-size balance sheet?

9. During the past year, Lite Company had net income of $5 million, and Scanlon Company had net income of $8 million. Both companies manufacture electrical components for the construction industry. What additional information would you need to compare the profitability of the two companies?

10. Under what circumstances can the profit margin be used to assess the profitability of a company? Can this ratio be used to compare the profitability of companies from different industries? Explain.

11. What is the relationship between asset turnover, return on assets, and profit margin?

12. Blare Company had a profit margin of 6.5 percent and an asset turnover of 2.40. What is Blare's return on assets?

13. What does the return on common stockholders' equity measure?

14. How does the quick ratio differ from the current ratio?

15. For each of the following ratios, is a high ratio or low ratio considered, in general, a positive sign?

a. Current ratio
b. Quick ratio
c. Operating-cash-flow-to-current-liabilities ratio
d. Accounts receivable turnover
e. Average collection period
f. Inventory turnover
g. Days' sales in inventory

16. What is the significance of the debt-to-equity ratio, and how is it computed?

17. What does the times-interest-earned ratio indicate, and how is it calculated?

18. What does the operating-cash-flow-to-capital-expenditures ratio measure?

19. Clair, Inc., earned $4.50 per share of common stock in the current year and paid dividends of $2.34 per share. The most recent market price per share of the common stock is $46.80. What is the company's (a) price-earnings ratio, (b) dividend yield, and (c) dividend payout ratio?

20. What are two inherent limitations of financial statement data?

DATA ANALYTICS

The assignments in this Data Analytics section are designed to familiarize you with the tools used in analyzing data and communicating the results. Appendix F provides an in-depth discussion of data analytics and blockchain technology.

DA12-1. Analyzing Trends in the Price-to-Earnings Ratio using Excel

Data Analytics

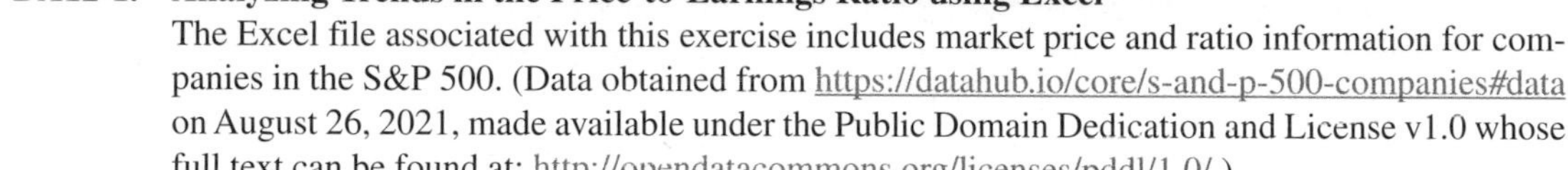

The Excel file associated with this exercise includes market price and ratio information for companies in the S&P 500. (Data obtained from https://datahub.io/core/s-and-p-500-companies#data on August 26, 2021, made available under the Public Domain Dedication and License v1.0 whose full text can be found at: http://opendatacommons.org/licenses/pddl/1.0/.)

For this exercise, we examine trends in the price-to-earnings ratio of S&P 500 companies by industry segment. The price-to-earnings ratio measures the amount an investor is willing to pay per share of stock for each dollar of earnings per share. An increase in this ratio generally means that an investor would have a higher expectation for company profits in the future. In the first analysis, we calculate the average value or mean of the price-to-earnings ratio for each segment. In the second analysis, we calculate the median value of the price-to-earnings ratio for each segment. Lastly, we compare the average and median ratio results and analyze the cause of the differences.

REQUIRED

Price-to Earnings Ratio

$$\frac{\text{Market price per share}}{\text{Earnings per share}}$$

1. Download Excel file DA12-1 found in myBusinessCourse.
2. Create a PivotTable (PivotTable 1) showing the average Price/Earnings ratio by sector. *Hint:* With your cursor in your data, select Insert, PivotChart. Add Sector to Rows and Price/Earnings to Values; select Average for the display of Price/Earnings by right-clicking on an amount in the PivotTable, clicking Value Field Settings, and selecting Average.
3. Remove the grand total row (which is irrelevant for this table). *Hint:* Click on the Design tab, Grand totals, Off for rows & columns.
4. Change display of your data to show two decimal places. *Hint:* Right-click on an amount in the PivotTable, click on number format, and make change.
5. Sort your PivotTable in the order of highest to lowest values. *Hint:* Right-click on an amount in the PivotTable; click Sort, Sort Largest to smallest.
6. Indicate which sector has the highest and which sector has the lowest average price/earnings ratio.
7. Copy original PivotTable, paste below the original to create PivotTable 2, change the calculation of price/earnings to now display maximum value, and sort Price/Earnings values from largest to smallest values. *Hint:* Right-click on an amount in the PivotTable, and click Value Field Settings.
8. Indicate which sector has the highest and which sector has the lowest maximum price/earnings ratio.
9. Copy original PivotTable, paste below PivotTable 2 to create PivotTable 3, change the calculation of price/earnings to now display minimum value, and sort Price/Earnings values from largest to smallest values. *Hint:* Click the i button next to Average of Price/Earnings and select Min.
10. Indicate which sector has the highest and which sector has the lowest minimum price/earnings ratio.
11. Read the following article, "Stuck in the Middle—Mean vs. Median," by Dr. Dieter Schremmer found at the following link: https://www.clinfo.eu/mean-median/.
12. Compute the median value of the Price/Earnings ratio for the Energy sector and for the Industrials sector. *Hint:* Median is not a calculation option within the PivotTables. Instead, double-click on the dollar amount in the PivotTable for Energy to open up a new sheet with the underlying data. In a new cell (at least two rows below the table) calculate the median of the Price/Earnings data: =MEDIAN(xx). Repeat steps for the Industrials sector.
13. Compute the difference between the Maximum Price/Earnings (see PivotTable 2) and the Minimum Price/Earnings (see PivotTable 3) for both sectors: Energy and Industrials.

14. Compare the median values obtained in part 12 to the average values listed in PivotTable 1 and answer the following question: What caused the differences between the mean and median values in your calculations?

DA12-2. Critically Analyzing a Visualization in Excel

The financial information in the Excel file associated with this exercise was obtained from 10-K reports for Costco Wholesale Corporation. In this exercise, we examine how changing the starting point (baseline) of the y-axis from 0.0 impacts the chart that is created. The chart that is created for Costco examines return on equity over a five-year period. The return on equity ratio measures the return of the stockholders' investment in the company. An increase in the ratio generally means that the company is more efficiently using its equity to generate profits.

REQUIRED

1. Download Excel file DA12-2 found in myBusinessCourse.
2. Calculate the return on equity for Costco for Year 2 through Year 6 in Excel. Carry your answers to three decimal places.
3. Create a line chart showing the return on equity for Year 2 through Year 6. Note that when you use the default setting, the y-axis starts at point 0.0. *Hint:* Highlight data; click Insert, Line. You may need to edit the data selections. Right-click inside the chart, Select Data. The Series (y-axis) should be the ROE; the Category (x-axis) should be Years 2–6.

   Return on equity
   $$\frac{\text{Net income}}{\text{Average stockholders' equity}}$$

4. Create a second line chart showing the return on equity for Year 2 through Year 6. For this second chart, change the scale of the y-axis to start at 0.17 and to end at 0.27. *Hint:* Right-click inside the y-axis scale and select Format Axis. Set Minimum bound as 0.17 and Maximum bound as 0.27 on the column chart icon tab.
5. Indicate which of the following descriptions best depicts the trends in Chart 1 and the description that best depicts the trends in Chart 2:
   a. Return on equity increased sharply from Year 2 to Year 4, stabilized for a year and dropped more rapidly in Year 5.
   b. Return on equity gradually increased from Year 2 to Year 4, and remained fairly stable through Year 6.
6. Compute the percentage change in ROE from Year 2 to Year 3, Year 3 to Year 4, Year 4 to Year 5, and Year 5 to Year 6 in Excel.
7. Compare Chart 1 to Chart 2.

DA12-3. Preparing Tableau Visualizations to Analyze the Use of Assets Through Asset Turnover

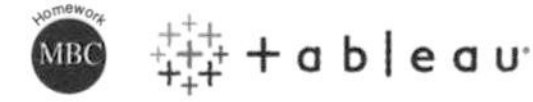

Refer to PF-26 in Appendix F. This problem uses Tableau to analyze asset utilization of S&P 500 companies in certain segments through the asset turnover ratio.

DA12-4. Preparing Tableau Visualizations to Decompose Return on Equity Using the DuPont Method: Part 1, Part II, Part III

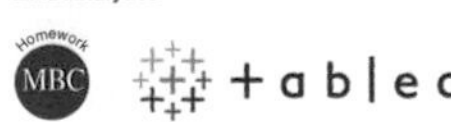

Refer to PF-29, PF-30, and PF-31 in Appendix F. This three-part problem uses Tableau to decompose the return on equity ratio of S&P 500 companies using the DuPont method. The final part of the problem includes the creation of an interactive dashboard.

Assignments with the MBC logo in the margin are available in myBusinessCourse. See the Preface of the book for details.

SHORT EXERCISES

Use the following financial data for Hi-Tech Instruments to answer Short Exercises 12-1 through 12-10:

For the Year Ended December 31 (Thousands of Dollars, except Earnings per Share)	
Sales revenue	$210,000
Cost of goods sold	125,000
Net income	8,300
Dividends	2,600
Earnings per share	4.15

HI-TECH INSTRUMENTS, INC.
Balance Sheets

(Thousands of Dollars)	December 31 Current Year	Prior Year
Assets		
Cash	$ 18,300	$ 18,000
Accounts receivable (net)	46,000	41,000
Inventory	39,500	43,700
Total Current Assets	103,800	102,700
Plant assets (net)	52,600	50,500
Other assets	15,600	13,800
Total Assets	$172,000	$167,000
Liabilities and Stockholders' Equity		
Notes payable—banks	$ 6,000	$ 6,000
Accounts payable	22,500	18,700
Accrued liabilities	16,500	21,000
Total Current Liabilities	45,000	45,700
9% Bonds payable	40,000	40,000
Total Liabilities	85,000	85,700
Common stock, $25 par value (2,000,000 shares)	50,000	50,000
Retained earnings	37,000	31,300
Total Stockholders' Equity	87,000	81,300
Total Liabilities and Stockholders' Equity	$172,000	$167,000

Industry Average Ratios for Competitors	
Quick ratio	1.3
Current ratio	2.4
Accounts receivable turnover	5.9 times
Inventory turnover	3.5 times
Debt-to-equity ratio	0.73
Gross profit percentage	42.8 percent
Profit margin	4.5 percent
Return on assets	7.6 percent

LO4 Homework MBC **SE12-1. Quick Ratio** Calculate the company's quick ratio and compare the result to the industry average.

LO4 Homework MBC **SE12-2. Current Ratio** Calculate the company's current ratio and compare the result to the industry average.

LO4 Homework MBC **SE12-3. Accounts Receivable Turnover** Calculate the company's accounts receivable turnover and compare the result to the industry average.

LO4 Homework MBC **SE12-4. Inventory Turnover** Calculate the company's inventory turnover and compare the result to the industry average.

LO4 Homework MBC **SE12-5. Debt-to-Equity Ratio** Calculate the company's debt-to-equity ratio and compare the result to the industry average.

LO4 Homework MBC **SE12-6. Gross Profit Percentage** Calculate the company's gross profit percentage and compare the result to the industry average.

LO4 Homework MBC **SE12-7. Profit Margin** Calculate the company's profit margin and compare the result to the industry average.

LO4 Homework MBC **SE12-8. Return on Assets** Calculate the company's return on assets and compare the result to the industry average.

SE12-9. Dividends per Share Calculate the company's dividend paid per share of common stock. What was the dividend payout ratio? LO4

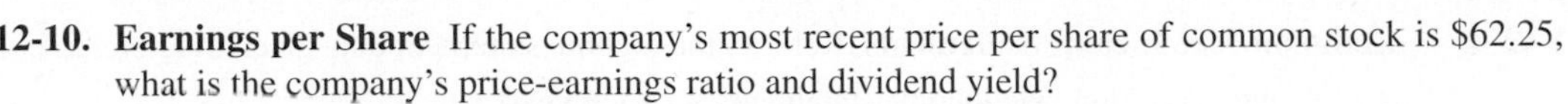

SE12-10. Earnings per Share If the company's most recent price per share of common stock is $62.25, what is the company's price-earnings ratio and dividend yield? LO4

SE12-11. Persistent Earnings Identify each of the following items as either (P) persistent or (T) transitory. LO1

a. Sale of merchandise
b. Settlement of a lawsuit
c. Interest income
d. Payment to vendors
e. Loss from expropriations of property by a foreign government

SE12-12. Horizontal Analysis Total assets were $1,000,000 in Year 3, $900,000 in Year 2, and $950,000 in Year 1. What was the percentage change from Year 1 to Year 2 and from Year 2 to Year 3? Was the change an increase or a decrease? LO2

SE12-13. Common-Size Income Statement A partial common-size income statement for Prag Company for three years is shown below. LO3

Item	Year 3	Year 2	Year 1
Net sales	100.0	100.0	100.0
Cost of goods sold	60.5	63.0	62.5
Other expenses	21.0	19.0	20.5

Did Prag's net income as a percentage of net sales increase, remain the same, or decrease over the three-year period?

SE12-14. Financial Statement Analysis Limitations Which of the following is not considered a limitation of financial statement analysis? LO5

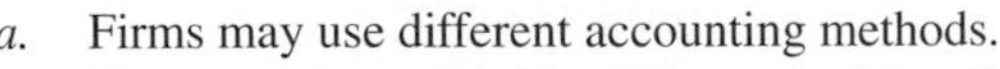

a. Firms may use different accounting methods.
b. Firms may be audited by different auditing firms.
c. Inflation may distort trend analysis.
d. It may be difficult to classify large conglomerate firms by industry.

SE12-15. Financial Statement Disclosures Which of the following is not a common form of financial statement disclosure? LO6 (Appendix 12A)

a. Notes to financial statements
b. Supplemental information
c. Parenthetical disclosure
d. Bullet points

EXERCISES

E12-1. Income Statement Sections During the current year, Dale Corporation sold a segment of its business at a gain of $210,000. Until it was sold, the segment had a current period operating loss of $75,000. The company had $850,000 income from continuing operations for the current year. Prepare the lower part of the income statement, beginning with the $850,000 income from continuing operations. Follow tax allocation procedures, assuming that all changes in income are subject to a 35 percent income tax rate. Disregard earnings per share disclosures. LO1

E12-2. Earnings per Share Lucky Corporation began the year with a simple capital structure consisting of 240,000 shares of outstanding common stock. On April 1, 5,000 additional common shares were issued, and another 30,000 common shares were issued on August 1. The company had net income for the year of $589,375. Calculate the earnings per share of common stock. LO4

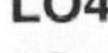

E12-3. Comparative Income Statements Consider the following income statement data from the Ross Company: LO2

	Current Year	Prior Year
Sales revenue	$550,000	$450,000
Cost of goods sold	336,000	279,000
Selling expenses	105,000	99,000
Administrative expenses	60,000	50,000
Income tax expense	7,800	5,400

a. Prepare a comparative income statement, showing increases and decreases in dollars and in percentages.
b. Comment briefly on the changes between the two years.

LO3 Homework MBC **E12-4. Common-Size Income Statements** Refer to the income statement data given in Exercise E12-3.

a. Prepare common-size income statements for each year.
b. Compare the common-size income statements and comment briefly.

LO4 Homework MBC **E12-5. Ratios Analyzing Firm Profitability** The following information is available for Buhler Company:

Annual Data	Current Year	Prior Year
Net sales	$8,600,000	$8,200,000
Gross profit on sales	3,050,000	2,736,000
Net income	567,600	488,000

December 31 Year-End Data	Current Year	Prior Year
Total assets	$6,500,000	$6,000,000
Stockholders' equity	4,000,000	3,200,000

Calculate the following ratios for the current year:

a. Gross profit percentage
b. Profit margin
c. Asset turnover
d. Return on assets
e. Return on common stockholders' equity (Buhler Company has no preferred stock.)

LO4 Homework MBC **E12-6. Working Capital and Short-Term Liquidity Ratios** Bell Company has a current ratio of 3.00 on December 31. On that date the company's current assets are as follows:

Cash	$ 29,000
Short-term investments	49,400
Accounts receivable (net)	170,000
Inventory	200,000
Prepaid expenses	11,600
Current assets	$460,000

Bell Company's current liabilities at the beginning of the year were $140,000 and during the year its operating activities provided a cash flow of $60,000.

a. What are the firm's current liabilities on December 31?
b. What is the firm's working capital on December 31?
c. What is the quick ratio on December 31?
d. What is Bell's operating-cash-flow-to-current-liabilities ratio?

LO4 Homework MBC **E12-7. Accounts Receivable and Inventory Ratios** Bell Company, whose current assets at December 31 are shown in Exercise E12-6A, had net sales for the year of $900,000 and cost of goods sold of $550,000. At the beginning of the year, Bell's accounts receivable (net) were $160,000 and its inventory was $195,000.

a. What is the company's accounts receivable turnover for the year?
b. What is the company's average collection period for the year?
c. What is the company's inventory turnover for the year?
d. What is the company's days' sales in inventory for the year?

LO4 Homework MBC **E12-8. Ratios Analyzing Long-Term Firm Solvency** The following information is available for Antler Company:

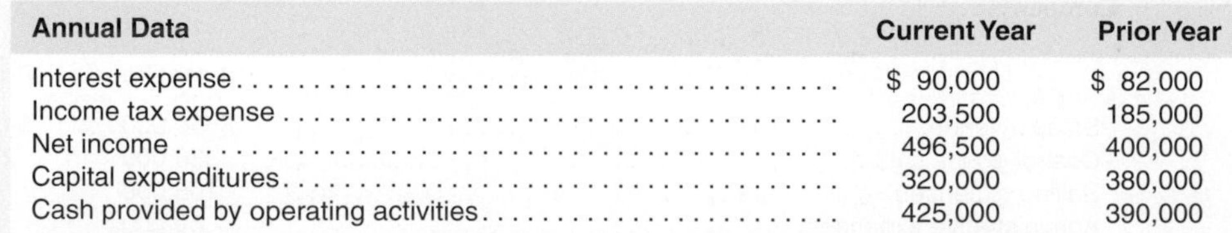

Annual Data	Current Year	Prior Year
Interest expense	$ 90,000	$ 82,000
Income tax expense	203,500	185,000
Net income	496,500	400,000
Capital expenditures	320,000	380,000
Cash provided by operating activities	425,000	390,000

December 31 Year-End Data	Current Year	Prior Year
Total liabilities	$2,400,000	$1,900,000
Total stockholders' equity	4,000,000	3,800,000

Calculate the following ratios for the current year:

a. Debt-to-equity ratio
b. Times-interest-earned ratio
c. Operating-cash-flow-to-capital-expenditures ratio

E12-9. Financial Ratios for Common Stockholders Kluster Corporation has only common stock outstanding. The firm reported earnings per share of $5.25 for the year. During the year, Kluster paid dividends of $2.10 per share. At year end the current market price of the stock was $63 per share. Calculate the following: **LO4** Homework MBC

a. Year-end price-earnings ratio
b. Dividend yield
c. Dividend payout ratio

E12-10. Financial Statement Limitations You have been asked to perform financial statement analysis on the Patton Company. The Patton Company is a large chain of retail outlets that sells a wide range of household items. Last year the company introduced its own credit card and is pleased that profit from this financing activity now accounts for more than 20 percent of the company's total profit. As part of your analysis you have chosen to compare the Patton Company to Johnson Stores, a much larger chain of stores. Johnson Stores sells household items and groceries, but it does not have its own credit card. Your analysis includes both horizontal trend analysis and vertical analysis. Identify some of the limitations from the description above. **LO5**

E12-11. Financial Statement Notes The notes to financial statements present information on significant accounting policies, complex or special transactions, details of reported amounts, commitments, contingencies, segments, quarterly data, and subsequent events. Indicate which type of note disclosure is illustrated by each of the following notes: **LO6 (Appendix 12A)**

a. The company has agreed to purchase seven EMB-120 aircraft and related spare parts. The aggregate cost of these aircraft is approximately $41,250,000, subject to a cost escalation provision. The aircraft are scheduled to be delivered over the next two fiscal years.
b. The company has deferred certain costs related to major accounting and information systems enhancements that are anticipated to benefit future years. Upon completion, the related cost is amortized over a period not exceeding five years.
c. The company has guaranteed loans and leases of independent distributors approximating $27,500,000 as of December 31 of the current year.
d. An officer of the company is also a director of a major raw material supplier of the company. The amount of raw material purchases from this supplier approximated $410,000 in the current year.

PROBLEMS

P12-1. Income Statement Format The following information from Belvidere Company's current operations is available: **LO1**

Administrative expenses	$ 73,000
Cost of goods sold	464,000
Sales revenue	772,000
Selling expenses	87,000
Interest expense	10,000
Loss from operations of discontinued segment	60,000
Gain on disposal of discontinued segment	40,000
Income taxes:	
Amount applicable to ordinary operations	60,000
Reduction applicable to loss from operations of discontinued segment	24,000
Amount applicable to gain on disposal of discontinued segment	16,000

Required

a. Prepare a multiple-step income statement. (Disregard earnings per share.)

b. Prepare a single-step income statement. (Disregard earnings per share.)

LO4 **P12-2. Earnings per Share** Leland Corporation began the year with 150,000 shares of common stock outstanding. On March 1 an additional 10,000 shares of common stock were issued. On August 1, another 16,000 shares of common stock were issued. On November 1, 6,000 shares of common stock were acquired as Treasury Stock. Leland Corporation's net income for the calendar year is $516,000.

Required

Calculate the company's earnings per share.

LO1, 4 **P12-3. Earnings per Share and Multiple-Step Income Statement** The following summarized data relate to Bowden Corporation's current operations:

Sales revenue	$760,000
Cost of goods sold	450,000
Selling expenses	65,000
Administrative expenses	72,000
Loss on sale of equipment	5,000
Income tax expense	42,000
Shares of common stock	
Outstanding at January 1	20,000 shares
Additional issued at May 1	7,000 shares
Additional issued at November 1	2,000 shares

Required

Prepare a multiple-step income statement for Bowden Corporation for the year. Include earnings per share disclosure at the bottom of the income statement.

LO2 **P12-4. Trend Percentages** Net sales, net income, and total asset figures for Vibrant Controls, Inc., for five consecutive years are given below (Vibrant manufactures pollution controls):

	Annual Amounts (Thousands of Dollars)				
	Year 1	Year 2	Year 3	Year 4	Year 5
Net sales	$71,500	$79,800	$85,275	$88,400	$94,700
Net income	3,200	3,650	3,900	4,250	4,790
Total assets	42,500	46,200	48,700	51,000	54,900

Required

a. Calculate trend percentages, using Year 1 as the base year.

b. Calculate the profit margin for each year. (Rates above 2.8 percent are considered good for manufacturers of pollution controls; rates above 6.4 percent are considered very good.)

c. Comment on the results of your analysis.

LO4 **P12-5. Changes in Various Ratios** Presented below is selected information for Brimmer Company:

	Current Year	Prior Year
Sales revenue	$920,000	$840,000
Cost of goods sold	575,000	545,000
Interest expense	20,000	20,000
Income tax expense	27,000	30,000
Net income	61,000	52,000
Cash flow from operating activities	65,000	55,000
Capital expenditures	45,000	45,000
Accounts receivable (net), December 31	126,000	120,000
Inventory, December 31	196,000	160,000
Stockholders' equity, December 31	450,000	400,000
Total assets, December 31	750,000	675,000

Required

a. Calculate the following ratios for the current year. The prior year results are given for comparative purposes.

		Prior Year
1.	Gross profit percentage	33.5 percent
2.	Return on assets	8.3 percent
3.	Profit margin	6.2 percent
4.	Return on common stockholders' equity (no preferred stock was outstanding)	13.9 percent
5.	Accounts receivable turnover	7.50
6.	Average collection period	48.7 days
7.	Inventory turnover	3.61
8.	Times-interest-earned ratio	4.80
9.	Operating-cash-flow-to-capital-expenditures ratio	1.22

b. Comment on the changes between the two years.

P12-6. Ratios from Comparative and Common-Size Data Consider the following financial statements for Waverly Company. **LO2, 3, 4**

During the current year, management obtained additional bond financing to enlarge its production facilities. The company faced higher production costs during the year for such things as fuel, materials, and freight. Because of temporary government price controls, a planned price increase on products was delayed several months.

As a holder of both common and preferred stock, you decide to analyze the financial statements:

WAVERLY COMPANY
Balance Sheets
(Thousands of Dollars)

	December 31	
	Current Year	**Prior Year**
Assets		
Cash and cash equivalents	$ 19,000	$ 12,000
Accounts receivable (net)	55,000	43,000
Inventory	120,000	105,000
Prepaid expenses	20,000	14,000
Plant and other assets (net)	471,000	411,000
Total Assets	$685,000	$585,000
Liabilities and Stockholders' Equity		
Current liabilities	$ 91,000	$ 82,000
10% Bonds payable	225,000	160,000
9% Preferred stock, $50 Par Value	75,000	75,000
Common stock, $10 Par Value	200,000	200,000
Retained earnings	94,000	68,000
Total Liabilities and Stockholders' Equity	$685,000	$585,000

WAVERLY COMPANY
Income Statements
(Thousands of Dollars)

	Current Year	**Prior Year**
Sales revenue	$820,000	$678,000
Cost of goods sold	545,000	433,920
Gross profit on sales	275,000	244,080
Selling and administrative expenses	175,000	149,200
Income before interest expense and income taxes	100,000	94,880
Interest expense	22,500	16,000
Income before income taxes	77,500	78,880
Income tax expense	22,900	21,300
Net income	$ 54,600	$ 57,580
Other financial data (thousands of dollars)		
Cash provided by operating activities	$ 65,200	$ 60,500
Preferred stock dividends	6,750	6,750

Required

a. Calculate the following for each year: current ratio, quick ratio, operating-cash-flow-to-current-liabilities ratio (current liabilities were $77,000,000 at January 1 of the prior year), inventory turnover (inventory was $87,000,000 at January 1 of the prior year), debt-to-equity ratio, times-interest-earned ratio, return on assets (total assets were $490,000,000 at January 1 of the prior year), and return on common stockholders' equity (common stockholders' equity was $235,000,000 at January 1 of the prior year).

b. Calculate common-size percentages for each year's income statement.

c. Comment on the results of your analysis.

LO4 **P12-7. Constructing Statements from Ratio Data** The following are the financial statements for Omicron Company, with almost all dollar amounts missing:

OMICRON COMPANY
Balance Sheet
December 31

Cash	$?	Current liabilities	$?
Accounts receivable (net)	?	8% Bonds payable	?
Inventory	?	Common stock	?
Equipment (net)	?	Retained earnings	950,000
Total Assets	$6,000,000	Total Liabilities and Stockholders' Equity	$6,000,000

OMICRON COMPANY
Income Statement
For the Year Ended December 31

Sales revenue	$?
Cost of goods sold	?
Gross profit	?
Selling and administrative expenses	?
Income before interest expense and income taxes	?
Interest expense	80,000
Income before income taxes	?
Income tax expense (30%)	?
Net income	$580,000

The following information is available about Omicron Company's financial statements:

1. Quick ratio, 0.95.
2. Inventory turnover (inventory at January 1 was $924,000), 5 times.
3. Profit margin, 8.0 percent.
4. Accounts receivable turnover (accounts receivable (net) at January 1 were $860,000), 8 times.
5. Gross profit percentage, 32 percent.
6. Return on common stockholders' equity (common stockholders' equity at January 1 was $3,300,000), 16 percent.
7. The interest expense relates to the bonds payable that were outstanding all year.

Required

Compute the missing amounts, and complete the financial statements of Omicron Company. *Hint:* Complete the income statement first.

LO4 **P12-8. Ratios Compared with Industry Averages** Because you own the common stock of Phantom Corporation, a paper manufacturer, you decide to analyze the firm's performance for the most recent year. The following data are taken from the firm's latest annual report:

December 31	Current Year	Prior Year
Quick assets	$ 700,000	$ 552,000
Inventory and prepaid expenses	372,000	312,000
Other assets	4,788,000	4,200,000
Total Assets	$5,860,000	$5,064,000
Current liabilities	$ 724,000	$ 564,000
10% Bonds payable	1,440,000	1,440,000
8% Preferred stock, $100 par value	480,000	480,000
Common stock, $10 par value	2,700,000	2,160,000
Retained earnings	516,000	420,000
Total Liabilities and Stockholders' Equity	$5,860,000	$5,064,000

For the current year, net sales amount to $11,280,000, net income is $575,000, and preferred stock dividends paid are $42,000.

Required

a. Calculate the following ratios for the current year:

1. Profit margin
2. Return on assets
3. Return on common stockholders' equity
4. Quick ratio
5. Current ratio
6. Debt-to-equity ratio

b. Trade association statistics and information provided by credit agencies reveal the following data on industry norms:

	Median	Upper Quartile
Profit margin	4.9 percent	8.6 percent
Return on assets	6.5 percent	11.2 percent
Return on common stockholders' equity	10.6 percent	17.3 percent
Quick ratio	1.0	1.8
Current ratio	1.8	3.0
Debt-to-equity ratio	1.08	0.66

Compare Phantom Corporation's performance with industry performance.

P12-9. **Ratios Compared with Industry Averages** Packard Plastics, Inc., manufactures various plastic and synthetic products. Financial statement data for the firm follow: LO4

	Current Year (Thousands of Dollars, except Earnings per Share)
Sales revenue	$825,000
Cost of goods sold	540,000
Net income	50,500
Dividends	15,000
Earnings per share	4.25

PACKARD PLASTICS, INC.
Balance Sheets
(Thousands of Dollars)

	December 31	
	Current Year	Prior Year
Assets		
Cash	$ 4,100	$ 2,700
Accounts receivable (net)	66,900	60,900
Inventory	148,000	140,000
Total Current Assets	219,000	203,600
Plant assets (net)	215,000	194,000
Other assets	13,900	3,900
Total Assets	$447,900	$401,500

PACKARD PLASTICS, INC.
Balance Sheets
(Thousands of Dollars)

	December 31	
	Current Year	Prior Year
Liabilities and Stockholders' Equity		
Notes payable—banks	$ 31,000	$ 25,000
Accounts payable	27,600	23,000
Accrued liabilities	25,100	24,800
Total Current Liabilities	83,700	72,800
10% Bonds payable	150,000	150,000
Total Liabilities	233,700	222,800
Common stock, $10 par value (12,500,000 shares)	125,000	125,000
Retained earnings	89,200	53,700
Total Stockholders' Equity	214,200	178,700
Total Liabilities and Stockholders' Equity	$447,900	$401,500

Required

a. Using the given data, calculate items 1 through 8 below for the current year. Compare the performance of Packard Plastics, Inc., with the following industry averages and comment on its operations.

	Median Ratios for Manufacturers of Plastic and Synthetic Products
1. Quick ratio	1.2
2. Current ratio	1.9
3. Accounts receivable turnover	7.9 times
4. Inventory turnover	7.8 times
5. Debt-to-equity ratio	0.95
6. Gross profit percentage	32.7 percent
7. Profit margin	3.5 percent
8. Return on assets	6.3 percent

b. Calculate the dividends paid per share of common stock. What was the dividend payout ratio?

c. If the most recent price per share of common stock is $50.25, what is the price-earnings ratio? The dividend yield?

LO2, 4 **P12-10. Financial Statement Notes: Quarterly Data** Quarterly data are presented below for Company A and Company B. One of these companies is Gibson Greetings, Inc., which manufactures and sells greeting cards. The other company is Hon Industries, Inc., which manufactures and sells office furniture. Both companies are on a calendar year basis.

	(Amounts in Thousands)				
	First Quarter	Second Quarter	Third Quarter	Fourth Quarter	Year
Company A					
Net sales	$186,111	$177,537	$203,070	$213,608	$780,326
Gross profit	55,457	53,643	64,024	69,374	242,498
Company B					
Net sales	$ 84,896	$ 83,796	$142,137	$235,336	$546,165
Gross profit	53,900	52,983	66,018	104,961	277,862

Required

a. Compute the percent of annual net sales generated each quarter by Company A. Round to the nearest percent.

b. Compute the percent of annual net sales generated each quarter by Company B. Round to the nearest percent.

c. Which company has the most seasonal business? Briefly explain.

d. Which company is Gibson Greetings, Inc.? Hon Industries, Inc.? Briefly explain.

e. Which company's interim quarterly data are probably most useful for predicting annual results? Briefly explain.

SERIAL PROBLEM: ANGEL CITY GREETINGS

(Note: This is a continuation of the Serial Problem: Angel City Greetings from Chapter 1 through Chapter 11.)

SP12. Kate is very pleased with the results of the first year of operations for Angel City Greetings. She ended the year on a high note, with the company's reputation for producing quality cards leading to more business than she can currently manage. Kate is considering expanding and bringing in several employees. In order to do this, she will need to find a larger location and also purchase more equipment. All this means additional financing. Kate has asked you to look at her year-end financial statements as if you were a banker considering giving Kate a loan. Comment on your findings and provide calculations to support your comments.

ANGEL CITY GREETINGS
Income Statement
Year Ended August 31

Sales revenue	$135,000
Cost of goods sold	72,000
Gross profit	63,000
Operating expenses	
Wages	18,000
Consulting	11,850
Insurance	1,200
Utilities	2,400
Depreciation	3,250
Total operating expenses	36,700
Income from operations	26,300
Interest expense	900
Income before income tax	25,400
Income tax expense	8,900
Net income	$ 16,500

ANGEL CITY GREETINGS
Balance Sheet
August 31

Assets	
Current assets	
Cash	$12,300
Accounts receivable	11,000
Inventory	16,000
Prepaid insurance	1,000
Total current assets	40,300
Equipment	17,500
Accumulated depreciation	3,250
Total assets	$54,550

ANGEL CITY GREETINGS Balance Sheet August 31	
Liabilities	
Current liabilities	
Accounts payable	$ 6,200
Unearned revenue	1,250
Other current liabilities	1,900
Total current liabilities	9,350
Note payable	15,000
Total liabilities	24,350
Stockholders' equity	
Common stock	500
Additional paid-in-capital	9,500
Preferred stock	5,000
Retained earnings	15,200
Total stockholders' equity	30,200
Total liabilities and stockholders' equity	$54,550

ANGEL CITY GREETINGS Statement of Cash Flows Year Ended August 31	
Cash flow from operating activities	
Net income	$16,500
Add depreciation	3,250
Increase in accounts receivable	(11,000)
Increase in inventory	(16,000)
Increase in prepaid expenses	(1,000)
Increase in accounts payable	6,200
Increase in unearned revenue	1,250
Increase in other current liabilities	1,900
Cash provided by operating activities	1,100
Cash flow from investing activities	
Purchase of equipment	(17,500)
Cash used by investing activities	(17,500)
Cash flow from financing activities	
Proceeds from bank note	15,000
Issuance of common stock	10,000
Issuance of preferred stock	5,000
Cash dividends	(1,300)*
Cash provided by financing activities	28,700
Net increase in cash	12,300
Cash at beginning of year	0
Cash at end of year	$12,300

*Kate issued cash dividends on both the common stock and the preferred stock. There are 50 preferred shares outstanding and 500 common shares outstanding. The dividends that Kate paid were $6 per share on the preferred shares and $2 per share on the common shares.

BEYOND THE NUMBERS

REPORTING AND ANALYSIS

Columbia Sportswear Company

BTN12-1. Financial Reporting Problem: Columbia Sportswear Company The financial statements for the Columbia Sportswear Company can be found in Appendix A at the end of this book.

You are considering an investment in Columbia Sportswear after a recent outdoor trip in which you really liked some of the clothes you purchased from the company. You decide to do an analysis of the company's financial statements in order to help you make an informed decision.

Required

a. Using the five-year selected financial data reported in the annual report, produce a five-year trend analysis, using 2016 as a base year, of (1) net sales, (2) net income, and (3) total assets. Comment on your findings.

b. Calculate the (1) gross profit percentage, (2) profit margin, and (3) return on assets for 2019 and 2020. Comment on Columbia Sportswear's profitability. (2018 total assets in thousands = $2,368,721)

c. Calculate the (1) current ratio, (2) quick ratio, and (3) operating-cash-flow-to-current-liabilities ratio for 2019 and 2020. (2018 current liabilities in thousands = $572,882) Comment on Columbia Sportswear's liquidity.

d. Calculate the debt-to-equity ratio for 2019 and 2020. Comment on Columbia Sportswear's solvency.

BTN12-2. **Comparative Analysis Problem: Columbia Sportswear Company vs Under Armour, Inc.** The financial statements for the Columbia Sportswear Company can be found in Appendix A at the end of this book, and the financial statements of Under Armour, Inc., can be found in Appendix B.

Columbia Sportswear Company
Under Armour, Inc.

Required

Based on the information from the financial statements of each company, do the following:

a. Calculate the percentage change in (1) net sales, (2) net income, (3) cash flow from operating activities, and (4) total assets from 2019 to 2020.

b. What conclusions can you draw from this analysis?

BTN12-3. **Business Decision Problem** Crescent Paints, Inc., a paint manufacturer, has been in business for five years. The company has had modest profits and has experienced few operating difficulties until this year, when president Alice Becknell discussed her company's working capital problems with you, a loan officer at Granite Bank. Becknell explained that expanding her firm has created difficulties in meeting obligations when they come due and in taking advantage of cash discounts offered by manufacturers for the timely payment of the company's accounts payable. She would like to borrow $50,000 from Granite Bank. At your request, Becknell submits the following financial data for the past two years:

	Year 5	Year 4
Sales revenue	$2,000,000	$1,750,000
Cost of goods sold	1,320,000	1,170,000
Net income	42,000	33,600
Dividends	22,000	18,000
December 31, Year 3, data		
Total assets	1,100,000	
Accounts receivable (net)	205,000	
Inventory	350,000	

CRESCENT PAINTS, INC.
Balance Sheets

	Dec. 31, Year 5	Dec. 31, Year 4
Assets		
Cash	$ 31,000	$ 50,000
Accounts receivable (net)	345,000	250,000
Inventory	525,000	425,000
Prepaid expenses	11,000	6,000
Total Current Assets	912,000	731,000
Plant assets (net)	483,000	444,000
Total Assets	$1,395,000	$ 1,175,000

CRESCENT PAINTS, INC. Balance Sheets	Dec. 31, Year 5	Dec. 31, Year 4
Liabilities and Stockholders' Equity		
Notes payable—banks	$ 100,000	$ 35,000
Accounts payable	244,000	190,000
Accrued liabilities	96,000	85,000
Total Current Liabilities	440,000	310,000
10% Mortgage payable	190,000	250,000
Total Liabilities	630,000	560,000
Common stock	665,000	535,000
Retained earnings	100,000	80,000
Total Stockholders' Equity	765,000	615,000
Total Liabilities and Stockholders' Equity	$1,395,000	$1,175,000

Calculate the following items for both years from the given data and then compare them with the median ratios for paint manufacturers provided by a commercial credit firm:

	Median Ratios for Paint Manufacturers
1. Current ratio	2.5
2. Quick ratio	1.3
3. Accounts receivable turnover	8.1
4. Average collection period	44.9 days
5. Inventory turnover	4.9
6. Debt-to-equity ratio	0.78
7. Return on assets	4.8%
8. Profit margin	2.4%

Required

Based on your analysis, decide whether and under what circumstances you would grant Becknell's request for a loan. Explain the reasons for your decision.

Honeywell International, Inc.
The Dow Chemical Company
Abbott Laboratories

BTN12-4. Financial Analysis Problem Listed below are selected financial data for three corporations: **Honeywell International, Inc.** (environmental controls), **The Dow Chemical Company** (chemicals and plastic products), and **Abbott Laboratories** (health care products). These data cover five years (Year 5 is the most recent year; net income in thousands):

	Year 5	Year 4	Year 3	Year 2	Year 1
Honeywell International, Inc.					
Net income	$278,900	$322,200	$246,800	$331,100	$381,900
Earnings per common share	$2.15	$2.40	$1.78	$2.35	$2.52
Dividend per common share	$1.00	$0.91	$0.84	$0.77	$0.70
The Dow Chemical Company					
Net income	$938,000	$644,000	$276,000	$942,000	$1,384,000
Earnings per common share	$3.88	$2.33	$0.99	$3.46	$5.10
Dividend per common share	$2.60	$2.60	$2.60	$2.60	$2.60
Abbott Laboratories					
Net income*	$1,399,100	$1,239,100	$1,088,700	$965,800	$859,800
Earnings per common share*	$1.69	$1.47	$1.27	$1.11	$0.96
Dividend per common share	$0.68	$0.60	$0.50	$0.42	$0.35

*Before accounting change

Required

a. Calculate the dividend payout ratio for each company for each of the five years.

b. Companies may differ in their dividend policy; that is, they may differ in whether they emphasize a constant dividend amount per share, a steady growth in dividend amount per share, a target or constant dividend payout ratio, or some other criterion. Based on the data available, identify what appears to be each of the above firms' dividend policy over the five-year period.

CRITICAL THINKING

BTN12-5. Accounting Research Problem: General Mills, Inc. The fiscal year 2020 annual report of General Mills, Inc., can be found at: https://investors.generalmills.com/financial-information/annual-reports/default.aspx.

General Mills, Inc.

Required

a. Calculate (or identify) the following financial ratios for 2019 and 2020:
1. Gross profit percentage
2. Profit margin
3. Asset turnover (2018, total assets = $30,624.0 million)
4. Return on assets (2018, total assets = $30,624.0 million)
5. Return on common stockholders' equity (2018, total stockholders' equity = $6,492.4 million)
6. Current ratio
7. Quick ratio
8. Operating-cash-flow-to-current-liabilities ratio (2018, current liabilities = $7,341.9 million)
9. Accounts receivable turnover (2018, accounts receivable = $1,684.2 million)
10. Average collection period
11. Inventory turnover (2018, inventory = $1,642.2 million)
12. Days' sales in inventory
13. Debt-to-equity ratio
14. Times-interest-earned ratio
15. Operating-cash-flow-to-capital-expenditures ratio
16. Earnings per share
17. Price-earnings ratio (Use year-end adjusted closing stock price of $60.98 for 2020 and $49.27 for 2019.)
18. Dividend yield
19. Dividend payout ratio

b. Comment briefly on the changes in the ratios computed above.

BTN12-6. Accounting Communication Activity Pete Hollingsworth is currently taking an accounting course and is confused about what his professor told the class about analyzing financial statements. Pete would like you to lead a study session on the topic. In order to help everyone out, you decide to write a short memo describing some of the key points.

Required

Include the following items in your memo:

a. What is meant by trend analysis and how is it helpful?

b. How are common-size statements constructed and what are their uses?

c. What are a few common profitability, liquidity, and solvency ratios and how are they interpreted?

d. What are some limitations of financial statement analysis?

BTN12-7. Accounting Ethics Case Chris Nelson, the new assistant controller for Grand Company, is preparing for the firm's year-end closing procedures. On December 30, the prior year, a memorandum from the controller directed Nelson to make a journal entry debiting Cash and crediting Long-Term Advances to Officers for $1,000,000. Not finding the $1,000,000 in the cash deposit prepared for the bank that day, Nelson went to the controller for a further explanation. In response, the controller took from her desk drawer a check for $1,000,000 payable to Grand Company from Jason Grand, chief executive officer of the firm. Attached to the check was a note from Jason Grand saying that if this check were not needed to return it to him next week.

"This check is paying off a $1,000,000 advance the firm made to Jason Grand six years ago," stated the controller. "Mr. Grand has done this every year since the advance; each time we have returned the check to him in January of the following year. We plan to do so again this time. In fact, when Mr. Grand retires in four years, I expect the board of directors will forgive this advance. However, if the firm really needed the cash, we would deposit the check."

"Then why go through this charade each year?" inquired Nelson.

"It dresses up our year-end balance sheet," replied the controller. "Certain financial statement ratios are improved significantly. Further, the notes to the financial statements don't have to reveal a related-party loan. Lots of firms engage in year-end transactions designed to dress up their financial statements."

Required

a. What financial statement ratios are improved by making the journal entry contained in the controller's memorandum?

b. Is the year-end handling of Jason Grand's advance an ethical practice? Discuss.

BTN12-8. Accounting Ethics Problem Accrual accounting is based on the principle that revenue should be reported when earned and that expenses associated with that revenue should be matched against the revenue in the same period. Some financial statement frauds violate this fundamental concept in order to overstate net income in the current year. Provide an example of how this may be accomplished.

BTN12-9. Working with the Takeaways Below are income statements and balance sheets for the Fango Company:

FANGO COMPANY
Income Statement
For the Years Ended December 31

(in millions)	Current Year	Prior Year
Sales revenue	$10,000	$9,500
Cost of goods sold	5,500	5,200
Gross profit	4,500	4,300
Selling and administrative expenses	2,800	2,700
Income from operations	1,700	1,600
Interest expense	300	250
Income before income taxes	1,400	1,350
Income tax expense	420	400
Net income	$ 980	$ 950

FANGO COMPANY
Balance Sheet
December 31

(in millions)	Current Year	Prior Year
Assets		
Current assets		
Cash and cash equivalents	$ 200	$ 400
Accounts receivable	900	800
Inventory	700	650
Other current assets	400	250
Total current assets	2,200	2,100
Property, plant, & equipment (net)	2,600	2,500
Other assets	5,700	5,900
Total assets	$10,500	$10,500
Liabilities and Stockholders' Equity		
Current liabilities	$ 3,000	$ 2,900
Long-term liabilities	5,000	5,400
Total liabilities	8,000	8,300
Stockholders' equity—common	2,500	2,200
Total liabilities and stockholders' equity	$10,500	$10,500

Required

Calculate the following ratios for the Fango Company for both years and discuss your findings:

1. Profitability
   a. Profit margin
   b. Return on common stockholders' equity (common stockholders' equity was $2,000 at the beginning of the prior year)

2. Liquidity
   a. Current ratio
   b. Accounts receivable turnover (accounts receivable was $780 at the beginning of the prior year)
   c. Inventory turnover (inventory was $620 at the beginning of the prior year)
3. Solvency
   a. Debt-to-equity ratio
   b. Times-interest-earned ratio

ANSWERS TO SELF-STUDY QUESTIONS

1. c **2.** c **3.** c **4.** b **5.** b **6.** c **7.** d, **8.** b **9.** c **10.** b **11.** c **12.** d

REVIEW SOLUTIONS

Solution 12.1

1. Persistent
2. Transitory
3. Transitory
4. Persistent
5. Transitory
6. Persistent

Solution 12.2

	Increase in Current Year	
	Amount	Percent
Sales revenue	$50,000	6.7 percent [($800,000 – $750,000)/$750,000]
Net income	20,000	20.0 percent [($120,000 – $100,000)/$100,000]
Total assets	10,000	3.4 percent [($300,000 – $290,000)/$290,000]

Solution 12.3

SANFORD COMPANY
Income Statement
For the Year Ended December 31

	Amount	Percent
Sales revenue	$13,500	100.0
Cost of goods sold	5,400	40.0
Gross profit	8,100	60.0
Selling and administrative expenses	1,350	10.0
Income from operations	6,750	50.0
Interest expense	675	5.0
Other expense	135	1.0
Income before income taxes	5,940	44.0
Income tax expense	2,295	17.0
Net income	$ 3,645	27.0

Solution 12.4

a. Gross profit percentage = ($30,000 – $10,500)/$30,000 = 65.0 percent
b. Profit margin = $4,500/$30,000 = 15.0 percent
c. Asset turnover = $30,000/$50,000 = 0.60
d. Return on assets = $4,500/$50,000 = 9.0 percent
e. Return on common stockholders' equity = ($4,500 – $500)/$35,000 = 11.4 percent

Solution 12.5

a. Working capital = $60,000 – $40,000 = $20,000
b. Current ratio = $60,000/$40,000 = 1.5
c. Operating-cash-flow-to-current-liabilities ratio = $55,000/$40,000 = 1.375
d. Accounts receivable turnover = $100,000/$15,000 = 6.67 times
e. Days' sales in inventory = 365/($70,000/$9,000) = 46.9 days

Solution 12.6

a. Debt-to-equity ratio = $180,000/$600,000 = 0.30
b. Times-interest-earned ratio = ($55,000 + $5,000 + $25,000)/$5,000 = 17.0 times
c. Operating-cash-flow-to-capital-expenditures ratio = $100,000/$30,000 = 3.33 times

Solution 12.7

a. Dividend yield = $1.50/$54.00 = 2.8 percent
b. Dividend payout ratio = $1.50/$4.50 = 33.3 percent

Solution 12.8

a.

1. Current ratio = $95,000/$45,200 = 2.10
2. Quick ratio = $31,000/$45,200 = 0.69
3. Average collection period:
   Accounts receivable turnover = $200,000/[($28,800 + $28,000)/2] = 7.04
   Average collection period = 365/7.04 = 51.8 days
4. Inventory turnover = $98,000/[($44,000 + $64,000)/2] = 1.81
5. Operating-cash-flow-to-current-liabilities ratio = $7,800/[($39,750 + $45,200)/2] = 0.18
6. Debt-to-equity ratio = $65,200/$105,800 = 0.62
7. Return on assets = $10,750/[($143,000 + $171,000)/2] = 6.8 percent
8. Return on common stockholders' equity = $10,750/[($89,250 + $105,800)/2] = 11.0 percent
9. Profit margin = $10,750/$200,000 = 5.4 percent

Although the firm's current ratio of 2.10 is below the industry median, it is still acceptable; however, the quick ratio of 0.69 is well below the industry median. This indicates that Knox's inventory (which is omitted from this calculation) is excessive. This is also borne out by the firm's inventory turnover of 1.81 times, which compares with the industry median of 2.3 times. The firm's average collection period of 51.8 days is significantly better than the industry median of 73 days, while the operating-cash-flow-to-current-liabilities ratio is close to the industry median. Knox's debt-to-equity ratio of 0.62 indicates that the firm has proportionately more debt in its capital structure than the median industry firm, which has a debt-to-equity ratio of 0.50. Knox's operations appear efficient as its return on assets, return on common stockholders' equity, and profit margin all exceed the industry medians.

b. Average number of shares outstanding = (4,000,000 + 3,000,000)/2 = 3,500,000 shares.
$4,200,000 dividends/3,500,000 shares = $1.20 dividend per share.
Dividend payout ratio = $1.20/$3.07 = 39.1 percent.

c. Price-earnings ratio = $25/$3.07 = 8.1.
Dividend yield = $1.20/$25 = 4.8 percent.

Appendix

Columbia Sportswear: Financial Statements

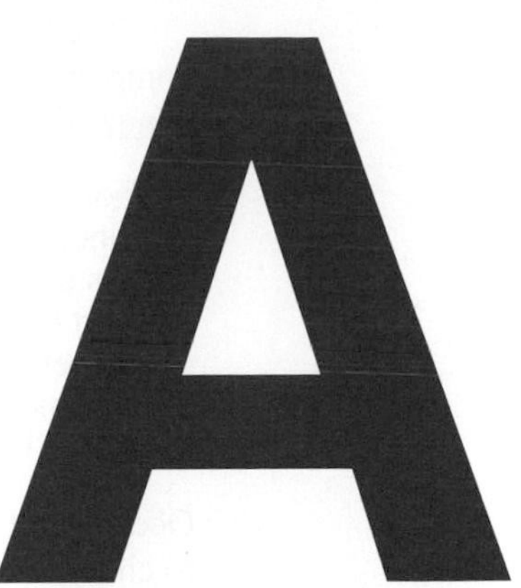

The law requires publicly traded companies to submit an audited annual report to the Securities and Exchange Commission (SEC) within two months of the close of their fiscal year. This annual report is called Form 10-K. Companies also provide their stockholders with an annual report that contains many of the items included in Form 10-K, along with a letter to the shareholders and public relations and marketing material. Although each annual report is different, all annual reports typically include the following elements:

- Letter to the Shareholders
- Management Discussion and Analysis
- Independent Auditor's Report
- Financial Statements
- Notes to Financial Statements
- Report on Internal Control
- Management's Certification of Financial Statements
- Supplemental Information

In addition, most publicly traded companies also provide a voluntary report on their corporate social responsibility commitments. Because this report is voluntary, its content varies to a greater degree from company to company. Most reports, however, discuss the company's commitment in the areas of both social and environmental impact.

The following pages include selected data from Columbia Sportswear's 2020 Annual Report. The complete annual report can be found at Columbia's website: https://investor.columbia.com/sec-filings/annual-reports. Appendix A is organized as follows:

Occasionally, companies restate financial data for previous years, which may cause specific amounts to change in their financial statements.

REPORT OF INDEPENDENT AUDITORS

Report of Independent Registered Public Accounting Firm

To the Shareholders and the Board of Directors of Columbia Sportswear Company

Opinion on the Financial Statements

We have audited the accompanying consolidated balance sheets of Columbia Sportswear Company and subsidiaries (the "Company") as of December 31, 2020 and 2019, the related consolidated statements of operations, comprehensive income, equity, and cash flows for each of the three years in the period ended December 31, 2020, and the related notes and the schedule listed in the Index at Item 15 (collectively referred to as the "financial statements"). In our opinion, the financial statements present fairly, in all material respects, the financial position of the Company as of December 31, 2020 and 2019, and the results of its operations and its cash flows for each of the three years in the period ended December 31, 2020, in conformity with accounting principles generally accepted in the United States of America.

We have also audited, in accordance with the standards of the Public Company Accounting Oversight Board (United States) (PCAOB), the Company's internal control over financial reporting as of December 31, 2020, based on criteria established in *Internal Control - Integrated Framework (2013)* issued by the Committee of Sponsoring Organizations of the Treadway Commission and our report dated February 25, 2021, expressed an unqualified opinion on the Company's internal control over financial reporting.

Basis for Opinion

These financial statements are the responsibility of the Company's management. Our responsibility is to express an opinion on the Company's financial statements based on our audits. We are a public accounting firm registered with the PCAOB and are required to be independent with respect to the Company in accordance with the U.S. federal securities laws and the applicable rules and regulations of the Securities and Exchange Commission and the PCAOB.

We conducted our audits in accordance with the standards of the PCAOB. Those standards require that we plan and perform the audit to obtain reasonable assurance about whether the financial statements are free of material misstatement, whether due to error or fraud. Our audits included performing procedures to assess the risks of material misstatement of the financial statements, whether due to error or fraud, and performing procedures that respond to those risks. Such procedures included examining, on a test basis, evidence regarding the amounts and disclosures in the financial statements. Our audits also included evaluating the accounting principles used and significant estimates made by management, as well as evaluating the overall presentation of the financial statements. We believe that our audits provide a reasonable basis for our opinion.

Critical Audit Matters

The critical audit matters communicated below are matters arising from the current-period audit of the financial statements that were communicated or required to be communicated to the audit committee and that (1) relate to accounts or disclosures that are material to the financial statements and (2) involved our especially challenging, subjective, or complex judgments. The communication of critical audit matters does not alter in any way our opinion on the financial statements, taken as a whole, and we are not, by communicating the critical audit matters below, providing separate opinions on the critical audit matters or on the accounts or disclosures to which they relate.

Goodwill – prAna Reporting Unit – Refer to Notes 2 and 6 to the Consolidated Financial Statements

Critical Audit Matter Description

The Company's evaluation of goodwill for impairment involves the comparison of the fair value of each reporting unit to its carrying value. The Company uses a combination of discounted cash flow analysis and market-based valuation methods, which requires management to make significant estimates and assumptions related to projected cash flow, discount rates, market-based multiples, and other operating performance measures. Changes in these assumptions could have a significant impact on either the fair value, the amount of any goodwill impairment charge, if any, or both. The goodwill balance was $68.6 million as of December 31, 2020, of which $54.2 million was allocated to the prAna Reporting Unit ("prAna"). The fair value of prAna exceeded its carrying value as of the measurement date and, therefore, no impairment was recognized.

Auditing management's estimates and assumptions related to projected cash flow, discount rates, market-based multiples, and other operating performance measures for prAna involved especially subjective judgment.

How the Critical Audit Matter Was Addressed in the Audit

Our audit procedures related to management's estimates and assumptions related to projected cash flow, discount rates, market-based multiples, and other operating performance measures for the prAna goodwill impairment analysis included the following, among others:

- We tested the effectiveness of internal controls over the prAna goodwill impairment analysis, including those over the forecasts for cash flow and other operating performance measures, and the selection of the discount rate and market-based multiples.
- We evaluated management's ability to accurately forecast cash flow and other operating performance measures by comparing actual results to management's historical forecasts.
- We evaluated the reasonableness of management's cash flow forecasts by comparing the forecasts to:
    - Historical cash flow.
    - Forecasted information included in Company press releases as well as in analyst and industry reports for the Company and certain of its peer companies.
- We evaluated the impact of changes in management's cash flow forecasts from the October 31, 2020 annual measurement date to December 31, 2020.
- To evaluate the reasonableness of the discount rate, with the assistance of our fair value specialists, we:
    - Developed a range of independent estimates of the discount rate and compared those to the discount rate selected by management to assess the appropriateness of the discount rate assumption.
    - Tested the inputs and source information underlying the determination of the discount rate by comparing to reputable third-party data or industry information and tested the mathematical accuracy of the calculation.
- With the assistance of our fair value specialists, we evaluated the reasonableness of the selection and application of valuation multiples management applied in i market-based valuation method through comparison to valuation multiples for guideline public companies.

Intangible Assets, Net – prAna Trademark– Refer to Notes 2 and 6 to the Consolidated Financial Statements

Critical Audit Matter Description

The Company has trademarks and trade names ("trademarks") that are indefinite-lived intangible assets. As of December 31, 2020, the carrying value of the intangible assets was $103.6 million, of which $70.5 million was attributed to prAna's trademark, after recognizing $17.5 million of impairment loss in the year ended December 31, 2020. The Company used the relief from royalty method to estimate fair value, which requires management to make significant estimates and assumptions related to projected sales, royalty rates and discount rates to estimate the net present value of future cash flows relating to the prAna trademark.

Auditing management's estimates and assumptions related to projected sales, royalty rates, and discount rates for prAna involved especially subjective judgment.

How the Critical Audit Matter Was Addressed in the Audit

Our audit procedures related to management's estimates and assumptions related to projected sales, royalty rates, and discount rates for the prAna trademark valuation included the following, among others:

- We tested the effectiveness of controls over intangible assets, including those over the forecasts of future sales, and the selection of the discount rate and royalty rate.
- We evaluated management's ability to accurately forecast future sales by comparing actual results to management's historical forecasts.
- We evaluated the reasonableness of management's sales forecasts by comparing the forecasts to:
    - Historical sales.
    - Forecasted information included in Company press releases as well as in analyst and industry reports for the Company and certain of its peer companies.

- We evaluated the impact of changes in management's forecasts from the October 31, 2020 annual measurement date to December 31, 2020.
- To evaluate the reasonableness of the (1) discount rate and (2) royalty rate, with the assistance of our fair value specialists, we:
  - Developed a range of independent estimates of the discount rate and compared those to the discount rate selected by management to assess the appropriateness of the discount rate assumption.
  - Tested the inputs and source information underlying the determination of the discount rate by comparing to reputable third-party data or industry information and tested the mathematical accuracy of the calculation.
  - Compared the royalty rate selected by management to rates from royalty agreements in the outdoor apparel industry for comparable companies and the Company's own contract royalty rates.

Long-lived Asset Valuation – Refer to Notes 2, 5 and 9 to the Consolidated Financial Statements

Critical Audit Matter Description

The Company evaluates retail location long-lived assets for impairment when events or changes in circumstances exist that may indicate that the carrying amounts of retail location long-lived assets are no longer recoverable. Events that result in an impairment review include plans to close a retail location or a significant decrease in the operating results of the retail location. When such an indicator occurs, the Company evaluates its retail location long-lived assets for impairment by comparing the undiscounted future cash flow expected to be generated by the location to the retail location long-lived asset's carrying amount. If the carrying amount of an asset exceeds the estimated undiscounted future cash flow, an analysis is performed to estimate the fair value of the asset. An impairment is recorded if the fair value of the retail location long-lived asset is less than the carrying amount.

The Company makes significant assumptions to evaluate retail location long-lived assets for possible indications of impairment. Changes in these assumptions could have a significant impact on the retail location long-lived assets identified for further analysis. For the year ended December 31, 2020, impairment charges from underperforming retail location long-lived assets were $7.0 million for lease right-of-use assets and $4.5 million for property, plant, and equipment.

Given the Company's evaluation of possible indications of impairment of retail location long-lived assets requires management to make significant assumptions, performing audit procedures to evaluate whether management appropriately identified events or changes in circumstances indicating that the carrying amounts of retail location long-lived assets may not be recoverable involved especially subjective judgment.

How the Critical Audit Matter Was Addressed in the Audit

Our audit procedures related to the evaluation of retail location long-lived assets for possible indications of impairment included the following, among others:

- We tested the effectiveness of controls over management's identification of possible circumstances that may indicate that the carrying amounts of retail location long-lived assets are no longer recoverable.
- We evaluated management's analysis of long-lived assets for indications of impairment analysis by:
  - Testing retail location long-lived assets for possible indications of impairment, including searching for locations with a history of losses, current period loss, or projected losses.
  - Performing inquiries of management regarding the process and assumptions used to identify potential indicators of impairment and evaluating the consistency of the assumptions with evidence obtained in other areas of the audit.

/s/ DELOITTE & TOUCHE LLP
Portland, Oregon
February 25, 2021

We have served as the Company's auditor since at least 1994; however, an earlier year could not be reliably determined.

FINANCIAL STATEMENTS

COLUMBIA SPORTSWEAR COMPANY

CONSOLIDATED BALANCE SHEETS

(in thousands)	December 31, 2020	December 31, 2019
ASSETS		
Current Assets:		
Cash and cash equivalents	$ 790,725	$ 686,009
Short-term investments	1,224	1,668
Accounts receivable, net of allowance of $ 21,810 and $ 8,925, respectively	452,945	488,233
Inventories, net	556,530	605,968
Prepaid expenses and other current assets	54,197	93,868
Total current assets	1,855,621	1,875,746
Property, plant and equipment, net	309,792	346,651
Operating lease right-of-use assets	339,244	394,501
Intangible assets, net	103,558	123,595
Goodwill	68,594	68,594
Deferred income taxes	96,126	78,849
Other non-current assets	63,636	43,655
Total assets	$ 2,836,571	$ 2,931,591
LIABILITIES AND EQUITY		
Current Liabilities:		
Accounts payable	$ 206,697	$ 255,372
Accrued liabilities	257,278	295,723
Operating lease liabilities	65,466	64,019
Income taxes payable	23,181	15,801
Total current liabilities	552,622	630,915
Non-current operating lease liabilities	353,181	371,507
Income taxes payable	49,922	48,427
Deferred income taxes	5,205	6,361
Other long-term liabilities	42,870	24,934
Total liabilities	1,003,800	1,082,144
Commitments and contingencies (Note 12)		
Shareholders' Equity:		
Preferred stock; 10,000 shares authorized; none issued and outstanding	—	—
Common stock (no par value); 250,000 shares authorized; 66,252 and 67,561 issued and outstanding, respectively	20,165	4,937
Retained earnings	1,811,800	1,848,935
Accumulated other comprehensive income (loss)	806	(4,425)
Total shareholders' equity	1,832,771	1,849,447
Total liabilities and shareholders' equity	$ 2,836,571	$ 2,931,591

See accompanying notes to consolidated financial statements

COLUMBIA SPORTSWEAR COMPANY

CONSOLIDATED STATEMENTS OF OPERATIONS

(in thousands, except per share amounts)	Year Ended December 31, 2020	2019	2018
Net sales	$ 2,501,554	$ 3,042,478	$ 2,802,326
Cost of sales	1,277,665	1,526,808	1,415,978
Gross profit	1,223,889	1,515,670	1,386,348
Selling, general and administrative expenses	1,098,948	1,136,186	1,051,152
Net licensing income	12,108	15,487	15,786
Income from operations	137,049	394,971	350,982
Interest income, net	435	8,302	9,876
Other non-operating income (expense), net	2,039	2,156	(141)
Income before income tax	139,523	405,429	360,717
Income tax expense	(31,510)	(74,940)	(85,769)
Net income	108,013	330,489	274,948
Net income attributable to non-controlling interest	—	—	6,692
Net income attributable to Columbia Sportswear Company	$ 108,013	$ 330,489	$ 268,256
Earnings per share attributable to Columbia Sportswear Company:			
Basic	$ 1.63	$ 4.87	$ 3.85
Diluted	$ 1.62	$ 4.83	$ 3.81
Weighted average shares outstanding:			
Basic	66,376	67,837	69,614
Diluted	66,772	68,493	70,401

See accompanying notes to consolidated financial statements

COLUMBIA SPORTSWEAR COMPANY

CONSOLIDATED STATEMENTS OF COMPREHENSIVE INCOME

(in thousands)	Year Ended December 31, 2020	2019	2018
Net income	$ 108,013	$ 330,489	$ 274,948
Other comprehensive income (loss):			
Unrealized holding gains (losses) on available-for-sale securities, net	4	56	(56)
Unrealized holding gains (losses) on derivative transactions (net of tax effects of $ 6,271, $830, and $(7,782), respectively)	(18,851)	(2,383)	24,262
Foreign currency translation adjustments (net of tax effects of $(388), $2,188, and $1,557, respectively)	24,078	2,064	(18,079)
Other comprehensive income (loss)	5,231	(263)	6,127
Comprehensive income	113,244	330,226	281,075
Comprehensive income attributable to non-controlling interest	—	—	7,480
Comprehensive income attributable to Columbia Sportswear Company	$ 113,244	$ 330,226	$ 273,595

See accompanying notes to consolidated financial statements

COLUMBIA SPORTSWEAR COMPANY

CONSOLIDATED STATEMENTS OF CASH FLOWS

(in thousands)	Year Ended December 31, 2020	2019	2018
Cash flows from operating activities:			
Net income	$ 108,013	$ 330,489	$ 274,948
Adjustments to reconcile net income to net cash provided by operating activities:			
Depreciation, amortization, and non-cash lease expense	146,601	121,725	58,230
Provision for uncollectible accounts receivable	19,156	(108)	3,908
Loss on disposal or impairment of intangible assets, property, plant and equipment, and right-of-use assets	31,342	5,442	4,208
Deferred income taxes	(11,263)	(1,808)	1,462
Stock-based compensation	17,778	17,832	14,291
Changes in operating assets and liabilities:			
Accounts receivable	22,885	(37,429)	(29,509)
Inventories, net	64,884	(84,058)	(94,716)
Prepaid expenses and other current assets	33,712	(15,068)	(9,771)
Other assets	(21,224)	(3,547)	(12,421)
Accounts payable	(49,275)	(10,419)	19,384
Accrued liabilities	(52,115)	18,863	66,900
Income taxes payable	9,082	(9,402)	(3,958)
Operating lease assets and liabilities	(52,112)	(54,197)	—
Other liabilities	8,613	7,137	(3,387)
Net cash provided by operating activities	276,077	285,452	289,569
Cash flows from investing activities:			
Purchases of short-term investments	(35,044)	(136,257)	(518,755)
Sales and maturities of short-term investments	36,631	400,501	352,127
Capital expenditures	(28,758)	(123,516)	(65,622)
Proceeds from sale of property, plant and equipment	—	—	19
Net cash provided by (used in) investing activities	(27,171)	140,728	(232,231)
Cash flows from financing activities:			
Proceeds from credit facilities	402,422	78,186	70,576
Repayments on credit facilities	(403,146)	(78,186)	(70,576)
Payment of line of credit issuance fees	(3,278)	—	—
Proceeds from issuance of common stock related to stock-based compensation	6,919	19,793	18,484
Tax payments related to stock-based compensation	(4,533)	(5,806)	(4,285)
Repurchase of common stock	(132,889)	(121,702)	(201,600)
Purchase of non-controlling interest	—	(17,880)	—
Cash dividends paid	(17,195)	(65,127)	(62,664)
Cash dividends paid to non-controlling interest	—	—	(19,949)
Net cash used in financing activities	(151,700)	(190,722)	(270,014)
Net effect of exchange rate changes on cash	7,510	(1,244)	(8,695)
Net increase (decrease) in cash and cash equivalents	104,716	234,214	(221,371)
Cash and cash equivalents, beginning of period	686,009	451,795	673,166
Cash and cash equivalents, end of period	$ 790,725	$ 686,009	$ 451,795
Supplemental disclosures of cash flow information:			
Cash paid during the year for income taxes	$ 14,687	$ 99,062	$ 77,408
Supplemental disclosures of non-cash investing and financing activities:			
Property, plant and equipment acquired through increase in liabilities	$ 3,831	$ 9,543	$ 11,831

See accompanying notes to consolidated financial statements

COLUMBIA SPORTSWEAR COMPANY

CONSOLIDATED STATEMENTS OF EQUITY

	Columbia Sportswear Company Shareholders' Equity					
	Common Stock					
(in thousands, except per share amounts)	Shares Outstanding	Amount	Retained Earnings	Accumulated Other Comprehensive Income (Loss)	Non-Controlling Interest	Total
BALANCE, JANUARY 1, 2018	69,995	$ 45,829	$ 1,585,009	$ (8,887)	$ 30,308	$ 1,652,259
Net income	—	—	268,256	—	6,692	274,948
Other comprehensive income (loss):						
Unrealized holding losses on available-for-sale securities, net	—	—	—	(56)	—	(56)
Unrealized holding gains on derivative transactions, net	—	—	—	23,195	1,067	24,262
Foreign currency translation adjustment, net	—	—	—	(17,800)	(279)	(18,079)
Cash dividends ($0.90 per share)	—	—	(62,664)	—	—	(62,664)
Dividends to non-controlling interest	—	—	—	—	(21,332)	(21,332)
Adoption of new accounting standards	—	—	14,600	(515)	—	14,085
Issuance of common stock related to stock-based compensation, net	600	14,199	—	—	—	14,199
Stock-based compensation expense	—	14,291	—	—	—	14,291
Repurchase of common stock	(2,349)	(74,319)	(127,281)	—	—	(201,600)
BALANCE, DECEMBER 31, 2018	68,246	—	1,677,920	(4,063)	16,456	1,690,313
Net income	—	—	330,489	—	—	330,489
Purchase of non-controlling interest	—	—	—	(99)	(16,456)	(16,555)
Other comprehensive income (loss):						
Unrealized holding gains on available-for-sale securities, net	—	—	—	56	—	56
Unrealized holding losses on derivative transactions, net	—	—	—	(2,383)	—	(2,383)
Foreign currency translation adjustment, net	—	—	—	2,064	—	2,064
Cash dividends ($0.96 per share)	—	—	(65,127)	—	—	(65,127)
Issuance of common stock related to stock-based compensation, net	558	13,987	—	—	—	13,987
Stock-based compensation expense	—	17,832	—	—	—	17,832
Repurchase of common stock	(1,243)	(26,882)	(94,347)	—	—	(121,229)
BALANCE, DECEMBER 31, 2019	67,561	4,937	1,848,935	(4,425)	—	1,849,447
Net income	—	—	108,013	—	—	108,013
Other comprehensive income (loss):						
Unrealized holding gains on available-for-sale securities, net	—	—	—	4	—	4
Unrealized holding losses on derivative transactions, net	—	—	—	(18,851)	—	(18,851)
Foreign currency translation adjustment, net	—	—	—	24,078	—	24,078
Cash dividends ($0.26 per share)	—	—	(17,195)	—	—	(17,195)
Issuance of common stock related to stock-based compensation, net	248	2,386	—	—	—	2,386
Stock-based compensation expense	—	17,778	—	—	—	17,778
Repurchase of common stock	(1,557)	(4,936)	(127,953)	—	—	(132,889)
BALANCE, DECEMBER 31, 2020	66,252	20,165	1,811,800	806	—	1,832,771

See accompanying notes to consolidated financial statements

NOTES TO FINANCIAL STATEMENTS

COLUMBIA SPORTSWEAR COMPANY

NOTES TO CONSOLIDATED FINANCIAL STATEMENTS

NOTE 1—BASIS OF PRESENTATION AND ORGANIZATION

Nature of the Business

Columbia Sportswear Company connects active people with their passions through its four well-known brands, Columbia, SOREL, Mountain Hardwear, and prAna, by designing, developing, marketing, and distributing its outdoor, active and everyday lifestyle apparel, footwear, accessories, and equipment products to meet the diverse needs of its customers and consumers.

Principles of Consolidation

The consolidated financial statements include the accounts of Columbia Sportswear Company, its wholly owned subsidiaries and entities in which it maintained a controlling financial interest (the "Company"). All significant intercompany balances and transactions have been eliminated in consolidation.

Estimates and Assumptions

The preparation of financial statements in conformity with GAAP requires management to make estimates and assumptions that affect the reported amounts of assets and liabilities and disclosure of contingent assets and liabilities at the date of the consolidated financial statements and the reported amounts of revenues and expenses during the reporting period. Actual results may differ from these estimates and assumptions. Some of the more significant estimates relate to revenue recognition, allowance for uncollectible accounts receivable, excess, close-out and slow moving inventory, impairment of long-lived assets, intangible assets and goodwill, and income taxes.

Recently Adopted Accounting Pronouncements

Effective January 1, 2020, the Company adopted Accounting Standards Update ("ASU") No. 2018-15, Intangibles - Goodwill and Other - Internal-Use Software (Subtopic 350-40) issued by the Financial Accounting Standards Board ("FASB") in August 2018, which clarifies certain aspects of accounting for implementation costs incurred in a cloud computing arrangement ("CCA") that is a service contract. Under the ASU, an entity would expense costs incurred in the preliminary-project and post-implementation-operation stages. The entity would also capitalize certain costs incurred during the application-development stage, as well as certain costs related to enhancements. The ASU does not change the accounting for the service component of a CCA. The Company adopted the standard using the prospective method and anticipates an increase in cloud-specific implementation assets as specific cloud initiatives are executed by the Company. These assets will generally be included in *Other non-current assets* in the Consolidated Balance Sheets and will amortize over their assessed useful lives or the term of the underlying cloud computing hosting contract, whichever is shorter. Upon the adoption of the standard, there was no immediate impact to the Company's financial position, results of operations or cash flows.

Effective January 1, 2020, the Company adopted ASU No. 2017-04, Intangibles - Goodwill and Other (Topic 350): Simplifying the Test for Goodwill Impairment issued by the FASB in January 2017, which simplifies the accounting for goodwill impairments by eliminating step two from the goodwill impairment test. Under this guidance, if the carrying amount of a reporting unit exceeds its estimated fair value, an impairment charge shall be recognized in an amount equal to that excess, limited to the total amount of goodwill allocated to that reporting unit. The impact of the new standard will depend on the specific facts and circumstances of future individual goodwill impairments, if any.

Effective January 1, 2020, the Company adopted ASU No. 2016-13, Financial Instruments - Credit Losses (Topic 326): Measurement of Credit Losses on Financial Instruments issued by the FASB in June 2016, as well as the clarifying amendments subsequently issued. The pronouncement changes the impairment model for most financial assets and requires the use of an "expected loss" model for instruments measured at amortized cost. Under this model, entities are required to estimate the lifetime expected credit loss on such instruments and record an allowance to offset the amortized cost basis of the financial asset, resulting in a net presentation of the amount expected to be collected on the financial asset. Upon adoption of the standard, there was no immediate impact to the Company's financial position, results of operations or cash flows. On an ongoing basis, the Company will contemplate forward-looking economic conditions in recording lifetime expected credit losses for the Company's financial assets measured at cost, such as the Company's trade receivables and certain short-term investments.

NOTE 2—SUMMARY OF SIGNIFICANT ACCOUNTING POLICIES

Cash and cash equivalents

Cash and cash equivalents are stated at fair value or at cost, which approximates fair value, and include investments with original maturities of 90 days or less at the date of acquisition. At December 31, 2020, *Cash and cash equivalents* consisted of cash, money

COLUMBIA SPORTSWEAR COMPANY

NOTES TO CONSOLIDATED FINANCIAL STATEMENTS—(Continued)

market funds, and United States government treasury bills. At December 31, 2019, *Cash and cash equivalents* consisted of cash, money market funds, United States government treasury bills, and commercial paper.

Investments

At December 31, 2020, *Short-term investments* consisted of money market funds and mutual fund shares held as part of the Company's deferred compensation plan expected to be distributed in the next twelve months. At December 31, 2019, *Short-term investments* consisted of mutual fund shares held as part of the Company's deferred compensation plan expected to be distributed in the next twelve months. Investments held as part of the Company's deferred compensation plan are classified as trading securities and are recorded at fair value with any unrealized gains and losses included in *SG&A expense*. Realized gains or losses from these trading securities are determined based on the specific identification method and are included in *SG&A expense*.

At December 31, 2020 and 2019, long-term investments included in *Other non-current assets* consisted of money market funds and mutual fund shares held to offset liabilities to participants in the Company's deferred compensation plan. The investments are classified as long-term because the related deferred compensation liabilities are not expected to be paid within the next year. These investments are classified as trading securities and are recorded at fair value with unrealized gains and losses reported as a component of operating income.

Accounts receivable

Accounts receivable have been reduced by an allowance for doubtful accounts. The Company maintains the allowance for estimated losses resulting from the inability of the Company's customers to make required payments. The allowance represents the current estimate of lifetime expected credit losses over the remaining duration of existing accounts receivable considering current market conditions and supportable forecasts when appropriate. The estimate is a result of the Company's ongoing evaluation of collectability, customer creditworthiness, historical levels of credit losses, and future expectations. Write-offs of accounts receivable were $8.0 million and $ 1.2 million for the years ended December 31, 2020 and 2019, respectively.

Inventories

Inventories consist primarily of finished goods and are carried at the lower of cost or net realizable value. Cost is determined using the first-in, first-out method. The Company periodically reviews its inventories for excess, close-out or slow moving items and makes provisions as necessary to properly reflect inventory value.

Property, plant and equipment

Property, plant and equipment are stated at cost, net of accumulated depreciation. Depreciation is provided using the straight-line method over the estimated useful lives of the assets. The principal estimated useful lives are: land improvements, 15 years; buildings and building improvements, 15-30 years; furniture and fixtures, 3-10 years; and machinery, software and equipment, 3-10 years. Leasehold improvements are depreciated over the lesser of the estimated useful life of the improvement, which is most commonly 7 years, or the remaining term of the underlying lease.

Improvements to property, plant and equipment that substantially extend the useful life of the asset are capitalized. Repair and maintenance costs are expensed as incurred. Internal and external costs directly related to the development of internal-use software during the application development stage, including costs incurred for third party contractors and employee compensation, are capitalized and depreciated over a 3-10 year estimated useful life.

Intangible assets and goodwill

Intangible assets with indefinite useful lives and goodwill are not amortized but are periodically evaluated for impairment. Intangible assets that are determined to have finite lives are amortized using the straight-line method over their estimated useful lives and are measured for impairment only when events or circumstances indicate the carrying value may be impaired. Intangible assets with finite lives include patents, purchased technology and customer relationships and have estimated useful lives which range from approximately 3 to 10 years.

Cloud computing arrangements

The Company's CCAs primarily relate to various enterprise resource planning systems, as well as other supporting systems. These assets are generally included in *Other non-current assets* in the Consolidated Balance Sheets and amortize on a straight-line basis over their assessed useful lives or the term of the underlying cloud computing hosting contract, whichever is shorter. As of December 31, 2020, CCAs in-service have useful lives which range from approximately ten months to five years. As of December 31, 2020, CCA assets consisted of capitalized implementation costs of $ 24.3 million and associated accumulated amortization of $1.9

COLUMBIA SPORTSWEAR COMPANY

NOTES TO CONSOLIDATED FINANCIAL STATEMENTS—(Continued)

million. Changes in these assets are recorded in *Other assets* within operating activities in the Consolidated Statements of Cash Flows.

Leases

The Company leases, among other things, retail space, office space, warehouse facilities, storage space, vehicles, and equipment. Generally, the base lease terms are between five and 10 years. Certain lease agreements contain scheduled rent escalation clauses and others include rental payments adjusted periodically depending on an index or rate. Certain retail space lease agreements provide for additional rents based on a percentage of annual sales in excess of stipulated minimums ("percentage rent"). Certain lease agreements require the Company to pay real estate taxes, insurance, common area maintenance, and other costs, collectively referred to as operating costs, in addition to base rent.

Certain lease agreements also contain lease incentives, such as tenant improvement allowances and rent holidays. Most leases include one or more options to renew, with renewal terms that can extend the lease term from one to 10 years or more. The exercise of lease renewal options is generally at the Company's sole discretion. The Company's lease agreements do not contain any material residual value guarantees or material restrictive covenants.

The Company determines if an arrangement is or contains a lease at contract inception. The Company recognizes a ROU asset and a lease liability at the lease commencement date. The lease liability is initially measured at the present value of the unpaid lease payments at the lease commencement date. Key estimates and judgments include how the Company determines (1) the discount rate it uses to discount the unpaid lease payments to present value, (2) the lease term and (3) lease payments.

ASC 842 requires a lessee to discount its unpaid lease payments using the interest rate implicit in the lease or, if that rate cannot be readily determined, its incremental borrowing rate. Generally, the Company cannot determine the interest rate implicit in the lease because it does not have access to the lessor's estimated residual value or the amount of the lessor's deferred initial direct costs. Therefore, the Company generally uses its incremental borrowing rate as the discount rate for the lease. The Company's incremental borrowing rate for a lease is the rate of interest it would have to pay on a collateralized basis to borrow an amount equal to the lease payments under similar terms. Because the Company does not generally borrow on a collateralized basis, it uses market-based rates as an input to derive an appropriate incremental borrowing rate, adjusted for the lease term and the effect on that rate of designating specific collateral with a value equal to the unpaid lease payments for that lease. The Company also contemplates adjusting the discount rate for the amount of the lease payments.

The Company's lease contracts may include options to extend the lease following the initial term or terminate the lease prior to the end of the initial term. In most instances, at the commencement of the leases, the Company has determined that it is not reasonably certain to exercise either of these options; accordingly, these options are generally not considered in determining the initial lease term. At the renewal of an expiring lease, the Company reassesses options in the contract that it is reasonably certain to exercise in its measurement of lease term.

For lease agreements entered into or reassessed after the adoption of ASC 842, the Company has elected the practical expedient to account for the lease and non-lease components as a single lease component. Therefore, for those leases, the lease payments used to measure the lease liability include all of the fixed consideration in the contract.

Variable lease payments associated with the Company's leases are recognized upon occurrence of the event, activity, or circumstance in the lease agreement on which those payments are assessed. Variable lease payments are presented in the Company's Consolidated Statements of Operations in the same line item as expense arising from fixed lease payments.

Leases with an initial term of 12 months or less are not recorded on the balance sheet; the Company recognizes lease expense for these leases on a straight-line basis over the lease term.

Concessions

In April 2020, the FASB issued a Staff Q&A, Topic 842 and 840: Accounting for Lease Concessions Related to the Effects of the COVID-19 Pandemic. The FASB staff indicated that it would be acceptable for entities to make an election to account for lease concessions related to the effects of the COVID-19 pandemic consistent with how they would be accounted for as though enforceable rights and obligations for those concessions existed in the original contract. The Company elected to account for lease concessions related to the effects of the COVID-19 pandemic in accordance with the Staff Q&A. For concessions that provide a deferral of payments with no substantive changes to the consideration in the original contract, the Company continues to recognize expense during the deferral period. For concessions in the form of lease abatements, the reduced lease payments are accounted for as reductions to variable lease expense.

COLUMBIA SPORTSWEAR COMPANY

NOTES TO CONSOLIDATED FINANCIAL STATEMENTS—(Continued)

Impairment of long-lived assets, intangible assets and goodwill

Long-lived assets, which include property, plant and equipment, lease right-of-use assets, capitalized implementation costs for cloud computing arrangements, and intangible assets with finite lives, are measured for impairment only when events or circumstances indicate the carrying value may be impaired. In these cases, the Company estimates the future undiscounted cash flows to be derived from the asset or asset group to determine whether a potential impairment exists. If the sum of the estimated undiscounted cash flows is less than the carrying value of the asset, the Company recognizes an impairment loss, measured as the amount by which the carrying value exceeds the estimated fair value of the asset.

The Company reviews and tests its intangible assets with indefinite useful lives and goodwill for impairment in the fourth quarter of each year and when events or changes in circumstances indicate that the carrying amount of such assets may be impaired. The Company's intangible assets with indefinite lives consist of trademarks and trade names. In the impairment test for goodwill, the estimated fair value of the reporting unit is compared with the carrying amount of that reporting unit. In the impairment tests for trademarks and trade names, the Company compares the estimated fair value of each asset to its carrying amount. For goodwill and trademarks and trade names, if the carrying amount exceeds its estimated fair value, the Company calculates an impairment as the excess of carrying amount over the estimate of fair value.

Impairment charges, if any, are classified as a component of *SG&A expense*.

Income taxes

Income taxes are based on amounts of taxes payable or refundable in the current year and on expected future tax consequences of events that are recognized in the financial statements in different periods than they are recognized in tax returns. As a result of timing of recognition and measurement differences between financial accounting standards and income tax laws, temporary differences arise between amounts of pre-tax financial statement income and taxable income and between reported amounts of assets and liabilities in the Consolidated Balance Sheets and their respective tax bases. Deferred income tax assets and liabilities reported in the Consolidated Balance Sheets reflect estimated future tax effects attributable to these temporary differences and to net operating loss and net capital loss carryforwards, based on tax rates expected to be in effect for years in which the differences are expected to be settled or realized. Realization of deferred tax assets is dependent on future taxable income in specific jurisdictions. Valuation allowances are used to reduce deferred tax assets to amounts considered likely to be realized.

Accrued income taxes in the Consolidated Balance Sheets include unrecognized income tax benefits relating to uncertain tax positions, including related interest and penalties, appropriately classified as current or noncurrent. The Company recognizes the tax benefit from an uncertain tax position if it is more likely than not that the tax position will be sustained on examination by the relevant taxing authority based on the technical merits of the position. The tax benefits recognized in the financial statements from such positions are then measured based on the largest benefit that has a greater than 50% likelihood of being realized upon ultimate settlement with the relevant tax authority. In making this determination, the Company assumes that the taxing authority will examine the position and that it will have full knowledge of all relevant information. The provision for income taxes also includes estimates of interest and penalties related to uncertain tax positions.

Derivatives

The effective portion of changes in fair values of outstanding cash flow hedges is recorded in *Other comprehensive income (loss)* until earnings are affected by the hedged transaction, and any ineffective portion is included in current income. In most cases, amounts recorded in *Other comprehensive income (loss)* will be released to earnings after maturity of the related derivative. The Consolidated Statements of Operations classification of effective hedge results is the same as that of the underlying exposure. Results of hedges of product costs are recorded in *Cost of sales* when the underlying hedged transactions affect earnings. Results of hedges of revenue are recorded in *Net sales* when the underlying hedged transactions affect earnings. Unrealized derivative gains and losses, which are recorded in assets and liabilities, respectively, are non-cash items and therefore are taken into account in the preparation of the Consolidated Statements of Cash Flows based on their respective balance sheet classifications.

Foreign currency translation

The assets and liabilities of the Company's foreign subsidiaries have been translated into United States dollars using the exchange rates in effect at period end, and the sales and expenses have been translated into United States dollars using average exchange rates in effect during the period. The foreign currency translation adjustments are included as a separate component of *Accumulated other comprehensive income (loss)* in the Consolidated Balance Sheets.

Revenue recognition

COLUMBIA SPORTSWEAR COMPANY

NOTES TO CONSOLIDATED FINANCIAL STATEMENTS—(Continued)

Revenues are recognized when the Company's performance obligations are satisfied as evidenced by transfer of control of promised goods to customers or consumers, in an amount that reflects the consideration the Company expects to be entitled to receive in exchange for those goods or services. Within the Company's wholesale channel, control generally transfers to the customer upon shipment to, or upon receipt by, the customer depending on the terms of sale with the customer. Within the Company's direct-to-consumer ("DTC") channel, control generally transfers to the consumer at the time of sale within retail stores and concession-based arrangements and upon shipment to the consumer with respect to e-commerce transactions.

The amount of consideration the Company expects to be entitled to receive and recognize as *Net sales* across both wholesale and DTC channels varies with changes in sales returns and other accommodations and incentives offered. The Company estimates expected sales returns and other accommodations, such as chargebacks and markdowns and records a sales reserve to reduce *Net sales.* These estimates are based on historical rates of product returns and claims, as well as events and circumstances that indicate changes to such historical rates. However, actual returns and claims in any future period are inherently uncertain and thus may differ from the estimates. As a result, the Company adjusts estimates of revenue at the earlier of when the most likely amount of consideration the Company expects to receive changes or when the amount of consideration becomes fixed. If actual or expected future returns and claims are significantly greater or lower than the sales reserves established, the Company records an adjustment to *Net sales* in the period in which it made such determination.

Licensing income, which is presented separately as *Net licensing income* on the Consolidated Statements of Operations and represents less than 1% of total revenue, is recognized over time based on the greater of contractual minimum royalty guarantees and actual, or estimated, sales of licensed products by the Company's licensees.

The Company expenses sales commissions when incurred, which is generally at the time of sale, because the amortization period would have been one year or less. These costs are recorded within *SG&A expenses*.

Revenue recognized from contracts with customers is recorded net of sales taxes, value added taxes, or similar taxes that are collected on behalf of local taxing authorities.

Shipping and handling costs

The Company treats shipping and handling activities as fulfillment costs, and as such recognize the costs for these activities at the time related revenue is recognized. The majority of these costs are recorded as *SG&A expenses*, and the direct costs associated with shipping goods to customers and consumers are recorded as *Costs of sales*. Shipping and handling fees billed to customers are recorded as *Net sales.* Shipping and handling costs recorded as a component of *SG&A expenses* and were $98.0 million, $89.2 million and $82.7 million for the years ended December 31, 2020, 2019 and 2018, respectively.

Cost of sales

Cost of sales consists of all direct product costs, including shipping, duties and importation costs, as well as specific provisions for excess, close-out or slow moving inventory. In addition, certain products carry life-time or limited warranty provisions for defects in quality and workmanship. *Cost of sales* includes a warranty reserve established for these provisions at the time of sale to cover estimated costs based on the Company's history of warranty repairs and replacements.

Selling, general and administrative expenses

SG&A expenses consists of personnel-related costs, advertising, depreciation and amortization, occupancy, and other selling and general operating expenses related to the Company's business functions.

Stock-based compensation

Stock-based compensation cost is estimated at the grant date based on the award's fair value and is recorded as expense when recognized. For stock options and service-based restricted units, stock-based compensation cost is recognized over the expected requisite service period using the straight-line attribution method. For performance-based restricted stock units, stock-based compensation cost is recognized based on the Company's assessment of the probability of achieving performance targets in the reporting period. The Company estimates forfeitures for stock-based awards granted, but which are not expected to vest.

Advertising costs

Advertising costs, including marketing and demand creation spending, are expensed in the period incurred and are included in *SG&A expenses*. Total advertising expense, including cooperative advertising costs, were $141.3 million, $166.4 million and $150.4 million for the years ended December 31, 2020, 2019 and 2018, respectively. Cooperative advertising costs are expensed when the related revenues are recognized and included in *SG&A expenses* when the Company receives an identifiable benefit in exchange for the

COLUMBIA SPORTSWEAR COMPANY

NOTES TO CONSOLIDATED FINANCIAL STATEMENTS—(Continued)

cost, the advertising may be obtained from a party other than the customer, and the fair value of the advertising benefit can be reasonably estimated.

Recently issued accounting pronouncements

Effective January 1, 2021, the Company adopted ASU No. 2019-12 , Income Taxes (Topic 740): Simplifying the Accounting for Income Taxes, which, among other things, removes specific exceptions for recognizing deferred taxes for investments, performing intraperiod allocation and calculating income taxes in interim periods, as well as targeted impacts to the accounting for taxes under hybrid tax regimes. At adoption, there was not a material impact to the Company's financial position, results of operations or cash flows.

NOTE 3—REVENUES

Disaggregated revenue

As disclosed below in Note 17, the Company has four geographic reportable segments: United States ("U.S."), Latin America and Asia Pacific ("LAAP"), Europe, Middle East and Africa ("EMEA") and Canada.

The following tables disaggregate our operating segment *Net sales* by product category and channel, which the Company believes provides a meaningful depiction how the nature, timing, and uncertainty of *Net sales* are affected by economic factors:

(in thousands)	Year Ended December 31, 2020				
	U.S.	LAAP	EMEA	Canada	Total
Product category net sales					
Apparel, Accessories and Equipment	$ 1,231,835	$ 320,616	$ 197,052	$ 118,116	$ 1,867,619
Footwear	371,948	103,873	101,855	56,259	633,935
Total	$ 1,603,783	$ 424,489	$ 298,907	$ 174,375	$ 2,501,554
Channel net sales					
Wholesale	$ 838,388	$ 198,083	$ 249,161	$ 117,628	$ 1,403,260
DTC	765,395	226,406	49,746	56,747	1,098,294
Total	$ 1,603,783	$ 424,489	$ 298,907	$ 174,375	$ 2,501,554

(in thousands)	Year Ended December 31, 2019				
	U.S.	LAAP	EMEA	Canada	Total
Product category net sales					
Apparel, Accessories and Equipment	$ 1,562,487	$ 395,002	$ 245,381	$ 138,292	$ 2,341,162
Footwear	380,520	134,280	121,691	64,825	701,316
Total	$ 1,943,007	$ 529,282	$ 367,072	$ 203,117	$ 3,042,478
Channel net sales					
Wholesale	$ 1,049,300	$ 272,389	$ 312,347	$ 148,760	$ 1,782,796
DTC	893,707	256,893	54,725	54,357	1,259,682
Total	$ 1,943,007	$ 529,282	$ 367,072	$ 203,117	$ 3,042,478

COLUMBIA SPORTSWEAR COMPANY

NOTES TO CONSOLIDATED FINANCIAL STATEMENTS—(Continued)

(in thousands)	Year Ended December 31, 2018				
	U.S.	LAAP	EMEA	Canada	Total
Product category net sales					
Apparel, Accessories and Equipment	$ 1,432,711	$ 400,240	$ 226,324	$ 131,783	$ 2,191,058
Footwear	295,765	129,912	124,430	61,161	611,268
Total	$ 1,728,476	$ 530,152	$ 350,754	$ 192,944	$ 2,802,326
Channel net sales					
Wholesale	$ 902,928	$ 267,002	$ 300,626	$ 141,467	$ 1,612,023
DTC	825,548	263,150	50,128	51,477	1,190,303
Total	$ 1,728,476	$ 530,152	$ 350,754	$ 192,944	$ 2,802,326

Performance obligations

For the years ended December 31, 2020 and 2019, *Net sales* recognized from performance obligations related to prior periods were not material. *Net sales* expected to be recognized in any future period related to remaining performance obligations is not material.

Contract balances

As of December 31, 2020 and 2019, contract liabilities included in *Accrued Liabilities* on the Consolidated Balance Sheets, which consisted of obligations associated with the Company's gift card and customer loyalty programs, were not material.

NOTE 4—CONCENTRATIONS

Trade receivables

The Company had one customer that accounted for approximately 14.3% and 13.9% of *Accounts receivable, net* at December 31, 2020 and 2019, respectively. No single customer accounted for 10% or more of *Net sales* for any of the years ended December 31, 2020, 2019 or 2018.

NOTE 5—PROPERTY, PLANT AND EQUIPMENT, NET

Property, plant and equipment, net consisted of the following:

(in thousands)	December 31, 2020	December 31, 2019
Land and improvements	$ 33,231	$ 26,951
Buildings and improvements	209,251	204,077
Machinery, software and equipment	388,808	383,881
Furniture and fixtures	96,521	96,303
Leasehold improvements	152,852	147,760
Construction in progress	3,376	10,771
	884,039	869,743
Less accumulated depreciation	(574,247)	(523,092)
	$ 309,792	$ 346,651

Depreciation expense for property, plant and equipment, net was $ 60.9 million, $59.8 million, and $58.2 million for the years ended December 31, 2020, 2019 and 2018, respectively.

Impairment charges for property, plant and equipment are included in *SG&A expense* and were $5.0 million, $0.4 million and $2.1 million for the years ended December 31, 2020, 2019 and 2018, respectively. Charges during the years ended December 31, 2020, 2019 and 2018 were recorded primarily for certain underperforming retail stores in the U.S., EMEA and LAAP regions.

COLUMBIA SPORTSWEAR COMPANY

NOTES TO CONSOLIDATED FINANCIAL STATEMENTS—(Continued)

NOTE 6—INTANGIBLE ASSETS, NET AND GOODWILL

Intangible assets, net consisted of the following:

(in thousands)	December 31, 2020	December 31, 2019
Intangible assets subject to amortization:		
Patents and purchased technology	$ 14,198	$ 14,198
Customer relationships	23,000	23,000
Gross carrying amount	37,198	37,198
Accumulated amortization:		
Patents and purchased technology	(14,198)	(13,311)
Customer relationships	(17,363)	(15,713)
Accumulated amortization	(31,561)	(29,024)
Net carrying amount	5,637	8,174
Intangible assets not subject to amortization	97,921	115,421
Intangible assets, net	$ 103,558	$ 123,595

Amortization expense for intangible assets subject to amortization was $ 2.5 million for the year ended December 31, 2020, and $ 3.0 million for the years ended December 31, 2020 and 2019.

Impairment charges for the intangible assets not subject to amortization are included in *SG&A expense* and were $17.5 million for the year ended December 31, 2020. The impairment of the prAna trademark and trade name intangible asset was determined as part of the annual impairment test. The fair value was estimated using a relief from royalty method under the income approach. Cash flow projections were developed in part from the Company's annual planning process. The discount rate is the estimated weighted-average costs of capital of the reporting unit from a market-participant perspective. The decline in estimated fair value from the fourth-quarter 2019 impairment test reflects a lower estimated royalty rate and a decline in forecasted revenues. There was no impairment recorded for intangible assets not subject to amortization for the years ended December 31, 2019 and 2018.

Substantially all of the Company's goodwill is recorded in the U.S. segment. The Company determined that goodwill was not impaired for the years ended December 31, 2020, 2019, and 2018.

The following table presents the estimated annual amortization expense for the years 2021 through 2025:

(in thousands)	
2021	$ 1,650
2022	1,650
2023	1,650
2024	688
2025	—

NOTE 7—SHORT-TERM BORROWINGS AND CREDIT LINES

Columbia Sportswear Company Credit Lines

In 2020, the Company entered into a credit agreement, maturing on December 30, 2025, which provides an unsecured, committed revolving credit facility that provides for funding up to $500.0 million. Interest, payable monthly, is based on the Company's option of either LIBOR plus an applicable margin or a base rate. Base rate is defined as the highest of the following, plus an applicable margin:

- the administrative agent's prime rate;
- the higher of the federal funds rate or the overnight bank funding rate set by the Federal Reserve Bank of New York, plus 0.50%; or
- the one-month LIBOR plus 1.00%.

COLUMBIA SPORTSWEAR COMPANY

NOTES TO CONSOLIDATED FINANCIAL STATEMENTS—(Continued)

This credit agreement requires the Company to comply with certain financial covenants covering the Company's funded debt ratio and asset coverage ratio. The credit agreement also includes customary covenants that, among other things, limit or restrict the ability of the Company and its subsidiaries to incur additional indebtedness and liens, engage in mergers, acquisitions and dispositions, and engage in transactions with affiliates, as well as restrict certain payments, including dividends and share buybacks.

At December 31, 2020, the Company was in compliance with all associated covenants and there was no balance outstanding. At December 31, 2019, there was no balance outstanding under the credit agreement in effect for such period.

Columbia Sportswear Company's Subsidiary Credit Lines

At December 21, 2020 and 2019, there was no balance outstanding under the Company's subsidiary credit lines.

The Company's Canadian subsidiary has available an unsecured and uncommitted line of credit, which is payable on demand, guaranteed by the Company, and provides for borrowing up to a maximum of CAD$30.0 million (approximately US$23.5 million) at December 31, 2020. The revolving line accrues interest at the Canadian prime rate for CAD overdraft borrowings or Bankers' Acceptance rate plus 150 basis points for Bankers' Acceptance loans.

The Company's European subsidiary has available two separate unsecured and uncommitted lines of credit, and an unsecured, committed line of credit, which are guaranteed by the Company, and provide for borrowing up to a maximum of €25.8 million, €0.6 million, and €4.4 million, respectively (combined approximately US$37.9 million), at December 31, 2020. Borrowings under the € 25.8 million line accrue interest at a base rate of 185 basis points plus 175 basis points. Borrowings under the €4.4 million and €0.6 million lines each accrue interest at 75 basis points.

The Company's Japanese subsidiary has available two separate unsecured and uncommitted overdraft facilities guaranteed by the Company providing for borrowing up to a maximum of ¥1.5 billion and US$7.0 million, respectively (combined approximately US$ 21.5 million) at December 31, 2020. Borrowings under the ¥1.5 billion overdraft facility accrue interest at the Tokyo Interbank Offered Rate plus 0.50 basis points and borrowings under the US$ 7.0 million overdraft facility accrue interest at 175 basis points.

The Company's Korean subsidiary has available an unsecured and uncommitted overdraft facility guaranteed by the Company providing for borrowing up to a maximum of US$20.0 million at December 31, 2020. Borrowings under the overdraft facility accrue interest at the Korea three month CD rate plus 175 basis points.

The Company's Chinese subsidiary has available an unsecured and uncommitted line of credit providing for borrowings up to a maximum of RMB 140.0 million at December 31, 2020. The Company's Chinese subsidiary also has an unsecured and uncommitted overdraft and clean advance facility, guaranteed by the Company that provides for borrowings of advances or overdrafts up to a maximum of US$20.0 million at December 31, 2020. Borrowings under the RMB 140.0 million line of credit accrue interest at the one year loan prime rate less 10 basis points. Borrowings under the US$20.0 million facility accrue interest on advances of RMB at 4.15%, advances of USD based on LIBOR plus 1.75% per annum or overdrafts of RMB based on 110% of the People's Bank of China rate. The combined available borrowings of the two facilities were approximately US$41.5 million at December 31, 2020.

NOTE 8—ACCRUED LIABILITIES

Accrued liabilities consisted of the following:

(in thousands)	December 31, 2020	December 31, 2019
Sales reserves	$ 83,175	$ 110,758
Accrued salaries, bonus, paid time off and other benefits	80,074	93,887
Accrued import duties	18,522	20,922
Taxes other than income taxes payable	15,002	15,496
Product warranties	14,745	14,466
Other	45,760	40,194
	$ 257,278	$ 295,723

COLUMBIA SPORTSWEAR COMPANY

NOTES TO CONSOLIDATED FINANCIAL STATEMENTS—(Continued)

A reconciliation of product warranties is as follows:

	Year Ended December 31,		
(in thousands)	**2020**	**2019**	**2018**
Balance at beginning of year	$ 14,466	$ 13,186	$ 12,339
Provision for warranty claims	3,033	5,152	5,054
Warranty claims	(3,128)	(3,810)	(3,942)
Other	374	(62)	(265)
Balance at end of year	$ 14,745	$ 14,466	$ 13,186

NOTE 9—LEASES

The components of lease cost consisted of the following:

	Year Ended December 31,	
(in thousands)	**2020**	**2019**
Operating lease cost[(1)]	$ 104,906	$ 78,609
Variable lease cost[(1)]	58,391	60,085
Short term lease cost[(1)]	9,600	9,013
	$ 172,897	$ 147,707

[(1)] For the year ended December 31, 2018, prior to the adoption of ASC 842 on January 1, 2019, rent expenses of $143.9 million and $1.6 million was included in *SG&A expense and Cost of sales, respectively.*

For the year ended December 31, 2020, operating lease cost included $ 16.5 million of accelerated amortization for retail locations that permanently closed during 2020 for which the related lease liabilities have not been extinguished as of December 31, 2020 due to ongoing negotiations with the landlords. In addition, for the year ended December 31, 2020, operating lease cost included $7.0 million of right-of-use asset impairment charges related to underperforming retail locations primarily in the U.S. segment for the year ended December 31, 2020. There was no impairment recorded for the year ended December 31, 2019.

In the periods presented, lease concessions reducing variable lease expense were not material.

The following table presents supplemental cash flow information:

	Year Ended December 31,	
(in thousands)	**2020**	**2019**
Cash paid for amounts included in the measurement of operating lease liabilities	$ 82,083	$ 77,350
Operating lease liabilities arising from obtaining ROU assets [(1)(2)]	22,416	471,396
Reductions to ROU assets resulting from reductions to operating lease liabilities	6,400	783

[(1)] The year ended December 31, 2019 reflects the impact from amount initially capitalized in conjunction with the adoption of ASC 842.
[(2)] Includes amounts added to the carrying amount of lease liabilities resulting from lease modifications and reassessments.

The following table presents supplemental balance sheet information related to leases:

	Year Ended December 31,	
	2020	**2019**
Weighted average remaining lease term	6.16 years	6.79 years
Weighted average discount rate	3.72 %	3.82 %

COLUMBIA SPORTSWEAR COMPANY

NOTES TO CONSOLIDATED FINANCIAL STATEMENTS—(Continued)

The following table presents the future maturities of liabilities as of December 31, 2020:

(in thousands)	
2021	$ 92,756
2022	73,936
2023	66,328
2024	58,726
2025	51,134
Thereafter	130,429
Total lease payments	473,309
Less: imputed interest	(54,662)
Total lease liabilities	418,647
Less: current obligations	(65,466)
Long-term lease obligations	$ 353,181

As of December 31, 2020, the Company has additional operating lease commitments that have not yet commenced of $ 3.9 million. These leases will commence in 2021 with lease terms of approximately two to 10 years.

NOTE 10—INCOME TAXES

Income Tax Provision

Consolidated income from continuing operations before income taxes consisted of the following:

	Year Ended December 31,		
(in thousands)	2020	2019	2018
United States operations	$ 29,154	$ 247,642	$ 224,430
Foreign operations	110,369	157,787	136,287
Income before income tax	$ 139,523	$ 405,429	$ 360,717

The components of the provision for income taxes consisted of the following:

	Year Ended December 31,		
(in thousands)	2020	2019	2018
Current:			
Federal	$ 18,435	$ 41,148	$ 59,213
State and local	4,929	7,458	9,959
Non-United States	26,897	30,930	28,700
	50,261	79,536	97,872
Deferred:			
Federal	(14,728)	(7,887)	(10,961)
State and local	(5,097)	(999)	(1,910)
Non-United States	1,074	4,290	768
	(18,751)	(4,596)	(12,103)
Income tax expense	$ 31,510	$ 74,940	$ 85,769

COLUMBIA SPORTSWEAR COMPANY

NOTES TO CONSOLIDATED FINANCIAL STATEMENTS—(Continued)

The following is a reconciliation of the statutory federal income tax rate to the effective rate reported in the financial statements:

	Year Ended December 31,		
(percent of income before tax)	**2020**	**2019**	**2018**
Provision for federal income taxes at the statutory rate	21.0 %	21.0 %	21.0 %
State and local income taxes, net of federal benefit	1.5	1.7	2.0
Non-United States income taxed at different rates	2.1	(0.1)	(0.1)
Foreign tax credits	(0.9)	(0.1)	—
Adjustment to deferred taxes	(1.2)	(2.1)	—
Global Intangible Low-Taxed Income	0.1	—	0.4
Research credits	(1.4)	(0.5)	(0.6)
Withholding taxes	0.5	0.3	0.4
Excess tax benefits from stock plans	(0.8)	(1.6)	(1.4)
Provision for income taxes related to tax reform	—	—	1.4
Other	1.7	(0.1)	0.7
Actual provision for income taxes	22.6 %	18.5 %	23.8 %

Deferred Income Tax Balances

Significant components of the Company's deferred taxes consisted of the following:

	December 31,	
(in thousands)	**2020**	**2019**
Deferred tax assets:		
Accruals and allowances	$ 47,667	$ 38,532
Capitalized inventory costs	38,832	34,389
Stock compensation	6,078	5,013
Net operating loss carryforwards	24,253	23,660
Depreciation and amortization	29,358	32,293
Tax credits	844	2,329
Foreign currency	2,418	—
Other	2,304	2,258
Gross deferred tax assets	151,754	138,474
Valuation allowance	(23,534)	(24,130)
Net deferred tax assets	128,220	114,344
Deferred tax liabilities:		
Depreciation and amortization	(16,206)	(15,738)
Prepaid expenses	(2,085)	(2,661)
Deferred tax liability associated with future repatriations	(19,008)	(19,847)
Foreign currency	—	(3,610)
Gross deferred tax liabilities	(37,299)	(41,856)
Total net deferred taxes	$ 90,921	$ 72,488

The Company has foreign net operating loss carryforwards of $ 89.1 million as of December 31, 2020, of which $ 72.7 million have an unlimited carryforward period and $16.5 million expire between 2025 and 2040. The net operating losses result in deferred tax assets of $ 24.3 million and $23.7 million and were subject to a valuation allowance of $21.2 million and $21.9 million at December 31, 2020 and 2019, respectively.

At December 31, 2020, the Company has accumulated undistributed earnings generated by the Company's foreign subsidiaries of

COLUMBIA SPORTSWEAR COMPANY

NOTES TO CONSOLIDATED FINANCIAL STATEMENTS—(Continued)

$320.8 million As $100.0 million of such earnings have previously been subject to the one-time transition tax on foreign earnings by the Tax Cuts and Jobs Act, any additional taxes due with respect to such earnings would generally be limited to foreign and state taxes and have been recorded as a deferred tax liability. However, the Company intends to indefinitely reinvest the earnings generated after January 1, 2018 and expects future domestic cash generation to be sufficient to meet future domestic cash needs.

Unrecognized Tax Benefits

The Company conducts business globally, and, as a result, the Company or one or more of its subsidiaries file income tax returns in the United States federal jurisdiction and various state and foreign jurisdictions. The Company is subject to examination by taxing authorities throughout the world, including such major jurisdictions as Canada, China, France, Japan, South Korea, Switzerland, and the United States. The Company has effectively settled Canadian tax examinations of all years through 2012, United States tax examinations of all years through 2013, Japanese tax examinations of all years through 2014, France tax examinations of all years through 2014, Swiss tax examinations of all years through 2014, Italy tax examinations of all years through 2016, and China tax examinations of all years through 2018. The Korean National Tax Service concluded an audit of the Company's 2009 through 2013 corporate income tax returns in 2014, and an audit of the Company's 2014 corporate income tax return in 2016. Due to the nature of the findings in both of these audits, the Company has invoked the Mutual Agreement Procedures outlined in the United States-Korean income tax treaty. The Company does not anticipate that adjustments relative to these findings, or any other ongoing tax audits, will result in material changes to its financial condition, results of operations or cash flows. Other than the findings previously noted, the Company is not currently under examination in any major jurisdiction.

A reconciliation of the beginning and ending amount of gross unrecognized tax benefits is as follows:

(in thousands)	December 31, 2020	2019	2018
Balance at beginning of year	$ 12,478	$ 11,064	$ 10,512
Increases related to prior year tax positions	1,903	4,374	490
Decreases related to prior year tax positions	(162)	(5,423)	(1,093)
Increases related to current year tax positions	906	4,991	1,818
Settlements	—	(1,464)	319
Expiration of statute of limitations	(632)	(1,064)	(982)
Balance at end of year	$ 14,493	$ 12,478	$ 11,064

Due to the potential for resolution of income tax audits currently in progress, and the expiration of various statutes of limitation, it is reasonably possible that the unrecognized tax benefits balance may change within the twelve months following December 31, 2020 by a range of zero to $5.4 million. Open tax years, including those previously mentioned, contain matters that could be subject to differing interpretations of applicable tax laws and regulations as they relate to the amount, timing, or inclusion of revenue and expenses or the sustainability of income tax credits for a given examination cycle.

Unrecognized tax benefits of $13.6 million, $11.5 million and $9.1 million would affect the effective tax rate if recognized at December 31, 2020, 2019 and 2018, respectively.

The Company recognizes interest expense and penalties related to income tax matters in *Income tax expense*. The Company recognized a net increase of accrued interest and penalties of $0.8 million in 2020, and a net reversal of accrued interest and penalties of $ 0.5 million in 2019 and a net increase of accrued interest and penalties of $0.4 million in 2018, all of which related to uncertain tax positions. The Company had $ 2.3 million and $ 1.5 million of accrued interest and penalties related to uncertain tax positions at December 31, 2020 and 2019, respectively.

NOTE 11—RETIREMENT SAVINGS PLANS

401(k) Profit-Sharing Plan

The Company has a 401(k) profit-sharing plan, which covers substantially all United States employees. Participation begins the first day of the quarter following completion of 30 days of service. The Company, with approval of the Board of Directors, may elect to make discretionary matching or non-matching contributions. Costs recognized for Company contributions to the plan were $10.1 million, $9.4 million and $8.9 million for the years ended December 31, 2020, 2019 and 2018, respectively.

COLUMBIA SPORTSWEAR COMPANY

NOTES TO CONSOLIDATED FINANCIAL STATEMENTS—(Continued)

Deferred Compensation Plan

The Company sponsors a nonqualified retirement savings plan for certain senior management employees whose contributions to the tax qualified 401(k) plan would be limited by provisions of the Internal Revenue Code. This plan allows participants to defer receipt of a portion of their salary and incentive compensation and to receive matching contributions for a portion of the deferred amounts. Costs recognized for Company matching contributions to the plan totaled $0.4 million, $0.5 million and $0.4 million for the years ended December 31, 2020, 2019 and 2018, respectively. Participants earn a return on their deferred compensation based on investment earnings of participant-selected investments. Deferred compensation, including accumulated earnings on the participant-directed investment selections, is distributable in cash at participant-specified dates or upon retirement, death, disability, or termination of employment.

The Company has purchased specific money market and mutual funds in the same amounts as the participant-directed investment selections underlying the deferred compensation liabilities. These investment securities and earnings thereon, held in an irrevocable trust, are intended to provide a source of funds to meet the deferred compensation obligations, subject to claims of creditors in the event of the Company's insolvency. Changes in the market value of the participants' investment selections are recorded as an adjustment to the investments and as unrealized gains and losses in *SG&A expense*. A corresponding adjustment of an equal amount is made to the deferred compensation liabilities and compensation expense, which is included in *SG&A expense*.

At December 31, 2020, and 2019, the long-term portion of the liability to participants under this plan was $18.7 million and $ 14.0 million, respectively, and was recorded in *Other long-term liabilities*. At December 31, 2020 and 2019, the current portion of the participant liability was $ 1.2 million and $ 1.7 million, respectively, and was recorded in *Accrued liabilities*. At December 31, 2020 and 2019, the fair value of the long-term portion of the investments related to this plan was $18.7 million and $ 14.0 million, respectively, and was recorded in *Other non-current assets*. At December 31, 2020 and 2019, the current portion of the investments related to this plan was $1.2 million and $ 1.7 million, respectively, and was recorded in *Short-term investments*.

NOTE 12—COMMITMENTS AND CONTINGENCIES

Litigation

The Company is involved in litigation and various legal matters arising in the normal course of business, including matters related to employment, retail, intellectual property, contractual agreements, and various regulatory compliance activities. Management has considered facts related to legal and regulatory matters and opinions of counsel handling these matters, and does not believe the ultimate resolution of these proceedings will have a material adverse effect on the Company's financial position, results of operations or cash flows.

Indemnities and Guarantees

During its normal course of business, the Company has made certain indemnities, commitments and guarantees under which it may be required to make payments in relation to certain transactions. These include (i) intellectual property indemnities to the Company's customers and licensees in connection with the use, sale or license of Company products, (ii) indemnities to various lessors in connection with facility leases for certain claims arising from such facility or lease, (iii) indemnities to customers, vendors and service providers pertaining to claims based on the negligence or willful misconduct of the Company, (iv) executive severance arrangements, and (v) indemnities involving the accuracy of representations and warranties in certain contracts. The duration of these indemnities, commitments and guarantees varies, and in certain cases, may be indefinite. The majority of these indemnities, commitments and guarantees do not provide for any limitation of the maximum potential for future payments the Company could be obligated to make. The Company has not recorded any liability for these indemnities, commitments and guarantees in the accompanying Consolidated Balance Sheets.

NOTE 13—SHAREHOLDERS' EQUITY

Since the inception of the Company's stock repurchase plan in 2004 through December 31, 2020, the Company's Board of Directors has authorized the repurchase of $1.1 billion of the Company's common stock. Shares of the Company's common stock may be purchased in the open market or through privately negotiated transactions, subject to market conditions, and generally settle subsequent to the trade date. The repurchase program does not obligate the Company to acquire any specific number of shares or to acquire shares over any specified period of time.

Under this program as of December 31, 2020, the Company had repurchased 26.8 million shares at an aggregate purchase price of $ 1,017.8 million and have $82.2 million remaining available. During the year ended December 31, 2020, the Company purchased an aggregate of $ 132.9 million of common stock under this program.

COLUMBIA SPORTSWEAR COMPANY

NOTES TO CONSOLIDATED FINANCIAL STATEMENTS—(Continued)

In January 2021, the Company's Board of Directors approved a $ 400.0 million increase in share repurchase authorization.

NOTE 14—STOCK-BASED COMPENSATION

At its Annual Meeting held on June 3, 2020, the Company's shareholders approved the Company's 2020 Stock Incentive Plan (the "2020 Plan"), and the 2020 Plan became effective on that date following such approval. The 2020 Plan replaced the Company's 1997 Stock Incentive Plan (the "Prior Plan") and no new awards will be granted under the Prior Plan. The terms and conditions of the awards granted under the Prior Plan will remain in effect with respect to awards granted under the Prior Plan. The Company has reserved 3.0 million shares of common stock for issuance under the 2020 Plan, plus up to an aggregate of 1.5 million shares of the Company's common stock that were previously authorized and available for issuance under the Prior Plan. At December 31, 2020, 4,169,642 shares were available for future grants under the 2020 Plan and up to 328,486 additional shares that were previously authorized and available for issuance under the Prior Plan may become available for future grants under the 2020 Plan. The 2020 Plan allows for grants of incentive stock options, non-statutory stock options, restricted stock awards, restricted stock units, and other stock-based or cash-based awards. The Company uses original issuance shares to satisfy share-based payments.

Stock Compensation

Stock-based compensation expense consisted of the following:

	Year Ended December 31,		
(in thousands)	2020	2019	2018
Cost of sales	$ 303	$ 278	$ 250
SG&A expense	17,475	17,554	14,041
Pre-tax stock-based compensation expense	17,778	17,832	14,291
Income tax benefits	(4,015)	(4,009)	(3,218)
Total stock-based compensation expense, net of tax	$ 13,763	$ 13,823	$ 11,073

The Company realized a tax benefit for the deduction from stock-based award transactions of $ 4.1 million, $9.9 million and $7.9 million for the years ended December 31, 2020, 2019 and 2018, respectively.

Stock Options

Options to purchase the Company's common stock are granted at exercise prices equal to or greater than the fair market value of the Company's common stock on the date of grant. Options generally vest and become exercisable ratably on an annual basis over a period of four years and expire ten years from the date of the grant.

The fair value of stock options is determined using the Black-Scholes model. Key inputs and assumptions used in the model include the exercise price of the award, the expected option term, the expected stock price volatility of the Company's stock over the option's expected term, the risk-free interest rate over the option's expected term, and the Company's expected annual dividend yield. The option's expected term is derived from historical option exercise behavior and the option's terms and conditions, which the Company believes provide a reasonable basis for estimating an expected term. The expected volatility is estimated based on observations of the Company's historical volatility over the most recent term commensurate with the expected term. The risk-free interest rate is based on the United States Treasury yield approximating the expected term. The dividend yield is based on the expected cash dividend payouts.

The weighted average assumptions for stock options granted and resulting fair value is as follows:

	Year Ended December 31,		
	2020	2019	2018
Expected option term	4.39 years	4.50 years	4.50 years
Expected stock price volatility	21.19%	27.14%	28.39%
Risk-free interest rate	1.14%	2.49%	2.47%
Expected annual dividend yield	1.13%	1.03%	1.15%
Weighted average grant date fair value per share	$14.67	$22.51	$18.86

COLUMBIA SPORTSWEAR COMPANY

NOTES TO CONSOLIDATED FINANCIAL STATEMENTS—(Continued)

The following table summarizes stock option activity under the Plan:

	Number of Shares	Weighted Average Exercise Price	Weighted Average Remaining Contractual Life	Aggregate Intrinsic Value [(1)] *(in thousands)*
Options outstanding at January 1, 2018	1,769,887	$ 44.22	6.69	$ 48,962
Granted	402,010	76.48		
Cancelled	(67,440)	60.75		
Exercised	(499,836)	36.98		
Options outstanding at December 31, 2018	1,604,621	53.86	6.95	48,703
Granted	395,653	93.98		
Cancelled	(68,275)	74.10		
Exercised	(452,325)	43.76		
Options outstanding at December 31, 2019	1,479,674	66.74	7.11	49,930
Granted	660,071	87.25		
Cancelled	(78,163)	83.76		
Exercised	(142,419)	48.58		
Options outstanding at December 31, 2020	1,919,163	$ 74.45	7.19	$ 29,489
Options vested and expected to vest at December 31, 2020	1,839,590	$ 73.88	7.12	$ 29,185
Options exercisable at December 31, 2020	806,320	$ 60.31	5.53	$ 22,620

[(1)]The aggregate intrinsic value above represents pre-tax intrinsic value that would have been realized if all options had been exercised on the last business day of the period indicated, based on the Company's closing stock price on that day.

Stock option compensation expense for the years ended December 31, 2020, 2019 and 2018 was $ 7.0 million, $6.2 million and $4.9 million, respectively. At December 31, 2020, unrecognized costs related to outstanding stock options totaled $11.5 million, before any related tax benefit. The unrecognized costs related to stock options are being amortized over the related vesting period using the straight-line attribution method. These unrecognized costs related to stock options are being amortized over a weighted average period of 2.33 years. The aggregate intrinsic value of stock options exercised was $ 4.9 million, $26.8 million and $22.4 million for the years ended December 31, 2020, 2019 and 2018, respectively. The total cash received as a result of stock option exercises for the years ended December 31, 2020, 2019 and 2018 was $6.9 million, $19.8 million and $ 18.5 million, respectively.

Restricted Stock Units

Service-based restricted stock units are granted at no cost to key employees and generally vest over a period of four years. Performance-based restricted stock units are granted at no cost to certain members of the Company's senior executive team, excluding the Chief Executive Officer. Performance-based restricted stock units granted after 2009 generally vest over a performance period of between two and three years. Restricted stock units vest in accordance with the terms and conditions established by the Compensation Committee of the Board of Directors, and are based on continued service and, in some instances, on individual performance or Company performance or both.

The fair value of service-based and performance-based restricted stock units is determined using the Black-Scholes model. Key inputs and assumptions used in the model include the vesting period, the Company's expected annual dividend yield and the closing price of the Company's common stock on the date of grant.

The weighted average assumptions for restricted stock units granted and resulting fair value are as follows:

	Year Ended December 31,		
	2020	2019	2018
Vesting period	3.79 years	3.76 years	3.77 years
Expected annual dividend yield	1.18%	0.97%	1.15%
Weighted average grant date fair value per restricted stock unit granted	$78.90	$94.58	$73.74

COLUMBIA SPORTSWEAR COMPANY

NOTES TO CONSOLIDATED FINANCIAL STATEMENTS—(Continued)

The following table summarizes the restricted stock unit activity under the Plan:

	Number of Shares	Weighted Average Grant Date Fair Value Per Share
Restricted stock units outstanding at January 1, 2018	449,475	$ 52.07
Granted	197,299	73.74
Vested[(1)]	(155,847)	50.97
Forfeited	(66,926)	53.19
Restricted stock units outstanding at December 31, 2018	424,001	62.38
Granted	177,618	94.58
Vested[(1)]	(163,195)	60.45
Forfeited	(33,320)	72.35
Restricted stock units outstanding at December 31, 2019	405,104	76.45
Granted	216,318	78.90
Vested[(1)]	(160,229)	68.72
Forfeited	(35,918)	79.36
Restricted stock units outstanding at December 31, 2020	425,275	$ 80.37

[(1)] The number of vested units includes shares withheld by the Company to pay up to maximum statutory requirements to taxing authorities on behalf of the employee. For the years ended December 31, 2020, 2019 and 2018, the Company withheld 54,543, 56,843 and 55,907 shares, respectively, to satisfy $4.5 million, $5.8 million and $4.3 million of employees' tax obligations, respectively.

Restricted stock unit compensation expense for the years ended December 31, 2020, 2019 and 2018 was $ 10.8 million, $11.6 million and $9.4 million, respectively. At December 31, 2020, unrecognized costs related to restricted stock units totaled $ 18.6 million, before any related tax benefit. The unrecognized costs related to restricted stock units are being amortized over the related vesting period using the straight-line attribution method. These unrecognized costs at December 31, 2020 are expected to be recognized over a weighted average period of 2.08 years. The total grant date fair value of restricted stock units vested during the years ended December 31, 2020, 2019 and 2018 was $11.0 million, $9.9 million and $7.9 million, respectively.

NOTE 15—EARNINGS PER SHARE

Earnings per share ("EPS") is presented on both a basic and diluted basis. Basic EPS is based on the weighted average number of common shares outstanding. Diluted EPS reflects the potential dilution that could occur if outstanding securities or other contracts to issue common stock were exercised or converted into common stock.

A reconciliation of the common shares used in the denominator for computing basic and diluted EPS is as follows:

	Year Ended December 31,		
(in thousands, except per share amounts)	2020	2019	2018
Weighted average common shares outstanding, used in computing basic earnings per share	66,376	67,837	69,614
Effect of dilutive stock options and restricted stock units	396	656	787
Weighted average common shares outstanding, used in computing diluted earnings per share	66,772	68,493	70,401
Earnings per share of common stock attributable to Columbia Sportswear Company:			
Basic	$ 1.63	$ 4.87	$ 3.85
Diluted	$ 1.62	$ 4.83	$ 3.81

Stock options and service-based restricted stock units, and performance-based restricted stock representing 1,122,935, 405,928 and 372,516 shares of common stock for the years ended December 31, 2020, 2019 and 2018, respectively, were outstanding but were excluded from the computation of diluted EPS because their effect would be anti-dilutive under the treasury stock method or because the shares were subject to performance conditions that had not been met.

COLUMBIA SPORTSWEAR COMPANY

NOTES TO CONSOLIDATED FINANCIAL STATEMENTS—(Continued)

NOTE 16—ACCUMULATED OTHER COMPREHENSIVE INCOME (LOSS)

Accumulated other comprehensive income (loss) on the Consolidated Balance Sheets is net of applicable taxes, and consists of unrealized holding gains and losses on available-for-sale securities, unrealized gains and losses on certain derivative transactions and foreign currency translation adjustments.

The following table sets forth the changes in *Accumulated other comprehensive income (loss)* attributable to the Company:

(in thousands)	Unrealized gains (losses) on available for sale securities	Unrealized holding gains (losses) on derivative transactions	Foreign currency translation adjustments	Total
Balance at January 1, 2018	$ (4)	$ (10,716)	$ 1,833	$ (8,887)
Other comprehensive income (loss) before reclassifications	(56)	23,065	(17,800)	5,209
Amounts reclassified from accumulated other comprehensive loss [1]	—	130	—	130
Net other comprehensive income (loss) during the year	(56)	23,195	(17,800)	5,339
Adoption of ASU 2017-12	—	(515)	—	(515)
Balance at December 31, 2018	(60)	11,964	(15,967)	(4,063)
Other comprehensive income before reclassifications	56	6,669	2,064	8,789
Amounts reclassified from accumulated other comprehensive loss [1]	—	(9,052)	—	(9,052)
Net other comprehensive income (loss) during the year	56	(2,383)	2,064	(263)
Purchase of non-controlling interest	—	(99)	—	(99)
Balance at December 31, 2019	(4)	9,482	(13,903)	(4,425)
Other comprehensive income (loss) before reclassifications	4	(7,218)	24,078	16,864
Amounts reclassified from accumulated other comprehensive income [1]	—	(11,633)	—	(11,633)
Net other comprehensive income (loss) during the year	4	(18,851)	24,078	5,231
Balance at December 31, 2020	$ —	$ (9,369)	$ 10,175	$ 806

[1] Amounts reclassified are recorded in *Net sales, Cost of sales,* or *Other operating income (expense), net* on the Consolidated Statements of Operations. Refer to Note 18 for further information regarding reclassifications.

NOTE 17—SEGMENT INFORMATION

The Company has four reportable geographic segments: U.S., LAAP, EMEA, and Canada, which are reflective of the Company's internal organization, management and oversight structure. Each geographic segment operates predominantly in one industry: the design, development, marketing, and distribution of outdoor, active and everyday lifestyle apparel, footwear, accessories, and equipment products. Intersegment net sales and intersegment profits, which are recorded at a negotiated mark-up and eliminated in consolidation, are not material. Unallocated corporate expenses consist of expenses incurred by centrally-managed departments, including global information services, finance, human resources and legal, as well as executive compensation, unallocated benefit program expense, trademark impairment charges, and other miscellaneous costs.

COLUMBIA SPORTSWEAR COMPANY

NOTES TO CONSOLIDATED FINANCIAL STATEMENTS—(Continued)

The following table presents financial information for the Company's reportable segments:

(in thousands)	Year Ended December 31, 2020	2019	2018
Net sales to unrelated entities:			
U.S.	$ 1,603,783	$ 1,943,007	$ 1,728,476
LAAP	424,489	529,282	530,152
EMEA	298,907	367,072	350,754
Canada	174,375	203,117	192,944
	$ 2,501,554	$ 3,042,478	$ 2,802,326
Segment income from operations:			
U.S.	$ 250,485	$ 456,656	$ 410,750
LAAP	35,875	80,138	80,967
EMEA	31,235	45,419	33,314
Canada	37,620	39,576	31,304
Total segment income from operations	355,215	621,789	556,335
Unallocated corporate expenses	(218,166)	(226,818)	(205,353)
Interest income, net	435	8,302	9,876
Other non-operating income (expense), net	2,039	2,156	(141)
Income before income tax	$ 139,523	$ 405,429	$ 360,717
Depreciation and amortization expense:			
U.S.	$ 25,852	$ 23,388	$ 21,938
LAAP	5,756	5,956	5,721
EMEA	3,739	4,036	4,260
Canada	2,825	3,009	3,076
Unallocated corporate expense	25,244	23,367	23,235
	$ 63,416	$ 59,756	$ 58,230
Accounts receivable, net:			
U.S.	$ 244,236	$ 248,211	
LAAP	83,671	101,995	
EMEA	66,780	82,500	
Canada	58,258	55,527	
	$ 452,945	$ 488,233	
Inventories, net:			
U.S.	$ 362,061	$ 398,192	
LAAP	94,448	105,978	
EMEA	60,124	58,731	
Canada	39,897	43,067	
	$ 556,530	$ 605,968	
Property, plant and equipment, net:			
U.S.	$ 245,690	$ 280,178	
Canada	25,992	27,800	
All other countries	38,110	38,673	
	$ 309,792	$ 346,651	

COLUMBIA SPORTSWEAR COMPANY

NOTES TO CONSOLIDATED FINANCIAL STATEMENTS—(Continued)

NOTE 18—FINANCIAL INSTRUMENTS AND RISK MANAGEMENT

In the normal course of business, the Company's financial position, results of operations and cash flows are routinely subject to a variety of risks. These risks include risks associated with financial markets, primarily currency exchange rate risk and, to a lesser extent, interest rate risk and equity market risk. The Company regularly assesses these risks and has established policies and business practices designed to mitigate them. The Company does not engage in speculative trading in any financial market.

The Company actively manages the risk of changes in functional currency equivalent cash flows resulting from anticipated non-functional currency denominated purchases and sales. Subsidiaries that use European euros, Canadian dollars, Japanese yen, Chinese renminbi, or Korean won as their functional currency are primarily exposed to changes in functional currency equivalent cash flows from anticipated United States dollar inventory purchases. Subsidiaries that use United States dollars and euros as their functional currency also have non-functional currency denominated sales for which the Company hedges the Canadian dollar and British pound. The Company manages these risks by using currency forward contracts formally designated and effective as cash flow hedges. Hedge effectiveness is generally determined by evaluating the ability of a hedging instrument's cumulative change in fair value to offset the cumulative change in the present value of expected cash flows on the underlying exposures. For forward contracts, prior to June 2019, the time value components ("forward points") were excluded from the determination of hedge effectiveness and included in current period *Cost of sales* for hedges of anticipated United States dollar inventory purchases and in *Net sales* for hedges of anticipated non-functional currency denominated sales on a straight-line basis over the life of the contract. Effective June 2019, the forward points are now included in the fair value of the cash flow hedge on a prospective basis. These costs or benefits will be included in *Accumulated other comprehensive income (loss)* until the underlying hedge transaction is recognized in either *Net sales* or *Cost of sales*, at which time, the forward points will also be recognized as a component of *Net income*.

The Company also uses currency forward contracts not formally designated as hedges to manage the consolidated currency exchange rate risk associated with the remeasurement of non-functional currency denominated monetary assets and liabilities by subsidiaries that use United States dollars, euros, Canadian dollars, yen, won, or renminbi as their functional currency. Non-functional currency denominated monetary assets and liabilities consist primarily of cash and cash equivalents, short-term investments, receivables, payables, deferred income taxes, and intercompany loans. The gains and losses generated on these currency forward contracts not formally designated as hedges are expected to be largely offset in *Other non-operating income (expense), net* by the gains and losses generated from the remeasurement of the non-functional currency denominated monetary assets and liabilities.

The following table presents the gross notional amount of outstanding derivative instruments:

	December 31,	
(in thousands)	2020	2019
Derivative instruments designated as cash flow hedges:		
Currency forward contracts	$ 417,707	$ 471,822
Derivative instruments not designated as hedges:		
Currency forward contracts	326,280	214,086

At December 31, 2020, $4.3 million of deferred net loss on both outstanding and matured derivatives recorded in *Other comprehensive income (loss)* are expected to be reclassified to *Net income* during the next twelve months as a result of underlying hedged transactions also being recorded in *Net sales* or *Cost of sales* in the Consolidated Statements of Operations. Actual amounts ultimately reclassified to *Net sales* or *Cost of sales* in the Consolidated Statements of Comprehensive Income are dependent on United States dollar exchange rates in effect against the euro, pound sterling, renminbi, Canadian dollar, and yen when outstanding derivative contracts mature.

At December 31, 2020, the Company's derivative contracts had a remaining maturity of less than four years. The maximum net exposure to any single counterparty, which is generally limited to the aggregate unrealized gain of all contracts with that counterparty, was less than $1.4 million at December 31, 2020. All of the Company's derivative counterparties have credit ratings that are investment grade or higher. The Company is a party to master netting arrangements that contain features that allow counterparties to net settle amounts arising from multiple separate derivative transactions or net settle in the case of certain triggering events such as a bankruptcy or major default of one of the counterparties to the transaction. The Company has not pledged assets or posted collateral as a requirement for entering into or maintaining derivative positions.

COLUMBIA SPORTSWEAR COMPANY

NOTES TO CONSOLIDATED FINANCIAL STATEMENTS—(Continued)

The following table presents the balance sheet classification and fair value of derivative instruments:

(in thousands)	Balance Sheet Classification	December 31, 2020	December 31, 2019
Derivative instruments designated as cash flow hedges:			
Derivative instruments in asset positions:			
Currency forward contracts	Prepaid expenses and other current assets	$ 947	$ 11,855
Currency forward contracts	Other non-current assets	1,126	4,159
Derivative instruments in liability positions:			
Currency forward contracts	Accrued liabilities	7,573	1,313
Currency forward contracts	Other long-term liabilities	6,590	768
Derivative instruments not designated as cash flow hedges:			
Derivative instruments in asset positions:			
Currency forward contracts	Prepaid expenses and other current assets	1,650	2,146
Derivative instruments in liability positions:			
Currency forward contracts	Accrued liabilities	2,268	953

The following table presents the statement of operations effect and classification of derivative instruments:

(in thousands)	Statement Of Operations Classification	Year Ended December 31, 2020	2019	2018
Currency Forward Contracts:				
Derivative instruments designated as cash flow hedges:				
Gain (loss) recognized in other comprehensive income (loss), net of tax	—	$ (7,218)	$ 6,669	$ 23,503
Gain reclassified from accumulated other comprehensive income (loss) to income for the effective portion	Net sales	191	338	62
Gain (loss) reclassified from accumulated other comprehensive income (loss) to income for the effective portion	Cost of sales	14,495	9,558	(7,604)
Gain reclassified from accumulated other comprehensive income (loss) to income as a result of cash flow hedge discontinuance	Other non-operating income (expense), net	817	—	—
Gain (loss) recognized in income for amount excluded from effectiveness testing and for the ineffective portion	Net sales	—	(43)	19
Gain recognized in income for amount excluded from effectiveness testing and for the ineffective portion	Cost of sales	—	2,380	7,009
Derivative instruments not designated as cash flow hedges:				
Gain (loss) recognized in income	Other non-operating income (expense), net	(2,865)	411	3,334

COLUMBIA SPORTSWEAR COMPANY

NOTES TO CONSOLIDATED FINANCIAL STATEMENTS—(Continued)

NOTE 19—FAIR VALUE MEASURES

Certain assets and liabilities are reported at fair value on either a recurring or nonrecurring basis. Fair value is defined as an exit price, representing the amount that the Company would receive to sell an asset or pay to transfer a liability in an orderly transaction between market participants, under a three-tier fair value hierarchy that prioritizes the inputs used in measuring fair value as follows:

Level 1	—	observable inputs such as quoted prices for identical assets or liabilities in active liquid markets;
Level 2	—	inputs, other than the quoted market prices in active markets, that are observable, either directly or indirectly; or observable market prices in markets with insufficient volume or infrequent transactions; and
Level 3	—	unobservable inputs for which there is little or no market data available, that require the reporting entity to develop its own assumptions.

The Company's assets and liabilities measured at fair value are categorized as Level 1 or Level 2 instruments. Level 1 instrument valuations are obtained from real-time quotes for transactions in active exchange markets involving identical assets. Level 2 instrument valuations are obtained from inputs, other than quoted market prices in active markets, that are directly or indirectly observable in the marketplace and quoted prices in markets with limited volume or infrequent transactions.

Assets and liabilities measured at fair value on a recurring basis as of December 31, 2020 are as follows:

(in thousands)	Level 1	Level 2	Level 3	Total
Assets:				
Cash equivalents:				
Money market funds	$ 119,378	$ —	$ —	$ 119,378
United States government treasury bills	—	234,982	—	234,982
Short-term investments:				
Money market funds	105	—	—	105
Mutual fund shares	1,119	—	—	1,119
Other current assets:				
Derivative financial instruments	—	2,597	—	2,597
Non-current assets:				
Money market funds	4,059	—	—	4,059
Mutual fund shares	14,657	—	—	14,657
Derivative financial instruments	—	1,126	—	1,126
Total assets measured at fair value	$ 139,318	$ 238,705	$ —	$ 378,023
Liabilities:				
Accrued liabilities:				
Derivative financial instruments	$ —	$ 9,841	$ —	$ 9,841
Other long-term liabilities				
Derivative financial instruments	—	6,590	—	6,590
Total liabilities measured at fair value	$ —	$ 16,431	$ —	$ 16,431

COLUMBIA SPORTSWEAR COMPANY

NOTES TO CONSOLIDATED FINANCIAL STATEMENTS—(Continued)

Assets and liabilities measured at fair value on a recurring basis at December 31, 2019 are as follows:

(in thousands)	Level 1	Level 2	Level 3	Total
Assets:				
Cash equivalents:				
Money market funds	$ 288,926	$ —	$ —	$ 288,926
United States government treasury bills	—	34,928	—	34,928
Commercial paper	—	33,587	—	33,587
Short-term investments:				
Mutual fund shares	1,668	—	—	1,668
Other current assets:				
Derivative financial instruments	—	14,001	—	14,001
Non-current assets:				
Money market funds	1,792	—	—	1,792
Mutual fund shares	12,172	—	—	12,172
Derivative financial instruments	—	4,159	—	4,159
Total assets measured at fair value	$ 304,558	$ 86,675	$ —	$ 391,233
Liabilities:				
Accrued liabilities:				
Derivative financial instruments	$ —	$ 2,266	$ —	$ 2,266
Other long-term liabilities:				
Derivative financial instruments	—	768	—	768
Total liabilities measured at fair value	$ —	$ 3,034	$ —	$ 3,034

Non-recurring Fair Value Measurements

The Company measured the fair value of certain trademark and trade name intangible assets and certain retail store long-lived assets consisting of property, plant and equipment, and lease right-of-use assets as part of impairment testing for the year ending December 31, 2020. The inputs used to measure the fair value of these assets are primarily unobservable inputs and, as such, considered Level 3 fair value measurements. See Notes 5, 6 and 9 for discussion of 2020 impairment charges.

SUPPLEMENTARY DATA—QUARTERLY FINANCIAL DATA
(Unaudited)

The following table summarizes the Company's quarterly financial data for the past two years ended December 31:

	2020			
(in thousands, except per share amounts)	**First Quarter**	**Second Quarter**	**Third Quarter**	**Fourth Quarter**
Net sales	$ 568,228	$ 316,611	$ 701,092	$ 915,623
Gross profit	271,714	146,230	342,908	463,037
Net income (loss)	213	(50,707)	62,751	95,756
Earnings (loss) per share:				
Basic	$ 0.00	$ (0.77)	$ 0.95	$ 1.45
Diluted	0.00	(0.77)	0.94	1.44

	2019			
(in thousands, except per share amounts)	**First Quarter**	**Second Quarter**	**Third Quarter**	**Fourth Quarter**
Net sales	$ 654,608	$ 526,210	$ 906,793	$ 954,867
Gross profit	336,729	253,591	446,695	478,655
Net income	74,177	23,029	119,258	114,025
Earnings per share:				
Basic	$ 1.09	$ 0.34	$ 1.76	$ 1.69
Diluted	1.07	0.34	1.75	1.67

Item 9. ***CHANGES IN AND DISAGREEMENTS WITH ACCOUNTANTS ON ACCOUNTING AND FINANCIAL DISCLOSURE***

None.

Item 9A. ***CONTROLS AND PROCEDURES***

Evaluation of Disclosure Controls and Procedures

We have evaluated, under the supervision and with the participation of management, including our Chief Executive Officer and the Chief Financial Officer, the effectiveness of our disclosure controls and procedures pursuant to Rule 13a-15(b) under the Securities Exchange Act of 1934, as amended (the "Exchange Act") as of the end of the period covered by this report. These disclosure controls and procedures require information to be disclosed in our Exchange Act reports to be (1) recorded, processed, summarized, and reported in a timely manner and (2) accumulated and communicated to our management, including our Chief Executive Officer and Chief Financial Officer.

Based on our evaluation, we, including, our Chief Executive Officer and Chief Financial Officer, have concluded that our disclosure controls and procedures were effective as of the end of the period covered by this Annual Report on Form 10-K.

Management's Report on Internal Control Over Financial Reporting

Our management is responsible for establishing and maintaining adequate internal control over financial reporting as defined in the Exchange Act Rule 13a-15(f). All internal control systems, no matter how well designed, have inherent limitations. Therefore, even those systems determined to be effective can provide only reasonable assurance with respect to financial statement preparation and presentation.

Under the supervision and with the participation of management, we have assessed the effectiveness of our internal control over financial reporting as of December 31, 2020. In making this assessment, we used the criteria set forth by the Committee of Sponsoring Organizations of the Treadway Commission in *Internal Control - Integrated Framework (2013)*. Based on our assessment, we, including our Chief Executive Officer and Chief Financial Officer, have concluded our internal control over financial reporting is effective as of December 31, 2020.

The effectiveness of our internal control over financial reporting as of December 31, 2020 has been audited by Deloitte & Touch LLP, an independent registered public accounting firm, as stated in its report, which is included in Item 8 in this annual report.

Changes in Internal Control Over Financial Reporting

There have not been any changes in our internal control over financial reporting that occurred during the quarter ended December 31, 2020 that have materially affected, or are reasonably likely to materially affect, our internal control over financial reporting.

Item 9B. ***OTHER INFORMATION***

None.

REPORT ON INTERNAL CONTROL

REPORT OF INDEPENDENT REGISTERED PUBLIC ACCOUNTING FIRM

To the Shareholders and the Board of Directors of Columbia Sportswear Company

Opinion on Internal Control over Financial Reporting

We have audited the internal control over financial reporting of Columbia Sportswear Company and subsidiaries (the "Company") as of December 31, 2020, based on criteria established in *Internal Control - Integrated Framework (2013)* issued by the Committee of Sponsoring Organizations of the Treadway Commission (COSO). In our opinion, the Company maintained, in all material respects, effective internal control over financial reporting as of December 31, 2020, based on criteria established in *Internal Control - Integrated Framework (2013)* issued by COSO.

We have also audited, in accordance with the standards of the Public Company Accounting Oversight Board (United States) (PCAOB), the consolidated financial statements as of and for the year ended December 31, 2020, of the Company and our report dated February 25, 2021, expressed an unqualified opinion on those financial statements.

Basis for Opinion

The Company's management is responsible for maintaining effective internal control over financial reporting and for its assessment of the effectiveness of internal control over financial reporting, included in the accompanying Report of Management. Our responsibility is to express an opinion on the Company's internal control over financial reporting based on our audit. We are a public accounting firm registered with the PCAOB and are required to be independent with respect to the Company in accordance with the U.S. federal securities laws and the applicable rules and regulations of the Securities and Exchange Commission and the PCAOB.

We conducted our audit in accordance with the standards of the PCAOB. Those standards require that we plan and perform the audit to obtain reasonable assurance about whether effective internal control over financial reporting was maintained in all material respects. Our audit included obtaining an understanding of internal control over financial reporting, assessing the risk that a material weakness exists, testing and evaluating the design and operating effectiveness of internal control based on the assessed risk, and performing such other procedures as we considered necessary in the circumstances. We believe that our audit provides a reasonable basis for our opinion.

Definition and Limitations of Internal Control over Financial Reporting

A company's internal control over financial reporting is a process designed to provide reasonable assurance regarding the reliability of financial reporting and the preparation of financial statements for external purposes in accordance with generally accepted accounting principles. A company's internal control over financial reporting includes those policies and procedures that (1) pertain to the maintenance of records that, in reasonable detail, accurately and fairly reflect the transactions and dispositions of the assets of the company; (2) provide reasonable assurance that transactions are recorded as necessary to permit preparation of financial statements in accordance with generally accepted accounting principles, and that receipts and expenditures of the company are being made only in accordance with authorizations of management and directors of the company; and (3) provide reasonable assurance regarding prevention or timely detection of unauthorized acquisition, use, or disposition of the company's assets that could have a material effect on the financial statements.

Because of its inherent limitations, internal control over financial reporting may not prevent or detect misstatements. Also, projections of any evaluation of effectiveness to future periods are subject to the risk that controls may become inadequate because of changes in conditions, or that the degree of compliance with the policies or procedures may deteriorate.

/s/ DELOITTE & TOUCHE LLP
Portland, Oregon
February 25, 2021

MANAGEMENT'S CERTIFICATION OF FINANCIAL STATEMENTS

EXHIBIT 32.1

SECTION 1350 CERTIFICATION

In connection with the Annual Report of Columbia Sportswear Company (the "Company") on Form 10-K for the period ended December 31, 2020 as filed with the Securities and Exchange Commission on the date hereof (the "Form 10-K"), I, Timothy P. Boyle, Chief Executive Officer of the Company, certify, pursuant to 18 U.S.C. Section 1350, as adopted pursuant to Section 906 of the Sarbanes-Oxley Act of 2002, that to my knowledge:

(1) The Form 10-K fully complies with the requirements of Section 13(a) or 15(d), as applicable, of the Securities Exchange Act of 1934 as of, and for, the periods presented in the Form 10-K; and

(2) The information contained in the Form 10-K fairly presents, in all material respects, the financial condition and results of the operation of the Company.

Dated: February 25, 2021

/s/ TIMOTHY P. BOYLE

Timothy P. Boyle
Chairman, President and Chief Executive Officer
(Principal Executive Officer)

SUPPLEMENTAL INFORMATION

PART II

Item 5. ***MARKET FOR REGISTRANT'S COMMON EQUITY, RELATED STOCKHOLDER MATTERS AND ISSUER PURCHASES OF EQUITY SECURITIES***

Market Information

Our common stock is traded on the NASDAQ Global Select Market under the symbol "COLM."

Holders

At February 12, 2021, we had 266 shareholders of record, although we have a much larger number of beneficial owners, whose shares of record are held by banks, brokers and other financial institutions

Quarterly dividends on our common stock, when declared by our Board of Directors, are paid in March, May, August, and November. In March 2020, our Board of Directors suspended quarterly dividend payments as part of a broader capital preservation effort during the ongoing COVID-19 pandemic.

Based on the strength of our balance sheet and confidence in our earnings recovery and long-term growth trajectory, our Board of Directors approved a regular quarterly cash dividend of $0.26 per share, payable on March 22, 2021 to shareholders of record on March 9, 2021.

Performance Graph

The line graph below compares the cumulative total shareholder return of our common stock with the cumulative total return of the Russell 1000 Index and Russell 1000 Textiles Apparel & Shoes Index for the period beginning December 31, 2015 and ending December 31, 2020. The graph and table assume that $100 was invested on December 31, 2015, and that any dividends were reinvested. Historical stock price performance should not be relied on as indicative of future stock price performance.

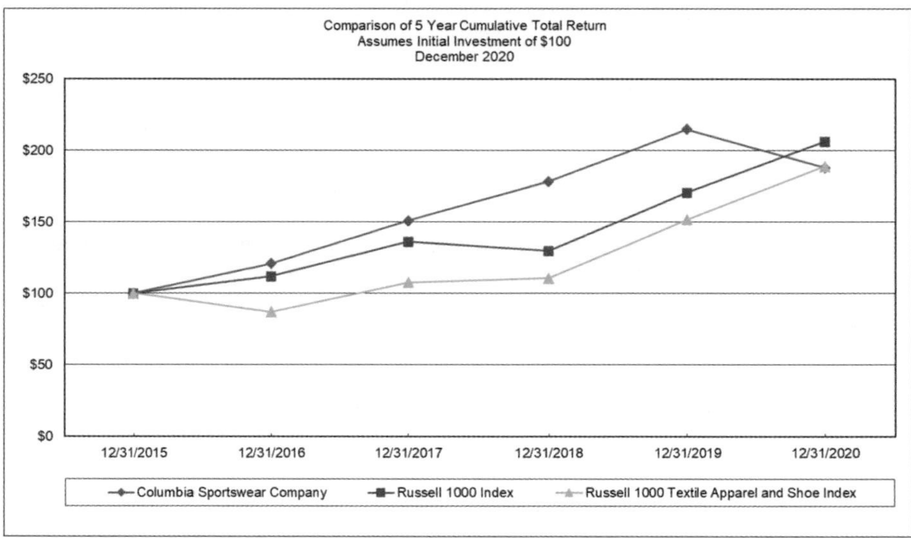

	12/31/2015	12/31/2016	12/31/2017	12/31/2018	12/31/2019	12/31/2020
Columbia Sportswear Company	$100.00	$121.02	$151.11	$178.63	$214.99	$188.17
Russell 1000 Index	$100.00	$112.05	$136.36	$129.83	$170.63	$206.40
Russell 1000 Textiles Apparel & Shoes Index	$100.00	$87.13	$107.64	$110.65	$151.70	$189.19

SELECTED FINANCIAL DATA INCLUDING EARNINGS PER SHARE

Issuer Purchases of Equity Securities

Since the inception of our share repurchase program in 2004 through December 31, 2020, our Board of Directors has authorized the repurchase of $1.1 billion of our common stock. Shares of our common stock may be purchased in the open market or through privately negotiated transactions, subject to market conditions. The repurchase program does not obligate us to acquire any specific number of shares or to acquire shares over any specified period of time. Under this program as of December 31, 2020, we have repurchased 26.8 million shares at an aggregate purchase price of $1,017.8 million, and have $82.2 million remaining available.

In March 2020, we suspended future share repurchases as part of a broader capital preservation effort during the ongoing COVID-19 pandemic. We did not repurchase any shares or common stock during the fourth quarter of 2020.

In 2021, we have reinstated our historical capital allocation strategy, which includes share repurchases. At its regular board meeting in January 2021, our Board of Directors approved an additional $400.0 million share repurchase authorization.

Item 6. ***SELECTED FINANCIAL DATA***

Selected Consolidated Financial Data

The selected consolidated financial data presented below for, and as of the end of, each of the years in the five-year period ended December 31, 2020 have been derived from our audited Consolidated Financial Statements. The selected consolidated financial data should be read in conjunction with the Item 7 and Item 8 of this annual report.

(in thousands, except per share amounts)	2020	2019	2018	2017	2016
Statement of Operations Data:					
Net sales	$ 2,501,554	$3,042,478	$ 2,802,326	$ 2,466,105	$ 2,377,045
Gross profit	1,223,889	1,515,670	1,386,348	1,159,962	1,110,348
Gross margin	48.9 %	49.8 %	49.5 %	47.0 %	46.7 %
Income from operations	137,049	394,971	350,982	262,969	256,508
Net income attributable to Columbia Sportswear Company[(1)]	108,013	330,489	268,256	105,123	191,898
Per Share of Common Stock Data:					
Earnings per share attributable to Columbia Sportswear Company:					
Basic	$ 1.63	$ 4.87	$ 3.85	$ 1.51	$ 2.75
Diluted	1.62	4.83	3.81	1.49	2.72
Cash dividends per share	0.26	0.96	0.90	0.73	0.69
Weighted average shares outstanding:					
Basic	66,376	67,837	69,614	69,759	69,683
Diluted	66,772	68,493	70,401	70,453	70,632
Balance Sheet Data:					
Inventories, net[(2)]	$ 556,530	$ 605,968	$ 521,827	$ 457,927	$ 487,997
Total assets[(2)(3)]	2,836,571	2,931,591	2,368,721	2,212,902	2,013,894
Non-current operating lease liabilities[(3)]	353,181	371,507	—	—	—

[(1)] The year-ended December 31, 2017 reflects the provisional impact from the enactment of the Tax Cuts and Jobs Act in December 2017.
[(2)] The year-ended December 31, 2018 reflects the impact from adoption of ASU 2014-09, *Revenue from Contracts with Customers*.
[(3)] The year-ended December 31, 2019 reflects the impact from the adoption of ASU 2016-02, *Leases*.

Under Armour Financial Statements

Appendix

The complete annual report for Under Armour is available at their website: https://about.underarmour.com/investor-relations/annualreport2020.

Under Armour, Inc. and Subsidiaries
Consolidated Balance Sheets
(In thousands, except share data)

	December 31, 2020	December 31, 2019
Assets		
Current assets		
Cash and cash equivalents	$ 1,517,361	$ 788,072
Accounts receivable, net	527,340	708,714
Inventories	895,974	892,258
Prepaid expenses and other current assets	282,300	313,165
Total current assets	3,222,975	2,702,209
Property and equipment, net	658,678	792,148
Operating lease right-of-use assets	536,660	591,931
Goodwill	502,214	550,178
Intangible assets, net	13,295	36,345
Deferred income taxes	23,930	82,379
Other long-term assets	72,876	88,341
Total assets	$ 5,030,628	$ 4,843,531
Liabilities and Stockholders' Equity		
Current liabilities		
Accounts payable	$ 575,954	$ 618,194
Accrued expenses	378,859	374,694
Customer refund liabilities	203,399	219,424
Operating lease liabilities	162,561	125,900
Other current liabilities	92,503	83,797
Total current liabilities	1,413,276	1,422,009
Long term debt	1,003,556	592,687
Operating lease liabilities, non-current	839,414	580,635
Other long-term liabilities	98,389	98,113
Total liabilities	3,354,635	2,693,444
Commitments and contingencies (see Note 10)		
Stockholders' equity		
Class A Common Stock, $0.0003 1/3 par value; 400,000,000 shares authorized as of December 31, 2020 and 2019; 188,603,686 shares issued and outstanding as of December 31, 2020 (2019: 188,289,680)	62	62
Class B Convertible Common Stock, $0.0003 1/3 par value; 34,450,000 shares authorized, issued and outstanding as of December 31, 2020 and 2019.	11	11
Class C Common Stock, $0.0003 1/3 par value; 400,000,000 shares authorized as of December 31, 2020 and 2019; 231,953,667 shares issued and outstanding as of December 31, 2020 (2019: 229,027,730)	77	76
Additional paid-in capital	1,061,173	973,717
Retained earnings	673,855	1,226,986
Accumulated other comprehensive loss	(59,185)	(50,765)
Total stockholders' equity	1,675,993	2,150,087
Total liabilities and stockholders' equity	$ 5,030,628	$ 4,843,531

Under Armour, Inc. and Subsidiaries
Consolidated Statements of Operations
(In thousands, except per share amounts)

	Year Ended December 31, 2020	2019	2018
Net revenues	$ 4,474,667	$ 5,267,132	$ 5,193,185
Cost of goods sold	2,314,572	2,796,599	2,852,714
Gross profit	2,160,095	2,470,533	2,340,471
Selling, general and administrative expenses	2,171,934	2,233,763	2,182,339
Restructuring and impairment charges	601,599	—	183,149
Income (loss) from operations	(613,438)	236,770	(25,017)
Interest expense, net	(47,259)	(21,240)	(33,568)
Other income (expense), net	168,153	(5,688)	(9,203)
Income (loss) before income taxes	(492,544)	209,842	(67,788)
Income tax expense (benefit)	49,387	70,024	(20,552)
Income (loss) from equity method investment	(7,246)	(47,679)	934
Net income (loss)	$ (549,177)	$ 92,139	$ (46,302)
Basic net income (loss) per share of Class A, B and C common stock	$ (1.21)	$ 0.20	$ (0.10)
Diluted net income (loss) per share of Class A, B and C common stock	$ (1.21)	$ 0.20	$ (0.10)
Weighted average common shares outstanding Class A, B and C common stock			
Basic	454,089	450,964	445,815
Diluted	454,089	454,274	445,815

Under Armour, Inc. and Subsidiaries
Consolidated Statements of Comprehensive Income (Loss)
(In thousands)

	Year Ended December 31,		
	2020	2019	2018
Net income (loss)	$ (549,177)	$ 92,139	$ (46,302)
Other comprehensive income (loss):			
Foreign currency translation adjustment	(5,060)	10,754	(18,535)
Unrealized gain (loss) on cash flow hedge, net of tax benefit (expense) of $1,791, $7,798, and $(7,936) for the years ended December 31, 2020, 2019, and 2018, respectively.	(18,075)	(21,646)	22,800
Gain (loss) on intra-entity foreign currency transactions	14,715	(886)	(5,041)
Total other comprehensive (loss)	(8,420)	(11,778)	(776)
Comprehensive income (loss)	$ (557,597)	$ 80,361	$ (47,078)

Under Armour, Inc. and Subsidiaries

Consolidated Statements of Stockholders' Equity
(In thousands)

	Class A Common Stock		Class B Convertible Common Stock		Class C Common Stock		Additional Paid-in-Capital	Retained Earnings	Accumulated Other Comprehensive Income	Total Equity
	Shares	Amount	Shares	Amount	Shares	Amount				
Balance as of December 31, 2017	185,257	61	34,450	11	222,375	74	872,266	1,184,441	(38,211)	$ 2,018,642
Exercise of stock options	2,084	1	—	—	2,127	—	6,747	—	—	6,748
Shares withheld in consideration of employee tax obligations relative to stock-based compensation arrangements	(23)	—	—	—	(140)	—	—	(2,564)	—	(2,564)
Issuance of Class A Common Stock, net of forfeitures	392	—	—	—	—	—	—	—	—	—
Issuance of Class C Common Stock, net of forfeitures	—	—	—	—	2,060	1	(4,168)	—	—	(4,167)
Impact of adoption of accounting standard updates	—	—	—	—	—	—	—	3,507	—	3,507
Stock-based compensation expense	—	—	—	—	—	—	41,783	—	—	41,783
Comprehensive income (loss)	—	—	—	—	—	—	—	(46,302)	(776)	(47,078)
Balance as of December 31, 2018	187,710	$ 62	34,450	$ 11	226,422	$ 75	$ 916,628	$ 1,139,082	$ (38,987)	$ 2,016,871
Exercise of stock options and warrants	441	—	—	—	293	—	2,101	—	—	2,101
Shares withheld in consideration of employee tax obligations relative to stock-based compensation arrangements	(15)	—	—	—	(227)	—	—	(4,235)	—	(4,235)
Issuance of Class A Common Stock, net of forfeitures	154	—	—	—	—	—	—	—	—	—
Issuance of Class C Common Stock, net of forfeitures	—	—	—	—	2,540	1	5,370	—	—	5,371
Impact of adoption of accounting standard updates	—	—	—	—	—	—	—	—	—	—
Stock-based compensation expense	—	—	—	—	—	—	49,618	—	—	49,618
Comprehensive loss	—	—	—	—	—	—	—	92,139	(11,778)	80,361
Balance as of December 31, 2019	188,290	$ 62	34,450	$ 11	229,028	$ 76	$ 973,717	$ 1,226,986	$ (50,765)	$ 2,150,087
Exercise of stock options	148	—	—	—	136	—	517	—	—	517
Shares withheld in consideration of employee tax obligations relative to stock-based compensation arrangements	(1)	—	—	—	(262)	—	—	(3,954)	—	(3,954)
Issuance of Class A Common Stock, net of forfeitures	166	—	—	—	—	—	—	—	—	—
Issuance of Class C Common Stock, net of forfeitures	—	—	—	—	3,052	1	4,225	—	—	4,226
Stock-based compensation expense	—	—	—	—	—	—	42,070	—	—	42,070
Equity Component value of convertible notes issuance, net	—	—	—	—	—	—	40,644	—	—	40,644
Comprehensive income (loss)	—	—	—	—	—	—	—	(549,177)	(8,420)	(557,597)
Balance as of December 31, 2020	188,603	$ 62	34,450	$ 11	231,954	$ 77	$ 1,061,173	$ 673,855	$ (59,185)	$ 1,675,993

Under Armour, Inc. and Subsidiaries
Consolidated Statements of Cash Flows
(In thousands)

	Year Ended December 31, 2020	2019	2018
Cash flows from operating activities			
Net income (loss)	$ (549,177)	$ 92,139	$ (46,302)
Adjustments to reconcile net income (loss) to net cash provided by operating activities			
Depreciation and amortization	164,984	186,425	181,768
Unrealized foreign currency exchange rate gain (loss)	(9,295)	(2,073)	14,023
Impairment charges	470,543	39,000	9,893
Amortization of bond premium	12,070	254	254
Gain on sale of MyFitnessPal platform	(179,318)	—	—
Loss on disposal of property and equipment	3,740	4,640	4,256
Stock-based compensation	42,070	49,618	41,783
Deferred income taxes	43,992	38,132	(38,544)
Changes in reserves and allowances	10,347	(26,096)	(234,998)
Changes in operating assets and liabilities:			
Accounts receivable	167,614	(45,450)	186,834
Inventories	15,306	149,519	109,919
Prepaid expenses and other assets	18,603	24,334	(107,855)
Other non-current assets	(259,735)	19,966	—
Accounts payable	(40,673)	59,458	26,413
Accrued expenses and other liabilities	318,532	(18,987)	134,594
Customer refund liability	(19,250)	(80,710)	305,141
Income taxes payable and receivable	2,511	18,862	41,051
Net cash provided by operating activities	212,864	509,031	628,230
Cash flows from investing activities			
Sale of MyFitnessPal platform	198,916	—	—
Purchase of businesses	(40,280)	—	—
Purchases of property and equipment	(92,291)	(145,802)	(170,385)
Sale of property and equipment	—	—	11,285
Purchase of equity method investment	—	—	(39,207)
Purchases of other assets	—	(1,311)	(4,597)
Net cash (used in) provided by investing activities	66,345	(147,113)	(202,904)
Cash flows from financing activities			
Proceeds from long term debt and revolving credit facility	1,288,753	25,000	505,000
Payments on long term debt and revolving credit facility	(800,000)	(162,817)	(695,000)
Purchase of capped call	(47,850)	—	—
Employee taxes paid for shares withheld for income taxes	(3,675)	(4,235)	(2,743)
Proceeds from exercise of stock options and other stock issuances	4,744	7,472	2,580
Other financing fees	100	63	306
Payments of debt financing costs	(5,219)	(2,553)	(11)
Net cash (used in) provided by financing activities	436,853	(137,070)	(189,868)
Effect of exchange rate changes on cash, cash equivalents and restricted cash	16,445	5,100	12,467
Net increase in cash, cash equivalents and restricted cash	732,507	229,948	247,925
Cash, cash equivalents and restricted cash			
Beginning of period	796,008	566,060	318,135
End of period	$ 1,528,515	$ 796,008	$ 566,060
Non-cash investing and financing activities			
Change in accrual for property and equipment	$ (13,875)	$ (8,084)	$ (14,611)
Other supplemental information			
Cash paid (received) for income taxes, net of refunds	24,443	23,352	(16,738)
Cash paid for interest, net of capitalized interest	28,626	18,031	28,586

The Language of Accountants: Debits and Credits

Road Map

LO	Learning Objective	Page	eLecture	Review	Assignments
LO1	**Describe the system of debits and credits and its use in recording transactions.**	C-2	C-1	C.1	SE1, SE2, SE3, SE4, SE5, SE6, SE7, E1, E2, E4, P1, P2, P3, P4, P5, P10
LO2	**Illustrate the adjusting process using debits and credits.**	C-11	C-2	C.2	SE8, SE9, P6, P7, P10
LO3	**Explain the adjusted trial balance and use it to prepare financial statements.**	C-16	C-3	C.3	SE10, SE12, P8, P10
LO4	**Describe the closing process and summarize the accounting cycle.**	C-19	C-4	C.4	SE11, E3, P8, P9, P10

SYSTEM OF DEBITS AND CREDITS

LO1 **Describe** the system of debits and credits and its use in recording transactions.

One basic characteristic of all accounts is that data entries separately record the increases and decreases to an account. In some accounts, such as the Cash account in **Exhibit C-2**, increases are recorded on the left side of the account and decreases are recorded on the right side. In other accounts, the reverse is true. The method of recording data entries in the accounts is a matter of convention; that is, a simple set of rules is followed, which involves debits and credits.

The terms **debit** and **credit** are used to refer to the left side and the right side, respectively, of an account as shown below:

(Any Type of Account)	
Debit Always the left side	**Credit** Always the right side

Hint: *A "Retained Earnings" account would be included in Exhibit C-1 for a continuing business that has not paid out its income with dividends. That account would have increases on the right and decreases on the left.*

Regardless of what amount is recorded in an account, a data entry made on the left side is a debit to the account; and, a data entry recorded on the right side is a credit to the account.

The system of debits and credits identifies which accounts are increased by debits (or by credits) and which accounts are decreased by debits (or by credits). **Exhibit C-1** summarizes these rules for each of the six primary categories of accounts: assets, liabilities, common stock, dividends, revenues, and expenses. Observe the following relations in **Exhibit C-1**:

1. *Debit* always refers to the left side of an account; *credit* always refers to the right side.
2. Increases in asset, dividend, and expense accounts are debit entries. Increases in liability, common stock, and revenue accounts are credit entries.
3. Decreases in asset, dividend, and expense accounts are credit entries. Decreases in liability, common stock, and revenue accounts are debit entries.
4. The **normal balance** of an account is the side on which increases to the account are recorded. Thus, asset, dividend, and expense accounts normally have debit balances, whereas liabilities, common stock, and revenue accounts normally have credit balances. This is because increases in an account are usually greater than, or equal to, the decreases to an account.

The pattern of increases and decreases for asset accounts is opposite that for liability, common stock, and revenue accounts. The pattern of increases and decreases for revenue accounts is to be expected because revenue is a temporary subdivision of stockholders' equity. Following the same logic, the pattern of increases and decreases for dividends and expenses is opposite that because dividends and expenses reduce stockholders' equity.

EXHIBIT C-1 **System of Increases and Decreases, Debits and Credits, and Normal Balances**

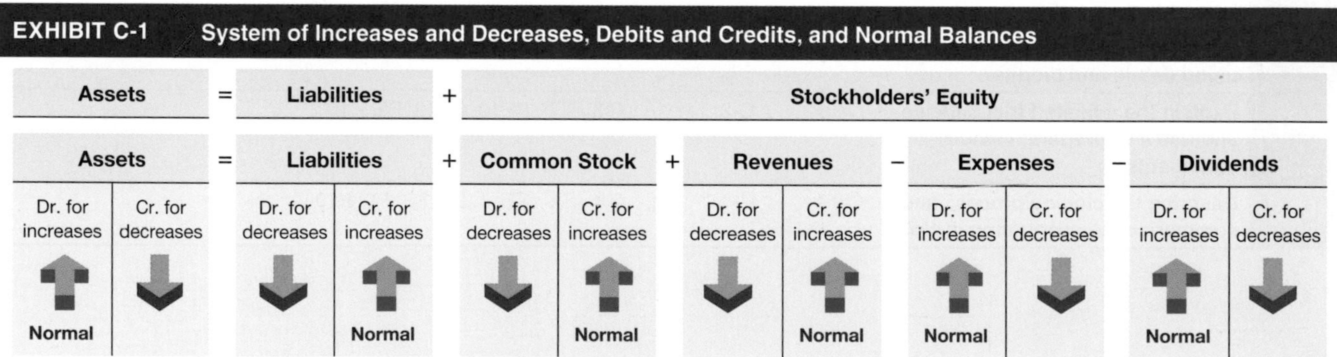

A **T-account** is a simplified form of an account. T-accounts are so named because they resemble the letter "T." A T-account with the December changes in the Cash account for DataForce is presented in **Exhibit C-2**.

EXHIBIT C-2 Cash T-account

Cash			
(1)	30,000	10,800	**(2)**
(4)	36,000	32,400	**(5)**
(6)	3,000	1,620	**(9)**
(7)	13,510	500	**(11)**
(8)	1,000		
(10)	2,400		
	85,910	45,320	
Bal.	40,590		

To compute the T-account balance, sum the numbers in each column and subtract the smaller total from the larger total. In this example, subtract 45,320 from 85,910 to compute the 40,590 balance.

A T-account consists of: (1) the account title (such as Cash), (2) amounts reflecting increases and decreases, and (3) cross-references to other accounting records. It is customary to reference (or link) the data entries in a T-account with a number or a letter to identify the related accounting transaction that originated the data. This permits a systematic review of the data entries in the event of a recording error. It also enables a company, and its independent auditor, to review the company's set of accounts and match the account information with the related accounting transactions. The numerical references in the Cash T-account are the ones used to identify the December transactions for DataForce from Chapter 2, **Exhibit 2-3**.

Illustration of the Recording Process

To illustrate how transactions are recorded using the system of debits and credits, we use the transactions of DataForce, which were summarized in Chapter 2, **Exhibit 2-3**. For each transaction, we **(1) analyze** the transaction using the accounting equation, **(2) journalize** the transaction, and **(3) post** journal entries to the general ledger (for simplicity, we use the T-account structure for each ledger account).

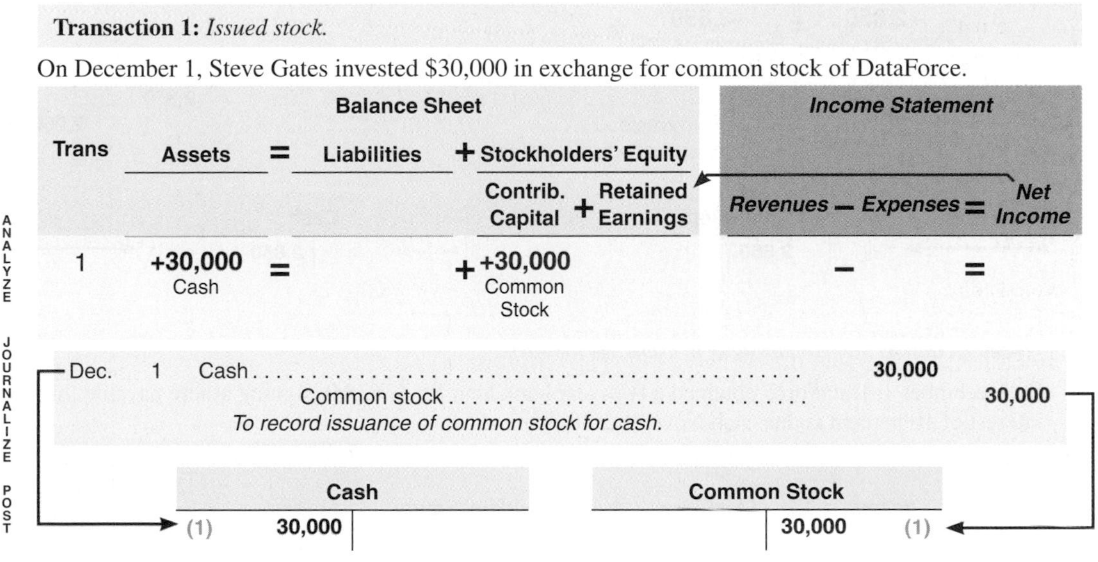

Transaction 2: *Paid rent in advance.*

On December 1, DataForce prepaid rent for the office covering the next six months, December of the current year through May of the following year. Monthly rent is $1,800; the total amount prepaid was $10,800 cash.

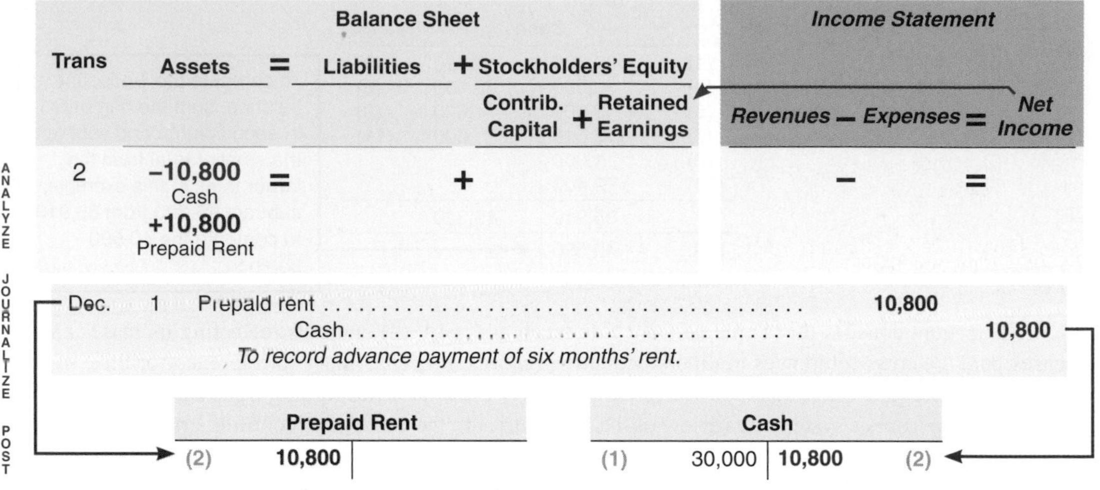

Transaction 3: *Purchased office supplies on account.*

On December 1, DataForce purchased $2,850 of office supplies on account.

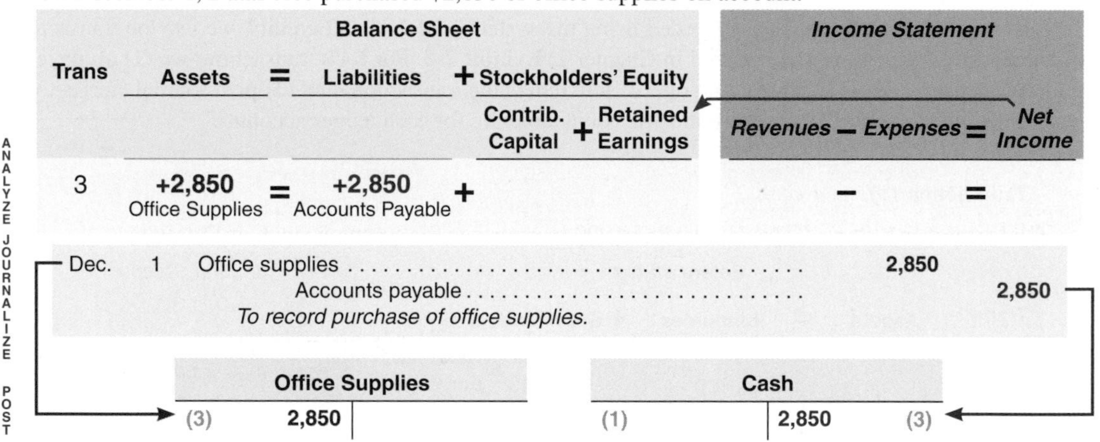

Transaction 4: *Signed bank note in exchange for cash.*

On December 1, DataForce obtained a two-year bank loan for $36,000, signing a note payable. Annual interest of 10 percent is due each November 30.

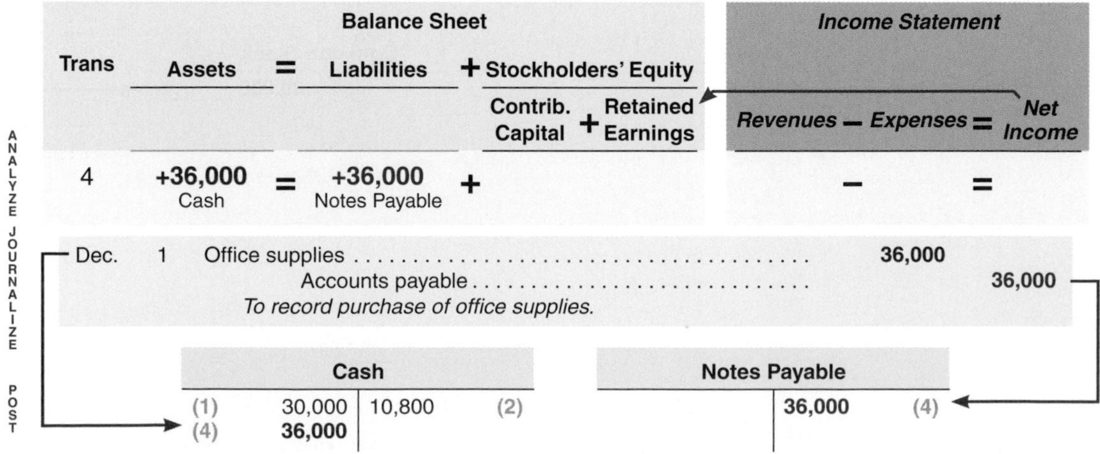

Transaction 5: *Purchased office equipment.*

On December 2, DataForce used cash to purchase $32,400 of office equipment.

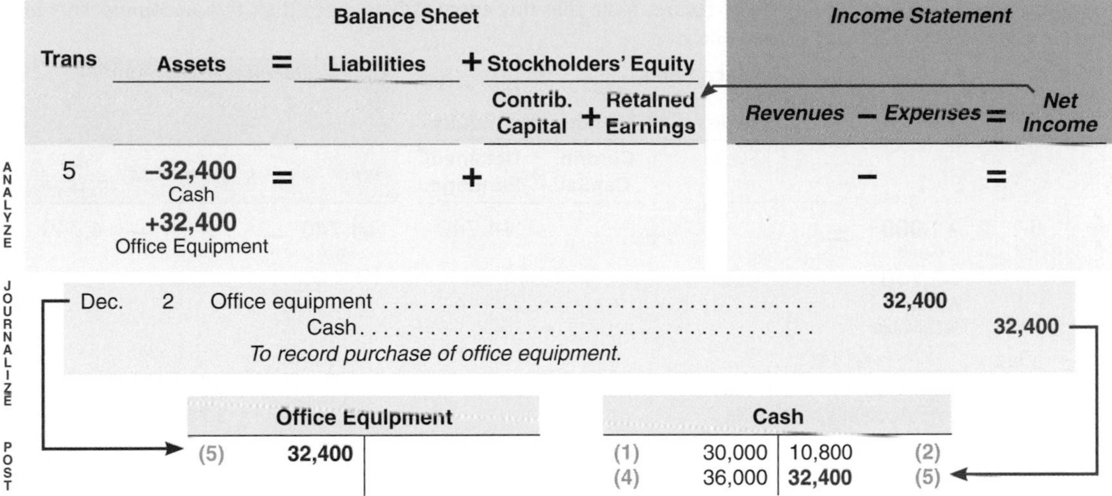

Transaction 6: *Received customer prepayment.*

On December 5, DataForce received a $3,000 advanced payment from a customer.

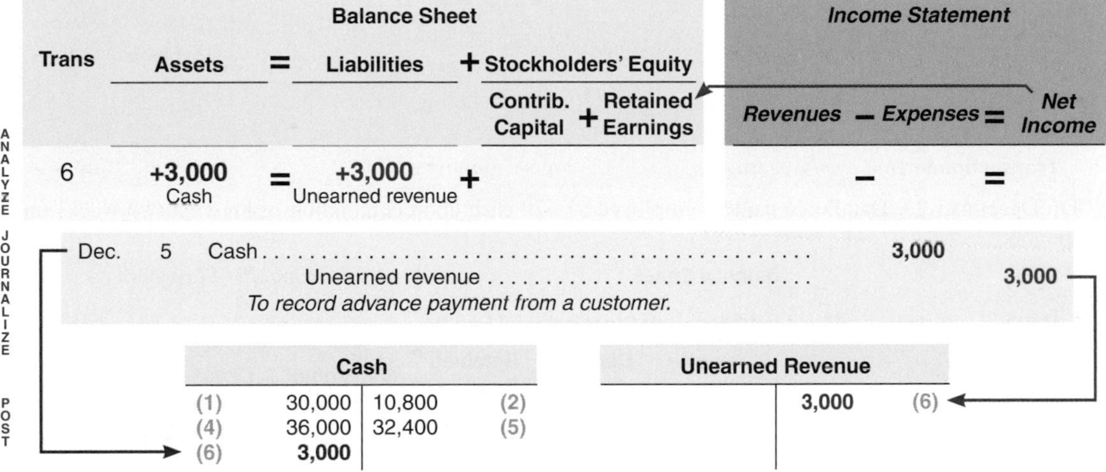

Transaction 7: *Performed services for customers.*

On December 6, DataForce performed services for several customers and was paid $13,510 cash.

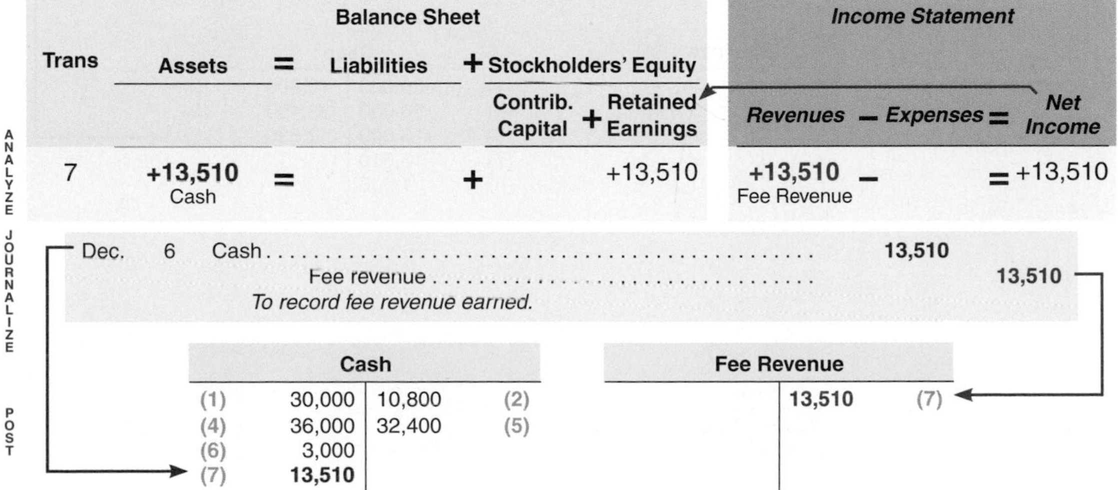

Transaction 8: *Performed services for cash and on account.*

On December 8, DataForce performed $4,740 of services for which it received $1,000 cash with the remaining $3,740 to be paid in the future. Note that this entry affects more than two accounts. This is referred to as a compound journal entry.

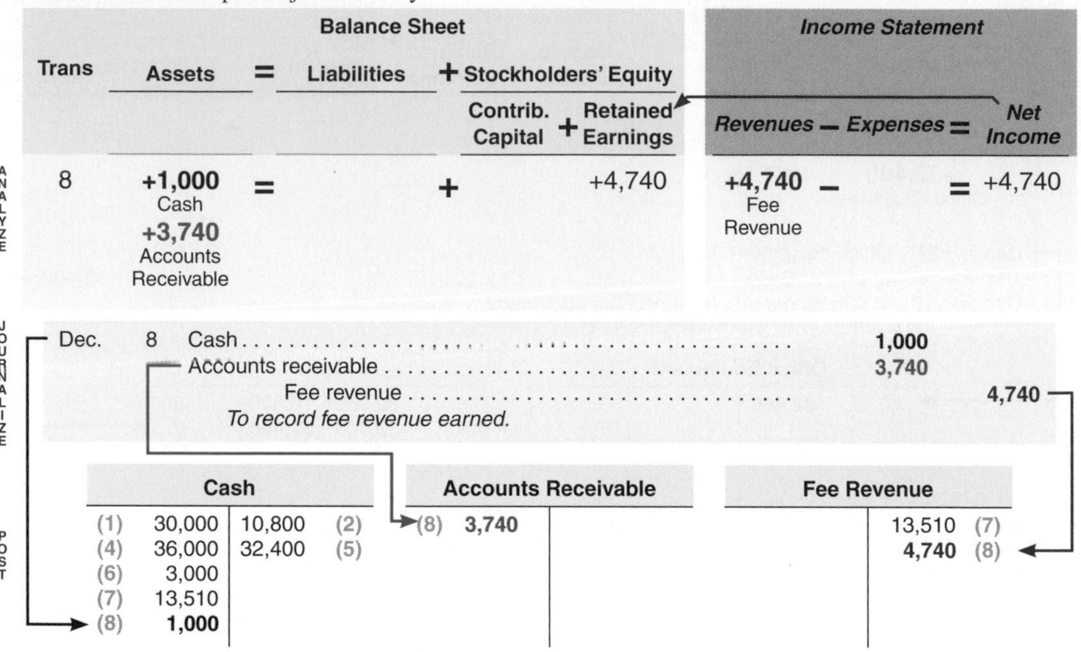

Transaction 9: *Paid employee wages.*

On December 23, DataForce paid its employee $1,620 cash upon completion of her first two weeks on the job.

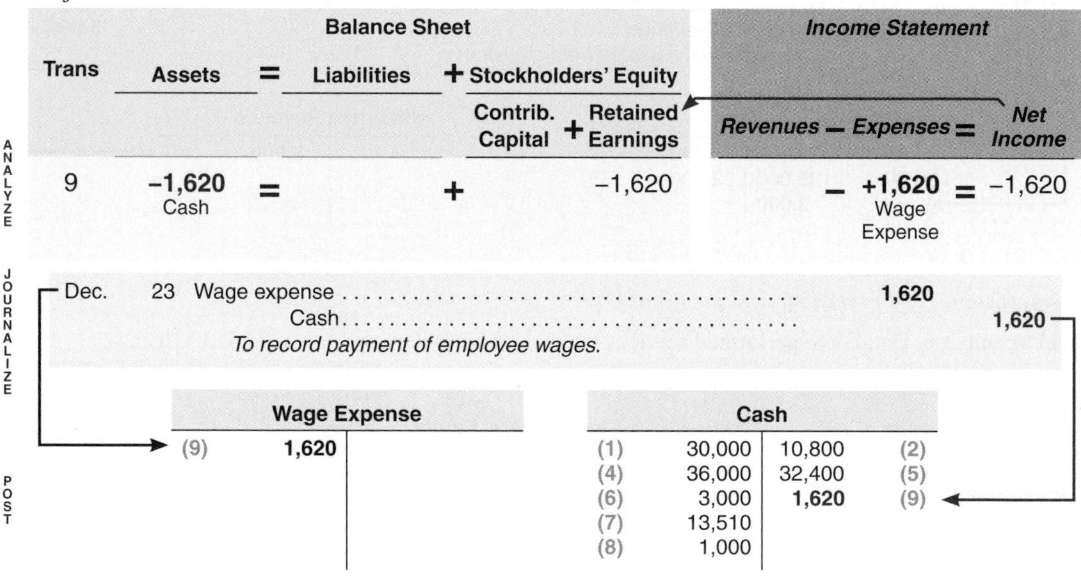

Transaction 10: *Received payment on account from customer.*

On December 27, DataForce received $2,400 cash from a customer for services previously performed on account.

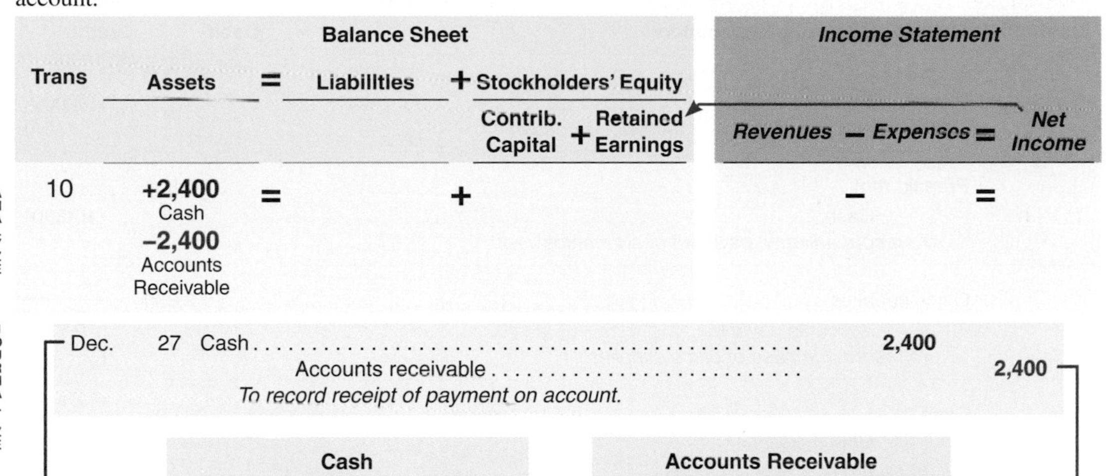

			Debit	Credit
Dec.	27	Cash	2,400	
		Accounts receivable		2,400
		To record receipt of payment on account.		

POST

Cash

	Debit	Credit	
(1)	30,000	10,800	(2)
(4)	36,000	32,400	(5)
(6)	3,000	1,620	(9)
(7)	13,510		
(8)	1,000		
(10)	**2,400**		

Accounts Receivable

	Debit	Credit	
(8)	3,740	**2,400**	(10)

Transaction 11: *Paid cash dividend.*

On December 30, DataForce paid a $500 cash dividend.

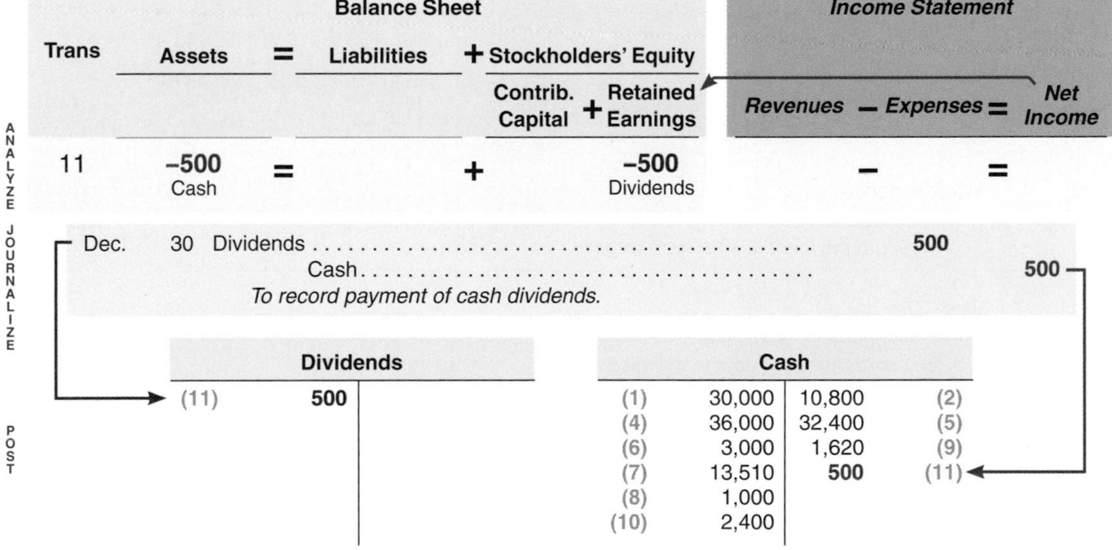

			Debit	Credit
Dec.	30	Dividends	500	
		Cash		500
		To record payment of cash dividends.		

Dividends

	Debit	Credit
(11)	**500**	

Cash

	Debit	Credit	
(1)	30,000	10,800	(2)
(4)	36,000	32,400	(5)
(6)	3,000	1,620	(9)
(7)	13,510	**500**	(11)
(8)	1,000		
(10)	2,400		

Summary Illustration of Journalizing and Posting Transactions

Exhibit C-3 presents the general journal for DataForce for the month of December. **Exhibit C-4** presents the general ledger for DataForce as of December 31. All journal entries appearing in **Exhibit C-3** have been posted to the general ledger accounts in **Exhibit C-4**. The accounts in DataForce's general ledger are grouped by category as follows: (1) assets, (2) liabilities, and (3) stockholders' equity, which includes: common stock, dividends, revenues, and expenses. Each general ledger account in **Exhibit C-4** has been totaled with the ending balance appearing in green.

EXHIBIT C-3 General Journal for DataForce

General Journal

	Date	Account Titles and Explanation	Debit	Credit
(1)	Dec. 1	Cash	30,000	
		Common stock		30,000
		To record issuance of common stock for cash.		
(2)	1	Prepaid rent	10,800	
		Cash		10,800
		To record advance payment of six months' rent.		
(3)	1	Office supplies	2,850	
		Accounts payable		2,850
		To record purchase of office supplies.		
(4)	1	Cash	36,000	
		Notes payable		36,000
		To record borrowing of funds.		
(5)	2	Office equipment	32,400	
		Cash		32,400
		To record purchase of office equipment.		
(6)	5	Cash	3,000	
		Unearned revenue		3,000
		To record a prepayment from a customer.		
(7)	6	Cash	13,510	
		Fee revenue		13,510
		To record fee revenue earned.		
(8)	8	Cash	1,000	
		Accounts receivable	3,740	
		Fee revenue		4,740
		To record fee revenue earned.		
(9)	23	Wage expense	1,620	
		Cash		1,620
		To record payment of employee wages.		
(10)	27	Cash	2,400	
		Accounts receivable		2,400
		To record receipt of payment on account.		
(11)	30	Dividends	500	
		Cash		500
		To record payment of cash dividends.		

EXHIBIT C-4 General Ledger for DataForce

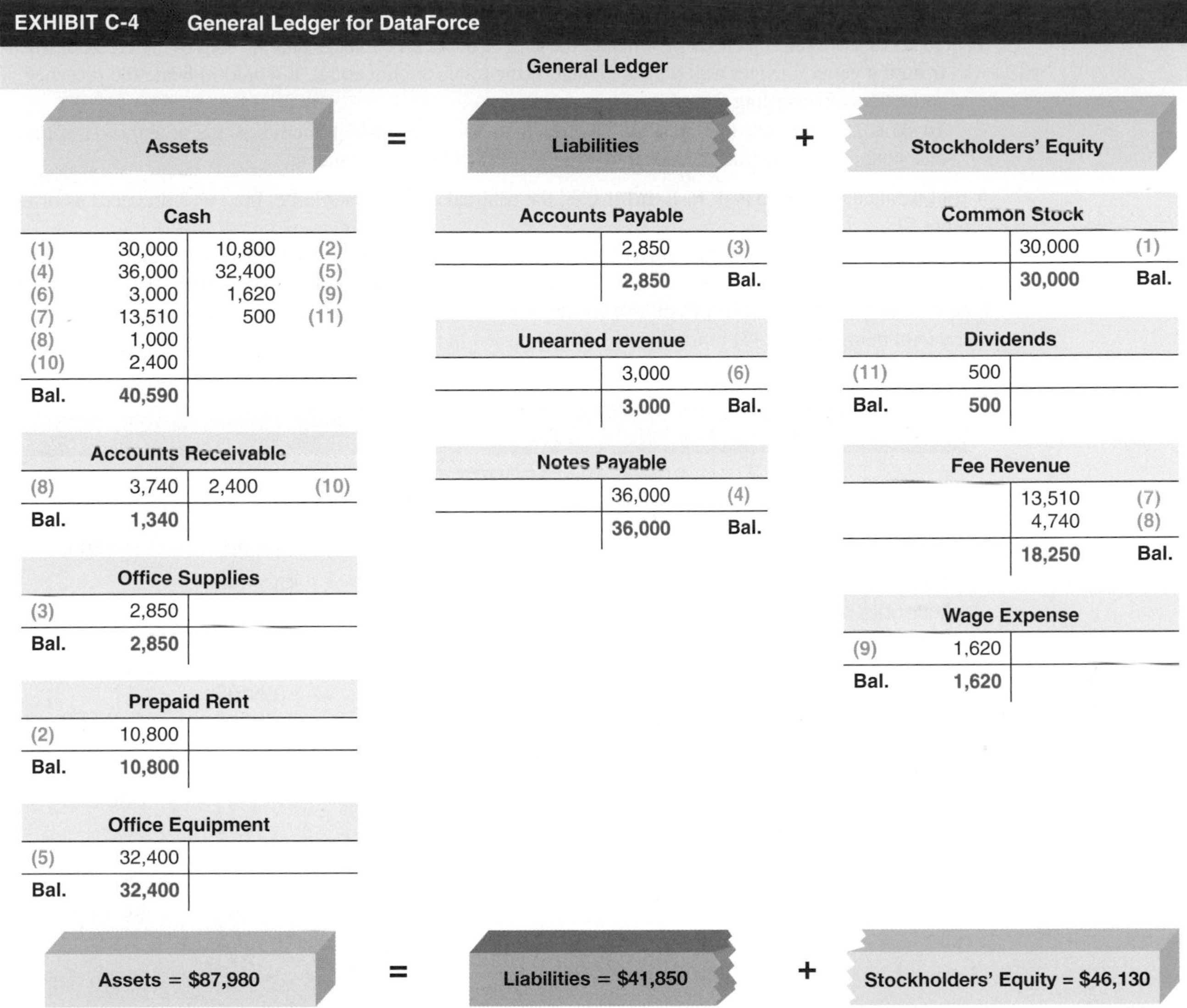

TRIAL BALANCE

A **trial balance** is a listing of all accounts from the general ledger with their respective debit or credit balance. A trial balance is prepared at the end of an accounting period after all transactions have been recorded. **Exhibit C-5** shows an unadjusted trial balance for DataForce, Inc., as of December 31. The sequence of the accounts and the dollar amounts are taken directly from the general ledger T-accounts in **Exhibit C-4** (which follow the order of the account numbering system). The debit and credit columns from the trial balance are in balance; that is, the $90,100 sum of the debit account balances equals the $90,100 sum of the credit account balances.

The two principal reasons for preparing a trial balance are:

1. To serve as an interim check on whether the sum of the debit balances and the sum of the credit balances from the general ledger accounts are equal. If the totals are not equal, it would indicate the presence of some type of recording error.
2. To show all general ledger account balances in one location, which facilitates the preparation of financial statements. The trial balance, however, is *not* a financial statement.

A trial balance must be dated. In **Exhibit C-5**, the trial balance of DataForce, Inc., was prepared as of December 31.

Although it is required that a trial balance be in balance—that is, that the total of the debit column equal the total of the credit column—this equality does not guarantee that the accounting data is error-free. Potential data errors could still exist as a consequence of (1) transactions not being journalized, (2) journal entries not being posted, (3) journal entries being posted in the wrong amount, and (4) journal entries being posted to the wrong accounts.

EXHIBIT C-5 Unadjusted Trial Balance for DataForce

DATAFORCE, INC.
Unadjusted Trial Balance
December 31

	Debit	Credit
Cash	$40,590	
Accounts receivable	1,340	
Office supplies	2,850	
Prepaid rent	10,800	
Office equipment	32,400	
Accounts payable		$ 2,850
Unearned revenue		3,000
Notes payable		36,000
Common stock		30,000
Dividends	500	
Fee revenue		18,250
Wage expense	1,620	
Totals	$90,100	$90,100

REVIEW C.1

Use the information for Miguel's Designs provided in Chapter 2, Review 2.3.

REQUIRED

a. Use the following accounts to create a general ledger using T-accounts.
    Cash
    Common Stock
    Accounts Receivable
    Equipment
    Accounts Payable
    Service Revenue
    Supplies Expense
    Advertising Expense
    Wage Expense
    Rent Expense

b. Prepare journal entries and post the accounting transactions to their general ledger T-accounts.

The solution is on pages C-33–C-34.

ACCOUNTING ADJUSTMENTS

Earlier in this appendix, we analyzed a series of accounting transactions for DataForce, Inc., that occurred during the month of December. Many of the account balances require an end-of-period adjustment to bring them to the correct balance for the preparation of DataForce's financial statements. For example, DataForce prepaid six months of rent for its office space on December 1. By December 31, one month's rent has expired, and thus, the prepaid rent account must be adjusted so that the account balance reflects the remaining amount of rent that is still prepaid. When it is time to prepare a company's financial statements, the company must review account balances and make any necessary end-of-period adjustments to bring those unadjusted accounts to their proper balances.

LO2 Illustrate the adjusting process using debits and credits.

The four types of accounting adjustments are discussed in **Chapter 3**. To illustrate how accounting adjustments are recorded using the system of debits and credits, we use the adjusting entries of DataForce, which are discussed in detail in **Chapter 3**.

Recognizing Previously Deferred Revenue

Deferred Revenues

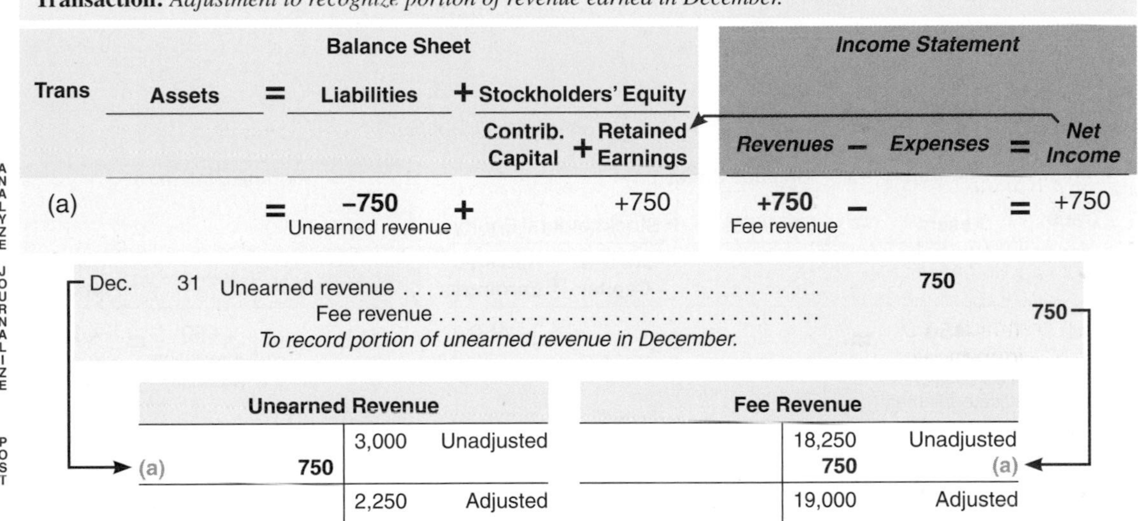

Transaction: *Adjustment to recognize portion of revenue earned in December.*

Trans	Assets	=	Liabilities	+	Contrib. Capital	+	Retained Earnings	Revenues	−	Expenses	=	Net Income
(a)		=	−750 Unearned revenue	+			+750	+750 Fee revenue	−		=	+750

			Debit	Credit
Dec.	31	Unearned revenue	750	
		Fee revenue		750
		To record portion of unearned revenue in December.		

Unearned Revenue

	Debit	Credit	
		3,000	Unadjusted
(a)	750		
		2,250	Adjusted

Fee Revenue

	Debit	Credit	
		18,250	Unadjusted
		750	(a)
		19,000	Adjusted

Recognizing Previously Deferred Expenses

Deferrred Expenses

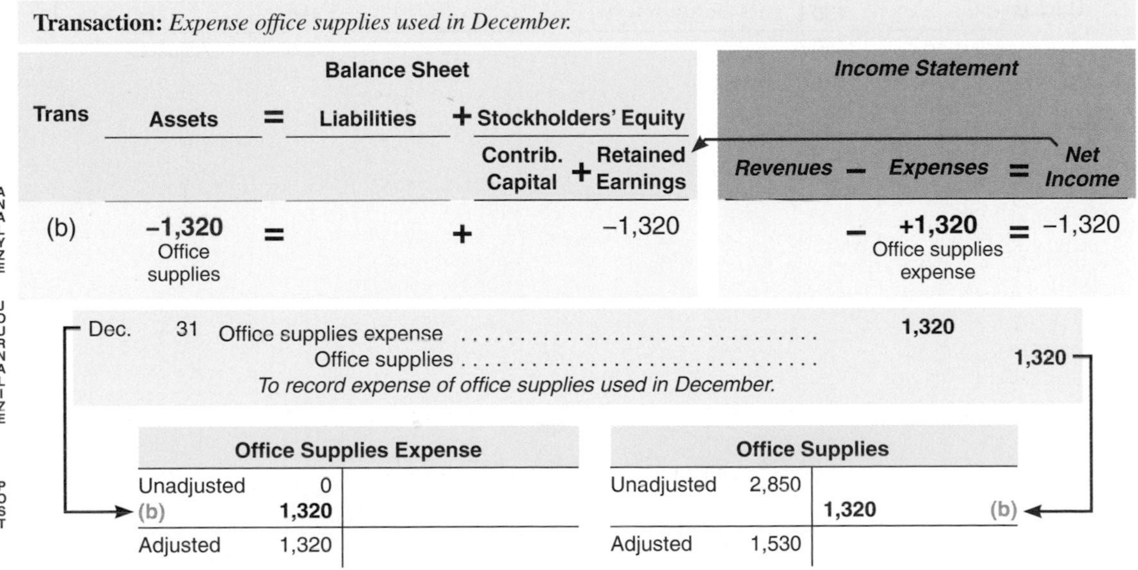

Transaction: *Expense office supplies used in December.*

Trans	Assets	=	Liabilities	+	Contrib. Capital	+	Retained Earnings	Revenues	−	Expenses	=	Net Income
(b)	−1,320 Office supplies	=		+			−1,320		−	+1,320 Office supplies expense	=	−1,320

			Debit	Credit
Dec.	31	Office supplies expense	1,320	
		Office supplies		1,320
		To record expense of office supplies used in December.		

Office Supplies Expense

	Debit	Credit
Unadjusted	0	
(b)	1,320	
Adjusted	1,320	

Office Supplies

	Debit	Credit	
Unadjusted	2,850		
		1,320	(b)
Adjusted	1,530		

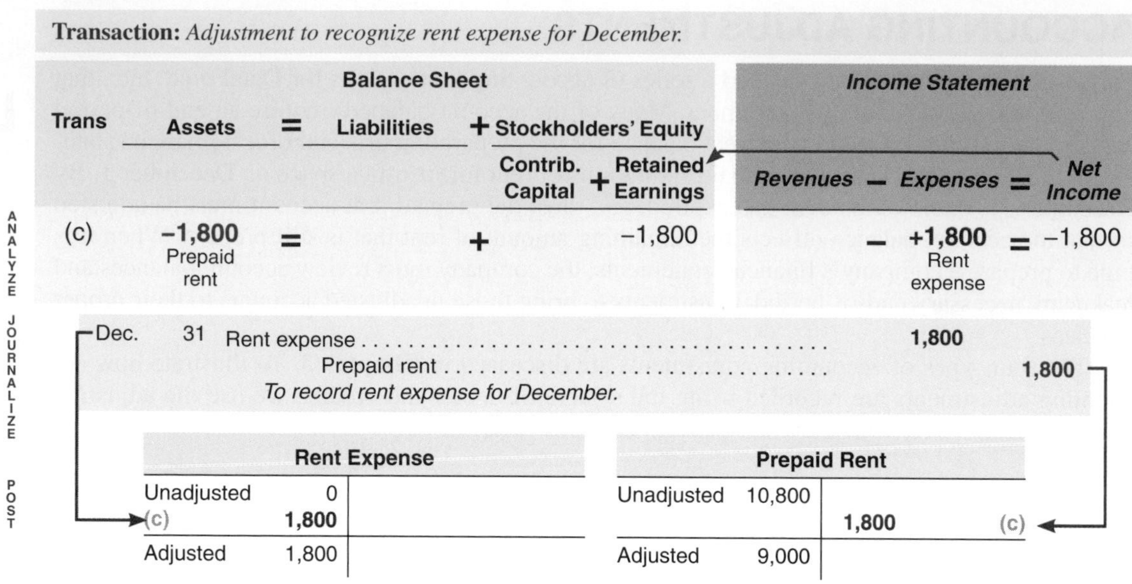
Transaction: *Adjustment to recognize rent expense for December.*
Balance Sheet
Trans
Assets = Liabilities + Stockholders' Equity
Contrib. Capital + Retained Earnings
Income Statement
Revenues − Expenses = Net Income
ANALYZE
(c) −1,800 Prepaid rent = + −1,800 − +1,800 Rent expense = −1,800
JOURNALIZE
Dec. 31 Rent expense 1,800
Prepaid rent 1,800
To record rent expense for December.
POST
Rent Expense
Unadjusted 0
(c) 1,800
Adjusted 1,800
Prepaid Rent
Unadjusted 10,800
1,800 (c)
Adjusted 9,000

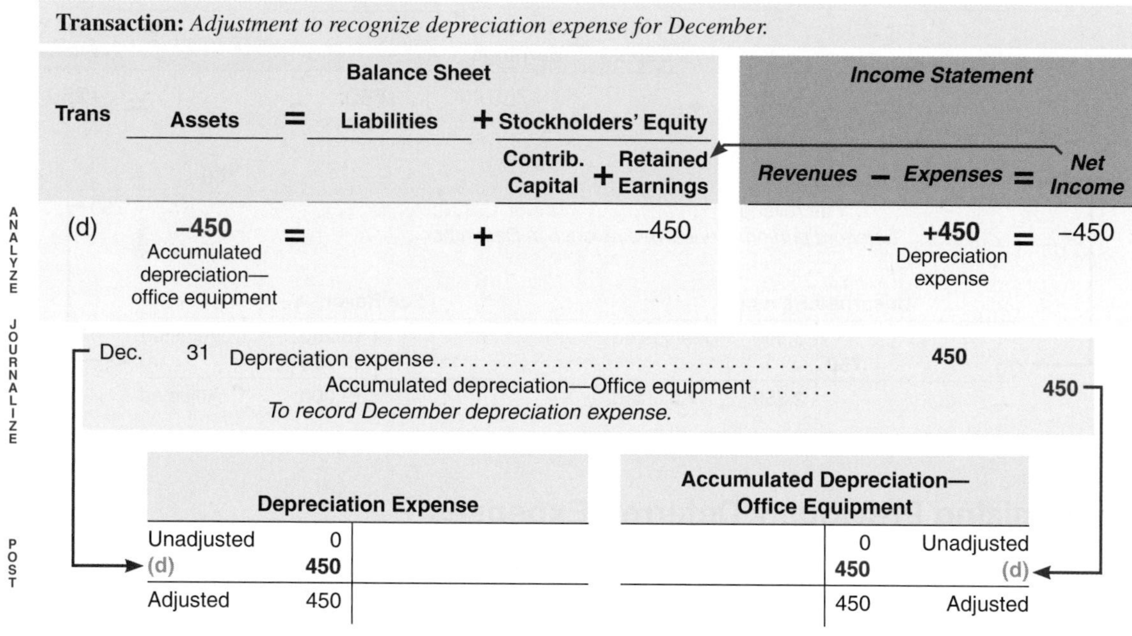
Transaction: *Adjustment to recognize depreciation expense for December.*
Balance Sheet
Trans
Assets = Liabilities + Stockholders' Equity
Contrib. Capital + Retained Earnings
Income Statement
Revenues − Expenses = Net Income
ANALYZE
(d) −450 Accumulated depreciation—office equipment = + −450 − +450 Depreciation expense = −450
JOURNALIZE
Dec. 31 Depreciation expense 450
Accumulated depreciation—Office equipment 450
To record December depreciation expense.
POST
Depreciation Expense
Unadjusted 0
(d) 450
Adjusted 450
Accumulated Depreciation—Office Equipment
0 Unadjusted
450 (d)
450 Adjusted

Recognizing Accrued Revenue

Accrued Revenues

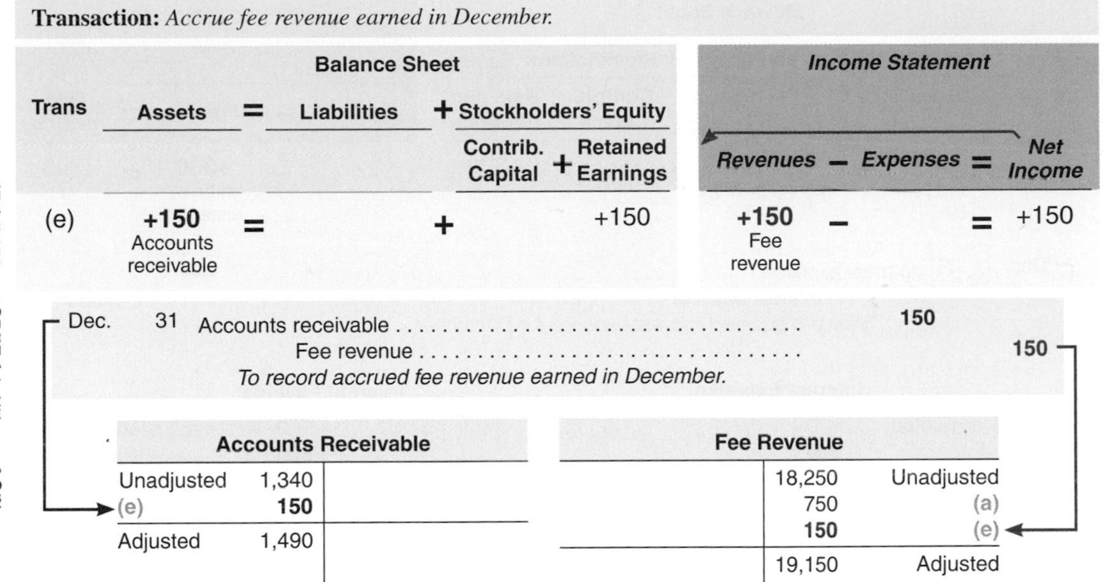

Recognizing Accrued Expenses

Accrued Expenses

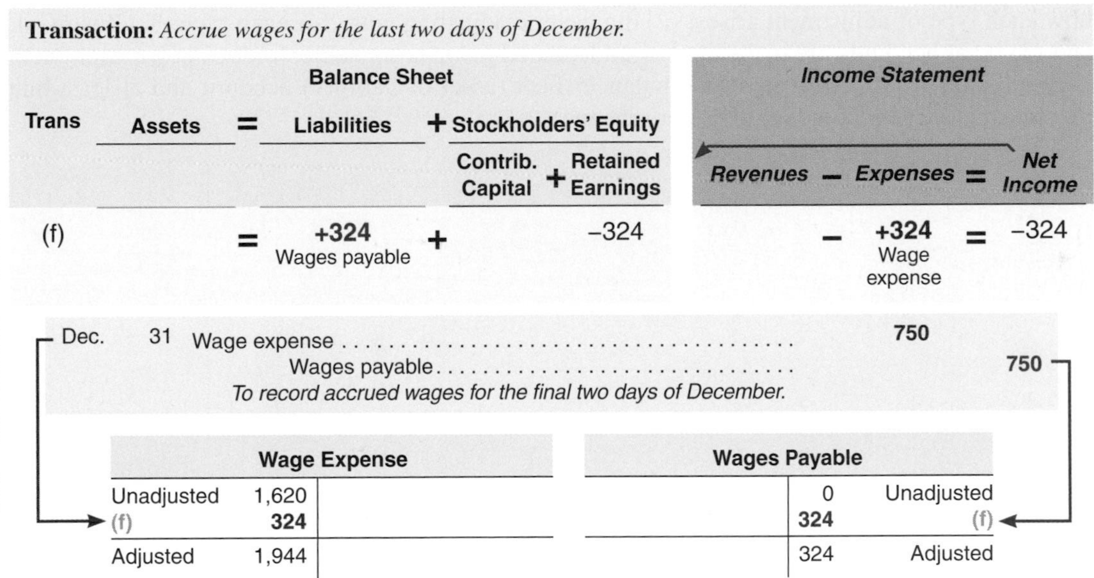

Transaction: Accrue wages for the last two days of December.
Balance Sheet
Trans
Assets = Liabilities + Stockholders' Equity
Contrib. Capital + Retained Earnings
Income Statement
Revenues − Expenses = Net Income
ANALYZE
(f) = +324 Wages payable + −324
− +324 Wage expense = −324
JOURNALIZE
Dec. 31 Wage expense 750
Wages payable 750
To record accrued wages for the final two days of December.
POST
Wage Expense
Unadjusted 1,620
(f) 324
Adjusted 1,944
Wages Payable
0 Unadjusted
324 (f)
324 Adjusted

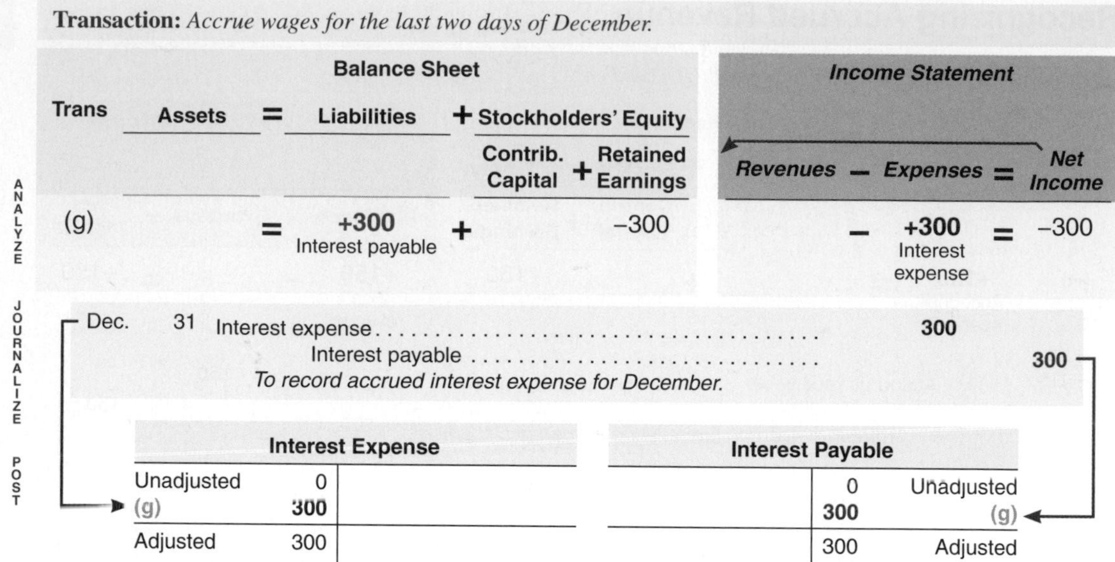

Summary of Accounting Adjustments

Exhibit C-6 summarizes the adjusting entries for DataForce as recorded in its general journal. These adjustments would be posted to the company's general ledger.

Exhibit C-7 lists the four types of accounting adjustments and also shows (1) examples of how each type of adjustment arises, (2) the generic adjusting entry for each type of adjustment, and (3) what accounts are overstated or understated *prior to* any adjustment. As we explained, each adjustment affects at least one balance sheet (asset or liability) account and at least one income statement account (expense or revenue).

EXHIBIT C-6 Adjusting Entries for DataForce

General Journal

Date	Account Titles and Explanation	Debit	Credit	
Dec. 31	Unearned revenue	750		(a)
	Fee revenue		750	
	To record portion of unearned revenue in December.			
Dec. 31	Supplies expense	1,320		(b)
	Office supplies		1,320	
	To record expense of office supplies used in December.			
Dec. 31	Rent expense	1,800		(c)
	Prepaid rent		1,800	
	To record rent expense for December.			
Dec. 31	Depreciation expense	450		(d)
	Accumulated depreciation—Office equipment		450	
	To record December depreciation.			
Dec. 31	Accounts receivable	150		(e)
	Fee revenue		150	
	To record accrued fee revenue earned in December.			
Dec. 31	Wage expense	324		(f)
	Wages payable		324	
	To record accrued wages for the final two days of December.			
Dec. 31	Interest expense	300		(g)
	Interest payable		300	
	To record accrued interest expense for December.			

EXHIBIT C-7 Four Types of Accounting Adjustments

Accounting Adjustment	Examples	Adjustment	Financial Statement Effect If the Adjustment is NOT Made: Balance Sheet	Financial Statement Effect If the Adjustment is NOT Made: Income Statement
Deferrals				
Deferred revenue	Recognize revenue earned on products or services for which cash was received in a prior period, such as unearned fee revenue.	**Increase Revenue** **Decrease Liability**	Liability overstated Equity understated	Revenue understated
Deferred expenses	Recognize expenses incurred for cash expenditures made in a prior period, such as depreciation of buildings and expiration of prepaid rent and insurance.	**Increase Expense** **Decrease Asset**	Asset overstated Equity overstated	Expense understated
Accruals				
Accrued revenue	Recognize revenue earned on sales for which the cash will be received in a later period, such as sales of products or services, and interest income.	**Increase Revenue** **Increase Asset**	Asset understated Equity understated	Revenue understated
Accrued expenses	Recognize expenses incurred for which cash will be paid in a later period, such as wages or interest.	**Increase Expense** **Increase Liability**	Liabilty understated Equity overstated	Expense understated

REVIEW C.2

Prepare the journal entries for each of the following end-of-year accounting adjustments.

1. Record depreciation expense adjustment of $700 on the company's buildings.
2. Record $1,500 for rent expense that was previously recorded as part of a $2,000 advance rent payment to the company's landlord.
3. Record $400 of revenue earned that was previously recorded as unearned revenue due to an advance payment from a customer.
4. Record $500 of accrued interest expense that applies to the company's bank loan. The $500 is part of the company's annual cash interest payment that is due next period.

The solution is on page C-34.

ADJUSTED TRIAL BALANCE AND FINANCIAL STATEMENTS

LO3 **Explain** the adjusted trial balance and use it to **prepare** the financial statements.

After the end-of-period adjustments are recorded in the general journal and posted to the general ledger, the company prepares an adjusted trial balance. The company then uses the adjusted trial balance to prepare financial statements.

Preparing the Adjusted Trial Balance

The **adjusted trial balance** lists all the general ledger account balances after the end-of-period adjustments have been posted. **Exhibit C-8** presents DataForce's adjusted trial balance as of December 31 in the two right-hand columns of the exhibit. This exhibit begins with the unadjusted trial balance, shown in the two left-hand columns, and lists the seven adjustments in the middle columns. For example, adjusting entry (b) adjusted office supplies for the $1,320 of supplies used in December. This adjustment is highlighted in **Exhibit C-8**. Office Supplies has a $2,850 debit balance in the unadjusted trial balance column. The adjustment of a $1,320 credit appears in the credit column of the adjustments. This leads to a $1,530 debit balance in the adjusted trial balance.

EXHIBIT C-8 **Adjusted Trial Balance for DataForce, Inc.**

DATAFORCE, INC.
Adjusted Trial Balance
December 31

	Unadjusted Trial Balance		Adjustments		Adjusted Trial Balance	
	Debit	**Credit**	**Debit**	**Credit**	**Debit**	**Credit**
Cash	$40,590				$40,590	
Accounts receivable	1,340		(e) $ 150		1,490	
Office supplies	2,850			(b) $1,320	1,530	
Prepaid rent	10,800			(c) 1,800	9,000	
Office equipment	32,400				32,400	
Accumulated depreciation—Office equipment				(d) 450		$ 450
Accounts payable		$ 2,850				2,850
Interest payable				(g) 300		300
Wages payable				(f) 324		324
Unearned revenue		3,000	(a) 750			2,250
Notes payable		36,000				36,000
Common stock		30,000				30,000
Dividends	500				500	
Fee revenue		18,250		(a) 750 (e) 150		19,150
Supplies expense			(b) 1,320		1,320	
Wage expense	1,620		(f) 324		1,944	
Rent expense			(c) 1,800		1,800	
Depreciation expense			(d) 450		450	
Interest expense			(g) 300		300	
Totals	$90,100	$90,100	$5,094	$5,094	$91,324	$91,324

The adjusting entry also affects supplies expense, as shown in the exhibit. Supplies expense has a zero balance in the unadjusted trial balance. The adjustment appears as a $1,320 debit in the adjustments column, leading to a $1,320 debit balance in the adjusted trial balance for supplies expense. Using this presentation, managers can readily see the adjustments made and their impact on the financial accounting numbers.

Preparing Financial Statements

The adjusted trial balance is used to prepare the income statement, the statement of stockholders' equity, and the balance sheet. (It is also helpful in preparing the statement of cash flows although other information is also necessary to complete this financial statement.) We illustrate the preparation of financial statements for DataForce in **Exhibit C-9**. Recall from Chapter 1 that financial statements are prepared in the following sequence: (1) the income statement, (2) the statement of stockholders' equity, (3) the balance sheet, and (4) the statement of cash flows.

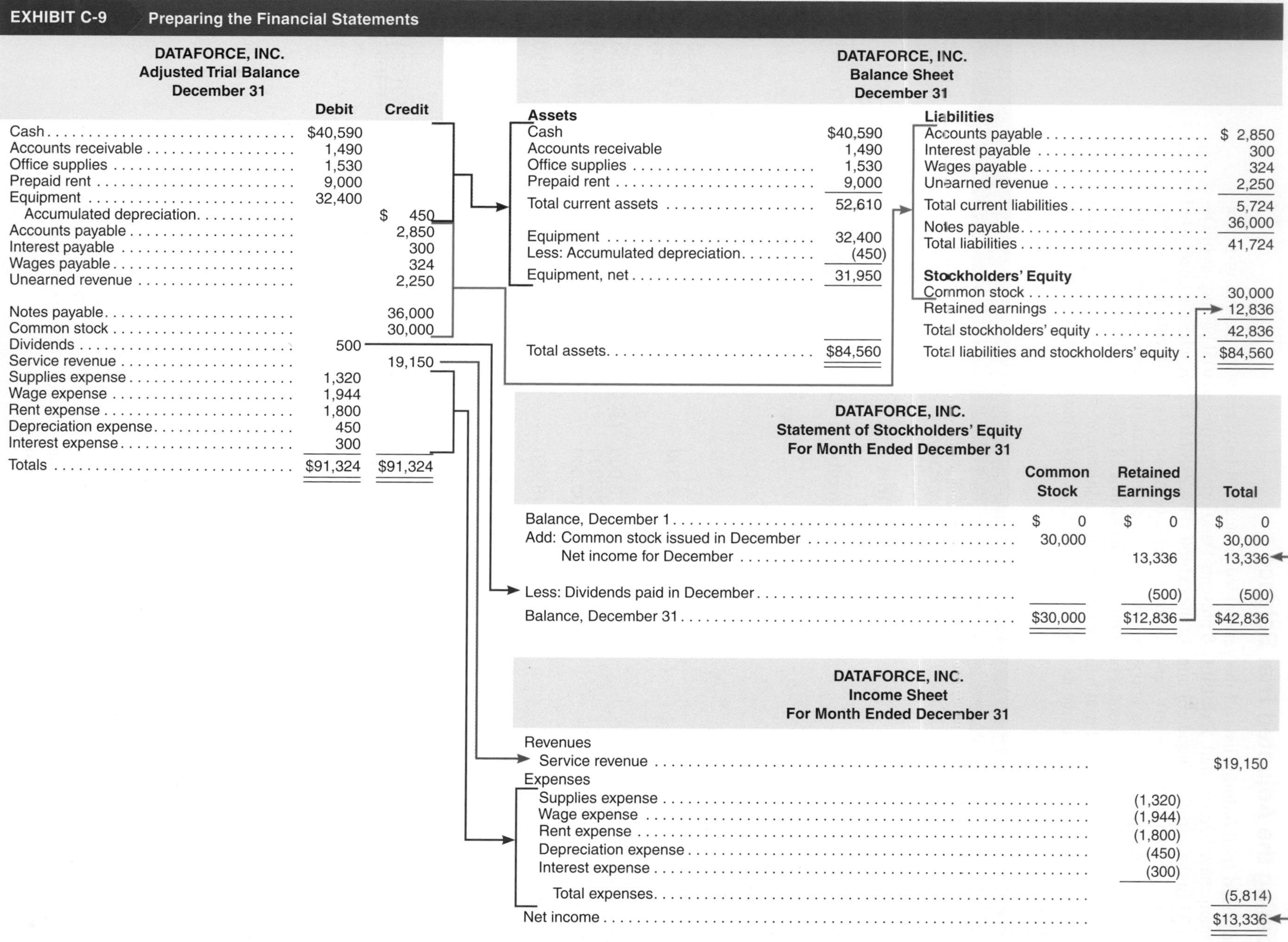

EXHIBIT C-9 Preparing the Financial Statements

DATAFORCE, INC.
Adjusted Trial Balance
December 31

	Debit	Credit
Cash	$40,590	
Accounts receivable	1,490	
Office supplies	1,530	
Prepaid rent	9,000	
Equipment	32,400	
Accumulated depreciation		$ 450
Accounts payable		2,850
Interest payable		300
Wages payable		324
Unearned revenue		2,250
Notes payable		36,000
Common stock		30,000
Dividends	500	
Service revenue		19,150
Supplies expense	1,320	
Wage expense	1,944	
Rent expense	1,800	
Depreciation expense	450	
Interest expense	300	
Totals	$91,324	$91,324

DATAFORCE, INC.
Balance Sheet
December 31

Assets		Liabilities	
Cash	$40,590	Accounts payable	$ 2,850
Accounts receivable	1,490	Interest payable	300
Office supplies	1,530	Wages payable	324
Prepaid rent	9,000	Unearned revenue	2,250
Total current assets	52,610	Total current liabilities	5,724
		Notes payable	36,000
Equipment	32,400	Total liabilities	41,724
Less: Accumulated depreciation	(450)		
Equipment, net	31,950	**Stockholders' Equity**	
		Common stock	30,000
		Retained earnings	12,836
		Total stockholders' equity	42,836
Total assets	$84,560	Total liabilities and stockholders' equity	$84,560

DATAFORCE, INC.
Statement of Stockholders' Equity
For Month Ended December 31

	Common Stock	Retained Earnings	Total
Balance, December 1	$ 0	$ 0	$ 0
Add: Common stock issued in December	30,000		30,000
Net income for December		13,336	13,336
Less: Dividends paid in December		(500)	(500)
Balance, December 31	$30,000	$12,836	$42,836

DATAFORCE, INC.
Income Sheet
For Month Ended December 31

Revenues		
Service revenue		$19,150
Expenses		
Supplies expense	(1,320)	
Wage expense	(1,944)	
Rent expense	(1,800)	
Depreciation expense	(450)	
Interest expense	(300)	
Total expenses		(5,814)
Net income		$13,336

REVIEW C.3

Cassi Company prepared the following adjusted trial balance to assist in the preparation of its December 31 year end financial statements.

CASSI COMPANY Adjusted Trial Balance December 31	Debit	Credit
Cash	$ 4,000	
Accounts receivable	15,000	
Supplies	18,000	
Prepaid rent	5,000	
Equipment	50,000	
Accumulated depreciation		$ 10,000
Accounts payable		8,000
Salaries payable		9,000
Dividends payable		2,000
Unearned revenue		5,000
Long-term debt		35,000
Common stock		15,000
Retained earnings		5,000
Sales revenue		52,000
Supplies expense	30,000	
Salaries expense	5,000	
Rent expense	6,000	
Depreciation expense	6,000	
Dividends	2,000	
Totals	$141,000	$141,000

REQUIRED

Prepare an income statement, a statement of stockholders' equity, and a balance sheet for Cassi Company using its December 31 adjusted trial balance. There were no changes in stockholders' equity during the year other than for net income and dividends.

The solution is on pages C-34–C-35.

CLOSING PROCESS

LO4 Describe the closing process and **summarize** the accounting cycle.

As discussed in Chapter 3, all accounts can be identified as either permanent accounts or temporary accounts. Permanent accounts are the accounts presented on the balance sheet. They consist of the asset, liability, and stockholders' equity accounts. The distinguishing feature of a permanent account is that any balance in the account at the end of an accounting period is carried forward to the following accounting period. Temporary accounts are used to gather information for a particular accounting period. Revenue, expense, and dividend accounts are temporary subdivisions of stockholders' equity. At the end of the accounting period, temporary account balances are transferred to Retained Earnings, which is a permanent stockholders' equity account. The process of transferring the balances in temporary accounts to Retained Earnings is referred to as the closing process or closing procedures.

A temporary account is *closed* when an entry is made that changes its account balance to zero—that is, the entry is equal in amount to the account's ending balance but is opposite to the balance as a debit or credit. An account that is closed is said to be closed *to* the account that receives the offsetting debit or credit. Thus, a closing entry simply transfers the balance of one account to another account. Because closing entries bring temporary account balances to zero, the temporary accounts are then ready to start accumulating data for the next accounting period. In essence, closing the temporary accounts prevents information from the current accounting period from being carried forward to a subsequent period, which enables financial statement users to make meaningful comparisons of revenue and expenses from one period to the next.

Journalizing and Posting the Closing Entries

The Retained Earnings account is used to close the temporary revenue, expense, and Dividends accounts. The closing entries occur only at the end of an accounting period and consist of three steps, which are graphically shown below.

1. **Close the revenue accounts.** Debit each revenue account for an amount equal to its current credit balance, and credit the Retained Earnings account for the total amount of earned revenue.
2. **Close the expense accounts.** Credit each expense account for an amount equal to its current debit balance, and debit the Retained Earnings account for the total amount of expenses.
3. **Close the Dividends account.** Debit the Retained Earnings account and credit the Dividends account for an amount equal to the balance in the Dividends account.

Closing Process for DataForce

Exhibit C-10 illustrates the closing entries for DataForce as recorded in the company's general journal. The financial information in these entries is posted to the appropriate general ledger accounts, which is represented using T-accounts.

EXHIBIT C-10 Closing Revenue, Expense, and Dividends Accounts—DataForce, Inc.

General Journal

	Date	Description	Debit	Credit
1	Dec. 31	Fee revenue	19,150	
		Retained earnings		19,150
		To close the revenue account.		
2	Dec. 31	Retained earnings	5,814	
		Supplies expense		1,320
		Wage expense		1,944
		Rent expense		1,800
		Depreciation expense		450
		Interest expense		300
		To close the expense accounts.		
3	Dec. 31	Retained earnings	500	
		Dividends		500
		To close the dividends account.		

The financial effect of posting these entries on the general ledger is diagrammed below.

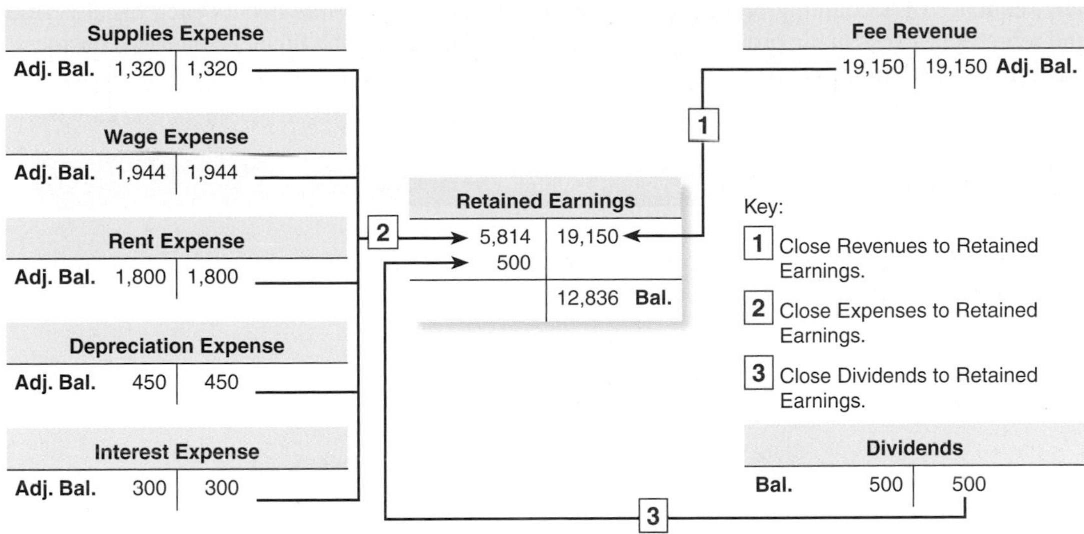

Preparing the Post-Closing Trial Balance

After closing entries are recorded in the general journal and posted to the general ledger, all of the temporary accounts have zero balances. At this point a **post-closing trial balance** is prepared. The post-closing trial balance provides evidence that an equality of debits and credits has been maintained in the general ledger throughout the adjusting and closing processes, and that the general ledger is in balance to start the next accounting period. Because the temporary accounts have been closed, only the balance sheet (or permanent) accounts appear in the post-closing trial balance. **Exhibit C-11** presents the post-closing trial balance for DataForce.

EXHIBIT C-11 Post-Closing Trial Balance for DataForce, Inc.

DATAFORCE, INC.
Post-Closing Trial Balance
December 31

	Debit	Credit
Cash	$40,590	
Accounts receivable	1,490	
Office supplies	1,530	
Prepaid rent	9,000	
Office equipment	32,400	
Accumulated depreciation—Office equipment		$ 450
Accounts payable		2,850
Interest payable		300
Wages payable		324
Unearned revenue		2,250
Notes payable		36,000
Common stock		30,000
Retained earnings		12,836
Totals	$85,010	$85,010

Summary of the Accounting Cycle

The sequence of accounting procedures known as the *accounting cycle* occurs each fiscal period and represents a systematic process for accumulating and reporting the financial data of a business. **Exhibit C-12** summarizes the five major steps in the accounting cycle as described in this and the preceding chapter.

EXHIBIT C-12 The Accounting Cycle: A Summary

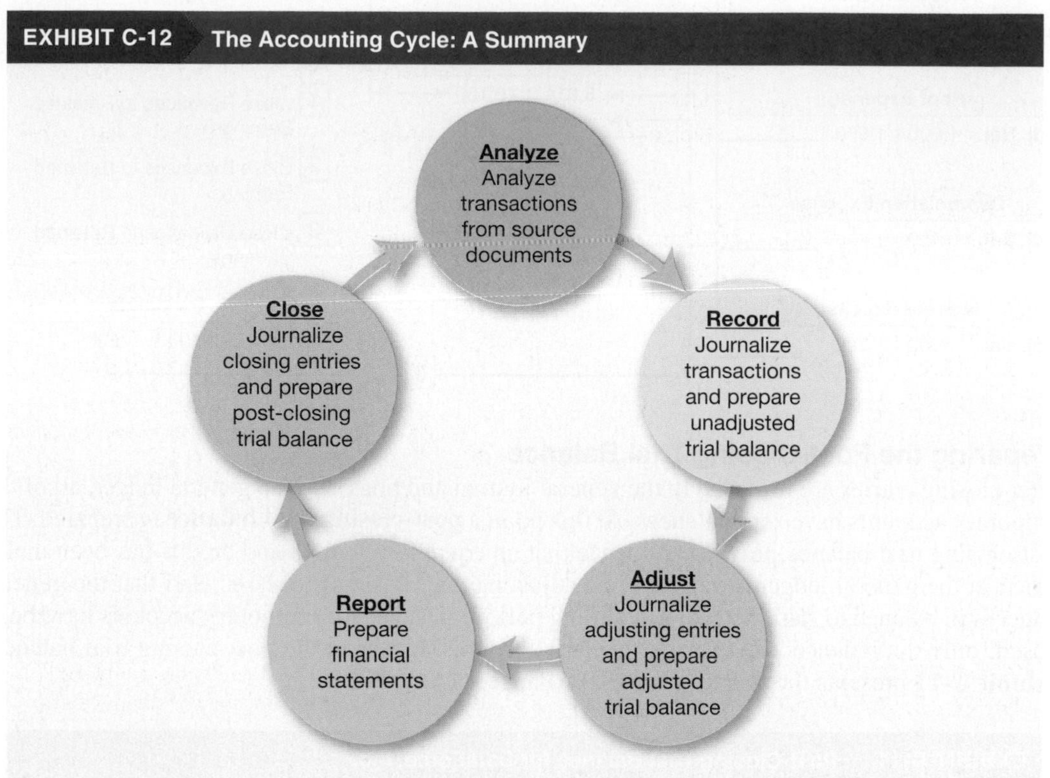

REVIEW C.4

Prior to closing its books, the Morgan Company has the following balances in its temporary accounts as of December 31.

	Debit	Credit
Sales revenue		$79,000
Cost of goods sold	$41,000	
Wage expense	22,000	
Rent expense	3,000	
Depreciation expense	2,000	
Interest expense	4,000	
Dividends	5,000	

REQUIRED

Prepare closing entries as of December 31 for the Morgan Company.

The solution is on pages C-35.

SUMMARY OF LEARNING OBJECTIVES

Describe the system of debits and credits and its use in recording transactions. (p. C-2) LO1

- The left side of an account is always the debit side; the right side of an account is always the credit side.
- Increases in assets, dividends, and expenses are debit entries; increases in liabilities, stockholders' equity, and revenues are credit entries. Decreases are the opposite.
- The normal balance of any account appears on the account side used for recording account increases.
- A trial balance serves as a mechanical check to evaluate the equality of the sum of the debit account balances and the sum of the credit account balances.
- A trial balance facilitates the preparation of the financial statements by showing all account balances in one concise record.

Illustrate the adjusting process using debits and credits. (p. C-11) LO2

- Adjusting entries are made to achieve the appropriate recognition of revenues and matching of expenses with revenues, and consist of four general types of adjustments:
  1. Allocating previously recorded assets to operating expenses to reflect the total expenses incurred during the period.
  2. Allocating previously recorded unearned revenue to revenue to reflect revenues earned during the period.
  3. Recording operating expenses to reflect expenses incurred during the period that have not yet been paid or recorded.
  4. Recording revenues to reflect revenue earned during the period that has not yet been received or recorded.

Explain the adjusted trial balance and use it to prepare financial statements. (p. C-16) LO3

- An income statement, statement of stockholders' equity, balance sheet, and statement of cash flows may be prepared from an adjusted trial balance and other information.
- The stockholders' equity accounts may need to be reviewed to obtain information regarding the beginning balances and additional capital contributions during the period for the statement of stockholders' equity.

Describe the closing process and summarize the accounting cycle. (p. C-19) LO4

- *Closing the books* means closing the revenue, expense, and dividend accounts by transferring the balances to the Retained Earnings account.

KEY TERMS

Adjusted trial balance (p. C-17)
Credit (entry) (p. C-2)
Debit (entry) (p. C-2)
Normal balance (p. C-2)
Post-closing trial balance (p. C-21)
T-account (p. C-3)
Trial balance (p. C-9)

SELF-STUDY QUESTIONS

(Answers to Self-Study Questions are at the end of this appendix.)

1. **Which of the following is true?** LO1 
   a. A debit will increase a liability account.
   b. A credit will increase an asset account.
   c. A credit will increase a revenue account.
   d. A debit will decrease an expense account.

LO1

2. **In applying the rules of debits and credits, which of the following statements is correct?**
   a. The word *debit* means to increase and the word *credit* means to decrease.
   b. Asset, expense, and common stock accounts are debited for increases.
   c. Liability, revenue, and common stock accounts are debited for increases.
   d. Asset, expense, and dividends are debited for increases.

LO1

3. **Which of these accounts has a normal debit balance?**
   a. Assets, expenses, dividends
   b. Assets, revenues, common stock
   c. Liabilities, revenues, common stock
   d. Assets, liabilities, dividends

LO1

4. **The general ledger includes accounts for all but which of the following?**
   a. Assets
   b. Expenses
   c. Dividends
   d. All of the above are in the general ledger

LO1

5. **Which of the following will cause a trial balance to be out of balance?**
   a. Mistakenly debiting an asset account instead of an expense account
   b. Posting $123 as $213 to both a debit and a credit account
   c. Posting the same transaction twice by mistake
   d. Posting only the debit part of a transaction

LO1

6. **‘`1289**

A journal entry that contains more than just two accounts is called:
   a. A posted journal entry
   b. An adjusting journal entry
   c. An erroneous journal entry
   d. A compound journal entry

LO1

7. **Posting refers to the process of transferring information from:**
   a. A journal to the general ledger accounts
   b. General ledger accounts to a journal
   c. Source documents to a journal
   d. A journal to source documents

LO2

8. **Which of the following is an example of an adjusting entry?**
   a. Recording the purchase of supplies on account
   b. Recording depreciation expense on a truck
   c. Recording the billing of customers for services rendered
   d. Recording the payment of wages to employees

LO4

9. **Which of the following is not an example of a closing entry?**
   a. Close each revenue account to the Retained Earnings account
   b. Close each expense account to the Retained Earnings account
   c. Close the Dividends account to the Retained Earnings account
   d. Close Unearned Revenue to Retained Earnings

QUESTIONS

1. Some accounting students believe that debits are good and credits are bad. Explain why this is not an accurate way to think about debits and credits.
2. What information is recorded in an account?
3. What does the term *debit* mean? What does the term *credit* mean?
4. How is the normal side of an account determined?
5. Describe the nature and purpose of a general journal.
6. What is the justification for the use of posting references?
7. Describe a compound journal entry.
8. Explain the terms *general ledger* and *trial balance*. What are the primary reasons for preparing a trial balance?
9. Define *permanent account*. Provide an example.
10. Define *temporary account*. Provide an example.
11. Which group of accounts is closed at the end of the accounting year? Why?

12. What is the purpose of a post-closing trial balance? Which of the following accounts should not appear in the post-closing trial balance: Cash, Unearned Revenue, Dividends, Depreciation Expense, Utilities Payable, Supplies Expense, Retained Earnings?

Assignments with the MBC logo in the margin are available in myBusinessCourse. See the Preface of the book for details.

SHORT EXERCISES

SEC-1. Normal Balances Indicate for each of the following accounts whether the normal balance is a debit or a credit: LO1

a. Accounts Receivable
b. Accounts Payable
c. Dividends
d. Wage Expense
e. Inventory
f. Interest Income
g. Retained Earnings

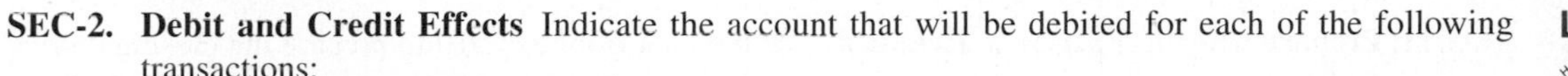

SEC-2. Debit and Credit Effects Indicate the account that will be debited for each of the following transactions: LO1

a. Issued common stock for cash
b. Borrowed money from a bank
c. Provided services on account
d. Purchased inventory on account
e. Collected cash from customers that owed a balance due

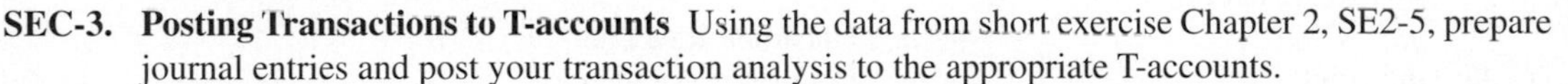

SEC-3. Posting Transactions to T-accounts Using the data from short exercise Chapter 2, SE2-5, prepare journal entries and post your transaction analysis to the appropriate T-accounts. LO1

SEC-4. Posting Transactions to T-accounts Using the data from short exercise Chapter 2, SE2-6, prepare journal entries and post your transaction analysis to the appropriate T-accounts. LO1

SEC-5. Prepare a Trial Balance The following balances were taken from the general ledger of Howser Corporation as of December 31. All balances are normal. Prepare a trial balance. LO1

Cash	$ 6,000	Accounts receivable	$10,800
Accounts payable	6,000	Common stock	36,000
Equipment	30,000	Dividends	2,400
Utilities expense	2,000	Administrative expense	8,000
Sales revenue	17,200		

SEC-6. Prepare a Corrected Trial Balance The following trial balance for Magill Company has errors that cause it to be out of balance. Prepare a corrected version of the trial balance for Magill Company. LO1

MAGILL COMPANY
Unadjusted Trial Balance
December 31

	Debit	Credit
Cash	$ 20,000	
Inventory		$ 85,000
Accounts receivable	30,000	
Accounts payable		12,000
Common stock		40,000
Retained earnings		58,000
Sales revenue	100,000	
Cost of goods sold	60,000	
Selling expenses	15,000	
Totals	$225,000	$195,000

SEC-7. The Account Which of the following is not part of the T-account? LO1

a. Title
b. Amount
c. Cross-reference
d. Analysis

LO2 **SEC-8. Accrual Adjusting Entries** Prepare adjusting journal entries for Sparky Electronics for the following items:

a. Salaries for employees in the amount of $2,500 have not been paid.
b. Interest expense of $1,200 for an outstanding note.
c. Work performed but not yet billed for $3,500.

LO2 **SEC-9. Analyze an Adjusted Trial Balance** The trial balance of Fisher Supplies contains the following balance sheet accounts that require adjustment. Identify the likely income statement account that will be used to adjust these accounts.

a. Prepaid Insurance
b. Accumulated Depreciation
c. Supplies
d. Unearned Revenue
e. Interest Payable

LO3 **SEC-10. Prepare an Income Statement from an Adjusted Trial Balance** The Century Company's adjusted trial balance contains the following balances as of December 31: Retained Earnings $8,500; Dividends $2,000; Sales $20,000; Cost of Goods Sold $8,000; Selling and Administrative Expenses $3,000; Interest Expense $1,500. Prepare an income statement for the year.

LO4 **SEC-11. Prepare Closing Entries to Retained** Use the data from SEC-10 to prepare the closing entries for The Century Company. Close the temporary accounts straight to retained earnings. The balance of $8,500 in the retained earnings account is from the beginning of the year. What is the ending retained earnings balance after posting the closing entries?

LO3 **SEC-12. Identify Financial Statements from Adjusted Trial Balance Accounts** Trownel Corp reports the following accounts in its adjusted trial balance. Identify which financial statement each account would appear on:

a. Cash
b. Sales
c. Accounts Payable
d. Unearned Revenue
e. Retained Earnings
f. Interest Income

EXERCISES

LO1 **EC-1. Nature of Accounts, Debit and Credit Rules** In columns, enter *debit* or *credit* to describe the journal entry necessary to increase and decrease the account shown on the left, and which side of the account represents its normal balance.

	Increase	Decrease	Normal Balance
Asset.	_____	_____	_____
Liability	_____	_____	_____
Common stock	_____	_____	_____
Dividends	_____	_____	_____
Revenue	_____	_____	_____
Expense	_____	_____	_____

LO1 **EC-2. The Account** The following transactions occurred during December, the first month of operations for Harris Company. Prepare journal entries and create a T-account for accounts payable that includes the following five transactions.

1. Purchased $500 of inventory on account.
2. Purchased $300 of inventory on account.
3. Paid suppliers $600.
4. Purchased $400 of inventory on account.
5. Paid suppliers $300.

LO4 **EC-3. Closing Entries** The adjusted trial balance prepared as of December 31, for Phyllis Howell & Company, Consultant, contains the following revenue and expense accounts:

	Debit	Credit
Service fees earned		$80,500
Rent expense	$20,800	
Salaries expense	52,000	
Supplies expense	5,600	
Depreciation expense	11,300	
Retained earnings		72,000
Dividends	10,000	

Prepare journal entries to close the accounts directly to Retained Earnings. After these entries are posted, what is the balance in the Retained Earnings account?

EC-4. Transaction Analysis and Trial Balance Using the transactions for Daniel Kelly in Chapter 2, E2-11, prepare journal entries and record the October transactions in T-accounts. Determine the balance in each account and prepare a trial balance as of October 31. **LO1**

PROBLEMS

PC-1. Transaction Analysis and the Effect of Errors on the Trial Balance The following T-accounts contain numbered entries for the May transactions of Carol Marsh, a market analyst, who opened her business on May 1 of the current year: **LO1**

	Cash		
(1)	13,000	4,800	(2)
(9)	3,700	810	(4)
		1,950	(6)
		600	(8)

	Common Stock		
		13,000	(1)

	Accounts Receivable		
(5)	6,400	3,700	(9)

	Dividends		
(8)	600		

	Office Supplies		
(3)	2,800		

	Professional Fees Earned		
		6,400	(5)

	Office Equipment		
(2)	4,800		

	Rent Expense		
(4)	810		

	Accounts Payable		
(6)	1,950	2,800	(3)
		270	(7)

	Utilities Expense		
(7)	270		

REQUIRED

a. Give a description of each of the nine numbered transactions entered in the above T-accounts. Example: (1) Carol Marsh invested $13,000 of her personal funds in her business.

b. The following trial balance, prepared from Marsh's data as of May 31, contains several errors. Itemize the errors and indicate the correct totals for the trial balance.

CAROL MARSH & COMPANY Unadjusted Trial Balance May 31	Debit	Credit
Cash	$ 8,450	
Accounts receivable	3,700	
Office supplies	2,800	
Office equipment	4,800	
Accounts payable		$ 1,120
Common stock		13,000
Dividends		600
Professional fees earned		6,400
Rent expense	810	
Totals	$20,560	$21,120

LO1 **PC-2.** **Transaction Analysis and Trial Balance** Pam Brown owns Art Graphics, a firm providing designs for advertisers and market analysts. On July 1, the business's general ledger showed the following normal account balances:

Homework MBC

Cash	$ 8,500	Accounts payable	$ 2,100
Accounts receivable	9,800	Notes payable	5,000
		Common stock	2,000
		Retained earnings	9,200
Total Assets	$18,300	Total Liabilities and Stockholders' Equity	$18,300

The following transactions occurred during the month of July:

July 1 Paid July rent, $670.
2 Collected $7,100 on account from customers.
3 Paid $2,500 installment due on the $5,000 noninterest-bearing note payable.
4 Billed customers for design services rendered on account, $16,550.
5 Rendered design services and collected from cash customers, $1,200.
6 Paid $1,400 to creditors on account.
7 Collected $12,750 on account from customers.
8 Paid a delivery service for delivery of graphics to commercial firms, $400.
9 Paid July salaries, $4,600.
10 Received invoice for July advertising expense, to be paid in August, $600.
11 Paid utilities for July, $350.
12 Paid stockholders a dividend of $2,000 cash.
13 Received invoice for supplies used in July, to be paid in August, $2,260.
14 Purchased computer for $4,300 cash to be used in the business starting next month.

REQUIRED

a. Set up accounts for the general ledger accounts with July 1 balances and enter the beginning balances. Also provide the following accounts: Equipment; Service Fees Earned; Rent Expense; Salaries Expense; Delivery Expense; Advertising Expense; Utilities Expense; Supplies Expense; and Dividends. Prepare journal entries and record the listed transactions in the appropriate T-accounts.

b. Prepare a trial balance as of July 31.

LO1 **PC-3.** **Transaction Analysis and Trial Balance** Outpost Fly-In Service, Inc., operates leased amphibious aircraft and docking facilities, equipping the firm to transport campers and hunters from Vancouver, Canada, to outpost camps owned by various resorts. On August 1, the firm's trial balance was as follows:

OUTPOST FLY-IN SERVICE, INC.
Unadjusted Trial Balance
August 1

	Debit	Credit
Cash	$52,600	
Accounts receivable	23,200	
Accounts payable		$ 1,700
Notes payable		3,000
Common stock		50,000
Retained earnings		21,100
Totals	$75,800	$75,800

During the month of August, the following transactions occurred:

Aug. 1 Paid August rental cost for aircraft, dockage, and dockside office, $5,000.
2 Paid insurance premium for August, $1,800.
3 Paid for August advertising in various sports magazines, $1,000.
4 Rendered fly-in services for various groups for cash, $13,750.
5 Billed the Canadian Ministry of Natural Resources for services in transporting mapping personnel, $3,200.
6 Received $17,400 on account from clients.
7 Paid $1,500 on accounts payable.
8 Billed various clients for services, $16,400.
9 Paid interest on a note payable for August, $25.
10 Paid August wages, $12,800.
11 Received invoice for the cost of fuel used during August, $3,200.
12 Paid a cash dividend, $4,500 (debit Retained Earnings).

REQUIRED

a. Set up accounts for each item in the August 1 trial balance and enter the beginning balances. Also provide accounts for the following items: Service Fees Earned, Wage Expense, Advertising Expense, Rent Expense, Fuel Expense, Insurance Expense, and Interest Expense. Prepare journal entries and record the transactions for August in the appropriate T-accounts, using the dates given.

b. Prepare a trial balance as of August 31.

PC-4. Transaction Analysis and the Effect of Errors on the Trial Balance LO1

The following T-accounts contain numbered entries for the May transactions of Flores Corporation, an architectural firm, which opened its offices on May 1 of the current year:

Cash

	Debit	Credit	
(1)	20,000	1,400	(4)
(10)	5,200	5,950	(7)
		1,000	(8)

Accounts Payable

	Debit	Credit	
(5)	310	1,530	(3)
(8)	1,000	290	(9)

Accounts Receivable

	Debit	Credit	
(6)	8,750	5,200	(10)

Common Stock

	Debit	Credit	
		20,000	(1)

Supplies

	Debit	Credit	
(3)	1,530	310	(5)

Professional Fees Earned

	Debit	Credit	
		8,750	(6)

Office Equipment

	Debit	Credit	
(2)	5,000		

Rent Expense

	Debit	Credit	
(4)	1,400		

Notes Payable

	Debit	Credit	
		5,000	(2)

Utilities Expense

	Debit	Credit	
(9)	290		

Salaries Expense

	Debit	Credit	
(7)	5,950		

REQUIRED

a. Give a description of each of the 10 numbered transactions entered in the above accounts. Example: (1) Flores Corporation issued common stock for cash, $20,000.

b. The following trial balance, prepared for Flores Corporation as of May 31, contains several errors. Itemize the errors, and indicate the correct totals for the trial balance.

FLORES CORPORATION
Unadjusted Trial Balance
May 31

	Debit	Credit
Cash	$61,850	
Accounts receivable	3,550	
Supplies	1,220	
Office equipment		$ 5,000
Accounts payable		510
Notes payable		50,000
Common stock		2,000
Professional fees earned		8,570
Rent expense	1,400	
Utilities expense	290	
Salaries expense	5,950	
Totals	$74,260	$66,080

LO1 PC-5. **Transaction Analysis and Trial Balance** James Behm, electrical contractor, began business on May 1. The following transactions occurred during the month of May:

May 1 Behm invested $18,000 of his personal funds in the business in exchange for common stock.
2 Purchased equipment on account, $4,200.
3 Returned $200 of equipment that was not satisfactory. The return reduced the amount owed to the supplier.
4 Purchased supplies on account, $860.
5 Purchased a truck for $10,500. Behm paid $5,500 cash and gave a note payable for the balance.
6 Paid rent for May, $875.
7 Paid fuel cost for truck, $60.
8 Billed customers for services rendered, $13,700.
9 Paid $3,000 on account for equipment purchased on May 2.
10 Paid utilities for May, $210.
11 Received invoice for May advertising, to be paid in June, $280.
12 Paid employees' wages, $3,350.
13 Collected $8,600 on accounts receivable.
14 Paid stockholders $1,500 cash as a dividend.
15 Paid interest for May on an outstanding note payable, $40.

REQUIRED

a. Prepare journal entries and record the above transactions in T-accounts, and key entries with the numbers of the transactions. The following accounts will be needed to record the transactions for May: Cash; Accounts Receivable; Supplies; Equipment; Truck; Accounts Payable; Notes Payable; Common Stock; Dividends; Service Revenue; Rent Expense; Wages Expense; Utilities Expense; Truck Expense; Advertising Expense; and Interest Expense.

b. Prepare a trial balance as of May 31.

LO2 PC-6. **Adjusting Entries** The following selected accounts appear in the Shaw Company's unadjusted trial balance as of December 31, the end of the fiscal year (all accounts have normal balances):

Prepaid advertising	$ 1,200	Unearned service fees	$ 5,400
Wages expense	43,800	Service fees earned	87,000
Prepaid insurance	3,420	Rental income	4,900

REQUIRED

Prepare the necessary adjusting entries in the general journal as of December 31, assuming the following:

1. Prepaid advertising at December 31 is $950.
2. Unpaid wages earned by employees in December are $1,600.
3. Prepaid insurance at December 31 is $2,750.
4. Unearned service fees at December 31 are $2,800.
5. Rent revenue of $1,300 owed by a tenant is not recorded at December 31.

PC-7. Adjusting Entries The following selected accounts appear in the Birch Company's unadjusted trial balance as of December 31, the end of the fiscal year (all accounts have normal balances): LO2

Homework MBC

Prepaid maintenance	$2,700	Commission fees earned	$86,000
Supplies	9,400	Rent expense	10,800
Unearned commission fees	8,500		

REQUIRED

Prepare the necessary adjusting entries in the general journal as of December 31, assuming the following:

1. On September 1, the company entered into a prepaid equipment maintenance contract. Birch Company paid $2,700 to cover maintenance service for six months, beginning September 1. The $2,700 payment was debited to Prepaid Maintenance.
2. Supplies on hand at December 31 are $3,200.
3. Unearned commission fees at December 31 are $4,000.
4. Commission fees earned but not yet billed at December 31 are $3,500. (*Note:* Debit Fees Receivable.)
5. Birch Company's lease calls for rent of $900 per month payable on the first of each month, plus an annual amount equal to 1 percent of annual commissions earned. This additional rent is payable on January 10 of the following year. (*Note:* Be sure to use the adjusted amount of commissions earned in computing the additional rent.)

PC-8. Financial Statements and Closing Entries The adjusted trial balance shown below is for Fine Consulting Service as of December 31. Byran Fine made no capital contributions during the year. LO3, 4

	Adjusted Trial Balance	
	Debit	**Credit**
Cash	$ 2,700	
Accounts receivable	3,270	
Supplies	5,060	
Prepaid insurance	1,500	
Equipment	6,400	
Accumulated depreciation—Equipment		$ 1,080
Accounts payable		845
Long-term notes payable		7,000
Common stock		3,000
Retained earnings		5,205
Dividends	2,900	
Service fees earned		62,400
Rent expense	15,000	
Salaries expense	33,400	
Supplies expense	4,700	
Insurance expense	3,250	
Depreciation expense—Equipment	720	
Interest expense	630	
Totals	$79,530	$79,530

REQUIRED

a. Prepare an income statement and a statement of stockholders' equity for the year, and a balance sheet as of December 31.

b. Prepare closing entries directly to Retained Earnings in general journal form.

LO4 **PC-9. Closing Entries** The adjusted trial balance shown below is for Bayou, Inc., at December 31:

	Adjusted Trial Balance	
	Debit	Credit
Cash	$ 3,500	
Accounts receivable	8,000	
Prepaid insurance	3,600	
Equipment	75,000	
Accumulated depreciation		$ 12,000
Accounts payable		600
Common stock		30,000
Retained earnings		14,100
Cash dividends	7,500	
Service fees earned		102,200
Miscellaneous income		4,200
Salaries expense	42,800	
Rent expense	12,900	
Insurance expense	1,800	
Depreciation expense	8,000	
Income tax expense	8,800	
Income tax payable		8,800
Totals	$171,900	$171,900

REQUIRED

a. Prepare closing entries directly to Retained Earnings in general journal form.
b. After the closing entries are posted, what is the ending balance in the Retained Earnings account?
c. Prepare a post-closing trial balance.

LO1, 2, 3, 4 **PC-10. Transaction Analysis, Trial Balance, and Financial Statements** Angela Mehl operates the Mehl Dance Studio. On June 1, the business's general ledger contained the following information:

Cash	$ 5,930	Accounts payable	$ 480
Accounts receivable	8,000	Notes payable	3,580
		Common stock	7,870
		Retained earnings	2,000
	$13,930		$13,930

The following transactions occurred during the month of June:

June
1 Paid June rent for practice studio, $975.
2 Paid June piano rental, $240 (Rent Expense).
3 Collected $5,320 from students on account.
4 Borrowed $1,500 and signed a promissory note payable due in six months.
5 Billed students for June instructional fees, $7,500.
6 Paid interest for June on notes payable, $30.
7 Paid $350 for advertising ballet performances.
8 Paid costume rental, $550 (Rent Expense).
9 Collected $2,100 admission fees from ballet performances given during the month.
10 Paid $480 owed on account.
11 Received invoice for June utilities, to be paid in July, $465.
12 Paid stockholders $900 cash as a dividend.
13 Purchased piano for $5,000 cash, to be used in business starting in July.

REQUIRED

a. Set up accounts for the general ledger with June 1 balances and enter the beginning balances. Also provide the following accounts: Piano; Dividends; Instructional Fees Earned; Performance Revenue; Rent Expense; Utilities Expense; Advertising Expense; and Interest Expense. Record the listed transactions in the accounts.
b. Prepare a trial balance as of June 30.
c. Prepare an income statement for the month of June.
d. Prepare a statement of stockholders' equity for the month of June.
e. Prepare a balance sheet as of June 30.
f. Prepare closing entries.
g. Prepare a post-closing trial balance.

ANSWERS TO SELF-STUDY QUESTIONS

1. c **2.** d **3.** a **4.** d **5.** d **6.** d **7.** a **8.** b **9.** d

REVIEW SOLUTIONS

Solution C.1

Date	Description	Post Ref.	Debit	Credit
October	Cash	1	40,000	
	Common stock	1		40,000
	Owner purchased shares for cash.			
	Rent expense	2	2,500	
	Cash	2		2,500
	Paid rent for office suite.			
	Equipment	3	10,000	
	Cash	3		10,000
	Purchased office equipment.			
	Supplies expense	4	500	
	Accounts payable	4		500
	Purchased supplies on account to be used in current month.			
	Advertising expense	5	300	
	Cash	5		300
	Purchased advertising.			
	Accounts receivable	6	7,800	
	Service revenue	6		7,800
	Performed design work on account.			
	Cash	7	3,500	
	Accounts receivable	7		3,500
	Received cash from previously billed work.			
	Accounts payable	8	350	
	Cash	8		350
	Paid cash towards accounts payable.			
	Wage expense	9	2,500	
	Cash	9		2,500
	Paid wages.			

Cash			
(1)	40,000	2,500	(2)
(7)	3,500	10,000	(3)
		300	(5)
		350	(8)
		2,500	(9)
Bal.	27,850		

Equipment			
(3)	10,000		

Common Stock			
		40,000	(1)

Supplies Expense			
(4)	500		

Advertising Expense			
(5)	300		

Accounts Receivable			
(6)	7,800	3,500	(7)
Bal.	4,300		

Accounts Payable			
(8)	350	500	(4)
		150	Bal.

Service Revenue			
		7,800	(6)

Wage Expense			
(9)	2,500		

Rent Expense			
(2)	2,500		

Solution C.2

		Debit	Credit
1.	Depreciation expense	$700	
	Accumulated depreciation—Buildings		$700
	To record depreciation expense on buildings.		
2.	Rent expense	$1,500	
	Prepaid rent		$1,500
	To record rent expense.		
3.	Unearned revenue	$400	
	Service fee revenue		$400
	To record revenue earned.		
4.	Interest expense	$500	
	Interest payable		$500
	To record interest payable.		

Solution C.3

THE CASSI COMPANY
Income Statement
For the Year Ended December 31

Sales revenues		$52,000
Expenses		
Supplies expense	$30,000	
Salaries expense	5,000	
Rent expense	6,000	
Depreciation expense	6,000	
Total expenses		47,000
Net income		$ 5,000

THE CASSI COMPANY
Statement of Stockholders' Equity
For the Year Ended December 31

	Common Stock	Retained Earnings	Total
Balance, December 1	$15,000	$5,000	$20,000
Add: Net income for December		5,000	5,000
Less: Dividends in December		(2,000)	(2,000)
Balance, December 31	$15,000	$8,000	$23,000

THE CASSI COMPANY
Balance Sheet
As of December 31

Assets			**Liabilities**		
Current assets			Current liabilities		
Cash	$ 4,000		Accounts payable	$ 8,000	
Accounts receivable	15,000		Salaries payable	9,000	
Supplies	18,000		Dividends payable	2,000	
Prepaid rent	5,000		Unearned revenue	5,000	
Total current assets		$42,000	Total current liabilities		$24,000
			Long-term debt		35,000
Equipment	50,000		Total liabilities		59,000
Less: Accumulated depreciation	(10,000)	40,000			
			Stockholders' Equity		
			Common stock	15,000	
			Retained earnings	8,000	
			Total stockholders' equity		23,000
Total Assets		$82,000	Total Liabilities and Stockholders' Equity		$82,000

Solution C.4

Date	Account	Debit	Credit
Dec. 31	Sales revenue	79,000	
	Retained earnings		79,000
	To close the revenue account.		
Dec. 31	Retained earnings	72,000	
	Cost of goods sold		41,000
	Wage expense		22,000
	Rent expense		3,000
	Depreciation expense		2,000
	Interest expense		4,000
	To close the expense accounts.		
Dec. 31	Retained earnings	5,000	
	Dividends		5,000
	To close the dividends account.		

Accounting for Investments and Consolidated Financial Statements

Appendix

D

Road Map

LO	Learning Objective	Page	eLecture	Assignments
LO1	**Describe debt and equity securities and how they may be acquired.**	D-2	D-1	
LO2	**Describe the accounting for various kinds of debt security investments.**	D-3	D-2	E1, E2, E3, P1, P2
LO3	**Describe the accounting for various kinds of equity security investments.**	D-9	D-3	E4, E5, E6, E7, P3, P4, P5
LO4	**Define parent-subsidiary relationships and discuss how their balance sheet data are consolidated.**	D-15	D-4	E8

INVESTMENTS

Debt and Equity Securities

LO1 Describe debt and equity securities and how they may be acquired.

The assets of a business may include investments in one or more types of debt or equity securities. For some businesses, such as insurance companies, investments in debt and equity securities constitute the major portion of a company's total assets. Investments in various debt and equity securities, for example, represent more than 50 percent of the assets of **Blue Cross Blue Shield**, a large insurance company.

A **debt security** refers to a financial instrument that creates a creditor relationship for the debtholder. Examples of debt securities include U.S. Treasury bills, notes, and bonds; U.S. government agency bonds, such as Fannie Mae and Ginnie Mae bonds; state and local government bonds; corporate bonds; and commercial paper. Bonds are long-term debt securities and are discussed in detail in Chapter 9. Long-term bonds have maturities of 30 years or more, while shorter term bonds range from one to four years. Commercial paper, on the other hand, refers to very short term (1 to 180 days), unsecured promissory notes issued by large corporations.

An **equity security** is a financial instrument that represents an ownership interest in a company. Shares of stock represent ownership interests in a corporation and are discussed in detail in Chapter 10. Investors owning a company's common stock have the most basic ownership rights, whereas owners of a company's preferred stock have some rights that take preference over the common stockholders, such as preferential treatment in the receipt of dividends and the receipt of assets in the event that a company liquidates.

Debt and equity securities may be acquired directly from the entity that issues the securities or through a secondary market. When corporations or government agencies need to borrow, they offer their debt securities for sale to the general public. This process is called floating an issue. When a corporation initially issues (sells) stock to the general public to raise money, the process is called an initial public offering (IPO). When companies need additional cash to fund their operations after initially going public, they may conduct additional sales of their shares through secondary public offerings.

More frequently, investors acquire debt and equity securities through the secondary capital market. The secondary capital market consists of individual and institutional investors desiring to buy or sell securities. Many debt and equity securities are bought and sold on organized exchanges. Stocks and bonds, for example, may trade on a national exchange such as the New York Stock Exchange or the London Stock Exchange. (Despite their names, both exchanges list both bonds and stocks.) Stocks and bonds may also trade in a less formal market known as the over-the-counter market. Many buyers and sellers typically use the services of a brokerage firm, such as **Charles Schwab** or **Fidelity Investments**, to facilitate the acquisition and disposition of their investments. In addition, online brokerages, such as Robinhood, are becoming increasingly popular.

Investments in Debt Securities

LO2 Describe the accounting for various kinds of debt security investments.

Investments in debt securities are placed in one of the following three investment categories:

- **Trading Securities**: Debt securities that management purchases with the intent to hold for only a short period of time.
- **Available-for-Sale Securities**: Debt securities that management does not intend to sell in the near future but also does not intend to hold until maturity.
- **Held-to-Maturity Securities**: Debt securities that management intends to hold until maturity.

The major accounting events concerning investments in debt securities are their purchase, the recognition of interest income, their balance sheet valuation, and their sale or redemption at maturity. **Exhibit D-1** summarizes the accounting guidelines for these events. Following Exhibit D-1, we illustrate these guidelines with examples.

EXHIBIT D-1 Accounting Guidelines for Investments in Debt Securities

Event/Accounting Guideline	Trading Securities	Available-for-Sale Securities	Held-to-Maturity Securities
1. Purchase Record at cost, which includes any broker's fees.	X	X	X
2. Recognition of Interest Income Interest accrues daily and is usually recorded when payment is received. Premium or discount on purchase price is not amortized.	X		
Interest accrues daily and is usually recorded when payment is received. Premium or discount on purchase price is amortized as an adjustment of interest income.		X	X
3. Balance Sheet Valuation Measure securities at fair value at balance sheet date. No valuation account to the asset account is used. Changes in fair value are reported in the income statement.	X		
Measure securities at fair value at balance sheet date. Use a valuation account to the asset account. Changes in fair value are reported in stockholders' equity.		X	
Measure securities at amortized cost at balance sheet date.			X
4. Sale or Redemption at Maturity Sale proceeds less investment's book value is a realized gain or loss.	X		
Sale proceeds less investment's amortized cost is a realized gain or loss.		X	
At maturity, the investment's book value will equal the redemption proceeds.			X

Purchase

Assume that the Warner Company purchases $300,000 face value of Natco Company 8 percent bonds at 98 on July 1, Year 1. (Recall from Chapter 9 that bond prices are quoted on a basis of $100 while their base value is actually $1,000. Thus, a bond said to sell for 98 is actually selling for $980. And, for a group of bonds with an aggregate maturity value of $100,000, this would imply a selling price of $98,000.) The bonds pay interest on December 31 and June 30 and mature in 10 years. The brokerage commission is $600. Warner's management considers the bond investment to be divided equally between trading securities, available-for-sale securities, and held-to-maturity securities. **Exhibit D-2** shows the financial statement effects of recording this debt investment. Note that the accounting for the purchase is the same regardless of the classification of the bond investment.

The Natco Company bonds are purchased the first day after an interest payment date, so there is no unpaid interest related to the bonds. If any more time had elapsed, however, the bond price would include an amount for the accrued but unpaid interest. This occurs because the bond seller is entitled to receive the interest earned up to the date of sale. As a result, the purchase price of a bond that is sold between interest payment dates includes not only the current market price but also any interest accrued since the last interest payment date. The bond buyer pays the accrued interest amount to the bond seller, increases the Bond Interest Receivable account for the amount of the accrued interest, and then collects it as part of the next interest payment received from the bond issuer. Because the accrued interest purchased by the bond buyer is collected with the next interest payment, the accrued interest is not treated as part of the initial cost of the bond investment.

EXHIBIT D-2 Purchase of Debt Securities

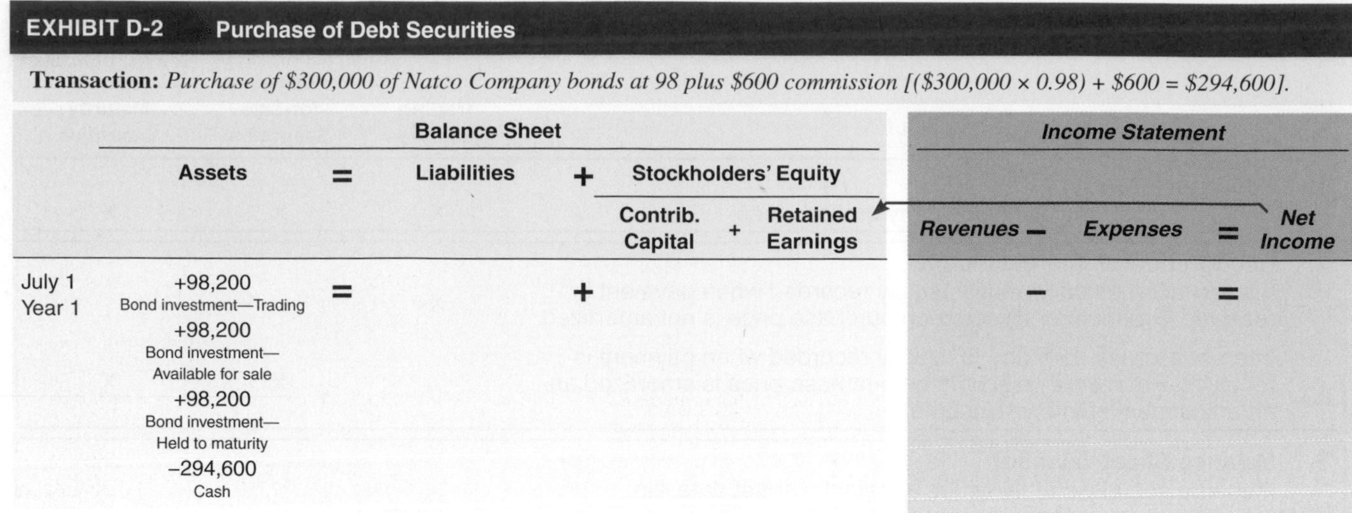

Transaction: *Purchase of $300,000 of Natco Company bonds at 98 plus $600 commission [($300,000 × 0.98) + $600 = $294,600].*

	Balance Sheet						Income Statement				
	Assets	=	Liabilities	+	Stockholders' Equity						
					Contrib. Capital	+	Retained Earnings	*Revenues*	−	*Expenses*	=	*Net Income*
July 1 Year 1	+98,200 Bond investment—Trading +98,200 Bond investment—Available for sale +98,200 Bond investment—Held to maturity −294,600 Cash	=		+					−		=	

Recognition of Interest Income

Each $100,000 of Natco Company bonds acquired on July 1, Year 1, was purchased at a $1,800 discount ($100,000 – $98,200). This means that the market rate of interest on July 1, Year 1 was higher than the 8 percent coupon rate offered on the bonds. For trading securities, any bond discount (or premium) is ignored in accounting for the periodic interest income because management plans to sell the securities in the near future. As such, the effect on net income from ignoring the bond discount (or premium) is immaterial.

PRINCIPLE ALERT

Materiality Concept Note the role played by the *materiality concept* in determining interest income on trading securities. Because of the short time period that trading securities are held by a company before being resold, accountants do not bother to amortize any discount or premium associated with the debt securities. This simplifies the accounting for these debt securities, yet it causes no significant distortion in the periodic reporting of interest income.

For available-for-sale securities and held-to-maturity securities, any bond discount (or premium) is amortized to interest income. This is done to make periodic interest income more accurately reflect the economic reality of the bond investment. The amortization of bond discount causes the periodic interest income to be higher than the semiannual cash receipt of interest. If the bonds had been purchased at a premium (more than their face value), the premium amortization would cause periodic interest income to be less than the semiannual cash receipt of interest.

Two amortization methods are available for use: the straight-line method and the effective interest method. We use the straight-line method here because the difference in the financial effect between the two methods is immaterial in this case. (See Chapter 9 for a discussion of the effective interest method.) The straight-line method of amortization writes off an equal amount of discount or premium each interest period. The Natco Company bonds, when purchased, had 10 years to maturity, with interest paid semi-annually. Consequently, there are 20 interest periods associated with the bonds. During each interest period, $90 ($1,800/20 periods) of discount will be amortized for the available-for-sale securities and the held-to-maturity securities. Each $100,000 (face value) of Natco bonds pays $4,000 interest semiannually (8 percent × $100,000 × ½-year). The entries to record interest income at December 31, Year 1, are shown in **Exhibit D-3**.

EXHIBIT D-3 Recognition of Interest Income on Debt Securities

Transaction: *Trading Debt Securities—Receipt of semiannual interest on $100,000 of trading bonds.*

	Balance Sheet							Income Statement				
	Assets	=	Liabilities	+	Stockholders' Equity							
					Contrib. Capital	+	Retained Earnings	Revenues	–	Expenses	=	Net Income
Dec. 31 Year 1	+4,000 Cash	=		+			+4,000 Retained earnings	+4,000 Bond interest income	–		=	+4,000

Transaction: *Available-for-Sale Debt Securities—Receipt of semiannual interest and discount amortization on $100,000 of available-for-sale bonds.*

	Balance Sheet							Income Statement				
	Assets	=	Liabilities	+	Stockholders' Equity							
					Contrib. Capital	+	Retained Earnings	Revenues	–	Expenses	=	Net Income
Dec. 31 Year 1	+4,000 Cash +90 Bond investment—Available for sale	=		+			+4,090 Retained earnings	+4,090 Bond interest income	–		=	+4,090

Transaction: *Held-to-Maturity Debt Securities—Receipt of semiannual interest and discount amortization on $100,000 of held-to-maturity bonds.*

	Balance Sheet							Income Statement				
	Assets	=	Liabilities	+	Stockholders' Equity							
					Contrib. Capital	+	Retained Earnings	Revenues	–	Expenses	=	Net Income
Dec. 31 Year 1	+4,000 Cash +90 Bond investment—Held to maturity	=		+			+4,090 Retained earnings	+4,090 Bond interest income	–		=	+4,090

Balance Sheet Valuation

Debt securities that the investor company intends to sell (trading securities) or may sell (available-for-sale securities) are reported on the balance sheet at their fair value. Debt that is held to maturity is not required to be reported at fair value. Generally Accepted Accounting Principles allow companies to use one of three methods to estimate the fair value of trading and available-for-sale debt investments. These methods are known as the fair value hierarchy, which is ranked by the quality and reliability of the resulting fair value estimates.

- **Level 1:** Quoted market prices in active markets for identical assets or liabilities. For example, there is an active public market for the bonds issued by Apple, Inc. Thus, the fair value of an investment in Apple's bonds would typically be estimated using their current market price. This is the preferred fair valuation method and is generally considered to arrive at the most reliable and accurate fair value estimates.
- **Level 2:** Quoted market prices in active markets for similar securities and model-based valuation methods. For example, if an investee's bonds are not traded in an active market, the investor might estimate their fair value using the bonds of a similar company that is traded in an active market.
- **Level 3:** When the fair value of the debt security cannot be determined based upon readily observable inputs (such as those used for Level 1 and Level 2 estimates), the investor company

uses so-called unobservable inputs. For example, the fair value may be based on the discounted present value of the bond's expected future cash flows. Because Level 3 estimates rely heavily on assumptions, they are generally considered the least reliable method of estimating fair values.

Assume that a general decline in market interest rates causes the Natco Company bonds to trade at 99.5 as of December 31, Year 1. **Exhibit D-4** shows the adjusting entries made on this date to record the relevant fair values.

EXHIBIT D-4 Balance Sheet Valuation for Debt Securities

Transaction: *Trading Debt Securities—Adjustment to trading debt securities to year-end fair value ($99,500 – $98,200 = $1,300 gain).*

	Balance Sheet						Income Statement				
	Assets	=	Liabilities	+	Stockholders' Equity						
					Contrib. Capital	+ Retained Earnings	Revenues	–	Expenses	=	Net Income
Dec. 31 Year 1	+1,300 Bond investment—Trading	=		+		+1,300 Retained earnings	+1,300 Unrealized gain on investments	–		=	+1,300

Transaction: *Available-for-Sale Debt Securities—Adjustment to available-for-sale debt securities to year-end fair value ($99,500 – $98,290 = $1,210 gain).*

	Balance Sheet						Income Statement				
	Assets	=	Liabilities	+	Stockholders' Equity						
					Contrib. Capital	+ Retained Earnings	Revenues	–	Expenses	=	Net Income
Dec. 31 Year 1	+1,210 Fair value adjustment to bond investment	=		+		+1,210 Unrealized gain/loss on investments		–		=	

Fair value changes in securities that are still owned are called **unrealized gains and losses.** Unrealized gains and losses that relate to trading securities are reported in the income statement. Thus, the $1,300 unrealized gain shown in **Exhibit D-4** is included in Warner's Year 1 income statement.

Unrealized gains and losses that relate to available-for-sale securities are excluded from the income statement. Instead, their net amount is reported as a separate component of stockholders' equity called Unrealized Gain/Loss on Investments (Equity). Unrealized Gain/Loss on Investments is included in comprehensive income that was discussed in Chapter 12. Because these unrealized gains and losses are not included in earnings, the investment's cost must be maintained in the accounts so that a total realized gain or loss can be determined when the investment is actually sold. Using the valuation account Fair Value Adjustment to Bond Investment permits the maintenance of the investment's cost in the Bond Investment—Available-for-Sale account.[1] After the adjustments shown in **Exhibit D-4**, the December 31, Year 1, balance sheet reports the bond investments as follows:

Hint: Although the accounting for debt trading securities calls for the recognition of any fair value changes as part of a company's current net income, those unrealized gains or losses are not reported as part of a company's net income for income tax purposes. The IRS does not require the reporting of any gains until they are realized and prohibits the reporting of any losses until realized (when a security is sold).

Bond investment—Trading (fair value)		$99,500
Bond investment—Available-for-sale (amortized cost)	$98,290	
Add: Fair value adjustment to bond investment	1,210	99,500
Bond investment—Held-to-maturity (amortized cost)		98,290

[1] The cost of trading securities must be maintained for income tax purposes. A fair value valuation account, therefore, may be used for maintaining the income tax records of trading securities.

Sale or Redemption at Maturity

To complete our illustration, assume that the trading and available-for-sale bond investments are both sold on July 1, Year 2, for $99,800 each (after recognizing interest income on June 30, Year 2). The remaining bond investment is held to maturity (June 30, Year 11), at which time the issuer redeems the bonds for their maturity value of $100,000. **Exhibit D-5** shows the financial statement effect of these events.

EXHIBIT D-5 Sale or Redemption at Maturity of Debt Securities

Transaction: *Trading Debt Securities—Sale of trading debt securities for $99,800 ($99,800 – $99,500 = $300 realized gain).*

	Balance Sheet							Income Statement				
	Assets	=	Liabilities	+	Stockholders' Equity							
					Contrib. Capital	+	Retained Earnings	Revenues	–	Expenses	=	Net Income
Jul. 1 Year 2	+99,800 Cash −99,500 Bond investment—Trading	=		+			+300 Retained earnings	+300 Gain on sale of investments	–		=	+300

Transaction: *Available-for-Sale Debt Securities—Sale of available-for-sale debt securities for $99,800 ($99,800 – $98,380 = $1,420 gain). Adjust fair valuation accounts to zero.*

	Balance Sheet							Income Statement				
	Assets	=	Liabilities	+	Stockholders' Equity							
					Contrib. Capital	+	Retained Earnings	Revenues	–	Expenses	=	Net Income
Jul. 1 Year 2	+99,800 Cash −98,380 Bond investment—Available for sale	=		+			+1,420 Retained earnings	+1,420 Gain on sale of investments	–		=	+1,420
Dec. 31 Year 2	−1,210 Fair value adjustment to bond investment	=		+			−1,210 Unrealized gain/loss on investments		–		=	

Transaction: *Held-to-Maturity Debt Securities—Redemption of bonds at maturity.*

	Balance Sheet							Income Statement				
	Assets	=	Liabilities	+	Stockholders' Equity							
					Contrib. Capital	+	Retained Earnings	Revenues	–	Expenses	=	Net Income
Jun. 30 Year 11	+100,000 Cash −100,000 Bond investment—Held to maturity	=		+					–		=	

In **Exhibit D-5**, the $300 gain on the sale of the trading securities is the difference between the $99,800 sales proceeds and the last recorded fair value of $99,500. By July 1, Year 2, another $90 of discount amortization would have been recorded on the available-for-sale securities, increasing their amortized cost to $98,380 ($98,290 + $90). The $1,420 gain that is recorded on their sale is the difference between the $99,800 sales proceeds and the amortized cost of $98,380. Because all available-for-sale bonds were sold, the related valuation account and unrealized gain/loss account are adjusted to zero balances at the next financial statement closing date (December 31, Year 2). The completion of the discount amortization on the held-to-maturity bonds brings their amortized cost to $100,000 on June 30, Year 11. Thus, there is no gain or loss associated with the redemption of the bonds at maturity.

Investments in Equity Securities

LO3 Describe the accounting for various kinds of equity security investments.

The accounting for equity securities depends upon the extent to which the investor company is able to influence or control the investee company (where the investee is the company whose stock the investor company owns). Accountants classify equity investments into one of three categories based on the level of the investor's influence or control over the investee.

- **Little or no influence (Passive)**: When an investor company owns only a small percentage of the investee's voting stock, it lacks the ability to exert influence or control over the investee's behavior. Investors buy small percentages of a company's stock when they wish to earn dividend income and capital gains from the investment. When an investor owns less than 20 percent of an investee's outstanding voting stock, they are judged to have little or no influence over the investee company. These are sometimes referred to as "passive" investments.
- **Significant influence**: When an investor company owns a significant portion of the investee's voting stock, it has the ability to exert significant influence over the investee. For example, it may be able to influence whether and how much dividends the investee pays. In the absence of evidence to the contrary, when an investor owns between 20 percent and 50 percent of an investee's outstanding voting stock, it is judged to have significant influence over the investee company.
- **Controlling**: When an investor owns a majority of the investee's voting stock, it is able to control strategic decisions made by the investees, such as the election of the majority of the board of directors and the hiring of executive management. For accounting purposes, when an investor owns more than 50 percent of an investee's outstanding voting stock, it is presumed to have control over the investee company.

The ownership percentages used to classify equity investments into the above categories are guidelines only and may be overcome by other factors. For example, an investor may control an investee with less than 50 percent ownership of its voting stock. For example, ownership of a large minority interest (such as 45 percent), with other owners widely dispersed and unorganized, may result in effective control. The guiding principle in the proper classification is the presence of significant influence on, or effective control over, the investee company.

The major accounting events associated with investments in equity securities are their purchase, the recognition of investment income, their balance sheet valuation, and their sale. **Exhibit D-6** summarizes the accounting guidelines for these events. Following **Exhibit D-6**, we discuss how companies determine a security's fair value and illustrate how to apply the guidelines in **Exhibit D-6**.

EXHIBIT D-6 Accounting Guidelines for Investments in Equity Securities

	Event/Accounting Guideline	Little or No Influence (Passive)	Significant Influence	Controlling
1.	**Purchase** Record at cost, which includes any broker's fees.	X	X	X
2.	**Recognition of Investment Income** Record dividend income when dividends are received.	X		
	Record equity in investee company's net income as investment income. Decrease investment account for dividends received.		X	X
3.	**Balance Sheet Valuation** Measure securities at fair value at balance sheet date. No valuation account to the investment account is used. Changes in fair value are reported in the income statement.	X		
	Report securities at book value (cost plus share of investee net income less dividends).		X	
	Eliminate investment account as part of consolidation procedures.			X
4.	**Sale** Sale proceeds less investment's book value is a realized gain or loss.	X	X	X

Purchase

Assume that Warner Company purchases 1,500 shares of common stock in each of three different companies—Ark, Inc.; Barcal, Inc.; and Call, Inc.—on January 1, Year 1. Each investment costs $15,000, including broker's fees. The shares acquired represent 10 percent of Ark's voting stock, 25 percent of Barcal's voting stock, and 60 percent of Call's voting stock.[2] Thus, the investment in Ark is passive, the investment in Barcal results in significant influence over the investee, and the investment in Call results in control of the investee. **Exhibit D-7** presents the financial statement effect of the purchase of these investments. Note that each stock investment is recorded at its acquisition cost.

EXHIBIT D-7 Purchase of Equity Securities

Transaction: *Record the purchase of 1,500 shares each of Ark, Inc., Barcal, Inc., and Call, Inc., common stock for $45,000 ($15,000 for each investment), including broker's fees.*

	Balance Sheet							Income Statement				
	Assets	=	Liabilities	+	Stockholders' Equity							
					Contrib. Capital	+	Retained Earnings	Revenues	−	Expenses	=	Net Income
Jan. 1, Year 1	+15,000 Stock investment—Passive (Ark) +15,000 Stock investment—Significant influence (Barcal) +15,000 Stock investment—Controlling (Call) −45,000 Cash	=		+					−		=	

Recognition of Investment Income

Now assume that each of the three companies earns net income of $10,000 in Year 1 and that each company also declares a cash dividend of $0.50 per share, which is received by Warner on December 31, Year 1. **Exhibit D-8** shows the financial statement effect of this information.

As shown in **Exhibit D-8**, the dividends of $750 received on the Ark investment is reported as Dividend Income. This is the proper treatment for cash dividends received on passive investments (Ark).

When the percentage ownership of voting stock reaches 20 percent or more, as is the case with the investment in Barcal stock, the **equity method** of accounting is used. Under the equity method, the investor company records as income or loss its proportionate share of the net income or net loss reported for the period by the investee company (Barcal), with an offsetting increase or decrease to the Stock Investment account. In addition, the receipt of any cash dividends from the investee company reduces the Stock Investment account. The equity method prevents an investor company from manipulating its own income by the influence it can exercise on the dividend policies of the investee company.

In **Exhibit D-8**, the equity method is used for the Barcal stock investment (25 percent ownership) and Call stock investment (60 percent ownership). At December 31, Year 1, the Income from the Stock Investments account and the Barcal Stock Investment account are increased by 25 percent of Barcal's Year 1 net income (25 percent × $10,000 = $2,500). The receipt of the $750 cash dividend from Barcal reduces the Barcal Stock Investment account. Similarly, the equity method causes a $6,000 increase (60 percent × $10,000 net income) in both the Income from Stock Investments account and the Call Stock Investment account at December 31, Year 1. The $750 cash dividend received from Call decreases the Call Stock Investment account.

A.K.A. Stock investments involving ownership interests of 20 to 50 percent of the outstanding voting shares are often referred to as **affiliate companies**.

[2] We assume that the costs of the investments in Barcal and Call are equal to the book value of the underlying net assets of the investee company. This assumption permits us to simplify the illustration of the accounting for these two investments.

EXHIBIT D-8 Recognition of Investment Income on Equity Securities

Transaction: *Passive Investment Securities—Record receipt of cash dividend from Ark, Inc.*

	Balance Sheet							Income Statement				
	Assets	=	Liabilities	+	Stockholders' Equity: Contrib. Capital	+	Retained Earnings	Revenues	−	Expenses	=	Net Income
Dec. 31 Year 1	+750 Cash	=		+			+750 Retained earnings	+750 Dividend income	−		=	+750

Transaction: *Significant Influence Securities—Record as income 25 percent of Barcal's Year 1 net income of $10,000 and receipt of cash dividend from Barcal, Inc.*

	Balance Sheet							Income Statement				
	Assets	=	Liabilities	+	Stockholders' Equity: Contrib. Capital	+	Retained Earnings	Revenues	−	Expenses	=	Net Income
Dec. 31 Year 1	+2,500 Stock investment—Significant influence (Barcal)	=		+			+2,500 Retained earnings	+2,500 Income from stock investments	−		=	+2,500
	(Investment balance = $15,000 + $2,500 = $17,500)											
Dec. 31 Year 1	+750 Cash −750 Stock investment—Significant influence (Barcal)	=		+					−		=	
	(Investment balance = $17,500 − $750 = $16,750)											

Transaction: *Controlling Equity Securities—Record as income 60 percent of Call's Year 1 net income of $10,000 and the receipt of cash dividend from Call, Inc.*

	Balance Sheet							Income Statement				
	Assets	=	Liabilities	+	Stockholders' Equity: Contrib. Capital	+	Retained Earnings	Revenues	−	Expenses	=	Net Income
Dec. 31 Year 1	+6,000 Stock investment—Controlling (Call)	=		+			+6,000 Retained earnings	+6,000 Income from stock investments	−		=	+6,000
	(Investment balance = $15,000 + $6,000 = $21,000)											
Dec. 31 Year 1	+750 Cash −750 Stock investment—Controlling (Call)	=		+					−		=	
	(Investment balance = $21,000 − $750 = $20,250)											

Balance Sheet Valuation

All passive investment securities are valued on the balance sheet at their fair value. These fair values are determined using the fair value hierarchy shown on page D-5, which is also used to determine the fair values of debt trading and available-for-sale securities. Recall that this hierarchy consists of three levels, ranked on the reliability of the resulting fair value estimates.

- **Level 1:** Quoted market prices in active markets for identical assets or liabilities.
- **Level 2:** Quoted market prices in active markets for similar securities and model-based valuation methods.
- **Level 3:** Unobservable inputs such as the discounted present value of future cash flows.

The choice of fair value method is based upon whether the passive equity investments are classified as **marketable securities** or **non-marketable securities.** Marketable equity securities are investments in companies whose shares are traded on organized public stock exchanges, such as the New York Stock Exchange (NYSE). These include large well-known companies such as Walmart, Starbucks and Columbia Sportswear. The fair value of marketable passive securities is based upon quoted market prices (Level 1) or quoted markets for similar securities (Level 2). Non-marketable equity securities are investments in stock issued by privately-held companies, which are typically much smaller and less well known. The fair value of non-marketable passive securities is based upon unobservable inputs, such as discounted cash flows (Level 3).

Assume that Natco uses the appropriate fair value method to determine that at December 31, Year 1, the fair value of the 1,500 shares of Ark common stock is $23,000. Since the original cost of Ark was $15,000, this indicates that there is an unrealized gain of $8,000 ($23,000 minus $15,000) on the investment. As shown in Exhibit D-9, this results in an $8,000 increase to the investment in Ark and an $8,000 unrealized gain reported in Warner's Year 1 income statement.

Stock investments accounted for by the equity method are not measured at year-end fair values. The year-end account balances remain as calculated using the equity method—that is, $16,750 for the Barcal investment and $20,250 for the Call investment. For controlling investments, the financial statements of the investee company are usually consolidated with the statements of the investor company; consequently, the investment account does not appear in the consolidated statements.

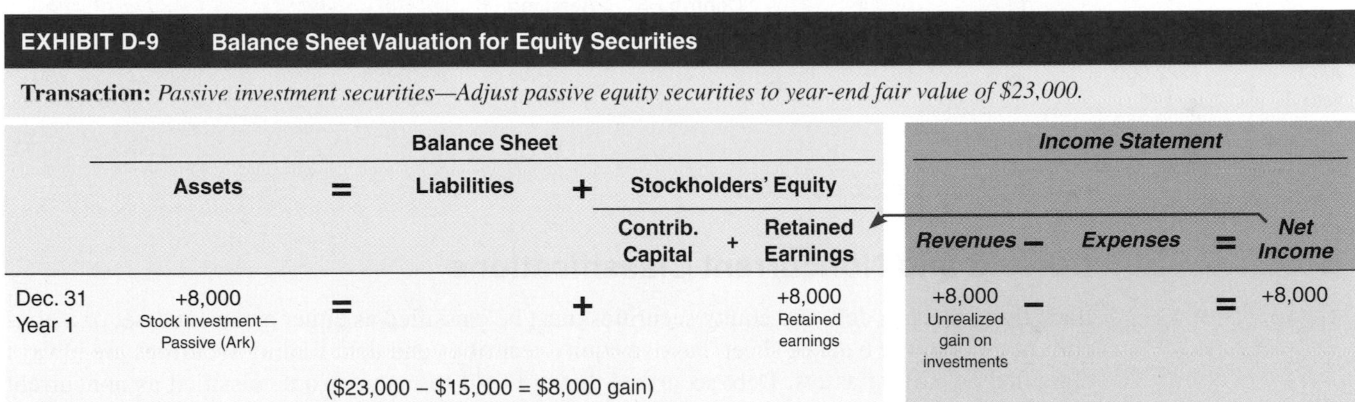

EXHIBIT D-9 Balance Sheet Valuation for Equity Securities

Transaction: *Passive investment securities—Adjust passive equity securities to year-end fair value of $23,000.*

	Assets	=	Liabilities	+	Contrib. Capital	+	Retained Earnings	Revenues	−	Expenses	=	Net Income
Dec. 31 Year 1	+8,000 Stock investment—Passive (Ark)	=		+			+8,000 Retained earnings	+8,000 Unrealized gain on investments	−		=	+8,000

($23,000 – $15,000 = $8,000 gain)

Sale

To complete our illustration, assume that all three stock investments are sold on July 1, Year 2. Each of the stock investments is sold for $22,000. **Exhibit D-10** shows the financial statement effect of these events. As shown in **Exhibit D-10**, each sale generates a different gain or loss. Even though the basic events relating to each of the stock investments were the same, the accounting guidelines result in quite different results.

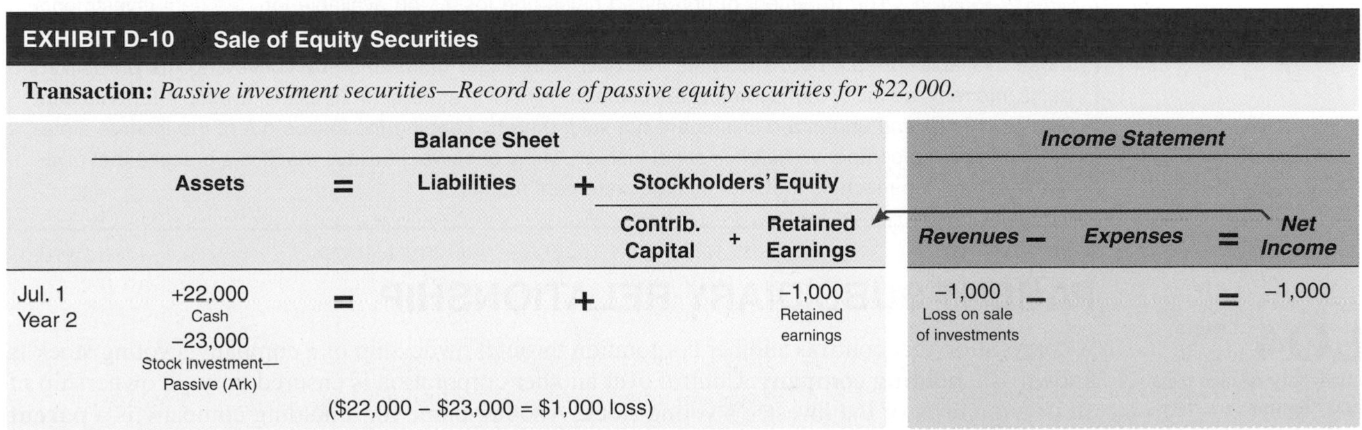

EXHIBIT D-10 Sale of Equity Securities

Transaction: *Passive investment securities—Record sale of passive equity securities for $22,000.*

	Assets	=	Liabilities	+	Contrib. Capital	+	Retained Earnings	Revenues	−	Expenses	=	Net Income
Jul. 1 Year 2	+22,000 Cash −23,000 Stock investment—Passive (Ark)	=		+			−1,000 Retained earnings	−1,000 Loss on sale of investments	−		=	−1,000

($22,000 – $23,000 = $1,000 loss)

continued

continued from previous page

EXHIBIT D-10 Sale of Equity Securities

Transaction: *Significant Influence Securities—Record sale of securities with significant influence for $22,000.*

	Balance Sheet						Income Statement			
	Assets	=	Liabilities	+	Stockholders' Equity: Contrib. Capital	+ Retained Earnings	Revenues	− Expenses	=	Net Income
Jul. 1 Year 2	+22,000 Cash −16,750 Stock Investment—Significant influence (Barcal)	=		+		+5,250 Retained earnings	+5,250 Gain on sale of investments	−	=	+5,250

($22,000 − $16,750 = $5,250 gain)

Transaction: *Controlling Equity Securities—Record sale of controlling equity securities for $22,000.*

	Balance Sheet						Income Statement			
	Assets	=	Liabilities	+	Stockholders' Equity: Contrib. Capital	+ Retained Earnings	Revenues	− Expenses	=	Net Income
Jul. 1 Year 2	+22,000 Cash −20,250 Stock investment—Controlling (Call)	=		+		+1,750 Retained earnings	+1,750 Gain on sale of investments	−	=	+1,750

($22,000 − $20,250 = $1,750 gain)

Current and Noncurrent Classifications

Each investment in debt and equity securities must be classified as either a current asset or a noncurrent asset in the balance sheet. Passive equity securities and debt trading securities are always classified as current assets. Debt securities that are held to maturity are classified as noncurrent assets until the last year before maturity. Debt securities that are available for sale may be classified as either current or noncurrent assets, depending on management's intentions regarding their sale. Equity securities that result in significant influence over the investee are usually classified as noncurrent assets, but a current classification is proper if management intends to sell the investments within the next year or operating cycle, whichever is longer. Controlling investments do not appear in consolidated financial statements as a separate account but rather are "consolidated" into the accounts of the parent company.

ACCOUNTING IN PRACTICE

Cherry Picking The treatment of unrealized gains and losses on available-for-sale debt investments permits management to engage in a practice known as "cherry picking." Management may select for sale those available-for-sale debt securities that have unrealized gains, thereby converting the unrealized gains into realized gains that appear in the company's income statement. Similarly, available-for-sale debt investments having unrealized losses are not sold, thereby keeping the losses out of the income statement and on the company's balance sheet instead. Many observers believe that it is a practice that gives management too much control over income statement results.

LO4 **Define** parent-subsidiary relationships and **discuss** how their balance sheet data are consolidated.

PARENT-SUBSIDIARY RELATIONSHIP

A corporation that controls another corporation through ownership of a company's voting stock is known as a **holding company**. Control over another corporation is ensured through ownership of all or a majority of the investee's voting stock. Another name for a holding company is a **parent company**, and the wholly owned or majority-held investees are called **subsidiaries**. The parent company and each subsidiary company are separate legal entities.

Consolidated Financial Statements

As separate legal entities, a parent company and its subsidiaries maintain their own accounting records and prepare separate financial statements primarily for internal purposes. In the parent company's separate financial statements, the ownership of a subsidiary's stock is reported as a stock investment accounted for by the equity method. When the parent company prepares financial statements for its stockholders and creditors, however, the financial statements of the parent company and its subsidiaries are combined and reported as a single set of **consolidated financial statements**.

The financial statements of the parent and the various subsidiaries are combined using the acquisition method of consolidated accounting. Under this method, the individual line item (stock investment—controlling) used to account for an investment in a subsidiary under the equity method is replaced by all the individual asset and liability accounts of the consolidated subsidiary. In other words, the cash account of the subsidiary is combined with the cash account of the parent, the accounts receivable of the subsidiary is combined with the accounts receivable of the parent, the accounts payable of the subsidiary is combined with the accounts payable of the parent, and so on. In addition, all transactions between the parent and the subsidiary are eliminated. Thus, only transactions with outside entities are reported in the consolidated financial statements. When the financial data of these legal entities are consolidated, the resulting statements represent the group as an economic entity, as shown in **Exhibit D-11**.

Consolidated financial statements are prepared in order to more accurately portray the economic activities and financial position of the reporting entity. Management of the parent company is tasked with managing all of the assets and liabilities of the entities under its control, not just those of the parent company. In addition, consolidation helps to avoid the problem of information overload in which investors and investment professionals receive more financial data than can be purposely processed. For example, the **General Electric Company** is made up of over 2,000 companies worldwide. A shareholder of General Electric would be overwhelmed to receive 2,000 individual company balance sheets, 2,000 individual company income statements, and 2,000 individual company statements of cash flows. Consolidated financial statements avoid this data problem for financial statement users by providing a single set of financial data for the economic entity.

EXHIBIT D-11 Parent-Subsidiary Relationship: Legal and Economic Entities

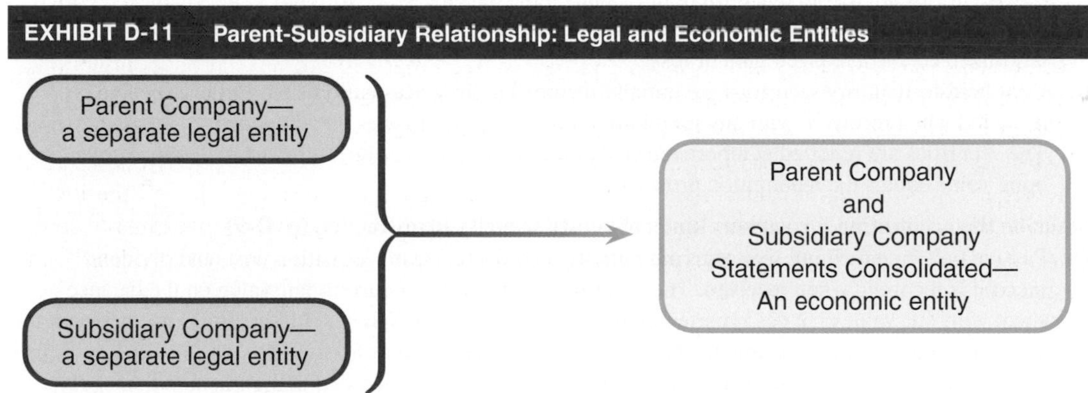

Consolidated financial statements present both the total assets controlled by a parent company and the aggregate results of the group's operations and cash flows. These amounts are difficult to perceive when viewing only the separate reports of the individual companies. Consolidated statements are particularly valuable to the managers and stockholders of the parent company. In addition, creditors, government agencies, and the general public are informed of the magnitude and scope of an economic enterprise through consolidated statements.

PRINCIPLE ALERT

Accounting Entity Concept The preparation of consolidated financial statements represents an application of the *accounting entity concept*. By viewing the parent company and its subsidiaries as a single economic entity, accountants ignore the legal boundaries of the separate companies. For consolidated financial statements, the overall economic entity is the accounting entity.

Limitations of Consolidated Statements

Consolidated statements have certain limitations. The status or performance of weak subsidiaries in a group can be "masked" through consolidation with more successful subunits. Rates of return, other ratios, and trend percentages calculated from consolidated statements may sometimes prove deceptive because they are really composite calculations. Stockholders and creditors of controlled companies who are interested in their legal rights and prerogatives should examine the separate financial statements of the relevant constituent companies.

Supplemental disclosures do improve the quality of consolidated statements, particularly those of conglomerates—that is, entities with diversified lines of business. U.S. GAAP stipulates that firms disclose information regarding revenues, income from operations, and identifiable assets for significant business segments.

SUMMARY OF LEARNING OBJECTIVES

LO1 Describe debt and equity securities and how they may be acquired. (p. D-2)

- A debt security refers to a financial instrument that creates a creditor relationship for the debtholder.
- An equity security is a financial instrument that represents an ownership interest in a company.
- Debt and equity securities may be acquired directly from the entity that issues the securities or through a secondary market.

LO2 Describe the accounting for various kinds of debt security investments. (p. D-3)

- Debt trading securities are initially recorded at their acquisition cost, and interest income is recorded when received. The securities are reported at current fair value on the balance sheet with fair value changes reported on the income statement. When sold, the difference between the sales proceeds and the investment's book value is a realized gain or loss.
- Debt available-for-sale securities are initially recorded at their acquisition cost. Interest income is recorded when received, with any premium or discount amortized as an adjustment to interest income. The securities are reported at current fair value on the balance sheet with fair value changes reported in stockholders' equity. When sold, the difference between the sales proceeds and the investment's amortized cost is a realized gain or loss.
- Debt held-to-maturity securities are initially recorded at their acquisition cost. Interest income is recorded when received, with any premium or discount amortized as an adjustment to interest income. The securities are reported at amortized cost at the balance sheet date. At maturity, the investment's book value equals the redemption proceeds.

LO3 Describe the accounting for various kinds of equity security investments. (p. D-9)

- Passive investment equity securities are initially recorded at their acquisition cost, and dividend income is recorded when received. The securities are reported at current fair value on the balance sheet with fair value changes reported on the income statement. When sold, the difference between the sales proceeds and the investment's book value is a realized gain or loss.
- Equity securities that result in significant influence arc initially recorded at their acquisition cost. Subsequent accounting uses the equity method: the investment account is increased by a proportionate share of the investee company's net income and decreased by the amount of any dividends received. When sold, the difference between the sales proceeds and the investment's book value is a realized gain or loss.
- Controlling equity securities are initially recorded at their acquisition cost. Subsequent accounting uses the equity method: the investment account is increased by a proportionate share of the investee company's net income and decreased by the amount of any dividends received. For financial reporting, however, the investment account is replaced by a subsidiary's individual assets and liabilities, producing consolidated financial statements. When sold, the difference between the sales proceeds and the investment's book value is a realized gain or loss.

LO4 Define parent-subsidiary relationships and discuss how their balance sheet data are consolidated. (p. D-15)

- A corporation that controls another corporation (the investee) by virtue of owning all, or a majority, of the investee's common stock is referred to as the parent company. The wholly owned or majority-owned investee is called the subsidiary.

- When a parent company prepares financial statements for its stockholders, the financial statements of the parent and its subsidiaries are combined and reported as a single set of consolidated financial statements.

KEY TERMS

Affiliate companies (p. D-9)
Available-for-Sale Securities (p. D-2)
Consolidated financial statements (p. D-13)
Controlling (p. D-8)
Debt security (p. D-2)
Equity method (p. D-9)
Equity security (p. D-2)
Held-to-Maturity Securities (p. D-2)
Holding company (p. D-12)
Little or no influence (Passive) (p. D-8)
Marketable securities (p. D-11)
Non-marketable securities (p. D-11)
Parent company (p. D-12)
Significant influence (p. D-8)
Subsidiaries (p. D-12)
Trading Securities (p. D-2)
Unrealized gains and losses (p. D-6)

SELF-STUDY QUESTIONS

(Answers for the Self-Study Questions are available at the end of this appendix.)

1. **Snyder, Inc. purchased $100,000 of Dane Company's 8 percent, 15-year bonds for $96,400 on January 1. Snyder plans to hold the bonds to maturity. Snyder records interest and straight-line amortization on interest dates (June 30 and December 31). At December 31, the bonds have a market value of $97,200. Snyder's balance sheet at December 31 should report the bonds at:** LO2
   a. $96,400. *c.* $97,200.
   b. $96,640. *d.* $96,160.

2. **A firm purchased noninfluential and noncontrolling stock investments for $65,000. During the year, the firm received dividends totaling $4,000 from these stock investments. At year-end, the stock portfolio had a quoted market value of $68,000. The increase in net income for the year (ignore income taxes) from these stock investments is:** LO3
   a. $1,000. *c.* $4,000.
   b. $3,000. *d.* $7,000.

3. **Artway Company purchased 30 percent of the voting stock of Barton Company for $60,000 on January 1. During the year, Barton Company earned $50,000 net income and paid $15,000 in dividends. At the end of the year, Artway Company's account, Stock Investment—Significant influence (Barton) should have a balance of:** LO3
   a. $110,000. *c.* $95,000.
   b. $70,500. *d.* $60,000.

4. **The proper category to classify an investment in equity securities depends on:** LO1
   a. management's intentions with regard to when to sell the investment.
   b. the relative size of the investment to the purchasing company's total assets.
   c. the ability of the purchasing company to influence the investee company.
   d. both *a* and *c*.

5. **Where would the account unrealized gain/loss on investment appear for trading debt security investment?** LO3
   a. Income Statement *c.* Statement of Cash Flows
   b. Equity section of the Balance Sheet *d.* It does not appear on any statement.

6. **Where would the account unrealized gain/loss on investment appear for an available-for-sale debt security investment?** LO3
   a. Income Statement *c.* Statement of Cash Flows
   b. Equity section of the Balance Sheet *d.* It does not appear on any statement.

7. **Controlling equity securities typically require the investor to acquire what percent of the investee company common stock?** LO1
   a. Under 20 percent *c.* Over 50 percent
   b. Between 20 and 50 percent *d.* 100 percent

LO2 **8. Jeffrey Company invested in debt securities. Jeffrey will initially record this investment at:**

a. Cost
b. Cost plus any accrued interest
c. Cost less any accrued interest
d. Maturity value

LO3 **9. Franz Co. acquired a 30 percent interest in Esik for $420,000 and appropriately applied the equity method. During the first year, Esik reported net income of $200,000 and paid cash dividends totaling $50,000. What amount will Franz report as it relates to the investment at the end of the first year on its income statement?**

a. Investment earnings totaling $60,000
b. Investment earnings totaling $45,000
c. Net investment earnings totaling $150,000
d. Dividend income totaling $15,000

LO3 **10. Blanc Co. received dividends from its common stock investments during the year ended December 31 as follows:**

- A cash dividend totaling $15,000 from its passive security investment in Fisher Corporation, when the market price of Fisher's shares was $20 per share
- A cash dividend of $10,000 from Myler Corp. in which Blanc Co. owns a 32 percent interest

How much dividend income should Blanc report in its income statement?

a. $25,000
b. $15,000
c. $10,000
d. $ 0

LO2 **11. At what value are held-to-maturity debt securities reported on the balance sheet?**

a. Acquisition cost
b. Market value
c. Amortized cost
d. Historical cost adjusted for a proportionate share of the affiliate's earnings, losses, and dividends

LO4 **12. Norma Travel, Inc. acquired an 80 percent interest in CruisesByBen on December 31 for $870,000. Norma has the ability to exercise significant influence on management decisions. The CruisesByBen stock is publicly traded. During the year, CruisesByBen reported net income of $160,000 and paid cash dividends of $40,000. How should Norma Travel account for its investment in CruisesByBen?**

a. Apply the equity method and report the investment at market value at year-end
b. Apply the equity method and perform a full consolidation
c. Apply mark-to-market accounting and consolidate the statements at year-end
d. Account for the investment as a trading security

LO1 **13. In classifying investments, how do held-to-maturity securities differ from other marketable securities?**

a. The investor plans to hold the securities until they mature.
b. The investor has the ability to exercise significant influence over management of the investee.
c. The investor has the ability to control the investee.
d. These securities have a high degree of liquidity.

QUESTIONS

1. Debt security investments are placed in one of three investment categories. What are these three categories?
2. Equity security investments are placed in one of three investment categories. What are these three categories?
3. Caldwell Company invests in bonds at a premium. Caldwell does not intend to sell the bonds in the near future, nor does it intend to hold the bonds to maturity. Should the bond premium be amortized? What measure should be used to report these bonds on the company's year-end balance sheet?
4. What measure should be used to report trading debt securities on the balance sheet? Available-for-sale debt securities? Held-to-maturity debt securities?
5. What is an unrealized gain? Unrealized loss?
6. Where are unrealized gains and losses related to trading debt securities reported in the financial statements? Where are unrealized gains and losses related to available-for-sale debt securities reported in the financial statements?

7. What is an equity investment that results in significant influence? Describe the accounting procedures used for such investments.
8. On January 1, Mower Company purchased 40 percent of the common stock of Starr Company for $250,000. During the year, Starr reported $80,000 of net income and paid $60,000 in cash dividends. At year-end, what amount should appear on Mower's balance sheet for its investment in Starr?
9. What accounting procedures are used when a stock investment represents more than 50 percent of the investee company's voting stock?
10. What is the purpose of consolidated financial statements?
11. What are the inherent limitations of consolidated financial statements?

Assignments with the MBC logo in the margin are available in myBusinessCourse. See the Preface of the book for details.

EXERCISES

ED-1. Accounting for Debt Securities—Trading Gressens Company had the following transactions and adjustments related to a bond investment: LO2

Year 1

Oct. 1 Purchased $500,000 face value of Skyline, Inc.'s 7 percent bonds at 97 plus a brokerage commission of $1,000. The bonds pay interest on September 30 and March 31 and mature in 20 years. Gressens expects to sell the bonds in the near future.

Dec. 31 Made the adjustment to record interest earned on investment in the Skyline bonds.

31 Made the adjustment to record the current fair value of the Skyline bonds. At December 31, the market value of the Skyline bonds was $490,000.

Year 2

Mar. 31 Received the semiannual interest payment on investment in the Skyline bonds.

Apr. 1 Sold the Skyline bond investment for $492,300 cash.

Determine the financial statement effect of the transactions and adjustments of the Gressens Company using the transaction analysis template.

ED-2. Accounting for Debt Securities—Available for Sale Hilyn Company had the following transactions and adjustments related to a bond investment: LO2

Year 1

Jan. 1 Purchased $800,000 face value of Cynad, Inc.'s 9 percent bonds at 99 plus a brokerage commission of $1,400. The bonds pay interest on June 30 and December 31 and mature in 15 years. Hilyn does not expect to sell the bonds in the near future, nor does it intend to hold the bonds to maturity.

June 30 Received the semiannual interest payment on the Cynad bonds and amortized the bond discount for six months. Hilyn uses the straight-line method to amortize bond discounts and premiums.

Dec. 31 Received the semiannual interest payment on the Cynad bonds and amortized the bond discount for six months.

31 Made the adjustment to record the current fair value of the Cynad bonds. At December 31, the market value of the Cynad bonds was $790,000.

Year 2

June 30 Received the semiannual interest payment on the Cynad bonds and amortized the bond discount for six months.

July 1 Sold the Cynad bond investment for $792,500 cash.

Dec. 31 Made the adjustment to eliminate balances from the Fair Value Adjustment to Bond Investment account and the Unrealized Gain/Loss on Investments (Equity) account.

Determine the financial statement effect of the transactions and adjustments of Hilyn Company using the transaction analysis template.

ED-3. Accounting for Debt Securities—Held-to-Maturity Kurl Company had the following transactions and adjustments related to a bond investment: LO2

Year 1

Jan. 1 Purchased $600,000 face value of Sphere, Inc.'s 9 percent bonds at 102 plus a brokerage commission of $900. The bonds pay interest on June 30 and December 31 and mature in 10 years. Kurl expects to hold the bonds to maturity.

June 30 Received the semiannual interest payment on the Sphere bonds and amortized the bond premium for six months. Kurl uses the straight-line method to amortize bond discounts and premiums.

Year 10

Dec. 31 Received the semiannual interest payment on the Sphere bonds and amortized the bond premium for six months.

31 Received the principal amount in cash on maturity date of the Sphere bonds.

Determine the financial statement effect of the transactions and adjustments of Kurl Company using the transaction analysis template.

LO3 **ED-4. Accounting for Equity Securities—Passive** The Glass Company had the following transactions and adjustment related to a stock investment:

Homework MBC

Year 1

Nov. 15 Purchased 6,000 shares of Erie, Inc.'s common stock at $12 per share plus a brokerage commission of $750. Glass expects to sell the stock in the near future.

Dec. 22 Received a cash dividend of $1.10 per share of common stock from Erie.

31 The year-end market price of the Erie common stock is $11.25 per share.

Year 2

Jan. 20 Sold all 6,000 shares of the Erie common stock for $66,900.

Determine the financial statement effect of the transactions and adjustment of the Glass Company using the transaction analysis template.

LO3 **ED-5. Accounting for Equity Securities—Significant Influence** The Dunn Company had the following transactions and adjustment related to a stock investment:

Year 1

Jan. 15 Purchased 12,000 shares of Van, Inc.'s common stock at $9 per share plus a brokerage commission of $900. These shares represent a 30 percent ownership of Van's common stock.

Dec. 31 Received a cash dividend of $1.25 per share of common stock from Van.

31 Made the adjustment to reflect income from the Van stock investment. Van's Year 1 net income is $80,000.

Year 2

Jan. 20 Sold all 12,000 shares of the Van common stock for $120,500.

Determine the financial statement effect of the transactions and adjustment of the Dunn Company using the transaction analysis template.

LO3 **ED-6. Accounting for Equity Securities—Significant Influence** On January 3, Mahony Farm purchased 20 percent of the outstanding stock of Watson Company for $80,000. The purchase gave Mahony the ability to exercise significant influence over Watson. During the year, Watson paid cash dividends totaling $70,000 and reported net income for the year of $90,000.

Homework MBC

Determine the financial statement effect of all transactions necessary for Mahony Farm using the transaction analysis template.

LO3 **ED-7. Accounting for Equity Securities—Passive** Microsoft, Inc. maintained a large investment in marketable securities valued at approximately $42 billion as of the beginning of the year. During the year, the securities produced investment income (dividends and interest income) totaling $2 billion. At year-end, the portfolio of marketable securities had appreciated to $43.5 billion.

Homework MBC

Calculate the income statement effect of the marketable securities if the entire portfolio is classified as passive securities.

LO4 **ED-8. Consolidation Accounting** Fletcher Company, a manufacturer of precision mining equipment, acquired 100 percent of the outstanding common stock of Denfork Company, a small mining company with several mines that extract rare earth materials.

a. How should Fletcher account for this acquisition during the year?

b. What adjustments are needed at year-end?

c. What limitations are present in this method of accounting?

PROBLEMS

PD-1. The Analysis of Bond Investments Columbia Company began operations in the current year and by year-end (December 31) had made six bond investments. Year-end information on these bond investments follows: LO2

Company	Face Value	Cost or Amortized Cost	Year-End Market Value	Classification
Ling, Inc.	$100,000	$102,400	$105,300	Trading
Wren, Inc.	$250,000	$262,500	$270,000	Trading
Olanamic, Inc..	$200,000	$197,000	$199,000	Available for sale
Fossil, Inc..	$150,000	$154,000	$160,000	Available for sale
Meander, Inc.	$100,000	$101,200	$102,400	Held to maturity
Resin, Inc..	$140,000	$136,000	$137,000	Held to maturity

REQUIRED

a. At what total amount will the trading bond investments be reported on the December 31 balance sheet?

b. At what total amount will the available-for-sale bond investments be reported on the December 31 balance sheet?

c. At what total amount will the held-to-maturity bond investments be reported on the December 31 balance sheet?

d. What total amount of unrealized holding gains or unrealized holding losses related to bond investments will appear on the income statement?

e. What total amount of unrealized holding gains or unrealized holding losses related to bond investments will appear in the stockholders' equity section of the December 31 balance sheet?

f. What total amount of fair value adjustment to bond investments will appear on the December 31 balance sheet? Which category of bond investments does the fair value adjustment relate to? Does the fair value adjustment increase or decrease the financial statement presentation of these bond investments?

PD-2. Accounting for Bond Investments The following transactions and adjustments relate to bond investments acquired by Bloom Corporation: LO2

Year 1

June 30 Purchased $200,000 face value of Dynamo, Inc.'s 20-year, 9 percent bonds dated June 30, Year 1, for $215,200 cash. Interest is paid December 31 and June 30. The investment is classified as an available-for-sale security.

Dec. 31 Received the semiannual interest payment from Dynamo and amortized the bond premium (straight-line method).

Dec. 31 Purchased $300,000 face value of Link, Inc.'s 10-year, 7 percent bonds dated December 31, Year 1, for $297,000 cash. Interest is paid June 30 and December 31. The investment is classified as a held-to-maturity security.

31 Made an adjustment to record the current fair value of the Dynamo bonds. At December 31, the market value was $216,000.

Year 2

June 30 Received the semiannual interest payment from Dynamo and amortized the bond premium.

30 Received the semiannual interest payment from Link and amortized the bond discount (straight-line method).

July 1 Sold the Dynamo bonds for $216,500.

Oct. 31 Purchased $60,000 face value of Taxco, Inc.'s 5-year, 8 percent bonds dated October 31, Year 2, for $60,500. Interest is paid April 30 and October 31. The investment is classified as a trading security.

Dec. 31 Received the semiannual interest payment from Link and amortized the bond discount.

31 Made an adjustment to record interest earned on the investment in Taxco bonds.

31 Made an adjustment to record the current fair value of the Taxco bonds. At December 31, the market value of the bonds was $59,200.

31 Made an adjustment to eliminate balances in the Fair Value Adjustment to Bond Investment account and the Unrealized Gain/Loss on Investments (Equity) account.

REQUIRED

Determine the financial statement effect of these transactions and adjustments using the transaction analysis template.

LO3  **PD-3. Accounting for Stock Investments—Passive** The following transactions and adjustments relate to a stock investment made by Steen Corporation:

Year 1

July	1	Purchased 1,000 shares of Polk, Inc.'s common stock for $66,200 cash. The investment is noninfluential and noncontrolling and is classified as a passive investment security.
Nov.	9	Received a cash dividend of 90 cents per share on the Polk stock.
Dec.	31	Made an adjustment to record the current fair value of the Polk stock. At December 31, the stock has a market value of $63.00 per share.

Year 2

Feb.	1	Sold the Polk stock for $62 per share.

REQUIRED

Determine the financial statement effect of these transactions and adjustments using the transaction analysis template.

LO3  **PD-4. Contrasting Entries for Stock Investments: Passive Securities and Securities with Significant Influence** On January 2, Year 1, Trubek Corporation purchased 10,000 shares of Forge Company common stock for $15 per share, including commissions and taxes. On December 31, Year 1, Forge announced its net income of $80,000 for the year and paid a dividend of $1.10 per share. At December 31, Year 1, the market value of Forge's stock was $19 per share. Trubek received its dividend on December 31, Year 1.

REQUIRED

a. Assume that the stock acquired by Trubek represents 15 percent of Forge's voting stock and is classified as a passive investment security. Using the transaction analysis template, determine the financial statement effect of this investment.

b. Assume that the stock acquired by Trubek represents 25 percent of Forge's voting stock. Using the transaction analysis template, determine the financial statement effect of this investment.

LO3  **PD-5. Accounting for Securities with Significant Influence** At the beginning of the year, the Carlton and United Brewery (CUB) of Melbourne, Australia, purchased a 30 percent ownership interest in Icehouse Brewery of Brisbane, Australia. The investment cost $30 million. At year-end, Icehouse Brewery declared and paid cash dividends to shareholders totaling $800,000, after reporting earnings of $5 million.

REQUIRED

a. Calculate the income statement effect of CUB's investment in Icehouse Brewery as of year-end.

b. Calculate the book value of CUB's equity investment in Icehouse Brewery at year-end.

c. Calculate the book value of CUB's equity investment in Icehouse Brewery at year-end assuming that Icehouse reported a loss of $3 million instead of a profit of $5 million and still paid its dividend of $800,000.

ANSWERS TO SELF-STUDY QUESTIONS

1. b **2.** d **3.** b **4.** c **5.** a **6.** b **7.** c **8.** c **9.** a **10.** b **11.** c **12.** b **13.** a

Appendix

E

Accounting and the Time Value of Money

Road Map

LO	Learning Objective	Page	eLecture	Assignments
LO1	**Describe the nature of interest and distinguish between simple and compound interest.**	E-2	E-1	E1
LO2	**Calculate future values.**	E-3	E-2	SE1, E2, E3, E6, E8, E9, E11, E12, E14
LO3	**Calculate present values.**	E-6	E-3	SE2, E4, E5, E7, E10, E13, E15

TIME VALUE OF MONEY CONCEPT

LO1 Describe the nature of interest and **distinguish** between simple and compound interest.

Would you rather receive a dollar now or a dollar one year from now? Most people would answer "a dollar now." Intuition tells us that a dollar received now is more valuable than the same amount received sometime in the future. Sound reasons exist, however, for choosing the option of receiving the money sooner rather than later, the most obvious of which concerns risk. Because the future is always uncertain, some event may prevent you from receiving the dollar at a later date. To avoid this risk, we choose the earlier date.

A second reason for choosing the earlier date is that the dollar has a **time value**—that is, the dollar received now could be invested such that one year from now, you could have not only the original dollar but also the interest income on the dollar for the past year. **Interest** is a payment for the use of money, much like a rent payment for the use of an apartment. Interest is calculated by multiplying an interest rate, usually stated as an annual rate, by a principal amount for a period of time. The **principal** amount represents the amount to be repaid. The amount of interest can be computed as either a simple interest amount or a compound interest amount.

Time Value of Money: Simple Interest Model

Simple interest involves calculating interest on only the principal amount owed without considering any interest already earned. Simple interest is calculated using the following well-known formula:

$$\textbf{Interest} = \mathbf{p \times i \times n}$$

where

p = principal (total amount)
i = interest rate for one period
n = time (number of periods)

For example, if you borrow $3,000 for four years at a simple interest rate of 6 percent annually, the amount of simple interest would total $720, calculated as $3,000 × 0.06 × 4.

Time Value of Money: Compound Interest Model

Compound interest differs from simple interest because it is calculated on both the principal and any previously earned interest that has not been paid. In other words, compound interest involves computing interest on interest, along with the principal amount.

As we can see in **Exhibit E-1**, simple interest only uses the original $3,000 principal to compute the annual interest in each of the four years. In contrast, compound interest uses the entire principal balance, including both the original $3,000 principal and the accumulated interest to date, to compute the next year's interest. This results in increasing interest each year, with the result in **Exhibit E-1** for compound interest yielding a larger ending balance by $67.43.

Because almost all businesses use compound interest, we will assume the use of compound interest in all of the illustrations in this appendix. Simple interest is generally only used in short-term credit arrangements, typically lasting less than a year.

EXHIBIT E-1 Illustration Comparing Simple Interest to Compound Interest

	Simple Interest Model			Compound Interest Model		
	Interest Calculation	Simple Interest	Principal Balance	Interest Calculation	Compound Interest	Principal Balance
Year 1 .	$3,000.00 × 6%	$180.00	$3,180.00	$3,000.00 × 6%	$180.00	$3,180.00
Year 2 .	$3,000.00 × 6%	$180.00	$3,360.00	$3,180.00 × 6%	$190.80	$3,370.80
Year 3 .	$3,000.00 × 6%	$180.00	$3,540.00	$3,370.80 × 6%	$202.25	$3,573.05
Year 4 .	$3,000.00 × 6%	$180.00	$3,720.00	$3,573.05 × 6%	$214.38	$3,787.43
		$720.00	→ $67.43 difference ←		$787.43	

FUTURE VALUE OF AN AMOUNT

The **future value** of a single sum is the amount that a specified investment will be worth at a future date if invested at a given rate of compound interest. For example, suppose that we decide to invest $6,000 in a savings account that pays 6 percent annual interest, and that we intend to leave the principal and interest in the account for five years. Assuming that interest is credited to the account at the end of each year, the balance in the account at the end of five years is determined using the following formula:

$$FV = PV \times (1 + i)^n$$

where

FV = future value of an amount
PV = present value (today's value)
i = interest rate for one period
n = number of periods

The future value in this case is $8,029, computed as [$6,000 × (1.06)^5] = ($6,000 × 1.33823).

It is often easier to solve time value of money problems with the aid of a time diagram, as illustrated in **Exhibit E-2**. Time diagrams are drawn to show the timing of the various cash inflows and outflows. Note in **Exhibit E-2** that our initial $6,000 cash inflow (the amount deposited in a savings account) allows us to withdraw $8,029 (a cash outflow) at the end of five years.

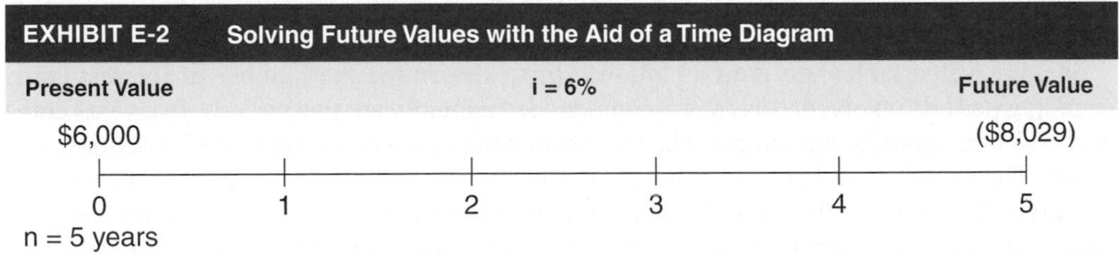

We can also calculate the future value of a single amount with the use of a table like **Table I**, which presents the future value of a single dollar after a given number of time periods. Simply stated, future value tables provide a multiplier for many combinations of time periods and interest rates that, when applied to the dollar amount of a present value, determines its future value.

TABLE I Future Value of $1

Period	1.0%	2.0%	3.0%	4.0%	5.0%	6.0%	7.0%	8.0%	9.0%	10.0%	11.0%	12.0%
1	1.01000	1.02000	1.03000	1.04000	1.05000	1.06000	1.07000	1.08000	1.09000	1.10000	1.11000	1.12000
2	1.02010	1.04040	1.06090	1.08160	1.10250	1.12360	1.14490	1.16640	1.18810	1.21000	1.23210	1.25440
3	1.03030	1.06121	1.09273	1.12486	1.15763	1.19102	1.22504	1.25971	1.29503	1.33100	1.36763	1.40493
4	1.04060	1.08243	1.12551	1.16986	1.21551	1.26248	1.31080	1.36049	1.41158	1.46410	1.51807	1.57352
5	1.05101	1.10408	1.15927	1.21665	1.27628	1.33823	1.40255	1.46933	1.53862	1.61051	1.68506	1.76234
6	1.06152	1.12616	1.19405	1.26532	1.34010	1.41852	1.50073	1.58687	1.67710	1.77156	1.87041	1.97382
7	1.07214	1.14869	1.22987	1.31593	1.40710	1.50363	1.60578	1.71382	1.82804	1.94872	2.07616	2.21068
8	1.08286	1.17166	1.26677	1.36857	1.47746	1.59385	1.71819	1.85093	1.99256	2.14359	2.30454	2.47596
9	1.09369	1.19509	1.30477	1.42331	1.55133	1.68948	1.83846	1.99900	2.17189	2.35795	2.55804	2.77308
10	1.10462	1.21899	1.34392	1.48024	1.62889	1.79085	1.96715	2.15892	2.36736	2.59374	2.83942	3.10585
11	1.11567	1.24337	1.38423	1.53945	1.71034	1.89830	2.10485	2.33164	2.58043	2.85312	3.15176	3.47855
12	1.12683	1.26824	1.42576	1.60103	1.79586	2.01220	2.25219	2.51817	2.81266	3.13843	3.49845	3.89598
13	1.13809	1.29361	1.46853	1.66507	1.88565	2.13293	2.40985	2.71962	3.06580	3.45227	3.88328	4.36349
14	1.14947	1.31948	1.51259	1.73168	1.97993	2.26090	2.57853	2.93719	3.34173	3.79750	4.31044	4.88711
15	1.16097	1.34587	1.55797	1.80094	2.07893	2.39656	2.75903	3.17217	3.64248	4.17725	4.78459	5.47357
16	1.17258	1.37279	1.60471	1.87298	2.18287	2.54035	2.95216	3.42594	3.97031	4.59497	5.31089	6.13039
17	1.18430	1.40024	1.65285	1.94790	2.29202	2.69277	3.15882	3.70002	4.32763	5.05447	5.89509	6.86604
18	1.19615	1.42825	1.70243	2.02582	2.40662	2.85434	3.37993	3.99602	4.71712	5.55992	6.54355	7.68997
19	1.20811	1.45681	1.75351	2.10685	2.52695	3.02560	3.61653	4.31570	5.14166	6.11591	7.26334	8.61276
20	1.22019	1.48595	1.80611	2.19112	2.65330	3.20714	3.86968	4.66096	5.60441	6.72750	8.06231	9.64629
25	1.28243	1.64061	2.09378	2.66584	3.38635	4.29187	5.42743	6.84848	8.62308	10.83471	13.58546	17.00006
30	1.34785	1.81136	2.42726	3.24340	4.32194	5.74349	7.61226	10.06266	13.26768	17.44940	22.89230	29.95992
35	1.41660	1.99989	2.81386	3.94609	5.51602	7.68609	10.67658	14.78534	20.41397	28.10244	38.57485	52.79962
40	1.48886	2.20804	3.26204	4.80102	7.03999	10.28572	14.97446	21.72452	31.40942	45.25926	65.00087	93.05097
50	1.64463	2.69159	4.38391	7.10668	11.46740	18.42015	29.45703	46.90161	74.35752	117.39085	184.56483	289.00219

Future value tables are used as follows. First, determine the number of interest compounding periods involved. (Five years compounded annually are five periods, five years compounded semiannually are ten periods, five years compounded quarterly are 20 periods, and so on.) The extreme left-hand column indicates the number of periods covered in the table.

Second, determine the interest rate per compounding period. Note that interest rates are usually quoted on an annual or *per year* basis. Therefore, only in the case of annual compounding is the quoted interest rate the interest rate per compounding period. In other cases, the rate per compounding period is the annual rate divided by the number of compounding periods in a year. For example, an interest rate of 10 percent per year would be 10 percent for one compounding period if compounded annually, 5 percent for two compounding periods if compounded semiannually, and 2 ½ percent for four compounding periods if compounded quarterly.

Finally, locate the factor that is to the right of the appropriate number of compounding periods and beneath the appropriate interest rate per compounding period. Multiply this factor by the number of dollars involved.

Note the logical progression among the various multipliers in **Table I**. All values are 1.0 or greater because the future value is always greater than the $1 present amount if the interest rate is greater than zero. Also, as the interest rate increases (moving from left to right in the table) or the number of periods increases (moving from top to bottom), the multipliers become larger.

Continuing with our example of calculating the future value of a $6,000 savings account deposit earning 6 percent annual compound interest for five years, and using the multipliers from Table I, we solve for the future value of the deposit as follows:

Principal	×	Factor	=	Future Value
$6,000	×	**1.33823**	=	**$8,029**

The factor 1.33823 is in the row for five periods and the column for 6 percent. Note that this factor is the same as the multiplier we determined using the future value formula in our calculation above.

Suppose, instead, that the interest is credited to the savings account semiannually rather than annually. In this situation, there are ten compounding periods, and we use a 3 percent rate (one-half the annual rate). The future value calculation using the **Table I** multipliers is as follows:

Principal	×	Factor	=	Future Value
$6,000	×	**1.34392**	=	**$8,064**

FUTURE VALUE OF AN ANNUITY

Using future value tables like **Table I**, we can calculate the future value of any single future cash flow or series of future cash flows. One frequent pattern of cash flows, however, is subject to a more convenient calculation. This pattern, known as an **annuity**, can be described as *equal amounts equally spaced over a period.*

For example, assume that $100 is to be deposited at the end of each of the next three years as an annuity into a savings account. When annuity cash flows occur at the end of each period, the annuity is called an **ordinary annuity**. As shown below in **Exhibit E-3**, the future value of this ordinary annuity can be calculated from **Table I** by calculating the future value of each of the three individual deposits and summing them (assuming 8 percent annual interest).

EXHIBIT E-3 Future Value of an Ordinary Annuity

Future Deposits (ordinary annuity)				FV Multiplier		
Year 1	**Year 2**	**Year 3**		**(Table I)**		**Future Value**
$100			×	1.16640	=	$1.1664
	$100		×	1.08000	=	1.0800
		$100	×	1.00000	=	1.0000
				Total future value		$324.64

Present Value			Future Value
	$100	$100	$100
0	1	2	3

Table II, on the other hand, provides a single multiplier for calculating the future value of a series of future cash flows that reflect an ordinary annuity. Referring to **Table II** in the 3 periods row and the 8 percent interest column, we see that the multiplier is 3.24640, equal to the sum of the three future value factors in **Exhibit E-3**. When applied to the $100 annuity amount, the multiplier gives a future value of $324.64, or $100 × 3.2464. As shown above, the same future value is derived from the several multipliers of **Table I**. For annuities of 5, 10, or 20 years, numerous calculations are avoided by using annuity tables like **Table II**.

TABLE II Future Value of an Ordinary Annuity of $1 per Period

Period	1%	2%	3%	4%	5%	6%	7%	8%	9%	10%	11%	12%
1	1.00000	1.00000	1.00000	1.00000	1.00000	1.00000	1.00000	1.00000	1.00000	1.00000	1.00000	1.00000
2	2.01000	2.02000	2.03000	2.04000	2.05000	2.06000	2.07000	2.08000	2.09000	2.10000	2.11000	2.12000
3	3.03010	3.06040	3.09090	3.12160	3.15250	3.18360	3.21490	3.24640	3.27810	3.31000	3.34210	3.37440
4	4.06040	4.12161	4.18363	4.24646	4.31013	4.37462	4.43994	4.50611	4.57313	4.64100	4.70973	4.77933
5	5.10101	5.20404	5.30914	5.41632	5.52563	5.63709	5.75074	5.86660	5.98471	6.10510	6.22780	6.35285
6	6.15202	6.30812	6.46841	6.63298	6.80191	6.97532	7.15329	7.33593	7.52333	7.71561	7.91286	8.11519
7	7.21354	7.43428	7.66246	7.89829	8.14201	8.39384	8.65402	8.92280	9.20043	9.48717	9.78327	10.08901
8	8.28567	8.58297	8.89234	9.21423	9.54911	9.89747	10.25980	10.63663	11.02847	11.43589	11.85943	12.29969
9	9.36853	9.75463	10.15911	10.58280	11.02656	11.49132	11.97799	12.48756	13.02104	13.57948	14.16397	14.77566
10	10.46221	10.94972	11.46388	12.00611	12.57789	13.18079	13.81645	14.48656	15.19293	15.93742	16.72201	17.54874
11	11.56683	12.16872	12.80780	13.48635	14.20679	14.97164	15.78360	16.64549	17.56029	18.53117	19.56143	20.65458
12	12.68250	13.41209	14.19203	15.02581	15.91713	16.86994	17.88845	18.97713	20.14072	21.38428	22.71319	24.13313
13	13.80933	14.68033	15.61779	16.62684	17.71298	18.88214	20.14064	21.49530	22.95338	24.52271	26.21164	28.02911
14	14.94742	15.97394	17.08632	18.29191	19.59863	21.01507	22.55049	24.21492	26.01919	27.97498	30.09492	32.39260
15	16.09690	17.29342	18.59891	20.02359	21.57856	23.27597	25.12902	27.15211	29.36092	31.77248	34.40536	37.27971
16	17.25786	18.63929	20.15688	21.82453	23.65749	25.67253	27.88805	30.32428	33.00340	35.94973	39.18995	42.75328
17	18.43044	20.01207	21.76159	23.69751	25.84037	28.21288	30.84022	33.75023	36.97370	40.54470	44.50084	48.88367
18	19.61475	21.41231	23.41444	25.64541	28.13238	30.90565	33.99903	37.45024	41.30134	45.59917	50.39594	55.74971
19	20.81090	22.84056	25.11687	27.67123	30.53900	33.75999	37.37896	41.44626	46.01846	51.15909	56.93949	63.43968
20	22.01900	24.29737	26.87037	29.77808	33.06595	36.78559	40.99549	45.76196	51.16012	57.27500	64.20283	72.05244
25	28.24320	32.03030	36.45926	41.64591	47.72710	54.86451	63.24904	73.10594	84.70090	98.34706	114.41331	133.33387
30	34.78489	40.56808	47.57542	56.08494	66.43885	79.05819	94.46079	113.28321	136.30754	164.49402	199.02088	241.33268
35	41.66028	49.99448	60.46208	73.65222	90.32031	111.43478	138.23688	172.31680	215.71075	271.02437	341.58955	431.66350
40	48.88637	60.40198	75.40126	95.02552	120.79977	154.76197	199.63511	259.05652	337.88245	442.59256	581.82607	767.09142
50	64.46318	84.57940	112.79687	152.66708	209.34800	290.33590	406.52893	573.77016	815.08356	1163.90853	1668.77115	2400.01825

If we decide to invest $50 at the end of each six months for three years at an 8 percent annual rate of return, we would use the factor for 6 periods at 4 percent, as follows:

Periodic Payment	×	**Factor**	=	**Future Value**
$50	×	**6.63298**	=	**$331.65**

PRESENT VALUE OF AN AMOUNT

LO3 Calculate present values.

We can generalize that (1) the right to receive an amount of money now—its **present value**—is normally worth more than the right to receive the same amount later—its future value; (2) the longer we must wait to receive an amount, the less attractive the receipt is; and (3) the difference between the present value of an amount and its future value is a function of interest (Principal × Interest Rate × Time). Further, the more risk associated with any situation, the higher the appropriate interest rate.

We support these generalizations with an illustration. What amount should we accept now that would be as valuable as receiving $100 one year from now ($100 represents the future value) if the appropriate interest rate is 10 percent? We recognize intuitively that with a 10 percent interest rate, we should accept less than \$100, or approximately \$91. We base this estimate on the realization that the \$100 received in the future must equal the present value (100 percent) plus 10 percent interest on the present value. Thus, in our example, the \$100 future receipt must be 1.10 times the present value. Dividing \$100 by 1.10, we obtain a present value of \$90.91. In other words, under the given conditions, we would do as well to accept \$90.91 now as to wait one year and receive \$100. To confirm the equality of a \$90.91 payment now with a \$100 payment one year later, we calculate the future value of \$90.91 at 10 percent for one year as follows:

$$\$90.91 \times 1.10 \times 1 \text{ year} = \$100 \text{ (rounded)}$$

Thus, we calculate the present value of a future receipt by discounting (deducting an interest factor) the future receipt back to the present at an appropriate interest rate. We present this schematically below:

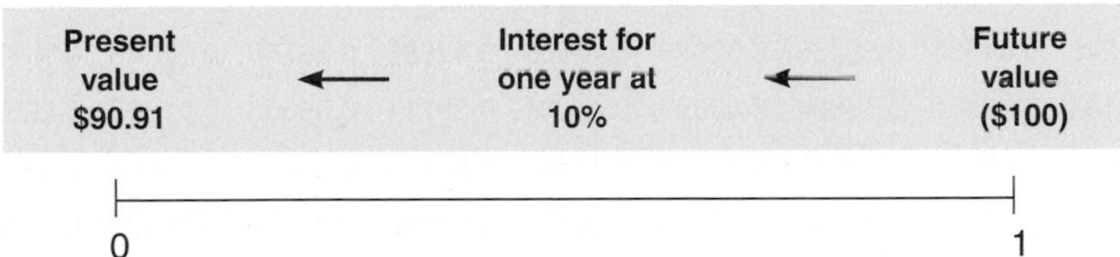

The formula for calculating the present value of a single amount is determined using the following formula:

$$PV = FV \times [1 \div (1 + i)^n]$$

where

PV = present value of an amount
FV = future value
i = interest rate for one period
n = number of periods

As can be seen from this formula, if either the time period or the interest rate is increased, the resulting present value would decrease. If more than one time period is involved, compound interest calculations are appropriate. **Exhibit E-4** illustrates the calculation of the present value of a single amount.

EXHIBIT E-4 Present Value of a Single Amount

How much must be deposited in a savings account today in order to have \$1,000 in four years if the savings account pays 12 percent annual interest?
$PV = \$1,000 \times [1 \div (1.12)^4] = (\$1,000 \times 0.63552) = \$636$

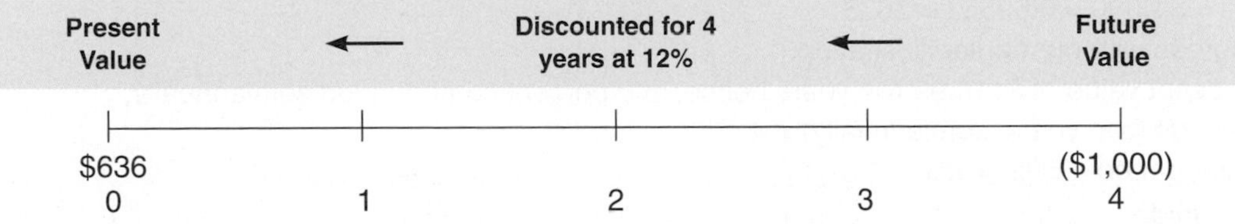

Table III can be used to calculate the present value amounts in a manner similar to the way we previously calculated future values using **Tables I** and **II**. As with the future value tables, present value tables provide a multiplier for many combinations of time periods and interest rates that, when applied to the dollar amount of a future cash flow or annuity, determines its present value.

TABLE III Present Value of $1

Period	1%	2%	3%	4%	5%	6%	7%	8%	9%	10%	11%	12%
1	0.99010	0.98039	0.97087	0.96154	0.95238	0.94340	0.93458	0.92593	0.91743	0.90909	0.90090	0.89286
2	0.98030	0.96117	0.94260	0.92456	0.90703	0.89000	0.87344	0.85734	0.84168	0.82645	0.81162	0.79719
3	0.97059	0.94232	0.91514	0.88900	0.86384	0.83962	0.81630	0.79383	0.77218	0.75131	0.73119	0.71178
4	0.96098	0.92385	0.88849	0.85480	0.82270	0.79209	0.76290	0.73503	0.70843	0.68301	0.65873	0.63552
5	0.95147	0.90573	0.86261	0.82193	0.78353	0.74726	0.71299	0.68058	0.64993	0.62092	0.59345	0.56743
6	0.94205	0.88797	0.83748	0.79031	0.74622	0.70496	0.66634	0.63017	0.59627	0.56447	0.53464	0.50663
7	0.93272	0.87056	0.81309	0.75992	0.71068	0.66506	0.62275	0.58349	0.54703	0.51316	0.48166	0.45235
8	0.92348	0.85349	0.78941	0.73069	0.67684	0.62741	0.58201	0.54027	0.50187	0.46651	0.43393	0.40388
9	0.91434	0.83676	0.76642	0.70259	0.64461	0.59190	0.54393	0.50025	0.46043	0.42410	0.39092	0.36061
10	0.90529	0.82035	0.74409	0.67556	0.61391	0.55839	0.50835	0.46319	0.42241	0.38554	0.35218	0.32197
11	0.89632	0.80426	0.72242	0.64958	0.58468	0.52679	0.47509	0.42888	0.38753	0.35049	0.31728	0.28748
12	0.88745	0.78849	0.70138	0.62460	0.55684	0.49697	0.44401	0.39711	0.35553	0.31863	0.28584	0.25668
13	0.87866	0.77303	0.68095	0.60057	0.53032	0.46884	0.41496	0.36770	0.32618	0.28966	0.25751	0.22917
14	0.86996	0.75788	0.66112	0.57748	0.50507	0.44230	0.38782	0.34046	0.29925	0.26333	0.23199	0.20462
15	0.86135	0.74301	0.64186	0.55526	0.48102	0.41727	0.36245	0.31524	0.27454	0.23939	0.20900	0.18270
16	0.85282	0.72845	0.62317	0.53391	0.45811	0.39365	0.33873	0.29189	0.25187	0.21763	0.18829	0.16312
17	0.84438	0.71416	0.60502	0.51337	0.43630	0.37136	0.31657	0.27027	0.23107	0.19784	0.16963	0.14564
18	0.83602	0.70016	0.58739	0.49363	0.41552	0.35034	0.29586	0.25025	0.21199	0.17986	0.15282	0.13004
19	0.82774	0.68643	0.57029	0.47464	0.39573	0.33051	0.27651	0.23171	0.19449	0.16351	0.13768	0.11611
20	0.81954	0.67297	0.55368	0.45639	0.37689	0.31180	0.25842	0.21455	0.17843	0.14864	0.12403	0.10367
25	0.77977	0.60953	0.47761	0.37512	0.29530	0.23300	0.18425	0.14602	0.11597	0.09230	0.07361	0.05882
30	0.74192	0.55207	0.41199	0.30832	0.23138	0.17411	0.13137	0.09938	0.07537	0.05731	0.04368	0.03338
35	0.70591	0.50003	0.35538	0.25342	0.18129	0.13011	0.09366	0.06763	0.04899	0.03558	0.02592	0.01894
40	0.67165	0.45289	0.30656	0.20829	0.14205	0.09722	0.06678	0.04603	0.03184	0.02209	0.01538	0.01075
50	0.60804	0.37153	0.22811	0.14071	0.08720	0.05429	0.03395	0.02132	0.01345	0.00852	0.00542	0.00346

Exhibit E-5 illustrates calculations of present values using the factors in **Table III**.

EXHIBIT E-5 Present Value of a Single Amount Using Present Value Tables

Calculate the present value of $1,000 four years hence, at 12 percent interest compounded annually:

Number of periods (one year, annually) = 4

Interest rate per period (12%/1) = 12%

Multiplier = 0.63552

Present value = $1,000 × 0.63552 = $636

(This result agrees with our earlier illustration.)

Calculate the present value of $116.99 two years hence, at 8 percent compounded semiannually:

Number of periods (two years, semiannually) = 4

Interest rate per period (8%/2) = 4%

Multiplier = 0.85480

Present value = $116.99 × 0.85480 = $100 (rounded)

PRESENT VALUE OF AN ANNUITY

We can also use present value tables like **Table III** to calculate the present value of any single future cash flow or series of future cash flows. For example, assume $100 is to be received at the end of each of the next three years as an annuity. As shown in **Exhibit E-6**, the present value of this ordinary annuity can be calculated from **Table III** by calculating the present value of each of the three individual receipts and summing them (assuming 5 percent annual interest).

EXHIBIT E-6 Present Value of an Ordinary Annuity

Future Receipts (ordinary annuity)				PV Multiplier		
Year 1	Year 2	Year 3		(Table III)		Present Value
$100			×	0.95238	=	$ 95.24
	$100		×	0.90703	=	90.70
		$100	×	0.86384	=	86.38
				Total present value		$272.32

Table IV, on the other hand, provides a single multiplier for calculating the present value of a series of future cash flows that represent an ordinary annuity. Referring to **Table IV** in the three periods row and the 5 percent interest column, we see that the multiplier is 2.72325, equal to the sum of the three present value factors in **Exhibit E-6**. When applied to the $100 annuity amount, the multiplier gives a present value of $272.32.

TABLE IV Present Value of an Ordinary Annuity of $1 per Period

Period	1%	2%	3%	4%	5%	6%	7%	8%	9%	10%	11%	12%
1	0.99010	0.98039	0.97087	0.96154	0.95238	0.94340	0.93458	0.92593	0.91743	0.90909	0.90090	0.89286
2	1.97040	1.94156	1.91347	1.88609	1.85941	1.83339	1.80802	1.78326	1.75911	1.73554	1.71252	1.69005
3	2.94099	2.88388	2.82861	2.77509	2.72325	2.67301	2.62432	2.57710	2.53129	2.48685	2.44371	2.40183
4	3.90197	3.80773	3.71710	3.62990	3.54595	3.46511	3.38721	3.31213	3.23972	3.16987	3.10245	3.03735
5	4.85343	4.71346	4.57971	4.45182	4.32948	4.21236	4.10020	3.99271	3.88965	3.79079	3.69590	3.60478
6	5.79548	5.60143	5.41719	5.24214	5.07569	4.91732	4.76654	4.62288	4.48592	4.35526	4.23054	4.11141
7	6.72819	6.47199	6.23028	6.00205	5.78637	5.58238	5.38929	5.20637	5.03295	4.86842	4.71220	4.56376
8	7.65168	7.32548	7.01969	6.73274	6.46321	6.20979	5.97130	5.74664	5.53482	5.33493	5.14612	4.96764
9	8.56602	8.16224	7.78611	7.43533	7.10782	6.80169	6.51523	6.24689	5.99525	5.75902	5.53705	5.32825
10	9.47130	8.98259	8.53020	8.11090	7.72173	7.36009	7.02358	6.71008	6.41766	6.14457	5.88923	5.65022
11	10.36763	9.78685	9.25262	8.76048	8.30641	7.88687	7.49867	7.13896	6.80519	6.49506	6.20652	5.93770
12	11.25508	10.57534	9.95400	9.38507	8.86325	8.38384	7.94269	7.53608	7.16073	6.81369	6.49236	6.19437
13	12.13374	11.34837	10.63496	9.98565	9.39357	8.85268	8.35765	7.90378	7.48690	7.10336	6.74987	6.42355
14	13.00370	12.10625	11.29607	10.56312	9.89864	9.29498	8.74547	8.24424	7.78615	7.36669	6.98187	6.62817
15	13.86505	12.84926	11.93794	11.11839	10.37966	9.71225	9.10791	8.55948	8.06069	7.60608	7.19087	6.81086
16	14.71787	13.57771	12.56110	11.65230	10.83777	10.10590	9.44665	8.85137	8.31256	7.82371	7.37916	6.97399
17	15.56225	14.29187	13.16612	12.16567	11.27407	10.47726	9.76322	9.12164	8.54363	8.02155	7.54879	7.11963
18	16.39827	14.99203	13.75351	12.65930	11.68959	10.82760	10.05909	9.37189	8.75563	8.20141	7.70162	7.24967
19	17.22601	15.67846	14.32380	13.13394	12.08532	11.15812	10.33560	9.60360	8.95011	8.36492	7.83929	7.36578
20	18.04555	16.35143	14.87747	13.59033	12.46221	11.46992	10.59401	9.81815	9.12855	8.51356	7.96333	7.46944
25	22.02316	19.52346	17.41315	15.62208	14.09394	12.78336	11.65358	10.67478	9.82258	9.07704	8.42174	7.84314
30	25.80771	22.39646	19.60044	17.29203	15.37245	13.76483	12.40904	11.25778	10.27365	9.42691	8.69379	8.05518
35	29.40858	24.99862	21.48722	18.66461	16.37419	14.49825	12.94767	11.65457	10.56682	9.64416	8.85524	8.17550
40	32.83469	27.35548	23.11477	19.79277	17.15909	15.04630	13.33171	11.92461	10.75736	9.77905	8.95105	8.24378
50	39.19612	31.42361	25.72976	21.48218	18.25593	15.76186	13.80075	12.23348	10.96168	9.91481	9.04165	8.30450

CALCULATIONS USING A SPREADSHEET

While present value tables can provide a handy method to solve some time value of money problems, they are not suitable for many real-world situations. For example, many real-world interest rates are not even integers like those appearing in **Table I** through **Table IV**, nor are many problems limited to the number of time periods appearing in the tables. While it is still possible to solve these problems with the provided formulas, financial calculators and spreadsheet programs provide a much quicker solution. We illustrate the calculation of bond issuance prices using a spreadsheet in Appendix 9A at the end of Chapter 9.

SUMMARY OF LEARNING OBJECTIVES

LO1 Describe the nature of interest and distinguish between simple and compound interest. (p. E-2)

- Interest is payment for the use of money over time.
- Simple interest is computed only on the principal.
- Compound interest is computed on the accumulated principal including any earned interest that has not been paid.

LO2 Calculate future values. (p. E-3)

- The future value of a single amount is the amount that a specified investment will be worth at a future date if invested at a given rate of compound interest.
- The formula for calculating the future value of a single amount is $FV = PV \times (1 + i)^n$.
- Future value tables provide a multiplier for many combinations of time periods and interest rates that, when applied to the dollar amount of a present value, determines its future value.
- An annuity represents a special case of a pattern of cash flows where the cash flow amounts are of equal amounts and equally spaced over time.
- A separate table is available that provides a multiplier for the future value of an annuity rather than using separate multipliers from the future value of $1 table.

LO3 Calculate present values. (p. E-6)

- The right to receive an amount of money now—its present value—is normally worth more than the right to receive the same amount later—its future value.
- The formula for calculating the present value of a single amount is $PV = FV \times [1 \div (1 + i)^n]$.
- A separate table is available that provides a multiplier for the present value of an annuity rather than using separate multipliers from the present value of $1 table.

KEY TERMS

Annuity (p. E-5)
Compound interest (p. E-2)
Future value (p. E-3)
Interest (p. E-2)
Ordinary annuity (p. E-5)
Present value (p. E-6)
Principal (p. E-2)
Simple interest (p. E-2)
Time value (p. E-2)

SELF-STUDY QUESTIONS

(Answers to Self-Study Questions are at the end of this appendix.)

1. **Calculate the future value of each of the following items.** LO2
   a. $50,000 deposited in a savings account for ten years if the annual interest rate is
      1. 12 percent compounded annually.
      2. 12 percent compounded semiannually.
      3. 12 percent compounded quarterly.

   b. $5,000 received at the end of each year for the next ten years if the money earns interest at the rate of 4 percent compounded annually.

   c. $3,000 received semiannually for the next five years if the money earns interest at the rate of 8 percent compounded semiannually.

   d. $1,000 deposited each year for the next ten years plus a single sum of $15,000 deposited today if the interest rate is 10 percent per year compounded annually.

2. **Calculate the present value of each of the following items.** LO3
   a. $90,000 ten years hence if the annual interest rate is
      1. 8 percent compounded annually.
      2. 8 percent compounded semiannually.
      3. 8 percent compounded quarterly.

   b. $1,000 received at the end of each year for the next eight years if money is worth 10 percent per year compounded annually.

   c. $600 received at the end of each six months for the next fifteen years if the interest rate is 8 percent per year compounded semiannually.

   d. $500,000 inheritance ten years hence if money is worth 10 percent per year compounded annually.

   e. $2,500 received each half year for the next ten years plus a single sum of $85,000 at the end of ten years if the interest rate is 12 percent per year compounded semiannually.

Assignments with the MBC logo in the margin are available in myBusinessCourse. See the Preface of the book for details.

EXERCISES

EE-1. Simple and Compound Interest LO1 Homework MBC

a. For each of the following notes, calculate the simple interest due at the end of the term.

Note	Principal	Rate	Term
1	$10,000	2%	6 years
2	$10,000	4%	4 years
3	$10,000	6%	3 years

b. Compute the amount of interest due at the end of the term for each of the above notes assuming interest is compounded annually.

EE-2. Future Value Computation At the beginning of the year you deposit $3,000 in a savings account. How much will accumulate in three years if you earn 8 percent compounded annually? LO2

EE-3. Future Value Computation You deposit $3,000 at the end of every year for three years. How much will accumulate in three years if you earn 8 percent compounded annually? LO2

EE-4. Present Value Computation You will receive $3,000 in three years. What is the present value if you can earn 8 percent interest compounded annually? LO3

EE-5. Present Value Computation You receive $3,000 at the end of every year for three years. What is the present value of these receipts if you earn 8 percent compounded annually? LO3

EE-6. Future Value Computation What amount will be accumulated in five years if $10,000 is invested today at 6 percent interest compounded annually? LO2

LO3 **EE-7. Present Value Computation** You are scheduled to be paid $10,000 in five years. What amount today is equivalent to the $10,000 to be received in five years assuming interest is compounded annually at 6 percent?

Homework MBC

LO2 **EE-8. Future Value Computation** What amount will be accumulated in five years if $10,000 is invested every six months beginning in six months and ending five years from today? Interest will accumulate at an annual rate of 10 percent compounded semiannually.

Homework MBC

LO2 **EE-9. Future Value Computation** You are scheduled to receive $10,000 every six months for ten periods beginning in six months. What amount in five years is equivalent to the future series of payments assuming interest compounds at the annual rate of 8 percent compounded semiannually?

Homework MBC

LO3 **EE-10. Present Value Computation** Zazzi, Inc., believes it will need $100,000 in five years to expand its operations. Zazzi can earn 5 percent, compounded annually if it deposits its money right now. How large of a deposit must Zazzi make to have the necessary $100,000 in five years?

Homework MBC

LO2 **EE-11. Future Value Computation** Peyton Company deposited $10,000 in the bank today, earning 8 percent interest. Peyton plans to withdraw the money in five years. How much money will be available to withdraw assuming that interest is compounded (a) annually, (b) semiannually, and (c) quarterly?

Homework MBC

LO2 **EE-12. Future Value Computation** Sam Smith deposited $5,000 in a savings account today. The deposit will earn interest at the rate of 8 percent. How much will be available for Sam to withdraw in three years, assuming interest is compounded (a) annually, (b) semiannually, and (c) quarterly?

Homework MBC

LO3 **EE-13. Present Value Computation** Pete Frost made a deposit into his savings account three years ago and earned interest at an annual rate of 8 percent. The deposit accumulated to $25,000. How much was initially deposited assuming that the interest was compounded (a) annually, (b) semiannually, and (c) quarterly?

Homework MBC

LO2 **EE-14. Future Value Computation** Kumari Jennings has decided to start saving for his daughter's college education by depositing $2,500 at the end of every year for 18 years. He has determined that he will be able to earn 6 percent interest compounded annually. He hopes to have at least $70,000 when his daughter starts college in eighteen years. Will his savings plan be successful?

Homework MBC

LO3 **EE-15. Present Value Computation** Kerry Bales won the state lottery and was given four choices for receiving her winnings.

Homework MBC

1. Receive $400,000 right now.
2. Receive $432,000 in one year.
3. Receive $40,000 at the end of each year for 20 years.
4. Receive $36,000 at the end of each year for 30 years.

Assuming Kerry can earn interest of 8 percent compounded annually, which option should Kerry choose?

ANSWERS TO SELF-STUDY QUESTIONS

1.

a.	1.	$ 50,000	×	3.10585	=	$155,293
	2.	$ 50,000	×	3.20714	=	$160,357
	3.	$ 50,000	×	3.26204	=	$163,102
b.		$ 5,000	×	12.00611	=	$ 60,031
c.		$ 3,000	×	12.00611	=	$ 36,018
d.		$ 1,000	×	15.93742	=	$ 15,937
		$ 15,000	×	2.59374	=	$ 38,906
						$ 54,843

2.

a.	1.	$ 90,000	×	0.46319	=	$ 41,687
	2.	$ 90,000	×	0.45639	=	$ 41,075
	3.	$ 90,000	×	0.45289	=	$ 40,760
b.		$ 1,000	×	5.33493	=	$ 5,335
c.		$ 600	×	17.29203	=	$ 10,375
d.		$500,000	×	0.38554	=	$192,770
e.		$ 2,500	×	11.46992	=	$ 28,675
		$ 85,000	×	0.31180	=	$ 26,503
						$ 55,178

Data Analytics and Blockchain Technology

Road Map

Learning Objectives		Page	eLecture	Assignments
1	**Define Big Data and describe its four attributes.**	F-2	F-1	1, 7, 8, 9, 10, 15, 32, 33, 34
2	**Identify and define the four types of data analytics.**	F-2	F-1	2, 7, 8, 9, 10, 15, 23, 24, 25, 32, 33, 34, 39, 40, 41
3	**Describe the use of data analytics within the accounting profession.**	F-3	F-2	15, 16, 17, 18, 19, 20, 21, 22, 23, 24, 25, 26, 27, 28, 29, 30, 31, 35, 36, 37, 38, 39, 40, 41
4	**Describe the analytics mindset.**	F-4	F-3	3, 16, 17, 18, 19, 20, 21, 22, 23, 24, 25, 26, 27, 28, 29, 30, 31, 35, 36, 37, 38, 39, 41
5	**Describe data visualization best practices.**	F-6	F-4	4, 5
6	**Describe how blockchain technology works and its use within the accounting profession.**	F-10	F-5	6, 11, 12, 13, 14

DATA ANALYTICS

LO1 Define Big Data and describe its four attributes.

Data analytics can broadly be defined as the process of examining sets of data with the goal of discovering useful information from patterns found in the data. Increasingly, this process is aided by computers running programs ranging from basic spreadsheet software, such as **Microsoft Excel** and **Google Sheets**, to specialized software, such as **Tableau** or **Power BI**. This technology can reveal trends and insights that would otherwise be lost in the overwhelming amount of data.

Big Data

The concept of data analytics is intertwined with the concept of **big data**. Although no precise definition exists for big data, a commonly accepted definition is that big data is a collection of data that is both extremely large and also extremely complex, thus making its analysis beyond the scope of traditional tools. Important attributes of big data, commonly referred to as the four V's, are Volume, Variety, Velocity, and Veracity. **Volume** refers to the amount of data. According to IDC (a market intelligence company), there were 33 available zettabytes of data globally in 2018. IDC predicted that the amount of data would increase to 175 zettabytes by 2025. (Just so you know, there are 21 zeros in one zettabyte.) Total amounts of data are growing because we are creating more data (through new technologies) and because we are able to store more data (using cloud storage services like Amazon Web Services [AWS] and Microsoft Azure). Massive data sets can't be managed on a single machine. They must be stored in clusters over multiple physical or virtual machines.

Variety refers to the source of data. Data can be structured, semi-structured, or unstructured. Structured data can be contained in rows and columns and stored in spreadsheets or relational databases. Although most accounting data is structured, it is estimated that less than 20 percent of all data is structured.

Unstructured data cannot be easily contained in rows and columns and is, therefore, difficult to search and analyze. Photos, video and audio files, and social media content are examples of unstructured data.

Semi-structured data has characteristics of both structured and unstructured data. It may include some defining details but doesn't completely conform to a rigid structure. For example, the words in an email are unstructured data. The email date and the addresses of the sender and the recipient are structured data. Artificial intelligence algorithms are used to process unstructured and semi-structured data in a way that makes the information useable.

Velocity refers to the speed at which the data is being produced. The amount of data is not only growing; it's growing exponentially as more people gain internet access, and more technology is created that connects humans to machines and machines to machines. Collecting and translating data (especially unstructured data) into usable information is complicated by how quickly new data is generated.

Veracity refers to the quality of the data. Data quality can be negatively affected by untrustworthy data sources, inconsistent or missing data, statistical biases, and human error. The veracity of unstructured data is especially difficult to determine. Machine learning, a type of artificial intelligence based on the idea that systems can learn from data and can identify patterns, is often used to assess data quality.

In summary, a set of data would be considered "big data" if:

- The data set is too large to be managed by traditional methods.
- The data set includes a variety of types of data (structured, semi-structured, and unstructured).
- The amount of data in the data set is expanding rapidly.
- The accuracy and reliability of the data may be uncertain.

LO2 Identify and define the four types of data analytics.

Types of Data Analytics

Data analytics can be categorized into four main types, ranging in sophistication from relatively straightforward to very complex. The first category is **descriptive analytics**, which describes what has happened over a given period of time. Simple examples include determining sales trends over a period of time and the relative effectiveness of various social media promotions based on click-through rates. Microsoft Excel and other spreadsheet programs include built-in functions that greatly simplify performing descriptive analytics.

Diagnostic analytics focuses more on why something occurred. This data analytics technique is used to monitor changes in data and often includes a certain amount of hypothesizing: Did the marketing campaign lead to the increase in sales? Did changing the beverage items affect food choices? Did the opening of competing restaurants negatively impact sales growth? Diagnostic analytics is useful because past performance is often a reliable predictor of future outcomes and can greatly aid in planning and forecasting.

Whereas descriptive and diagnostic analytics use data to try to understand what happened and why, **predictive analytics** uses data to try to determine what *will* happen. The movie ***Moneyball*** made the general manager of the **Oakland Athletics**, Billy Beane, famous for using predictive analytics to make personnel decisions in professional baseball. In his evaluation of baseball players, Beane used data to predict player performance so he could assemble the team with the greatest likelihood of winning the World Series. Banks also use predictive analytics to identify and prevent fraudulent transactions by monitoring customer credit card transactions and red flagging those that deviate from a customer behavior profile that was developed from previous transaction and geographic data.

Prescriptive analytics moves beyond what is going to happen to suggesting a course of action for what *should* happen to optimize outcomes. The forecasts created using predictive analytics can be used to make recommendations for future courses of action. For example, if we own a sports bar and determine there is a high likelihood of our local sports team winning the championship this year, we should expand the bar area and add more big-screen televisions to maximize revenues. **Exhibit F-1** summarizes the four types of data analytics.

EXHIBIT F-1 The Four Types of Data Analytics

Type of Data Analytics	Purpose	Example
Descriptive	To explain what happened	What were sales by month last year?
Diagnostic	To understand why it happened	Did the new advertising campaign cause sales to increase last quarter?
Predictive	To predict what will happen	Does this credit card charge deviate (amount, location, etc.) from past purchases by this credit card holder?
Prescriptive	To determine what should happen	How many servers should be on the schedule for game nights?

Data Analytics in the Accounting Profession

LO3 Describe the use of data analytics within the accounting profession.

Accountants are already preparing descriptive analytic reports regularly. Comparative income statements, sales reports by location, inventory valuation reports, and ratio calculations (average collection periods, days' sales in inventory, etc.) are all examples of descriptive analytics.

Budget variance reports and segment reports by region or product line prepared by accountants can be used for diagnostic analytics. Accountants may also work with sales and production managers to analyze the reasons behind changes in operating results. A distributor might want to know how much of the increase in overall sales last year was caused by the transfer of two of its representatives to other sales regions. A grocery store manager might want to know if the winter storm last month impacted sales in all or just some of the various departments. A production manager might work with the accounting department to determine any correlation between equipment repair costs and the number of units produced over the last two years.

Data analytics should not be limited to only descriptive and diagnostic analysis. Accountants can provide even more value by employing predictive and prescriptive analytics. Accountants can obtain data from a variety of company sources, including enterprise resource planning systems, customer relationship management systems, and point-of-sale systems, to aid them in obtaining insight into future outcomes and providing guidance for future actions. The area of credit granting provides an example. Predictive analytics can help compute credit scores to predict the likelihood of future payments. As a result, prescriptive analytics can aid in suggesting terms for granting credit. Predictive analytics can also be used to help analyze outstanding accounts receivables and determine estimated credit losses based on how much time has elapsed since the credit sale took place.

Many other opportunities exist for accountants to utilize data analytics. Tax accountants can apply data analysis to unique tax issues to suggest optimal tax strategies. Accountants serving as investment advisors can use big data to find patterns in consumer behavior that others can use to build analytic models for identifying investment opportunities.

Perhaps no area of accounting can benefit more from an understanding of data analytics than auditing. Auditors employ data analytics to shift from the sample-based audit model to one based on continuous modeling of much larger data sets. This allows auditors to identify the riskiest areas of an audit by focusing on outliers and exceptions.

The major accounting firms have fully embraced the power of data analytics. **PricewaterhouseCoopers** (PWC), **Deloitte**, **Ernst & Young** (EY), and **KPMG** all devote significant staffing resources to provide data analytics services to their clients. These firms claim they can help their clients optimize their data assets to aid in faster and better decisions. For example, PWC provides a flowchart starting with the building of a data foundation and applies advanced analytics to improving business performance, ultimately leading to opportunities for innovation.

While computers and software are instrumental in the entire process, the human element is the most critical factor in the success of any data analytics program. One commonality among surveys of top company managers is the value placed on data analytics for the company's future. Another commonality is the need for professionals trained in data analytics to help the company attain its goals.

In order to be useful, data needs to be analyzed. Technology has provided the analyst with powerful tools that allow big data to provide insights that would not have been possible in the past. Still, the most important tool in the analytics toolkit comes from the analyst. Without critical thinking and good judgement, the value would remain locked within the data.

The Analytics Mindset[1]

LO4 Describe the analytics mindset.

The analytics mindset consists of a four-step process of (1) asking the right questions; (2) extracting, transforming, and loading the necessary data; (3) applying appropriate data analytics techniques; and (4) interpreting and presenting the results. **Exhibit F-2** summarizes the steps and requirements of an analytics mindset.

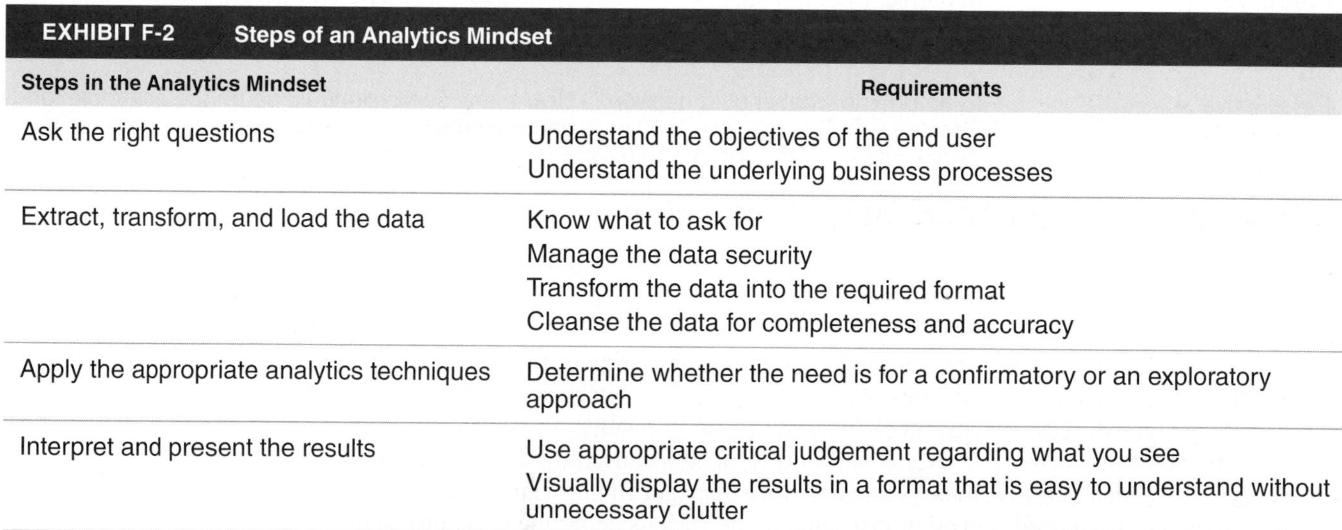

EXHIBIT F-2 Steps of an Analytics Mindset

Steps in the Analytics Mindset	Requirements
Ask the right questions	Understand the objectives of the end user Understand the underlying business processes
Extract, transform, and load the data	Know what to ask for Manage the data security Transform the data into the required format Cleanse the data for completeness and accuracy
Apply the appropriate analytics techniques	Determine whether the need is for a confirmatory or an exploratory approach
Interpret and present the results	Use appropriate critical judgement regarding what you see Visually display the results in a format that is easy to understand without unnecessary clutter

Note that while technology is imbedded in this process, the process still begins and ends with the human element of asking the right questions and interpreting the results. Nothing is more critical than the first step of knowing what to ask. The right questions guide the process to find the right data to analyze and interpret.

Asking the right questions requires a few prerequisites. First, you need to know the audience that the analysis is for and what their objectives are. Next, you need to understand the context

[1] The analytics mindset discussed here is an approach developed by the Ernst & Young Foundation.

underlying the problem. For example, to analyze a marketing question you should understand the industry characteristics and the consumer demographics. Without this knowledge, you may not select the correct indicators to analyze.

Along with knowing the right questions to ask, an analytical mindset requires you to form an idea of what to expect from the data. For example, when analyzing inventory salability, you would expect to see certain associated movements in sales and receivables.

After your questions are formed, you need to determine the data needed to aid in finding answers to those questions. This requires a knowledge of the data characteristics of the four V's previously mentioned. With this knowledge you can begin the data extraction process. Here you will need to know what data to ask for, how to manage data security, and what form the data will take.

Once you have the data, you will need to transform it into a format suitable for analysis. This is often referred to as data cleaning. Data is rarely found in the form of a nicely organized Excel spreadsheet. Rather, the data will often need to be converted into a proper format and tested for completeness and accuracy. Further, unnecessary data should be removed from the data set.

The data should then be loaded into the proper analysis tool, such as **Tableau** or Microsoft's **Power BI**. Once loaded, the data should again be cleansed to be sure it is ready for analysis in the chosen software.

It is necessary to determine the appropriate technique to analyze the data within the analysis tool. There are a multitude of ways that the data can be analyzed. Possible choices include computing ratios between associated measures, identifying trends among various measures, creating comparisons between dates, and sorting measures. The proper technique to use will be guided by the questions being asked.

In your interpretation of the data, you should ask yourself what do you see and is this what you expected? In other words, do these results make sense or did the results create new questions that require further analysis?

Eventually, the results must be packaged into a presentation that can be shared with the intended audience. Software such as Tableau, Power BI, or Excel can greatly enhance these presentations through their ability to create **visualizations** and **dashboards**. These visualizations can take many forms, from simple tables to bar or pie charts, to more sophisticated scatter plots, map charts, heat maps, and more. Dashboards are created by combining multiple visualizations. Interactive dashboards allow users to filter out or drill down on content included in the charts and tables, on demand.

Data Analytic Tools

Technologies used by organizations to analyze data and communicate information to users are known as Business Intelligence (BI) tools. Data warehousing (data storage), data mining (extracting usable insights from data), and reporting and querying software are all BI tools.

Excel and Tableau are two popular BI tools that you will be using in the exercises and problems at the end of this Appendix.

Although Excel and Tableau can be used in similar ways, there are some important differences. Excel is a software application that is used for creating, organizing, and analyzing data. Tableau is a data visualization tool. Although calculations can be performed in Tableau, those calculations are made to create new fields for use in visualizations, not as support for accounting transactions. For example, Excel might be used to calculate sales commission amounts, which are then inputted into the accounting system. Tableau would not be used for that purpose.

Users in both Excel[2] and Tableau can

- Connect with different data sources
- Create visualizations and dashboards
- Work with big data sets

Tableau has much stronger interactivity tools and a more comprehensive selection of chart options. Excel generally has more flexibility and more extensive analytics tools.[3]

[2] Full functionality in Excel is only available if you have Excel 2010 or newer and you are running a 64-bit version of Windows. To determine the version of Windows on your computer, go to Settings>System>About. The version will be listed in the Device specifications section.

[3] Pan and Blankley, Excel vs. Tableau: See your data differently, *Journal of Accountancy*, February 29, 2020.

Python and **R** are popular programming languages that are used for data analysis, particularly when working with big data sets. Although these are programming languages and not application software (Business Intelligence tools), they are relatively easy to code compared to other languages and can be used to write software programs that perform powerful data analyses and visualizations.

ACCESSING EXCEL AND TABLEAU

Excel, if not available to you through your school, can be accessed for free by creating a Microsoft account at https://office.live.com/start/Excel.aspx. A free version of Tableau (Tableau Public) is available to you at https://public.tableau.com/en-us/s/. Tableau Public has most of the functions of Tableau Desktop (the full version). However, you can't save your workbooks locally if you're using Tableau Public. Instead, all workbooks are saved online and are accessible to any Tableau user unless you elect to hide your visualizations. Hiding visualizations is done in Settings after you've registered for Tableau on the Tableau website. Walk-through videos are available for every exercise and problem at cambridgepub.com. Tableau tutorial videos are available at https://www.tableau.com/learn/training/.

Data Visualization

LO5 Describe data visualization best practices.

As noted previously, the final step in the analytics mindset is to present your results. This is often done in the form of a visualization. While it is possible to present results as a bunch of tables full of numbers, visualizations with imagery are often a far better means to convey the raw numbers. Visualizations can be thought of as a blending of the art of design with the science of data.

There is an unlimited number of ways that data can be presented; however, certain best practices exist that can serve as a guide when building a visualization. For example, the exact same data on GDP levels are shown in the three charts in **Exhibit F-3**, but each displays the data differently. The table presents the raw data; however, the reader cannot easily rank the different economies. The two bar charts both show the same data; however, the one all in blue makes it far easier to compare economies by showing the data in sorted order. Also, note that adding multiple colors to the other bar chart does nothing to aid the reader, rather it just adds confusion.

EXHIBIT F-3 Different Displays of the Same Data

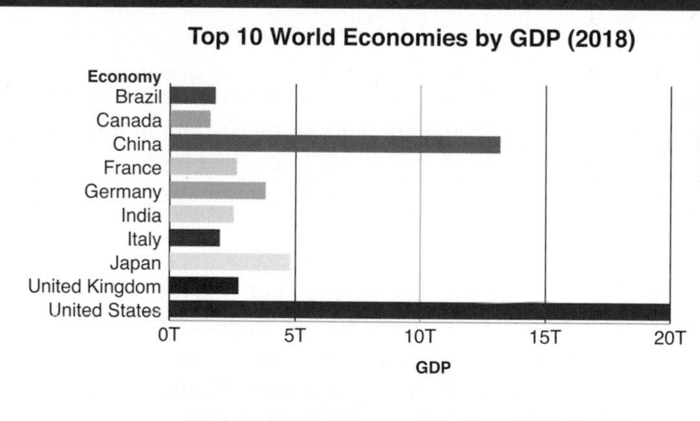

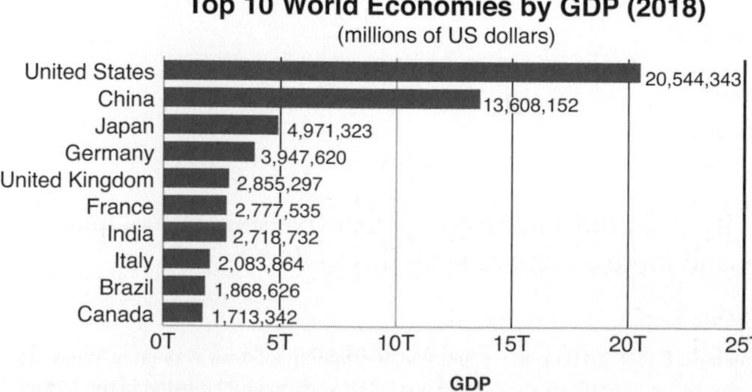

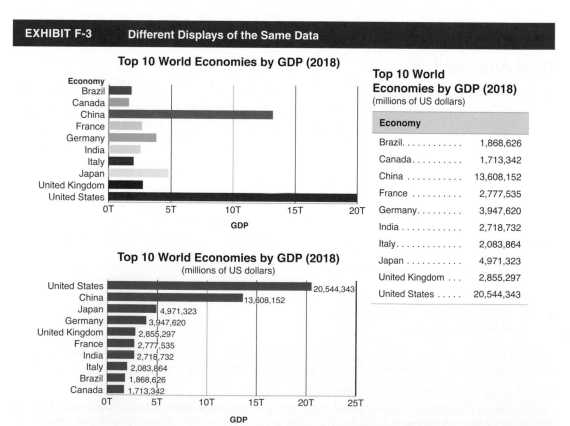

Top 10 World Economies by GDP (2018)
(millions of US dollars)

Economy	
Brazil	1,868,626
Canada	1,713,342
China	13,608,152
France	2,777,535
Germany	3,947,620
India	2,718,732
Italy	2,083,864
Japan	4,971,323
United Kingdom	2,855,297
United States	20,544,343

Visualizations can be divided into two primary categories, exploratory and explanatory. **Exploratory visualizations** are meant to allow the reader to explore the data presented in order to do additional analysis. Exploratory visualizations would normally include interactive tools like filters that allow the user to change the level of data displayed. This can be useful when the problem is not clearly defined, and the reader wishes to gain a further understanding of the data.

In contrast to exploratory visualizations, **explanatory visualizations** are used to convey information to the audience. A classic example of such a visualization was prepared in 1854 by the British physician Dr. John Snow. Dr. Snow plotted cholera deaths in central London on a map that also showed the location of water pumps. The visualization identified the relationship between these deaths and the Broad Street water pump and lead to a change in the water and waste systems. Dr. Snow's visualization is shown in **Exhibit F-4**.

EXHIBIT F-4 Cholera Deaths in London in 1854

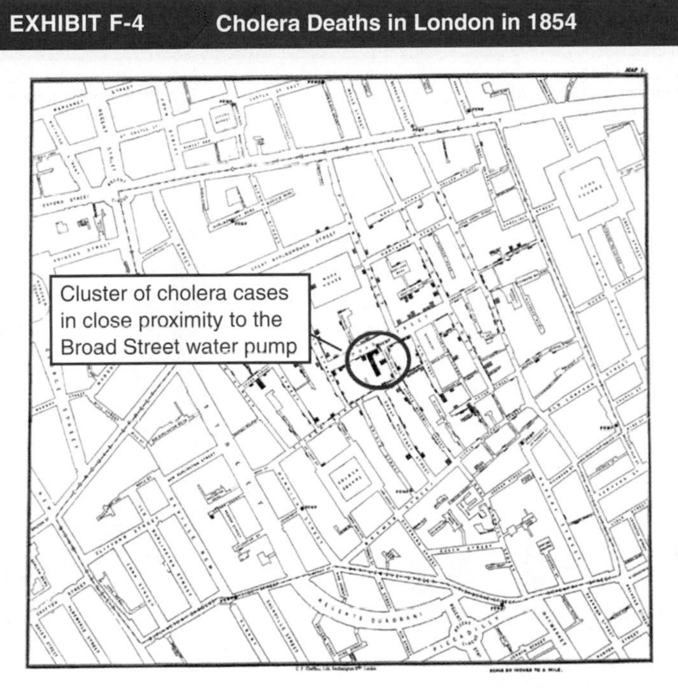

Good visualization design can be enhanced by considering how our brains process visual details such as form, position, and color.

For example, items that are different from the rest become the focus of attention as shown in **Exhibit F-5**. An item that is longer, wider, or in a different orientation will stand out, as will an item that is of a different size, shape, in a different position, or has a different hue or intensity of color.

EXHIBIT F-5 Displays that Emphasize How Differences Focus Our Attention

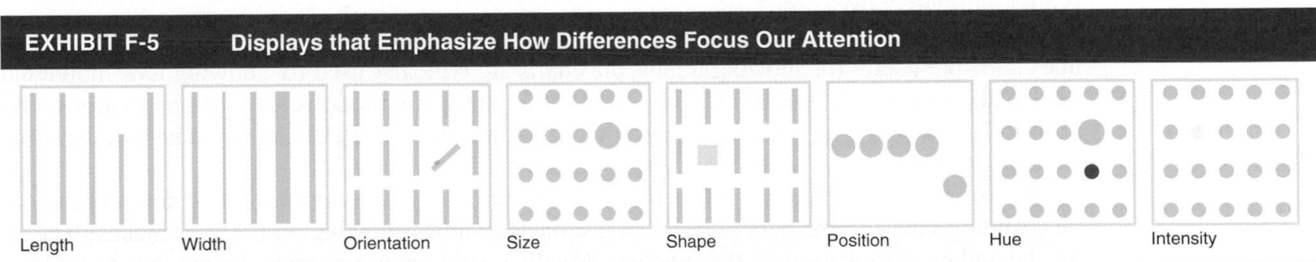

While the use of color can help an item to stand out, it is important to use color correctly. The use of too much color can add to visual clutter. And it's important that color is used consistently, such as always representing a certain year or category. The choice of color is also important since color can convey meanings that differ from one culture to another. For example, red may mean good luck, and green may mean jealousy.

Good visualization design requires the removal of items that detract from the message that we are trying to communicate. **Visual clutter** confuses the audience and lessens the chance that they will be able to easily understand the information that is being conveyed. The concept that less is more is the essence of the visualization design principles developed by Edward Tufte, a statistician and professor emeritus at Yale University. Tufte uses the term chart-junk to refer to any unnecessary or confusing elements included in information displays. His principles show that "excellence in statistical graphics consists of ideas communicated with clarity, precision and efficiency."[4]

Exhibit F-6 illustrates **Tufte's principles**. Note in the first visualization all of the visual clutter only serves to distract the audience from seeing the main point that the United States is the largest economy based on its GDP. Now notice how much cleaner the second visualization is after removing the distracting yellow background, the color coding of each economy, the redundant labeling, and the unnecessary grid lines.

EXHIBIT F-6 Illustration of Tufte's Principles

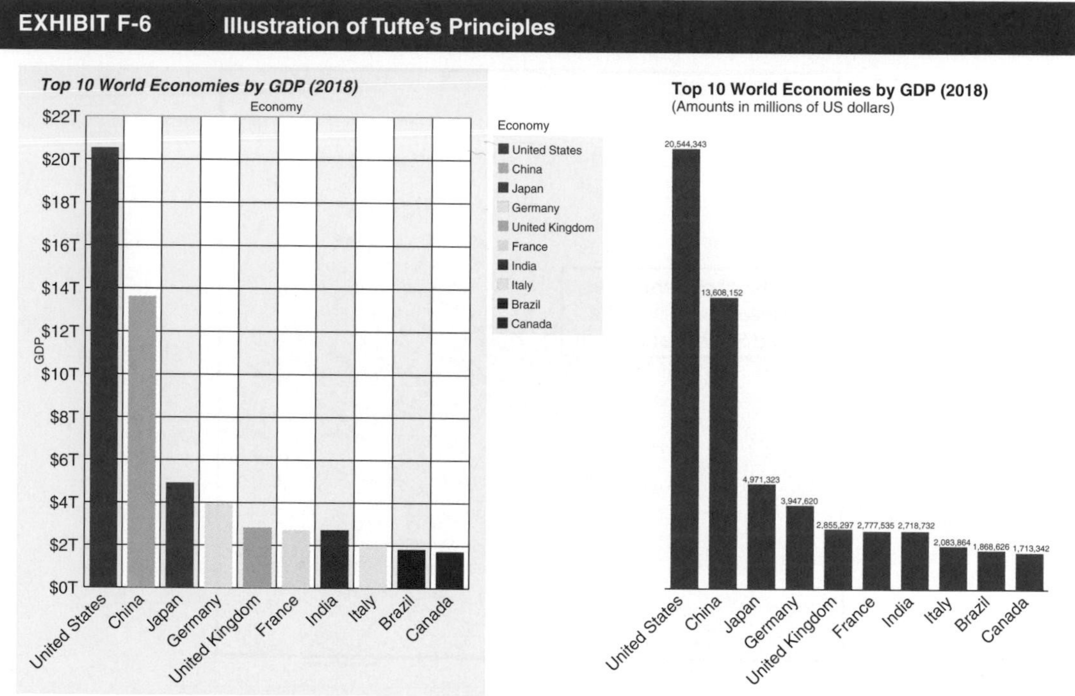

Good visualization construction also involves choosing the most effective chart type depending on what information is being presented.

The starting point for all of the visualizations we will be discussing is a simple table of data. While the table is excellent for looking up values and can precisely communicate numerical values, visualizations in the form of charts provide the audience an easier method to see what the analyst is attempting to convey.

Among the most used chart types, column and bar charts are best for showing comparisons, line charts are useful for showing trends, pie charts are typically used for showing how individual parts make up a whole, and scatter plots are best for showing relationships and distributions. **Exhibit F-7**, reprinted with permission from the author, provides an excellent tool to help in choosing the correct chart type.[5]

Column (vertical) charts and **bar** (horizontal) charts are best used to compare different categories. Adding labels to the bars rather than just having values showing on the axes makes it easier for the audience to determine these values. Finally, avoid using too many colors that just add to visual clutter.

As a general rule, **line charts** are best for illustrating changes over time and work best with continuous data. Best practices include clearly labeling the axes so the audience knows what is being shown, removing excess clutter such as grid lines and redundant labeling, and avoiding comparing more than five to seven lines.

---

[4] E.R. Tufte, *The Visual Display of Quantitative Information* (Graphics Press, Cheshire, CT 2001).

[5] Abela, Andrew V. (2013). *Advanced Presentations by Design: Creating Communication that Drives Action*. John Wiley & Sons.

EXHIBIT F-7 Chart Types

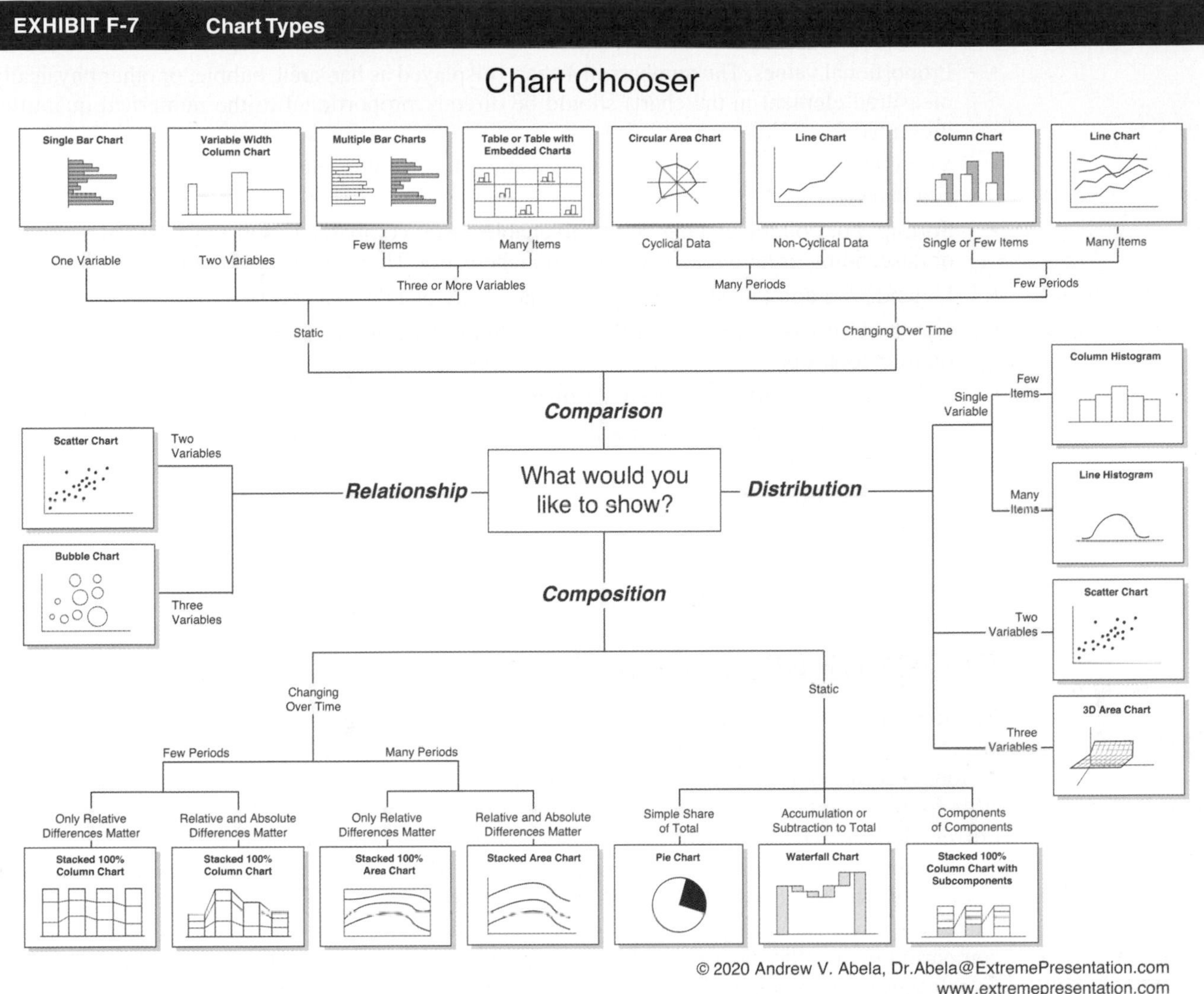

Pie charts are best used to show parts of a whole. Be sure the parts add up to 100 percent. Pie charts work best when there are just a few categories. If there are many categories of similar size, consider using a bar or column chart instead. Finally, avoid the temptation to get "fancy" with 3-D imagery and tilting the pie chart.

Scatter plots are useful if the goal is to show correlations between two variables. They are also useful for showing data distributions and clustering, which can identify anomalies and outliers. A **bubble chart** can extend the capability of a scatter plot by adding an additional dimension through changing the size of each bubble in the scatter plot. The more data that is included in a scatter plot or bubble chart, the better are the comparisons that can be made. If the elements being graphed are distributed over a very wide range, the horizontal axis can be converted from a linear to a logarithmic scale (where the numbers on the horizontal axis increase by multiples of a number). Bubble charts should use only circles rather than other shapes. Bubble charts should be scaled based on the area of the circle and not the diameter.

A **map chart** is a good choice if the data being conveyed in the visualization includes geographic locations. Map charts are best at showing relative differences in numerical values among geographic locations rather than precise differences since the values are usually portrayed as differences in a color gradient.

There are several general rules to follow regardless of the chart type. The following list was found from a search of best practices for data visualization charts.[6]

[6] https://eazybi.com/blog/data_visualization_and_chart_types/

- Time axis. When using time in charts, set it on the horizontal axis. Time should run from left to right. Do not skip values (time periods), even if there are no values.
- Proportional values. The numbers in a chart (displayed as bar, area, bubble, or other physically measured element in the chart) should be directly proportional to the numerical quantities presented.
- Visual clutter. Remove any excess information, lines, colors, and text from a chart that do not add value.
- Sorting. For column and bar charts, to enable easier comparison, sort your data in ascending or descending order by the value, not alphabetically. This applies also to pie charts.
- Legend. You don't need a legend if you have only one data category.
- Labels. Use labels directly on the line, column, bar, pie, etc., whenever possible, to avoid indirect look-up.
- Colors. In any chart, don't use more than six colors.
- Colors. For comparing the same value at different time periods, use the same color in a different intensity (from light to dark).
- Colors. For different categories, use different colors. The most widely used colors are black, white, red, green, blue, and yellow.
- Colors. Keep the same color palette or style for all charts in the series and the same axes and labels for similar charts to make your charts consistent and easy to compare.

BLOCKCHAIN TECHNOLOGY

LO6 Describe how blockchain technology works and its use within the accounting profession.

Blockchain technology differs from the traditional accounting ledger in a fundamental way that has immense implications for the accounting profession. A traditional ledger system is a closed system controlled at a centralized location with individuals at the centralized location responsible for the maintenance and integrity of the ledger. In contrast, a blockchain is an open, decentralized ledger, where the ledger is distributed across multiple computers called **nodes**. The blockchain ledger is managed autonomously by the distributed nodes such that data is authenticated by mass collaboration rather than by a central authority. Each node on the blockchain maintains a complete copy of all past transactions that have been added to the ledger. Thus, by comparing to the other nodes' copies, the ledger is continuously synchronized. Unlike traditional accounting ledgers, none of the nodes has any special rights that differ from those of the other nodes.

Blockchains get their name because new ledger data are periodically bundled into blocks, which are then added to previous blocks to form a chain. Each block can contain a cryptocurrency exchange, as is the case with **Bitcoin**, but other possibilities include sales transactions, equity trades, loan payments, election votes—pretty much any contract transaction. In addition, the block contains a **time stamp** and a **hash #**, which together form a cryptographic signature associated with the previous blocks. This time stamp and hash make the blockchain essentially tamper-proof because the blocks cannot be changed without the change being apparent to all other nodes. While the chain propagates in only a single chronological order, it can be audited in both directions. **Exhibit F-8** is a visual depiction of the blockchain process.

The accounting profession has seen changes arising from a vast array of technological innovations, from computer spreadsheets to general ledger software to enterprise resource systems. Blockchain technology represents another innovation in the way accounting is and will be performed. The invention of double-entry accounting, the bedrock of financial accounting, allowed managers to trust their own financial recordkeeping. Unfortunately, the same level of trust does not exist with outsiders, which is why companies rely on independent auditors for an opinion on the integrity of an entity's financial statements. These audits are often very time consuming and costly.

Accountants working in the traditional centralized-ledger environment are likely to spend a large amount of time reconciling accounts and amounts. This involves comparing balances at their company with external documents from outside entities, including banks, brokerages, and business partners, among others. In addition to the time-consuming process of acquiring all the needed sources of information and performing the comparisons, additional time and effort are often needed to reconcile any differences. In a blockchain's distributed ledger system, all node participants can continually confirm all transactions, greatly reducing the effort involved in periodic reconciliations.

EXHIBIT F-8 Blockchain Process

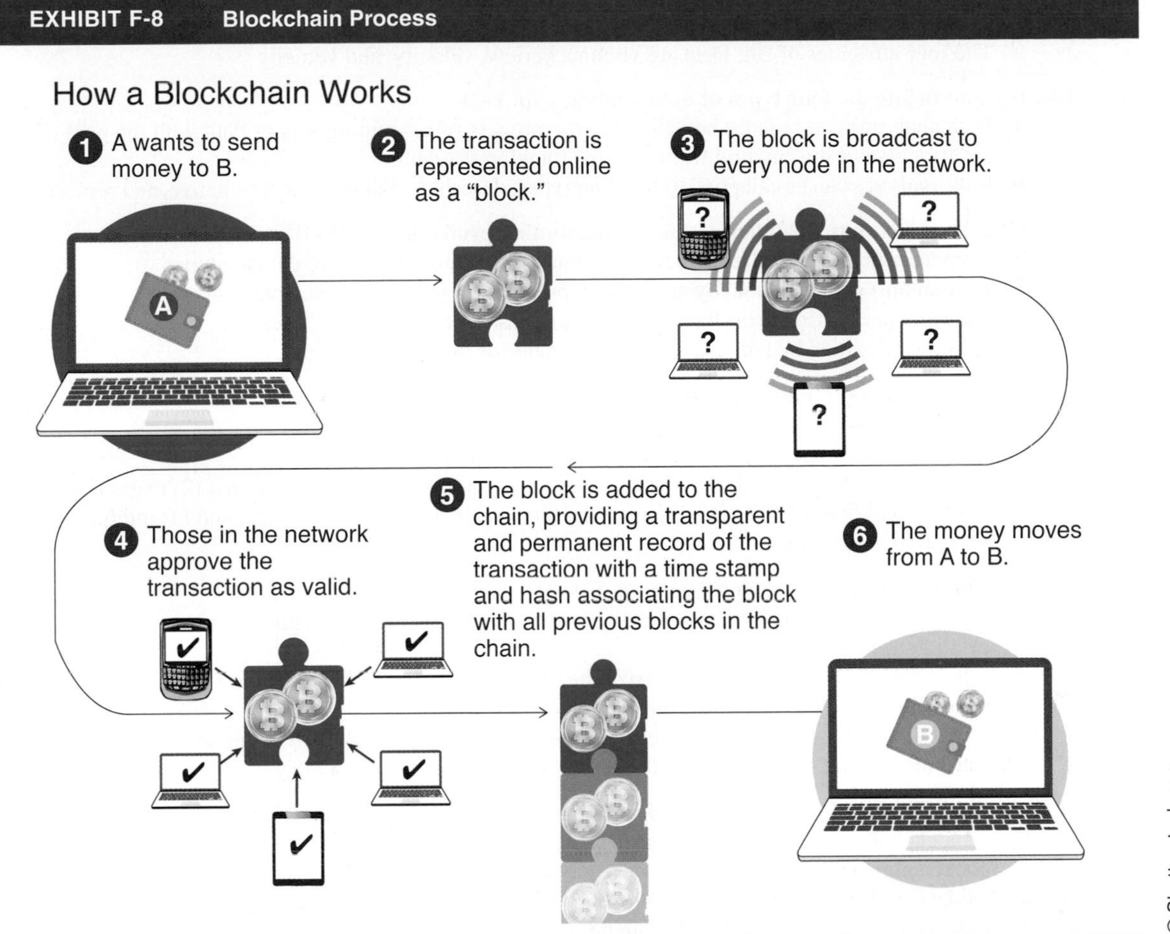
How a Blockchain Works
1 A wants to send money to B.
2 The transaction is represented online as a "block."
3 The block is broadcast to every node in the network.
4 Those in the network approve the transaction as valid.
5 The block is added to the chain, providing a transparent and permanent record of the transaction with a time stamp and hash associating the block with all previous blocks in the chain.
6 The money moves from A to B.
A
B
© Shutterstock.com

Accountants working in the traditional environment are expected to produce internal, ad hoc reports. This often requires considerable effort reconciling internal documents, perhaps from multiple departments or divisions. In a blockchain environment, accountants spend far less time verifying transactional data, freeing up time for more valuable advisory activities.

As a final example of the many ways blockchain technology will change the way accountants work, consider the traditional closing of the books at the end of each period. Instead of needing to acquire the necessary data, verify its accuracy, and make all the necessary adjustments, one could envision a far more automated process with the use of blockchain technology. Financial statements could be updated continuously from data provided by the blockchain, making the period-ending closing process much less time consuming.

Blockchain technology is widely viewed as the next major step in financial accounting. Instead of keeping separate records documenting each transaction, transactions can be written directly into the decentralized ledger. Thus, each transaction is distributed and cryptographically signed to ensure against later falsification or destruction. This has the potential to allow auditors to automatically verify much of the data in a traditional audit, freeing them to provide value in more important areas, such as the analysis of complex transactions or operational efficiencies.

Some accountants may worry that these evolving technologies will diminish the need for accountants. If history is any indication, the opposite is likely. The accountant's role in the financial process will certainly change, but this change will be evolution, not extinction. Information will still need to be interpreted and categorized before entering the blockchain, and this is where future accountants will provide their value. The Big Four accounting firms realize this and are at the forefront in research on how blockchain technology will be used.

SUMMARY

LO1 **Define Big Data and describe its four attributes. (p. F-2)**

- Big data is a collection of data that is both extremely large and also extremely complex, thus making its analysis beyond the scope of traditional tools.
- The four attributes of Big Data are volume, variety, velocity, and veracity.

LO2 **Identify and define the four types of data analytics. (p. F-2)**

- Data analytics can broadly be defined as the process of examining sets of data with the goal of discovering useful information from patterns found in the data.
- Data analytics can be categorized into four types: descriptive, diagnostic, predictive, and prescriptive.

LO3 **Describe the use of data analytics within the accounting profession. (p. F-3)**

- Many accountants are already performing descriptive and diagnositc data analytics.
- Accountants can add value by performing predictive and prescriptive data analytics.
- The large accounting firms have devoted large resources to data analytics.
- Being well trained in data analytics is important for future accountants.

LO4 **Describe the analytics mindset. (p. F-4)**

- Analytics is the process of deriving value from the data.
- An analytics mindset requires critical thinking and judgement.
- The four steps of the analytics mindset include (1) asking the right questions; (2) extracting, transforming, and loading the data; (3) applying the proper analytics techniques; and (4) interpreting and presenting the results.

LO5 **Describe data visualization best practices. (p. F-6)**

- Form, position, and color can be used to have elements stand out without any conscious effort by the audience.
- Tufte's principles of design emphasize the elimination of visual clutter that serves to distract from the ability of a visualization to convey its message.
- Use of the proper chart type can help the intended audience to visualize comparisons, compositions, distributions, and relationships in the data.

LO6 **Describe how blockchain technology works and its use within the accounting profession. (p. F-10)**

- A blockchain represents a decentralized ledger system and each decentralized computer on the blockchain is called a node.
- Unlike a traditional ledger system where authority for maintenance and integrity rests at a centralized location, each node on the blockchain has the same rights as each other node.
- Each block in the blockchain contains information, such as transaction details, along with a time stamp and a hash linking the block to previous blocks in a chronological order.
- Blockchains are essentially tamperproof because alteration to a block by a node would be apparent to every other node on the blockchain.
- Blockchain technology represents another innovation that will change the way accountants perform their work. Blockchain technology will fundamentally change the way audits are performed, and greatly reduce the time and effort spent on tasks, such as reconciling source documents, producing ad hoc reports, and performing period-ending book closings.

KEY CONCEPTS AND TERMS

Bar charts (p. F-8)
Big data (p. F-2)
Blockchain technology (p. F-10)
Bubble chart (p. F-9)
Column chart (p. F-8)
Dashboards (p. F-5)
Data analytics (p. F-2)
Descriptive analytics (p. F-2)
Diagnostic analytics (p. F-3)
Explanatory visualizations (p. F-7)
Exploratory visualizations (p. F-7)
Hash # (p. F-10)
Line charts (p. F-8)
Map chart (p. F-9)
Nodes (p. F-10)
Pie chart (p. F-9)
Predictive analytics (p. F-3)
Prescriptive analytics (p. F-3)
Scatter plots (p. F-9)
Time stamp (p. F-10)
Tufte's principles (p. F-8)
Variety (p. F-2)
Velocity (p. F-2)
Veracity (p. F-2)
Visual clutter (p. F-7)
Visualizations (p. F-5)
Volume (p. F-2)

VIDEO RESOURCES FOR TABLEAU

Many assignments require the use of Tableau. For anyone new to Tableau, the following videos are recommended. In addition to these videos, Tableau offers many more free training videos on its website under the learning tab.

A general introduction to the software. (25 minutes). https://www.tableau.com/learn/tutorials/on-demand/getting-started?playlist=484034

An introduction to the Tableau interface. (4 minutes). https://www.tableau.com/learn/tutorials/on-demand/tableau-interface?playlist=484034

Gaining an understanding of relationships in order to connect to outside data. Stop at 14 minutes and 33 seconds. https://www.tableau.com/learn/tutorials/on-demand/relationships?playlist=484036

A general introduction to visual analytics. (6 minutes). https://www.tableau.com/learn/tutorials/on-demand/getting-started-visual-analytics?playlist=484037

How to use sorting. (5 minutes). https://www.tableau.com/learn/tutorials/on-demand/sorting?playlist=484037

An introduction to filtering. (2 minutes). https://www.tableau.com/learn/tutorials/on-demand/ways-filter?playlist=484037

A deeper look at filtering. (7 minutes). https://www.tableau.com/learn/tutorials/on-demand/using-filter-shelf?playlist=484037

Using interactive filters. (4 minutes). https://www.tableau.com/learn/tutorials/on-demand/interactive-filters?playlist=484037

An introduction to formatting. (7 minutes). https://www.tableau.com/learn/tutorials/on-demand/formatting?playlist=484037

The formatting pane. (7 minutes). https://www.tableau.com/learn/tutorials/on-demand/formatting-pane?playlist=484037

An introduction to calculation in Tableau. (3 minutes). https://www.tableau.com/learn/tutorials/on-demand/getting-started-calculations?playlist=484040

Calculation syntax in Tableau. (4 minutes). https://www.tableau.com/learn/tutorials/on-demand/calculation-syntax?playlist=484040

MULTIPLE CHOICE

1. Which of the following are four characteristics of big data? **LO1**

a. Volume, variety, vagueness, veracity
b. Volume, variety, velocity, veracity
c. Volume, validate, velocity, veracity
d. Volume, variety, velocity, vulnerability

2. Which of the following are the four categories of data analytics? **LO2**

a. Descriptive, diagnostic, predictive, prescriptive
b. Expressive, diagnostic, predictive, prescriptive
c. Descriptive, analytical, predictive, prescriptive
d. Descriptive, diagnostic, prognostic, prescriptive

3. What is the correct order of the steps in the analytics mindset? **LO4**

a. Extract, transform, and load the data; ask the right questions; apply the proper analytics techniques; interpret and present the results.
b. Ask the right questions; extract, transform, and load the data; apply the proper analytics techniques; interpret and present the results.
c. Ask the right questions; extract, transform, and load the data; interpret and present the results; apply the proper analytics techniques.
d. Ask the right questions; apply the proper analytics techniques; extract, transform, and load the data; interpret and present the results.

LO5  **4.** Charts are used in visualizations to convey the following primary types of information:
a. comparisons, compositions, distributions, and relationships.
b. comparisons, historical, distributions, and relationships.
c. comparisons, compositions, forecasts, and relationships.
d. geographical, compositions, distributions, and relationships.

LO5 **5.** Which of the following statements is not true regarding the use of color in a chart?
a. Use at most six different colors in a chart.
b. To show changes in an item over time use a color gradient rather than different colors.
c. Always use color in a chart to differentiate items.
d. Use the same color palette in a chart series.

LO6 **6.** The glue that binds blocks in a blockchain consists of what?
a. Time stamps
b. Sequential numbering
c. Regulatory approval
d. Hashes
e. Both *a.* and *d.*

Assignments with the MBC logo in the margin are available in myBusinessCourse. See the Preface of the book for details.

EXERCISES

LO1, 2 **EF-7. Public accounting firms and data analytics.** Go to PWC.com and select "Services" and then "Data and Analytics." Choose a topic and write about how PWC is using data analytics to help its clients.

LO1, 2 **EF-8. Public accounting firms and data analytics.** Go to KPMG.com and select "Insights." Under "Areas of interest," select "Special Attention" and then "Data and Analytics." Choose a topic and write about how KPMG is using data analytics to help its clients.

LO1, 2 **EF-9. Public accounting firms and data analytics.** Go to Deloitte.com and select "Services" and then "Analytics." Choose a topic and write about how Deloitte is using data analytics to help its clients.

LO1, 2 **EF-10. Public accounting firms and data analytics.** Go to EY.com and enter Big data and analytics in the search bar. Choose a topic and write about how Ernst & Young is using data analytics to help its clients.

LO6 **EF-11. Public accounting firms and blockchain technology.** Go to PWC.com and search for "blockchain." Choose a topic and write about how PWC is using blockchain to help its clients.

LO6 **EF-12. Public accounting firms and blockchain technology.** Go to KPMG.com and search for "blockchain." Choose a topic and write about how KPMG is using blockchain to help its clients.

LO6 **EF-13. Public accounting firms and blockchain technology.** Go to Deloitte.com and search for "blockchain." Select "Blockchain—Perspectives, insights, and analysis." Choose a topic and write about how Deloitte is using blockchain to help its clients.

LO6 **EF-14. Public accounting firms and blockchain technology.** Go to EY.com and search for "blockchain." Choose a topic and write about how Ernst & Young is using blockchain to help its clients.

PROBLEMS

Problems PF-15 through PF-16 use data on employee statistics. The data is contained in the Excel file Employee Data Tableau.xlsx and is accessible on myBusinessCourse.

LO1, 2, 3 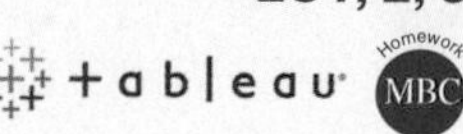 **PF-15. Using Tableau to create summary statistics.** Go to myBusinessCourse and download the Excel file **Employee Data Tableau.xlsx**. Connect Tableau Public to this Excel file. Go to the worksheet and drag the measures "Education," "Jobcat," and "Jobtime" up to Dimensions. Compare the average salaries by gender and minority status by dragging "Gender" to Rows and "Minority" to Columns and then "Salary" to the canvas. Change salary from a sum to an average.

a. How do average salaries compare by gender and minority status?

Next, explore how education level affects this relation by dragging "Education" to Columns. It may be easier to make this comparison by switching the order of "Minority" and "Education" on the Columns bar.

b. Does education level affect how average salaries compare by gender and minority status?

Next, change salary from average to maximum.

c. Does education level affect how maximum salaries compare by gender and minority status?

PF-16. Using Tableau to calculate a visualization. Starting with the results from PF-15, change salary back to average. Select the side-by-side bar chart (ninth selection) from the "show me" selections.

Based on this visualization of the data, what can you say about relative salaries for males and females and for caucasians and minorities?

LO3,4

Problems PF-17 through PF-19 use data on executive compensation from S&P 500 companies for the years 2015 through 2019. The data is contained in the Excel file Compensation Data 2015_2019 SP500.xlsx that is available on myBusinessCourse.

PF-17. Executive Compensation Visualizations with Tableau—Part I. As a researcher in executive compensation you desire to learn more about the compensation differences between men and women in the roles of Chief Executive Officer (CEO) and Chief Financial Officer (CFO). Data including salary and total compensation, including salary, bonus, stock option awards, and miscellaneous income, for both men and woman serving as CEOs and CFOs for S&P 500 companies for the five years 2015 through 2019 is contained in the Excel file **Compensation Data 2015_2019 SP500.xlsx**. First connect to this file with Tableau and change the Year field from a number to a date type. Next create the following visualizations:

LO3, 4

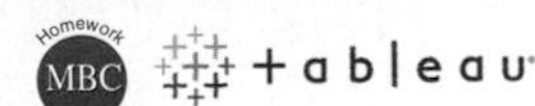

a. A crosstab showing median salary by gender for the entire database. One method to accomplish this is to drag the dimension Gender to the rows shelf and then drag the measure Salary directly to the canvas. Next change the measure of Salary from Sum to Median. Do men or women have a higher median salary and by how much?

b. Create a crosstab that separates CEO median total compensation (Measure Comp1) by gender and Sector. Also show how many individual CEOs are shown by gender and sector. One method to accomplish this is to drag the dimension Sector Name to the columns shelf and the dimensions Position and Gender to the rows shelf. Next drag the measures Comp1 and WRDS(Count) directly to the canvas. Finally change the measure of Comp1 to median. In the consumer Staples sector, how many men and how many women are CEOs, and what is their median total compensation? Note that the totals shown are combined for all five years.

c. Create a separate visualization in the form of a vertical bar chart that displays CEO total compensation by sector, position, and gender. Provide interactive filters for Year, Position, Gender, and Sector Name. Finally, use colors to highlight gender. Within the information technology sector, how much higher is the median compensation for male CEOs than for female CEOs in 2019? What is the name of the highest paid female CEO in this segment and where does she work? One method to accomplish this is to drag the dimensions Sector Name, Position, and Gender to the columns shelf. Next drag the measure Comp1 to the rows shelf and change the measure to Median. Drag Year, Position, Gender, and Sector Name to the Filters shelf and then select Show Filter from each dimension pull down arrow. Select CEO from the Position filter and 2018 from the Year filter. Finally drag Gender to the Color card and WRDS (Count) and Comp1 to the Label card. To see the data behind each of the bars simply hover over the bar and right click and then select Full Data.

d. Save the file for future use.

PF-18. Executive Compensation Visualizations with Tableau—Part II. To further your research in executive compensation you would like to see the location by state, the level of executive compensation, and also where females hold the position of CFO.

LO3, 4

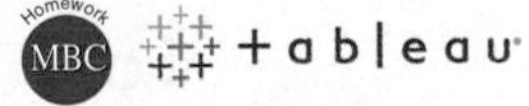

a. Create a map visualization that shows the location of companies that employ female CFOs. In 2016, which state had the highest level of median compensation for a female CFO? Who was the CFO, how much was she paid, and what company did she work for? One way to accomplish this is to first create a map by holding the control key on a Windows machine or the command key on a Mac and select the measures Latitude and Longitude, and then select the map from the Show Me menu. Next drag Total Comp 1 over the Color card and change the measure to Median. Drag the dimension State over the Detail card and the measure WRDS(Count) over the Label card. Drag Gender, Position, Sector Name, and Year to the Filter shelf and select to show these filters. Select 2016 from the Year filter, CFO from the Position filter, and Female from the Gender filter. The state of Washington should appear the darkest indicating the highest median compensation. Click on this state and then click on the View data icon in the top right corner. Select the Full Data tab.

b. Save the file for future use.

LO3, 4

PF-19. Executive Compensation Visualizations with Tableau—Part III. In order to present your findings, you decide to construct a dashboard in Tableau that integrates the visualizations you created in problems PF-17 and PF-18. You wish to allow the user of the dashboard to interact by having the bar chart serve as a filter for the map visualization.

a. Create a dashboard with the bar chart visualization created in problem PF-17 on the top and the map visualization created in problem PF-18 on the bottom. Make the bar chart serve as a filter for the map. What state had the most female CFOs in 2018 from the financials sector and what companies did they work for? How many male CFOs worked in the financials sector in 2018 in that state? Who was the only female CEO in the real estate sector in 2018 and in what state did she work and for what company? What was her total compensation in 2018? How many male CEOs were there in the real estate sector in 2018, and what state employed the largest number? One way to create this dashboard is to open a new dashboard and drag in the bar chart visualization to the top and the map visualization under it. Next click on the bar chart visualization and click on the funnel icon to turn it on as a filter. In order to see the number of individuals in each bar, you can go back to the bar chart and modify the visualization by dragging WRDS(Count) over the Tooltip card.

b. Save the file for future use.

Problems PF-20 through PF-22 use financial statement data for S&P 500 companies for the years 2015 through 2019. The data is contained in the Excel file Compustat SP500 2015_2019.xlsx that is available on myBusinessCourse.

LO3, 4

PF-20. Building Basic Tableau Financial Accounting Visualizations.

a. Connect the Tableau software to the Excel file **Compustat SP500 2015_2019.xlsx**. This file consists of four worksheets. First bring in the Balance sheet worksheets and then join both the cash flow statement and the income statement worksheets to the balance sheet worksheets using both of the fields company name and year.

b. What is the sum of net income for all firms in the database for all years combined? One way to determine this is to drag the measure Net income to the canvas.

c. How many unique companies are included in the database? One way to determine this is to drag the dimension Company name to the rows shelf and then select Measure Count (Distinct) from the pull-down menu on the Company name pill.

d. How many distinct firms are there in each segment? One way to determine this is to drag the dimension Segment to the Columns shelf in the visualization created in part *c*. The totals for each segment will appear if the Show marks label is checked in the Label card.

e. What is the sum of total assets for all companies in each segment for the year 2018? One way to determine this is to drag the dimension Segment to the Columns shelf and then drag the Total Assets measure to the Rows shelf. Next drag the Year dimension to the filters shelf, select year as the filter, click next, and then check 2018. Totals for total assets can be seen in the tool tip by hovering over any bar or by checking Show marks label in the Label card.

f. What firm had the most sales in 2018? What segment was this firm in? One way to determine this is to drag the dimension Company name to the rows shelf and drag the measure Sales to the columns shelf. Next drag the Year dimension to the filters shelf, select year as the filter, click next, and then check 2018. Segments can be highlighted by dragging the dimension Segment over the color card. Finally sort the Company names by Sales by clicking the sort icon in the tool bar.

g. Save the file for future use.

LO3, 4

PF-21. Tableau Visualizations to Analyze Accounting Performance Measures. You recently joined a firm as a junior financial analyst, and you would like to make a good impression by showing your manager the power of visualizations for analyzing data. In order to get a feel for the Tableau software and the dataset you created of financial statement data for S&P 500 firms, you decided to create a few very basic visualizations.

Two widely used ratios to analyze company performance are gross profit percentage and return on sales. You would like to create a visualization that compares these two ratios by segment and further compares segment performance to the median values of these ratios for the entire database of companies.

a. Because of the way cost of goods sold is reported for companies in the real estate segment you decide to exclude this segment from the visualization. After excluding real estate, for the year 2017, which segment reported the highest median value for gross profit percentage and for return on sales?

b. Did any segment report a higher median return on sales than the upper band of the 95 percent confidence interval of overall median return on sales in 2015?

c. Which company had the highest gross profit percentage in 2018 for the segment with the highest median gross profit percentage?

PF-22. Using Tableau to Analyze Inventory. You have learned of the importance of a company being able to sell its products in a timely fashion, and that the ratio of days sales in inventory provides this useful information. You decide a dashboard would be helpful in seeing whether this ratio is improving or declining in the consumer discretionary and the consumer staples segments between 2017 and 2018. You build two sheets that are included in the dashboard. The first sheet shows the level of the ratio for each segment for the two years in question. The second sheet shows the change in the ratio between the two years.

LO3, 4

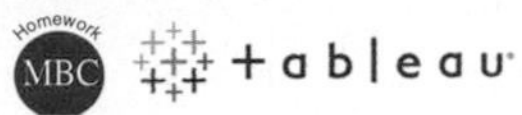

Has the ratio days sales in inventory improved or declined in the consumer discretionary and the consumer staples segments between 2017 and 2018. By how much?

PF-23. Using Tableau for Accounts Receivable Aging—Hugo Enterprises. Hugo Enterprises has been performing its aging of accounts receivable (see Chapter 6) manually; however, the task is becoming too time consuming. The company has recently acquired Tableau for some data visualizations; however, it was mentioned that the software could be used for receivables aging. You have been asked to perform Hugo's accounts receivable aging using Tableau.

LO2, 3, 4

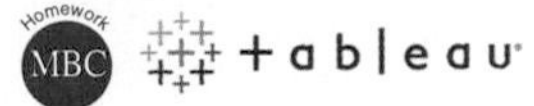

- The Excel file **Hugo Aging Tableau.xlsx** can be found on myBusinessCourse with Hugo's accounts receivable amounts and due dates.
- The first step is to link the Excel file to Tableau. Within Tableau, within the Connect column on the left, select Microsoft Excel. Locate **Hugo Aging Tableau.xlsx** and then click Open.
- If the file needs to be cleaned up for further use, select the checkbox for using the built-in Data Interpreter. This particular file has already been completely cleaned up, so no further work is required here. Now there should appear three columns with customer, amount, and due date data.
- Click on Sheet 1 (this can be renamed) in order to begin creating the aging table.
- A calculated field will need to be created that computes the number of days each invoice is past due. Select Analysis and then select Create Calculated Field. Name this measure Past Due. Next use the formula DateDiff('day',[Due Date],#2023-12-31#). Note the formula is case sensitive and then click OK.
- We now want to put these past due amounts into groupings. We will do this by creating bins and each of the bins will be 30 days. Right-click on the newly created Past Due pill from the Measures shelf on the left of the screen and then select Create and then select Bins. Change the size of the bins to 30 and click OK. A Past Due bin now shows up under Dimensions on the top left of the screen. Double-click the Past Due (bin) in the Dimensions shelf to see a list of the aging groups. To fill in the table with invoice amounts, simply double-click on the Amount measure in the Measures shelf.
- In order to see the data that makes up each total in the aging table, simply click on the amount and then select the view data icon on the top right corner and select Full Data at the bottom of the pop-up window.
- In order to see a visualization of the data, simply select an appropriate chart from the show me selections.

a. What is Hugo's total dollar value of the invoices that are between 31 and 60 days past due?

b. What is its largest invoice within the 91- to 120-day grouping?

PF-24. Using Tableau for Accounts Receivable Aging—Javier Enterprises. Javier Enterprises has been performing its aging of accounts receivable (see Chapter 6) manually; however, the task is becoming too time consuming. The company has recently acquired Tableau for some data visualizations; however, it was mentioned that the software could be used for receivables aging. You have been asked to perform Javier's accounts receivable aging using Tableau.

LO2, 3, 4

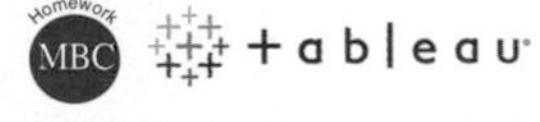

- The Excel file **Javier Aging Tableau.xlsx** can be found on myBusinessCourse with Javier's accounts receivable amounts and due dates.
- The first step is to link the Excel file to Tableau. Within Tableau, within the Connect column on the left, select Microsoft Excel. Locate **Javier Aging Tableau.xlsx** and then click Open.
- If the file needs to be cleaned up for further use, select the checkbox for using the built-in Data Interpreter. This particular file has already been completely cleaned up, so no further work is required here. Now there should appear three columns with customer, amount, and due date data.

- Click on Sheet 1 (this can be renamed) in order to begin creating the aging table.
- A calculated field will need to be created that computes the number of days each invoice is past due. Select Analysis and then select Create Calculated Field. Name this measure Past Due. Next use the formula DateDiff('day',[Due Date],#2023-12-31#). Note the formula is case sensitive and then click OK.
- We now want to put these past due amounts into groupings. We will do this by creating bins, and each of the bins will be 30 days. Right-click on the newly created Past Due bill from the Measures shelf on the left of the screen and then select Create and then select Bins. Change the size of the bins to 30 and click OK. A Past Due bin now shows up under Dimensions on the top left of the screen. Double-click the Past Due (bin) in the Dimensions shelf to see a list of the aging groups. To fill in the table with invoice amounts, simply double-click on the Amount measure in the Measures shelf.
- In order to see the data that makes up each total in the aging table, simply click on the amount and then select the view data icon on the top right corner and select Full Data at the bottom of the pop-up window.
- In order to see a visualization of the data, simply select an appropriate chart from the show me selections.

a. What is Javier Enterprises' total dollar value of the invoices that are between 31 and 60 days past due?

b. What is its largest invoice within the 91- to 120-day grouping?

LO2, 3, 4 **PF-25.** **Using Tableau for Fraud Detection.** Benford's Law represents a powerful tool in the forensic accountant's toolkit to aid in the detection of fraud. Benford's Law is a mathematical law that recognizes the leading (first) digit in many real-life number sets is distributed in a certain manner, and often not in the manner that a fraudster would expect. Specifically the number 1 occurs as the first digit approximately 30 percent of the time, with each succeeding digit appearing less often as follows: 1–30%, 2–18%, 3–12%, 4–10%, 5–8%, 6–7%, 7–6%, 8–5%, and 9–5%. Fraudsters who are unaware of this natural ordering will often arrange digits in a random order that deviates from Benford's Law.

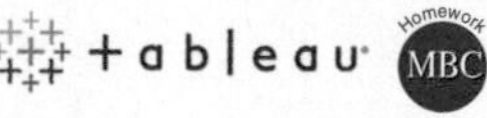

In Part A of this problem you will use Tableau to show how a natural data set of GDP by country conforms to Benford's Law and how a random set of numbers does not. In Part B you will use the same data used in an actual court case to convict a fraudster of embezzlement. Finally, in Part C you will use Benford's Law to test a new reimbursement procedure for possible fraud. A video demonstrating the Tableau tools used in this problem is available on myBusinessCourse.

Part A Use Tableau to show how a natural data set of GDP by country conforms to Benford's Law and how a random set of numbers does not.

- Download the file **GDP Tableau.xlsx** from myBusinessCourse. The file contains World Bank GDP data by country for 2018, along with a separate column of random numbers that was generated in Excel using the command =RAND()*1000.
- After you have uploaded the workbook to Tableau, create two calculated fields.
- The first calculated field will pull the first digit from each country's GDP amount. Choose Analysis > Create Calculated Field and name the calculation First Integer. Then either type or paste the following formula in the formula area: LEFT(STR([GDP]),1)
- Next create a second calculated field named Benfords Law by typing or pasting the following in the formula area: LOG(INT([First Integer])+1)- LOG(INT([First Integer]))
- To create the visualization, drag First Integer from the Dimensions area to Columns and drag Number of Records from the Measures area to Rows. Click Sum(Number of Records) on Rows to show the pull-down menu and choose Quick Table Calculation > Percent of Total. The visualization should now show a bar chart with the bars conforming to Benford's Law.
- While it is relatively easy to see that the data conforms to Benford's Law, with a little more work the visualization can be significantly enhanced. To do this, drag Benfords Law from the Measures area of the Data pane to Detail on the Marks card, and then click Benfords Law on the Marks card and choose Measure > Minimum.
- Next switch from the current Data pane to the Analytics pane and then drag Distribution Band over the chart and drop it on the cell icon in the pop-up. A dialog box will appear. Under computation change the value to percentages of 90,100,110 and select Percent of to be Min(Benfords Law). Choose a fill line as the thick black line and then click OK.
- Finally click on the Label icon in the Marks section and select the Show marks labels box.

a. Does the GDP data appear to conform to Benford's Law?

Now return to the Data pane and create a new calculated field for the random numbers by naming the calculation Random Values and typing or pasting the following formula in the formula area: LEFT(STR([Random]),1)

- Drag the Min(Benfords Law) pill out of the Marks area to remove the bands and drag Random Values from the Dimensions area on top of First Integer to replace it in the visualization. If both pills remain in the columns section, simply drag First Integer away.

b. Do the random values appear to conform with Benford's Law?

Part B Use the same data used in an actual court case to convict a fraudster of embezzlement.

In the 1993 court case *State of Arizona v. Wayne James Nelson* Benford's Law was used to convict the defendant of defrauding the state of nearly $2 million by diverting money to a nonexistent vendor. Nelson tried to make the checks appear random; however, he was unaware that these check amounts should actually follow Benford's Law much closer than the random distribution he created. Download the file **Arizona Fraud.xlsx** from myBusinessCourse and follow the same procedure as you did in Part A above and use Tableau to show how the data conforms to Benford's Law.

a. From a casual observation of the checks, can you detect anything suspect?
b. After using Benford's Law, does the list of checks appear suspect?

Part C Use Benford's Law to test a new reimbursement procedure for possible fraud.

Wally's Enterprises has been reimbursing its employees for business expenses after the employee submits detailed evidence of the expense, such as paid receipts. Management has recently changed the reimbursement policy because of the time spent checking all the submitted evidence, with an especially high volume of smaller reimbursement requests. The new policy only requires evidence be submitted if the reimbursement request exceeds $50. As the company's internal auditor, you are concerned that this policy change may result in fraudulent reimbursement requests. In order to test the new policy, you have gathered a random sample of 100 reimbursement requests from both before and after the policy change. This data is located in the file **Expense Reimbursement.xlsx** in myBusinessCourse. Download this file and using Tableau, apply Benford's Law to test whether the new policy appears to have resulted in any fraud.

a. Do the reimbursement requests prior to the policy change appear to follow Benford's Law?
b. Do the reimbursement requests occurring after the policy change appear to follow Benford's Law?
c. What, if anything, leads you to believe that fraud may be occurring?

Problems PF-26 through PF-31 use financial statement data for S&P 500 companies for the years 2015 through 2019. The data is contained in the Excel file Compustat SP500 2015_2019.xlsx. The file can be downloaded from myBusinessCourse.

PF-26. Using Tableau to Analyze Fixed Assets. One of the ratios that provides information on how well a company utilizes its assets is the ratio asset turnover. As part of your analysis of different segments of the S&P 500 you would like to have a visualization that ranks companies within various segments by their asset turnover.

LO3, 4

a. For the year 2019 what firm in the consumer discretionary segment had the second highest asset turnover? How did the same firm rank in 2018? Did the segment Consumer Discretionary or Consumer Staples have a higher median level of asset turnover in 2017? One way to determine this is to create a visualization by first creating a calculated field of the ratio asset turnover and then dragging the dimensions Segment and Company Name to the rows shelf and the ratio asset turnover to the columns shelf. Using the pull-down arrow of the ratio's pill, change the measure to median. Next sort the horizontal bar chart by Company Name. Drag the dimension Year to the filter shelf and select Show filter. Finally switch from the Data pane to the Analytics pane and drag Median with 95% Cl on the canvas and place the distribution band on Pane.
b. Save the file for future use.

PF-27. Using Tableau to Analyze Liquidity. A popular ratio for analyzing a company's short-term liquidity is the current ratio. In your continuing analysis of S&P 500 companies, you have decided to build a simple visualization that uses color highlighting and tooltip labeling to show current ratios by segment over the five-year period 2015 through 2019. You also desire to do some further analysis in Excel, so you will want to export this data as a crosstab to Excel. Finally, you want to include your visualization in a PowerPoint presentation.

LO3, 4

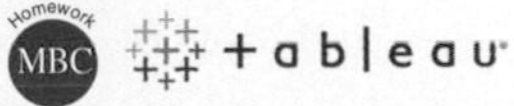

a. What segment has the highest current ratio in each year? One way to create this visualization is to first create the calculated field current ratio. Next drag the dimension Year to the Columns shelf and the ratio Current ratio to the Rows shelf. Next change the ratio's measure to median. Finally drag the dimension Segment over the Color card. In order to export the data as a cross-tab to Excel click on the worksheet tab in the menu bar and choose Export > Crosstab to excel. If you would prefer to see the data as a crosstab in Tableau, right-click on the Tableau workbook icon and choose Duplicate as crosstab. Finally, to export the visualization to PowerPoint, select File from the menu bar and choose Export as PowerPoint.

b. Save the file for future use.

LO3, 4

PF-28. Using Tableau to Analyze Dividend Policy. Many equity investors are particularly interested in the dividend paying policy of a company. Two ratios that provide information in this regard are the dividend payout ratio and the dividend yield. As an analyst you would like to build a visualization that looks at these two ratios together and in particular which segments outperform the S&P500 in general.

a. For the year 2015, did any segment outperform or underperform the median S&P500 company for both the dividend payout and dividend yield by more than a 95 percent confidence level? One way to determine this is to first create calculated fields for both dividend yield and dividend payout and then build a scatter graph visualization with median dividend payout on the columns shelf and median dividend yield on the rows shelf. Next drag Segment to the Color card to color highlight the segments. Drag Year to the filter shelf in order to filter on Year. Finally, switch to the Analytics pane and drag Median with 95% Cl to the canvas.

b. Save the file for future use.

LO3, 4

PF-29. Using Tableau to Study ROE with the Dupont Method—Part I. One of the basic tools in any analyst's toolkit is the DuPont method of Return on Equity (ROE) decomposition. You would like to build a series of visualizations to exploit the DuPont method to find value in equities. To do this you will need visualizations that show, by segment, both ROE and the components of ROE, namely Return on Sales (ROS), Asset Turnover (AT), and Leverage (LEV).

a. Which segment had the highest ROE in both 2017 and 2018? Which component of ROE was mostly responsible? The first step in determining this is to create calculated fields for ROE, ROS, AT, and LEV. The next step is to create a vertical bar chart visualization by dragging the dimensions Segment and Year to the Columns shelf and the median measure of the four new calculated fields to the Rows shelf. The dimension Year needs to be dragged to the filter shelf with the years 2017 and 2018 selected. Finally, Segment can be dragged over the Color card to highlight by color.

b. Which segment showed the largest gain and the largest decline in ROE between 2017 and 2018? This is best shown on a dashboard by combining two separate visualizations. The first visualization in the form of a vertical bar chart can be constructed by dragging the dimensions Segment and Year to the Column shelf and the measure of Median ROE to the rows shelf. The dimension Year should be dragged to the filters shelf and the years 2017 and 2018 selected. To make segments easier to see in the visualization, Segment can be dragged over the Color card to highlight by color. The second visualization, which will show the change in the ratio between 2017 and 2018, can be accomplished by first dragging the dimensions Segment and Year to the Columns shelf and also dragging the dimension Year to the filters shelf and selecting the years 2017 and 2018. Next drag the ratio ROE to the rows shelf and change its measure to median. In order to show the change between years use the pull-down arrow on the ratio's pill and select Quick table calculation and then Difference. Finally, right-click on the year 2017 on the horizontal axis and select hide. To make segments easier to see in the visualization, Segment can be dragged over the Color card to highlight by color. As the last step, create a new dashboard and drag the two visualizations in.

c. Save the file for future use.

LO3, 4

PF-30. Using Tableau to Study ROE with the Dupont Method—Part II. You wish to continue your analysis of segment ROE by looking at trends within segments and then identifying which companies rank the highest for ROE within those segments.

a. For the period 2015 through 2019, which segments showed the best positive trends in ROE growth? One way to create a line chart visualization showing this trend is to drag the dimensions Segment and Year to the Columns shelf and drag the Median measure of ROE to the Rows shelf. To make segments easier to see in the visualization, Segment can be dragged over the Color card to highlight by color. Finally, switch to the Analytics pane and drag Trend line to the canvas, selecting "linear."

b. For the segments identified in part *a*, which firms reported the highest ROE in 2019? A horizontal bar chart visualization can be created by dragging the dimensions Segment and Company name to the Rows shelf and the Median measure of ROE to the columns shelf. Segment and Year can be dragged to the filters shelf to allow filtering on these two dimensions. Finally, to aid in the analysis, the company names can be sorted by clicking on the sort icon located on the tool bar.

c. Save the file for future use.

PF-31. Using Tableau to Study ROE with the Dupont Method—Part III. To complete your analysis of the DuPont method, you would like to have an interactive dashboard that allows the user to select any of the S&P 500 companies and see its segment, its change in ROE between 2017 and 2018, along with the changes in each of the items making up components of ROE. **LO3, 4**

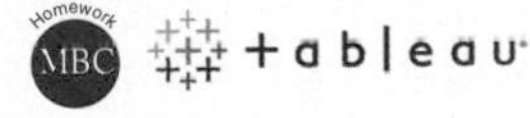

a. How much did Alphabet's (the parent company of Google) ROE improve between 2017 and 2018 and which component showed the largest increase? Pick any other company and answer the same question. One approach to build this dashboard is to first create five visualizations. The first horizontal bar chart visualization can be created by dragging the dimensions Company name and Year to the Rows shelf and the measure ROE to the Columns shelf. The dimension Year needs to be dragged to the filters shelf and the years 2017 and 2018 selected. Next drag the dimension Company name to the filters shelf and click on Show filter from the pills pull-down menu. To allow segments to be highlighted by color in the visualization, Segment can be dragged over the Color card. This process can be repeated to create separate visualizations for the components of ROE, namely ROS, AT, and LEV. The fifth visualization, a line chart, can be created by dragging the dimension Year to the Columns shelf and the measures Net Income, Stockholders Equity, Sales, and Total Assets to the rows shelf. The dimension Year should be dragged to the filters shelf and the years 2017 and 2018 selected. The dimension Company name should also be dragged to the filters shelf and then have Show filter selected. Finally, to allow segments to be highlighted by color in the visualization, Segment can be dragged over the Color card. Now that each of the visualizations are complete, create a dashboard by dragging the first four visualizations, one under the other, on the left side of the dashboard and drag the fifth visualization to the right side of the dashboard. Convert the filter of Company name to a Single Value drop-down floating filter by selecting those two options and position the filter at the top of the dashboard.

b. Save the file for future use.

PF-32. Using Microsoft Excel for descriptive analytics. Go to myBusinessCourse and download the Excel file **Employee Data Excel.xlsx**. You will need to have the Analysis Toolpak add-in installed in Excel. It can be found under the Tools tab. If it does not appear, select Excel Add-ins under the Tools tab, and then check Analysis Toolpak. From the Excel ribbon, select Data and then Data Analysis. From the pop-up window, choose Descriptive Statistics and then click OK. Select the salary column as the input range and check the box for labels in the first row. Choose "New Worksheet" as the output option, click summary statistics, and click OK. Report the following: **LO1, 2**

a. Mean (average) salary
b. Median salary
c. Minimum salary
d. Maximum salary
e. Number of salary observations in the database

PF-33. Using the Microsoft Excel PivotTable function for descriptive analytics. Go to myBusinessCourse and download the Excel file **Employee Data Excel.xlsx**. Place your cursor anywhere in the table of data. From the Excel ribbon, select Insert and then Pivot Table. The entire table should be selected automatically along with the choice to output the PivotTable to a new worksheet. Select OK. From the PivotTable Fields section, select and drag "Gender" and "Minority" to the "Rows" box below. Select and drag the variable "Education" to the "Columns" box. Select and drag the variable "Salary" to the "Values" box. Change the sum of salary to the average of salary by clicking the "i" icon to the right of the "Sum of Salary," choosing "Average," and then clicking OK. Report the following: **LO1, 2**

a. Does additional education appear to be associated with a higher average salary?
b. Do males (1) or females (0) appear to earn higher average salaries?
c. Do minorities (1) or nonminorities (0) appear to earn higher average salaries? Does this hold for both genders?
d. What is the average salary of the entire population? What is the average salary of the entire population of males? What is the average salary of the entire population of females? What is the average salary of the entire population of male minorities? What is the average salary of the entire population of female minorities?

LO1, 2

PF-34. Using Microsoft Excel for diagnostic analytics. Go to myBusinessCourse and download the Excel file **Employee Data Excel.xlsx**. You will need to have the Analysis Toolpak add-in installed in Excel. It can be found under the Tools tab. If it does not appear, you will need to select Excel Add-ins under the Tools tab and then check Analysis Toolpak. From the Excel ribbon, select Data and then Data Analysis. From the pop-up window, choose "Regression," and then click OK. Select values in the "Salary" column as the Input Y Range and values in the columns for "Gender" through "Education" for the Input X Range. Choose "New Worksheet" as the output option, and then click OK. Report the following:

a. A measure on how well the independent variables gender, minority, and education are able to explain the variation in average salary is the adjusted R Squared. What percentage of the variation in average salaries is described by these variables?

b. The *t* Stat is a measure of how an individual independent variable explains variation in the dependent variable average salary. An absolute value greater than 2 is generally considered a significant value in explaining variation. What do the *t* Stats tell us about the ability of the variables gender, minority, and education to explain average salary?

Problems PF-35 through PF-38. will be using the Excel file Compensation Data 2015_2019 SP500.xlsx **that can be downloaded from myBusinessCourse.**

LO3, 4

PF-35. Building a basic Excel PivotTable. You have been tasked by a compensation consulting firm to research compensation amounts being paid to executives in large public companies. In particular you wish to learn more about amounts being paid to CEOs and CFOs within certain industries and how these amounts differ by gender. You have gathered a large database of amounts paid by the S&P500 companies during the period 2015 through 2019.

a. Your first task is to build a PivotTable that separately shows the average salaries paid to CEOs and CFOs by gender on the rows and these amounts by industry segment on the columns. You do not need to separate the data by year at this time. What was the average salary paid to female CEOs in the healthcare segment? How does this compare to male CEOs in the same segment? Were there more male or female CFOs in the Consumer Staples segment?

b. What was the total average salary of all CEOs and CFOs in the information technology segment? Did CEOs or CFOs get paid more? Did males or females get paid more?

LO3, 4

PF-36. Sorting, grouping, and filtering a basic PivotTable. You have been asked to construct a basic PivotTable that shows by position and gender the average salary, average total compensation, and number of executives in each of the industry segments.

a. Construct a PivotTable with Position, Gender, and Sector name on the rows and the average salary, average total compensation, and the count of executives in the columns. To make things easier to read, sort the Sector names by the average of salaries. What sector paid its female CEOs the highest average salary and how many female CEOs made up this calculation? Answer the same question for female CFOs.

b. Rather than combining all five years together you would like to answer similar questions for a single year. Add the year measure to the filter and select 2017. Repeat the questions from part *a*, but this time report the lowest paying segment.

c. Copy the entire PivotTable to the right on the same worksheet, but this time sort by the count of the executives rather than by the average salary. Again, filter by year, but this time select 2018. Which industry segment employs the second most male CFOs?

d. You would like for the reader of these PivotTables to interact with them so that they can answer specific questions regarding the data within the PivotTables. In order to add interactivity, insert four slicers, one for position and one for gender, one for years and one for segment. Connect each slicer to both of the PivotTables through the report connections. Also, make each slicer multi-select. What was the average salary and number of male CFOs in the consumer staples segment in 2018?

e. Finally, you are interested in how much of an executive's total compensation is from salary. Rather than doing the calculation for each industry segment, you decide to create a calculated field of salary as a percentage of total compensation. What percentage of the female CFOs in the industrials segment during 2016 was from salary?

LO3, 4

PF-37. Adding a PivotChart to a PivotTable. Your audience is having difficulty reading through all the numbers in the PivotTables and would like an easier method to visualize the data. In particular they are interested in seeing the relative salaries among the executives within the various industry segments.

a. Create a PivotTable with position, gender, and sector name in the rows and the average of salary for values. Format the average of salary using number format as currency with zero decimal places. Sort the rows using the field sector name by the value average of salary. Add slicers for gender, year, position, and sector name. Finally, add a PivotChart in the form of a bar chart and give it the title "Salary by position, gender, and industry" and add data labels to the bars. Observe how making selections in the slicers updates both the PivotTable and the PivotChart. Select female CFOs in 2017. What industry segment paid the fifth highest average salary? Answer the same question for male CFOs in 2016.

PF-38. Creating a PivotTable Dashboard. Your audience was happy with the PivotTable produced in Problem PF-37, however they would like to see several visualizations at one time. Specifically, they would like to see total compensation by industry, number of executives by industry, and the state locations where these executives are employed. You decide to make a dashboard with a bar PivotChart of total compensation by industry, a pie PivotChart for the number of executives by industry, and a column PivotChart with the top five states by number of executives. **LO3, 4**

a. Create the dashboard described previously. Add slicers for gender, position, and year and link the slicers to all of the PivotTables and PivotCharts. Format the dashboard so as to create a visually pleasing layout that is easy to read. In 2018, for male CEOs, how many executives were there and what was the average salary paid in the information technology segment? Also, in 2018, what state employed the most male CEOs?

PF-39. Using Excel for Accounts Receivable Aging—Bella Co. Bella Co. has been performing its aging of accounts receivable (see Chapter 6) manually; however, the task is becoming too time consuming. The CFO has heard that the PivotTable function within Microsoft Excel could make the task much easier; however, she has never used this technique before. You have been asked to perform Bella's accounts receivable aging using an Excel PivotTable. **LO2, 3, 4**

- The Excel file **Bella Aging Pivot.xlsx** can be found on myBusinessCourse with Bella's accounts receivable amounts and due dates.
- Assume that you are performing the aging as of December 31, 2023, the date already entered in cell G1.
- Create new data within column D for the number of days that each invoice is past the due date by entering in cell D2 the formula of cell G1 as an absolute reference minus the cell C2 as a relative reference =$G$1-C2. Next copy this formula down column D to include the entire list of receivables. We now have a list that identifies for each invoice the number of days past due.
- In order to create the PivotTable, simply place the cursor anywhere within columns A through D and select Insert; then select PivotTable. A pop-up should appear with the table range including all the data from columns A through D already selected and the location of the PivotTable being a new worksheet. If this is correct, click OK.
- In the new PivotTable worksheet, locate the PivotTable Fields to the right of the worksheet. Drag the Days Past field down to the rows section and the Amount field down to the values section.
- Finally, in order to do some groupings, place the cursor within the data in column A and right-click and select Group. In the Grouping pop-up, change the starting value to 1, the ending value to 180, and the by value to 30, and click OK. The aging table should appear.
- To add visual impact, a column chart can be added to the worksheet. In order to see all the invoices that make up any grouping, simply place the cursor on the dollar value of the grouping and double-click.

a. What is Bella's total dollar value of the invoices that are between 61 and 90 days past due?
b. What is its largest invoice within the 151- to 180-day grouping?

PF-40. Using Excel for Accounts Receivable Aging—Remus Co. Remus Co. has been performing its aging of accounts receivable (see Chapter 6) manually; however, the task is becoming too time consuming. The CFO has heard that the PivotTable function within Microsoft Excel could make the task much easier; however, she has never used this technique before. You have been asked to perform Remus' accounts receivable aging using an Excel PivotTable. **LO2, 3**

- The Excel file **Remus Again Pivot.xlsx** can be found on myBusinessCourse with Remus' accounts receivable amounts and due dates.
- Assume that you are performing the aging as of December 31, 2023, the date already entered in cell G1.

- Create new data within column D for the number of days that each invoice is past the due date by entering in cell D2 the formula of cell G1 as an absolute reference minus the cell C2 as a relative reference =$G$1-C2. Next copy this formula down column D to include the entire list of receivables. We now have a list that identifies for each invoice the number of days past due.
- In order to create the PivotTable, simply place the cursor anywhere within columns A through D and select Insert; then select PivotTable. A pop-up should appear with the table range including all the data from columns A through D already selected and the location of the PivotTable being a new worksheet. If this is correct, click OK.
- In the new PivotTable worksheet, locate the PivotTable Fields to the right of the worksheet. Drag the Days Past field down to the rows section and the Amount field down to the values section.
- Finally, in order to do some groupings, place the cursor within the data in column A and right-click and select Group. In the Grouping pop-up, change the starting value to 1, the ending value to 180, and the by value to 30, and click OK. The aging table should appear.
- To add visual impact, a column chart can be added to the worksheet. In order to see all the invoices that make up any grouping, simply place the cursor on the dollar value of the grouping and double-click.

a. What is Remus' total dollar value of the invoices that are between 61 and 90 days past due?
b. What is its largest invoice within the 151- to 180-day grouping?

LO2, 3, 4 **PF-41. Using Excel for Fraud Detection.** Benford's Law represents a powerful tool in the forensic accountant's toolkit to aid in the detection of fraud. Benford's Law is a mathematical law that recognizes the leading (first) digit in many real-life number sets is distributed in a certain manner, and often not in the manner that a fraudster would expect. Specifically, the number 1 occurs as the first digit approximately 30 percent of the time, with each succeeding digit appearing less often as follows: 1–30%, 2–18%, 3–12%, 4–10%, 5–8%, 6–7%, 7–6%, 8–5%, and 9–5%. Fraudsters who are unaware of this natural ordering will often arrange digits in a random order that deviates from Benford's Law.

In Part A of this problem, you will use Microsoft Excel to show how a natural data set of GDP by country conforms to Benford's Law and how a random set of numbers does not. In Part B you will use the same data used in an actual court case to convict a fraudster of embezzlement. Finally, in Part C you will use Benford's Law to test a new reimbursement procedure for possible fraud.

Part A Use Microsoft Excel to show how a natural data set of GDP by country conforms to Benford's Law and how a random set of numbers does not.

- Download the Excel file **GDP Excel.xlxs** from myBusinessCourse. The file contains World Bank GDP data by country for 2018.
- In order to use Benford's Law, you need to first extract the leading digit from each country's GDP amount. To do this, place the cursor in cell C2 and input the formula =Left(B2,1). Copy this formula down column C for each country.
- Next in cells F2 through F10 input the numbers 1 through 9. In cell G2 input the formula =COUNTIF(c2:$C$205,F2) and copy the formula down for each number 1 through 9. This formula goes through the entire range of extracted first digits in column C and records the count of these digits in the cell if it matches the number in column F.
- Sum the column total in cell G11.
- Next determine the percentage that each leading digit appears by dividing the amount in column G by the total of these amounts in cell G11 and place this figure in column H.
- In column I compute the predicted occurrences of each digit (given above) by placing the formula =Log10(1/F2+1) in cell I2 and copying the formula down the column.
- Finally create a Combo chart to visualize these results by highlighting cells H1:I10 and selecting Combo chart.

a. Do the naturally occurring GDP amounts appear to follow Benford's law?

- Next replace the GDP amounts with random numbers to see if random numbers also obey Benford's Law.
- Input the formula =Rand()*1000 in cell B2 and copy this formula down the column.
- Observe the results in the table and the chart. Try to recalculate the spreadsheet several times to obtain different sets of random numbers.

b. Do random numbers appear to follow Benford's Law?

Part B Use the same data used in an actual court case to convict a fraudster of embezzlement.

In the 1993 court case *State of Arizona v. Wayne James Nelson* Benford's Law was used to convict the defendant of defrauding the state of nearly $2 million by diverting money to a nonexistent vendor. Nelson tried to make the checks appear random; however, he was unaware that these check amounts should actually follow Benford's Law much closer than the distribution he created. Download the file **Arizona Fraud.xlsx** from myBusinessCourse and follow the same procedure as you did in Part A above to use Excel to show how the data conforms to Benford's Law.

a. From a casual observation of the checks, can you detect anything suspect?
b. After using Benford's Law, does the list of checks appear suspect?

Part C Use Benford's Law to test a new reimbursement procedure for possible fraud.

Jimmy's Enterprises has been reimbursing its employees for business expenses after the employee submits detailed evidence of the expense, such as paid receipts. Management has recently changed the reimbursement policy because of the time spent checking all the submitted evidence, with an especially high volume of smaller reimbursement requests. The new policy requires evidence be submitted only if the reimbursement request exceeds $50. As the company's internal auditor, you are concerned that this policy change may result in fraudulent reimbursement requests. In order to test the new policy, you have gathered a random sample of 100 reimbursement requests from both before and after the policy change. This data is located in the file **Expense Reimbursement.xlxs** in myBusinessCourse. Download this file and within Excel use Benford's Law to test whether the new policy appears to have resulted in any fraud.

a. Do the reimbursement requests prior to the policy change appear to follow Benford's Law?
b. Do the reimbursement requests occurring after the policy change appear to follow Benford's Law?
c. What, if anything, leads you to believe that fraud may be occurring?

Index

D

E

F

G

H

I

J

K

L

P

Q

R

S